Lecture Notes in Computer Science 12826

Tal Malkin · Chris Peikert (Eds.)

Advances in Cryptology – CRYPTO 2021

41st Annual International Cryptology Conference, CRYPTO 2021
Virtual Event, August 16–20, 2021
Proceedings, Part II

 Springer

Editors
Tal Malkin ⓘ
Columbia University
New York City, NY, USA

Chris Peikert ⓘ
University of Michigan
Ann Arbor, MI, USA

ISSN 0302-9743   ISSN 1611-3349   (electronic)
Lecture Notes in Computer Science
ISBN 978-3-030-84244-4   ISBN 978-3-030-84245-1   (eBook)
https://doi.org/10.1007/978-3-030-84245-1

LNCS Sublibrary: SL4 – Security and Cryptology

This Springer imprint is published by the registered company Springer Nature Switzerland AG
The registered company address is: Gewerbestrasse 11, 6330 Cham, Switzerland

Preface

The 41st International Cryptology Conference (Crypto 2021), sponsored by the International Association of Cryptologic Research (IACR), was held during August 16–20, 2021. Due to the ongoing COVID-19 pandemic, and for the second consecutive year, Crypto was held as an online-only virtual conference, instead of at its usual venue of the University of California, Santa Barbara. In addition, six affiliated workshop events took place during the days immediately prior to the conference.

The Crypto conference continues its substantial growth pattern: this year's offering received a record-high 430 submissions for consideration, of which 103 (also a record) were accepted to appear in the program. The two program chairs were not allowed to submit a paper, and Program Committee (PC) members were limited to two submissions each. Review and extensive discussion occurred from late February through mid-May, in a double-blind, two-stage process that included an author rebuttal phase (following the initial reviews) and extensive discussion by reviewers. We thank the 58-person PC and the 390 external reviewers for their efforts to ensure that, during the continuing COVID-19 pandemic and unusual work and life circumstances, we nevertheless were able to perform a high-quality review process.

The PC selected four papers to receive recognition via awards, along with invitations to the Journal of Cryptology, via a voting-based process that took into account conflicts of interest (the program chairs did not vote).

- The Best Paper Award went to "On the Possibility of Basing Cryptography on EXP $\neq$ BPP" by Yanyi Liu and Rafael Pass.
- The Best Paper by Early Career Researchers Award, along with an Honorable Mention for Best Paper, went to "Linear Cryptanalysis of FF3-1 and FEA" by Tim Beyne.
- Honorable Mentions for Best Paper also went to "Efficient Key Recovery for all HFE Signature Variants" by Chengdong Tao, Albrecht Petzoldt, and Jintai Ding; and "Three Halves Make a Whole? Beating the Half-Gates Lower Bound for Garbled Circuits" by Mike Rosulek and Lawrence Roy.

In addition to the regular program, Crypto 2021 included two invited talks, by Vanessa Teague on "Which e-voting problems do we need to solve?" and Jens Groth on "A world of SNARKs." The conference also carried forward the long-standing tradition of having a rump session, organized in a virtual format.

The chairs would also like to thank the many other people whose hard work helped ensure that Crypto 2021 was a success:

- Vladimir Kolesnikov (Georgia Institute of Technology)—Crypto 2021 general chair.
- Daniele Micciancio (University of California, San Diego), Thomas Ristenpart (Cornell Tech), Yevgeniy Dodis (New York University), and Thomas Shrimpton (University of Florida)—Crypto 2021 Advisory Committee.

- Carmit Hazay (Bar Ilan University)—Crypto 2021 workshop chair.
- Bertram Poettering and Antigoni Polychroniadou—Crypto 2021 rump session chairs.
- Kevin McCurley, for his critical assistance in setting up and managing the HotCRP paper submission and review system, conference website, and other technology.
- Kevin McCurley, Kay McKelly, and members of the IACR's emergency pandemic team for their work in designing and running the virtual format.
- Anna Kramer and her colleagues at Springer.

July 2021

Tal Malkin
Chris Peikert

Organization

General Chair

Vladimir Kolesnikov   Georgia Institute of Technology, USA

Program Committee Chairs

Tal Malkin   Columbia University, USA
Chris Peikert   University of Michigan and Algorand, Inc., USA

Program Committee

Abhi Shelat	Northeastern University, USA
Andrej Bogdanov	Chinese University of Hong Kong, Hong Kong
Antigoni Polychroniadou	JP Morgan AI Research, USA
Brice Minaud	Inria and École Normale Supérieure, France
Chaya Ganesh	Indian Institute of Science, India
Chris Peikert	University of Michigan and Algorand, Inc., USA
Claudio Orlandi	Aarhus University, Denmark
Daniele Venturi	Sapienza University of Rome, Italy
David Cash	University of Chicago, USA
David Wu	University of Virginia, USA
Dennis Hofheinz	ETH Zurich, Switzerland
Divesh Aggarwal	National University of Singapore, Singapore
Dominique Unruh	University of Tartu, Estonia
Elena Andreeva	Technical University of Vienna, Austria
Elena Kirshanova	Immanuel Kant Baltic Federal University, Russia
Fabrice Benhamouda	Algorand Foundation, USA
Fang Song	Portland State University, USA
Frederik Vercauteren	KU Leuven, Belgium
Ghada Almashaqbeh	University of Connecticut, USA
Itai Dinur	Ben-Gurion University, Israel
Jean-Pierre Tillich	Inria, France
Jeremiah Blocki	Purdue University, USA
John Schanck	University of Waterloo, Canada
Jonathan Bootle	IBM Research, Switzerland
Joseph Jaeger	University of Washington, USA
Junqing Gong	East China Normal University, China
Lisa Kohl	CWI Amsterdam, The Netherlands
Manoj Prabhakaran	IIT Bombay, India
Marcel Keller	CSIRO's Data61, Australia
Mariana Raykova	Google, USA

Mike Rosulek	Oregon State University, USA
Mor Weiss	Bar-Ilan University, Israel
Muthuramakrishnan Venkitasubramaniam	University of Rochester, USA
Ni Trieu	Arizona State University, USA
Nir Bitansky	Tel Aviv University, Israel
Nuttapong Attrapadung	AIST, Japan
Omer Paneth	Tel Aviv University, Israel
Paul Grubbs	NYU, Cornell Tech and University of Michigan, USA
Peihan Miao	University of Illinois at Chicago, USA
Peter Schwabe	Max Planck Institute for Security and Privacy, Germany, and Radboud University, The Netherlands
Ran Canetti	BU, USA, and Tel Aviv University, Israel
Romain Gay	IBM Research, Switzerland
Ron Steinfeld	Monash University, Australia
Rosario Gennaro	City University of New York, USA
Ryo Nishimaki	NTT Secure Platform Laboratories, Japan
Sandro Coretti	IOHK, Switzerland
Sikhar Patranabis	Visa Research, USA
Sina Shiehian	UC Berkeley and Stony Brook University, USA
Siyao Guo	NYU Shanghai, China
Stanislaw Jarecki	University of California, Irvine, USA
Tal Malkin	Columbia University, USA
Tarik Moataz	Aroki Systems, USA
Thomas Peters	UC Louvain, Belgium
Thomas Peyrin	Nanyang Technological University, Singapore
Tianren Liu	University of Washington, USA
Viet Tung Hoang	Florida State University, USA
Xavier Bonnetain	University of Waterloo, Canada
Yu Yu	Shanghai Jiao Tong University, China

Additional Reviewers

Aaram Yun	Akshayaram Srinivasan
Aarushi Goel	Akshima
Aayush Jain	Alain Passelègue
Abhishek Jain	Alex Bienstock
Adrien Benamira	Alex Lombardi
Agnes Kiss	Alexander Golovnev
Aishwarya Thiruvengadam	Alexander Hoover
Ajith Suresh	Alexander May
Akin Ünal	Alexandre Wallet
Akinori Kawachi	Alexandru Cojocaru
Akira Takahashi	Alice Pellet-Mary
Akshay Degwekar	Alin Tomescu

Amin Sakzad
Amit Singh Bhati
Amitabh Trehan
Amos Beimel
Anat Paskin-Cherniavsky
Anca Nitulescu
André Chailloux
Andre Esser
André Schrottenloher
Andrea Coladangelo
Andreas Hülsing
Antonin Leroux
Antonio Florez-Gutierrez
Archita Agarwal
Ariel Hamlin
Arka Rai Choudhuri
Arnab Roy
Ashrujit Ghoshal
Ashutosh Kumar
Ashwin Jha
Atsushi Takayasu
Aurore Guillevic
Avijit Dutta
Avishay Yanay
Baiyu Li
Balazs Udvarhelyi
Balthazar Bauer
Bart Mennink
Ben Smith
Benjamin Diamond
Benjamin Fuller
Benny Applebaum
Benoît Cogliati
Benoit Libert
Bertram Poettering
Binyi Chen
Bo-Yin Yang
Bogdan Ursu
Bruno Freitas dos Santos
Bryan Parno
Byeonghak Lee
Carl Bootland
Carles Padro
Carmit Hazay
Carsten Baum
Cecilia Boschini

Chan Nam Ngo
Charles Momin
Charlotte Bonte
Chen Qian
Chen-Da Liu-Zhang
Chenkai Weng
Chethan Kamath
Chris Brzuska
Christian Badertscher
Christian Janson
Christian Majenz
Christian Matt
Christina Boura
Christof Paar
Christoph Egger
Cody Freitag
Dahmun Goudarzi
Dakshita Khurana
Damian Vizar
Damiano Abram
Damien Stehlé
Damien Vergnaud
Daniel Escudero
Daniel Jost
Daniel Masny
Daniel Tschudi
Daniel Wichs
Dario Catalano
Dario Fiore
David Gerault
David Heath
Debbie Leung
Dean Doron
Debapriya Basu Roy
Dima Kogan
Dimitrios Papadopoulos
Divya Gupta
Divya Ravi
Dominique Schröder
Eduardo Soria-Vazquez
Eldon Chung
Emmanuela Orsini
Eran Lambooij
Eran Omri
Eshan Chattopadhyay
Estuardo Alpirez Bock

Evgenios Kornaropoulos

Eysa Lee

Fabio Banfi

Felix Engelmann

Felix Günther

Ferdinand Sibleyras

Fermi Ma

Fernando Virdia

Francesco Berti

François-Xavier Standaert

Fuyuki Kitagawa

Gaëtan Cassiers

Gaëtan Leurent

Gayathri Annapurna Garimella

Geoffroy Couteau

Georg Fuchsbauer

Ghous Amjad

Gildas Avoine

Giorgos Panagiotakos

Giorgos Zirdelis

Giulio Malavolta

Guy Rothblum

Hamidreza Khoshakhlagh

Hamza Abusalah

Hanjun Li

Hannah Davis

Haoyang Wang

Hart Montgomery

Henry Corrigan-Gibbs

Hila Dahari

Huijia Lin

Ian McQuoid

Ignacio Cascudo

Igors Stepanovs

Ilan Komargodski

Ilia Iliashenko

Ingrid Verbauwhede

Itamar Levi

Ittai Abraham

Ivan Damgård

Jack Doerner

Jacob Schuldt

James Bartusek

Jan Czajkowski

Jan-Pieter D'Anvers

Jaspal Singh

Jean Paul Degabriele

Jesper Buus Nielsen

Jesús-Javier Chi-Domínguez

Ji Luo

Jian Guo

Jiaxin Pan

Jiayu Xu

Joanne Adams-Woodage

João Ribeiro

Joël Alwen

Julia Hesse

Julia Len

Julian Loss

Junichi Tomida

Justin Holmgren

Justin Thaler

Kai-Min Chung

Katerina Sotiraki

Katharina Boudgoust

Kathrin Hövelmanns

Katsuyuki Takashima

Kazuhiko Minematsu

Keita Xagawa

Kevin Yeo

Kewen Wu

Khoa Nguyen

Koji Nuida

Kristina Hostáková

Laasya Bangalore

Lars Knudsen

Lawrence Roy

Lejla Batina

Lennart Braun

Léo Colisson

Leo de Castro

Léo Ducas

Léo Perrin

Lin Lyu

Ling Song

Luca De Feo

Luca Nizzardo

Lucjan Hanzlik

Luisa Siniscalchi

Łukasz Chmielewski

Maciej Obremski

Madalina Bolboceanu

Mahimna Kelkar

Maria Eichlseder

María Naya-Plasencia

Marilyn George

Marios Georgiou

Mark Abspoel

Mark Simkin

Mark Zhandry

Markulf Kohlweiss

Marshall Ball

Marta Mularczyk

Martin Albrecht

Martin Hirt

Mary Wooters

Masayuki Abe

Matteo Campanelli

Matthias Fitzi

Mia Filic

Michael Reichle

Michael Rosenberg

Michael Walter

Michele Orru

Miguel Ambrona

Mingyuan Wang

Miran Kim

Miruna Rosca

Miyako Ohkubo

Mohammad Hajiabadi

Mohammad Hossein Faghihi Sereshgi

Monosij Maitra

Morgan Shirley

Mridul Nandi

Muhammed F. Esgin

Mustafa Khairallah

Naomi Ephraim

Nathan Manohar

Naty Peter

Navid Alamati

Ngoc Khanh Nguyen

Nicholas Spooner

Nicholas-Philip Brandt

Nico Döttling

Nicolas Resch

Nicolas Sendrier

Nikolaos Makriyannis

Nikolas Melissaris

Nils Fleischhacker

Nina Bindel

Nirvan Tyagi

Niv Gilboa

Noah Stephens-Davidowitz

Olivier Blazy

Olivier Bronchain

Omri Shmueli

Orfeas Stefanos Thyfronitis Litos

Orr Dunkelman

Oxana Poburinnaya

Patrick Derbez

Patrick Longa

Patrick Towa

Paul Rösler

Paul Zimmermann

Peter Gazi

Peter Rindal

Philippe Langevin

Pierre Briaud

Pierre Meyer

Pierrick Gaudry

Pierrick Mèaux

Po-Chu Hsu

Prabhanjan Ananth

Prashant Vasudeval

Pratik Sarkar

Pratik Soni

Pratyay Mukherjee

Pratyush Mishra

Qian Li

Qiang Tang

Qipeng Liu

Quan Quan Tan

Rachit Garg

Radu Titiu

Rajeev Raghunath

Rajendra Kumar

Ran Cohen

Raymond K. Zhao

Riad Wahby

Rishab Goyal

Rishabh Bhadauria

Rishiraj Bhattacharyya

Ritam Bhaumik

Robi Pedersen

Rohit Chatterjee
Rolando La Placa
Roman Langrehr
Rongmao Chen
Rupeng Yang
Ruth Ng
Saba Eskandarian
Sabine Oechsner
Sahar Mazloom
Saikrishna Badrinarayanan
Sam Kim
Samir Hodzic
Sanjam Garg
Sayandeep Saha
Schuyler Rosefield
Semyon Novoselov
Serge Fehr
Shai Halevi
Shashank Agrawal
Sherman S. M. Chow
Shi Bai
Shifeng Sun
Shivam Bhasin
Shota Yamada
Shuai Han
Shuichi Katsumata
Siang Meng Sim
Somitra Sanadhya
Sonia Belaïd
Sophia Yakoubov
Srinivas Vivek
Srinivasan Raghuraman
Sruthi Sekar
Stefano Tessaro
Steve Lu
Steven Galbraith
Stjepan Picek
Sumegha Garg
Susumu Kiyoshima
Sven Maier
Takahiro Matsuda
Takashi Yamakawa
Tal Moran
Tamer Mour
Thom Wiggers

Thomas Agrikola
Thomas Attema
Thomas Debris-Alazard
Thomas Decru
Tiancheng Xie
Tim Beyne
Titouan Tanguy
Tommaso Gagliardoni
Varun Maram
Vassilis Zikas
Venkata Koppula
Vincent Zucca
Virginie Lallemand
Ward Beullens
Wei Dai
Willy Quach
Wouter Castryck
Xiao Liang
Xiao Wang
Xiong Fan
Yael Kalai
Yan Bo Ti
Yann Rotella
Yannick Seurin
Yaobin Shen
Yashvanth Kondi
Yfke Dulek
Yiannis Tselekounis
Yifan Song
Yilei Chen
Yixin Shen
Yongsoo Song
Yu Long Chen
Yu Sa
Yue Guo
Yuncong Hu
Yupeng Zhang
Yuriy Polyakov
Yuval Ishai
Zahra Jafargholi
Zeyong Li
Zhengfeng Ji
Zichen Gui
Zuoxia Yu
Zvika Brakerski

Contents – Part II

Lattice Cryptography

Lattice Cryptanalysis

Multi-party Computation

Game-Theoretic Fairness Meets Multi-party Protocols: The Case of Leader Election

Kai-Min Chung[1]([⊠]), T.-H. Hubert Chan[2], Ting Wen[2], and Elaine Shi[3]

[1] Academia Sinica, Taipei City, Taiwan
kmchung@iis.sinica.edu.tw
[2] The University of Hong Kong, Pokfulam, Hong Kong
hubert@cs.hku.hk
[3] Carnegie Mellon University, Pittsburgh, USA
runting@cs.cmu.edu

Abstract. Suppose that n players want to elect a random leader and they communicate by posting messages to a common broadcast channel. This problem is called leader election, and it is fundamental to the distributed systems and cryptography literature. Recently, it has attracted renewed interests due to its promised applications in decentralized environments. In a game theoretically fair leader election protocol, roughly speaking, we want that even a majority coalition cannot increase its own chance of getting elected, nor hurt the chance of any honest individual. The folklore tournament-tree protocol, which completes in logarithmically many rounds, can easily be shown to satisfy game theoretic security. To the best of our knowledge, no sub-logarithmic round protocol was known in the setting that we consider.

We show that by adopting an appropriate notion of approximate game-theoretic fairness, and under standard cryptographic assumption, we can achieve $(1 - 1/2^{\Theta(r)})$-fairness in r rounds for $\Theta(\log \log n) \leq r \leq \Theta(\log n)$, where n denotes the number of players. In particular, this means that we can approximately match the fairness of the tournament tree protocol using as few as $O(\log \log n)$ rounds. We also prove a lower bound showing that logarithmically many rounds are necessary if we restrict ourselves to "perfect" game-theoretic fairness and protocols that are "very similar in structure" to the tournament-tree protocol.

Although leader election is a well-studied problem in other contexts in distributed computing, our work is the first exploration of the round complexity of *game-theoretically fair* leader election in the presence of a possibly majority coalition. As a by-product of our exploration, we suggest a new, approximate game-theoretic fairness notion, called "approximate sequential fairness", which provides a more desirable solution concept than some previously studied approximate fairness notions.

Author ordering is randomized. See our online full version [15] for full details and proofs.

© International Association for Cryptologic Research 2021
T. Malkin and C. Peikert (Eds.): CRYPTO 2021, LNCS 12826, pp. 3–32, 2021.
https://doi.org/10.1007/978-3-030-84245-1_1

1 Introduction

Suppose that Murphy and Moody simultaneously solve a long-standing open problem in cryptography and they each submit a paper with identical result to CRYPTO'21. The amazing CRYPTO'21 program committee recommends a hard merge of the two papers. Murphy and Moody decide to flip a random coin over the Internet to decide who gets to present the result at the prestigious CRYPTO'21 conference, to be held on the beautiful virtual beaches of Santa Barbara. Murphy and Moody both want to make sure that the outcome of the coin toss is fair, even when the other player may be behaving selfishly. There is good news and bad news. The bad news is that a famous lower bound by Cleve [16] proved that a strong notion of fairness, henceforth called *unbiasability*, is impossible in any n-player coin toss protocol in the presence of corrupt majority. Specifically, for any r-round protocol, a coalition controlling half or more of the players can implement an efficient attack that biases the outcome by $\Omega(\frac{1}{r})$. This impossibility result also holds in the two-party setting where one of the parties can be corrupt. This strong unbiasability notion is also the *de facto* notion in the long line of work on multi-party computation [8,13,26]. The good news is that Cleve's lower bound is not a deal-breaker for Murphy and Moody. In fact, they can simply run Blum's celebrated coin toss protocol [10]: each player picks a random bit and posts a commitment of the bit to a public bulletin board (e.g., a broadcast channel, a blockchain); then both parties open their committed bits and the XOR of the two bits is used to decide the winner. If either player ever aborts from the protocol or opens the commitment wrongly, it automatically forfeits and the other is declared the winner. Blum's protocol is *not* unbiasable, i.e., a player can indeed misbehave and bias the coin—however, the bias will simply benefit the other player and hurt itself. Although not explicitly stated in Blum's original paper, in fact, his celebrated protocol achieves a *game-theoretic* notion of fairness which is strictly weaker than the de facto unbiasability notion. Specifically, no player can benefit itself or hurt the other by deviating from the protocol, and thus the honest protocol is a Nash equilibrium in which no player would be incentivized to deviate.

The above example shows that in the two-party setting, adopting a game theoretic notion of fairness allows us to circumvent the impossibility of fairness in the corrupt majority setting [16]. Therefore, a natural question is whether such game theoretic notions can also help us in the multi-party setting. Surprisingly, this very natural question has traditionally been overlooked in the long line of work on multi-party protocols. Only very recently, an elegant work by Chung et al. [14] initiated the study of game-theoretic fairness in a multi-party setting. Unfortunately, Chung et al. [14] proved broad impossibility results (in the corrupt majority setting) for a particular formulation of the multi-party coin toss problem for natural game-theoretic fairness notions. Specifically, suppose that n parties want to toss a *binary* coin, and each player has preference for either the bit 0 or 1. If the outcome agrees with a player's preference, it obtains a utility 1; otherwise, it obtains a utility of 0. Chung et al. [14] showed that roughly speaking, unless all players but one prefer the same coin, the following natural fairness notions can be ruled out in the corrupt majority setting: 1) *maximin fairness*, which requires that no coalition can harm any honest individual; and 2) *cooperative strategy proofness* (also called *CSP-fairness* for short), which requires that no coalition can benefit itself.

Philosophically, if a protocol satisfies maximin fairness and CSP fairness, then no individual should be incentivized to deviate from this equilibrium, no matter whether the coalition/individual is greedy and profit-seeking, malicious and aiming to harm others, or paranoid and aiming to defend itself in the worst-possible scenario. Such protocols are also said to be *incentive compatible*.

1.1 Leader Election: Another Formulation of Multi-party Coin Toss

In this paper, we revisit the question of game-theoretically fair multi-party coin toss. Specifically, we consider an alternative formulation. Instead of tossing a binary coin, we consider the problem of *leader election* which can be viewed as tossing an n-way coin among n parties. Suppose that all parties prefer to be elected: the elected leader gains a utility of 1 (or equivalently, a utility of an arbitrary positive value), whereas everyone else gains a utility of 0. This natural utility notion is often encountered in practical applications as we mention in Sect. 1.3. Intriguingly, for this formulation, the theoretical landscape appears starkly different from the binary-coin case[1]. The broad impossibility results of Chung et al. [14] for the binary case no longer apply. A folklore approach henceforth called the tournament-tree protocol [6,31] establishes the feasibility of a logarithmic round, game-theoretically fair leader election protocol, even in the presence of majority coalitions:

- Each pair of players duels with each other to select a winner using Blum's coin toss [10]; again, aborting is treated as forfeiting.
- Now the $\frac{n}{2}$ winners of the previous iteration form pairs and run the same protocol to elect $\frac{n}{4}$ winners.
- After logarithmically many rounds, the final winner is called the leader.

Like Blum's protocol, the tournament-tree protocol also does not satisfy unbiasability, since anyone can abort and bias the outcome in a direction that harms itself. However, one can show that it indeed satisfies the aforemnetioned maximin fairness and CSP fairness notions, i.e., no coalition can harm an honest individual or benefit itself. In light of this folklore protocol, one important and natural open question is to understand the *round complexity* of game-theoretically fair, multi-party leader election in the corrupt majority setting. Specifically, *can we have an n-party, game-theoretically fair leader election protocol that tolerates majority coalitions, and completes in o(log n) number of rounds?* A naïve idea is to directly collapse the tournament-tree protocol to two rounds—in the first round, all players commit all random coins they ever need to use in the protocol; and in the second round, they open all random coins. It turns out that this naïve approach completely fails in the sense that a majority coalition can have a definitive winning strategy (see the online full version [15]).

---

[1] Game theoretically fair leader election and binary coin toss are different in nature partly due to the different utility functions.

Throughout this paper, we shall consider the *plain setting without trusted setup*, and allowing *standard cryptographic assumptions*. This rules out naïve solutions such as having the trusted setup choose the coin toss outcome, or using Verifiable Delay Functions [11,12]. Also, recall that in the honest majority setting, the standared multi-party computation literature gives us constant-round solutions [7,18] that achieves the stronger notion of unbiasability. Therefore, we will focus on the corrupt majority setting. We also stress that the game-theoretic fairness notions we consider are stronger than in some previous contexts. For example, a strictly weaker notion is called *resilience*, which requires that an honest player is elected with constant probability [19,20,35,36]. The resilience notion may be sufficient in certain contexts, however, it does not provide *incentive compatibility* like our notions.

1.2   Our Results and Contributions

We initiate the study of the round complexity of game-theoretically fair, multiparty leader election. Below, we first describe our new upper bound result and techniques informally, and then we will discuss the interesting definitional subtleties we encountered and our definitional contributions—it turns out that even defining an *approximate* notion of (game-theoretic) fairness is rather non-trivial, and the notions that existed in the literature appear somewhat lacking.

New upper bounds and techniques. Roughly speaking, we prove that one can *approximately* match the fairness of the tournament-tree protocol, in as small as $O(\log \log n)$ rounds. Specifically, we give the following parametrized result that allows one to trade off the round complexity and approximation factor.

Theorem 1 (Informal: round-efficient, game theoretically fair leader election). *For $r \in [C_0 \log \log n, C_1 \log n]$ where C_0 and C_1 are suitable constants, r-round protocols exist that achieve $\left(1 - \frac{1}{2^{\Theta(r)}}\right)$-approximate fairness in the presence of a coalition of size at most $\left(1 - \frac{1}{2^{\Theta(r)}}\right) \cdot n$.*

In the above, roughly speaking, 1-fairness means perfect fairness and 0-fairness means no fairness. Observe that if we plug in $r = \Theta(\log \log n)$, we can achieve $(1 - o(1))$-fairness against coalitions of size $n - o(n)$. It is also interesting to contrast our result with the classical notion of approximate unbiasability—it is well-known that r-round protocols cannot achieve better than $O(1/r)$-unbiasability in the presence of a majority coalition [16]. In contrast, our approximation factor, i.e., $\frac{1}{2^{\Theta(r)}}$, is exponentially sharper than the case of approximate unbiasability. We review more related work on ϵ-unbiasability in the online full version [15].

The techniques for achieving our upper bound are intriguing and somewhat surprising at first sight. We describe a novel approach that combines combinatorial techniques such as extractors, as well as cryptographic multiparty computation (MPC). Intriguingly, for designing game theoretically secure protocols, some of our classical insights in the standard MPC literature do not apply.

Several aspects of our protocol design are counter-intuitive at first sight. For example, jumping ahead, we defend against "a *large* coalition benefitting itself" using (non-trivial) combinatorial techniques; but these combinatorial techniques provide no meaningful defense against a *small* coalition benefitting itself—it is initially surprising that small coalitions turn out to be more challenging to defend against. To defend against a small coalition, we employ a special *honest-majority* MPC protocol as part of our final construction. The fact that an honest-majority MPC can provide meaningful guarantees in a corrupt majority setting is initially surprising too. Of course, weaving together the combinatorial and the cryptographic techniques also has various subtleties as we elaborate on in subsequent sections. We believe our design paradigm can potentially lend to the design of other game-theoretically fair protocols.

New definition of approximate fairness. It turns out that how to define a good *approximate* fairness notion requires careful thought. The most natural (but somewhat flawed) way to define $(1-\epsilon)$-fairness is to require that even a majority coalition cannot increase its own chances by more than an ϵ factor, or reduce an honest individual's chance by more than ϵ. Throughout the paper, we allow the coalition's *action space* to include *arbitrary deviations from the prescribed protocol*, as long as the coalition is subject to probabilistic polynomial-time (p.p.t.) computations. We consider a multiplicative notion of error, i.e., we want that a coalition A's expected utility is at most $\frac{|A|}{(1-\epsilon)\cdot n}$ where $\frac{|A|}{n}$ is the coalition's fair share had it played honestly; moreover, we want that any honest individual's expected utility is at least $(1-\epsilon)/n$ where $1/n$ is its utility if everyone participated honestly. We prefer a multiplicative notion to an additive notion, because in practical settings, the game may be repeated many times and the absolute value of the utility may not be as informative or meaningful. The relative gain or loss often matters more.

Indeed, some earlier works considered such an approximate fairness notion—for example, Pass and Shi [33] considered such a notion in the context of consensus protocols; they want that a (minority) coalition cannot act selfishly to increase its own gains by more than ϵ^2. We realize, however, that such an approximate notion is somewhat flawed and may fail to rule out some undesirable protocols. Specifically, consider a protocol in which some bad event happens with small but non-negligible probability, and if the bad event happens, it makes sense for the coalition to deviate. For example, consider a contrived example.

Example. Suppose that Alice and Bob run Blum's coin toss except that with ϵ probability, Bob sends all his random coins for the commitment to Alice in the first round. If this small-probability bad event happens, Alice should choose a coin that lets her win. This is not a desirable protocol because with small but non-negligible probability, it strongly incentivizes Alice to deviate.

However, the above protocol is not ruled out by the aforementioned notion of approximate fairness: since the probability of the bad event is small, the a-

---

² Pass and Shi [33] do not consider the threat of a coalition targeting an individual.

priori motivation for Alice or Bob to deviate is indeed small. In the online full version [15], we give another (arguably less contrived) counter-example that also violates sequential fairness.

We propose a new approximate fairness notion called *sequential approximate fairness* that avoids this drawback, and characterizes a more desirable space of solution concepts. At a very high level, our new notion says, it is not enough for a coalition to not have *a-priori* noticeable incentives to deviate, rather, we want the following stronger guarantee: *except with negligible probability, at no point during the protocol execution should a coalition have noticeable (i.e., ϵ) incentive to deviate, even after having observed the history of the execution so far.*

Remark 1. In the online full version [15], we show that the non-sequential approximate fairness notion is in fact equivalent to a multiplicative approximate variant of the Rational Protocol Design (RPD) notion proposed by Garay et al. [22–24]. However, as mentioned, we believe that our new *sequential* approximate notion provides a better solution concept.

Lower bound. The tournament-tree protocol achieves perfect fairness (i.e., $\epsilon = 0$) in an ideal "commit-and-immediately-open" model. That is, the protocol proceeds in $\log n$ iterations where each iteration consists of a commitment and a subsequent opening for every player. In the online full version [15], we prove a lower bound showing that in the operational model of the tournament-tree protocol, i.e., if we insist on perfect fairness (assuming idealized commitments) as well as immediate opening of committed values, unfortunately $\Theta(\log n)$ rounds is optimal. This lower bound provides a useful sanity check and guideline for protocol design. In comparison, our protocol achieves sub-logarithmic round complexity by introducing the approximate fairness relaxation and general cryptographic techniques. It is an open direction to precisely characterize the minimal conditions/assumptions under which sub-logarithmic rounds become possible.

Theorem 2 (Informal: some relaxations in our design are necessary). *Assume the ideal commitment model. If commitments must be opened immediately in the next round and perfect fairness is required, then $\Omega(\log n)$ rounds is necessary.*

Our work complements the recent prior work of Chung et al. [14] and makes a new step forward at understanding the mathematical landscape of game-theoretically fair, multi-party coin toss. Unlike the *de facto* unbiasability notion, however, our understanding of game-theoretic fairness in multi-party protocols is only just beginning, and there are numerous open questions. We describe some open questions in the online full version [15].

1.3   Motivating Applications and Scope of Our Work

Our work should be viewed as an *initial theoretical exploration* of the round complexity of game-theoretically fair leader-election. We do not claim practicality;

however, it is indeed an exciting future direction to design practical variants of our ideas.

Having said this, interestingly, the original inspiration that led the formulation of this problem as well as our game theoretic notions comes from emerging decentralized applications [5,6,9,31]. In a decentralized environment, often pseudonyms or public keys are cheap to create, and thus it may well be that many pseudonyms are controlled by the same entity, i.e., *the classical honest majority assumption is not reasonable*. Some works orthogonal and complementary to our paper [30] aim to make it more costly to establish identities in decentralized applications, nonetheless, even with such DoS-defense mechanisms, honest majority may not be a reasonable assumption.

A line of work [5,9] considered how to achieve a "financially fair" n-party lottery over cryptocurrencies such as Bitcoin and Ethereum. These works adopt game-theoretic fairness notions similar in spirit to ours, but they rely on collateral and penalty mechanisms to achieve fairness. In comparison, in our model, we aim to achieve fairness *without having to rely on additional assumptions such as collateral and penalty*. A couple recent works [6,31] also pointed out that collateral and penalty mechanism can be undesirable and should be minimized in mechanism design in decentralized blockchain environments.

Leader election is also needed in decentralized smart contracts where one may want to select a service provider among a pool to provide some service, e.g., act as the block proposer, generate a verifiable random beacon, or verifiably perform some computational task, in exchange for rewards. In this case, providers may wish to get elected to earn a profit. A coalition may also wish to monopolize the eco-system by harming and driving away smaller players (potentially even at the cost of near-term loss). Conversely, a small player may be concerned about protecting itself in worst-possible scenarios. Our game-theoretic notion guarantees that no matter which of objectives a player or coalition has, it has no noticeable incentive to deviate from the honest protocol. In such blockchain settings, typically the blockchain itself can serve as a broadcast channel, and a round can be a confirmation delay of the blockchain[3].

2 Technical Overview

In this section, we will go through a few stepping stones to derive an $O(\log \log n)$-round protocol achieving $(1 - o(1))$-approximate fairness. We defer the fully parametrized version to the subsequent formal sections.

---

[3] Why and how blockchain can formally realize/approximate a broadcast channel is outside the scope of our paper, and has been extensively studied in a line of works on distributed consensus. We simply assume broadcast as given, a modeling approach that has been adopted in the long line of work on multi-party computation. In fact, our protocol execution model is no different from the standard literature on multi-party computation—see Sect. 2.1.

2.1 Leader Election Protocol

A leader election protocol (also called lottery) involves n players which exchange messages over *pairwise private channels* as well as a *common broadcast channel*. The protocol execution proceeds in synchronous rounds: in every round, players first receive new messages, then they perform some local computation, and send new messages. We assume a *synchronous network* where messages posted by honest players can be received by honest recipients in the immediate next round. At the end of the final round, everyone can apply an a-priori fixed function f over all messages on the broadcast channel to determine a unique leader from $[n]$, i.e., the result is *publicly verifiable*. For *correctness*, we require that in an honest execution where all players faithfully follow the protocol, the elected leader be chosen uniformly at random from $[n]$.

A subset of the players (often called a coalition) may decide to deviate from the honest strategy. Such a coalition can perform a *rushing* attack: during a round, players in the coalition (also called corrupt players) can wait to read all messages sent by honest players in this round, then decide what messages they should send in the same round.

Throughout the paper, we assume that an execution of the protocol is parametrized with a security parameter κ, since the protocol may adopt cryptographic primitives. We assume that the number of players n is a polynomially bounded function in κ; without loss of generality we assume that $n \geq \kappa$.

2.2 Non-sequential Approximate Fairness

For simplicity, we first present an overview of our upper bound using the *non-sequential* notion of approximate fairness. However, in subsequent formal sections, we will actually define a better solution concept called *sequential approximate fairness*, and prove our protocols secure under this better solution concept.

Chung et al. [14] considered game theoretic fairness in a setting where n parties wish to toss a binary coin. They considered *perfect* fairness notions and coined them cooperative-strategy-proofness and maximin fairness, respectively. Below we give the natural approximate versions of these notions:

- *CSP-fairness:* we say that a leader election protocol achieves $(1 - \epsilon)$-cooperative-strategy-proofness against a (non-uniform p.p.t.) coalition $A \subset [n]$, iff no matter what (non-uniform p.p.t.) strategy A adopts, its expected utility is at most $\frac{|A|}{(1-\epsilon)n}$. We often write CSP-fairness in place of "cooperative strategy proofness" for short.
- *Maximin fairness:* we say that a leader election protocol achieves $(1 - \epsilon)$-maximin-fairness against a (non-uniform p.p.t.) coalition $A \subset [n]$, iff no matter what (non-uniform p.p.t.) strategy A adopts, any honest individual's expected utility is at least $(1 - \epsilon)/n$.

Approximate maximin-fairness and approximate CSP-fairness are not equivalent—we give more explanations in the online full version [15].

Remark 2 (Coalition-resistant notions of equilibrium). In our definitions, we consider the deviation of a single coalition. This definitional approach is standard in game theory [1–4,19–21,25,29,36,38], since the philosophy is to capture the notion of an approximate equilibrium in the sense that no coalition has noticeable incentives to deviate. Our equilibrium notion is coalition-resistant. In comparison, the standard notion of (approximate) Nash equilibrium typically considers deviation of a single player, and therefore is weaker than our notions in this sense.

Remark 3 (Choice of ϵ). In our formal results later, we will use $\epsilon = o(1)$—in fact, our result will be parametrized. For simplicity, in the informal roadmap, it helps to think of $\epsilon = 1\%$.

2.3 A Strawman Scheme

Although *in our final scheme we do NOT use random oracles* (RO), it is instructive to think about a strawman scheme with an RO. Interestingly, this approach is inspired by recent proof-of-stake consensus protocols [17,28].

Strawman: RO-based committee election + tournament tree

1. Every player $i \in [n]$ broadcasts a bit $x_i \in \{0,1\}$, and we use $\mathrm{RO}(x_1, \ldots, x_n)$ to elect committee of size $\log^9 n$. If a player i fails to post a bit, we treat $x_i := 0$.
2. The committee runs the tournament-tree protocol to elect a final leader.

One can easily show that this approach achieves $(1 - \epsilon)$-CSP-fairness against any coalition A containing *at least $\epsilon/2$ fraction of the players*—we call a coalition at least $\epsilon/2$ fraction in size a *large coalition*. The argument is as follows. Since the second step, i.e., tournament tree, is in some sense "ideal", to increase its expected utility, the coalition $A \subset [n]$ must include as many of its own members in the committee as possible. Suppose that $\epsilon = 1\%$. For a fixed RO query, the probability that it selects a *bad* committee, i.e., one with more than $\frac{|A|}{(1-\epsilon)\cdot n}$ fraction of coalition players, is negligibly small by the Chernoff bound. Since the coalition is computationally bounded and can make at most polynomially many queries to RO, by the union bound, except with negligible probability, all of its RO queries select a good committee.

Unfortunately, this scheme suffers from a couple serious flaws:

- *Drawback 1: NOT approximately maximin-fair:* a coalition A can harm an individual $i \notin A$ as follows: wait till everyone not in A broadcasts their bits, and then try different combinations of bits for those in A to find a combination that excludes the player i from the committee. This attack can succeed with $1 - o(1)$ probability if $|A| = \Theta(\log n)$.
- *Drawback 2: NOT approximately CSP-fair against a small coalition:* a profit-seeking individual i is incentivized to deviate in the following manner: i can

wait for everyone else to post bits before posting its own bit denoted x_i. In this way it can increase its advantage roughly by a factor of 2 since it can try two choices of x_i. This attack can be extended to work for small coalitions too.

The second drawback is somewhat surprising at first sight, since we proved the strawman scheme to be CSP-fair against large coalitions (i.e., at least $\epsilon/2$ fraction in size). The reason is because the Chernoff bound proof gives only statistical guarantees about a population, but does not give meaningful guarantees about an individual or a very small group of players.

Remark 4. In the above strawman, one can also replace the committee election with a single iteration of Feige's lightest bin protocol [20]. The resulting protocol would still be $(1 - \epsilon)$-CSP-fair, although it suffers from exactly the same drawbacks as the RO-based strawman. The upgrade techniques described in Sect. 2.4, however, is compatible only with the RO-based approach—and this is why we start with the RO-based approach. However, intriguingly, we will indeed make use of the lightest bin protocol later in Sect. 2.5 where we show how to get rid of the RO.

2.4   Warmup: A Game Theoretically Fair, RO-Based Protocol

We now discuss how to fix the two drawbacks in the previous strawman scheme. We will still have an RO in the resulting warmup scheme; however, in the immediate next subsection, we will discuss techniques for removing the RO, and obtain our final construction.

The first drawback is due to a potentially large coalition A choosing its coins (after examining honest coins) to exclude some individual $i \notin A$ from the committee. The second drawback is due to a small coalition A containing less than ϵ fraction of the players choosing its coins to help its members get included. To tackle these drawbacks, our idea is to introduce virtual identities henceforth called v-ids for short. Basically, we will use the RO to select a committee consisting of v-ids. When the RO's inputs are being jointly selected, we make sure that 1) a potentially large coalition A has no idea what each honest individual's v-id is and thus A has no idea which v-id to target; and 2) a small coalition has no idea what its own v-ids are, and thus it has no idea which v-ids to help.

To achieve this, each player i's final v-id will be the xor of two shares: a share chosen by the player itself henceforth called the *unmasked* v-id, and a share jointly chosen by a special, honest-majority protocol, henceforth called the *mask*. In the beginning, the player itself commits to its own unmasked v-id, and the MPC protocol jointly commits to each player's mask. Next, the players jointly choose the inputs to the RO. Finally, each player reveals its own unmasked v-id, and then the MPC protocol reconstructs all players' masks.

Special honest-majority MPC. Instantiating these ideas correctly, however, turns out to be rather subtle. A generic honest-majority MPC protocol does not guarantee anything when there is a large coalition. In our case, when the coalition is large, it can fully control the mask value. However, we do need that even with $(1 - \epsilon)n$-sized coalitions, the mask value must be uniquely determined at the end of the sharing phase, and reconstruction is guaranteed. More specifically, we want our special, honest-majority MPC to satisfy the following properties for some small $\eta \in (0, 1)$ (think of $\eta = \epsilon/2$):

- If $|A| \le \eta n$, we want that at the end of this sharing phase, A has no idea what its own masks are;
- As long as $|A| < (1 - 2\eta)n$, at the end of the sharing phase, the mask value to be reconstructed is uniquely determined, and moreover, reconstruction is guaranteed to be successful.

The following $\mathcal{F}^{\eta}_{\mathrm{mpc}}$ ideal functionality describes what we need from the honest-majority MPC. For simplicity, in our informal overview, we will describe our protocols assuming the existence of this $\mathcal{F}^{\eta}_{\mathrm{mpc}}$ ideal functionality. Later in Sect. 4.2, we will instantiate it with an actual, constant-round cryptographic protocol using bounded concurrent MPC techniques [32]. Technically, the real-world cryptographic instantiation does not securely emulate $\mathcal{F}_{\mathrm{mpc}}$ by a standard simulation-based notion; nonetheless, we prove in the online full version [15] that the fairness properties we care about in the ideal-world protocol (using idealized cryptography) extend to the real-world protocol (using actual cryptography).

$\mathcal{F}^{\eta}_{\mathrm{mpc}}$: special, honest-majority MPC functionality

Sharing phase. Upon receiving **share** from all honest players, choose a random string coins. If the coalition size $|A| \ge \eta n$, the adversary is asked to overwrite the variable coins to any value of its choice. Send **ok** to all honest players.

Reconstruction phase. Upon receiving **recons** from all honest players: if $|A| \ge (1 - 2\eta)n$, the adversary may, at this point, overwrite the string coins to its choice. Afterwards, in any case, send coins to all honest players.

Our warmup RO-based protocol. Now, it helps to describe our protocol first, then we explain the additional subtleties. We describe our warmup protocol using an idealized commitment scheme, as well as the $\mathcal{F}_{\mathrm{mpc}}$ functionality described earlier.

Our warmup RO-based protocol

1. Every player $i \in [n]$ commits to a randomly selected unmasked v-id $y_i \in \{0, 1\}^v$ where $2^v = n \cdot \mathrm{poly} \log n$.
2. Send **share** to $\mathcal{F}^{\epsilon/2}_{\mathrm{mpc}}$ and receive **ok** from $\mathcal{F}_{\mathrm{mpc}}$.
3. Every player $i \in [n]$ broadcasts a bit x_i. Let x be the concatenation of all of $\{x_i\}_{i \in [n]}$ in increasing order of the players' indices—here for any player j who has aborted, its x_j is treated as 0.
4. Every player $i \in [n]$ now opens its committed unmasked v-id $y_i \in \{0, 1\}^v$.

5. All honest players send recons to $\mathcal{F}_{\mathrm{mpc}}^{\epsilon/2}$, and they each receive a mask vector z from $\mathcal{F}_{\mathrm{mpc}}^{\epsilon/2}$.
6. Parse $z := (z_1, \ldots, z_n)$ where each $z_j \in \{0,1\}^v$ for $j \in [n]$. We now view $y_i \oplus z_i$ player i's final v-id. A player i is a member of the committee $\mathcal{C}$ iff 1) it correctly committed and opened its unmasked v-id y_i; 2) its final v-id $y_i \oplus z_i$ is chosen by $RO(\mathbf{x})$; and 3) its final v-id $y_i \oplus z_i$ does not collide with anyone else's final v-id—we may assume that anyone who aborted has the final v-id $\bot$.
7. The committee $\mathcal{C}$ runs the tournament-tree protocol to elect a leader.

Additional subtleties. At this moment, it helps to point out a few additional subtleties.

1. *Unique reconstruction even under a majority coalition.* First, recall that even in the presence of a $(1-\epsilon)$-coalition, we wanted our $\mathcal{F}_{\mathrm{mpc}}$ to guarantee uniqueness of the reconstructed mask z at the end of the sharing phase. This is important because we do not want the coalition to see the RO's outputs and then choose the mask vector z a-posteriori to exclude some honest individual from the final committee or to include all of the coalition members.
2. *The need for collision detection.* Second, notice that the protocol prevents colliding final v-ids from being elected into the final committee. Such a collision detection mechanism is necessary since otherwise, the following attack would be possible[4]: a 99% coalition can make all of its members choose the same final v-id—it can do that because it controls its members' unmasked v-ids as well as the mask value. Now, the 99% coalition can choose its input bits to the RO to help this particular final v-id. In this way, with high probability, all coalition members can be elected into the final committee.
3. *Proving sequential approximate fairness.* Last but not the least, so far we have only focused on the non-sequential notion of fairness, and it turns out that proving the sequential notion is much more subtle. In our formal proofs later (see Sect. 5 and the online full version [15]), we will do a round-by-round argument to show that except with negligible probability, in no round of the protocol would the coalition have noticeable incentive to deviate.

Since this warmup construction is not our final scheme, we will not formally prove the warmup construction. Instead, we now explain how to get rid of the RO to get our final scheme.

2.5   Final Construction: Removing the Random Oracle

To remove the RO, our idea is to replace the committee election with a two-phase approach, where the first phase uses a single iteration of Feige's lightest-bin protocol [20] and the second phase uses a combinatorial object called a

---

[4] We describe this attack for illustration purposes to help understanding. Of course, we will later prove our final construction secure against all possible p.p.t. coalition strategies.

sampler [37] in place of the RO. We briefly describe the intuition below. The actual scheme, calculations, and proofs are more involved especially for getting the more general, parametrized result, and we defer the full description to the subsequent formal sections.

Background. We will rely on a combinatorial object called a *sampler* which is known to be equivalent to a seeded extractor [37][5]. A sampler, denoted as Samp, is a combinatorial object with the following syntax and properties: given an input $x \in \{0,1\}^u$, Samp(x) returns d sample points $z_1, \ldots, z_d \in \{0,1\}^v$ from its output space. A sampler is supposed to have good, random-sampling-like properties. Consider a predicate function $f : \{0,1\}^v \to \{0,1\}$. The *population mean* of f over its inputs is defined as is $\frac{1}{2^v} \sum_{z \in \{0,1\}^v} f(z)$. The d sample points define a *sample mean* $\frac{1}{d} \sum_{j=1}^{d} f(z_j)$, which ideally should be close to the population mean. An (ϵ_s, δ_s)-averaging sampler Samp guarantees that for any f, at least a $1 - \delta_s$ fraction of the inputs will lead to a sample mean that differs from the population mean by at most ϵ_s additively.

Intuition. A flawed idea is to directly replace the RO in the warmup scheme with a sampler. To do so, the nature of our proof for this specific step will have to change: in the warmup scheme, we relied on the fact that the coalition can make only polynomially many queries to RO in our fairness proof. With a sampler, however, we must make a combinatorial argument here that does not depend on the adversary's computational bounds (although to reason about other parts of the scheme involving the commitment and the MPC, we still need to make computational assumptions on the adversarial coalition). Specifically, we want to argue that no matter which subset of players form a coalition, as long as the coalition's size is, say, between $0.01n$ and $0.99n$, then almost all honest inputs x_H *resist even the worst-case attack*, in the sense that there does not exist a x_A such that $x = (x_H, x_A)$ would form a bad input to Samp[6]. Here x is said to be a bad input to Samp if Samp(x) selects a committee in which the fraction of coalition players is noticeably higher than $|A|/n$.

Suppose that we want to select a $\log^9 n$-sized committee, and the final v-id space is of size $n \log^3 n$. In this case, we would need the sampler to select roughly $d = \log^{12} n$ output points. A calculation using the probabilistic method suggests that in this case, we cannot start with n players who jointly select the input to the sampler—if so, there would simply be too many combinations the adversarial coalition could try for its own input bits; and the number of bad inputs to the sampler simply is not sparse enough to defeat so many adversarial combinations.

The parameters would work out, however, if we start out with, say, $\log^3 n$ players who jointly choose the input to the sampler. In our subsequent formal sections, we will select parameters that work with the best known explicit sampler construction [27, 34, 37].

---

[5] We stress that our construction does not need a common reference string as the seed.

[6] Throughout the paper, for $S \subseteq [n]$, we use $x_S := \{x_i\}_{i \in S}$ to denote the coordinates of the vector x corresponding to all players in S.

Our idea. Given the above intuition, our idea is to adopt a *two-phase committee election* approach. We first down-select to a preliminary committee of size $\log^3 n$, and then the preliminary committee jointly choose input bits to a sampler to select a *final committee* among *all* players, and the final committee runs the tournament tree protocol to elect a leader among the final committee. We sketch the protocol below while deferring a more formal description to Sect. 4:

- *Commitment phase.* As before, players commit to their unmasked v-ids and use an honest-majority MPC to jointly commit to a mask first.
- *Preliminary committee election.* First, we elect a $\log^3 n$-sized *preliminary committee* such that the fraction of honest players on the preliminary committee approximately matches the fraction of honest players in the overall population. Here we do not care about the threat where a potentially large coalition seek to exclude a specific individual or a small coalition or individual try to include itself. It turns out that this can be accomplished by running a single iteration of Feige's elegant lightest bin protocol [20] in the plain model.
- *Final committee election.* Next, the preliminary committee jointly selects an input to the sampler, which is used to select $\log^9 n$ final v-ids among the space of all possible v-ids—these final v-ids would form the *final* committee. At this moment, the players open their unmasked v-ids, and reconstruct the mask that was secret shared earlier by the MPC. The players' final v-ids are now revealed, and the final committee determined.
- *Leader election.* Finally, the elected, poly-logarithmically sized final committee runs the tournament-tree protocol to elect a final leader.

3   Defining Sequential Approximate Fairness

3.1   Sequential Approximate Fairness

The non-sequential fairness notions mentioned in Sect. 2.2 does not rule out some undesirable protocols that may offer incentives for a coalition to deviate with non-negligible probability. Recall the example given in Sect. 1 where two parties run Blum's coin toss except that with some small ϵ probability, Bob broadcasts all its private coins in the first round. If the small (but non-negligible) probability bad event happens, Alice should deviate and choose her coins to definitively win. However, *a-priori* Alice does not have much incentive to deviate: since the bad event happens with only ϵ probability, her a-priori probability if winning is at most $\epsilon \cdot 1 + (1 - \epsilon) \cdot \frac{1}{2} = (1 + \epsilon) \cdot \frac{1}{2}$, and this is only an ϵ fraction more than her fair share. Nonetheless, we do want to rule out such bad protocols since such a protocol has a non-negligible probability ϵ of creating incentives for Alice to deviate.

We propose a better solution concept called sequential approximate fairness. Roughly speaking, we require that even if the coalition is allowed to re-evaluate whether to deviate at the beginning of every round in the protocol, except with negligible probability, no p.p.t. coalition (of size at most $(1 - \epsilon)n$) should have ϵ incentive to deviate at any time.

When we try to formalize this notion of sequential rationality, we encounter another subtlety: since our protocols will rely on cryptographic commitment schemes, our definitions should capture the fact that the coalition is polynomially bounded. For example, it could be that there *exists* a set of execution prefixes that account for non-negligible probability mass, such that if A deviated conditioned on having observed those prefixes, it would have gained noticeably. However, it might be that these prefixes are computationally infeasible to recognize, since recognizing them might involve, say, breaking cryptographic commitments. As a result, our definitions actually stipulate that, for any *polynomially bounded* coalition strategy that *wants to deviate with non-negligible probability* at some point in the execution, deviating will not *conditionally* improve the coalition's utility by more than a noticeable amount.

To formally define our sequentially approximately fair notions, we first introduce some probability notations.

Probability notation. In this paper, we use the acronym p.p.t. to mean expected probabilistic polynomial-time. Let Π denote the original honest protocol. However, a non-uniform p.p.t. coalition $A \subset [n]$ might deviate from the original protocol and we use S to denote the strategy of A. As a special case, we use the notation $A(\Pi)$ to mean that the coalition A simply follows the honest protocol and does not deviate. Let κ be the security parameter. We use the notation $tr \leftarrow \mathsf{Exec}^{A(S)}$ to denote a random sample of the protocol execution, where the honest players $[n]\backslash A$, interact with the coalition A which adopts the strategy S. The random experiment $\mathsf{Exec}^{A(S)}$ produces an *execution trace tr* (also called a *trace* for short), which consists of all the messages and the internal states of all players throughout the entire execution. Once the coalition A's strategy S is fixed, all players' internal states and messages in all rounds would be uniquely determined by all players' randomness in all rounds—thus one can also equivalently think of tr as the sequence of *all* players' random coins in all rounds.

An event $\mathsf{Evt}(tr)$ is identified with its indicator function that takes a trace tr and returns either 1 (meaning the event happens) or 0. For example, we use $W^A(tr) = 1$ to indicate that one player in A is elected as the leader in the end.

We use $\Pr[\mathsf{Exec}^{A(S)}(1^\kappa) : \mathsf{Evt}] := \Pr[tr \leftarrow \mathsf{Exec}^{\Pi,A(S)}(1^\kappa) : \mathsf{Evt}(tr)]$ to denote the probability that when the coalition A adopts strategy S, the event Evt happens. Similarly, given events Evt_1 and Evt_2, we use $\Pr[\mathsf{Exec}^{A(S)}(1^\kappa) : \mathsf{Evt}_1 \mid \mathsf{Evt}_2]$ to denote the conditional probability that when the coalition A adopts strategy S and conditioning on the event Evt_2, event Evt_1 also happens. The same notation extends to expectation $\mathbf{E}[\cdot]$.

Deviation event. Given a strategy S of the coalition A, we define the deviation event $\mathsf{Dev}^{A(S)}(tr)$ as follows:

- for each round $r = 1, 2, \ldots$: replay the trace tr (which contains all players' random coins) till the beginning of round r, immediately after the coalition A has observed all honest nodes' round-r messages; at this moment, check whether the strategy S adopted by A would deviate from the honest protocol

Π in round r (i.e., whether S would send a message that differs from what the honest strategy would have sent, suppose that the random coins of S have been fixed by the trace tr); if yes, return 1;
– return 0 if the strategy S adopted by A does not actually deviate from Π till the end.

Intuitively, we say that a protocol satisfies sequential CSP-fairness against the coalition A iff either A never wants to deviate except with negligible probability (condition 1 in Definition 1); or conditioned on deviating, A does not do noticeably better (condition 2 in Definition 1).

Definition 1 (Sequential CSP-fairness). *Let $\epsilon \in (0,1)$. We say that a leader election protocol Π achieves $(1 - \epsilon)$-sequential-CSP-fairness against a (non-uniform p.p.t.) coalition $A \subseteq [n]$ iff for any strategy S by A, there exist a negligible function $\mathsf{negl}(\cdot)$, such that and for all κ, at least one of the following holds—recall that W^A is the event that one of the coalition members in A is elected leader:*

1. $\Pr\left[\mathsf{Exec}^{A(S)}(1^\kappa) : \mathsf{Dev}^{A(S)}\right] \leq \mathsf{negl}(\kappa),$
2. $\Pr\left[\mathsf{Exec}^{A(S)}(1^\kappa) : W^A \mid \mathsf{Dev}^{A(S)}\right] \leq \frac{1}{1-\epsilon} \cdot \Pr\left[\mathsf{Exec}^{A(\Pi)}(1^\kappa) : W^A \mid \mathsf{Dev}^{A(S)}\right] + \mathsf{negl}(\kappa).$

In the above, the left-hand-side $\Pr\left[\mathsf{Exec}^{A(S)}(1^\kappa) : W^A \mid \mathsf{Dev}^{A(S)}\right]$ means the conditional probability that $A(S)$, i.e., a coalition A adopting strategy S, is elected leader, conditioned on $\mathsf{Dev}^{A(S)}$, i.e., that $A(S)$ decided to deviate from honest behavior. The right-hand-side $\Pr\left[\mathsf{Exec}^{A(\Pi)}(1^\kappa) : W^A \mid \mathsf{Dev}^{A(S)}\right]$ means *the conditional probability for A to win, had A continued to adopt the honest strategy throughout, even though $A(S)$ had wanted to deviate at some point in the protocol*—the conditional probability is calculated when conditioning on traces where $A(S)$ would have deviated[7]. Intuitively, Condition 2 above says that conditioned on the strategy S deciding to deviate, the coalition A cannot benefit itself noticeably in comparison with just executing honestly to the end.

We can similarly define the sequential approximate maximin fairness.

Definition 2 (Sequential maximin fairness). *Let $\epsilon \in (0,1)$. We say that a leader election protocol Π achieves $(1-\epsilon)$-sequential-maximin-fairness against a (non-uniform p.p.t.) coalition $A \subseteq [n]$ iff for any strategy S by A, there exist a negligible function $\mathsf{negl}(\cdot)$, such that for all κ, at least one of the following holds:*

---

[7] Note that the event $\mathsf{Dev}^{A(S)}(tr)$ is well-defined, even if tr is sampled from $\mathsf{Exec}^{A(\Pi)}$, i.e., an execution in which A adopts the honest strategy. In this case, $\mathsf{Dev}^{A(S)}(tr)$ means the following: had A instead adopted the strategy S rather than the honest strategy Π, is there a round in which S would have started to deviate from the honest protocol, given that all players' randomness in all rounds is fixed by tr.

1. $\Pr\left[\mathsf{Exec}^{A(S)}(1^{\kappa}) : \mathsf{Dev}^{A(S)}\right] \leq \mathsf{negl}(\kappa),$

2. *for any $i \notin A$, let W^i be the event that player i is elected as the leader, it holds that*

$$\Pr\left[\mathsf{Exec}^{A(S)}(1^{\kappa}) : W^i \mid \mathsf{Dev}^{A(S)}\right] \geq (1-\epsilon) \cdot \Pr\left[\mathsf{Exec}^{A(\Pi)}(1^{\kappa}) : W^i \mid \mathsf{Dev}^{A(S)}\right] - \mathsf{negl}(\kappa).$$

The following fact says that the sequentially rational notions implies the corresponding non-sequential counterparts defined earlier in Sect. 2.2.

Fact 1 (Sequential notions are stronger). *Let $\epsilon(n, \kappa) \in (0,1)$ be a nonnegligible function. If a leader election protocol satisfies $(1 - \epsilon)$-sequential-CSP-fairness (or $(1 - \epsilon)$-sequential-maximin-fairness resp.) against the coalition $A \subseteq [n]$, then for $\epsilon'(n, \kappa) = \epsilon(n, \kappa) + \mathsf{negl}(\kappa)$ where $\mathsf{negl}(\cdot)$ is some negligible function, then, the same protocol also satisfies non-sequential $(1 - \epsilon')$-CSP-fairness (or non-sequential $(1 - \epsilon')$-maximin-fairness resp.) against A.*

Proof. Deferred to the online full version [15].

We show that if the slack ϵ is constrained to being negligibly small, then in fact the non-sequential notions imply the sequential notions too. However, this direction is not true when the slack ϵ may be non-negligible.

Fact 2. *If a protocol Π satisfies $(1 - \mathsf{negl}(\kappa))$-CSP-fairness (or $(1 - \mathsf{negl}(\kappa))$-maximin-fairness resp.) against the coalition $A \subset [n]$ for some negligible function $\mathsf{negl}(\cdot)$, then Π satisfies $(1 - \mathsf{negl}'(\kappa))$-sequential-CSP-fairness (or $(1 - \mathsf{negl}(\kappa))$-sequential-maximin-fairness resp.) against A for some negligible function $\mathsf{negl}'(\cdot)$.*

Proof. Deferred to the online full version [15].

3.2   Fairness of the Tournament Tree Protocol

Instantiated with a suitable cryptographic commitment protocol (described in the online full version [15]), the folklore tournament-tree protocol satisfies $(1 - \mathsf{negl}(\kappa))$-sequential-CSP-fairness and $(1 - \mathsf{negl}(\kappa))$-sequential-maximin-fairness against coalitions of arbitrarily sizes, as stated below:

Theorem 3 (Tournament-tree protocol). *Suppose that n is the number of players and κ is the security parameter. Then, the tournament-tree protocol, when instantiated with a suitable publicly verifiable, non-malleable commitment scheme as defined in the online full version [15], satisfies $(1 - \mathsf{negl}(\kappa))$-sequential-CSP-fairness and $(1 - \mathsf{negl}(\kappa))$-sequential-maximin-fairness against coalitions of arbitrarily sizes. Moreover, the number of rounds is $O(\log n)$.*

Proof. Deferred to the online full version [15].

4   Formal Description of Our Scheme

4.1   Description of Our Scheme Assuming Idealized Cryptography

Our scheme makes use of an (ϵ_s, δ_s)-averaging sampler which we define in the online full version [15]. We will first describe our scheme assuming idealized commitments $\mathcal{F}_{\text{comm}}$ and an ideal MPC functionality $\mathcal{F}_{\text{mpc}}$ described earlier in Sect. 2.4. Later in Sect. 4.2, we will instantiate the ideal cryptographic primitives with actual cryptography. In the scheme below, committing to a value is performed by sending it to $\mathcal{F}_{\text{comm}}$, and opening is performed by instructing $\mathcal{F}_{\text{comm}}$ to send the opening to everyone.

Our leader election protocol (assuming idealized cryptography)

Parameters. For some $r := r(n)$, suppose that we would like to achieve round complexity $O(r)$ satisfying $C_0 \log \log n < r(n) < C_1 \log n$, where C_0 and C_1 are suitable constants. We set the parameters as follows:

- Let $B := \frac{n}{2^{9r}}$ such that the expected number of players in a bin (assuming honest behavior) is $\frac{n}{B} = 2^{9r}$ in the preliminary committee election.
- The parameters of the sampler are chosen as below: v is chosen such that $\frac{2^v}{n} = 2^{0.5r}$. Let $\epsilon_s := 2^{-6r}$, and $\delta_s := 2^{-(1-\frac{\psi}{2})|\mathcal{U}|}$, where ψ denotes a lower bound on the fraction of honest players, we shall assume $\psi \geq \frac{1}{2^{\Theta(r)}}$, which means that $|A| \leq (1 - \frac{1}{2^{\Theta(r)}})n$. Let $d = (|\mathcal{U}|/\epsilon_s)^{\tilde{c}}$, where $\tilde{c}$ is the universal constant specified in the online full version [15].
- Let $\eta := 1/2^{0.2r}$.

Our protocol.

1. *Elect the preliminary committee $\mathcal{U}$ using lightest bin.* Everyone $i \in [n]$ broadcasts a random index $\beta_i \in [B]$ indicating its choice of bin where B denotes the number of bins. The bin with the lightest load is selected as the preliminary committee $\mathcal{U}$. Break ties with lexicographically the smallest bin.
2. *Elect the final committee $\mathcal{C}$.* Let $\text{Samp} : \{0,1\}^{|\mathcal{U}|} \to \{\{0,1\}^v\}^d$ denote an explicit (ϵ_s, δ_s)-averaging sampler. If it is not the case that $|\mathcal{U}| \geq \log \frac{1}{\delta_s} + c \cdot v$ (see the online full version [15]), simply abort with the exception param_error and output player 1 as the leader.
   (a) Every player sends **share** to $\mathcal{F}^\eta_{\text{mpc}}$, and receives **ok** from $\mathcal{F}^\eta_{\text{mpc}}$.
   (b) Every player $i \in [n]$ commits to a randomly selected unmasked v-id henceforth denoted $y_i \in \{0,1\}^v$.
   (c) Every player in the preliminary committee $i \in \mathcal{U}$ broadcasts a bit x_i. Let x be the concatenation of all of $\{x_i\}_{i \in \mathcal{U}}$ in increasing order of the players' indices—here for any player j who has aborted, its x_j is treated as 0.
   (d) Every player $i \in [n]$ now opens the committed string $y_i \in \{0,1\}^v$.

(e) Input **recons** to $\mathcal{F}_{\mathrm{mpc}}^{\eta}$, and receive a mask vector z from $\mathcal{F}_{\mathrm{mpc}}^{\eta}$.

(f) Parse $z := (z_1, \ldots, z_n)$ where each $z_j \in \{0,1\}^v$ for $j \in [n]$. We now view $y_i \oplus z_i$ as player i's finalized v-id, which corresponds to a point in the output range of the sampler Samp. The final committee $\mathcal{C}$ is defined as a *multiset* constructed as follows: for $j \in [d]$, if there is exactly one player $i \in [n]$ who opened y_i and whose final v-id $y_i \oplus z_i = \mathsf{Samp}_j(x)$, then add i to $\mathcal{C}$.

3. *Elect leader among final committee.* The final committee run the tournament-tree protocol to elect a final leader.[a] In case the final committee is empty, simply output player 1 as the leader.

---

[a] When the ideal $\mathcal{F}_{\mathrm{comm}}$ and $\mathcal{F}_{\mathrm{mpc}}^{\eta}$ are instantiated with actual cryptography later in Sect. 4.2, the opening/reconstruction messages will be posted to the broadcast channel such that the elected leader can be determined from the collection of messages posted to the broadcast channel.

4.2 Instantiating the Scheme with Real-World Cryptography

Our final protocol replaces the ideal commitment and $\mathcal{F}_{\mathrm{mpc}}$ with actual cryptography. To achieve this, we take an intermediate step and consider an **IdealZK**-hybrid protocol where **IdealZK** is an idealized zero-knowledge proof functionality which we formally define in the online full version [15]. We first instantiate the ideal commitment and $\mathcal{F}_{\mathrm{mpc}}$ using a protocol in the **IdealZK**-hybrid world, and then we use the elegant techniques of Pass [32] to instantiate the protocol with actual cryptography with only $O(1)$ round blowup, while allowing bounded concurrent composition *without any common reference string or trusted setup*. In our case, the total number of concurrent sessions of the cryptographic protocols is a-priori known given n.

Instantiating the ideal commitments with non-malleable commitments. We will instantiate the ideal commitments using a publicly verifiable, non-malleable commitment (NMC) scheme which is defined in the online full version [15]. Basically, to commit to a string, a player invokes n instances of NMC, one for each of the n recipients. To open a previously committed string, post the openings corresponding to all n instances, and the opening is successful iff all n instances open to the same string. We may assume that messages are posted to the broadcast channel and it can be publicly checked what a commitment opens to. An honest committer's commitment will always successfully open even when the receiver is malicious.

Instantiating the $\mathcal{F}_{\mathrm{mpc}}$ with bounded concurrent zero-knowledge proofs. To instantiate $\mathcal{F}_{\mathrm{mpc}}$ with actual cryptography, we first instantiate it in **IdealZK**-hybrid world. Then, we use the bounded concurrent zero-knowledge proofs of Pass [32] to replace the **IdealZK** instances with actual zero-knowledge proofs.

Therefore, it suffices to describe how to replace $\mathcal{F}_{\mathrm{mpc}}$ with a protocol Π_{mpc} in the **IdealZK**-hybrid world. This protocol actually does not realize $\mathcal{F}_{\mathrm{mpc}}$ with full simulation security[8]. Yet, we can later prove that when we replace $\mathcal{F}_{\mathrm{mpc}}$ with this protocol, the game theoretic fairness properties we care about extend to the real-world protocol.

Π_{mpc}: **instantiating $\mathcal{F}_{\mathrm{mpc}}^{\eta}$ in the IdealZK-hybrid world**

Let comm be a perfectly binding and computationally hiding (non-interactive) commitment scheme. We assume that committing to a string is accomplished by committing to each individual bit. Let $\eta \in (0,1)$ be a parameter.

Sharing phase.

1. Every player i chooses a random string $\mathsf{coins}_i \in \{0,1\}^{vn}$. It splits coins_i into a $\lceil \eta \cdot n \rceil$-out-of-$n$ Shamir secret shares, and let $\mathsf{coins}_{i,j}$ be the j-th share. Next, for each $j \in [n]$, player i computes the commitment $\overline{\mathsf{coins}}_{i,j} := \mathsf{comm}(\mathsf{coins}_{i,j}, \rho_{i,j})$ where $\rho_{i,j}$ denotes some fresh randomess consumed by the commitment scheme, and it posts the commitment message $\{\overline{\mathsf{coins}}_{i,j}\}_{j \in [n]}$ to the broadcast channel.

2. Player i does the following for each $j \in [n]$:
   - invokes an **IdealZK** instance denoted **IdealZK**$_{i,j}$ to prove that the commitment message $\{\overline{\mathsf{coins}}_{i,k}\}_{k \in [n]}$ it has posted is computed correctly, by supplying to **IdealZK**$_{i,j}$ 1) the statement $\{\overline{\mathsf{coins}}_{i,k}\}_{k \in [n]}$ and 2) all the random coins used in computing the commitment message. **IdealZK**$_{i,j}$ checks the following NP relation: all the commitments are computed correctly, and moreover, the openings form a valid $\lceil \eta n \rceil$-out-of-n secret sharing.
   - gives player j the opening $(\mathsf{coins}_{i,j}, \rho_{i,j})$.

3. A player $i \in [n]$ does the following: for every $j \in [n]$, if player i
   - has seen a message $\{\overline{\mathsf{coins}}_{j,k}\}_{k \in [n]}$ posted by j;
   - has received the message $(\{\overline{\mathsf{coins}}_{j,k}\}_{k \in [n]}, 1)$ from **IdealZK**$_{j,i}$ where the statement must match the message posted by j; and
   - has received a correct opening $(\mathsf{coins}_{j,i}, \rho_{j,i})$ w.r.t. the i-th coordinate of j's posted message $\{\overline{\mathsf{coins}}_{j,k}\}_{k \in [n]}$, that is, $\overline{\mathsf{coins}}_{j,i}$.

   then, it posts the tuple (ok, j) to the broadcast channel.

4. Every player i does the following: for every $j \in [n]$ who has obtained an approval message ok from at least $(1 - \eta)n$ players, add j to the set S. If $|S| \geq \eta n$, then let $\mathsf{succ} := 1$; else let $\mathsf{succ} := 0$. Output ok.

Reconstruction phase. If $\mathsf{succ} = 0$, simply output the **0** vector. Else continue with the following.

---

[8] The reason we do not fully simulate $\mathcal{F}_{\mathrm{mpc}}$ is due to technicalities arising from the requirement that the outcome of the leader election be publicly computable from all the messages posted to the broadcast channel.

1. For every player $j \in S$, if the current player i posted (ok, j) during the sharing phase, then let $(\text{coins}_{j,i}, \rho_{j,i})$ be the correct opening received from j during the sharing phase, post $(j, \text{coins}_{j,i}, \rho_{j,i})$ to the broadcast channel.
2. For every tuple $(j, \text{coins}_{j,k}, \rho_{j,k})$ received from some player $k \in [n]$, if $j \in S$ and $(\text{coins}_{j,k}, \rho_{j,k})$ is a valid opening w.r.t. the k-th coordinate of j's commitment message posted during the sharing phase, then accept this share $(k, \text{coins}_{j,k})$ of coins_j.

   For every $j \in S$, use all accepted shares to reconstruct coins_j. Output $z := \bigoplus_{j \in S} \text{coins}_j$ if the reconstruction of every coins_j for $j \in S$ is successful; else output the vector $\mathbf{0}$.

Theorem 4 (Main theorem). *Assume the existence of enhanced trapdoor permutations and collision resistant hash functions. Then, there exists an $O(r)$-round leader election protocol that achieves $(1 - 2^{-\Theta(r)})$-sequential-maximin-fairness against a non-uniform p.p.t. coalition of size at most $(1 - 2^{-\Theta(r)}) \cdot n$, and $(1 - 2^{-\Theta(r)})$-sequential-CSP-fairness against a non-uniform p.p.t. coalition of arbitrary size.*

Proof. The theorem results from the construction presented in this section. The detailed proofs are presented in Sect. 5 and the online full version [15]. □

5 Proofs for the Ideal-World Protocol

5.1 Bounding the Preliminary Committee's Size

Since the preliminary committee $\mathcal{U}$ is chosen from a lightest bin, it is immediate that $|\mathcal{U}| \leq \lfloor \frac{n}{B} \rfloor$. The next lemma states that there is a sufficient number of honest players in $\mathcal{U}$ with high probability.

Lemma 1 (Sufficient honest players in the preliminary committee). *Suppose for some $\psi \in (0, 0.5)$, there are at least $\psi \cdot n$ honest players. Let $|\mathcal{U}_H|$ denote the number of honest players in the preliminary committee $\mathcal{U}$. Then, for $\gamma \in (0, 1)$, the following holds:*

$$\Pr\left[|\mathcal{U}_H| \leq (1 - \gamma) \cdot \frac{\psi n}{B}\right] \leq B \cdot \exp\left(-\gamma^2 \cdot \frac{\psi n}{2B}\right).$$

In particular, if $\frac{n}{B} = 2^{9r}$ and $C_0 \log \log n \leq r \leq C_1 \log \log n$ for appropriate constants C_0 and C_1, and $\psi \geq 2^{-r}$, then the number of honest players in the preliminary committee is at least $0.9 \psi n / B$, except with $\exp(-2^{7r})$ probability.

Proof. By the Chernoff bound, except with probability $\exp\left(-\gamma^2 \cdot \frac{\psi n}{2B}\right)$, the number of honest players in any particular bin is greater than $(1 - \gamma) \cdot \frac{\psi n}{B}$. The union bound over all the B bins gives the required result.

The following fact makes sure that the sampler needed by our protocol exists except with doubly-exponentially small in r probability as long as at least a $\psi(n) \geq 1/2^r$ fraction of the players are honest.

Fact 3. *Suppose that the honest fraction $\psi \geq \frac{1}{2^r}$ and that our protocol uses the aforementioned parameters. We have that $|\mathcal{U}| \geq \log(1/\delta_s) + c \cdot v$ except with $\exp(-\Omega(2^{7r}))$ probability.*

Proof. Since we choose $\delta_s := 2^{-(1-\frac{\psi}{2})|\mathcal{U}|}$, the expression to verify can be rewritten as $|\mathcal{U}| \geq (1 - \psi/2)|\mathcal{U}| + c \cdot v$, which is equivalent to:

$$0.5\psi \cdot |\mathcal{U}| \geq c \cdot v = c \cdot (\log n + 0.5r).$$

Due to Lemma 1, the size of the preliminary committee is at least $\frac{0.9\psi n}{B}$, except $\exp(-\Omega(2^{7r}))$ probability. Therefore, it suffices to show that

$$0.5\psi \cdot 0.9\psi n/B \geq 0.45 \cdot 2^{-2r} \cdot 2^{9r} \geq c \cdot (\log n + 0.5r),$$

where the last inequality holds as long as $r \geq C_0 \log\log n$ for a sufficiently large constant C_0.

5.2   Terminology and Notations

We first present proofs for our protocol in Sect. 4 assuming idealized $\mathcal{F}_{comm}$ and $\mathcal{F}_{mpc}$. However, we shall assume that the tournament-tree protocol is instantiated with real cryptography as explained in the online full version [15], since we will use the tournament-tree protocol's fairness properties as a blackbox in our proofs. In the online full version [15], we prove that the relevant security properties extend to the real-world protocol when the idealized cryptographic primitives are instantiated with actual cryptography.

Recall that A denotes the coalition; we often refer to players in A as corrupt and players outside A as honest. Further, we often use the notation $H := [n]\backslash A$ to denote the set of honest players. For $S \subseteq [n]$, we use the notation $x_S := \{x_i\}_{i \in S}$ and y_S is also similarly defined.

5.3   Composition of the Final Committee

Lemma 2 (Final committee composition). *Suppose that the honest fraction $\psi \geq 2\eta = 2 \cdot \frac{1}{2^{0.2r}}$ and that our protocol uses the aforementioned parameters. Fix $\mathcal{N}$ to be an arbitrary set of (distinct) final v-ids in the sampler's output range $\{0,1\}^v$ where $|\mathcal{N}| \leq n$. Let $\mathcal{C}_\mathcal{N}$ be the (multi-)set of final v-ids in $\mathcal{N}$ chosen by $\mathsf{Samp}(x)$. Let[9] $\epsilon_0 = \epsilon_s \cdot \frac{2^v}{|\mathcal{N}|}$. Then, conditioned on no param_error and $|\mathcal{U}_H| \geq 0.9\psi \cdot n/B$, with probability at least $1 - \exp(-\Omega(2^{7r}))$ over the choice of x_H, $\mathcal{C}_\mathcal{N}$ has size in the range $[1 - \epsilon_0, 1 + \epsilon_0] \cdot d \cdot \frac{|\mathcal{N}|}{2^v}$.*

---

[9] Note that ϵ_0 would be very large if $\mathcal{N}$ is too tiny, but our usage later will guarantee that $\mathcal{N}$ is not too tiny.

Alternatively, suppose there is some upper bound $|\mathcal{N}| \leq N$, and we set $\epsilon_0 = \epsilon_s \cdot \frac{2^v}{N}$. Then, with conditional probability at least $1 - \exp(-\Omega(2^{7r}))$ under the events, $\mathcal{C}_\mathcal{N}$ has size at most $(1 + \epsilon_0) \cdot d \cdot \frac{N}{2^v}$.

Proof. Let the final committee $\mathcal{C}_\mathcal{N}$ be the multi-set of v-ids in $\mathcal{N}$ chosen by the $\mathsf{Samp}(x)$. We shall show that, using the sampler theorem in the online full version [15], except with probability $p := \exp(-\Omega(2^{6r}))$ over the choice of x_H,

$$|\mathcal{C}_\mathcal{N}| \in [1 - \epsilon_0, 1 + \epsilon_0] \cdot d \cdot \frac{|\mathcal{N}|}{2^v}. \tag{1}$$

Observing that $\epsilon_s = \epsilon_0 \cdot \frac{|\mathcal{N}|}{2^v}$, by the property of the (ϵ_s, δ_s)-averaging sampler, except for at most $2^{|\mathcal{U}|} \cdot \delta_s = 2^{0.5\psi|\mathcal{U}|}$ number of *bad* inputs to the sampler, the size of $\mathcal{C}_\mathcal{N}$ satisfies (1).

We say that some choice of $x_{H \cap \mathcal{U}}$ is *bad* if there exists a corrupt choice of $x_{A \cap \mathcal{U}}$ such that the combination of $x_{H \cap \mathcal{U}}$ and $x_{A \cap \mathcal{U}}$ (arranged in the right order) will lead to $\mathcal{C}_\mathcal{N}$ such that (1) is violated. Otherwise, we say that $x_{H \cap \mathcal{U}}$ is *good*. Note that if $x_{H \cap \mathcal{U}}$ is good, it means that no matter how the adversary chooses $x_{A \cap \mathcal{U}}$, it cannot make $\mathcal{C}_\mathcal{N}$ violate (1).

Since honest players choose their $x_{H \cap \mathcal{U}}$ at random, we next claim that the fraction of bad $x_{H \cap \mathcal{U}}$ is bounded by $2^{-0.3\psi|\mathcal{U}|} \leq 2^{-0.27\psi^2 \cdot n/B} \leq 2^{-\Omega(2^{7r})}$. The claim is true; otherwise, the number of bad inputs to the sampler is at least $2^{-0.3\psi|\mathcal{U}|} \cdot 2^{0.9\psi|\mathcal{U}|} = 2^{0.6\psi|\mathcal{U}|}$ and thus we have reached a contradiction. Finally, a union bound over all the above bad events shows that except with probability at most $\exp(-\Omega(2^{7r}))$, $\mathcal{C}_\mathcal{N}$ respects the range in (1).

The alternative case when there is an upper bound $|\mathcal{N}| \leq N$ uses the same argument, but we just need one direction of the inequality from the sampler. $\qed$

The above Lemma 2 immediately implies the following bound on the final committee size.

Lemma 3 (Final committee not too large). *Suppose that the honest fraction $\psi > 2\eta = 2 \cdot \frac{1}{2^{0.2r}}$ and that our protocol uses the aforementioned parameters. Let $\epsilon_0 = \epsilon_s \cdot \frac{2^v}{n} = 2^{-5.5r}$. Then, with probability at least $1 - \exp(-\Omega(2^{6r}))$, the final committee $\mathcal{C}$ has size at most $(1 + \epsilon_0) \cdot d \cdot \frac{n}{2^v} \leq 2^{O(r)}$, and the protocol does not throw $\mathsf{param\_error}$. In particular, with probability at least $1 - \exp(-\Omega(2^{6r}))$, the protocol has round complexity at most $O(r)$.*

Proof. Due to Lemma 1, except with $\exp(-\Omega(2^{7r}))$ probability, $|\mathcal{U}_H| \geq 0.9\psi \cdot n/B \geq 0.9\psi \cdot |\mathcal{U}|$. Further, due to Fact 3, $\mathsf{param\_error}$ does not happen except with $\exp(-\Omega(2^{7r}))$ probability. Conditioned on these bad events not happening, we now use Lemma 2. In this case, the n players can choose at most n final v-ids, i.e., $|\mathcal{N}| \leq n$. The range in (1) implies that except with $\exp(-\Omega(2^{6r}))$ over the choice of x_H, the final committee $\mathcal{C}$ has size at most:

$$d(\frac{n}{2^v} + \epsilon_s) = (1 + \epsilon_0) \cdot d \cdot \frac{n}{2^v} \leq d \cdot (2^{-0.5r} + 2^{-6r})$$

$$= (1 + 2^{-5.5r}) \cdot (|\mathcal{U}|/\epsilon_s)^{\tilde{c}} \cdot 2^{-0.5r} \leq (1 + 2^{-5.5r}) \cdot 2^{15r\tilde{c}} \cdot 2^{-0.5r}.$$

We shall consider the following bad events in our proofs. Recall that conditioned on any coin used in the lightest-bin protocol for the preliminary committee election, the protocol still has independent randomness x chosen by the preliminary committee as input for the averaging sampler, the unmasked v-ids y chosen by all players, as well as the mask vector z.

- Event param_error. Recall that this happens when the preliminary comittee selected does not have the desirable properties; by Lemma 1 and Fact 3, this bad event happens with probability at most $\exp(-\Omega(2^{7r}))$.
- Event bad_1: out of the d samples from the (ϵ_s, δ_s)-sampler, at least $(1 + \epsilon_0) \cdot d \cdot \frac{n}{2^v}$ number of them correspond to corrupt players' final v-ids, where $\epsilon_0 := 2^{-6r} \cdot 2^{0.5r}$ is defined as in Lemma 3. Assuming the honest fraction $\psi \geq 2\eta$, by Lemma 3, $\Pr[\mathsf{bad}_1] \leq \exp(-\Omega(2^{6r}))$. Moreover, observe that bad_1 is determined by x, y_A, and z_A, and is independent of y_H and z_H.
- Event bad_2: the final committee $\mathcal{C}$ has size greater than $(1 + \epsilon_0) \cdot d \cdot \frac{n}{2^v}$. Again assuming $\psi \geq 2\eta$, Lemma 3 implies that $\Pr[\mathsf{bad}_2] \leq \exp(-\Omega(2^{6r}))$. Observe that bad_2 depends on x, y, and z.

Lemma 4 (Influence of an honest player in the final committee). *Suppose that $|A| < (1 - 2\eta)n$, i.e., $\frac{h}{n} = \psi > 2\eta \geq \frac{1}{2^r}$. For an honest player $i \notin A$, let M_i be its multiplicity in the final committee $\mathcal{C}$. Define a random variable Υ_i that equals $\frac{M_i}{|\mathcal{C}|}$, if none of the bad events bad events param_error or bad_1 or bad_2 happens; otherwise, Υ_i equals 0.*

Then, $\mathbf{E}[\Upsilon_i] \geq \frac{1}{n}\left(1 - 2^{-0.48r}\right)$, where the expectation is taken over the randomness used in the entire execution.

Proof. For ease of notation, the rest of the proof conditions on the event that during the preliminary committee election, param_error does not happen; observe that this bad event happens with probability at most $\exp(-\Omega(2^{7r}))$, by Lemma 1 and Fact 3. Hence, at the end, we just need to multiply any conditional expectation by a factor of $1 - \exp(-\Omega(2^{7r}))$. Recall that we identify an event with its $\{0, 1\}$-indicator random variable.

We next give a lower bound on $\mathbf{E}[M_i | \overline{\mathsf{bad}_1}]$. Since y_H is opened in the last but second step and as long as $|A| < (1 - 2\eta)n$, the reconstruction of z is fully determined before selecting input to the sampler, we may equivalently imagine that y_H is chosen at the end, independently of x, y_A, and z. Since the event bad_1 does not happen, there are at least $d - (1+\epsilon_0) \cdot d \cdot \frac{n}{2^v} = d(1 - (1+\epsilon_0)\frac{n}{2^v}) \geq d(1 - 2^{-0.49r})$ available slots for the honest players' final v-ids, where the inequality follows from $1 + \epsilon_0 \leq 2^{0.01r}$.

For each such slot, player i can get it if it chooses this slot and none of the other honest players choose it; this happens with probability $\frac{1}{2^v} \cdot (1 - \frac{1}{2^v})^{h-1} \geq \frac{1}{2^v}(1 - \frac{n}{2^v}) = \frac{1}{2^v}(1 - 2^{-0.5r})$. Therefore, conditioned on any choice of x, y_A, z, by just using the randomness of y_H, we can conclude that $\mathbf{E}_{y_H}[M_i | \overline{\mathsf{bad}_1}] \geq \frac{d}{2^v} \cdot (1 - 2^{-0.49r})(1 - 2^{-0.5r}) \geq \frac{d}{2^v}(1 - 2^{-0.485r})$, where the last inequality holds for large enough $r = \Omega(1)$.

Since this holds conditioned any choice of x, y_A, z, we have the desired lower bound on $\mathbf{E}[M_i | \overline{\mathsf{bad}_1}]$.

We next give a lower bound for the following quantity:

$$\mathbf{E}[M_i \cdot \overline{\mathsf{bad_1}} \cdot \overline{\mathsf{bad_2}}] = \mathbf{E}[M_i|\overline{\mathsf{bad_1}}] \cdot \Pr[\overline{\mathsf{bad_1}}] - \mathbf{E}[M_i \cdot \overline{\mathsf{bad_1}} \cdot \mathsf{bad_2}]$$

$$\geq \frac{d}{2^v}(1 - 2^{-0.485r}) \cdot \Pr[\overline{\mathsf{bad_1}}] - d\Pr[\mathsf{bad_2}]$$

We use $\mathbf{E}[M_i \cdot \overline{\mathsf{bad_1}} \cdot \mathsf{bad_2}] \leq d\Pr[\mathsf{bad_2}] \leq d \cdot \Pr[\mathsf{bad_2}] \leq d \cdot \exp(-\Omega(2^{6r})) \leq \frac{d}{2^v} \cdot \exp(-\Omega(2^{5r}))$ where the last inequality holds because $2^v = n \cdot 2^{0.5r}$ and we assume that $r \geq C_0 \log\log n$ for some suitably large constant C_0. Therefore, we have $\mathbf{E}[M_i \cdot \overline{\mathsf{bad_1}} \cdot \overline{\mathsf{bad_2}}] \geq \frac{d}{2^v}\left(1 - 2^{-0.485r}\right) \cdot \left(1 - \exp(-\Omega(2^{6r}))\right) - \frac{d}{2^v} \cdot \exp(-\Omega(2^{5r})) \geq \frac{d}{2^v}(1 - 2^{-0.483r})$. Finally, we have

$$\mathbf{E}[\Upsilon_i|\overline{\mathsf{bad_1}} \cdot \overline{\mathsf{bad_2}}] = \mathbf{E}\left[\frac{M_i}{|\mathcal{C}|}|\overline{\mathsf{bad_1}} \cdot \overline{\mathsf{bad_2}}\right] \geq \frac{\mathbf{E}[M_i|\overline{\mathsf{bad_1}} \cdot \overline{\mathsf{bad_2}}]}{(1 + \epsilon_0) \cdot d \cdot \frac{n}{2^v}}$$

$$\geq \frac{1}{n}(1 - 2^{-0.483r})(1 - \epsilon_0) \cdot \Pr[\overline{\mathsf{bad_1}} \cdot \overline{\mathsf{bad_2}}]^{-1}$$

$$\geq \frac{1}{n}(1 - 2^{-0.481r}) \cdot \Pr[\overline{\mathsf{bad_1}} \cdot \overline{\mathsf{bad_2}}]^{-1}.$$

Hence, we have the lower bound $\mathbf{E}[\Upsilon_i] \geq \mathbf{E}[\Upsilon_i \cdot \overline{\mathsf{bad_1}} \cdot \overline{\mathsf{bad_2}}] \geq \frac{1}{n}(1 - 2^{-0.481r})$.

Finally, recalling so far we have assume that param_error does not happen. Therefore, multiplying the above by $(1 - \Pr[\mathsf{param\_error}]) = 1 - \exp(-\Omega(2^{7r}))$ gives the desired lower bound for the expectation of Υ_i.

Lemma 5 (Sufficient honest players without collision). *Suppose $n = g + t < V$. There are V bins, of which t bins are bad and the rest are good. Suppose each of g balls is thrown into a bin uniformly at random independently. Let Z be the number of good bins containing exactly one ball. For any $0 < \alpha < 1$, except with probability $\exp(-\Theta(\alpha^2 g(1 - \frac{n}{V})))$, we have $Z \geq g(1 - \frac{2n}{V} - 2\alpha)$.*

Proof. Consider throwing the g balls one by one independently into the bins. For $1 \leq i \leq g$, let $X_i \in \{0, 1\}$ be the indicator random variable for the event that when the i-th ball is thrown, it goes to an empty good bin. Observe that no matter what happens to the first $i - 1$ balls, the event $X_i = 1$ happens with probability at least $1 - \frac{n}{V}$. Hence, $S := \sum_{i=1}^{g} X_i$ stochastically dominates the binomial distribution $\mathsf{Binom}(g, 1 - \frac{n}{V})$ with g trials and success rate $1 - \frac{n}{V}$. By stochastic dominance and the Chernoff bound,

$$\Pr\left[S \leq (1 - \alpha) \cdot g(1 - \frac{n}{V})\right] \leq \exp\left(-\Theta(\alpha^2 g(1 - \frac{n}{V}))\right)$$

Hence, except with probability $\exp(-\Theta(\alpha^2 g(1 - \frac{n}{V})))$, we have that $S \geq (1 - \alpha) \cdot g(1 - \frac{n}{V}) \geq g(1 - \frac{n}{V} - \alpha)$.

Finally, observe what happens to the number Z of good bins having exactly one ball as the g balls are thrown one by one. When $X_i = 1$, Z increases by 1; when $X_i = 0$, Z either remains the same or decreases by 1. Hence, at the end, the number Z of good bins having exactly one ball satisfies $Z \geq S - (g - S) = 2S - g$. The result follows.

Lemma 6 (Sufficient honest players in the final committee). *Suppose that $|A| < (1 - 2\eta)n$. Let $G \subseteq H$ denote an arbitrary subset of honest players with $g = |G|$, where $\frac{g}{n} \geq 1/2^r$. Except with probability $\exp(-\Omega(2^r))$, the number of players from G that are in the final committee[10] is at least $g \cdot \frac{d}{2^v} \cdot (1 - 2^{-0.48r})$.*

As a direct corollary, no matter how large A is, as long as the coalition A adopts the honest strategy, then, for any subset $G \subseteq [n]$ of at least $n/2^r$ players, except with probability $\exp(-\Omega(2^r))$, the number of players from G that are in the final committee is at least $g \cdot \frac{d}{2^v} \cdot (1 - 2^{-0.48r})$.

Proof. Let $V = 2^v$, and so $\frac{n}{V} = \frac{1}{2^{0.5r}}$. Since $|A| < (1 - 2\eta)n$, the mask z to be reconstructed later is fully determined before selecting input x to the sampler—in this case, we can imagine that y_G is chosen and revealed at the end, independent of x, $y_{[n]\backslash G}$, and z. Setting $\alpha := \frac{1}{2^r}$ in Lemma 5, we have, except with probability $p \leq \exp\left(-\Omega(\frac{1}{2^{2r}} \cdot g \cdot (1 - 2^{-0.5r}))\right) \leq \exp\left(-\Omega(\frac{n}{2^{3r}})\right)$, the number of players in G whose final v-id has no collision is at least $Z := g(1 - 2 \cdot 2^{-0.5r} - 2 \cdot 2^{-r}) \geq \frac{g}{2}$. Recall that $r \leq C_1 \log n$, and, as long as the constant C_1 is sufficiently small, we have that $n > 2^{4r}$, and thus $p \leq \exp(-\Omega(2^r))$.

Setting $\epsilon_0 := \epsilon_s \cdot \frac{2^v}{|Z|} \leq 2 \cdot 2^{-6r} \cdot 2^{1.5r}$, and using Lemma 2, we can show that except with probability $\exp(-\Omega(2^r))$, the number of players from G in the final committee is at least $(1 - \epsilon_0) \cdot d \cdot \frac{Z}{2^v} \geq g \cdot \frac{d}{2^v} \cdot (1 - 2^{-0.48r})$.

5.4   Maximin Fairness

In this section, we will prove the following lemma.

Lemma 7 (Ideal-world protocol: maximin fairness). *The ideal-world protocol (i.e., instantiated with $\mathcal{F}_{\text{comm}}$ and $\mathcal{F}_{\text{mpc}}$) satisfies $(1 - 2^{-0.4r}) = (1 - 2^{-\Theta(r)})$-sequential-maximin-fairness against any non-uniform p.p.t. coalition[11] of size at most $(1 - 2\eta)n = (1 - 2^{-\Theta(r)})n$.*

Proof. Due to a lemma proven in the online full version [15], we can do a round-by-round analysis. Let r^* be the first round in which the coalition deviates. Let $\widetilde{r}$ be the round in which all players reconstruct the mask vector z. Throughout, we may assume that $A < (1 - 2\eta)n$. Further, for each round r^*, we may assume that $\Pr[\text{Dev}^{r^*}]$ is non-negligible where Dev^{r^*} denotes the event that A deviates first in round r^*. We want to show that conditioned on this non-negligible probability event Dev^{r^*}, A cannot conditionally harm an honest individual noticeably, or conditionally increase its own winning probability noticeably.

Easy case: $r^* > \widetilde{r}$. This means the coalition A will deviate only in the tournament tree protocol, whose sequential maximin fairness holds according to Theorem 3. This means each honest player can only be hurt negligibly more.

Easy case: $r^* = \widetilde{r}$. As mentioned earlier, as long as $|A| < (1 - 2\eta)n$, in this round, no matter what A does, reconstruction of z is guaranteed and the reconstructed value is unique.

---

[10] Throughout, a player with multiplicity μ in the final committee is counted μ times.
[11] Recall that the tournament-tree protocol is still instantiated with real cryptography.

Slightly more complicated case: $r^* = \tilde{r} - 1$. This is the case when the coalition A deviates in the round in which the unmasked v-ids y are opened. Since we are using an ideal $\mathcal{F}_{\text{comm}}$, the only possible deviation in round $r^* = \tilde{r} - 1$ is if some member of the coalition $i \in A$ fails to open its committed its y_i value.

We consider two cases.

- First, suppose that $|A| \geq \eta n$. This means that the adversarial coalition already knows the committed mask z at the end of the sharing phase. In this case, the z mask to be reconstructed is uniquely determined at the end of the sharing phase. In the round $r^* = \tilde{r} - 1$, to harm any specific honest individual, A's best strategy is the following: for every final v-id in the space $\{0, 1\}^v$, if one or more player(s) in A happen(s) to have that final v-id, make exactly one of them open its y_i value, such that there is no internal collision among the coalition A. Due to the sequential fairness of the tournament-tree protocol (i.e., Theorem 3), conditioned on the history of the protocol till the end of round $\tilde{r}$, every honest final committee member's winning probability is at least $\frac{1}{|C|} - \mathsf{negl}(\kappa)$, no matter how A behaves in any round greater than $\tilde{r}$. Therefore, avoiding internal collision but otherwise opening every final v-id is A's best strategy for harming any specific honest player.

  Note that opening the coalition members' unmasked v-ids in an internal-collision-avoiding manner like above does not change whether any honest individual is included in the final committee, but it may increase the final committee size (in comparison with the case when A continues to play honestly). Due to Lemma 6, and since A has acted honestly so far, except with negligible probability, the final committee size is at least $\frac{nd}{2^v}(1 - 2^{-0.48r})$.

  Now, suppose A excludes its members from the final committee due to internal collision. Observe that actually this decision could have been made before the input x to the Samp is chosen. Since there are at most n finalized v-ids with no collision, by Lemma 3, except with $\exp(-2^{\Omega(r)})$ probability (which is negligible if $r \geq C_0 \log \log n$ for a sufficiently large C_0), the final committee has size at most $\frac{nd}{2^v}(1 + 2^{-5.5r})$.

  Therefore, except with negligible probability, for any honest i, the coalition A can only reduce Υ_i by a $1 - 2^{-\Theta(r)}$ factor.

- Second, suppose that $|A| < \eta n$. In this case, A has no information about the mask z, and Dev^{r^*} is independent of z. Further, z is guaranteed to be reconstructed later. In this case, we can reprove Lemma 4 almost identically except that instead of using the randomness y_H, we now use the randomness z_H; further, notice that bad_1 is independent of z_H, and even when conditioning on the non-negligible probability event Dev^{r^*}, the probabilities of bad_1 and bad_2 are still negligible. Therefore, we get that even when conditioning on Dev^{r^*}, for any honest i, the expectation of Υ_i is at least $\frac{1}{n} \cdot (1 - 2^{-0.48r})$ no matter how A behaves during round $\tilde{r}$ and after. Had A continued to play honestly, using the randomness of z, we know that even when conditioning on Dev^{r^*}, the expectation of Υ_i is at least $1/n - \mathsf{negl}(\kappa)$ where the $\mathsf{negl}(\kappa)$ term is due to the negligibly small probability of bad_1 and bad_2 in which case Υ_i is defined to be 0. (see Lemma 4).

Therefore, deviating in round $\tilde{r}$ will not reduce any honest individual's conditional winning probability by a $1 - 2^{-\Theta(r)}$ multiplicative factor.

Remaining case: $r^* < \tilde{r} - 1$. The rest of the proof focuses on this remaining case. Recall that we assume $\Pr[\mathsf{Dev}^{r^*}] \geq \frac{1}{\mathsf{poly}(n)}$. Let $\mathsf{LEIdeal}$ denote a randomized execution of our ideal-world leader-election protocol described in Sect. 4.1.

Conditioning on the event Dev^{r^*}, we prove maximin fairness assuming that the coalition A contains no more than a $1 - 2\eta$ fraction of the players. Fix any $i \notin A$. Now, observe the following:

1. Recall that we may assume Dev^{r^*} happens with non-negligible probability. Following the proof of Lemma 4, and observing that before round $\tilde{r}$, the randomness y_H remains hidden and is independent of whatever that has happened so far, we have:

$$\mathbf{E}\left[tr \leftarrow \mathsf{LEIdeal} : \Upsilon_i | \mathsf{Dev}^{r^*}(tr) \right] \geq \frac{1}{n} \cdot \left(1 - 2^{-0.48r} \right). \tag{2}$$

   The only difference in the argument is that both the probabilities $\Pr[\mathsf{bad}_1 | \mathsf{Dev}^{r^*}]$ and $\Pr[\mathsf{bad}_2 | \mathsf{Dev}^{r^*}]$ are at most $\mathsf{poly}(n) \cdot \exp(-\Omega(2^{6r}))$, which is still negligible, because we assume that $r = \Omega(\log \log n)$ is sufficiently large. Indeed, for sufficiently large n, $\mathsf{poly}(n) \cdot \exp(-\Omega(2^{6r})) \leq \exp(-\Omega(2^{5.99r}))$, and the proof works as before.

2. We next consider the proof of Lemma 6, but now we conditioned on Dev^{r^*} (which has non-negligible probability). Suppose all players in A actually play honestly. Define bad_3 to be the event that the final committee has size less than $\frac{nd}{2^v} \cdot (1 - 2^{-0.48r})$. Lemma 6 states that $\Pr[\mathsf{bad}_3] \leq \exp(-\Omega(2^r))$. Since Dev^{r^*} has non-negligible probability, we have $\Pr[\mathsf{bad}_3 | \mathsf{Dev}^{r^*}] \leq \mathsf{poly}(n) \cdot \exp(-\Omega(2^r)) \leq \exp(-\Omega(2^{0.99r})) \leq \mathsf{negl}(\kappa)$, where the last inequalities hold for large enough $n \geq \kappa$ because $r \geq \Omega(\log \log n)$.
   This implies that an honest continuation of the execution would lead to a conditional expectation of Υ_i of at most

$$\frac{d/2^v}{n \cdot \frac{d}{2^v} \cdot (1 - 2^{-0.48r})} + \mathsf{negl}(\kappa) \leq \frac{1}{n} \cdot (1 + 2^{-0.47r}) + \mathsf{negl}(\kappa) \leq \frac{1}{n} \cdot (1 + 2^{-0.46r})$$

Summarizing the above, the ideal protocol is $(1 - 2^{-0.4r})$-sequential-maximin-fair for any coalition that is at most $(1 - 2\eta)n = (1 - 2^{-\Theta(r)})n$ in size.

Deferred materials. We defer to the online full version [15] 1) proofs of CSP fairness for the ideal-world protocol, 2) proofs for the real-world protocol, and 3) our full lower bound proof. The online full version [15] also contain additional preliminaries, additional proofs for our sequential approximate fairness notion, relationship to the RPD notion [22–24], as well as proofs for the folklore tournament-tree protocol.

Acknowledgment. This work is partially supported by NSF under the award numbers CNS-1601879 and CNS-1561209, a Packard Fellowship, an ONR YIP award, and the Hong Kong RGC under the grants 17200418 and 17201220.

References

1. Abraham, I., Dolev, D., Halpern, J.Y.: Distributed protocols for leader election: a game-theoretic perspective. ACM Trans. Econ. Comput. **7**(1), 1–26 (2019)
2. Alistarh, D., Aspnes, J.: Sub-logarithmic test-and-set against a weak adversary. In: Peleg, D. (ed.) DISC 2011. LNCS, vol. 6950, pp. 97–109. Springer, Heidelberg (2011). https://doi.org/10.1007/978-3-642-24100-0_7
3. Alistarh, D., Attiya, H., Gilbert, S., Giurgiu, A., Guerraoui, R.: Fast randomized test-and-set and renaming. In: Lynch, N.A., Shvartsman, A.A. (eds.) DISC 2010. LNCS, vol. 6343, pp. 94–108. Springer, Heidelberg (2010). https://doi.org/10.1007/978-3-642-15763-9_9
4. Alistarh, D., Gelashvili, R., Vladu, A.: How to elect a leader faster than a tournament. In: PODC (2015)
5. Andrychowicz, M., Dziembowski, S., Malinowski, D., Mazurek, L.: Secure multi-party computations on bitcoin. Commun. ACM **59**(4), 76–84 (2016)
6. Bartoletti, M., Zunino, R.: Constant-deposit multiparty lotteries on bitcoin. In: Brenner, M., et al. (eds.) FC 2017. LNCS, vol. 10323, pp. 231–247. Springer, Cham (2017). https://doi.org/10.1007/978-3-319-70278-0_15
7. Beaver, D., Micali, S., Rogaway, P.: The round complexity of secure protocols. In: STOC (1990)
8. Ben-Or, M., Goldwasser, S., Wigderson, A.: Completeness theorems for non-cryptographic fault-tolerant distributed computation. In: STOC (1988)
9. Bentov, I., Kumaresan, R.: How to use bitcoin to design fair protocols. In: Garay, J.A., Gennaro, R. (eds.) CRYPTO 2014. LNCS, vol. 8617, pp. 421–439. Springer, Heidelberg (2014). https://doi.org/10.1007/978-3-662-44381-1_24
10. Blum, M.: Coin flipping by telephone a protocol for solving impossible problems. SIGACT News **15**(1), 23–27 (1983)
11. Boneh, D., Bonneau, J., Bünz, B., Fisch, B.: Verifiable delay functions. In: Shacham, H., Boldyreva, A. (eds.) CRYPTO 2018. LNCS, vol. 10991, pp. 757–788. Springer, Cham (2018). https://doi.org/10.1007/978-3-319-96884-1_25
12. Boneh, D., Bünz, B., Fisch, B.: A survey of two verifiable delay functions. Cryptology ePrint Archive, Report 2018/712 (2018)
13. Chaum, D., Crépeau, C., Damgård, I.: Multiparty unconditionally secure protocols (extended abstract). In: STOC (1988)
14. Chung, K.-M., Guo, Y., Lin, W.-K., Pass, R., Shi, E.: Game theoretic notions of fairness in multi-party coin toss. In: Beimel, A., Dziembowski, S. (eds.) TCC 2018. LNCS, vol. 11239, pp. 563–596. Springer, Cham (2018). https://doi.org/10.1007/978-3-030-03807-6_21
15. Chung, K.-M., Chan, T.-H.H., Wen, T., Shi, E.: Game-theoretic fairness meets multi-party protocols: the case of leader election. Online full version of this paper. https://eprint.iacr.org/2020/1591
16. Cleve, R.: Limits on the security of coin flips when half the processors are faulty. In: STOC (1986)
17. Daian, P., Pass, R., Shi, E.: Snow White: robustly reconfigurable consensus and applications to provably secure proof of stake. In: Goldberg, I., Moore, T. (eds.) FC 2019. LNCS, vol. 11598, pp. 23–41. Springer, Cham (2019). https://doi.org/10.1007/978-3-030-32101-7_2
18. Damgård, I., Ishai, Y.: Constant-round multiparty computation using a black-box pseudorandom generator. In: Shoup, V. (ed.) CRYPTO 2005. LNCS, vol. 3621, pp. 378–394. Springer, Heidelberg (2005). https://doi.org/10.1007/11535218_23

19. Dodis, Y.: Fault-tolerant leader election and collective coin-flipping in the full information model (2006, manuscript)
20. Feige, U.: Non-cryptographic selection protocols. In: FOCS (1999)
21. Gallager, R.G., Humblet, P.A., Spira, P.M.: A distributed algorithm for minimum-weight spanning trees. ACM Trans. Program. Lang. Syst. **5**(1), 66–77 (1983)
22. Garay, J., Katz, J., Tackmann, B., Zikas, V.: How fair is your protocol? A utility-based approach to protocol optimality. In: PODC (2015)
23. Garay, J.A., Katz, J., Maurer, U., Tackmann, B., Zikas, V.: Rational protocol design: cryptography against incentive-driven adversaries. In: FOCS (2013)
24. Garay, J.A., Tackmann, B., Zikas, V.: Fair distributed computation of reactive functions. In: Moses, Y. (ed.) DISC 2015. LNCS, vol. 9363, pp. 497–512. Springer, Heidelberg (2015). https://doi.org/10.1007/978-3-662-48653-5_33
25. Giakkoupis, G., Woelfel, P.: On the time and space complexity of randomized test-and-set. In: PODC (2012)
26. Goldreich, O., Micali, S., Wigderson, A.: How to play any mental game. In: ACM Symposium on Theory of Computing (STOC) (1987)
27. Guruswami, V., Umans, C., Vadhan, S.P.: Unbalanced expanders and randomness extractors from Parvaresh-Vardy codes. J. ACM **56**(4), 20:1–20:34 (2009)
28. Kiayias, A., Russell, A., David, B., Oliynykov, R.: Ouroboros: a provably secure proof-of-stake blockchain protocol. In: Katz, J., Shacham, H. (eds.) CRYPTO 2017. LNCS, vol. 10401, pp. 357–388. Springer, Cham (2017). https://doi.org/10.1007/978-3-319-63688-7_12
29. Korach, E., Kutten, S., Moran, S.: A modular technique for the design of efficient distributed leader finding algorithms. In: PODC, pp. 163–174 (1985)
30. Maram, D., et al.: Candid: can-do decentralized identity with legacy compatibility, sybil-resistance, and accountability. https://eprint.iacr.org/2020/934
31. Miller, A., Bentov, I.: Zero-collateral lotteries in bitcoin and ethereum. In: EuroS&P Workshops (2017)
32. Pass, R.: Bounded-concurrent secure multi-party computation with a dishonest majority. In: STOC (2004)
33. Pass, R., Shi, E.: Fruitchains: a fair blockchain. In: PODC (2017)
34. Reingold, O., Vadhan, S.P., Wigderson, A.: Entropy waves, the zig-zag graph product, and new constant-degree expanders and extractors. In: FOCS (2000)
35. Russell, A., Saks, M., Zuckerman, D.: Lower bounds for leader election and collective coin-flipping in the perfect information model. In: STOC (1999)
36. Russell, A., Zuckerman, D.: Perfect information leader election in $\log^* n + o(1)$ rounds. In: FOCS (1998)
37. Vadhan, S.P.: Pseudorandomness (foundations and trends in theoretical computer science) (2012)
38. Zuckerman, D.: Randomness-optimal sampling, extractors, and constructive leader election. In: STOC (1996)

Computational Hardness of Optimal Fair Computation: Beyond Minicrypt

Hemanta K. Maji[✉] and Mingyuan Wang

Department of Computer Science, Purdue University, West Lafayette, USA
{hmaji,wang1929}@purdue.edu

Abstract. Secure multi-party computation allows mutually distrusting parties to compute securely over their private data. However, guaranteeing output delivery to honest parties when the adversarial parties may abort the protocol has been a challenging objective. As a representative task, this work considers two-party coin-tossing protocols with guaranteed output delivery, a.k.a., fair coin-tossing.

In the information-theoretic plain model, as in two-party zero-sum games, one of the parties can force an output with certainty. In the commitment-hybrid, any r-message coin-tossing protocol is $1/\sqrt{r}$-unfair, i.e., the adversary can change the honest party's output distribution by $1/\sqrt{r}$ in the statistical distance. Moran, Naor, and Segev (TCC–2009) constructed the first $1/r$-unfair protocol in the oblivious transfer-hybrid. No further security improvement is possible because Cleve (STOC–1986) proved that $1/r$-unfairness is unavoidable. Therefore, Moran, Naor, and Segev's coin-tossing protocol is optimal. However, is oblivious transfer necessary for optimal fair coin-tossing?

Maji and Wang (CRYPTO–2020) proved that any coin-tossing protocol using one-way functions in a black-box manner is at least $1/\sqrt{r}$-unfair. That is, optimal fair coin-tossing is impossible in Minicrypt. Our work focuses on tightly characterizing the hardness of computation assumption necessary and sufficient for optimal fair coin-tossing within Cryptomania, outside Minicrypt. Haitner, Makriyannis, Nissim, Omri, Shaltiel, and Silbak (FOCS–2018 and TCC–2018) proved that better than $1/\sqrt{r}$-unfairness, for any constant r, implies the existence of a key-agreement protocol.

We prove that any coin-tossing protocol using public-key encryption (or, multi-round key agreement protocols) in a black-box manner must be $1/\sqrt{r}$-unfair. Next, our work entirely characterizes the additional power of secure function evaluation functionalities for optimal fair coin-tossing. We augment the model with an idealized secure function evaluation of f, a.k.a., the f-hybrid. If f is complete, that is, oblivious transfer is

The research effort is supported in part by an NSF CRII Award CNS–1566499, NSF SMALL Awards CNS–1618822 and CNS–2055605, the IARPA HECTOR project, MITRE Innovation Program Academic Cybersecurity Research Awards (2019–2020, 2020–2021), a Ross-Lynn Research Scholars Grant (2021–2022), a Purdue Research Foundation (PRF) Award (2017–2018), and The Center for Science of Information, an NSF Science and Technology Center, Cooperative Agreement CCF–0939370.

T. Malkin and C. Peikert (Eds.): CRYPTO 2021, LNCS 12826, pp. 33–63, 2021.
https://doi.org/10.1007/978-3-030-84245-1_2

possible in the f-hybrid, then optimal fair coin-tossing is also possible in the f-hybrid. On the other hand, if f is not complete, then a coin-tossing protocol using public-key encryption in a black-box manner in the f-hybrid is at least $1/\sqrt{r}$-unfair.

Keywords: Fair computation · Optimal fair coin-tossing · Cryptomania · Black-box separation · Hardness of computation results · Secure function evaluation functionalities

1 Introduction

Secure multi-party computation [31,75] allows mutually distrusting parties to compute securely over their private data. However, guaranteeing output delivery to honest parties when the adversarial parties may abort during the protocol execution has been a challenging objective. A long line of highly influential works has undertaken the task of defining security with guaranteed output delivery (i.e., *fair computation*) and fairly computing functionalities [1–5,10,11,14,33,34,39,60]. This work considers the case when honest parties are not in the majority. In particular, as is standard in this line of research, the sequel relies on the representative task of two-party secure coin-tossing, an elegant functionality providing uncluttered access to the primary bottlenecks of achieving security in any specific adversarial model.

In the *information-theoretic plain model*, one of the parties can fix the coin-tossing protocol's output (using attacks in two-player zero-sum games, or games against nature [65]). If the parties additionally have access to the commitment functionality (a.k.a., the information-theoretic *commitment-hybrid*), an adversary is forced to follow the protocol honestly (otherwise, the adversary risks being identified), or abort the protocol execution prematurely. Against such adversaries, referred to as *fail-stop adversaries* [20], there are coin-tossing protocols [6,12,13,19] where a fail-stop adversary can change the honest party's output distribution by at most $\mathcal{O}(1/\sqrt{r})$, where r is the round-complexity of the protocol. That is, these protocols are $\mathcal{O}(1/\sqrt{r})$-*insecure*. In a ground-breaking result, Moran, Naor, and Segev [61] constructed the first secure coin-tossing protocol in the oblivious transfer-hybrid [24,67,68] that is $\mathcal{O}(1/r)$-insecure. No further security improvements are possible because Cleve [19] proved that $\mathcal{O}(1/r)$-insecurity is unavoidable; hence, the protocol by Moran, Naor, and Segev is *optimal*.

Incidentally, all fair computation protocols (not just coin-tossing, see, for example, [1–5,10,11,14,33,34,39,60]) rely on the oblivious transfer functionality to achieve $\mathcal{O}(1/r)$-insecurity. A fundamental principle in theoretical cryptography is to securely realize cryptographic primitives based on the minimal computational hardness assumptions. Consequently, the following question is natural.

Is oblivious transfer necessary for optimal fair computation?

Towards answering this fundamental research inquiry, recently, Maji and Wang [59] proved that any coin-tossing protocol that uses one-way functions in a *black-box manner* [7,44,69] must incur $\Omega(1/\sqrt{r})$-insecurity. This result proves the qualitative optimality of the coin tossing protocols of [6,12,13,19] in Minicrypt [42] because the commitment functionality is securely realizable by the black-box use of one-way functions [38,62,63]. Consequently, the minimal hardness of computation assumption enabling optimal fair coin-tossing must be outside Minicrypt.

Summary of our results. This work studies the insecurity of fair coin-tossing protocols outside Minicrypt, within (various levels of) Cryptomania [42]. Our contributions are two-fold.

1. First, we generalize the (fully) black-box separation of Maji and Wang [59] to prove that any coin-tossing protocol using public-key encryption in a fully black-box manner must be $\Omega(1/\sqrt{r})$-insecure.
2. Finally, we prove a dichotomy for two-party secure (possibly, *randomized* output) function evaluation functionalities. For any secure function evaluation functionality f, either (A) optimal fair coin-tossing exists in the information-theoretic f-hybrid, or (B) any coin-tossing protocol in the f-hybrid, even using public-key encryption algorithms in a black-box manner, is $\Omega(1/\sqrt{r})$-insecure.

Remark 1. In the information-theoretic f-hybrid model, parties have access to a trusted party faithfully realizing the functionality f. However, this functionality is realized *unfairly*. That is, the trusted party delivers the output to the adversary first. If the adversary wants, it can abort the protocol and block the output delivery to the honest parties. Otherwise, it can also permit the delivery of the output to the honest parties and continue with the protocol execution. We highlight that the fair f-hybrid (where the adversary cannot block output delivery to the honest parties), for any f where both parties influence the output, straightforwardly yields *perfectly or statistically secure* fair coin-tossing protocol.[1]

Our hardness of computation results hold even for a game-theoretic definition of fairness as well (which extends to the stronger simulation-based security definition). Section 1.1 summarizes our contributions. As shown in Fig. 1, our results

---

[1] Suppose $f = \mathrm{XOR}$. In a *fair* f-hybrid, the adversary cannot block the output delivery to the honest parties. So, parties input random bits to the f-functionality and agree on the output. This protocol has 0-insecurity. A similar protocol (using a deterministic extractor for independent small-bias sources) can extract the fair output from any f where both parties have influence on the output distribution. Consider the following "collaborative randomness generation" followed by "extraction" protocol. (a) Invoke (in parallel) a bidirectional influence functionality multiple times with random inputs. The output of each invocation in *not* entirely determined by one of the parties. Consequently, these samples have average min-entropy. (b) Non-interactively, parties use these fair output samples to extract this entropy to obtain the (common) fair coin toss (using convolution/XOR, or traversal of an appropriate expander graph).

	Secure Construction	Adversarial Attack
Pessiland	Fail-stop Adversary:	In General: constant-unfair [37]
		Fail-stop Adversary: $1/\sqrt{r}$-unfair [20]
Minicrypt	One-way Functions: $1/\sqrt{r}$-unfair [6,12,13,19]	$1/\sqrt{r}$-unfair [59]
Cryptomania	Public-key Encryption:	$1/\sqrt{r}$-unfair [This work]
	PKE + f-hybrid, $f \not\rightarrow$ OT:	$1/\sqrt{r}$-unfair [This work]
	Oblivious Transfer: $1/r$-unfair [61]	$1/r$-unfair [19]

Fig. 1. The first column summarizes of the most secure fair coin-tossing protocols in Impagliazzo's worlds [42]. Corresponding to each of these worlds, the second column has the best attacks on these fair coin-tossing protocols. All the adversarial attacks are fail-stop attackers except for the general attack in pessiland.

further reinforce the widely-held perception that oblivious transfer is necessary for optimal fair coin-tossing. Our work nearly squeezes out the entire remaining space left open in the state-of-the-art after the recent breakthrough of [59], which was the first advancement on the quality of the attacks on fair coin-tossing protocols since [20] after almost three decades. However, there are fascinating problems left open by our work; Sect. 6 discusses one.

Positioning the technical contributions. Information-theoretic lower-bounding techniques that work in the plain model and also extend to the f-hybrid are rare. Maji and Wang [59] proved that optimal coin-tossing is impossible in the information-theoretic model even if parties can access a random oracle. This work extends the potential-based approach of [59] to f-hybrid information-theoretic models, such that oblivious transfer is impossible in the f-hybrid and parties additionally have access to a public-key encryption oracle.

$$
\begin{array}{c|c|c|c|}
 & 0 & 1 & 2 \\
\hline
0 & z_0 & z_0 & z_1 \\
\hline
1 & z_3 & z_4 & z_1 \\
\hline
2 & z_3 & z_2 & z_2 \\
\hline
\end{array}
$$

Fig. 2. The Kushilevitz Function [51], where Alice holds input $x \in \{0,1,2\}$ and Bob holds input $y \in \{0,1,2\}$. For example, the output is z_0 if $x = 0$ and $y \in \{0,1\}$.

For the discussion below, consider f to be the Kushilevitz function [51] (see Fig. 2). One cannot realize this function securely in the information-theoretic plain model even against honest-but-curious adversaries [9,49,50,57]. Furthermore, oblivious transfer is impossible in the f-hybrid [46,47]. The characterization of the *exact power* of making ideal f-invocations is not entirely well-understood.

Invocations of the ideal f-functionality are *non-trivially useful*. For example, one can realize the commitment functionality in the f-hybrid model [58] (even with Universally Composable (UC) security [15,16] against malicious adversaries). The f-functionality is also known to securely implement other secure function evaluation functionalities as well [71]. All these functionalities would otherwise be impossible to securely realize in the plain model [17,52,66]. Consequently, it is plausible that one can even implement optimal fair coin-tossing without implementing oblivious transfer in the f-hybrid model.

Our technical contribution is an information-theoretic lower-bounding technique that precisely characterizes the power of any f-hybrid vis-à-vis its ability to implement optimal fair coin-tossing. The authors believe that these techniques shall be of independent interest to characterize the power of performing ideal f-invocations in general.

1.1 Our Contribution

This section provides an informal summary of our results and positions our contributions relative to the state-of-the-art. To facilitate this discussion, we need to introduce a minimalistic definition of coin-tossing protocols. An (r, X)-*cointossing* protocol is a two-party r-message interactive protocol where parties agree on the final output $\in \{0, 1\}$, and the expected output of an honest execution of the protocol is X. A coin-tossing protocol is ϵ-*unfair* if one of the parties can change the honest party's output distribution by ϵ (in the statistical distance).

Maji and Wang [59] proved that the existence of optimal coin-tossing protocols is outside Minicrypt [42], where one-way functions and other private-key cryptographic primitives exist (for example, pseudorandom generator [40, 41,43], pseudorandom function [29,30], pseudorandom permutation [55], statistically binding commitment [62], statistically hiding commitment [38,63], zero-knowledge proof [32], and digital signature [64,70]). Public-key cryptographic primitives like public-key encryption, (multi-message) key-agreement protocols, and secure oblivious transfer protocol are in Cryptomania [44] (outside Minicrypt). Although the existence of a secure oblivious transfer protocol suffices for optimal fair coin-tossing, it was unknown whether weaker hardness of computation assumptions (like public-key encryption and (multi-message) key-agreement protocols [27]) suffice for optimal fair coin-tossing or not. Previously, Haitner, Makriyannis, Nissim, Omri, Shaltiel, and Silbak [35,36], for any constant r, prove that r-message coin-tossing protocols imply key-agreement protocols, if they are less than $1/\sqrt{r}$-insecure.

Result I. Towards this objective, we prove the following result.

Corollary 1 (Separation from Public-key Encryption). *Any (r, X)-cointossing protocol that uses a public-key encryption scheme in a fully black-box manner is $\Omega(X(1 - X)/\sqrt{r})$-unfair.*

We emphasize that X may depend on the message complexity r of the protocol, which, in turn, depends on the security parameter. For example, consider an ensemble of fair coin-tossing protocols with round complexity r and expected output $X = 1/r$. This result shows a fail-stop adversary that changes the honest party's output distribution by $1/r^{3/2}$ in the statistical distance.

This hardness of computation result extends to the fair computation of any multi-party functionality (possibly with inputs) such that the output has some entropy, and honest parties are not in the majority (using a standard partition argument). At a high level, this result implies that relying on stronger hardness of computation assumptions like the existence of public-key cryptography provides no "fairness-gains" for coin-tossing protocols than only using one-way functions.

This result's heart is the following *relativized separation* in the information-theoretic setting (refer to Theorem 5). There exists an oracle PKE_n [56] that enables the secure public-key encryption of n-bit messages. However, we prove that any (r, X)-coin-tossing protocol where parties have oracle access to the PKE_n oracle (with polynomial query complexity) is $\Omega(X(1 - X)/\sqrt{r})$-unfair. This relativized separation translates into a fully black-box separation using by-now-standard techniques in this field [69]. Conceptually, this black-box separation indicates that optimal fair coin-tossing requires a hardness of computation assumption that is *stronger* than the existence of a secure public-key encryption scheme.

Gertner, Kannan, Malkin, Reingold, and Vishwanathan [27] showed that the existence of a public-key encryption scheme with additional (seemingly innocuous) properties (like the ability to efficiently sample a public-key without knowing the private-key) enables oblivious transfer. Consequently, our oracles realizing public-key encryption must avoid any property enabling oblivious transfer (even unforeseen ones). This observation highlights the subtlety underlying our technical contributions. For example, our set of oracles permit testing whether a public-key or cipher-text is valid or not. Without this test, oblivious transfer and, in turn, optimal fair coin-tossing is possible. Surprisingly, these test oracles are also sufficient to rule out the possibility of oblivious transfer.

Since public-key encryption schemes imply key agreement protocols, our results prove that optimal fair coin-tossing is black-box separated from key agreement protocols as well.

Result II. Let $f: X \times Y \to \mathbb{R}^Z$ be a two-party secure symmetric function evaluation functionality, possibly with randomized output. The function takes private inputs x and y from the parties and samples an output $z \in Z$ according to the probability distribution $p_f(z|x, y)$. The *information-theoretic f-hybrid* is an information-theoretic model where parties have additional access to the (unfair) f-functionality.

Observe that if f is the (symmetrized) oblivious transfer functionality,[2] then the Moran, Naor, and Segev protocol [61] is an optimal fair coin-tossing protocol in the (unfair) f-hybrid. More generally, if f is a functionality such that there is an oblivious transfer protocol in the f-hybrid, one can emulate the Moran, Naor, and Segev optimal coin-tossing protocol; consequently, optimal coin-tossing exists in the f-hybrid. Kilian [47] characterized all functions f such that there exists a secure oblivious transfer protocol in the f-hybrid, referred to as *complete* functions.

Our work explores whether a function f that is *not complete* may enhance the security of fair coin-tossing protocols.

Corollary 2 (Dichotomy of Functions). *Let f be an arbitrary 2-party symmetric function evaluation functionality, possibly with randomized output. Then, exactly one of the following two statements holds.*

1. *For all $r \in \mathbb{N}$ and $X \in [0,1]$, there exists an optimal (r, X)-coin-tossing protocol in the f-hybrid (a.k.a., $\mathcal{O}(1/r)$-unfair protocol).*
2. *Any (r, X)-coin-tossing protocol that uses public-key encryption protocols in a black-box manner in the f-hybrid is $\Omega(X(1-X)/\sqrt{r})$-unfair.*

For example, Corollary 1 is implied by the stronger version of our result by using a constant-valued f, a trivial function evaluation. For more details, refer to Theorem 6. In our model, we emphasize that parties can perform an arbitrary number of f-invocations in parallel in every round.

Let us further elaborate on our results. Consider a function f that has a secure protocol in the information-theoretic plain model, referred to as *trivial* functions. For deterministic output, trivial functions' full characterization is known [9,49,50,57]. For randomized output, the characterization of trivial functions is not known currently. Observe that trivial functions are definitely not complete; otherwise, a secure oblivious transfer protocol shall exist in the information-theoretic plain model, which is impossible. For every $t \in \mathbb{N}$, there are functions f_t such that any secure protocol for f_t requires t rounds of interactive communication in the information-theoretic plain model. For the randomized output case, the authors know of functions such that $|X| = |Y| = 2$ and $|Z| = (t+1)$ that need t-round protocols for secure computation, which is part of ongoing independent research. Compiling out the f_t-hybrid using such a t-round secure computation protocol allows only for an $\Theta(X(1-X)/\sqrt{rt})$-insecurity, which yields a useless bound for $t = \Omega(r)$. Consequently, compiling out the trivial functions is inadequate.

It is also well-known that functions of *intermediate* complexity exist [9,49,50,57], which are neither complete nor trivial (for example, the Kushilevitz function, refer to Fig. 2). In fact, there are randomized functions (refer to Fig. 3) of intermediate complexity such that $|X| = |Y| = 2$ and $|Z| = 3$ [23].

---

[2] In the symmetrized oblivious transfer functionality, the sender has input $(x_0, x_1) \in \{0,1\}^2$, and the receiver has input $(b, r) \in \{0,1\}^2$. The symmetric oblivious transfer functionality returns $x_b \oplus r$ to both the parties. If the receiver picks $r \xleftarrow{\$} \{0,1\}$, then this functionality hides the receiver's choice bit b from the sender.

$$\frac{1}{54} \begin{pmatrix} (18,18,18) & (36,12,6) \\ (21,3,30) & (42,2,10) \end{pmatrix}$$

Fig. 3. A randomized functionality of intermediate complexity with $X = Y = \{0,1\}$ and $Z = \{0,1,2\}$. For instance, when $x = 0$ and $y = 0$, the distribution of the output over Z is $(18/54, 18/54, 18/54)$, i.e., a uniform distribution over Z.

Our result claims that even an intermediate function f is useless for optimal fair coin-tossing; it is as useless as one-way functions or public-key encryption. Therefore, our results' technical approach must treat each f-hybrid invocation as one step in the protocol. We highlight that the intermediate functions are useful in securely realizing other non-trivial functionalities as well [58,71]. However, for fair coin-tossing, they are useless.

1.2 Prior Works

Deterministic secure function evaluation. In this paper, we focus on two-party secure function evaluation functionalities that provide the same output to the parties. Consider a deterministic function $f \colon X \times Y \to Z$. The *unfair ideal functionality* implementing f takes as input x and y from two parties and delivers the output $f(x,y)$ to the adversary. The adversary may choose to block the output delivery to the honest party, or permit the delivery of the output to the honest party.

In this document, we consider security against a semi-honest information-theoretic adversary, i.e., the adversary follows the protocol description honestly but is curious to find additional information about the other party's private input. There are several natural characterization problems in this scenario. The functions that have perfectly secure protocols in the information-theoretic plain model, a.k.a., the *trivial functions*, are identical to the set of *decomposable functions* [9,50]. For every $t \in \mathbb{N}$, there are infinitely many functions that require t-rounds for their secure evaluation. Interestingly, relaxing the security from perfect to statistical security, does not change this characterization [49,57].

Next, Kilian [46] characterized all deterministic functions f that enable oblivious transfer in the f-hybrid, the *complete functions*. Any functions that has an "embedded OR-minor" (refer to Definition 4) is complete. Such functions, intuitively, are the most powerful functions that enable general secure computation of arbitrary functionalities.

The sets of trivial and complete functions are not exhaustive (for $|Z| > 3$ [18,48]). There are functions of *intermediate* complexity, which are neither trivial nor complete (see, for example, Fig. 2). The power of the f-hybrid, for an intermediate f, was explored by [71] using restricted forms of protocols.

Randomized secure function evaluation. A two-party randomized function $f(x,y) \colon X \times Y \to \mathbb{R}^Z$ is a function that, upon receipt of the inputs x and y, samples an output according to the distribution $p_f(z|x,y)$ over the samples space Z. Kilian [47] characterized all complete randomized functions. Any function that has an "embedded generalized OR-minor" (refer to Definition 4) is complete. Recently, [23] characterized functions with 2-round protocols. Furthermore, even for $|X| = |Y| = 2$ and $|Z| = 3$, there are random function evaluations that are of intermediate complexity [23].

In the field of black-box separation, the seminal work of Impagliazzo and Rudich [44] first proposed the notion of black-box separation between cryptographic primitives. Since then, there has been many influential works [25–28, 69, 72, 74] in this line of research. Below, we elaborate on a few works that are most relevant to us.

Firstly, for the fair coin-tossing in the random oracle model, the work of Dachman-Soled, Lindell, Mahmoody, and Malkin [21] showed that when the message complexity is small, random oracle can be compiled away and hence is useless for fair coin-tossing. In another work, Dachman-Soled, Mahmoody, and Malkin [22] studied a restricted type of protocols that they called "function-oblivious" and showed that for this particular type of protocols, random oracles cannot yield optimal fair coin-tossing. Recently, Maji and Wang [59] resolved this problem in the full generality. They showed that any r-message coin-tossing protocol in the random oracle model must be $\Omega(1/\sqrt{r})$-unfair.

In a recent work of Haitner, Nissim, Omri, Shaltiel, and Silbak [36] and Haitner, Makriyannis, and Omri [35], they proved that, for any constant r, the existence of an r-message fair coin-tossing protocol that is more secure than $1/\sqrt{r}$ implies the existence of (infinitely often) key agreement protocols.

1.3 Technical Overview

In this section, we present a high-level overview of our proofs. We start by recalling the proofs of Maji and Wang [59].

Before we begin, we need to introduce the notion of Alice and Bob's *defense coins*. At any instance of the protocol evolution, Alice has a private defense coin $\in \{0, 1\}$, referred to as the Alice defense coin, which she outputs if Bob aborts the protocol. Similarly, Bob has a Bob defense coin. When Alice prepares a next message of the protocol, she updates her defense coin. However, when Bob prepares a next message of the protocol, Alice's defense coin remains unchanged. Analogously, Bob updates his defense coin when preparing his next messages in the protocol.

Abstraction of Maji and Wang [59] Technique. Consider an arbitrary fair coin-tossing protocol $\pi^{\mathcal{O}}$ where Alice and Bob have black-box access to some oracle $\mathcal{O}$. In their setting, $\mathcal{O}$ is a random oracle. Let r and X be the message complexity and the expected output of this protocol. They used an inductive approach to prove this protocol is $(c \cdot X(1 - X)/\sqrt{r})$-insecure as follows ($c$ is a universal constant).

For every possible first message of this protocol, they consider two attacks (refer to Fig. 4). Firstly, parties can attack by immediately abort upon this first message. Secondly, parties can defer their attack to the remaining sub-protocol,

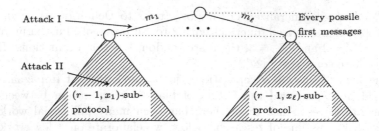

Fig. 4. An intuitive illustration of the approach of Maji and Wang [59].

which has only $r-1$ messages. Suppose when the first message is m_i, the remaining sub-protocol has expected output x_i. Additionally, the expectation of Alice and Bob defense is a_i and b_i. The effectiveness of the first attack is precisely

$$|x_i - a_i| + |x_i - b_i|,$$

where $|x_i - a_i|$ is the change of Alice's output if Bob aborts, and analogously, $|x_i - b_i|$ is the change of Bob's output if Alice aborts. On the other hand, by the inductive hypothesis, we know the effectiveness of the second attack is at least

$$c \cdot x_i(1 - x_i)/\sqrt{r - 1}.$$

Now, they employed a key inequality by [45] (refer to Imported Lemma 1) and show that the maximum of these two quantities is lower bounded by

$$\frac{c}{\sqrt{r}} \cdot \left(x_i(1 - x_i) + (x_i - a_i)^2 + (x_i - b_i)^2 \right).$$

Define potential function $\Phi(x, a, b) := x(1 - x) + (x - a)^2 + (x - b)^2$. Maji and Wang noted that if Jensen's inequality holds, i.e.,

$$\underset{i}{\mathrm{E}}\left[\Phi(x_i, a_i, b_i)\right] \geq \Phi\left(\underset{i}{\mathrm{E}}\left[x_i\right], \underset{i}{\mathrm{E}}\left[a_i\right], \underset{i}{\mathrm{E}}\left[b_i\right]\right), \tag{1}$$

then the proof is complete. This is because the overall effectiveness of the attack is lower bounded by

$$\underset{i}{\mathrm{E}}\left[\max\left(|x_i - a_i| + |x_i - b_i|, \; c \cdot x_i(1 - x_i)/\sqrt{r - 1}\right)\right]$$

(Expectation of the most effective attack)

$$\geq \underset{i}{\mathrm{E}}\left[\frac{c}{\sqrt{r}} \cdot \Phi(x_i, a_i, b_i)\right] \qquad \text{(The key inequality of [45])}$$

$$\geq \frac{c}{\sqrt{r}} \cdot \Phi\left(\underset{i}{\mathrm{E}}\left[x_i\right], \underset{i}{\mathrm{E}}\left[a_i\right], \underset{i}{\mathrm{E}}\left[b_i\right]\right) \qquad \text{(Jensen's inequality)}$$

$$\geq \frac{c}{\sqrt{r}} \cdot X(1 - X). \qquad (\because \underset{i}{\mathrm{E}}\left[x_i\right] = X)$$

To prove Eq. 1, they noted that $\Phi(x, a, b)$ could be rewritten as

$$\Phi(x, a, b) = x + (x - a - b)^2 - 2ab.$$

Observe that x and $(x-a-b)^2$ are convex functions, and hence Jensen's inequality holds. The only problematic term is ab. To resolve this, they noted that suppose we have the following guarantee.

Conditioned on the partial transcript,
Alice private view and Bob private view are (close to) independent.[3]

Then we shall have $\underset{i}{\mathbb{E}}\,[a_i b_i] \approx \underset{i}{\mathbb{E}}\,[a_i]\,\underset{i}{\mathbb{E}}\,[b_i]$ (refer to Claim 1).[4] Consequently, Eq. 1 shall hold and the proof is done.

Note that the argument thus far is oblivious to the fact that the oracle in use is a random oracle. For any oracle $\mathcal{O}$, if we have the guarantee above, this proof will follow.

In particular, when the oracle in use is the random oracle, Maji and Wang observed that, standard techniques (namely, the heavy querier [8]) do ensure that Alice private view and Bob private view are (close to) independent. This completes their proof.

Extending to f-hybrid. When f is a complete function, one can build oblivious transfer protocol in the f-hybrid model and, consequently, by the MNS protocol [61], optimal fair coin-tossing does exist in the f-hybrid model.

On the other hand, if f is not complete, Kilian [47] showed that f must satisfy the cross product rule (refer to Definition 4). This implies that conditioned on the partial transcript, which includes ideal calls to f, Alice and Bob private view are (perfectly) independent (refer to Lemma 3). Therefore, the proof strategy of Maji and Wang [59] is applicable.

Extending to Public-key Encryption. Our proof for the public-key encryption follows from the ideas of Mahmoody, Maji, and Prabhakaran [56]. First, we define a collection of oracles PKE_n (refer to Sect. 5.1), with respect to which public-key encryption exists. To prove that optimal fair coin-tossing protocol does not exist, it suffices to ensure that Alice and Bob private view are (close to) independent. However, since with the help of PKE_n oracle, Alice and Bob can agree on a secret key such that a third party, Eve, who sees the transcript and may ask polynomially many queries to the oracle, cannot learn any information about the key. It is impossible to ensure the independence of the private views by only invoking a *public* algorithm.

To resolve this, [56] showed that one could compile any protocol π in the PKE_n oracle to be a new protocol π' in the PKE_n oracle where parties never

---

[3] For a joint distribution (X, Y), one may measure the closeness of X and Y being independent by the statistical distance between (X, Y) and $X \times Y$.

[4] In particular, if Alice private view and Bob private view are *perfectly* independent, we shall have $\underset{i}{\mathbb{E}}\,[a_i b_i] = \underset{i}{\mathbb{E}}\,[a_i]\,\underset{i}{\mathbb{E}}\,[b_i]$.

query the decryption oracle (refer to Imported Theorem 1). This compiler satisfies that given a local view of Alice (resp., Bob) in protocol π, one could simulate the local view of Alice (resp., Bob) in protocol π' and vice versa. Therefore, instead of considering a fair coin-tossing protocol in the PKE_n oracle model, one could consider a fair coin-tossing protocol in the PKE_n oracle model where parties never query the decryption oracle. And [56] showed that, when the parties do not call the decryption oracle, there does exist a public algorithm, namely the *common information learner*, who can find all the correlation between Alice and Bob (refer to Imported Theorem 2). And conditioned on the partial transcript with the additional information from the common information learner, Alice and Bob private view are (close to) independent. Therefore, we can continue with the proof-strategy of Maji and Wang [59].

2   Preliminaries

For a randomized function $f \colon \mathcal{X} \to \mathcal{Y}$, we shall use $f(x; s)$ for f evaluated with input x and randomness s.

We use uppercase letters for random variables, (corresponding) lowercase letters for their values, and calligraphic letters for sets. For a joint distribution (A, B), A and B represent the marginal distributions, and $A \times B$ represents the product distribution where one samples from the marginal distributions A and B independently. For two random variables A and B distributed over a (discrete) sample space Ω, their *statistical distance* is defined as $\mathsf{SD}\,(A, B) := \frac{1}{2} \cdot \sum_{\omega \in \Omega} |\Pr[A = w] - \Pr[B = w]|$.

For a sequence $(X_1, X_2, \ldots)$, we use $X_{\leq i}$ to denote the joint distribution $(X_1, X_2, \ldots, X_i)$. Similarly, for any $(x_1, x_2, \ldots) \in \Omega_1 \times \Omega_2 \times \cdots$, we define $x_{\leq i} := (x_1, x_2, \ldots, x_i) \in \Omega_1 \times \Omega_2 \times \cdots \times \Omega_i$. Let $(M_1, M_2, \ldots, M_r)$ be a joint distribution over sample space $\Omega_1 \times \Omega_2 \times \cdots \times \Omega_r$, such that for any $i \in \{1, 2, \ldots, n\}$, M_i is a random variable over Ω_i. A (real-valued) random variable X_i is said to be $M_{\leq i}$ *measurable* if there exists a deterministic function $f \colon \Omega_1 \times \cdots \times \Omega_i \to \mathbb{R}$ such that $X_i = f(M_1, \ldots, M_i)$. A random variable $\tau \colon \Omega_1 \times \cdots \times \Omega_r \to \{1, 2, \ldots, r\}$ is called a *stopping time*, if the random variable $\mathbb{1}_{\tau \leq i}$ is $M_{\leq i}$ measurable, where $\mathbb{1}$ is the indicator function. For a more formal treatment of probability spaces, σ-algebras, filtrations, and martingales, refer to, for example, [73].

The following inequality shall be helpful for our proof.

Theorem 1 (Jensen's inequality). *If f is a multivariate convex function, then $\mathbb{E}[f(\boldsymbol{X})] \geq f(\mathbb{E}[\boldsymbol{X}])$, for all probability distributions $\boldsymbol{X}$ over the domain of f.*

In particular, $f(x, y, z) = (x - y - z)^2$ is a tri-variate convex function where Jensen's inequality applys.

3   Fair Coin-Tossing Protocol in the f-hybrid Model

Let $f \colon \mathcal{X} \times \mathcal{Y} \to \mathcal{Z}$ be an arbitrary (possibly randomized) function. As standard in the literature, we shall restrict to f such that the input domain $\mathcal{X}$ and $\mathcal{Y}$ and the range $\mathcal{Z}$ are of constant size. A two-party protocol in the f-hybrid model is defined as follows.

Definition 1 (f-hybrid Model [15,53]). *A protocol between Alice and Bob in the f-hybrid model is identical to a protocol in the plain model except that both parties have access to a trusted party realizing f. At any point during the execution, the protocol specifies which party is supposed to speak.*

- *Alice/Bob message. If Alice is supposed to speak, she shall prepare her next message as a deterministic function of her private randomness and the partial transcript.If Bob is supposed to speak, his message is prepared in a similar manner.*
- *Trusted party message. At some point during the execution, the protocol might specify that the trusted party shall speak next. In this case, the protocol shall also specify a natural number ℓ, which indicates how many instances of f should the trusted party compute. Alice (resp., Bob) will prepare her inputs $\boldsymbol{x} = (x_1, \ldots, x_\ell)$ (resp., $\boldsymbol{y} = (y_1, \ldots, y_\ell)$) and send it privately to the trusted party. The trusted party shall compute $(f(x_1, y_1), \ldots, f(x_\ell, y_\ell))$ and send it as the next message.*

In this paper, we shall restrict to fail-stop adversarial behavior.

Definition 2 (Fail-stop Attacker in the f-hybrid Model). *A fail-stop attacker follows the protocol honestly and might prematurely abort. She might decide to abort when it is her turn to speak. Furthermore, during the trusted party message, she shall always receive the trusted party message first and, based on this message, decide whether to abort or not. If she decides to abort, this action prevents the other party from receiving the trusted party message.*

In particular, we shall focus on fair coin-tossing protocols in the f-hybrid model.

Definition 3 (Fair Coin-tossing in the f-hybrid Model). *An (X_0, r)-fair coin-tossing in the f-hybrid model is a two-party protocol between Alice and Bob in the f-hybrid model such that it satisfies the following.*

- *X_0-Expected Output. At the end of the protocol, parties always agree on the output $\in \{0, 1\}$ of the protocol. The expectation of the output of an honest execution is $X_0 \in (0, 1)$.*
- *r-Message Complexity. The total number of messages of the protocol is (at most) r. This includes both the Alice/Bob message and the trusted party message.*
- *Defense Preparation. Anytime a party speaks, she shall also prepare a defense coin based on her private randomness and the partial transcript. Her latest defense coin shall be her output when the other party decides to abort. To ensure that parties always have a defense to output, they shall prepare a defense before the protocol begins.*
- *Insecurity. The insecurity is defined as the maximum change a fail-stop adversary can cause to the expectation of the other party's output.*

For any (randomized) functionality f, Kilian [47] proved that if f *does not* satisfy the following cross product rule, f is complete for information-theoretic semi-honest adversaries. That is, for any functionality g, there is a protocol in the f-hybrid model that realizes g, which is secure against information-theoretic semi-honest adversaries. In particular, this implies that there is a protocol in the f-hybrid model that realizes oblivious transfer.

Definition 4 (Cross Product Rule). *A (randomized) functionality* $f\colon \mathcal{X} \times \mathcal{Y} \to \mathcal{Z}$ *is said to satisfy the cross product rule if for all* $x_0, x_1 \in \mathcal{X}$, $y_0, y_1 \in \mathcal{Y}$, *and* $z \in \mathcal{Z}$ *such that*

$$\Pr[f(x_0, y_0) = z] > 0 \quad and \quad \Pr[f(x_1, y_0) = z] > 0,$$

we have

$$\Pr[f(x_0, y_0) = z] \cdot \Pr[f(x_1, y_1) = z] = \Pr[f(x_1, y_0) = z] \cdot \Pr[f(x_0, y_1) = z].$$

We recall the MNS protocol by Moran, Naor, and Segev [61]. The MNS protocol makes black-box uses of the oblivious transfer as a subroutine to construct optimal-fair coin-tossing protocols. In particular, their protocol enjoys the property that any fail-stop attack during the oblivious transfer subroutine is an entirely ineffective attack. Therefore, the MNS protocol, combined with the results of Kilian [47], gives us the following theorem.

Theorem 2 ([47,61]). *Let* f *be a (randomized) functionality that is complete. For any* $X_0 \in (0, 1)$ *and* $r \in \mathbb{N}^*$, *there is an* (X_0, r)-*fair coin-tossing protocol in the* f-*hybrid model that is (at most)* $\mathcal{O}(1/r)$-*insecure against fail-stop attackers.*

Remark 2 (On the necessity of the unfairness of f). We emphasize that it is necessary that in the f-hybrid model, f is realized *unfairly*. That is, the adversary receives the output of f before the honest party does. If f is realized fairly, i.e., both parties receive the output simultaneously, it is possible to construct perfectly-secure fair coin-tossing. For instance, let f be the XOR function. Consider the protocol where Alice samples $x \xleftarrow{\$} \{0, 1\}$, Bob samples $y \xleftarrow{\$} \{0, 1\}$, and the trusted party broadcast $f(x, y)$, which is the final output of the protocol. Trivially, one can verify that this protocol is perfectly-secure.

Intuitively, the results of Kilian [47] and Moran, Naor, and Segev [61] showed that when f is a functionality that does not satisfy the cross product rule, a secure protocol realizing f can be used to construct optimal-fair coin-tossing.

In this work, we complement the above results by showing that when f is a functionality that does satisfy the cross product rule, a fair coin-tossing protocol in the f-hybrid model is (qualitatively) as insecure as a fair coin-tossing protocol in the information-theoretic model. In other words, f is completely useless for fair coin-tossing. Our results are summarized as the following theorem.

Theorem 3 (Main Theorem for f-**hybrid).** *Let* f *be a randomized functionality that is* not *complete. Any* (X_0, r)-*fair coin-tossing protocol in the* f-*hybrid model is (at least)* $\Omega\left(\frac{X_0(1-X_0)}{\sqrt{r}}\right)$-*insecure.*

4 Proof of Theorem 3

4.1 Properties of Functionalities

Let f be a functionality that satisfies the cross product rule. We start by observing some properties of f. Firstly, let us recall the following definition.

Definition 5 (Function Isomorphism [57]). *Let $f: \mathcal{X} \times \mathcal{Y} \to \mathcal{Z}$ and $g: \mathcal{X} \times \mathcal{Y} \to \mathcal{Z}'$ be any two (randomized) functionalities. We say $f \leq g$ if there exist deterministic mappings $M_A: \mathcal{X} \times \mathcal{Z}' \to \mathcal{Z}$ and $M_B: \mathcal{Y} \times \mathcal{Z}' \to \mathcal{Z}$ such that, for all $x \in \mathcal{X}$, $y \in \mathcal{Y}$, and randomness s,*

$$M_A\left(x, g(x, y; s)\right) = M_B\left(y, g(x, y; s)\right)$$

and

$$\mathsf{SD}\left(f(x, y)\,,\, M_A\left(x, g(x, y)\right)\right) = 0.$$

We say f and g are isomorphic (i.e., $f \cong g$) if $f \leq g$ and $g \leq f$.

Intuitively, f and g are isomorphic if securely computing f can be realized by one ideal call to g without any further communication and vise versa. As an example, the (deterministic) XOR functionality $\begin{bmatrix} 0 & 1 \\ 1 & 0 \end{bmatrix}$ is isomorphic to $\begin{bmatrix} 0 & 1 \\ 2 & 3 \end{bmatrix}$.

Given two isomorphic functionalities f and g, it is easy to see that there is a natural bijection between protocols in the f-hybrid model and g-hybrid model.

Lemma 1. *Let f and g be two functionalities such that $f \cong g$. For every fair coin-tossing protocol π in the f-hybrid model, there is a fair coin-tossing protocol π' in the g-hybrid model such that*

- *π and π' have the same message complexity r and expected output X_0.*
- *For every fail-stop attack strategy for π, there exists a fail-stop attack strategy for π' such that the insecurities they cause are identical and vice versa.*

Proof (Sketch). Given any protocol π in the f-hybrid model between A and B, consider the protocol π' in the g-hybrid model between A' and B'. In π', A' simply simulates A and does what A does. Except when the trusted party sends the output of g, A' uses the mapping M_A to recover the output of f and feeds it to A. B' behaves similarly. Easily, one can verify that these two protocols have the same message complexity and expected output. Additionally, for every fail-stop adversary A* for π, there is a fail-stop adversary (A*)' for π' that simulates A* in the same manner, which deviates the output of Bob by the same amount.

We are now ready to state our next lemma.

Lemma 2 (Maximally Renaming the Outputs of f). *Let $f: \mathcal{X} \times \mathcal{Y} \to \mathcal{Z}$ be a (randomized) functionality that is not complete. There exists a functionality $f': \mathcal{X} \times \mathcal{Y} \to \mathcal{Z}'$ such that $f \cong f'$ and f' satisfies the following strict cross product rule. That is, for all $x_0, x_1 \in \mathcal{X}$, $y_0, y_1 \in \mathcal{Y}$, and $z' \in \mathcal{Z}'$, we have*

$$\Pr[f'(x_0, y_0) = z'] \cdot \Pr[f'(x_1, y_1) = z'] = \Pr[f'(x_1, y_0) = z'] \cdot \Pr[f'(x_0, y_1) = z'].$$

The proof of this lemma follows from standard argument. We refer the reader to the full version for a complete proof.

Following the example above, the XOR functionality $\begin{bmatrix} 0 & 1 \\ 1 & 0 \end{bmatrix}$ satisfies the cross product rule, i.e., XOR is not complete, but it does not satisfy the strict cross product rule since

$$\Pr[\mathsf{XOR}(0,0) = 1] \cdot \Pr[\mathsf{XOR}(1,1) = 1] \neq \Pr[\mathsf{XOR}(1,0) = 1] \cdot \Pr[\mathsf{XOR}(0,1) = 1].$$

On the other hand, functionality $\begin{bmatrix} 0 & 1 \\ 2 & 3 \end{bmatrix}$ is isomorphic to XOR and does satisfy the strict cross product rule.

By Lemma 1, the insecurity of a fair coin-tossing protocol in the f-hybrid model is identical to a fair coin-tossing protocol in the f'-hybrid model when $f \cong f'$. Therefore, in the rest of this section, without loss of generality, we shall always assume f is maximally renamed according to Lemma 2 such that it satisfies the strict cross product rule.

4.2 Notations and the Technical Theorem

Let π be an (X_0, r)-fair coin-tossing protocol in the f-hybrid model. We shall use R^{A} and R^{B} to denote the private randomness of Alice and Bob. We use random variable M_i to denote the ith message of the protocol, which could be either an Alice/Bob message or a trusted party message. Let X_i be the expected output of the protocol conditioned on the first i messages of the protocol. In particular, this definition is consistent with the definition of X_0.

For an arbitrary i, we consider both Alice aborts and Bob aborts the ith message. Suppose the ith message is Alice's message. Alice abort means that she aborts without sending this message to Bob. Conversely, Bob abort means he aborts in his next message immediately after receiving this message. On the other hand, if this is a trusted party message, then both a fail-stop Alice and a fail-stop Bob can abort this message. This prevents the other party from receiving the message. We refer to the defense output of Alice when Bob aborts the ith message as Alice's i^{th} defense. Similarly, we define the ith defense of Bob. Let D_i^{A} (resp., D_i^{B}) be the expectation of Alice's (resp., Bob's) i^{th} defense conditioned on the first i messages.

Now, we are ready to define our score function.

Definition 6. *Let π be a fair coin-tossing protocol in the f-hybrid model with message complexity r. Let τ be a stopping time. Let $\mathsf{P} \in \{\mathsf{A}, \mathsf{B}, \mathsf{T}\}$ be the party who sends the last message.[5] We define the score function as follows.*

$$\mathsf{Score}\,(\pi, \tau) := \mathbb{E}\left[\mathbb{1}_{(\tau \neq r) \vee (\mathsf{P} \neq \mathsf{A})} \cdot \left|X_\tau - D_\tau^{\mathsf{A}}\right| + \mathbb{1}_{(\tau \neq r) \vee (\mathsf{P} \neq \mathsf{B})} \cdot \left|X_\tau - D_\tau^{\mathsf{B}}\right|\right].$$

The following remarks, similar to [45,59], provide additional perspectives.

---

[5] We use A, B, and T to stand for Alice, Bob, and the trusted party, respectively.

Remark 3. 1. In the information-theoretic plain model, for every message of the protocol, one usually only consider the attack by the sender of this message. The attack by the receiver, who may abort immediately after receiving this message, usually is ineffective. This is because the sender is not lagging behind in terms of the progress of the protocol. However, in the f-hybrid model, we have trusted party messages, which reveal information regarding both parties' private randomness. Therefore, both parties' defenses may lag behind, and both parties' attacks could be effective. Hence, in our definition of the score function, for every message we pick in the stopping time, we consider the effectiveness of both parties' attacks.

2. The last message of the protocol is a boundary case of the above argument. Suppose Alice sends the last message of the protocol, Bob does not have the opportunity to abort after receiving this message. Similarly, if this is a Bob message, Alice cannot attack this message. On the other hand, if the last message is a trusted party message, then both parties could potentially attack this message. This explains the indicator function in our definition.

3. Finally, given a stopping time τ^* that witnesses a high score. We can always find a fail-stop attack strategy that deviates the expected output of the other party by $\frac{1}{4} \cdot$ Score (π, τ^*) in the following way. For Alice, we shall partition the stopping time τ^* by considering whether $X_\tau \geq D_\tau^{\mathsf{B}}$ or not. Similarly, we partition τ^* for Bob. These four attacks correspond to either Alice or Bob favoring either 0 or 1. The quality of these four attacks sums up to be Score (π, τ^*). Hence, one of these four fail-stop attacks might be at least $\frac{1}{4} \cdot$ Score (π, τ^*) effective.

The score function measures the effectiveness of a fail-stop attack corresponds to a stopping time τ. We are interested in the effectiveness of the most devastating fail-stop attacks. This motivates the following definition.

Definition 7. *Let π be a fair coin-tossing protocol in the f-hybrid model. Define*

$$\mathsf{Opt}\,(\pi) := \max_{\tau}\,\mathsf{Score}\,(\pi, \tau).$$

Now, we are ready to state our main theorem, which shows that the most devastating fail-stop attack is guaranteed to achieve a high score. In light of the remarks above, Theorem 4 directly implies Theorem 3.

Theorem 4. *For any (X_0, r)-fair coin-tossing protocol π in the f-hybrid model, we have*

$$\mathsf{Opt}\,(\pi) \geq \Gamma_r \cdot X_0\,(1 - X_0)\,,$$

where $\Gamma_r := \sqrt{\frac{\sqrt{2}-1}{r}}$.

4.3   Inductive Proof of Theorem 4

In this section, we shall prove Theorem 4 by using mathematical induction on the message complexity r. Let us first state some useful lemmas.

Firstly, we note that in the f-hybrid model, where f is a (randomized) functionality that satisfies the strict cross product rule, Alice view and Bob view are always independent conditioned on the partial transcript.

Lemma 3 (Independence of Alice and Bob view). *For any i and partial transcript $m_{\leq i}$, conditioned on this partial transcript, the joint distribution of Alice and Bob private randomness is identical to the product of the marginal distribution. That is,*

$$\mathsf{SD}\Big((R^{\mathsf{A}}, R^{\mathsf{B}}) | M_{\leq i} = m_{\leq i} \;,\; (R^{\mathsf{A}} | M_{\leq i} = m_{\leq i}) \times (R^{\mathsf{B}} | M_{\leq i} = m_{\leq i}) \Big) = 0.$$

In particular, this lemma implies the following claim.

Claim 1. *Let π be an arbitrary fair coin-tossing protocol in the f-hybrid model. Suppose there are ℓ possible first messages, namely, $m_1^{(1)}, m_1^{(2)}, \ldots, m_1^{(\ell)}$, each happens with probability $p^{(1)}, p^{(2)}, \ldots, p^{(\ell)}$. Suppose conditioned on the first message being $M_1 = m_1^{(i)}$, the expected defense of Alice and Bob are $d_1^{\mathsf{A},(i)}$ and $d_1^{\mathsf{B},(i)}$ respectively. Then we have*

$$\sum_{i=1}^{\ell} p^{(i)} \cdot d_1^{\mathsf{A},(i)} d_1^{\mathsf{B},(i)} = D_0^{\mathsf{A}} \cdot D_0^{\mathsf{B}}.$$

Lemma 3 and Claim 1 can be proven in a straightforward manner. We omit it due to space constraint. A proof can be found in the full version. Finally, the following lemma from [45] shall be helpful as well.

Imported Lemma 1 ([45]). *For all $P \in [0,1]$ and $Q \in [0, 1/2]$, if P and Q satisfy that*

$$Q \leq \frac{P}{1 + P^2},$$

then for all $x, \alpha, \beta \in [0,1]$, we have

$$\max\left(P \cdot x(1-x) , |x - \alpha| + |x - \beta| \right) \geq Q \cdot \left(x(1-x) + (x - \alpha)^2 + (x - \beta)^2 \right).$$

In particular, for any integer $r \geq 1$, the constraints are satisfied, if we set $P = \Gamma_r$ and $Q = \Gamma_{r+1}$, where $\Gamma_r := \sqrt{\frac{\sqrt{2}-1}{r}}$.

Base case: $r = 1$. We are now ready to prove Theorem 4. Let us start with the base case. In the base case, the protocol consists of only one message. Recall that the last message of the protocol is a boundary case of our score function. It might not be the case that both parties can attack this message. Hence, we prove it in different cases.

Case 1: Alice message. Suppose this message is an Alice message. In this case, we shall only consider the attack by Alice. By definition, with probability X_0, Alice will send a message, conditioned on which the output shall be 1. And with probability $1 - X_0$, Alice will send a message, conditioned on which the output shall be 0. On the other hand, the expectation of Bob's defense will remain the same as D_0^B. Therefore, the maximum of the score shall be

$$X_0 \cdot \left|1 - D_0^B\right| + (1 - X_0) \cdot \left|0 - D_0^B\right|,$$

which is

$$\geq X_0 \left(1 - X_0\right).$$

In particular, this is

$$\geq \Gamma_1 \cdot X_0 \left(1 - X_0\right).$$

Case 2: Bob message. This case is entirely analogous to case 1.

Case 3: Trusted party message. In this case, we shall consider the effectiveness of the attacks by both parties. Suppose there are ℓ possible first message by the trusted party, namely, $m_1^{(1)}, m_1^{(2)}, \ldots, m_1^{(\ell)}$, each happens with probability $p^{(1)}, p^{(2)}, \ldots, p^{(\ell)}$. Conditioned on first message being $M_1 = m_1^{(i)}$, the output of the protocol is $x_1^{(i)}$. We must have $x_1^{(i)} \in \{0, 1\}$ since the protocol has ended and parties shall agree on the output. Furthermore, let the expected defense of Alice and Bob be $d_1^{A,(i)}$ and $d_1^{B,(i)}$. Therefore, the maximum of the score will be

$$\sum_{i=1}^{\ell} p^{(i)} \cdot \left(\left| x_1^{(i)} - d_1^{A,(i)} \right| + \left| x_1^{(i)} - d_1^{B,(i)} \right| \right).$$

We have

$$\sum_{i=1}^{\ell} p^{(i)} \cdot \left(\left| x_1^{(i)} - d_1^{A,(i)} \right| + \left| x_1^{(i)} - d_1^{B,(i)} \right| \right)$$

$$\geq \sum_{i=1}^{\ell} p^{(i)} \cdot \left(x_1^{(i)} \left(1 - x_1^{(i)}\right) + \left(x_1^{(i)} - d_1^{A,(i)} \right)^2 + \left(x_1^{(i)} - d_1^{B,(i)} \right)^2 \right)$$

$$\text{(Since } x_1^{(i)} \in \{0, 1\})$$

$$= \sum_{i=1}^{\ell} p^{(i)} \cdot \left(x_1^{(i)} + \left(x_1^{(i)} - d_1^{A,(i)} - d_1^{B,(i)} \right)^2 - 2 d_1^{A,(i)} d_1^{B,(i)} \right)$$

$$\text{(Identity Transformation)}$$

$$\geq X_0 + \left(X_0 - D^A - D^B \right)^2 - \sum_{i=1}^{\ell} p^{(i)} \cdot 2 d_1^{A,(i)} d_1^{B,(i)}$$

$$\text{(Jensen's inequality on convex function } F(x, y, z) := (x - y - z)^2)$$

$$= X_0 + \left(X_0 - D^A - D^B \right)^2 - 2 D_0^A \cdot D_0^B \qquad \text{(Claim 1)}$$

$$= X_0 \left(1 - X_0\right) + \left(X_0 - D_0^{\mathsf{A}}\right)^2 + \left(X_0 - D_0^{\mathsf{B}}\right)^2 \quad \text{(Identity Transformation)}$$
$$\geq X_0 \left(1 - X_0\right)$$
$$\geq \Gamma_1 \cdot X_0 \left(1 - X_0\right)$$

This completes the proof of the base case.

Inductive Step. Suppose the statement is true for message complexity r. Let π be an arbitrary protocol with message complexity $r + 1$. Suppose there are ℓ possible first messages, namely, $m_1^{(1)}, m_1^{(2)}, \ldots, m_1^{(\ell)}$, each happens with probability $p^{(1)}, p^{(2)}, \ldots, p^{(\ell)}$. Conditioned on first message being $M_1 = m_1^{(i)}$, the output of the protocol is $x_1^{(i)}$ and the expected defense of Alice and Bob are $d_1^{\mathsf{A},(i)}$ and $d_1^{\mathsf{B},(i)}$ respectively. Note that conditioned on the first message being $M_1 = m_1^{(i)}$, the remaining protocol $\pi^{(i)}$ becomes a protocol with expected output $x_1^{(i)}$ and message complexity r. By our inductive hypothesis, we have

$$\mathsf{Opt}\left(\pi^{(i)}\right) \geq \Gamma_r \cdot x_1^{(i)} \left(1 - x_1^{(i)}\right).$$

On the other hand, we could also pick the first message $m_1^{(i)}$ as our stopping time, which yields a score of

$$\left| x_1^{(i)} - d_1^{\mathsf{A},(i)} \right| + \left| x_1^{(i)} - d_1^{\mathsf{B},(i)} \right|.$$

Therefore, the stopping time that witnesses the largest score yields (at least) a score of

$$\max\left(\Gamma_r \cdot x_1^{(i)} \left(1 - x_1^{(i)}\right) \, , \, \left| x_1^{(i)} - d_1^{\mathsf{A},(i)} \right| + \left| x_1^{(i)} - d_1^{\mathsf{B},(i)} \right| \right)$$
$$\geq \Gamma_{r+1} \cdot \left(x_1^{(i)} \left(1 - x_1^{(i)}\right) + \left(x_1^{(i)} - d_1^{\mathsf{A},(i)} \right)^2 + \left(x_1^{(i)} - d_1^{\mathsf{B},(i)} \right)^2 \right)$$

$$\text{(Imported Lemma 1)}$$

Therefore, $\mathsf{Opt}\left(\pi\right)$ is lower bounded by

$$\sum_{i=1}^{\ell} p^{(i)} \cdot \Gamma_{r+1} \cdot \left(x_1^{(i)} \left(1 - x_1^{(i)}\right) + \left(x_1^{(i)} - d_1^{\mathsf{A},(i)} \right)^2 + \left(x_1^{(i)} - d_1^{\mathsf{B},(i)} \right)^2 \right)$$
$$= \Gamma_{r+1} \cdot \sum_{i=1}^{\ell} p^{(i)} \cdot \left(x_1^{(i)} + \left(x_1^{(i)} - d_1^{\mathsf{A},(i)} - d_1^{\mathsf{B},(i)} \right)^2 - 2 d_1^{\mathsf{A},(i)} d_1^{\mathsf{B},(i)} \right)$$

$$\text{(Identity Transformation)}$$

$$\geq \Gamma_{r+1} \cdot \left(X_0 + \left(X_0 - D^{\mathsf{A}} - D^{\mathsf{B}} \right)^2 - \sum_{i=1}^{\ell} p^{(i)} \cdot 2 d_1^{\mathsf{A},(i)} d_1^{\mathsf{B},(i)} \right)$$

$$\text{(Jensen's inequality on convex function } F(x, y, z) := (x - y - z)^2)$$

$$= \Gamma_{r+1} \cdot \left(X_0 + (X_0 - D^{\mathsf{A}} - D^{\mathsf{B}})^2 - 2D_0^{\mathsf{A}} \cdot D_0^{\mathsf{B}} \right) \tag{Claim 1}$$

$$= \Gamma_{r+1} \cdot \left(X_0(1 - X_0) + (X_0 - D_0^{\mathsf{A}})^2 + (X_0 - D_0^{\mathsf{B}})^2 \right)$$

(Identity Transformation)

$$\geq \Gamma_{r+1} \cdot X_0(1 - X_0)$$

This completes the proof of the inductive step.

5 Black-Box Uses of Public-Key Encryption is Useless for Optimal Fair Coin-Tossing

In this section, we prove that public-key encryption used in a black-boxed manner shall not enable optimal fair coin-tossing. Our objective is to prove the existence of an oracle, with respect to which public-key encryption exists, but optimal fair coin-tossing does not.

5.1 Public-Key Encrytion Oracles

Let n be the security parameter. We follow the work of [56] and define the following set of functions.

- Gen: $\{0,1\}^n \to \{0,1\}^{3n}$. This function is a random injective function.
- Enc: $\{0,1\}^{3n} \times \{0,1\}^n \to \{0,1\}^{3n}$. This function is uniformly randomly sampled among all functions that are injective with respect to the second input. That is, when the first input is fixed, this function is injective.
- Dec: $\{0,1\}^n \times \{0,1\}^{3n} \to \{0,1\}^n \cup \{\bot\}$. This function is the uniquely determined by functions Gen and Enc as follows. Dec takes as inputs a secret-key $sk \in \{0,1\}^n$ and a ciphertext $c \in \{0,1\}^{3n}$. If there exists a message $m \in \{0,1\}^n$ such that $\mathsf{Enc}(\mathsf{Gen}(sk), m) = c$, define $\mathsf{Dec}(sk, c) := m$. Otherwise, define $\mathsf{Dec}(sk, c) := \bot$. Note that such message m, if exists, must be unique, because Enc is injective with respect to the second input.
- Test$_1$: $\{0,1\}^{3n} \to \{0,1\}$. This function is uniquely determined by function Gen. It takes as an input a public-key $pk \in \{0,1\}^{3n}$. If there exists a secret-key $sk \in \{0,1\}^n$ such that $\mathsf{Gen}(sk) = pk$, define $\mathsf{Test}_1(pk) := 1$. Otherwise, define $\mathsf{Test}_1(pk) := 0$.
- Test$_2$: $\{0,1\}^{3n} \times \{0,1\}^{3n} \to \{0,1\}$. This function is uniquely determined by function Enc. It takes as inputs a public-key $pk \in \{0,1\}^{3n}$ and a ciphertext $c \in \{0,1\}^{3n}$. If there exists a message m such that $\mathsf{Enc}(pk, m) = c$, define $\mathsf{Test}_2(pk, c) := 1$. Otherwise, define $\mathsf{Test}_2(pk, c) := 0$.

We shall refer to this collection of oracles the PKE oracle. Trivially, the PKE oracle enables public-key encryption. We shall prove that it does not enable optimally-fair coin-tossing.

Remark 4. We stress that it is necessary to include the test functions Test_1 and Test_2. As shown by [27,54], public-key encryption with additional features could be used to construct oblivious transfer protocols, which, in turn, could be used to construct optimally-fair coin-tossing protocols [61].[56] proved that with the test functions Test_1 and Test_2, Alice's and Bob's private views can only be correlated as a disjoint union of independent views, which is not sufficient to realize oblivious transfer.We refer the readers to [56] for more details.

5.2   Our Results

We shall prove the following theorem.

Theorem 5 (Main theorem for PKE Oracle). *There exists a universal polynomial $p(\cdot, \cdot, \cdot, \cdot)$ such that the following holds. Let π be any fair coin-tossing protocol in the PKE oracle model, where Alice and Bob make at most m queries. Let X_0 be the expected output, and r be the message complexity of π. There exists an (information-theoretic) fail-stop attacker that deviates the expected output of the other party by (at least)*

$$\Omega\left(\frac{X_0\left(1 - X_0\right)}{\sqrt{r}}\right).$$

This attacker shall ask at most $p\left(n, m, r, \frac{1}{X_0(1-X_0)}\right)$ additional queries.

It is instructive to understand why Theorem 3 does not imply Theorem 5. One may be tempted to model the public-key encryption primitive as an idealized secure function evaluation functionality to prove this implication. The idealized functionality for public-key encryption delivers sender's message to the receiver, while hiding it from the eavesdropper. So, the "idealized public-key encryption" functionality is a three-party functionality where the sender's input is delivered to the receiver; the eavesdropper has no input or output. This idealized effect is easily achieved given secure point-to-point communication channels, which we assume in our work. The non-triviality here is that our result is with respect to an *oracle* that implements the public-key encryption functionality. An oracle for public-key encryption is not necessarily used just for secure message passing. Section 6 has a discussion elaborating the difference between an "ideal functionality" and an "oracle implementing the ideal functionality."

Remark 5. As usual in the literature [21,22,59], we shall only consider *instant protocols*. That is, once a party aborts, the other party shall not make any additional queries to defend, but directly output her current defense coin. We refer the reader to [21] for justification and more details on this assumption.

In fact, our proof technique is sufficient to prove the following stronger theorem.

Theorem 6. *There exists a universal polynomial $p(\cdot, \cdot, \cdot, \cdot)$ such that the following holds. Let f be any (randomized) functionality that is not complete. Let π be any fair coin-tossing protocol in the f-hybrid model where parties have access to the PKE oracle model. Assume Alice and Bob make at most m queries. Let X_0 be the expected output, and r be the message complexity of π. There exists an (information-theoretic) fail-stop attacker that deviates the expected output of the other party by (at least)*

$$\Omega\left(\frac{X_0(1-X_0)}{\sqrt{r}}\right).$$

This attacker shall ask at most $p\left(n, m, r, \frac{1}{X_0(1-X_0)}\right)$ additional queries.

Our proof strategy consists of two steps, similar to that of [56].

1. Given a protocol in the PKE oracle model, we shall first convert it into a protocol where parties do not invoke the decryption queries. By Imported Theorem 1 proven in [56], we can convert it in a way such that the insecurity of these two protocols in the presence of a semi-honest adversary is (almost) identical. In particular, this ensures that the insecurity of fair coin-tossing protocol in the presence of a fail-stop adversary is (almost) identical.
2. Next, we shall extend the results of [59], where they proved a fair coin-tossing protocol in the random oracle model is highly insecure, to the setting of PKE oracles without decryption oracle. Intuitively, The proof of [59] only relied on the fact that in the random oracle model, there exists a public algorithm [8] that asks polynomially many queries and decorrelate the private view of Alice and Bob. Mahmoody, Maji, and Prabhakaran [56] proved that (summarized as Imported Theorem 2) the PKE oracles without the decryption oracle satisfies the similar property. Hence, the proof of [59] extends naturally to this setting.

Together, these two steps prove Theorem 5. The first step is summarized in Sect. 5.3. The second step is summarized in Sect. 5.4.

5.3 Reduction from PKE Oracle to Image Testable Random Oracle

A (keyed version of) *image-testable random oracles* is a collection of pairs of oracles $(R^{\mathsf{key}}, T^{\mathsf{key}})$ parameterized by a key such that the following holds.

- $R^{\mathsf{key}} \colon \{0,1\}^n \to \{0,1\}^{3n}$ is a randomly sampled injective function.
- $T^{\mathsf{key}} \colon \{0,1\}^{3n} \to \{0,1\}$ is uniquely determined by function R^{key} as follows. Define $T^{\mathsf{key}}(\beta) := 1$ if there exists an $\alpha \in \{0,1\}^n$ such that $R^{\mathsf{key}}(\alpha) = \beta$. Otherwise, define $T^{\mathsf{key}}(\beta) = 0$.

Observe that the PKE oracle without the decryption oracle Dec is exactly a (keyed version of) image-testable random oracles with the keys drawn from $\{\bot\} \cup \{0,1\}^{3n}$. If the key is $\bot$, it refers to the pair of oracles $(\mathsf{Gen}, \mathsf{Test}_1)$. If the key $\in \{0,1\}^{3n}$, it refers to the pair of oracles $(\mathsf{Enc}(\mathsf{key}, \cdot), \mathsf{Test}_2(\mathsf{key}, \cdot))$. We shall refer to the PKE oracle without the decryption oracle Dec as ITRO. We shall use the following imported theorem, which is implicitly proven in [56].

Imported Theorem 1 ([56]). *There exists a universal polynomial $p(\cdot, \cdot)$ such that the following holds. Let π be a fair coin-tossing protocol in the PKE oracle model. Let X_0 and r be the expected output and message complexity. Suppose Alice and Bob ask (at most) m queries. For any $\epsilon > 0$, there exists a fair coin-tossing protocol π' in the ITRO model such that the following holds.*

- *Let X_0' and r' be the expected output and message complexity of π'. Then, $r' = r$ and $|X_0' - X_0| < \epsilon$.*
- *Parties asks at most $p(m, 1/\epsilon)$ queries in protocol π'.*
- *For any semi-honest adversary $\mathcal{A}'$ for protocol π', there exists a semi-honest adversary $\mathcal{A}$ for protocol π, such that the view of $\mathcal{A}$ is ϵ-close to the view of $\mathcal{A}'$. And vice versa. In particular, this implies that if π' is α-insecure. π is (at least) $(\alpha - \epsilon)$-insecure.*

The intuition behind this theorem is the following. To avoid the uses of decryption oracle, parties are going to help each other decrypt. In more detail, suppose Alice generates a ciphertext using Bob's public key. Whenever the probability that Bob invokes the decryption oracle on this ciphertext is non-negligibly high, Alice will directly reveal the message to Bob. Hence, Bob does not need to use the decryption oracle. This shall not harm the security as a semi-honest Bob can recover the message by asking polynomially many additional queries. We refer the readers to [56] for more details.

Looking forward, we shall prove that any fair coin-tossing protocol in the ITRO model is $\Omega\left(\frac{X_0'(1-X_0')}{\sqrt{r}}\right)$-insecure. By setting ϵ to be $1/\mathsf{poly}$ for some sufficiently large polynomial, we shall guarantee that

$$ \epsilon = o\left(\frac{X_0(1-X_0)}{\sqrt{r}}\right). $$

This guarantees that the insecurity of the protocol in the PKE oracle model is (qualitatively) identical to the insecure of the protocol in the ITRO model.

5.4   Extending the Proof of [59] to Image Testable Random Oracle

We first recall the following theorem from [56].

Imported Theorem 2 (Common Information Learner [56]). *There exists a universal polynomial $p(\cdot, \cdot)$ such that the following holds. Let π be any two-party protocol in the ITRO model, in which both parties make at most m queries. For all threshold $\epsilon \in (0, 1)$, there exists a public algorithm, called the common information learner, who has access to the transcript between Alice and Bob. After receiving each message, the common information learner performs a sequence of queries and obtain its corresponding answers from the ITRO. Let M_i denote the ith message of the protocol. Let H_i denote the sequence of query-answer pairs asked by the common information learner after receiving the message M_i. Let T_i be the union of the ith message M_i and the ith common information learner*

message H_i. Let V_i^A (resp., V_i^B) denote Alice's (resp., Bob's) private view imme-
diately after message T_i, which includes her private randomness, private queries,
and the public partial transcript. The common information learner guarantees
that the following conditions are simultaneously satisfied.

- **Cross-product Property.** *Fix any round i,*

$$\operatorname*{E}_{t_{\leq i} \leftarrow T_{\leq i}} \left[\mathsf{SD} \left(\left(V_i^A, V_i^B \middle| T_{\leq i} = t_{\leq i} \right), \left(V_i^A \middle| T_{\leq i} = t_{\leq i} \right) \times \left(V_i^B \middle| T_{\leq i} = t_{\leq i} \right) \right) \right] \leq \epsilon.$$

Intuitively, it states that on average, the statistical distance between (1) the
joint distribution of Alice and Bob's private view, and (2) the product of
the marginal distributions of Alice's private views and Bob's private views is
small.

- **Efficient Property.** *The expected number of queries asked by the common*
information learner is bounded by $p(m, 1/\epsilon)$.

This theorem, combined with proof of [59] gives the following theorem.

Theorem 7. *There exists a universal polynomial $p(\cdot, \cdot, \cdot, \cdot)$ such that the follow-*
ing holds. Let π be a protocol in the ITRO model, where Alice and Bob make at
most m queries. Let X_0 and r be the expected output and message complexity.
Then, there exists an (information-theoretic) fail-stop adversary that deviates
the expected output of the other party by

$$\Omega \left(\frac{X_0 (1 - X_0)}{\sqrt{r}} \right).$$

This attacker asks at most $p \left(n, m, r, \frac{1}{X_0(1-X_0)} \right)$ additional queries.

Below, we briefly discuss why Imported Theorem 2 is sufficient to prove this
theorem. The full proof is analogous to [59] and the proof of the results in the
f-hybrid model. Hence we omit it here.

On a high level, the proof goes as follows. We prove Theorem 7 by induction.
Conditioned on the first message, the remaining protocol becomes an $(r - 1)$-
message protocol, and one can apply the inductive hypothesis. For every possible
first message i, we consider whether to abort immediately or defer the attack
to the remaining sub-protocol. By invoking Imported Lemma 1, we obtain a
potential function, which characterizes the insecurity of the protocol with first
message being i. This potential function will be of the form

$$\Phi(x_i, a_i, b_i) = x_i(1 - x_i) + (x_i - a_i)^2 + (x_i - b_i)^2,$$

where x_i, a_i, and b_i stands for the expected output, expected Alice defense, and
expected Bob defense, respectively. To complete the proof, [59] showed that it
suffices to prove the following Jensen's inequality.

$$\operatorname*{E}_i \left[\Phi(x_i, a_i, b_i) \right] \geq \Phi \left(\operatorname*{E}_i \left[x_i \right], \operatorname*{E}_i \left[a_i \right], \operatorname*{E}_i \left[b_i \right] \right).$$

To prove this, one can rewrite $\Phi(x, a, b)$ as

$$\Phi(x, a, b) = x + (x - a - b)^2 - 2ab.$$

We note that x and $(x - a - b)^2$ are convex functions, and hence Jensen's inequality holds. As for the term ab, we shall have

$$\mathop{\mathrm{E}}_i [a_i b_i] \approx \mathop{\mathrm{E}}_i [a_i] \cdot \mathop{\mathrm{E}}_i [b_i]$$

as long as, conditioned on every possible first message i, Alice's private view is (almost) independent to Bob's private view. This is exactly what Imported Theorem 2 guarantees except for a small error depending on ϵ, which we shall set to be sufficiently small. Therefore, the proof shall follow.

6   Open Problems

In this work, we proved that access to ideal invocations to the secure function evaluation functionalities like the Kushilevitz function [51] (Fig. 2) does not enable optimal fair coin-tossing. However, we do *not* resolve the following stronger statement. Suppose there exists an oracle relative to which there exists a secure protocol for the Kushilevitz function. Is optimal fair coin-tossing impossible relative to this oracle?

To appreciate the distinction between these two statements, observe that there may be additional ways to use the "oracle implementing Kushilevitz function" than *merely* facilitating the secure computing of the Kushilevitz function. More generally, there may be implicit consequences implied by the existence of such an oracle. For example, "the existence of an efficient algorithm for 3SAT" not only allows solving 3SAT problems, but it also allows efficiently solving any problem in PH because the entire PH collapses to P.

This problem is incredibly challenging and one of the major open problems in this field. The technical tools developed in this paper also bring us closer to resolving this problem.

References

1. Agrawal, S., Prabhakaran, M.: On fair exchange, fair coins and fair sampling. In: Canetti, R., Garay, J.A. (eds.) CRYPTO 2013, Part I. LNCS, vol. 8042, pp. 259–276. Springer, Heidelberg (2013). https://doi.org/10.1007/978-3-642-40041-4_15
2. Alon, B., Omri, E.: Almost-optimally fair multiparty coin-tossing with nearly three-quarters malicious. In: Hirt, M., Smith, A. (eds.) TCC 2016, Part I. LNCS, vol. 9985, pp. 307–335. Springer, Heidelberg (2016). https://doi.org/10.1007/978-3-662-53641-4_13
3. Asharov, G.: Towards characterizing complete fairness in secure two-party computation. In: Lindell, Y. (ed.) TCC 2014. LNCS, vol. 8349, pp. 291–316. Springer, Heidelberg (2014). https://doi.org/10.1007/978-3-642-54242-8_13

4. Asharov, G., Beimel, A., Makriyannis, N., Omri, E.: Complete characterization of fairness in secure two-party computation of boolean functions. In: Dodis, Y., Nielsen, J.B. (eds.) TCC 2015, Part I. LNCS, vol. 9014, pp. 199–228. Springer, Heidelberg (2015). https://doi.org/10.1007/978-3-662-46494-6_10
5. Asharov, G., Lindell, Y., Rabin, T.: A full characterization of functions that imply fair coin tossing and ramifications to fairness. In: Sahai, A. (ed.) TCC 2013. LNCS, vol. 7785, pp. 243–262. Springer, Heidelberg (2013). https://doi.org/10.1007/978-3-642-36594-2_14
6. Awerbuch, B., Blum, M., Chor, B., Goldwasser, S., Micali, S.: How to implement Bracha's O (log n) byzantine agreement algorithm (1985)
7. Baecher, P., Brzuska, C., Fischlin, M.: Notions of black-box reductions, revisited. In: Sako, K., Sarkar, P. (eds.) ASIACRYPT 2013, Part I. LNCS, vol. 8269, pp. 296–315. Springer, Heidelberg (2013). https://doi.org/10.1007/978-3-642-42033-7_16
8. Barak, B., Mahmoody-Ghidary, M.: Merkle puzzles are optimal - an $O(n^2)$-query attack on any key exchange from a random oracle. In: Halevi, S. (ed.) CRYPTO 2009. LNCS, vol. 5677, pp. 374–390. Springer, Heidelberg (2009). https://doi.org/10.1007/978-3-642-03356-8_22
9. Beaver, D.: Perfect privacy for two-party protocols. In: DIMACS (1989)
10. Beimel, A., Lindell, Y., Omri, E., Orlov, I.: 1/p-secure multiparty computation without honest majority and the best of both worlds. In: Rogaway, P. (ed.) CRYPTO 2011. LNCS, vol. 6841, pp. 277–296. Springer, Heidelberg (2011). https://doi.org/10.1007/978-3-642-22792-9_16
11. Beimel, A., Omri, E., Orlov, I.: Protocols for multiparty coin toss with dishonest majority. In: Rabin, T. (ed.) CRYPTO 2010. LNCS, vol. 6223, pp. 538–557. Springer, Heidelberg (2010). https://doi.org/10.1007/978-3-642-14623-7_29
12. Blum, M.: Coin flipping by telephone - a protocol for solving impossible problems (1982)
13. Broder, A.Z., Dolev, D.: Flipping coins in many pockets (byzantine agreement on uniformly random values). In: 25th FOCS, pp. 157–170. IEEE Computer Society Press, October 1984
14. Buchbinder, N., Haitner, I., Levi, N., Tsfadia, E.: Fair coin flipping: tighter analysis and the many-party case. In: Klein, P.N. (ed.) 28th SODA, pp. 2580–2600. ACM-SIAM, January 2017
15. Canetti, R.: Security and composition of multiparty cryptographic protocols. J. Cryptol. 13(1), 143–202 (2000)
16. Canetti, R.: Universally composable security: a new paradigm for cryptographic protocols. In: 42nd FOCS, pp. 136–145. IEEE Computer Society Press, October 2001
17. Canetti, R., Kushilevitz, E., Lindell, Y.: On the limitations of universally composable two-party computation without set-up assumptions. In: Biham, E. (ed.) EUROCRYPT 2003. LNCS, vol. 2656, pp. 68–86. Springer, Heidelberg (2003). https://doi.org/10.1007/3-540-39200-9_5
18. Chor, B., Kushilevitz, E.: A zero-one law for Boolean privacy (extended abstract). In: 21st ACM STOC, pp. 62–72. ACM Press, May 1989
19. Cleve, R.: Limits on the security of coin flips when half the processors are faulty (extended abstract). In: 18th ACM STOC, pp. 364–369. ACM Press, May 1986
20. Cleve, R., Impagliazzo, R.: Martingales, collective coin flipping and discrete control processes (extended abstract) (1993)

21. Dachman-Soled, D., Lindell, Y., Mahmoody, M., Malkin, T.: On the black-box complexity of optimally-fair coin tossing. In: Ishai, Y. (ed.) TCC 2011. LNCS, vol. 6597, pp. 450–467. Springer, Heidelberg (2011). https://doi.org/10.1007/978-3-642-19571-6_27

22. Dachman-Soled, D., Mahmoody, M., Malkin, T.: Can optimally-fair coin tossing be based on one-way functions? In: Lindell, Y. (ed.) TCC 2014. LNCS, vol. 8349, pp. 217–239. Springer, Heidelberg (2014). https://doi.org/10.1007/978-3-642-54242-8_10

23. Data, D., Prabhakaran, M.: Towards characterizing securely computable two-party randomized functions. In: Abdalla, M., Dahab, R. (eds.) PKC 2018, Part I. LNCS, vol. 10769, pp. 675–697. Springer, Cham (2018). https://doi.org/10.1007/978-3-319-76578-5_23

24. Even, S., Goldreich, O., Lempel, A.: A randomized protocol for signing contracts. In: Chaum, D., Rivest, R.L., Sherman, A.T. (eds.) CRYPTO 1982, pp. 205–210. Plenum Press, New York (1982)

25. Gennaro, R., Gertner, Y., Katz, J.: Lower bounds on the efficiency of encryption and digital signature schemes. In: 35th ACM STOC, pp. 417–425. ACM Press, June 2003

26. Gennaro, R., Trevisan, L.: Lower bounds on the efficiency of generic cryptographic constructions. In: 41st FOCS, pp. 305–313. IEEE Computer Society Press, November 2000

27. Gertner, Y., Kannan, S., Malkin, T., Reingold, O., Viswanathan, M.: The relationship between public key encryption and oblivious transfer. In: 41st FOCS, pp. 325–335. IEEE Computer Society Press, November 2000

28. Gertner, Y., Malkin, T., Reingold, O.: On the impossibility of basing trapdoor functions on trapdoor predicates. In: 42nd FOCS, pp. 126–135. IEEE Computer Society Press, October 2001

29. Goldreich, O., Goldwasser, S., Micali, S.: How to construct random functions (extended abstract). In: 25th FOCS, pp. 464–479. IEEE Computer Society Press, October 1984

30. Goldreich, O., Goldwasser, S., Micali, S.: How to construct random functions. J. ACM **33**(4), 792–807 (1986)

31. Goldreich, O., Micali, S., Wigderson, A.: How to play any mental game or a completeness theorem for protocols with honest majority. In: Aho, A. (ed.) 19th ACM STOC, pp. 218–229. ACM Press, May 1987

32. Goldreich, O., Micali, S., Wigderson, A.: Proofs that yield nothing but their validity or all languages in NP have zero-knowledge proof systems. J. ACM **38**(3), 691–729 (1991)

33. Gordon, S.D., Hazay, C., Katz, J., Lindell, Y.: Complete fairness in secure two-party computation. In: Ladner, R.E., Dwork, C. (eds.) 40th ACM STOC, pp. 413–422. ACM Press, May 2008

34. Gordon, S.D., Katz, J.: Partial fairness in secure two-party computation. In: Gilbert, H. (ed.) EUROCRYPT 2010. LNCS, vol. 6110, pp. 157–176. Springer, Heidelberg (2010). https://doi.org/10.1007/978-3-642-13190-5_8

35. Haitner, I., Makriyannis, N., Omri, E.: On the complexity of fair coin flipping. In: Beimel, A., Dziembowski, S. (eds.) TCC 2018, Part I. LNCS, vol. 11239, pp. 539–562. Springer, Cham (2018). https://doi.org/10.1007/978-3-030-03807-6_20

36. Haitner, I., Nissim, K., Omri, E., Shaltiel, R., Silbak, J.: Computational two-party correlation: a dichotomy for key-agreement protocols. In: Thorup, M. (ed.) 59th FOCS, pp. 136–147. IEEE Computer Society Press, October 2018

37. Haitner, I., Omri, E.: Coin flipping with constant bias implies one-way functions. In: Ostrovsky, R. (ed.) 52nd FOCS, pp. 110–119. IEEE Computer Society Press, October 2011

38. Haitner, I., Reingold, O.: Statistically-hiding commitment from any one-way function. In: Johnson, D.S., Feige, U. (eds.) 39th ACM STOC, pp. 1–10. ACM Press, June 2007

39. Haitner, I., Tsfadia, E.: An almost-optimally fair three-party coin-flipping protocol. In: Shmoys, D.B. (ed.) 46th ACM STOC, pp. 408–416. ACM Press, May/June (2014)

40. Håstad, J.: Pseudo-random generators under uniform assumptions. In: 22nd ACM STOC, pp. 395–404. ACM Press, May 1990

41. Håstad, J., Impagliazzo, R., Levin, L.A., Luby, M.: A pseudorandom generator from any one-way function. SIAM J. Comput. **28**(4), 1364–1396 (1999)

42. Impagliazzo, R.: A personal view of average-case complexity. In: Proceedings of the Tenth Annual Structure in Complexity Theory Conference (1995)

43. Impagliazzo, R., Levin, L.A., Luby, M.: Pseudo-random generation from one-way functions (extended abstracts). In: 21st ACM STOC, pp. 12–24. ACM Press, May 1989

44. Impagliazzo, R., Rudich, S.: Limits on the provable consequences of one-way permutations. In: 21st ACM STOC, pp. 44–61. ACM Press, May 1989

45. Khorasgani, H.A., Maji, H.K., Wang, M.: Coin tossing with lazy defense: hardness of computation results. Cryptology ePrint Archive, Report 2020/131 (2020). https://eprint.iacr.org/2020/131

46. Kilian, J.: A general completeness theorem for two-party games. In: 23rd ACM STOC, pp. 553–560. ACM Press, May 1991

47. Kilian, J.: More general completeness theorems for secure two-party computation. In: 32nd ACM STOC, pp. 316–324. ACM Press, May 2000

48. Kreitz, G.: A zero-one law for secure multi-party computation with ternary outputs. In: Ishai, Y. (ed.) TCC 2011. LNCS, vol. 6597, pp. 382–399. Springer, Heidelberg (2011). https://doi.org/10.1007/978-3-642-19571-6_23

49. Künzler, R., Müller-Quade, J., Raub, D.: Secure computability of functions in the IT setting with dishonest majority and applications to long-term security. In: Reingold, O. (ed.) TCC 2009. LNCS, vol. 5444, pp. 238–255. Springer, Heidelberg (2009). https://doi.org/10.1007/978-3-642-00457-5_15

50. Kushilevitz, E.: Privacy and communication complexity. In: 30th FOCS, pp. 416–421. IEEE Computer Society Press, October/November 1989

51. Kushilevitz, E., Nisan, N.: Communication complexity. Google Scholar Digital Library Digital Library (1997)

52. Lindell, Y.: Lower bounds for concurrent self composition. In: Naor, M. (ed.) TCC 2004. LNCS, vol. 2951, pp. 203–222. Springer, Heidelberg (2004). https://doi.org/10.1007/978-3-540-24638-1_12

53. Lindell, Y.: How to simulate it - a tutorial on the simulation proof technique. Tutor. Found. Cryptogr. **277–346**, (2017)

54. Lindell, Y., Omri, E., Zarosim, H.: Completeness for symmetric two-party functionalities - revisited. In: Wang, X., Sako, K. (eds.) ASIACRYPT 2012. LNCS, vol. 7658, pp. 116–133. Springer, Heidelberg (2012). https://doi.org/10.1007/978-3-642-34961-4_9

55. Luby, M., Rackoff, C.: How to construct pseudorandom permutations from pseudorandom functions. SIAM J. Comput. **17**(2), 373–386 (1988)

56. Mahmoody, M., Maji, H.K., Prabhakaran, M.: On the power of public-key encryption in secure computation. In: Lindell, Y. (ed.) TCC 2014. LNCS, vol. 8349, pp. 240–264. Springer, Heidelberg (2014)

57. Maji, H.K., Prabhakaran, M., Rosulek, M.: Complexity of multi-party computation problems: the case of 2-party symmetric secure function evaluation. In: Reingold, O. (ed.) TCC 2009. LNCS, vol. 5444, pp. 256–273. Springer, Heidelberg (2009). https://doi.org/10.1007/978-3-642-00457-5_16

58. Maji, H.K., Prabhakaran, M., Rosulek, M.: A zero-one law for cryptographic complexity with respect to computational UC security. In: Rabin, T. (ed.) CRYPTO 2010. LNCS, vol. 6223, pp. 595–612. Springer, Heidelberg (2010). https://doi.org/10.1007/978-3-642-14623-7_32

59. Maji, H.K., Wang, M.: Black-box use of one-way functions is useless for optimal fair coin-tossing. In: Micciancio, D., Ristenpart, T. (eds.) CRYPTO 2020, Part II. LNCS, vol. 12171, pp. 593–617. Springer, Cham (2020). https://doi.org/10.1007/978-3-030-56880-1_21

60. Makriyannis, N.: On the classification of finite boolean functions up to fairness. In: Abdalla, M., De Prisco, R. (eds.) SCN 2014. LNCS, vol. 8642, pp. 135–154. Springer, Cham (2014). https://doi.org/10.1007/978-3-319-10879-7_9

61. Moran, T., Naor, M., Segev, G.: An optimally fair coin toss. In: Reingold, O. (ed.) TCC 2009. LNCS, vol. 5444, pp. 1–18. Springer, Heidelberg (2009). https://doi.org/10.1007/978-3-642-00457-5_1

62. Naor, M.: Bit commitment using pseudorandomness. J. Cryptol. 4(2), 151–158 (1991)

63. Naor, M., Ostrovsky, R., Venkatesan, R., Yung, M.: Perfect zero-knowledge arguments for NP using any one-way permutation. J. Cryptol. 11(2), 87–108 (1998)

64. Naor, M., Yung, M.: Universal one-way hash functions and their cryptographic applications. In: 21st ACM STOC, pp. 33–43. ACM Press, May 1989

65. Papadimitriou, C.H.: Games against nature (extended abstract). In: 24th FOCS, pp. 446–450. IEEE Computer Society Press, November 1983

66. Prabhakaran, M., Rosulek, M.: Cryptographic complexity of multi-party computation problems: classifications and separations. In: Wagner, D. (ed.) CRYPTO 2008. LNCS, vol. 5157, pp. 262–279. Springer, Heidelberg (2008). https://doi.org/10.1007/978-3-540-85174-5_15

67. Rabin, M.O.: How to exchange secrets by oblivious transfer. Technical Memo TR-81 (1981)

68. Rabin, M.O.: How to exchange secrets with oblivious transfer. Cryptology ePrint Archive, Report 2005/187 (2005). http://eprint.iacr.org/2005/187

69. Reingold, O., Trevisan, L., Vadhan, S.: Notions of reducibility between cryptographic primitives. In: Naor, M. (ed.) TCC 2004. LNCS, vol. 2951, pp. 1–20. Springer, Heidelberg (2004).https://doi.org/10.1007/978-3-540-24638-1_1

70. Rompel, J.: One-way functions are necessary and sufficient for secure signatures. In: 22nd ACM STOC, pp. 387–394. ACM Press, May 1990

71. Rosulek, M., Shirley, M.: On the structure of unconditional UC hybrid protocols. In: Beimel, A., Dziembowski, S. (eds.) TCC 2018, Part II. LNCS, vol. 11240, pp. 98–126. Springer, Cham (2018). https://doi.org/10.1007/978-3-030-03810-6_4

72. Rudich, S.: The use of interaction in public cryptosystems (extended abstract). In: Feigenbaum, J. (ed.) CRYPTO 1991. LNCS, vol. 576, pp. 242–251. Springer, Heidelberg (1992). https://doi.org/10.1007/3-540-46766-1_19

73. Schilling, R.L.: Measures, integrals and martingales (2017)

74. Simon, D.R.: Finding collisions on a one-way street: can secure hash functions be based on general assumptions? In: Nyberg, K. (ed.) EUROCRYPT 1998. LNCS, vol. 1403, pp. 334–345. Springer, Heidelberg (1998). https://doi.org/10.1007/BFb0054137

75. Yao, A.C.-C.: Protocols for secure computations (extended abstract). In: 23rd FOCS, pp. 160–164. IEEE Computer Society Press, November 1982

YOSO: You Only Speak Once

Secure MPC with Stateless Ephemeral Roles

Craig Gentry[1]([✉]), Shai Halevi[1], Hugo Krawczyk[1], Bernardo Magri[2],
Jesper Buus Nielsen[2], Tal Rabin[1,3], and Sophia Yakoubov[4]

[1] Algorand Foundation, New York, USA
hugo@ee.technion.ac.il
[2] Concordium Blockchain Research Center, Aarhus University, Aarhus, Denmark
[3] UPenn, Philadelphia, USA
[4] Aarhus University, Aarhus, Denmark

Abstract. The inherent difficulty of maintaining stateful environments over long periods of time gave rise to the paradigm of *serverless computing*, where mostly stateless components are deployed on demand to handle computation tasks, and are torn down once their task is complete. Serverless architecture could offer the added benefit of improved resistance to targeted denial-of-service attacks, by hiding from the attacker the physical machines involved in the protocol until after they complete their work. Realizing such protection, however, requires that the protocol only uses stateless parties, where each party sends only one message and never needs to speaks again. Perhaps the most famous example of this style of protocols is the Nakamoto consensus protocol used in Bitcoin: A peer can win the right to produce the next block by running a local lottery (mining) while staying covert. Once the right has been won, it is executed by sending a *single* message. After that, the physical entity never needs to send more messages.

We refer to this as the You-Only-Speak-Once (YOSO) property, and initiate the formal study of it within a new model that we call the YOSO model. Our model is centered around the notion of *roles*, which are stateless parties that can only send a single message. Crucially, our modelling separates the protocol design, that only uses roles, from the role-assignment mechanism, that assigns roles to actual physical entities. This separation enables studying these two aspects separately, and our YOSO model in this work only deals with the protocol-design aspect.

We describe several techniques for achieving YOSO MPC; both computational and information theoretic. Our protocols are synchronous and provide guaranteed output delivery (which is important for application domains such as blockchains), assuming honest majority of roles in every

J. B. Nielsen—Partially funded by The Concordium Foundation; The Danish Independent Research Council under Grant-ID DFF-8021-00366B (BETHE); The Carlsberg Foundation under the Semper Ardens Research Project CF18-112 (BCM).
S. Yakoubov—Funded by the European Research Council (ERC) under the European Unions's Horizon 2020 research and innovation programme under grant agreement No 669255 (MPCPRO).

T. Malkin and C. Peikert (Eds.): CRYPTO 2021, LNCS 12826, pp. 64–93, 2021.
https://doi.org/10.1007/978-3-030-84245-1_3

time step. We describe a practically efficient computationally-secure protocol, as well as a proof-of-concept information theoretically secure protocol.

Keywords: Blockchains · Secure MPC · Stateless Parties · YOSO

1   Introduction

A somewhat surprising feature of our networked world is just how hard it is to keep a working stateful execution environment over long periods of time. Even in non-adversarial settings, it is a major challenge to keep a server operational and connected through software updates, local physical events, and global infrastructure interruptions. This becomes even harder in adversarial environments. Consider for example a network adversary targeting a specific protocol, watching the communication network and mounting a targeted denial of service (DoS) attack on any machine that sends a message in this protocol. In high-stake environments, one also must worry about near-instant malicious compromise, unleashed by well equipped adversaries with a stash of zero-day exploits.

One approach for mitigating this issue is the paradigm of *serverless computing*, where mostly-stateless components are deployed on demand to handle computation tasks, and are torn down once their task is complete. In addition to economic benefits, a protocol built from such components could offer better resistance against strong adversaries by hiding the physical machines that play a role in the protocol, until after they complete their work and send their messages. To realize this protection, however, the protocol must utilize only stateless components, making it harder to design.

Perhaps the best-known example of this style of protocol is the Nakamoto consensus protocol used in Bitcoin [19]. A salient property of the Bitcoin design is that a peer can win the right to produce the next block by running a local lottery (mining), while staying covert. Once the right has been won, it is executed by sending a *single* message. After that, the physical entity never needs to send another message. Another example is the Algorand consensus protocol [8] with its player-replaceability property.

In this work we initiate a formal study of protocols of this style, which we refer to as You-Only-Speak-Once (YOSO). An important conceptual contribution of our work is the (relatively) clean modeling of such protocols, centered around their use of *roles* (which is the name we use for those one-time stateless parties). Crucially, our modeling separates the protocol design using roles from the role-assignment functionality that assigns the roles to actual physical machines.

This separation lets us study the protocol design problem on its own, freeing us from having to specify the role-assignment implementation which is necessarily very system dependent: a proof-of-work blockchain will have very different role-assignment mechanisms from a proof-of-stake blockchain, and a traditional cloud environment will use yet different mechanisms. However, all these systems could use the same protocol for secure computation once the roles have been properly assigned. On the technical side we make the following contributions:

- We present a formal model for defining and studying such protocols, called the YOSO model, which in particular codifies the separation between role-assignment and protocol execution and formally defines the notion of only speaking once. The YOSO model is cast within the UC framework [5] and therefore can draw on the existing body of research on UC security. An overview of the model is provided in Sect. 2. For a more detailed treatment see the full version of the paper [14].
- We also devise tools for working in the YOSO model, and describe two different secure MPC protocols. Our main solution presented in Sect. 3 is an information theoretic proof-of-concept protocol that provides statistical security.[1] Additionally, in the full version [14] we also describe a computationally-secure protocol. Both protocols are synchronous and provide guaranteed output delivery (which is important for our application domain), assuming an honest majority of roles in every protocol step.
- We show that an information theoretic secure YOSO MPC can be compiled into a natural UC secure protocol running on a toy model of a blockchain with role assignment. This is meant as a sanity check of the abstract role-based YOSO model. It shows that protocols developed in this model can indeed be compiled to practice. We show that if we start with a static-secure (analogously, adaptive-secure) YOSO protocol, we can get a static-secure (analogously, adaptive-secure) UC protocol with essentially the same corruption threshold.

1.1   The YOSO Model

We introduce the YOSO model to make it easy to start studying YOSO MPC independently of blockchain and role assignment.

Role-based computation. In the YOSO model, participants in protocols are called *roles* rather than parties or nodes or machines. The reason for the name "roles" is that we usually think of these one-time parties as playing some role in a protocol. Some examples of roles include "Party #3 in the 2nd VSS protocol on the 8th round", "the prover in the 6th NIZK", etc. Formally, a role is just a stateless party that can only send a single message before it is destroyed, and a protocol is an interaction between roles. Throughout this manuscript we use the following terminology:

Roles: are abstract formal entities that perform the protocol actions and communicate with other roles.

Nodes/Machines: refer to stateful long-living entities that the adversary can identify and target for corruption. These can be physical or virtual machines, that would typically have some identifying characteristics such as an IP address that can be used by the adversary to attack them.

---

[1] As we explain below, the restrictions of working in the YOSO model are so severe that a priory it was not clear to us that information-theoretical security is even possible in the "$2t + 1$ regime". Indeed this work began as an attempt to prove that no such protocols exist.

We sometimes use the term *parties*, but only in informal discussions and in contexts where the distinction between roles and machines is immaterial.

Importantly, roles are detached from machines, and mapping of machines to roles happens at execution time. A protocol in the YOSO model will inevitably be executed alongside a role-assignment functionality, and the security of the protocol will rely on the guarantees provided by that functionality. Ideally, this assignment should be unknown to the attacker until after the machine plays its role and sends a message, hence limiting the adversary's ability to target the role for corruption.

The YOSO model can be used with different role-assignment functionalities with different guarantees. In this work we mainly consider a simple random-assignment functionality: it assigns each role to a random machine from among a universe of available ones, and hides that assignment from the adversary (unless the chosen machine is already corrupted). An adversary that corrupts machines will therefore be unable to predict which roles will be corrupted; upon corruption of a machine the adversary will be handed the random roles that are mapped to that machine. This allows for a simplified view of the adversary where all corruptions are random.

1.2 MPC in the YOSO Model

A compelling motivation for these protocols is scalable computation in the presence of an adaptive fail-stop adversary (a powerful DoS adversary, as noted earlier). Imagine a large number—perhaps millions—of nodes that want to engage in a secure computation in the presence of such an adversary. Assuming that the DoS adversary cannot take down more than some threshold of the nodes, then running an MPC protocol among all of them would yield the desired result. However, running classical MPC protocols among a large number of nodes is expensive. All of the nodes typically need to communicate with all of their peers, creating a prohibitive communication load. YOSO MPC enables the computation to be run by a small subset of the nodes, with an independent subset—or committee—participating in every round. YOSO MPC thwarts an adaptive DoS adversary because the adversary is unable to predict which fail-stops will be useful to foil the security; thus it creates the opportunity for execution of the protocol with small committees resulting in communication that is sub-linear in the number of nodes in the network.

As a more concrete example of a scenario where such scalable computation would be necessary, consider "MPC as a service". That is, an outsourced computation service where clients submit inputs for a joint computation so that the privacy of the inputs and the correctness of the output are guaranteed, even if a fraction of the provider's servers are adversarially controlled. However, while full corruption of servers is expensive, dedicated denial of service against targeted servers is an easier attack to carry out, and the protocol should be able to withstand it. YOSO MPC offers a solution that remains secure under these realistic conditions.

Role Assignment for YOSO MPC. In order to reap the benefits of such scalable YOSO MPC, it is important to assign YOSO MPC roles to machines in a scalable way without revealing the role assignment before the roles need to speak. Furthermore, the assigned machines should be able to receive secret messages (even while the message senders do not know their identities). This is challenging since, being able to speak only once, the machine having won a role cannot first make a public key available, and then receive messages and execute its role in the protocol. This would involve speaking at least twice.

One solution that was recently proposed by Benhamouda *et al.* [3] involves the use of nominating committees: each machine has a public key for an encryption scheme allowing the rerandomization of public keys. For each role R there will be a delegator role D. (We call R the delegate, and D the delegator.) First a machine is assigned a delegator role D using, e.g., cryptographic sortition (or just by solving some puzzle). Then the delegator D will pick, uniformly at random, another machine to play the delegate role R. It will take that machine's public key pk_i, rerandomize it into $\widetilde{pk}_i$, and publish $\widetilde{pk}_i$. Note that $\widetilde{pk}_i$ does not reveal the identity of the machine that was assigned to R; however, it enables other roles to send secret messages to the delegate R by encrypting to $\widetilde{pk}_i$. Finally, the delegate R will execute the role.

One drawback of this approach is that the role R will be corrupt if the delegator is corrupt *or* if the delegate is corrupt. This essentially doubles the corruption budget of the adversary. It is an interesting research direction to develop more practical and more secure role assignment mechanisms. However, this is orthogonal to the design of MPC protocols which will be run by the roles, which is the focus of our work. In the full version [14] we give a toy example of compiling a YOSO protocol to run on top of a blockchain with role assignment to illuminate this compelling use case.

Parameters of YOSO MPC Protocols. When designing a YOSO MPC protocol there is a number of interesting parameters to consider. In addition to the many "generic" aspects of MPC (such as corruption type and threshold, hardness assumptions, trusted setup, security guarantees, etc.) YOSO MPC protocols have some new parameters in their design.

- *Future/Past Horizon:* When a role speaks, it may send private messages to roles intended to speak in future rounds. The future horizon describes how far into the future a role may need to speak (similarly past horizon is how far back a role may need to listen). The method of assigning roles impacts and is impacted by the future and past horizons and should be taken into consideration. For example, for proof-of-stake systems it is undesirable to assign roles in advance using the current stake distribution. Or if roles are assigned on the fly parties would need to read the history of communication far into the past. One should therefore try to use as short a future/past horizon as possible.
- *Dynamic and Static Execution Time:* Static execution time refers to the ability to know ahead of time when a role would speak in the protocol,

contrasted with the dynamic case where the time to speak is only determined at run-time. As YOSO protocols are ideal for serverless architectures where servers are only running when they need to act, static execution time may save resources (e.g. cloud rental).

A related distinction (in the dynamic case) is whether only the role itself can determine when it is going to speak, or whether it can be determined publicly. (This could make a difference, e.g., in agreement protocols that must accumulate enough votes before moving to the next phase, where we may want to know if we still need to wait for the vote from the role or can we assume that it crashed and will never vote.)

YOSO MPC from Additive Homomorphic Threshold Encryption. Our first technical contribution is a YOSO MPC protocol in the computational setting with guaranteed output delivery in a synchronous model, tolerating a dishonest minority of roles at any given round. Specifically, in every round we will have some number n of roles that will form an honest-majority committee. As stated, it falls to the role-assignment functionality to supply us with committees with honest majority; in this work we allow ourselves to just assume that we have them.

Given a supply of committees with honest majority, our construction is based on the CDN protocol [10]. Informally, CDN requires a system-wide public key pk for an additively homomorphic threshold encryption scheme, where the secret key sk is shared among the committee members (with each member i holding sk_i). The participants then perform the entire computation using additive homomorphism, interspersed with public decryption of masked intermediate values. The protocol uses Beaver triples that are generated on-the-fly to support multiplications; the secret key shares are used to open values in every round of Beaver triple use, and to obtain the computation output at the end.

We note that CDN is already almost a YOSO protocol: the only state the participants need is the secret key shares sk_i, and the only messages that they send are their decryption shares (with the ciphertexts all being public). Providing the participants with shares of the global secret key sk can be done, e.g., using the proactive handover protocol of Benhamouda *et al.* [3], which is a YOSO protocol. In each protocol round, committee members get their decryption shares, and then the committee decrypts the current batch of ciphertexts and reshares sk to the next committee.

To get a YOSO protocol, we also need to generate the Beaver triples YOSO-style. We will use two committees—C_A and C_B—to generate many triples of the form $(\mathsf{Enc}(a), \mathsf{Enc}(b), \mathsf{Enc}(ab))$, which will be consumed by future committees during multiplications. We first have members P_i of committee C_A individually choose random a_i's and publish the ciphertexts $\overline{a_i} = \mathsf{Enc}(a_i)$ along with NIZK proofs that these are valid ciphertexts. All parties can use additive homomorphism to obtain $\overline{a}$, an encryption of the sum a of the a_i's. Then members P_j of committee C_B will individually choose random b_j's and set $\overline{b_j} = \mathsf{Enc}(b_j)$, then use additive homomorphism to compute $\overline{c_j}$, an encryption of $b_j a$. P_j then publishes $(\overline{b_j}, \overline{c_j})$, along with proofs that they were generated properly. All parties can use additive homomorphism to obtain $\overline{b}$ and $\overline{c}$, encryptions of the sums b of the b_j's and c of the $b_j a$'s, respectively. $(\overline{a}, \overline{b}, \overline{c})$ form a Beaver triple. Note that as long as all the NIZK proofs are valid and there is at least one honest party in each committee C_A, C_B, the triple is indeed a Beaver triple for the values $a = \sum_i a_i$ and $b = \sum_j b_j$ which are unknown to the adversary.[2]

We describe the complete CDN-based protocol Π_{CDN}, and prove its security, in the full version [14]. For now, we state the following informal theorem.

Theorem. (informal) *Any multiparty function F can be securely implemented by the CDN YOSO protocol in a synchronous network with authenticated broadcast channel, resilient against a fraction $\tau < 1/2$ of random Byzantine corruptions.*

We note that another approach for achieving computational security would be to leverage *fully* homomorphic encryption (FHE). This requires an FHE scheme with a one-message threshold decryption procedure, and also one whose secret key could be maintained proactively using a YOSO protocol. Proactive maintenance of the secret key can be achieved, e.g., using the YOSO handover protocol of Benhamouda *et al.* [3], and one-round decryption can be achieved using the techniques from Asharov *et al.* [1] and Mukherjee-Wichs [18] (after a one-time trusted setup to generate the required evaluation key). In terms of complexity, an FHE-based solution may be more efficient in number of rounds and total communication, but it requires much more local computation, more per-round communication, and a more complicated trusted setup.

YOSO MPC from Information Theoretic Techniques. Our second (and main) technical contribution is a proof-of-concept information theoretic YOSO protocol with guaranteed output delivery in a synchronous model, tolerating any dishonest minority of roles at any given committee. This protocol does not need any trusted setup, but it relies on secure point-to-point channels between roles,[3] as well as a totally-ordered broadcast. One consequence of this protocol is statistically unbiased coin-flip in the YOSO model, which (together with appropriate role-assignment) implies unbiased public randomness in public blockchains via a YOSO protocol.

We begin by observing that YOSO is easy in the semi-honest model, in fact semi-honest BGW [2] is basically already a YOSO protocol. The BGW protocol only uses secret sharing and reconstruction: secret sharing can be done to a future committee (instead of the current one) over point-to-point channels, and reconstruction can be done publicly. When implementing a circuit, each multiplication gate has two committees, one for each round in the multiplication

---

[2] If we have many honest parties in C_A, C_B (say m of them in each committee), then we can improve efficiency and get $\Omega(m)$ triples at roughly the same bandwidth using standard techniques.

[3] We note again that such secure point-to-point channels would have to be implemented somehow, even though the receiving role may not have been assigned yet to a machine. This task falls to the role-assignment functionality, which we do not specify in this work.

protocol. For a gate with large fan-out, the gate committee will reshare their shares to the committees of all the downstream gates.

It is only when switching to the malicious model that things get hard, as YOSO seems to rule out many common information-theoretic techniques. In particular, patterns such as "committing" to a value and then being challenged on it, or even just using the same secret value in many parts of the protocol, seem to inherently require a party to stick around and speak more than once. The same can be said for cut-and-choose techniques that have a party generating multiple values, being challenged to open (say) half of them, and if they are all valid then the other half is used in the protocol.

It is also easy to see that simplistic solutions such as one party sending all its secret state to another will not help: It would allow the adversary to get this secret value if either the sender or the receiver are corrupted, hence amplifying the adversary's power. A more promising avenue is to let a party share its secret state with future committees (maybe more than one), and have these committees emulate it in the future as needed. However, ensuring that a message from one party is recoverable intact by future committees is challenging; this is essentially a verifiable-secret-sharing (VSS) functionality. Ensuring that the party shares *the same message* to multiple committees poses more challenges still. In Sect. 3 we address these challenges by gradually developing stronger and stronger primitives that build on each other. Here we just give a hint for some of the observations that enable these tools, and the various steps that go into the construction.

*Step 1, Future Broadcast (*FBcast*).* In Sect. 3.2 we describe a Future Broadcast construction that enables a party to prepare a message that should be sent in a future round. This may be complicated in general, since we need to ensure that the message delivered in the future is in fact the message of the party creating it, the kind of authenticity often requires VSS. But in our context we observe that we only need to ensure this authenticity for messages of honest parties, as faulty parties can say whatever they want at any time. Hence, for the FBcast primitive we can assume an honest dealer, which makes the design a lot easier.

Observe that in the computational setting this is straightforward to achieve. A party shares its value using a Shamir secret sharing and also provides every share holder with a digital signature on the share. When the value is reconstructed only shares with valid signatures are taken into the interpolation, if they all lie on a degree-t polynomial then the constant term is taken as the broadcasted message. In the IT setting we show that if the dealer is honest, information theoretic MACs are sufficient to replace digital signatures in this construction.

*Step 2, Distributed Commitment (*DC*).* In this construction we want to offer some guarantees for reconstructing a value at a later time also in the case when the dealer is faulty. DC enables a dealer to commit in a distribute manner to a value and at a later time either open the committed value or null. This is exactly the functionality of a commitment in the computational setting, but it is achieved in the IT distributed setting.

To deliver DC we fortify the IT MACs into IT signatures (IT-SIG). An IT-SIG offers a holder of the signature on a value some assurances that in fact the value will be verified when presented. Our techniques build on the VSS interactive tools of Rabin and Ben-Or [22] adjusted to the YOSO model. We transform the IT-SIG from [22] into one where a party knows in advance all the messages that it may need to send in the future. This makes it possible to replace the multiple speaking rounds in the original protocol, by having each party share its future messages using FBcast (Sect. 3.3). The IT-SIGs provide enough of the digital signature properties for the purpose of realizing distributed commitments (Sect. 3.4).

*Step 3, Duplicate DC (*DupDC*) and VSS.* Proceeding towards VSS, we again turn to Rabin and Ben-Or [22], who utilize DC to achieve VSS via a cut-and-choose proof. The complication in using in the YOSO model is that in this proof one value needs to be used multiple times. In the YOSO model, this requires creating duplicates of the same committed value, each to be used in a different step of the proof. Letting the dealer run multiple DC's does not work as the dealer might be faulty and share different values. Thus, we would need the dealer to prove that all the committed values are the same. This will create a problem because for the proof to go through the committee holding the sharing would need to talk. Once they talk they have exhausted their one opportunity to speak and now the duplicate of the value has been wasted. Thus, we need to create a mechanism that duplicates values without "wasting" them. Surprisingly, we observe that our DC protocol allows the share holders themselves to create duplicates of the commitment. This avoids the need for additional proofs, the committee of shareholders is mostly honest so all the duplicates will be the same by design (see Sect. 3.5). Here, yet again, we can make all elements of the proof public, thus informing all parties of the result of the computation. This enables us to finalize the design of the VSS (Sect. 3.6).

To eventually complete the design of the MPC we would also need duplicates of the VSS as the same value might go into multiple gates and the committee holding the value can only speak once. Luckily, we can derive the duplicates of the VSS directly from the duplicates of the DC.

*Step 4, Augmented VSS (*AugVSS*).* We need one more level of sharing which we call Augmented VSS. In this level of sharing we add the property that not only is a secret s shared via VSS but also that all the shares that define the sharing of s are VSSed. This will enable the MPC.

Step 5, Secure-MPC. Once we have AugVSS, getting information-theoretic secure-MPC can be done using standard techniques that need to be adapted to the YOSO model. We maintain the variant throughout the computation that the values on the wires are AugVSS. Hence we prove:

Theorem. (informal) *Any multiparty function F can be securely implemented by an information-theoretic YOSO protocol in a synchronous network with broadcast and secure point-to-point channels, resilient against a fraction $\tau < 1/2$ of random Byzantine corruptions. The protocol additionally tolerates any number of chosen, Byzantine corruptions of input roles and output roles.*

It is crucial, for practical purposes, that we can tolerate chosen corruptions of input roles and output roles. Often the inputs and outputs are given by known clients that could more easily be targeted by an attack.

Epilogue, Public Randomness. The cut-and-choose protocols in our design are described using access to public randomness (which defines the challenges in those protocols). But where can we get this public randomness? Producing true randomness in a distributed setting seems to require MPC, creating a circular problem. Yet, we can show that our protocols remain secure when using *unpredictable* (high min-entropy) values, rather than truly random ones. Producing public unpredictable values in the honest-majority setting is much easier, and can even be done in a YOSO fashion. Thus, we can complete the MPC without the need for true randomness.

Of course, once we are able to get full-blown MPC, we can use it to produce completely uniform public randomness. This in particular solves the problem of obtaining public uniform randomness on a public blockchain using a YOSO protocol, a problem that was explored by a few previous works [6,7].

On the impossibility of Garay et al. [12]. In [12] it was shown that any protocol in the information theoretic model with a sublinear message complexity (in the number of parties) cannot withstand adaptive corruptions of a fraction equal or greater than $1 - \sqrt{0.5}$ of the total number of parties. Yet, we claim that our IT protocol can withstand less than $n/2$ adaptive corruptions. This is not a contradiction. Our proof proceeds in two steps. In the first we prove that our IT protocol is adaptively secure without the assumption of sublinear message complexity. In the second part, when we prove the protocol that has sublinear message complexity, we need to combine our IT protocol with some role-assignment mechanism. This inevitably takes our protocol out of the IT model, making the lower bound of [12] not applicable.[4]

YOSO can be Realized. Our YOSO protocols are abstract in that they only consider abstract roles; we abstract away role assignment and machines. To show that protocols designed in our abstract YOSO model can be used in practice, we show how to compile these abstract protocols into concrete protocols that use physical machines, assuming an underlying role-assignment service. To that end, we define a simple UC functionality $\mathcal{F}_{RA}$, modeling a system with role assignment: That functionality "spits out" a sequence of random public keys,

---

[4] Specifically, the implementation of our communication channels which are needed to enable the solution can only be achieved in the computational setting (in our specific case we assume a PKI and more).

where the corresponding secret key is known by a random, secret node in the system.

Assuming access to this role-assignment functionality, in addition to a broadcast channel and point-to-point channels *between physical machines in the system* (modeled as ideal functionalities $\mathcal{F}_{BC}$, $\mathcal{F}_{SPP}$), we show how to compile any abstract protocol Π in the YOSO model into a concrete protocol in the UC hybrid model with functionalities $\mathcal{F}_{RA}$, $\mathcal{F}_{BC}$, and $\mathcal{F}_{SPP}$. (These functionalities can then be implemented using an underlying blockchain, e.g., as described in [3].)

We prove two results: (1) We show that an abstract YOSO protocol Π that IT YOSO-implements a secure function evaluation of F against t *random*, static corruptions, can be compiled using hybrid functionalities $\mathcal{F}_{BC}$ and $\mathcal{F}_{SPP}$ into a UC secure protocol Π' for the $\mathcal{F}_{RA}$-hybrid model that tolerates ρ *chosen*, static corruptions for any $\rho < t$. (2) We show the same for adaptive security.

We can get security against chosen corruptions from security against random corruptions because the adversary does not know the role-to-machine association chosen by $\mathcal{F}_{RA}$. Intuitively, corrupting a machine just corrupts random roles.

1.3 Related Work

Protocols built out of ephemeral one-time roles became popular over the last decade with the emergence of public blockchains, whose defining feature is not relying on long-term participants with fixed identities. In particular, starting with Nakamoto's consensus protocol [19], these protocols became popular for achieving agreement in different settings, e.g., [4,8,17,20].

Only very recently did we start seeing attempts at using this style of protocols for other cryptographic tasks: Benhamouda *et al.* [3] described how to use such protocols for long-term maintenance of secrets on public blockchains, and mentioned the possibility of using these secrets for various tasks, including for general-purpose secure computation. Blum *et al.* [4] described how to implement input-free protocols in this model (such as coin tossing), and also described informally an FHE-based solution for functions with input (similar to the one sketched in Sect. 1.2 above).

Choudhuri *et al.* [9] described general-purpose secure-MPC protocols of this style (that they call *fluid*), where the participants need to volunteer for roles (in our terminology we would call it a volunteer-based role-assignment functionality). Such protocols can be tweaked and casted as YOSO protocols with a volunteer-based role assignment. However, the protocols of [9] only guarantee security with abort, making their use extremely fragile as a single corruption can abort the protocol. Moreover, volunteer-based role assignment seems susceptible to an adversary filling the volunteering parties with faulty parties by volunteering many times.

2   YOSO for the Working Cryptographer

The YOSO model can be cast within the UC framework [5] by identifying the roles in YOSO protocols with the party identifiers of the UC framework. This means that the roles are executed by the UC model, which completely abstracts away how these roles are actually assigned to physical machines; in fact, there is not even a notion of physical machines left. We then introduce a notion of random corruptions that are out of the control of the adversary. This can be used to model a set of roles which, in the now abstracted away real world, are hidden inside random physical machines, and the adversary can corrupt machines of its choosing.

Below we always use the term roles rather than parties, just to stress that we are in the YOSO model. This terminology is for didactic purposes only; a role in our formal model is identical to a party in the normal UC framework. The "speak once" aspect is enforced by our execution model, as we now explain.

2.1   YOSO Wrappers

To force roles to only speak once, we are explicitly "yosofying" them with a YOSO wrapper. Namely, our execution model postulates a wrapper around each role, that kills it immediately after the first time that it speaks. When that happens, the wrapper sends a SPOKE token to the environment, the adversary and all its sub-routines (sub-protocols and ideal functionalities). Thereafter it responds with a SPOKE token to the environment whenever activated, and only sends SPOKE to the sub-routines that it is connected to.

Defining what it means for a role to "speak for the first time" is somewhat nontrivial. The main issue to tackle is whether sending messages to functionalities constitute speaking. To see the issue, consider a protocol Π (that implements some functionality $\mathcal{F}$), in which a role R must listen for many incoming messages before deciding to send a message. In this case, the $\mathcal{F}$-hybrid model could have the role R sending its input to $\mathcal{F}$ very early, but the implementation would have R actually speaking much later.

To account for that, we let functionalities reply to parties with the special SPOKE token. The functionality can freely choose when to send this token, and the YOSO wrapper will kill the role as soon as it receives a SPOKE token from any functionality. For example, a communication-channel functionality will reply with a SPOKE token as soon as a party sends anything on it, while a higher-level functionality may trigger a SPOKE token based on some input from the adversary. Note that when a communication channel outputs SPOKE to a role, the role will pass it on to all its sub-routines and then its environment/outer protocol. Hence the entire composed role will be crashed.

We denote the "yosofied" role R by $\mathsf{YoS}(R)$, and the protocol that we get by yosofying all the roles in Π is denoted by $\mathsf{YoS}(\Pi)$.

2.2 Random Corruptions

In addition to the usual corruptions of the UC model we also model random corruptions in the YOSO model—that is, corruptions out of the control of the adversary.

We do this without changing the UC framework itself. Recall that in UC a corruption is implemented by the adversary just writing (corrupt, cp) on the backdoor tape of the party, where cp is some auxiliary information like the type of corruption: Byzantine, semi-honest, *et cetera*. There is no explicit mechanism in UC for limiting how many parties are corrupted or with which flavor. However, we often choose to analyze protocols under a restricted set of corruptions. This is simple to do by only quantifying over adversaries adhering to this restriction. This is easy to formulate for settings like "only semi-honest corruptions" or "at most a minority of the parties". However, it seems to be trickier for random corruptions: if the adversary corrupts a role R, how can we know that R was chosen at random? We need a precise meaning for this in order to be able to make precise security claims. For this purpose, we introduce a simple notion called the corruption controller ($\mathcal{CC}$), that runs as part of the environment. If an adversary wants to do a random corruption, it asks the environment, which will pass the request to the $\mathcal{CC}$. Then, the $\mathcal{CC}$ will sample the corruption and inform the adversary which role was corrupted (via the environment). If the environment sees the adversary is not respecting the decision of the $\mathcal{CC}$, then the environment will make a random guess in the security game. This enforces that no distinguishing advantage comes from executions violating the will of the $\mathcal{CC}$. We then only prove security under the class of environments having such a $\mathcal{CC}$ and using it as intended. We call this the class of controlled environments.

These random corruptions can be mixed freely with other corruption types, but it is illustrative to consider a generalization of the usual adversary structures to random corruptions. We codify the corruption power of the adversary by means of a *corruption structure*.

Let Role be the set of (names of) roles in the system. A corruption structure on Role is a set of probability distributions over $2^{|\text{Role}|}$. A static adversary would choose at the beginning of the execution a specific corruption distribution $C \in \mathcal{C}$ and give it to the $\mathcal{CC}$ via the environment. Then the $\mathcal{CC}$ samples $c \leftarrow C$ and give it to the adversary via the environment, and each role R $\in$ Role can now be corrupted if R $\in c$. Note that a corruption structure with only point distributions (i.e. with a single probability-one pattern $c \in C$) corresponds exactly to standard static corruptions with these allowed patterns, coinciding with the notion of general adversary structure of Hirt and Maurer [15]. We stress that corruption structure represents our *assumption* about the corruption power of the adversary when designing the protocol. It is up to the role-assignment functionality to ensure that realistic adversaries will be unlikely to exceed this power.

When considering adaptive corruptions several choices are possible. We consider two in this work called sample corruptions and point corruptions. In sample corruptions the adversary gives a distribution on a set of roles and gets one of them corrupted, within some bound. In point corruptions the adversary can ask permission to corrupt a given role with some limited probability. If the corruption fails the role stays honest forever after. It is interesting future work to explore the relation between different notions of random corruptions.

2.3 YOSO Security

The notion of a protocol realizing a functionality is borrowed from the UC model. Namely, we say that Π YOSO-realizes (implements) $\mathcal{F}$ for some class of environments (possibly using random corruptions) if $\mathsf{YoS}(\Pi)$ UC-realizes $\mathcal{F}$. The considered class of environments should be a subset of the controlled environments.

It is easy to see that UC composition still holds for controlled environments. If an environment is composed with a protocol or simulator to define a new environment, as happens in the proof of the UC theorem, then this composed environment still uses the $\mathcal{CC}$ of the original one. The same holds when one composes an environment with a simulator. Therefore we get UC composition also for controlled environments.

YOSO composition then follows directly from UC composition. Let Π be a protocol for the $\mathcal{G}$-hybrid model and assume that Π YOSO-realises $\mathcal{F}$. Assume that Γ YOSO-realises $\mathcal{G}$. As usual in the UC framework let $\Pi^{\mathcal{G}\rightarrow\Gamma}$ be the protocol Π with calls to $\mathcal{G}$ replaced by calls to Γ. It follows that $\Pi^{\mathcal{G}\rightarrow\Gamma}$ YOSO-realises $\mathcal{F}$. To see this, note that the premises give us that $\mathsf{YoS}(\Pi)$ UC-realises $\mathcal{F}$ and that $\mathsf{YoS}(\Gamma)$ UC-realises $\mathcal{G}$. By the usual UC theorem we get that $\mathsf{YoS}(\Pi)^{\mathcal{G}\rightarrow\mathsf{YoS}(\Gamma)}$ UC-realises $\mathcal{F}$. Then use that by construction $\mathsf{YoS}(\Pi)^{\mathcal{G}\rightarrow\mathsf{YoS}(\Gamma)} = \mathsf{YoS}(\Pi^{\mathcal{G}\rightarrow\Gamma})$. This follows by the way the YoS wrapper passes around the SPOKE token to shut down entire composed parties.

2.4 Common Features, Functionalities, and Models

Synchrony. To simplify the treatment of synchronous clocks, we assume that in every round the environment sends a TICK message to all the roles *and also to all the functionalities* and the adversary, in addition to any other inputs that it wants to provide them. We use the model in [16] for this.

Communication Channels and PKI. We assume an authenticated broadcast channel denoted $\mathcal{F}_{\mathsf{BC}}$, and usually also secure point-to-point channels $\mathcal{F}_{\mathsf{SPP}}$ (or at least authenticated channels $\mathcal{F}_{\mathsf{PP}}$). These functionalities are defined more or less as usual in the UC framework, except that in our case they return a SPOKE token to any role immediately in the step following the receipt of message from it.[5] These functionalities are formally presented in the full version [14]. We also sometimes use a PKI functionality, which is specified in Fig. 1.

YOSO Secure Function Evaluation. We consider secure function evaluation in the YOSO model. We assume that the roles of a protocol Π are divided into

---

[5] We allow a role to send messages on multiple channels in the same step, then it will receive SPOKE tokens from all of them in the next step.

On the first input TICK sample $(pk_R, sk_R) \leftarrow$ Gen for all R $\in$ Correct $\cup$ Crash. Output pk to $\mathcal{O}$. For all R $\in$ Leaky output sk_R to $\mathcal{O}$. For each R $\in$ Malicious query $\mathcal{O}$ to get the keys (pk_R, sk_R) for R. Then for each R $\in$ Correct output $(sk_R, \{ pk_{R'} \}_{R' \in \text{Role}})$ to R.

Fig. 1. The ideal functionality $\mathcal{F}_{\text{Gen}}$ for a very simple PKI setup with key generator Gen.

input roles, output roles and computation roles. The input roles receive inputs from the environment and the output roles will deliver the outputs back. The computation nodes carry out intermediary steps of the computation and do not interact with the environment.

As usual for UC-like models, to formulate the assertion that a function F could be computed securely we need to wrap that function by a compatible functionality $\mathcal{F}^F_{\text{MPC}}$, as described in [14]. Importantly, we assume that the roles receiving the output *do not speak in an implementation* (so $\mathcal{F}^F_{\text{MPC}}$ never sends SPOKE tokens to the output roles). Otherwise these output roles would not be able to contribute the result to the higher-level protocol.

By default, we assume that the roles receiving the inputs and the roles giving the outputs can be corrupted using the usual chosen corruptions. This is reasonable since in most of the meaningful high-level protocols, like elections, the inputs to the protocol are given by known machines that might be subject to targeted DoS attacks. Computation nodes however, are only subject to random corruptions; when running in the "real world" with a concrete role assignment mechanism, we get to execute computation roles on random machines.

We then say that Π YOSO securely implements F with a fraction τ random corruptions if Π implements $\mathcal{F}^F_{\text{MPC}}$ against any number of chosen corruptions of input roles and output roles and random corruptions of up to a fraction τ of the computation roles.

The IT YOSO Model. We define the standard IT YOSO model to be the model with broadcast and secure point-to-point channels, unbounded environments, and poly-time protocols, ideal functionalities and simulators.

The Computational YOSO Model. The computational YOSO model is equipped with an authenticated broadcast channel, perhaps authenticated point-to-point channels, a PKI functionality (such as the one from Fig. 1), and poly-time environments, protocols, ideal functionalities and simulators.

3   The Information-Theoretic $t < \frac{n}{2}$ MPC Protocol

In this section we describe an MPC protocol in the information theoretic YOSO model for a fraction $\tau < 1/2$ of random Byzantine corruptions.

Theorem 1. *For any multiparty function F, there exists a poly-time protocol Π described below running with the network $(\mathcal{F}_{\text{BC}}, \mathcal{F}_{\text{SPP}})$ which YOSO-realizes* *the ideal functionality $\mathcal{F}_{\mathrm{MPC}}^F$ in the information theoretic YOSO model. The protocol tolerates any number of chosen, Byzantine corruptions of input roles and output roles, and for any $\tau < 1/2$ it tolerates adaptive, Byzantine, random τ-point-corruptions of computation nodes.*

Recall that the reason we allow chosen corruptions of input roles and output roles is that in a real-life setting we cannot reasonably assume that it is unknown which machines will give input or get the outputs. So input and output roles could be targeted. On the other hand, we want to model that computation roles are run on random, secret machines, so we only allow random corruptions of computation nodes. Recall that τ-point corruptions just means that the adversary can point to a role R and ask for a corruption. Then the role is made corrupted with probability τ, and with probability $1 - \tau$ it will remain honest forever after. The type of random corruption it not essential for our proof. The reason why we prove security against point corruptions is that this is the type of corruption needed for the compilation result shown in the full version [14].

Below we will phrase the protocol in terms of disjoint *committees* of size n. We call the roles in a committee *parties*. Let c be the number of committees that we need. We then start with $N = cn$ computation roles $R_1, \ldots, R_N$. We call the committees $C_1, \ldots, C_c$ where $C_j = \{P_1^j, \ldots, P_n^j\}$ and $P_i^j = R_{i+(j-1)n}$. We call P_i^j *party i in committee j*. Notice that this grouping of roles into committees is static. This does not affect security as the adversary cannot bias corruption towards a specific committee. Each party is still subject only to τ-point corruptions. If we set $\tau < 1/2$ then we can clearly pick n large enough that we can conclude from a tail bound that all committees have at most $t < n/2$ corrupted parties except with negligible probability. For the rest of the section we then assume that this has been done. From this point on the only assumption we need for security is that each committee has $t < n/2$ corrupted parties.

Note that we allow any number of corruptions among input roles and output roles. However, input roles and output roles are not part of committees, so this does not violate the honest majority assumption for committees.

Our protocol is adaptively secure. We will, however, below mainly prove static security and only briefly discuss adaptive security. The reason is that for point corruptions, the distinction between adaptive corruptions and static corruptions is minimal. An adaptive point corruption just means that the adversary chooses to be oblivious to whether a party is corrupt or not until the point corruption. This gives it no new powers over static corruptions. Note, in particular, that corruption control component $\mathcal{CC}$ could sample before the UC execution starts for each role R_i a bit b_i which is 1 with probability τ. If later the adversary does a point corruption of R_i it will become corrupted if and only if $b_i = 1$. Therefore, even in the adaptive case, the corruptions can be thought of as being static: they were chosen before the execution started. The only complication in proving adaptive security compared to proving static security is then that in the adaptive case, the simulator will not know b_i until the adversary does a point corruption of R_i. Below we phrase the proof in terms of static security. The proof can be adapted to the adaptive case using standard techniques.

The challenge in designing an information-theoretic MPC protocol in the YOSO model is in replacing the actions of parties that interact and speak multiple times in regular MPC protocols with parties (more precisely, roles) that speak only once. For this we introduce several tools and components for YOSO adaptation that may be useful for other protocols as well. A first such tool is *Future Broadcast* (FBcast) that allows a party P, that in the standard model would speak in several rounds, to send its future messages to future roles that will transmit the messages (either privately or through broadcast) when the time for those messages to be delivered comes. For example, consider a non-YOSO protocol where a party P transmits a message m at round i and a message m' at round $i + 3$. In the YOSO adaptation, the role representing the actions of P in round i will transmit m at round i and also, in the same round, apply FBcast(m') to pass message m' to a role that will speak m' in round $i + 3$. Note that this procedure is possible only in cases where the future message is known in advance. An interesting point to observe is that correctness of FBcast (in particular, in terms of correctness of messages sent "into the future"), needs only be guaranteed for original senders of m' that are honest as faulty ones can choose to speak any message of their choice whenever they speak. The sender P_i^j uses FBcast(m') to replace its own sending of m' in the future. In the emulated protocol a corrupt P_i^j could send $m'' \neq m'$ at this future point. So it is tolerable that FBcast(m') may open to $m'' \neq m'$ in the future when P_i^j is corrupt.

As a first application of FBcast, we use it to adapt the IT-SIGs of [21,22] to the YOSO model and then use this YOSOfied primitive to build a Distributed Commitment (DC) protocol in the YOSO model. In it, a party (honest or faulty) commits to a value that it can later choose to reveal or not, but it cannot change the committed value. Furthermore, it is guaranteed that values committed by honest parties are always revealed correctly. We then use DC as an essential ingredient in the design of a YOSO Verifiable Secret Sharing (VSS) scheme which in turn is a central component of our YOSO information-theoretic MPC solution.

In various steps in our protocol we need access to some form of randomness and for clarity of presentation we will assume the presence of a beacon functionality. However, in actuality we need something much weaker than a truly random source to deliver our results, it is enough that the challenge cannot be guessed. Thus, we can have a very simple implementation of the beacon (see full version [14]). We denote this functionality as $\mathcal{F}_{\mathsf{UPBeacon}}$ to reflect that it is an unpredictable beacon. During the analysis we at first assume it returns uniformly random elements. At the end we then return to why it is enough that it is unpredictable and how to implement it.

The solutions presented in this section make essential and repeated use of secret sharing techniques. In all cases, the underlying scheme is Shamir's scheme over a given field, and we assume all committees into which secrets are shared to have at least $t + 1$ honest parties where $t + 1 > n/2$. Thus, the polynomials defining shares are of degree t.

3.1   Information Theoretic and Homomorphic MAC

Message authentication codes (MAC) are used for verifying the authenticity of messages between a sender and receiver that share a secret key. Following the construction of [22] we have the following two protocols.

Three-party Setting. There exists (i) a sender S holding a message m, it chooses a key K and generates its corresponding MAC tag M computed under a key K; (ii) S sends the pair (m, M) to a receiver R; (iii) S sends the key K to a verifier V. The verification procedure combines the pair (m, M) held by R with the key K held by V.

For our purposes, we consider an information theoretic MAC function with the following properties: (i) producing a correct MAC without knowing the key succeeds with negligible probability even for an unbounded attacker; (ii) message hiding: nothing is learned about the message m from the key K; (iii) homomorphic: the MAC function is homomorphic with respect to appropriate group operations in the following sense. If $M_i = \mathsf{MAC}_{K_i}(m_i), i = 1, 2$, and the keys K_1, K_2 were computed by the same party (they might need to be correlated) then $M_1 + M_2 = \mathsf{MAC}_{K_1 +' K_2}(m_1 + m_2)$.

Such a MAC can be implemented as follows (all elements and operations are over a finite field, e.g., $\mathbb{Z}_p$): $K_i = (a, b_i)$, $M_i = am_i + b_i$ and $K_i +' K_j = (a, b_i + b_j)$. In the sequel, we will say that keys that share the same coefficient a but differ in b_i are *correlated*.

MAC with Distributed Public Verification. In the above setting, to verify a MAC one has to trust V to provide the correct key. In the scenarios in this paper, we often do not trust any single party individually, but rather can only count on committees with a majority of honest participants. Thus, we extend the basic 3-party scheme to one where the role of V is instantiated by an n-party committee $V = \{V_1, \ldots, V_n\}$. Given a message m that S hands to R, S creates a MAC for m as follows. For $i = 1, \ldots, n$, S chooses keys K_i, computes $M_i = \mathsf{MAC}_{K_i}(m)$, and provides all M_i to R and K_i to V_i. When m needs to be verified, R first broadcasts m and the values M_i. Then, each V_i broadcasts K_i and the value m is accepted (i.e., the MAC validates) if and only if it holds that $M_i = \mathsf{MAC}_{K_i}(m)$ for at least $t + 1$ values of i.

The scheme guarantees that if S follows the protocol and $t + 1 > (n - 1)/2$ members of V are honest, then only a message m originating from S will be accepted. Note that the validation of m is public once R and members of V broadcast their values.

When the MAC in use is homomorphic, we have that if S MACs messages m_1, m_2 in the above way, with the same R and same committee V, then the message $m = m_1 + m_2$ can be validated as follows. R outputs m and $M_i = M_i^{(1)} + M_i^{(2)}$, $i = 1, \ldots, n$, and each V_i outputs $K_i^{(1)} +' K_i^{(2)}$. Here, $M_i^{(1)}, M_i^{(2)}$ are the MAC values received by R for m_1 and m_2, respectively, and $K_i^{(1)}, K_i^{(2)}$ are the keys received by V_i for m_1 and m_2, respectively. We therefore say that this MAC procedure is *homomorphic*.

This protocol is inherently YOSO as each party speaks only once and we refer to it in the following as IT-MAC.

3.2 Future Broadcast

We introduce *Future Broadcast* (FBcast), a fundamental primitive in the YOSO setting that allows an *honest* party P that speaks at time t to prepare a message m for broadcasting at a future time t'. This is accomplished by having P simply secret share m to a committee that will broadcast m at time t', hence bypassing the limitation of speaking only once. To guarantee that the message can be reconstructed (in the case that P is honest and the committee has an honest majority), FBcast implements a robust secret sharing scheme. Namely, a scheme where correct reconstruction is guaranteed as long as the sharing was done correctly and at least $t + 1$ honest parties provide their shares (i.e., bad shares from corrupt parties can be identified and eliminated). In settings where digital signatures are available, robust secret sharing is implemented by having the dealer sign its shares. In our information-theoretic setting, we achieve a similar effect using the IT-MAC procedure from Sect. 3.1 for verifying share integrity.

FBcast.Share (Executed by S on input m)	FBcast.Reveal(with public verification)
Set two n-party committees, ShareHolder and ShareVerifier. 1. Compute a (t, n)-secret sharing $(m_1, \ldots, m_n)$ of m for $t = (n-1)/2$. 2. Generate keys $K_{i,j}$, $1 \le i, j \le n$ and compute $M_{i,j} = \mathsf{MAC}_{K_{i,j}}(m_i)$. 3. For $i = 1, \ldots, n$: Send $m_i, M_{i,1}, \ldots, M_{i,n}$ to ShareHolder$_i$; Send $K_{1,i}, \ldots, K_{n,i}$ to ShareVerifier$_i$.	1. ShareHolder$_i$ bcasts $m_i, M_{i,1}, \ldots, M_{i,n}$. 2. ShareVerifier$_i$ bcasts $K_{1,i}, \ldots, K_{n,i}$. 3. Accept m_i iff $M_{i,j} = \mathsf{MAC}_{K_{i,j}}(m_i)$ for at least $t + 1$ of the keys. 4. If there are at least $t + 1$ accepted shares and they all define a single polynomial of degree t then output the constant term. Otherwise, output "fail".

Fig. 2. Future broadcast protocol

The FBcast protocol is presented in Fig. 2. Its first phase, FBcast.Share, is executed by a party S on input message m. It consists of S secret sharing m with a committee ShareHolder where in addition to its share, each ShareHolder$_i$ receives an IT-MAC of the share computed by S using the above distributed MAC procedure. An additional committee, ShareVerifier, receives the MAC keys from S. When the value m needs to be broadcast in the future, FBcast.Reveal is performed following the distributed verification procedure: the ShareHolder members first broadcast their shares together with their MAC values, followed by a broadcast of keys held by ShareVerifier (note that ShareVerifier must speak after ShareHolder hence requiring two separate committees). Shares that do not pass verification are discarded and if those that remain interpolate to a single polynomial of degree t, the secret is reconstructed, otherwise reconstruction fails.

We denote by FBcast.Share$_S(m)$ the sharing by S of a value m and FBcast.Reveal$_S(m)$ the revealing of m (executed by two committees), and refer to the whole protocol execution as FBcast$_S(m)$.

Analysis. We show that FBcast satisfies the requirement that if S is honest and used m as input to FBcast.Share then m will be reconstructed when FBcast.Reveal is executed. For this we need to show that only m_i's that originated from S are accepted and that there are sufficiently many accepted shares to interpolate the polynomial. If m_i is accepted then the MAC was verified by a key broadcast by at least one honest ShareVerifier. As S is honest, only m_i's created by S are accepted by an honest party. Furthermore, each share broadcasted by an honest ShareHolder is accepted as there will be at least $t+1$ honest ShareVerifiers whose broadcasted keys satisfy the MAC. By construction, no party speaks twice.

Homomorphism of FBcast. Note that when used with a homomorphic MAC, FBcast inherits the homomorphic property of the distributed MAC scheme from Sect. 3.1. We denote this fact as $\mathsf{FB}_P(m_1) + \mathsf{FB}_P(m_2) = \mathsf{FB}_P(m_1 + m_2)$ for any messages m_1 and m_2 shared by the same party P. Yet, as the keys need to be correlated the creator of the MAC needs to know in advance what two values will be added. This is easily achievable in our protocols.

3.3 Homomorphic IT-SIG

Our protocols would benefit from a signature functionality in order to construct a VSS protocol. Of course in the information theoretic setting we cannot achieve the full properties of a signature, but we can achieve enough of the functionality to deliver the result. The property which we need is the following. Assume again the setting from the IT-MAC (Sect. 3.1). We would want to assure R that the message that it holds will be accepted by the committee V. In essence, that it has a "signature" on the message that it holds.

Unlike the transformation of the basic IT-MAC from [22] that did not require modification to comply with the YOSO model, the IT-SIG construction from that paper does require changes as it has interaction. Our protocol IT-SIG is described in Fig. 3. It consists of two phases, IT-SIG.Setup and IT-SIG.Reveal. In IT-SIG.Setup, a sender S provides a receiver R with a value m and also provides verification information to a committee V of n verifiers $V_1, \ldots, V_n$. The goal is for R to disclose m in the IT-SIG.Reveal phase in a way that allows to *publicly verify* the correctness of m with the help of committee V and with the following guarantees, assuming that V contains an honest majority:

- If S and R are honest then the correct value m is disclosed and verified during IT-SIG.Reveal and no information on m is revealed prior to that.
- If both S and R are corrupt we make no requirement at all.
- If only S is corrupt, at the end of IT-SIG.Setup, R holds a value m' that will pass verification in IT-SIG.Reveal.

IT-SIG.Setup	IT-SIG.Reveal

1. On input m, the sender S:
  (a) Generates keys $K_{i,j}$, $1 \leq i \leq n, 1 \leq j \leq \kappa$ (for security parameter κ), and computes $M_{i,j} = \mathsf{MAC}_{K_{i,j}}(m)$.
  (b) Transfers $(m, \{M_{i,j}\}_{1\leq i\leq n, 1\leq j\leq \kappa})$ to receiver R and $\{K_{i,j}\}_{1\leq j\leq \kappa}$ to V_i.
  (c) Executes $\mathsf{FBcast.Share}_S(m)$, and $\mathsf{FBcast.Share}_S(K_{i,j})$, $1\leq i \leq n, 1 \leq j \leq \kappa$.
2. Party V_i:
  (a) Chooses half of the indices at random, denoted by INX_i.
  (b) Broadcasts $K_{i,j}$ for $j \in INX_i$.
  (c) Executes $\mathsf{FBcast.Share}_{V_i}(K_{i,j})$, $j \notin INX_i$.
3. Execute $\mathsf{FBcast.Reveal}_S(K_{i,j})$ $j \in INX_i$ for all i; denote by $\bar{K}_{i,j}$ the reconstructed values.
4. If there exist indexes i and j for which $\mathsf{MAC}_{\bar{K}_{i,j}}(m) \neq M_{i,j}$ then R asks that $\mathsf{FBcast.Reveal}_S(m)$ be executed to reveal $\bar{m}$. If $\bar{m} = \bot$ set $\bar{m}$ to a default value.
	1. If $\bar{m}$ was revealed in IT-SIG.Setup output this as S's message.
	2. R broadcasts $(m, \{M_{i,j}\}_{1\leq i\leq n, j\notin INX_i})$.
	3. Set the number of votes for m to be the number of i's for which $\bar{K}_{i,j} \neq K_{i,j}$ for some $j \in INX_i$ from the setup.
	4. For all i's not counted in the previous step, execute $\mathsf{FBcast.Reveal}_{V_i}(K_{i,j})$ for $j \notin INX_i$. If $\mathsf{MAC}_{K_{i,j}}(m) = M_{i,j}$ for any one of the recovered values then increment the vote by "1".
	5. If vote is at least $t + 1$ then output m as S's message. Otherwise, output $\bot$.

Fig. 3. Information theoretic SIG

– If only R is corrupt, no value other than the m that originated with S in IT-SIG.Setup can pass verification in IT-SIG.Reveal.

In addition, the protocol needs to satisfy the YOSO model where parties speak only once. We build it so that R speaks only once (either in IT-SIG.Setup or in IT-SIG.Reveal) while in the case of S and the parties in V, from which the logic of the protocol requires more than one message, we resort to FBcast for distributing their future messages so that a different committee broadcasts them when needed, and all parties speak only once.

Analysis. The following assumes an honest majority in committee V and that at most one of R and S is corrupted.

– Corrupt S: We need to show that at the end of IT-SIG.Setup, R holds a value m' that can pass verification in IT-SIG.Reveal. We split our analysis into two cases. First, if a value $\bar{m}$ is revealed during Step 4 of IT-SIG.Setup we set m' to $\bar{m}$ and the rest follows trivially as this value will be outputted in IT-SIG.Reveal. Otherwise, we set m' to the value m received from S and show that m' will have at least $t + 1$ votes in IT-SIG.Reveal. Indeed, for each honest V_i, either $\bar{K}_{i,j} \neq K_{i,j}$ for some $j \in INX_i$ and thus their vote is counted; otherwise, it holds that $\mathsf{MAC}_{K_{i,j}}(m) = M_{i,j}$ for all $j \in INX_i$ as R did not complain against these values. Thus, with (overwhelming) probability $1/\binom{\kappa}{\kappa/2}$ due to the cut-and-choose technique, there exists a $j \notin INX_i$ such that $\mathsf{MAC}_{K_{i,j}}(m) = M_{i,j}$, and hence a vote for i will be counted. This guarantees at least $t + 1$ votes for the value $m = m'$.

- Corrupt R: In this case we show that only the m that originated with S will pass verification in IT-SIG.Reveal. If the message associated with S is set to the value derived from FBcast.Reveal$_S(m)$ in the setup, it is certainly a message that originated with S. If it is set to the message published by R, then that message must get $t + 1$ "votes". Votes can be generated by corrupt V_i publishing incorrect keys in Step 2b of IT-SIG.Setup; however, there are at most t such corrupt V_i. The only other way to generate a vote for an incorrect m is to forge a MAC M, which happens with negligible probability.

- If S and R are honest, then due to the message hiding property of the MAC function, no information on m is revealed until IT-SIG.Reveal is executed. Indeed, the only case where R requests to broadcast m prior to IT-SIG.Reveal is when the keys broadcasted by S do not verify the MACs; this cannot be the case when S and R are both honest.

Homomorphism of IT-SIGs. The homomorphic properties of the MAC construction from Sect. 3.1, imply similar properties for IT-SIG in Fig. 3 when the underlying MAC function is homomorphic. Namely, if m, m' are messages on which the (same) sender S runs IT-SIG.Setup with the same set V of verifiers and with correlated keys (i.e., corresponding keys use the same coefficient a in the scheme from Sect. 3.1), then an IT-SIG on $m + m'$ can be verified with committee V using the MAC keys held by V for m and for m'. This homomorphic property is used in an essential way when performing additions/multiplications in an arithmetic circuit as described in Sect. 3.11. A consequence of the need for correlated keys is that if two messages may need to be added in the future, this fact needs to be known at the time of generating the IT-SIG for both m_1 and m_2. In our application this is always the case as the need for additions is determined by the specific circuit being computed.

3.4   Distributed Commitment (DC)

The FB protocol does not offer any guarantees in the case when the dealer is faulty. Here, we introduce the *distributed commitment protocol* DC, shown in Fig. 4, that strengthens FB by providing better guarantees when the dealer is corrupt. DC consists of two phases, DC.Commit and DC.Reveal. In DC.Commit, a committer C commits to a value m that may later be revealed in DC.Reveal. More precisely, if C is honest, then as in the case of FB, the revealed value is m, and m is hidden until it is revealed. However, if C is corrupt, the execution of DC.Commit determines a single value m such that the output of DC.Reveal is guaranteed to be either $\perp$ or m (where m itself can be $\perp$). In other words, C can choose to prevent reconstruction, but if it allows for it to happen then it can only be to a value it committed to at the end of DC.Commit. Reconstruction is public, namely, there will be public agreement on the output of DC.Reveal. In essence, this is analogous to a regular commitment in the computational setting where the committer is bound to the value but has the option not to reveal it.

DC.Commit (executed by C on input m)	DC.Reveal
Let ShareHolder and ShareVerifier be two n-party committees. 1. Committer C computes a t-secret sharing of m, $(m_1, \ldots, m_n)$ for $t \geq (n-1)/2$. 2. For $i = 1, \ldots, n$: C executes IT-SIG.Setup on input m_i with ShareHolder$_i$ as receiver R and the set ShareVerifier acting as the set of verifiers V (same ShareVerifier committee is used in all the invocations).	1. For $i = 1, \ldots, n$, run IT-SIG.Reveal with ShareHolder$_i$ as receiver R; let $\bar{m}_i$ to the output of this execution. 2. Take all $\bar{m}_i$ that are not $\perp$ and interpolate a polynomial through these points. If the polynomial is of degree t or less output its constant term, otherwise output $\perp$.

Fig. 4. Distributed commitment

Protocol DC uses the IT-SIGs (Fig. 3) in an essential way. In particular, in Step 3 of DC.Commit, for each m_i, C executes IT-SIG.Setup(m_i) with ShareHolder$_i$ acting as the receiver and with ShareVerifier as the set V of verifiers. The n executions (one for each m_i) are performed in parallel using the same set ShareVerifier in all these executions.

Analysis. We show that at the end of DC.Commit a value m (or $\perp$) is determined, and during DC.Reveal, if C is honest m will be revealed, and if C is corrupt, either m or $\perp$ will be revealed.

In DC.Commit, C executes IT-SIG.Setup with at least $t+1$ honest parties acting as receivers R. For these honest parties, due to the properties of IT-SIG.Setup, it is guaranteed that the value they hold will be accepted in IT-SIG.Reveal. We claim that at the end of DC.Commit, a single value m is committed to, such that the output in DC.Reveal is either m or $\perp$ (where m itself can be $\perp$). To show this, we define m as the constant term of a polynomial of degree at most t interpolated through the set of shares held by the honest parties (this value might be $\perp$ if the points interpolate to a polynomial of a higher degree than t). We now show that if a value is outputted in DC.Reveal it can only be m. When C is honest then only shares that were created by C are accepted and thus the polynomial will interpolate properly during DC.Reveal. If C is faulty we know that at least the shares of the honest parties will be included in the set of shares being interpolated and this is a set of at least $t+1$ shares. Thus, the message which is opened can only be m or $\perp$, with the latter happening only if the shares m_i did not correspond to points on a polynomial of degree at most t.

We denote by $DC_P(m)$ the output of the execution of DC.Commit by party P on message m.

Homomorphism of DC. Due to the homomorphic properties of the IT-SIG and FBcast, we have that for any two values m and m' committed by the same honest party P, it holds that $DC_P(m) + DC_P(m') = DC_P(m + m')$. The same considerations for ensuring the homomorphism of IT-SIG described in Sect. 3.3 hold here too (i.e., the DC operations need to be performed by the same committer using correlated keys). In particular, if this property may be required in the future for two messages m, m', then this fact needs to be known at the time of running DC.Commit on these values (fortunately, for our application this requirement does hold). The question might be raised if we know that m and m' will be added why compute individual DC.Commit for both rather than the sum. In many instances we will need to utilize all three values in different computations.

3.5 Duplicate DC

In our protocols, we often need to use a committed value multiple times, thus requiring the decommitting parties in the DC protocol to act in more than one round, a violation of the YOSO model. One possible solution is for the committer C to commit twice (or more) onto different committees to the same value and provide a proof of equality for the committed values; yet this proof of equality will "waste" the sharing, which is what we need to prevent. Thus, we avoid proofs of equality by having the parties in ShareHolder and ShareVerifier reshare the values that they receive in IT-SIG.Setup. It suffices that honest parties share their shares correctly to guarantee that all duplicates commit to the same value. We are using in an essential way the fact that it is the shareholders and verifiers that reshare their values rather than C, and that we can rely on a majority of honest shareholders.

We define protocol DupDC that allows for the duplication of a DC-committed value m. Let d be the number of duplicates needed. In a first committing phase, DupDC.Commit, committer C runs DC.Commit with a committee ShareHolder, sharing its input m so that ShareHolder$_i$ receives a share m_i. To generate d duplicates, for each i, $1 \leq i \leq n$, C runs d copies of IT-SIG.Setup on m_i, each copy with an independent set of MAC keys. The same ShareVerifier committee is used for all invocations. The d copies are verified by ShareHolder$_i$, acting as receiver R, as specified by IT-SIG.Setup. Finally, in the last step of DupDC.Commit, the ShareHolder$_i$'s and ShareVerifiers execute d independent FBcast.Share for all the values that they holds, onto $2d$ separate committees.

The DupDC.Reveal phase follows DC.Reveal where the opening of m_i is implemented via share reconstruction by one of the d ShareHolder committees to which m_i was shared. Additional information that needs to be broadcast and verified as specified by IT-SIG.Reveal is performed via FBcast.Reveal by the FBcast committees created by ShareHolder$_i$ during DupDC.Commit.

Analysis. It is straightforward to check that if the original committer C was honest, all duplicated values are correct DC commitments and they will open to the same committed value during DupDC.Reveal. If C is dishonest, but ShareHolder$_i$ is honest, and verification against a ShareVerifier committee fails during the IT-SIG.Setup actions, then the committed value is set to the one that is FBcast.Reveal as part of Step 4 in IT-SIG.Setup. Otherwise, the value m_i can be reconstructed correctly by any of the d sharings of m_i shared by ShareHolder$_i$. Since there is a majority ($t + 1$ or more) of honest shareholders in each of the d ShareHolder committees, it is guaranteed that only the committed value or $\perp$ will be reconstructed in each of the d copies.

It follows from the properties of the DC and FBcast protocols. We note that C still has the option of not opening any subset of these duplicate commitments, but all those that will be open will be open to the same value. Note that if the verification fails for one of the duplicates and a value $\bar{m}$ is revealed then it is used for all duplicates.

3.6   Verifiable Secret Sharing Scheme

The distributed commitment DC functionality ensures that the committer, even a corrupt one, is committed to a single value at the end of DC.Commit. However, a corrupt committer can prevent reconstruction of the committed value during DC.Reveal. In our applications, we need a commitment scheme with the property that if the commitment phase is successful then reconstruction of the committed value is guaranteed. We achieve this via *Verifiable Secret Sharing* (VSS), a protocol where a dealer secret shares a value s during a VSS.Share phase so that s is guaranteed to be reconstructed during VSS.Reveal from any subset of shareholders that includes $t + 1$ honest ones. This is the case even for corrupt dealers that were not disqualified during VSS.Share.

First, we introduce a procedure used in our VSS design as well as part of the MPC protocol. The goal is to guarantee that two parties that are supposed to share the same value s, had in fact done so. We describe the protocol using generic sharing that can be instantiated with any of the sharing protocols discussed in this paper, including DC, VSS, and its variants.

Protocol Share Equality Test.

1. Party P_1 shares two values a_1, ρ_1 and P_2 shares values a_2, ρ_2.
2. Value r is obtained from an unpredictable beacon $\mathcal{F}_{\text{UPBeacon}}$
3. The values $a_1 + r \cdot \rho_1$ and $a_2 + r \cdot \rho_2$ are reconstructed from their sharings.
4. If the reconstruction succeeds and the reconstructed values are equal, conclude the test was successful and $a_1 = a_2$. In any other case reject the test.

It follows using a standard argument that if $a_1 \neq a_2$ then there is at most a single challenge r that will make the proof pass, implying a probability error of $|\mathbb{F}|^{-1}$ for unpredictable r. Therefore, an unpredictability beacon $\mathcal{F}_{\text{UPBeacon}}$ suffices (see the full version [14] for details).

Protocol VSS.Share proceeds as follows.

1. The dealer D chooses a random polynomial $f(x)$, s.t. $f(0) = s$ and an additional random polynomial $r(x)$, both of degree t. Let the coefficients of $f(x)$ and $r(x)$ be, respectively, f_j, r_j for $0 \leq j \leq t$.
2. Given a set ShareHolder $= \{P_1, \ldots, P_n\}$, D computes $s_i = f(i), \rho_i = r(i)$ for $1 \leq i \leq n$ and transfers these values privately to P_i.
3. In the same step as above, D performs DupDC.Committo all the values f_j, r_j. Due to the homomorphic properties of DC, this results in implicit $DC_D(s_i)$ and $DC_D(\rho_i)$ sharings (shares of f_j, r_j allow the ShareHolder committee to compute values s_i, ρ_i for all i).

4. P_i performs DupDC.Commit(s_i) to obtain two copies of $DC_{P_i}(s_i)$ (particular applications, such as MPC, may require more copies) and performs $DC_{P_i}(\rho_i)$, all with homomorphically correlated keys. Additionally, P_i shares the ρ_i to one of the committees to which it duplicates the s_i.
5. Run the above *Equality Test* on the sharings of D and P_i of value s_i and auxiliary ρ_i (in the case of D, the committee uses the implicit DC commitment of s_i, ρ_i).
6. If the values are not equal execute DC.Reveal of D's sharing of s_i. If it returns $\perp$ disqualify the dealer.

Protocol VSS.Reveal proceeds as follows.

1. Execute DC.Reveal for all s_i shared by P_i
2. Interpolate a polynomial using all these share and output the constant term.

Analysis. The VSS protocol needs to ensure that all of the dealer's shares s_i are points on a polynomial of degree at most t and that the value s_i shared by P_i is the same as the one received from D. The former property is enforced via the DC-sharing of polynomial coefficients by D (it ensures the degree of the polynomial and the implicit DC sharing of shares s_i and ρ_i) while the latter uses the equality test to compare the sharings of D and P_i.

Homomorphism of VSS. VSS inherits the homomorphic properties of DC, importantly, in the case of VSS, these properties hold even if the VSS was performed by two different dealers as long as it was done into *the same set of shareholders*. Namely, for two secrets m_1 and m_2, and two dealers D_1 and D_2, we have $VSS_{D_1}(m_1) + VSS_{D_2}(m_2) = VSS(m_1 + m_2)$. Note that the right-hand side VSS is not associated to a specific dealer as it combines sharings of D_1 and D_2. The reason the homomorphism holds across dealers is due to the homomorphic properties of $DC_{P_i}(\cdot)$ (that only hold for same committer) and the fact that the same P_i's act in both VSS dealings as shareholders.

3.7 Duplicate VSS

As in the case of DC, we also need duplicates of VSS values as a value will need to be part of various computations. Recall that a VSS is a sharing of a value s where each share s_i of the sharing is shared as $DC_{P_i}(s_i)$. It is easy to see that duplicating the $DC_{P_i}(s_i)$ commitments results in duplicate VSSs.

3.8 Augmented VSS

In our application, particularly for the multiplication protocol, we need an *Augmented VSS* (AugVSS), where not only the secret given as input is shared with VSS but also the shares resulting from $VSS(s)$ are shared with VSS.

AugVSS is achieved via the following computation. The dealer D holding a value s defines a polynomial $f(x) = f_t x^t + \dots + f_1 x + f_0$ where $f_0 = s$. It carries out $\mathsf{VSS}(f_\ell)$ for $0 \leq \ell \leq t$. Through the homomoprhic properties of the VSS, this implicitly creates a $\mathsf{VSS}(s_i)$ where $s_i = f(i)$.

It can easily be verified that AugVSS is also additively homomorphic, inheriting this property from the homomorphic properties of the VSS. Furthermore, an AugVSS of a value m can be added to a VSS of a value m' creating a VSS sharing of $m + m'$.

3.9   Duplicate AugVSS

Unlike the previous duplications, e.g. duplicate VSS, where we need to simply have another copy of the value, the duplicate AugVSS needs to provide a stronger guarantee. It needs to have a sharing of the same value but with a different polynomial. The need for this will become evident when we describe the MPC protocol. AugVSS is modified as follows.

A single duplicate VSS is carried out for the constant term, $\mathsf{DupVSS}(f_0)$. In addition, two sets of values $f_t, ..., f_1$ and $f'_t, ... f'_1$ are chosen. Each set in combination with f_0 defines a different polynomial with the same constant term. The protocol from above is executed on both these sets to create two duplicates. If more copies are needed additional coefficients need to be chosen.

3.10   Proof of Local Multiplication (PLM)

In the following protocol, a prover P shares values a, b and c using VSS and proves that $a \cdot b = c$. The proof uses two committees, C and C'.

1. P performs $\mathsf{VSS}_P(a)$ and $\mathsf{VSS}_P(c)$ onto committee C, and $\mathsf{VSS}_P(b)$ onto committee C'. In addition, P chooses a random value b' and executes $\mathsf{VSS}_P(b')$ onto committee C' and $\mathsf{VSS}_P(a \cdot b')$ onto committee C.
2. Receive random e from $\mathcal{F}_{\mathsf{UPBeacon}}$;
3. Committee C' reconstructs using VSS.Reveal the value $r = e \cdot b + b'$;
4. Committee C reconstructs using VSS.Reveal the value $d = r \cdot a - e \cdot c - a \cdot b'$
5. Accept the proof if $d = 0$ and reject otherwise.

It follows using a standard argument that if $c \neq ab$ then $d \neq 0$ except with probability $|\mathbb{F}|^{-1}$. In particular, there is a single e which will let the proof pass. Hence it is enough that e cannot be guessed with non-negligible probability. The rest of the argument for the correctness of the proof follows from the properties of the VSS.

3.11   YOSO MPC

Using the tools developed up to now we can show how to do secure function evaluation (or MPC) in the YOSO model. That is, we are given an arithmetic circuit $\mathcal{C}$, with m secret inputs provided by m parties (roles), and we show how to privately compute the circuit on the inputs, in the YOSO model.

Let $\mathcal{C}$ be a given arithmetic circuit with m inputs $x_1, \ldots, x_m$ and gates $g_1, \ldots, g_\ell$. For the YOSO computation of $\mathcal{C}$, we show how to create, given a gate g_i with input values v_{i1}, v_{i2}, both shared with DupAugVSS, a committee C_i that will hold a DupAugVSS sharing of the output of the gate. In addition, there will be a collection of d duplicates of the AugVSS of the gate's output, where d is the number of gates to which this output enters as an input.

With a lot of attention to details and committee selection we could do the addition of the MPC without interaction. However, to simplify the description of the protocol and to make the addition and multiplication more uniform we will describe things in the same manner.

Gate input setup: As we are looking at a single gate we refer to the committee computing the gate as C. The parties in this committee are $P_1, \ldots, P_n$. Assume that the value on one input wire is a and the second is b.

The parties in the committee C needs to receive its shares of the values on the input wires. As we assume that the values a and b of input wires are shared using AugVSS this means that the share a_i and b_i of party P_i are shared using a VSS. These values are reconstructed towards P_i. Once P_i receives these two shares it shares them using DupVSS. In addition, P_i proves that it shared the values which it received, and this is done using the proof of equality of sharing from Sect. 3.6.

Addition: An addition gate can be implemented without interaction. However, for simplicity, we take advantage of the fact that (as needed for multiplication gates) input wires are shared using DupAugVSS, hence we can use the homomophic properties of AugVSS to implement addition.

Multiplication: 1. Party P_i holding shares a_i and b_i of the input wires, shares the value $\gamma_i = a_i \cdot b_i$ using DupAugVSS. The sharing of these values needs to be done onto different committees as specified by the PLM protocol.

   2. It executes the PLM protocol to prove that γ_i is the product of its two input shares (Sect. 3.10).

   3. For any i for which the DupAugVSS or the PLM procedures fail, the committee that holds a_i and b_i uses VSS.Reveal to publicly reconstruct these values. Later, when the protocol uses the value γ_i, its value is set to the product $a_i \cdot b_i$ of the reconstructed values.

   4. The linear combination of the AugVSS of the γ_i's define the AugVSS of $c = a \cdot b = \Sigma_{i=1}^{2t+1} \lambda_i (\gamma_i = a_i \cdot b_i)$. This also creates the VSS$(c_i) = \Sigma_{j=1}^{2t+1} \lambda_j \mathsf{VSS}(\gamma_{j,i})$ for the appropriate Lagrange coefficients.

Security argument. The multiplication protocol follows the design of [13]. The correctness of the AugVSS sharing of the multiplication $c = a \cdot b$ follows from: (i) the fact that AugVSS(γ_i) completed in a proper manner and its homomorphic properties (ii) the correctness of the PLM; (iii) the public availability of γ_i values for those i where verification failed (these values are available because in AugVSS of the input values of the wires, not only the secret is shared but also its shares). (iv) the existence of Lagrange coefficients λ_i for which $c = a \cdot b = \Sigma_{i=1}^{2t+1} \lambda_i (a_i \cdot b_i)$.

Formalizing security follows standard arguments. In particular, the simulator proceeds as follows. Use the AugVSS's to reconstruct the inputs of the corrupted parties. Input these to $\mathcal{F}_{\mathrm{MPC}}^{F}$ where F denotes the function computed by $\mathcal{C}$. Use dummy inputs of the honest parties in the simulation. Run the simulated protocol honestly with these dummy inputs. When processing an output gate, learn the correct output from $\mathcal{F}_{\mathrm{MPC}}^{F}$. Then from the t simulated shares of the corrupted parties and the output acting as share $t+1$ compute the matching shares of the honest parties. Then send these in the simulation. Furthermore, the simulation of the IT-MAC and IT-SIG are straightforward.

To prove adaptive security the simulator will for each committee C_j start out with a set C_j of size t playing the role of the corrupted parties and will simulate as in the static case with C_j being corrupted. If party P_i^j in C_j becomes corrupted and $\mathsf{P}_i^j \notin C_j$ then the simulator will swap P_i^j with an honest party in C_j and then patch the view of the party to get a simulated state of P_i^j. If P_i^j holds a share on a random, unknown polynomial of degree at most t, the share will just be simulated by a random field element. If P_i^j holds a share on a random, known polynomial of degree at most t, as is the case for a reconstructed output of the computation, then the simulator will know the output and will, with the additional t simulated shares of C_j, have $t+1$ simulated shares. From these it can compute the corresponding simulated share of P_i^j and claim this as the state of P_i^j. In general the adaptive patching follows using standard techniques from MPC and can be done along the lines of [11] where the patching technique is used to prove [2] adaptive secure in the UC model.

References

1. Asharov, G., Jain, A., López-Alt, A., Tromer, E., Vaikuntanathan, V., Wichs, D.: Multiparty computation with low communication, computation and interaction via threshold FHE. In: Pointcheval, D., Johansson, T. (eds.) EUROCRYPT 2012. LNCS, vol. 7237, pp. 483–501. Springer, Heidelberg (2012). https://doi.org/10.1007/978-3-642-29011-4_29
2. Ben-Or, M., Goldwasser, S., Wigderson, A.: Completeness theorems for non-cryptographic fault-tolerant distributed computation (extended abstract). In: Simon, J. (ed.) Proceedings of the 20th Annual ACM Symposium on Theory of Computing, Chicago, Illinois, USA, 2–4 May 1988, pp. 1–10 (1988)
3. Benhamouda, F., et al.: Can a public blockchain keep a secret? In: Pass, R., Pietrzak, K. (eds.) TCC 2020. LNCS, vol. 12550, pp. 260–290. Springer, Cham (2020). https://doi.org/10.1007/978-3-030-64375-1_10
4. Blum, E., Katz, J., Liu Zhang, C.-D., Loss, J.: Asynchronous byzantine agreement with subquadratic communication. IACR Cryptology ePrint Archive, 2020:851 (2020)
5. Canetti, R.: Universally composable security: a new paradigm for cryptographic protocols. In: 42nd FOCS, pp. 136–145. IEEE Computer Society Press, October 2001
6. Cascudo, I., David, B.: SCRAPE: scalable randomness attested by public entities. In: Gollmann, D., Miyaji, A., Kikuchi, H. (eds.) ACNS 2017. LNCS, vol. 10355, pp. 537–556. Springer, Cham (2017). https://doi.org/10.1007/978-3-319-61204-1_27

7. Cascudo, I., David, B.: ALBATROSS: publicly attestable batched randomness based on secret sharing. IACR Cryptology ePrint Archive, 2020:644 (2020)
8. Chen, J., Micali, S.: Algorand: a secure and efficient distributed ledger. Theor. Comput. Sci. **777**, 155–183 (2019)
9. Choudhuri, A.R., Goel, A., Green, M., Jain, A., Kaptchuk, G.: Fluid MPC: secure multiparty computation with dynamic participants. IACR Cryptology ePrint Archive, 2020:754 (2020)
10. Cramer, R., Damgård, I., Nielsen, J.B.: Multiparty computation from threshold homomorphic encryption. In: Pfitzmann, B. (ed.) EUROCRYPT 2001. LNCS, vol. 2045, pp. 280–300. Springer, Heidelberg (2001). https://doi.org/10.1007/3-540-44987-6_18
11. Damgård, I., Nielsen, J.B.: Adaptive versus static security in the UC model. In: Chow, S.S.M., Liu, J.K., Hui, L.C.K., Yiu, S.M. (eds.) ProvSec 2014. LNCS, vol. 8782, pp. 10–28. Springer, Cham (2014). https://doi.org/10.1007/978-3-319-12475-9_2
12. Garay, J.A., Ishai, Y., Ostrovsky, R., Zikas, V.: The price of low communication in secure multi-party computation. In: Katz, J., Shacham, H. (eds.) CRYPTO 2017, Part I. LNCS, vol. 10401, pp. 420–446. Springer, Cham (2017). https://doi.org/10.1007/978-3-319-63688-7_14
13. Gennaro, R., Rabin, M.O., Rabin, T.: Simplified VSS and fast-track multiparty computations with applications to threshold cryptography. In: Coan, B.A., Afek, Y. (eds.) 17th ACM PODC, pp. 101–111. ACM, June/July 1998
14. Gentry, C., et al.: YOSO: you only speak once/secure MPC with stateless ephemeral roles. IACR Cryptology ePrint Archive, 2021:210 (2021)
15. Hirt, M., Maurer, U.M.: Player simulation and general adversary structures in perfect multiparty computation. J. Cryptol. **13**(1), 31–60 (2000)
16. Katz, J., Maurer, U., Tackmann, B., Zikas, V.: Universally composable synchronous computation. In: Sahai, A. (ed.) TCC 2013. LNCS, vol. 7785, pp. 477–498. Springer, Heidelberg (2013). https://doi.org/10.1007/978-3-642-36594-2_27
17. Micali, S.: Very simple and efficient byzantine agreement. In: Papadimitriou, C.H. (ed.) ITCS 2017. LIPIcs, vol. 4266, pp. 6:1–6:1, 67, January 2017
18. Mukherjee, P., Wichs, D.: Two round multiparty computation via multi-key FHE. In: Fischlin, M., Coron, J.-S. (eds.) EUROCRYPT 2016, Part II. LNCS, vol. 9666, pp. 735–763. Springer, Heidelberg (2016). https://doi.org/10.1007/978-3-662-49896-5_26
19. Nakamoto, S.: Bitcoin: a peer-to-peer electronic cash system (2009)
20. Pass, R., Shi, E.: The sleepy model of consensus. In: Takagi, T., Peyrin, T. (eds.) ASIACRYPT 2017, Part II. LNCS, vol. 10625, pp. 380–409. Springer, Cham (2017). https://doi.org/10.1007/978-3-319-70697-9_14
21. Rabin, T.: Robust sharing of secrets when the dealer is honest or cheating. J. ACM **41**(6), 1089–1109 (1994)
22. Rabin, T., Ben-Or, M.: Verifiable secret sharing and multiparty protocols with honest majority (extended abstract). In: Proceedings of the 21st Annual ACM Symposium on Theory of Computing, pp. 73–85. ACM (1989)

Fluid MPC: Secure Multiparty Computation with Dynamic Participants

Arka Rai Choudhuri[1][✉], Aarushi Goel[1], Matthew Green[1], Abhishek Jain[1], and Gabriel Kaptchuk[2]

[1] Johns Hopkins University, Baltimore, USA
{achoud,aarushig,mgreen,abhishek}@cs.jhu.edu
[2] Boston University, Boston, USA
kaptchuk@bu.edu

Abstract. Existing approaches to secure multiparty computation (MPC) require all participants to commit to the entire duration of the protocol. As interest in MPC continues to grow, it is inevitable that there will be a desire to use it to evaluate increasingly complex functionalities, resulting in computations spanning several hours or days.

Such scenarios call for a *dynamic* participation model for MPC where participants have the flexibility to go offline as needed and (re)join when they have available computational resources. Such a model would also democratize access to privacy-preserving computation by facilitating an "MPC-as-a-service" paradigm—the deployment of MPC in volunteer-operated networks (such as blockchains, where dynamism is inherent) that perform computation on behalf of clients.

In this work, we initiate the study of *fluid MPC*, where parties can dynamically join and leave the computation. The minimum commitment required from each participant is referred to as *fluidity*, measured in the number of rounds of communication that it must stay online. Our contributions are threefold:

- We provide a formal treatment of fluid MPC, exploring various possible modeling choices.
- We construct information-theoretic fluid MPC protocols in the honest-majority setting. Our protocols achieve *maximal fluidity*, meaning that a party can exit the computation after receiving and sending messages in one round.
- We implement our protocol and test it in multiple network settings.

1   Introduction

Secure multiparty computation (MPC) [6,10,32,48] allows a group of parties to jointly compute a function while preserving the confidentiality of their inputs. The increasing practicality of MPC protocols has recently spurred demand for its use in a wide variety of contexts such as studying the wage gap in Boston [37] and student success [8].

Given the increasing popularity of MPC, it is inevitable that more ambitious applications will be explored in the near future—like complex simulations

© International Association for Cryptologic Research 2021
T. Malkin and C. Peikert (Eds.): CRYPTO 2021, LNCS 12826, pp. 94–123, 2021.
https://doi.org/10.1007/978-3-030-84245-1_4

on secret initial conditions or training machine learning algorithms on *massive, distributed datasets*. Because the circuit representations of these functionalities can be extremely deep, evaluating them could take several hours or even days, even with highly efficient MPC protocols. While MPC has been studied in a variety of settings over the years, nearly all previous work considers *static* participants who must commit to participating for the entire duration of the computation. However, this requirement may not be reasonable for large, long duration computations such as above because the participants may be limited in their computational resources or in the amount of time that they can devote to the computation at a stretch. Indeed, during such a long period, it is more realistic to expect that some participants may go offline either to perform other duties (or undergo maintenance), or due to connectivity problems.

To accommodate increasingly complex applications and participation from parties with fewer computational resources, MPC protocols must be designed to support *flexibility*. In this work, we formalize the study of MPC protocols that can support *dynamic* participation – where parties can join and leave the computation without interrupting the protocol. Not only would this remove the need for parties to commit to entire long running computations, but it would also allow fresh parties to join midway through, shepherding the computation to its end. It would also reduce reliance on parties with very large computational resources, by enabling parties with low resources to contribute in long computations. This would effectively yield a *weighted*, privacy preserving, distributed computing system.

Highly dynamic computational settings have already started to appear in practice, *e.g.* Bitcoin [42], Ethereum [9], and TOR [21]. These networks are powered by volunteer nodes that are free to come and go as they please, a model that has proven to be wildly successful. Designing networks to accommodate high churn rates means that anyone can participate in the protocol, no matter their computational power or availability. Building MPC protocols that are amenable to this setting would be an important step towards replicating the success of these networks. This would allow the creation of volunteer networks capable of *private computation*, creating an "MPC-as-a-service" [3] system and democratizing access to privacy preserving computation.

Fluid MPC. To bring MPC to highly dynamic settings, we formalize the study of *fluid MPC*. Consider a group of clients that wish to compute a function on confidential inputs, but do not have the resources to conduct the full computation themselves. These clients share their inputs in a privacy preserving manner with some initial *committee* of (volunteer) servers. Once the computation begins, both the clients and the initial servers may exit the protocol execution. Additionally, other servers, even those not present during the input stage, can simply "sign-up" to join part-way through the protocol execution. The resulting protocol should still provide the security properties we expect from MPC.

We consider a model in which the computation is divided into an *input* stage, an *execution* stage, and an *output* stage. We illustrate this in Fig. 1. During the input stage, a set of clients prepare their inputs for computation and hand them over to the first committee of servers. The execution stage is further divided into a sequence of *epochs*. During each epoch, a committee of servers are responsible for doing some part of the computation, and then the intermediary state of the computation is securely transferred to a new committee. Once the full circuit has been evaluated, there is an output stage where the final results are recovered by the clients.

In order to see how well suited a particular protocol is to this dynamic setting, we introduce the notion of *fluidity* of a protocol. Fluidity captures the minimum commitment required from each server participating in the execution stage, measured in communication rounds. More specifically, fluidity is the number of communication rounds within an epoch.

A protocol with worse fluidity might require that servers remain active to send, receive, or act as passive observers on many rounds of communication. In this sense, MPC protocols designed for static participants have the worst possible fluidity—all participants must remain active throughout the lifetime of the entire protocol. In this work, we focus on protocols with only a single round of communication per epoch, which we say achieve *maximal fluidity*. Note that such protocols must have no intra-committee communication, as the communication round must be used to transfer state.

Recall that the idea of flexibility is central to the goal of Fluid MPC. Achieving maximal fluidity is ideal for fluid MPC protocols, as they give the most flexibility to the servers participating in the protocol. It allows owners of computational resources to contribute spare cycles to MPC during downtime, and a quick exit (without disrupting computation) when they are needed for another, possibly a more important task. Maximal fluidity is important to achieving this vision. Moreover, since one of our motivations behind introducing this model is evaluation of deep circuits, an important goal of this work is also to design protocol that not only achieve maximal fluidity, but also where the computation done by the servers in each epoch is independent of the size of the function/circuit.

There are several other modeling choices that can significantly impact feasibility and efficiency of a fluid MPC protocol—many of which are non-trivial and unique to this setting. For instance: when and how are the identities of the servers in the committee of a particular epoch fixed? What requirements are there on the churn rate of the system? How does the adversary's corruption model interact with the dynamism of the protocol participants? We have already seen from the extensive literature on consensus networks that different networks make different, reasonable assumptions and arrive at very different protocols.

We discuss these modeling choices and provide a formal treatment of fluid MPC in Sect. 3. For the constructions we give in this work, we assume that the identities of the servers in a committee are made known during the previous epoch.

Applications. We imagine that fluid MPC will be most useful for applications that involve long-running computations with deep circuits. In such a setting, being able to temporarily enlist dynamic computing resources could facilitate privacy-preserving computations that are difficult or impossible with limited

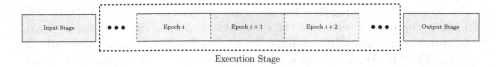

Fig. 1. Computation model of fluid MPC. A set of clients initiate the computation with the input stage. During the execution stage, servers come and go, doing small amounts of work during the compute phases and transferring state in the hand-off phase. Finally, once the entire circuit has been evaluated, the output parties recover the outputs during the output stage.

static resources. This model would be especially valuable in scientific computing, where deep circuits are common and resources can be scarce. Consider, for example, an optimization problem with many constraints over distributed medical datasets. Using a fluid MPC protocol makes it more feasible to perform such a computation with limited resources: the privacy provided by MPC can help clear important regulatory or legal impediments that would otherwise prevent stakeholders from contributing data to the analysis, and a dynamic participation model can allow stakeholders to harness computing resources as they become available.

Prior Work: Player Replaceability. In recent years, the notion of *player replaceability* has been studied in the context of Byzantine Agreement (BA) [11,40]. These works design BA protocols where after every round, the "current" set of players can be replaced with "new" ones without disrupting the protocol. This idea has been used in the design of blockchains such as Algorand [30], where player replaceability helps mitigate targeted attacks on chosen participants after their identity is revealed.

Our work can be viewed as extending this line of research to the setting of MPC. We note that unlike BA where the parties have no private states – and hence, do not require state transfer for achieving player replaceability – the MPC setting necessitates a state transfer step to accommodate player churn. Maximal fluidity captures the best possible scenario where this process is performed in a *single* round.

1.1 Our Contributions

In this work, we initiate the study of fluid MPC. We state our contributions below.

Model. We provide a formal treatment of fluid MPC, exploring possible modeling choices in the setting of dynamic participants.

Protocols With Maximal Fluidity. We construct information-theoretic fluid MPC protocols that achieve maximal fluidity. We consider adversaries that (adaptively) corrupt any minority of the servers in each committee.

We begin by observing that the protocol by Genarro, Rabin and Rabin [28], which is an optimized version of the classical semi-honest BGW protocol [6] can be adapted to the fluid MPC setting in a surprisingly simple manner. We call this protocol Fluid-BGW. This protocol also achieves division of work, in the sense that the amount of work that each committee is required to do is independent of the depth of the circuit.

To achieve security against malicious adversaries, we extend the "additive attack" paradigm of [26] to the fluid MPC setting, showing that any malicious adversarial strategy on semi-honest fluid MPC protocols (with a specific structure and satisfying a weak notion of privacy against malicious adversaries[1]) is limited to injecting additive values on the intermediate wires of the circuit. We use this observation to build an *efficient* compiler (in a similar vein as recent works of [12,43]) that transforms such semi-honest fluid MPC protocols into ones that achieve security with abort against malicious adversaries. Our compiler enjoys two salient properties:

- It *preserves fluidity* of the underlying semi-honest protocol.
- It incurs a *multiplicative overhead of only* 2 (for circuits over large fields) in the communication complexity of the underlying protocol.

Applying our compiler to Fluid-BGW yields a maximally fluid MPC protocol that achieves security with abort against malicious adversaries.

We note that, while we consider a slightly restrictive setting where the adversary is limited to corrupting a minority of servers in each committee, there is evidence that our assumption might hold in practice if we, e.g., leverage certain blockchains. The work of [7] (see also [29]) explores a similar problem of dynamism in the context of secret-sharing with a similar honest-majority assumption as in our work. They show that in certain blockchain networks, it is possible to leverage the honest-majority style assumption (which is crucial to the security of such blockchains) to elect committees of servers with an honest majority of parties. The same mechanism can also be used in our work (we discuss this in more detail in Sect. 3.2). Moreover, the honest majority assumption is necessary for achieving information-theoretic security (or for using assumptions weaker than oblivious transfer), for the same reasons as in standard (static) MPC.

Implementation. We implement Fluid-BGW and our malicious compiler in C++, building off the code-base of [12,16]. We run our implementation across multiple network settings and give concrete measurements. Due to space constraints, we discuss our implementation and experimental results in the full version of the paper [13].

---

[1] It was observed in [26] that almost all known secret sharing based semi-honest protocols in the static model naturally satisfy this weak privacy property. We observe that the fluid version of BGW continues to satisfy this property. Further, we conjecture that most secret-sharing based approaches in the fluid MPC setting would also yield semi-honest protocols that achieve this property.

1.2 Related Work

Proactive Multiparty Computation. The proactive security model, first introduced in [44], aims to model the persistent corruption of parties in a distributed computation, and the continuous race between parties for corruption and recovery. To capture this, the model defines a "mobile" adversary that is not restricted in the total number of corruptions, but can corrupt a subset of parties in different time periods, and the parties periodically reboot to a clean state to mitigate the total number of corruptions. Prior works have investigated the feasibility of proactive security both in the context of secret sharing [35, 39] and general multiparty computation [4, 22, 44].

While both fluid MPC and Proactive MPC (PMPC) consider dynamic models, the motivation behind the two models are completely different. This in turn leads to different modeling choices. Indeed, the dynamic model in PMPC considers slow-moving adversaries, modeling a spreading computer virus where the set of participants are fixed through the duration of the protocol. This is in contrast to the Fluid MPC model where the dynamism is derived from participants leaving and joining the protocol execution as desired. As such, the primary objective of our work is to construct protocols that have maximal fluidity while simultaneously minimizing the computational complexity in each epoch. Neither of these goals are a consideration for protocols in the PMPC setting. Furthermore, unlike PMPC, fluid MPC captures the notion of volunteer servers that sign-up for computation proportional to the computational resources available to them.

The difference in motivation highlighted above also presents different constraints in protocol design. For instance, unlike PMPC, the size of private states of parties is a key consideration in the design of fluid MPC; we discuss this further in Sect. 2. We do note, however, that some ideas from the PMPC setting, such as state re-randomization are relevant in our setting as well.

Transferable MPC. In [14], Clark and Hopkinson consider a notion of Transferable MPC (T-MPC) where parties compute partial outputs of their inputs and transfer these shares to other parties to continue computation while maintaining privacy. Unlike our setting, the sequence of transfers, and the computation at each step is determined completely by the circuit structure. In the constructed protocol, each partial computation involves multiple rounds of interaction and therefore does not achieve fluidity; additionally parties cannot leave during computation sacrificing on dynamism.

Concurrent and Independent Work. Two independent and concurrent works [7, 33] also model dynamic computing environments by considering protocols that progress in discrete stages denoted as epochs, which are further divided into computation and hand-off phases. These works study and design *secret sharing* protocols in the dynamic environment. In contrast, our work focuses on the broader goal of *multi-party computation* protocols for all functionalities.

Furthermore, we focus on building protocols that achieve maximal fluidity. While this goal is not considered in [33], [7] can be seen as achieving maximal fluidity for secret sharing. In choosing committees for each epoch, [33] consider an approach similar to ours where the committee is announced at the start of the hand-off phase of each epoch. [7] leverage properties in the blockchain to implement a committee selection procedure that ensures an honest majority in each committee.

Lastly, both of these works consider a security model incomparable to ours. Specifically, they consider security with guaranteed output delivery for secret sharing against computationally bounded adversaries, whereas we consider MPC with security with abort against computationally unbounded adversaries.

Malicious Security Compilers for MPC. There has been a recent line of exciting work [1,2,12,23,36,38,41,43] in designing concretely efficient compiler that upgrade security from semi-honest to malicious in the honest majority setting. Some of these compilers rely on the additive attack paradigm introduced in [26]. We take a similar approach, but adapt and extend the additive attack paradigm to the fluid MPC setting.

2   Technical Overview

We start by briefly discussing some specifics of the model in which we will present our construction. A detailed formal description of our model is provided in Sect. 3.

As discussed earlier, we consider a client-server model where computation proceeds in three phases – input stage, execution stage and output stage (see Fig. 1). The execution stage proceeds in epochs, where different committees of servers perform the computation. Each epoch ℓ is further divided into two phases: (1) *computation phase*, where the servers in the committee (denoted as $\mathcal{S}^\ell$) perform computation, and (2) *hand-off* phase, where the servers in $\mathcal{S}^\ell$ transfer their states to the incoming committee $\mathcal{S}^{\ell+1}$. We require that at the start of the hand-off phase of epoch ℓ, everyone is aware of committee $\mathcal{S}^{\ell+1}$. We consider security in the presence of an adversary who can corrupt a minority of servers in every committee.

For the remainder of the technical overview, we describe our ideas for the simplified case where all the committees are disjoint and the size of the committees remain the same across all epochs, denoted as n. Neither of these restrictions are necessary for our protocols, and we refer the reader to the technical sections for further details.

Main Challenges. Designing protocols that are well suited to the fluid MPC setting requires overcoming challenges that are not standard in the static setting. While some of these challenges have been considered previously in isolation in other contexts, the main difficulty is in addressing them at the same time.

1. **Fluidity.** The primary focus of our work is the fluidity of protocols, a measure of how long the servers must remain online in order to contribute to the computation. The fluidity of a protocol is the number of rounds of interaction

in a single epoch, and we say that a protocol achieves maximal fluidity if there is only a *single* round in each epoch. Designing protocols with maximal fluidity means that the computation phase of an epoch must be "silent" (i.e., non-interactive), and the hand-off phase must complete in a single round.

2. **Small State Complexity.** In many classical MPC protocols, the private state held by each party is quite large, often proportional to the size of the circuit (see, e.g. [19]). We refer to this as the *state complexity* of the protocol. While state complexity is generally not considered an important measure of a protocol's efficiency, in the fluid MPC setting it takes on new importance. Because the state held by the servers must be transferred between epochs, the state complexity of a protocol contributes directly to its communication complexity. Protocols with large state complexity, say proportional to the size of the circuit, would require each committee to perform a large amount of work, undermining any advantage of fluidity. Therefore, special attention must be paid to minimize the state complexity of the protocol in the fluid MPC setting.

3. **Secure State Transfer.** As mentioned earlier, we consider adversaries that can corrupt a minority of servers in every committee. As such, state cannot be naively handed off between committees in a one-to-one manner. To illustrate why this is true, consider secret sharing based protocols where the players collectively hold a t-out-of-n secret sharing of the wire values and iteratively compute on these shares. If states were transferred by having each server in committee $\mathcal{S}^i$ choose a unique server in $\mathcal{S}^{i+1}$ (as noted, we assume for convenience that $|\mathcal{S}^i| = |\mathcal{S}^{i+1}|$) and simply sending that new server their state, the adversary would see $2t$ shares of the transferred state, t shares from $\mathcal{S}^i$ and another t shares from $\mathcal{S}^{i+1}$, thus breaking the privacy of the protocol. Fluid MPC protocols must therefore incorporate mechanisms to securely transfer the protocol state between committees.

In this work, we focus our attention on protocols that achieve maximal fluidity. Designing such protocols requires careful balancing between these three factors. In particular, the need for small state complexity makes it difficult to use many of the efficient MPC techniques known in the literature, as we will discuss in more detail below.

Adapting Optimized Semi-honest BGW [28] to Fluid MPC. Despite the challenges involved in the design of fluid MPC protocols, we observe that the protocol by Gennaro et al. [28], which is an optimized version of the semi-honest BGW [6] protocol can be adapted to the fluid MPC setting in a surprisingly simple manner.

Recall that in [28], the parties collectively compute over an arithmetic circuit representation of the functionality that they wish to compute, using Shamir's secret sharing scheme. For each intermediate wire in the circuit, the following invariant is maintained: the shares held by the parties correspond to a t-of-n secret sharing of the value induced by the inputs on that wire. Evaluating addition gates requires the parties to simply add their shares of the incoming wires,

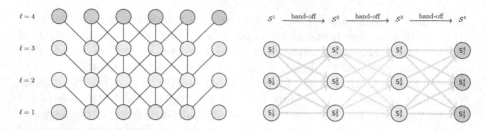

Fig. 2. Left: Part of the circuit partitioned into different layers, indicated by the different colors. **Right:** A visual representation of the flow of information during the modified version of BGW presented in Sect. 2, running with committees of size 3, which achieves maximal fluidity. $\mathcal{S}^\ell = \{S_1^\ell, S_2^\ell, S_3^\ell,\}$ denotes the set of active servers in each committee corresponding to level ℓ, indicated by the same color.

leveraging the linearity of the secret sharing scheme. For evaluating multiplication gates, the parties first locally multiply their shares of the incoming wires, resulting in a distributed degree $2t$ polynomial encoding of the value induced on the output wire of the gate. Then, each party computes a fresh t-out-of-n sharing of this degree $2t$ share and sends one of these *share-of-share* to every other party. Finally, the parties locally interpolate these received shares and as a result, all the parties hold a t-out-of-n sharing of the product. Thus, every multiplication gate requires only one round of communication.

We observe that adapting this version of semi-honest BGW to fluid MPC setting, which we will refer to as Fluid-BGW, is straightforward. The key observation is that the degree reduction procedure of this protocol *simultaneously* re-randomizes the state, so that only a *single round of communication* is required to accomplish both goals. In each epoch, the servers will evaluate all the gates in a *single layer* of the circuit, which may contain both addition and multiplication gates (see Fig. 2). More specifically, for each epoch ℓ:

Computation Phase: The servers in $\mathcal{S}^\ell$ interpolate the shares-of-shares (received from the previous committee) to obtain a degree t sharing for full intermediary state (for each gate in that layer). Then, they locally evaluate each gate in layer ℓ, possibly increasing the degree of the shares that they hold. Finally, they compute a t-out-of-n secret sharing of the *entire* state they hold, including multiplied shares, added shares and any "old" values that may be needed later in the circuit.

Hand-off Phase: The servers in $\mathcal{S}^\ell$ then send one share of each sharing to each active server in $\mathcal{S}^{\ell+1}$.

The computation phase is non-interactive and the hand-off phase consists of only a single round of communication, and therefore the above protocol achieves maximal fluidity.

Recall that we consider adversaries who can corrupt a minority of t servers in *each committee*, a significant departure from the classical setting in which a *total* of t parties can be corrupted. At first glance, it may seem as though the adversary can gain significant advantage by corrupting (say) the first t parties in committee $\mathcal{S}^{\ell}$ and the last t parties in committee $\mathcal{S}^{\ell+1}$. However, since computing shares-of-shares essentially re-randomizes the state, at the end of the hand-off phase of epoch ℓ, the adversary is aware of the (1) nt shares-of-shares that were sent to the last t corrupt servers during the hand-off phase of epoch ℓ and (2) $(n-t) \times t$ shares-of-shares that the first t corrupt servers in $\mathcal{S}^{\ell}$ sent to the $(n-t)$ honest servers in $\mathcal{S}^{\ell+1}$. This is in fact no different than regular BGW. Since the partial information that the adversary has about the states of the $(n-t)$ honest servers in $\mathcal{S}^{\ell+1}$ only corresponds to t shares of their individual states, privacy is ensured.

Compiler for Malicious Security. Having established the feasibility of semi-honest MPC with maximal fluidity, we now describe our ideas for transforming semi-honest fluid MPC protocols into ones that achieve security against malicious adversaries. Our goal is to achieve two salient properties: (1) *fluidity preservation*, i.e., preserve the fluidity of the underlying protocol, (2) *multiplicative overhead of 2* in the complexity of the underlying protocol.

Shortcomings of Natural Solutions. Consider a natural way of achieving malicious security: after each gate evaluation, the servers perform a check that the gate was properly evaluated, as is done in the malicious-secure version of BGW [6]. However, known techniques for implementing gate-by-gate checks rely on primitives such as verifiable secret sharing (among others) that require *additional interaction* between the parties. Such a strategy is therefore incompatible with our goal of achieving maximal fluidity, which requires a single round hand-off phase. Even computational techniques like non-interactive zero knowledge proofs do not appear to be directly applicable as they may require a committee to have access to all prior rounds of communication in order to verify that the received messages were correctly computed.

Starting Idea: Consolidated Checks. Since performing gate-by-gate checks is not well-suited to fluid MPC, we consider a *consolidated check* approach to malicious security, where the correctness of the computation (of the entire circuit) is checked *once*. This approach has previously been studied in the design of efficient MPC protocols [12,20,23,25,26,34,43]. In this line of work, [26] made an important observation, that *linear-based MPC protocols* (a natural class of semi-honest honest-majority MPC protocols) are secure *up to additive attacks*, meaning any strategy followed by a malicious adversary is equivalent to injecting an additive error on each wire in the circuit. They use this observation to first compile the circuit into another circuit that automatically detects errors, e.g., AMD circuits and then run a semi-honest protocol on this modified circuit to get malicious security. Many other works [25,27] follow suit.

Assuming that the same observation caries over to the fluid MPC setting, for feasibility, one could consider running a semi-honest, maximally fluid MPC protocol on such transformed circuits. However, transforming a circuit into an AMD circuit incurs very high overhead in practice. In order to design a more efficient compiler that only incurs an overhead of 2, we turn towards the approach taken by some of the more recent malicious security compilers [12,23,34,43]. In some sense, the ideas used in these works can be viewed as a more efficient implementation of the same idea as above (without using AMD circuits).

Roughly speaking, in the approach taken by these recent compilers, for every shared wire value z in the circuit, the parties also compute a secret sharing of a MAC on z. At the end of the protocol, the parties verify validity of all the MACs in one shot. Given the observation from [26], it is easy to see that the parties can generate a single, secret MAC key r at the beginning of the protocol and compute $MAC(r, z) = rz$ for each wire z in the circuit. It holds that if the adversary injects an additive error δ on the wire value z, to surpass the check, they must inject a corresponding additive error of $\hat{\delta} = r\delta$ on the MAC. Because r is uniformly distributed and unknown to all servers, this can only happen with probability negligible in the field size. While previously, this approach has primarily been used for improving the efficiency of MPC protocols, we use it in this work for also maximizing fluidity.

Verifying the MACs requires revealing the key r, but this is only done at the *end* of the protocol, as revealing r too early would allow the adversary to forge MACs. Furthermore, to facilitate efficient MAC verification, the parties finish the protocol with the following "condensed" check: they generate random coefficients α_k and use them to compute linear combinations of the wire values and MACs as follows:

$$u = \sum_{k \in [|C|]} \alpha_k \cdot z_k \text{ and } v = \sum_{k \in [|C|]} \alpha_k \cdot r z_k.$$

Finally, they reconstruct the key r and interactively verify if $v = ru$, before revealing the output shares.

To build on this approach, we first need to show that *linear-based fluid MPC protocols* are also secure up to additive attacks against malicious adversaries. We prove this to be true in the full version of the paper and show that the semi-honest Fluid-BGW satisfies the structural requirement of linear-based fluid MPC protocols. At first glance, it would appear that we can then directly implement the above mechanism to the fluid MPC setting as follows: in the output stage, parties interactively generate shares of α_k, locally compute this linear combination, reconstruct r, and perform the equality check.

To see where this approach falls short, consider the state complexity of this protocol. To perform the consolidated check, parties in the output stage require shares of *all wires in the circuit*, namely z_k and $r z_k$ for $k \in [|C|]$, which must have been passed along as part of the state between each consecutive pair of committees. This means that the state complexity of the protocol is proportional to the *size of the circuit*, which (as discussed earlier) would undermine the advantages of the fluid MPC model. More concretely, this approach would incur at least $|C|$ multiplicative overhead in the communication of the underlying protocol – far higher than our goal of achieving constant overhead.

Incrementally Computing Linear Combination. In order to implement the above consolidated check approach in the fluid MPC setting, we require a method for computing the aforementioned aggregated values that does not require access to the entire intermediate computation during the output stage. Towards this, we observe that the servers can *incrementally* compute u and v throughout the protocol. This can be done by having each committee incorporate the part of u and v corresponding to the *gates evaluated by the previous committee* into the partial sum. That is, committee $\mathcal{S}^\ell$ is responsible for (1) evaluating the gates on layer ℓ, (2) computing the MACs for gates on layer ℓ, and (3) computing the partial linear combination for all the gates *before* layer $\ell - 1$.

Let the output of the kth gate on the ith layer of the circuit be denoted as z_k^i. Apart from the shares of $z_k^{\ell-1}$ and $rz_k^{\ell-1}$ (for $k \in [w]$), the servers computing layer ℓ of the circuit $\mathcal{S}^\ell$ also receive shares of

$$u_{\ell-2} = \sum_{i \leq \ell-2} \sum_{k \in [w]} \alpha_k^i \cdot z_k^i \text{ and } v_{\ell-2} = \sum_{i \leq \ell-2} \sum_{k \in [w]} \alpha_k^i \cdot rz_k^i$$

from $\mathcal{S}^{\ell-1}$ during hand-off, where α_k^i is a random value associated with the gate outputting z_k^i. While $u_{\ell-2}$ and $v_{\ell-2}$ represent the consolidated check for all gates in the circuit *before* layer $\ell - 1$. $\mathcal{S}^\ell$ then computes shares of

$$u_{\ell-1} = u_{\ell-2} + \sum_{k \in [w]} \alpha_k^{\ell-1} \cdot z_k^{\ell-1} \text{ and } v_{\ell-1} = v_{\ell-2} + \sum_{k \in [w]} \alpha_k^{\ell-1} \cdot rz_k^{\ell-1}$$

in addition to shares of the outputs of gates on layer ℓ (z_k^ℓ and rz_k^ℓ) and transfer $u_{\ell-1}$ and $v_{\ell-1}$ to $\mathcal{S}^{\ell+1}$ during hand-off. Note that the final $u = u_d$ and $v = v_d$, where d is the depth of the circuit. This leaves the following main question: how do the servers agree upon the values of α_k^ℓ?

Notice that $|\{\alpha_k^\ell\}_{k\in[w],\ell\in[d]}| = |C|$, therefore generating shares of all the α_k^ℓ values at the beginning of the protocol and passing them forward will, again, yield a protocol that has an excessively large state complexity. Another natural solution might be to have the servers generate α_k^ℓ as and when they need them. However, because our goal is to maintain maximal fluidity, the servers in $\mathcal{S}^j$ for some fixed j cannot generate α_k^j, as this would require communication *within* $\mathcal{S}^j$.

Instead, consider a protocol in which the servers in $\mathcal{S}^{j-1}$ do the work of generating the shares of α_k^j. Each server in $\mathcal{S}^{j-1}$ generates a random value and shares it, sending one share to each server in $\mathcal{S}^j$. The servers in $\mathcal{S}^j$ then combine these shares using a Vandermonde matrix to get correct shares of α_k^j, as suggested by [5]. While this approach achieves maximal fluidity and requires a small state complexity, it incurs a multiplicative overhead of n in the complexity of the underlying semi-honest protocol.[2]

---

[2] In the static setting, this technique allows for batched randomness generation, by generating $O(n)$ sharings with $O(n^2)$ messages. In the fluid MPC setting, however, the number of servers *cannot* be known in advance and may not correspond to the width of the circuit. Therefore, such amortization techniques are not applicable.

Efficient Compiler. We now describe our ideas for achieving multiplicative overhead of only 2 (for circuits over large fields). In our compiler, we use the above intuition, having each committee, evaluate gates for its layer, compute MACs for the previous layer, and incrementally add to the sum. In the input stage, the clients generate a sharing of a secret random MAC key r, and secret random values $\beta, \alpha_1, \ldots, \alpha_w$. Over the course of the protocol, the servers will incrementally compute values

$$u = \sum_{\ell \in [d]} \sum_{k \in [w]} (\alpha_k(\beta)^\ell) \cdot z_k^\ell \text{ and } v = \sum_{\ell \in [d]} \sum_{k \in [w]} (\alpha_k(\beta)^\ell) \cdot r z_k^\ell$$

where z_k^ℓ is the output of the kth gate on level ℓ, $(\beta)^\ell$ is β raised to the ℓth power, and $\alpha_k(\beta)^\ell$ is the "random" coefficient associated with it. At the end of the protocol, the parties verify whether $v = ru$.

Notice that at the beginning of the execution stage, the servers do not have shares of $(\alpha_k(\beta)^\ell)$ for $\ell > 0$, but they have the necessary information to compute a valid sharing of this coefficient in parallel with the normal computation, namely $\beta, \alpha_1, \ldots, \alpha_w$. To compute the coefficients, we require that the servers computing layer ℓ are given shares of $(\alpha_k(\beta)^{\ell-1})$ and β by the previous set of servers, in addition to the shares of the actual wire values. The servers in $\mathcal{S}^\ell$ then use these shares to compute shares of (1) the values z_k^ℓ on outgoing wires from the gates on layer ℓ, (2) the partial sums by adding the values computed in the previous layer $u_{\ell-1} = u_{\ell-2} + (\alpha_k(\beta)^{\ell-1}) \cdot z_k^{\ell-1}$ and $v_{\ell-1} = v_{\ell-2} + (\alpha_k(\beta)^{\ell-1}) \cdot r z_k^{\ell-1}$, and (3) the coefficients for the next layer $(\alpha_k(\beta)^\ell) = \beta \cdot \alpha_k(\beta)^{\ell-1}$. All of this information can be securely transferred to the next committee.

We give a simplified sketch to illustrate why this check is sufficient. Let $\epsilon_{z,k}^\ell$ (and $\epsilon_{rz,k}^\ell$ resp.) be the additive error introduced by the adversary on the computation of z_k^ℓ ($r z_k^\ell$ resp.).

As before, the check succeeds if

$$r \cdot \sum_{\ell \in [d]} \sum_{k \in [w]} (\alpha_k(\beta)^\ell)(z_k^\ell + \epsilon_{z,k}^\ell) = \sum_{\ell \in [d]} \sum_{k \in [w]} (\alpha_k(\beta)^\ell)(r z_k^\ell + \epsilon_{rz,k}^\ell)$$

Let the qth gate on level m be the first gate where the adversary injects errors $\epsilon_{z,q}^m$ and $\epsilon_{rz,q}^m$. The above equality can be re-written as.

$$\alpha_q \left[\sum_{\ell=m}^{d} ((\beta)^\ell \epsilon_{rz,q}^\ell) - r \sum_{\ell=m}^{d} ((\beta)^\ell \epsilon_{z,q}^\ell) \right] =$$

$$r \cdot \sum_{\ell=m}^{d} \sum_{\substack{k \in [w] \\ k \neq q}} (\alpha_k(\beta)^\ell)(z_k^\ell + \epsilon_{z,k}^\ell) - \sum_{\ell=m}^{d} \sum_{\substack{k \in [w] \\ k \neq q}} (\alpha_k(\beta)^\ell)(r z_k^\ell + \epsilon_{rz,k}^\ell)$$

This holds only if either (1) $\sum_{\ell=m}^{d} ((\beta)^\ell \epsilon_{z,q}^\ell) = 0$ and $\sum_{\ell=m}^{d} ((\beta)^\ell \epsilon_{rz,q}^\ell) = 0$. The key point is that since these are polynomials in β with degree at most d, the probability that β is equal to one of its roots is $d/|\mathbb{F}|$. Or if (2)

$r = \sum_{\ell=m}^{d}((\beta)^{\ell}\epsilon_{rz,q}^{\ell})(\sum_{\ell=m}^{d}((\beta)^{\ell}\epsilon_{z,q}^{\ell}))^{-1}$. Since r is uniformly distributed, this happens only with probability $1/|\mathbb{F}|$.

This analysis is significantly simplified for clarity and the full analysis is included in the full version of the paper [13]. Note that the adversary can inject additive errors on r and β, since these values are also re-shared between sets of servers. Also, since the α values for the gates on level $\ell > 0$ are computed using a multiplication operation, the adversary can potentially inject additive errors on these values as well. However, we observe that the additive errors on the value of β and consequently on the α values associated with the gates on higher levels, does not hamper the correctness of output. But the errors on the value of r, do need to be taken into consideration. The analysis in the full version of the paper addresses how these errors can be handled, making it non-trivial and notationally complicated, but the core intuition remains the same.

We note that we are not the first to consider generating multiple random values by raising a single random value to consecutively larger powers. In particular, [20] performs consolidated checks by taking a linear combination of all wire values, the coefficients for which need to be generated securely, i.e. be randomly distributed and authenticated. But this generation is expensive, so they generate a single secure value and derive all other values by raising it to consecutively larger powers. A consequence of this technique is that once the single secure value is revealed, the exponentiations are done locally and therefore precludes any introduction of errors in this computation for the honest parties. Although this technique might seem similar to ours, our specific implementation is different and for a different purpose, namely, achieving maximal fluidity together with small constant multiplicative overhead.

Implementation Overview. Due to space constraints, discussion of our implementation does not fit in this version of this work, so we briefly discuss it here. We implement Fluid-BGW with our malicious security compiler in C++, using libscapi [16] and the code written for [12] as a starting point. We implement several minor optimizations for our implementation. For instance, we preprocess the circuit so the players always know the maximum number of random values that will be needed in future layers for the malicious security compiler. This allows the player to never pass on unnecessary information. We run our protocol both on a single large server, to benchmark its computational performance, and using the AWS C4.large instances spread between North Virginia, Germany and India, replicating the WAN deployment in [12]. We report both per-layer timing results and total runtime for between 3 and 20 servers per epoch.

3   Fluid MPC

In this section, we give a formal treatment of the fluid MPC setting. We start by describing the model of computation and then turn to the task of defining security. Our goals in this section are twofold: first, we illustrate that there are many possible modeling parameters to choose from in the fluid MPC setting. Second, we highlight the modeling choices that we make for the protocols we describe in later sections. Before beginning, we reiterate that the functionalities considered in this setting can be represented by circuits where the depth of such circuits are large.

Model of Computation. We consider a *client-server* model of computation where a set of clients $\mathcal{C}$ want to compute a function over their private inputs. The clients delegate the computation of the function to a set of servers $\mathcal{S}$. Unlike the traditional client-server model [15,17,18] where every server is required to participate in the entire computation (and hence, remain online for its entire duration), we consider a dynamic model of computation where the servers can volunteer their computational resources for *part of the computation* and then potentially go offline. That is, the set of servers is not fixed in advance.

We adopt terminology from the execution model used in the context of permissionless blockchains [24,45,46]. The protocol execution is specified by an interactive Turing Machine (ITM) $\mathcal{E}$ referred to as the *environment*. The environment $\mathcal{E}$ represents everything that is external to the protocol execution. The environment generates inputs to all the parties, reads all the outputs and additionally can interact in an arbitrary manner with an adversary $\mathcal{A}$ during the execution of the protocol.

Protocols in this execution model proceed in rounds, where at the start of each round, the environment $\mathcal{E}$ can specify an input to the parties, and receive an output from the corresponding parties at the end of the round. We also allow the environment $\mathcal{E}$ to spawn new parties at any point during the protocol. The parties have access to point-to-point and broadcast channels. In addition, we assume fully synchronous message channels, where the adversary does not have control over the delivery of messages. This is the commonly considered setting for MPC protocols.

3.1 Modeling Dynamic Computation

In a fluid MPC protocol, computation proceeds in three stages:

Input Stage: In this stage, the environment $\mathcal{E}$ hands the input to the clients at the start of the protocol, who then pre-process their inputs and hand them off to the servers for computation.

Execution Stage: This is the main stage of computation where only the servers participate in the computation of the function.

Output Stage: This is the final stage where only the clients participate in order to reconstruct the output of the function. The output is then handed to the environment.

The clients only participate in the input and output stages of the protocol. Consequently, we require that the computational complexity of both the input and the output stages is *independent* of the depth of the functionality (when represented as a circuit) being computed by the protocol. Indeed, a primary goal of this work is to offload the computation work to the servers and a computation-intensive input/output phase would undermine this goal.

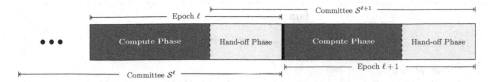

Fig. 3. Epochs ℓ and $\ell + 1$

We wish to capture dynamism for the bulk of the computation, and thus model dynamism in the *execution stage* of the protocol (rather than the input and output stages). In the following, we highlight the key modeling choices for the protocols we present in the full version of the paper by displaying them in bold font in color.

Epoch. We model the progression of the execution stage in discrete steps referred to as *epochs*. In each epoch ℓ, only a subset of servers $\mathcal{S}^\ell$ participate in the computation. We refer to this set of servers $\mathcal{S}^\ell$ as the **committee** for epoch ℓ. An epoch is further divided into two phases, illustrated in Fig. 3:

    Computation Phase: Every epoch begins with a computation phase where the servers in the committee $\mathcal{S}^\ell$ perform computation over their local states, possibly involving multiple rounds of interaction with each other.

    Hand-off Phase: The epoch then transitions to a hand-off phase where the committee $\mathcal{S}^\ell$ transfers the protocol state to the next committee $\mathcal{S}^{\ell+1}$. As with the computation phase, this phase may involve multiple rounds of interaction. When this phase is completed, epoch $\ell + 1$ begins.

Fluidity. We define the notion of *fluidity* to measure the minimum commitment that a server needs to make for participating in the execution stage.

Definition 1 (Fluidity). *Fluidity is defined as the number of* rounds *of interaction within an epoch.*

Clearly, the fewer the number rounds in an epoch, the more "fluid" the protocol. We say that a protocol has **maximal fluidity** when the number of rounds in an epoch is 1. We emphasize that this is only possible when the computation phase of an epoch is completely *non-interactive*, i.e., the servers only perform local computation on their states without interacting with each other. This is because the hand-off phase must consist of at least one round of communication. *In this work, we aim to design protocols with maximal fluidity.*

3.2 Committees

We now explore modeling choices for committees. We address three key aspects of a committee – its formation, size and possible overlap with other committees. Along the way, we also discuss how long a server needs to remain *online*.

Functionality $f_{\mathsf{committee}}$

Hardcoded: Sampling function $\mathsf{Sample} : \mathcal{P} \mapsto \mathcal{P}$.

1. Set $\mathcal{P} := \emptyset$
2. When party P_i sends input $\mathsf{nominate}$, $\mathcal{P} := \mathcal{P} \cup \{\mathsf{P}_i\}$.
3. When the environment sends input elect, compute $\mathcal{P}' \leftarrow \mathsf{Sample}(\mathcal{P})$ and broadcast $\mathcal{P}'$ as the selected committee.

Fig. 4. Functionality for committee formation.

Committee Formation. From our above discussion on computation progressing in epochs, we consider two choices for *committee formation*:

Static. In the most restrictive choice, the environment determines right at the start, which servers will participate in the protocol, *and* the epoch(s) they will be participating in. This in turn determines the committee for every epoch. This means that the servers must commit to their resources ahead of time. We view this choice to be too restrictive and shall not consider it for our model.

On-the-fly. In the other choice, committees are determined dynamically such that committee for epoch $\ell + 1$ is determined and known to everyone at the start of the hand-off phase of epoch ℓ. We consider the functionality $f_{\mathsf{committee}}$ described in Figure 4 to capture this setting.

In an epoch ℓ, if the environment $\mathcal{E}$ provides input $\mathsf{nominate}$ to a party at the start of the round, it relays this message to $f_{\mathsf{committee}}$ to indicate that it wants to be considered in the committee for epoch $\ell + 1$. The functionality computes the committee using the sampling function Sample, from the set of parties $\mathcal{P}$ that have been "nominated." The environment $\mathcal{E}$ is also allowed a separate input elect that specifies the cut-off point for the functionality to compute the committee. The cut-off point corresponds to the start of the hand-off phase of epoch ℓ where the parties in $\mathcal{S}^\ell$ are made aware of the committee $\mathcal{S}^{\ell+1}$ via a broadcast from $f_{\mathsf{committee}}$.

We consider two possible committee choices in this dynamic setting below.

Volunteer Committees. One can view the servers as "volunteers" who sign up to participate in the execution stage whenever they have computational resources available. Essentially anyone, who wants to, can join (up until the cut-off point) in aiding with the computation. This can be implemented by simply setting the sampling function Sample in $f_{\mathsf{committee}}$ to be the identity function, i.e. a party is included in the committee for epoch $\ell + 1$ if and only if it sent a $\mathsf{nominate}$ to $f_{\mathsf{committee}}$ during the computation phase of epoch ℓ.

Elected Committees. One could envision other sampling functions that implement a *selection* process using a participation criterion such as the cryptographic sortition [30] considered in the context of proof of stake blockchains. The work of [7] considers the function Sample that is additionally parameterized by a probability p; for each party in $\mathcal{P}$, Sample independently flips a coin that outputs 1 with probability p, and only includes the party in the final committee if the corresponding coin toss results in the value 1. To ensure that all parties are considered in the selection process, one can simply require that every party sends a nominate to $f_{\text{committee}}$ in each epoch. Committee election has also been studied in different network settings; e.g., the recent work of [47] provides methods for electing committees over TOR [21].

Both of the above choices have direct consequences on the corruption model. The former choice of volunteer committees models protocols that are accessible to anyone who wants to participate. However, an adversary could misuse this accessibility to corrupt a large fraction of (maybe even all) participants of a committee. As such, we view this as an *optimistic* model since achieving security in this model can require placing severe constraints on the global corruption threshold.

The latter choice of elected committees can, by design, be viewed as a semi-closed system since not everyone who "volunteers" their resources are selected to participate in the computation. However, by using an appropriate sampling function, this selection process can potentially ensure that the number of corruptions in each committee are kept within a desired threshold.

We envision that the choice of the specific model (i.e. the sampling function Sample) is best determined by the environment the protocol is to be deployed in and the corruption threshold one is willing to tolerate. (We discuss the latter implication in Section 3.3.) Our protocol design is agnostic to this choice and only requires that the committee $\mathcal{S}^\ell$ knows committee $\mathcal{S}^{\ell+1}$ at the start of the hand-off phase.

Participant Activity. We say that a server is *active* within an epoch if it either (a) performs some protocol computation, or (b) sends/receives protocol messages. Clearly, a server S is active during epoch ℓ only if it belongs to $\mathcal{S}^\ell \cup \mathcal{S}^{\ell+1}$. When extending this notion to a committee, we say committee $\mathcal{S}^\ell$ is active from the beginning of the hand-off phase in epoch $\ell - 1$ to the end of the hand-off phase in epoch ℓ (see Fig. 3).

We say that a server is "online" if it is active (in the above sense) or simply passively listening to broadcast communication. A protocol may potentially require a server to be online throughout the protocol and keep its local state up-to-date as a function of all the broadcast protocol messages (possibly for participation at a later stage). In such a case, while a server may not be performing active computation throughout the protocol, it would nevertheless have to commit to being present and listening throughout the protocol. To minimize the amount of online time of participants, ideally one would like servers to be online only when active.

Committee Sizes. In view of modeling committee members signing up as and when they have available computational resources, we allow for variable committee sizes in each epoch. This simply follows from allowing the environment $\mathcal{E}$ to determine how many parties it provides the nominate input. For simplicity, we describe our protocol in the technical sections for the simplified setting where the committee sizes in each epoch are equal and indicate how it extends to the variable committee size setting. An alternative choice would be to require the committee to have a fixed size, or change sizes at some prescribed rate. These choices might be more reasonable under the requirement that servers announce their committee membership at the start of the protocol.

Committee Overlap. In our envisioned applications, participants with available computational resources will sign up more often to be a part of a committee (see Remark 1). In view of this, we make no restriction on committee overlap, i.e., we allow a server to volunteer to be in multiple epoch committees. As we discuss below, this has some bearing on modeling security for the protocol.

Remark 1 (Weighted Computation). We note that our model naturally allows for a form of *weighted computation*, where the amount of work performed by a participant is proportional to its available resources. This is because a participant (i.e., a server) can choose to participate in a number of epochs proportional to its available resources.

3.3   Security

As in traditional MPC, there are various choices for modeling corruption of parties to determine the number of parties that can be corrupted (i.e., honest vs dishonest majority) as well as the time of corruption (i.e., static vs adaptive corruption). The environment $\mathcal{E}$ can determine to corrupt a party, and on doing so, hands the local state of the corrupted party to the adversary $\mathcal{A}$. For a semi-honest (passive) corruption, $\mathcal{A}$ is only able to continue viewing the local state, but for a malicious (active) corruption, $\mathcal{A}$ takes full control of the party and instructs its behavior subsequently.

Corruption Threshold. We consider an *honest-majority* model for fluid MPC where we restrict $(\mathcal{A}, \mathcal{E})$ to the setting where the adversary $\mathcal{A}$ controls any minority of the clients as well as any minority of servers in every committee in an epoch.

   We discuss the impact of the choice of committee formation on corruption threshold:

- **Volunteer Committee.** In the volunteer setting, ensuring honest majority in each epoch may be difficult; as such we view it as an optimistic model. In the extreme case, honest-majority per epoch can be enforced by assuming the global corruption threshold to be $N/2E$ where E is the total number of epochs and N is the total number of parties across all epochs.
- **Elected Committee.** In the elected committee model, the committee selection process may enforce an honest majority amongst the selected participants in every epoch. The work of [7] enforces this via a cryptographic sortition

process in proof-of-stake blockchains where an honest majority of stake is assumed (in fact they require a larger stake fraction to be honest for their committee selection).

An alternative model is where an adversary may control a majority of clients and additionally a majority of servers in one or more epochs. We leave the study of such a model for future work.

Corruption Timing. Given that the protocol progresses in discrete steps, and knowledge of committees may not be known in advance, it is important to model when an adversary can specify the list of corrupted parties. For clients, this is straightforward: we assume that the environment $\mathcal{E}$ specifies the list of corrupted clients at the start of the protocol, i.e. we assume static corruption for the clients. Since the servers perform the bulk of the computation, and their participation is already dynamic, there are various considerations for corruption timing. We consider two main aspects below: *point of corruption* and *effect on prior epochs*.

Point of corruption: When the committee $\mathcal{S}^\ell$ is determined at the start of hand-off phase of epoch $\ell - 1$, the adversary can specify the corrupted servers from $\mathcal{S}^\ell$ in either:
1. a *static* manner, where the environment $\mathcal{E}$ is only allowed to list the set of corrupted servers when the committee $\mathcal{S}^\ell$ is determined; or
2. an *adaptive* manner, where the environment $\mathcal{E}$ can corrupt servers in $\mathcal{S}^\ell$ adaptively up until the end of epoch ℓ, i.e. while they are active.

Effect on prior epochs: We consider the effect of the adversary corrupting parties during epoch ℓ on prior epochs.
1. *No retroactive effect:* In this setting, the corruption of servers during epoch ℓ has no bearing on any epoch $j < \ell$, i.e. the adversary does not learn any additional information about epoch j at epoch ℓ. This model can be achieved in two ways:

    Erasure of states: If servers in $\mathcal{S}^j$ erase their respective local states at the end of epoch j, then even if the server were to participate in epoch ℓ (i.e. $\mathcal{S}^j \cap \mathcal{S}^\ell \neq \emptyset$), the adversary would not gain any additional information when the environment $\mathcal{E}$ hands over the local state.

    Disjoint committees: If the sets of servers in each epoch are disjoint, by corrupting servers in epoch ℓ, the adversary cannot learn anything about prior epochs.

    We note that for any protocol that is oblivious to the real identities of the servers (i.e. the protocol doesn't assume any prior state from the servers), the two methods of achieving *no retroactive effect*, i.e. erasures and disjoint committees are equivalent. This follows from the fact that servers do not have to keep state in order to rejoin computation, and therefore from the point of view of the protocol and for all purposes, are equivalent to new servers.[3]

---

[3] We would like to point out that if one were to implement point-to-point channels via a PKI, this equivalence may not hold.

2. *Retroactive effect:* In this setting, the adversary is allowed limited information from prior epochs. Specifically, when corrupting a server $S \in \mathcal{S}^\ell$ in epoch ℓ, the adversary learns private states of the server in all prior epochs (if the server has been in a committee before). Therefore, the S is then assumed to have been (passively) corrupt in every epoch $j < \ell$. In order to prevent the adversary from arbitrarily learning information about prior epochs, the adversary is limited to corrupting servers in epoch ℓ as long as corrupting a server S and its retroactive effect of considering S to be corrupted in all prior epochs does not cross the corruption threshold in *any* epoch.

One could consider models with various combinations of the aforementioned aspects. We will narrow further discussion to two models of the adversary:

Definition 2 (R-adaptive Adversary). *We say that the $(\mathcal{A}, \mathcal{E})$ results in an R-adaptive adversary $\mathcal{A}$ if the environment $\mathcal{E}$ can statically corrupt a set T of the clients (at the start of the protocol) and corrupt the servers in an adaptive manner with retroactive effect. Specifically, in epoch ℓ, the environment $\mathcal{E}$ can adaptively choose to corrupt a set of servers $T^\ell \subset [n_\ell]$ from the set $\mathcal{S}^\ell$, where T^ℓ corresponds to a canonical mapping based on the ordering of servers in $\mathcal{S}^\ell$. On $\mathcal{E}$ corrupting the server, $\mathcal{A}$ learns its entire past state and can send messages on its behalf in epoch ℓ. The set of servers that $\mathcal{E}$ can corrupt, and its corresponding retroactive effect, will be determined by the corruption threshold τ specifying that $\forall \ell, \; |T^\ell| < \tau \cdot n_\ell$.*

Definition 3 (NR-adaptive Adversary). *We say that the $(\mathcal{A}, \mathcal{E})$ results in an NR-adaptive adversary $\mathcal{A}$ if the environment $\mathcal{E}$ can statically corrupt a set T of the clients (at the start of the protocol) and corrupt the servers in an adaptive manner with no retroactive effect. The corruption process is similar to the case of R-adaptive adversaries, except that the environment $\mathcal{E}$ can corrupt any server in epoch ℓ as long as the number of corrupted servers in epoch ℓ are within the corruption threshold. As mentioned earlier, any protocol that achieves security against such an adversary necessarily requires either (a) erasure of state, or (b) disjoint committees.*

While our security definition will be general, and encompass both adversarial models, we will consider protocols in the model with **R-adaptive** adversary.

In the above discussions, we have considered corruptions only when servers are *active*. One could also consider a seemingly stronger model where the adversary can corrupt servers when they are *offline*, i.e. no longer *active*. We remark below that our model already captures offline corruption.

Remark 2 (Offline Corruption). If servers are *offline* once they are no longer *active* i.e. they are not passively listening to protocol messages, then offline corruptions in the retroactive effect model is the same as adaptive corruptions during (and until the end of) the epoch due to the fact that the server's protocol state has not changed since the last time it was active. Going forward, since honest parties do go offline when they are no longer active, we do not specify offline corruptions as they are already captured by our model.

Remark 3 (Un-corrupting parties). It might be desirable to consider a model in which a server is initially corrupted by the adversary, but then the adversary eventually decided to "un-corrupt" that server, returning it to honest status. This kind of "mobile adversary" has been studied in some prior works [31]. We note that this can be captured in our model by just having the adversary "un-corrupt" a server by making that server leave the computation at the end of the epoch and rely on the natural churn of the network to replace that server.

Defining Security. We consider a network of m-clients and N-servers $\mathcal{S}$ and denote by $(\overrightarrow{n} = (n_1, \ldots, n_E), E)$ the partitioning of the servers into E tuples (corresponding to epochs) where the ℓ-th tuple has n_ℓ parties (corresponding to committee in the ℓ-th epoch), i.e. $\mathcal{S}^\ell \subset \mathcal{S}$ such that $\forall \ell \in [E], |\mathcal{S}^\ell| = n_\ell$.

Similar to the **client-server** setting, defined in [15,17,18], only the m clients have an input (and receive output), computing a function $f : X_1 \times \cdots \times X_m \to Y_1 \times \cdots \times Y_m$, where for each $i \in [m]$, X_i and Y_i are the input and output domains of the i-th client.

We provide a definition of fluid MPC that corresponds to the classical security notion in the MPC literature called security with abort, but note that other commonly studied security notions can also be defined in this setting in a straightforward manner. The security of a protocol (with respect to a functionality f) is defined by comparing the real-world execution of the protocol with an ideal-world evaluation of f by a trusted party. More concretely, it is required that for every adversary $\mathcal{A}$, which attacks the real execution of the protocol, there exist an adversary Sim, also referred to as a simulator in the ideal-world such that no environment $\mathcal{E}$ can tell whether it is interacting with $\mathcal{A}$ and parties running the protocol or with Sim and parties interacting with f. As mentioned earlier, the environment $\mathcal{E}$ (i) determines the inputs to the parties running the protocol in each round; (ii) sees the outputs to the protocol; and (iii) interacts in an arbitrary manner with the adversary $\mathcal{A}$. In this context, one can view the environment $\mathcal{E}$ as an interactive distinguisher.

It should be noted that it is only the clients that have inputs to the protocol π. While the servers have no input, the environment $\mathcal{E}$, in any round, can provide it with the input nominate upon which the server relays this message to the ideal functionality to indicate it is volunteering for the committee in the subsequent epoch. These servers have no output, so do not relay any information back to $\mathcal{E}$.

In the **real execution** of the $(\overrightarrow{n}, E)$-party protocol π for computing f in the presence of $f_{\text{committee}}$ proceeds first with the environment passing the inputs to all the clients, who then pre-process their inputs and hand it off to the servers in $\mathcal{S}^1$. The protocol then proceeds in epochs as described earlier in the presence of an adversary $\mathcal{A}$ and environment $\mathcal{E}$. $\mathcal{E}$ at the start of the protocol chooses a subset of clients $T \subset [m]$ to corrupt and hands their local states to $\mathcal{A}$. As discussed, the corruption of the clients is static, and thus fixed for the duration of the protocol. The honest parties follow the instructions of π. Depending on whether $\mathcal{A}$ is R-adaptive or NR-adaptive, $\mathcal{E}$ proceeds with adaptively corrupting servers and handing over their states to $\mathcal{A}$ who then sends messages on their behalf.

The execution of the above protocol defines $\mathsf{REAL}_{\pi,\mathcal{A},T,\mathcal{E},f_{\mathsf{committee}}}(z)$, a random variable whose value is determined by the coin tosses of the adversary and the honest players. This random variable contains (a) the output of the adversary (which may be an arbitrary function of its view); (b) the outputs of the uncorrupted clients; and (c) list of all the corrupted servers $\left\{T^\ell\right\}_{\ell\in[E]}$.

The **ideal world execution** is defined similarly to prior works. We formally define the ideal execution for the case of retroactive adaptive security, and the analogous definition for non-retroactive adaptive security can be obtained by appropriate modifications. Roughly, in the ideal world execution, the participants have access to a trusted party who computes the desired functionality f. The participants send their inputs to this trusted party who computes the function and returns the output to the participants.

More formally, an ideal world execution for a function f in the presence of $f_{\mathsf{committee}}$ with adversary Sim proceeds as follows:

- **Clients send inputs to the trusted party:** The clients send their inputs to the trusted party, and we let x_i' denote the value sent by client C_i. The adversary Sim sends inputs on behalf of the corrupted clients.
- **Corruption Phase of servers:** The trusted party initializes $\ell = 1$. Until Sim indicates the end of the current phase (see below), the following steps are executed:
  1. Trusted party sends ℓ to Sim and initializes an *append-only* list $\mathsf{Corrupt}^\ell$ to be $\emptyset$.
  2. Sim then sends pairs of the form (j, i) where j denotes epoch number and i denotes the *index of the corrupted server* in epoch $j \leq \ell$. Upon receiving this, the trusted party appends i to the list $\mathsf{Corrupt}^j$. This step can be repeated multiple times.
  3. Sim sends continue to the trusted party, and the trusted party increments ℓ by 1.
  Sim may also send an abort message to the trusted party in this phase in which case the trusted party sends $\perp$ to all honest clients and stops. Else, Sim sends next phase to the trusted party to indicate the end of the current phase.
  The following steps are only executed if the Sim has not already sent an abort message to the trusted.
- **Trusted party sends output to the adversary:** The trusted party computes $f(x_1', \ldots, x_m') = (y_1, \ldots, y_m)$ and sends $\{y_i\}_{i\in T}$ to the adversary Sim.
- **Adversary instructs trust party to abort or continue:** This is formalized by having the adversary send either a continue or abort message to the trusted party. In the latter case, the trusted party sends to each uncorrupted client C_i its output value y_i. In the former case, the trusted party sends the special symbol $\perp$ to each uncorrupted client.
- **Outputs:** Sim outputs an arbitrary function of its view, and the honest parties output the values obtained from the trusted party.

Sim also interacts with the environment $\mathcal{E}$ in an identical manner to the real execution interaction between $\mathcal{E}$ and $\mathcal{A}$. In particular this means, Sim cannot rewind $\mathcal{E}$ or look at its internal state. The above ideal execution defines a random variable $\mathsf{IDEAL}_{\pi,\mathsf{Sim},T,\mathcal{E},f_{\mathsf{committee}}}(z)$ whose value is determined by the coin tosses of the adversary and the honest players. This random variable containing the (a) output of the ideal adversary Sim; (b) output of the honest parties after an ideal execution with the trusted party computing f where Sim has control over the adversary's input to f; and (c) the lists $\left\{\mathsf{Corrupt}^{\ell}\right\}_{\ell}$ of corrupted servers output by the trusted party. If Sim sends abort in the *corruption phase of the server*, the trusted party outputs the lists that have been updated until the point the abort message was received from Sim.

Having described the real and the ideal worlds, we now define security.

Definition 4. *Let $f : X_1 \times \cdots \times X_m \rightarrow Y_1 \times \cdots \times Y_m$ be a functionality and let π be a fluid MPC protocol for computing f with m clients, N servers and E epochs. We say that π achieves (τ, μ) retroactive adaptive security (resp. non-retroactive adaptive security) if for every probabilistic adversary $\mathcal{A}$ in the real world there exists a probabilistic simulator Sim in the ideal world such that for every probabilistic environment $\mathcal{E}$ if $\mathcal{A}$ is R-adaptive (resp. NR-adaptive) controlling a subset of servers $T^{\ell} \subseteq \mathcal{S}^{\ell}$, $\forall \ell \in [E]$ s.t. $|T^{\ell}| < \tau \cdot n_{\ell}$ and less than $\tau \cdot m$ clients, it holds that for all auxiliary input $z \in \{0,1\}^*$*

$$\mathsf{SD}\left(\mathsf{IDEAL}_{f,\mathsf{Sim},T,\mathcal{E},f_{\mathsf{committee}}}(z), \mathsf{REAL}_{\pi,\mathcal{A},T,\mathcal{E},f_{\mathsf{committee}}}(z)\right) \leq \mu$$

where $\mathsf{SD}(X,Y)$ is the statistical distance between distributions X and Y.

When μ is a negligible function of some security parameter λ, we say that the protocol π is τ-secure.

Remark 4. We note that the above definitions do not explicitly state whether the adversary behaves in (a) a semi-honest manner, where the messages that it sends on behalf of the parties are computed as per protocol specification; or (b) a malicious manner, where it can deviate from the protocol specification. Our intention is to give a general definition independent of the type of adversary. In the subsequent description, we will appropriately prefix the adversary with semi-honest/malicious to indicate the power of the adversary.

This Work. We summarize the fluid MPC model that we focus on in the full version of this paper [13], in the definition below.

Definition 5 (Maximally-Fluid MPC with R-Adaptive Security). *We say that a Fluid MPC protocol π is a* **Maximally-Fluid MPC with R-Adaptive Security** *if it additionally satisfies the following properties:*

- *Fluidity: It has maximal fluidity.*
- *Volunteer Based Sign-up Model: Committee for epoch $\ell+1$ is determined and known to everyone at the start of the hand-off phase of epoch ℓ where the sampling function for $f_{\mathsf{committee}}$ is the identity function. Each epoch can have variable committee sizes, and the committees themselves can arbitrarily overlap. A server is only required to be online during epochs where it is active.*

– **Malicious R-Adaptive Security:** *It achieves security as per Definition 4 against malicious R-adaptive adversaries who control any minority ($\tau < 1/2$) of clients and any minority of servers in every committee in an epoch.*

As we have just shown, there are many interesting, reasonable modeling choices that can be made in the study of fluid MPC. While our specific model name may be heavy-handed, we want to ensure that our modeling choices are clear throughout this work. Additionally, we hope to emphasize that our work is an initial foray in the study of fluid MPC and much is to be done to fully understand this setting.

4 Results in Full Version of the Paper

In the full version of this work [13], we construct a Maximally-Fluid MPC with R-Adaptive Security (see Definition 5). In this section, we outline the sequence of steps used for obtaining this result, and include the main theorems we prove for completeness.

1. We start by adapting the additive attack paradigm of [26] to the fluid MPC setting. In particular, we formally define a class of secret sharing based fluid MPC protocols, called "linear-based fluid MPC protocols". We then focus on "weakly private" linear-based fluid MPC protocols, which are semi-honest protocols that additionally achieve a weak notion of privacy against a malicious R-adaptive (see Definition 2) adversary. We show that such weakly private protocols are also secure against a malicious R-adaptive adversary up to "additive attacks". Formally, we prove the following theorem:

Theorem 1. *Let Π be a Fluid MPC protocol computing a (possibly randomized) m-client circuit $C : \left(\mathbb{F}^{in}\right)^m \to \mathbb{F}^{out}$ using N servers that is a linear-based Fluid MPC with respect to a t-out-of-n secret sharing scheme, and is weakly-private against malicious R-adaptive adversaries controlling at most $t_\ell < n_\ell/2$ servers in committee $\mathcal{S}_\ell$ (for each $\ell \in [d]$) and $t < m/2$ clients, where d is the depth of the circuit C and n_ℓ are the number of servers in epoch ℓ. Then, Π is a $1/2$-secure Fluid MPC with R-Adaptive Security with d epochs for computing the additively corruptible version $\tilde{f}_C$ of C.*

2. Next, we present a general compiler that can transform any linear based fluid MPC protocol that is secure against a malicious R-adaptive adversary up to additive attacks, into a protocol that achieves security with abort against a malicious R-adaptive adversary. Our resulting protocol only incurs a constant multiplicative overhead in the communication complexity of the original protocol and also preserves its fluidity. Formally, we prove the following theorem:

Theorem 2. *Let $C : \left(\mathbb{F}^{in}\right)^m \to \mathbb{F}^{out}$ be a (possibly randomized) m-client circuit. Let $\tilde{C}$ be the robust circuit corresponding to C. Let Π be a Fluid MPC protocol computing $\tilde{C}$ using N servers that is linear-based with respect to a t-out-of-n*

*secret sharing scheme, and is weakly-private against malicious **R-adaptive** adversaries controlling at most $t_\ell < n_\ell/2$ servers in committee S_ℓ (for each $\ell \in [d+1]$) and $t < m/2$ clients, where d is the depth of the circuit C and n_ℓ is the number of servers in epoch ℓ. Then, the there exists a protocol that is a $1/2$-secure **Fluid MPC with R-Adaptive Security** with $d + 1$ epochs for computing C. Moreover, this protocol preserves the fluidity of Π and only adds a constant multiplicative overhead to the communication complexity of Π.*

3. Finally, we adapt the semi-honest protocol of Genarro, Rabin and Rabin [28], which is an optimized version of the classical semi-honest BGW protocol [6], to the fluid MPC setting and show that this protocol is both linear-based and weakly private against a malicious **R-adaptive** adversary, and achieves maximal fluidity. Using Theorem 1, we establish that this linear-based weakly private protocol is also secure against a malicious **R-adaptive** adversary up to additive attacks. Finally, we apply the compiler from Theorem 2 to this protocol to obtain a maximally fluid MPC protocol secure against malicious **R-adaptive** adversaries. Concretely, the following corollary holds directly from the two theorems above:

Corollary 1. *There exists an information-theoretically secure **Maximally-Fluid MPC with R-Adaptive Security** (See Definition 5) for any $f \in P/Poly$.*

Acknowledgements. The fourth author would like to thank Amit Sahai and Sunoo Park for insightful discussions on dynamism in MPC. The fifth author would like to thank Shaanan Cohney for early discussions around blockchains and MPC.

Arka Rai Choudhuri, Aarushi Goel and Abhishek Jain were supported in part by DARPA/ARL Safeware Grant W911NF-15-C-0213, NSF CNS-1814919, NSF CAREER 1942789, Samsung Global Research Outreach award and Johns Hopkins University Catalyst award. Arka Rai Choudhuri is also supported by NSF Grants CNS-1908181 and Office of Naval Research Grant N00014-19-1-2294. Matthew Green is supported by NSF under awards CNS-1653110 and CNS-1801479, the Office of Naval Research under contract N00014-19-1-2292, DARPA under Contract No. HR001120C0084, and a Security and Privacy research award from Google. Abhishek Jain was additionally supported in part by an Office of Naval Research grant N00014-19-1-2294. Gabriel Kaptchuk is supported by the National Science Foundation under Grant #2030859 to the Computing Research Association for the CIFellows Project. Significant portions of this work were done while Gabriel Kaptchuk was at Johns Hopkins University and supported by NSF CNS-1329737. Any opinions, findings and conclusions or recommendations expressed in this material are those of the author(s) and do not necessarily reflect the views of the United States Government or DARPA.

References

1. Araki, T., et al.: Optimized honest-majority MPC for malicious adversaries - breaking the 1 billion-gate per second barrier. In: 2017 IEEE Symposium on Security and Privacy, San Jose, CA, USA, 22–26 May 2017, pp. 843–862. IEEE Computer Society Press (2017)

2. Araki, T., Furukawa, J., Lindell, Y., Nof, A., Ohara, K.: High-throughput semi-honest secure three-party computation with an honest majority. In: Weippl, E.R., Katzenbeisser, S., Kruegel, C., Myers, A.C., Halevi, S. (eds.) ACM CCS 2016, Vienna, Austria, 24–28 October 2016, pp. 805–817. ACM Press (2016)
3. Barak, A., Hirt, M., Koskas, L., Lindell, Y.: An end-to-end system for large scale P2P MPC-as-a-service and low-bandwidth MPC for weak participants. In: Proceedings of the 2018 ACM SIGSAC Conference on Computer and Communications Security, CCS 2018, pp. 695–712. ACM, New York (2018). http://doi.acm.org/10.1145/3243734.3243801
4. Baron, J., El Defrawy, K., Lampkins, J., Ostrovsky, R.: How to withstand mobile virus attacks, revisited. In: Halldórsson, M.M., Dolev, S. (eds.) 33rd ACM PODC, Paris, France, 15–18 July 2014, pp. 293–302. ACM (2014)
5. Beerliová-Trubíniová, Z., Hirt, M.: Efficient multi-party computation with dispute control. In: Halevi, S., Rabin, T. (eds.) TCC 2006. LNCS, vol. 3876, pp. 305–328. Springer, Heidelberg (2006). https://doi.org/10.1007/11681878_16
6. Ben-Or, M., Goldwasser, S., Wigderson, A.: Completeness theorems for non-cryptographic fault-tolerant distributed computation (extended abstract). In: 20th ACM STOC, Chicago, IL, USA, 2–4 May 1988, pp. 1–10. ACM Press (1988)
7. Benhamouda, F., et al.: Can a blockchain keep a secret? Cryptology ePrint Archive, Report 2020/464 (2020). https://eprint.iacr.org/2020/464
8. Bogdanov, D., Kamm, L., Kubo, B., Rebane, R., Sokk, V., Talviste, R.: Students and taxes: a privacy-preserving study using secure computation. Proc. Priv. Enhancing Technol. 2016(3), 117–135 (2016)
9. Buterin, V., et al.: A next-generation smart contract and decentralized application platform. White Paper 3(37) (2014)
10. Chaum, D., Crépeau, C., Damgård, I.: Multiparty unconditionally secure protocols (abstract). In: Pomerance, C. (ed.) CRYPTO 1987. LNCS, vol. 293, pp. 462–462. Springer, Heidelberg (1988). https://doi.org/10.1007/3-540-48184-2_43
11. Chen, J., Micali, S.: Algorand: a secure and efficient distributed ledger. Theor. Comput. Sci. 777, 155–183 (2019)
12. Chida, K., et al.: Fast large-scale honest-majority MPC for malicious adversaries. In: Shacham, H., Boldyreva, A. (eds.) CRYPTO 2018, Part III. LNCS, vol. 10993, pp. 34–64. Springer, Cham (2018). https://doi.org/10.1007/978-3-319-96878-0_2
13. Choudhuri, A.R., Goel, A., Green, M., Jain, A., Kaptchuk, G.: Fluid MPC: secure multiparty computation with dynamic participants. Cryptology ePrint Archive, Report 2020/754 (2020). https://eprint.iacr.org/2020/754
14. Clark, M.R., Hopkinson, K.M.: Transferable multiparty computation with applications to the smart grid. IEEE Trans. Inf. Forensics Secur. 9(9), 1356–1366 (2014)
15. Cramer, R., Damgård, I., Ishai, Y.: Share conversion, pseudorandom secret-sharing and applications to secure computation. In: Kilian, J. (ed.) TCC 2005. LNCS, vol. 3378, pp. 342–362. Springer, Heidelberg (2005). https://doi.org/10.1007/978-3-540-30576-7_19
16. Cryptobiu: cryptobiu/libscapi, May 2019. https://github.com/cryptobiu/libscapi
17. Damgård, I., Ishai, Y.: Constant-round multiparty computation using a black-box pseudorandom generator. In: Shoup, V. (ed.) CRYPTO 2005. LNCS, vol. 3621, pp. 378–394. Springer, Heidelberg (2005). https://doi.org/10.1007/11535218_23
18. Damgård, I., Ishai, Y.: Scalable secure multiparty computation. In: Dwork, C. (ed.) CRYPTO 2006. LNCS, vol. 4117, pp. 501–520. Springer, Heidelberg (2006). https://doi.org/10.1007/11818175_30

19. Damgård, I., Nielsen, J.B.: Scalable and unconditionally secure multiparty computation. In: Menezes, A. (ed.) CRYPTO 2007. LNCS, vol. 4622, pp. 572–590. Springer, Heidelberg (2007). https://doi.org/10.1007/978-3-540-74143-5_32

20. Damgård, I., Pastro, V., Smart, N., Zakarias, S.: Multiparty computation from somewhat homomorphic encryption. In: Safavi-Naini, R., Canetti, R. (eds.) CRYPTO 2012. LNCS, vol. 7417, pp. 643–662. Springer, Heidelberg (2012). https://doi.org/10.1007/978-3-642-32009-5_38

21. Dingledine, R., Mathewson, N., Syverson, P.: Tor: the second-generation onion router. In: Proceedings of the 13th Conference on USENIX Security Symposium, SSYM 2004, vol. 13, pp. 21–21. USENIX Association, Berkeley (2004). http://dl.acm.org/citation.cfm?id=1251375.1251396

22. Eldefrawy, K., Ostrovsky, R., Park, S., Yung, M.: Proactive secure multiparty computation with a dishonest majority. In: Catalano, D., De Prisco, R. (eds.) SCN 2018. LNCS, vol. 11035, pp. 200–215. Springer, Cham (2018). https://doi.org/10.1007/978-3-319-98113-0_11

23. Furukawa, J., Lindell, Y.: Two-thirds honest-majority MPC for malicious adversaries at almost the cost of semi-honest. In: Cavallaro, L., Kinder, J., Wang, X., Katz, J. (eds.) ACM CCS 2019, 11–15 November 2019, pp. 1557–1571. ACM Press (2019)

24. Garay, J., Kiayias, A., Leonardos, N.: The bitcoin backbone protocol: analysis and applications. In: Oswald, E., Fischlin, M. (eds.) EUROCRYPT 2015, Part II. LNCS, vol. 9057, pp. 281–310. Springer, Heidelberg (2015). https://doi.org/10.1007/978-3-662-46803-6_10

25. Genkin, D., Ishai, Y., Polychroniadou, A.: Efficient multi-party computation: from passive to active security via secure SIMD circuits. In: Gennaro, R., Robshaw, M. (eds.) CRYPTO 2015, Part II. LNCS, vol. 9216, pp. 721–741. Springer, Heidelberg (2015). https://doi.org/10.1007/978-3-662-48000-7_35

26. Genkin, D., Ishai, Y., Prabhakaran, M., Sahai, A., Tromer, E.: Circuits resilient to additive attacks with applications to secure computation. In: Shmoys, D.B. (ed.) 46th ACM STOC, New York, NY, USA, 31 May–3 June 2014, pp. 495–504. ACM Press (2014)

27. Genkin, D., Ishai, Y., Weiss, M.: Binary AMD circuits from secure multiparty computation. In: Hirt, M., Smith, A. (eds.) TCC 2016, Part I. LNCS, vol. 9985, pp. 336–366. Springer, Heidelberg (2016). https://doi.org/10.1007/978-3-662-53641-4_14

28. Gennaro, R., Rabin, M.O., Rabin, T.: Simplified VSS and fast-track multiparty computations with applications to threshold cryptography. In: Coan, B.A., Afek, Y. (eds.) 17th ACM PODC, Puerto Vallarta, Mexico, 28 June–2 July 1998, pp. 101–111. ACM (1998)

29. Gentry, C., Halevi, S., Magri, B., Nielsen, J.B., Yakoubov, S.: Random-index PIR and applications. Cryptology ePrint Archive, Report 2020/1248 (2020). https://eprint.iacr.org/2020/1248

30. Gilad, Y., Hemo, R., Micali, S., Vlachos, G., Zeldovich, N.: Algorand: scaling byzantine agreements for cryptocurrencies. In: Proceedings of the 26th Symposium on Operating Systems Principles, Shanghai, China, 28–31 October 2017, pp. 51–68 (2017)

31. Gilad, Y., Hemo, R., Micali, S., Vlachos, G., Zeldovich, N.: Algorand: scaling byzantine agreements for cryptocurrencies. Cryptology ePrint Archive, Report 2017/454 (2017). http://eprint.iacr.org/2017/454

32. Goldreich, O., Micali, S., Wigderson, A.: How to play any mental game or a completeness theorem for protocols with honest majority. In: Aho, A. (ed.) 19th ACM STOC, New York City, NY, USA, 25–27 May 1987, pp. 218–229. ACM Press (1987)

33. Goyal, V., Kothapalli, A., Masserova, E., Parno, B., Song, Y.: Storing and retrieving secrets on a blockchain. Cryptology ePrint Archive, Report 2020/504 (2020). https://eprint.iacr.org/2020/504

34. Goyal, V., Song, Y., Zhu, C.: Guaranteed output delivery comes free in honest majority MPC. In: Micciancio, D., Ristenpart, T. (eds.) CRYPTO 2020, Part II. LNCS, vol. 12171, pp. 618–646. Springer, Cham (2020). https://doi.org/10.1007/978-3-030-56880-1_22

35. Herzberg, A., Jarecki, S., Krawczyk, H., Yung, M.: Proactive secret sharing or: how to cope with perpetual leakage. In: Coppersmith, D. (ed.) CRYPTO 1995. LNCS, vol. 963, pp. 339–352. Springer, Heidelberg (1995). https://doi.org/10.1007/3-540-44750-4_27

36. Ikarashi, D., Kikuchi, R., Hamada, K., Chida, K.: Actively private and correct MPC scheme in $t<n/2$ from passively secure schemes with small overhead. Cryptology ePrint Archive, Report 2014/304 (2014). http://eprint.iacr.org/2014/304

37. Lapets, A., Volgushev, N., Bestavros, A., Jansen, F., Varia, M.: Secure MPC for analytics as a web application. In: 2016 IEEE Cybersecurity Development (SecDev), pp. 73–74. IEEE (2016)

38. Lindell, Y., Nof, A.: A framework for constructing fast MPC over arithmetic circuits with malicious adversaries and an honest-majority. In: Thuraisingham, B.M., Evans, D., Malkin, T., Xu, D. (eds.) ACM CCS 2017, Dallas, TX, USA, 31 October–2 November 2017, pp. 259–276. ACM Press (2017)

39. Maram, S.K.D., et al.: CHURP: dynamic-committee proactive secret sharing. In: ACM Conference on Computer and Communications Security, pp. 2369–2386. ACM (2019)

40. Micali, S.: Very simple and efficient byzantine agreement. In: Papadimitriou, C.H. (ed.) ITCS 2017, Berkeley, CA, USA, 9–11 January 2017, vol. 4266, pp. 6:1–6:1. LIPIcs (2017)

41. Mohassel, P., Rosulek, M., Zhang, Y.: Fast and secure three-party computation: the garbled circuit approach. In: Ray, I., Li, N., Kruegel, C. (eds.) ACM CCS 2015, Denver, CO, USA, 12–16 October 2015, pp. 591–602. ACM Press (2015)

42. Nakamoto, S.: Bitcoin: a peer-to-peer electronic cash system, 2008 (2008). http://www.bitcoin.org/bitcoin.pdf

43. Nordholt, P.S., Veeningen, M.: Minimising communication in honest-majority MPC by batchwise multiplication verification. In: Preneel, B., Vercauteren, F. (eds.) ACNS 2018. LNCS, vol. 10892, pp. 321–339. Springer, Cham (2018). https://doi.org/10.1007/978-3-319-93387-0_17

44. Ostrovsky, R., Yung, M.: How to withstand mobile virus attacks (extended abstract). In: Logrippo, L. (ed.) 10th ACM PODC, Montreal, QC, Canada, 19–21 August 1991, pp. 51–59. ACM (1991)

45. Pass, R., Seeman, L., Shelat, A.: Analysis of the blockchain protocol in asynchronous networks. In: Coron, J.-S., Nielsen, J.B. (eds.) EUROCRYPT 2017, Part II. LNCS, vol. 10211, pp. 643–673. Springer, Cham (2017). https://doi.org/10.1007/978-3-319-56614-6_22

46. Pass, R., Shi, E.: FruitChains: a fair blockchain. In: Schiller, E.M., Schwarzmann, A.A. (eds.) 36th ACM PODC, Washington, DC, USA, 25–27 July 2017, pp. 315–324. ACM (2017)

47. Wails, R., Johnson, A., Starin, D., Yerukhimovich, A., Gordon, S.D.: Stormy: statistics in tor by measuring securely. In: Cavallaro, L., Kinder, J., Wang, X., Katz, J. (eds.) ACM CCS 2019, 11–15 November 2019, pp. 615–632. ACM Press (2019)
48. Yao, A.C.C.: How to generate and exchange secrets (extended abstract). In: 27th FOCS, Toronto, Ontario, Canada, 27–29 October 1986, pp. 162–167. IEEE Computer Society Press (1986)

Secure Computation from One-Way Noisy Communication, or: Anti-correlation via Anti-concentration

Shweta Agrawal[1(✉)], Yuval Ishai[2], Eyal Kushilevitz[2], Varun Narayanan[3], Manoj Prabhakaran[4], Vinod Prabhakaran[3], and Alon Rosen[5]

[1] Indian Institute of Technology Madras, Chennai, India
shweta@iitm.ac.in
[2] Technion, Haifa, Israel
{yuvali,eyalk}@cs.technion.ac.il
[3] Tata Institute of Fundamental Research, Mumbai, India
vinodmp@tifr.res.in
[4] Indian Institute of Technology Bombay, Mumbai, India
mp@cse.iitb.ac.in
[5] IDC Herzliya, Herzliya, Israel
alon.rosen@idc.ac.il

Abstract. Can a sender encode a pair of messages (m_0, m_1) jointly, and send their encoding over (say) a binary erasure channel, so that the receiver can decode exactly one of the two messages and the sender does not know which one?

Garg et al. (Crypto 2015) showed that this is information-theoretically impossible. We show how to circumvent this impossibility by assuming that the receiver is computationally bounded, settling for an inverse-polynomial security error (which is provably necessary), and relying on *ideal obfuscation*. Our solution creates a "computational anti-correlation" between the events of receiving m_0 and receiving m_1 by exploiting the *anti-concentration* of the binomial distribution.

The ideal obfuscation primitive in our construction can either be directly realized using (stateless) tamper-proof hardware, yielding an unconditional result, or heuristically instantiated in the plain model using existing indistinguishability obfuscation schemes.

As a corollary, we get similar feasibility results for *general secure computation* of sender-receiver functionalities by leveraging the completeness of the above "random oblivious transfer" functionality.

1 Introduction

Starting with the pioneering work of Wyner [57], who showed that the wiretap channel can be used for secure communication, a long line of work in cryptography studied the usefulness of noisy channels for general cryptographic tasks [12,13,22,35,48,51,55,56]. A major landmark in this line of work is a full characterization of the "complete" channels on which oblivious transfer, and

© International Association for Cryptologic Research 2021
T. Malkin and C. Peikert (Eds.): CRYPTO 2021, LNCS 12826, pp. 124–154, 2021.
https://doi.org/10.1007/978-3-030-84245-1_5

hence secure two-party computation, can be based [20,21]. In a nutshell, almost all nontrivial noisy channels are complete in this sense.

However, most cryptographic constructions from noisy channels crucially require interaction, and while this is not always a barrier, there are applications in which interaction is inherently unidirectional. Indeed, secure communication in this setting was the topic of Wyner's work, and is a central theme in the big body of work on "physical layer security" [14,50]. Given only one-way noisy communication, any functionality that can be securely realized can be expressed as a randomized mapping $f : \mathcal{A} \to \mathcal{B}$ that takes an input $a \in \mathcal{A}$ from a *sender S* and delivers an output $b = f(a)$ to a *receiver R*. Note that, here the randomness is internal to the functionality, and is neither known to nor can be influenced by the sender or the receiver. We will give examples for useful functionalities of this type in Sect. 1.3.

The goal is to realize such sender-receiver functionalities assuming that S and R are given access to a *channel* $\mathcal{C} : \mathcal{X} \to \mathcal{Y}$. Such channels are usually simpler than the target function f, and can be plausibly assumed to be available to the parties. Well-known examples of "simple" channels that correspond to naturally occurring processes are the *binary erasure channel (BEC)*, which erases each transmitted bit with some fixed probability $0 < p < 1$, and the *binary symmetric channel (BSC)* which flips each bit with probability $0 < p < 1/2$.

1.1   Complete Channels

The general study of secure computation from one-way noisy communication was initiated by Garg et al. [25], who showed that one-way communication over BEC or BSC suffices for realizing any *deterministic* sender-receiver functionality. This includes zero-knowledge proofs as a useful special case. For general, possibly randomized, functionalities, they showed that the following random string-OT functionality (ROT) described below (where a_0, a_1 are strings), is complete:

$$\mathcal{C}_{\mathsf{ROT}}(a_0, a_1) = \begin{cases} (a_0, \bot) & \text{w.p. } \frac{1}{2} \\ (\bot, a_1) & \text{w.p. } \frac{1}{2}, \end{cases}$$

This was recently extended to the case when a_0, a_1 are bits [2], albeit at the (necessary) cost of allowing an inverse polynomial, rather than negligible, error.

Note that in ROT the receiver must learn *exactly* one of the two messages but the sender should not be able to guess which one. This makes the secure realization of ROT highly non-trivial. Indeed, ROT appears to be significantly more powerful than BEC and BSC, and it is not clear how to realize it by a naturally occurring process. While BEC and BSC merely erase or flip bits of information *randomly and independently*, ROT induces a strong *anti-correlation* between events, namely the receipt of a_0 and the receipt of a_1.

Can the anti-correlation inherent in ROT be generated "out of thin air" by invoking simple channels such as BEC or BSC? This question was already addressed by Garg et al. [25], who showed that the simple noisy channels are indeed *not* complete. In fact, ROT cannot be securely realized from such channels even if one considers semi-honest parties (who do not deviate from the protocol) and allows a small constant security error.[1]

It is instructive to sketch the proof of this impossibility result. We consider the more general case of a *string* erasure channel (SEC) that erases each input string with probability p. The proof relies on a classical correlation inequality due to Harris and Kleitman [33,43], asserting that for any two *monotone* Boolean functions $f_0, f_1 : \{0,1\}^n \to \{0,1\}$ and for any product distribution R over $\{0,1\}^n$, the events $f_0(R) = 1$ and $f_1(R) = 1$ are *not* anti-correlated. That is,

$$\Pr[f_0(R) = 1 \land f_1(R) = 1] \geq \Pr[f_0(R) = 1] \cdot \Pr[f_1(R) = 1].$$

Now, by the receiver's security requirement, even if we condition on a "typical" joint encoding x of (a_0, a_1) that the sender transmits over the SEC channel, the receiver's output should be distributed almost as prescribed by the ROT functionality. In particular, if p_i is the probability that the receiver can confidently decode a_i conditioned on x being sent, and E_i is the corresponding conditional event, then $p_0 \approx p_1 \approx 0.5$. Letting n denote the number of invocations of the SEC, $r \subseteq [n]$ represent the set of received symbols, and $f_i(r)$ indicate whether E_i occurs on received set r, the Harris-Kleitman inequality implies that $\Pr[E_0 \land E_1] \geq p_0 \cdot p_1 \approx 0.25$, contradicting the sender's security requirement.

The above impossibility result is purely information-theoretic and does not give rise to a constructive attack. In particular, the functions f_i are monotone because information is monotone: more received symbols mean more confidence. While there are examples for non-monotonicity of information in a computational setting, for instance in the context of generalized secret sharing [45], it is not clear that this has any relevance to the current setting. In fact, Garg et al. [25] showed an efficient attack that rules out computationally secure protocols with *negligible* security error. This leaves open the possibility of obtaining ROT from naturally-occurring channels with a small constant, or better yet *inverse-polynomial*, error.

1.2   Our Results

In this work, we show that the impossibility result for ROT from SEC and other simple channels *can* be circumvented, if one is willing to settle for security against a computationally bounded receiver and to allow for inverse-polynomial error. On the one hand, both of these relaxations are necessary in light of the above mentioned impossibility results but, on the other hand, we still find the positive result to be unexpected, even with these relaxations.

Our main result is cast in a generic model that assumes "ideal obfuscation," enabling the sender to give the receiver an *oracle access* to an obfuscated program. In this generic model, we can unconditionally obtain information-theoretic security by assuming that a malicious receiver is restricted to polynomially many

---

[1] The argument in [25] implicitly relies on the technical assumption that the ROT protocol is *Las Vegas*, in the sense that if the receiver does output a message a_b, then this message is correct; all existing protocols in this setting, including those presented in this work, satisfy this requirement.

queries to the program, but is otherwise computationally unbounded. Before discussing the question of instantiating the generic model, we state the main result.

Theorem 1 (Informal). *There is a one-way secure computation (OWSC) protocol for ROT over the binary erasure channel (BEC) as well as the binary symmetric channel (BSC) using ideal obfuscation, with inverse-polynomial statistical security error against a semi-honest sender and a query-bounded malicious receiver.*

Building on Theorem 1, we can leverage the completeness of ROT for sender-receiver functionalities [25] to obtain the following general completeness result:

Theorem 2 (Informal). *BEC and BSC are (each) complete for OWSC using ideal obfuscation, with inverse-polynomial statistical security against a semi-honest sender and a query-bounded malicious receiver.*

Instantiating ideal obfuscation. A direct way of implementing the ideal obfuscation in our construction is by sending (stateless) tamper-proof hardware to the receiver. To obtain a plain-model instantiation, a natural approach is to use *indistinguishability obfuscation* (iO) [6,30] instead of ideal obfuscation. Following the first candidate construction of Garg et al. [24], iO has been studied extensively [1,4,7,8,15,16,19,26,27,37,38,46,54] and has been constructed from well-studied assumptions in the recent breakthrough work of Jain, Lin and Sahai [38]. Unfortunately, we were unable to prove that our protocols remain (computationally) secure when replacing ideal obfuscation by iO, and consider this to be a highly plausible conjecture. Since iO is "best possible" obfuscation [30], it follows that if *some* instantiation of ideal obfuscation in our protocols is secure then its instantiation with *any* iO scheme is secure. Concretely, we make the following conjecture.

Conjecture 1 (Informal). Replacing ideal obfuscation by any secure iO scheme in the protocol establishing Theorem 1 results in a OWSC protocol for ROT over BEC or BSC that has inverse-polynomial *computational* security against a semi-honest sender and a malicious receiver.

While there are strong negative results for instantiating ideal notions of obfuscation [6,28], these results require at least one of the building blocks to be "contrived." They are not known to apply to any combination of a natural (unbroken) iO candidate and natural application. We believe that Conjecture 1 is qualitatively similar to the leap of faith one makes when heuristically instantiating natural protocols in generic models such as the Random Oracle Model [9] or the Generic Group Model [53]. Arguably, the leap of faith in our case is quite conservative because of the simple and "non-cryptographic" functions to which we apply ideal obfuscation. This should be contrasted with typical applications of obfuscation in cryptography, and also with heuristic iO candidates whose security needs to hold even for contrived pairs of equivalent circuits. See Sect. 1.5 for further discussion.

Assuming Conjecture 1, we can obtain a plain-model variant of Theorem 2 with security against a *malicious* sender by using OWSC for non-interactive zero knowledge to effectively emulate an honest sender behavior.

Theorem 3 (Informal). *Suppose* iO *exists and Conjecture 1 holds. Then, BEC and BSC are (each) complete for OWSC, with inverse-polynomial computational security against malicious sender and receiver.*

We leave open the question of eliminating Conjecture 1 or, better yet, basing the conclusion of Theorem 3 on a weaker or incomparable assumption to iO.

1.3   Why Base on One-Way Noisy Communication?

Several important cryptographic tasks can be captured as sender-receiver functionalities. A natural example, already given in [25] is that of randomly generating "puzzles" without giving any of the parties an advantage in solving them. For instance, the sender can transmit to a receiver a random Sudoku challenge, or a random image of a one-way function, while the receiver is guaranteed that the sender has no advantage in solving the puzzle. More generally, one could use secure realizations of sender-receiver functionalities to unidirectionally generate trusted parameters such as RSA moduli or common reference strings. Unlike the common interactive solutions to such problems, here we consider a setting that allows for completely non-interactive solutions.

Another example of a useful sender-receiver functionality is randomized *blind signatures*, which can be captured by a randomized function that takes a message and a signing key from the sender and delivers a signature on some randomized function of the message to the receiver (for instance by adding a random serial number to a given dollar amount). Randomized blind signatures are a fundamental building block for e-cash applications. They can also be used for non-interactive certified PKI generation, where an authority can issue to a user signed public keys, while only the users learn the corresponding secret keys.

Non-interactive zero-knowledge (NIZK), which is constructed in the common random string model, can also be implemented in the sender-receiver model, by modeling it as a deterministic function that takes an NP-statement and a witness from the sender and outputs the statement along with the output of the verification predicate to the receiver. As noted by Garg et al. [25], NIZK over a one-way noisy channel provides a truly non-interactive solution to zero knowledge proofs, where no trusted common randomness is available to the parties. Moreover, this solution can achieve useful properties of interactive zero-knowledge protocols such as non-transferability and deniability, which are impossible to achieve in the standard non-interactive setting.

While the above applications require security against a malicious sender, it is also meaningful (and non-trivial) to implement protocols that are secure against semi-honest senders. Such protocols can be generically compiled to be secure against malicious senders by invoking NIZK in the sender-receiver model. Note that NIZK by itself is not sufficient for realizing many non-trivial functionalities, including the ones mentioned above. For this, it is necessary (and sufficient) to have a secure realization of semi-honest ROT.

Applications notwithstanding, understanding the cryptographic power of noisy channels with one-way communication is a fundamental question from the theoretical standpoint.

1.4   Technical Overview

To present the new idea underlying our constructions, we focus on a protocol for realizing ROT using a string erasure channel (SEC), with erasure probability $p = 0.5$. This can be extended to BEC and BSC as required by Theorem 1. To realize ROT, we want the symbols that the sender transmits over the SEC to partition the probability space into two events E_0 and E_1, such that $\Pr[E_0] \approx \Pr[E_1] \approx 0.5$, and in each event E_i the receiver can learn a_i but not a_{1-i}.

The protocol begins by having the sender transmit a random n-tuple $\boldsymbol{x} \in \Sigma^n$ over a large alphabet Σ that makes the probability of predicting an erased symbol negligible. It sends $\boldsymbol{x}$ over the SEC. It then picks a small secret "test set" $S \subset [n]$ and sends to the receiver an obfuscated program $F = F_{S,\boldsymbol{x},a}$ that expects the receiver to report all of the symbols it received from the channel. (When instantiating the ideal obfuscation, the sender needs to communicate the obfuscated program over a reliable channel; however, the latter can be implemented with constant rate over any standard noisy channel.) After checking that each unerased symbol reported by the receiver matches the corresponding symbol in $\boldsymbol{x}$, the program F counts how many symbols from the secret set S were reported; if this number is bigger than $|S|/2$ it outputs a_1, otherwise it outputs a_0 (Fig. 1).

Sender input: $a = (a_0, a_1)$.
Sender: Sample random $\boldsymbol{x} \in \Sigma^n$ and send $\boldsymbol{x}$ over SEC.
Sender: Sample random $S \subset [n]$ of size $\sqrt{n}$ and send an obfuscation of $F = F_{S,\boldsymbol{x},a}$ over reliable channel.
Receiver: Output $F(\boldsymbol{y})$, where $\boldsymbol{y}$ is the sequence of non-erased symbols.

Fig. 1. ROT from String Erasure Channel (SEC)

The erasures induced by the channel are independent of $\boldsymbol{x}$, and so whether the receiver outputs a_0 or a_1 is independent of the sender's view. Thus, the protocol is secure even against a computationally unbounded semi-honest sender.

For security against the receiver, we consider two cases. If the channel delivers a minority of the symbols from S, then an honest receiver can legitimately obtain a_0 from F, and even a dishonest receiver will need a super-polynomial number of calls to F to guess even one of the missing symbols.

On the other hand, what if the channel delivers a majority of the symbols from S, which occurs with probability ≈ 0.5? In this case, a dishonest receiver can obtain both messages by first acting honestly, legitimately obtaining a_1, and then invoking F again and obtaining a_0 by just "forgetting" some of the received symbols. The latter attack seems inherently impossible to defend against. How can we expect a receiver who obtained few symbols from S to prove its ignorance?

It turns out, however, that there is a surprisingly simple solution: F will not deliver a_0 when the total reported number of received symbols is significantly below $n/2$. In other words, F does not trust a receiver who claims to be too unlucky. Intuitively, the reason this simple approach works is that S is both small and secret. So without knowledge of S, for every symbol in S that the receiver tries to "forget" it needs to unwillingly forget a large number of additional received symbols. By choosing the size of S and the "unluckiness" threshold carefully, we can ensure that successfully mounting the above "forgetting" attack is computationally infeasible except for a bad event that occurs with inverse-polynomial probability.

The analysis however requires more care and crucially relies, in addition to standard Chernoff-style concentration inequalities, on a simple *anti-concentration* phenomenon: the binomial distribution with n trials is almost always $\Omega(n^{1/2})$-far from its mean. Metaphorically speaking, the events E_0 and E_1 that are separated by this anti-concentration can be viewed as "computational black holes" whose disjoint gravity zones cover almost the entire probability space.

In a bit more detail, for a transmitted $x \in \Sigma^n$ and set $V \subseteq [n]$ indicating non-erased coordinates, let $x|_V$ denote the vector x with all coordinates outside of V replaced by a special erasure symbol $\perp$. Set the "unluckiness" threshold to be $n/2 - n^{0.51}$ and the size of S to be $\sqrt{n}$. Define the function F as:

$$F_{S,x,a}\left(y|_V\right) = \begin{cases} (\perp, \perp) & \text{if } \left(y|_V \neq x|_V\right) \vee \left(|V| < n/2 - n^{0.51}\right), \\ (a_0, \perp) & \text{otherwise if } |V \cap S| < |S|/2, \\ (\perp, a_1) & \text{otherwise.} \end{cases}$$

where $y|_V$ denotes a n-tuple of presumably received symbols.

An honest receiver, who always feeds $y|_V = x|_V$ to F, gets unlucky with negligible probability. This is because, over the random erasures of the SEC, $\Pr\left[|V| \geq n/2 - n^{0.51}\right] > 1 - \text{negl}(n)$, and conditioned on this event, $|V \cap S|$ is symmetrically distributed around $|S|/2$. In particular, the output of F is almost equally likely to be a_0 as it is to be a_1.

A dishonest receiver, on the other may attempt to learn both a_0 and a_1 by feeding $y|_U$ to F, where $U \neq V$ does not correspond to the set of non-erased coordinates. This is not a problem if $y|_U \neq x|_U$ as in such a case F will output $(\perp, \perp)$, but there is always a chance that the receiver can come up with $y|_U = x|_U$. Here we have two possible cases:

U is not contained in V. This case can be ruled out when $|\Sigma|$ is super-polynomially large, as it requires the receiver to correctly guess a randomly sampled x_i for $i \in U \setminus V$.

U **is a strict subset of** V. In this case, one cannot prevent the receiver from feeding an input $y|_U = x|_U$, as this merely amounts to erasing symbols from the received string $x|_V$. Here, the only hope for the receiver to obtain both a_0 and a_1 is to be able to transition from the case $|V \cap S| \geq |S|/2$ to the case $|U \cap S| < |S|/2$. Note that, by anti-concentration, in this case $|V \cap S|$ is likely larger than $|S|/2$ by $\Omega(\sqrt{|S|})$ and, moreover, S is secret, hence the receiver cannot just find such U by only removing few elements of V in an exhaustive search. On the other hand, if the receiver tries to forget many symbols from the unknown S by just forgetting many symbols from V, it will hit the unlucky zone where F returns $(\perp, \perp)$.

To prevent attacks as in the first case, it is imperative that the obfuscation of F hide x. Avoiding attacks as in the second case, on the other hand, requires the obfuscation to hide S. What type of obfuscation would be sufficient for hiding x and S? Ideal obfuscation limits the receiver to black-box access to F. Intuitively, this means that the receiver's attempts to mount the above attacks are restricted to random guesses, as x and S are information theoretically hidden.

1.5   Discussion

The unconditional result given by Theorem 1 (and subsequent theorems that build on it) captures the main contribution of this work. Our use of ideal obfuscation is technically equivalent to having a single, stateless, tamper-proof hardware token shipped from the sender to the receiver. In fact, unlike current candidates for cryptographic obfuscation, such an approach may be efficient enough to be implemented. Thus, our results can be cast as part of a long line of theory-oriented works on cryptography using tamper-proof hardware (see [5,29,32,40], along many others).

From a complexity theoretic point of view, the ideal obfuscation primitive can be viewed as a (succinctly described) *oracle* generated by the sender, such that security holds unconditionally with respect to any *query-bounded* receiver that has access to this oracle. For instance, this is the model used in works on zero-knowledge PCP [36,42,47]. Alternatively, it can be seen as a second, "resettable" sender, analogously to the multi-prover proof model [10,11,31,39].

An unusual aspect of our main feasibility result that separates it from almost all nontrivial applications of obfuscation in cryptography is that it is based on *ideal obfuscation alone*, without making any additional assumptions such as the existence of one-way functions (or alternatively $NP \not\subseteq$ io-BPP [44]). In particular, the functions we obfuscate are simple, explicit and "non-cryptographic."

We also note the analogy with the Random Oracle Model (ROM) methodology: there is a long tradition in cryptography of using a construction in an idealized "generic" model, such as the ROM [9], as a stepping stone towards heuristic plain-model realizations. The latter are obtained by using concrete hash functions as a substitute for the random oracle. For example, constructions of transparent SNARGs for NP follow this approach [49]. Our proposal is analogous: heuristically instantiate the ideal obfuscation by using any iO construction from the literature. There are strong negative results for instantiating ideal notions of obfuscation [6]. These are in a sense analogous to similar negative results for instantiating the ROM [18]. However, similarly to ROM instantiations, we do not see a reason why these negative results should apply to a combination of a *natural* application and a *natural* iO construction that was not designed with a counterexample in mind.

Finally, most solutions for natural cryptographic tasks that were initially cast in idealized models were later followed by plain-model constructions under simple and plausible cryptographic assumptions. We expect the current work to follow a similar path.

2 Preliminaries

Notation. We write $x \leftarrow \mathcal{X}$ to denote the process of freshly sampling a uniformly random element x from a finite set $\mathcal{X}$. We denote the i-th coordinate of a vector $\boldsymbol{x} \in \mathcal{X}^n$ by either x_i or $\boldsymbol{x}(i)$. For a vector $\boldsymbol{x} \in \mathcal{X}^n$ and set $A \subseteq [n]$, the restriction of $\boldsymbol{x}$ to A, denoted by $\boldsymbol{x}|_A$, is the length n vector in $(\mathcal{X} \cup \{\bot\})^n$ with all the coordinates outside of A replaced by a special erasure symbol $\bot$. That is, $\boldsymbol{x}|_A (i) = \boldsymbol{x}(i)$ if $i \in A$ and $\boldsymbol{x}|_A (i) = \bot$ otherwise. The notation $\binom{[n]}{k}$ denotes the family of all subsets of $[n]$ with size k.

2.1 Sender-Receiver Functionalities and Channels

We study secure computation tasks that are made possible by one-way communication over a noisy channel. Such tasks can be captured by *sender-receiver* functionalities, that take an input from a *sender* S and deliver a (possibly) randomized output to a *receiver* R. In the randomized case, the randomness is picked by the functionality and is not revealed to the sender or the receiver. More precisely, a sender-receiver functionality is a randomized mapping $f : \mathcal{A} \to \mathcal{B}$ that takes an input $a \in \mathcal{A}$ from a sender S and delivers an output $b = f(a)$ to a receiver R. We will sometimes refer to f simply as a *function*.

In order to realize f, we assume that S and R are given parallel access to a *channel* $\mathcal{C} : \mathcal{X} \to \mathcal{Y}$. A channel is also a sender-receiver functionality but is usually much simpler than the target function f. We define three channels of interest below.

- **BSC.** $\mathcal{C}^p_{\mathsf{BSC}}$ denotes the *Binary Symmetric Channel* (BSC) with crossover probability p: i.e., for input $x \in \{0, 1\}$, the output $\mathcal{C}^p_{\mathsf{BSC}}(x)$ is $1 - x$ with probability p and is x otherwise.
- **SEC and BEC.** $\mathcal{C}^p_{\mathsf{SEC}}$ denotes the *String Erasure Channel* (SEC) which takes an input string of a fixed length and outputs $\bot$ with probability p and x otherwise. When the string length is 1, $\mathcal{C}^p_{\mathsf{SEC}}$ is called a *Binary Erasure Channel* (BEC), and denoted by $\mathcal{C}^p_{\mathsf{BEC}}$. When $p = \frac{1}{2}$, we may omit it from the notation.
- **ROT.** The *(String) Randomized Oblivious Transfer* channel $\mathcal{C}_{\mathsf{ROT}}$ takes as input a pair of fixed-length strings (x_0, x_1) and outputs $(x_0, \bot)$ or $(\bot, x_1)$ with probability $\frac{1}{2}$ each.

For brevity, we shall write $\mathcal{C}(x_1, \ldots, x_m)$ to denote $(\mathcal{C}(x_1), \ldots, \mathcal{C}(x_m))$, i.e., the outcome of m independent invocations of a channel $\mathcal{C}$.

2.2   Secure Computation with One-Way Communication

A secure protocol for $f : \mathcal{A} \rightarrow \mathcal{B}$ over a channel $\mathcal{C}$ is formalized via the standard definitional framework of reductions in secure computation. Our definitions are in fact simpler because of the non-interactive setting. We start with the simplest case of defining *information-theoretic* security against *semi-honest* parties for a *finite* function f, ignoring computational complexity. We then describe extensions to malicious parties, computational security, and infinite families of functions.

OWSC protocols. A one-way secure computation protocol for f over $\mathcal{C}$ specifies a randomized encoder that maps the sender's input a into a sequence of channel inputs $\boldsymbol{x}$, and a decoder that maps the receiver's channel outputs $\boldsymbol{y}$ into an output b. Up to an error bound parameter ϵ, the protocol should satisfy the following security requirements: (i) given the sender's view, which consists of an input a and the messages $\boldsymbol{x}$ that it fed into the channel, the receiver's output should be distributed as $f(a)$, and (ii) the view of the receiver, namely the messages $\boldsymbol{y}$ it received from the channel, can be simulated from $f(a)$. Note that (i) captures receiver security against a semi-honest sender *as well as correctness*, while (ii) captures sender security against the receiver. Also note that since the receiver does not send messages, whether it is semi-honest or malicious does not make a difference. We formalize the above security requirements below, using Δ to denote statistical distance.

Definition 1 (One-way secure computation: semi-honest sender). *Given a randomized function $f : \mathcal{A} \rightarrow \mathcal{B}$ and a channel $\mathcal{C} : \mathcal{X} \rightarrow \mathcal{Y}$, a pair of randomized functions $\langle \mathsf{S}, \mathsf{R} \rangle$, where $\mathsf{S} : \mathcal{A} \rightarrow \mathcal{X}^n$ and $\mathsf{R} : \mathcal{Y}^n \rightarrow \mathcal{B}$, is said to be an ϵ-secure OWSC protocol for f over $\mathcal{C}$ (with semi-honest sender) if there exists a simulator $\mathcal{S}_\mathsf{R} : \mathcal{B} \rightarrow \mathcal{Y}^n$, such that for all $a \in \mathcal{A}$, the following hold:*

$$\Delta\left((\mathsf{S}(a), f(a)), (\mathsf{S}(a), \mathsf{R}(\mathcal{C}(\mathsf{S}(a))))\right) \leq \epsilon \quad \text{(Security against semi-honest sender)}$$
$$\Delta\left(\mathcal{S}_\mathsf{R}(f(a)), \mathcal{C}(\mathsf{S}(a))\right) \leq \epsilon \quad \text{(Security against receiver)}$$

OWSC for malicious parties. In the case of a malicious sender, our security requirement coincides with the standard notion of universally composable (UC) security [17], but with simplifications implied by the communication model. The extra security requirement in this case is that for any strategy of the sender (for choosing $\boldsymbol{x}$), a simulator is able to extract a valid input. Formally, an OWSC protocol for f over $\mathcal{C}$ is *secure against malicious parties* if, in addition to the requirements in Definition 1, there exists a randomized simulator $\mathcal{S}_\mathsf{S} : \mathcal{X}^n \rightarrow \mathcal{A}$ such that for every $\boldsymbol{x} \in \mathcal{X}^n$,

$$\Delta\left(f(\mathcal{S}_\mathsf{S}(\boldsymbol{x})), \mathsf{R}(\mathcal{C}(\boldsymbol{x}))\right) \leq \epsilon \quad \text{(Security against malicious sender)}$$

Note that the first condition of Definition 1 is retained to imply correctness when the sender is honest, and the second condition implies security against malicious receiver as well.

OWSC with computational security. We can naturally relax the above definition of (statistical) ϵ-secure OWSC to a *computationally (T, ϵ)-secure* OWSC, for a distinguisher size bound T, by replacing each statistical distance bound $\Delta(A, B) \leq \epsilon$ by the condition that for all circuits C of size T, $|\Pr[C(A) = 1] - \Pr[C(B) = 1]| \leq \epsilon$.

Universal Protocols and Complete channels for OWSC. So far, we considered OWSC protocols for a concrete finite function f and with a concrete level of security. However, in a cryptographic context, one is often interested in a single "universal" protocol in which the sender and the receiver are given a circuit $\hat{f}$, representing a function f, and a security parameter 1^λ as common inputs (in addition to the sender being given an input a for f). More generally, one may consider any computational model – i.e., a representation of the function – instead of circuits (e.g., in the context of information-theoretic security, it will be useful to consider weaker representation models such as branching programs).

In a *polynomial time* universal protocol $\Pi = \langle \mathsf{S}, \mathsf{R} \rangle$, both S and R run in time polynomial in λ. Protocol Π is said to be a universal ϵ-secure (resp., (T, ϵ)-secure) OWSC protocol for $\mathcal{F}$ over $\mathcal{C}$, if for all $\hat{f} \in \mathcal{F}$ with $|\hat{f}| \leq \lambda$, the protocol obtained from Π by fixing the common inputs to $(\hat{f}, 1^\lambda)$ is an $\epsilon(\lambda)$-secure (resp., $(T(\lambda), \epsilon(\lambda))$-secure) OWSC for f over $\mathcal{C}$, where f denotes the function represented by $\hat{f}$.

While $\mathcal{F}$ above can be a narrow class of functions (e.g., string OTs), we shall be particularly interested in the case where it is a general computational model like circuits or branching programs. If a channel $\mathcal{C}$ enables such a universal protocol, we say that $\mathcal{C}$ is *OWSC-complete* for the corresponding computational model. We will distinguish between completeness with inverse-polynomial error and completeness with negligible error, depending on how fast the error vanishes with λ. We will also distinguish between completeness with statistical vs. computational security and between semi-honest vs. malicious senders.

Definition 2 (OWSC-complete channel). *For a computational model $\mathcal{F}$, we say that $\mathcal{C}$ is* OWSC-complete with inverse-polynomial statistical error *if, for every $c > 0$, there is a polynomial-time universal ϵ-secure OWSC protocol for $\mathcal{F}$ over $\mathcal{C}$, where $\epsilon(\lambda) = \mathcal{O}(\frac{1}{\lambda^c})$. We say that $\mathcal{C}$ is* OWSC-complete with negligible statistical error *if there exists a polynomial-time universal ϵ-secure OWSC protocol for $\mathcal{F}$ over $\mathcal{C}$ for some negligible function ϵ.*

We say that $\mathcal{C}$ is computational OWSC-complete with inverse-polynomial statistical error *(resp., negligible statistical error) if, for every $c > 0$, there exists a polynomial-time universal OWSC protocol Π such that for every polynomial $T(\lambda)$, Π is a (T, ϵ)-secure OWSC protocol for $\mathcal{F}$ over $\mathcal{C}$, where $\epsilon(\lambda) = \mathcal{O}(\frac{1}{\lambda^c})$ (resp., ϵ is negligible).*

Completeness as defined above is said to be against malicious parties *if the definition of secure OWSC used is against malicious parties, with the simulator $\mathcal{S}_S$ being polynomial time.*

As discussed above, useful instantiations of $\mathcal{F}$ include circuits, branching programs, and string-ROT. We will assume statistical security against semi-honest parties by default, and will explicitly indicate when security is computational or against malicious parties.

OWSC using ideal obfuscation. Our results, which are information-theoretic in nature, make use of obfuscation as an ideal primitive. An OWSC protocol for f over $\mathcal{C}$ *using ideal obfuscation* is defined similarly to the above except that, in addition to its inputs $\boldsymbol{x}$ for the channel $\mathcal{C}$, the sender specifies a function F (using, say, a circuit $\hat{F}$), to which the receiver is only given (bounded) oracle access. An *honest* receiver can make a single query q to F after observing the outputs $\boldsymbol{y}$ of $\mathcal{C}$, and then compute the output b based on $\boldsymbol{y}$ and $F(q)$. To define security, we extend the syntax of Definition 1 by adding a *query bound* parameter Q. The definition of ϵ-security against the receiver is modified to (Q, ϵ)-security as follows. The simulator $\mathcal{S}_R$ is now an interactive algorithm that interacts with an arbitrary Q-bounded R^*. Given input b (output of f), $\mathcal{S}_R$ first generates and sends to R^* a simulated channel output $\boldsymbol{y}$, and then provides a simulated response for each F-query made by R^*. We require that for *every Q-bounded* R^* and sender input $a \in \mathcal{A}$, the following holds:

$$\Delta\left([\mathcal{S}_R(f(a)) \leftrightarrow \mathsf{R}^*], [F \leftrightarrow \mathsf{R}^*(\mathcal{C}(x)) \mid (\hat{F}, x) \leftarrow \mathsf{S}(a))] \right) \le \epsilon$$

(Security against a query-bounded receiver)

Here $[\mathcal{S}_R(f(a)) \leftrightarrow \mathsf{R}^*]$ is the ideal-world transcript of the interaction of $\mathcal{S}_R(f(a))$ with R^*, and $[F \leftrightarrow \mathsf{R}^*(\mathcal{C}(x))]$ denotes the real-world transcript of R^* interacting with the channel $\mathcal{C}$ and F, on sender input a. Note that in the latter F denotes the function corresponding to $\hat{F}$ generated by $\mathsf{S}(a)$. The completeness notions in Definition 2 are adapted to the ideal obfuscation setting by requiring that *for every polynomial query bound $Q(\lambda)$, there is an appropriate ϵ such that Π is a universal (Q, ϵ)-secure OWSC protocol.*

2.3 Probability Preliminaries

We state an anti-concentration bound for binomial distribution, which we crucially use in the analysis of all our constructions. The statement of the lemma is quoted verbatim from [52, Theorem 4.6].

Lemma 1 (Anti-concentration). *Let $0 < p < 1$, and $X = X_1 + \ldots + X_n$, where, for each $i \in [n]$, X_i is independently and identically distributed as Bernoulli(p). There exists $\Theta_p > 0$ depending only on p (where $\Theta_{\frac{1}{2}} = 1$), such that, for all $0 \le k \le n$, we have $\Pr[X = k] \le \dfrac{\Theta_p}{\sqrt{n}}$.*

Following is a standard concentration inequality required for the analysis of our protocols.

Lemma 2 (Chernoff bound). *Let $0 < p < 1$, and $X_1, \ldots, X_n$ be random variables such that for each $i \in [n]$, X_i is independently and identically distributed as Bernoulli(p). Further, let $X = X_1 + X_2 + \ldots + X_n$. When μ denotes the expected value of X, i.e., $\mu = \mathbb{E}(X) = p \cdot n$,*

$$(i) \ \Pr[X \geq (1 + \delta)\mu] \leq e^{-\frac{\delta^2}{2+\delta}\mu} \text{ for all } \delta > 0,$$

$$(ii) \ \Pr[X \leq (1 - \delta)\mu] \leq e^{-\mu\frac{\delta^2}{2}} \text{ for all } \delta \in (0,1).$$

In particular, for all $\eta \in \left(\frac{1}{2}, 1\right)$, for sufficiently large n,

$$(iii) \ \Pr[X \in [p(n - n^\eta), p(n + n^\eta)]] \geq 1 - 2e^{-\frac{1}{4p}n^{2\eta-1}} = 1 - \mathrm{negl}(n).$$

Proof: (iii) follows from applying (i) and (ii) by setting $\mu = p \cdot n$ and $\delta = \frac{n^{\eta-1}}{p}$. Note that $\delta \in (0,1)$ for sufficiently large n.   □

3   ROT from SEC Using Ideal Obfuscation

In this section, we prove that ROT can be realized using a string erasure channel (with erasure probability $p = 0.5$), assuming ideal obfuscation, following the sketch discussed in Sect. 1.4. In more detail, we prove:

Theorem 4 (ROT from SEC using ideal obfuscation). *There exists an OWSC protocol for string-ROT over SEC using ideal obfuscation, with inverse-polynomial statistical security against a semi-honest sender and a query-bounded receiver.*

More concretely, for any constant $c > 0$, there exists an OWSC protocol which, for all $\lambda, t \in \mathbb{N}$, realizes t-bit string ROT with ϵ-security against a semi-honest sender and a polynomial query-bounded receiver, using n invocations of ℓ-bit SEC and an ideal obfuscation of a circuit $\hat{F}$, when $\epsilon = \mathcal{O}(\frac{1}{\lambda^c})$, $n = \mathcal{O}(\lambda^{8c})$, $\ell = \omega(\log \lambda)$, and $|\hat{F}| = \mathcal{O}(t + \lambda^{16c})$.

Proof: An OWSC protocol $\langle S, R \rangle$ for t-bit string ROT over ℓ-bit SEC is provided in Fig. 2. The proof follows the argument sketched in the technical overview (See Sect. 1.4). We will use the following lemmas to prove the theorem; they are formally proved in the full version of this work [3] using the anti-concentration bound (Lemma 1) and Chernoff bound (Lemma 2).

Lemma 3. *Let $\eta > \frac{1}{2}$, and U, V be arbitrary subsets of $[n]$ such that $|U|, |V| \in [\frac{n-n^\eta}{2}, \frac{n+n^\eta}{2}]$ and $V \subseteq U$. For all $\delta \in (\eta - \frac{1}{2}, \frac{1}{2})$, and for sufficiently large n,*

$$\Pr_{S \leftarrow \binom{[n]}{\sqrt{n}}} \left[|S \cap V| \leq \frac{\sqrt{n}}{2} \ \middle| \ |S \cap U| \geq \frac{\sqrt{n}}{2} + n^\delta \right] \leq e^{-\frac{n^\delta}{4}+6}.$$

Lemma 4. *Let* $k \in [\frac{n-n^{\eta}}{2}, \frac{n+n^{\eta}}{2}]$ *and* $0 < \delta < \min(\frac{1}{4}, 1 - \eta)$. *For sufficiently large* n *such that* $\frac{\sqrt{n}}{2}$ *is an integer, for any* $S \subset [n]$ *with* $|S| = \sqrt{n}$,

$$\Pr_{U \leftarrow \binom{[n]}{k}} \left[|S \cap U| \in \left[\frac{\sqrt{n}}{2} - n^{\delta}, \frac{\sqrt{n}}{2} + n^{\delta} \right] \right] \leq 2n^{\delta - \frac{1}{4}} e^3.$$

Correctness. For any $\boldsymbol{x} = (x_1, \ldots, x_n)$ such that $x_i \in \{0, 1\}^{\ell}$, the output of $\mathcal{C}_{\mathsf{SEC}}$ on input $\boldsymbol{x}$ is $\mathcal{C}_{\mathsf{SEC}}(\boldsymbol{x}) = \boldsymbol{x}|_U$, where U is a uniformly random subset of $[n]$. Hence, when $|S| = \sqrt{n}$ is an odd number, by symmetry, the event $|U \cap S| \leq \frac{|S|}{2} = \frac{\sqrt{n}}{2}$ occurs with probability $\frac{1}{2}$. By Lemma 2, with all but negligible probability, $|U| \geq \frac{n}{2} - n^{0.51}$. Hence, by a union bound, $F_{S, \boldsymbol{x}, a_0, a_1}(\boldsymbol{x}|_U) = (a_0, \bot)$ with probability $\frac{1}{2} - \mathsf{negl}(n)$ and $F_{S, \boldsymbol{x}, a_0, a_1}(\boldsymbol{x}|_U) = (\bot, a_1)$ with probability $\frac{1}{2} - \mathsf{negl}(n)$. This proves the correctness of the protocol.

Security. Next, we argue that the protocol presented in Fig. 2 achieves sender and receiver privacy. To argue receiver privacy against (even a computationally unbounded) semi-honest sender, we need to show that for all (a_0, a_1), it holds that:

$$\Delta\left((\mathsf{S}(a_0, a_1), \mathcal{C}_{\mathsf{ROT}}(a_0, a_1)), (\mathsf{S}(a_0, a_1), \mathsf{R}(\mathcal{C}_{\mathsf{SEC}}(\mathsf{S}(a_0, a_1)))) \right) \leq \mathsf{negl}(n)$$

Note that the erasures induced by the string erasure channel are independent of the input to the channel. Hence, as we already observed, for any $\boldsymbol{x}$ sent by the sender, the receiver R obtains $\boldsymbol{x}|_U$, where U is a uniformly random subset of $[n]$, independent of $\boldsymbol{x}$ (as well as single query access to $F_{S, \boldsymbol{x}, a_0, a_1}$). By definition of F, the output of an honest receiver, viz. $F_{S, \boldsymbol{x}, a_0, a_1}(\boldsymbol{x}|_U)$, is only a function of the size of the sets U and $U \cap S$. Thus, whether the receiver outputs $(a_0, \bot)$ or $(\bot, a_1)$ is independent of the view of the sender. Receiver privacy now follows from the fact that the receiver is correct with negligible error.

To argue sender privacy, we need to construct a simulator $\mathcal{S}_{\mathsf{R}} : \mathcal{B} \rightarrow \mathcal{Y}^n$ as an interactive algorithm that interacts with an arbitrary Q-bounded R*. In the sequel, for ease of presentation, for $a_0, a_1 \in \{0, 1\}^t$, we will denote $(\bot, a_1)$ by $(1, a_1)$ and $(a_0, \bot)$ by $(0, a_0)$ (i.e., we will use the format (index revealed, message at the revealed index)). Given input (b, a_b) for a random bit b, $\mathcal{S}_{\mathsf{R}}$ first generates and sends to R* a simulated channel output $\boldsymbol{y}$, and then provides a simulated response for each F-query made by R*.

Simulator $\mathcal{S}_{\mathsf{R}}(b, a_b)$:

1. Sample $S \leftarrow \binom{[n]}{\sqrt{n}}$.
2. Let $\boldsymbol{x} = (x_1, \ldots, x_n)$, where $x_i \leftarrow \{0, 1\}^{\ell}$ for $i \in [n]$.
3. Sample $U \leftarrow 2^{[n]}$ conditioned on
   (a) $|U \cap S| \geq \frac{\sqrt{n}}{2}$ if $b = 0$,
   (b) $|U \cap S| < \frac{\sqrt{n}}{2}$ if $b = 1$.
4. Output $\boldsymbol{x}|_U$ to R*.

Next, the simulator answers Q queries by R^* to F_{S,x,a_0,a_1} as follows: Upon query $\boldsymbol{y}|_V$, if $\left(|V| \geq \frac{n}{2} - n^{0.51}\right) \wedge (\boldsymbol{y}|_V = \boldsymbol{x}|_V)$ it outputs (b, a_b). If not, it outputs $\perp$.

We will argue that the statistical distance between the simulated transcript resulting from the interaction of $\mathcal{S}_\mathsf{R}(b, a_b)$ with R^* and the real view of R^* on sender input (a_0, a_1) is at most $O(n^{-\frac{1}{8}})$. The distribution on $\boldsymbol{x}|_U$ received by R^* is identical when it interacts with S or with the simulator $\mathcal{S}_\mathsf{R}$. It remains to argue that R^* cannot make a query which $\mathcal{S}_\mathsf{R}(b, a_b)$ cannot simulate (except with probability $O(n^{\frac{-1}{8}})$).

First, we argue that,

$$\Pr\left[|U| \in \left[\frac{n}{2} - n^{0.51}, \frac{n}{2} + n^{0.51}\right] \text{ and } |U \cap S| \notin \left[\frac{\sqrt{n}}{2}, \frac{\sqrt{n}}{2} + n^{\frac{1}{8}}\right]\right]$$

$$\geq 1 - O(n^{\frac{-1}{8}}). \quad (1)$$

To see this, observe that by Lemma 2, with all but negligible probability, $|U| \in \left[\frac{n}{2} - n^{0.51}, \frac{n}{2} + n^{0.51}\right]$. Conditioned on this event, by Lemma 4, probability with which $|U \cap S| \in [\frac{\sqrt{n}}{2} - n^{\frac{1}{8}}, \frac{\sqrt{n}}{2} + n^{\frac{1}{8}}]$ is $O(n^{-\frac{1}{8}})$.

Now we show that in the above event, the simulator answers any query by R^* as in the real world, except with negligible probability. To see this, note that the simulator has access to a_b, and the only cases in which it *cannot* answer correctly is when R^* makes a query to $\hat{F}$ whose output is $(1 - b, a_{1-b})$. We argue that this does not happen, except with negligible probability. Consider the following cases:

Case 1: $|U \cap S| < \frac{\sqrt{n}}{2}$. R^* is given $\boldsymbol{x}|_U$ where $F_{S,x,a_0,a_1}(\boldsymbol{x}|_U) = (\perp, a_1)$. To recover a_0, R^* must output $(\boldsymbol{y}|_V)$ such that $|V \cap S| \geq \frac{\sqrt{n}}{2}$ and $\boldsymbol{y}|_V = \boldsymbol{x}|_V$. However, since $\forall i \in [n]$, x_i is uniform in $\{0,1\}^\ell$, the probability of guessing even a single string x_i is negligible. Thus in this case, R^* succeeds with probability at most $2^{-\ell}$, which is negligible.

Case 2: $|U \cap S| \geq \frac{\sqrt{n}}{2} + n^{\frac{1}{8}}$. R^* is given $\boldsymbol{x}|_U$ s.t. $F_{S,x,a_0,a_1}(\boldsymbol{x}|_U) = (a_0, \perp)$. To recover the other output a_0, R^* must output $(\boldsymbol{y}|_V)$ such that $|V \cap S| < \frac{\sqrt{n}}{2}$ and $\boldsymbol{y}|_V = \boldsymbol{x}|_V$. As before, for any $i \notin U$, it can guess x_i correctly only with negligible probability. By Lemma 3, when $|U| \leq \frac{n}{2} + n^{0.51}$ (this happens with overwhelming probability by Lemma 2), for all $V \subseteq U$ such that $|U| \geq \frac{n}{2} - n^{0.51}$, the probability that $|V \cap S| < \frac{\sqrt{n}}{2}$ is negligible. Thus in this case also, R^* succeeds in coming up with a query that makes F_{S,x,a_0,a_1} output $(1 - b, a_{1-b})$ with at most negligible probability.

Thus, by taking a union bound, we can conclude that the simulator can answer the queries of a poly(λ)-bounded R^* except with negligible probability.

Finally, we show the bound on the circuit $|\hat{F}|$ in the theorem statement. Each position of the input $\boldsymbol{y}$ is encoded using $\ell + 1$ bits, with say, the first bit used as a flag denoting if it is $\perp$. Then a circuit of size $\mathcal{O}(n^2)$ on the n flag bits suffices for computing the two threshold conditions on $|V|$ and $|V \cap S|$ used in F, and a circuit of size $\mathcal{O}(n\ell)$ suffices to compute the equality condition $\boldsymbol{x}|_V = \boldsymbol{y}|_V$. The output is encoded, say, as (b, a_b) for $b \in \{0,1\}$ with an additional flag to indicate if it is $(\bot, \bot)$. Each of these $t + 2$ output bits can be computed as a function of two bits from a_0 and a_1 and the three condition bits computed above. So overall $\hat{F}$ is of size $\mathcal{O}(t + n^2 + n\ell))$. The theorem now follows by setting $n = \lambda^{8c}$. This concludes the proof. $\qquad\square$

ROT from String Erasure Channel

Function F

Parameters: $S \subseteq [n]$ with $|S| = \sqrt{n}$, $\boldsymbol{x} = (x_1, \ldots, x_n)$, where $x_i \in \{0,1\}^\ell$ for $i \in [n]$, $a_0, a_1 \in \{0,1\}^t$.

Input: $\boldsymbol{y} = (y_1, \ldots, y_n)$, where, for all $i \in [n]$, $y_i \in \{0,1\}^\ell$ or $y_i = \bot$. We write $\boldsymbol{y}|_V$ to indicate that $V = \{i | y_i \neq \bot\}$.

$F_{S,\boldsymbol{x}}\left(\boldsymbol{y}|_V, a_0, a_1\right)$

$$= \begin{cases} (\bot, a_1), & \text{if } \left(|V| \geq \frac{n}{2} - n^{0.51}\right) \wedge \left(\boldsymbol{y}|_V = \boldsymbol{x}|_V\right) \wedge (|V \cap S| < \frac{\sqrt{n}}{2}), \\ (a_0, \bot), & \text{if } \left(|V| \geq \frac{n}{2} - n^{0.51}\right) \wedge \left(\boldsymbol{y}|_V = \boldsymbol{x}|_V\right) \wedge (|V \cap S| \geq \frac{\sqrt{n}}{2}), \quad (2) \\ (\bot, \bot), & \text{otherwise.} \end{cases}$$

We write $F_{S,\boldsymbol{x},a_0,a_1}(\cdot)$ to denote $F_{S,\boldsymbol{x}}(\cdot, a_0, a_1)$.

Sender $S(a_0, a_1)$		Receiver R
(inputs $a_0, a_1 \in \{0,1\}^t$)	$\boldsymbol{x}$ sent over $\mathcal{C}_{\mathsf{SEC}}$	(with 1-query access to F)
1. Sample $S \leftarrow \binom{[n]}{\sqrt{n}}$	$\xrightarrow{\hspace{2cm}}$	1. Receive $\mathcal{C}_{\mathsf{SEC}}(\boldsymbol{x}) = \boldsymbol{x}|_U$
2. Let $\boldsymbol{x} = (x_1, \ldots, x_n)$, where each $x_i \leftarrow \{0,1\}^\ell$.	$\hat{F}$ given as oracle to R	where $U \leftarrow 2^{[n]}$.
3. Output $(\hat{F}, \boldsymbol{x})$ where $\hat{F}$ is a circuit for $F_{S,\boldsymbol{x},a_0,a_1}$.		2. Output $F\left(\boldsymbol{x}|_U\right)$.

Fig. 2. The OWSC protocol $\langle \mathsf{S}, \mathsf{R} \rangle$ for realizing ROT over the string erasure channel assuming ideal obfuscation.

4   Completeness of BEC and BSC Using Ideal Obfuscation

In this section, we show that the binary erasure channel and the binary symmetric channel are (each) complete, assuming ideal obfuscation. In Sect. 4.1, we construct the string erasure channel from the binary erasure channel and from the binary symmetric channel. We then appeal to a composition theorem 5 to argue that BEC/BSC can be used to construct ROT. Finally, in Sect. 4.2 we discuss completeness of BEC/BSC for general sender-receiver functionalities.

4.1 String Erasure Channel from BEC/BSC

In this section, we provide constructions of string erasure channel from binary erasure channel and from binary symmetric channel using ideal obfuscation.[2]

We first define a quantity that will be used in the construction and analysis of the following protocols. Let $0 < p < 1$, and $X_1, \ldots, X_n$ be random variables such that for each $i \in [n]$, X_i is independently and identically distributed as Bernoulli(p). Further, let $X = X_1 + X_2 + \ldots + X_n$. Define

$$\mathsf{Centre}(p, n) = \max \left\{ t \in [n] : \Pr[X < t] \leq \frac{1}{2} \right\}.$$

Claim 1. *For $\Theta_p > 0$ that depends only on p (as described in Lemma 1),*

$$\Pr[X \leq \mathsf{Centre}(p, n)] \in \left(\frac{1}{2}, \frac{1}{2} + \frac{\Theta_p}{\sqrt{n}} \right].$$

Proof: $\Pr[X = \mathsf{Centre}(p, n)] \leq \frac{\Theta_p}{\sqrt{n}}$ by the anti-concentration bound in Lemma 1. Claim follows from this and the definition of $\mathsf{Centre}(p, n)$. □

We now proceed to formally state and prove the first main result in this section.

Lemma 5 (SEC from BEC using ideal obfuscation). *There exists an OWSC protocol for SEC over BEC using ideal obfuscation, with inverse-polynomial statistical security against a semi-honest sender and a query-bounded receiver.*

More concretely, for all $p \in (0, 1)$ and $c > 0$, there exists an OWSC protocol which, for all $\lambda, \ell \in \mathbb{N}$, realizes ℓ-bit SEC with ϵ-security against a semi-honest sender and a polynomial query-bounded receiver, using n invocations of the BEC with erasure probability p and an ideal obfuscation of a circuit $\hat{F}$, when $\epsilon = \mathcal{O}(\frac{1}{\lambda^c})$, $n = \mathcal{O}(\lambda^{4c})$, and $|\hat{F}| = \mathcal{O}(\ell \cdot \lambda^{8c})$.

Proof: The OWSC protocol $\langle S, R \rangle$ for an ℓ-bit SEC over BEC with erasure probability $p \in (0, 1)$ is provided in Fig. 3. We argue correctness and security below.

Correctness. Since $\mathcal{C}_{\mathsf{BEC}}^p$ erases each bit in x with probability p independently, the number of non-erasures $|U|$ is distributed according to Binomial$(n, 1 - p)$. Hence, by Claim 1, the probability with which receiver reports an erasure is

$$\Pr[|U| \leq \mathsf{Centre}(1 - p, n)] \in \left(\frac{1}{2}, \frac{1}{2} + \frac{\Theta_{1-p}}{\sqrt{n}} \right).$$

---

[2] We remark that OWSC of SEC over BEC with inverse polynomial statistical security exists without using ideal obfuscation. Such a protocol can be obtained following the ideas in [2], where an OWSC protocol was constructed for string-ROT over bit-ROT with inverse polynomial statistical security. We do not explore the possibility of building such an OWSC protocol for SEC over BSC. Instead, we stick to constructions using ideal obfuscation since our next step towards realizing OWSC of ROT over BEC/BEC, i.e. of constructing OWSC of ROT over SEC, anyway uses ideal obfuscation.

String Erasure Channel from Binary Erasure Channel

Function F

- *Parameters:* $\boldsymbol{x} \in \{0,1\}^n$ and $a \in \{0,1\}^\ell$.
- *Input:* $\boldsymbol{y}|_V$ such that $V \subseteq [n]$ and $y_i \in \{0,1\}^n$ for all $i \in V$.

$$F_{\boldsymbol{x}}(\boldsymbol{y}|_V, a) = \begin{cases} a, & \text{if } (\boldsymbol{y}|_V = \boldsymbol{x}|_V) \wedge (|V| > \mathsf{Centre}(1-p, n)), \\ \bot, & \text{otherwise.} \end{cases}$$

We write $F_{\boldsymbol{x},a}(\cdot)$ to denote $F_{\boldsymbol{x}}(\cdot, a)$.

Sender $S(a \in \{0,1\}^\ell)$	$\boldsymbol{x}$ sent over $\mathcal{C}_{\mathsf{BEC}}^p$	Receiver R
		(with 1-query access to F)
1. $\boldsymbol{x} \leftarrow \{0,1\}^n$.	$\hat{F}$ given as oracle to R	1. Receive $\boldsymbol{x}|_U = \mathcal{C}_{\mathsf{BEC}}^p(\boldsymbol{x})$.
2. Output $(\hat{F}, \boldsymbol{x})$ where $\hat{F}$ is a circuit for $F_{\boldsymbol{x},a}$.		2. Output $F(\boldsymbol{x}|_U)$.

Fig. 3. Protocol $\langle S, R \rangle$ for realizing ℓ-bit string-Erasure Channel using n invocations of a binary erasure channel with erasure probability $p \in (0,1)$.

Thus, the input string a is output with probability $\frac{1}{2}$ (with inverse polynomial bias), which proves correctness of SEC.

Security. We first prove the statistical security against a computationally unbounded semi-honest sender by arguing that for all $a \in \{0,1\}^\ell$

$$\Delta\left((S(a), \mathcal{C}_{\mathsf{SEC}}(a)), (S(a), R(\mathcal{C}_{\mathsf{BEC}}^p(S(a))))\right) \leq \frac{\Theta_{1-p}}{\sqrt{n}}.$$

The erasure pattern over n uses of the channel is independent of the sender's input $\boldsymbol{x}$. Consequently, whether the receiver outputs a or $\bot$ is independent of the view of the sender. The bound on the statistical distance now follows from the correctness of the protocol.

To argue security against the receiver, we need to construct a simulator $\mathcal{S}_R : \mathcal{B} \to \mathcal{Y}^n$ as an interactive algorithm that interacts with an arbitrary $\mathrm{poly}(n)$-bounded R*. Given input $a \in \{0,1\}^\ell \cup \{\bot\}$, $\mathcal{S}_R$ first generates and sends to R* a simulated channel output $\boldsymbol{y}$, and then provides a simulated response for each $\hat{F}$-query made by R*.

Simulator $\mathcal{S}_R(a)$: Simulator constructs $\boldsymbol{y}$ as follows:

1. Sample $\boldsymbol{x} \leftarrow \{0,1\}^n$
2. Sample erasure pattern $[n] \setminus U$ (as generated on n independent uses of $\mathcal{C}_{\mathsf{BEC}}^p$) under the conditioning $|U| > \mathsf{Centre}(1-p, n)$ if $a \neq \bot$ and under the conditioning $|U| \leq \mathsf{Centre}(1-p, n)$ if $a = \bot$.
3. Output $\boldsymbol{x}|_U$ to R*.

For Q queries by R^* to F, the simulator replies to a query $\boldsymbol{y}|_V$ follows:

- *Case 1:* If $|U| > \mathsf{Centre}(1-p,n)$, simulator outputs $F_{\boldsymbol{x},a}(\boldsymbol{y}|_V)$ as it has access to $x, a,$ and U.
- *Case 2:* If $|U| \leq \mathsf{Centre}(1-p,n)$, simulator simply outputs $\perp$.

Since the distribution on $\boldsymbol{x}|_U$ received by R^* is identical when it interacts with S or with the simulator $\mathcal{S}_\mathsf{R}$, it is sufficient to argue that R^* cannot make any query which $\mathcal{S}_\mathsf{R}$ cannot correctly respond to, except with probability $O(n^{\frac{-1}{4}})$. In case 1, when $|U| > \mathsf{Centre}(1-p,n)$, the simulator/predictor can honestly compute $F_{\boldsymbol{x},a}(\boldsymbol{y}|_V)$ and the query is answered correctly. In case 2, the simulator/predictor fails if R^* makes a query $\boldsymbol{y}|_V$ such that $F_{\boldsymbol{x},a}(\boldsymbol{y}|_V) = a$. Define the set

$$\mathsf{Bad} = \left\{ U : |U| \in \left[\mathsf{Centre}(1-p,n) - n^\delta, \mathsf{Centre}(1-p,n) \right) \right\}.$$

Since $[n] \setminus U$ is the erasure pattern during n independent uses of $\mathcal{C}_\mathsf{BEC}^p$, $|U|$ is distributed according to the Binomial$(n, 1-p)$ distribution independent of $\boldsymbol{x}$. Hence, for all $\boldsymbol{x} \in \{0,1\}^n$, by applying the anti-concentration bound in Lemma 1 together with a union bound,

$$\Pr[\mathsf{Bad}] = \Pr_U \left[|U| \in \left[\mathsf{Centre}(1-p,n) - n^\delta, \mathsf{Centre}(1-p,n) \right) \right] \leq \frac{\Theta_{1-p}}{\sqrt{n}} \cdot n^\delta.$$

We will show that, except under the event Bad (which happens with probability at most $\Theta_{1-p} \cdot n^{-\frac{1}{4}}$, when $\delta = \frac{1}{4}$), R^* outputs a query $\boldsymbol{y}|_V$ such that $F_{\boldsymbol{x},a}(\boldsymbol{y}|_V) = a$ with negligible probability. Taking a union bound over poly(n) queries, we achieve the desired security condition.

It suffices to show that for all $a \in \{0,1\}^\ell$ and computationally unbounded algorithms Adv that take $\boldsymbol{x}|_U$ as input,

$$\Pr_{\boldsymbol{x} \leftarrow \{0,1\}^n, U} \left[F_{\boldsymbol{x}}(\boldsymbol{y}|_V, a) \neq \perp \, \middle| \, \neg \mathsf{Bad}, \boldsymbol{y}|_V = \mathsf{Adv}(\boldsymbol{x}|_U), F_{\boldsymbol{x}}(\boldsymbol{y}|_V, a) = \perp \right] = \mathrm{negl}(n). \tag{3}$$

The event '$\neg\mathsf{Bad}$ and $F_{\boldsymbol{x}}(\boldsymbol{y}|_V, a) = \perp$' is the same as '$|U| \leq \mathsf{Centre}(1-p,n) - n^\delta$'. Hence,

$$\Pr_{\boldsymbol{x} \leftarrow \{0,1\}^n, U} \left[F_{\boldsymbol{x}}(\boldsymbol{y}|_V, a) \neq \perp \, \middle| \, \neg\mathsf{Bad}, \boldsymbol{y}|_V = \mathsf{Adv}(\boldsymbol{x}|_U), F_{\boldsymbol{x}}(\boldsymbol{y}|_V, a) = \perp \right]$$

$$\leq \Pr_{\boldsymbol{x} \leftarrow \{0,1\}^n, U} \left[|V \setminus U| \geq n^\delta \text{ and } \boldsymbol{y}|_{V \setminus U} = \boldsymbol{x}|_{V \setminus U} \, \middle| \right.$$

$$\left. |U| \leq \mathsf{Centre}(1-p,n) - n^\delta, \boldsymbol{y}|_V = \mathsf{Adv}(\boldsymbol{x}|_U) \right]$$

$$\leq \Pr_{x_i \leftarrow \{0,1\}, \forall i \in [n^\delta]} \left[y_i = x_i, \forall i \in [n^\delta] \right] = 2^{-n^\delta}.$$

The function F can be realized using $\ell + 1$ Boolean circuits (to compute each bit of the output encoded with one extra bit to report $\perp$). When the input is appropriately encoded, the Boolean circuits need to compute a thresholding function on n-bit inputs (quadratic blow-up), and equality check for $\mathcal{O}(n)$-bit inputs (linear blow-up). Hence, the size of $\hat{F}$ is $\mathcal{O}(\ell \cdot n^2)$. The lemma now follows by setting $n = \lambda^4 c$. This concludes the proof. $\qquad\square$

We would like to remark that the above construction can also be used to realize string erasure channel with erasure probability $\frac{1}{2}$ from another string erasure channel (possibly of different string length) with arbitrary probability of erasure (ℓ'-bit $\mathcal{C}^p_{\mathsf{SEC}}$ for $0 < p < 1$). We can then put this result together with the result in Theorem 4 to show that ROT can be realized from general SEC (See Sect. 4.2).

Using a similar construction we can realize string erasure channel from binary symmetric channel using ideal obfuscation. Formally, we prove the following lemma:

Lemma 6 (SEC from BSC using ideal obfuscation). *For $p \in (0, \frac{1}{2})$, there exists an OWSC protocol for SEC over BSC with crossover probability p using ideal obfuscation, with inverse-polynomial statistical security against a semi-honest sender and a query-bounded receiver.*

More concretely, for all $p \in (0, \frac{1}{2})$ and $c > 0$, there exists an OWSC protocol which, for all $\lambda, \ell \in \mathbb{N}$, realizes ℓ-bit SEC with ϵ-security against a semi-honest sender and a polynomial query-bounded receiver, using n invocations of the BSC with crossover probability p and an ideal obfuscation of a circuit $\hat{F}$, when $\epsilon = \mathcal{O}(\frac{1}{\lambda^c})$, $n = \mathcal{O}(\lambda^{4c})$, and $|\hat{F}| = \mathcal{O}(\ell \cdot \lambda^{8c})$.

Proof: The OWSC protocol $\langle \mathsf{R}, \mathsf{S} \rangle$ for SEC over BSC is provided in Fig. 4. We argue correctness and security below.

Correctness. Since $\mathcal{C}^p_{\mathsf{BSC}}$ flips each bit in x with probability p independently, $|x \oplus y|$ is distributed according to $\mathsf{Binomial}(n, p)$. Hence, by Claim 1,

$$\Pr\left[|x \oplus y| \leq \mathsf{Centre}(p, n)\right] \in \left(\frac{1}{2}, \frac{1}{2} + \Theta_p \cdot n^{-\frac{1}{2}}\right).$$

Thus, the input string a is output with probability $\frac{1}{2}$ (with inverse polynomial bias), which proves correctness of SEC.

Security. We first argue statistical security against a computationally unbounded semi-honest sender by showing that for all $a \in \{0, 1\}^\ell$

$$\Delta\left((\mathsf{S}(a), \mathcal{C}_{\mathsf{SEC}}(a)), (\mathsf{S}(a), \mathsf{R}(\mathcal{C}^p_{\mathsf{BSC}}(\mathsf{S}(a))))\right) \leq \Theta_p \cdot n^{-\frac{1}{2}}.$$

Observe that the noise added by the BSC is independent of the sender's input x. Consequently, whether the receiver outputs a or $\bot$ is independent of the view of the sender. The bound on the statistical distance now follows from the correctness of the protocol.

To argue security against the receiver, we need to construct a simulator $\mathcal{S}_{\mathsf{R}} : \mathcal{B} \to \mathcal{Y}^n$ as an interactive algorithm that interacts with an arbitrary $\mathsf{poly}(n)$-bounded R^*. Given input $a \in \{0, 1\}^\ell \cup \{\bot\}$, $\mathcal{S}_{\mathsf{R}}$ first generates and sends to R^* a simulated channel output y, and then provides a simulated response for each F-query made by R^*.

Simulator $\mathcal{S}_{\mathsf{R}}(a)$: Simulator constructs y as follows:

1. Sample $x \leftarrow \{0, 1\}^n$.

String Erasure Channel from Binary Symmetric Channel

Function F

- *Parameters:* $x \in \{0,1\}^n$ and $a \in \{0,1\}^\ell$.
- *Input:* $y \in \{0,1\}^n$.

$$F_x(y,a) = \begin{cases} a, & \text{if } |x \oplus y| \leq \mathsf{Centre}(p,n), \\ \bot, & \text{otherwise.} \end{cases}$$

We write $F_{x,a}(\cdot)$ to denote $F_x(\cdot, a)$.

Sender $\mathsf{S}(a \in \{0,1\}^\ell)$

1. $x \leftarrow \{0,1\}^n$.
2. Output $(\hat{F}, x)$ where $\hat{F}$ is a circuit for $F_{x,a}$.
   (x will be sent to R over $\mathcal{C}^p_{\mathsf{BSC}}$, and $\hat{F}$ will be used as the oracle for R, below.)

Receiver R with 1 query oracle access to F

1. Receive $y = \mathcal{C}^p_{\mathsf{BSC}}(x)$.
2. Output $F(y)$.

Fig. 4. The protocol $\langle \mathsf{S}, \mathsf{R} \rangle$ for realizing ℓ-bit String-Erasure Channel using n invocations of a binary symmetric channel with crossover probability p.

2. Sample $y = \mathcal{C}^p_{\mathsf{BSC}}(x)$ conditioned on $|x \oplus y| \leq \mathsf{Centre}(p,n)$ if $a \neq \bot$ and $|x \oplus y| > \mathsf{Centre}(p,n)$ if $a = \bot$.
3. Output y to R*.

For Q queries by R* to $\hat{F}$, the simulator replies to a query $\hat{y}$ follows:

- *Case 1:* If $|x \oplus y| \leq \mathsf{Centre}(p,n)$, simulator outputs $F_{x,a}(\hat{y})$ as it has access to x and a.
- *Case 2:* If $|x \oplus y| > \mathsf{Centre}(p,n)$, simulator simply outputs $\bot$.

Since the distribution on $x|_U$ received by R* is identical when it interacts with S or with the simulator $\mathcal{S}_\mathsf{R}$, it is sufficient to argue that R* cannot make any query which $\mathcal{S}_\mathsf{R}$ cannot correctly respond to (except with probability $O(n^{\frac{-1}{4}})$). In case 1, when $|U| > \mathsf{Centre}(1-p,n)$, the simulator/predictor can honestly compute $F_{x,a}(y|_V)$ and the query is answered correctly. In case 2, the simulator/predictor fails if R* makes a query $y|_V$ such that $F_{x,a}(y|_V) = a$. Define the set

$$\mathsf{Bad} = \left\{ (x,y) \in \{0,1\}^{2n} : |x \oplus y| \in (\mathsf{Centre}(p,n), \mathsf{Centre}(p,n) + n^\delta] \right\}.$$

In the sequel, we will denote $\mathsf{Centre}(p,n)$ by t. When $x \leftarrow \{0,1\}^n$ and $y = \mathcal{C}^p_{\mathsf{BSC}}(x)$, $|x \oplus y|$ is the number of bits noise added by $\mathcal{C}^p_{\mathsf{BSC}}$. Hence, it is distributed according to the Binomial(n, p) distribution. By applying the anti-concentration bound in Lemma 1 together with a union bound, we get

$$\Pr_{(\boldsymbol{x}\leftarrow\{0,1\}^n, \boldsymbol{y}=\mathcal{C}^p_{\mathsf{BSC}}(\boldsymbol{x}))}[\mathsf{Bad}] = \Pr_{\boldsymbol{x}\leftarrow\{0,1\}^n, \boldsymbol{y}=\mathcal{C}^p_{\mathsf{BSC}}(\boldsymbol{x})}\left[|\boldsymbol{x}\oplus\boldsymbol{y}| \in (t, t+n^\delta]\right] \le \Theta_p \cdot n^{\delta-\frac{1}{2}}.$$

We will show that, except under the event Bad (which happens with probability at most $\Theta_{1-p} \cdot n^{-\frac{1}{4}}$, when $\delta = \frac{1}{4}$), R^* outputs a query $\boldsymbol{y}|_V$ such that $F_{\boldsymbol{x},a}(\boldsymbol{y}|_V) = a$ with negligible probability. Taking a union bound over $\mathrm{poly}(n)$ queries, we achieve the desired security condition.

It suffices to show that for all $a \in \{0,1\}^\ell$ and computationally unbounded algorithms Adv that take $\boldsymbol{y}$ as input,

$$\Pr_{\boldsymbol{x}\leftarrow\{0,1\}^n, \boldsymbol{y}=\mathcal{C}^p_{\mathsf{BSC}}(\boldsymbol{x})}[F_{\boldsymbol{x},a}(\hat{\boldsymbol{y}}) \ne \bot \,|\, \neg\mathsf{Bad}, F_{\boldsymbol{x},a}(\hat{\boldsymbol{y}}) = \bot, \hat{\boldsymbol{y}} = \mathsf{Adv}(\boldsymbol{y})] = \mathrm{negl}(n). \qquad (4)$$

The event '$\neg\mathsf{Bad}$ and $F_{\boldsymbol{x},a}(\hat{\boldsymbol{y}}) = \bot$' is the same as '$|\boldsymbol{x}\oplus\boldsymbol{y}| \ge \mathsf{Centre}(p,n) + n^\delta$'. We complete the argument by appealing to the following claim.

Claim 2. *For any computationally unbounded algorithm A, for sufficiently large values of n,*

$$\Pr_{\boldsymbol{x}\leftarrow\{0,1\}^n, \boldsymbol{y}=\mathcal{C}^p_{\mathsf{BSC}}(\boldsymbol{x})}\left[F_{\boldsymbol{x}}(\hat{\boldsymbol{y}}, a) \ne \bot \,\big|\, |\boldsymbol{x}\oplus\boldsymbol{y}| \ge \mathsf{Centre}(p,n) + n^\delta, \hat{\boldsymbol{y}} \leftarrow A(\boldsymbol{y})\right]$$

$$\le 3e^{-\frac{(1-2p)^2}{4}n^\delta}.$$

Proof: Let $t = \mathsf{Centre}(p,n)$ and $V = \{i \in [n] : \hat{y}_i \oplus y_i = 1\}$. For $\boldsymbol{x}\leftarrow\{0,1\}^n, \boldsymbol{y} = \mathcal{C}^p_{\mathsf{BSC}}(\boldsymbol{x})$, and $\hat{\boldsymbol{y}} \leftarrow A(\boldsymbol{y})$,

$$\Pr\left[F_{\boldsymbol{x},a}(\hat{\boldsymbol{y}}) \ne \bot \,\big|\, |\boldsymbol{x}\oplus\boldsymbol{y}| \ge t+n^\delta\right]$$

$$= \Pr\left[|\boldsymbol{x}\oplus\hat{\boldsymbol{y}}| \le t \,\big|\, |\boldsymbol{x}\oplus\boldsymbol{y}| \ge t+n^\delta\right]$$

$$= \Pr\left[|(\boldsymbol{x}\oplus\boldsymbol{y})\oplus(\boldsymbol{y}\oplus\hat{\boldsymbol{y}})| \le t \,\big|\, |\boldsymbol{x}\oplus\boldsymbol{y}| \ge t+n^\delta\right]$$

$$\le \Pr\left[\sum_{i\in V}(x_i \oplus y_i) - \left(|V| - \sum_{i\in V}(x_i \oplus y_i)\right) \ge n^\delta \,\bigg|\, |\boldsymbol{x}\oplus\boldsymbol{y}| \ge t+n^\delta\right]$$

$$= \Pr\left[\sum_{i\in V}(x_i \oplus y_i) \ge \frac{|V|+n^\delta}{2} \,\bigg|\, |\boldsymbol{x}\oplus\boldsymbol{y}| \ge t+n^\delta\right].$$

Since $\boldsymbol{x}$ is uniformly distributed, $\boldsymbol{x}\oplus\boldsymbol{y}$ is independent of $\boldsymbol{y}$ and, therefore, independent of $(\boldsymbol{y}, \hat{\boldsymbol{y}}, V)$. Conditioned on V (and suppressing this conditioning in the steps below), we have, for all $V \subseteq [n]$,

$$\Pr\left[\sum_{i\in V}(x_i \oplus y_i) \ge \frac{|V|+n^\delta}{2}, |\boldsymbol{x}\oplus\boldsymbol{y}| \ge t+n^\delta\right] \le \Pr\left[\sum_{i\in V}(x_i \oplus y_i) \ge \frac{|V|+n^\delta}{2}\right],$$

where $x_i \oplus y_i$, $i \in V$, are independent and identically distributed with distribution Bernoulli(p). This probability is clearly zero if $|V| < n^\delta$. For $|V| \geq n^\delta$, by the Chernoff bound in Lemma 2,

$$\Pr\left[\sum_{i \in V}(x_i \oplus y_i) \geq \frac{|V| + n^\delta}{2}\right] \leq \Pr\left[\sum_{i \in V}(x_i \oplus y_i) \geq \frac{|V|}{2}\right]$$

$$= \Pr\left[\sum_{i \in V}(x_i \oplus y_i) \geq \left(1 + \left(\frac{1}{2p} - 1\right)\right)p \cdot |V|\right]$$

$$\leq e^{-\frac{\left(\frac{1}{2p} - 1\right)^2}{\frac{1}{2p} + 1} p \cdot |V|} \leq e^{-\frac{(1-2p)^2}{4}n^\delta}.$$

Moreover, since $|\boldsymbol{x} \oplus \boldsymbol{y}|$ is Binomial(n, p), we have $\Pr[|\boldsymbol{x} \oplus \boldsymbol{y}| < \mathsf{Centre}(p, n)] < \frac{1}{2}$, which along with the anti-concentration bound in Lemma 1, gives

$$\Pr\left[|\boldsymbol{x} \oplus \boldsymbol{y}| \geq t + n^\delta\right] \geq \frac{1}{2} - \frac{\Theta_p}{\sqrt{n}} \cdot (1 + n^\delta) \geq \frac{1}{3},$$

for sufficiently large n since $\delta < \frac{1}{2}$. This proves the claim.   □

The function F can be realized using $\ell + 1$ Boolean circuits (to compute each bit of the output encoded with one extra bit to report $\perp$). When the input is appropriately encoded, the Boolean circuits need to compute a XOR and thresholding function on n-bit input (quadratic blow-up). Hence, the size of $\hat{F}$ is $\mathcal{O}(\ell \cdot n^2)$. The lemma now follows by setting $n = \lambda^4 c$. This concludes the proof.   □

4.2   Completeness of BEC/BSC Using Ideal Obfuscation

We can put together the results in Sect. 4.1 (that the string erasure channel (SEC) can be constructed using the binary erasure and binary symmetric channels, using ideal obfuscation) with the result from Sect. 3 (that ROT can be constructed using SEC, using ideal obfuscation), to obtain the following.

Theorem 5 (ROT from BEC or BSC using ideal obfuscation). *There exists an OWSC protocol* $\Pi_{\mathrm{ROT}}^{\mathrm{BEC}}$ *(respectively,* $\Pi_{\mathrm{ROT}}^{\mathrm{BSC}}$*) for ROT over BEC (respectively, BSC) using ideal obfuscation, with inverse-polynomial statistical security against a semi-honest sender and a polynomial query-bounded receiver.*

Proof: We shall compose the OWSC protocol for ROT over SEC from Theorem 4 with the protocol from Lemma 5 (respectively, from Lemma 6). For this, we need to argue that OWSC protocols compose. The security definition of OWSC (Definition 1) could be seen as a specialization of the UC security notion, to the one-way communication setting, and a semi-honest sender, in a $(\mathcal{C}, \mathcal{B})$-hybrid model, where $\mathcal{C}$ is the channel, and $\mathcal{B}$ is a functionality that takes a circuit from the sender and provides the receiver with black-box access to it (for a bounded number of queries). To see this is indeed the case, note that when the sender is (passively) corrupt, a simulator for passive-security should merely forward the sender's input a to the functionality, resulting in the receiver obtaining $f(a)$; hence the environment's views in the ideal and real executions (in addition to a, which is universally quantified over) are simply $(S(a), R(C(S(a))))$ and $(S(a), f(a))$.

When the receiver is (possibly actively) corrupt, its view includes an output from the channel C and its interaction with the oracle B; the security definition for OWSC in this case is the same as for UC security, by treating the receiver as the environment (the input a is part of the corrupt receiver's view in the OWSC definition, due to the universal quantifier over a).

Before we can apply composition, note that we have a mixed corruption model with *fixed roles*. That is, the party playing the sender in all of the protocols or functionalities is the same (i.e., corrupting one corrupts all), and similarly for the receiver. Hence we have only two non-trivial corruption scenarios: all the senders are passively corrupt, or all the receiver's are actively corrupt. In either case, the protocol for ROT from SEC, as well as the protocol for SEC from BEC (or BSC) satisfies the corresponding security guarantee. We note that in a corruption scenario, if UC or passive security holds for each protocol instance, then, it holds for the composed protocol for the same corruption scenario (this is implicit in the proof of composition theorems for static adversaries, which fixes a corruption scenario and derives a simulator for the composed protocol from individual simulators for the constituent protocols).

Finally, note that in the composed secure protocol, there are several instances of B invoked by the sender (and each one accessed a bounded number of times by the receiver). These multiple instances, with programs, say $F_1, \cdots, F_n$ can be replaced by a single instance of B to which the sender inputs a combined program F such that $F(i, x) = F_i(x)$. Thus we obtain an OWSC protocol using ideal obfuscation for ROT from either BEC or BSC.   □

We are now ready to show that the binary erasure channel and the binary symmetric channel are complete, using ideal obfuscation. To generalize the above construction to arbitrary functionalities, we rely on a previous result by Garg et al. [25], which showed that ROT is complete for arbitrary finite functionalities even for the case of malicious parties, with statistical security. Combined with our reductions from ROT to BSC and BEC, we get a similar completeness result for BEC/BSC with inverse-polynomial error.

In more detail, we claim that:

Theorem 6 (Completeness of BEC/BSC using ideal obfuscation: semi-honest sender). *BEC and BSC are (each) complete for OWSC using ideal obfuscation, with inverse-polynomial statistical security against a semi-honest sender and a polynomial query-bounded receiver.*

Proof: [Proof sketch] Analogously to [2], let us first consider the setting of semi-honest parties. In this case, we may combine the reduction from ROT to BEC/BSC with Yao's garbled circuits [58] as follows. Given a randomized sender receiver functionality $F(a; r)$, define a deterministic (two-way) functionality $\tilde{F}$ that takes (a, r_1) from the sender and r_2 from the receiver, and outputs $F(a; r_1 \oplus r_2)$ to the receiver. Using Yao's protocol to securely evaluate $\tilde{F}$ with uniformly random choices of r_1, r_2, we get a secure reduction of F to OT where the receiver's inputs are random. We may now replace the random choices of the receiver by leveraging a ROT channel, and then apply the reduction from ROT to BEC/BSC.

The above compiler makes use of Yao's garbled circuits, which assume the existence of one way functions. In the setting of ideal obfuscation, we may obtain an unconditional result as follows. First, note that for the case of branching programs, we may use information theoretic garbled circuits [23, 34, 41]. For the case of circuits, we use a result of Goyal et al. [32] which implies unconditionally secure garbled circuits from ideal obfuscation. In more detail, [32] show how to obtain unconditionally secure computation from hardware tokens. Our setting requires only a degenerate "single-use" version of the construction of Goyal et al., that replaces symmetric encryption with a one-time pad.   □

5   OWSC in the Plain Model and Against Malicious Adversaries

In this section, we address the question of implementing our protocols in the plain model. We also show how to augment a plain model OWSC protocol to be secure against active corruption (of the sender, as the receiver is always passive), using a NIZK proof.

5.1   OWSC in the Plain Model

Recall that an OWSC protocol Π using ideal obfuscation uses oracle access to a function F (specified as a circuit $\hat{F}$). We denote by $\Pi[\mathcal{O}]$ the protocol in the plain model that is obtained by communicating $\mathcal{O}(\hat{F})$ instead of providing the oracle. Here, for the purpose of error-free communication, we use an error correcting (or erasure correcting, resp.) code to encode $\mathcal{O}(\hat{F})$ before sending it over BSC (resp., BEC).

As discussed earlier, given the statistical nature of the functions used in the protocols $\Pi_{\text{ROT}}^{\text{BEC}}$ and $\Pi_{\text{ROT}}^{\text{BSC}}$, it is conceivable that there *exists* an obfuscation scheme $\mathcal{O}$ such that the protocols $\Pi_{\text{ROT}}^{\text{BEC}}$ and $\Pi_{\text{ROT}}^{\text{BSC}}$ can be converted to secure protocols in the plain model by using this obfuscation scheme to replace the ideal obfuscation scheme. We state this as a conjecture below.[3]

---

[3] We remark that a more general conjecture about obfuscation of a generalized notion of "evasive" functions is plausible, and would in turn imply Conjecture 2. As such a generalization is somewhat tangential to the focus of this work, we do not present this formalization here.

Conjecture 2. There exists an obfuscation scheme $\mathcal{O}$ such that $\Pi_{\mathrm{ROT}}^{\mathrm{BEC}}[\mathcal{O}]$ and $\Pi_{\mathrm{ROT}}^{\mathrm{BSC}}[\mathcal{O}]$ are OWSC protocols (in the plain model) for ROT, over BEC and BSC respectively, with inverse-polynomial security against a semi-honest sender and a computationally bounded receiver.

Interestingly, if *any* such scheme as conjectured above exists, then an indistinguishability obfuscation (iO) scheme can be used in its place. More formally, we have the following theorem. Its proof follows standard ideas and is deferred to the full version.

Theorem 7. *Suppose Conjecture 2 holds, with an obfuscation scheme $\mathcal{O}$. Further, suppose there is an iO scheme iO for all polynomial sized circuits. Let* $\mathrm{pad}(\hat{F})$ *be a padded version of the circuit $\hat{F}$ which is of the same size as $\mathcal{O}(\hat{F})$. Then* $\Pi_{\mathrm{ROT}}^{\mathrm{BEC}}[i\mathcal{O} \circ \mathrm{pad}]$ *and* $\Pi_{\mathrm{ROT}}^{\mathrm{BSC}}[i\mathcal{O} \circ \mathrm{pad}]$ *are OWSC protocols (in the plain model) for ROT, over BEC and BSC respectively, with inverse-polynomial security against a semi-honest sender and a computationally bounded receiver.*

5.2 Security Against Malicious Sender

In this section, we argue that BEC and BSC are (each) complete even against malicious adversaries in the plain model, assuming Conjecture 2. The key observation here is that UC-secure OWSC protocols for NIZK exist over BEC as well as over BSC, as shown by Garg et al. [25, Lemma 3]. We show that such a NIZK can be used to turn the ROT protocols $\Pi_{\mathrm{ROT}}^{\mathrm{BEC}}[\mathcal{O}]$ and $\Pi_{\mathrm{ROT}}^{\mathrm{BSC}}[\mathcal{O}]$ to be secure against malicious senders. We then appeal to another result of Garg et al. [25] which shows that for general (possibly randomized) functionalities, the ROT channel is complete.

To obtain security against malicious senders, we need to ensure that the receiver's output is of the form $(a_0, \bot)$ with probability $\frac{1}{2}$ and $(\bot, a_1)$ otherwise (except for a small inverse polynomial error). The strings (a_0, a_1) may be probabilistic, but should be extracted by a simulator. For this, we show that it is enough for the sender to additionally provide a NIZK proof of the fact that the program communicated is indeed an obfuscation $\mathcal{O}(\hat{F})$ of a valid function $\hat{F}$ as specified by the protocol. Recall that in the original protocol, the receiver is supposed to feed the message it received over the channel (BEC or BSC) to the obfuscated program and output whatever the program outputs. In the modified ROT protocol, if the verification of the NIZK proof fails, or if the program outputs an error, then the receiver outputs $(a, \bot)$ or $(\bot, a)$ (for some fixed a) with probability $\frac{1}{2}$ each.

We briefly sketch why this modification yields a OWSC for ROT that is secure against a malicious sender (we defer further details to the full version [3]). If the NIZK proof fails or if the program outputs an error, the protocol corresponds to an ideal ROT execution in which the sender sends (a, a) as its input. We need to analyze the behavior of the protocol when this does not happen. Note that the program $\hat{F}$ contains a string x that the sender is supposed to send over the channel, but a malicious sender may send a different string x'. If x' differs from x in a lot of positions, then with all but negligible probability the program outputs an error, captured by the above case. On the other hand, if x' agrees with x in most places, then *conditioned on the program not outputting an error*, it can be shown that the output continues to be of the form $(a_0, \perp)$ or $(\perp, a_1)$ with almost equal probabilities, as in the original analysis. A formal analysis of this modification is provided in the full version of this work [3].

It remains to argue that BEC and BSC are complete, even in the plain model, assuming Conjecture 2. Recall that in Sect. 4.2, we argued that BEC and BSC are complete for OWSC assuming ideal obfuscation, by composing OWSC protocols over ROT for general sender-receiver functionalities with OWSC protocols over BEC/BSC for ROT using ideal obfuscation. The argument for the plain model remains the same, except that we now use the ROT protocols in the plain model. Using standard garbled circuits based on one way functions in the compiler described by Theorem 6, we obtain:

Theorem 8 (Completeness of BEC/BSC against malicious adversary).
Suppose Conjecture 2 holds and one-way functions exist. Then BEC and BSC are (each) complete for OWSC with inverse-polynomial security against a malicious sender and a computationally bounded receiver.

Acknowledgements. We thank the anonymous Crypto reviewers for their careful reading and many helpful comments. This Research was supported by Ministry of Science and Technology, Israel and Department of Science and Technology, Government of India, and in part by the International Centre for Theoretical Sciences (ICTS) during a visit for participating in the program-Foundational Aspects of Blockchain Technology (ICTS/Prog-fabt2020/01). In addition, S. Agrawal was supported by the DST "Swarnajayanti" fellowship, and Indo-French CEFIPRA project; Y. Ishai was supported by ERC Project NTSC (742754), NSF-BSF grant 2015782, ISF grant 2774/20, and BSF grant 2018393; E. Kushilevitz was supported by ISF grant 2774/20, BSF grant 2018393, and NSF-BSF grant 2015782; V. Narayanan and V. Prabhakaran were supported by the Department of Atomic Energy, Government of India, under project no. RTI4001, DAE OM No. 1303/4/2019/R&D-II/DAE/1969 dated 7.2.2020; M. Prabhakaran was supported by the Dept. of Science and Technology, India via the Ramanujan Fellowship; V. Prabhakaran was supported by the Science & Engineering Research Board, India through project MTR/2020/000308; A. Rosen was supported in part by ISF grant No. 1399/17 and Project PROMETHEUS (Grant 780701). This work was conducted in part when the first and second author were visiting the Simons Institute for Theory of Computing.

References

1. Agrawal, S.: Indistinguishability obfuscation without multilinear maps: new methods for bootstrapping and instantiation. In: EUROCRYPT. Springer (2019)
2. Agrawal, S., et al.: Cryptography from one-way communication: on completeness of finite channels. In: Moriai, S., Wang, H. (eds.) ASIACRYPT 2020. LNCS, vol. 12493, pp. 653–685. Springer, Cham (2020). https://doi.org/10.1007/978-3-030-64840-4_22

3. Agrawal, S., et al.: Secure computation from one-way noisy communication, or: anti-correlation via anti-concentration. ePrint (2021)
4. Ananth, P., Jain, A., Sahai, A.: Indistinguishability obfuscation without multilinear maps: iO from LWE, bilinear maps, and weak pseudorandomness. Cryptology ePrint Archive, Report 2018/615 (2018). https://ia.cr/2018/615
5. Applebaum, B.: Bootstrapping obfuscators via fast pseudorandom functions. In: Sarkar, P., Iwata, T. (eds.) ASIACRYPT 2014. LNCS, vol. 8874, pp. 162–172. Springer, Heidelberg (2014). https://doi.org/10.1007/978-3-662-45608-8_9
6. Barak, B., et al.: On the (im)possibility of obfuscating programs. J. ACM **59**(2), 6:1–6:48 (2012)
7. Bartusek, J., Guan, J., Ma, F., Zhandry, M.: Return of GGH15: provable security against zeroizing attacks. In: Beimel, A., Dziembowski, S. (eds.) TCC 2018. LNCS, vol. 11240, pp. 544–574. Springer, Cham (2018). https://doi.org/10.1007/978-3-030-03810-6_20
8. Bartusek, J., Ishai, Y., Jain, A., Ma, F., Sahai, A., Zhandry, M.: Affine determinant programs: a framework for obfuscation and witness encryption. In: ITCS, vol. 151, pp. 82:1–82:39 (2020)
9. Bellare, M., Rogaway, P.: Random oracles are practical: a paradigm for designing efficient protocols. In: CCS, pp. 62–73 (1993)
10. Ben-Or, M., Goldwasser, S., Kilian, J., Wigderson, A.: Multi-prover interactive proofs: how to remove intractability assumptions. In: STOC, pp. 113–131. ACM (1988)
11. Ben-Sasson, E., Chiesa, A., Forbes, M.A., Gabizon, A., Riabzev, M., Spooner, N.: Zero knowledge protocols from succinct constraint detection. In: Kalai, Y., Reyzin, L. (eds.) TCC 2017. LNCS, vol. 10678, pp. 172–206. Springer, Cham (2017). https://doi.org/10.1007/978-3-319-70503-3_6
12. Bennett, C.H., Brassard, G., Crepeau, C., Maurer, U.M.: Generalized privacy amplification. IEEE Trans. Inf. Theor. **41**(6), 1915–1923 (1995)
13. Bennett, C.H., Brassard, G., Robert, J.-M.: Privacy amplification by public discussion. SIAM J. Comput. **17**(2), 210–229 (1988)
14. Bloch, M., Barros, J.: Physical-Layer Security: from Information Theory to Security Engineering. Cambridge University Press, Cambridge (2011)
15. Brakerski, Z., Döttling, N., Garg, S., Malavolta, G.: Candidate iO from homomorphic encryption schemes. In: Canteaut, A., Ishai, Y. (eds.) EUROCRYPT 2020. LNCS, vol. 12105, pp. 79–109. Springer, Cham (2020). https://doi.org/10.1007/978-3-030-45721-1_4
16. Brakerski, Z., Döttling, N., Garg, S., Malavolta, G.: Factoring and pairings are not necessary for iO: circular-secure LWE suffices. IACR Cryptology ePrint Archive (2020)
17. Canetti, R.: Universally composable security: a new paradigm for cryptographic protocols. Cryptology ePrint Archive, Report 2000/067 (2005). Extended abstract in FOCS 2001
18. Canetti, R., Goldreich, O., Halevi, S.: The random oracle methodology, revisited. J. ACM **51**(4), 557–594 (2004)
19. Chen, Y., Vaikuntanathan, V., Wee, H.: GGH15 beyond permutation branching programs: proofs, attacks, and candidates. In: Shacham, H., Boldyreva, A. (eds.) CRYPTO 2018. LNCS, vol. 10992, pp. 577–607. Springer, Cham (2018). https://doi.org/10.1007/978-3-319-96881-0_20
20. Crepeau, C., Kilian, J.: Achieving oblivious transfer using weakened security assumptions. In: FOCS, pp. 42–52 (1988)

21. Crépeau, C., Morozov, K., Wolf, S.: Efficient unconditional oblivious transfer from almost any noisy channel. In: Blundo, C., Cimato, S. (eds.) SCN 2004. LNCS, vol. 3352, pp. 47–59. Springer, Heidelberg (2005). https://doi.org/10.1007/978-3-540-30598-9_4

22. Damgård, I., Kilian, J., Salvail, L.: On the (im)possibility of basing oblivious transfer and bit commitment on weakened security assumptions. In: Stern, J. (ed.) EUROCRYPT 1999. LNCS, vol. 1592, pp. 56–73. Springer, Heidelberg (1999). https://doi.org/10.1007/3-540-48910-X_5

23. Feige, U., Kilian, J., Naor, M.: A minimal model for secure computation (extended abstract). In: STOC, pp. 554–563 (1994)

24. Garg, S., Gentry, C., Halevi, S., Raykova, M., Sahai, A., Waters, B.: Candidate indistinguishability obfuscation and functional encryption for all circuits. SIAM J. Comput. 45, 882–929 (2016)

25. Garg, S., Ishai, Y., Kushilevitz, E., Ostrovsky, R., Sahai, A.: Cryptography with one-way communication. In: Gennaro, R., Robshaw, M. (eds.) CRYPTO 2015. LNCS, vol. 9216, pp. 191–208. Springer, Heidelberg (2015). https://doi.org/10.1007/978-3-662-48000-7_10

26. Garg, S., Miles, E., Mukherjee, P., Sahai, A., Srinivasan, A., Zhandry, M.: Secure obfuscation in a weak multilinear map model. In: Hirt, M., Smith, A. (eds.) TCC 2016. LNCS, vol. 9986, pp. 241–268. Springer, Heidelberg (2016). https://doi.org/10.1007/978-3-662-53644-5_10

27. Gay, R., Pass, R.: Indistinguishability obfuscation from circular security. In: STOC 2021, pp. 736–749 (2021)

28. Goldwasser, S., Kalai, Y.T.: On the impossibility of obfuscation with auxiliary input. In: FOCS, pp. 553–562 (2005)

29. Goldwasser, S., Kalai, Y.T., Rothblum, G.N.: One-time programs. In: Wagner, D. (ed.) CRYPTO 2008. LNCS, vol. 5157, pp. 39–56. Springer, Heidelberg (2008). https://doi.org/10.1007/978-3-540-85174-5_3

30. Goldwasser, S., Rothblum, G.N.: On best-possible obfuscation. In: Vadhan, S.P. (ed.) TCC 2007. LNCS, vol. 4392, pp. 194–213. Springer, Heidelberg (2007). https://doi.org/10.1007/978-3-540-70936-7_11

31. Goyal, V., Ishai, Y., Mahmoody, M., Sahai, A.: Interactive locking, zero-knowledge PCPs, and unconditional cryptography. In: Rabin, T. (ed.) CRYPTO 2010. LNCS, vol. 6223, pp. 173–190. Springer, Heidelberg (2010). https://doi.org/10.1007/978-3-642-14623-7_10

32. Goyal, V., Ishai, Y., Sahai, A., Venkatesan, R., Wadia, A.: Founding cryptography on tamper-proof hardware tokens. In: Micciancio, D. (ed.) TCC 2010. LNCS, vol. 5978, pp. 308–326. Springer, Heidelberg (2010). https://doi.org/10.1007/978-3-642-11799-2_19

33. Harris, T.E.: A lower bound for the critical probability in a certain percolation process. Math. Proc. Cambridge Philos. Soc. 56(1), 13–20 (1960)

34. Ishai, Y., Kushilevitz, E.: Private simultaneous messages protocols with applications. In: ISTCS 1997, pp. 174–184. IEEE Computer Society (1997)

35. Ishai, Y., Kushilevitz, E., Ostrovsky, R., Prabhakaran, M., Sahai, A., Wullschleger, J.: Constant-rate oblivious transfer from noisy channels. In: Rogaway, P. (ed.) CRYPTO 2011. LNCS, vol. 6841, pp. 667–684. Springer, Heidelberg (2011). https://doi.org/10.1007/978-3-642-22792-9_38

36. Ishai, Y., Mahmoody, M., Sahai, A.: On efficient zero-knowledge PCPs. In: Cramer, R. (ed.) TCC 2012. LNCS, vol. 7194, pp. 151–168. Springer, Heidelberg (2012). https://doi.org/10.1007/978-3-642-28914-9_9

37. Jain, A., Lin, H., Sahai, A.: Simplifying constructions and assumptions for $i\mathcal{O}$. Cryptology ePrint Archive, Report 2019/1252 (2019). https://eprint.iacr.org/2019/1252

38. Jain, A., Lin, H., Sahai, A.: Indistinguishability obfuscation from well-founded assumptions. In: STOC 2021, pp. 60–73 (2021)

39. Kalai, Y.T., Raz, R.: Interactive PCP. In: ICALP, pp. 536–547 (2008)

40. Katz, J.: Universally composable multi-party computation using tamper-proof hardware. In: Naor, M. (ed.) EUROCRYPT 2007. LNCS, vol. 4515, pp. 115–128. Springer, Heidelberg (2007). https://doi.org/10.1007/978-3-540-72540-4_7

41. Kilian, J.: Founding cryptography on oblivious transfer. In: STOC, pp. 20–31 (1988)

42. Kilian, J., Petrank, E., Tardos, G.: Probabilistically checkable proofs with zero knowledge. In: STOC, pp. 496–505. ACM (1997)

43. Kleitman, D.J.: Families of non-disjoint subsets. J. Comb. Theory 1(1), 153–155 (1966)

44. Komargodski, I., Moran, T., Naor, M., Pass, R., Rosen, A., Yogev, E.: One-way functions and (im)perfect obfuscation. In: FOCS 2014, pp. 374–383 (2014)

45. Komargodski, I., Naor, M., Yogev, E.: Secret-sharing for NP. J. Cryptol. 30(2), 444–469 (2017)

46. Ma, F., Zhandry, M.: The MMap strikes back: obfuscation and new multilinear maps immune to CLT13 zeroizing attacks. In: Beimel, A., Dziembowski, S. (eds.) TCC 2018. LNCS, vol. 11240, pp. 513–543. Springer, Cham (2018). https://doi.org/10.1007/978-3-030-03810-6_19

47. Mahmoody, M., Xiao, D.: Languages with efficient zero-knowledge PCPs are in SZK. In: Sahai, A. (ed.) TCC 2013. LNCS, vol. 7785, pp. 297–314. Springer, Heidelberg (2013). https://doi.org/10.1007/978-3-642-36594-2_17

48. Maurer, U.M.: Perfect cryptographic security from partially independent channels. In: STOC, pp. 561–571 (1991)

49. Micali, S.: Computationally sound proofs. SIAM J. Comput. 30(4), 1253–1298 (2000)

50. Vincent Poor, H., Schaefer, R.F.: Wireless physical layer security. Proc. Nat. Acad. Sci. 114(1), 19–26 (2017)

51. Ranellucci, S., Tapp, A., Winkler, S., Wullschleger, J.: On the efficiency of bit commitment reductions. In: Lee, D.H., Wang, X. (eds.) ASIACRYPT 2011. LNCS, vol. 7073, pp. 520–537. Springer, Heidelberg (2011). https://doi.org/10.1007/978-3-642-25385-0_28

52. Sedgewick, R., Flajolet, P.: An Introduction to the Analysis of Algorithms. Pearson Education, London (2013)

53. Shoup, V.: Lower bounds for discrete logarithms and related problems. In: Fumy, W. (ed.) EUROCRYPT 1997. LNCS, vol. 1233, pp. 256–266. Springer, Heidelberg (1997). https://doi.org/10.1007/3-540-69053-0_18

54. Wee, H., Wichs, D.: Candidate obfuscation via oblivious LWE sampling. In: Canteaut, A., Standaert, F.-X. (eds.) EUROCRYPT 2021. LNCS, vol. 12698, pp. 127–156. Springer, Cham (2021). https://doi.org/10.1007/978-3-030-77883-5_5

55. Winter, A., Nascimento, A.C.A., Imai, H.: Commitment capacity of discrete memoryless channels. In: Paterson, K.G. (ed.) Cryptography and Coding 2003. LNCS, vol. 2898, pp. 35–51. Springer, Heidelberg (2003). https://doi.org/10.1007/978-3-540-40974-8_4

56. Wullschleger, J.: Oblivious transfer from weak noisy channels. In: Reingold, O. (ed.) TCC 2009. LNCS, vol. 5444, pp. 332–349. Springer, Heidelberg (2009). https://doi.org/10.1007/978-3-642-00457-5_20

57. Wyner, A.D.: The wire-tap channel. Bell Syst. Tech. J. **54**(8), 1355–1387 (1975)
58. Yao, A.C.-C.: How to generate and exchange secrets (extended abstract). In: FOCS, pp. 162–167 (1986)

Broadcast-Optimal Two Round MPC with an Honest Majority

Ivan Damgård[1(✉)], Bernardo Magri[1,2(✉)], Divya Ravi[1(✉)],
Luisa Siniscalchi[1,2(✉)], and Sophia Yakoubov[1(✉)]

[1] Aarhus University, Aarhus, Denmark
{ivan,magri,divya,lsiniscalchi,sophia.yakoubov}@cs.au.dk
[2] Concordium Blockchain Research Center, Aarhus, Denmark

Abstract. This paper closes the question of the possibility of two-round MPC protocols achieving different security guarantees with and without the availability of broadcast in any given round. Cohen *et al.* [CGZ20] study this question in the dishonest majority setting; we complete the picture by studying the honest majority setting.

In the honest majority setting, given broadcast in both rounds, it is known that the strongest guarantee—guaranteed output delivery—is achievable [GLS15]. We show that, given broadcast in the first round only, guaranteed output delivery is still achievable. Given broadcast in the second round only, we give a new construction that achieves identifiable abort, and we show that fairness—and thus guaranteed output delivery—are not achievable in this setting. Finally, if only peer-to-peer channels are available, we show that the weakest guarantee—selective abort—is the only one achievable for corruption thresholds $t > 1$ and for $t = 1$ and $n = 3$. On the other hand, it is already known that selective abort can be achieved in these cases. In the remaining cases, i.e., $t = 1$ and $n \geq 4$, it is known [IKP10,IKKP15] that guaranteed output delivery (and thus all weaker guarantees) are possible.

1 Introduction

In this paper we advance the study of round-optimal secure computation, focusing on secure computation with active corruptions, an honest majority, and some setup (e.g. a public key infrastructure). It is known that in this setting, secure computation is possible in two rounds (whereas one round is clearly not enough). However, most known two-round protocols in the honest majority setting either only achieve the weakest security guarantee (selective abort) [ACGJ19], or make use of a broadcast channel in both rounds [GLS15]. Since broadcast channels are expensive, it is important to try to minimize their use (while achieving strong security guarantees).

The only step in this direction is the protocol of Cohen *et al.* [CGZ20]. They achieve secure computation with unanimous abort for a dishonest majority

---

S. Yakoubov and Divya Ravi—Funded by the European Research Council (ERC) under the European Unions's Horizon 2020 research and innovation programme under grant agreement No 669255 (MPCPRO) and 803096 (SPEC).

T. Malkin and C. Peikert (Eds.): CRYPTO 2021, LNCS 12826, pp. 155–184, 2021.
https://doi.org/10.1007/978-3-030-84245-1_6

(and thus also for an honest majority) with broadcast in the second round only, and they also show that unanimous abort is the strongest achievable guarantee in this setting. Finally, Cohen *et al.* showed that, given a dishonest majority, selective abort is the strongest achievable security guarantee with broadcast in the first round only.

We make a study analogous to the work of Cohen *et al.* but in the honest majority setting. Like Cohen *et al.*, we consider all four broadcast patterns: broadcast in both rounds, broadcast in the second round only, broadcast in the first round only, and no broadcast at all. Gordon *et al.* [GLS15] showed that, given broadcast in both rounds, the strongest guarantee—guaranteed output delivery—is achievable. For each of the other broadcast patterns, we ask:

> What is the strongest achievable security guarantee in this broadcast pattern, given an honest majority?

We consider the following security guarantees:

Selective Abort (SA): A secure computation protocol achieves *selective abort* if every honest party either obtains the output, or aborts.

Unanimous Abort (UA): A secure computation protocol achieves *unanimous abort* if either *all* honest parties obtain the output, or they all (unanimously) abort.

Identifiable Abort (IA): A secure computation protocol achieves *identifiable abort* if either all honest parties obtain the output, or they all (unanimously) abort, *identifying one corrupt party*.

Fairness (FAIR): A secure computation protocol achieves *fairness* if either all parties obtain the output, or none of them do. In particular, an adversary cannot learn the output if the honest parties do not also learn it.

Guaranteed Output Delivery (GOD): A secure computation protocol achieves *guaranteed output delivery* if all honest parties will learn the computation output no matter what the adversary does.

Some of these guarantees are strictly stronger than others. In particular, guaranteed output delivery implies identifiable abort (since an abort never happens), which implies unanimous abort, which in turn implies selective abort. Similarly, guaranteed output delivery implies fairness, which implies unanimous abort. Fairness and identifiable abort are incomparable. In a fair protocol, in case of an abort, both corrupt and honest parties get less information: corrupt parties are guaranteed to learn nothing if the protocol aborts, but honest parties may not learn anything about corrupt parties' identities. On the other hand, in a protocol with identifiable abort, in case of an abort corrupt parties may learn the output, but honest parties will identify at least one corrupt party.

In Table 1, we summarize our results. Like the impossibility results of Cohen *et al.*, all of our impossibility results hold given arbitrary setup (such as a common reference string, a public key infrastructure, and correlated randomness). Our feasibility results use only a PKI and CRS. Below we give a very brief

Table 1. Feasibility and impossibility for two-round MPC in the honest majority setting with different guarantees and broadcast patterns. The R1 column describes whether broadcast is available in round 1; the R2 column describes whether broadcast is available in round 2. Arrows indicate implication: the possibility of a stronger security guarantee implies the possibility of weaker ones in the same setting, and the impossibility of a weaker guarantee implies the impossibility of stronger ones in the same setting.

Broadcast Pattern		t	selective abort	unanimous abort	identifiable abort	fairness	guaranteed output delivery
R1	R2						
BC	BC		✓ ⟵	✓ ⟵	✓ [GLS15]	✓ ⟵	✓ [GLS15]
P2P	BC	$1 < t < \frac{n}{2}$	✓ ⟵	✓ ⟵	✓ (Thm 9)	✗ (Thm 2) for $t > 1$ ⟶ ✗ for $t > 1$; ✗ (Cor 3) for $n \leq 3t$ ⟶ ✗ for $n \leq 3t$	
BC	P2P		✓ ⟵	✓ ⟵	✓ (Thm 7)	✓ ⟵	✓ (Thm 7)
P2P	P2P		✓ [ACGJ19]	✗ (Cor 1) for $t > 1$ ⟶ ✗ for $t > 1$		✗ (Thm 2) for $t > 1$ ⟶ ✗ for $t > 1$; ✗ (Cor 3) for $n \leq 3t$ ⟶ ✗ for $n \leq 3t$	
P2P	P2P	$t = 1, n = 3$	✓ [ACGJ19]	✗ (Cor 2) ⟶ ✗		✗ (Cor 2) ⟶ ✗	
		$t = 1, n = 4$	✓ ⟵	✓ ⟵	✓ ([IKKP15])	✓ ⟵	✓ ([IKKP15])
		$t = 1, n \geq 5$	✓ ⟵	✓ ⟵	✓ ([IKP10])	✓ ⟵	✓ ([IKP10])

description of our results. It turns out that going from dishonest to honest majority allows for stronger security guarantees in some, but not all cases. In Sect. 1.1 we give a longer overview of our results, and the techniques we use.

No Broadcast In this setting, we show that if the adversary controls two or more parties ($t > 1$), or if $t = 1, n = 3$, selective abort is the best achievable guarantee. This completes the picture, since (1) selective abort can indeed be achieved by the results of Ananth *et al.* [ACGJ19], and (2) for $t = 1, n \geq 4$, guaranteed output delivery can be achieved by the results of Ishai *et al.* [IKP10], [IKKP15].

Broadcast in the First Round Only In this setting, we show that guaranteed output delivery—the strongest guarantee—can be achieved.

Broadcast in the Second Round Only In this setting, we show that fairness is impossible if $t \geq n/3$, or if $t > 1$ (again, in the remaining case of $t = 1, n \geq 4$, guaranteed output delivery can be achieved). If fairness is ruled out, the best one can hope for is identifiable abort, and we show this can indeed be achieved given an honest majority.

To achieve identifiable abort with broadcast in the second round only, we introduce a new tool called *one-or-nothing secret sharing*, which we believe to be of independent interest. One-or-nothing secret sharing is a flavor of secret sharing that allows a dealer to share a *vector* of secrets. Once the shares are distributed to the receivers, they can vote on which secret to reconstruct by publishing "ballots". Each receiver either votes for the secret she wishes to reconstruct, or abstains (by publishing a special equivocation ballot). If only one secret is voted for, and gets sufficiently many votes, the ballots enable reconstruction of that secret. On the other hand, if receivers disagree about which secret to reconstruct, nothing is revealed. This could have applications to voting scenarios where, though some voters may remain undecided, unanimity among the decided voters is important.

1.1 Technical Overview

In this section we summarize our results given each of the broadcast patterns in more detail.

No Broadcast (P2P-P2P). Without a broadcast channel, we show that only the weakest guarantee—selective abort—is achievable. Ananth *et al.* [ACGJ19] give a protocol for secure computation with selective abort in this setting; we prove that secure computation with unanimous abort is not achievable, implying impossibility for all stronger guarantees. More specifically, we get the following two results:

Result 1 (Cor 1: P2P-P2P, UA, $t > 1$) *Secure computation of general functions with unanimous abort cannot be achieved in two rounds of peer-to-peer communication for corruption threshold $t > 1$.*

Result 2 (Cor 2: P2P-P2P, UA, $t = 1$, $n = 3$) *Secure computation of general functions with unanimous abort cannot be achieved in two rounds of peer-to-peer communication for corruption threshold $t = 1$ when $n = 3$[1].*

We prove the first result by focusing on broadcast, where only one party (the dealer) has an input bit, and all parties should output that bit. We show that computing broadcast with unanimous abort in two peer-to-peer rounds with $t > 1$ is impossible[2].

The only case not covered by these two results is $t = 1$ and $n \geq 4$. However for this case, it follows from results by Ishai *et al.* [IKP10] and [IKKP15] that the strongest guarantee—guaranteed output delivery—is achievable in two rounds of peer-to-peer communication.

For completeness, we note that the case of $n = 2$ and $t = 1$ is special. We are no longer in an honest majority setting, so fairness is known to be impossible [Cle86]. The other three guarantees are possible and equivalent.

---

[1] Patra and Ravi [PR18] give a similar result in the absence of a PKI and correlated randomness; our impossibility result is stronger, as it holds even given arbitrary correlated randomness.

[2] It is well known that computing broadcast with guaranteed output delivery requires t rounds, but this of course does not imply the same for broadcast with unanimous abort.

Broadcast in the First Round Only (BC-P2P). We show that any *first-round extractable* two broadcast-round protocol (where the simulator demonstrating security of the protocol can extract parties' inputs from their first-round messages and it is efficient to check whether a given second-round message is correct) can be run over one broadcast round followed by one peer-to-peer round without any loss in security. Since the protocol of Gordon et al. [GLS15] satisfies these properties, we conclude that guaranteed output delivery is achievable in the honest majority setting as long as broadcast is available in the first round.

Result 3 (Thm 7: BC-P2P, GOD, $n \geq 2t+1$) *Secure computation of general functions with guaranteed output delivery is possible in two rounds of communication, only the first of which is over a broadcast channel, for corruption threshold t such that $n \geq 2t + 1$.*

Broadcast in the Second Round Only (P2P-BC). When broadcast is available in the second round, not the first, it turns out that fairness (and hence guaranteed output delivery) cannot be achieved. More specifically, we obtain the following two results:

Result 4 (Cor 3: P2P-BC, FAIR, $n \leq 3t$) *Secure computation of general functions with fairness cannot be achieved in two rounds of communication, only the second of which is over a broadcast channel, for corruption threshold t such that $n \leq 3t$.*

Result 5 (Thm 2: P2P-BC, FAIR, $t > 1$) *Secure computation of general functions with fairness cannot be achieved in two rounds of communication, only the second of which is over a broadcast channel, for corruption threshold $t > 1$.*

Both these results are shown using the same basic idea, namely if the protocol is fair, we construct an attack in which corrupt players send inconsistent messages in the first round and then use the second round messages to obtain two different outputs, corresponding to different choices of their own input—which, of course, violates privacy.

Combining the two results, we see that fairness is unachievable when broadcast is only available in the second round (the only case not covered is $t = 1, n \geq 4$ where guaranteed output delivery is possible, as discussed above). We therefore turn to the next-best guarantee, which is identifiable abort; in Sect. 8, we show how to achieve it for $n > 2t$.

Result 6 (Thm 9: P2P-BC, ID, $n > 2t$) *Secure computation of general functions with identifiable abort is achievable in two rounds of communication, only the second of which is over a broadcast channel, for corruption threshold t such that $n > 2t$.*

To show this result, we use a high-level strategy adopted from Cohen et al. Namely, we start from any protocol that achieves identifiable abort for honest majority given two rounds of broadcast, and compile this into a protocol that works when the first round is limited to peer-to-peer channels. While Cohen *et al.* achieve unanimous abort this way, we aim for the stronger guarantee of identifiable abort, since we assume honest majority.

To explain our technical contribution, let us follow the approach of Cohen *et al.* and see where we get stuck. The idea is to have each party broadcast a garbled circuit in the second round. This garbled circuit corresponds to the code they would use to compute their second-round message in the underlying protocol (given their input and all the first-round messages they receive). In the first round (over peer-to-peer channels), the parties additively secret share all the labels for their garbled circuit, and send their first-round message from the underlying protocol to each of their peers. In the second round (over broadcast), for each bit of first-round message she receives, each party forwards her share of the corresponding label in everyone else's garbled circuit. Cohen *et al.* used this approach to achieve unanimous abort for dishonest majority.

However, even assuming honest majority, this will not be sufficient for identifiable abort. The main issue is that corrupt parties may send inconsistent messages in the first round. This problem cannot be solved just by requiring each party to sign their first-round messages, because P_i may send an invalid signature—or nothing at all—to P_j. P_j then cannot do what she was supposed to in the second round; so, all she can do is to complain, but she cannot demonstrate any proof that P_i cheated. All honest parties now agree that either P_i or P_j is corrupt, but there is no way to tell which one. This is not an issue if we aim for unanimous abort; however, if we aim for identifiable abort, we must either find out who to blame or compute the correct output anyway, without any further interaction.

We solve this problem by introducing a new primitive we call *one-or-nothing* secret sharing. This special kind secret sharing allows a dealer to share several values simultaneously. (In our case, the values would be two garbled circuit labels for a given bit b.) The share recipients can then "vote" on which of the values to reconstruct; if they aren't sure (in our case, they wouldn't be sure if they didn't get b in the first round), they are able to "abstain", which essentially means casting their vote with the majority. As long as there are no contradictory votes and a minority of abstain votes, reconstruction of the appropriate value succeeds; otherwise, the privacy of all values is guaranteed.

We use this primitive to share the labels for the garbled circuits as sketched above. If all reconstructions succeed, we get the correct output. Otherwise, we can identify a corrupt player. By requiring parties to sign their first-round messages, we can ensure that if there are contradicting votes, all parties can agree that some party P_i sent inconsistent messages in the first round. If there is a majority of abstains, this proves that some particular P_i sent an invalid first-round message to at least one honest party.

1.2 Related Work

The quest for optimal round-complexity for secure computation protocols is a well-established topic in cryptography. Starting with the first feasibility results from almost 35 years ago [Yao86, GMW87, BGW88, CCD88] a lot of progress has been made in improving the round complexity of protocols [GIKR01, Lin01, CD01] [IK02, IKP10, IKKP15, GLS15, PR18, ACGJ18, CGZ20]. In this section we detail the prior work that specifically targets the two-round setting. We divide the discussion into two: impossibility and feasibility results.

Table 2. Previous impossibility results. Each row in this table describes a setting where MPC is known to be *impossible*. "UA" stand for unanimous abort, and "IA" for identifiable abort.

Result	n	t	Guarantee	CRS?	PKI?	CR?	R1	R2
[GIKR02]	any	$t \geq 2$	fairness	✓	✗	✗	BC + P2P	BC + P2P
[GLS15]	$n = 3$	$t = 1$	fairness	✓	✗	✗	BC	BC
[PR18]	$n = 3$	$t = 1$	fairness	✓	✗	✗	BC + P2P	BC + P2P
[PR18]	$n = 3$	$t = 1$	UA	✓	✗	✗	P2P	P2P
[CGZ20]	$n = 3$	$t = 2$	UA	✓	✓	✓	BC	P2P
[CGZ20]	$n = 3$	$t = 2$	IA	✓	✓	✓	P2P	BC

Impossibility Results. Table 2 summarizes the known lower bounds on two-round secure computation. Gennaro *et al.* [GIKR02] shed light on the optimal round-complexity for general MPC protocols achieving fairness without correlated randomness (e.g., PKI). Their model allows for communication over both authenticated point-to-point channels and a broadcast channel. They show that in this setting, three rounds are necessary for a protocol with at least $t \geq 2$ corrupt parties by focusing on the computation of exclusive-or and conjunction functions. In a slightly different model, where the parties can communicate only over a broadcast channel, Gordon *et al.* [GLS15] show that the existence of a fair two-round MPC protocol for an honest majority would imply a virtual black-box program obfuscation scheme, which would contradict the well-known impossibility result of Barak *et al.* [BGI+01].

Patra and Ravi [PR18] investigate the three party setting. They show that three rounds are necessary for generic secure computation achieving unanimous abort when parties *do not* have access to a broadcast channel, and that the same three are necessary for fairness even when parties do have a broadcast channel. Badrinarayanan *et al.* [BMMR21] study broadcast-optimal three-round MPC with guaranteed output delivery given an honest majority and CRS, and show that use of broadcast in the first two rounds is necessary.

It is well known that in the dishonest majority setting fairness cannot be achieved for generic computation [Cle86]. Cohen *et al.* [CGZ20] study the feasibility of two round secure computation with unanimous and identifiable abort in the dishonest majority setting. Their results show that considering arbitrary setup (e.g., a PKI) and communication over point-to-point channels, achieving unanimous abort in two rounds is not possible even if the parties are additionally allowed to communicate over a broadcast channel only in the first round, and achieving identifiable abort in two rounds is not possible even if the parties are additionally allowed to communicate over a broadcast channel only in the second round.

Table 3. Protocols for secure MPC with two-rounds. "UA" stands for unanimous abort, "FS-GOD" for guaranteed output delivery against fail-stop adversaries, "SM-GOD" for guaranteed output delivery against semi-malicious adversaries, and "M-GOD" for guaranteed output delivery against malicious adversaries.

Result	n	t	Guarantee	PKI?	CRS?	1st round	2nd round	Assumptions
[IKP10]	$n \geq 5$	$t = 1$	GOD	✗	✗	P2P	P2P	PRG
[IKKP15]	$n = 3$	$t = 1$	SA	✗	✗	P2P	P2P	PRG
[IKKP15]	$n = 4$	$t = 1$	GOD	✗	✗	P2P	P2P	injective OWF
[GLS15]	any	$t < \frac{n}{2}$	M-GOD	✓	✓	BC + P2P	BC + P2P	dFHE
[PR18]	$n = 3$	$t = 1$	UA	✗	✗	BC + P2P	BC + P2P	GC, NICOM, eNICOM, PRG
[ACGJ18]	any	$t < \frac{n}{2}$	UA	✗	✗	BC + P2P	BC + P2P	OWF
[ACGJ18]	any	$t < \frac{n}{2}$	FS-GOD	✓	✗	BC + P2P	BC + P2P	OWF
[ACGJ18]	any	$t < \frac{n}{2}$	FS-GOD	✗	✗	BC + P2P	BC + P2P	OWF, SH-OT
[ACGJ18]	any	$t < \frac{n}{2}$	FS-GOD / SM-GOD	✓	✗	BC	BC	OWF
[GS18]	any	$t < n$	UA	✗	✓	BC	BC	2-round OT
[CGZ20]	any	$t < n$	SA	✗	✓	P2P	P2P	2-round OT
[CGZ20]	any	$t < n$	UA	✗	✓	P2P	BC	2-round OT
[CGZ20]	any	$t < n$	IA	✗	✓	BC	BC	2-round OT

Feasibility Results. Table 3 summarizes known two-round secure computation constructions. While three rounds are necessary for fair MPC [GIKR02] for $t \geq 2$ (without correlated randomness), Ishai *et al.* [IKP10] show that it is possible to build generic two-round MPC with guaranteed output delivery when only a *single* party is corrupt ($t = 1$) for $n \geq 5$. Later, [IKKP15] showed the same for $n = 4$, and that selective abort is also possible for $n = 3$.

The work of [GLS15] gives a three round generic MPC protocol that guarantees output delivery and is secure against a minority of semi-honest fail-stop adversaries where parties only communicate over point-to-point channels; the same protocol can be upgraded to be secure against malicious adversaries if the parties are also allowed to communicate over a broadcast channel. The use of broadcast channel in the last round can be avoided (and point-to-point channels can be used instead), as shown by Badrinarayanan *et al.* [BMMR21]. Moreover, assuming a PKI, the protocol of [GLS15] can be compressed to only two rounds.

For $n = 3$ and $t = 1$, Patra and Ravi [PR18] present a tight upper bound achieving unanimous abort in the setting with point-to-point channels and a broadcast channel. The protocol leverages garbled circuits, (equivocal) non-interactive commitment scheme and a PRG. In the same honest majority setting but for arbitrary n, Ananth *et al.* [ACGJ18] build four variants of a two-round protocol. Two of these variants are in the plain model (without setup), with both point-to-point channels and broadcast available in both rounds. The first achieves security with unanimous abort and relies on one-way functions, and the second achieves guaranteed output delivery against fail-stop adversaries and additionally relies on semi-honest oblivious transfer. Their other two protocols require a PKI; and achieve guaranteed output delivery against fail-stop and semi-malicious adversaries.

Finally, Cohen et al. [CGZ20] present a complete characterization of the feasibility landscape of two-round MPC in the dishonest majority setting, for all broadcast patterns. In particular, they show protocols (without a PKI) for the cases of point-to-point communication in both rounds, point-to-point in the first round and broadcast in the second round, and broadcast in both rounds. The protocols achieve security with selective abort, unanimous abort and identifiable abort, respectively. All protocols rely on two-round oblivious transfer.

2 Secure Multiparty Computation (MPC) Definitions

2.1 Security Model

We follow the real/ideal world simulation paradigm and we adopt the security model of Cohen, Garay and Zikas [CGZ20]. As in their work, we state our results in a stand-alone setting.[3]

Real-world. An n-party protocol $\Pi = (P_1, \ldots, P_n)$ is an n-tuple of probabilistic polynomial-time (PPT) interactive Turing machines (ITMs), where each party P_i is initialized with input $x_i \in \{0,1\}^*$ and random coins $r_i \in \{0,1\}^*$. We let $\mathcal{A}$ denote a special PPT ITM that represents the adversary and that is initialized with input that contains the identities of the corrupt parties, their respective private inputs, and an auxiliary input. The protocol is executed in rounds (i.e., the protocol is synchronous), where each round consists of the send phase and the receive phase, where parties can respectively send the messages from this round to other parties and receive messages from other parties. In every round parties can communicate either over a broadcast channel or a fully connected point-to-point (P2P) network, where we additionally assume all communication to be private and ideally authenticated. (Given a PKI and a broadcast channel, such a fully connected point-to-point network can be instantiated.)

During the execution of the protocol, the corrupt parties receive arbitrary instructions from the adversary $\mathcal{A}$, while the honest parties faithfully follow the instructions of the protocol. We consider the adversary $\mathcal{A}$ to be rushing, i.e., during every round the adversary can see the messages the honest parties sent before producing messages from corrupt parties.

At the end of the protocol execution, the honest parties produce output, the corrupt parties produce no output, and the adversary outputs an arbitrary function of its view. The view of a party during the execution consists of its input, random coins and the messages it sees during the execution.

---

[3] We note that our security proofs can translate to an appropriate (synchronous) composable setting with minimal changes.

Definition 1 (Real-world execution). *Let $\Pi = (P_1, \ldots, P_n)$ be an n-party protocol and let $\mathcal{I} \subseteq [n]$, of size at most t, denote the set of indices of the parties corrupted by $\mathcal{A}$. The joint execution of Π under $(\mathcal{A}, \mathcal{I})$ in the real world, on input vector $x = (x_1, \ldots, x_n)$, auxiliary input aux and security parameter λ, denoted $\mathrm{REAL}_{\Pi, \mathcal{I}, \mathcal{A}(\mathsf{aux})}(x, \lambda)$, is defined as the output vector of $P_1, \ldots, P_n$ and $\mathcal{A}(\mathsf{aux})$ resulting from the protocol interaction.*

Ideal-world. We describe ideal world executions with selective abort (sl-abort), unanimous abort (un-abort), identifiable abort (id-abort), fairness (fairness) and guaranteed output delivery (god).

Definition 2 (Ideal Computation). *Consider type $\in \{$sl-abort, un-abort, id-abort, fairness, god$\}$. Let $f : (\{0,1\}^*)^n \to (\{0,1\}^*)^n$ be an n-party function and let $\mathcal{I} \subseteq [n]$, of size at most t, be the set of indices of the corrupt parties. Then, the joint ideal execution of f under $(\mathcal{S}, \mathcal{I})$ on input vector $x = (x_1, \ldots, x_n)$, auxiliary input aux to $\mathcal{S}$ and security parameter λ, denoted $\mathrm{IDEAL}_{f, \mathcal{I}, \mathcal{S}(\mathsf{aux})}^{\mathsf{type}}(x, \lambda)$, is defined as the output vector of $P_1, \ldots, P_n$ and $\mathcal{S}$ resulting from the following ideal process.*

1. Parties send inputs to trusted party: *An honest party P_i sends its input x_i to the trusted party. The simulator $\mathcal{S}$ may send to the trusted party arbitrary inputs for the corrupt parties. Let x_i' be the value actually sent as the input of party P_i.*

2. Trusted party speaks to simulator: *The trusted party computes $(y_1, \ldots, y_n) = f(x_1', \ldots, x_n')$. If there are no corrupt parties or type = god, proceed to step 4.*
   (a) *If type $\in \{$sl-abort, un-abort, id-abort$\}$: The trusted party sends $\{y_i\}_{i \in \mathcal{I}}$ to $\mathcal{S}$.*
   (b) *If type = fairness: The trusted party sends ready to $\mathcal{S}$.*

3. Simulator $\mathcal{S}$ responds to trusted party:
   (a) *If type = sl-abort: The simulator $\mathcal{S}$ can select a set of parties that will not get the output as $\mathcal{J} \subseteq [n] \backslash \mathcal{I}$. (Note that $\mathcal{J}$ can be empty, allowing all parties to obtain the output.) It sends $(\mathrm{abort}, \mathcal{J})$ to the trusted party.*
   (b) *If type $\in \{$un-abort, fairness$\}$: The simulator can send abort to the trusted party. If it does, we take $\mathcal{J} = [n] \backslash \mathcal{I}$.*
   (c) *If type = id-abort: If it chooses to abort, the simulator $\mathcal{S}$ can select a corrupt party $i^* \in \mathcal{I}$ who will be blamed, and send (abort, i^*) to the trusted party. If it does, we take $\mathcal{J} = [n] \backslash \mathcal{I}$.*

4. Trusted party answers parties:
   (a) *If the trusted party got abort from the simulator $\mathcal{S}$,*
       i. *It sets the abort message abortmsg, as follows:*
          - *if type $\in \{$sl-abort, un-abort, fairness$\}$, we let abortmsg $= \bot$.*
          - *if type $=$ id-abort, we let abortmsg $= (\bot, i^*)$.*
       ii. *The trusted party then sends abortmsg to every party P_j, $j \in \mathcal{J}$, and y_j to every party P_j, $j \in [n] \backslash \mathcal{J}$.*
       Note that, if type = god, we will never be in this setting, since $\mathcal{S}$ was not allowed to ask for an abort.

(b) Otherwise, it sends y to every P_j, $j \in [n]$.

5. Outputs: *Honest parties always output the message received from the trusted party while the corrupt parties output nothing. The simulator S outputs an arbitrary function of the initial inputs $\{x_i\}_{i \in \mathcal{I}}$, the messages received by the corrupt parties from the trusted party and its auxiliary input.*

Security Definitions. We now define the security notion for protocols.

Definition 3. *Consider* type $\in \{$sl-abort, un-abort, id-abort, fairness, god$\}$. *Let $f : (\{0,1\}^*)^n \to (\{0,1\}^*)^n$ be an n-party function. A protocol Π t-securely computes the function f with* type *security if for every PPT real-world adversary $\mathcal{A}$ there exists a PPT simulator S such that for every $\mathcal{I} \subseteq [n]$ of size at most t, it holds that*

$$\left\{\text{REAL}_{\Pi,\mathcal{I},\mathcal{A}(\text{aux})}(x,\lambda)\right\}_{x \in (\{0,1\}^*)^n, \lambda \in \mathbb{N}} \overset{c}{\equiv} \left\{\text{IDEAL}^{\text{type}}_{f,\mathcal{I},S(\text{aux})}(x,\lambda)\right\}_{x \in (\{0,1\}^*)^n, \lambda \in \mathbb{N}}.$$

2.2 Notation

In this paper, we focus on two-round secure computation protocols. Rather than viewing a protocol Π as an n-tuple of interactive Turing machines, it is convenient to view each Turing machine as a sequence of three algorithms: frst-msg_i, to compute P_i's first messages to its peers; snd-msg_i, to compute P_i's second messages; and output_i, to compute P_i's output. Thus, a protocol Π can be defined as $\{(\text{frst-msg}_i, \text{snd-msg}_i, \text{output}_i)\}_{i \in [n]}$.

The syntax of the algorithms is as follows:

- $\text{frst-msg}_i(x_i, r_i) \to (\text{msg}^1_{i \to 1}, \ldots, \text{msg}^1_{i \to n})$ produces the first-round messages of party P_i to all parties. Note that a party's message to itself can be considered to be its state.
- $\text{snd-msg}_i(x_i, r_i, \text{msg}^1_{1 \to i}, \ldots, \text{msg}^1_{n \to i}) \to (\text{msg}^2_{i \to 1}, \ldots, \text{msg}^2_{i \to n})$ produces the second-round messages of party P_i to all parties.
- $\text{output}_i(x_i, r_i, \text{msg}^1_{1 \to i}, \ldots, \text{msg}^1_{n \to i}, \text{msg}^2_{1 \to i}, \ldots, \text{msg}^2_{n \to i}) \to y_i$ produces the output returned to party P_i.

When the first round is over broadcast channels, we consider frst-msg_i to return only one message—msg^1_i. Similarly, when the second round is over broadcast channels, we consider snd-msg_i to return only msg^1_i.

Throughout our negative results, we omit the randomness r, and instead focus on deterministic protocols, modeling the randomness implicitly as part of the algorithm.

3 No Broadcast: Impossibility of Unanimous Abort

For our negative results in the setting where no broadcast is available, we leverage related negative results for broadcast (or byzantine agreement). To show that guaranteed output delivery is impossible in two rounds of peer-to-peer communication, we can use the fact that broadcast cannot be realized in two rounds for $t > 1$ [FL82,DS83]. To show the impossibility of weaker guarantees such as unanimous abort in this setting, we prove that a weaker flavor of broadcast, called *(weak) detectable* broadcast [FGMv02]—where all parties either learn the broadcast bit, or unanimously abort—cannot be realized in two rounds either.

We state the definitions of *broadcast* and *detectable broadcast* (from Fitzi *et al.* [FGMv02]) below.

Definition 4 (Broadcast). *A protocol among n parties, where the dealer $D = P_1$ holds an input value $x \in \{0,1\}$ and every other party $P_i, i \in [2, \ldots, n]$ outputs a value $y_i \in \{0,1\}$, achieves* broadcast *if it satisfies the following two conditions:*

Validity: *If the dealer D is honest then all honest parties P_i output $y_i = x$.*
Consistency: *All honest parties output the same value $y_2 = \cdots = y_n = y$.*

Definition 5 (Detectable Broadcast). *A protocol among n parties achieves* detectable broadcast *if it satisfies the following three conditions:*

Correctness: *All honest parties unanimously accept or unanimously reject the protocol. If all honest parties accept then the protocol achieves broadcast.*
Completeness: *If all parties are honest then all parties accept.*
Fairness: *If any honest party rejects the protocol then the adversary gets no information about the dealer's input x.*

We additionally define *weak detectable broadcast*.

Definition 6 (Weak Detectable Broadcast). *A protocol among n parties achieves* weak detectable broadcast *if it satisfies only the correctness and completeness requirements of detectable broadcast.*

An alternative way of viewing broadcast, through the lens of secure computation, is by considering the simple broadcast function $f_{bc}(x, \bot, \ldots, \bot) = (\bot, x, \ldots, x)$ which takes an input bit x from the dealer $D = P_1$, and outputs that bit to all other parties. *Broadcast* (Definition 4) is exactly equivalent to computing f_{bc} with guaranteed output delivery; *detectable broadcast* (Definition 5) is equivalent to computing it with fairness; and *weak detectable broadcast* (Definition 6) is equivalent to computing it with unanimous abort.

Theorem 1. *Weak detectable broadcast cannot be achieved in two rounds of peer-to-peer communication for corruption threshold $t > 1$.*

Proof. We prove Thm 1 by contradiction. We let

$$\Pi_{wdbc} = \{(\texttt{frst-msg}_i, \texttt{snd-msg}_i, \texttt{output}_i)\}_{i \in [1, \ldots, n]}$$

be the description of the two-round weak detectable broadcast protocol. We use the notation we introduce for two-round secure computation in Sect. 2.2, and consider the weak detectable broadcast protocol to be a secure computation with unanimous abort of f_{bc}. We let $x_1 = x$ denote the bit being broadcast by the dealer $D = P_1$, and $x_i = \perp$ for $i \in [2, \ldots, n]$ be placeholders for other parties' inputs. We assume that $\mu = negl$ is the negligible probability with which security of Π_{wdbc} fails.

Below we consider an execution of Π_{wdbc} and a sequence of scenarios involving different adversarial strategies with two corruptions ($t = 2$). The dealer $D = P_1$ is corrupt in all of these; at most one of the receiving parties $P_2, \ldots, P_n$ is corrupt at a time. We argue that each subsequent strategy clearly requires certain parties to output certain values, by the definition of weak detectable broadcast. In the last strategy, we see a contradiction, where some parties must output both 0 and 1. Therefore, Π_{wdbc} could not have been a weak detectable broadcast protocol. In all of the strategies below, we let $\text{msg}_{b,i \to j}$ denote a party P_i's bth-round message to party P_j; we only specify how these messages are generated when this is done dishonestly.

Scenario 1: D is corrupt.

   Round 1: D behaves honestly using input $x = 0$.

   Round 2: D behaves honestly using input $x = 0$.

By completeness (which holds since everyone behaved honestly), all honest parties must accept the protocol. By correctness, the protocol must thus achieve broadcast. By validity, all honest parties must output 0. Since completeness, correctness and validity hold with probability at least $1 - \mu$, we can infer that honest parties must output 0 with probability at least $1 - \mu$.

Scenario 2_M: D and P_2 are corrupt.

   Round 1: D computes two different sets of messages, using different inputs $x = 0$ and $x = 1$, as follows:

$$(\text{msg}_{1 \to 1}^{1,(0)}, \ldots, \text{msg}_{1 \to n}^{1,(0)}) \leftarrow \texttt{frst-msg}_1(x = 0)$$

$$(\text{msg}_{1 \to 1}^{1,(1)}, \ldots, \text{msg}_{1 \to n}^{1,(1)}) \leftarrow \texttt{frst-msg}_1(x = 1)$$

D sends $\text{msg}_{1 \to 3}^{1,(0)}, \ldots, \text{msg}_{1 \to n}^{1,(0)}$ to parties $P_3, \ldots, P_n$. P_2 behaves honestly.

   Round 2: D behaves honestly using input $x = 0$. P_2 computes two different sets of second-round messages, as follows:

$$(\text{msg}_{2 \to 1}^{2,(0)}, \ldots, \text{msg}_{2 \to n}^{2,(0)}) \leftarrow \texttt{snd-msg}_2(\perp, \text{msg}_{1 \to 2}^{1,(0)}, \text{msg}_{2 \to 2}^1, \ldots, \text{msg}_{n \to 2}^1)$$

$$(\text{msg}_{2 \to 1}^{2,(1)}, \ldots, \text{msg}_{2 \to n}^{2,(1)}) \leftarrow \texttt{snd-msg}_2(\perp, \text{msg}_{1 \to 2}^{1,(1)}, \text{msg}_{2 \to 2}^1, \ldots, \text{msg}_{n \to 2}^1)$$

P_2 sends $\text{msg}_{2 \to n}^{2,(1)}$ to P_n (pretending, essentially, that D dealt a 1), and $\text{msg}_{2 \to i}^{2,(0)}$ to other parties P_i (pretending that D dealt a 0).

$P_3, \ldots, P_{n-1}$ must accept and output 0 with probability at least $1 - \mu$, since their views are identical to those in the previous scenario. By correctness, P_n must also accept when other honest parties accept. By consistency, P_n must also output 0. Since correctness or consistency break with probability at most μ, P_n outputs 0 with probability at least $1 - 2\mu$.

Scenario 2_H: D is corrupt.

Round 1: D sends $\mathsf{msg}_{1\to 2}^{1,(1)}$ to P_2, and $\mathsf{msg}_{1\to i}^{1,(0)}$ to other parties P_i.

Round 2: D continues to represent $x = 1$ towards P_2 and $x = 0$ towards the others.

P_n must accept and output 0 with probability at least $1 - 2\mu$, since its view is the same as in the previous scenario. By correctness, $P_2, \ldots, P_{n-1}$ must also accept when P_n accepts. By consistency, $P_2, \ldots, P_{n-1}$ must also output 0. Since correctness or consistency break with probability at most μ, $P_2, \ldots, P_{n-1}$ output 0 with probability at least $1 - 3\mu$.

Now, skipping ahead, we generalize, for $k \in [3, \ldots, n-1]$:

Scenario k_M: D and P_k are corrupt.

Round 1: D sends $\mathsf{msg}_{1\to i}^{1,(1)}$ to $P_2, \ldots, P_{k-1}$, and $\mathsf{msg}_{1\to i}^{1,(0)}$ to the other parties $P_{k+1}, \ldots, P_n$. P_k acts honestly.

Round 2: D continues to represent $x = 1$ to $P_2, \ldots, P_{k-1}$ and $x = 0$ to $P_{k+1}, \ldots, P_n$. In the second round P_k acts analogously to P_2 in scenario 2_M; i.e., P_k uses $\mathsf{msg}_{1\to k}^{1,(0)}$ to compute $(\mathsf{msg}_{k\to 1}^{2,(0)}, \ldots, \mathsf{msg}_{k\to n-1}^{2,(0)})$ (which it sends to $P_2, \ldots, P_{n-1}$), and $\mathsf{msg}_{1\to k}^{1,(1)}$ to compute $\mathsf{msg}_{k\to n}^{2,(1)}$ (which it sends to P_n).

$P_2, \ldots, P_{n-1}$ must accept and output 0 with probability at least $1 - (2(k-1) - 1)\mu = 1 - (2k - 3)\mu$, since their views are identical to those in the previous scenario (namely Scenario $(k-1)_H$). By correctness, P_n must also accept when other honest parties accept. By consistency, P_n must also output 0. Since correctness or consistency break with probability at most μ, P_n outputs 0 with probability at least $1 - (2k - 3)\mu - \mu = 1 - 2(k - 1)\mu$.

Scenario k_H: D is corrupt.

Round 1: D sends $\mathsf{msg}_{1\to i}^{1,(1)}$ to $P_2, \ldots, P_k$, and $\mathsf{msg}_{1\to i}^{1,(0)}$ to the other parties $P_{k+1}, \ldots, P_n$.

Round 2: D continues to represent $x = 1$ to $P_2, \ldots, P_k$ and $x = 0$ to $P_{k+1}, \ldots, P_n$.

P_n must accept and output 0 with probability at least $1 - 2(k - 1)\mu$, since its view is the same as in the previous scenario. By correctness, $P_2, \ldots, P_{n-1}$ must also accept. By consistency, $P_2, \ldots, P_{n-1}$ must also output 0. Since correctness or consistency break with probability at most μ, $P_2, \ldots, P_{n-1}$ output 0 with probability at least $1 - 2(k - 1)\mu - \mu = 1 - (2k - 1)\mu$.

We end with Scenarios n_M, n_H.

Scenario n_M: D and P_n are corrupt.

Round 1: D behaves honestly using input $x = 1$. P_n behaves honestly.

Round 2: D behaves honestly using input $x = 1$. P_n pretends D dealt a 0 towards, e.g., only P_2. More precisely, P_n uses $\mathsf{msg}_{1\to n}^{1,(0)}$ to compute $\mathsf{msg}_{n\to 2}^{2,(0)}$ (which it sends to P_2), and $\mathsf{msg}_{1\to n}^{1,(1)}$ to compute $(\mathsf{msg}_{n\to 3}^{2,(1)}, \ldots, \mathsf{msg}_{n\to n-1}^{2,(1)})$ (which it sends to $P_3, \ldots, P_{n-1}$).

P_2 must accept and output 0 with probability at least $1 - (2(n-1) - 1)\mu = 1 - (2n - 3)\mu$, since its view is the same as in the previous scenario (namely, Scenario $(n-1)_H$). By correctness, $P_3, \ldots, P_{n-1}$ must also accept. By consistency, $P_3, \ldots, P_{n-1}$ must also output 0. This must happen with probability at least $1 - (2n - 3)\mu - \mu = 1 - 2(n-1)\mu$.

Scenario n_H: D is corrupt.

  Round 1: D behaves honestly using input $x = 1$.

  Round 2: D behaves honestly using input $x = 1$.

In Scenario n_H, on the one hand, by completeness (which holds as everyone behaved honestly), all honest parties must accept the protocol; by validity, all honest parties must output 1. On the other hand, since the view of $P_3, \ldots, P_{n-1}$ is the same as their respective views in the previous scenario, they must output 0 with probability at least $1 - 2(n-1)\mu$, which is overwhelming. This is a contradiction.

The impossibility of realizing weak detectable broadcast in two rounds for $t > 1$ clearly implies that there exists a function (specifically, f_{bc}) which is impossible to compute with unanimous abort for $t > 1$ in two rounds of peer-to-peer communication.

Corollary 1 (P2P-P2P, UA, $t > 1$). *There exist functions f such that no n-party two-round protocol can compute f with unanimous abort against $t > 1$ corruptions in two rounds of peer-to-peer communication.*

4 Broadcast in the Second Round: Impossibility of Fairness

In this section, we show that it is not possible to design fair protocols tolerating $t > 1$ corruptions when broadcast is available only in the second round.

Theorem 2 (P2P-BC, FAIR, $t > 1$). *There exist functions f such that no n-party two-round protocol can compute f with fairness against $t > 1$ corruptions while making use of broadcast only in the second round (i.e. where the first round is over point-to-point channels and second round uses both broadcast and point-to-point channels).*

In our proof we use the function $f_{\mathtt{mot}}$, which is defined below. Let P_1 hold as input a bit $X_1 = b \in \{0, 1\}$, and every other party P_i ($i \in \{2, \ldots, n\}$) hold as input a pair of strings, denoted as $X_i = (x_i^0, x_i^1)$.

$$f_{\mathtt{mot}}\big(X_1 = b, X_2 = (x_2^0, x_2^1), \ldots, X_n = (x_n^0, x_n^1)\big) = (x_2^b, x_3^b, \ldots, x_n^b).$$

Proof. We prove Thm 2 by contradiction. Let Π be a protocol that computes $f_{\mathtt{mot}}$ with fairness by using broadcast only in the second round. Consider an execution of Π where X_i denotes the input of P_i. We describe a sequence of scenarios $C_1, \ldots, C_n, C_n^*$. In each scenario, P_1 and at most one other party is corrupt. In all the scenarios, the corrupt parties behave honestly (in particular, they use their honest inputs), but may drop incoming or outgoing messages.

At a high-level, the sequence of scenarios is designed so that corrupt P_1 drops her first-round message to one additional honest party in each scenario. We show that in each scenario, the adversary manages to obtain the output computed with respect to $X_1 = b$ and (at least some of) the honest parties' inputs. This leads to a contradiction, because the final scenario involves no first-round messages from P_1 related to its input $X_1 = b$, but the adversary is still able to learn x_i^b corresponding to some honest P_i. In particular, this implies that the adversary is able to re-compute second-round messages from P_1 with different choices of input X_1, obtaining multiple outputs (on different inputs).

Before describing the scenarios in detail, we define some useful notation. Let $(X_1, \ldots, X_n)$ denote a specific combination of inputs that are fixed across all scenarios. Let $\mu = negl$ denote the negligible probability with which the security of Π breaks. We assume, without loss of generality, that the second round of Π involves broadcast communication alone (as given a PKI and a broadcast channel, point-to-point communication can be realized by broadcasting encryptions of the private messages using the public key of the recipient). Let $\widetilde{\mathsf{msg}}_i^2$ denote P_i's second-round broadcast message, computed honestly given that P_i did not receive the private message (i.e. the communication over point-to-point channel) from P_1 in the first round.

Scenario C_1: P_1 is corrupt.
  Round 1: P_1 behaves honestly (i.e. follows the instructions of Π).
  Round 2: P_1 behaves honestly.

Since everyone behaved honestly, it follows from correctness that P_1 obtains the output $y = f_{\mathsf{mot}}(x_1, \ldots, x_n) = (x_2^b, x_3^b, \ldots, x_n^b)$ with probability at least $1 - \mu$.

Scenario C_2: P_1 and P_2 are corrupt.
  Round 1: P_1 and P_2 behave honestly.
  Round 2: P_1 remains silent. P_2 pretends she did not receive a first-round message from P_1. In more detail, P_2 sends $\widetilde{\mathsf{msg}}_2^2$ over broadcast channel.

The adversary's view subsumes her view in the previous scenario, so the adversary learns the output $y = (x_2^b, x_3^b, \ldots, x_n^b)$ which allows her to learn x_i^b corresponding to each honest P_i. It follows from the security of Π that honest parties also obtain x_i^b corresponding to each honest P_i (i.e. for $i \in [n] \backslash \{1, 2\}$) with probability at least $1 - \mu$. If not, then either correctness or fairness is violated, which contradicts our assumption that Π is secure.

Scenario C_3: P_1 and P_3 are corrupt.
  Round 1: P_1 behaves honestly, but does not send a message to P_2. P_3 behaves honestly.
  Round 2: P_1 remains silent. P_3 pretends that she did not receive a first-round message from P_1 (i.e. she sends $\widetilde{\mathsf{msg}}_3^2$ via broadcast).

The adversary's view subsumes the view of an honest P_3 in Scenario C_2 (which includes $\widetilde{\mathsf{msg}}_2^2$); so, the adversary learns $\{x_i^b\}_{i \in [n] \backslash \{1,2\}}$ with probability at least $1 - \mu$. By the fairness of Π, when the adversary obtains this information, honest parties $P_2, P_4, P_5, \ldots, P_n$ must also learn x_i^b corresponding to each honest P_i (i.e. for $i \in [n] \backslash \{1,3\}$).[4] Since the fairness of Π breaks with probability at most μ, parties $P_2, P_4, P_5, \ldots, P_n$ learn $\{x_i^b\}_{i \in [n] \backslash \{1,3\}}$ with probability at least $1 - 2\mu$.

Scenario C_4: P_1 and P_4 are corrupt.
> **Round 1:** P_1 behaves honestly, except that she does not send a message to P_2 and P_3. P_4 behaves honestly.
> **Round 2:** P_1 remains silent. P_4 pretends that she did not receive a first-round message from P_1 (i.e. she sends $\widetilde{\mathsf{msg}}_4^2$ via broadcast).

The adversary's view subsumes the view of an honest P_4 in Scenario C_3 (which includes $\widetilde{\mathsf{msg}}_j^2$, where $j \in \{2,3\}$). Therefore, the adversary learns $\{x_i^b\}_{i \in [n] \backslash \{1,3\}}$ with probability at least $1 - 2\mu$. By the security of Π, honest $P_2, P_3, P_5, \ldots, P_n$ must also obtain x_i^b corresponding to each honest P_i (i.e. for $i \in [n] \backslash \{1,4\}$). Since the security of Π breaks with probability at most μ, parties $P_2, P_3, P_5, \ldots, P_n$ learn $\{x_i^b\}_{i \in [n] \backslash \{1,4\}}$ with probability at least $1 - 3\mu$.

Generalizing the above for $k = 3$ to n:

Scenario C_k: P_1 and P_k are corrupt.
> **Round 1:** P_1 behaves honestly, except that she does not send a message to $P_2, P_3, \ldots, P_{k-1}$. P_k behaves honestly.
> **Round 2:** P_1 remains silent. P_k pretends that she did not receive a first-round message from P_1 (i.e. she sends $\widetilde{\mathsf{msg}}_k^2$ via broadcast).

The adversary's view subsumes the view of an honest P_k in Scenario C_{k-1} (which includes messages $\widetilde{\mathsf{msg}}_j^2$, where $j \in \{2, \ldots, k-1\}$). Thus, the adversary learns $\{x_i^b\}_{i \in [n] \backslash \{1,k-1\}}$ with probability at least $1 - (k-2)\mu$. By the security of Π, honest parties should obtain x_i^b corresponding to each honest P_i (i.e. for $i \in [n] \backslash \{1,k\}$). Since the security of Π breaks with probability at most μ, honest parties learn the values x_i^b with probability at least $1 - (k-2)\mu - \mu = 1 - (k-1)\mu$.

Finally, we describe the last scenario:

Scenario C_n^*: P_1 and P_n are corrupt.
> **Round 1:** P_1 remains silent. P_n behaves honestly.
> **Round 2:** P_1 and P_n remain silent.

The adversary's view subsumes her view in Scenario C_n (which includes messages $\widetilde{\mathsf{msg}}_j^2$, where $j \in \{1, \ldots, n-1\}$). Thus, in Scenario C_n^*, the adversary is able to learn $\{x_i^b\}_{i \in [n] \backslash \{1,n-1\}}$ with probability at least $1 - (n-1)\mu$. This leads us to the

---

[4] Note that we conclude that the honest parties learn x_2^b, which the adversary may, for some reason, not have learned. This is because in the ideal functionality, output is considered as a single unit of information; fairness requires that if the adversary learns *any* output it could not have obtained solely from its own inputs, then the honest parties must learn the *entire* output.

final contradiction: C_n^* does not involve any message from P_1 related to the input $X_1 = b$, but the adversary was able to obtain $\{x_i^b\}_{i \in [n] \setminus \{1, n-1\}}$. This implies that the adversary can compute $\{x_i^{b'}\}_{i \in [n] \setminus \{1, n-1\}}$ with respect to any input $X_1 = b'$ of her choice. This "residual attack" breaks the privacy property of the protocol, as it allows the adversary to learn both input strings of an honest P_i. (which is not allowed as per the ideal realization of $f_{\texttt{mot}}$).

Lastly, we note that the above proof requires that the function computed is such that each party receives the output. This is because the inference in Scenario C_k ($k \in [n]$) relies on the adversary obtaining output on behalf of P_k.

5   Completing the Picture: Impossibility Results for $n \leq 3t$

In the previous two sections, we showed the impossibility of unanimous abort when no broadcast is available, and the impossibility of fairness when broadcast is only available in the second round. However, both of those impossibility results only hold for $t > 1$. In this section, using different techniques, we extend those results to the case when $t = 1$ and $n = 3$. In our impossibility results in this section, we use a property which we call *last message resiliency*.

Definition 7 (Last Message Resiliency).   *A protocol is t-last message resiliency if, in an honest execution, any protocol participant P_i can compute its output without using t of the messages it received in the last round.*

More formally, consider a protocol Π = $\{(\texttt{frst-msg}_i, \texttt{snd-msg}_i, \texttt{output}_i)\}_{i \in [1, \ldots, n]}$. The protocol is t-last message resilient if, for each $i \in [1, \ldots, n]$ and each $S \subseteq \{1, \ldots, n\} \setminus \{i\}$ such that $|S| \leq t$, the output function $\texttt{output}_i$ returns the correct output even without second round messages from parties $P_i, i \in S$. That is, for all security parameters λ, for all sets $S \subseteq \{1, \ldots, n\} \setminus \{i\}$ such that $|S| \leq t$, for all inputs $x_1, \ldots, x_n$,

$$\Pr \left(\begin{array}{c} \texttt{output}_i(x_i, \texttt{msg}^1_{1 \to i}, \ldots, \texttt{msg}^1_{n \to i}, \tilde{\texttt{msg}}^2_{1 \to i}, \ldots, \tilde{\texttt{msg}}^2_{n \to i}) \\ \neq \texttt{output}_i(x_i, \texttt{msg}^1_{1 \to i}, \ldots, \texttt{msg}^1_{n \to i}, \texttt{msg}^2_{1 \to i}, \ldots, \texttt{msg}^2_{n \to i}) \end{array} \right) = negl(\lambda)$$

over the randomness used in the protocol, where, for $j \in [1, \ldots, n]$,

$$(\texttt{msg}^1_{j \to 1}, \ldots, \texttt{msg}^1_{j \to n}) \leftarrow \texttt{frst-msg}_j(x_j),$$

$$(\texttt{msg}^2_{j \to 1}, \ldots, \texttt{msg}^2_{j \to n}) \leftarrow \texttt{snd-msg}_j(x_j, \texttt{msg}^1_{1 \to j}, \ldots, \texttt{msg}^1_{n \to j}),$$

and

$$\tilde{\texttt{msg}}^2_{j \to i} = \begin{cases} \texttt{msg}^2_{j \to i}, & \textit{if } j \notin S, \\ \bot & \textit{otherwise.} \end{cases}$$

Theorem 3. *Any protocol Π which achieves secure computation with unanimous abort with corruption threshold t and whose last round can be executed over peer-to-peer channels must be t-last message resilient.*

Proof. We prove this by contradiction. Assume Π achieves unanimous abort, and is not t-resilient. Then, by definition, there exist inputs $x_1, \ldots, x_n$, an $i \in [1, \ldots, n]$ and a subset $S \subseteq \{1, \ldots, n\} \backslash \{i\}$ (such that $|S| \leq t$) where, with non-negligible probability,

$$\text{output}_i(x_i, \text{msg}^1_{1 \to i}, \ldots, \text{msg}^1_{n \to i}, \tilde{\text{msg}}^2_{1 \to i}, \ldots, \tilde{\text{msg}}^2_{n \to i})$$
$$\neq \text{output}_i(x_i, \text{msg}^1_{1 \to i}, \ldots, \text{msg}^1_{n \to i}, \text{msg}^2_{1 \to i}, \ldots, \text{msg}^2_{n \to i})$$

(where the messages are produced in the way described in Definition 7).

The adversary can use this by corrupting P_j, $j \in S$; it will behave honestly, except in the last round, where $P_j, j \in S$ will not send messages to P_i. (Note that the ability to send last round messages to some parties but not others relies on the fact that the last round is over peer-to-peer channels.) With non-negligible probability, P_i will receive an incorrect output (e.g. an abort). However, this cannot occur in a protocol with unanimous abort; all other honest parties must accept the protocol and produce the correct output (since their views are the same as in an entirely honest execution), so P_i must as well.

Theorem 4. *Any protocol Π which achieves secure computation with fairness with corruption threshold t must be t-last message resilient.*

Proof. We prove this by contradiction. Assume Π achieves fairness, and is not t-resilient. Then, by definition, there exist inputs $x_1, \ldots, x_n$, an $i \in [1, \ldots, n]$ and a subset $S \subseteq \{1, \ldots, n\} \backslash \{i\}$ (such that $|S| \leq t$) where, with non-negligible probability,

$$\text{output}_i(x_i, \text{msg}^1_{1 \to i}, \ldots, \text{msg}^1_{n \to i}, \tilde{\text{msg}}^2_{1 \to i}, \ldots, \tilde{\text{msg}}^2_{n \to i})$$
$$\neq \text{output}_i(x_i, \text{msg}^1_{1 \to i}, \ldots, \text{msg}^1_{n \to i}, \text{msg}^2_{1 \to i}, \ldots, \text{msg}^2_{n \to i}).$$

(where the messages are produced in the way described in Definition 7).

The adversary can use this by corrupting P_j, $j \in S$. As in the previous proof, it will behave honestly, except in the last round, where $P_j, j \in S$ will not send messages to P_i. With non-negligible probability, P_i will receive an incorrect output (e.g. an abort), while the rushing adversary will learn the output, since it will have all of the messages it would have gotten in a fully honest execution of the protocol. This violates fairness.[5]

Theorem 5. *There exists a function f such that any protocol Π securely realizing f with corruption threshold t such that $n \leq 3t$ and whose first round can be executed over peer-to-peer channels cannot be t-last message resilient.*

Proof. Consider the function f_{mot} described in the proof of Thm 2, where party P_1 provides as input a choice bit $X_1 = b \in \{0, 1\}$ and every other party P_i provides as input a pair of strings i.e. $X_i = (x_i^0, x_i^1)$.

---

[5] Note that while P_i does not learn the output, other honest parties might. However, even one honest party not receiving the output is a violation of fairness if the adversary learns the output.

Consider an adversary corrupting P_1. The adversary should clearly be unable to recompute the function with multiple inputs, e.g., with respect to both $X_1 = 0$ and $X_1 = 1$ (as this will allow it to learn both the input strings of the honest parties which is in contrast to an ideal execution, where it can learn exactly one of the input strings).

We now show that, in a t-last message resilient (where $n \leq 3t$) two-round protocol Π where the first round is over peer-to-peer channels, P_1 can always learn both of those outputs. Consider a corrupt P_1, and partition the honest parties into two sets of equal size (assuming for simplicity that the number of honest parties is even): S_0 and S_1. Note that $|S_0| = |S_1| = \frac{n-t}{2} \leq t$.

P_1 uses $X_1 = 0$ to compute its first round messages to S_0; it uses $X_1 = 1$ to compute its first round messages to S_1. (Note that the ability to send first round messages based on different inputs relies on the fact that the first round is over peer-to-peer channels.) All other parties behave honestly. Because the protocol Π is t-last message resilient, and because S_1 contains t or fewer parties, P_1 has enough second round messages excluding those it received from S_1 to compute its output. Note that all second round messages except for those received from S_1 are distributed exactly as in an honest execution with $X_1 = 0$; therefore, by last message resiliency, P_1 learns $(x_2^0, x_3^0, \ldots, x_n^0)$ (as per the definition of $f_{\mathtt{mot}}$). Similarly, by excluding second round messages it received from S_0, P_1 learns the output $(x_2^1, x_3^1, \ldots, x_n^1)$ i.e. the output computed based on $X_1 = 1$. This is clearly a violation of privacy.

Corollary 2 (P2P-P2P, UA, $n \leq 3t$). *Secure computation of general functions with unanimous abort cannot be achieved in two rounds of peer-to-peer communication for corruption threshold t such that $n \leq 3t$.*

This corollary follows directly from Theorems 3 and 5.

Remark 1. Note that for $t > 1$, Cor 2 is subsumed by Cor 1. However, Cor 2 covers the case of $t = 1$ and $n = 3$, closing the question of unanimous abort with honest majority in two rounds of peer-to-peer communication.

Corollary 3. (P2P-BC, FAIR, $n \leq 3t$). *Secure computation of general functions with fairness cannot be achieved in two rounds the first of which is over peer-to-peer channels for corruption threshold t such that $n \leq 3t$.*

This corollary follows from Theorems 4 and 5.

6 Broadcast in the First Round: Guaranteed Output Delivery

In this section, we argue that *any* protocol that achieves guaranteed output delivery in two rounds of broadcast also achieves guaranteed output delivery when broadcast is available in the first round only. We first show that if the protocol achieves guaranteed output delivery with corruption threshold t in two rounds of broadcast, it achieves the same guarantee with threshold $t-1$ when the second round is over peer-to-peer channels. We next show that if the first-round messages commit corrupt parties to their inputs, the second round can be run over peer-to-peer channels with no loss in corruption budget.

Theorem 6. *Let Π_{bc}^{god} be a two broadcast-round protocol that securely computes the function f with guaranteed output delivery against an adversary corrupting t parties. Then Π_{bc}^{god} achieves the same guarantee when the second round is run over peer-to-peer channels but with $t - 1$ corruptions.*

Proof (Sketch). Let $\tilde{\Pi}_{bc}^{god}$ denote the protocol where the second round is run over peer-to-peer channels but with $t - 1$ corruptions. Towards a contradiction, assume $\tilde{\Pi}_{bc}^{god}$ is not secure against $(t-1)$ corruptions; in particular, assume that there is an adversary $\tilde{\mathcal{A}}$ that breaks security.

We first observe that $\tilde{\mathcal{A}}$ certainly can't cause honest parties to abort in $\tilde{\Pi}_{bc}^{god}$ by sending them incorrect things in the second round, since Π_{bc}^{god} achieves guaranteed output delivery, meaning that honest parties do not abort no matter what $\tilde{\mathcal{A}}$ does. Therefore, all $\tilde{\mathcal{A}}$ can hope for is to cause disagreement in $\tilde{\Pi}_{bc}^{god}$. In particular, $\tilde{\mathcal{A}}$ can send different second-round messages to different honest parties, hoping that honest parties end up with outputs computed on different corrupt party inputs. However, if $\tilde{\mathcal{A}}$ could do that, we could use $\tilde{\mathcal{A}}$ to build an adversary $\mathcal{A}$ that breaks the security of Π_{bc}^{god} by corrupting one additional honest party, mentally sending different messages to it, and obtaining the output on two different sets of its own inputs.

Suppose $\tilde{\mathcal{A}}$ can make a pair of honest parties in $\tilde{\Pi}_{bc}^{god}$—P_i and P_j—obtain different outputs by sending different second-round messages to them. Then, we construct our adversary $\mathcal{A}$ for Π_{bc}^{god} as follows. $\mathcal{A}$ corrupts the same $t - 1$ parties as $\tilde{\mathcal{A}}$, as well as one additional honest party—P_i—who will behave semi-honestly. $\mathcal{A}$ uses the second-round messages sent by $\tilde{\mathcal{A}}$ to P_j as her broadcast second-round messages in Π_{bc}^{god}. However, $\mathcal{A}$ also computes what P_i's output would have been if she had broadcast the second-round messages sent by $\tilde{\mathcal{A}}$ to P_i. This allows $\mathcal{A}$ to obtain the output on behalf of P_i on two different sets of inputs, breaking the security of Π_{bc}^{god} (and completing the proof). ∎

Theorem 7. *Let Π_{bc}^{god} be a two broadcast-round protocol that securely computes the function f with guaranteed output delivery with the additional constraint that a simulator can extract inputs from the first-round messages and it is efficient to check whether a given second-round message is correct. Then Π_{bc}^{god} achieves the same guarantee when the second round is run over point-to-point channels.*

Proof (Sketch). Starting from the protocol Π_{bc}^{god} it is possible to define another protocol Π_{bcp2p}^{god} that has the following modifications: (1) the second round messages of Π_{bc}^{god} are sent over point-to-point channels and (2) the honest parties compute their output based on all the first round messages and the subset C of second round messages that are generated correctly. (Observe that $|C| \geq n - t$, because at least $n - t$ parties are honest.)

Relying on the GOD security of $\Pi_{\text{bc}}^{\text{god}}$, it is possible to claim that $\Pi_{\text{bcp2p}}^{\text{god}}$ also achieves GOD. This follows from two important observations. First, since the input is extracted from the first round of $\Pi_{\text{bcp2p}}^{\text{god}}$ which is over broadcast, the adversary cannot cause disagreement among the honest parties with respect to her input (i.e. she cannot send messages based on different inputs to different honest parties). Second, in $\Pi_{\text{bcp2p}}^{\text{god}}$ the honest parties are always able to compute the output; otherwise, the honest parties in $\Pi_{\text{bc}}^{\text{god}}$ would not have been able to compute an output when $\mathcal{A}$ does not send any second round message, which contradicts GOD security.

Next, we observe that the two broadcast-round protocol of Gordon et al. [GLS15] has the two properties required by Thm 7. The protocol of Gordon et al. [GLS15] uses zero knowledge proofs to compile a semi-malicious protocol into a fully malicious one. The zero knowledge proofs accompanying the first round messages can be used for input extraction; the zero knowledge proofs accompanying the second round messages can be used to efficiently determine which of these second round messages are generated correctly.

7   One-or-Nothing Secret Sharing

In Sect. 8, we will show a protocol that achieves security with identifiable abort in the honest majority setting in two rounds, only the second of which is over broadcast. In this section, we introduce an important building block for that protocol which we call *one-or-nothing secret sharing*.

We define one-or-nothing secret sharing as a new flavor of secret sharing wherein the dealer can share a *vector* of secrets. While traditional secret sharing schemes are designed for receivers to eventually publish their shares and recover the entirety of what was shared, one-or-nothing secret sharing is designed for receivers to eventually recover *at most one* of the shared values. While reconstruction usually requires each party to contribute its entire share, in one-or-nothing secret sharing, each party instead *votes* on the index of the value to reconstruct by producing a "ballot" based on its secret share. If two parties vote for different indices, the set of published ballots should reveal nothing about any of the values. However, some parties are allowed to equivocate—they might be unsure which index they wish to vote for, so they will support the preference of the majority. If a majority votes for the same index, and the rest equivocate, the ballots enable the recovery of the value at that index.

Our secure computation construction in Sect. 8 uses one-or-nothing secret sharing to share labels for garbled circuits. However, we imagine one-or-nothing secret sharing might be of independent interest, e.g. in voting scenarios where unanimity among the decided voters is important.

7.1   Definitions

Syntax. The natural syntax for a one-or-nothing secret sharing scheme consists of a tuple of three algorithms $(\texttt{share}, \texttt{vote}, \texttt{reconstruct})$.

$\mathtt{share}(x^{(1)}, \ldots, x^{(l)}) \to (s, s_1, \ldots, s_n)$ is an algorithm that takes l values $x^{(1)}$, $\ldots, x^{(l)}$, and produces the secret shares $s_1, \ldots, s_n$, as well as the public share s.

$\mathtt{vote}(s, s_i, v) \to \bar{s}_i$ is an algorithm that takes the public share s, a secret share s_i, and a vote v, where $v \in \{1, \ldots, l, \bot\}$ can either be an index of a value, or it can be $\bot$ if party i is unsure which value it wants to vote for. It outputs a public ballot $\bar{s}_i$.

$\mathtt{reconstruct}(s, \bar{s}_1, \ldots, \bar{s}_n) \to \{x^{(v)}, \bot\}$ is an algorithm that takes the public share s, all of the ballots $\bar{s}_1, \ldots, \bar{s}_n$, and outputs either the value $x^{(v)}$ which received a majority of votes, or outputs $\bot$.

Non-Interactive One-or-Nothing Secret Sharing. We modify this natural syntax to ensure that each party can vote even if they have not received a secret share. This is important in case e.g. the dealer is corrupt, and chooses not to distribute shares properly. We call such a scheme a *non-interactive* one-or-nothing secret sharing scheme. A non-interactive one-or-nothing secret sharing scheme consists of a tuple of four algorithms ($\mathtt{setup}, \mathtt{share}, \mathtt{vote}, \mathtt{reconstruct}$).

$\mathtt{setup}(1^\lambda) \to \mathsf{sk}$ is an algorithm that produces a key shared between the dealer and one of the receivers. (This can be non-interactively derived by both dealer and receiver by running $\mathtt{setup}$ on randomness obtained from e.g. key exchange.)

$\mathtt{share}(\mathsf{sk}_1, \ldots, \mathsf{sk}_n, x^{(1)}, \ldots, x^{(l)}) \to s$ is an algorithm that takes the n shared keys $\mathsf{sk}_1, \ldots, \mathsf{sk}_n$ and the l values $x^{(1)}, \ldots, x^{(l)}$, and produces a public share s.

$\mathtt{vote}(\mathsf{sk}_i, v) \to \bar{s}_i$ is an algorithm that takes a secret share s_i and a vote v, where $v \in \{1, \ldots, l, \bot\}$ can either be an index of a value, or it can be $\bot$ if party i is unsure which value it wants to vote for. It outputs a public ballot $\bar{s}_i$.

$\mathtt{reconstruct}(s, \bar{s}_1, \ldots, \bar{s}_n) \to \{x^{(v)}, \bot\}$ is an algorithm that takes the public share s, all of the ballots $\bar{s}_1, \ldots, \bar{s}_n$, and outputs either the value $x^{(v)}$ which received a majority of votes, or outputs $\bot$.

Security. We require three properties of one-or-nothing secret sharing: *correctness*, *privacy* (which requires that if fewer than $t + 1$ parties vote for an index, the value at that index stays hidden) and *contradiction-privacy* (which requires that if two parties vote for different indices, all values stay hidden). Below we define these formally for *non-interactive* one-or-nothing secret sharing.

Definition 8 (One-or-Nothing Secret Sharing: Correctness). *Informally, this property requires that when at least $n - t$ parties produce their ballot using the same v (and the rest produce their ballot with $\bot$), $\mathtt{reconstruct}$ returns $x^{(v)}$. (When $t = \frac{n}{2} - 1$, $n - t$ is a majority.)*

More formally, a one-or-nothing secret sharing scheme is correct *if for any security parameter $\lambda \in \mathbb{N}$, any vector of secrets $(x^{(1)}, \ldots, x^{(l)})$, any index $v \in [l]$*

and any subset $S \subseteq [n], |S| \geq n - t,$

$$\Pr \left[x = x^{(v)} : \begin{array}{c} \mathrm{sk}_i \leftarrow \mathrm{setup}(1^\lambda) \ for \ i \in [n] \\ s \leftarrow \mathrm{share}(\mathrm{sk}_1, \ldots, \mathrm{sk}_n, x^{(1)}, \ldots, x^{(l)}) \\ \overline{s}_i \leftarrow \mathrm{vote}(\mathrm{sk}_i, v) \ for \ i \in S \\ \overline{s}_i \leftarrow \mathrm{vote}(\mathrm{sk}_i, \bot) \ for \ i \in [n] \backslash S \\ x \leftarrow \mathrm{reconstruct}(s, \overline{s}_1, \ldots, \overline{s}_n) \end{array} \right] \geq 1 - negl(\lambda),$$

where the probability is taken over the random coins of the algorithms.

Definition 9 (One-or-Nothing Secret Sharing: Privacy). *Informally, this property requires that when no honest parties produce their ballot using* v*, then the adversary learns nothing about* $x^{(v)}$*.*

More formally, a one-or-nothing secret sharing scheme is private *if for any security parameter* $\lambda \in \mathbb{N}$*, for every PPT adversary* $\mathcal{A}$*, it holds that*

$$\Pr[\mathcal{A} \ wins] \leq \frac{1}{2} + negl(\lambda)$$

in the following experiment:

Definition 10 (One-or-Nothing Secret Sharing: Contradiction-Privacy). *Informally, this property requires that if two different parties produce their ballots using different votes* $v_i \neq v_j$ *such that* $v_i \neq \bot$ *and* $v_j \neq \bot$*, then the adversary should learn nothing at all.*

More formally, a one-or-nothing secret sharing scheme is contradiction-private *if for any security parameter* $\lambda \in \mathbb{N}$*, for every PPT adversary* $\mathcal{A}$*, it holds that*

$$\Pr[\mathcal{A} \ wins] \leq \frac{1}{2} + negl(\lambda)$$

in the following experiment:

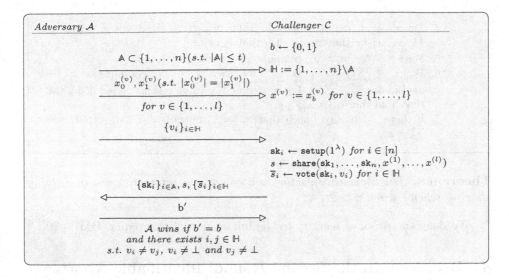

7.2   Constructions

A first attempt would be to additively share all the values $x^{(1)}, \ldots, x^{(l)}$. However, this fails because if all of the honest parties compute vote on $\perp$ (by e.g. publishing both their additive shares), the adversary will be able to reconstruct all of the values, violating privacy (Definition 9).

Instead, we instantiate a non-interactive one-or-nothing secret sharing scheme as follows, using a symmetric encryption scheme $\mathsf{SKE} = (\mathsf{keygen}, \mathsf{enc}, \mathsf{dec})$ (defined in the full version of this paper [DMR+20]).

Figure 7.1: Non-Interactive One-or-Nothing Secret Sharing

$\mathsf{setup}(1^\lambda) \to \mathsf{sk}$: Choose $l+1$ symmetric encryption keys $\mathsf{k}^{(1)}, \ldots, \mathsf{k}^{(l)}, \mathsf{k}^{(\perp)}$ using $\mathsf{SKE.keygen}(1^\lambda)$. Let $\mathsf{sk} = (\mathsf{k}^{(1)}, \ldots, \mathsf{k}^{(l)}, \mathsf{k}^{(\perp)})$.

$\mathsf{share}(\mathsf{sk}_1, \ldots, \mathsf{sk}_n, x^{(1)}, \ldots, x^{(l)}) \to s$:

1. Compute $(x_1^{(v)}, \ldots, x_n^{(v)})$ as the additive sharing of $x^{(v)}$ for $v \in [l]$.
2. Compute $(x_{i \to 1}^{(v)}, \ldots, x_{i \to n}^{(v)})$ as the threshold sharing of $x_i^{(v)}$ with threshold t for $v \in [l]$, $i \in [n]$.
3. Parse $(\mathsf{k}_i^{(1)}, \ldots, \mathsf{k}_i^{(l)}, \mathsf{k}_i^{(\perp)}) = \mathsf{sk}_i$ for $i \in [n]$.
4. Compute $c_i^{(v)} = \mathsf{enc}(\mathsf{k}_i^{(v)}, x_i^{(v)})$ for $v \in [l]$, $i \in [n]$.
5. Compute $c_{i \to j}^{(v)} = \mathsf{enc}(\mathsf{k}_i^{(\perp)}, \mathsf{enc}(\mathsf{k}_j^{(v)}, x_{i \to j}^{(v)}))$ for $v \in [l]$, $i \in [n]$, $j \in [n]$.
6. Output $s = (\{c_i^{(v)}\}_{i \in [n], v \in [l]}, \{c_{i \to j}^{(v)}\}_{i,j \in [n], v \in [l]})$.

$\mathsf{vote}(\mathsf{sk}_i, v) \to \overline{s}_i$ where $v \in \{1, \ldots, l, \perp\}$: Output $\overline{s}_i = (v, \mathsf{k}_i^{(v)})$.

$\mathsf{reconstruct}(s, \overline{s}_1, \ldots, \overline{s}_n) \to \{x^{(v)}, \perp\}$:

1. Parse $(\{c_i^{(v)}\}_{i \in [n], v \in [l]}, \{c_{i \to j}^{(v)}\}_{i,j \in [n], v \in [l]}) = s$.
2. Parse $(v_i, \mathsf{k}_i) = \overline{s}_i$ for $i \in [n]$.
3. If there does not exist a $v \in \{1, \ldots, l\}$ such that at least $(n-t)$ parties vote for v and everyone else votes for $\perp$, output $\perp$.

4. Let $v \neq \bot$ denote the only value which received votes; let $S \subseteq \{1, \ldots, n\}$ be the set of i such that $v_i = v$.
5. For $i \in S$ (so, $v_i = v$), compute $x_i = \mathsf{dec}(\mathtt{k}_i, c_i^{(v)})$.
6. For $i \notin S$ (so, $v_i = \bot$), for each $j \in S$, compute $x_{i \to j} = \mathsf{dec}\big(\mathtt{k}_i, \mathsf{dec}(\mathtt{k}_j, c_{i \to j}^{(v)})\big)$. Let x_i denote the value reconstructed using the threshold shares $\{x_{i \to j}\}_{j \in S}$.
7. If there exists any i such that $x_i = \bot$, output $\bot$. Else, output $x = \sum_{i=1}^{n} x_i$.

Theorem 8. *The above construction is a secure non-interactive one-or-nothing sharing scheme when $n > 2t$.*

We defer the proof of security to the full version of this paper [DMR+20].

8   Broadcast in the Second Round: Identifiable Abort

In this section, we show a protocol achieving secure computation with identifiable abort in two rounds, with the first round only using peer-to-peer channels, when $t < \frac{n}{2}$.

One could hope that executing a protocol Π_{bc} that requires two rounds of broadcast over one round of peer-to-peer channels followed by one round of broadcast will simply work, just like in the case of one round of broadcast followed by one round of peer-to-peer channels (Sect. 6). However, this is not the case. When the first round is over peer-to-peer channels, the danger is that corrupt parties might send inconsistent messages to honest parties in that round. Allowing honest parties to compute their second-round messages based on inconsistent first-round messages might violate security. So, we must somehow guarantee that all honest-party second-round messages are based on the same set of first-round messages.

Our protocol follows the structure of the protocols described by Cohen *et al.* [CGZ20]. It is described as a compiler that takes a protocol Π_{bc} which achieves the desired guarantees given two rounds of broadcast, and achieves those same guarantees in the broadcast pattern we are interested in, which has broadcast available in the second round only. In the compiler of Cohen *et al.*, to ensure that honest parties base their second-round messages on the same view of the first round, parties garble and broadcast their second-message functions. In more detail, in the first round the parties secret share all the labels for their garbled circuit using additive secret sharing, and send their first-round message from the underlying protocol to each of their peers. In the second round (over broadcast), each party sends their garbled second-message function, and for each bit of first-round message she receives, she forwards her share of the corresponding label in everyone else's garbled circuit. The labels corresponding to *the same set of first-round messages* are reconstructed for each party's garbled second-message function, thus guaranteeing consistency.

We use a similar approach. However, as mentioned in the introduction, there are other challenges to address when our goal is identifiable (as opposed to unanimous) abort. In the techniques of Cohen *et al.*, in the second round, for each bit of every first-round message, every party P_i must forward to everyone else exactly one of a pair of shares of labels which P_i should have obtained from every other party P_j. However, since the first round is over peer-to-peer channels, P_i can claim that it didn't get the shares of labels from P_j, and the computation must still complete (i.e. the correct label needs to be reconstructed), since it is unclear who to blame—P_i or P_j [6]

An alternative approach might be to use *threshold* secret sharing instead of additive secret sharing to share the garbled labels. In order to ensure that honest parties can either identify a cheater or reconstruct at least one of each pair of labels, we would need to set our secret sharing threshold to be at most $n - t$. However, when $t = \frac{n}{2} - 1$, the adversary only needs one additional honest party's share to reconstruct any given label. If she sends different first-round messages to different honest parties, they will contribute shares of different labels, enabling the adversary to reconstruct both labels for some input wires. This allows the adversary to violate honest parties' privacy.

This is where our *non-interactive one-or-nothing secret sharing* primitive comes into play. Parties can use it to secret share the pair of labels for each wire of their garbled circuit *by only broadcasting one value—the public share—in the second round*. By the non-interactive design of the one-or-nothing secret sharing scheme, parties don't even need to have seen the public share to contribute to reconstruction, so no party can claim to be unable to contribute. The privacy properties of the scheme guarantee that at most one label per wire will be recovered. Moreover, if an honest party is not sure which label share to choose (which may happen if she did not get a valid first-round message of Π_{bc}), she can still enable the recovery of the appropriate label (by contributing an equivocation ballot).

We also have to consider how to identify an adversary that sends different first-round messages *from the underlying protocol* to different honest parties. We thus require each party P_i to sign these first-round messages; each other party P_j will only act upon first-round messages from P_i with valid signatures, and echo those messages (and signatures). In this way, we can identify P_i as a cheater as long as she included valid signatures with her inconsistent messages. If she did not, then either enough parties will complain about P_i to implicate her, or the equivocation ballots will allow the computation to complete anyway.

At a very high level, our protocol can be described as follows. In the first round, the parties send their first-round message of Π_{bc} along with a signature to each of their peers. In the second round (over broadcast), the parties do the following: (1) compute a garbling of their second-message function; (2) secret share all the labels for their garbled circuit using the one-or-nothing secret sharing; (3) vote for the share of the corresponding label (based on the first-round message

---

[6] Note that this is not an issue in the protocol with unanimous abort of Cohen *et al.* since if the reconstruction of the label fails, the honest parties can simply abort.

received) in everyone else's garbled circuit; (4) compute a zero-knowledge proof to ensure the correctness of the actions taken in the second round; and (5) echo all the first-round messages of Π_{bc} with the corresponding signatures received from the other parties in the first round.

Intuitively, our protocol achieves identifiable abort due to the following. First, if a corrupt party is not caught, she must have sent a first-round message with a valid signature to at least one honest party; otherwise, $n - t > t$ parties would claim to have a conflict with her, which implicates her as a cheater (since at least one honest party is clearly accusing her). Second, she must *not* have sent two different first-round messages with valid signatures; otherwise, those two contradictory signatures would implicate her. Third, the zero-knowledge proof in the second round ensures that every corrupt party garbles and shares its garbled circuit labels correctly. We can conclude that, by the correctness property of the secret sharing scheme, if no party is caught, then one label from each label pair is reconstructed, and the underlying protocol Π_{bc} can be carried out.

We state the theorem below, and defer the formal description of the protocol to the full version of this paper [DMR+20].

Theorem 9 (P2P-BC, ID, $n > 2t$). *Let $\mathcal{F}$ be an efficiently computable n-party function and let $n > 2t$. Let Π_{bc} be a two broadcast-round protocol that securely computes $\mathcal{F}$ with identifiable abort with the additional constraint that the straight-line simulator can extract inputs from the first-round messages. Assuming a setup with CRS and PKI, and that $(\mathtt{garble}, \mathtt{eval}, \mathtt{simGC})$ is a secure garbling scheme, $(\mathtt{gen}, \mathtt{sign}, \mathtt{ver})$ is a digital signature scheme, $(\mathtt{share}, \mathtt{vote},$ $\mathtt{reconstruct}, \mathtt{verify})$ is a one-or-nothing secret sharing scheme, $(\mathtt{keygen},$ $\mathtt{keyagree})$ is a non-interactive key agreement scheme and $(\mathtt{setupZK}, \mathtt{prove},$ $\mathtt{verify}, \mathtt{simP}, \mathtt{simP.Extract})$ is a secure non-interactive zero-knowledge proof system. Then, there exists a protocol that securely computes $\mathcal{F}$ with identifiable abort over two rounds, the first of which is over peer-to-peer channels, and the second of which is over a broadcast channel.*

Remark 2. Note that when the underlying protocol Π_{bc} is instantiated using the protocols of Gordon *et al.* or Cohen *et al.* [GLS15, CGZ20], then our construction relies only on CRS and PKI (and does not require correlated randomness).

References

[ACGJ18] Ananth, P., Choudhuri, A.R., Goel, A., Jain, A.: Round-optimal secure multiparty computation with honest majority. In: Shacham, H., Boldyreva, A. (eds.) CRYPTO 2018, Part II. LNCS, vol. 10992, pp. 395–424. Springer, Cham (2018). https://doi.org/10.1007/978-3-319-96881-0_14

[ACGJ19] Ananth, P., Choudhuri, A.R., Goel, A., Jain, A.: Two round information-theoretic MPC with malicious security. In: Ishai, Y., Rijmen, V. (eds.) EUROCRYPT 2019, Part II. LNCS, vol. 11477, pp. 532–561. Springer, Cham (2019). https://doi.org/10.1007/978-3-030-17656-3_19

[BGI+01] Barak, B., et al.: On the (im)possibility of obfuscating programs. In: Kilian, J. (ed.) CRYPTO 2001. LNCS, vol. 2139, pp. 1–18. Springer, Heidelberg (2001). https://doi.org/10.1007/3-540-44647-8_1

[BGW88] Ben-Or, M., Goldwasser, S., Wigderson, A.: Completeness theorems for non-cryptographic fault-tolerant distributed computation (extended abstract). In: 20th ACM STOC. ACM Press, May 1988

[BMMR21] Badrinarayanan, S., Miao, P., Mukherjee, P., Ravi, D.: On the round complexity of fully secure solitary MPC with honest majority. Cryptology ePrint Archive, Report 2021/241 (2021). https://eprint.iacr.org/2021/241

[CCD88] Chaum, D., Crépeau, C., Damgård, I.: Multiparty unconditionally secure protocols (extended abstract). In: 20th ACM STOC. ACM Press, May 1988

[CD01] Cramer, R., Damgård, I.: Secure distributed linear algebra in a constant number of rounds. In: Kilian, J. (ed.) CRYPTO 2001. LNCS, vol. 2139, pp. 119–136. Springer, Heidelberg (2001). https://doi.org/10.1007/3-540-44647-8_7

[CGZ20] Cohen, R., Garay, J., Zikas, V.: Broadcast-optimal two-round MPC. In: Canteaut, A., Ishai, Y. (eds.) EUROCRYPT 2020, Part II. LNCS, vol. 12106, pp. 828–858. Springer, Cham (2020). https://doi.org/10.1007/978-3-030-45724-2_28

[Cle86] Cleve, R.: Limits on the security of coin flips when half the processors are faulty (extended abstract). In: 18th ACM STOC. ACM Press, May 1986

[DMR+20] Damgård, I., Magri, B., Ravi, D., Siniscalchi, L., Yakoubov, S.: Broadcast-optimal two round MPC with an honest majority. Cryptology ePrint Archive, Report 2020/1254 (2020). https://eprint.iacr.org/2020/1254

[DS83] Dolev, D., Raymond Strong, H.: Authenticated algorithms for byzantine agreement. SIAM J. Comput. 12(4), 656–666 (1983)

[FGMv02] Fitzi, M., Gisin, N., Maurer, U., von Rotz, O.: Unconditional byzantine agreement and multi-party computation secure against dishonest minorities from scratch. In: Knudsen, L.R. (ed.) EUROCRYPT 2002. LNCS, vol. 2332, pp. 482–501. Springer, Heidelberg (2002). https://doi.org/10.1007/3-540-46035-7_32

[FL82] Fischer, M.J., Lynch, N.A.: A lower bound for the time to assure interactive consistency. Inf. Process. Lett. 14(4), 183–186 (1982)

[GIKR01] Gennaro, R., Ishai, Y., Kushilevitz, E., Rabin, T.: The round complexity of verifiable secret sharing and secure multicast. In: 33rd ACM STOC. ACM Press, July 2001

[GIKR02] Gennaro, R., Ishai, Y., Kushilevitz, E., Rabin, T.: On 2-round secure multiparty computation. In: Yung, M. (ed.) CRYPTO 2002. LNCS, vol. 2442, pp. 178–193. Springer, Heidelberg (2002). https://doi.org/10.1007/3-540-45708-9_12

[GLS15] Dov Gordon, S., Liu, F.-H., Shi, E.: Constant-round MPC with fairness and guarantee of output delivery. In: Gennaro, R., Robshaw, M. (eds.) CRYPTO 2015, Part II. LNCS, vol. 9216, pp. 63–82. Springer, Heidelberg (2015). https://doi.org/10.1007/978-3-662-48000-7_4

[GMW87] Goldreich, O., Micali, S., Wigderson, A.: How to play any mental game or a completeness theorem for protocols with honest majority. In: 19th ACM STOC. ACM Press, May 1987

[GS18] Garg, S., Srinivasan, A.: Two-round multiparty secure computation from minimal assumptions. In: Nielsen, J.B., Rijmen, V. (eds.) EUROCRYPT 2018, Part II. LNCS, vol. 10821, pp. 468–499. Springer, Cham (2018). https://doi.org/10.1007/978-3-319-78375-8_16

[IK02] Ishai, Y., Kushilevitz, E.: Perfect constant-round secure computation via perfect randomizing polynomials. In: Widmayer, P., Eidenbenz, S., Triguero, F., Morales, R., Conejo, R., Hennessy, M. (eds.) ICALP 2002. LNCS, vol. 2380, pp. 244–256. Springer, Heidelberg (2002). https://doi.org/10.1007/3-540-45465-9_22

[IKKP15] Ishai, Y., Kumaresan, R., Kushilevitz, E., Paskin-Cherniavsky, A.: Secure computation with minimal interaction, revisited. In: Gennaro, R., Robshaw, M. (eds.) CRYPTO 2015, Part II. LNCS, vol. 9216, pp. 359–378. Springer, Heidelberg (2015). https://doi.org/10.1007/978-3-662-48000-7_18

[IKP10] Ishai, Y., Kushilevitz, E., Paskin, A.: Secure multiparty computation with minimal interaction. In: Rabin, T. (ed.) CRYPTO 2010. LNCS, vol. 6223, pp. 577–594. Springer, Heidelberg (2010). https://doi.org/10.1007/978-3-642-14623-7_31

[Lin01] Lindell, Y.: Parallel coin-tossing and constant-round secure two-party computation. In: Kilian, J. (ed.) CRYPTO 2001. LNCS, vol. 2139, pp. 171–189. Springer, Heidelberg (2001). https://doi.org/10.1007/3-540-44647-8_10

[PR18] Patra, A., Ravi, D.: On the exact round complexity of secure three-party computation. In: Shacham, H., Boldyreva, A. (eds.) CRYPTO 2018, Part II. LNCS, vol. 10992, pp. 425–458. Springer, Cham (2018). https://doi.org/10.1007/978-3-319-96881-0_15

[Yao86] Yao, A.C.-C.: How to generate and exchange secrets (extended abstract). In: 27th FOCS. IEEE Computer Society Press, October 1986

Three-Round Secure Multiparty Computation from Black-Box Two-Round Oblivious Transfer

Arpita Patra[1]($\boxtimes$) and Akshayaram Srinivasan[2]

[1] Indian Institute of Science, Bangalore, India
arpita@iisc.ac.in
[2] Tata Institute of Fundamental Research, Mumbai, India

Abstract. We give constructions of three-round secure multiparty computation (MPC) protocols for general functions that make *black-box* use of a two-round oblivious transfer (OT). For the case of semi-honest adversaries, we make use of a two-round, semi-honest secure OT in the plain model. This resolves the round-complexity of black-box (semi-honest) MPC protocols from minimal assumptions and answers an open question of Applebaum et al. (ITCS 2020). For the case of malicious adversaries, we make use of a two-round maliciously-secure OT in the common random/reference string model that satisfies a (mild) variant of adaptive security for the receiver.

1 Introduction

Secure Multiparty Computation (MPC) is a fundamental cryptographic primitive that allows a set of mutually distrusting parties to compute a joint function of their private inputs. The security guarantee provided here is that any adversary corrupting an arbitrary subset of the participating parties cannot learn anything about the inputs of the honest parties except what is leaked from the output of the function. The seminal feasibility results of Yao [36] and Goldreich, Micali, and Wigderson [20] showed that any multiparty functionality can be securely computed.

An important line of research in this area aims to construct efficient MPC protocols that minimizes the *number of rounds of communication*. The work of Beaver, Micali, and Rogaway [5] initiated this research direction and gave a construction of a constant-round protocol for computing general functions. On the lower bounds side, it is known that a single-round of communication is insufficient for securely computing most functionalities and hence, the minimum number of rounds needed to securely compute general functions is two.

A recent line of work has led to constructions of round-optimal (i.e., two-round) secure multiparty computation protocols under various cryptographic assumptions. The work of Garg et al. [14] gave a construction of such a protocol based on indistinguishability obfuscation [4,15] and subsequent work of Gordon et al. [21] improved the assumption to a witness encryption scheme [16]. Later,

© International Association for Cryptologic Research 2021
T. Malkin and C. Peikert (Eds.): CRYPTO 2021, LNCS 12826, pp. 185–213, 2021.
https://doi.org/10.1007/978-3-030-84245-1_7

Mukherjee and Wichs [31] (and the subsequent works [9,33]) gave a protocol based on the Learning with Errors assumption [35], Garg and Srinivasan [18] gave a construction from Bilinear maps and Boyle et al. [7,8] gave a construction from the Decisional Diffie-Hellman (DDH) assumption. Finally, the works of Benhamouda and Lin [6] and Garg and Srinivasan [19] gave constructions of two-round MPC protocols based on the minimal assumption that two-round oblivious transfer (OT) exists.

Black-Box Round Complexity. A cryptographic protocol P is said to make *black-box* use of an underlying primitive Q if P only makes input/output calls to Q and is agnostic to how Q is implemented. Apart from being a fundamental theoretical question, black-box protocols tend to be more efficient than their non-black-box counterparts and are usually viewed as the first step towards practicality. Unfortunately, the constructions of two-round MPC protocols from [6,19] made non-black-box use of a two-round OT. On the other hand, a recent work of Applebaum et al. [3] showed that such non-black-box use is inherent by providing a black-box separation between these two primitives. As far as positive results are concerned, we do know of 4-round MPC protocols making black-box use of a two-round OT from [2,17,30]. These works left open the following intriguing question (which was explicitly mentioned in [3]):

Can we construct a three-round secure multiparty computation protocol for general functions making black-box use of a two-round OT?

1.1   Our Results

In this work, we give a near complete answer to the above question. For the case of semi-honest adversaries, we fully resolve the problem and show that two-round OT is black-box complete for three-round MPC. Specifically,

Informal Theorem 1. *Let f be an arbitrary multiparty functionality. There exists a three-round protocol that securely computes f against semi-honest adversaries corrupting an arbitrary subset of the parties. The protocol makes black-box use of a two-round, semi-honest secure OT and is in the plain model. The computational cost of the protocol grows polynomially with the circuit size of f and the security parameter.*

For the case of malicious adversaries, we give a three-round MPC protocol that makes black-box use of two-round, malicious-secure OT that additionally satisfies an equivocality property for the receiver's message. Specifically, we require the existence of a special algorithm that can equivocate the first round receiver OT message to both bits 0 and 1. Such equivocality property is implied by a two-round OT that is secure against a malicious adversary that can adaptively corrupt the receiver or, it can be obtained from black-box use of a dual-mode public-key encryption scheme [34]. The main theorem we show for malicious adversaries is the following:

Informal Theorem 2. *Let f be an arbitrary multiparty functionality. There exists a three-round protocol that UC-realizes f (with unanimous abort) against malicious adversaries corrupting an arbitrary subset of the parties. The protocol makes black-box use of a two-round, UC-secure OT against malicious adversaries with equivocal receiver security and is in the common random/reference string model. The computational cost of the protocol grows polynomially with the circuit size of f and the security parameter.*

We note that the work of Garg and Srinivasan [19] gave a generic transformation from any two-round, malicious-secure OT to one that additionally satisfies the equivocal receiver property. Unfortunately, this transformation makes non-black-box use of a PRG (but makes black-box use of OT). We leave open the interesting problem of obtaining a black-box transformation, or showing that such non-black-box use is inherent.

2   Technical Overview

In this section, we give a high-level overview of the main techniques used in the construction our MPC protocols in the semi-honest and the malicious setting.

Starting Point. Our work builds on the recent results of [6,19] which gave constructions of a two-round MPC protocol from two-round OT. The key technical contribution in these works is the design of a round-collapsing compiler that takes a larger round protocol for securely computing the required functionality and squishes the number of rounds to two. Specifically, instead of the parties interacting with each other as in the larger round protocol, the round-collapsing compiler gave a mechanism wherein the garbled circuits generated by each party performs this interaction. The interaction between garbled circuits is enabled by making use of a two-round OT. Unfortunately, these constructions [6,19] require non-black-box use of cryptographic primitives.

If we look closely into these constructions, we observe that there is only one place where non-black-box use of cryptography is needed. Specifically, the garbled circuits which perform the interaction on behalf of the parties use the code of the underlying larger round protocol. Thus, if the larger round protocol makes use of cryptographic primitives such as an OT, then the squished protocol makes non-black-box use of these primitives. On the other hand, if the larger round protocol only made use of information-theoretic operations, then the resultant two-round protocol makes black-box use of cryptography. Unfortunately, the negative results in [29] rules out information-theoretic secure computation protocols for most functions in the dishonest majority setting. Furthermore, the work of Applebaum et al. [3] showed that such non-black-box use of OT is inherent if we want to construct a two-round MPC protocol. However, their work left open the problem of constructing a black-box three-round MPC protocol based on two-round OT.

The work of Garg, Ishai, and Srinivasan [17] observed that if the parties apriori shared random OT correlations, then one can use the results of [26,

28] to construct an information-theoretic MPC protocol in the OT correlations model. Now, squishing the number of rounds of such a protocol using the round-collapsing compiler of [6,19] gives rise to an MPC protocol that makes black-box use of cryptography. Garg et al. [17] also gave a method of generating such correlations in a single round using a primitive called *non-interactive OT*. This gives rise to the following three-round protocol that makes black-box use of cryptographic operations: use the first round to generate random OT correlations relying on non-interactive OT, and use the next two rounds to implement the round-collapsing compiler of [6,19]. However, a non-interactive OT is a very strong primitive and it is not known whether this can be constructed generically from a two-round OT.

Double Selection Functionality. If we abstract out the other details from [17], then the main ingredient needed to instantiate the black-box version of the round-collapsing compiler is a three-round protocol for a special multiparty functionality that we call as the *double selection*. In this functionality, only three of the n parties, say, P_1, P_2 and P_3 have private inputs. The input of P_1 is given by two bits (α, r), the input of P_2 is given by two bits (x_0, x_1) and the input of P_3 is given by two strings (y_0, y_1). The functionality first computes $x_\alpha \oplus r$ and then computes $y_{x_\alpha \oplus r}$ and delivers $(x_\alpha \oplus r, y_{x_\alpha \oplus r})$ to every party (and not just to P_1, P_2, and P_3.). In other words, the functionality first selects x_α from (x_0, x_1), XORs x_α with r and then again selects $y_{x_\alpha \oplus r}$ from (y_0, y_1) and hence, the name double selection. The work of Garg et al. [17] can be viewed as giving a three-round protocol for the double selection functionality based on non-interactive OT. The goal of this work is to give such a protocol based only on black-box use of a two-round OT.

We first note that if we relax the requirement to say that, only one of $\{P_1, P_2, P_3\}$ gets the output at the end of the third round, then based on prior work, it is possible to design a black-box three-round protocol for this relaxed functionality. Indeed, one can express the double selection functionality as a degree-3 polynomial (over $\mathbb{F}_2$) and use the protocol from [2] to securely evaluate a degree-3 polynomial. Additionally, it is not too hard to see that if we invoke such a protocol thrice, then we can enable each one of $\{P_1, P_2, P_3\}$ to get the output of the double selection functionality at the end of the third round. However, the main technical challenge here is to enable each of the n parties and not just $\{P_1, P_2, P_3\}$, to reconstruct the output at the end of the third round. This requirement is equivalent to constructing a three-party protocol with a special property called as *publicly-decodable transcript* [3]. Roughly speaking, this property requires the existence of an efficient algorithm that takes the transcript of the three-party protocol and gives the output of the double selection functionality. For the sake of simplicity, let us restrict ourselves to protocols where the last round (i.e., the third round) message contains the output in the clear. We now explain how to construct such a protocol making black-box use of two-round OT.

Key Idea: "Cascading OT." Since the last round message of the protocol contains the output of the functionality in the clear, this implies that there exists some party that can compute this output at the end of the second round and then broadcast this value to all the parties in the third round. This seems particularly challenging if we restrict ourselves to making black-box use of a two-round OT. Indeed, this implies that we need a mechanism to compute the output of a degree-3 function in two rounds using a two-round OT that only enables degree-2 computation. This apparent mismatch in the degree is the key challenge that we need to tackle.

This is where our idea of "cascading OT" comes into the picture. Specifically, in our protocol, one of the parties, say P_3, computes a sender OT message with respect to a receiver OT message generated by P_1 (that encodes P_1's input). The sender inputs used by P_3 to generate this message are in fact, two other sender OT messages computed by P_3, each with respect to a receiver OT message generated by P_2 (that encodes P_2's input). Thus, the "inner" sender OT message encodes a degree two computation of P_2 and P_3's inputs and the "outer" sender OT message encodes a degree-3 computation of P_1, P_2 and P_3's inputs. This idea of cascading two sender OT messages by P_3 allows P_1 to compute a degree-3 function in two rounds and thus, enabling us to solve the degree mismatch problem. Let us first see how to implement this "cascading OT" idea in the semi-honest setting and later explain the additional challenges that arise in the malicious setting.

2.1   Semi-honest Setting

In the first round, P_1 computes two receiver OT messages: otr that encodes α as the choice bit and otr′ that encodes r as the choice bit. In parallel, P_2 computes two receiver OT messages otr_0 that encodes its input x_0 and otr_1 that encodes x_1. P_1 broadcasts (otr, otr′) and P_2 broadcasts $(\mathsf{otr}_0, \mathsf{otr}_1)$ in the first round. In the second round, P_3 chooses a random bit mask and computes two sender OT messages: ots_0 with respect to otr_0 using $(y_0 \oplus \mathsf{mask}, y_1 \oplus \mathsf{mask})$ as its sender inputs and ots_1 with respect to otr_1 using again $(y_0 \oplus \mathsf{mask}, y_1 \oplus \mathsf{mask})$ as its inputs. It then computes the "cascading" sender OT message ots with respect to otr using $(\mathsf{ots}_0, \mathsf{ots}_1)$ as its two sender messages. Additionally, it computes ots′ with respect to otr′ with $(\mathsf{mask}, y_1 \oplus y_0 \oplus \mathsf{mask})$ as its sender messages. It then sends (ots, ots′) to P_1 in the second round.

Now, the randomness used in generating otr enables P_1 to recover ots_α from ots. However, recall that ots_α is generated with respect to otr_α and the randomness used for generating this message is available with P_2. Thus, to enable P_1 to decrypt ots_α, in the second round, P_2 computes a sender OT message with respect to otr with the input and randomness used for computing otr_0 and otr_1 as the two sender inputs. Thus, P_1 can first recover x_α and the randomness used for generating otr_α from P_2's second round message and then obtain $y_{x_\alpha} \oplus \mathsf{mask} := x_\alpha(y_1 \oplus y_0) \oplus y_0 \oplus \mathsf{mask}$ from ots_α. P_1 also computes $r(y_1 \oplus y_0) \oplus \mathsf{mask}$ from ots′ using the randomness used in generating otr′. It adds these two values to get $y_{x_\alpha \oplus r}$. In the last round, P_1 broadcasts $(x_\alpha \oplus r, y_{x_\alpha \oplus r})$. This protocol satisfies correctness and we can show that this protocol is secure against semi-honest adversaries by relying on the semi-honest security of the two-round OT.

From Double Selection to General Functions. To give a protocol for general functions, we can use the reduction from general functions to double selection implicit in the work of [17]. Alternatively, we can use the above idea of cascading OT to give a three-round secure protocol for a related degree-3 function called as 3MULTPlus. We can then rely on completeness results from [3,8,17] who showed a round-preserving black-box reduction from a semi-honest protocol for computing general functions to a secure protocol for 3MULTPlus functionality. In the main body, we construct a protocol for securely computing 3MULTPlus and directly rely on the above completeness theorem to give a self-contained version of our semi-honest MPC result.

2.2   Malicious Setting

In the malicious setting, many other challenges arise and we now explain our ideas to solve them.

Challenge-1: Attack by a malicious P_3. Let us start with the bare-bones version of the malicious protocol which is just the semi-honest protocol but with all the OT invocations replaced with a malicious secure version. On inspection, we see that a corrupt P_3 can completely break the security of this protocol. Specifically, P_3 can compute ots_0 and ots_1 on two different pairs of inputs, say using $(\mathsf{mask}, \mathsf{mask})$ and $(1 \oplus \mathsf{mask}, 1 \oplus \mathsf{mask})$ respectively and compute ots' on inputs $(\mathsf{mask}, \mathsf{mask})$. Depending on the message received from P_1 in the last round, corrupt P_3 learns the value α. In order to prevent such an attack, we need a mechanism to ensure that P_3 uses consistent inputs to compute both ots_0 and ots_1.

One way to ensure consistency of P_3's inputs is to ask P_3 to give a zero-knowledge proof that the inputs used in both these computations are consistent. However, a naïve way of implementing such a zero-knowledge proof makes non-black-box use of cryptographic primitives which we want to avoid. To give a "black-box" zero-knowledge proof, we make use of "MPC-in-the-head" approach of Ishai et al. [25].

Solution: "MPC-in-the-head" Approach. To convey the main idea, we first explain a simple solution that blows-up the number of rounds and later show how to squish the number of rounds. P_3 imagines m-servers in its head (for some appropriately chosen parameter m). It then shares y_0, y_1, mask among these m servers using a threshold linear secret sharing scheme with a threshold parameter t. For each $i \in [m]$, P_3 computes $\{\mathsf{ots}_0^i, \mathsf{ots}_1^i, \mathsf{ots}^i, \mathsf{ots}'^i\}$ using the shares given to the i-th server. Specifically, the values $(y_0, y_1, \mathsf{mask})$ in the original computation are replaced with the shares $(y_0^i, y_1^i, \mathsf{mask}^i)$ given to the i-th server. P_3 sends $\{\mathsf{ots}^i, \mathsf{ots}'^i\}_{i \in [m]}$ to P_1 in the second round. P_1 now chooses a random subset T of $[m]$ of size t and asks P_3 to reveal the shares and the randomness used in the computation of $(\mathsf{ots}^i, \mathsf{ots}'^i)$ for every $i \in T$. P_1 now checks if these computations are correct. If they are all correct, then for each $i \in [m]$, P_1 recovers the share of the output and reconstructs the output. Here, we are crucially relying on the fact $x_\alpha(y_1 \oplus y_0) \oplus y_0 \oplus \mathsf{mask}$ and $r(y_1 \oplus y_0) \oplus \mathsf{mask}$ recovered by P_1 in the bare-bones protocol are linear functions of y_0, y_1, mask and the secret sharing scheme used by P_3 supports linear operations on the shares. This ensures that P_1 can recover the correct output from the shares. However, this idea seems to blow-up the number of rounds to 4. To squish the number of rounds to 2, we make use of a trick from [27], wherein P_1, in the first round, uses a t-out-of-m OT to commit to its set T and P_3 in the second round uses the m sets of inputs, randomness as its sender inputs.

We can now show that if a malicious P_3 is using inconsistent inputs in "many" server executions then it gets caught with overwhelming probability. On the other hand, if P_3 is using inconsistent inputs in a "small" number of server executions, then we can rely on the error correcting properties of the secret sharing scheme to recover the correct output.[1]

Need for Equivocal Receiver Security. Here, another technical issue arises and to solve this, we need the OT to satisfy the equivocality property on the receiver's message. To see why this additional property is required, consider the case where P_2 is honest but P_1 is corrupted. Since the adversary is rushing, the honest P_2 sends both $\mathsf{otr}_0, \mathsf{otr}_1$ before receiving $\mathsf{otr}, \mathsf{otr}'$. Recall that in the second round, P_2 generates a sender OT message with respect to otr with the input and the randomness used in otr_0 and otr_1 as its OT inputs. Unfortunately, this leads to the following issue during simulation. We cannot know the value of x_α unless we receive otr from the corrupt P_1. This value is obtained only after we send both $\mathsf{otr}_0, \mathsf{otr}_1$. However, since x_α and the randomness used in generating otr_α are needed to compute the sender OT message from P_2, we need to generate otr_α in a way that it correctly encodes x_α. To solve this issue, we rely on the equivocality property of the receiver's message. Specifically, since the first round OT message of the receiver can be equivocated to both bits 0 and 1, we use the equivocal simulator to generate randomness that is consistent with the encoding of x_α. We then use this randomness to generate the second round OT message. As mentioned earlier, this property is satisfied by any two-round OT that is secure against adversaries that can adaptively corrupt the receiver, or it can be obtained from a dual-mode public-key encryption scheme [34].

Challenge-2: Attack by Malicious P_2. In the previous step, we prevented a malicious P_3 from breaking the security of the protocol. However, we observe that a malicious P_2 can still break the security of the protocol by mounting an input dependent abort. Specifically, a corrupt P_2 can generate the second round OT message with respect to otr such that only one of its two sender inputs contains the correct randomness used in generating $(\mathsf{otr}_0, \mathsf{otr}_1)$. It sets the other sender input to be some junk value. If the input α of P_1 corresponds to the position that contains the junk value, then P_1 aborts at the end of the second round. This enables P_2 to learn the value α. The first natural idea to prevent this attack is to use a zero-knowledge proof to show that P_2 is using the correct inputs in generating the sender OT message. However, unlike the previous step,

---

[1] Here, we need to additionally ensure that malicious P_3 is generating the shares correctly. Hence, we make use of a pairwise verifiable secret sharing based on bivariate polynomials and do additional checks on the shares to ensure that the sharing is done correctly.

the relation that we want to prove (or equivalently, the functionality computed by the MPC) involves a cryptographic statement and in those cases, the "MPC-in-the-head" approach leads to non-black-box use of cryptographic primitives. Thus, we need a new approach to deal with this issue.

Solution: Using an OT-Combiner. We first observe that if the input α of P_1 was uniformly random, then the probability that a corrupt P_2 can guess α to force P_1 to abort is $1/2$. For $\kappa = \Omega(\lambda)$ (where λ is the security parameter), consider invoking the above protocol κ times on independently chosen random P_1 inputs $(\alpha_1, \ldots, \alpha_\kappa)$. Then, the probability that corrupt P_2 can guess more than λ of these inputs is negligible. Given this observation, consider the following two-party functionality:

1. The input of P_1 is given by two bits (α, r) and the input of P_2 is given by two other bits (x_0, x_1).
2. P_1 and P_2 also share $\kappa = \Omega(\lambda)$ random OT correlations with P_1 acting as the receiver and P_2 acting as the sender. Additionally, a corrupt P_2 might learn λ of these receiver correlations. We call these as "leaky" OT correlations.
3. At the end of the protocol, we want both P_1 and P_2 to learn $(x_\alpha \oplus r)$.

A statistically secure protocol for the above functionality is obtained by first implementing the information-theoretic OT combiner protocol from [12] to extract "pure" OT correlations from the above "leaky" OT correlations and then use the information-theoretic two-party protocols [24,26,28] in the OT correlations model to securely compute $x_\alpha \oplus r$. Unfortunately, this protocol does not run in two rounds. To squish the number of rounds, we apply the round collapsing compiler of [6,19] to this larger round protocol and use the protocol from the first step (the one that suffers from input dependent abort) to set up the leaky OT correlations. Since the above protocol is statistical, the squished protocol only makes black-box use of cryptographic operations. Additionally, to enable the party P_3 to output $y_{x_\alpha \oplus r}$, we use the following observation about the compiler given in [19]: even if a party is not participating in the protocol, the garbled circuit generated by the party can listen to the protocol transcript and thus, learn the output. This observation allows the garbled circuit generated by P_3 to listen to the protocol between P_1 and P_2 and obtain $x_\alpha \oplus r$. This garbled circuit can then output $y_{x_\alpha \oplus r}$. This allows us to obtain a three-round black-box protocol for the double selection functionality that does not suffer from input dependent abort.

From Double Selection to General Functions. To give a protocol for general functions, we use the techniques in [17] to show that double selection is black-box complete for designing three-round secure protocols against malicious adversaries. Specifically, we apply the round-collapsing compiler to statistically secure protocols in the OT correlations model [26,28] and use the above protocol to implement the double selection functionality. This gives rise to a three-round MPC protocol that makes black-box use of a two-round, malicious-secure OT with equivocal receiver security.

3   Preliminaries

We recall some standard cryptographic definitions in this section. Let λ denote the security parameter. We give the standard definition for negligible functions, computational indistinguishability and the UC framework [11] in the full version.

3.1   Oblivious Transfer

In this paper, we consider a 1-out-of-2 OT, similar to [1,10,13,22,32,34] where one party, the *sender*, has input composed of two strings (s_0, s_1) and the input of the second party, the *receiver*, is a bit β. The receiver should learn s_β and nothing regarding $s_{1-\beta}$, while the sender should gain no information about β.

Semi-honest Secure Two-Round OT. A two-round semi-honest OT protocol $\langle S, R \rangle$ is defined by three probabilistic algorithms $(\mathsf{OT}_1, \mathsf{OT}_2, \mathsf{OT}_3)$ as follows. The receiver runs the algorithm OT_1 with the security parameter 1^λ, and a bit $\beta \in \{0,1\}$ as input and the random tape set to ω and obtains otr. The receiver then sends otr to the sender, who obtains ots by evaluating $\mathsf{OT}_2(\mathsf{otr}, (s_0, s_1))$ (with a uniform random tape), where $s_0, s_1 \in \{0,1\}^\lambda$ are the sender's input messages. The sender then sends ots to the receiver who obtains s_β by evaluating $\mathsf{OT}_3(\mathsf{ots}, (\beta, \omega))$.

- **Correctness.** For every choice bit $\beta \in \{0,1\}$ and the random tape ω of the receiver, and any input messages s_0 and s_1 of the sender we require that, if $\mathsf{otr} := \mathsf{OT}_1(1^\lambda, \beta; \omega)$, $\mathsf{ots} \leftarrow \mathsf{OT}_2(\mathsf{otr}, (s_0, s_1))$, then $\mathsf{OT}_3(\mathsf{ots}, (\beta, \omega)) = s_\beta$ with probability 1.
- **Receiver's security.** We require that, $\{\mathsf{otr} : \omega \leftarrow \{0,1\}^*, \mathsf{otr} := \mathsf{OT}_1(1^\lambda, 0; \omega)\} \overset{c}{\approx} \{\mathsf{otr} : \omega \leftarrow \{0,1\}^*, \mathsf{otr} := \mathsf{OT}_1(1^\lambda, 1; \omega)\}$.
- **Sender's security.** We require that for any choice of $\beta \in \{0,1\}$ and any strings $K_0, K_1, L_0, L_1 \in \{0,1\}^\lambda$ with $L_0 = L_1 = K_\beta$, we have that, $\{\beta, \omega \leftarrow \{0,1\}^*, \mathsf{OT}_2(1^\lambda, \mathsf{otr}, K_0, K_1)\} \overset{c}{\approx} \{\beta, \omega \leftarrow \{0,1\}^*, \mathsf{OT}_2(1^\lambda, \mathsf{otr}, L_0, L_1)\}$ where $\mathsf{otr} := \mathsf{OT}_1(1^\lambda, \beta; \omega)$.

Remark 1. We note that we can relax the correctness requirement to have a negligible probability of error. For the sake of simplicity of exposition, we stick to protocols having perfect correctness.

Maliciously Secure Two-Round OT with Equivocal Receiver Security. We consider the stronger notion of oblivious transfer with security against malicious adversaries in the common random/reference string model. In addition to the standard security against malicious receivers, we need this protocol to satisfy a special property called equivocal receiver security introduced in [19]. Informally, this property says that the first round message of the receiver can be equivocated to both choice bits 0 and 1. In terms of syntax, we supplement the syntax of semi-honest OT with an algorithm K_{OT} that takes the security parameter 1^λ as input and outputs the common random/reference string crs. Also, the three algorithms $\mathsf{OT}_1, \mathsf{OT}_2$ and OT_3 additionally take crs as input.

Furthermore, instead of using the entire random tape of OT_1 algorithm as input to OT_3, we let the OT_1 algorithm to output some secret information which is then used by OT_3.

- **Correctness.** For every $\beta \in \{0,1\}$ and any input messages s_0 and s_1 of the sender, we require that, if $\mathsf{crs} \leftarrow K_{\mathsf{OT}}(1^\lambda)$, $(\mathsf{otr}, \mu) \leftarrow \mathsf{OT}_1(\mathsf{crs}, \beta)$, $\mathsf{ots} \leftarrow \mathsf{OT}_2(\mathsf{crs}, \mathsf{otr}, (s_0, s_1))$, then $\mathsf{OT}_3(\mathsf{crs}, \mathsf{ots}, (\beta, \mu)) = s_\beta$ with probability 1.
- **Equivocal Receiver's security.** We require the existence of a PPT simulator $\mathsf{Sim}_R = (\mathsf{Sim}_R^1, \mathsf{Sim}_R^2)$ such that for any sequence of $(\beta_1, \ldots, \beta_n)$ where each $\beta_i \in \{0,1\}$ and $n = \mathsf{poly}(\lambda)$, we have:

$$\left\{ (\mathsf{crs}, \{(\mathsf{otr}^i, \mu_{\beta_i}^i)\}_{i \in [n]}) : (\mathsf{crs}, \mathsf{td}) \leftarrow \mathsf{Sim}_R^1(1^\lambda), \{(\mathsf{otr}^i, \mu_0^i, \mu_1^i) \leftarrow \right.$$
$$\left. \mathsf{Sim}_R^2(\mathsf{crs}, \mathsf{td})\}_{i \in [n]} \right\} \stackrel{c}{\approx} \left\{ (\mathsf{crs}, \{\mathsf{OT}_1(\mathsf{crs}, \beta_i)\}_{i \in [n]}) : \mathsf{crs} \leftarrow K_{\mathsf{OT}}(1^\lambda) \right\}.$$

- **Checking Validity of Receiver's Key.** There is a deterministic polynomial time algorithm $\mathsf{CheckValid}$ that takes as input $\mathsf{crs}, \mathsf{otr}, \beta, \mu$ and outputs 1 if and only if there exists some $\omega \in \{0,1\}^*$ such that $(\mathsf{otr}, \mu) := \mathsf{OT}_1(\mathsf{crs}, \beta; \omega)$.
- **Sender's security.** We require the existence of PPT algorithm $\mathsf{Sim}_S = (\mathsf{Sim}_S^1, \mathsf{Sim}_S^2)$ such that for any choice of $K_0^i, K_1^i \in \{0,1\}^\lambda$ for $i \in [n]$ where $n = \mathsf{poly}(\lambda)$, PPT adversary $\mathcal{A}$ and any PPT distinguisher D, we have:

$$\left| \Pr[\mathrm{Expt}_1 = 1] - \Pr[\mathrm{Expt}_2 = 1] \right| \leq \mathsf{negl}(\lambda).$$

$\mathrm{Expt}_1:$
$\mathsf{crs} \leftarrow K_{\mathsf{OT}}(1^\lambda)$
$\{\mathsf{otr}^i\}_{i \in [n]} \leftarrow \mathcal{A}(\mathsf{crs})$

$\left\{\mathsf{ots}^i \leftarrow \mathsf{OT}_2(\mathsf{crs}, \mathsf{otr}^i, (K_0^i, K_1^i))\right\}_{i \in [n]}$
Output $D(\mathsf{crs}, \{\mathsf{ots}^i\}_{i \in [n]})$

$\mathrm{Expt}_2:$
$(\mathsf{crs}, \mathsf{td}) \leftarrow \mathsf{Sim}_S^1(1^\lambda)$
$\{\mathsf{otr}^i\}_{i \in [n]} \leftarrow \mathcal{A}(\mathsf{crs})$
$\beta_i := \mathsf{Sim}_S^2(\mathsf{crs}, \mathsf{td}, \mathsf{otr}^i) \ \forall i \in [n]$
$L_0^i := K_{\beta_i}^i$ and $L_1^i := K_{\beta_i}^i$
$\left\{\mathsf{ots}^i \leftarrow \mathsf{OT}_2(\mathsf{crs}, \mathsf{otr}, (L_0^i, L_1^i))\right\}_{i \in [n]}$
Output $D(\mathsf{crs}, \{\mathsf{ots}^i\}_{i \in [n]})$

Remark 2. We note that a two-round malicious secure OT with equivocal receiver security implies a standard two-round malicious OT that implements the ideal OT functionality.

We recall the definitions of garbled circuits, non-interactive secure computation and some properties of symmetric bivariate polynomial in the full version.

4   3-Round Semi-honest MPC

In this section, we give a three-round, semi-honest secure protocol for computing arbitrary multiparty functionalities making black-box use of a two-round, semi-honest secure OT in the plain model. We do this in two steps. In the first step, we give a three round protocol for securely computing the $\mathcal{F}_{\mathsf{3MULTPlus}}$ functionality (described below) against semi-honest adversaries. In the second step, we extend it for the case of general functions by relying on the results from [3,8,17].

4.1   First Step: Protocol for $\mathcal{F}_{3\mathsf{MULTPlus}}$

Let us first recall the $\mathcal{F}_{3\mathsf{MULTPlus}}$ functionality. It is a n-party functionality that takes input from 3 parties and delivers output to every party. Specifically, let us denote the parties that provide inputs to this functionality by P_1, P_2, and P_3. The input of P_i for $i \in \{1, 2, 3\}$ is given by $(x_i, y_i) \in \{0, 1\} \times \{0, 1\}$. The output of the functionality is given by $x_1 \cdot x_2 \cdot x_3 + y_1 + y_2 + y_3$ (where $+$ and $\cdot$ are over $\mathbb{F}_2$). The main theorem that we show in this subsection is:

Theorem 3. *There is an efficient three-round protocol $\Pi_{3\mathsf{MULTPlus}}$ (Fig. 1) that makes black-box use of a two-round, semi-honest OT and securely computes the $\mathcal{F}_{3\mathsf{MULTPlus}}$ functionality against semi-honest adversaries corrupting an arbitrary subset of the parties. The protocol is in the plain model.*

Building $\Pi_{3\mathsf{MULTPlus}}$. In Fig. 1, we describe a three-round protocol for securely computing $\mathcal{F}_{3\mathsf{MULTPlus}}$ against semi-honest adversaries making black-box access to a 2-round semi-honest OT. We give an informal description below.

At a high-level, the degree-3 computation is achieved by cascading OT messages i.e., generating a sender OT message where the inputs are themselves two other sender OT messages. Since OT enables degree-2 computation, cascading OT enables us to compute the result of a degree-3 computation. The main novelty lies in being able to do this in 2 rounds for OTs that are run in parallel. The last round is spent on a single broadcast of a value by each party and subsequent local accumulation of these broadcasted values to obtain the final result. We elaborate on this idea below.

In the first round, P_1, acting as a receiver, publishes an OT receiver message otr that encodes its input x_1. In parallel, P_2, first splits x_2 into two additive shares $(x_{2,0}, x_{2,1})$ and then publishes two OT receiver messages, $\mathsf{otr}_0, \mathsf{otr}_1$ where otr_b encodes $x_{2,b}$. In the second round, P_3 splits its input x_3 into two additive shares, $x_{3,0}, x_{3,1}$. It then prepares two OT sender messages with respect to the receiver messages $\mathsf{otr}_0, \mathsf{otr}_1$ where the sender inputs used in both these messages are given by $(x_{3,0}, x_{3,1})$. Let these OT messages be denoted by $\mathsf{ots}_0, \mathsf{ots}_1$. The crux of our construction is then to use $\mathsf{ots}_0, \mathsf{ots}_1$ as the sender inputs in response to P_1's receiver message otr. With this sender message, P_1 can retrieve ots_{x_1}, but in order to decode ots_{x_1}, it needs the receiver's input and randomness used for ots_{x_1}, which are held by P_2. Responding to P_1's receiver message otr, P_2 computes a sender OT message with input $((x_{2,0}, \omega_{2,0}), (x_{2,1}, \omega_{2,1}))$. Using this message, P_1 can retrieve x_{2,x_1} and the corresponding randomness while $x_{2,1-x_1}$ and the matching randomness are hidden. Deducing from the OT correctness, we conclude that P_1 at the end of the second round can compute $x_{3,x_{2,x_1}}$ which can be written as $x_{2,x_1}(x_{3,0} + x_{3,1}) + x_{3,0} = (x_1 \cdot x_2 + x_{2,0}) \cdot x_3 + x_{3,0}$, since $x_{2,x_1} = x_1(x_{2,0} + x_{2,1}) + x_{2,0}$. To cancel out the extra multiplicative term $x_{2,0} \cdot x_3$ in the expression, another OT instance is needed between P_2, P_3, where P_3 enacts a receiver with input x_3 and P_2 enacts a sender with input $x_{2,0,0}, x_{2,0,1}$ which are an additive secret sharing of $x_{2,0}$. Once all the OTs conclude in the first two rounds, each of P_1, P_2 and P_3 accumulates their appropriate local data (which includes their other input y_i) and this can be shown to be an additive secret sharing of the output. In the final round, each party broadcasts this value and this enables every party to compute the final result via plain addition. Lastly, each of these three parties distributes shares of 0 amongst P_1, P_2, P_3 to be added to their local sum before broadcast. This step is required for simulation in the case where there exists more than one honest party in the set P_1, P_2, P_3.

Protocol $\Pi_{3\text{MULTPlus}}$

Inputs: P_i for $i \in [3]$ inputs (x_i, y_i).
Output: For each $i \in [n]$, P_i outputs $x_1 x_2 x_3 + y_1 + y_2 + y_3$.
Primitive: A two-round semi-honest secure OT protocol $(\text{OT}_1, \text{OT}_2, \text{OT}_3)$.

Round-1: In the first round,
- P_1 chooses a random string $\omega \leftarrow \{0,1\}^*$ and computes $\text{otr} := \text{OT}_1(1^\lambda, x_1; \omega)$.
- P_2 chooses two random strings $\omega_0, \omega_1 \leftarrow \{0,1\}^*$. It chooses random bits $x_{2,0}, x_{2,1} \leftarrow \{0,1\}$ subject to $x_2 = x_{2,1} + x_{2,0}$. It computes $\text{otr}_0 := \text{OT}_1(1^\lambda, x_{2,0}; \omega_0)$ and $\text{otr}_1 := \text{OT}_1(1^\lambda, x_{2,1}; \omega_1)$.
- P_3 chooses a random string $\omega' \leftarrow \{0,1\}^*$ and computes $\text{otr}_3 := \text{OT}_1(1^\lambda, x_3; \omega')$.
- P_1 broadcasts otr, P_2 broadcasts $(\text{otr}_0, \text{otr}_1)$ and P_3 broadcasts otr_3.
- For every $i \in [3]$, P_i chooses a random additive secret sharing of 0 given by $(\delta_1^i, \delta_2^i, \delta_3^i)$ and sends the share δ_j^i to party P_j for $j \in [3] \setminus \{i\}$ via private channels.[a]

Round-2: In the second round,
- P_2 computes $\text{ots} \leftarrow \text{OT}_2(\text{otr}, (x_{2,0}, \omega_0), (x_{2,1}, \omega_1))$. It then chooses random bits $x_{2,0,0}, x_{2,0,1} \leftarrow \{0,1\}$ subject to $x_{2,0} = x_{2,0,0} + x_{2,0,1}$. It computes $\text{ots}_3 \leftarrow \text{OT}_2(\text{otr}_3, x_{2,0,0}, x_{2,0,1})$.
- P_3 chooses random bits $x_{3,0}, x_{3,1} \leftarrow \{0,1\}$ subject to $x_3 = x_{3,0} + x_{3,1}$. For each $b \in \{0,1\}$, it first computes $\text{ots}_b \leftarrow \text{OT}_2(\text{otr}_b, x_{3,0}, x_{3,1})$. It then computes $\overline{\text{ots}} \leftarrow \text{OT}_2(\text{otr}, \text{ots}_0, \text{ots}_1)$.
- P_2 broadcasts $(\text{ots}, \text{ots}_3)$ and P_3 broadcasts $\overline{\text{ots}}$.

Round-3: In the last round,
- For each $i \in [3]$, P_i computes $\delta_i = \delta_i^1 + \delta_i^2 + \delta_i^3$.
- P_2 sets $z_2 := x_{2,0,0} + y_2 + \delta_2$.
- P_3 computes $x_{2,0,x_3} := \text{OT}_3(\text{ots}_3, (x_3, \omega'))$ and sets $z_3 = x_{2,0,x_3} + x_{3,0} + y_3 + \delta_3$.
- P_1 computes $(x_{2,x_1}, \omega_{x_1}) := \text{OT}_3(\text{ots}, (x_1, \omega))$ and $\text{ots}_{x_1} := \text{OT}_3(\overline{\text{ots}}, (x_1, \omega))$. It then computes $x_{3,x_{2,x_1}} := \text{OT}_3(\text{ots}_{x_1}, (x_{2,x_1}, \omega_{x_1}))$. It then sets $z_1 := x_{3,x_{2,x_1}} + y_1 + \delta_1$.
- P_1 broadcasts z_1, P_2 broadcasts z_2 and P_3 broadcasts z_3.

Output: Every party outputs $z_1 + z_2 + z_3$.

---

[a] We can simulate a single round of private channel messages in two rounds over public channels by making use of a two-round OT.

Fig. 1. Protocol $\Pi_{3\text{MULTPlus}}$

We show the correctness and security in Lemma 1–2.

Lemma 1 (Correctness). *Protocol* $\Pi_{\mathsf{3MULTPlus}}$ *correctly computes* $\mathcal{F}_{\mathsf{3MULTPlus}}$.

Proof. We first observe that $x_{2,0,x_3}$ computed by P_3 in Round-3 is equal to $x_3(x_{2,0,0} + x_{2,0,1}) + x_{2,0,0} = x_3 \cdot x_{2,0} + x_{2,0,0}$. Therefore, $z_3 = x_3 \cdot x_{2,0} + x_{2,0,0} + x_{3,0} + y_3 + \delta_3$. We then observe that x_{2,x_1} and ots_{x_1} computed by P_1 are equal to $x_1 \cdot x_2 + x_{2,0}$ and $\mathsf{OT}_2(\mathsf{OT}_1(1^\lambda, x_{2,x_1}; \omega_{x_1}), x_{3,0}, x_{3,1})$ respectively. Therefore, $x_{3,x_{2,x_1}}$ computed by P_1 is equal to $x_{2,x_1}(x_{3,0} + x_{3,1}) + x_{3,0} = (x_1 \cdot x_2 + x_{2,0}) \cdot x_3 + x_{3,0}$. This implies that $z_1 = (x_1 \cdot x_2 + x_{2,0}) \cdot x_3 + x_{3,0} + y_1 + \delta_1$. Finally, we observe that $(\delta_1, \delta_2, \delta_3)$ form an additive secret sharing of 0. Hence,

$$
\begin{aligned}
z_1 + z_2 + z_3 &= ((x_1 \cdot x_2 + x_{2,0}) \cdot x_3 + x_{3,0} + y_1 + \delta_1) \\
&\quad + (x_{2,0,0} + y_2 + \delta_2) + (x_3 \cdot x_{2,0} + x_{2,0,0} + x_{3,0} + y_3 + \delta_3) \\
&= x_1 \cdot x_2 \cdot x_3 + y_1 + y_2 + y_3
\end{aligned}
$$

This completes the proof of correctness.

Lemma 2 (Security). *Protocol* $\Pi_{\mathsf{3MULTPlus}}$ *securely computes* $\mathcal{F}_{\mathsf{3MULTPlus}}$ *against a semi-honest adversary corrupting an arbitrary subset of parties.*

We defer the proof to the full version.

4.2 Second Step: Protocol for Arbitrary Functions

We recall the theorem about completeness of $\mathcal{F}_{\mathsf{3MULTPlus}}$ from [3, Theorem 6.4].

Theorem 4 ([3,8,17]). *Let f be an n-party functionality. There exists a protocol Π_f for securely computing f against a semi-honest adversary (corrupting an arbitrary subset of parties), where Π_f makes parallel calls to the $\mathcal{F}_{\mathsf{3MULTPlus}}$ functionality and uses no further interaction. The protocol Π_f can either be: (1) computationally secure using a black-box PRG, where the complexity of the parties is polynomial in n, the security parameter λ and the circuit size of f, or alternatively (2) perfectly secure, where the complexity of the parties is polynomial in n and the branching program size of f.*

From Theorem 3 and the UC composition theorem [11], we get the following.

Corollary 1. *Let f be an n-party functionality. There is a three-round protocol that makes black-box use of a two-round, semi-honest secure OT and securely computes f against a semi-honest adversary corrupting an arbitrary subset of parties. The complexity of the parties is polynomial in n, the security parameter λ and the circuit size of f.*

5   3-Round Malicious MPC

In this section, we give a construction of a 3-round protocol that computes any multiparty functionality with UC-security against malicious adversaries. The protocol makes black-box use of a two-round, malicious-secure OT with equivocal receiver security. We do this in three steps. In the first step, we define a special n-party functionality called double selection and give a two-round, black-box protocol that securely computes this functionality. However, this protocol satisfies only a weaker notion of security which is security with input dependent abort. In the second step, we use the protocol from the first step and give a three-round protocol that securely computes this double selection functionality with standard security. In the final step, we show how to bootstrap the protocol from the second step to a black-box, three-round protocol for general functions.

5.1   First Step: Special Functionality with Input Dependent Abort

In this subsection, we define a special n-party functionality $\mathcal{F}_{\mathsf{dSelPri}}^{\dagger}$ in Fig. 2 and give a black-box, two-round protocol that computes $\mathcal{F}_{\mathsf{dSelPri}}^{\dagger}$. This functionality captures input-dependent abort attack that can be launched by a corrupt P_2 against P_1, causing loss of input privacy of P_1.

Functionality $\mathcal{F}_{\mathsf{dSelPri}}^{\dagger}$

$\mathcal{F}_{\mathsf{dSelPri}}^{\dagger}$ is parameterized by an n-party function $\mathsf{dSelPri}$ whose description follows. $\mathsf{dSelPri}$ receives $(\alpha, r) \in \{0,1\} \times \{0,1\}$ from P_1, $(y_0, y_1) \in \{0,1\} \times \{0,1\}$ from P_2 and for every $3 \leq i \leq n$, it receives $(z_0^i, z_1^i) \in \{0,1\}^{\lambda} \times \{0,1\}^{\lambda}$ from P_i. $\mathsf{dSelPri}$ delivers $(y_\alpha, \{z_{y_\alpha \oplus r}^i\}_{3 \leq i \leq n})$ to P_1 and the other parties do not get any outputs. Let x_i be the input of party P_i to $\mathsf{dSelPri}$ (note that x_i for different parties maybe of different lengths) and let $\mathcal{S}$ be the adversary. The functionality $\mathcal{F}_{\mathsf{dSelPri}}^{\dagger}$ proceeds as follows:

1. Each party P_i (and $\mathcal{S}$ on behalf of P_i if P_i is corrupted) sends (input, sid, P_i, x_i) to the functionality.
2. If P_2 is corrupted then $\mathcal{S}$ may send (predicate, sid, EQ_β) where EQ_β is the equality predicate that takes the first component of P_1's input α and outputs 1 iff $\beta = \alpha$.
3. Upon receiving the inputs from all parties, evaluate out $:= \mathsf{dSelPri}(x_1, \ldots, x_n)$. If P_1 is corrupted, the functionality delivers out to $\mathcal{S}$.
4. If P_1 is not corrupted, then on receiving (generateOutput, sid) from $\mathcal{S}$, the ideal functionality computes pred $= \mathsf{EQ}_\beta(\alpha)$ (if (predicate, sid, EQ_β) is received; if such a message is not received, it sets pred $= 0$). If pred $= 0$, it gives (output, sid, P_1, out) to P_1. Else, if pred $= 1$, it sends (output, sid, P_1, abort). (And ignores the message if inputs from all parties in $\{P_1, \ldots, P_n\}$ have not been received.) On the other hand, if (abort, sid) is received then, it sends (output, sid, P_1, abort) to P_1.

Fig. 2. Functionality $\mathcal{F}_{\mathsf{dSelPri}}^{\dagger}$

We show the following theorem, which implies the subsequent corollary via the results from [24,26].

Theorem 5. *There exists a two-round protocol* $\Pi^\dagger_{\mathsf{dSelPri}}$ *(Fig. 4) that UC-realizes* $\mathcal{F}^\dagger_{\mathsf{dSelPri}}$ *in the* $\mathcal{F}_{(m,p)\text{-}\mathsf{RaOT}}$ *(Fig. 3) hybrid model making black-box access to a two-round, malicious-secure OT with equivocal receiver security.*

Corollary 2. *There exists a two-round protocol* $\Pi^\dagger_{\mathsf{dSelPri}}$ *that UC-realizes the functionality* $\mathcal{F}^\dagger_{\mathsf{dSelPri}}$ *making black-box access to a two-round, malicious-secure OT with equivocal receiver security.*

Functionality $\mathcal{F}_{(m,p)\text{-}\mathsf{RaOT}}$

Let $\mathcal{S}$ be an adversary.

- A party P_i (and $\mathcal{S}$ on behalf of P_i if P_i is corrupted) sends (receiver, sid, P_i).
- Another party P_j (and $\mathcal{S}$ on behalf of P_j if P_j is corrupted) sends (sender, sid, P_j, $(s_1, \ldots, s_m)$) to the functionality where $s_j \in \{0,1\}^*$ for each $j \in [m]$.
- On receiving both these messages, for each $j \in [m]$, the functionality independently sets $s'_j = s_j$ with probability p and sets $s'_j = \perp$ with probability $1 - p$.
- On receiving (generateOutput, sid) from $\mathcal{S}$ (if P_j is corrupted), the functionality delivers (output, sid, $(s'_1, \ldots, s'_m)$) to P_i.

Fig. 3. Functionality $\mathcal{F}_{(m,p)\text{-}\mathsf{RaOT}}$

Building $\Pi^\dagger_{\mathsf{dSelPri}}$**.** We begin with the description of a protocol that computes a simplified version of the function dSelPri in the face of a semi-honest adversary, assuming P_3 as the lone provider of a pair z_0, z_1. This version, in fact, is identical to the first two rounds of the construction for "double-selection" functionality implementing "cascaded OT" described in Sect. 2.1.

Now, to make the idea work against a malicious adversary, we inspect the roles of the various parties and try to see the kind of attack that they can mount. P_1's role only includes preparing two OT receiver messages and therefore a corrupt P_1 is taken care by the sender security of the OT against malicious receivers. Next, a corrupt P_2 plays the role of two receivers to P_3 and one sender to P_1, where the messages and matching randomnesses used for the former role are fed as input in the latter role. While OT's sender security takes care, and in effect, fixes P_2's input through the receiver messages, there is still a scope for P_2 to launch a selective failure or input-dependent attack against P_1 by selectively choosing only one of the OT sender inputs correctly. This allows it to learn P_1's input α, by simply observing whether P_1 aborts or not. But the functionality $\mathcal{F}^\dagger_{\mathsf{dSelPri}}$ allows this attack, and preventing this attack is taken care in the next section. This brings us to the last case where P_3 can be corrupt.

P_3 prepares three OT sender messages, wherein the third instance takes the result of first two instances as input and in addition, the inputs to the first two instances need to be identical, namely $(z_0 + \mathsf{mask}, z_1 + \mathsf{mask})$. Tackling a corrupt P_3 clearly requires to step beyond OT receiver security against malicious senders. Here, we deploy MPC-in-the-head approach [25] for the consistency check, where P_3 prepares states of m virtual parties in its head that jointly hold a secret sharing of z_0, z_1, mask. The sharing is pairwise checkable and adheres to a threshold that dictates its security. A bivariate polynomial based sharing scheme fits the bill. Next, the i-th virtual party's state includes the OT sender messages that are prepared by simply replicating P_3's computation on the i-th shares of z_0, z_1, mask. Now, the goal is to open some number of the states to P_1 for checking and we need to ensure that this number (a) is not big enough to violate P_3's privacy, (b) but is enough to either catch a corrupt P_3 or error-correct the faults. Here, we invoke a 2-party NISC between P_1 and P_2 for computing the Rabin OT functionality $\mathcal{F}_{(m,p)\text{-RaOT}}$, where P_3 inputs the m states. $\mathcal{F}_{(m,p)\text{-RaOT}}$ ensures each state is chosen to be revealed to P_1 independently with probability p. Using Chernoff bounds, we can conclude that the probability that more than the threshold number of states are revealed to P_1 is negligible. Consequently, the secrets z_0, z_1, mask are safe from P_1 with overwhelming probability. On the other hand, a corrupt P_3 either gets caught with overwhelming probability when it prepares a "large" number of wrong states and in the case where it ends up maligning small number of states, we rely on error correction to ensure the recovery of information. Since the NISC realizing $\mathcal{F}_{(m,p)\text{-RaOT}}$ makes black-box use of a two-round OT [24,26], our final construction is black-box, as desired.

Protocol $\Pi^\dagger_{\mathsf{dSelPri}}$

Inputs: P_1 inputs $(\alpha, r) \in \{0,1\} \times \{0,1\}$, P_2 inputs $(y_0, y_1) \in \{0,1\} \times \{0,1\}$. For every $3 \le i \le n$, P_i inputs $(z_0^i, z_1^i) \in \{0,1\}^\lambda \times \{0,1\}^\lambda$.

Output: P_1 outputs $(y_\alpha, \{z_{y_\alpha \oplus r}^i\}_{3 \le i \le n})$.

Primitives: (a) A malicious-secure two-round OT with equivocal receiver security $(K_{\mathsf{OT}}, \mathsf{OT}_1, \mathsf{OT}_2, \mathsf{OT}_3)$ (see Section 3.1). We use OT_1^* to denote an algorithm that takes a crs and $q(\lambda)$-bit string (for some polynomial $q(\cdot)$) as input and applies OT_1 to each bit of that string. (b) Functionality $\mathcal{F}_{(m,p)\text{-RaOT}}$ where $m = 3\lambda + 1$ and $p = \lambda/2m$.

Common Random/Reference String Generation: For each $i \in [n]$, sample $\mathsf{crs}^i \leftarrow K_{\mathsf{OT}}(1^\lambda)$. Set the crs to be $(\mathsf{crs}^1, \ldots, \mathsf{crs}^n)$.

Round-1: In the first round,

- P_1 computes $(\mathsf{otr}, \mu) \leftarrow \mathsf{OT}_1(\mathsf{crs}^1, \alpha)$ and $(\overline{\mathsf{otr}}, \overline{\mu}) \leftarrow \mathsf{OT}_1(\mathsf{crs}^1, r)$. For each $i \in [3, n]$, P_1 sends $(\mathsf{receiver}, i, P_1)$ to the $\mathcal{F}_{(m,p)\text{-RaOT}}$ functionality.
- For each $b \in \{0,1\}$, P_2 computes $(\mathsf{otr}_b, \mu_b) \leftarrow \mathsf{OT}_1(\mathsf{crs}^2, y_b)$.
- For each $i \in [3, n]$, P_i does the following:
  - It chooses $\mathsf{mask}^i \leftarrow \{0,1\}^\lambda$ uniformly at random.

- It chooses three random degree-λ symmetric bivariate polynomials S_0^i, S_1^i, S_2^i over $\mathsf{GF}(2^\lambda)$ such that $S_0^i(0,0) = z_0^i$, $S_1^i(0,0) = z_1^i$ and $S_2^i(0,0) = \mathsf{mask}^i$.
- For each $j \in [m]$ and for each $\gamma \in [0,2]$, let $f_\gamma^{i,j}(x) = S_\gamma^i(x,j)$ (where we associate j with the j-th element in $\mathsf{GF}(2^\lambda)$).
- For each $j \in [m]$ and for each $\gamma \in [0,2]$, it computes $(\mathsf{otr}_\gamma^{i,j}, \mu_\gamma^{i,j}) := \mathsf{OT}_1^*(\mathsf{crs}^i, f_\gamma^{i,j}(x))$.

  – P_1 broadcasts $(\mathsf{otr}, \overline{\mathsf{otr}})$, P_2 broadcasts $(\mathsf{otr}_0, \mathsf{otr}_1)$ and for each $i \in [3,n]$, P_i broadcasts $\{\mathsf{otr}_\gamma^{i,j}\}_{j \in [m], \gamma \in [0,2]}$ to every party.

Round-2: In the second round,

  – P_2 computes $\mathsf{ots} \leftarrow \mathsf{OT}_2(\mathsf{crs}^1, \mathsf{otr}, (y_0, \mu_0), (y_1, \mu_1))$.
  – For every $i \in [3,n]$, P_i does the following for each $j \in [m]$,
  - For each $b \in \{0,1\}$, it chooses $\tau_b^{i,j} \leftarrow \{0,1\}^*$ and computes $\mathsf{ots}_b^{i,j} := \mathsf{OT}_2(\mathsf{crs}^2, \mathsf{otr}_b, f_0^{i,j}(0) + f_2^{i,j}(0), f_1^{i,j}(0) + f_2^{i,j}(0); \tau_b^{i,j})$.
  - It chooses random $\tau^{i,j} \leftarrow \{0,1\}^*$ and computes $\mathsf{ots}^{i,j} := \mathsf{OT}_2(\mathsf{crs}^1, \mathsf{otr}, \mathsf{ots}_0^{i,j}, \mathsf{ots}_1^{i,j}; \tau^{i,j})$.
  - It chooses random $\overline{\tau}^{i,j} \leftarrow \{0,1\}^*$ and computes $\overline{\mathsf{ots}}^{i,j} \leftarrow \mathsf{OT}_2(\mathsf{crs}^1, \overline{\mathsf{otr}}, -f_2^{i,j}(0), f_1^{i,j}(0) - f_0^{i,j}(0) - f_2^{i,j}(0); \overline{\tau}^{i,j})$.
  - It sets the string $s^{i,j} = (\{f_\gamma^{i,j}(x), \mu_\gamma^{i,j}\}_{\gamma \in [0,2]}, \{\mathsf{ots}_b^{i,j}, \tau_b^{i,j}\}_{b \in \{0,1\}}, \tau^{i,j}, \overline{\tau}^{i,j})$. It then sends $(\mathsf{sender}, i, P_i, (s^{i,1}, \ldots, s^{i,m}))$ to the $\mathcal{F}_{(m,p)\text{-RaOT}}$ functionality.

  – P_2 sends ots and for every $i \in [3,n]$, P_i sends $(\{\mathsf{ots}^{i,j}, \overline{\mathsf{ots}}^{i,j}\}_{j \in [m]})$ to P_1 via private channels (which can implemented in two rounds over a public-channel model using a two-round OT).

Output: To compute the output, P_1 does the following: For each $i \in [3,n]$,

  – It receives $(\mathsf{output}, i, (\overline{s}^{i,1}, \ldots, \overline{s}^{i,m}))$ as the output from $\mathcal{F}_{(m,p)\text{-RaOT}}$.
  – Let $J_i \subseteq [m]$ such that for each $j \in J_i$, $\overline{s}_j^i \neq \perp$.
  – For each $j \in J_i$:
  - It parses $\overline{s}^{i,j}$ as $(\{f_\gamma^{i,j}(x), \mu_\gamma^{i,j}\}_{\gamma \in [0,2]}, \{\mathsf{ots}_b^{i,j}, \tau_b^{i,j}\}_{b \in \{0,1\}}, \tau^{i,j}, \overline{\tau}^{i,j})$.
  - For each $\gamma \in [0,2]$, it checks if $\mathsf{CheckValid}(\mathsf{crs}^i, \mathsf{otr}_\gamma^{i,j}, (f_\gamma^{i,j}(x), \mu_\gamma^{i,j}))$ (see Sect. 3.1 for $\mathsf{CheckValid}$) outputs 1 and if $f_\gamma^{i,j}(x)$ is a degree-λ polynomial.
  - For every $k \in J_i \setminus \{j\}$ and $\gamma \in [0,2]$, it checks if $f_\gamma^{i,j}(k) = f_\gamma^{i,k}(j)$.
  - It checks if $\mathsf{ots}^{i,j} := \mathsf{OT}_2(\mathsf{crs}^1, \mathsf{otr}, \mathsf{ots}_0^{i,j}, \mathsf{ots}_1^{i,j}; \tau^{i,j})$ and $\overline{\mathsf{ots}}^{i,j} \leftarrow \mathsf{OT}_2(\mathsf{crs}^1, \overline{\mathsf{otr}}, -f_2^{i,j}(0), f_1^{i,j}(0) - f_0^{i,j}(0) - f_2^{i,j}(0); \overline{\tau}^{i,j})$.
  - It also checks if $\mathsf{ots}_b^{i,j} := \mathsf{OT}_2(\mathsf{crs}^2, \mathsf{otr}_b, f_0^{i,j}(0) + f_2^{i,j}(0), f_1^{i,j}(0) + f_2^{i,j}(0); \tau_b^{i,j})$ for each $b \in \{0,1\}$.
  - If any of the above checks fail, it aborts.
  – It computes $(y_\alpha, \mu_\alpha) := \mathsf{OT}_3(\mathsf{crs}^1, \mathsf{ots}, (\alpha, \mu))$. It then runs $\mathsf{CheckValid}(\mathsf{crs}^2, \mathsf{otr}_\alpha, (y_\alpha, \mu_\alpha))$. If the algorithm outputs 1, then it proceeds. Otherwise, it aborts.
  – For each $j \in [m]$,
  - It computes $\mathsf{ots}_\alpha^{i,j} := \mathsf{OT}_3(\mathsf{crs}^1, \mathsf{ots}^{i,j}, (\alpha, \mu))$.
  - It then computes $\mathsf{Sh}_{y_\alpha}^{i,j} := \mathsf{OT}_3(\mathsf{crs}^2, \mathsf{ots}_\alpha^{i,j}, (y_\alpha, \mu_\alpha))$.
  - It also computes $\overline{\mathsf{Sh}}_r^{i,j} := \mathsf{OT}_3(\mathsf{crs}^1, \overline{\mathsf{ots}}^{i,j}, (r, \overline{\mu}))$.
  – It computes z_i as the Reed-Solomon decoding of $\{\mathsf{Sh}_{y_\alpha}^{i,j} + \overline{\mathsf{Sh}}_r^{i,j}\}_{j \in [m]}$, correcting at most λ errors.

  It outputs $(y_\alpha, \{z_i\}_{i \in [3,n]})$.

Fig. 4. Protocol $\Pi_{\mathsf{dSelPri}}^\dagger$

The following lemma proves Theorem 5. We defer the proof to the full version.

Lemma 3. *Let $\mathcal{A}$ be an (possibly malicious) adversary corrupting an arbitrary subset of parties in the protocol $\Pi_{\mathsf{dSelPri}}^{\dagger}$. There exists a simulator Sim such that for any environment $\mathcal{Z}$, $\mathrm{EXEC}_{\mathcal{F}_{\mathsf{dSelPri}}^{\dagger},\mathsf{Sim},\mathcal{Z}} \overset{c}{\approx} \mathrm{EXEC}_{\Pi_{\mathsf{dSelPri}}^{\dagger},\mathcal{A},\mathcal{Z}}$*

5.2 Conforming Protocols and the Round-Collapsing Compiler

The steps 2 and 3 of building a maliciously-secure MPC protocol for a general function require the usage of a conforming protocol introduced in [19]. In this subsection, we recall this notion and present a slightly modified version given in [17]. Further, these two steps will build upon the round-collapsing compiler of [19].

Specification of a Conforming Protocol. Consider an n-party deterministic[2] MPC protocol Φ between parties $P_1, \ldots, P_n$ with inputs $x_1, \ldots, x_n$, respectively computing some function $f(x_1, \ldots, x_n)$. For each $i \in [n]$, we let $x_i \in \{0,1\}^m$ denote the input of party P_i. A conforming protocol Φ is defined by functions pre, post, and computations steps or what we call *actions* $\phi_1, \cdots \phi_T$. The protocol Φ proceeds in three stages: pre-processing, computation and output.

- **Pre-processing phase:** For each $i \in [n]$, party P_i first samples $v_i \in \{0,1\}^{\ell}$ (where ℓ is the parameter of the protocol) as the output of a randomized function $\mathsf{pre}(1^{\lambda}, i)$ and sets z_i as $z_i = (x_i \oplus v_i[(i-1)\ell/n + 1, (i-1)\ell/n + m]) \| 0^{\ell/n - m}$, where $v_i[(i-1)\ell/n + 1, (i-1)\ell/n + m]$ denotes the bits of the string v_i in the positions $[(i-1)\ell/n + 1, (i-1)\ell/n + m]$. P_i retains v_i as the secret information and broadcasts z_i to every other party. We require that $v_i[k] = 0$ for all $k \in [\ell] \backslash \{(i-1)\ell/n + 1, \ldots, i\ell/n\}$.[3]
- **Computation phase:** For each $i \in [n]$, party P_i sets $\mathsf{st} := (z_1 \| \cdots \| z_n)$. Next, for each $t \in \{1 \cdots T\}$ parties proceed as follows:
  1. Parse action ϕ_t as (i, f, g, h) where $i \in [n]$ and $f, g, h \in [\ell]$.
  2. Party P_i computes *one* NAND gate as $\mathsf{st}[h] = \mathsf{NAND}\big(\mathsf{st}[f] \oplus v_i[f], \mathsf{st}[g] \oplus v_i[g]\big) \oplus v_i[h]$ and broadcasts $\mathsf{st}[h]$ to every other party.
  3. Every party P_j for $j \neq i$ updates $\mathsf{st}[h]$ to the bit value received from P_i. We require that for all $t, t' \in [T]$ such that $t \neq t'$, if $\phi_t = (\cdot, \cdot, \cdot, h)$ and $\phi_{t'} = (\cdot, \cdot, \cdot, h')$ then $h \neq h'$. Also, we denote $A_i \subset [T]$ to be the set of rounds in which P_i sends a bit. Namely, $A_i = \{t \in T \mid \phi_t = (i, \cdot, \cdot, \cdot)\}$.
- **Output phase:** For each $i \in [n]$, party P_i outputs $\mathsf{post}(\mathsf{st})$.

We now recall the following theorem proved in [17,19].

---

[2] Randomized protocols can be handled by including the randomness used by a party as part of its input.

[3] Here, we slightly differ from the formulation used in [17,19]. In their work, pre is defined to additionally take x_i as input and outputs (z_i, v_i). However, the transformation from any protocol to a conforming protocol given in these works has the above structure where the last $\ell/n - m$ bits of z_i are 0 and the first m bits of z_i is the XOR of x_i and $v_i[(i-1)\ell/n + 1, (i-1)\ell/n + m]$.

Theorem 6 ([17,19]). *Any MPC protocol Π can be transformed into a conforming protocol Φ while inheriting the correctness and the security of the original protocol. Furthermore, the post function of Φ is just a projection function (i.e., it outputs some bits of st)[4] and the simulated message z_i (for every honest party) is $(r_i \| 0^{\ell/n-m})$ where r_i is a uniformly chosen random string of length m (independent of other simulated messages).*

5.3 Second Step: Special Functionality with Standard Security

In this subsection, we define the n-party version of the double-selection functionality $\mathcal{F}_{\mathsf{dSel}}$ in Fig. 5 and give a three-round protocol for securely realizing this functionality. The main theorem we prove in this subsection is given below.

Functionality $\mathcal{F}_{\mathsf{dSel}}$

$\mathcal{F}_{\mathsf{dSel}}$ is parameterized by an n-party function dSel whose description follows. dSel receives $(\alpha, r) \in \{0,1\} \times \{0,1\}$ from P_1 and $(y_0, y_1) \in \{0,1\} \times \{0,1\}$ from P_2. For every $3 \leq i \leq n$, dSelPri receives $(z_0^i, z_1^i) \in \{0,1\}^\lambda \times \{0,1\}^\lambda$ from P_i. dSel delivers $(y_\alpha \oplus r, \{z_{y_\alpha \oplus r}^i\}_{3 \leq i \leq n})$ to every party (and this is where dSelPri differs from dSel). Let x_i be the input of party P_i to dSel (note that x_i for different parties maybe of different lengths) and let S be the adversary. $\mathcal{F}_{\mathsf{dSel}}$ proceeds as follows:

1. For each $i \in [3, n]$, P_i (and S on behalf of P_i if P_i is corrupted) sends (input, sid, P_i, x_i) to the functionality.
2. If either of P_1 or P_2 is honest, then for each $i \in \{1, 2\}$, P_i (and S on behalf of P_i if P_i is corrupted) sends (input, sid, P_i, x_i) to the functionality.
3. If P_1 and P_2 are both corrupted, S sends (Corrupt, sid, β) where $\beta \in \{0, 1\}$.
4. Upon receiving the inputs from all parties, the functionality computes:

$$\mathsf{out} := \begin{cases} (y_\alpha \oplus r, \{z_{y_\alpha \oplus r}^i\}_{i \in [3,n]}) & \text{If } P_1 \text{ or } P_2 \text{ is honest.} \\ (\beta, \{z_\beta^i\}_{i \in [3,n]}) & \text{If } P_1 \text{ and } P_2 \text{ are corrupt.} \end{cases}$$

5. The functionality delivers (output, sid, out) to S. On receiving (generateOutput, sid) from S, the functionality delivers (output, sid, P_i, out) to every honest P_i. On the other hand, if S sends (abort, sid), then the functionality sends (output, sid, P_i, abort) to every honest P_i. (And ignores the message if inputs from all parties in $\{P_1, \ldots, P_n\}$ have not been received.)

Fig. 5. Functionality $\mathcal{F}_{\mathsf{dSel}}$

Theorem 7. *There exists a three-round protocol Π_{dSel} (Fig. 7) that UC-realizes the $\mathcal{F}_{\mathsf{dSel}}$ functionality. Π_{dSel} makes black-box use of a two-round malicious-secure OT with equivocal receiver security in the $\mathcal{F}_{\mathsf{dSelPri}}^\dagger$-hybrid model.*

---

[4] We note that this property can be generically added to any conforming protocol by expanding the computation phase to include more actions that compute the output of the protocol.

Building Π_{dSel}. The primary challenge in Π_{dSel}, over $\Pi_{\text{dSelPri}}^{\dagger}$, is to keep any corrupt P_2's behaviour, as an OT sender, in check. We resort to an OT combiner protocol [12,23], that guarantees generation of a secure OT correlation given a number of leaky OTs, as formalized by functionality $\mathcal{F}_{\kappa\text{-LeakyOT}}$ in Fig. 6.

Functionality $\mathcal{F}_{\kappa\text{-LeakyOT}}$

Let $\mathcal{S}$ be an adversary corrupting at most one among $\{P_1, P_2\}$.

- A party P_1 (and $\mathcal{S}$ on behalf of P_1 if P_1 is corrupted) sends (receiver, sid, $P_1, \alpha_1, \ldots, \alpha_\kappa$).
- Another party P_2 (and $\mathcal{S}$ on behalf of P_2 if P_2 is corrupted) sends (sender, sid, $P_2, (K, \{(s_0^i, s_1^i)\}_{i \in [\kappa]})$) to the functionality where $K \subseteq [\kappa]$ is a set of size at most λ and $s_b^i \in \{0, 1\}$ for each $i \in [\kappa]$ and $b \in \{0, 1\}$.
- On receiving both these messages, the functionality computes $\text{out}_1 := \{(\alpha_i, s_{\alpha_i}^i)\}_{i \in [\kappa]}$ and $\text{out}_2 := \{\alpha_i\}_{i \in K}$.
- For $i \in \{1, 2\}$, if P_i is corrupted, the functionality delivers (output, sid, P_i, out_i) to $\mathcal{S}$. On receiving (generateOutput, sid) from $\mathcal{S}$ (if either of P_1 or P_2 is corrupted), the functionality delivers (output, sid, P_i, out_i) to every honest P_i. On the other hand, if $\mathcal{S}$ sends (abort, sid), it sends (output, sid, P_i, abort) to every honest P_i.

Fig. 6. Functionality $\mathcal{F}_{\kappa\text{-LeakyOT}}$

In keeping with the goal of publishing a masked version of P_1's selected input of P_2, i.e. $y_\alpha + r$, we slightly stretch the goal of OT combiner from realizing a secure OT correlation to realizing a simple two-party functionality captured by $\mathcal{F}_{\text{OTplus}}$. $\mathcal{F}_{\text{OTplus}}$ gets two bits (α, r) from the receiver and two bits (s_0, s_1) from the sender and delivers $(s_\alpha \oplus r)$ to both parties. An information-theoretic protocol for securely realizing $\mathcal{F}_{\text{OTplus}}$ in the $\mathcal{F}_{\kappa\text{-LeakyOT}}$-hybrid model is guaranteed from an OT combiner protocol followed by a secure computation protocol in the OT-hybrid model [24,28].

Theorem 8 ([12,24,28]). *Let $\kappa = \Omega(\lambda)$ and consider the $\mathcal{F}_{\kappa\text{-LeakyOT}}$ functionality described in Fig. 6. There exists a statistically secure protocol that UC-realizes the $\mathcal{F}_{\text{OTplus}}$ functionality making a single call to the $\mathcal{F}_{\kappa\text{-LeakyOT}}$ functionality. Furthermore, the inputs to $\mathcal{F}_{\kappa\text{-LeakyOT}}$ given by an honest receiver in the above protocol are uniformly chosen $(\alpha_1, \ldots, \alpha_\kappa)$ and the inputs given by an honest sender are $(\varnothing, \{(s_0^i, s_1^i)\}_{i \in [\kappa]})$ where $\{(s_0^i, s_1^i)\}_{i \in [\kappa]}$ are uniformly chosen.*

While Theorem 8 guarantees a protocol for $\mathcal{F}_{\text{OTplus}}$, it may be a multi-round protocol and it is not clear how Π_{dSel} can use this for its goal to realize $\mathcal{F}_{\text{dSel}}$. Here, we invoke the round-collapsing compiler of [17,19] on a conforming protocol obtained from the protocol implied by Theorem 8 in $\mathcal{F}_{\kappa\text{-LeakyOT}}$-hybrid model. To be specific, Theorem 8 implies the following protocol for realizing $\mathcal{F}_{\text{OTplus}}$:

- **Call to $\mathcal{F}_{\kappa\text{-LeakyOT}}$ functionality.** The honest P_1 samples uniform bits $(\alpha_1, \ldots, \alpha_\kappa)$ as input to the functionality. The honest P_2 samples uniform bits $\{(s_0^i, s_1^i)\}_{i \in [\kappa]}$ and sends $(\varnothing, \{(s_0^i, s_1^i)\}_{i \in [\kappa]})$ to the functionality.
- **Protocol Π_{OTplus}.** Using the output of $\mathcal{F}_{\kappa\text{-LeakyOT}}$ functionality, P_1 and P_2 interact with each other using the *statistically-secure* protocol Π_{OTplus} (from

Theorem 8) that realizes the $\mathcal{F}_{\mathsf{OTplus}}$ functionality. In this protocol, P_1's input is given by $((\alpha, r), (s_{\alpha_1}^1, \alpha_1), \ldots, (s_{\alpha_\kappa}^\kappa, \alpha_\kappa))$ and P_2's input is given by $((y_0, y_1), (s_0^1, s_1^1), \ldots, (s_0^\kappa, s_1^\kappa))$ (where (α, r) are the P_1's inputs to the $\mathcal{F}_{\mathsf{OTplus}}$ functionality and y_0, y_1 are P_2's inputs). Without loss of generality, we assume that the last message from P_1 to P_2 contains the output of $\mathcal{F}_{\mathsf{OTplus}}$.

Let Φ be the conforming protocol obtained as a result of the transformation given in Theorem 6 to the protocol Π_{OTplus} (as above). We assume w.l.o.g. that the input of P_1 in Φ is of the form $(s_{\alpha_1}^i, \ldots, s_{\alpha_\kappa}^i, \alpha_1, \ldots, \alpha_k, \alpha, r)$ and that of P_2 is $(\{s_0^i, s_1^i\}_{i \in [\kappa]}, y_0, y_1)$. We further assume w.l.o.g. that at the end of the computation phase of Φ, $\mathsf{st}[\ell/2]$ (for each $i \in \{1, 2\}$) contains the output of the protocol (i.e., $v_1[\ell/2] = v_2[\ell/2] = 0$) and post just outputs this bit (if either party has not aborted and this information is public from st).

Now to enable Π_{dSel} to achieve the larger goal of publishing "doubly-selected" inputs of $P_3, \ldots, P_n$, all that is needed from $P_3, \ldots, P_n$ is to take part in Φ and listen to the conversation. That is, the garbled circuits generated by P_1 and P_2 will perform the interaction as dictated by the protocol Φ while the garbled circuits generated by all other parties will listen to this interaction. By the virtue of listening to this interaction, the last garbled circuit of every party in $\{P_3, \ldots, P_n\}$ will output the labels for st that has $(s_\alpha \oplus r)$ at the position $\ell/2$. Specifically, we introduce another layer of garbled circuits for the parties P_3 to P_n that takes st as input, has z_0^i, z_1^i hardwired and outputs $z_{\mathsf{st}[\ell/2]}^i$ if st does not indicate an abort of P_1 or P_2. W.l.o.g., we can assume that st contains this information on abort. To tackle a malicious behaviour of P_i, we make them commit to z_0^i, z_1^i via OT receiver messages in the first round and reveal the opening information via the garbled circuit.

There are two missing blocks now: (a) how to create the correlation of a $\mathcal{F}_{\kappa\text{-LeakyOT}}$ functionality (since Φ runs given the output of $\mathcal{F}_{\kappa\text{-LeakyOT}}$) and (b) how to release the labels corresponding to the initial public joint state for every party's garbled circuit in 3 rounds. Both are resolved through κ calls to $\mathcal{F}_{\mathsf{dSelPri}}^\dagger$ functionality (recall that κ is the OT combiner parameter). Π_{dSel} runs κ copies of $\mathcal{F}_{\mathsf{dSelPri}}^\dagger$ with the input of P_1 in the k-th copy being $\{\alpha_k, v_1[k]\}_{k \in [\kappa]}$ (where v_1 is the private state of P_1 as per the round-collapsing compiler and α_k is uniformly chosen), the input of P_2 being a random pair of bits (s_0^k, s_1^k) and the inputs for the rest of parties being equal to a pair of secret keys for a SKE scheme (looking ahead, these keys will enable release of the first set of labels). These κ executions of $\mathcal{F}_{\mathsf{dSelPri}}^\dagger$ lead to P_1 and P_2 sharing κ-random OT correlations. It is these κ random OT correlations that serve as the input and output of the leaky OT functionality. Specifically, as argued in the proof, we show that a corrupt P_2 cannot guess more than λ among $(\alpha_1, \ldots, \alpha_\kappa)$ without triggering an abort by an honest P_1 with overwhelming probability. In other words, the size of the set K that a corrupt P_2 sends to the $\mathcal{F}_{\kappa\text{-LeakyOT}}$ functionality is at most λ. This allows us to use the security of the conforming protocol Φ to argue the security of the round-collapsed protocol.

We now explain how to release the labels corresponding to the initial public joint state for every party's garbled circuit in 3 rounds. This is where we use the secret keys in the calls to $\mathcal{F}_{\mathsf{dSelPri}}^\dagger$. Recall that P_1 gets P_j's secret key corresponding to the bit $s_{\alpha_k}^k \oplus v_1[k]$ from $\mathcal{F}_{\mathsf{dSelPri}}^\dagger$ at the end of round-2. In round-3, P_1 sends this secret key and P_j sends a pair of encryptions, encrypting b-th label under b-th key for $b \in \{0,1\}$. Putting these two things together, all parties can recover the label for P_j's circuit corresponding to the bit $s_{\alpha_k}^k \oplus v_1[k]$. This way all the parties obtain the labels for the first set of garbled circuits. This will trigger evaluation of the bunch of circuits emulating Φ.

Lastly, we consider the $\mathcal{F}_{\mathsf{dSelPri}}^\dagger$ functionality instantiated with $n+1$ parties with P_2 additionally playing the role of P_{n+1}. Specifically, the inputs of party P_2 includes (y_0, y_1) as well as (z_0^2, z_1^2).

Protocol Π_{dSel}

Inputs: P_1 inputs $(\alpha, r) \in \{0,1\} \times \{0,1\}$, P_2 inputs $(y_0, y_1) \in \{0,1\} \times \{0,1\}$. For every $3 \le i \le n$, P_i inputs $(z_0^i, z_1^i) \in \{0,1\}^\lambda \times \{0,1\}^\lambda$.

Output: Every party outputs $(y_\alpha \oplus r, \{z_{y_\alpha \oplus r}^i\}_{3 \le i \le n})$.

Primitives and Functionalities: (a) A malicious-secure, two-round OT with equivocal receiver security $(K_{\mathsf{OT}}, \mathsf{OT}_1, \mathsf{OT}_2, \mathsf{OT}_3)$ (see Section 3.1). We use OT_1^* to denote an algorithm that takes a crs and $q(\lambda)$-bit string (for some polynomial $q(\cdot)$) as input and applies OT_1 to each bit of that string. (b) Functionality $\mathcal{F}_{\mathsf{dSelPri}}^\dagger$. (c) The conforming protocol Φ obtained as a result of the transformation in Theorem 6 to Π_{OTplus} as discussed. (d) Garbling scheme $(\mathsf{Garble}, \mathsf{Eval})$ (e) A symmetric-key Encryption Scheme $(\mathsf{Gen}, \mathsf{Enc}, \mathsf{Dec})$.

Common Random/Reference String: For each $i \in [n]$, sample $\mathsf{crs}^i \leftarrow K_{\mathsf{OT}}(1^\lambda)$ and output $\{\mathsf{crs}^i\}_{i \in [n]}$ as the common random/reference string.

Round-1: In the first round,

- P_1 and P_2 run $\mathsf{pre}(1^\lambda, 1)$ and $\mathsf{pre}(1^\lambda, 2)$ to get v_1 and v_2 respectively. For each $i \in [3,n]$, P_i sets $v_i = 0^\ell$.
- P_1 chooses κ random bits $\alpha_1, \ldots, \alpha_\kappa$ and P_2 chooses random pairs of bits (s_0^k, s_1^k) for each $k \in [\kappa]$.
- For each $i \in [2,n]$ and for each $k \in [\kappa]$, P_i chooses two random secret keys $(sk_0^{i,k}, sk_1^{i,k})$ using $\mathsf{Gen}(1^\lambda)$.
- For each $k \in [\kappa]$, P_1 sends $(\mathsf{input}, k, P_1, (\alpha_k, v_1[k]))$, P_2 sends $(\mathsf{input}, k, P_2, (s_0^k, s_1^k))$ and for each $i \in [2,n]$, P_i sends $(\mathsf{input}, k, P_i, (sk_0^{i,k}, sk_1^{i,k}))$ to $\mathcal{F}_{\mathsf{dSelPri}}^\dagger$.
- For each $i \in [3,n]$, for each $b \in \{0,1\}$, P_i computes $(\mathsf{otr}_b^i, \mu_b^i) \leftarrow \mathsf{OT}_1^*(\mathsf{crs}^i, z_b^i)$.
- For each $i \in [3,n]$, P_i broadcasts $\{\mathsf{otr}_b^i\}_{b \in \{0,1\}}$ to every other party.

Round-2: In the second round,

- P_1 sets $x_1^{\mathsf{part}} := (\alpha_1, \ldots, \alpha_\kappa, \alpha, r)$ and P_2 sets $x_2 := (\{s_0^k, s_1^k\}_{k \in [\kappa]}, y_0, y_1)$.
- P_1 and P_2 respectively set $z_1^{\mathsf{part}} := (x_1^{\mathsf{part}} \oplus v_1[\kappa+1, 2\kappa+2]) \| 0^{\ell/2 - (2\kappa+2)}$ and $z_2 := (x_2 \oplus v_2[\ell/2+1, \ell/2+2\kappa+2]) \| 0^{\ell/2 - (2\kappa+2)}$.
- For each $i \in \{1,2\}$ and for each t such that $\phi_t = (i, f, g, h)$ (A_i is the set of such values of t), for each $\alpha, \beta \in \{0,1\}$, P_i computes $(\mathsf{otr}^{i,t,\alpha,\beta}, \mu^{i,t,\alpha,\beta}) \leftarrow \mathsf{OT}_1(\mathsf{crs}^i, v_i[h] \oplus \mathsf{NAND}(v_i[f] \oplus \alpha, v_i[g] \oplus \beta))$.
- P_1 broadcasts $(z_1^{\mathsf{part}}, \{\mathsf{otr}^{i,t,\alpha,\beta}\}_{t \in A_1, \alpha, \beta \in \{0,1\}})$ and P_2 broadcasts $(z_2, \{\mathsf{otr}^{i,t,\alpha,\beta}\}_{t \in A_2, \alpha, \beta \in \{0,1\}})$ to every other party.

Round-3: In the final round, each party P_i does the following:

- If $i = 1$, P_1 receives for each $k \in [\kappa]$, $(\text{output}, k, P_1, (x_1[k],$ $\{sk^{i,k}_{x_1[k] \oplus v_1[k]}\}_{i \in [2,n]}))$ from $\mathcal{F}^{\dagger}_{\text{dSelPri}}$ where $x_1[k] = s^k_{\alpha_k}$ [a]
- P_i sets $\mathsf{st} := 0^{\kappa} \| (z^{\text{part}}_1 \| z_2)$.
- If $i \in [3,n]$, P_i computes $(\widetilde{\mathsf{ChkC}}^i, \mathsf{lab}^{i,T+1}) \leftarrow \mathsf{Garble}(1^{\lambda}, \mathsf{ChkC}^i[\{z^i_b, \mu^i_b\}_{b \in \{0,1\}}])$.
- If $i \in \{1,2\}$, P_i sets $\mathsf{lab}^{i,T+1} = \{\bot, \bot\}_{k \in [\ell]}$.
- **for** each t from T down to 1,
  1. Parse ϕ_t as (i^*, f, g, h).
  2. If $i = i^*$ then it computes (where $C^{i,t}$ is described in Figure 8) $(\widetilde{C}^{i,t}, \mathsf{lab}^{i,t}) \leftarrow \mathsf{Garble}(1^{\lambda}, C^{i,t}[v_i, \{\mu^{i,t,\alpha,\beta}\}_{\alpha,\beta}, \bot, \mathsf{lab}^{i,t+1}])$.
  3. If $i \neq i^*$ then for every $\alpha, \beta \in \{0,1\}$, it sets $\mathsf{ots}^{i^*,t,\alpha,\beta} \leftarrow \mathsf{OT}_2(\mathsf{crs}^{i^*}, \mathsf{otr}^{i^*,t,\alpha,\beta}_h, \mathsf{lab}^{i,t+1}_{h,0}, \mathsf{lab}^{i,t+1}_{h,1})$ and computes $(\widetilde{C}^{i,t}, \mathsf{lab}^{i,t}) \leftarrow \mathsf{Garble}(1^{\lambda}, C^{i,t}[v_i, \bot, \{\mathsf{ots}^{i^*,t,\alpha,\beta}\}_{\alpha,\beta}, \mathsf{lab}^{i,t+1}])$.
- Each P_i sends $(\{\widetilde{C}^{i,t}\}_{t \in [T]}, \{\mathsf{lab}^{i,1}_{k,\mathsf{st}[k]}\}_{k \in [\kappa+1,\ell]})$ to every other party and if $i \in [3,n]$, it also sends $\widetilde{\mathsf{ChkC}}^i$. In addition, P_1 sends $\{\mathsf{lab}^{1,1}_{k,x_1[k] \oplus v_1[k]}, x_1[k] \oplus v_1[k], \{sk^{i,k}_{x_1[k] \oplus v_1[k]}\}_{i \in [2,n]}\}_{k \in [\kappa]}$ and for each $i \in [2,n]$, P_i sends $\{\mathsf{Enc}(sk^{i,k}_0, \mathsf{lab}^{i,1}_{k,0}), \mathsf{Enc}(sk^{i,k}_1, \mathsf{lab}^{i,1}_{k,1})\}_{k \in [\kappa]}$.

Output. Each party P_i does the following:

- It sets $\mathsf{st}[k] = x_1[k] \oplus v_1[k]$ for each $k \in [\kappa]$ receiving the value from P_1's broadcast.
- For each $j \in [2,n]$ and $k \in [\kappa]$, it recovers $\mathsf{lab}^{j,1}_{k,\mathsf{st}[k]} \leftarrow \mathsf{Dec}(sk^{j,k}_{\mathsf{st}[k]}, \mathsf{Enc}(sk^{i,k}_{\mathsf{st}[k]}, \mathsf{lab}^{i,1}_{k,\mathsf{st}[k]}))$.
- Let $\widetilde{\mathsf{lab}}^{1,1} := \{\{\mathsf{lab}^{1,1}_{k,x_1[k] \oplus v_1[k]}\}_{k \in [\kappa]}, \{\mathsf{lab}^{1,1}_{k,\mathsf{st}[k]}\}_{k \in [\kappa+1,\ell]}\}$.
- For each $j \in [2,n]$, let $\widetilde{\mathsf{lab}}^{j,1} := \{\mathsf{lab}^{j,1}_{k,\mathsf{st}[k]}\}_{k \in [\ell]}$.
- **for** each t from 1 to T **do:**
  1. Parse ϕ_t as (i^*, f, g, h).
  2. Compute $((\alpha, \beta, \gamma), \mu, \widetilde{\mathsf{lab}}^{i^*,t+1}) := \mathsf{Eval}(\widetilde{C}^{i^*,t}, \widetilde{\mathsf{lab}}^{i^*,t})$.
  3. Set $\mathsf{st}[h] := \gamma$.
  4. **for** each $j \neq i^*$ **do:**
     (a) Compute $(\mathsf{ots}, \{\mathsf{lab}^{j,t+1}_k\}_{k \in [\ell] \setminus \{h\}}) := \mathsf{Eval}(\widetilde{C}^{j,t}, \widetilde{\mathsf{lab}}^{j,t})$.
     (b) Recover $\mathsf{lab}^{j,t+1}_h := \mathsf{OT}_3(\mathsf{crs}^{i^*}, \mathsf{ots}, (\gamma, \mu))$.
     (c) Set $\widetilde{\mathsf{lab}}^{j,t+1} := \{\mathsf{lab}^{j,t+1}_k\}_{k \in [\ell]}$.
- For each $j \in [3,n]$,
  - Compute $(z^j, \mu^j) := \mathsf{Eval}(\widetilde{\mathsf{ChkC}}^j, \widetilde{\mathsf{lab}}^{j,T+1})$
  - Run $\mathsf{CheckValid}(\mathsf{crs}^j, \mathsf{otr}^j_{\mathsf{st}[\ell/2]}, (z^j, \mu^j))$.
- If any of runs of the $\mathsf{CheckValid}$ algorithm outputs 0 then abort. Otherwise, output $(\mathsf{st}[\ell/2], \{z^j_{\mathsf{st}[\ell/2]}\}_{j \in [3,n]})$.

---

[a] This message is received in the end of round-2, since $\Pi^{\dagger}_{\text{dSelPri}}$ is a 2-round protocol.

Fig. 7. Protocol Π_{dSel}

Circuit $C^{i,t}$ and ChkC^i

Input of $C^{i,t}$: st
Hard-coded Information of $C^{i,t}$: v_i, $\{\mu^{i,t,\alpha,\beta}\}_{\alpha,\beta}$, $\{\text{ots}^{t,\alpha,\beta}\}_{\alpha,\beta}$, and lab $=$ $\{\text{lab}_{k,0}, \text{lab}_{k,1}\}_{k \in [\ell]}$.
Code of $C^{i,t}$:
- Let $\phi_t = (i^*, f, g, h)$.
- if $i = i^*$ then:
  - Compute $\text{st}[h] := \text{NAND}(\text{st}[f] \oplus v_i[f], \text{st}[g] \oplus v_i[g]) \oplus v_i[h]$.
  - Output $((\text{st}[f], \text{st}[g], \text{st}[h]), \mu^{i,t,\text{st}[f],\text{st}[g]}, \{\text{lab}_{k,\text{st}[k]}\}_{k \in [\ell]})$.
- else: Output $(\text{ots}^{i^*,t,\text{st}[f],\text{st}[g]}, \{\text{lab}_{k,\text{st}[k]}\}_{k \in [\ell] \setminus \{h\}})$.

Input of ChkC^i: st

Hard-coded Information of ChkC^i: $\{z_b^i, \mu_b^i\}_{b \in \{0,1\}}$.
Code of ChkC^i:
- Check from st if P_1 or P_2 have not aborted. We assume w.l.o.g. that this information is public from st.
- If no abort occurs, then output $z^i_{\text{st}[\ell/2]}, \mu^i_{\text{st}[\ell/2]}$. Otherwise, output $\bot$.

Fig. 8. Circuit $C^{i,t}$ and ChkC^i

Lemma 4. *Let $\mathcal{A}$ be an (possibly malicious) adversary corrupting an arbitrary subset of parties in the protocol Π_{dSel}. There exists a simulator Sim such that for any environment $\mathcal{Z}$, $\text{EXEC}_{\mathcal{F}_{\text{dSel}},\text{Sim},\mathcal{Z}} \stackrel{c}{\approx} \text{EXEC}_{\Pi_{\text{dSel}},\mathcal{A},\mathcal{Z}}$*

We defer the proof of this lemma to the full version.

5.4 Third Step: Bootstrapping from Special to General Functions

In this section, we build a 3-round MPC protocol for any multiparty function f in the $\mathcal{F}_{\text{dSel}}$-hybrid model. The main theorem shown here is the following.

Theorem 9. *Let f be a n-party functionality. There exists a protocol Π_f (Fig. 9) that UC-realizes f in three rounds against malicious adversaries corrupting an arbitrary number of parties. Π_f makes black-box use of a two-round, malicious-secure OT with equivocal receiver security and is in $\mathcal{F}_{\text{dSel}}$-hybrid model.*

Building Π_f. The protocol Π_f is obtained as a result of applying the round-collapsing compiler in [17,19] to perfect/statistical protocols in the OT-correlations model (e.g., [26,28]) which have the following structure.

- **Generating OT Correlations.** Every pair of parties invoke a certain number of OT executions on uniformly chosen random inputs.
- **Protocol Π.** The parties augment their inputs with the OT correlations generated in the previous phase. The parties then use the perfect/statistical protocol from [26,28] in the OT correlations model to securely compute f.

Let Φ be the conforming protocol obtained as a result of the transformation in Theorem 6 to Π. For every $i, j \in [n]$ such that $i \neq j$, let κ be the number of random OT correlations required between party P_i (acting as the receiver) and P_j (acting as the sender) in the protocol Φ. The building blocks we use for Π_f are the conforming protocol Φ, a two-round, malicious-secure OT with equivocal receiver security, a garbling scheme for circuits and a symmetric key encryption. Further, we assume without loss of generality, that the first $(n-1)\kappa$ bits of the augmented input of party P_i in Φ contains the bits obtained from every other party (acting as sender) in the OT correlations generation phase. Specifically, the first κ bits are the received bits from P_1 (if $i \neq 1$) and the second set of κ bits are the received bits from P_2 (if $i \neq 2$) and so on. We denote a function GetIndex that takes i, j, k as inputs (where $i, j \in [n]$, $i \neq j$ and $k \in [\kappa]$) and returns an index ind $\in [\ell]$ of the state st of the conforming protocol that corresponds to the received bit in the k-th OT correlation between P_i (acting as the receiver) and P_j (acting as the sender). We now present an information description of Π_f.

Building on the round-collapsing compiler of [17,19], the main challenge in Π_f is in making the first set of labels for the joint state available within 3 rounds. Unlike [17,19], the input to the conforming protocol in our case not only includes the actual inputs of the parties, but also the OT correlations. The generation of the latter (to be specific, the output bit of an OT) is completed only at the end of round-2. As a result, the public state of a party can be made available to all only in round-3 and the labels for the joint state in round-4. We overcome this challenge using the double selection $\mathcal{F}_{\mathsf{dSel}}$ functionality. The double selection functionality allows the parties to learn the labels corresponding to masked value of the correlation bits at the end of round-3 allowing them to trigger the evaluation of garbled circuits at the end of round-3.

Protocol Π_f

Inputs: P_i for $i \in [n]$ inputs x_i.

Output: Every party outputs $f(x_1, \ldots, x_n)$.

Primitives and Functionalities: (a) A malicious-secure two-round OT with equivocal receiver security $(K_{\mathsf{OT}}, \mathsf{OT}_1, \mathsf{OT}_2, \mathsf{OT}_3)$ (see Section 3.1), (b) Functionality $\mathcal{F}_{\mathsf{dSel}}$ (c) The conforming protocol Φ obtained as a result of the transformation in Theorem 6 to Π as discussed (c) Garbling scheme $(\mathsf{Garble}, \mathsf{Eval})$ (d) A symmetric-key Encryption Scheme $(\mathsf{Gen}, \mathsf{Enc}, \mathsf{Dec})$.

Common Random/Reference String: For each $i \in [n]$, sample $\mathsf{crs}^i \leftarrow K_{\mathsf{OT}}(1^\lambda)$ and output $\{\mathsf{crs}^i\}_{i \in [n]}$ as the common random/reference string.

Round-1: In the first round,

- Each P_i runs $\mathsf{pre}(1^\lambda, i)$ to get v_i.
- For each $i, j \in [n]$ and $i \neq j$ and for each $k \in [\kappa]$, the parties invoke an instance of functionality $\mathcal{F}_{\mathsf{dSel}}$ as follows:
  - P_i, taking the role of P_1, sends $(\mathsf{input}, (i, j, k), P_i, (\alpha_k^{i,j}, r_k^{i,j}))$ to $\mathcal{F}_{\mathsf{dSel}}$ where $\alpha_k^{i,j}$ is a uniformly chosen bit and $r_k^{i,j} := v_i[\mathsf{GetIndex}(i, j, k)]$.
  - P_j, taking the role of P_2, sends $(\mathsf{input}, (i, j, k), P_j, (y_{k,0}^{i,j}, y_{k,1}^{i,j}))$ to $\mathcal{F}_{\mathsf{dSel}}$ where $y_{k,0}^{i,j}, y_{k,1}^{i,j}$ are uniformly chosen bits.
  - For every $s \in [n]$, P_s inputs $(\mathsf{input}, (i, j, k), P_s, (sk_{k,0}^{s,i,j}, sk_{k,1}^{s,i,j}))$ to $\mathcal{F}_{\mathsf{dSel}}$ where $sk_{k,0}^{s,i,j}, sk_{k,1}^{s,i,j}$ are sampled using $\mathsf{Gen}(1^\lambda)$.

Round-2: In the second round, every P_i does the following

- It sets $x_i^{\mathsf{part}} := (x_i, \{\alpha_k^{i,j}, y_{k,0}^{j,i}, y_{k,1}^{j,i}\}_{j \in [n] \setminus \{i\}, k \in [\kappa]})$.
- It sets $z_i^{\mathsf{part}} := x_i^{\mathsf{part}} \oplus v_i[(i-1)\ell/n + (n-1)\kappa + 1, i\ell/n]$.
- For each $i \in [n]$ and for each t such that $\phi_t = (i, f, g, h)$ (A_i is the set of such values of t), for each $\alpha, \beta \in \{0, 1\}$, it computes: $(\mathsf{otr}^{i,t,\alpha,\beta}, \mu^{i,t,\alpha,\beta}) \leftarrow \mathsf{OT}_1(\mathsf{crs}^i, v_i[h] \oplus \mathsf{NAND}(v_i[f] \oplus \alpha, v_i[g] \oplus \beta))$.
- It broadcasts $(z_i^{\mathsf{part}}, \{\mathsf{otr}^{i,t,\alpha,\beta}\}_{t \in A_i, \alpha, \beta \in \{0,1\}})$.

Round-3: In the final round, each party P_i does the following:

- It sets $\mathsf{st} = \left((0^{(n-1)\kappa} \| z_1^{\mathsf{part}}) \| \ldots \| (0^{(n-1)\kappa} \| z_n^{\mathsf{part}})\right)$.
- It sets $\mathsf{lab}^{i,T+1} := \{\mathsf{lab}_{k,0}^{i,T+1}, \mathsf{lab}_{k,1}^{i,T+1}\}_{k \in [\ell]}$ where for each $k \in [\ell]$ and $b \in \{0, 1\}$, $\mathsf{lab}_{k,b}^{i,T+1} := \bot$.
- **for** each t from T down to 1,
  1. Let ϕ_t as (i^*, f, g, h).
  2. If $i = i^*$, then it computes $(\widetilde{C}^{i,t}, \mathsf{lab}^{i,t}) \leftarrow \mathsf{Garble}(1^\lambda, C^{i,t}[v_i, \{\mu^{i,t,\alpha,\beta}\}_{\alpha,\beta}, \bot, \mathsf{lab}^{i,t+1}])$ (where $C^{i,t}$ is described in Figure 8).
  3. If $i \neq i^*$ then for every $\alpha, \beta \in \{0, 1\}$, it sets $\mathsf{ots}^{i^*,t,\alpha,\beta} \leftarrow \mathsf{OT}_2(\mathsf{crs}^{i^*}, \mathsf{otr}^{i^*,t,\alpha,\beta}, \mathsf{lab}_{h,0}^{i,t+1}, \mathsf{lab}_{h,1}^{i,t+1})$ and computes $(\widetilde{C}^{i,t}, \mathsf{lab}^{i,t}) \leftarrow \mathsf{Garble}(1^\lambda, C^{i,t}[v_i, \bot, \{\mathsf{ots}^{i,t,\alpha,\beta}\}_{\alpha,\beta}, \mathsf{lab}^{i,t+1}])$ (where $C^{i,t}$ is described in Figure 8).
- Each P_i broadcasts $\{\widetilde{C}^{i,t}\}_{t \in [T]}$, and for each $j \in [n]$ and $k \notin [(j-1)\ell/n + 1, (j-1)\ell/n + (n-1)\kappa]$, P_i broadcasts $\mathsf{lab}_{k,\mathsf{st}[k]}^{i,1}$. In addition, P_i broadcasts for each $j, j' \in [n]$ such that $j \neq j'$ and $k \in [\kappa]$, $\left(\mathsf{ct}_{k,0}^{i,j,j'} = \mathsf{Enc}(sk_{k,0}^{i,j,j'}, \mathsf{lab}_{\mathsf{GetIndex}(j,j',k),0}^{i,1}), \mathsf{ct}_{k,1}^{i,j,j'} = \mathsf{Enc}(sk_{k,1}^{i,j,j'}, \mathsf{lab}_{\mathsf{GetIndex}(j,j',k),1}^{i,1})\right)$.

Output: Each party P_i does the following:

- For each $j, j' \in [n]$ such that $j \neq j'$ and for each $k \in [\kappa]$, let $\eta :=$ GetIndex(i, j, k) and do the following:
  1. Receive $(\text{output}, (j, j', k), P_i, (z_\eta, \{sk_{k, z_\eta}^{s, j, j'}\}_{s \in [n]}))$ from $\mathcal{F}_{\text{dSel}}$ functionality.
  2. Reset $\text{st}[\eta] = z_\eta$.
  3. For each $s \in [n]$, set $\text{lab}_{\eta, \text{st}[\eta]}^{s, 1} \leftarrow \text{Dec}(sk_{k, \text{st}[\eta]}^{s, j, j'}, \text{ct}_{k, \text{st}[\eta]}^{s, j, j'})$.

- For every $j \in [n]$, let $\widetilde{\text{lab}}^{j, 1} = \{\text{lab}_{k, \text{st}[k]}^{j, 1}\}_{k \in [\ell]}$, where $\{\text{lab}_{k, \text{st}[k]}^{j, 1}\}_{k \in [(j-1)\ell/n+1, (j-1)\ell/n+(n-1)\kappa]}$ are decrypted as above and the rest received from P_j's round-3 message.

- **for** each t from 1 to T **do:**
  1. Parse ϕ_t as (i^*, f, g, h).
  2. Compute $((\alpha, \beta, \gamma), \mu, \widetilde{\text{lab}}^{i^*, t+1}) := \text{Eval}(\widetilde{C}^{i^*, t}, \widetilde{\text{lab}}^{i^*, t})$.
  3. Set $\text{st}[h] := \gamma$.
  4. **for** each $j \neq i^*$ **do:**
     (a) Compute $(\text{ots}, \{\text{lab}_{k, \text{st}[k]}^{j, t+1}\}_{k \in [\ell] \setminus \{h\}}) := \text{Eval}(\widetilde{C}^{j, t}, \widetilde{\text{lab}}^{j, t})$.
     (b) Recover $\text{lab}_{h, \text{st}[h]}^{j, t+1} := \text{OT}_3(\text{crs}^{i^*}, \text{ots}, (\gamma, \mu))$.
     (c) Set $\widetilde{\text{lab}}^{j, t+1} := \{\text{lab}_{k, \text{st}[k]}^{j, t+1}\}_{k \in [\ell]}$.

- Output $\text{post}(\text{st}, v_i)$.

Fig. 9. Protocol Π_f

Lemma 5. *Let $\mathcal{A}$ be an (possibly malicious) adversary corrupting an arbitrary subset of parties in the protocol Π_f. There exists a simulator Sim such that for any environment $\mathcal{Z}$, $\text{EXEC}_{\mathcal{F}_f, \text{Sim}, \mathcal{Z}} \overset{c}{\approx} \text{EXEC}_{\Pi_f, \mathcal{A}, \mathcal{Z}}$*

We give the proof of this lemma in the full version.

References

1. Aiello, B., Ishai, Y., Reingold, O.: Priced oblivious transfer: how to sell digital goods. In: Pfitzmann, B. (ed.) EUROCRYPT 2001. LNCS, vol. 2045, pp. 119–135. Springer, Heidelberg (2001). https://doi.org/10.1007/3-540-44987-6_8

2. Ananth, P., Choudhuri, A.R., Jain, A.: A new approach to round-optimal secure multiparty computation. In: Katz, J., Shacham, H. (eds.) CRYPTO 2017, Part I. LNCS, vol. 10401, pp. 468–499. Springer, Cham (2017). https://doi.org/10.1007/978-3-319-63688-7_16

3. Applebaum, B., Brakerski, Z., Garg, S., Ishai, Y., Srinivasan, A.: Separating two-round secure computation from oblivious transfer. In: Vidick, T. (ed.) 11th Innovations in Theoretical Computer Science Conference, ITCS 2020, Seattle, Washington, USA, 12–14 January 2020, volume 151 of LIPIcs, pp. 71:1–71:18. Schloss Dagstuhl - Leibniz-Zentrum für Informatik (2020)

4. Barak, B., et al.: On the (im)possibility of obfuscating programs. In: Kilian, J. (ed.) CRYPTO 2001. LNCS, vol. 2139, pp. 1–18. Springer, Heidelberg (2001). https://doi.org/10.1007/3-540-44647-8_1

5. Beaver, D., Micali, S., Rogaway, P.: The round complexity of secure protocols (extended abstract). In: 22nd ACM STOC, pp. 503–513. ACM Press, May 1990

6. Benhamouda, F., Lin, H.: k-round multiparty computation from k-round oblivious transfer via garbled interactive circuits. In: Nielsen, J.B., Rijmen, V. (eds.) EUROCRYPT 2018, Part II. LNCS, vol. 10821, pp. 500–532. Springer, Cham (2018). https://doi.org/10.1007/978-3-319-78375-8_17

7. Boyle, E., Gilboa, N., Ishai, Y.: Group-based secure computation: optimizing rounds, communication, and computation. In: Coron, J.-S., Nielsen, J.B. (eds.) EUROCRYPT 2017, Part II. LNCS, vol. 10211, pp. 163–193. Springer, Cham (2017). https://doi.org/10.1007/978-3-319-56614-6_6

8. Boyle, F., Gilboa, N., Ishai, Y., Lin, H., Tessaro, S.: Foundations of homomorphic secret sharing. In: ITCS 2018, pp. 21:1–21:21, January 2018

9. Brakerski, Z., Perlman, R.: Lattice-based fully dynamic multi-key FHE with short ciphertexts. In: Robshaw, M., Katz, J. (eds.) CRYPTO 2016, Part I. LNCS, vol. 9814, pp. 190–213. Springer, Heidelberg (2016). https://doi.org/10.1007/978-3-662-53018-4_8

10. Cachin, C., Crépeau, C., Marcil, J.: Oblivious transfer with a memory-bounded receiver. In: 39th FOCS, pp. 493–502. IEEE Computer Society Press, November 1998

11. Canetti, R.: Universally composable security: a new paradigm for cryptographic protocols. In: 42nd FOCS, pp. 136–145. IEEE Computer Society Press, October 2001

12. Cascudo, I., Damgård, I., Farràs, O., Ranellucci, S.: Resource-efficient OT combiners with active security. In: Kalai, Y., Reyzin, L. (eds.) TCC 2017, Part II. LNCS, vol. 10678, pp. 461–486. Springer, Cham (2017). https://doi.org/10.1007/978-3-319-70503-3_15

13. Ding, Y.Z., Harnik, D., Rosen, A., Shaltiel, R.: Constant-round oblivious transfer in the bounded storage model. In: Naor, M. (ed.) TCC 2004. LNCS, vol. 2951, pp. 446–472. Springer, Heidelberg (2004). https://doi.org/10.1007/978-3-540-24638-1_25

14. Garg, S., Gentry, C., Halevi, S., Raykova, M.: Two-round secure MPC from indistinguishability obfuscation. In: Lindell, Y. (ed.) TCC 2014. LNCS, vol. 8349, pp. 74–94. Springer, Heidelberg (2014). https://doi.org/10.1007/978-3-642-54242-8_4

15. Garg, S., Gentry, C., Halevi, S., Raykova, M., Sahai, A., Waters, B.: Candidate indistinguishability obfuscation and functional encryption for all circuits. In: 54th FOCS, pp. 40–49. IEEE Computer Society Press, October 2013

16. Garg, S., Gentry, C., Sahai, A., Waters, B.: Witness encryption and its applications. In: Boneh, D., Roughgarden, T., Feigenbaum, J. (eds.) 45th ACM STOC, pp. 467–476. ACM Press, June 2013

17. Garg, S., Ishai, Y., Srinivasan, A.: Two-round MPC: information-theoretic and black-box. In: Beimel, A., Dziembowski, S. (eds.) TCC 2018, Part I. LNCS, vol. 11239, pp. 123–151. Springer, Cham (2018). https://doi.org/10.1007/978-3-030-03807-6_5

18. Garg, S., Srinivasan, A.: Garbled protocols and two-round MPC from bilinear maps. In: 58th FOCS, pp. 588–599. IEEE Computer Society Press (2017)

19. Garg, S., Srinivasan, A.: Two-round multiparty secure computation from minimal assumptions. In: Nielsen, J.B., Rijmen, V. (eds.) EUROCRYPT 2018. LNCS, vol. 10821, pp. 468–499. Springer, Cham (2018). https://doi.org/10.1007/978-3-319-78375-8_16

20. Goldreich, O., Micali, S., Wigderson, A.: How to play any mental game or A completeness theorem for protocols with honest majority. In: Aho, S. (ed.) 19th ACM STOC, pp. 218–229. ACM Press, May 1987

21. Dov Gordon, S., Liu, F.-H., Shi, E.: Constant-round MPC with fairness and guarantee of output delivery. In: Gennaro, R., Robshaw, M. (eds.) CRYPTO 2015, Part II. LNCS, vol. 9216, pp. 63–82. Springer, Heidelberg (2015). https://doi.org/10.1007/978-3-662-48000-7_4

22. Halevi, S., Kalai, Y.T.: Smooth projective hashing and two-message oblivious transfer. J. Cryptol. **25**(1), 158–193 (2012). https://doi.org/10.1007/s00145-010-9092-8

23. Harnik, D., Kilian, J., Naor, M., Reingold, O., Rosen, A.: On robust combiners for oblivious transfer and other primitives. In: Cramer, R. (ed.) EUROCRYPT 2005. LNCS, vol. 3494, pp. 96–113. Springer, Heidelberg (2005). https://doi.org/10.1007/11426639_6

24. Ishai, Y., Kushilevitz, E., Ostrovsky, R., Prabhakaran, M., Sahai, A.: Efficient non-interactive secure computation. In: Paterson, K.G. (ed.) EUROCRYPT 2011. LNCS, vol. 6632, pp. 406–425. Springer, Heidelberg (2011). https://doi.org/10.1007/978-3-642-20465-4_23

25. Ishai, Y., Kushilevitz, E., Ostrovsky, R., Sahai, A.: Zero-knowledge from secure multiparty computation. In: Johnson, D.S., Feige, U. (eds.) 39th ACM STOC, pp. 21–30. ACM Press, June 2007

26. Ishai, Y., Prabhakaran, M., Sahai, A.: Founding cryptography on oblivious transfer – efficiently. In: Wagner, D. (ed.) CRYPTO 2008. LNCS, vol. 5157, pp. 572–591. Springer, Heidelberg (2008). https://doi.org/10.1007/978-3-540-85174-5_32

27. Jain, A., Kalai, Y.T., Khurana, D., Rothblum, R.: Distinguisher-dependent simulation in two rounds and its applications. In: Katz, J., Shacham, H. (eds.) CRYPTO 2017, Part II. LNCS, vol. 10402, pp. 158–189. Springer, Cham (2017). https://doi.org/10.1007/978-3-319-63715-0_6

28. Kilian, J.: Founding cryptography on oblivious transfer. In: 20th ACM STOC, pp. 20–31. ACM Press, May 1988

29. Kushilevitz, E.: Privacy and communication complexity. In: 30th FOCS, pp. 416–421. IEEE Computer Society Press, October/November 1989

30. Lin, H., Liu, T., Wee, H.: Information-theoretic 2-round MPC without round collapsing: adaptive security, and more. In: Pass, R., Pietrzak, K. (eds.) TCC 2020, Part II. LNCS, vol. 12551, pp. 502–531. Springer, Cham (2020). https://doi.org/10.1007/978-3-030-64378-2_18

31. Mukherjee, P., Wichs, D.: Two round multiparty computation via multi-key FHE. In: Fischlin, M., Coron, J.-S. (eds.) EUROCRYPT 2016, Part II. LNCS, vol. 9666, pp. 735–763. Springer, Heidelberg (2016). https://doi.org/10.1007/978-3-662-49896-5_26

32. Naor, M., Pinkas, B.: Efficient oblivious transfer protocols. In: Rao Kosaraju, S. (ed.) 12th SODA, pp. 448–457. ACM-SIAM, January 2001

33. Peikert, C., Shiehian, S.: Multi-key FHE from LWE, revisited. In: Hirt, M., Smith, A. (eds.) TCC 2016-B, Part II. LNCS, vol. 9986, pp. 217–238. Springer, Heidelberg (2016). https://doi.org/10.1007/978-3-662-53644-5_9

34. Peikert, C., Vaikuntanathan, V., Waters, B.: A framework for efficient and composable oblivious transfer. In: Wagner, D. (ed.) CRYPTO 2008. LNCS, vol. 5157, pp. 554–571. Springer, Heidelberg (2008). https://doi.org/10.1007/978-3-540-85174-5_31

35. Regev, O.: On lattices, learning with errors, random linear codes, and cryptography. In: Gabow, H.N., Fagin, R. (eds.) 37th ACM STOC, pp. 84–93. ACM Press, May 2005

36. Yao, A.C.-C.: How to generate and exchange secrets (extended abstract). In: 27th FOCS, pp. 162–167. IEEE Computer Society Press, October 1986

On the Round Complexity of Black-Box Secure MPC

Yuval Ishai[1]([✉]), Dakshita Khurana[2], Amit Sahai[3],
and Akshayaram Srinivasan[4]

[1] Technion, Haifa, Israel
yuvali@cs.technion.ac.il
[2] UIUC, Champaign, US
dakshita@illinois.edu
[3] UCLA, Los Angeles, US
sahai@cs.ucla.edu
[4] Tata Institute of Fundamental Research, Mumbai, India
akshayaram.srinivasan@tifr.res.in

Abstract. We consider the question of minimizing the *round complexity* of secure multiparty computation (MPC) protocols that make a *black-box* use of simple cryptographic primitives with security against any number of malicious parties. In the plain model, previous black-box protocols required a high constant number of rounds (>15). This is far from the known lower bound of 4 rounds for protocols with black-box simulators.

When allowing random oblivious transfer (OT) correlations, 2-round protocols making black-box use of a pseudorandom generator were known. However, such protocols were obtained via a round-collapsing "protocol garbling" technique that has poor concrete efficiency and makes non-black-box use of an underlying maliciously secure protocol.

We improve this state of affairs by presenting the following types of black-box protocols.

- **4-round "pairwise MPC" in the plain model.** This round-optimal protocol enables each ordered pair of parties to compute a function of both inputs whose output is delivered to the second party. The protocol makes black-box use of any public-key encryption (PKE) with pseudorandom public keys. As a special case, we get a black-box round-optimal realization of secure (copies of) OT between every ordered pair of parties.
- **2-round MPC from OT correlations.** This round-optimal protocol makes a black-box use of any *general* 2-round MPC protocol satisfying an augmented notion of *semi-honest* security. In the two-party case, this yields new kinds of 2-round black-box protocols.
- **5-round MPC in the plain model.** This protocol makes a black-box use of PKE with pseudorandom public keys, and 2-round oblivious transfer with "semi-malicious" security.

A key technical tool for the first result is a novel combination of split-state non-malleable codes (Dziembowski, Pietrzak, and Wichs, JACM'18) with standalone secure *two-party* protocols to construct *non-malleable two-party protocols*. The second result is based on a new round-optimized

T. Malkin and C. Peikert (Eds.): CRYPTO 2021, LNCS 12826, pp. 214–243, 2021.
https://doi.org/10.1007/978-3-030-84245-1_8

variant of the "IPS compiler" (Ishai, Prabhakaran and Sahai, Crypto'08). The third result is obtained via a specialized combination of these two techniques.

1 Introduction

Minimizing the *round complexity* of cryptographic protocols has been a central theme of research in the past few decades. Much of this research focused on the question of minimizing the round complexity of protocols for *secure multiparty computation* (MPC), both in the general case as well as for special tasks of interest such as zero-knowledge proofs, oblivious transfer (OT), or coin-tossing. This question is motivated not only by its direct relevance to the latency of protocols running over real-life networks, but also as an intriguing theoretical challenge that often inspires new ideas and serves as a test bed for new techniques.

The round complexity of MPC. We consider the standard setting of MPC with *an arbitrary number* of *malicious* parties, namely parties that are corrupted by a central adversary who may arbitrarily change their behavior. What do we know about the round complexity of MPC in this setting? Allowing a *common random string* (CRS) setup, it was recently shown [13,28] that *2-round* MPC protocols are possible under the (minimal) assumption that 2-round OT exists in the CRS model. This round complexity is clearly optimal, even in the easier setting of *semi-honest* adversaries who send messages as instructed by the protocol. In the *plain model*, without any setup, a long line of works [6,9,10,15,19,27,40,54] has culminated in *4-round* protocols that rely on the minimal assumption that a 4-round OT protocol exists [19]. This round complexity is known to be optimal for protocols that admit a *black-box simulator* [27,30,52]. All of the above 4-round protocols are of this kind.

Black-box constructions. Another central research theme in cryptography is obtaining *black-box constructions* of higher-level primitives from simpler lower-level primitives. A black-box construction of X from Y, also known as a (fully) black-box *reduction* from X to Y [59], specifies an implementation of X that only has oracle access to the input-output relation of Y, without being given any explicit representation of Y, e.g., in the form of a Boolean circuit or a Turing Machine. Moreover, it is required that the security reduction be black-box in the sense that any adversary A_X "attacking" X can be used as a black-box to obtain an adversary A_Y who obtains a similar advantage in attacking Y. Originating from the pioneering work of Impagliazzo and Rudich [43], a long line of works study the landscape of black-box reductions between natural cryptographic primitives. More relevant to our work is the effort to replace known instances of *non-black-box* constructions, where X requires access to the *code* of Y, by black-box constructions.

In the MPC context, early examples of results along this line include a black-box construction of constant-round *honest-majority* MPC protocols from one-way functions [22] (replacing an earlier non-black-box construction from [12]) and a black-box construction of malicious-secure OT from semi-honest OT [39] (replacing a non-black-box construction of [31]). Beyond the theoretical interest in understanding the tightness of the relation between primitives, the goal of replacing non-black-box constructions by black-box counterparts is strongly motivated by asymptotic and concrete *efficiency*. A well-known example in the context of MPC is the non-black-box *OT extension* construction of Beaver [11], which was replaced by a much more efficient black-box construction from [44] that is commonly used as a basis for fast MPC implementations. We use the term *black-box MPC* to refer generically to an MPC protocol obtained via a black-box construction from simple low-level primitives (such as OT) that can be easily and efficiently constructed from standard cryptographic assumptions.

Round complexity of *black-box* MPC. Interestingly, all of the round-optimal MPC protocols in the standard setting we consider, including those mentioned above, make *non-black-box* use of the underlying primitives. In the case of 2-round MPC protocols in the CRS model, this is known to be inherent (even for the easier goal of semi-honest security), at least for black-box constructions from 2-round OT or any other *2-party* protocol [7]. However, no such impossibility result is known for 4-round MPC protocols in the *plain model*.

In the two-party case, a 4-round black-box protocol is known for *one-sided* functionalities that deliver output to only one of the two parties [24,57]. The most general protocol of this kind makes a black-box use of any public-key encryption (**PKE**) with pseudorandom public keys, which can be easily constructed from most standard cryptographic assumptions [24]. This implies a similar 5-round protocol for two-sided functionalities.

In contrast, for a general number of parties, all known constant-round protocols are either complex and inefficient, or resort to idealized models such as the Random Oracle (RO) model to achieve better efficiency but only heuristic security. Despite the significant body of work on the round complexity of black-box MPC and related primitives in the plain model, the best exact round complexity that follows from existing works [32,49,60] is greater than 15 (see Sect. 1.2). Recent attempts to minimize round complexity [6,9,10,15,19,27,54] have led to complex protocols that make heavy non-black-box use of cryptography. This gap gives rise to the first motivating question for our work.

What is the minimal round complexity of black-box MPC in the plain model?
Must we necessarily resort to idealized models to achieve simplicity and/or efficiency?

Round complexity of black-box protocol transformations. It turns out that if "plain model" is relaxed to allow a simple setup in the form of random *OT correlations* between each pair of parties, the first part of the above question has been settled. Concretely, given an OT correlation setup, which can be generated with good concrete efficiency [14,44], there is a 2-round MPC protocol making a black-box use of a pseudorandom generator [26]. However, this 2-round protocol is quite complex and inefficient, as it is obtained by applying a heavily non-black-box "protocol garbling" transformation [13,28] to an underlying multiround (information-theoretic) MPC protocol. This not only hurts asymptotic and concrete efficiency, but also rules out applying this transformation while respecting a black-box use of an underlying primitive. The latter includes a black-box use of an algebraic structure (e.g., a big finite field), a cryptographic primitive (e.g., homomorphic encryption or even a random oracle), or an ideal functionality oracle (e.g., OT or its arithmetic variant OLE). This is similar to the classical non-black-box protocol transformation from semi-honest MPC to malicious MPC, due to Goldreich, Micali, and Wigderson [31], which is limited in the same way.

In contrast, "black-box protocol transformations" from weak MPC protocols to stronger ones, commonly known as "MPC-in-the-head" transformations [46,49,50], have successfully avoided these limitations. In a nutshell, such transformations obtain a strong MPC protocol for f (say, with malicious security) by making a black-box use of any weak MPC protocol (say, with semi-honest security) for a *related* functionality f'. The relation between f and f' needs to be restricted in some way. Typically, f' is a next-message function of (an information-theoretic) weak MPC protocol for f.

This black-box protocol transformation paradigm, systematically studied in [48], has not only given rise to new theoretical feasibility and efficiency results, but it has also led to practical zero-knowledge proof systems [5,29], digital signatures [16,51], and MPC protocols [41]. The question we ask is whether one can obtain a similar black-box protocol transformation in the context of 2-round MPC with OT correlation setup:

> Are there useful kinds of "black-box protocol transformations" from 2-round semi-honest MPC to 2-round malicious MPC with OT correlation setup?

This question is particularly motivated in the two-party case, where there are many different techniques for efficient 2-round semi-honest protocols that make black-box use of algebraic or cryptographic primitives.

1.1 Our Contributions

We make progress on the aforementioned questions by obtaining the following types of round-efficient black-box protocols.

Black-box 4-Round "Pairwise MPC" in the Plain Model. Our first result addresses the first question by settling the round complexity of black-box MPC for a restricted but useful class of functionalities. Concretely, we get a 4-round black-box protocol for any *pairwise* MPC functionality that enable each ordered pair of parties to simultaneously compute a function of their inputs, whose output is delivered to the second party. The protocol makes a black-box use of any public-key encryption (PKE) with pseudorandom public keys (which can be instantiated based on CDH, LWE and LPN), similar to the 4-round 2-party OT protocol of [24].

Informal Theorem 1. *Let f be a pairwise MPC functionality. Assume the existence of a public-key encryption with pseudorandom public keys. There exists a four round black-box MPC protocol in the plain model that securely implements f against static corruptions of all-but-one parties.*

The central challenge in the pairwise MPC setting is to develop two-party protocols that remain secure *when executed in parallel*. We develop new black-box protocols for this setting, starting with the case of OT protocols, and generalizing via the result of [45] to any two-party functionality. To this end, a technical contribution of our work is a novel combination of split-state non-malleable codes [18,23] with standalone secure *two-party* protocols to obtain black-box, *non-malleable* two-party protocols.

The resulting pairwise MPC can be used to generate OT correlations in a preprocessing phase, as required by the 2-round black-box protocol of [26]. This results in a 6-round MPC protocol making black-box use of PKE with pseudorandom public keys. While this already constitutes a major improvement over the state of the art, it is still two rounds away from the 4-round lower bound. Perhaps more importantly, as discussed above, the [26] approach employs a round-collapsing "protocol garbling" that limits its efficiency and applicability to protocols that make black-box use of algebraic or cryptographic primitives. Motivated by both limitations, we would like to replace the protocol garbling technique by a black-box protocol transformation that takes advantage of OT correlations.

An "IPS-style Compiler" for 2-round MPC. Our second main contribution is a new black-box protocol transformation obtained via a round-optimized variant of the "IPS compiler" [49]. This transformation uses a 2-round honest-majority MPC protocol from [47,58] to transform in a black-box way any 2-round MPC protocol with an augmented variant of *semi-honest* security to obtain a 2-round MPC protocol with malicious security. The transformation relies on a special form of OT correlations (denoted as watchlist correlations) that can be generated via the above mentioned pairwise MPC functionality. Specifically, the watchlist correlations model outputs an n-party correlation between $(n-1)$ senders and a single receiver, where each sender S_i for $i \in [n-1]$ obtains a random set of m strings $x_{i,1}, \ldots, x_{i,m}$, and the receiver obtains a random subset $K \subset [m]$ of a fixed size, as well as the values $\{x_{i,j}\}_{i \in [n-1], j \in [k]}$. Combined with our first main result, this yields the same kind of 6-round black-box protocol obtained via [26], but with the advantage of making a black-box use of an augmented semi-honest protocol (as opposed to a non-black-box use of a malicious protocol incurred by the protocol garbling technique).

The augmented semi-honest security requirement combines the so-called *semi-malicious* security [8], which is satisfied by most natural 2-round semi-honest protocols, with a form of *adaptive security with erasures*. The latter is satisfied by all natural information-theoretic protocols (with standard forms of setup), as well as by computationally secure protocols with pre-processing. Concretely, we show the protocol from [26] in the OT correlations model and the protocol from [55] in the OLE correlations model satisfy augmented semi-honest security and thus, can be used in our compiler.

Informal Theorem 2. *Let f be an arbitrary multiparty functionality. Consider the client-server MPC protocol from [47] that securely computes f. Let f' be* *the function computed by the servers in this protocol. There exists a black-box transformation from a two-round MPC protocol for f' satisfying augmented semi-honest security to a two-round malicious secure protocol for computing f in the watchlist correlations model.*

Towards concretely efficient 2-sided NISC. An interesting use case for the above result is the 2-round, secure *two-party* protocol in which *both* parties get an output. This should be contrasted with the standard notion of non-interactive secure computation (NISC) [45] that applies to one-sided functionalities. Note that this kind of *2-sided NISC* cannot be obtained by simply running two parallel instances of standard NISC, since even if we ignore parallel composition issues, there is no mechanism to enforce consistency between the inputs used in these instances (unless we rely on zero-knowledge proofs and make non-black-box use of cryptography). The only alternative black-box approach to 2-sided NISC over OT correlations we are aware of is via the protocol garbling technique that garbles the code of a malicious secure protocol and thus, has prohibitive computational and communication cost. Even in the 1-sided case, existing protocols from [1,17,42,45,56] are heavily tailored to specific garbling techniques and do not make a black-box use of an underlying semi-honest protocol.

We note that techniques developed in the context of an "IPS-style compiler" in the two-round setting gives new approach for constructing protocols for the 2-sided NISC problem. Specifically, if we use [47,58] as the outer protocol and use the simple two-sided version of Yao's protocol (using Boolean garbling in the OT correlations model) as the inner protocol, we obtain a 2-sided NISC protocol that is secure against malicious adversaries in the OT correlations model.[1] In Sect. 8.5 of the full version, we suggest some optimizations to improve the concrete efficiency.

Black-box 5-Round MPC in the Plain Model. Our third and final result uses a specialized combination of the previous contributions to get "one round away" from settling the main open question about the round complexity of black-box MPC. Concretely, we get a 5-round MPC protocol that makes a black-box use of PKE with pseudorandom public keys (as in the first contribution), along with any 2-round OT protocol with "semi-malicious" security. The latter security requirement is a very mild strengthening of semi-honest security in the context of 2-round OT protocols, and is satisfied by most 2-round OT protocols from the literature (for instance, it can be instantiated from standard assumptions such as DDH, LWE, QR).

Informal Theorem 3. *Let f be an arbitrary multiparty functionality. Assume the existence of a public key encryption with pseudorandom public keys and a two-round oblivious transfer protocol with semi-malicious security. There exists a five-round black-box protocol in the plain model that securely implements f against malicious adversaries that statically corrupts upto all-but-one parties.*

---

[1] As we noted before, for the case of constant number of parties, watchlist correlations reduces to standard OT correlations.

1.2   Related Work

In this subsection, we give a brief overview of the two main approaches taken by prior work obtaining black-box MPC protocols in the plain model.

Coin tossing based approach. The main idea in this approach is to use a black-box simulatable coin tossing protocol to setup a CRS and then use black-box MPC protocols (such as [GIS18]) in the CRS model. Roughly, to generate the CRS, the idea is for each party to commit to a random string r_i and in a later step, for all parties to reveal their coins. To ensure that malicious parties cannot set their randomness as a function of that of other honest players, players should use a (concurrent) non-malleable commitment in the commit phase.

But the main bottleneck to obtaining such a coin tossing protocol is achieving simulatability. To achieve the simulation guarantee and allow a simulator to "force" the output of the coin toss to be a certain value[2], one would need to rely zero-knowledge protocols, which if applied naively make non-black-box use of cryptography. Even if one were able to achieve simulation-based guarantees via a specific protocol, one would need to tailor this to prove statements about construction of bounded concurrent non-malleable commitment w.r.t. commitment against synchronising adversaries, for which no round efficient black-box constructions exist. More specifically, [35] gives a black-box protocol but the number of rounds of this protocol is greater than 18 (the coin tossing requires at least two more rounds. [36] gives a 3-round black-box construction of NMCom but is only secure in the standalone setting. The other round efficient constructions of concurrent NMCom [20,21,37,53] make non-black use of cryptography.

IPS compiler based approach. The IPS compiler [49] gives a black-box MPC protocol in the OT hybrid model. The main challenge in instantiating this approach in the plain model is in constructing a protocol that securely realizes the ideal OT functionality. In particular, we need a protocol that realizes the ideal OT functionality between every ordered pair of parties. [60] gave a non-constant round black-box way to realize this which was improved by [32] who gave a constant round protocol. The main component in the constant round protocol is again a constant round black-box bounded concurrent non-malleable commitment wrt replacement (which is weaker than the traditional definition of non-malleable commitment wrt commitment). Even if we rely on a three-round black-box version of such a non-malleable commitment from [34], the OT protocol requires at least 12 rounds of communication. A straightforward way of combining this with the IPS approach incurs at least four more rounds.

2   Technical Overview

In this section, we provide an overview of the key technical ideas used in constructing a four round, black-box pairwise MPC in the plain model. One of the

---

[2] Note that this corresponds to the programmability requirement.

key building blocks used in this construction is a watchlist protocol. We give a construction of this protocol based on any public-key encryption with pseudorandom public keys and we elaborate on this next.

2.1 The Watchlist Protocol

We start by describing the ideal version of the watchlist functionality. The watchlist functionality is nothing but an implementation of a k-out-of-m oblivious transfer between each ordered pair of parties. Specifically, each ordered pair P_i and P_j execute a k-out-of-m OT where P_i acts as a receiver and P_j acts as a sender. We observe that the k-out-of-m OT is a one-sided functionality and hence, this can be realized if parties have pairwise access to independent copies of the ideal OT functionality [45,49]. We call this as simultaneous secure OT and would like to securely realize this ideal functionality in the plain model in the presence of *arbitrary malicious* corruptions.

A Starting Point. A natural first attempt is to just have each pair of parties simultaneously execute a two-party secure protocol computing the k-out-of-m OT functionality. Such a protocol can be realized based on black-box use of any public key encryption scheme with pseudorandom public keys [24,57].

Unfortunately, this *does not* securely emulate access to independent copies of the ideal OT functionality between pairs of participants, because this protocol satisfies only *stand-alone* security. It is easy to achieve OT that composes under parallel repetition with *fixed roles*, i.e., where many OT sessions are executed in parallel, and an adversary either corrupts multiple senders or multiple receivers but does *not* simultaneously corrupt (subsets of) senders and receivers. In particular, the stand-alone secure construction of OT from pseudorandom public keys in [24] already achieves this notion of parallel composition.

But in the (more general) simultaneous setting, an adversarial party P_i^* participates in many OT sessions simultaneously, as sender in some sessions and receiver in others. This gives P_i^* the opportunity to generate its own (e.g., sender) message in some OT session as a function of a message generated by an honest sender in a different OT session, thereby possibly making its own input depend on the input(s) of honest player(s). Clearly, this is disallowed by the ideal simultaneous OT functionality; but not prevented by standalone OT. Our first step towards addressing this vulnerability is to ensure that adversarial inputs are independent of the inputs of honest players.

As discussed in the introduction, we develop a novel approach to achieving such independence. In particular, we construct "non-malleable OT" that satisfies the following guarantees.

- **Receiver Security under Parallel Composition.** For every adversarial sender $\mathcal{A}^*$ that corrupts the OT sender (or resp., multiple senders in any parallel composition of the OT protocol), there exists a simulator that simulates the view of $\mathcal{A}^*$ with black-box access to (resp., copies of) the ideal OT functionality. This follows automatically from simulation-based security against malicious senders (resp., in the parallel composition setting) of the underlying two-party secure protocol $\Pi_{\mathcal{F}}$.

- **Non-Malleability.** Informally, here we consider a man-in-the-middle adversary MIM that acts as a receiver in a subset of OT sessions (that we refer to as "left" sessions) and as sender in a different subset of OT sessions (that we refer to as "right" sessions).

  We require the existence of a *simulator-extractor* Sim-Ext, that given the inputs of all honest receivers (participating in all right sessions), is able to extract all the implicit inputs used by the MIM *in all its right sessions*. Crucially, Sim-Ext *does not* have access to the inputs of honest senders (participating in the left sessions).

  This is the key property that prevents an adversarial sender from "copying" the inputs of honest senders, or more generally, generating its inputs as a function of honest senders' inputs. Achieving this property will be a key technical focus of our work.

In what follows, we provide an overview of our construction of non-malleable OT. Then, in Sect. 2.1, we discuss why any non-malleable OT protocol satisfying these properties almost directly implies pairwise ideal OT functionality (or, simultaneous secure OT), and therefore also securely realizes watchlists.

Towards Non-Malleable OT. We take inspiration from recent works that use non-malleable codes (introduced in [23]) to build cryptographic primitives like non-malleable commitments [36], and non-malleable multi-prover interactive proofs [33].

In more detail, we will build non-malleable OT by combining *parallel composable* two-party secure computation with (an) appropriate (variant of) split-state non-malleable codes. Such codes are specified by encoding and decoding algorithms (Enc, Dec). The encoding algorithm Enc is a randomized algorithm that encodes any message m into a codeword consisting of two parts or "states" (L, R), and the decoding algorithm Dec on input a codeword returns the underlying message. The security property is that for every pair of tampering functions (f, g) with no fixed points, the (distribution of) $\widetilde{m} \leftarrow \mathsf{Dec}(f(\mathsf{L}), g(\mathsf{R}))$, where $(\mathsf{L}, \mathsf{R}) \leftarrow \mathsf{Enc}(m)$, is independent of m. We now describe (a simplified variant of) our construction.

Our Construction. For simplicity, we will focus on the special case of implementing non-malleable 1-*out-of-*2 *OT*, but our techniques immediately extend to the more general setting of k-out-of-m OT. To prevent obvious copying attacks, we will assign to each party a unique tag or identity.

Our construction of non-malleable OT simply involves *executing a secure two-party protocol Π* between a sender $\mathcal{S}$ and a receiver $\mathcal{R}$, for a special functionality $\mathcal{F}$. Before describing this functionality, we discuss the inputs of participants to this functionality.

The sender $\mathcal{S}$ with on input $(\mathsf{m}_0, \mathsf{m}_1)$ and tag encodes these messages using an appropriate split-state non-malleable code (Enc, Dec). Specifically, $\mathcal{S}$ computes

$L_0, R_0 \leftarrow \mathsf{Enc}(m_0 \| \mathsf{tag})$ and $L_1, R_1 \leftarrow \mathsf{Enc}(m_1 \| \mathsf{tag})$. The receiver $\mathcal{R}$ obtains as input a choice bit $b \in \{0, 1\}$, and samples uniformly random $c \in \{0, 1\}$. $\mathcal{S}$ and $\mathcal{R}$ then invoke a two-party secure protocol $\Pi_{\mathcal{F}}$ to compute functionality $\mathcal{F}$ described in Fig. 1. In addition, $\mathcal{S}$ sends tag to $\mathcal{R}$.

Sender Inputs: $m_0, L_0, R_0, m_1, L_1, R_1, \mathsf{tag}$. **Receiver Inputs:** b, c.

The functionality $\mathcal{F}(m_0, L_0, R_0, m_1, L_1, R_1, b, c, \mathsf{tag})$ is defined as follows.

1. If $\mathsf{Dec}(L_0, R_0) \neq (m_0 \| \mathsf{tag})$ or $\mathsf{Dec}(L_1, R_1) \neq (m_1 \| \mathsf{tag})$, output $\perp$.
2. If $c = 0$, output (m_b, L_0, L_1) and output (m_b, R_0, R_1), otherwise.

Fig. 1. The functionality $\mathcal{F}$

We note that the ideal functionality $\mathcal{F}$ reveals m_b to $\mathcal{R}$, and in addition, reveals either *only* (L_0, L_1) or *only* (R_0, R_1). Because any split-state non-malleable code is also a 2-out-of-2 secret sharing scheme [4], the shares L_{1-b} and R_{1-b} each statistically hide m_{1-b} from $\mathcal{R}$. It is also clear that protocol Π makes only black-box use of the underlying two-party computation protocol.

We show that (an appropriate k-out-of-m variant of) the protocol sketched above securely realizes non-malleable OT, even when Π itself is only parallel composable secure (but may be completely malleable).

Proving Sender Non-Malleability. For ease of exposition, let's consider a simpler man-in-the-middle adversary (MIM) that participates in a single left session as receiver, and a single right session as sender. We will also assume that the MIM never sends messages that cause an honest party to abort. Additionally, the underlying secure two-party protocol Π will be a round optimal (four round) protocol with sequential messages, and has the following specific structure. Namely, it will require the receiver to commit to its input b in the first round of the protocol, and at the same time, it will be *delayed-input* w.r.t. receiver input c, which will be chosen by the receiver immediately before the third round begins. Finally, it will require the inputs $(m_0, m_1, L_0, R_0, L_1, R_1, \mathsf{tag})$ of the sender to be committed in the second round of the protocol, *before c is chosen by the receiver*.

First Attempt: An Alternate Extraction Mechanism. One possible way to extract sender inputs from the right execution, is to execute the simulator of the underlying two-party protocol Π. Unfortunately, this fails because Π is only parallel composable secure, and extracting from the right execution automatically reveals honest sender inputs from the left execution.

Instead, we will use the specific way that sender inputs are encoded to introduce an *alternate* extraction mechanism. Specifically, one could imagine rewinding the third and the fourth round message of Π, using inputs $c = 0$ and $c = 1$ on behalf of the honest receiver in the real and rewinding threads, respectively.

By our assumption, the adversary is non-aborting. Therefore, we expect to obtain outputs $(\widetilde{L}_0, \widetilde{L}_1)$ and $(\widetilde{R}_0, \widetilde{R}_1)$ in the right session in the real and rewinding threads respectively. At this point, we can use the decoder of the non-malleable code to obtain $(\widetilde{m}_0, \widetilde{m}_1)$, which, by correctness of the two-party protocol, should correspond to the implicit inputs of the MIM in the right session.

It doesn't seem like this argument gives us much (yet): rewinding the MIM's third and fourth rounds would also end up rewinding the third and the fourth rounds of the left execution with (possibly different) inputs $\widetilde{c}, \widehat{c}$ used by the MIM in the main and rewinding threads. Thus, it may seem like we are back to square one: it may not be possible to hide the inputs of the honest sender in the presence of such rewinding.

Towards Resolving the Extraction Bottleneck: 1-Rewind Sender Security. To tackle this problem, our first step will be to require that Π satisfy a stronger security property: *1-rewind sender security*. Roughly, this means that any adversarial receiver $\mathcal{R}^*$ that rewinds the honest sender one time in the third and fourth rounds, using (possibly different) inputs $\widetilde{c}, \widehat{c}$ in the main and rewinding threads, does not recover any information beyond the output of $\mathcal{F}$ on inputs $(m_0, m_1, L_0, L_1, R_0, R_1, b, \widetilde{c})$ and $(m_0, m_1, L_0, L_1, R_0, R_1, b, \widehat{c})$. We formalize this by requiring the existence of a specific type of simulator: this simulator generates a view for $\mathcal{R}^*$ in the main thread given only $(m_{\widetilde{b}}, L_0, L_1)$ and a view for $\mathcal{R}^*$ in the rewinding thread given only $(m_{\widetilde{b}}, R_0, R_1)$ (or vice-versa). Now, it may seem like this type of simulator may not be very meaningful, since the sum total of this information could essentially allow the receiver to recover $m_{1-\widetilde{b}}$ by combining $L_{1-\widetilde{b}}$ with $R_{1-\widetilde{b}}$.

However, the fact that (L_0, L_1) and (R_0, R_1) are made available in *separate* threads can be exploited argue that the MIM's input must be independent of $m_{1-\widetilde{b}}$, as we discuss next.

Alternative Simulation. Let us go back to our alternate extraction mechanism discussed earlier, where w.l.o.g. the third and fourth round messages of Π are rewound with (honest) receiver input set to $c = 0$ in the main and $c = 1$ in the rewinding thread, respectively. This means that in the main thread, the challenger obtains output $(\widetilde{L}_0, \widetilde{L}_1)$ in the right session. In the rewind thread, setting $c = 1$, the challenger obtains outputs $(\widetilde{R}_0, \widetilde{R}_1)$. Meanwhile the real and rewinding left executions will simulated using only $(m_{\widetilde{b}}, L_0, L_1)$ and $(m_{\widetilde{b}}, R_0, R_1)$ (or vice-versa) respectively, as described above. *This means that in the main thread, the MIM outputs $(\widetilde{L}_0, \widetilde{L}_1)$ as a function of only $(m_{\widetilde{b}}, L_0, L_1)$, and in the rewinding thread, the MIM outputs $(\widetilde{R}_0, \widetilde{R}_1)$ as a function of only $(m_{\widetilde{b}}, R_0, R_1)$.*[3]

We formalize this intuition to argue that the MIM's behaviour naturally gives rise to a split-state tampering function family. Here, one tampering function corresponds to the MIM's functionality in the main thread, and the other

---

[3] Actually, the MIM may also output $(\widetilde{L}_0, \widetilde{L}_1)$ as a function of only $(m_{\widetilde{b}}, R_0, R_1)$, and $(\widetilde{R}_0, \widetilde{R}_1)$ as a function of only $(m_{\widetilde{b}}, L_0, L_1)$. We use codes satisfying an additional *symmetric decoding* property to account for this case.

corresponds to the MIM's functionality in the rewinding thread. This allows us to rely on the non-malleability of the underlying encoding scheme to switch from generating $L_{1-\tilde{b}}, R_{1-\tilde{b}}$ as an encoding of m_{1-b}, to generating it as an encoding of a dummy value.

This completes a simplified description of the main ideas in our protocol. We swept several details under the rug but point out one important detail below.

Many-many Non-malleability. Recall that we simplified things earlier, to focus on a setting where the MIM participates in a single left session as receiver and a single right session as sender. For our application to watchlists, we require security against adversaries that participate in *multiple* left and right sessions.

To achieve security in this setting, we will rely on *many-many* non-malleable codes (that are implied by one-many non-malleable codes [18]) that achieve security in the presence of multiple tamperings of a single codeword [18]. Moreover, in order to deal with adversaries that may abort arbitrarily, we will modify the functionality $\mathcal{F}$. Instead of encoding (m_0, m_1) a single time, the sender generates λ (where λ is the security parameter) fresh encodings $\{(L_b^i, R_b^i)\}_{i \in [\lambda], b \in \{0,1\}}$ of m_0 and m_1. The receiver picks λ choice bits $c_1, \ldots, c_\lambda$ instead of a single bit c. The functionality $\mathcal{F}$ checks if for every $i \in [\lambda], b \in \{0, 1\}$, $\{(L_b^i, R_b^i)\}_{i \in [\lambda], b \in \{0,1\}}$ encode m_b. If the check fails, $\mathcal{F}$ outputs $\bot$. If it passes, then for every $i \in [\lambda]$, it outputs (L_0^i, L_1^i) if $c_i = 0$ and otherwise, outputs (R_0^i, R_1^i).

This helps ensure that for every adversary MIM that completes a main thread (without aborting) given honest receiver input $c = c_1, \ldots, c_\lambda$, there is (w.h.p.) a rewinding thread with a different choice $c' = c'_1, \ldots, c'_\lambda$ of honest receiver input, that is also completed by the MIM. We then rely on any index i for which $c_i \neq c'_i$ to carry out the argument described above. Additional details of our non-malleable OT protocol can be found in Sect. 5.1 in the full version.

From Non-Malleable OT to Watchlists. We note that that our OT protocol, as described above, prohibits an adversarial sender from generating its generating its inputs as a function of honest senders' inputs.

One could ask for an even stronger property, requiring the inputs of adversarial receivers to be independent of the honest receivers' inputs. At first glance, this stronger property appears to be necessary, since pairwise access to ideal OTs would actually enforce that all adversarial receiver inputs are independent of the inputs of honest receivers.

But upon taking a closer look, we realize that non-malleable OT as described in the previous section actually suffices to construct watchlists with security in the real/ideal paradigm. Intuitively, this is because the outputs of honest parties are affected only by the inputs of the adversarial senders, and are unaffected by the inputs of adversarial receivers. In other words, even if adversarial receivers manage to have their inputs depend on the inputs of the honest receivers, this cannot affect the joint distribution of their view and the outputs of honest parties in the ideal world. We formalize this intuition and show that non-malleable OT generically implies a protocol for securely realizing the watchlist functionality.

The only missing ingredient in our description is the 1-rewind sender secure protocol, which we describe next.

Constructing a 1-Rewind Sender Secure Protocol. In our actual construction of non-malleable OT, the receiver inputs $(c_1, \ldots c_\lambda)$ do not need to remain hidden from a corrupted sender. In particular, all we need is for the protocol to allow for delayed *function* selection, where the function to be computed (defined by $c_1, \ldots, c_\lambda$) is selected by the receiver in the third round. Given this, the 1-rewinding security property translates to requiring that any corrupt receiver which rewinds the third and the fourth round messages of the sender by providing (possibly) different functions learns nothing beyond the output of these two functions on sender and receiver inputs that were fixed in the first two rounds.

We will design such a 2-party protocol for NC1 circuits[4] by relying on a different variant [45,46,49] of the IPS paradigm. Specifically, we will use the same 2-client m-server outer protocol [58] that was discussed at the beginning of the overview, and combine it an inner protocol that is based a variant of Yao's garbled circuits [61]. Yao's protocol also allows for the garbled circuits to be generated in the final round, which immediately gives us the delayed function selection property. Importantly, since we only care about parallel composable security in the resulting two-party protocol, parallel composable but possibly malleable 1-rewind secure OT will suffice to implement watchlists in this setting. We slightly generalize the works of [24,57] to obtain a maliciously secure OT that satisfies 1-rewind sender security and makes black-box use of a PKE with pseudorandom public keys. We refer the reader to Appendix C of the full version for the details of constructing the secure computation protocol and to Appendix D of the full version for the construction of a 1-rewind sender secure OT protocol.

Immediate Application: Black-Box Simultaneous Two-Party Computation. Plugging the resulting simultaneous OT protocol in place of ideal OT, into the non-interactive two-party secure black-box computation protocol of [45], yields a round optimal two-party *simultaneous* secure computation, from black-box use of any PKE with pseudorandom public keys.

Organization. Due to lack of space, we include our construction of non-malleable OT in the body of the paper, and defer remaining protocols to the full version.

3 Preliminaries and Definitions

Let λ denote the security parameter. A function $\mu(\cdot) : \mathbb{N} \to \mathbb{R}^+$ is said to be negligible if for any polynomial $\mathsf{poly}(\cdot)$ there exists λ_0 such that for all $\lambda > \lambda_0$

---

[4] We show in Sect. 5.1 of the full version that 1-rewind secure 2PC for NC1 circuits suffices to obtain non-malleable OT.

we have $\mu(\lambda) < \frac{1}{\mathsf{poly}(\lambda)}$. We will use $\mathsf{negl}(\cdot)$ to denote an unspecified negligible function and $\mathsf{poly}(\cdot)$ to denote an unspecified polynomial function. We use Δ to denote the statistical distance.

For a probabilistic algorithm A, we denote $A(x; r)$ to be the output of A on input x with the content of the random tape being r. When r is omitted, $A(x)$ denotes a distribution. For a finite set S, we denote $x \leftarrow S$ as the process of sampling x uniformly from the set S. We will use PPT to denote Probabilistic Polynomial Time algorithm.

3.1 Non-malleable Codes

We will use non-malleable codes in the split-state model, that are one-many secure and satisfy a special augmented non-malleability [2] property, as discussed below.

Definition 1. (One-many augmented split-state non-malleable codes). *Fix any polynomials $\ell(\cdot), p(\cdot)$. An $\ell(\cdot)$-augmented non-malleable code with error $\epsilon(\cdot)$ for messages $m \in \{0,1\}^{p(\lambda)}$ consists of algorithms* NM.Code, NM.Decode *where* NM.Code$(m) \rightarrow (L, R)$ *such that for every $m \in \{0,1\}^{p(\lambda)}$,*

$$\mathsf{NM.Decode}(\mathsf{NM.Code}(m)) = m$$

and for every set of functions $f = (f_1, f_2, \ldots f_{\ell(\lambda)}), g = (g_1, g_2, \ldots g_{\ell(\lambda)})$ there exists a random variable $\mathcal{D}_{f,g}$ on $\{\{0,1\}^{p(\lambda)} \cup \mathsf{same}^*\}^{\ell(\lambda)}$ which is independent of the randomness in NM.Code *such that for all messages $m \in \{0,1\}^{p(\lambda)}$ it holds that*

$$\Delta\left(\left(\mathsf{R}, \{\mathsf{NM.Decode}\big(f_i(\mathsf{L}), g_i(\mathsf{R})\big)_{i \in [\ell(\lambda)]}\}\right), (\mathsf{replace}(\mathcal{D}_{f,g}, m)))\right) \leq \epsilon(\lambda)$$

$$\Delta\left(\left(\mathsf{R}, \{\mathsf{NM.Decode}\big(g_i(\mathsf{R}), f_i(\mathsf{L})\big)_{i \in [\ell(\lambda)]}\}\right), (\mathsf{replace}(\mathcal{D}_{f,g}, m)))\right) \leq \epsilon(\lambda)$$

where $(\mathsf{L}, \mathsf{R}) \leftarrow$ NM.Code(m) *and the function* $\mathsf{replace} : \{0,1\}^* \times \{0,1\}^* \rightarrow \{0,1\}$ *replaces all occurrences of* same* *in its first input with its second input s, and outputs the result.*

It was shown in [3,34,38] that the CGL one-many non-malleable codes constructed in [18] are also one-many *augmented* non-malleable codes. But we point out that in this definition, we also require messages obtained by decoding the tampered codewords with *left and right shares interchanged* to be unrelated with the original message. It is easy to see that this property is satisfied by any non-malleable code with symmetric decoding (i.e. where NMDec(L, R) = NMDec(R, L)). This property can be achieved, as observed in [33], by modifying any split-state code to attach a special symbol "ℓ" to the left part of the codeword, and a special symbol "r" to the right part of the codeword. This yields the following imported theorem:

Theorem 1. (Imported.) *[33, 34] For every polynomial $\ell(\cdot)$, there exists a polynomial $q(\cdot)$ such that for every $\lambda \in \mathbb{N}$, there exists an explicit ℓ-augmented, split-state non-malleable code satisfying Definition 1 with efficient encoding and decoding algorithms with code length $q(\lambda)$, rate $q(\lambda)^{-\Omega(1)}$ and error $2^{-q(\lambda)^{\Omega(1)}}$.*

3.2   Low-Depth Proofs

We will describe how any computation that can be verified by a family of poly-nomial sized ciruits can be transformed into a proof that is verifiable by a family of circuits in NC1. Let R be an efficiently computable binary relation. Let L be the language consisting of statements in R, i.e. for which $R(x) = 1$.

Definition 2 (Low-Depth Non-Interactive Proofs). *A low-depth non-interactive proof with perfect completeness and soundness for a relation R consists of an (efficient) prover P and a verifier V that satisfy:*

- **Perfect completeness.** *A proof system is perfectly complete if an honest prover can always convince an honest verifier. For all $x \in L$ we have*

$$\Pr[V(\pi) = 1 | \pi \leftarrow P(x)] = 1$$

- **Perfect soundness.** *A proof system is perfectly sound if it is infeasible to convince an honest verifier when the statement is false. For all $x \notin L$ and all (even unbounded) adversaries $\mathcal{A}$ we have*

$$Pr[V(x, \pi) = 1 | \pi \leftarrow \mathcal{A}(x)] = 0.$$

- **Low depth.** *The verifier V can be implemented in NC1.*

We outline a simple construction of a low-depth non-interactive proof, borrowed from [25]. The prover P executes the verification circuit on x and generates the proof as the sequential concatenation (in some specified order) of the bit values assigned to the individual wires of the circuit computing R. The verifier V proceeds by checking consistency of the values assigned to the internal wires of the circuit for each gate. In particular for each gate in the verification circuit the verifier checks if the wire vales provided in the proof represent a correct evaluation of the gate. Since the verification corresponding to each gate can be done independent of every other gate and in constant depth, we have that V itself is constant depth.

Looking ahead, our construction of non-malleable OT makes use of a (malleable) two-party computation protocol for NC1 that must verify validity of a non-malleable code. We rely on low-depth proofs to ensure that the two-party computation protocol only performs NC1 computations.

3.3   1-Rewind Sender-Secure Two-Party Computation

Let us consider a protocol Π between two parties, namely, the sender § and the receiver $\mathcal{R}$. The sender holds a private input $x_\S$ and the receiver holds a private input $x_\mathcal{R}$ and they wish to compute some function of their private inputs securely with the receiver obtains the output of the function. We want this protocol to satisfy:

– (Delayed-function selection) The function to be securely computed is only decided in the third round by the receiver $\mathcal{R}$. That is, the third round message contains the explicit description of the function f to be computed and the first two messages depend only on the size of the function.

– (1-Rewinding Security) Any malicious receiver that rewinds the third and fourth rounds of the protocol once (by possibly giving different functions f_0, f_1) cannot learn anything about the sender's inputs except the output on these two functions.

The syntax of the protocol and the two properties are formalized below.

Syntax. The special two party protocol Π is given by a tuple of algorithms $(\Pi_1, \Pi_2, \Pi_3, \Pi_4, \text{out}_\Pi)$. Π_1 and Π_3 are the next message functions run by the receiver $\mathcal{R}$ and Π_2 and Π_4 are the next message functions run by the sender §. At the end of the protocol, $\mathcal{R}$ runs out_Π on the transcript, its input and the random tape to get the output of the protocol. We use π_r to denote the message sent in the protocol Π in round r for every $r \in [4]$.

Definition 3. *Let* $\Pi = (\Pi_1, \Pi_2, \Pi_3, \Pi_4, \text{out}_\Pi)$ *be a 4-round protocol between a receiver* $\mathcal{R}$ *and a sender* § *with the receiver computing the output at the end of the fourth round. We say that* Π *is a 1-rewinding sender secure protocol with delayed function selection for* NC^1 *circuits if it satisfies:*

– **Delayed Function Selection.** *The first and second message functions* Π_1, Π_2 *take as input the size of the function* $f \in \mathsf{NC}^1$ *to be securely computed and are otherwise, independent of the function description. The third round message from* $\mathcal{R}$ *contains the explicit description of the function* f *to be computed.*

– **Receiver Security.** *For every malicious PPT adversary* $\mathcal{A}$ *that corrupts the sender, there exists an expected polynomial (black-box) simulator* $\mathsf{Sim}_\mathcal{R} = (\mathsf{Sim}_\mathcal{R}^1, \mathsf{Sim}_\mathcal{R}^2)$ *such that for all choices of honest receiver input* $x_\mathcal{R}$ *and the function* $f \in \mathsf{NC}^1$, *the joint distribution of the view of* $\mathcal{A}$ *and* $\mathcal{R}$*'s output in the real execution is computationally indistinguishable to the output of the ideal experiment described in Fig. 2.*

– **1-Rewinding Sender Security.** *For every malicious adversary* $\mathcal{A}$, *corrupting the receiver, there exists an expected polynomial time simulators* $\mathsf{Sim}_§ = (\mathsf{Sim}_§^1, \mathsf{Sim}_§^2)$ *such that for every choice of sender's input* $x_§$, *we have:*

$$\mathsf{Expt}_1(\mathcal{A}, \Pi, x_\mathcal{R}, x_§) \overline{\mathsf{Expt}_2}(\mathcal{A}, \mathsf{Sim}_§, x_\mathcal{R}, x_§)$$

where Expt_1 *and* Expt_2 *are defined in Fig. 3.*

- The honest receiver $\mathcal{R}$ sends $x_\mathcal{R}$ and f to the ideal functionality.
- Initialize $\mathcal{A}$ with uniform random tape r.
- $\text{Sim}^1_\mathcal{R}$ on input f, interacts with $\mathcal{A}$ and outputs $\pi_1, \pi_2, x_\mathcal{S}$ and sk.
- Send $x_\mathcal{S}$ to the ideal functionality.
- $\text{Sim}^2_\mathcal{R}$ on input sk, interacts with $\mathcal{A}$ and outputs π_3 and π_4. $\text{Sim}^2_\mathcal{R}$ may send an abort to the ideal functionality.
- Output $(r, \pi_1, \pi_2, \pi_3, \pi_4)$ and the output of the honest $\mathcal{R}$.

Fig. 2. Ideal experiment in the receiver security game

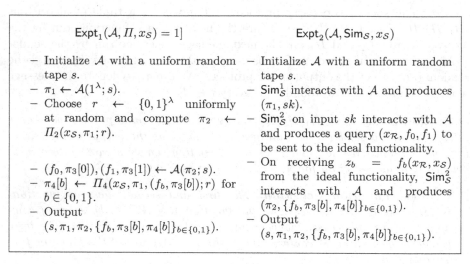

Fig. 3. Descriptions of Expt_1 and Expt_2.

4 Non-Malleable Oblivious Transfer

4.1 Definition

We define *non-malleable* OT which considers a man-in-the-middle adversary that generates OT messages as a function of those generated by honest players. The non-malleability property ensures that no PPT adversarial sender can generate its OT inputs as a function of the (secret) inputs of honest senders.

Definition 4 (ℓ non-malleable $\binom{m}{k}$ Oblivious Transfer). *An ℓ non-malleable $\binom{m}{k}$ Oblivious Transfer is a protocol between a sender $\mathcal{S}$ with inputs $\{m_i\}_{i \in [m]}$ and a receiver $\mathcal{R}$ with input $K \subset [m]$ where $|K| = k$, that satisfies the following:*

- **Correctness.** *For every* $i \in [m], \mathsf{m}_i \in \{0,1\}^\lambda$ *and* $K \subset [m]$ *such that* $|K| = k$,

$$\mathsf{Out}_\mathcal{R} \langle \mathcal{S}(\{\mathsf{m}_i\}_{i \in [m]}), \mathcal{R}(K) \rangle = \{m_i\}_{i \in K}$$

- **(Parallel Composable) Receiver Security.** *For every PPT sender* $\mathcal{S}^*$ *and every pair* K, K' *of* k-*sized subsets of* $[m]$, *we require*

$$\mathsf{View}_{\mathcal{S}^*} \langle \mathcal{S}^*, \mathcal{R}(K) \rangle \approx_c \mathsf{View}_{\mathcal{S}^*} \langle \mathcal{S}^*, \mathcal{R}(K') \rangle$$

Additionally, we require that there exists a PPT extractor Sen.Ext *that on input any transcript* τ *and with black-box access to any PPT sender* $\mathcal{S}^*$ *outputs* $\{(\mathsf{m}_{i,j}^*)\}_{i \in [m], j \in [\ell]}$ *where* $\mathsf{m}_{i,j}^*$ *denotes the* i^{th} *implicit input used by* $\mathcal{S}^*$ *in the* j^{th} *session of* τ *(if any input is not well-defined, it outputs* $\perp$ *in its place)*[5].

- **Non-Malleability.** *Consider any PPT adversary (denoted by* MIM*) that interacts with upto* ℓ *senders* $\mathcal{S}_1, \dots, \mathcal{S}_\ell$ *on the left, where for every* $j \in [\ell]$, $\mathcal{S}_j$ *has input* $\{\mathsf{m}_{i,j} \in \{0,1\}^n\}_{i \in [m]}$, *and upto* ℓ *receivers* $\mathcal{R}_1, \dots, \mathcal{R}_\ell$ *on the right, where for every* $j \in [\ell]$, $\mathcal{R}_j$ *has input* K_j.
We denote by $\mathsf{View}_{\mathsf{MIM}} \langle \{\mathcal{S}_j(\{\mathsf{m}_{i,j}\}_{i \in [m]})\}_{j \in [\ell]}, \{\mathcal{R}_j(K_j)\}_{j \in [\ell]} \rangle$ *the view of the* MIM *in this interaction, and denote the* i^{th} *implicit input used by the* MIM *in the* j^{th} *right session by* $\mathsf{m}_{i,j}'$ [6]. *We denote by* $\mathsf{Real}_{\mathsf{MIM}} \langle \{\mathcal{S}_j(\{\mathsf{m}_{i,j}\}_{i \in [m]})\}_{j \in [\ell]}, \{\mathcal{R}_j(K_j)\}_{j \in [\ell]} \rangle$ *the joint distribution of* $\{(\mathsf{m}_{i,j}')\}_{i \in [m], j \in [\ell]}$ *and* $\mathsf{View}_{\mathsf{MIM}} \langle \{\mathcal{S}_j(\{\mathsf{m}_{i,j}\}_{i \in [m]})\}_{j \in [\ell]}, \{\mathcal{R}_j(K_j)\}_{j \in [\ell]} \rangle$. *Then, we require that there exists a simulator-extractor pair,* $(\mathsf{Sim}_{\mathsf{OT}}, \mathsf{Ext}_{\mathsf{OT}})$ *that outputs*

$$\mathsf{Ideal}_{\mathsf{MIM}}(\{\mathsf{m}_{i,j}\}_{i \in [m], j \in [\ell]}, \{K_j\}_{j \in [\ell]}) = \mathsf{Sim}_{\mathsf{OT}}^{\mathsf{MIM}, \{\mathsf{OT}(\{\mathsf{m}_{i,j}\}_{i \in [m]}, \cdot)\}_{j \in [\ell]}}(\sigma, \{\widetilde{K}_j\}_{j \in [\ell]}),$$

for $(\sigma, \{\widetilde{K}_j\}_{j \in [\ell]}) \leftarrow \mathsf{Ext}_{\mathsf{OT}}^{\mathsf{MIM}}(\{K_j\}_{j \in [\ell]})$, *s.t. for all honest inputs* $\{\mathsf{m}_{i,j}\}_{i \in [m], j \in [\ell]}$, $\{K_j\}_{j \in [\ell]}$, *we have*

$$\mathsf{Real}_{\mathsf{MIM}} \langle \{\mathcal{S}_j(\{\mathsf{m}_{i,j}\}_{i \in [m]})\}_{j \in [\ell]}, \{\mathcal{R}_j(K_j)\}_{j \in [\ell]} \rangle \approx_c \mathsf{Ideal}_{\mathsf{MIM}}(\{\mathsf{m}_{i,j}\}_{i \in [m], j \in [\ell]}, \{K_j\}_{j \in [\ell]}).$$

4.2 Construction

In this subsection, we construct ℓ non-malleable m-choose-k OT. Here, ℓ denotes the number of executions that an MIM adversary may participate in. Our construction is described in Figure 4, and makes use of the following:

- A 4 round two-party secure computation protocol Π with delayed-function selection and 1-rewinding sender security.
- An information-theoretic $m(\lambda) \cdot \ell(\lambda)$ non-malleable secret sharing scheme.
- A low-depth proof for P.
- An existentially unforgeable signature scheme with algorithms denoted by Signature.Setup, Signature.Sign and Signature.Verify.

We describe our protocol formally in Fig. 4. The correctness of this protocol follows from correctness of the underlying oblivious transfer, non-malleable codes and signature scheme. In what follows, we prove security of this protocol.

---

[5] This property guarantees parallel composability, and is satisfied by most natural rewinding-based protocols.

[6] If any of these is not well-defined, we denote it by $\perp$.

Inputs: Sender $\mathcal{S}$ has inputs $\{m_j\}_{j \in m}$ and receiver $\mathcal{R}$ has input a set $K \subseteq [m]$ where $|K| = k$.

Protocol: $\mathcal{S}$ and $\mathcal{R}$ do the following.

1. $\mathcal{S}$ samples $(vk, sk) \leftarrow$ Signature.Setup(1^λ), then does the following.
   - For each $i \in [\lambda], j \in [m]$, pick uniform randomness $r_{i,j}$ and compute $(\mathsf{L}_{i,j}, \mathsf{R}_{i,j}) = \mathsf{NM.Code}((vk|m_j); r_{i,j})$.
   - Set $x = (vk, \{(\mathsf{L}_{i,j}, \mathsf{R}_{i,j}, m_j)\}_{i \in [\lambda], j \in [m]})$ and $\mathcal{L} = \{(vk, \{(\mathsf{L}_{i,j}, \mathsf{R}_{i,j}, m_j)\}_{i \in [\lambda], j \in [m]}) : \forall i \in [\lambda], j \in [m], \mathsf{NM.Decode}(\mathsf{L}_{i,j}, \mathsf{R}_{i,j}) = (vk|m_j)\}$. Compute $\mathsf{ldp} = \mathsf{LDP.Prove}(x, \mathcal{L})$.
2. For each $i \in [\lambda]$, $\mathcal{R}$ picks $c_i \leftarrow \{0, 1\}$.
3. Both parties engage in the protocol Π to compute functionality $\mathcal{F}$ where:
   - $\mathcal{R}$ plays the receiver with input K committed in round 1 and delayed function $(c_1, \ldots, c_\lambda)$ chosen in round 3.
   - $\mathcal{S}$ plays the sender with input (x, ldp), where x is parsed as $(vk, \{m_j, (\mathsf{L}_{i,j}, \mathsf{R}_{i,j})\}_{i \in [\lambda], j \in [m]}$.
   - The functionality $\mathcal{F}$ on input $(vk, \{m_j, \mathsf{L}_{i,j}, \mathsf{R}_{i,j}\}_{i \in [\lambda], j \in [m]}, K, \{c_i\}_{i \in [\lambda]})$ generates an output as follows:
     - If $\mathsf{LDP.Verify}(x, \mathsf{ldp}) \neq 1$, output $\perp$.
     - Otherwise set $\mathsf{out} = vk, \{m_j\}_{j \in K}$. Additionally, for every $i \in [\lambda]$, if $c_i = 0$, append $(\{\mathsf{L}_{i,j}\}_{j \in [m]})$ to out, else append $(\{\mathsf{R}_{i,j}\}_{j \in [m]})$ to out.
     - Output out.
   Additionally, $\mathcal{S}$ signs messages generated according to Π, denoted by (Π_2, Π_4). It sets $\sigma_2 = \mathsf{Signature.Sign}(\Pi_2, sk)$, $\sigma_4 = \mathsf{Signature.Sign}(\Pi_4, sk)$. It sends (σ_2, σ_4) to $\mathcal{R}$.
4. $\mathcal{R}$ obtains output out and parses $\mathsf{out} = (vk, \{m_j\}_{j \in K}, \cdot)$. It outputs $\{m_j\}_{j \in K}$ iff $\mathsf{Signature.Verify}(\sigma_2, \Pi_2, vk) \wedge \mathsf{Signature.Verify}(\sigma_4, \Pi_4, vk) = 1$, otherwise $\perp$.

Fig. 4. $\ell(\lambda)$ Non-Malleable $m(\lambda)$-choose-$k(\lambda)$ Oblivious Transfer

Theorem 2. *Let λ denote the security parameter, and $m = m(\lambda), k = k(\lambda), \ell = \ell(\lambda)$ be arbitrary fixed polynomials. There exists a 4 round ℓ non-malleable $\binom{m}{k}$ oblivious transfer protocol satisfying Definition 4 that makes black-box use of any 4 round two-party secure computation protocol Π satisfying Definition 3, and any existentially unforgeable signature scheme.*

By relying on our 4 round two-party secure computation protocol satisfying Definition 3 based on black-box use of any public-key encryption with pseudo-random public keys, we obtain the following Corollary.

Corollary 1. *Let λ denote the security parameter, and $m = m(\lambda), k = k(\lambda), \ell = \ell(\lambda)$ be arbitrary polynomials. There exists a 4 round ℓ non-malleable $\binom{m}{k}$ OT protocol satisfying Definition 4 that makes black-box use of any public-key encryption with pseudo-random public keys.*

4.3 Security

We consider any man-in-the-middle adversary that participates as an OT receiver in upto $\ell(\lambda)$ executions of this protocol on the right, and participates as an OT sender in upto $\ell(\lambda)$ executions on the left.

We will prove that there exists a PPT algorithm Sim-Ext, that with black-box access to the MIM, to ℓ copies of the ideal OT functionality $\mathbf{OT} = \{OT_j(\{m_{i,j}\}_{i\in[m]}, \cdot)\}_{j\in[\ell]}$ and with input $\{K_j\}_{j\in[\ell]}$, simulates an execution of the protocol with the MIM and extracts all the inputs $\{(\{\widetilde{m}_{i,j}\}_{i\in[m]})\}_{j\in[\ell]}$ used by the MIM in the executions where the MIM is sender. We will prove that Sim-Ext outputs $\mathsf{Ideal}_{\mathsf{MIM}}(\{m_{i,j}\}_{i\in[m],j\in[\ell]}, \{K_j\}_{j\in[\ell]})$ such that

$$\mathsf{Real}_{\mathsf{MIM}}\langle\{\mathcal{S}_j(\{m_{i,j}\}_{i\in[m]})\}_{j\in[\ell]}, \{\mathcal{R}_j(K_j)\}_{j\in[\ell]}\rangle \approx_c \mathsf{Ideal}_{\mathsf{MIM}}(\{m_{i,j}\}_{i\in[m],j\in[\ell]}, \{K_j\}_{j\in[\ell]})$$

To prove indistinguishability, we define a sequence of hybrid experiments, where the first one outputs the distribution $\mathsf{Real}_{\mathsf{MIM}}\langle\{\mathcal{S}_j(\{m_{i,j}\}_{i\in[m]})\}_{j\in[\ell]},$ $\{\mathcal{R}_j(K_j)\}_{j\in[\ell]}$ and the final one outputs the distribution $\mathsf{Ideal}_{\mathsf{MIM}}$ $(\{m_{i,j}\}_{i\in[m],j\in[\ell]}, \{K_j\}_{j\in[\ell]})$. Formally, these hybrids are defined as follows:

Hyb_0 : This corresponds to an execution of the MIM with ℓ honest senders $\{\mathcal{S}_j\}_{j\in[\ell]}$ on the left, each using inputs $\{m_{i,j}\}_{i\in[m]}$ respectively and ℓ honest receivers on the right with inputs $(\{K_j\}_{j\in[\ell]})$ respectively. The output of this hybrid is $\mathsf{Real}_{\mathsf{MIM}}\langle\{\mathcal{S}_j(\{m_{i,j}\}_{i\in[m]})\}_{j\in[\ell]}, \{\mathcal{R}_j(K_j)\}_{j\in[\ell]}$.

Hyb_1 : This experiment modifies Hyb_1 by introducing an additional abort condition. Specifically, the experiment first executes the complete protocol corresponding to the real execution of the MIM exactly as in Hyb_0 to obtain the distribution $\mathsf{Real}_{\mathsf{MIM}}\langle\{\mathcal{S}_j(\{m_{i,j}\}_{i\in[m]})\}_{j\in[\ell]}, \{\mathcal{R}_j(K_j)\}_{j\in[\ell]}\rangle$.

Let $p(\lambda)$ denote the probability that the MIM completes this execution without aborting. Set $\gamma(\lambda) = \max(\lambda, p^{-2}(\lambda))$. With the first two rounds of the transcript fixed, the rewind the right execution up to $\gamma(\lambda)$ times, picking inputs $(c_1^j, \ldots, c_\lambda^j)$ for each of the ℓ receivers $\{\mathcal{R}_j\}_{j\subset[\ell]}$ independently and uniformly at random in every run. If there exists a rewinding thread where the MIM completes the protocol execution, denote the inputs chosen by the challenger on behalf of the honest receiver in this rewinding thread by $(c'^j_1, \ldots, c'^j_\lambda)$. For every $j \in [\ell]$, let index $\alpha_j \in [\lambda]$ be such that $c^j_{\alpha_j} = 0$ and $c'^j_{\alpha_j} = 1$. Additionally for every $j \in [\ell], i \in [m]$, use $(\widetilde{\mathsf{L}}^j_{\alpha_j,i}, \widetilde{\mathsf{R}}^j_{\alpha_j,i})$ obtained as output from the main and rewinding executions respectively to compute $\widetilde{m}^j_i = \mathsf{NM.Decode}(\widetilde{\mathsf{L}}^j_{\alpha_j,i}, \widetilde{\mathsf{R}}^j_{\alpha_j,i})$.

If no such rewinding thread exists, or if there exists $j \in [\ell]$ for which there does not exist $\alpha \in [\lambda]$ such that $c^j_\alpha = 0$ and $c'^j_\alpha = 1$, then set $\widetilde{m}^j_i = \bot$ for all $i \in [m]$. Now, the output of this hybrid is the joint distribution

$$\mathsf{View}_{\mathsf{MIM}}\langle\{\mathcal{S}_j(\{m^j_i\}_{i\in[m]})\}_{j\in[\ell]}, \{\mathcal{R}^j(K^j)\}_{j\in[\ell]}\rangle, \{\widetilde{m}^j_i\}_{j\in[\ell],i\in[m]}.$$

Lemma 1. *For every unbounded distinguisher $\mathcal{D}$ we have*

$$\left| \Pr[\mathcal{D}(\mathsf{Hyb}_0) = 1] - \Pr[\mathcal{D}(\mathsf{Hyb}_1) = 1] \right| = \mathsf{negl}(\lambda)$$

Proof. Since the MIM's inputs $\{(\widetilde{m}_i^j\}_{j\in[\ell]}$ are committed in round 2 of the protocol, then conditioned on the adversary providing a non-aborting transcript in a rewinding execution in Hyb_1, by simulation security of the 2pc, $\{(\widetilde{m}_i^j\}_{j\in[\ell]}$ are correctly extracted.

Therefore, to prove this lemma it suffices to show that such a rewinding execution (with a non-aborting transcript) can be found within $\gamma(\lambda)$ attempts, except with probability $\mathsf{negl}(\lambda)$. To see this, we observe that the probability of a non-aborting transcript is $p(\lambda)$, and therefore, the probability that all $\gamma(\lambda)$ trials abort is $(1 - p(\lambda))^{\ell(\lambda)} \le \exp^{p^{-1}(\lambda)} = \mathsf{negl}(\lambda)$.

Hyb_2: This experiment modifies Hyb_2 to execute the simulator of Π in all sessions where the MIM is a receiver. Specifically, in these executions, instead of the honest sender strategy with input $\{m_i^j\}_{i\in[m],j\in[\ell]}$, we execute the simulator $\mathsf{Sim\text{-}2PC}_{\mathsf{Sen}}^{\mathsf{MIM},\mathcal{F}(\mathsf{inp}_{\mathcal{S}^j},\cdot)}$ where

$$\mathsf{inp}_{\mathcal{S}^j} = (\{m_i^j, \mathsf{L}_{1,i}^j, \ldots, \mathsf{L}_{\lambda,i}^j, \mathsf{R}_{1,i}^j, \ldots, \mathsf{R}_{\lambda,i}^j\}_{i\in[m]}).$$

$\mathsf{Sim\text{-}2PC}_{\mathsf{Sen}}$ expects round 1 and round 3 messages from the MIM, and the MIM in turn expects corresponding messages from the receiver in the right execution. Receiver messages for the right execution are generated using honest receiver strategy with inputs K^j fixed, and inputs $c_1^j, \ldots, c_\lambda^j$ chosen uniformly at random, exactly as in Hyb_1. Denote the view of the MIM by

$$\mathsf{View}_{\mathsf{Sim}^{\{\mathcal{F}(\mathsf{inp}_{\mathcal{S}^j},\cdot)\}_{j\in[\ell]}}}\langle\{\mathcal{R}^j(K^j)\}_{j\in[\ell]}\rangle,$$

where for every $j \in [\ell]$, $\mathsf{inp}_{\mathcal{S}^j}$ is as defined above.

Next, with the first two rounds of the transcript fixed, the challenger rewinds the right execution up to $\ell(\lambda)$ times, picking inputs $(c_1^j, \ldots, c_\lambda^j)$ for $\mathcal{R}^j$ independently and uniformly at random in every run, and generating messages in the left execution by running the simulator $\mathsf{Sim\text{-}2PC}_{\mathsf{Sen}}$ each time.

If there exists a rewinding execution where the MIM completes the protocol, denote the inputs chosen by the challenger on behalf of the honest receiver in this rewinding thread by $(c'^j_1, \ldots, c'^j_\lambda)$. For every $j \in [\ell]$, let index $\alpha_j \in [\lambda]$ be such that $c^j_{\alpha_j} = 0$ and $c'^j_{\alpha_j} = 1$. Additionally for every $j \in [\ell], i \in [m]$, use $(\widetilde{\mathsf{L}}_{\alpha_j,i}^j, \widetilde{\mathsf{R}}_{\alpha_j,i}^j)$ obtained as output from the main and rewinding executions respectively to compute $\widetilde{m}_i^j = \mathsf{NM.Decode}(\widetilde{\mathsf{L}}_{\alpha_j,i}^j, \widetilde{\mathsf{R}}_{\alpha_j,i}^j)$. If no such rewinding thread exists, or if there exists $j \in [\ell]$ for which there does not exist $\alpha \in [\lambda]$ such that $c_\alpha^j = 0$ and $c'^j_\alpha = 1$, then set $\widetilde{m}_i^j = \bot$ for all $i \in [m]$. The output of this hybrid is the joint distribution:

$$\mathsf{View}_{\mathsf{Sim}^{\{\mathcal{F}(\mathsf{inp}_{\mathcal{S}^j},\cdot)\}_{j\in[\ell]}}}\langle\{\mathcal{R}^j(K^j)\}_{j\in[\ell]}\rangle, \{\widetilde{m}_i^j\}_{j\in[\ell],i\in[m]},$$

where for every $j \in [\ell]$, $\mathsf{inp}_{\mathcal{S}^j}$ is as defined above.

Lemma 2. *Assuming 1-rewinding secure two party computation, for every efficient distinguisher $\mathcal{D}$ we have*

$$\left| \Pr[\mathcal{D}(\mathsf{Hyb}_1) = 1] - \Pr[\mathcal{D}(\mathsf{Hyb}_2) = 1] \right| = \mathsf{negl}(\lambda)$$

Proof. We consider a sequence of sub-hybrids $\mathsf{Hyb}_{1,0}, \mathsf{Hyb}_{1,1}, \ldots \mathsf{Hyb}_{1,\ell}$ where for every $j \in [\ell]$, $\mathsf{Hyb}_{1,j}$ is identical to $\mathsf{Hyb}_{1,j-1}$, except that instead of executing the honest sender strategy using honest sender inputs $\{m_i^j\}_{i \in [m]}$, we execute the simulator in the jth left execution, where $\mathsf{Sim\text{-}2PC}_{\mathsf{Sen}}^{\mathsf{MIM}, \mathcal{F}(\mathsf{inp}_{\mathcal{S}^j}, \cdot)}$ where

$$\mathsf{inp}_{\mathcal{S}^j} = (\{m_i^j, \mathsf{L}_{1,i}^j, \ldots, \mathsf{L}_{\lambda,i}^j, \mathsf{R}_{1,i}^j, \ldots, \mathsf{R}_{\lambda,i}^j\}_{i \in [m]})$$

Suppose the lemma is not true. Then for every large enough $\lambda \in \mathbb{N}$ there exists $j^*(\lambda) \in [\ell(\lambda)]$, a polynomial $p(\cdot)$ and a distinguisher $\mathcal{D}$ such that for infinitely many $\lambda \in \mathbb{N}$,

$$\left| \Pr[\mathcal{D}(\mathsf{Hyb}_{1,j^*-1}) = 1] - \Pr[\mathcal{D}(\mathsf{Hyb}_{1,j^*}) = 1] \right| = \frac{1}{q(\lambda)}$$

We derive a contradiction by building a reduction $\mathcal{A}$ that on input λ, obtains $j^*(\lambda)$ as advice and with black-box access to the MIM and to $\mathcal{D}$ contradicts 1-rewinding security of the two party computation protocol. $\mathcal{A}$ proceeds as follows:

- $\mathcal{A}$ first creates receiver $\mathcal{R}'$ that interacts with the external challenger as follows.
  - Generate the first round messages according to receiver strategy with inputs $\{K^j\}_{j \in [\ell]}$ for the right execution. Obtain first round messages from the MIM, and output the MIM's message in the j^{*th} left execution to the challenger of the 2pc.
  - Obtain the second round message for the left execution externally from the 2pc challenger, and forward this to the MIM as $\mathcal{S}^{j^*}$'s message in the j^{*th} left execution. Obtain the second round message from the MIM for the right execution.
  - Generate the third round message for the right execution according to honest receiver strategy, and obtain the third round message from the MIM. Output the MIM's message in left session j^* to the challenger.
  - Obtain the fourth round message for the left execution externally from the challenger, and forward this to the MIM as $\mathcal{S}$'s message in the j^{*th} left execution. Obtain the fourth round message from the MIM for the right execution.
- Next, $\mathcal{A}$ rewinds $\mathcal{R}'$ once, as follows.
  - Generate the third round message according to honest receiver strategy, and obtain the third round message from the MIM. Output the MIM's message in session j^* to the challenger.
  - Obtain the fourth round message for the left execution externally from the challenger, and forward this to the MIM as $\mathcal{S}$'s message in the j^{*th} left execution. Obtain the fourth round message from the MIM from the left execution.
  - If none of the executions abort, for every $j \in [\ell]$, find $\alpha_j \in [\lambda]$ such that $c_{\alpha_j}^j = 0$ and $c'^j_{\alpha_j} = 1$. and use it to compute $\tilde{m}_i^j = \mathsf{NM.Decode}(\tilde{\mathsf{L}}_{\alpha_j,i}^j, \tilde{\mathsf{R}}_{\alpha_j,i}^j)$ for $i \in [m], j \in [\ell]$. Else, set $\tilde{m}_i^j = \bot$ for $i \in [m], j \in [\ell]$

- $\mathcal{A}$ outputs the entire view of $\mathcal{R}'$ together with $\{\tilde{m}_i^j\}_{i\in[m],j\in[\ell]}$. If the challenger used honest sender messages, we denote the distribution output by $\mathcal{A}$ in this experiment by Dist_1 and if the challenger used simulated messages, we denote the distribution output by $\mathcal{A}$ in this experiment by Dist_2.

If the challenger's messages correspond to the real sender $\mathcal{S}$, then the distribution output by $\mathcal{A}$ conditioned on not aborting corresponds to Hyb_1, and if the challenger's messages correspond to $\mathsf{Sim\text{-}2PC}_{\mathsf{Sen}}$, then the distribution output by $\mathcal{A}$ conditioned on not aborting corresponds to Hyb_2.

By assumption, for infinitely many $\lambda \in \mathbb{N}$,

$$\left| \Pr[\mathcal{D}(\mathsf{Hyb}_1) = 1] - \Pr[\mathcal{D}(\mathsf{Hyb}_2) = 1] \right| = \frac{1}{q(\lambda)}$$

Since the MIM completes any run of the protocol without aborting with probability at least $p(\lambda)$, and because aborts are independent of the distinguishing advantage, for infinitely many $\lambda \in \mathbb{N}$:

$$\left| \Pr[\mathcal{D} = 1 \ \wedge \ \neg\mathsf{abort}|\mathsf{Hyb}_1] - \Pr[\mathcal{D} = 1 \ \wedge \ \neg\mathsf{abort}|\mathsf{Hyb}_2] \right| \geq \frac{1}{p(\lambda) \cdot q(\lambda)}$$

where $\neg\mathsf{abort}$ denotes the event that an execution that is completed in the main thread, is also completed without aborting in one rewinding execution.

This implies that for infinitely many $\lambda \in \mathbb{N}$:

$$\left| \Pr[\mathcal{D}(\mathsf{Dist}_1) = 1] - \Pr[\mathcal{D}(\mathsf{Dist}_2) = 1] \right| \geq \frac{1}{p(\lambda) \cdot q(\lambda)},$$

and thus $\mathcal{D}$ contradicts 1-rewinding security of the two party computation protocol.

Hyb_3: This hybrid is the same as Hyb_2 except whenever the challenger obtains as output a verification key in one of the right sessions that is identical to a verification key used in one of the left sessions, the hybrid outputs $\bot$. By existential unforgeability of the signature scheme, given any PPT adversary MIM, Hyb_2 and Hyb_3 are statistically indistinguishable.

Hyb_4: This hybrid is the same as Hyb_3 except that $\mathsf{inp}_{\mathcal{S}^j}$ is set differently. Specifically, for every $j \in [\ell], i \in [m]$ and $\alpha \in [\lambda]$, we set $(\mathsf{L}_{\alpha,i}^j, \mathsf{R}_{\alpha,i}^j) \leftarrow \mathsf{NM.Sim}(1^{p(\lambda)})$, and set

$$\mathsf{inp}_{\mathcal{S}^j} = (\{m_i^j, \mathsf{L}_{1,i}^j, \ldots, \mathsf{L}_{\lambda,i}^j, \mathsf{R}_{1,i}^j, \ldots, \mathsf{R}_{\lambda,i}^j\}_{i\in[m]}).$$

We note that at this point, the functionality $\{\mathcal{F}(\mathsf{inp}_{\mathcal{S}^j}, \cdot)\}_{j\in[\ell]}$ can be perfectly simulated with access to the ideal functionality $\{\mathsf{OT}^j(m_i^j, m_i^j, \cdot)\}_{j\in[\ell]}$. Therefore, the output of this hybrid is identical to the ideal view $\mathsf{Ideal}_{\mathsf{MIM}}(\{m_i^j\}_{i\in[m],j\in[\ell]}, \{K^j\}_{j\in[\ell]})$.

Lemma 3. *Assuming* $m(\lambda) \cdot \ell(\lambda)$ *symmetric non-malleable codes, for every unbounded distinguisher $\mathcal{D}$ we have:*

$$\left| \Pr[\mathcal{D}(\mathsf{Hyb}_4) = 1] - \Pr[\mathcal{D}(\mathsf{Hyb}_3) = 1] \right| = \mathsf{negl}(\lambda)$$

Proof. We prove indistinguishability between Hyb_3 and Hyb_4 by considering a sequence of sub-hybrids, $\{\mathsf{Hyb}_{3,i,j,k}\}_{i\in[1,m],j\in[1,\ell],k\in[0,\lambda]}$ where:

- $\mathsf{Hyb}_3 = \mathsf{Hyb}_{3,0,\ell,\lambda}$, $\mathsf{Hyb}_4 = \mathsf{Hyb}_{3,m,\ell,\lambda}$,
- for $i \in [m]$, $\mathsf{Hyb}_{3,i-1,\ell,\lambda} = \mathsf{Hyb}_{3,i,1,0}$
- for $j \in [\ell]$, $\mathsf{Hyb}_{3,i,j-1,\lambda} = \mathsf{Hyb}_{3,i,j,0}$,
- for every $i \in [m], j \in [\ell], k \in [\lambda]$, $\mathsf{Hyb}_{3,i,j,k}$ is identical to $\mathsf{Hyb}_{3,i,j,k-1}$ except that $\mathsf{Hyb}_{3,i,j,k}$ samples $(\mathsf{L}^j_{k,i}, \mathsf{R}^j_{k,i}) \leftarrow \mathsf{NM.Code}(0)$.

Suppose the lemma is not true. Then there exists $i^* \in [m], j^* \in [\ell], k^* \in [\lambda]$, an unbounded distinguisher $\mathcal{D}$ and a polynomial $p(\cdot)$ such that for large enough $\lambda \in \mathbb{N}$,

$$\left| \Pr[\mathcal{D}(\mathsf{Hyb}_{3,i^*,j^*,k^*}) = 1] - \Pr[\mathcal{D}(\mathsf{Hyb}_{3,i^*,j^*,k^*-1}) = 1] \right| = \frac{1}{p(\lambda)} \quad (1)$$

We now define a pair of tampering functions $(f_{\mathsf{MIM}}, g_{\mathsf{MIM}})$, and additional function h_{MIM} as follows:

- $f_{\mathsf{MIM}}, g_{\mathsf{MIM}}$ and h_{MIM} share common state that is generated as follows:
  - Execute $\mathsf{Sim\text{-}2PC}^{\mathsf{MIM}}_{\mathsf{Sen}}$, using honest $\mathcal{R}$ strategy in the right executions with input $\{K^j\}_{j\in[\ell]}$ and uniformly chosen $\{c^j_1, \dots c^j_\lambda\}_{j\in[\ell]}$, until $\mathsf{Sim\text{-}2PC}_{\mathsf{Sen}}$ generates a query to the ideal functionality $\mathcal{F}$ at the end of round 3.
  - At this point, $\mathsf{Sim\text{-}2PC}^{\mathsf{MIM}}_{\mathsf{Sen}}$ outputs a view and transcript of the MIM until the third round, as well as $\{\widetilde{K}^j, \widetilde{c}^j_1, \dots, \widetilde{c}^j_\lambda\}_{j\in[\ell]}$ that correspond to the receiver's inputs in the left execution.
  - Rewind the third round once with uniformly and independently chosen $\{c'^j_1, \dots, c'^j_\lambda\}_{j\in[\ell]}$. If for every $j \in [\ell(\lambda)]$, there exists $\alpha_j \in [\lambda]$ such that $c^j_{\alpha_j} = 0$ and $c'^j_{\alpha_j} = 1$, continue, otherwise abort.
  - Obtain the rewinding view (with the same prefix of the first two rounds), as well as $(\overline{c}_1, \dots, \overline{c}_n)$ that correspond to the receiver's input in the left session in this rewinding execution. If $\widetilde{c}^j_k \neq \overline{c}^j_k$, continue. Otherwise, abort.
  - Generate $(\mathsf{L}^j_{k,i}, \mathsf{R}^j_{k,i})$ for every $(i,j,k) \in [m] \times [\ell] \times [\lambda] \setminus \{i^*, j^*, k^*\}$ according to $\mathsf{Hyb}_{3,i^*,j^*,k^*-1}$ (this is identical to setting them according to $\mathsf{Hyb}_{3,i^*,j^*,k^*}$).
  - Output
    the view of the MIM until round 3 in the main the rewinding threads, including (i^*, j^*, k^*), the values $(\mathsf{L}^j_{k,i}, \mathsf{R}^j_{k,i})_{(i,j,k)\in[m]\times[\ell]\times[\lambda]\setminus\{i^*,j^*,k^*\}}$.
  - Additionally, output the receiver's inputs $\{\widetilde{K}^j, \widetilde{c}^j_1, \dots, \widetilde{c}^j_\lambda\}_{j\in[\ell]}$ and the sender's inputs $\{sk^j, vk^j, \{\mathsf{m}^j_i\}_{i\in[m]}\}_{j\in[\ell]}$.
- Next, the function h_{MIM} on input L, sets $\mathsf{L}^{j^*}_{k^*,i^*} = \mathsf{L}$, $\mathsf{R}^{j^*}_{k^*,i^*} = 0$.
  Now, using hardwired values $\{vk^j, \{\mathsf{m}^j_i\}_{i\in[m]}\}_{j\in[\ell]}$, $\{\widetilde{K}^j, \widetilde{c}^j_1, \dots, \widetilde{c}^j_\lambda\}_{j\in[\ell]}$ as well as the values $(\mathsf{L}^j_{k,i}, \mathsf{R}^j_{k,i})_{(i,j,k)\in[m]\times[\ell]\times[\lambda]\setminus\{i^*,j^*,k^*\}}$, it computes

$$\mathsf{out} = \{\mathcal{F}^j(vk^j, \{\mathsf{m}_i, \mathsf{L}^j_{k,i}, \mathsf{R}^j_{k,i}\}_{i\in[m],k\in[\lambda]}, \widetilde{K}^j, \{\widetilde{c}^j_k\}_{k\in[\lambda]})\}_{j\in[\ell]}.$$

It then invokes Sim-2PC$_{\mathsf{Sen}}$ on out to generate the fourth round message of the protocol transcript in the main thread if $\widetilde{c}_{k^*}^{j^*} = 0$, and generates the fourth round message of the protocol transcript in the rewinding thread if $\overline{c}_{k^*}^{j^*} = 0$. It outputs the resulting transcript as the view of the MIM.

- The function f_{MIM} on input L, sets $\mathsf{L}_{k^*,i^*}^{j^*} = \mathsf{L}, \mathsf{R}_{k^*,i^*}^{j^*} = 0$.
  Now, using hardwired values $\{vk^j, \{m_i^j\}_{i \in [m]}\}_{j \in [\ell]}$, $\{\widetilde{K}^j, \widetilde{c}_1^j, \dots, \widetilde{c}_\lambda^j\}_{j \in [\ell]}$ as well as the values $(\mathsf{L}_{k,i}^j, \mathsf{R}_{k,i}^j)_{(i,j,k) \in [m] \times [\ell] \times [\lambda] \setminus \{i^*, j^*, k^*\}}$, it computes

$$\mathsf{out} = \{\mathcal{F}^j vk^j, \{m_i, \mathsf{L}_{k,i}^j, \mathsf{R}_{k,i}^j\}_{i \in [m], k \in [\lambda]}, \widetilde{K}^j, \{\widetilde{c}_k^j\}_{k \in [\lambda]})\}_{j \in [\ell]}.$$

It then invokes Sim-2PC$_{\mathsf{Sen}}$ on out to generate the fourth round message of the protocol transcript in the main thread if $\widetilde{c}_{k^*}^{j^*} = 0$, and generates the fourth round message of the protocol transcript in the rewinding thread if $\overline{c}_{k^*}^{j^*} = 0$. It outputs the values $\{\mathsf{L}_{\alpha_j,i}^j\}_{i \in [m], j \in [\ell]}$ or $\{\mathsf{R}_{\alpha_j,i}^j\}_{i \in [m], j \in [\ell]}$ obtained from the MIM.

- The function g_{MIM} on input R, sets $\mathsf{R}_{k^*,i^*}^{j^*} = \mathsf{R}, \mathsf{L}_{k^*,i^*}^{j^*} = 0$.
  Now, using hardwired values $\{vk^j, \{m_i^j\}_{i \in [m]}\}_{j \in [\ell]}$, $\{\widetilde{K}^j, \widetilde{c}_1^j, \dots, \widetilde{c}_\lambda^j\}_{j \in [\ell]}$ as well as the values $(\mathsf{L}_{k,i}^j, \mathsf{R}_{k,i}^j)_{(i,j,k) \in [m] \times [\ell] \times [\lambda] \setminus \{i^*, j^*, k^*\}}$, it computes

$$\mathsf{out} = \{\mathcal{F}^j vk^j, \{m_i, \mathsf{L}_{k,i}^j, \mathsf{R}_{k,i}^j\}_{i \in [m], k \in [\lambda]}, \widetilde{K}^j, \{\widetilde{c}_k^j\}_{k \in [\lambda]})\}_{j \in [\ell]}.$$

It then invokes Sim-2PC$_{\mathsf{Sen}}$ on out to generate the fourth round message of the protocol transcript in the main thread if $\widetilde{c}_{k^*}^{j^*} = 1$, and generates the fourth round message of the protocol transcript in the rewinding thread if $\overline{c}_{k^*}^{j^*} = 1$. It outputs the values $\{\mathsf{L}_{\alpha_j,i}^j\}_{i \in [m], j \in [\ell]}$ or $\{\mathsf{R}_{\alpha_j,i}^j\}_{i \in [m], j \in [\ell]}$ obtained from the MIM.

By security augmented non-malleable codes,

$$\Big(\mathsf{L}, \mathsf{NM.Decode}\big(f_{\mathsf{MIM}}(\mathsf{L}), g_{\mathsf{MIM}}(\mathsf{R})\big)\Big|(\mathsf{L}, \mathsf{R} \leftarrow \mathsf{NM.Code}(m_{i^*}^{j^*}))\Big) \approx_\epsilon$$
$$\Big(\mathsf{L}, \mathsf{NM.Decode}\big(f_{\mathsf{MIM}}(\mathsf{L}), g_{\mathsf{MIM}}(\mathsf{R})\big)\Big|(\mathsf{L}, \mathsf{R} \leftarrow \mathsf{NM.Code}(0))\Big) \text{ and}$$
$$\Big(\mathsf{L}, \mathsf{NM.Decode}\big(g_{\mathsf{MIM}}(\mathsf{R}), f_{\mathsf{MIM}}(\mathsf{L})\big)\Big|(\mathsf{L}, \mathsf{R} \leftarrow \mathsf{NM.Code}(m_{i^*}^{j^*}))\Big) \approx_\epsilon$$
$$\Big(\mathsf{L}, \mathsf{NM.Decode}\big(g_{\mathsf{MIM}}(\mathsf{R}), f_{\mathsf{MIM}}(\mathsf{L})\big)\Big|(\mathsf{L}, \mathsf{R} \leftarrow \mathsf{NM.Code}(0))\Big)$$

By the data processing inequality, this implies that for every function $h(\cdot)$,

$$\Big(h(\mathsf{L}), \mathsf{NM.Decode}\big(f_{\mathsf{MIM}}(\mathsf{L}), g_{\mathsf{MIM}}(\mathsf{R})\big)\Big|(\mathsf{L}, \mathsf{R} \leftarrow \mathsf{NM.Code}(m_{i^*}^{j^*}))\Big) \approx_\epsilon$$
$$\Big(h(\mathsf{L}), \mathsf{NM.Decode}\big(f_{\mathsf{MIM}}(\mathsf{L}), g_{\mathsf{MIM}}(\mathsf{R})\big)\Big|(\mathsf{L}, \mathsf{R} \leftarrow \mathsf{NM.Code}(0))\Big) \text{ and}$$
$$\Big(h(\mathsf{L}), \mathsf{NM.Decode}\big(g_{\mathsf{MIM}}(\mathsf{R}), f_{\mathsf{MIM}}(\mathsf{L})\big)\Big|(\mathsf{L}, \mathsf{R} \leftarrow \mathsf{NM.Code}(m_{i^*}^{j^*}))\Big) \approx_\epsilon$$
$$\Big(h(\mathsf{L}), \mathsf{NM.Decode}\big(g_{\mathsf{MIM}}(\mathsf{R}), f_{\mathsf{MIM}}(\mathsf{L})\big)\Big|(\mathsf{L}, \mathsf{R} \leftarrow \mathsf{NM.Code}(0))\Big)$$

Setting $h = h_{\mathsf{MIM}}$, for f_{MIM} and g_{MIM} defined above, these distributions correspond exactly to the outputs of $\mathsf{Hyb}_{3,i^*,j^*,k^*-1}$ and $\mathsf{Hyb}_{3,i^*,j^*,k^*}$ respectively, whenever $\widetilde{c}_{k^*}^{j^*} \neq \overline{c}_{k^*}^{j^*}$. Whenever $\widetilde{c}_{k^*}^{j^*} = \overline{c}_{k^*}^{j^*}$, the distributions $\mathsf{Hyb}_{3,i^*,j^*,k^*-1}$ and $\mathsf{Hyb}_{3,i^*,j^*,k^*}$ are statistically indistinguishable because they jointly only depend on one of the shares, L or R. Since $\epsilon(\lambda) = \mathsf{negl}(\lambda)$, this contradicts Eq. (1), completing our proof.

5   Summary of Results

In this section, we provide a theorem statement capturing two of our main results. See full version for the proof.

Theorem 3. *Let f be an arbitrary multiparty functionality.*

- *In the watchlist correlations model, assuming black-box access to a pseudorandom generator, there exists a two-round protocol that computes f against static, malicious adversaries satisfying security with selective abort. For f in NC1, a similar protocol exists unconditionally.*
- *Further assuming black-box access to a public-key encryption with pseudorandom public keys and a two-round oblivious transfer with semi-malicious security, there exists a protocol that securely computes f in five rounds in the plain model against static, malicious corruptions of all-but-one players satisfying security with selective abort.*

The communication and computation costs of both the protocols are $\mathsf{poly}(\lambda, n, |f|)$, where $|f|$ denotes the size of the circuit computing f, and where communication is over a broadcast channel.

Acknowledgements. Y. Ishai was supported by ERC Project NTSC (742754), NSF-BSF grant 2015782, BSF grant 2018393, and ISF grant 2774/20. D. Khurana was supported from a DARPA SIEVE award. A. Sahai was supported in part from a DARPA SIEVE award, NTT Research, NSF Frontier Award 1413955, BSF grant2012378, a Xerox Faculty Research Award, a Google Faculty Research Award, an equipment grant from Intel, and an Okawa Foundation Research Grant. This material is based upon work supported by the Defense Advanced Research Projects Agency through Award HR00112020024. Work done in part when A. Srinivasan was at UC Berkeley and supported in part by AFOSR Award FA9550-19-1-0200, AFOSR YIP Award, NSF CNS Award 1936826, DARPA/ARL SAFEWARE Award W911NF15C0210, a Hellman Award and research grants by the Sloan Foundation, Okawa Foundation, Visa Inc., and Center for Long-Term Cybersecurity (CLTC, UC Berkeley). The views expressed are those of the authors and do not reflect the official policy or position of the funding agencies.

References

1. Afshar, A., Mohassel, P., Pinkas, B., Riva, B.: Non-interactive secure computation based on cut-and-choose. In: Nguyen, P.Q., Oswald, E. (eds.) EUROCRYPT 2014. LNCS, vol. 8441, pp. 387–404. Springer, Heidelberg (2014). https://doi.org/10.1007/978-3-642-55220-5_22

2. Aggarwal, D., Agrawal, S., Gupta, D., Maji, H.K., Pandey, O., Prabhakaran, M.: Optimal computational split-state non-malleable codes. In: Kushilevitz, E., Malkin, T. (eds.) TCC 2016-A, Part II. LNCS, vol. 9563, pp. 393–417. Springer, Heidelberg (2016). https://doi.org/10.1007/978-3-662-49099-0_15

3. Aggarwal, D., et al.: Stronger leakage-resilient and non-malleable secret sharing schemes for general access structures. In: Boldyreva, A., Micciancio, D. (eds.) CRYPTO 2019, Part II. LNCS, vol. 11693, pp. 510–539. Springer, Cham (2019). https://doi.org/10.1007/978-3-030-26951-7_18

4. Aggarwal, D., Dziembowski, S., Kazana, T., Obremski, M.: Leakage-resilient non-malleable codes. In: Dodis, Y., Nielsen, J.B. (eds.) TCC 2015, Part I. LNCS, vol. 9014, pp. 398–426. Springer, Heidelberg (2015). https://doi.org/10.1007/978-3-662-46494-6_17

5. Ames, S., Hazay, C., Ishai, Y., Venkitasubramaniam, M.: Ligero: lightweight sublinear arguments without a trusted setup. In: Thuraisingham, B.M., Evans, D., Malkin, T., Xu, D. (eds.) ACM CCS 2017, pp. 2087–2104. ACM Press (2017)

6. Ananth, P., Choudhuri, A.R., Jain, A.: A new approach to round-optimal secure multiparty computation. In: Katz, J., Shacham, H. (eds.) CRYPTO 2017, Part I. LNCS, vol. 10401, pp. 468–499. Springer, Cham (2017). https://doi.org/10.1007/978-3-319-63688-7_16

7. Applebaum, B., Brakerski, Z., Garg, S., Ishai, Y., Srinivasan, A.: Separating two-round secure computation from oblivious transfer. In: Vidick, T. (ed.) 11th Innovations in Theoretical Computer Science Conference, ITCS 2020, January 12–14, 2020, Seattle, Washington, USA. LIPIcs, vol. 151, pp. 71:1–71:18. Schloss Dagstuhl - Leibniz-Zentrum für Informatik (2020)

8. Asharov, G., Jain, A., López-Alt, A., Tromer, E., Vaikuntanathan, V., Wichs, D.: Multiparty computation with low communication, computation and interaction via threshold FHE. In: Pointcheval, D., Johansson, T. (eds.) EUROCRYPT 2012. LNCS, vol. 7237, pp. 483–501. Springer, Heidelberg (2012). https://doi.org/10.1007/978-3-642-29011-4_29

9. Badrinarayanan, S., Goyal, V., Jain, A., Kalai, Y.T., Khurana, D., Sahai, A.: Promise zero knowledge and its applications to round optimal MPC. In: Shacham, H., Boldyreva, A. (eds.) CRYPTO 2018, Part II. LNCS, vol. 10992, pp. 459–487. Springer, Cham (2018). https://doi.org/10.1007/978-3-319-96881-0_16

10. Badrinarayanan, S., Goyal, V., Jain, A., Khurana, D., Sahai, A.: Round optimal concurrent MPC via strong simulation. In: Kalai, Y., Reyzin, L. (eds.) TCC 2017, Part I. LNCS, vol. 10677, pp. 743–775. Springer, Cham (2017). https://doi.org/10.1007/978-3-319-70500-2_25

11. Beaver, D.: Correlated pseudorandomness and the complexity of private computations. In: Miller, G.L. (ed.) Proceedings of the Twenty-Eighth Annual ACM Symposium on the Theory of Computing, Philadelphia, Pennsylvania, USA, May 22–24, 1996, pp. 479–488. ACM (1996). https://doi.org/10.1145/237814.237996

12. Beaver, D., Micali, S., Rogaway, P.: The round complexity of secure protocols (extended abstract). In: STOC, pp. 503–513 (1990)

13. Benhamouda, F., Lin, H.: k-round multiparty computation from k-round oblivious transfer via garbled interactive Circuits. In: Nielsen, J.B., Rijmen, V. (eds.) EUROCRYPT 2018, Part II. LNCS, vol. 10821, pp. 500–532. Springer, Cham (2018). https://doi.org/10.1007/978-3-319-78375-8_17

14. Boyle, E., Couteau, G., Gilboa, N., Ishai, Y., Kohl, L., Scholl, P.: Efficient pseudorandom correlation generators: silent OT extension and more. In: Boldyreva, A., Micciancio, D. (eds.) CRYPTO 2019, Part III. LNCS, vol. 11694, pp. 489–518. Springer, Cham (2019). https://doi.org/10.1007/978-3-030-26954-8_16

15. Brakerski, Z., Halevi, S., Polychroniadou, A.: Four round secure computation without setup. In: Kalai, Y., Reyzin, L. (eds.) TCC 2017, Part I. LNCS, vol. 10677, pp. 645–677. Springer, Cham (2017). https://doi.org/10.1007/978-3-319-70500-2_22

16. Chase, M., et al.: Post-quantum zero-knowledge and signatures from symmetric-key primitives. In: Proceedings of the 2017 ACM SIGSAC Conference on Computer and Communications Security, pp. 1825–1842 (2017)

17. Chase, M., et al.: Reusable non-interactive secure computation. In: Boldyreva, A., Micciancio, D. (eds.) CRYPTO 2019, Part III. LNCS, vol. 11694, pp. 462–488. Springer, Cham (2019). https://doi.org/10.1007/978-3-030-26954-8_15

18. Chattopadhyay, E., Goyal, V., Li, X.: Non-malleable extractors and codes, with their many tampered extensions. In: Wichs, D., Mansour, Y. (eds.) 48th ACM STOC, pp. 285–298. ACM Press (2016)

19. Choudhuri, A.R., Ciampi, M., Goyal, V., Jain, A., Ostrovsky, R.: Round optimal secure multiparty computation from minimal assumptions. In: TCC 2020, Part II, pp. 291–319 (2020)

20. Ciampi, M., Ostrovsky, R., Siniscalchi, L., Visconti, I.: Concurrent non-malleable commitments (and more) in 3 rounds. In: Robshaw, M., Katz, J. (eds.) CRYPTO 2016, Part III. LNCS, vol. 9816, pp. 270–299. Springer, Heidelberg (2016). https://doi.org/10.1007/978-3-662-53015-3_10

21. Ciampi, M., Ostrovsky, R., Siniscalchi, L., Visconti, I.: Four-round concurrent non-malleable commitments from one-way functions. In: Katz, J., Shacham, H. (eds.) CRYPTO 2017, Part II. LNCS, vol. 10402, pp. 127–157. Springer, Cham (2017). https://doi.org/10.1007/978-3-319-63715-0_5

22. Damgård, I., Ishai, Y.: Constant-round multiparty computation using a black-box pseudorandom generator. In: Shoup, V. (ed.) CRYPTO 2005. LNCS, vol. 3621, pp. 378–394. Springer, Heidelberg (2005). https://doi.org/10.1007/11535218_23

23. Dziembowski, S., Pietrzak, K., Wichs, D.: Non-malleable codes. J. ACM 65(4), 20:1–20:32 (2018). https://doi.org/10.1145/3178432

24. Friolo, D., Masny, D., Venturi, D.: A black-box construction of fully-simulatable, round-optimal oblivious transfer from strongly uniform key agreement. In: Hofheinz, D., Rosen, A. (eds.) TCC 2019. LNCS, vol. 11891, pp. 111–130. Springer, Cham (2019). https://doi.org/10.1007/978-3-030-36030-6_5

25. Garg, S., Gentry, C., Halevi, S., Raykova, M., Sahai, A., Waters, B.: Candidate indistinguishability obfuscation and functional encryption for all circuits. In: 54th FOCS, pp. 40–49. IEEE Computer Society Press (2013)

26. Garg, S., Ishai, Y., Srinivasan, A.: Two-round MPC: information-theoretic and black-box. In: Beimel, A., Dziembowski, S. (eds.) TCC 2018. LNCS, vol. 11239, pp. 123–151. Springer, Cham (2018). https://doi.org/10.1007/978-3-030-03807-6_5

27. Garg, S., Mukherjee, P., Pandey, O., Polychroniadou, A.: The exact round complexity of secure computation. In: EUROCRYPT, pp. 448–476 (2016)

28. Garg, S., Srinivasan, A.: Two-round multiparty secure computation from minimal assumptions. In: Nielsen, J.B., Rijmen, V. (eds.) EUROCRYPT 2018, Part II. LNCS, vol. 10821, pp. 468–499. Springer, Cham (2018). https://doi.org/10.1007/978-3-319-78375-8_16

29. Giacomelli, I., Madsen, J., Orlandi, C.: Zkboo: faster zero-knowledge for boolean circuits. In: 25th {usenix} Security Symposium ({usenix} Security, vol. 16, pp. 1069–1083 (2016)

30. Goldreich, O., Krawczyk, H.: On the composition of zero-knowledge proof systems. SIAM J. Comput. 25(1), 169–192 (1996)

31. Goldreich, O., Micali, S., Wigderson, A.: How to play any mental game or a completeness theorem for protocols with honest majority. In: Aho, A. (ed.) 19th ACM STOC, pp. 218–229. ACM Press (1987)

32. Goyal, V.: Constant round non-malleable protocols using one way functions. In: Fortnow, L., Vadhan, S.P. (eds.) 43rd ACM STOC, pp. 695–704. ACM Press (2011)

33. Goyal, V., Jain, A., Khurana, D.: Witness signatures and non-malleable multi-prover zero-knowledge proofs. IACR Cryptology ePrint Archive 2015, vol. 1095 (2015). http://eprint.iacr.org/2015/1095

34. Goyal, V., Kumar, A., Park, S., Richelson, S., Srinivasan, A.: Non-malleable commitments from non-malleable extractors. Manuscript, Accessed via Personal Communication (2018)

35. Goyal, V., Lee, C.K., Ostrovsky, R., Visconti, I.: Constructing non-malleable commitments: a black-box approach. In: 53rd FOCS, pp. 51–60. IEEE Computer Society Press (2012)

36. Goyal, V., Pandey, O., Richelson, S.: Textbook non-malleable commitments. In: STOC, pp. 1128–1141 (2016)

37. Goyal, V., Richelson, S., Rosen, A., Vald, M.: An algebraic approach to non-malleability. In: 55th FOCS, pp. 41–50. IEEE Computer Society Press (2014)

38. Goyal, V., Srinivasan, A., Zhu, C.: Multi-source non-malleable extractors and applications. Cryptology ePrint Archive, Report 2020/157 (2020). https://eprint.iacr.org/2020/157

39. Haitner, I., Ishai, Y., Kushilevitz, E., Lindell, Y., Petrank, E.: Black-box constructions of protocols for secure computation. SIAM J. Comput. **40**(2), 225–266 (2011). https://doi.org/10.1137/100790537

40. Halevi, S., Hazay, C., Polychroniadou, A., Venkitasubramaniam, M.: Round-optimal secure multi-party computation. In: Shacham, H., Boldyreva, A. (eds.) CRYPTO 2018, Part II. LNCS, vol. 10992, pp. 488–520. Springer, Cham (2018). https://doi.org/10.1007/978-3-319-96881-0_17

41. Hazay, C., Ishai, Y., Marcedone, A., Venkitasubramaniam, M.: Leviosa: lightweight secure arithmetic computation. In: Cavallaro, L., Kinder, J., Wang, X., Katz, J. (eds.) CCS 2019, pp. 327–344. ACM (2019). https://doi.org/10.1145/3319535.3354258

42. Hazay, C., Ishai, Y., Venkitasubramaniam, M.: Actively secure garbled circuits with constant communication overhead in the plain model. In: Kalai, Y., Reyzin, L. (eds.) TCC 2017, Part II. LNCS, vol. 10678, pp. 3–39. Springer, Cham (2017). https://doi.org/10.1007/978-3-319-70503-3_1

43. Impagliazzo, R., Rudich, S.: Limits on the provable consequences of one-way permutations. In: Goldwasser, S. (ed.) CRYPTO 1988. LNCS, vol. 403, pp. 8–26. Springer, New York (1990). https://doi.org/10.1007/0-387-34799-2_2

44. Ishai, Y., Kilian, J., Nissim, K., Petrank, E.: Extending oblivious transfers efficiently. In: Boneh, D. (ed.) CRYPTO 2003. LNCS, vol. 2729, pp. 145–161. Springer, Heidelberg (2003). https://doi.org/10.1007/978-3-540-45146-4_9

45. Ishai, Y., Kushilevitz, E., Ostrovsky, R., Prabhakaran, M., Sahai, A.: Efficient non-interactive secure computation. In: Paterson, K.G. (ed.) EUROCRYPT 2011. LNCS, vol. 6632, pp. 406–425. Springer, Heidelberg (2011). https://doi.org/10.1007/978-3-642-20465-4_23

46. Ishai, Y., Kushilevitz, E., Ostrovsky, R., Sahai, A.: Zero-knowledge from secure multiparty computation. In: Johnson, D.S., Feige, U. (eds.) 39th ACM STOC, pp. 21–30. ACM Press (2007)

47. Ishai, Y., Kushilevitz, E., Paskin, A.: Secure multiparty computation with minimal interaction. In: Rabin, T. (ed.) CRYPTO 2010. LNCS, vol. 6223, pp. 577–594. Springer, Heidelberg (2010). https://doi.org/10.1007/978-3-642-14623-7_31

48. Ishai, Y., Kushilevitz, E., Prabhakaran, M., Sahai, A., Yu, C.H.: Secure protocol transformations. In: Robshaw, M., Katz, J. (eds.) CRYPTO 2016. LNCS, vol. 9815, pp. 430–458. Springer, Heidelberg (2016). https://doi.org/10.1007/978-3-662-53008-5_15

49. Ishai, Y., Prabhakaran, M., Sahai, A.: Founding cryptography on oblivious transfer – efficiently. In: Wagner, D. (ed.) CRYPTO 2008. LNCS, vol. 5157, pp. 572–591. Springer, Heidelberg (2008). https://doi.org/10.1007/978-3-540-85174-5_32

50. Ishai, Y., Prabhakaran, M., Sahai, A.: Secure arithmetic computation with no honest majority. In: Reingold, O. (ed.) TCC 2009. LNCS, vol. 5444, pp. 294–314. Springer, Heidelberg (2009). https://doi.org/10.1007/978-3-642-00457-5_18

51. Katz, J., Kolesnikov, V., Wang, X.: Improved non-interactive zero knowledge with applications to post-quantum signatures. In: Lie, D., Mannan, M., Backes, M., Wang, X. (eds.) CCS 2018, pp. 525–537. ACM (2018).https://doi.org/10.1145/3243734.3243805

52. Katz, J., Ostrovsky, R.: Round-optimal secure two-party computation. In: Franklin, M. (ed.) CRYPTO 2004. LNCS, vol. 3152, pp. 335–354. Springer, Heidelberg (2004). https://doi.org/10.1007/978-3-540-28628-8_21

53. Khurana, D.: Round optimal concurrent non-malleability from polynomial hardness. In: Kalai, Y., Reyzin, L. (eds.) TCC 2017, Part II. LNCS, vol. 10678, pp. 139–171. Springer, Cham (2017). https://doi.org/10.1007/978-3-319-70503-3_5

54. Khurana, D., Sahai, A.: Two-message non-malleable commitments from standard sub-exponential assumptions. IACR Cryptology ePrint Archive 2017, 291 (2017). http://eprint.iacr.org/2017/291

55. Lin, H., Liu, T., Wee, H.: Information-theoretic 2-round MPC without round collapsing: adaptive security, and more. In: Pass, R., Pietrzak, K. (eds.) TCC 2020. LNCS, vol. 12551, pp. 502–531. Springer, Cham (2020). https://doi.org/10.1007/978-3-030-64378-2_18

56. Mohassel, P., Rosulek, M.: Non-interactive secure 2PC in the offline/online and batch settings. In: Coron, J., Nielsen, J.B. (eds.) EUROCRYPT 2017, Part III. LNCS, vol. 10212, pp. 425–455. Springer, Cham (2017). https://doi.org/10.1007/978-3-319-56617-7_15

57. Ostrovsky, R., Richelson, S., Scafuro, A.: Round-optimal black-box two-party computation. In: Gennaro, R., Robshaw, M. (eds.) CRYPTO 2015, Part II. LNCS, vol. 9216, pp. 339–358. Springer, Heidelberg (2015). https://doi.org/10.1007/978-3-662-48000-7_17

58. Paskin-Cherniavsky, A.: Secure Computation with Minimal Interaction. Ph.D. thesis, Technion (2012). http://www.cs.technion.ac.il/users/wwwb/cgi-bin/tr-get.cgi/2012/PHD/PHD-2012-16.pdf

59. Reingold, O., Trevisan, L., Vadhan, S.: Notions of reducibility between cryptographic primitives. In: Naor, M. (ed.) TCC 2004. LNCS, vol. 2951, pp. 1–20. Springer, Heidelberg (2004). https://doi.org/10.1007/978-3-540-24638-1_1

60. Wee, H.: Black-box, round-efficient secure computation via non-malleability amplification. In: 51st FOCS, pp. 531–540. IEEE Computer Society Press (2010)

61. Yao, A.C.C.: How to generate and exchange secrets (extended abstract). In: 27th FOCS, pp. 162–167. IEEE Computer Society Press (1986)

ATLAS: Efficient and Scalable MPC in the Honest Majority Setting

Vipul Goyal[1,2]([⊠]), Hanjun Li[3], Rafail Ostrovsky[4], Antigoni Polychroniadou[5], and Yifan Song[1]

[1] Carnegie Mellon University, Pittsburgh, USA
goyal@cs.cmu.edu, yifans2@andrew.cmu.edu
[2] NTT Research, Sunnyvale, USA
[3] University of Washington, Seattle, USA
[4] UCLA, Los Angeles, USA
rafail@cs.ucla.edu
[5] J.P. Morgan AI Research, New York, USA

Abstract. In this work, we address communication, computation, and round efficiency of unconditionally secure multi-party computation for arithmetic circuits in the honest majority setting. We achieve both algorithmic and practical improvements:

– The best known result in the semi-honest setting has been due to Damgård and Nielsen (CRYPTO 2007). Over the last decade, their construction has played an important role in the progress of efficient secure computation. However despite a number of follow-up works, any significant improvements to the basic semi-honest protocol have been hard to come by. We show 33% improvement in communication complexity of this protocol. We show how to generalize this result to the malicious setting, leading to the best known unconditional honest majority MPC with malicious security.

– We focus on the round complexity of the Damgård and Nielsen protocol and improve it by a factor of 2. Our improvement relies on a novel observation relating to an interplay between Damgård and Nielsen multiplication and Beaver triple multiplication. An implementation of our constructions shows an execution run time improvement compared to the state of the art ranging from 30% to 50%.

1 Introduction

Secure Multi-Party Computation (MPC) allows $n \geq 2$ parties to compute a function on privately held inputs, such that the desired output is correctly computed and is the only new information released. This should hold even if t out of n parties have been corrupted by a semi-honest or malicious adversary. Since its introduction in the 1980s [Yao82, GMW87], a lot of research has been done to improve the efficiency of MPC protocols. Thanks to these efforts, MPC has rapidly moved from theory to practice.

H. Li—Work done in part while at CMU.

T. Malkin and C. Peikert (Eds.): CRYPTO 2021, LNCS 12826, pp. 244–274, 2021.
https://doi.org/10.1007/978-3-030-84245-1_9

In this work, our focus is on honest majority protocols in the presence of a malicious adversary. We note that the fastest known implementations of MPC have come in the honest majority setting, which does not necessarily require public key operations. For example, the recent work of Chida et al. [CGH+18] showed that their secure-with-abort protocol can evaluate 1 million multiplication gates within 1 s for up to 7 parties, 4 s for 50 parties, and 8 s for 110 parties. Another attractive feature of the honest majority setting is that it allows one to achieve the stronger properties of fairness and guaranteed output delivery which are otherwise impossible with dishonest majority.

For over a decade, the most efficient MPC protocol with semi-honest security in the honest majority setting has been the protocol of Damgård and Nielsen [DN07], hereafter known as the DN protocol. By using the Shamir secret sharing scheme [Sha79], addition gates can be evaluated without any communication. To evaluate a multiplication gate, each party only needs to communicate 6 field elements. In the computational setting, the communication complexity can be reduced to 3 field elements by using pseudo-random generators [NV18] (improved further to 1.5 elements by Boneh et al. [BBCG+19] for a constant number of parties). Due to its simplicity and efficiency, many subsequent works have used the DN protocol to achieve security-with-abort [GIP+14, CGH+18, NV18, BBCG+19, GSZ20] or guaranteed output delivery [BSFO12, GSZ20].

Despite the important role played by the DN protocol in the honest majority setting, any improvement to the basic protocol has been hard to come by unless one resorts to other approaches using computational assumptions. An exception is the recent work of Goyal et al. [GSZ20] who proposed a marginal improvement over DN of 6 field elements per multiplication gate to 5.5 field elements.

1.1 Our Contributions

We propose ATLAS, an unconditionally secure MPC protocol in the honest majority setting with reduced communication complexity over the celebrated DN protocol even in the honest but curious setting, as well as malicious setting. Our protocol ATLAS enjoys the following efficiency improvements over the DN protocol:

- We improve the basic DN protocol leading to a communication complexity of 4 field elements per multiplication gate per party. Our results are in the information-theoretic setting assuming a majority of the parties are honest and the adversary is semi-honest. This leads to the most communication-efficient semi-honest MPC protocol with honest majority.
- We note that the recent works [BBCG+19, GSZ20] compiled the DN protocol to get security-with-abort without increasing the communication complexity. We show that our protocol continues to satisfy the properties needed for this compilation to work. It allows us to present a secure-with-abort protocol with only 4 field elements per multiplication gate per party in the information-theoretic setting.

- Next, we focus on the round complexity of the DN protocol. Instead of evaluating multiplication gates of the same layer in parallel, we show how to evaluate all multiplication gates in a two-layer circuit in parallel. This allows us to improve the concrete efficiency even further and reduce the number of rounds by a factor of 2. The achieved amortized communication cost per multiplication gate in this setting is 4.5 field elements per party but halving the number of rounds.
- In the computational setting, where one can use pseudo-random generators based on any one-way function (in practice, one can use an AES based PRG in counter-mode), we show how to further reduce the communication complexity by making black-box use of any pseudo-random generator. The concrete efficiency can be improved to 2 field elements per party per gate in both semi-honest and secure-with-abort settings, and 2.5 field elements for the variant with the improvement of round complexity.

We implement ATLAS in the information-theoretic setting and compare with the previously best-known results [CGH+18, GSZ20] in the setting of security-with-abort. We measure the running time for circuits with 1 million and 10 million multiplication gates, with circuit depth from 20 to 10,000, and the number of parties from 3 to 21. By combining improvements on both communication and round complexity, our protocol shows around 2x speedup comparing with the protocol in [CGH+18], and around 1.4x speedup comparing with the protocol in [GSZ20] in all tested cases.

1.2   Other Related Works

The notion of MPC was first introduced in [Yao82, GMW87] in 1980s. Feasibility results for MPC were obtained by [Yao82, GMW87, CDVdG87] under cryptographic assumptions, and by [BOGW88, CCD88] in the information-theoretic setting. Subsequently, a large number of works have focused on improving the efficiency of MPC protocols in various settings.

A series of works focus on improving the communication efficiency of MPC with guaranteed output delivery in the settings with different thresholds on the number of corrupted parties. In the setting of honest majority setting, assuming the existence of a broadcast channel, the works [BSFO12, GSZ20] have shown that guaranteed output delivery can be achieved efficiently. In the setting where $t < n/3$, a rich line of works [HMP00, HM01, DN07, BTH08, GLS19] have focused on improving the asymptotic communication complexity in this setting. In the setting where $t < (1/3 - \epsilon)n$, packed secret sharing can be used to hide a batch of values, resulting in more efficient protocols. E.g., Damgård et al. [DIK10] introduced a protocol with communication complexity of $O(C \log C \log n \cdot \kappa + D_M^2 \mathrm{poly}(n, \log C)\kappa)$ bits.

A rich line of works have also focused on the performance of MPC in practice for two parties [LP12, NNOB12], or three parties [FLNW17, ABF+17].

2 Technical Overview

We give an overview of our techniques in this section. In the following, we will use n to denote the number of parties and t to denote the number of corrupted parties. In the setting of the honest majority, we have $n = 2t + 1$. Our construction is based on the standard Shamir Secret Sharing Scheme [Sha79]. We will use $[x]_d$ to denote a degree-d Shamir sharing, or a $(d + 1)$-out-of-n Shamir sharing. It requires at least $d + 1$ shares to reconstruct the secret and any d shares do not leak any information about the secret.

2.1 Review: The Secure-with-abort MPC Protocol in [GSZ20]

In [GIP+14], Genkin et al. showed that the best-known semi-honest protocol [DN07] (hereafter referred to as the DN protocol) is secure up to an additive attack in the presence of a fully malicious adversary. An additive attack means that the adversary is able to change the multiplication result by adding an arbitrary fixed value. As one corollary, the DN protocol provides full privacy of honest parties before reconstructing the output. Therefore, a straightforward strategy to achieve security-with-abort is to (1) run the DN protocol until the output phase, (2) check the correctness of the computation, and (3) reconstruct the output only if the check passes.

In the DN protocol [DN07], all parties compute a degree-t Shamir sharing for each wire. Since the Shamir secret sharing scheme is linearly homomorphic, addition gates can be evaluated without interaction. Therefore, to achieve security-with-abort, the main task is to verify the multiplications. In [GSZ20], Goyal et al. show that multiplications can be verified with sub-linear communication complexity in the number of multiplications. This allows Goyal et al. to obtain the first secure-with-abort MPC protocol which achieves the same concrete efficiency per gate as the best-known semi-honest protocol [DN07].

To make a further improvement in the concrete efficiency, we focus on the multiplication protocol in [DN07] (hereafter referred to as the DN multiplication protocol). Our idea is to reuse the correlated-randomness required in the DN multiplication protocol.

Review of the DN Multiplication Protocol. To evaluate a multiplication gate, all parties first need to prepare a pair of random sharings $([r]_t, [r]_{2t})$ of the same secret r, where the first sharing is a degree-t Shamir sharing and the second sharing is a degree-$2t$ Shamir sharing. Such a pair of sharings is referred to as a pair of double sharings. In [DN07], preparing a pair of random double sharings requires the communication of 4 elements per party.

For a multiplication gate, suppose the input sharings are denoted by $[x]_t, [y]_t$. To compute $[z]_t := [x \cdot y]_t$, a pair of random double sharings $([r]_t, [r]_{2t})$ is consumed. All parties first agree on a special party P_{king}. Then, all parties run the following steps:

1. All parties locally compute $[e]_{2t} := [x]_t \cdot [y]_t + [r]_{2t}$.

2. P_{king} collects all shares of $[e]_{2t}$ and reconstructs the secret e. Then P_{king} sends the value e to all other parties.

3. After receiving e from P_{king}, all parties locally compute $[z]_t := e - [r]_t$.

Correctness follows from the properties of the Shamir secret sharing scheme. Note that each party needs to send an element to P_{king}, and P_{king} needs to send an element to each party. The communication complexity of this protocol is 2 elements per party. Including the communication cost for preparing double sharings, the overall cost per multiplication gate is 6 elements per party.

2.2   Reducing the Communication Complexity via t-wise Independence

Starting Point. In [GSZ20], Goyal et al. observe that in the second step of the DN multiplication protocol, P_{king} can alternatively distribute a degree-t Shamir sharing $[e]_t$. Then in the last step, all parties can still compute $[z]_t := [e]_t - [r]_t$. This observation leads to an improvement from 6 elements to 5.5 elements. We refer the readers to Sect. 4.2 for more discussion.

Our main observation is that, when P_{king} is an honest party, the corrupted parties only receive several random elements from P_{king} if $[e]_t$ is a random degree-t Shamir sharing. In particular, it holds even if the corrupted parties know the whole sharings $[r]_t$ and $[r]_{2t}$. This is because the corrupted parties only receive t shares of a random degree-t sharing $[e]_t$ from P_{king}, which are uniformly random and independent of the secret. Therefore for an honest P_{king}, we do not need the double sharings to be uniformly random at all. While for a corrupted P_{king}, we still need to use random double sharings, we can split the tasks of handling multiplication gates as P_{king} to all parties. In this way, at least half of multiplication gates are handled by honest P_{king}'s. We show that it allows us to reduce the cost of preparing double sharings by a factor of 2.

Relying on t-wise Independence. Suppose we have n multiplication gates and we let each party behave as P_{king} for 1 multiplication gate. When P_{king} is a corrupted party, we still need to use a pair of random double sharings to protect the secrecy of the result. If P_{king} is an honest party, as argued above, the double sharings do not need to be random.

Our idea is to generate n pairs of double sharings such that any t pairs of them are independent and uniformly random. This guarantees that the double sharings used for multiplication gates handled by corrupted parties are uniformly random, which ensures the security of the MPC protocol. On the other hand, given these double sharings, the other double sharings used for multiplication gates handled by honest parties can be fixed and determined. It means that we only need to prepare t pairs of random and independent double sharings for n multiplication gates.

To this end, all parties agree on a fixed hyper-invertible matrix of size $n \times t$, denoted by $\boldsymbol{M}$. The main property of $\boldsymbol{M}$ is that any $t \times t$ sub-matrix of $\boldsymbol{M}$ is invertible. Since the Shamir secret sharing scheme is a linear homomorphism, a linear combination of several pairs of double sharings is still a pair of double sharings. All parties first prepare t pairs of random double sharings using the protocol in [DN07], denoted by

$$([r^{(1)}]_t, [r^{(1)}]_{2t}), \ldots, ([r^{(t)}]_t, [r^{(t)}]_{2t}).$$

Then, we expand these t pairs of double sharings to n pairs by computing

$$([\tilde{r}^{(1)}]_t, \ldots, [\tilde{r}^{(n)}]_t)^{\mathrm{T}} = M([r^{(1)}]_t, \ldots, [r^{(t)}]_t)^{\mathrm{T}}$$
$$([\tilde{r}^{(1)}]_{2t}, \ldots, [\tilde{r}^{(n)}]_{2t})^{\mathrm{T}} = M([r^{(1)}]_{2t}, \ldots, [r^{(t)}]_{2t})^{\mathrm{T}}.$$

We point out that this expansion can be done locally without interaction. Note that for all $i \in [n]$, $([\tilde{r}^{(i)}]_t, [\tilde{r}^{(i)}]_{2t})$ is a pair of double sharings. Let $\mathcal{C}$ denote the set of corrupted parties. According to the property of M, there is a one-to-one map from $\{([\tilde{r}^{(i)}]_t, [\tilde{r}^{(i)}]_{2t})\}_{i \in \mathcal{C}}$ to $\{([r^{(i)}]_t, [r^{(i)}]_{2t})\}_{i \in [t]}$. Since the input double sharings are independent and uniformly random, we conclude that the double sharings in $\{([\tilde{r}^{(i)}]_t, [\tilde{r}^{(i)}]_{2t})\}_{i \in \mathcal{C}}$ are independent and uniformly random.

When $([\tilde{r}^{(i)}]_t, [\tilde{r}^{(i)}]_{2t})$ is used to evaluate a multiplication gate, we require the party P_i to act as P_{king}. In this way, the multiplication gates handled by corrupted parties will use double sharings in $\{([\tilde{r}^{(i)}]_t, [\tilde{r}^{(i)}]_{2t})\}_{i \in \mathcal{C}}$, which are independent and uniformly random. We are able to show that the security still holds.

Concrete Efficiency of Our Improved Multiplication Protocol. Recall that in [DN07], preparing a pair of random double sharings requires the communication of 4 elements per party. Relying on t-wise independence, we only need to prepare t pairs of random double sharings for n multiplications. Thus, the amortized communication cost per pair of double sharings is $4 \cdot t/n \approx 2$ elements per party. Including the communication cost of the multiplication protocol in [DN07], which is 2 elements per party, the overall cost per multiplication is 4 elements per party.

In Sect. 4.2, we show that our multiplication protocol can be directly used in the secure-with-abort MPC protocol in [GSZ20]. It yields a secure-with-abort MPC protocol with the concrete efficiency of 4 elements per party per gate.

2.3 Reducing the Number of Rounds via Beaver Triples

In the secure-with-abort MPC protocol in [GSZ20], multiplication gates in the same layer of the circuit are evaluated in parallel. Therefore, the number of rounds is linear in the depth of the circuit. To further improve the concrete efficiency, we pay our attention to the round complexity. We note that the question of obtaining information theoretic constant round protocols for a general circuit has been opened for many years. In particular, it has been shown in [DNPR16] that the dependency on the depth in the round complexity is inherent for the DN protocol. Given this, we managed to reduce the number of rounds by a factor of 2 while maintaining the communication efficiency.

To this end, we first consider a two-layer circuit, and try to evaluate all multiplication gates in parallel.

Starting Point. For a two-layer circuit, an input sharing of a multiplication gate in the second layer may come from three places:

- This sharing is an input sharing of the circuit.
- This sharing is an output sharing of an addition gate in the first layer.
- This sharing is an output sharing of a multiplication gate in the first layer.

Note that an addition gate can be evaluated without interaction. Therefore for the first two cases, all parties can locally compute this sharing. However, for the third case, communication is required to evaluate this multiplication gate in the first layer. Therefore, the question becomes how to evaluate multiplication gates in the second layer *without learning the output sharings of multiplication gates in the first layer.*

A Beaver triple [Bea92] consists of three degree-t Shamir sharings $([a]_t, [b]_t, [c]_t)$ such that $c = a \cdot b$. Usually, a Beaver triple is used to transform one multiplication to two reconstructions. Concretely, given two sharings $[x]_t, [y]_t$, suppose we want to compute $[z]_t$ such that $z = x \cdot y$. Since

$$z = x \cdot y$$
$$= (x + a - a) \cdot (y + b - b)$$
$$= (x + a) \cdot (y + b) - (x + a) \cdot b - (y + b) \cdot a + a \cdot b,$$

we can compute

$$[z]_t := (x + a) \cdot (y + b) - (x + a) \cdot [b]_t - (y + b) \cdot [a]_t + [c]_t.$$

Therefore, the task of computing $[z]_t$ becomes to reconstruct two degree-t Shamir sharings $[x]_t + [a]_t$ and $[y]_t + [b]_t$. Observe that, if we set $u = x + a$ and $v = y + b$, the above equation allows us to locally compute a degree-t Shamir sharing of $z := (u - a) \cdot (v - b)$ using a Beaver triple $([a]_t, [b]_t, [c]_t)$ once u and v are publicly known.

Beaver-triple Friendly Form. We say a sharing is in the *Beaver-triple friendly form,* if it can be written as $u - [a]_t$, where u is a public element and $[a]_t$ is a degree-t Shamir sharing. Now suppose for each multiplication gate in the second layer, the input sharings are in the Beaver-triple friendly form, say $u - [a]_t$ and $v - [b]_t$. Given the Beaver triple $([a]_t, [b]_t, [c]_t)$, one can *non-interactively* compute the output sharing of this gate by

$$[z]_t := u \cdot v - u \cdot [b]_t - v \cdot [a]_t + [c]_t.$$

Note that the Beaver triple $([a]_t, [b]_t, [c]_t)$ can be prepared without learning u, v. Therefore, if for each multiplication gate in the second layer, the input sharings are in the Beaver-triple friendly form $u - [a]_t, v - [b]_t$, and $[a]_t, [b]_t$ are learnt *before evaluating the first layer*, we can prepare the Beaver triple $([a]_t, [b]_t, [c]_t)$ without evaluating the first layer, and then non-interactively evaluate multiplication gates in the second layer after learning u, v from the first layer.

Of course, the question remains: since the input sharings of the second layer come from the output sharings of the first layer, how do we ensure that the output sharings of the first layer are in the Beaver-triple friendly form?

Evaluating a Two-Layer Circuit. We observe that the original DN multiplication protocol in [DN07] satisfies our requirement! Concretely, to evaluate a multiplication gate with input sharings $[x]_t, [y]_t$ all parties need to first prepare a pair of random double sharings $([r]_t, [r]_{2t})$. In the last step of the DN multiplication protocol, P_{king} sends the reconstruction result of $[e]_{2t} := [x]_t \cdot [y]_t + [r]_{2t}$ to all parties, and all parties can compute the degree-t Shamir sharing $[z]_t := e - [r]_t$. In particular, the output sharing is in the Beaver-triple friendly form, and the sharing $[r]_t$ is prepared before evaluating this multiplication gate. Therefore, we will use the original DN multiplication protocol to evaluate multiplication gates in the first layer.

For a multiplication gate in the second layer, suppose that the two input wires are both the outputs of multiplication gates in the first layer. Let $e_1 - [r_1]_t$ and $e_2 - [r_2]_t$ denote these two output sharings. Now observe that e_1 and e_2 will already be public as part of evaluating the first layer. So to compute a degree-t Shamir sharing of $(e_1 - r_1)(e_2 - r_2)$, all we need is $[r_1 \cdot r_2]_t$. If we can pre-compute and distribute $([r_1]_t, [r_2]_t, [r_1 \cdot r_2]_t)$, we are done! Of course, since r_1 and r_2 are also used in the multiplication gates in the first layer, we simultaneously need to compute degree-$2t$ Shamir sharings of r_1 and r_2 as well. Fortunately, this does not affect the security of the second layer. In other words, the outputs of the first layer feed nicely into the second layer making the second layer non-interactive. At the same time, we are able to ensure that these two different types of multiplication protocols do not destroy the security of each other despite sharing randomness.

As we discussed above, the input sharing of a multiplication gate in the second layer may come from two other places: (1) it may be an input sharing of this two-layer circuit, or (2) it may be an output sharing of an addition gate in the first layer. In both cases, all parties can locally compute this sharing before evaluating the multiplication gates in the first layer. Let $[x]_t$ denote such an input sharing. Note that $[x]_t = 0 - (-[x]_t)$ is already in the Beaver-triple friendly form. Therefore, all the input sharings of multiplication gates in the second layer are in the Beaver-triple friendly form. But now, the problem is that $[x]_t$ is not known before the circuit evaluation starts (unlike $[r_1]_t$ and $[r_2]_t$), and hence $[x]_t$ cannot be part of a Beaver triple pre-computed before the evaluation. Fortunately, as observed earlier, parties hold $[x]_t$ before evaluating any multiplication gates in the first layer. Now our idea is to prepare the Beaver triples for the second layer dependent on $[x]_t$ *in parallel with* the multiplications in the first layer.

After preparing Beaver triples for the second layer and computing the output sharings of the multiplication gates in the first layer, all parties can locally compute the degree-t Shamir sharings associated with the output wires of this two-layer circuit. These sharings will be fed to the next two-layer circuit, which is sufficient to start the evaluation since the original DN multiplication protocol does not require any special property of the input sharings. Therefore in the evaluation of the whole circuit, these two types of multiplication protocols are alternatively used in every two layers.

Improving the Communication Complexity. While the above helps us make progress, it does not achieve our final goal. In particular, using the original DN protocol requires the communication of 6 elements per party per gate. We note that for multiplications in different layers, we have different requirements:

- For multiplication gates in the first layer, we need the output sharings to have the Beaver-triple friendly form.
- For multiplication gates in the second layer, we compute the Beaver triples in the form of $([a]_t, [b]_t, [c]_t)$. We only need to obtain the degree-t sharing of $[c]_t$ for each Beaver triple.

Therefore for multiplication gates in the second layer, we can use our improved multiplication protocol to compute Beaver triples, which requires the communication of 4 elements per party per multiplication. For multiplication gates in the first layer, however, P_{king} needs to send the same values to all parties. It seems like our trick of using t-wise independence does not work in this scenario.

Having a closer look at our trick of using t-wise independence, for a multiplication gate handled by an honest party, the secret r of the random double sharings is fixed given the double random sharings used for multiplication gates handled by corrupted parties. Revealing the reconstruction result of $[e]_{2t} := [x]_t \cdot [y]_t + [r]_{2t}$ may leak the multiplication result to the adversary. Therefore, to be able to reveal the reconstruction result, r needs to be uniformly random for every multiplication gate. However, we note that r being uniformly random is not equivalent to the pair of double sharings $([r]_t, [r]_{2t})$ being uniformly random.

Therefore, we want to decouple the relation between r and the double sharings. Note that a pair of double sharings $([r]_t, [r]_{2t})$ is equivalent to a pair of sharings $([r]_t, [o]_{2t})$, where the first sharing is a degree-t Shamir sharing of r and the second sharing is a degree-$2t$ Shamir sharing of zero $o = 0$. To see this, given $([r]_t, [r]_{2t})$, we can set $[o]_{2t} := [r]_{2t} - [r]_t$; given $([r]_t, [o]_{2t})$, we can set $[r]_{2t} := [r]_t + [o]_{2t}$. When using a pair of sharings $([r]_t, [o]_{2t})$, the DN multiplication protocol becomes:

1. All parties locally compute $[e]_{2t} := [x]_t \cdot [y]_t + [r]_t + [o]_{2t}$.
2. P_{king} collects all shares of $[e]_{2t}$ and reconstructs the secret e. Then P_{king} sends the value e to all other parties.
3. After receiving e from P_{king}, all parties locally compute $[z]_t := e - [r]_t$.

Note that $[o]_{2t}$ is only used to compute $[e]_{2t}$. When P_{king} is an honest party, $[o]_{2t}$ does not need to be a uniformly random degree-$2t$ sharing of 0. Thus, we can use t-wise independent $[o]_{2t}$'s with uniformly random degree-t sharings $[r]_t$'s.

In [DN07], it has been shown that preparing a random degree-t random sharing requires the communication of 2 elements per party. In Sect. 4.3, following from the same idea of preparing random degree-t Shamir sharings, we show that preparing a random degree-$2t$ sharing of 0 requires the communication of 2 elements per party as well. Then, using our idea of t-wise independence, we expand

t random degree-$2t$ sharings of 0 to n sharings with t-wise independence. In this way, the communication cost of preparing correlated-randomness for one multiplication in the first layer is $2 + 2 \cdot t/n \approx 3$ elements. Including the communication cost of the multiplication protocol in [DN07], which is 2 elements per party, the overall cost per multiplication in the first layer is 5 elements per party.

Recall that for multiplication gates in the second layer, we will use our improved multiplication protocol to compute Beaver triples, which requires the communication of 4 elements per party per gate. To evaluate the whole circuit, we first partition it into a sequence of two-layer sub-circuits. Then we use the above strategy to evaluate each two-layer sub-circuit in a predetermined topological order. Assuming that the number of multiplication gates in the first layer is roughly the same as the number of multiplication gates in the second layer, the concrete efficiency is $(4 + 5)/2 = 4.5$ elements per party per gate.

Achieving Security-with-abort. We note that the correctness of the computation requires the following two points:

- $P_{\texttt{king}}$ parties send the same values to all other parties for multiplication gates in the first layer of all sub-circuits.
- All multiplication tuples are correctly computed.

In the verification phase, all parties first check whether they receive the same values, which corresponds to the first point above. This is done by checking a random linear combination of the values they receive. Then, all parties use the verification of multiplications in [GSZ20] to efficiently check the correctness of all multiplication tuples. In Sect. 4.3, we show that the communication complexity of the verification phase is sub-linear in the number of multiplication gates. Therefore, the concrete efficiency of our protocol is the same as that for each multiplication gate, i.e., 4.5 elements per party per gate. In particular, comparing with the protocol in [GSZ20], we reduce the number of rounds by a factor of 2.

2.4 Using PRG to Reduce Communication Complexity

We note that the communication complexity can be further reduced by relying on pseudo-random generators. This trick has been used in previous works such as [BBCG+19, LN17, NV18].

At a high-level, each pair of parties will first agree on a random seed, which is unknown to other parties. When some party P_i needs to distribute a degree-t sharing, one can think that P_i first sends random elements to the first t parties as their shares. Then P_i reconstructs the whole sharing using the secret and the first t shares, and distributes the shares to the rest of parties. Relying on the PRG, P_i does not need to send shares to the first t parties. Instead, each of the first t parties and P_i will simply run the PRG on their common seed and take the same piece from the output as the share. In this way, the cost of distributing a degree-t sharing can be reduced by a factor of 2. For a degree-$2t$ sharing, one can think that P_i first sends random elements to all other parties as their shares. Then P_i reconstructs the whole sharing using the secret and the $2t$ shares distributed to other parties. Finally, P_i can compute its own share. Relying on PRG, P_i does not need to communicate with any party. Instead, each party and P_i simply run the PRG on their common seed and take the same piece from the output as the share. In this way, distributing a degree-$2t$ sharing can be done at no cost. Regarding the security, notice that the corrupted parties learn nothing about the secret of a sharing distributed by an honest party even if the shares of corrupted parties are determined by themselves. This is because the corrupted parties only learn t shares of either a degree-t Shamir sharing or a degree-$2t$ Shamir sharing, which are independent of the secret value.

As a result, for our first improvement of using t-wise independence, the concrete efficiency can be improved to 2 elements per party per gate. For our second improvement of using Beaver triples, the communication efficiency can be improved to 2.5 elements per party per gate. More details can be found in the full version of this paper [GLO+21].

3   Preliminaries

3.1   Model

In this work, we focus on functions that can be represented as arithmetic circuits over a finite field $\mathbb{F}$ (with $|\mathbb{F}| \geq 2n)^1$ with input, addition, multiplication, and output gates. Let $\phi = \log |\mathbb{F}|$ be the size of an element in $\mathbb{F}$. We use κ to denote the security parameter and let $\mathbb{K}$ be an extension field of $\mathbb{F}$ (with $|\mathbb{K}| \geq 2^\kappa$). For simplicity, we assume that κ is the size of an element in $\mathbb{K}$. Let c_I, c_M, c_O be the number of input gates, multiplication gates, and output gates respectively. We set $C = c_I + c_M + c_O$ to be the size of the circuit.

For the secure multi-party computation, we use the *client-server* model. In the client-server model, clients provide inputs to the functionality and receive outputs, and servers can participate in the computation but do not have inputs or get outputs. Each party may have different roles in the computation. Note that, if every party plays a single client and a single server, this corresponds to a protocol in the standard MPC model. Let c denote the number of clients and $n = 2t + 1$ denote the number of servers. For all clients and servers, we assume that every two of them are connected via a secure (private and authentic) synchronous channel so that they can directly send messages to each other. The communication complexity is measured by the number of bits via private channels.

An adversary $\mathcal{A}$ can corrupt at most c clients and t servers, provide inputs to corrupted clients, and receive all messages sent to corrupted clients and servers. Corrupted clients and servers can deviate from the protocol arbitrarily. We refer the readers to the full version of this paper [GLO+21] for the security definition.

---

[1] The requirement of the field size is due to the use of so-called hyper-invertible matrices in our construction. See more discussion in Section 3.2 of [BTH08].

Benefits of the Client-Server Model. In our construction, the clients only participate in the input phase and the output phase. The main computation is conducted by the servers. For simplicity, we use $\{P_1, \ldots, P_n\}$ to denote the n servers, and refer to the servers as parties. Let C denote the set of all corrupted parties and $\mathcal{H}$ denote the set of all honest parties. One benefit of the client-server model is the following theorem shown in [GIP+14].

Theorem 1 (Lemma 5.2 [GIP+14]). *Let Π be a protocol computing a c-client circuit C using $n = 2t + 1$ parties. Then, if Π is secure against any adversary controlling exactly t parties, then Π is secure against any adversary controlling at most t parties.*

This theorem allows us to only consider the case where the adversary controls exactly t parties. Therefore in the following, we assume that there are exactly t corrupted parties.

3.2 Secret Sharing

In this work, we will use the standard Shamir Secret Sharing Scheme [Sha79]. Let n be the number of parties and $\mathbb{F}$ be a finite field of size $|\mathbb{F}| \geq n + 1$. Let $\alpha_1, \ldots, \alpha_n$ be n distinct non-zero elements in $\mathbb{F}$.

A *degree-d* Shamir sharing of $x \in \mathbb{F}$ is a vector $(x_1, \ldots, x_n)$ which satisfies that there exists a polynomial $f(\cdot) \in \mathbb{F}[X]$ of degree at most d such that $f(0) = x$ and $f(\alpha_i) = x_i$ for $i \in \{1, \ldots, n\}$. Each party P_i holds a share x_i and the whole sharing is denoted by $[x]_d$.

We will utilize two properties of the Shamir secret sharing scheme.

- Linear Homomorphism:

$$\forall \ [x]_d, [y]_d, \ [x + y]_d = [x]_d + [y]_d.$$

- Multiplying two degree-d sharings yields a degree-$2d$ sharing. The secret value of the new sharing is the product of the original two secrets.

$$\forall \ [x]_d, [y]_d, \ [x \cdot y]_{2d} = [x]_d \cdot [y]_d.$$

3.3 Useful Building Blocks

In this part, we briefly summarize the functionalities that will be used in our main construction. These three functionalities can be efficiently instantiated from [DN07, GSZ20]. We refer the readers to the full version of this paper [GLO+21] for the descriptions of these functionalities.

- The first functionality $\mathcal{F}_{\text{rand}}$ allows all parties to prepare a random degree-t Shamir sharing. An instantiation of $\mathcal{F}_{\text{rand}}$ can be found in [DN07, GSZ20] (Protocol 2 in Section 3.3 of [GS20]). At a high-level, the idea is to let each party generate and distribute a random degree-t Shamir sharing to all parties. Then, all parties locally apply (the transpose of) a Vandermonde matrix, as a randomness extractor, on their shares to obtain $n-t$ random degree-t Shamir sharings. The amortized communication cost per sharing is 2 elements per party.

- The second functionality $\mathcal{F}_{\text{doubleRand}}$ allows all parties to prepare a pair of sharings $([r]_t, [r]_{2t})$ of the same random element r, where the first sharing is a random degree-t Shamir sharing, and the second sharing is a random degree-$2t$ Shamir sharing. We refer to such a pair of sharings as a pair of *double sharings*. An instantiation of $\mathcal{F}_{\text{doubleRand}}$ can be found in [DN07,GSZ20] (Protocol 4 in Section 3.4 of [GS20]). At a high-level, the idea is to let each party generate and distribute a pair of random double sharings to all parties. Then, all parties locally apply (the transpose of) a Vandermonde matrix, as a randomness extractor, on their shares to obtain $n-t$ pairs of random double sharings. The amortized communication cost per pair of random double sharings is 4 elements per party.

- The third functionality $\mathcal{F}_{\text{coin}}$ allows all parties to generate a random element. An instantiation of $\mathcal{F}_{\text{coin}}$ can be found in [GSZ20] (Protocol 6 in Section 3.5 of [GS20]). At a high-level, the idea is to first invoke $\mathcal{F}_{\text{rand}}$ to obtain a random degree-t Shamir sharing. Then all parties exchange their shares and reconstruct the secret as their output, which is a random field element. The communication complexity of the instantiation is $O(n^2\kappa)$ bits.

4   ATLAS: Our Unconditional MPC Construction

In this section, we will introduce two improvements to the secure-with-abort MPC protocol in [GSZ20].

- The first improvement reduces the communication cost per multiplication gate per party from 5.5 elements to 4 elements.
- The second improvement reduces the communication cost per multiplication gate per party from 5.5 elements to 4.5 elements *and reduce the number of rounds by a factor of* 2.

Our core idea is to reuse the correlated-randomness prepared for multiplication gates.

We first give a short review of the construction in [GSZ20]. Then we introduce our two improvements. We refer the readers to the full version of this paper [GLO+21] for further reducing the communication complexity by using a pseudo-random generator.

4.1   Review of the Secure-with-abort MPC Protocol in [GSZ20]

In [GIP+14], Genkin et al. showed that several semi-honest MPC protocols are secure up to an additive attack in the presence of a fully malicious adversary. An additive attack means that the adversary is able to change the multiplication result by adding an arbitrary fixed value. As one corollary, these semi-honest protocols provide full privacy of honest parties before reconstructing the output.

Therefore, a straightforward strategy to achieve security-with-abort is to (1) run a semi-honest protocol till the output phase, (2) check the correctness of the computation, and (3) reconstruct the output only if the check passes.

Fortunately, the best-known semi-honest protocol in this setting [DN07] is secure up to an additive attack. At a high-level, the semi-honest protocol in [DN07] computes a degree-t Shamir sharing for each wire. Since the Shamir secret sharing scheme is linear homomorphic, addition gates can be evaluated without interaction. Therefore, the main concern is multiplication gates. In [GSZ20], this kind of attack is modeled in the functionality $\mathcal{F}_{\text{mult}}$, which takes two degree-t Shamir sharings $[x]_t, [y]_t$ and outputs the multiplication result $[x \cdot y]_t$. The description of $\mathcal{F}_{\text{mult}}$ can be found in Functionality 1. The original multiplication protocol in [DN07] requires 6 elements per party per gate. Goyal et al. [GSZ20] improve this protocol and reduce the communication cost to 5.5 elements.

Functionality 1. $\mathcal{F}_{\text{mult}}$

1. Let $[x]_t, [y]_t$ denote the input sharings. $\mathcal{F}_{\text{mult}}$ receives from honest parties their shares of $[x]_t, [y]_t$. Then $\mathcal{F}_{\text{mult}}$ reconstructs the secrets x, y. $\mathcal{F}_{\text{mult}}$ further computes the shares of $[x]_t, [y]_t$ held by corrupted parties, and sends these shares to the adversary.

2. $\mathcal{F}_{\text{mult}}$ receives from the adversary a value d and a set of shares $\{z_i\}_{i \in \mathcal{C}}$.

3. $\mathcal{F}_{\text{mult}}$ computes $x \cdot y + d$. Based on the secret $z := x \cdot y + d$ and the t shares $\{z_i\}_{i \in \mathcal{C}}$, $\mathcal{F}_{\text{mult}}$ reconstructs the whole sharing $[z]_t$ and distributes the shares of $[z]_t$ to honest parties.

Since $\mathcal{F}_{\text{mult}}$ does not guarantee the correctness of the multiplications, all parties need to verify the multiplications computed by $\mathcal{F}_{\text{mult}}$ at the end of the protocol. The functionality $\mathcal{F}_{\text{multVerify}}$ takes N multiplication tuples as input and outputs to all parties a single bit b indicating whether all multiplication tuples are correct. The description of $\mathcal{F}_{\text{multVerify}}$ can be found in Functionality 2.

In [GSZ20], Goyal et al. provide an instantiation of $\mathcal{F}_{\text{multVerify}}$ which has communication complexity $O(n^2 \cdot \log C \cdot \kappa)$ bits, where n is the number of parties and κ is the security parameter. Note that it is sub-linear in the number of multiplication tuples. Relying on $\mathcal{F}_{\text{mult}}, \mathcal{F}_{\text{multVerify}}$, Goyal et al. [GSZ20] construct a secure-with-abort MPC protocol with communication complexity $O(Cn\phi + n^2 \cdot \log C \cdot \kappa)$ bits. In particular, the concrete efficiency per multiplication gate is the same as the communication cost of the instantiation of $\mathcal{F}_{\text{mult}}$, i.e., 5.5 elements per party.

Functionality 2. $\mathcal{F}_{\mathrm{multVerify}}$

1. Let N denote the number of multiplication tuples. The multiplication tuples are denoted by

$$([x^{(1)}]_t, [y^{(1)}]_t, [z^{(1)}]_t), ([x^{(2)}]_t, [y^{(2)}]_t, [z^{(2)}]_t), \ldots, ([x^{(N)}]_t \cdot [y^{(N)}]_t, [z^{(N)}]_t).$$

2. For all $i \in [N]$, $\mathcal{F}_{\mathrm{multVerify}}$ receives from honest parties their shares of $[x^{(i)}]_t, [y^{(i)}]_t, [z^{(i)}]_t$. Then $\mathcal{F}_{\mathrm{multVerify}}$ reconstructs the secrets $x^{(i)}, y^{(i)}, z^{(i)}$. $\mathcal{F}_{\mathrm{multVerify}}$ further computes the shares of $[x^{(i)}]_t, [y^{(i)}]_t, [z^{(i)}]_t$ held by corrupted parties and sends these shares to the adversary.
3. For all $i \in [N]$, $\mathcal{F}_{\mathrm{multVerify}}$ computes $d^{(i)} = z^{(i)} - x^{(i)} \cdot y^{(i)}$ and sends $d^{(i)}$ to the adversary.
4. Finally, let $b \in \{\mathtt{abort}, \mathtt{accept}\}$ denote whether there exists $i \in [N]$ such that $d^{(i)} \neq 0$. $\mathcal{F}_{\mathrm{multVerify}}$ sends b to the adversary and waits for its response.
   - If the adversary replies $\mathtt{continue}$, $\mathcal{F}_{\mathrm{multVerify}}$ sends b to honest parties.
   - If the adversary replies $\mathtt{abort}$, $\mathcal{F}_{\mathrm{multVerify}}$ sends $\mathtt{abort}$ to honest parties.

4.2 Reducing the Communication Complexity via t-wise Independence

Our first improvement comes from a new protocol for $\mathcal{F}_{\mathrm{mult}}$. The amortized communication cost of our new protocol is 4 elements per party. Relying on the secure-with-abort MPC protocol [GSZ20] which uses $\mathcal{F}_{\mathrm{mult}}, \mathcal{F}_{\mathrm{multVerify}}$ as building blocks, we directly obtain a secure-with-abort MPC protocol with the same asymptotic communication complexity, i.e., $O(Cn\phi + n^2 \cdot \log C \cdot \kappa)$ bits. In particular, the concrete efficiency per multiplication gate is 4 elements per party. Our new protocol is based on the multiplication protocol in [DN07]. We first give a quick review of the multiplication protocol in [DN07].

Review of the Multiplication Protocol in [DN07]. To evaluate a multiplication gate, all parties need to prepare a pair of random double sharings $([r]_t, [r]_{2t})$. This is done by invoking $\mathcal{F}_{\mathrm{doubleRand}}$ introduced in Sect. 3.3. Recall that the amortized communication complexity of the instantiation of $\mathcal{F}_{\mathrm{doubleRand}}$ in [DN07, GSZ20] is 4 elements per party.

For a multiplication gate, suppose the input sharings are denoted by $[x]_t, [y]_t$. To compute $[z]_t := [x \cdot y]_t$, a pair of random double sharings $([r]_t, [r]_{2t})$ is consumed. All parties first agree on a special party P_{king}. P_{king} will help do the reconstruction in the multiplication protocol. Then, all parties run the following steps:

1. All parties locally compute $[e]_{2t} := [x]_t \cdot [y]_t + [r]_{2t}$.
2. P_{king} collects all shares of $[e]_{2t}$ and reconstructs the secret e. Then P_{king} sends the value e to all other parties.
3. After receiving e from P_{king}, all parties locally compute $[z]_t := e - [r]_t$.

The correctness follows from the properties of the Shamir secret sharing scheme. Note that each party needs to send an element to P_{king}, and P_{king} needs to send an element to each party. The communication complexity of this protocol is 2 elements per party. Including the communication cost for preparing double sharings, the overall cost per multiplication gate is 6 elements per party.

In [GSZ20], Goyal et al. observe that in the second step, P_{king} can alternatively distribute a degree-t Shamir sharing $[e]_t$. Then in the last step, all parties can still compute $[z]_t := [e]_t - [r]_t$. Furthermore, since e does not need to be private, P_{king} can set the shares of (a predetermined set of) t parties to be 0 in $[e]_t$. This means that P_{king} need not to communication these shares at all, reducing the communication by half. This observation allows Goyal et al. to reduce the communication cost from 6 elements to 5.5 elements.

Our Observation. As [GSZ20], we require P_{king} to distribute a degree-t Shamir sharing $[e]_t$ in the second step. However, we further require P_{king} to generate a random sharing $[e]_t$. In this way, when P_{king} is an honest party, corrupted parties only receive t shares of a random degree-t sharing $[e]_t$ from P_{king}, which are uniform and independent of the secret. As discussed in Sect. 2, it means that we do not need to use uniform double sharings when P_{king} is honest.

For n multiplication gates, our idea is to let each party behave as P_{king} for one multiplication gate. Note that only t out of n multiplications are handled by corrupted P_{king}'s. To make sure that all parties still use a pair of random double sharings when P_{king} is corrupted, the n pairs of double sharings for these n multiplication gates only need to be t-wise independent. To this end, we will first generate t pairs of random double sharings, and then expand them to n pairs of double sharings with t-wise independence.

Specifically, all parties agree on an $n \times t$ hyper-invertible matrix $\boldsymbol{M}$. Let $([r^{(1)}]_t, [r^{(1)}]_{2t}), \ldots, ([r^{(t)}]_t, [r^{(t)}]_{2t})$ be t pairs of random double sharings prepared by $\mathcal{F}_{\text{doubleRand}}$. All parties execute EXPAND (Protocol 3) to expand these t pairs into n pairs of t-wise independent double sharings.

Protocol 3. EXPAND

1. All parties agree on an $n \times t$ hyper-invertible matrix $\boldsymbol{M}$. All parties locally compute

$$([\tilde{r}^{(1)}]_t, \ldots, [\tilde{r}^{(n)}]_t)^{\mathrm{T}} = \boldsymbol{M}([r^{(1)}]_t, \ldots, [r^{(t)}]_t)^{\mathrm{T}}$$
$$([\tilde{r}^{(1)}]_{2t}, \ldots, [\tilde{r}^{(n)}]_{2t})^{\mathrm{T}} = \boldsymbol{M}([r^{(1)}]_{2t}, \ldots, [r^{(t)}]_{2t})^{\mathrm{T}}$$

2. All parties output $\{([\tilde{r}^{(i)}]_t, [\tilde{r}^{(i)}]_{2t}, P_i)\}_{i=1}^{n}$, where $([\tilde{r}^{(i)}]_t, [\tilde{r}^{(i)}]_{2t}, P_i)$ will be used for a multiplication gate handled by P_i.

Recall that $\mathcal{C}$ denotes the set of all corrupted parties. By the property of hyper-invertible matrices, there is a one-to-one map from $\{([\tilde{r}^{(i)}]_t, [\tilde{r}^{(i)}]_{2t})\}_{i \in \mathcal{C}}$ to $\{[r^{(i)}]_t, [r^{(i)}]_{2t}\}_{i=1}^t$. Thus, $\{([\tilde{r}^{(i)}]_t, [\tilde{r}^{(i)}]_{2t})\}_{i \in \mathcal{C}}$ are t pairs of random double sharings.

ATLAS Multiplication Protocol. To evaluate a multiplication gate, a pair of double sharings $([r]_t, [r]_{2t}, P_i)$ is consumed. All parties execute MULT (Protocol 4).

Protocol 4. MULT

1. Let $([r]_t, [r]_{2t}, P_i)$ be the random double sharings which will be used in the protocol. Let $[x]_t, [y]_t$ denote the input sharings.
2. All parties locally compute $[e]_{2t} = [x]_t \cdot [y]_t + [r]_{2t}$.
3. P_i collects all shares and reconstructs the secret $e = x \cdot y + r$. Then P_i randomly generates a degree-t Shamir sharing $[e]_t$ and distributes the shares to other parties.
4. All parties locally compute $[z]_t = [e]_t - [r]_t$.

To show the security of ATLAS multiplication protocol, we consider the scenario where all parties evaluate *a sequence of N multiplication gates*. In particular, the input sharings of each multiplication gate can depend on the input sharings or output sharings of the previous multiplication gates. The functionality $\mathcal{F}'_{\text{mult}}$ appears in Functionality 5, which invokes $\mathcal{F}_{\text{mult}}$ for each multiplication gate. One can view $\mathcal{F}'_{\text{mult}}$ as an interface of $\mathcal{F}_{\text{mult}}$. It allows us to replace the invocation of $\mathcal{F}_{\text{mult}}$ in the secure-with-abort MPC protocol [GSZ20] by the invocation of $\mathcal{F}'_{\text{mult}}$, and thus directly use ATLAS multiplication protocol in the protocol [GSZ20]. The protocol ATLAS-MULT appears in Protocol 6.

Functionality 5. $\mathcal{F}'_{\text{mult}}$

1. $\mathcal{F}'_{\text{mult}}$ receives N from all parties.
2. From $i = 1$ to N, let $[x^{(i)}]_t, [y^{(i)}]_t$ denote the input sharings of the i-th multiplication gate. $\mathcal{F}'_{\text{mult}}$ invokes $\mathcal{F}_{\text{mult}}$ on $[x^{(i)}]_t, [y^{(i)}]_t$.

Lemma 1. *The protocol* ATLAS-MULT *securely computes the functionality* $\mathcal{F}'_{mult}$ *in the* $\mathcal{F}_{doubleRand}$-*hybrid model in the presence of a fully malicious adversary controlling t corrupted parties.*

Protocol 6. ATLAS-MULT

1. All parties set N to be the number of multiplication gates to be evaluated.
2. All parties invoke $\mathcal{F}_{\text{doubleRand}}$ to prepare $N \cdot t/n$ pairs of random double sharings, and invoke EXPAND to obtain N pairs of double sharings in the form of $([r]_t, [r]_{2t}, P_j)$
3. From $i = 1$ to N, let $[x^{(i)}]_t, [y^{(i)}]_t$ denote the input sharings of the i-th multiplication gate. Suppose $([r]_t, [r]_{2t}, P_j)$ is the first pair of unused double sharings. All parties invoke MULT on $[x^{(i)}]_t, [y^{(i)}]_t$ and $([r]_t, [r]_{2t}, P_j)$.

We refer the readers to the full version of this paper [GLO+21] for the proof of Lemma 1.

Using $\mathcal{F}'_{mult}$ in the MPC protocol in [GSZ20]. In the secure-with-abort MPC protocol in [GSZ20], all parties invoke $\mathcal{F}_{\text{mult}}$ for each multiplication gate. Note that $\mathcal{F}'_{\text{mult}}$ invoke $\mathcal{F}_{\text{mult}}$ for each multiplication. Therefore, we view $\mathcal{F}'_{\text{mult}}$ as an interface of $\mathcal{F}_{\text{mult}}$. All parties initialize $\mathcal{F}'_{\text{mult}}$ in the beginning of the protocol with the number of multiplications they need to compute (which is determined by the circuit). Then we replace each invocation of $\mathcal{F}_{\text{mult}}$ by $\mathcal{F}'_{\text{mult}}$.

Note that every t pairs of random double sharings generated by $\mathcal{F}_{\text{doubleRand}}$ are expanded to n pairs of double sharings. Therefore, the communication cost per pair of double sharings is $4 \cdot t/n \approx 2$ elements per party. The overall cost per multiplication gate is 4 elements per party. Therefore, when using ATLAS-MULT to instantiate $\mathcal{F}'_{\text{mult}}$, we obtain a secure-with-abort MPC protocol with communication complexity of $O(Cn\phi + n^2 \cdot \log C \cdot \kappa)$ bits. In particular, the concrete efficiency per multiplication gate is 4 elements per party.

Remark 1. It has been observed in many previous works (e.g., [CGH+18, GSZ20]) that the DN multiplication protocol can be extended to compute an inner-product operation *with the same communication complexity as a multiplication operation*. An inner-product operation is to compute the summation of the coordinate-wise multiplications between two vectors. At a high-level, given two vectors of input sharings $([x^{(1)}]_t, [x^{(2)}]_t, \ldots, [x^{(\ell)}]_t), ([y^{(1)}]_t, [y^{(2)}]_t, \ldots, [y^{(\ell)}]_t)$, the goal is to compute a degree-t Shamir sharing of $z = \sum_{i=1}^{\ell} x^{(i)} \cdot y^{(i)}$. Since all parties can locally compute a degree-$2t$ Shamir sharing $[z]_{2t} = \sum_{i=1}^{\ell} [x^{(i)}]_t \cdot [y^{(i)}]_t$, all parties can use the same technique as the DN multiplication protocol to do degree reduction.

We note that our technique of using t-wise independent double sharings also works in this extension. As a result, we obtain an inner-product protocol with communication complexity of 4 elements per party, which is secure up to an additive attack (see Functionality 7 in Section 4 of [GS20] for the description of the corresponding functionality).

4.3   Reducing the Number of Rounds via Beaver Triples

For the secure-with-abort MPC protocol in [GSZ20], multiplication gates in the same layer of the circuit are evaluated in parallel. Therefore, the number of rounds is linear in the depth of the circuit. To further improve the concrete efficiency, we pay our attention to the round complexity. In this part, we show that multiplication gates in a two-layer circuit can be evaluated in parallel. It allows us to reduce the number of rounds by a factor of 2. The amortized communication cost per multiplication gate is 4.5 elements per party.

An Overview of Our Approach. We first start with a two-layer circuit. At a high-level, we use Beaver triples to evaluate multiplications in the second layer. Recall that a Beaver triple consists of three degree-t Shamir sharings $([a]_t, [b]_t, [c]_t)$ such that $c = a \cdot b$. Usually, a Beaver triple is used to transform one multiplication to two reconstructions. Concretely, given two sharings $[x]_t, [y]_t$, suppose we want to compute $[z]_t$ such that $z = x \cdot y$. Since

$$z = x \cdot y = (x + a - a) \cdot (y + b - b)$$
$$= (x + a) \cdot (y + b) - (x + a) \cdot b - (y + b) \cdot a + a \cdot b,$$

we can compute

$$[z]_t := (x + a) \cdot (y + b) - (x + a) \cdot [b]_t - (y + b) \cdot [a]_t + [c]_t.$$

Therefore, the task of computing $[z]_t$ becomes to reconstruct two degree-t Shamir sharings $[x]_t + [a]_t$ and $[y]_t + [b]_t$. Observe that, if we set $u = x + a$ and $v = y + b$, the above equation allows us to locally compute a degree-t Shamir sharing of $z := (u - a) \cdot (v - b)$ using a Beaver triple $([a]_t, [b]_t, [c]_t)$. In particular, the values u, v *can be learnt after* preparing the Beaver triple. For multiplications in the second layer, our idea is to transform each input sharing to the form of $u - [a]_t$, where u is a public element and $[a]_t$ is a degree-t Shamir sharing. We refer to this form as the *Beaver-triple friendly form*. Moreover, the sharing $[a]_t$ is known to all parties *before evaluating the first layer*. In this way, for an multiplication gate in the second layer with input sharings $u - [a]_t$ and $v - [b]_t$, we can prepare the Beaver triple $([a]_t, [b]_t, [c]_t)$ *in parallel with* the multiplications in the first layer.

We note that an input sharing of a multiplication gate in the second layer may come from three places:

- This sharing is an input sharing of the circuit.
- This sharing is an output sharing of an addition gate in the first layer.
- This sharing is an output sharing of a multiplication gate in the first layer.

Note that an addition gate can be evaluated without interaction. For the first two cases, all parties can locally compute this sharing. Let $[x]_t$ denote such a sharing. Note that $[x]_t = 0 - (-[x]_t)$ is already in the Beaver-triple friendly form, and $(-[x]_t)$ is known before evaluating the first layer. For the third case, we want the output sharing of a multiplication gate in the first layer to have the Beaver-triple friendly form $u - [a]_t$, and $[a]_t$ is known before evaluating this gate. We note that the original multiplication protocol in [DN07] satisfies our requirement. Recall that in the original multiplication protocol in [DN07]:

1. P_{king} reconstructs a degree-$2t$ Shamir sharing $[e]_{2t} := [x]_t \cdot [y]_t + [r]_{2t}$ and sends e to other parties.
2. All parties locally compute $[z]_t := e - [r]_t$.

In particular, the random double sharings $([r]_t, [r]_{2t})$ are prepared before evaluating this gate.

In summary, a two-layer circuit can be evaluated as follows:

- For each input sharing in the second layer, all parties transform it to the Beaver-triple friendly form, denoted by $u - [a]_t$, such that $[a]_t$ is known to all parties.
- For each multiplication gate in the first layer, suppose $[x]_t, [y]_t$ are the input sharings. All parties use the original multiplication protocol in [DN07] to compute $[z]_t$, where $z = x \cdot y$. For each multiplication gate in the second layer, suppose $u - [a]_t, v - [b]_t$ are the input sharings. All parties use our multiplication protocol MULT on $[a]_t, [b]_t$ to compute $[c]_t$, where $c = a \cdot b$. Note that these two kinds of multiplications can be computed in parallel.
- For each multiplication gate in the second layer, suppose $u - [a]_t, v - [b]_t$ are the input sharings. Note that we have learnt u, v when evaluating the first layer, and we have computed the Beaver triple $([a]_t, [b]_t, [c]_t)$. Therefore, all parties compute $[z]_t := u \cdot v - u \cdot [b]_t - v \cdot [a]_t + [c]_t$.

We note that the original multiplication protocol in [DN07] requires the communication of 6 elements per party. Next, we show how to reduce the communication cost to 5 elements without breaking the form of the output sharing.

Improving the Original Multiplication Protocol in [DN07]. Recall that in the original multiplication protocol in [DN07]:

1. P_{king} reconstructs a degree-$2t$ Shamir sharing $[e]_{2t} := [x]_t \cdot [y]_t + [r]_{2t}$ and sends e to other parties.
2. All parties locally compute $[z]_t := e - [r]_t$.

To keep the form of the output sharing, P_{king} cannot replace e by a degree-t Shamir sharing $[e]_t$. Furthermore, to protect the secrecy of the multiplication result $x \cdot y$, r need to be uniformly random. Our main observation is that r being uniform is not equivalent to the double sharings $([r]_t, [r]_{2t})$ being uniform. To this end, we first decouple the relation between r and $([r]_t, [r]_{2t})$. Note that a pair of double sharings $([r]_t, [r]_{2t})$ is equivalent to a pair of sharings $([r]_t, [o]_{2t})$, where the first sharing is a degree-t Shamir sharing of r and the second sharing is a degree-$2t$ Shamir sharing of $o = 0$. To see this, given $([r]_t, [r]_{2t})$, we can set $[o]_{2t} := [r]_{2t} - [r]_t$; given $([r]_t, [o]_{2t})$, we can set $[r]_{2t} := [r]_t + [o]_{2t}$. When using a pair of sharings $([r]_t, [o]_{2t})$, the multiplication protocol becomes:

1. All parties locally compute $[e]_{2t} := [x]_t \cdot [y]_t + [r]_t + [o]_{2t}$.
2. P_{king} collects all shares of $[e]_{2t}$ and reconstructs the secret e. Then P_{king} sends the value e to all other parties.
3. After receiving e from P_{king}, all parties locally compute $[z]_t := e - [r]_t$.

Note that $[o]_{2t}$ is only used to compute $[e]_{2t}$. When P_{king} is an honest party, $[o]_{2t}$ does not need to be a uniformly random degree-$2t$ sharing of 0. Thus, following the same argument as that in Sect. 4.2, we can use t-wise independent $[o]_{2t}$'s with uniformly random degree-t sharings $[r]_t$'s.

The Improved Multiplication Protocol. For a sequence of n multiplication gates, all parties first prepare n random degree-t Shamir sharings using $\mathcal{F}_{\text{rand}}$, denoted by

$$[r^{(1)}]_t, \ldots, [r^{(n)}]_t.$$

Recall that the amortized communication cost of the instantiation of $\mathcal{F}_{\text{rand}}$ in [DN07, GS20] is 2 elements per sharing per party. For random degree-$2t$ Shamir sharings of 0, we model the functionality $\mathcal{F}_{\text{zero}}$ in Functionality 7. We refer the readers to the full version of this paper [GLO+21] for an instantiation of $\mathcal{F}_{\text{zero}}$ with communication complexity of 2 elements per sharing per party.

Functionality 7. $\mathcal{F}_{\text{zero}}$

1. $\mathcal{F}_{\text{zero}}$ receives from the adversary the set of shares $\{r_i\}_{i \in \mathcal{C}}$.
2. $\mathcal{F}_{\text{zero}}$ randomly samples t elements as the shares of the first t honest parties. Based on the secret $o = 0$, the t shares of the first t honest parties, and the t shares $\{r_i\}_{i \in \mathcal{C}}$ of corrupted parties, $\mathcal{F}_{\text{zero}}$ reconstructs the whole sharing $[o]_{2t}$. $\mathcal{F}_{\text{zero}}$ distributes the shares of $[o]_{2t}$ to honest parties.

All parties invoke $\mathcal{F}_{\text{zero}}$ to prepare t random degree-$2t$ Shamir sharings of 0, denoted by

$$[o^{(1)}]_t, \ldots, [o^{(t)}]_t.$$

These t sharings are expanded to n sharings with t-wise independence. As EXPAND, we will use a predetermined $n \times t$ hyper-invertible matrix $\boldsymbol{M}$. The protocol EXPANDZERO appears in Protocol 8.

For the i-th multiplication gate, we will use $([r^{(i)}]_t, [\tilde{o}^{(i)}]_{2t}, P_i)$ and P_i will act as P_{king}. The protocol MULTDN appears in Protocol 9. As for the amortized communication cost per gate:

- Preparing one random degree-t Shamir sharing using $\mathcal{F}_{\text{rand}}$ requires to communicate 2 elements per party.
- Preparing one t-wise independent degree-$2t$ Shamir sharing of 0 using $\mathcal{F}_{\text{zero}}$ and EXPANDZERO requires to communicate $2 \cdot t/n$ elements per party.
- The protocol MULTDN requires to communicate 2 elements per party.

Protocol 8. EXPANDZERO

1. All parties agree on an $n \times t$ hyper-intertible matrix $\boldsymbol{M}$. All parties locally compute

$$([\tilde{o}^{(1)}]_{2t}, \ldots, [\tilde{o}^{(n)}]_{2t})^{\mathrm{T}} = \boldsymbol{M}([o^{(1)}]_{2t}, \ldots, [o^{(t)}]_{2t})^{\mathrm{T}}$$

2. All parties output $\{([\tilde{o}^{(i)}]_{2t}, P_i)\}_{i=1}^{n}$, where $([\tilde{o}^{(i)}]_{2t}, P_i)$ will be used for a multiplication gate handled by P_i.

In summary, the amortized communication cost per gate is 5 elements per party.

Protocol 9. MULTDN

1. Let $([r]_t, [o]_{2t}, P_i)$ be the random sharings which will be used in the protocol. Let $[x]_t, [y]_t$ denote the input sharings.
2. All parties locally compute $[e]_{2t} = [x]_t \cdot [y]_t + [r]_t + [o]_{2t}$.
3. P_i collects all shares and reconstructs the secret $e = x \cdot y + r$. Then P_i sends e to other parties.
4. All parties locally compute $[z]_t = e - [r]_t$.

Evaluating a Two-Layer Circuit. Given a two-layer circuit, we assume that all parties hold a degree-t Shamir sharing for each input wire in the beginning. As described above, we will use MULTDN to evaluate multiplication gates in the first layer. For multiplication gates in the second layer, note that all parties only need to obtain the output sharings. Therefore, we can use MULT, which only requires 4 elements per gate per party, to evaluate multiplication gates in the second layer.

Suppose there are N_1 multiplication gates in the first layer, and N_2 multiplication gates in the second layer. We assume that all parties have prepared the correlated randomness associated with these multiplication gates, i.e., N_1 pairs of sharings in the form of $([r]_t, [o]_t, P_i)$, and N_2 pairs of sharings in the form of $([r]_t, [r]_{2t}, P_i)$. In the main protocol, these sharings are prepared together at the beginning of the protocol. Then all parties execute EVALUATE (Protocol 10) to compute the output sharings of this circuit.

Protocol 10. EVALUATE

1. All parties start with holding a degree-t Shamir sharing for each input wire of this circuit. For each multiplication gate in the second layer, we will transform the input sharings to the Beaver-triple friendly form $u - [a]_t$. Consider the following three cases.
   - If this sharing is an input sharing of the circuit, denoted by $[x]_t$, all parties set $u := 0$ and $[a]_t := -[x]_t$.
   - If this sharing is an output sharing of an addition gate in the first layer, all parties first locally compute this sharing, denoted by $[x]_t$, and then set $u := 0$ and $[a]_t := -[x]_t$.
   - If this sharing is an output sharing of a multiplication gate in the first layer, suppose $([r]_t, [o]_{2t}, P_i)$ are associated with this gate. All parties set $[a]_t := [r]_t$. The value u, which corresponds to e in MULTDN, will be computed when this multiplication gate is evaluated.
2. For each multiplication gate with input sharings $[x]_t, [y]_t$ in the first layer, all parties invoke MULTDN to compute $[z]_t$ where $z := x \cdot y$. For each multiplication gate with input sharings $(u - [a]_t), (v - [b]_t)$ in the second layer, where all parties have learnt the sharings $[a]_t, [b]_t$, all parties invoke MULT to compute $[c]_t$ where $c := a \cdot b$.
3. For each multiplication gate in the first layer, let e be the reconstruction result distributed by P_{king} in MULTDN. If the output sharing of this gate is used as an input sharing of a multiplication gate in the second layer, all parties set $u := e$ for this input sharing.
4. Finally, for each multiplication gate with input sharings $(u - [a]_t), (v - [b]_t)$ in the second layer, all parties locally compute

$$[z]_t := u \cdot v - u \cdot [b]_t - v \cdot [a]_t + [c]_t$$

as the output sharing of this gate.

Main Protocol. Now we are ready to present the main protocol. Recall that we are in the client-server model. In particular, all the inputs belong to the clients, and only the clients receive the outputs. The functionality $\mathcal{F}_{\text{main}}$ appears in Functionality 11.

As [GSZ20], our protocol includes 4 phases:

- Input Phase: The clients will share their inputs to the parties.
- Computation Phase: The whole circuit will be partitioned into a sequence of two-layer sub-circuits. We will evaluate each sub-circuit using EVALUATE.
- Verification Phase: To check the correctness of the computation, we will check that
   • All parties receive the same values when using MULTDN to evaluate multiplication gates in the first layer of each sub-circuit.
   • Multiplication tuples computed by MULTDN and MULT are correct.
- Output Phase: All parties reconstruct the outputs to the clients.

Functionality 11. $\mathcal{F}_{\text{main}}$

1. $\mathcal{F}_{\text{main}}$ receives from all clients their inputs.
2. $\mathcal{F}_{\text{main}}$ evaluates the circuit and computes the output. $\mathcal{F}_{\text{main}}$ first sends the output of corrupted clients to the adversary.
   - If the adversary replies `continue`, $\mathcal{F}_{\text{main}}$ distributes the output to honest clients.
   - If the adversary replies `abort`, $\mathcal{F}_{\text{main}}$ sends `abort` to honest clients.

To check that all parties receive the same values when using MULTDN, all parties will compute a random linear combination of the values they received in MULTDN and exchange their results. If a party receives different values, this party will abort. We will use the functionality $\mathcal{F}_{\text{coin}}$ introduced in Sect. 3.3 to generate a random element. The protocol CHECKCONSISTENCY appears in Protocol 12. Recall that the communication complexity of the instaniation of $\mathcal{F}_{\text{coin}}$ in [GSZ20] is $O(n^2\kappa)$ bits. The communication complexity of CHECKCONSISTENCY is $O(n^2\kappa)$ bits.

Protocol 12. CHECKCONSISTENCY$(N, \{x^{(1)}, \ldots, x^{(N)}\})$

1. All parties invoke $\mathcal{F}_{\text{coin}}$ to generate a random element $r \in \mathbb{K}$. All parties locally compute
$$x := x^{(1)} + x^{(2)} \cdot r + \ldots + x^{(N)} \cdot r^{N-1}.$$
2. All parties exchange their results x's and check whether they are the same. If a party P_i receives different x's, P_i aborts.

Lemma 2. *If there exists two honest parties who receive different set of values* $\{x^{(1)}, \ldots, x^{(N)}\}$, *then with overwhelming probability, at least one honest party will abort in the protocol* CHECKCONSISTENCY.

We refer the readers to the full version of this paper [GLO+21] for the proof of Lemma 2.

To check that multiplication tuples computed by MULTDN and MULT are correct, we will use $\mathcal{F}_{\text{multVerify}}$ from [GSZ20]. The protocol MAIN appears in Protocol 13.

Theorem 2. *Let c be the number of clients and $n = 2t+1$ be the number of parties. The protocol* MAIN *securely computes* $\mathcal{F}_{\text{main}}$ *with abort in the* $\{\mathcal{F}_{\text{rand}}, \mathcal{F}_{\text{zero}}, \mathcal{F}_{\text{doubleRand}}, \mathcal{F}_{\text{coin}}, \mathcal{F}_{\text{multVerify}}\}$-*hybrid model in the presence of a fully malicious adversary controlling up to c clients and t parties.*

Protocol 13. MAIN

1. **Input Phase:**
   For each client input x, client randomly samples a degree-t sharing $[x]_t$ and distributes the shares to all parties.
2. **Computation Phase – Preparing Correlated Randomness:**
   All parties start with holding a degree-t sharing for each input gate. The circuit is partitioned into a sequence of two-layer sub-circuits. Let N_1 denote the number of multiplications in the first layer of all sub-circuits, and N_2 denote the number of multiplications in the second layer of all sub-circuits. All parties prepare the correlated randomness as follows:
   - All parties invoke $\mathcal{F}_{\mathrm{rand}}$ to prepare N_1 random degree-t Shamir sharings. Then all parties invoke $\mathcal{F}_{\mathrm{zero}}$ to prepare $N_1 \cdot t/n$ random degree-$2t$ Shamir sharings of 0, and invoke EXPANDZERO to obtain N_1 degree-$2t$ Shamir sharings of 0. These sharings are transformed to N_1 pairs of sharings in the form of $([r]_t, [o]_{2t}, P_i)$.
   - All parties invoke $\mathcal{F}_{\mathrm{doubleRand}}$ to prepare $N_2 \cdot t/n$ pairs of random double sharings. Then all parties invoke EXPAND to obtain N_2 pairs of double sharings in the form of $([r]_t, [r]_{2t}, P_i)$.
3. **Computation Phase – Evaluating Two-Layer Circuits:**
   All sub-circuits are evaluated in a predetermined topological order. For each sub-circuit with all the input sharings prepared, all parties invoke EVALUATE to compute the output sharings.
4. **Verification Phase:**
   - Suppose $e^{(1)}, \ldots, e^{(N_1)}$ are the values all parties received in MULTDN invoked in EVALUATE. All parties invoke CHECKCONSISTENCY to check that they receive the same values.
   - Suppose $\{([x^{(i)}]_t, [y^{(i)}]_t, [z^{(i)}]_t)\}_{i=1}^{N_1}$ denote the multiplication tuples computed by MULTDN invoked in EVALUATE, and $\{([a^{(i)}]_t, [b^{(i)}]_t, [c^{(i)}]_t)\}_{i=1}^{N_2}$ denote the multiplication tuples computed by MULT invoked in EVALUATE. All parties invoke $\mathcal{F}_{\mathrm{multVerify}}$ to check the correctness of these $N_1 + N_2$ multiplication tuples.
5. **Output Phase:**
   For each output gate, suppose $[x]_t$ is the sharing associated with this gate and client is the client who should receive this output. All parties send their shares of $[x]_t$ to client. client checks whether the shares of $[x]_t$ is consistent. If not, client aborts. Otherwise, client reconstructs the result x.

We refer the readers to the full version of this paper [GLO+21] for the proof of Theorem 2.

Analysis of the Concrete Efficiency. In MAIN, all multiplication gates in the first layer of all sub-circuits are evaluated by MULTDN, which requires 5 elements per party per gate. All multiplication gates in the second layer of all sub-circuits are evaluated by MULT, which requires 4 elements per party per gate. Assuming that the number of multiplication gates in the first layer is roughly the same as the number of multiplication gates in the second layer, the concrete efficiency of MAIN is 4.5 elements per party per gate. Note that each sub-circuit is evaluated within one round of multiplication. Therefore, we reduce the number of rounds by a factor of 2. The overall communication complexity is the same as that in [GSZ20], i.e., $O(Cn\phi + n^2 \cdot \log C \cdot \kappa)$ bits.

5 Experimental Evaluation

In this section, we evaluate and compare the concrete efficiency of our proposed improvements. As a baseline for comparison, we use the publicly available implementation of [CGH+18]. We also use a setup similar to [CGH+18].

Experiment Setup. We run each party on an independent C4.large instance (2 cores with 2.9 GHz and 3.75 GB RAM) on Amazon AWS. The instances are all located in the same region (i.e. a *LAN* configuration). Throughout our experiments, we use the 61-bit Mersenne field, and we report the average of 5 executions as [CGH+18].

Our benchmark consists of two sets of synthetic arithmetic circuits. The first set has 4 circuits of 1 million multiplication gates, ranging from 20 layers to 10,000 layers. The second set has 2 circuits of 10 million multiplication gates, each with 20 layers and 100 layers. Together, the two sets cover scenarios ranging from wide-and-shallow circuits to narrow-and-deep ones. We generate these two sets of synthetic arithmetic circuits by using the code from [CGH+18]. We show running time on these circuits with 3 to 21 parties.

Benchmark Results. In Table 1 and Table 2, we compare the running time of four protocols: the baseline from [CGH+18], the secure-with-abort protocol from [GSZ20], our improved protocol using t-wise independence (abbreviated as t-wise), and the further improved version with round compression (abbreviated as round-compression). The orders of the protocols shown in both tables are based on the running times. Table 1 shows results for circuits of 1 million multiplication gates, and Table 2 shows results for circuits of 10 million multiplication gates. Note that in Table 2, the baseline implementation runs out of memory when running with 11, 15, or 21 parties. We put N/A in those cases.

We observe that when the circuit depth D is small relative to its size (e.g. $D = 20, 100$), the t-wise version achieves better speedup than the round-compression version. When D is large (e.g. $D = 1,000, 10,000$), the round-compression version achieves significant further speedup.

This is because when D is small, communication bandwidth is the bottleneck of running times. The t-wise version effectively reduces the number of bytes communicated in each round, hence speeds up the running time. The overhead of the round-compression version when D is small surpasses its improvement in running time. However, when D is large, round latency becomes the bottleneck of running times, and improvements on communication complexity become

Table 1. This table shows running times (in milliseconds) for circuits with 1 million multiplication gates and of various depths. The columns show running times for different number of parties.

Depth	version	3	5	7	9	11	15	21
20	[CGH+18]	1126	1235	1642	1739	2029	2315	2762
20	[GSZ20]	763	857	1007	1068	1177	1301	1528
20	round-compression	642	709	810	858	974	989	1118
20	t-wise	545	622	711	752	842	917	1047
20	speedup vs [CGH+18]	2.1x	2.0x	2.3x	2.3x	2.4x	2.5x	2.6x
20	speedup vs [GSZ20]	1.4x	1.4x	1.4x	1.4x	1.4x	1.4x	1.5x
100	[CGH+18]	1122	1174	1591	1729	2033	2442	2915
100	[GSZ20]	696	887	1096	1122	1230	1430	1830
100	round-compression	655	719	839	849	914	1050	1190
100	t-wise	535	618	770	820	910	1038	1250
100	speedup vs [CGH+18]	2.1x	1.9x	2.1x	2.1x	2.2x	2.4x	2.3x
100	speedup vs [GSZ20]	1.3x	1.4x	1.4x	1.4x	1.4x	1.4x	1.5x
1k	[CGH+18]	1480	1802	2510	2793	3232	4053	5093
1k	[GSZ20]	1146	1358	1748	1920	2332	2744	3543
1k	t-wise	939	1136	1490	1618	1983	2389	3108
1k	round-compression	855	976	1195	1268	1511	1700	2100
1k	speedup vs [CGH+18]	1.7x	1.8x	2.1x	2.2x	2.1x	2.4x	2.4x
1k	speedup vs [GSZ20]	1.3x	1.4x	1.5x	1.5x	1.5x	1.6x	1.7x
10k	[CGH+18]	4470	6444	9641	10702	15040	18398	24693
10k	[GSZ20]	4457	5892	8747	9850	12832	18630	23026
10k	t-wise	4333	5641	8570	9327	12323	16580	22220
10k	round-compression	2477	3252	4713	5173	6633	8713	11719
10k	speedup vs [CGH+18]	1.8x	2.0x	2.0x	2.1x	2.3x	2.1x	2.1x
10k	speedup vs [GSZ20]	1.8x	1.8x	1.9x	1.9x	1.9x	2.1x	2.0x

less significant. The round-compression version in this case achieves significant speedup by reducing the round complexity.

In practice, we can have a switch in the code to decide whether to use the t-wise version or the round-compression version according to the size and depth of each input circuit. By combining the two improvements, we achieve around 2 times speedup compared with [CGH+18] in the overall running time, which includes both communication and computation time, in all cases, and around 1.4 times speedup compared with [GSZ20].

Table 2. This table shows running times (in milliseconds) for circuits with 10 million multiplication gates and of various depths. The columns show running times for different number of parties.

D	version	3	5	7	9	11	15	21
20	[CGH+18]	11312	15118	17265	18988	N/A	N/A	N/A
20	[GSZ20]	7374	8795	10487	10883	11860	13520	15298
20	round-compression	5959	7176	8577	8846	9454	10538	11353
20	t-wise	5568	6461	7309	7892	8628	9524	10450
20	speedup vs [CGH+18]	2.0x	2.3x	2.4x	2.4x	N/A	N/A	N/A
20	speedup vs [GSZ20]	1.3x	1.4x	1.4x	1.4x	1.4x	1.4x	1.5x
100	[CGH+18]	12279	15434	17797	19273	N/A	N/A	N/A
100	[GSZ20]	7502	8220	10480	10845	12467	13112	14766
100	round-compression	6799	7319	8333	8867	9545	10396	11309
100	t-wise	5503	6076	7254	7818	8849	9144	10250
100	speedup vs [CGH+18]	2.2x	2.5x	2.5x	2.5x	N/A	N/A	N/A
100	speedup vs [GSZ20]	1.4x	1.4x	1.4x	1.4x	1.4x	1.4x	1.4x

Acknowledgements. V. Goyal, H. Li, Y. Song—Supported in part by the NSF award 1916939, DARPA SIEVE program, a gift from Ripple, a DoE NETL award, a JP Morgan Faculty Fellowship, a PNC center for financial services innovation award, and a Cylab seed funding award.

R. Ostrovsky—Supported in part by DARPA under Cooperative Agreement HR0011-20-2-0025, NSF grant CNS-2001096, US-Israel BSF grant 2015782, Google Faculty Award, JP Morgan Faculty Award, IBM Faculty Research Award, Xerox Faculty Research Award, OKAWA Foundation Research Award, B. John Garrick Foundation Award, Teradata Research Award, Lockheed-Martin Research Award and Sunday Group. The views and conclusions contained herein are those of the authors and should not be interpreted as necessarily representing the official policies, either expressed or implied, of DARPA, the Department of Defense, or the U.S. Government. The U.S. Government is authorized to reproduce and distribute reprints for governmental purposes not withstanding any copyright annotation therein.

A. Polychroniadou—This paper was prepared in part for information purposes by the Artificial Intelligence Research group of JPMorgan Chase & Co and its affiliates ("JP Morgan"), and is not a product of the Research Department of JP Morgan. JP Morgan makes no representation and warranty whatsoever and disclaims all liability, for the completeness, accuracy or reliability of the information contained herein. This document is not intended as investment research or investment advice, or a recommendation, offer or solicitation for the purchase or sale of any security, financial instrument, financial product or service, or to be used in any way for evaluating the merits of participating in any transaction, and shall not constitute a solicitation under any jurisdiction or to any person, if such solicitation under such jurisdiction or to such person would be unlawful. 2020 JPMorgan Chase & Co. All rights reserved.

References

[ABF+17] Araki, T., et al.: Optimized honest-majority MPC for malicious adversaries - breaking the 1 billion-gate per second barrier. In: 2017 IEEE Symposium on Security and Privacy (SP), pp. 843–862. IEEE (2017)

[BBCG+19] Boneh, D., Boyle, E., Corrigan-Gibbs, H., Gilboa, N., Ishai, Y.: Zero-knowledge proofs on secret-shared data via fully linear PCPs. In: Boldyreva, A., Micciancio, D. (eds.) CRYPTO 2019. LNCS, vol. 11694, pp. 67–97. Springer, Cham (2019). https://doi.org/10.1007/978-3-030-26954-8_3

[Bea92] Beaver, D.: Efficient multiparty protocols using circuit randomization. In: Feigenbaum, J. (ed.) CRYPTO 1991. LNCS, vol. 576, pp. 420–432. Springer, Heidelberg (1992). https://doi.org/10.1007/3-540-46766-1_34

[BOGW88] Ben-Or, M., Goldwasser, S., Wigderson, A.: Completeness theorems for non-cryptographic fault-tolerant distributed computation. In: Proceedings of the Twentieth Annual ACM Symposium on Theory of Computing, pp. 1–10. ACM (1988)

[BSFO12] Ben-Sasson, E., Fehr, S., Ostrovsky, R.: Near-linear unconditionally-secure multiparty computation with a dishonest minority. In: Safavi-Naini, R., Canetti, R. (eds.) CRYPTO 2012. LNCS, vol. 7417, pp. 663–680. Springer, Heidelberg (2012). https://doi.org/10.1007/978-3-642-32009-5_39

[BTH08] Beerliová-Trubíniová, Z., Hirt, M.: Perfectly-secure MPC with linear communication complexity. In: Canetti, R. (ed.) TCC 2008. LNCS, vol. 4948, pp. 213–230. Springer, Heidelberg (2008). https://doi.org/10.1007/978-3-540-78524-8_13

[CCD88] Chaum, D., Crépeau, C., Damgård, I.: Multiparty unconditionally secure protocols. In: Proceedings of the Twentieth Annual ACM Symposium on Theory of Computing, pp. 11–19. ACM (1988)

[CDVdG87] Chaum, D., Damgård, I.B., van de Graaf, J.: Multiparty computations ensuring privacy of each party's input and correctness of the result. In: Pomerance, C. (ed.) CRYPTO 1987. LNCS, vol. 293, pp. 87–119. Springer, Heidelberg (1988). https://doi.org/10.1007/3-540-48184-2_7

[CGH+18] Chida, K., et al.: Fast large-scale honest-majority MPC for malicious adversaries. In: Shacham, H., Boldyreva, A. (eds.) CRYPTO 2018. LNCS, vol. 10993, pp. 34–64. Springer, Cham (2018). https://doi.org/10.1007/978-3-319-96878-0_2

[DIK10] Damgård, I., Ishai, Y., Krøigaard, M.: Perfectly secure multiparty computation and the computational overhead of cryptography. In: Gilbert, H. (ed.) EUROCRYPT 2010. LNCS, vol. 6110, pp. 445–465. Springer, Heidelberg (2010). https://doi.org/10.1007/978-3-642-13190-5_23

[DN07] Damgård, I., Nielsen, J.B.: Scalable and unconditionally secure multiparty computation. In: Menezes, A. (ed.) CRYPTO 2007. LNCS, vol. 4622, pp. 572–590. Springer, Heidelberg (2007). https://doi.org/10.1007/978-3-540-74143-5_32

[DNPR16] Damgård, I., Nielsen, J.B., Polychroniadou, A., Raskin, M.: On the communication required for unconditionally secure multiplication. In: Robshaw, M., Katz, J. (eds.) CRYPTO 2016. LNCS, vol. 9815, pp. 459–488. Springer, Heidelberg (2016). https://doi.org/10.1007/978-3-662-53008-5_16

[FLNW17] Furukawa, J., Lindell, Y., Nof, A., Weinstein, O.: High-throughput secure three-party computation for malicious adversaries and an honest majority. In: Coron, J.-S., Nielsen, J.B. (eds.) EUROCRYPT 2017. LNCS, vol. 10211, pp. 225–255. Springer, Cham (2017). https://doi.org/10.1007/978-3-319-56614-6_8

[GIP+14] Genkin, D., Ishai, Y., Prabhakaran, M.M., Sahai, A., Tromer, E.: Circuits resilient to additive attacks with applications to secure computation. In: Proceedings of the Forty-sixth Annual ACM Symposium on Theory of Computing. STOC 2014, pp. 495–504. ACM, New York (2014)

[GLO+21] Goyal, V., Li, H., Ostrovsky, R., Polychroniadou, A., Song, Y.: ATLAS: efficient and scalable MPC in the honest majority setting. Cryptology ePrint Archive, Report 2021/833 (2021)

[GLS19] Goyal, V., Liu, Y., Song, Y.: Communication-efficient unconditional MPC with guaranteed output delivery. In: Boldyreva, A., Micciancio, D. (eds.) CRYPTO 2019. LNCS, vol. 11693, pp. 85–114. Springer, Cham (2019). https://doi.org/10.1007/978-3-030-26951-7_4

[GMW87] Goldreich, O., Micali, S., Wigderson, A.: How to play any mental game. In: Proceedings of the Nineteenth Annual ACM Symposium on Theory of Computing, pp. 218–229. ACM (1987)

[GS20] Goyal, V., Song, Y.: Malicious security comes free in honest-majority MPC. Cryptology ePrint Archive, Report 2020/134 (2020). https://eprint.iacr.org/2020/134

[GSZ20] Goyal, V., Song, Y., Zhu, C.: Guaranteed output delivery comes free in honest majority MPC. In: Micciancio, D., Ristenpart, T. (eds.) CRYPTO 2020. LNCS, vol. 12171, pp. 618–646. Springer, Cham (2020). https://doi.org/10.1007/978-3-030-56880-1_22

[HM01] Hirt, M., Maurer, U.: Robustness for free in unconditional multi-party computation. In: Kilian, J. (ed.) CRYPTO 2001. LNCS, vol. 2139, pp. 101–118. Springer, Heidelberg (2001). https://doi.org/10.1007/3-540-44647-8_6

[HMP00] Hirt, M., Maurer, U., Przydatek, B.: Efficient secure multi-party computation. In: Okamoto, T. (ed.) ASIACRYPT 2000. LNCS, vol. 1976, pp. 143–161. Springer, Heidelberg (2000). https://doi.org/10.1007/3-540-44448-3_12

[LN17] Lindell, Y., Nof, A.: A framework for constructing fast MPC over arithmetic circuits with malicious adversaries and an honest-majority. In: Proceedings of the 2017 ACM SIGSAC Conference on Computer and Communications Security, pp. 259–276. ACM (2017)

[LP12] Lindell, Y., Pinkas, B.: Secure two-party computation via cut-and-choose oblivious transfer. J. Cryptol. 25(4), 680–722 (2012). https://doi.org/10.1007/s00145-011-9107-0

[NNOB12] Nielsen, J.B., Nordholt, P.S., Orlandi, C., Burra, S.S.: A new approach to practical active-secure two-party computation. In: Safavi-Naini, R., Canetti, R. (eds.) CRYPTO 2012. LNCS, vol. 7417, pp. 681–700. Springer, Heidelberg (2012). https://doi.org/10.1007/978-3-642-32009-5_40

[NV18] Nordholt, P.S., Veeningen, M.: Minimising communication in honest-majority MPC by batchwise multiplication verification. In: Preneel, B., Vercauteren, F. (eds.) ACNS 2018. LNCS, vol. 10892, pp. 321–339. Springer, Cham (2018). https://doi.org/10.1007/978-3-319-93387-0_17

[Sha79] Shamir, A.: How to share a secret. Commun. ACM **22**(11), 612–613 (1979)

[Yao82] Yao, A.C.: Protocols for secure computations. In: 1982 23rd Annual Symposium on Foundations of Computer Science. SFCS'08, pp. 160–164. IEEE (1982)

Unconditional Communication-Efficient MPC via Hall's Marriage Theorem

Vipul Goyal[1,2]([⊠]), Antigoni Polychroniadou[3], and Yifan Song[1]

[1] Carnegie Mellon University, Pittsburgh, USA
goyal@cs.cmu.edu, yifans2@andrew.cmu.edu
[2] NTT Research, Sunnyvale, USA
[3] J.P. Morgan AI Research, New York, USA

Abstract. The best known n party unconditional multiparty computation protocols with an optimal corruption threshold communicates $O(n)$ field elements per gate. This has been the case even in the semi-honest setting despite over a decade of research on communication complexity in this setting. Going to the slightly sub-optimal corruption setting, the work of Damgård, Ishai, and Krøigaard (EUROCRYPT 2010) provided the first protocol for a single circuit achieving communication complexity of $O(\log |C|)$ elements per gate. While a number of works have improved upon this result, obtaining a protocol with $O(1)$ field elements per gate has been an open problem.

In this work, we construct the first unconditional multi-party computation protocol evaluating a single arithmetic circuit with amortized communication complexity of $O(1)$ elements per gate.

1 Introduction

Secure Multi-Party Computation (MPC) enables a set of n parties to mutually run a protocol that computes some function f on their private inputs without compromising the privacy of their inputs or the correctness of the outputs [Yao82, GMW87, CCD88, BOGW88]. An important distinction in designing

---

V. Goyal and Y. Song—Supported in part by the NSF award 1916939, DARPA SIEVE program, a gift from Ripple, a DoE NETL award, a JP Morgan Faculty Fellowship, a PNC center for financial services innovation award, and a Cylab seed funding award.

A. Polychroniadou—This paper was prepared in part for information purposes by the Artificial Intelligence Research group of JPMorgan Chase & Co and its affiliates ("JP Morgan"), and is not a product of the Research Department of JP Morgan. JP Morgan makes no representation and warranty whatsoever and disclaims all liability, for the completeness, accuracy or reliability of the information contained herein. This document is not intended as investment research or investment advice, or a recommendation, offer or solicitation for the purchase or sale of any security, financial instrument, financial product or service, or to be used in any way for evaluating the merits of participating in any transaction, and shall not constitute a solicitation under any jurisdiction or to any person, if such solicitation under such jurisdiction or to such person would be unlawful. 2020 JPMorgan Chase & Co. All rights reserved.

© International Association for Cryptologic Research 2021
T. Malkin and C. Peikert (Eds.): CRYPTO 2021, LNCS 12826, pp. 275–304, 2021.
https://doi.org/10.1007/978-3-030-84245-1_10

MPC protocols is that of the power of the adversary. An adversary in a semi-honest protocol follows the protocol's specification but tries to learn information from the received messages, and an adversary in a malicious protocol is allowed to deviate from the protocol's specification in arbitrary ways.

In this work, our focus is on the communication complexity of information theoretic protocols evaluating an arithmetic circuit in the presence of semi-honest or malicious adversaries. The "dream" in the unconditional setting is to get as close to $|C|$ as possible (or even below) where $|C|$ is the circuit size. The best known protocols in the so called optimal threshold regime tolerating $t = (n-1)/2$ corrupted parties require communicating $O(n \cdot |C|)$ field elements (ignoring circuit independent terms) [DN07, GIP+14, CGH+18, NV18, BBCG+19, GSZ20, BGIN20]. There are no constructions known beating this barrier even in the semi-honest setting despite over a decade of research.

Moving to Sub-optimal Corruption Threshold. In a remarkable result, Damgård et al. [DIK10] showed an unconditional MPC protocol with communication complexity of $O(\log |C| \cdot n/k)$ per gate (ignoring circuit independent terms) tolerating $t' = (n-1)/3 - k + 1$ corrupted parties. This was later extended by Genkin et al. [GIP15] to obtain a construction tolerating $t' = (n-1)/2 - k + 1$ corrupted parties with also a constant factor improvement in the communication complexity. These works rely on the packed secret sharing technique introduced by Franklin and Yung [FY92] where k secrets are packed into a single secret sharing. An incomparable result was given by Garay et al. [GIOZ17] who obtained a protocol with communication complexity $O(\log^{1+\delta} n \cdot |C|)$ where δ is any positive constant. If one was interested in evaluating the same circuit multiple times on different inputs, *Franklin and Yung* [FY92] showed how to use packed secret sharing to evaluate k copies of the circuit with *amortized* communication complexity of $O(n/k)$ elements per gate or $O(1)$ elements when $k = O(n)$. However in case of a single circuit evaluation, the works mentioned [GIP15, GIOZ17] remains the best known.

To our knowledge, there is no known unconditional MPC protocol which only requires communicating $O(1)$ field elements per gate for any corruption threshold (assuming the number of corrupted parties is at least super-constant). This raises the following natural question:

Is it possible to construct information theoretic MPC protocols for computing a single arithmetic circuit with communication complexity $O(1)$ field elements per gate?

We answer the above question in the affirmative by constructing an information theoretic n-party protocol based on packed secret sharing for an arithmetic circuit over a finite field $\mathbb{F}$ of size $|\mathbb{F}| \geq 2n$. Our communication complexity amortized over the multiplication gates within the same circuit (rather than amortized over multiple circuits) is $O(n/k)$ field elements per multiplication gate. Informally, we prove the following:

Theorem 1 (informal). *Assume a point-to-point channel between every pair or parties. For all $1 \leq k \leq t$ where $t = \lfloor (n-1)/2 \rfloor$, there exists an information theoretic n-party MPC protocol which securely computes a single arithmetic circuit in the presence of a semi-honest (malicious) adversary controlling up to $t - k + 1$ parties with an communication complexity of $O(n/k)$ field elements per multiplication gate. For the case where $k = O(n)$, the achieved communication complexity is $O(1)$ elements per gate. In addition, our finite field $\mathbb{F}$ is of size $|\mathbb{F}| \geq 2n$.*

Our formal theorem for semi-honest security with perfect security can be found in Theorem 6 and we refer the readers to the full version of this paper [GPS21] for the formal theorem for malicious security (with abort and statistical security). In order to achieve these results, we introduce a set of combinatorial lemmas which could be of independent interest. In particular, we marry packed secret sharing with techniques from graph theory. A key technical challenge with using packed secret sharing in the context of a single circuit is to make sure that all the required secrets for a batch of gates appear in a single packed secret sharing. In addition, one needs to ensure that these secrets appear in the correct order. Our key technical contributions in this paper relate to performing secure permutations of the secrets efficiency by using techniques from perfect matching in bipartite graphs. In particular, we make an extensive use of Hall's Marriage Theorem.

2   Technical Overview

In the following, we will use $n = 2t + 1$ to denote the number of parties. Let $1 \leq k \leq t$ be an integer. We consider the scenario where an adversary is allowed to corrupt $t' = t - k + 1$ parties. For simplicity, we focus on the semi-honest setting. We will discuss how to achieve malicious security at a later point.

Our construction will use the packed secret-sharing technique introduced by Franklin and Yung [FY92]. This is a generalization of the standard Shamir secret sharing scheme [Sha79]. It allows to secret-share a batch of secrets within a single Shamir sharing. In the case that $t' = t - k + 1$, we can use a degree-t Shamir sharing, which requires $t + 1$ shares to reconstruct the whole sharing, to store k secrets such that any t' shares are independent of the secrets. We refer to such a sharing as a degree-t packed Shamir sharing. Let x be a vector of dimension k. We use $[x]$ to denote a degree-t packed Shamir sharing of the secrets x.

In this work, we are interested in the information-theoretic setting. Our goal is to construct a semi-honest MPC protocol for a *single* arithmetic circuit over a finite field $\mathbb{F}$ (of size $|\mathbb{F}| \geq 2n$), such that the amortized communication complexity (of each party) per gate is $O(n/k)$ elements. Note that when $k = O(n)$, the amortized communication complexity per gate becomes $O(1)$ elements.

2.1   Background: Using the Packed Secret-Sharing Technique in MPC

In the information-theoretic setting, a general approach to construct an MPC protocol is to compute a secret sharing for each wire of the circuit. The circuit is evaluated gate by gate, and the problem is reduced to compute the output sharing of an addition gate or a multiplication gate given the input sharings. When the corruption threshold can be relaxed to $t' = t - k + 1$ where $t = \frac{n-1}{2}$, a natural way of using the packed secret-sharing technique [FY92] is to compute $k \geq 1$ copies of the same circuit (i.e., a SIMD circuit): by storing the value related to the i-th copy in the i-th position of the secret sharing for each wire, all copies of the same circuit are evaluated simultaneously. Moreover, the communication complexity of a single operation for packed secret sharings is usually the same as that for standard secret sharings. Effectively, the amortized communication complexity per copy is reduced by a factor of k.

In 2010, Damgård et al. [DIK10] provided the first protocol of using packed secret-sharing technique to evaluate *a single circuit*. The original work focuses on the corruption threshold $t' < (1/3 - \epsilon)n$ and perfect security. It is later extended by [GIP15] to the setting of security with abort against $t' < (1/2 - \epsilon)n$ corrupted parties with a constant factor improvement in the communication complexity[1]. At a high-level, the idea is to divide the gates of the same type in each layer into groups of k. Each group of gates will be evaluated at the same time. For each group of gates, all parties need to prepare the input sharings by using the output sharings from previous layers. Unlike the case when evaluating a SIMD circuit, input sharings for each group of gates do not come for free:

- The secrets needed to be in a single sharing may be scattered in different output sharings of previous layers.
- Even if we have all the secrets in a single sharing, we need the secrets to be in the correct order so that the i-th secret is the input of the i-th gate.

The naive approach of preparing a single input sharing by collecting the secret one by one would require $O(k)$ operations, which eliminates the benefit of using the packed secret-sharing technique. In [DIK10], they solve this problem by compiling the circuit into a special form of a universal circuit such that it can be viewed as k copies of the same circuit. In particular, the compilation uses the so-called Beneš network, which increases the circuit size by a factor of $\log |C|$, where $|C|$ is the circuit size. As a result, the amortized communication complexity per gate is $O(\log |C| \cdot n/k)$ elements.

Our work aims to remove the $\log |C|$ factor in the communication complexity and achieves the same communication efficiency as that for the evaluation of many copies of the same circuit. In this paper, we describe our idea from the bottom up:

---

[1] While the semi-honest version of the protocol in [GIP15] can use a field $\mathbb{F}$ of size $O(n)$, the maliciously secure protocol requires to use a large enough field since the error probability is proportional to the field size.

1. We start with the basic protocols to evaluate input gates, addition gates, multiplication gates, and output gates using the packed Shamir sharing scheme. These protocols are simple variants of the protocols in [DN07], which focuses on the adversary that can corrupt t parties.
2. To use these protocols to evaluate addition gates and multiplication gates, we need the secrets in the input packed Shamir sharings to have the correct order. Assuming each input sharing contains all the secrets we want, we discuss how to permute the secrets in each input sharing to the correct order.
3. Next, we show how to collect the secrets of an input packed Shamir sharing from the output sharings of previous layers. Our solution requires that each output wire from each layer is only used once in the computation, as an input wire to a single layer. This requirement can be met by further requiring that there is a fan-out gate right after each gate that copies the output wire the number of times it is used in later layers.
4. After that, we discuss how to evaluate fan-out gates efficiently.
5. Finally, we discuss how to achieve malicious security.

Our key techniques lie on the second point and the third point. We will focus on these two points in the technical overview, which are in Sect. 2.2 and Sect. 2.3. We will briefly discuss the last two points in Sect. 2.4 and Sect. 2.6.

2.2 Performing an Arbitrary Permutation on the Secrets of a Single Sharing

During the computation, we may encounter the scenario that the order of the secrets is not what we want. For example, when $k = 2$ and we want to compute two multiplication gates with input secrets $(x_1, y_1), (x_2, y_2)$, ideally we want all parties to hold two packed Shamir sharings of $\boldsymbol{x} = (x_1, x_2)$ and $\boldsymbol{y} = (y_1, y_2)$ so that when we use the multiplication protocol with these two packed Shamir sharing, we can obtain a packed Shamir sharing of the secret $\boldsymbol{x} * \boldsymbol{y} = (x_1 \cdot y_1, x_2 \cdot y_2)$. During the computation, however, all parties may hold two packed Shamir sharings of $\boldsymbol{x} = (x_1, x_2)$ and $\boldsymbol{y}' = (y_2, y_1)$. In particular, the secrets in the second sharing are not in the order we want. Using these two packed Shamir sharings in the multiplication protocol, we can only obtain a packed Shamir sharing of $\boldsymbol{x} * \boldsymbol{y}' = (x_1 \cdot y_2, x_2 \cdot y_1)$ instead of the correct result $\boldsymbol{x} * \boldsymbol{y} = (x_1 \cdot y_1, x_2 \cdot y_2)$.

To solve it, we need to construct a protocol which allows all parties to perform an arbitrary permutation on the secrets of a single sharing. Let $p(\cdot)$ be a permutation over $\{1, 2, \ldots, k\}$. We use F_p to denote the linear map which maps $\boldsymbol{x} = (x_1, x_2, \ldots, x_k)$ to $\tilde{\boldsymbol{x}} = (x_{p(1)}, x_{p(2)}, \ldots, x_{p(k)})$. Given the input sharing $[\boldsymbol{x}]$, the goal is to compute a degree-t packed Shamir sharing $[F_p(\boldsymbol{x})]$.

We first review the approach in [DIK10] for permuting the secrets of $[\boldsymbol{x}]$:

1. All parties prepare two random degree-t packed Shamir sharings $([\boldsymbol{r}], [\tilde{\boldsymbol{r}}])$, where $\tilde{\boldsymbol{r}} = F_p(\boldsymbol{r})$ and $p(\cdot)$ is the permutation we want to perform.
2. All parties locally compute $[\boldsymbol{e}] := [\boldsymbol{x}] + [\boldsymbol{r}]$ and send their shares to the first party P_1.

3. P_1 reconstructs the secrets e and computes $\tilde{e} = F_p(e)$. P_1 generates a random degree-t packed Shamir sharing $[\tilde{e}]$ and distributes the shares to other parties.
4. All parties locally compute $[\tilde{x}] := [\tilde{e}] - [\tilde{r}]$.

To see the correctness, note that in the second step we have $e = x + r$. Therefore,

$$\tilde{x} = F_p(x) = F_p(e - r) = F_p(e) - F_p(r) = \tilde{e} - \tilde{r}.$$

The communication complexity of this protocol is $O(n/k)$ elements per secret (excluding the cost for the preparation of $([r], [\tilde{r}])$).

As noted in [DIK10], the main issue of this approach is how to *efficiently* prepare a pair of random sharings $([r], [\tilde{r}])$. Although there are known techniques to prepare random sharings $([r], [\tilde{r}])$ for *a fixed* permutation p such that the amortized communication complexity per pair is $O(n)$ elements where in turn the amortized cost per secret is $O(n/k)$ elements, these techniques suffer a large overhead (at least $O(n^2)$ elements) that is independent of the number of sharings we want to prepare. It means that the overhead of preparing random sharings depends on the number of different permutations we want to perform. In the worst case where each time we need to perform a different permutation, the overhead of each pair of random sharings is as large as $O(n^2)$ elements, which eliminates the benefit of using the packed Shamir sharing scheme. In [DIK10], this issue is solved by compiling the circuit such that only $O(\log n)$ different permutations are needed in the computation with the cost of blowing up the circuit size by a factor of $O(\log |C|)$, where $|C|$ is the circuit size. This approach does not achieve our goal since the amortized communication complexity per gate becomes $O(\log |C| \cdot n/k)$ elements. To generate random sharings for m permutations, our idea is to first generate random sharings for a limited number $(O(n^2))$ of different permutations which are related to the input permutations, and then transform them to the random sharings for the desired permutations (the input permutations). In this way, since we only need to prepare random sharings for $O(n^2)$ different permutations, we do not suffer the quadratic overhead in the communication complexity even if all the input permutations are different. Moreover, we do not need to compile the circuit and therefore do not suffer the $O(\log |C|)$ factor in the communication complexity as that in [DIK10]. As a result, the amortized communication complexity of our permutation protocol is $O(n/k)$ elements per secret.

Before introducing our idea, we first introduce a useful functionality $\mathcal{F}_{\text{select}}$, which selects secrets from one or more packed Shamir sharings and outputs a single sharing which contains the chosen secrets. Later on, we will use $\mathcal{F}_{\text{select}}$ to solve the above issue of preparing random sharings for permutations. Concretely, $\mathcal{F}_{\text{select}}$ takes as input k degree-t packed Shamir sharings $\{[x^{(i)}]\}_{i=1}^k$ (which do not need to be distinct) and outputs a degree-t packed Shamir sharing of y such that $y_i = x_i^{(i)}$. Effectively, $\mathcal{F}_{\text{select}}$ chooses the i-th secret of $[x^{(i)}]$ and generates a new degree-t packed Shamir sharing $[y]$ that contains the chosen secrets. Note that *the secrets we choose are from different positions and the positions of these secrets remain unchanged in the output sharing*. To realize $\mathcal{F}_{\text{select}}$, we observe that y can be computed by $\sum_{i=1}^k e^{(i)} * x^{(i)}$, where $e^{(i)}$ is a constant vector where the i-th entry is 1 and all other entries are 0, and $*$ denotes the coordinate-wise multiplication operation. We realize $\mathcal{F}_{\text{select}}$ by extending the basic protocol for multiplication gates as described in Sect. 4.2. The amortized communication complexity of $\mathcal{F}_{\text{select}}$ is $O(n/k)$ elements per secret.

Using $\mathcal{F}_{select}$ to Generate Random Sharings for Permuting Secrets. For all $i, j \in \{1, 2, \ldots, k\}$, we say a pair of degree-t packed Shamir sharings $([\boldsymbol{x}], [\boldsymbol{y}])$ contains an (i, j)-component if $x_i = y_j$. To perform a permutation $p(\cdot)$, we need to prepare two random degree-t packed Shamir sharings $([\boldsymbol{r}], [F_p(\boldsymbol{r})])$. We can view $([\boldsymbol{r}], [F_p(\boldsymbol{r})])$ as a composition of an $(i, p(i))$-component for all $i \in [k]$.

Now we introduce a new approach for preparing random sharings $([\boldsymbol{r}], [F_p(\boldsymbol{r})])$:

1. Let $q_1, q_2, \ldots, q_k$ be k different permutations over $\{1, 2, \ldots, k\}$ such that for all $i \in [k]$, $q_i(i) = p(i)$.
2. All parties prepare a pair of random sharings for each permutation q_i, denoted by $([\boldsymbol{r}^{(i)}], [F_{q_i}(\boldsymbol{r}^{(i)})])$. Since $q_i(i) = p_i$, $([\boldsymbol{r}^{(i)}], [F_{q_i}(\boldsymbol{r}^{(i)})])$ contains an $(i, p(i))$-component.
3. To prepare $([\boldsymbol{r}], [F_p(\boldsymbol{r})])$, we can use $\mathcal{F}_{\text{select}}$ to select the $(i, p(i))$-component from $([\boldsymbol{r}^{(i)}], [F_{q_i}(\boldsymbol{r}^{(i)})])$ for all $i \in [k]$. More concretely, for $[\boldsymbol{r}]$, we use $\mathcal{F}_{\text{select}}$ to select the i-th secret of $[\boldsymbol{r}^{(i)}]$ for all $i \in [k]$. For $[F_p(\boldsymbol{r})]$, we use $\mathcal{F}_{\text{select}}$ to select the $p(i)$-th secret of $[F_{q_i}(\boldsymbol{r}^{(i)})]$ for all $i \in [k]$.

While this way of preparing a single pair of random sharings for the permutation p requires k pairs of random sharings for k permutations $q_1, \ldots, q_k$, we note that *the unused components of $([\boldsymbol{r}^{(i)}], [F_{q_i}(\boldsymbol{r}^{(i)})])$ can potentially be used to prepare random sharings for other permutations*.

In general, when we want to prepare random sharings for m permutations $p_1(\cdot), p_2(\cdot), \ldots, p_m(\cdot)$, relying on $\mathcal{F}_{\text{select}}$, it is sufficient to alternatively prepare random sharings for m permutations $q_1(\cdot), q_2(\cdot), \ldots, q_m(\cdot)$ such that:

- For all $i, j \in \{1, 2, \ldots, k\}$, the number of permutations $p \in \{p_1, p_2, \ldots, p_m\}$ which satisfies that $p(i) = j$ is equal to the number of permutations $q \in \{q_1, q_2, \ldots, q_m\}$ which satisfies that $q(i) = j$.

Then, from $i = 1$ to m, a pair of random sharings for the permutation p_i can be prepared by using $\mathcal{F}_{\text{select}}$ to choose the first unused $(j, p_i(j))$-component for all $j \in [k]$.

The major benefit of this approach is that *we can limit the number of different permutations in $\{q_1, q_2, \ldots, q_m\}$* as we show in Theorem 2.

Theorem 2. *Let $m, k \geq 1$ be integers. For all m permutations $p_1, p_2, \ldots, p_m$ over $\{1, 2, \ldots, k\}$, there exists m permutations $q_1, q_2, \ldots, q_m$ over $\{1, 2, \ldots, k\}$ such that:*

- *For all $i, j \in \{1, 2, \ldots, k\}$, the number of permutations $p \in \{p_1, p_2, \ldots, p_m\}$ such that $p(i) = j$ is the same as the number of permutations $q \in \{q_1, q_2, \ldots, q_m\}$ such that $q(i) = j$.*

– $q_1, q_2, \ldots, q_m$ *contain at most k^2 different permutations.*

Moreover, $q_1, q_2, \ldots, q_m$ can be found within polynomial time given $p_1, p_2, \ldots, p_m$.

Recall that the issue of using known techniques to prepare random sharings for $p_1, p_2, \ldots, p_m$ is that there will be an overhead of $O(n^2)$ elements per different permutation in $p_1, p_2, \ldots, p_m$. Relying on $\mathcal{F}_{\text{select}}$, we only need to prepare random sharings for permutations $q_1, \ldots, q_m$, which contain at most $k^2 \leq n^2$ different permutations. In this way, the overhead is independent of the number of permutations and the circuit size. Recall that the amortized communication complexity for each pair of random sharings is $O(n/k)$ elements per secret, and our protocol for $\mathcal{F}_{\text{select}}$ and the permutation protocol from [DIK10] also have the same amortized communication complexity, i.e., $O(n/k)$ elements per secret. Therefore, the overall communication complexity to perform an arbitrary permutation on the secrets of a single secret sharing is $O(n/k)$ elements per secret.

Using Hall's Marriage Theorem to Prove Theorem 2. We note that Theorem 2 has a close connection to graph theory. We first introduce two basic notions.

– For a graph $G = (V, E)$, we say G is a bipartite graph if there exists a partition (V_1, V_2) of V such that all edges are between vertices in V_1 and vertices in V_2. Such a graph is denoted by $G = (V_1, V_2, E)$.
– For a bipartite graph $G = (V_1, V_2, E)$ where $|V_1| = |V_2|$, a perfect matching is a subset of edges $\mathcal{E} \in E$ which satisfies that each vertex in the sub-graph $(V_1, V_2, \mathcal{E})$ has degree exactly 1.

Note that a permutation p over $\{1, 2, \ldots, k\}$ corresponds to a perfect matching in a bipartite graph: the set of vertices are $V_1 = V_2 = \{1, 2, \ldots, k\}$, and the set of edges are $\mathcal{E} = \{(i, p(i))\}_{i=1}^k$.

We first construct a bipartite graph $G = (V_1, V_2, E)$ where $V_1 = V_2 = \{1, 2, \ldots, k\}$ and E contains all edges in the perfect matching that $p_1, p_2, \ldots, p_m$ correspond to. Strictly speaking, G is a multi-graph since a pair of vertices may have multiple edges. Note that Theorem 2 is equivalent to decomposing G into m perfect matching such that the number of different perfect matching is bounded by k^2. Our idea of finding these m perfect matching is to repeat the following steps until E becomes empty:

1. We first find a perfect matching $\mathcal{E} \subset E$ in G.
2. We repeatedly remove $\mathcal{E}$ from E until $\mathcal{E}$ is no longer a subset of E. The number of times that $\mathcal{E}$ is removed from E is the number of times that $\mathcal{E}$ appears in the output perfect matching.

Note that the number of different perfect matches is the same as the number of iterations of the above two steps. Suppose the first step always succeeds. The second step guarantees that in each iteration, we will completely use up the edges between one pair of vertices in E. Since there are at most k^2 different pairs of vertices, the above process will terminate within k^2 iterations.

For the first step, we use Hall's Marriage Theorem to prove the existence of a perfect matching.

Theorem 3 (Hall's Marriage Theorem). *For a bipartite graph* (V_1, V_2, E) *such that* $|V_1| = |V_2|$, *there exists a perfect matching iff for all subset* $V_1' \subset V_1$, *the number of the neighbors of vertices in* V_2 *is at least* $|V_1'|$.

Hall's Marriage Theorem is a well-known theorem in graph theory which has many applications in mathematics and computer science. It provides a necessary and sufficient condition of the existence of a perfect matching in a bipartite graph. In addition, there are known efficient polynomial-time algorithms to find a perfect matching in a bipartite graph, e.g. the Hopcroft-Karp algorithm.

To prove the existence of a perfect matching, we show that the graph G at the beginning of each iteration satisfies the necessary and sufficient condition in Hall's Marriage Theorem. We say a bipartite graph $G' = (V_1', V_2', E')$ is d-regular if the degree of each vertex in $V_1' \bigcup V_2'$ is d. A well-known corollary of Hall's Marriage Theorem states that:

Corollary 1. *There exists a perfect matching in a d-regular bipartite graph.*

Therefore, it is sufficient to show that the graph G at the beginning of each iteration is a d-regular bipartite graph. Recall that in the beginning, the set of edges E contains all edges in the perfect matching that $p_1, p_2, \ldots, p_m$ correspond to. Since by definition, the degree of each vertex in a perfect matching is exactly 1, the degree of each vertex in G is m, which means that G is a m-regular bipartite graph. In each iteration, we first find a perfect matching in Step 1 and then repeatedly remove this perfect matching from E in Step 2. Each time of removing a perfect matching reduces the degree of each vertex in G by 1. Thus, G is still a d-regular bipartite graph after each remove of a perfect matching. Therefore, the graph G at the beginning of each iteration is a d-regular bipartite graph.

2.3 Obtaining Input Sharings for Multiplication Gates and Addition Gates

So far, we have introduced how to perform a permutation to the secrets of a single sharing to obtain the correct order. However, this only solves the problem when we have all the values we want in a single sharing. During the computation, such a sharing does not come for free since the values we want may be scattered in one or more output sharings of previous layers. This requires us to collect the secrets from those sharings and generate a single sharing for these secrets efficiently.

Our starting point is the functionality $\mathcal{F}_{\text{select}}$. Recall that $\mathcal{F}_{\text{select}}$ allows us to select secrets from one or more sharings and generate a new sharing for the chosen secrets if the secrets we select are *in different positions*. To use $\mathcal{F}_{\text{select}}$, we consider what we call the *non-collision* property stated in Property 1.

Property 1 (Non-collision). For each input sharing of each layer, the secrets of this input sharing come from different positions in the output sharings of previous layers.

Note that if we can guarantee the non-collision property, then we can use $\mathcal{F}_{\text{select}}$ to generate the input sharing we want. Unfortunately, this property does not hold in general. A counterexample is that we need the same secret twice in a single input sharing. Then these two secrets will always come from the same position. To solve this problem, we require that

- every output wire of the input layer and all intermediate layers is used exactly once as an input wire of a later layer (which may not be the next layer).

Note that this requirement can be met without loss of generality by assuming that there is a fan-out gate right after each (input, addition, or multiplication) gate that copies the output wire the number of times it is used in later layers. In the next subsection, we will discuss how to evaluate fan-out gates efficiently. With this requirement, there is a bijective map between the output wires (of the input layer and all intermediate layers) and the input wires (of the output layer and all intermediate layers).

Note that only meeting this requirement is not enough: it is still possible that two secrets of a single input sharing come from the same position but in two different output sharings. Our idea is to perform a permutation on each output sharing to achieve the non-collision property.

Since every output wire from every layer is only used once as an input wire of another layer, the number of output sharings in the circuit is the same as the number of input sharings in the circuit. Let m denote the number of output packed Shamir sharings of the input layer and all intermediate layers in the circuit. Then the number of input packed Shamir sharings of the output layer and all intermediate layers is also m. We label all the output sharings by $1, 2, \ldots, m$ and all the input sharings also by $1, 2, \ldots, m$. Consider a matrix $\boldsymbol{N} \in \{1, 2, \ldots, m\}^{m \times k}$ where $\boldsymbol{N}_{i,j}$ is the index of the input sharing that the j-th secret of the i-th output sharing wants to go to. Then for all $\ell \in \{1, 2, \ldots, m\}$, there are exactly k entries of $\boldsymbol{N}$ which are equal to ℓ. We will prove the following theorem.

Theorem 4. Let $m \geq 1, k \geq 1$ be integers. Let $\boldsymbol{N}$ be a matrix of dimension $m \times k$ in $\{1, 2, \ldots, m\}^{m \times k}$ such that for all $\ell \in \{1, 2, \ldots, m\}$, the number of entries of $\boldsymbol{N}$ which are equal to ℓ is k. Then, there exists m permutations $p_1, p_2, \ldots, p_m$ over $\{1, 2, \ldots, k\}$ such that after performing the permutation p_i on the i-th row of $\boldsymbol{N}$, the new matrix $\boldsymbol{N}'$ satisfies that each column of $\boldsymbol{N}'$ is a permutation over $(1, 2, \ldots, m)$. Furthermore, the permutations $p_1, p_2, \ldots, p_m$ can be found within polynomial time.

Jumping ahead, when we apply p_i to the i-th output sharing for all $i \in \{1, 2, \ldots, m\}$, Theorem 4 guarantees that for all $j \in \{1, 2, \ldots, k\}$ the j-th secrets of all output sharings want to go to different input sharings. Note that this ensures the non-collision property. During the computation, we will perform the permutation p_i on the i-th output sharing right after it is computed. Note that when preparing an input sharing, the secrets we need only come from the output sharings which have been computed. The secrets of these output sharings have been properly permuted such that the secrets we want are in different positions. Therefore, we can use $\mathcal{F}_{\text{select}}$ to choose these secrets and obtain the desired input sharing.

Using Hall's Marriage Theorem to Prove Theorem 4. Let $\boldsymbol{N}$ be the matrix in Theorem 4. Our idea is to repeat the following steps:

1. In the ℓ-th iteration, for each row of $\boldsymbol{N}$, we pick a value in the last $k - \ell + 1$ entries of this row (so that the first $\ell - 1$ entries will not be chosen), such that the values we pick in all rows form a permutation over $\{1, 2, \ldots, m\}$.
2. For each row of $\boldsymbol{N}$, we swap the ℓ-th entry with the value we picked in this row. In this way, the ℓ-th column of $\boldsymbol{N}$ is a permutation over $\{1, 2, \ldots, m\}$.

Note that in each iteration, we switch two elements in each row. At the end of the above process, we can compute the permutation for each row based on the elements we switched in each iteration.

To make this idea work, we need to show that we can always find the values which form a permutation over $\{1, 2, \ldots, m\}$ in Step 1. We transform this problem to finding a perfect matching in a bipartite graph. We explain our solution for the first iteration.

Consider a graph $G = (V_1, V_2, E)$ where $V_1 = V_2 = \{1, 2, \ldots, m\}$. For each entry $N_{i,j}$, there is an edge $(i, N_{i,j})$ in E. Then picking a value in each row is equivalent to picking an edge for each vertex in V_1. The chosen values forming a permutation over $\{1, 2, \ldots, m\}$ is equivalent to the chosen edges forming a perfect matching in G. To prove the existence of a perfect matching, we show that the graph G is a k-regular bipartite graph and rely on the corollary (Corollary 1) of Hall's Marriage Theorem. For all vertex $i \subset V_1$, there is an edge $(i, N_{i,j})$ in E for each entry in the i-th row of $\boldsymbol{N}$. Therefore, the degree of the vertex i is k. For all vertex $j \in V_2$, the degree of j equals to the number of entries in $\boldsymbol{N}$ which equal to j. Note that there are exactly k entries which equals to j. Thus, the degree of the vertex j is k. Therefore G is a k-regular graph. By Corollary 1, there exists a perfect matching in G. The same arguments work for other iterations. We refer the readers to Sect. 4.3 for more details.

It is worth noting that we use Hall's Marriage Theorem to solve two different problems:

- In Theorem 2, we use Hall's Marriage Theorem to find a different set of permutations $q_1, q_2, \ldots, q_m$ given the permutations $p_1, p_2, \ldots, p_m$ and limit the number of different permutations in $q_1, q_2, \ldots, q_m$.
- In Theorem 4, we use Hall's Marriage Theorem to find a permutation for each output sharing to achieve the non-collision property (Property 1).

2.4   Handling Fan-Out Gates

We briefly discuss how to evaluate fan-out gates efficiently. We first model the problem as follows: given a degree-t packed Shamir sharing $[\boldsymbol{x}]$ along with a vector $(n_1, n_2, \ldots, n_k) \in \mathbb{N}^k$, where $n_i \geq 1$ is the number of times that x_i is used in later layers, the goal is to compute $\frac{n_1+n_2+...+n_k}{k}$ degree-t packed Shamir sharings which contain n_i copies of the value x_i for all $i \in \{1, 2, \ldots, k\}$. (For simplicity, we assume that $n_1 + n_2 + \ldots + n_k$ is a multiple of k. We refer the readers to Sect. 5.1 for how we handle the edge case.)

Our idea is to compute the output sharings one by one. For each output sharing $[y]$, all values of y come from x, which means that we may write y as a linear function of x. Let F be a linear map such that $y = F(x)$. To compute $[y]$, we can prepare a pair of random sharings $([r], [F(r)])$ and use the same method to compute $[y]$ as that for permutations. Then we face the same problem that naively preparing the random sharings $([r], [F(r)])$ suffer an overhead which depends on the number of different linear maps F. In the worst case where we need a different linear map for different output packed Shamir sharing, the overhead of preparing each pair of random sharings is as large as $O(n^2)$ elements, which eliminate the benefit of using the packed Shamir sharing scheme.

We follow the same idea as that for permutation to prepare the random sharings $([r], [F(r)])$: Given m different linear maps $F_1, F_2, \ldots, F_m$, we will prepare random sharings for m other linear maps $G_1, G_2, \ldots, G_m$ and then recompose the components in the random sharings for $G_1, G_2, \ldots, G_m$ to obtain random sharings for $F_1, F_2, \ldots, F_m$. The main difficulty is that it is unclear how to define a component. Our solution includes the following additional steps:

– We require the secrets of the output packed Shamir sharings to be in a specific order.
– To compute each output packed Shamir sharing $[y]$, we first permute the secrets of $[x]$ based on y.

These two steps allow us to properly define a component in a way that we can efficiently find $G_1, G_2, \ldots, G_m$ such that the above idea works. The description of the ideal functionality for fan-out gates is presented in Sect. 4.4. We refer the readers to the full version of this paper [GPS21] for more details about our protocol for fan-out gates.

2.5   Overview of Our Semi-honest Protocol

So far, we have introduced all the building blocks we need in our semi-honest protocol. To evaluate a single circuit:

1. All parties first transform the circuit to a good form in the sense that the number of gates of each type in each layer is a multiple of k. The transformation is done locally by running a deterministic algorithm. Unlike [DIK10], our transformation only increases the circuit size by a constant factor and an additive term $O(k \cdot \text{Depth})$, where the latter term comes from the fact that the number of gates in each layer is a multiple of k after the transformation. The same term (or a larger term) also exists in [DIK10, GIP15]. We refer the readers to Sect. 5.1 for more details.
2. All parties preprocess the circuit to determine how the wire values should be packed. Also, all parties compute a permutation for each output sharing for

the non-collision property (see Property 1 in Sect. 2.3). This step is also done locally. We refer the readers to Sect. 5.2 for more details.
3. Finally, all parties evaluate the circuits using the protocols we described above. We refer the readers to Sect. 5.3 for more details.

Note that only the third step requires communication. We briefly analyze the communication complexity. For each group of k gates, all parties use the basic protocol to evaluate these gates. The communication complexity of the basic protocol is $O(n)$ elements. To prepare the input sharings for this group of k (addition, multiplication, or output) gates, we need to evaluate fan-out gates, perform permutations to achieve the non-collision property, use $\mathcal{F}_{\text{select}}$ to collect the secrets of the input sharings, and perform permutations again to obtain the correct orders. Since each operation requires $O(n)$ elements, the amortized communication complexity per gate is $O(n/k)$ elements.

2.6 Achieving Malicious Security

We briefly discuss how to compile our semi-honest protocol to a fully malicious one. Our main observation is that most of our semi-honest protocols have already achieved perfect privacy *against a fully malicious adversary*, namely the executions of these protocols do not leak any information to the adversary. Also, the deviation of a fully malicious adversary can be reduced to the following two kinds of attacks:

- An adversary can distribute an inconsistent degree-t packed Shamir sharing.
- An adversary can add additive errors to the secrets of the output sharing.

To achieve malicious security, our idea is to first run our semi-honest protocol before the output phase, check whether the above two kinds of attacks are launched by the adversary, and finally reconstruct the output.

To this end, for each semi-honest protocol, we first construct a functionality which allows the adversary to launch the above two kinds of attacks, and prove that our semi-honest protocol securely (with abort) computes the new functionality against a fully malicious adversary. Then we construct protocols to check whether the above two kinds of attacks are launched by the adversary. We view the computation as a composition of two parts: (1) evaluation of the basic gates, i.e., addition gates and multiplication gates, and (2) network routing, i.e., computing input sharings of each layer using the output sharings from previous layers.

- For the first part, since addition gates are computed without interaction, it is sufficient to only check the correctness of multiplications. We extend the recent sub-linear verification techniques [BBCG+19, GSZ20] which are used in the honest majority setting (i.e., the corruption threshold $t' = t$) to our setting (i.e., the corruption threshold $t' = t - k + 1$).
- For the second part, it includes evaluating fan-out gates, performing permutations to achieve the non-collision property, using $\mathcal{F}_{\text{select}}$ to collect the secrets

of the input sharings, performing permutations again to obtain the correct orders. We note that the network routing does not change the secret values. Instead, its goal is to create new sharings which contain the secret values we want in the correct positions. Thus, it is sufficient to only focus on the front sharing before the network routing and the end sharing after the network routing, and check whether they have the same values.

Finally, when both checks pass, all parties reconstruct the output as the semi-honest protocol. We refer the readers to the full version of this paper [GPS21] for more details.

Remark 1. We note that the multiplication protocol is an exception in the sense that it cannot be reduced directly to the additive attacks we mention above. In fact, the work [GIP15] showed that a malicious attack can only be reduced to a linear attack, where the error in the output secret can depend on the input secrets. Our observation is that the linear attack is due to the inconsistency of the input sharings. If the input sharings are consistent, then the linear attack in [GIP15] degenerates to an additive attack to the final result. To model such a security property, we use a weaker functionality for the multiplication protocol, which does not guarantee the correctness of the multiplication result when the input sharings are inconsistent. The verification is done by first checking the consistency of all sharings. If the verification passes, then the attack of an adversary degenerates to additive attacks, which allows us to use the efficient verification protocol for multiplication gates in previous works. We refer the readers to the full version of this paper [GPS21] for more discussion.

3   Preliminaries

3.1   The Model

In this work, we use the *client-server* model for the secure multi-party computation. In the client-server model, clients provide inputs to the functionality and receive outputs, and servers can participate in the computation but do not have inputs or get outputs. Each party may have different roles in the computation. Note that, if every party plays a single client and a single server, this corresponds to a protocol in the standard MPC model. Let c denote the number of clients and $n = 2t + 1$ denote the number of servers. For all clients and servers, we assume that every two of them are connected via a secure (private and authentic) synchronous channel so that they can directly send messages to each other. The communication complexity is measured by the number of bits via private channels.

We focus on functions that can be represented as arithmetic circuits over a finite field $\mathbb{F}$ with input, addition, multiplication, and output gates. We use κ to denote the security parameter, C to denote the circuit, and $|C|$ for the size of the circuit. We assume that the field size is $|\mathbb{F}| \geq 2n$.

Let $1 \leq k \leq t$ be an integer. An adversary $\mathcal{A}$ can corrupt at most c clients and $t' = t - k + 1$ servers, provide inputs to corrupted clients, and receive all messages sent to corrupted clients and servers. Corrupted clients and servers can deviate from the protocol arbitrarily. One benefit of the client-server model is that it is sufficient to only consider maximum adversaries, i.e., adversaries which corrupt $t' = t - k + 1$ parties. We refer the readers to the full version of this paper [GPS21] for more details about the security definition and the benefit of the client-server model. In the following, we assume that there are exactly $t' = t - k + 1$ corrupted parties.

3.2 Packed Shamir Secret Sharing Scheme

In this work, we will use the packed secret-sharing technique introduced by Franklin and Yung [FY92]. This is a generalization of the standard Shamir secret sharing scheme [Sha79]. Let n be the number of parties and k be the number of secrets that are packed in one sharing. Let $\alpha_1, \ldots, \alpha_n, \beta_1, \ldots, \beta_k$ be $n + k$ distinct non-zero elements in $\mathbb{F}$.

A *degree-d* ($d \geq k - 1$) packed Shamir sharing of $x = (x_1, \ldots, x_k) \in \mathbb{F}^k$ is a vector $(w_1, \ldots, w_n)$ which satisfies that, there exists a polynomial $f(\cdot) \in \mathbb{F}[X]$ of degree at most d such that $\forall i \in [k], f(\beta_i) = x_i$ and $\forall i \in [n], f(\alpha_i) = w_i$. The i-th share w_i is held by party P_i. Reconstructing a degree-d packed Shamir sharing requires $d + 1$ shares and can be done by Lagrange interpolation. For a random degree-d packed Shamir sharing of x, any $d - k + 1$ shares are independent of the secret x.

We will use $[x]$ to denote a degree-t packed Shamir sharing of $x \in \mathbb{F}^k$, and $\langle x \rangle$ to denote a degree-$2t$ packed Shamir sharing. Recall that the number of corrupted parties is at most $t - k + 1$. Therefore, using degree-t packed Shamir sharings is sufficient to protect the privacy of the secrets. In the following, operations (addition and multiplication) between two packed Shamir sharings are coordinate-wise.

We recall two properties of the packed Shamir sharing scheme:

- Linear Homomorphism: For all $x, y \in \mathbb{F}^k$, $[x + y] = [x] + [y]$.
- Multiplication: Let $*$ denote coordinate-wise multiplication. For all $x, y \in \mathbb{F}^k$, $\langle x * y \rangle = [x] \cdot [y]$.

These two properties directly follow from the computation of the polynomials.

For a constant vector $v \in \mathbb{F}^k$ which is known by all parties, sometimes it is convenient to transform it to a degree-t packed Shamir sharing. This can be done by constructing a polynomial $f(\cdot) \in F[X]$ of degree $k - 1$ such that for all $i \in [k], f(\beta_i) = v_i$. The i-th share of $[v]$ is defined to be $f(\alpha_i)$ as usual.

3.3 Generating Random Sharings

In our work, we adopt the notion of an abstract definition of a general linear secret sharing scheme (GLSSS) in [CCXY18]. We will make use of a functionality $\mathcal{F}_{\text{rand}}$ introduced in [PS21], which allows all parties to prepare a random sharing for a given $\mathbb{F}$-linear secret sharing scheme.

In [PS21], Polychroniadou and Song proposed an instantiation of $\mathcal{F}_{\text{rand}}$ which is secure against an adversary that corrupts t parties. We note that their protocol can be extended to any corruption threshold (with different communication complexity). In particular, in our setting where $t' = t - k + 1$, if the share size of the given $\mathbb{F}$-linear secret sharing scheme is sh field elements in $\mathbb{F}$, the communication complexity of generating N random sharings is $O(N \cdot n \cdot \text{sh} + n^3 \cdot \kappa)$ elements in $\mathbb{F}$. We refer the readers to the full version of this paper [GPS21] for more details.

3.4   Permutation Matrix, Bipartite Graph and Hall's Marriage Theorem

Definition 1 (Permutation Matrix). *Let $k \geq 1$ be an integer. A matrix $M \in \{0,1\}^{k \times k}$ is a permutation matrix if for each row and each column, there is exactly one entry which is 1.*

For a permutation $p(\cdot)$ over $\{1, 2, \ldots, k\}$, let M_p be a permutation matrix such that for all $i, j \in \{1, \ldots, k\}$, $(M_p)_{i,j} = 1$ iff $p(i) = j$. Note that for each permutation matrix M', there exists a permutation $p(\cdot)$ such that $M' = M_p$.

Definition 2 (Balanced Matrix). *Let $k \geq 1$ be an integer. A matrix $M \in \mathbb{N}^{k \times k}$ is a balanced matrix if for each row and each column, the summation of all the entries is the same.*

Note that for all permutations $p(\cdot)$ over $\{1, 2, \ldots, k\}$, the permutation matrix M_p is a balanced matrix since the summation of the entries in each row and each column is 1.

Definition 3 (Bipartite Graph). *A graph $G = (V, E)$ is a bipartite graph if there exists a partition (V_1, V_2) of V such that for all edge $(v_i, v_j) \in E$, $v_i \in V_1$ and $v_j \in V_2$.*

In the following, we will use (V_1, V_2, E) to denote a bipartite graph. We say a bipartite graph (V_1, V_2, E) is d-regular if the degree of each vertex in $V_1 \bigcup V_2$ is d.

Definition 4 (Perfect Matching). *For a bipartite graph (V_1, V_2, E) such that $|V_1| = |V_2|$, a perfect matching is a subset of edges $\mathcal{E} \in E$ which satisfies that each vertex in the sub-graph $(V_1, V_2, \mathcal{E})$ has degree 1.*

Theorem 3 (Hall's Marriage Theorem). *For a bipartite graph (V_1, V_2, E) such that $|V_1| = |V_2|$, there exists a perfect matching iff for all subset $V_1' \subset V_1$, the number of the neighbors of vertices in V_2 is at least $|V_1'|$.*

In this work, we will make use of the following two well-known corollaries of Hall's Marriage Theorem. For completeness, we also provide proofs for the corollaries in the full version of this paper [GPS21].

Corollary 1. *There exists a perfect matching in a d-regular bipartite graph.*

Corollary 2. *Let $k \geq 1$ be an integer. For all non-zero balanced matrix $N \in \mathbb{N}^{k \times k}$, there exists a permutation matrix M such that for all $i, j \in \{1, 2, \ldots, k\}$, $N_{i,j} \geq M_{i,j}$.*

4 Circuit Evaluation - Against a Semi-honest Adversary

In this section, we discuss how to evaluate a general circuit by using the packed Shamir sharing scheme. For simplicity, we assume the adversary is semi-honest. Recall that we are in the client-server model where there are c clients and $n = 2t + 1$ parties (servers). Recall that $1 \leq k \leq t$ is an integer. An adversary is allowed to corrupt $t' = t - k + 1$ parties. We will use the degree-t packed Shamir sharing scheme, which can store k secrets within one sharing. Recall that $\mathcal{C}$ denotes the set of corrupted parties and $\mathcal{H}$ denotes the set of honest parties.

4.1 Basic Protocols for Input Gates, Addition Gates, Multiplication Gates, and Output Gates

We distinguish input gates and output gates belonging to different clients. For each client, we assume the number of input gates belonging to this client and the number of output gates belonging to this client are multiples of k. For each layer, we assume that the number of addition gates and the number of multiplication gates are multiples of k. In Sect. 5, we will show how to compile a general circuit to meet this requirement.

Evaluating Input Gates and Output Gates. The functionalities $\mathcal{F}_{\text{input-semi}}$ and $\mathcal{F}_{\text{output-semi}}$ are described in Functionality 1 and Functionality 2 respectively. We refer the readers to the full version of this paper [GPS21] for the protocols that realize $\mathcal{F}_{\text{input-semi}}$ and $\mathcal{F}_{\text{output-semi}}$. The communication complexity of each protocol is $O(n)$ field elements.

Functionality 1: $\mathcal{F}_{\text{input-semi}}$

1. Suppose $x \in \mathbb{F}^k$ is the input associated with the input gate which belongs to the Client. $\mathcal{F}_{\text{input-semi}}$ receives the input x from the Client.
2. $\mathcal{F}_{\text{input-semi}}$ receives from the adversary a set of shares $\{s_i\}_{i \in \mathcal{C}}$. $\mathcal{F}_{\text{input-semi}}$ samples a random degree-t packed Shamir sharing $[x]$ such that for all $P_i \in \mathcal{C}$, the i-th share of $[x]$ is s_i.
3. $\mathcal{F}_{\text{input-semi}}$ distributes the shares of $[x]$ to honest parties.

Functionality 2: $\mathcal{F}_{\text{output-semi}}$

1. Suppose $[x]$ is the sharing associated with the output gate which belongs to the Client. $\mathcal{F}_{\text{output-semi}}$ receives the shares of $[x]$ from honest parties.
2. $\mathcal{F}_{\text{output-semi}}$ recovers the whole sharing $[x]$, and sends the shares of corrupted parties to the adversary.
3. $\mathcal{F}_{\text{output-semi}}$ reconstructs x and sends it to the Client.

Evaluating Addition Gates and Multiplication Gates. In the following, we use $[x], [y]$ to denote the input degree-t packed Shamir sharings.

For an addition gate, all parties want to compute $[x + y]$. Note that this can be done by computing $[x + y] := [x] + [y]$, i.e., each party locally adds its shares of $[x], [y]$. The correctness follows from the property that packed Shamir sharing is linearly homomorphic.

Recall that $*$ denotes the coordinate-wise multiplication. For a multiplication gate, all parties want to compute a degree-t packed Shamir sharing of $z := x * y$. We summarize the functionality $\mathcal{F}_{\text{mult-semi}}$ in Functionality 3.

Functionality 3: $\mathcal{F}_{\text{mult-semi}}$

1. Suppose $[x], [y]$ are the input degree-t packed Shamir sharings. $\mathcal{F}_{\text{mult-semi}}$ receives the shares of $[x], [y]$ from honest parties.
2. $\mathcal{F}_{\text{mult-semi}}$ recovers the whole sharings $[x], [y]$ and reconstructs the secrets x, y. $\mathcal{F}_{\text{mult-semi}}$ computes $z := x * y$.
3. $\mathcal{F}_{\text{mult-semi}}$ receives from the adversary a set of shares $\{s_i\}_{i \in \mathcal{C}}$. $\mathcal{F}_{\text{mult-semi}}$ samples a random degree-t packed Shamir sharing $[z]$ such that for all $P_i \in \mathcal{C}$, the i-th share of $[z]$ is s_i.
4. $\mathcal{F}_{\text{mult-semi}}$ distributes the shares of $[z]$ to honest parties.

A multiplication gate can be evaluated by a natural extension of the DN multiplication protocol in [DN07]. The main observation is that all parties can locally compute a degree-$2t$ packed Shamir sharing $\langle z \rangle = \langle x * y \rangle = [x] \cdot [y]$. The only task is to reduce the degree of $\langle z \rangle$. Following the approach in [DN07], this can be achieved by preparing a pair of two random sharings $([r], \langle r \rangle)$ of the same secrets r. We refer the readers to the full version of this paper [GPS21] for the protocol that realizes $\mathcal{F}_{\text{mult-semi}}$. The communication complexity of m invocations of $\mathcal{F}_{\text{mult-semi}}$ is $O(m \cdot n + n^3 \cdot \kappa)$ field elements.

4.2 Performing an Arbitrary Permutation on the Secrets of a Single Sharing

During the computation, we may encounter the scenario that the order of the secrets is not what we want (see more discussion in Sect. 2.2). To solve it, we need a functionality which allows us to perform an arbitrary permutation on the secrets of a single sharing. Let $p(\cdot)$ be a permutation over $\{1, 2, \ldots, k\}$. Recall that each permutation $p(\cdot)$ maps to a permutation matrix $M_p \in \{0, 1\}^{k \times k}$ where $(M_p)_{i,j} = 1$ iff $p(i) = j$. To permute a vector $x = (x_1, x_2, \ldots, x_k)$ to $\tilde{x} = (x_{p(1)}, x_{p(2)}, \ldots, x_{p(k)})$, it is equivalent to computing $\tilde{x} = M_p \cdot x$. We model the functionality $\mathcal{F}_{\text{permute-semi}}$ in Functionality 4.

Functionality 4: $\mathcal{F}_{\text{permute-semi}}$

1. $\mathcal{F}_{\text{permute-semi}}$ receives a permutation p and the shares of a degree-t packed Shamir sharing $[x]$ from honest parties.
2. $\mathcal{F}_{\text{permute-semi}}$ reconstructs the secrets x from the shares of honest parties, and computes $\tilde{x} = M_p \cdot x$.
3. $\mathcal{F}_{\text{permute-semi}}$ receives from the adversary a set of shares $\{s_i\}_{i \in C}$. $\mathcal{F}_{\text{permute-semi}}$ samples a random degree-t packed Shamir sharing $[\tilde{x}]$ such that for all $P_i \in C$, the i-th share of $[\tilde{x}]$ is s_i.
4. $\mathcal{F}_{\text{permute-semi}}$ distributes the shares of $[\tilde{x}]$ to honest parties.

We follow the techniques in [DIK10] to realize $\mathcal{F}_{\text{permute-semi}}$ by making use of a pair of random degree-t packed Shamir sharings $([r], [M_p \cdot r])$. We refer the readers to Sect. 2.2 for an overview of these techniques. As we discussed in Sect. 2.2, the main issue of this approach is how to how to *efficiently* prepare a pair of random sharings $([r], [\tilde{r}])$. To generate random sharings for m permutations, our idea is to first generate random sharings for a limited number $(O(n^2))$ of different permutations which are related to the input permutations, and then transform them to the random sharings for the desired permutations (the input permutations).

Before moving forward, we first introduce a useful functionality $\mathcal{F}_{\text{select}}$, which selects secrets from one or more packed Shamir sharings and outputs a single sharing which contains the chosen secrets. Later on, we will use $\mathcal{F}_{\text{select}}$ to solve the above issue of preparing random sharings for permutations.

Selecting Secrets from One or More Packed Shamir Sharings. Concretely, we want to realize the functionality $\mathcal{F}_{\text{select-semi}}$, which takes as input k degree-t packed Shamir sharings $[x^{(1)}], [x^{(2)}], \ldots, [x^{(k)}]$ (which do not need to be distinct) and a permutation $p(\cdot)$ over $\{1, 2, \ldots, k\}$, and outputs a degree-t packed Shamir sharing $[y]$ such that for all $i \in [k]$, $y_{p(i)} = x^{(i)}_{p(i)}$, where $x^{(i)}_j$ is the j-th value of $\boldsymbol{x}^{(i)}$. Effectively, $\mathcal{F}_{\text{select-semi}}$ chooses the $p(1)$-th secret of $[\boldsymbol{x}^{(1)}]$, the $p(2)$-th secret of $[\boldsymbol{x}^{(2)}]$, ..., the $p(k)$-th secret of $[\boldsymbol{x}^{(k)}]$ and generates a new degree-t packed Shamir sharing $[\boldsymbol{y}]$ which contains the chosen secrets. Note that the positions of the chosen secrets remain the same. Therefore, we require p to be a permutation so that the chosen secrets come from different positions. The description of $\mathcal{F}_{\text{select-semi}}$ appears in Functionality 5.

Functionality 5: $\mathcal{F}_{\text{select-semi}}$

1. $\mathcal{F}_{\text{select-semi}}$ receives from honest parties their shares of k degree-t packed Shamir sharings $[\boldsymbol{x}^{(1)}], [\boldsymbol{x}^{(2)}], \ldots, [\boldsymbol{x}^{(k)}]$. $\mathcal{F}_{\text{select-semi}}$ also receives a permutation p from honest parties.
2. $\mathcal{F}_{\text{select-semi}}$ reconstructs $\boldsymbol{x}^{(1)}, \boldsymbol{x}^{(2)}, \ldots, \boldsymbol{x}^{(k)}$. Then $\mathcal{F}_{\text{select-semi}}$ sets $\boldsymbol{y} = (y_1, y_2, \ldots, y_k)$ such that for all $i \in [k]$, $y_{p(i)} = x^{(i)}_{p(i)}$, where $x^{(i)}_j$ is the j-th value of $\boldsymbol{x}^{(i)}$.
3. $\mathcal{F}_{\text{select-semi}}$ receives from the adversary a set of shares $\{s_i\}_{i \in \mathcal{C}}$. $\mathcal{F}_{\text{select-semi}}$ samples a random degree-t packed Shamir sharing $[\boldsymbol{y}]$ such that for all $P_i \in \mathcal{C}$, the i-th share of $[\boldsymbol{y}]$ is s_i.
4. $\mathcal{F}_{\text{select-semi}}$ distributes the shares of $[\boldsymbol{y}]$ to honest parties.

For all $i \in [k]$, let $\boldsymbol{e}_i \in \{0,1\}^k$ denote the vector where the i-th entry is 1 and for all $j \neq i$, the j-th entry is 0. Recall that in Sect. 3.2 we show how to transform a constant vector to a degree-t packed Shamir sharing. Let $[\boldsymbol{e}_i]$ denote the degree-t packed Shamir sharing of $\boldsymbol{e}_i$.

To realize $\mathcal{F}_{\text{select-semi}}$, note that $[\boldsymbol{e}_{p(i)}] \cdot [\boldsymbol{x}^{(i)}]$ is a degree-$2t$ packed Shamir sharing of $\boldsymbol{e}_{p(i)} * \boldsymbol{x}^{(i)}$. Also note that $\boldsymbol{y} = \sum_{i=1}^k \boldsymbol{e}_{p(i)} * \boldsymbol{x}^{(i)}$. Therefore, all parties can locally compute $\langle \boldsymbol{y} \rangle = \sum_{i=1}^k [\boldsymbol{e}_{p(i)}] \cdot [\boldsymbol{x}^{(i)}]$. And the only task is to reduce the degree of $\langle \boldsymbol{y} \rangle$. Note that this can be achieved by the same technique as MULT. The description of the protocol SELECT appears in Protocol 6. The communication complexity of m invocations of SELECT is $O(m \cdot n + n^3 \cdot \kappa)$ field elements.

Lemma 1. *Protocol* SELECT *securely computes* $\mathcal{F}_{select\text{-}semi}$ *in the* $\mathcal{F}_{rand}$*-hybrid model against a semi-honest adversary who controls* $t' = t - k + 1$ *parties.*

We refer the readers to the full version of this paper [GPS21] for more discussion about Lemma 1.

Using $\mathcal{F}_{select-semi}$ *to Generate Random Sharings for Permuting Secrets.* For all $i, j \in \{1, 2, \ldots, k\}$, we say a pair of degree-t packed Shamir sharings $([\boldsymbol{x}], [\boldsymbol{y}])$ contains an (i, j)-component if the secrets of these two sharings satisfy that $x_i = y_j$.

Protocol 6: SELECT

1. Let $[\boldsymbol{x}^{(1)}], [\boldsymbol{x}^{(2)}], \ldots, [\boldsymbol{x}^{(k)}]$ denote the k input packed Shamir sharings and $p(\cdot)$ denote the permutation. The goal is to generate a degree-t packed Shamir sharing $[\boldsymbol{y}]$ such that for all $i \in [k]$, $y_{p(i)} = x_{p(i)}^{(i)}$. Recall that $\boldsymbol{e}_i \in \{0,1\}^k$ denote the vector where the i-th entry is 1 and for all $j \neq i$, the j-th entry is 0. For all $i \in [k]$, all parties agree on the whole sharing $[\boldsymbol{e}_i]$ based on the transformation in Section 3.2.
2. All parties invoke $\mathcal{F}_{\text{rand}}$ to prepare a pair of random sharings $([\boldsymbol{r}], \langle \boldsymbol{r} \rangle)$.
3. All parties locally compute $\langle \boldsymbol{e} \rangle := \sum_{i=1}^{k} [\boldsymbol{e}_{p(i)}] \cdot [\boldsymbol{x}^{(i)}] + \langle \boldsymbol{r} \rangle$.
4. All parties send their shares of $\langle \boldsymbol{e} \rangle$ to the first party P_1.
5. P_1 reconstructs the secrets $\boldsymbol{e}$, generates a random degree-t packed Shamir sharing $[\boldsymbol{e}]$, and distributes the shares to other parties.
6. All parties locally compute $[\boldsymbol{y}] := [\boldsymbol{e}] - [\boldsymbol{r}]$.

To perform a permutation $p(\cdot)$, we need to prepare two random degree-t packed Shamir sharings $([\boldsymbol{r}], [\boldsymbol{M}_p \cdot \boldsymbol{r}])$. We can view $([\boldsymbol{r}], [\boldsymbol{M}_p \cdot \boldsymbol{r}])$ as a composition of a $(1, p(1))$-component, a $(2, p(2))$-component, $\ldots$, and a $(k, p(k))$-component.

Let m denote the number of permutations we want to prepare random sharings for. These permutations are denoted by $p_1(\cdot), p_2(\cdot), \ldots, p_m(\cdot)$. Our idea is as follows:

1. We first find m permutations $q_1(\cdot), q_2(\cdot), \ldots, q_m(\cdot)$ such that:
   - For all $i, j \in \{1, 2, \ldots, k\}$, the number of permutations $p \in \{p_1, p_2, \ldots, p_m\}$ which satisfies that $p(i) = j$ is equal to the number of permutations $q \in \{q_1, q_2, \ldots, q_m\}$ which satisfies that $q(i) = j$.
2. All parties prepare random sharings for permutations $q_1, q_2, \ldots, q_m$.
3. From $i = 1$ to m, a pair of random sharings for the permutation p_i is prepared by using $\mathcal{F}_{\text{select-semi}}$ to choose the first unused $(j, p_i(j))$-component from the random sharings for $q_1, q_2, \ldots, q_m$ for all $j \in [k]$.

We refer the readers to Sect. 2.2 for a more detailed explanation.

The major benefit of this approach is that *we can limit the number of different permutations in* $\{q_1, q_2, \ldots, q_m\}$ as we show below. More concretely, we will prove the following theorem:

Theorem 2. *Let $m, k \geq 1$ be integers. For all m permutations $p_1, p_2, \ldots, p_m$ over $\{1, 2, \ldots, k\}$, there exists m permutations $q_1, q_2, \ldots, q_m$ over $\{1, 2, \ldots, k\}$ such that:*

- *For all $i, j \in \{1, 2, \ldots, k\}$, the number of permutations $p \in \{p_1, p_2, \ldots, p_m\}$ such that $p(i) = j$ is the same as the number of permutations $q \in \{q_1, q_2, \ldots, q_m\}$ such that $q(i) = j$.*
- $q_1, q_2, \ldots, q_m$ *contain at most k^2 different permutations.*

Moreover, $q_1, q_2, \ldots, q_m$ can be found within polynomial time given $p_1, p_2, \ldots, p_m$.

The proof of Theorem 2 can be found in the full version of this paper [GPS21].

Preparing Random Sharings for Different Permutations. We are ready to introduce the functionality and its implementation for preparing random sharings for different permutations. The functionality $\mathcal{F}_{\text{rand-perm-semi}}$ appears in Functionality 7.

Functionality 7: $\mathcal{F}_{\text{rand-perm-semi}}$

1. $\mathcal{F}_{\text{rand-perm-semi}}$ receives from honest parties m permutations $p_1, p_2, \ldots, p_m$ over $\{1, 2, \ldots, k\}$.
2. For all $i \in [m]$, $\mathcal{F}_{\text{rand-perm-semi}}$ receives from the adversary a set of shares $\{(u_j^{(i)}, v_j^{(i)})\}_{j \in \mathcal{C}}$. $\mathcal{F}_{\text{rand-perm-semi}}$ samples a random vector $r^{(i)} \in \mathbb{F}^k$ and samples two degree-t packed Shamir sharings $([r^{(i)}], [M_{p_i} \cdot r^{(i)}])$ such that for all $P_j \in \mathcal{C}$, the j-th share of $([r^{(i)}], [M_{p_i} \cdot r^{(i)}])$ is $(u_j^{(i)}, v_j^{(i)})$.
3. For all $i \in [m]$, $\mathcal{F}_{\text{rand-perm-semi}}$ distributes the shares of $([r^{(i)}], [M_{p_i} \cdot r^{(i)}])$ to honest parties.

For a fixed permutation $p(\cdot)$ over $\{1, 2, \ldots, k\}$, we show how to use $\mathcal{F}_{\text{rand}}$ to prepare a pair of random sharings $([r], [M_p \cdot r])$ in the full version of this paper [GPS21]. The communication complexity of preparing m pairs of random sharings in the form of $([r], [M_p \cdot r])$ for a fixed permutation $p(\cdot)$ is $O(m \cdot n + n^3 \cdot \kappa)$ elements in $\mathbb{F}$. We describe the protocol for $\mathcal{F}_{\text{rand-perm-semi}}$ in Protocol 8. The communication complexity of using RAND-PERM to prepare random sharings for m permutations is $O(m \cdot n + n^5 \cdot \kappa)$ field elements.

Lemma 2. *Protocol* RAND-PERM *securely computes* $\mathcal{F}_{\text{rand-perm-semi}}$ *in the* $(\mathcal{F}_{\text{rand}}, \mathcal{F}_{\text{select-semi}})$*-hybrid model against a semi-honest adversary who controls* $t' = t - k + 1$ *parties.*

The proof of Lemma 2 can be found in the full version of this paper [GPS21].

Realizing $\mathcal{F}_{\text{permute-semi}}$. Now we are ready to present the protocol for $\mathcal{F}_{\text{permute-semi}}$. The protocol PERMUTE uses $\mathcal{F}_{\text{rand-perm-semi}}$ to prepare the random sharings for the permutation we want to perform and then follows the techniques in [DIK10]. In PERMUTE, we will prepare a random degree-$2t$ packed Shamir sharing of $\mathbf{0} \in \mathbb{F}^k$, which is used as a random mask for the shares of honest parties (see the proof of Lemma 3). This is not needed for semi-honest security but will be helpful when we consider a fully malicious adversary at a later point.

We show how to use $\mathcal{F}_{\text{rand}}$ to prepare a random degree-$2t$ packed Shamir sharing of $\mathbf{0} \in \mathbb{F}^k$ in the full version of this paper [GPS21]. The communication complexity of preparing m random degree-$2t$ packed Shamir sharings of $\mathbf{0}$ is $O(m \cdot n + n^3 \cdot \kappa)$ elements in $\mathbb{F}$. The description of PERMUTE appears in Protocol 9. The communication complexity of m invocations of PERMUTE is $O(m \cdot n + n^5 \cdot \kappa)$ field elements.

Protocol 8: RAND-PERM

1. Let $p_1, p_2, \ldots, p_m$ be the permutations over $\{1, 2, \ldots, k\}$ that all parties want to prepare random sharings for.
2. All parties use a deterministic algorithm that all parties agree on to compute m permutations $q_1, q_2, \ldots, q_m$ such that
   - For all $i, j \in \{1, 2, \ldots, k\}$, the number of permutations $p \in \{p_1, p_2, \ldots, p_m\}$ such that $p(i) = j$ is the same as the number of permutations $q \in \{q_1, q_2, \ldots, q_m\}$ such that $q(i) = j$.
   - $q_1, q_2, \ldots, q_m$ contain at most k^2 different permutations.

   The existence of such an algorithm is guaranteed by Theorem 2.
3. Suppose $q'_1, q'_2, \ldots, q'_{k^2}$ denote the different permutations in $q_1, q_2, \ldots, q_m$. For all $i \in \{1, 2, \ldots, k^2\}$, let n'_i denote the number of times that q'_i appears in $q_1, q_2, \ldots, q_m$. All parties invoke $\mathcal{F}_{\text{rand}}$ to prepare n'_i pairs of random sharings in the form $([r], [M_{q'_i} \cdot r])$ for all $i \in \{1, 2, \ldots, k^2\}$. Note that we have prepared a pair of random sharings for each permutation q_i for all $i \in [m]$. Let $([r^{(i)}], [M_{q_i} \cdot r^{(i)}])$ denote the random sharings for the permutation q_i.
4. For all $i, j \in \{1, 2, \ldots, k\}$, all parties initiate an empty list $L_{i,j}$. From $\ell = 1$ to m, for all $i, j \in \{1, 2, \ldots, k\}$, if $([r^{(\ell)}], [M_{q_\ell} \cdot r^{(\ell)}])$ contains an (i, j)-component, all parties insert $([r^{(\ell)}], [M_{q_\ell} \cdot r^{(\ell)}])$ into the list $L_{i,j}$.
5. From $\ell = 1$ to m, all parties prepare a pair of random sharings for p_ℓ as follows:
   - From $i = 1$ to k, let $([r^{(\ell_i)}], [M_{q_{\ell_i}} \cdot r^{(\ell_i)}])$ denote the first pair of sharings in the list $L_{i,p_\ell(i)}$, and then remove it from $L_{i,p_\ell(i)}$. Note that $([r^{(\ell_i)}], [M_{q_{\ell_i}} \cdot r^{(\ell_i)}])$ contains an $(i, p_\ell(i))$-component, which is not used when preparing random sharings for $p_1, p_2, \ldots, p_{\ell-1}$.
   - Let I denote the identity permutation over $\{1, 2, \ldots, k\}$.
   - All parties invoke $\mathcal{F}_{\text{select-semi}}$ with
   $$[r^{(\ell_1)}], [r^{(\ell_2)}], \ldots, [r^{(\ell_k)}]$$
   and the permutation I. The output is denoted by $[v^{(\ell)}]$.
   - All parties invoke $\mathcal{F}_{\text{select-semi}}$ with
   $$[M_{q_{\ell_1}} \cdot r^{(\ell_1)}], [M_{q_{\ell_2}} \cdot r^{(\ell_2)}], \ldots, [M_{q_{\ell_k}} \cdot r^{(\ell_k)}]$$
   and the permutation p_ℓ. The output is denoted by $[\tilde{v}^{(\ell)}]$. Note that for all $i \in [k]$, $v_i^{(\ell)} = r_i^{(\ell_i)} = (M_{q_{\ell_i}} \cdot r^{(\ell_i)})_{q_{\ell_i}(i)} = (M_{q_{\ell_i}} \cdot r^{(\ell_i)})_{p_\ell(i)} = \tilde{v}_{p_\ell(i)}^{(\ell)}$.
6. All parties take $([v^{(1)}], [\tilde{v}^{(1)}]), ([v^{(2)}], [\tilde{v}^{(2)}]), \ldots, ([v^{(m)}], [\tilde{v}^{(m)}])$ as output.

Lemma 3. *Protocol* PERMUTE *securely computes* $\mathcal{F}_{permute\text{-}semi}$ *in the* $(\mathcal{F}_{rand}, \mathcal{F}_{rand\text{-}perm\text{-}semi})$-*hybrid model against a semi-honest adversary who controls* $t' = t - k + 1$ *parties.*

The proof of Lemma 3 can be found in the full version of this paper [GPS21].

Protocol 9: PERMUTE

1. Let $[x]$ denote the input degree-t packed Shamir sharing and $p(\cdot)$ denote the permutation all parties want to perform on x.
2. All parties invoke $\mathcal{F}_{\text{rand-perm-semi}}$ with p to prepare a pair of random sharings $([r], [M_p \cdot r])$. All parties invoke $\mathcal{F}_{\text{rand}}$ to prepare a random degree-$2t$ packed Shamir sharing $\langle 0 \rangle$.
3. All parties locally compute $\langle e \rangle := [x] + [r] + \langle 0 \rangle$.
4. All parties send their shares of $\langle e \rangle$ to the first party P_1.
5. P_1 reconstructs the secrets e, and computes $\tilde{e} = M_p \cdot e$. Then P_1 generates a random degree-t packed Shamir sharing $[\tilde{e}]$, and distributes the shares to other parties.
6. All parties locally compute $[\tilde{x}] := [\tilde{e}] - [M_p \cdot r]$.

4.3 Obtaining Input Sharings for Multiplication Gates and Addition Gates

So far, we have introduced how to evaluate multiplication gates and addition gates using the packed Shamir sharing scheme. In the case that the secrets of an input sharing are not in the correct order, we have shown how to efficiently perform a permutation to obtain the correct order. During the computation, however, input sharings of multiplication gates and addition gates do not come for free. When evaluating the multiplication gates and addition gates in some layer, the secrets we want to be in a single sharing may be scattered in one or more output sharings from the previous layers. This requires us to collect the secrets from those sharings and generate a single sharing for these secrets efficiently. Our idea is to achieve the *non-collision* property:

Property 1 (Non-collision). For each input sharing of each layer, the secrets of this input sharing come from different positions in the output sharings of previous layers.

As we discussed in Sect. 2.3, with this property, we can use $\mathcal{F}_{\text{select-semi}}$ to choose the secrets and generates the input sharing we want. To avoid the case that we need the same secret twice in a single input sharing, which makes the non-collision property impossible to achieve, we further require that

– every output wire of the input layer and all intermediate layers is used exactly once as an input wire of a later layer (which may not be the next layer).

Note that this requirement can be met without loss of generality by assuming that there is a fan-out gate right after each (input, addition, or multiplication) gate that copies the output wire the number of times it is used in later layers. To achieve the non-collision property, our idea is to perform a permutation on each output sharing.

In the following, when we use the term "output sharings", we refer to the output sharings from the input layer and all intermediate layers. When we use the term "input sharings", we refer to the input sharings of the output layer and all intermediate layers. We further assume that the number of the input wires and the number of the output wires of each layer are multiples of k, where recall that k is the number of secrets we can store in a single packed Shamir sharing. In Sect. 5, we will show how to compile a general circuit to meet this requirement.

Let m denote the number of output sharings in the circuit. Then the number of input sharings is also m. We will label all the output sharings by $1, 2, \ldots, m$ and all the input sharings also by $1, 2, \ldots, m$. Consider a matrix $N \in \{1, 2, \ldots, m\}^{m \times k}$ where $N_{i,j}$ is the index of the input sharing that the j-th secret of the i-th output sharing wants to go to. Then for all $\ell \in \{1, 2, \ldots, m\}$, there are exactly k entries of N which are equal to ℓ. And the secrets at those positions are the secrets we want to collect for the ℓ-th input sharing. We will prove the following theorem.

Theorem 4. *Let $m \geq 1, k \geq 1$ be integers. Let N be a matrix of dimension $m \times k$ in $\{1, 2, \ldots, m\}^{m \times k}$ such that for all $\ell \in \{1, 2, \ldots, m\}$, the number of entries of N which are equal to ℓ is k. Then, there exists m permutations $p_1, p_2, \ldots, p_m$ over $\{1, 2, \ldots, k\}$ such that after performing the permutation p_i on the i-th row of N, the new matrix N' satisfies that each column of N' is a permutation over $(1, 2, \ldots, m)$. Furthermore, the permutations $p_1, p_2, \ldots, p_m$ can be found within polynomial time.*

The proof of Theorem 4 can be found in the full version of this paper [GPS21].

When we apply p_i to the i-th output sharing for all $i \in \{1, 2, \ldots, m\}$, Theorem 4 guarantees that for all $j \in \{1, 2, \ldots, k\}$ the j-th secrets of all output sharings need to go to different input sharings. Note that this ensures the non-collision property. During the computation, we will perform the permutation p_i on the i-th output sharing right after it is computed. Note that when preparing an input sharing, the secrets we need only come from the output sharings which have been computed. The secrets of these output sharings have been properly permuted such that the secrets we want are in different positions. Therefore, we can use $\mathcal{F}_{\text{select-semi}}$ to choose these secrets and obtain the desired input sharing.

4.4 Handling Fan-Out Gates

In the last subsection, we discussed how to prepare the input sharings for multiplication gates and addition gates. Our solution requires that

- every output wire of the input layer and all intermediate layers is used exactly once as an input wire of a later layer (which may not be the next layer).

This requirement can be met by inserting fan-out gates in each layer, which copy each output wire the number of times it is used in later layers. Specifically, we consider a functionality $\mathcal{F}_{\text{fan-out-semi}}$ which takes as input a degree-t packed Shamir sharing of $x = (x_1, x_2, \ldots, x_k) \in \mathbb{F}^k$ along with a vector

$(n_1, n_2, \ldots, n_k) \in \mathbb{N}^k$, where $n_i \geq 1$ is the number of times that x_i is used in later layers, and outputs $\frac{n_1+n_2+\ldots+n_k}{k}$ degree-t packed Shamir sharings which contain n_i copies of the value x_i for all $i \in \{1, 2, \ldots, k\}$. We assume that $\sum_{i=1}^{k} n_i$ is a multiple of k. In Sect. 5, we will show how to compile a general circuit to meet this requirement. The description of $\mathcal{F}_{\text{fan-out-semi}}$ appears in Functionality 10.

Functionality 10: $\mathcal{F}_{\text{fan-out-semi}}$

1. $\mathcal{F}_{\text{fan-out-semi}}$ receives from honest parties the shares of $[x]$ and a vector $(n_1, n_2, \ldots, n_k)$.
2. $\mathcal{F}_{\text{fan-out-semi}}$ reconstructs the secrets $x = (x_1, x_2, \ldots, x_k)$. Then $\mathcal{F}_{\text{fan-out-semi}}$ initiates an empty list L. From $i = 1$ to k, $\mathcal{F}_{\text{fan-out-semi}}$ inserts n_i times of x_i into L.
3. Let $m = \frac{n_1+n_2+\ldots+n_k}{k}$. From $i = 1$ to m,
   (a) $\mathcal{F}_{\text{fan-out-semi}}$ sets $x^{(i)}$ to be the vector of the first k elements in L, and then removes the first k elements in L.
   (b) $\mathcal{F}_{\text{fan-out-semi}}$ receives from the adversary a set of shares $\{s_j^{(i)}\}_{j \in \mathcal{C}}$. $\mathcal{F}_{\text{fan-out-semi}}$ generates a degree-t packed Shamir sharing $[x^{(i)}]$ such that the j-th share of $[x^{(i)}]$ is $s_j^{(i)}$.
   (c) $\mathcal{F}_{\text{fan-out-semi}}$ distributes the shares of $[x^{(i)}]$ to honest parties.

We refer the readers to the full version of this paper [GPS21] for the protocol that realizes $\mathcal{F}_{\text{fan-out-semi}}$. Our protocol prepares the output sharings of $\mathcal{F}_{\text{fan-out-semi}}$ one by one. Therefore, the communication complexity only depends on the number of output sharings *even if the output sharings come from different invocations with different input sharings*. The communication complexity of computing m output sharings is $O(m \cdot n + n^5 \cdot \kappa)$ field elements.

5 Main Protocol - Against a Semi-honest Adversary

In this section, we will introduce our main protocol of using packed Shamir sharing to evaluate a general circuit C against a *semi-honest* adversary. We first discuss how to compile a general circuit to meet the requirements we assume in Sect. 4. Then we give the main protocol and analyze its security and communication complexity.

5.1 Transforming a General Circuit C

We will prove the following theorem.

Theorem 5. *Given an arithmetic circuit C with input coming from c clients, there exists an efficient algorithm which takes C as input and outputs an arithmetic circuit C' with the following properties:*

- For all input x, $C(x) = C'(x)$.
- In the input layer and the output layer, the number of input gates belonging to each client and the number of output gates belonging to each client are multiples of k. In each intermediate layer, the number of addition gates and the number of multiplication gates are multiples of k.
- After grouping the gates that have the same type in each layer, the number of times that the output wires of each group are used in later layers is a multiple of k.
- Circuit size: $|C'| = O(|C| + k \cdot (c + \text{Depth}))$, where c is the number of clients that provide inputs and Depth is the depth of C.

In the full version of this paper [GPS21], we explain why the properties we assume in Sect. 4 can be met by applying the transformation in Theorem 5 and then formally prove this theorem.

5.2   Preprocessing Phase

In this part, we describe how parties preprocess the circuit before doing the computation. During the computation phase, a batch of k wire values are stored in a single packed Shamir sharing. The main task of the preprocessing phase is to determine how the wire values should be packed. Also, all parties need to compute a permutation for each output sharing using the algorithm in Theorem 4. These permutations are used to achieve the non-collision property. See Sect. 4.3 for more details. The preprocessing phase only depends on the circuit C and does not need any communication. We refer the readers to the full version of this paper [GPS21] for the description of the protocol PREPROCESS.

5.3   Main Protocol - Against Semi-honest Adversary

We are ready to introduce our main protocol. At a high-level, given the preprocessed circuit,

- all parties use $\mathcal{F}_{\text{input-semi}}, \mathcal{F}_{\text{output-semi}}, \mathcal{F}_{\text{mult-semi}}$ (see Sect. 4.1) to evaluate input gates, output gates, multiplication gates, and addition gates in each layer;
- for the input layer and all intermediate layers, all parties use $\mathcal{F}_{\text{fan-out-semi}}$ to evaluate fan-out gates (see Sect. 4.4);
- for each output sharing, all parties use $\mathcal{F}_{\text{permute-semi}}$ to perform the permutation associated with this sharing (see Sect. 4.2) to achieve the non-collision property (see Sect. 4.3);
- to prepare each input sharing for the next layer, all parties use $\mathcal{F}_{\text{select-semi}}$ to choose the secrets it wants from the output sharings from previous layers (see Sect. 4.2), and then use $\mathcal{F}_{\text{permute-semi}}$ to permute the secrets to the correct order (see Sect. 4.2).

The ideal functionality $\mathcal{F}_{\text{main-semi}}$ appears in Functionality 11. The main protocol is introduced in Protocol 12.

Functionality 11: $\mathcal{F}_{\text{main-semi}}$

1. $\mathcal{F}_{\text{main-semi}}$ receives the input from all clients. Let x denote the input.
2. $\mathcal{F}_{\text{main-semi}}$ computes $C(x)$ and distributes the output to all clients.

Protocol 12: MAIN-SEMI

1. **Circuit Transformation Phase.** Let C denote the evaluated circuit. All parties preprocess the circuit by running the PREPROCESS protocol. Let C' denote the circuit after transformation.
2. **Input Phase.** Let $\text{Client}_1, \text{Client}_2, \ldots, \text{Client}_c$ denote the clients who provide inputs.
   (a) Input Secret-sharing Phase: For every group of k input gates of Client_i, Client_i invokes $\mathcal{F}_{\text{input-semi}}$ to share its inputs $\boldsymbol{x}^{(i)}$ to the parties.
   (b) Handling Fan-out Gates: For the output sharing $[\boldsymbol{x}]$ of each group of input gates, let n_i denote the number of times that the i-th secret of $\boldsymbol{x}$ is used in later layers. All parties invoke $\mathcal{F}_{\text{fan-out-semi}}$ with input $[\boldsymbol{x}]$ and $(n_1, n_2, \ldots, n_k)$.
   (c) Achieving Non-Collision Property for the next layers: For each output sharing $[\boldsymbol{y}]$ of the input layer, let p denote the permutation associated with it. All parties invoke $\mathcal{F}_{\text{permute-semi}}$ with input $[\boldsymbol{y}]$ and p.
3. **Evaluation Phase.** All parties evaluate the circuit layer by layer as follows:
   (a) Permute Input Sharings from Previous Layers: For each input sharing $[\boldsymbol{x}]$, let $[\boldsymbol{x}^{(i)}]$ denote the output sharing from previous layers which contains the i-th secret x_i, and let q_i denote the position of x_i in $[\boldsymbol{x}^{(i)}]$. According to the non-collision property, $q_1, q_2, \ldots, q_k$ is a permutation of $(1, 2, \ldots, k)$. Let $q(\cdot)$ be a permutation over $\{1, 2, \ldots, k\}$ such that $q(i) = q_i$. All parties invoke $\mathcal{F}_{\text{select-semi}}$ on $[\boldsymbol{x}^{(1)}], [\boldsymbol{x}^{(2)}], \ldots, [\boldsymbol{x}^{(k)}]$ and the permutation q. Let $[\boldsymbol{x}']$ denote the output of $\mathcal{F}_{\text{select-semi}}$. Then, all parties invoke $\mathcal{F}_{\text{permute-semi}}$ with input $[\boldsymbol{x}']$ and q to obtain $[\boldsymbol{x}]$.
   (b) Evaluating Multiplication Gates and Addition Gates: For each group of multiplication gates with input sharings $[\boldsymbol{x}], [\boldsymbol{y}]$, all parties invoke $\mathcal{F}_{\text{mult-semi}}$ with input $[\boldsymbol{x}], [\boldsymbol{y}]$. For each group of addition gates with input sharings $[\boldsymbol{x}], [\boldsymbol{y}]$, all parties locally compute $[\boldsymbol{x} + \boldsymbol{y}] = [\boldsymbol{x}] + [\boldsymbol{y}]$.
   (c) Handling Fan-out Gates: For the output sharing $[\boldsymbol{x}]$ of each group of multiplication gates or addition gates, all parties follow the same step as Step 2.(b) to handle fan-out gates.
   (d) Achieving Non-Collision Property: Follow Step 2.(c).
4. **Output Phase.**
   (a) Permute Input Sharings from Previous Layers: For each input sharing $[\boldsymbol{x}]$, all parties follow the same step as Step 3.(a) to prepare $[\boldsymbol{x}]$.
   (b) Reconstruct the Output: For each group of output gates belonging to Client_i $(i \geq 1)$, let $[\boldsymbol{x}]$ denote the input sharing. All parties invoke $\mathcal{F}_{\text{output-semi}}$ with input $[\boldsymbol{x}]$ to let Client_i learn the result $\boldsymbol{x}$.

Lemma 4. *Protocol* MAIN-SEMI *securely computes* $\mathcal{F}_{main\text{-}semi}$ *in the* $(\mathcal{F}_{input\text{-}semi}, \mathcal{F}_{fan\text{-}out\text{-}semi}, \mathcal{F}_{permute\text{-}semi}, \mathcal{F}_{select\text{-}semi}, \mathcal{F}_{mult\text{-}semi}, \mathcal{F}_{output\text{-}semi})$-*hybrid model against a semi-honest adversary who controls* $t' = t - k + 1$ *parties.*

The proof of Lemma 4 can be found in the full version of this paper [GPS21]. The overall communication complexity of our protocol MAIN-SEMI is $O(|C| \cdot n/k + n \cdot (c + \text{Depth}) + n^5 \cdot \kappa)$ field elements. In the full version of this paper [GPS21], we provide the analysis of the communication complexity of our protocol in details. Together with Lemma 4, we have the following theorem.

Theorem 6. *In the client-server model, let c denote the number of clients, and $n = 2t + 1$ denote the number of parties (servers). Let κ denote the security parameter, and $\mathbb{F}$ denote a finite field. For an arithmetic circuit C over $\mathbb{F}$ and for all $1 \leq k \leq t$, there exists an information-theoretic MPC protocol which securely computes the arithmetic circuit C in the presence of a semi-honest adversary controlling up to c clients and $t - k + 1$ parties. The communication complexity of this protocol is $O(|C| \cdot n/k + n \cdot (c + \text{Depth}) + n^5 \cdot \kappa)$ elements in $\mathbb{F}$.*

References

[BBCG+19] Boneh, D., Boyle, E., Corrigan-Gibbs, H., Gilboa, N., Ishai, Y.: Zero-knowledge proofs on secret-shared data via fully linear PCPs. In: Boldyreva, A., Micciancio, D. (eds.) CRYPTO 2019. LNCS, vol. 11694, pp. 67–97. Springer, Cham (2019). https://doi.org/10.1007/978-3-030-26954-8_3

[BGIN20] Boyle, E., Gilboa, N., Ishai, Y., Nof, A.: Efficient fully secure computation via distributed zero-knowledge proofs. In: Moriai, S., Wang, H. (eds.) ASIACRYPT 2020. LNCS, vol. 12493, pp. 244–276. Springer, Cham (2020). https://doi.org/10.1007/978-3-030-64840-4_9

[BOGW88] Ben-Or, M., Goldwasser, S., Wigderson, A.: Completeness theorems for non-cryptographic fault-tolerant distributed computation. In: Proceedings of the Twentieth Annual ACM Symposium on Theory of Computing, pp. 1–10. ACM (1988)

[CCD88] Chaum, D., Crépeau, C., Damgard, I.: Multiparty unconditionally secure protocols. In: Proceedings of the Twentieth Annual ACM Symposium on Theory of Computing, pp. 11–19. ACM (1988)

[CCXY18] Cascudo, I., Cramer, R., Xing, C., Yuan, C.: Amortized complexity of information-theoretically secure MPC revisited. In: Shacham, H., Boldyreva, A. (eds.) CRYPTO 2018. LNCS, vol. 10993, pp. 395–426. Springer, Cham (2018). https://doi.org/10.1007/978-3-319-96878-0_14

[CGH+18] Chida, K., et al.: Fast large-scale honest-majority MPC for malicious adversaries. In: Shacham, H., Boldyreva, A. (eds.) CRYPTO 2018. LNCS, vol. 10993, pp. 34–64. Springer, Cham (2018). https://doi.org/10.1007/978-3-319-96878-0_2

[DIK10] Damgård, I., Ishai, Y., Krøigaard, M.: Perfectly secure multiparty computation and the computational overhead of cryptography. In: Gilbert, H. (ed.) EUROCRYPT 2010. LNCS, vol. 6110, pp. 445–465. Springer, Heidelberg (2010). https://doi.org/10.1007/978-3-642-13190-5_23

[DN07]   Damgård, I., Nielsen, J.B.: Scalable and unconditionally secure multiparty computation. In: Menezes, A. (ed.) CRYPTO 2007. LNCS, vol. 4622, pp. 572–590. Springer, Heidelberg (2007). https://doi.org/10.1007/978-3-540-74143-5_32

[FY92]   Franklin, M., Yung, M.: Communication complexity of secure computation (extended abstract). In: Proceedings of the Twenty-Fourth Annual ACM Symposium on Theory of Computing. STOC 1992, pp. 699–710. Association for Computing Machinery, New York (1992)

[GIOZ17] Garay, J., Ishai, Y., Ostrovsky, R., Zikas, V.: The price of low communication in secure multi-party computation. In: Katz, J., Shacham, H. (eds.) CRYPTO 2017. LNCS, vol. 10401, pp. 420–446. Springer, Cham (2017). https://doi.org/10.1007/978-3-319-63688-7_14

[GIP+14] Genkin, D., Ishai, Y., Prabhakaran, M.M., Sahai, A., Tromer, E.: Circuits resilient to additive attacks with applications to secure computation. In: Proceedings of the Forty-Sixth Annual ACM Symposium on Theory of Computing. STOC 2014, pp. 495–504. ACM, New York (2014)

[GIP15]   Genkin, D., Ishai, Y., Polychroniadou, A.: Efficient multi-party computation: from passive to active security via secure SIMD circuits. In: Gennaro, R., Robshaw, M. (eds.) CRYPTO 2015. LNCS, vol. 9216, pp. 721–741. Springer, Heidelberg (2015). https://doi.org/10.1007/978-3-662-48000-7_35

[GMW87]   Goldreich, O., Micali, S., Wigderson, A.: How to play any mental game. In: Proceedings of the Nineteenth Annual ACM Symposium on Theory of Computing, pp. 218–229. ACM (1987)

[GPS21]   Goyal, V., Polychroniadou, A., Song, Y.: Unconditional communication-efficient MPC via Hall's marriage theorem. Cryptology ePrint Archive, Report 2021/834, 2021. https://eprint.iacr.org/2021/834

[GSZ20]   Goyal, V., Song, Y., Zhu, C.: Guaranteed output delivery comes free in honest majority MPC. In: Micciancio, D., Ristenpart, T. (eds.) CRYPTO 2020. LNCS, vol. 12171, pp. 618–646. Springer, Cham (2020). https://doi.org/10.1007/978-3-030-56880-1_22

[NV18]   Nordholt, P.S., Veeningen, M.: Minimising communication in honest-majority MPC by batchwise multiplication verification. In: Preneel, B., Vercauteren, F. (eds.) ACNS 2018. LNCS, vol. 10892, pp. 321–339. Springer, Cham (2018). https://doi.org/10.1007/978-3-319-93387-0_17

[PS21]   Polychroniadou, A., Song, Y.: Constant-overhead unconditionally secure multiparty computation over binary fields. Appears in Eurocrypt (2021). https://eprint.iacr.org/2020/1412

[Sha79]   Shamir, A.: How to share a secret. Commun. ACM **22**(11), 612–613 (1979)

[Yao82]   Yao, A.C.: Protocols for secure computations. In: 1982 23rd Annual Symposium on Foundations of Computer Science. SFCS'08, pp. 160–164. IEEE (1982)

Non-interactive Secure Multiparty Computation for Symmetric Functions, Revisited: More Efficient Constructions and Extensions

Reo Eriguchi[1,2(✉)], Kazuma Ohara[2], Shota Yamada[2], and Koji Nuida[2,3]

[1] The University of Tokyo, Tokyo, Japan
reo-eriguchi@g.ecc.u-tokyo.ac.jp
[2] National Institute of Advanced Industrial Science and Technology, Tokyo, Japan
{ohara.kazuma,yamada-shota}@aist.go.jp
[3] Kyushu University, Fukuoka, Japan
nuida@imi.kyushu-u.ac.jp

Abstract. Non-interactive secure multiparty computation (NIMPC) is a variant of secure computation which allows each of n players to send only a single message depending on his input and correlated randomness. Abelian programs, which can realize any symmetric function, are defined as functions on the sum of the players' inputs over an abelian group and provide useful functionalities for real-world applications. We improve and extend the previous results in the following ways:

- We present NIMPC protocols for abelian programs that improve the best known communication complexity. If inputs take any value of an abelian group $\mathbb{G}$, our protocol achieves the communication complexity $O(|\mathbb{G}|(\log|\mathbb{G}|)^2)$ improving $O(|\mathbb{G}|^2 n^2)$ of Beimel et al. (Crypto 2014). If players are limited to inputs from subsets of size at most d, our protocol achieves $|\mathbb{G}|(\log|\mathbb{G}|)^2(\max\{n,d\})^{(1+o(1))t}$ where t is a corruption threshold. This result improves $|\mathbb{G}|^3(nd)^{(1+o(1))t}$ of Beimel et al. (Crypto 2014), and even $|\mathbb{G}|^{\log n+O(1)}n$ of Benhamouda et al. (Crypto 2017) if $t = o(\log n)$ and $|\mathbb{G}| = n^{\Theta(1)}$.
- We propose for the first time NIMPC protocols for linear classifiers that are more efficient than those obtained from the generic construction.
- We revisit a known transformation of Benhamouda et al. (Crypto 2017) from Private Simultaneous Messages (PSM) to NIMPC, which we repeatedly use in the above results. We reveal that a sub-protocol used in the transformation does not satisfy the specified security. We also fix their protocol with only constant overhead in the communication complexity. As a byproduct, we obtain an NIMPC protocol for indicator functions with asymptotically optimal communication complexity with respect to the input length.

© International Association for Cryptologic Research 2021
T. Malkin and C. Peikert (Eds.): CRYPTO 2021, LNCS 12826, pp. 305–334, 2021.
https://doi.org/10.1007/978-3-030-84245-1_11

1   Introduction

Secure multiparty computation enables n players P_i ($i \in [n] := \{1, 2, \ldots, n\}$), each holding an input $x_i \in \mathcal{X}_0$, to jointly compute a function while keeping their inputs as secret as possible. NIMPC (Non-Interactive secure Multi-Party Computation) [2,3] is a variant of secure computation with a restricted interaction pattern, which assumes an external output player called an evaluator and allows each player to send only a single message depending on his input and pre-distributed correlated randomness to the evaluator.

Since it requires no interaction between the players, this model is especially well suited to a situation where the players cannot simultaneously participate in a protocol due to physical limitations. In spite of its limitations, NIMPC still provides useful functionalities in real-world scenarios such as voting, auctions, and statistical surveys using histograms. NIMPC is also of theoretical interest due to its various applications to other important models of secure computation [4,10,11].

To define the notion of security, an adversary is supposed to collude with a set of players $C \subseteq [n]$ as well as the evaluator. In NIMPC for a function h, it is impossible to prevent him from computing h on all possible inputs of the corrupted players combined with the inputs of the honest players. More formally, for the inputs of the honest players $x_{\overline{C}} = (x_i)_{i \in \overline{C}}$, the adversary can always evaluate the function $h|_{\overline{C}, x_{\overline{C}}}(x_C) = h(x_C, x_{\overline{C}})$ for all possible $x_C = (x_i)_{i \in C}$, which is called the residual function [12]. Thus, the security requirement of NIMPC is that the adversary learns the residual function $h|_{\overline{C}, x_{\overline{C}}}$ and nothing more. An NIMPC protocol is called t-robust if it can withstand collusion of at most t players and the evaluator. If $t = n$, we say that it is fully robust. The efficiency of NIMPC protocols is measured by the communication complexity defined as the maximum bit length of randomness and messages.

Fully robust NIMPC for the class of all the functions with input domain $\mathcal{X}_0^n$ is known to be possible [1,3,15,17]. However, due to the lower bound [17], it necessarily has the communication complexity proportional to $|\mathcal{X}_0|^n$, which is very inefficient when n is large. Therefore, it is important to construct efficient NIMPC protocols for specific functions of practical use. The aim of this paper is reducing the communication complexity as much as possible and specifically, making it as close as possible to the lower bound [17].

Above all, symmetric functions realize useful functionalities including voting and statistical surveys using histograms. The notion of abelian programs is a generalization of symmetric functions introduced in [3]. Technically, an abelian program h takes n elements from an abelian group $\mathbb{G}$ as inputs and outputs $h(x_1, \ldots, x_n) = f(\sum_{i \in [n]} x_i)$ for some function $f : \mathbb{G} \to \{0, 1\}$.

The authors of [3] propose a fully robust NIMPC protocol with communication complexity $O(|\mathbb{G}|^2 n^2)$ for abelian programs allowing inputs to take any value of $\mathbb{G}$. Since NIMPC protocols do not satisfy the same level of robustness in general if players are limited to inputs from smaller domains, they also propose a t-robust protocol with communication complexity $|\mathbb{G}|^3 (nd)^{t+O(1)}$ for abelian programs with input domains of size at most d. Benhamouda, Krawczyk, and Rabin [6] construct a fully robust protocol with communication complexity $|\mathbb{G}|^{\log n + O(1)} n$ when input spaces are arbitrary subsets. However, from the viewpoint of the lower bound $n^{-1}|\mathbb{G}|$ [17], there is still room for improvement especially in the exponent with respect to $|\mathbb{G}|$. To evaluate a histogram for m intervals, for example, we have to choose $d = m$ and the direct product $\mathbb{G} = (\mathbb{Z}_{n+1})^m$ of m copies of the cyclic group of size $n + 1$ [3], which is of size $n^{(1+o(1))m}$. Hence, reducing the exponent with respect to $|\mathbb{G}|$ will have a large effect on the communication complexity.

Abelian programs are also applicable to linear classifiers, which perform classification based on a weighted sum of inputs and cover popular methods such as support vector machines [7,8] and logistic regression. Indeed, if the weights are public, the players can locally multiply their inputs by the weights and then execute a protocol for a certain abelian program. However, the weights are often kept private to protect the intellectual property of learned models in practice. To the best of our knowledge, there is no NIMPC protocol for linear classifiers that does not reveal weights to players other than those obtained from the generic construction.

1.1 Our Results

The contributions of this paper are threefold. First, we present efficient NIMPC protocols for abelian programs that improve the best known communication complexity. Secondly, we propose for the first time NIMPC protocols for linear classifiers that are more efficient than those obtained from the generic construction. Thirdly, we revisit a known transformation [6] (hereinafter referred to as the BKR transformation), which transforms any 0-robust NIMPC protocol, also known as PSM (Private Simultaneous Messages) protocol [9,13], into a t-robust one. The transformation is repeatedly used in the above two results to limit players to inputs from smaller domains. We reveal that their NIMPC protocol used in the transformation does not satisfy even 1-robustness and we also fix their protocol.

Efficient NIMPC Protocols for Abelian Programs. We propose a fully robust NIMPC protocol with communication complexity $O(|\mathbb{G}|(\log |\mathbb{G}|)^2)$ for abelian programs allowing inputs to take any value of $\mathbb{G}$. Our protocol improves the previous result $O(|\mathbb{G}|^2 n^2)$ [3]. Note that it is impossible to cut down on the exponent with respect to $|\mathbb{G}|$ anymore due to the lower bound [17]. For abelian programs with limited input domains, we apply the BKR transformation to our protocol with the extended input domain in a non-straightforward way. This is the first time that the BKR transformation, which originally aims at lifting the level of robustness, has been used to restrict input domains. As a result, we obtain a t-robust protocol with communication complexity $|\mathbb{G}|(\log |\mathbb{G}|)^2 p^{t+O(1)}$ if input domains are of size at most d, where p is the smallest prime power such that $p \geq \max\{n, d\}$. This protocol is more efficient than the previous protocol of [3] and even than that of [6] if $t = o(\log n)$ and $|\mathbb{G}| = n^{\Theta(1)}$ (Table 1).

Table 1. Comparison of the existing t-robust NIMPC protocols for abelian programs. Let n be the number of players, $\mathbb{G}$ be an abelian group, d be a positive integer at most $|\mathbb{G}|$, and p be the smallest prime power such that $p \geq \max\{n, d\}$. We suppose $t = n$ if the symbol t does not appear in the complexity.

Reference	Input domain	Communication complexity
[3]	$\mathbb{G}^n$	$O(|\mathbb{G}|^2 n^2)$
Ours (Theorem 1)		$O(|\mathbb{G}|(\log|\mathbb{G}|)^2)$
[3]		$|\mathbb{G}|^3 (nd)^{t+O(1)}$
[6]	$\prod_{i \in [n]} S_i,$	$|\mathbb{G}|^{\log n + O(1)} n$
Ours (Corollary 1)	where $S_i \subseteq \mathbb{G}$ and $|S_i| \leq d$	$|\mathbb{G}|(\log|\mathbb{G}|)^2 p^{t+O(1)}$

New NIMPC Protocols for Linear Classifiers. We define the class of linear classifiers as functions computing $f(\sum_{i \in [n]} w_i x_i)$ on a weighted sum of inputs for some weights $\boldsymbol{w} = (w_i)_{i \in [n]}$ over a finite field $\mathbb{F}_q$ and some function $f : \mathbb{F}_q \to \{0, 1\}$. Our definition can be naturally extended to functions outputting many bits and can also deal with real-valued inputs by choosing a sufficiently large prime q. We propose a fully robust NIMPC protocol with communication complexity $O(q \log q)$ for this class when inputs take any value of $\mathbb{F}_q$. Note that the multiplicative factor of q is unavoidable due to the lower bound from [17]. In our protocol, no information on the weights is leaked other than what is implied by the residual function. Applying the BKR transformation, we also obtain a t-robust protocol with communication complexity $p^{t+O(1)} q \log q$ for linear classifiers with input domains of size at most d, where p is the smallest prime power such that $p \geq \max\{n, d\}$.

Revisiting the BKR Transformation. We have used the BKR transformation in the above two results to restrict input domains. However, we revisit the transformation and reveal that their fully robust NIMPC protocol for what they call outputting-message functions, which is used as a building block in the transformation, does not satisfy even 1-robustness. We also fix their protocol with only constant overhead in the communication complexity. Therefore, the statements of [6] still hold true but it is necessary to use our modified protocol for outputting-message functions when applying the BKR transformation. As a byproduct of that modification, we obtain a fully robust NIMPC protocol for the class of indicator functions. An indicator function decides whether a tuple of inputs $x \in \mathcal{X}_0^n$ is equal to some fixed $a \in \mathcal{X}_0^n$, where $\mathcal{X}_0$ is a fixed domain. Our protocol has communication complexity $O((\log|\mathcal{X}_0|)n)$ improving the best known result $O((\log|\mathcal{X}_0|)^2 n)$ [17] and is asymptotically optimal with respect to the input length according to the lower bound [17].

1.2   Related Work

It is known that NIMPC for indicator functions is used as a building block to construct protocols for any given class of functions [3]. For the class of all the functions from $\mathcal{X}_0^n$ to a finite set $\mathcal{Z}$, our result on indicator functions implies a fully robust protocol with communication complexity $O(|\mathcal{X}_0|^n (\log |\mathcal{X}_0|)(\log |\mathcal{Z}|)n)$ improving the previous results [3, 15, 17]. Recently, however, the authors of [1] propose an asymptotically optimal protocol achieving $O(|\mathcal{X}_0|^n (\log |\mathcal{Z}|))$ without using indicator functions. For the class consisting only of a single function $f : \mathcal{X}_0^n \to \{0, 1\}$, a t-robust protocol has been proposed in [5] by applying the BKR transformation to an efficient PSM protocol for f. If $t < n/2$, it is more efficient than the protocol obtained from indicator functions. Nevertheless, it makes sense to construct efficient protocols for indicator functions if we aim at an intermediate class of functions rather than the above two extreme ones.

For boolean symmetric functions, the authors of [6] devise a more efficient t-robust NIMPC protocol with communication complexity $n^{\log \log n + \log t + O(1)}$ than those obtained from abelian programs.

2   Technical Overview

In this section, we provide an overview of our NIMPC protocols. We give more detailed descriptions and security proofs in the following sections.

2.1   Efficient NIMPC Protocols for Abelian Programs

An abelian program h takes n inputs from an abelian group $\mathbb{G}$ and outputs $h(x_1, \ldots, x_n) = f(\sum_{i \in [n]} x_i)$ for some function $f : \mathbb{G} \to \{0, 1\}$. We start by explaining how to construct an efficient fully robust NIMPC protocol for the class of abelian programs in which inputs take any value of $\mathbb{G}$. Our protocol is in part based on the result of Beimel et al. [3, Theorem 7.2], which has presented a protocol tailored to abelian programs over the cyclic group $\mathbb{Z}_{n+1} = \{0, 1, \ldots, n\}$ of size $n + 1$. They consider a special map $\sigma : x \mapsto x + 1 \mod (n + 1)$ from $\mathbb{Z}_{n+1}$ to itself and view every element $g \in \mathbb{Z}_{n+1}$ as the g-th iteration of σ, i.e., $\sigma^g := \sigma \circ \cdots \circ \sigma$ (g times). They then reduce computing abelian programs to composing the maps σ^{x_i} corresponding to the players' inputs x_i. To hide the inputs and achieve robustness, they randomize the operation of that composition by using Kilian's technique [14]. However, there is no such map as σ in a general abelian group, which is why the previous result is only applicable to $\mathbb{Z}_{n+1}$.

Construction Based on the Regular Representation. To represent elements of an abelian group $\mathbb{G}$, we make the most use of the regular representation of $\mathbb{G}$. Observe that the g-th iteration of σ is equivalent to the map $x \mapsto x + g \mod (n + 1)$. Generalizing it, we view an element $g \in \mathbb{G}$ as a permutation $\sigma_g : \mathbb{G} \ni x \mapsto x + g \in \mathbb{G}$, which is further viewed as a linear map from the $|\mathbb{G}|$-dimensional vector space over $\mathbb{F}_2 = \{0, 1\}$ to itself translating every basis e_x to e_{x+g}, where $e_x \in \mathbb{F}_2^{|\mathbb{G}|}$ is the unit vector such that the entry indexed by $x \in \mathbb{G}$ is one. Then, the summation of inputs corresponds to the composition of the associated linear maps. Furthermore, if we appropriately represent the associated function $f : \mathbb{G} \to \{0, 1\}$ as a vector, we can express the whole computation of the abelian program as a certain matrix-vector product. As in [3], we use the randomization technique [14] to securely perform that linear algebra operation. However, there still remain two problems in the above protocol: (1) the resultant communication complexity is $O(|\mathbb{G}|^2 \log |\mathbb{G}|)$ since the protocol has to communicate $O(|\mathbb{G}|)$ permutations over $\mathbb{G}$, each of which is expressed as $O(|\mathbb{G}| \log |\mathbb{G}|)$ bits and (2) it only works for the specific abelian program since it reveals partial information on the truth table, e.g., $|f^{-1}(1)|$. Regarding the first problem, we cut down the number of matrices with the help of the fundamental theorem of finite abelian groups. Since it implies that all the group elements are generated by $O(\log |\mathbb{G}|)$ elements, players can compute their messages from only $O(\log |\mathbb{G}|)$ permutations corresponding to the generators. To hide the value of $|f^{-1}(1)|$, we carefully choose a group extension $\mathbb{H} \supsetneq \mathbb{G}$ and extend $f : \mathbb{G} \to \{0, 1\}$ to $\tilde{f} : \mathbb{H} \to \{0, 1\}$ so that $|\tilde{f}^{-1}(1)|$ is constant regardless of f. The details are given in Sect. 4.

Limiting Inputs. To construct a protocol for abelian programs with limited input domains, we use the BKR transformation in a non-straightforward way. Note that it has been originally devised to obtain t-robust NIMPC protocols from 0-robust ones. Clearly, the above fully robust protocol for abelian programs with the extended input domain satisfies 0-robustness. Since 0-robustness is not affected by what the input domain is, that protocol is itself a 0-robust protocol for abelian programs with *limited* input domain. We then apply the BKR transformation and lift the level of robustness to $t > 0$ with some overhead in communication complexity.

2.2   New NIMPC Protocols for Linear Classifiers

We formally define linear classifiers as the class of all the functions of the form $h_{f,w} : \mathbb{F}_q^n \ni (x_i)_{i \in [n]} \mapsto f(\sum_{i \in [n]} w_i x_i) \in \{0, 1\}$, where $\mathbb{F}_q$ is the fixed finite field of size q, $f : \mathbb{F}_q \to \{0, 1\}$, and $w = (w_i)_{i \in [n]} \in \mathbb{F}_q^n$.

To begin with, we fix f and treat $k = |f^{-1}(1)|$ as public information. We show a construction of a fully robust protocol for the class consisting only of the specific function $\{h_{f,w}\}$. Let $f^{-1}(1) = \{u_1, \ldots, u_k\}$ and set $u = (u_j)_{j \in [k]} \in \mathbb{F}_q^k$. The main idea of our construction is to use the fact that $f(\sum_{i \in [n]} w_i x_i) = 1$ if and only if at least one entry of $u_0 = (u_j - \sum_{i \in [n]} w_i x_i)_{j \in [k]}$ is zero. We must ensure that the evaluator learns the number of zeros in u_0 and nothing more. We randomly choose a permutation π over $[k]$ and k non-zero elements $r_i \in \mathbb{F}_q \backslash \{0\}$ $(i \in [k])$ and define $\tilde{u} = (r_j u_{\pi(j)})_{j \in [k]}$. We then send each P_i the vector $\tilde{u}_i = (r_j w_i)_{j \in [k]}$ along with a random vector $s_i \in \mathbb{F}_q^k$ for masking his input, who in turn sends his message $\tilde{u}_i x_i + s_i$ to the evaluator. We let the evaluator receive $\tilde{u} + \sum_{i \in [n]} s_i$ in advance and after receiving the messages, he outputs $f(\sum_{i \in [n]} w_i x_i)$ according to the number of zeros in $\tilde{u} - \sum_{i \in [n]} \tilde{u}_i x_i$.

However, as mentioned above, this protocol assumes the dimension $k = |f^{-1}(1)|$ of the vectors is public, which is why it does not work for the class of all the linear classifiers. Our solution to hide k is *padding* the vector u with certain $q - k$ elements u_j $(k < j \le q)$ to ensure that its dimension should be q. Specifically, we carefully select these $q - k$ elements from an extension field of $\mathbb{F}_q$

so that the protocol satisfies correctness. We also propose a protocol for linear classifiers with limited input domains by applying the BKR transformation as in the case of abelian programs. The details are given in Sect. 5.

2.3 Revisiting the BKR Transformation

As a building block for the BKR transformation, the authors of [6] propose a fully robust NIMPC protocol for what they call outputting-message functions. We reveal that their protocol does not satisfy even 1-robustness. Technically, they define an outputting-message function for a message m, a vector $\boldsymbol{u}$, and a matrix $\boldsymbol{A} = [\boldsymbol{a}_1, \ldots, \boldsymbol{a}_n]$ as the function outputting m if $\boldsymbol{u} = \boldsymbol{A}[x_1, \ldots, x_n]^\top$ holds and $\bot$ otherwise.

The main issue is in their procedures for securely testing the equality $\boldsymbol{u} = \boldsymbol{A}[x_1, \ldots, x_n]^\top$. In their protocol, each P_i receives a random vector $\boldsymbol{s}_i$ and sends $\boldsymbol{\nu}_i := \boldsymbol{a}_i x_i + \boldsymbol{s}_i$ as part of his message. The evaluator receives $\boldsymbol{\nu}_0 := \boldsymbol{u} + \sum_{i \in [n]} \boldsymbol{s}_i$ in advance and then tests whether $\boldsymbol{\nu}_0 = \sum_{i \in [n]} \boldsymbol{\nu}_i$ holds. However, consider the collusion of the player P_1 and the evaluator. If $\boldsymbol{d} := \boldsymbol{u} - \sum_{i \neq 1} \boldsymbol{a}_i x_i$ and $\boldsymbol{a}_1$ are linearly independent, they should learn nothing at all since the residual function outputs nothing but $\bot$. Nevertheless, they actually obtain the vector $\boldsymbol{d} = \boldsymbol{\nu}_0 - \sum_{i \neq 1} \boldsymbol{\nu}_i - \boldsymbol{s}_1$.

We fix their protocol with only constant overhead in the communication complexity. Our main idea is randomizing $\boldsymbol{d}$ to ensure for P_1 and the evaluator not to learn more than the linear independence relation between $\boldsymbol{d}$ and $\boldsymbol{a}_1$, which is the only information revealed by the residual function. Specifically, we choose an invertible matrix $\boldsymbol{T}$ uniformly at random and redefine $\boldsymbol{\nu}_0 = \boldsymbol{T}\boldsymbol{u} + \sum_{i \in [n]} \boldsymbol{s}_i$. We additionally give $\boldsymbol{T}\boldsymbol{a}_i$ to each P_i as randomness. Now, P_1 and the evaluator only learns $\boldsymbol{\nu}_0 - \sum_{i \neq 1} \boldsymbol{\nu}_i - \boldsymbol{s}_1 = \boldsymbol{T}\boldsymbol{d}$, which does not reveal more than the linear independence relation between $\boldsymbol{d}$ and $\boldsymbol{a}_1$ due to the randomness of $\boldsymbol{T}$. Note that our modification increases the communication complexity of their protocol only by a constant factor. We present the formal statements in Sect. 6.

Finally, as a byproduct of that modification, we obtain a fully robust protocol for indicator functions with asymptotically optimal communication complexity with respect to the input length. Roughly speaking, we embed every input domain to a subset of a fixed finite field and translate the condition $(x_i)_{i \in [n]} = (a_i)_{i \in [n]}$ to the equality test $\boldsymbol{u} = \boldsymbol{I}_n[x_1, \ldots, x_n]^\top$, where $\boldsymbol{u} = [a_1, \ldots, a_n]^\top$ and $\boldsymbol{I}_n$ is the identity matrix of size n. We show that an NIMPC protocol for that equality test is obtained from our modified protocol for outputting-message functions.

3 Preliminaries

Notations. For a set $\mathcal{X} = \mathcal{X}_1 \times \cdots \times \mathcal{X}_n$ and $C \subseteq [n]$, we define $\mathcal{X}_C = \prod_{i \in C} \mathcal{X}_i$. For $x \in \mathcal{X}$, we define x_C as the restriction $(x_i)_{i \in C}$ of x to $\mathcal{X}_C$. Let $\overline{C}$ be the complement of $C \subseteq [n]$ and $x_{\overline{C}} \in \mathcal{X}_{\overline{C}}$. For a function $h : \mathcal{X} \to \mathcal{Z}$, we define the residual function $h|_{\overline{C}, x_{\overline{C}}} : \mathcal{X}_C \to \mathcal{Z}$ of h for $\overline{C}$ and $x_{\overline{C}}$ as the sub-function of h obtained by restricting the input variables indexed by $\overline{C}$ to $x_{\overline{C}}$, that is, $h|_{\overline{C}, x_{\overline{C}}}(x_C) = h(x_C, x_{\overline{C}})$.

For a finite set S, we write $s \leftarrow_\$ S$ if we choose a uniformly random element s from S. For two distributions $\mathcal{D}, \mathcal{D}'$ on S, we write $\mathcal{D} \equiv \mathcal{D}'$ if they are perfectly identical to each other. Define $\mathfrak{S}_S$ as the set of all the permutations over S. We simply write $\mathfrak{S}_N$ if S is clear from the context, where $N = |S|$. For $\pi \in \mathfrak{S}_S$ and a finite field $\mathbb{K}$, we define a permutation matrix $\boldsymbol{U}_\pi$ as the square matrix over $\mathbb{K}$ of size $|S|$ whose (i,j)-th entry is 1 if $j = \pi(i)$ and 0 otherwise, where we assume that the sets indexing the rows and columns are both S. It holds that $\boldsymbol{U}_\pi^{-1} = \boldsymbol{U}_{\pi^{-1}} = \boldsymbol{U}_\pi^\top$ and $\boldsymbol{U}_\pi \boldsymbol{U}_\tau = \boldsymbol{U}_{\tau \circ \pi}$, where π^{-1} is the inverse of π and $\tau \circ \pi$ is the composition of $\pi, \tau \in \mathfrak{S}_S$, i.e., $(\tau \circ \pi)(i) = \tau(\pi(i))$ for all $i \in S$. For $i \in S$, let $\boldsymbol{e}_i = (a_j)_{j \in S} \in \mathbb{K}^N$ denote the i-th unit vector, i.e., $a_i = 1$ and $a_j = 0$ for all $j \neq i$.

For $r_i \in \mathbb{K}$ ($i \in [N]$), let $\mathrm{diag}(r_1, \ldots, r_N) \in \mathbb{K}^{N \times N}$ denote a diagonal matrix whose (i,i)-th entry is r_i for $i \in [N]$. Throughout the paper, all vectors are column vectors unless otherwise indicated. For a tuple of vectors $(\boldsymbol{v}_i)_{i \in [N]}$ where $\boldsymbol{v}_i \in \mathbb{K}^k$, we define $\mathrm{Ker}((\boldsymbol{v}_i)_{i \in [N]}) = \{(x_i)_{i \in [N]} \in \mathbb{K}^N \mid \sum_{i \in [N]} \boldsymbol{v}_i x_i = \boldsymbol{0}\}$. For a subset $\mathcal{S} \subseteq \mathbb{K}^N$, we denote by $\mathcal{S}^\perp$ the orthogonal complement of $\mathcal{S}$, i.e., $\mathcal{S}^\perp = \{(\delta_i)_{i \in [N]} \in \mathbb{K}^N \mid \forall (x_i)_{i \in [N]} \in \mathcal{S}, \ \sum_{i \in [N]} \delta_i x_i = 0\}$. We define $\mathrm{GL}_k(\mathbb{K})$ as the set of all the invertible k-by-k matrices, i.e., $\mathrm{GL}_k(\mathbb{K}) = \{\boldsymbol{T} \in \mathbb{K}^{k \times k} \mid \det(\boldsymbol{T}) \neq 0\}$.

3.1   Non-interactive Secure Multiparty Computation

In NIMPC, we consider n players P_i ($i \in [n]$), each holding an input, and an external output player P_0 called an evaluator. In this paper, we focus on NIMPC with correlated randomness, in which each player locally computes a message from his input and randomness and then sends it to the evaluator.

Definition 1 (NIMPC: syntax and correctness). *Let $\mathcal{X}_i$ ($i \in [n]$) and $\mathcal{Z}$ be finite sets. Let $\mathcal{X} = \prod_{i \in [n]} \mathcal{X}_i$ and $\mathcal{H}$ be a class of functions from $\mathcal{X}$ to $\mathcal{Z}$. Let $\mathcal{R}_i$ ($i \in \{0\} \cup [n]$) and $\mathcal{M}_i$ ($i \in [n]$) be finite sets. An NIMPC protocol for $\mathcal{H}$ is a triplet $\Pi = (\mathsf{Gen}, \mathsf{Enc}, \mathsf{Dec})$, where:*

- *$\mathsf{Gen} : \mathcal{H} \to \mathcal{R}_0 \times \mathcal{R}_1 \times \cdots \times \mathcal{R}_n$ is a randomized function;*
- *Enc is an n-tuple of deterministic functions $(\mathsf{Enc}_1, \ldots, \mathsf{Enc}_n)$, where $\mathsf{Enc}_i : \mathcal{X}_i \times \mathcal{R}_i \to \mathcal{M}_i$;*
- *$\mathsf{Dec} : \mathcal{R}_0 \times \mathcal{M}_1 \times \cdots \times \mathcal{M}_n \to \mathcal{Z}$ is a deterministic function satisfying the following correctness requirement: for any $x = (x_1, \ldots, x_n) \in \mathcal{X}$ and any $h \in \mathcal{H}$, it holds that*

$$\Pr[(R_0, R_1, \ldots, R_n) \leftarrow \mathsf{Gen}(h) : \mathsf{Dec}(R_0, \mathsf{Enc}(x, R)) = h(x)] = 1,$$

where $\mathsf{Enc}(x, R) = (\mathsf{Enc}_1(x_1, R_1), \ldots, \mathsf{Enc}_n(x_n, R_n))$.

The online communication complexity $\mathsf{CC}_{\mathsf{on}}(\Pi)$ of Π is the maximum of $\log |\mathcal{M}_1|, \ldots, \log |\mathcal{M}_n|$. The offline communication complexity $\mathsf{CC}_{\mathsf{off}}(\Pi)$ of Π is $\log |\mathcal{R}_0|, \log |\mathcal{R}_1|, \ldots, \log |\mathcal{R}_n|$. The communication complexity $\mathsf{CC}(\Pi)$ of Π is defined as the maximum of $\mathsf{CC}_{\mathsf{on}}(\Pi)$ and $\mathsf{CC}_{\mathsf{off}}(\Pi)$.

To define the security requirements of NIMPC, we consider an adversary who colludes with a set of players $C \subseteq [n]$ as well as the evaluator. In this setting, it is impossible to prevent the adversary from learning the residual function $h|_{\overline{C}, x_{\overline{C}}}$ for the inputs $x_{\overline{C}}$ of the honest players. Indeed, he is allowed to compute $h(x_C, x_{\overline{C}})$ for every input x_C from the correlated randomness of C and the messages of $\overline{C}$. We say that an NIMPC protocol is C-robust if the adversary's view is perfectly simulated by some simulator with oracle access to the residual function.

Definition 2 (NIMPC: robustness). *For a subset $C \subseteq [n]$, we say that an NIMPC protocol Π for $\mathcal{H}$ is C-robust if there exists a simulator Sim with oracle access to a residual function such that, for every $h \in \mathcal{H}$ and $x_{\overline{C}} \in \mathcal{X}_{\overline{C}}$, we have*
$$\mathsf{Sim}^{h|_{\overline{C}, x_{\overline{C}}}}(C) \equiv (R_0, R_C = (R_i)_{i \in C}, M_{\overline{C}} = (M_i)_{i \in \overline{C}}), \text{ where } (R_0, R_1, \ldots, R_n) \leftarrow$$
$\mathsf{Gen}(h)$ and $M_i = \mathsf{Enc}_i(x_i, R_i)$.

For an integer $0 \leq t \leq n$, we say that Π is t-robust if it is C-robust for every $C \subseteq [n]$ of size at most t. We say that Π is fully robust if it is n-robust.

3.2 Abelian Programs

Let $\mathbb{G}$ be a finite abelian group and $S_1, \ldots, S_n$ be subsets of $\mathbb{G}$. Let $\mathcal{X}_i = S_i$ for $i \in [n]$ and $\mathcal{X} = \mathcal{X}_1 \times \cdots \times \mathcal{X}_n$. Define the abelian program $h_f : \mathcal{X} \to \{0, 1\}$ associated with $f : \mathbb{G} \to \{0, 1\}$ as $h_f(x_1, \ldots, x_n) = f(\sum_{i \in [n]} x_i)$. We then define $\mathcal{A}_{\mathbb{G}}^{S_1, \ldots, S_n}$ be the class of all the abelian programs, that is, $\mathcal{A}_{\mathbb{G}}^{S_1, \ldots, S_n} = \{h_f : \mathcal{X} \to \{0, 1\} \mid f : \mathbb{G} \to \{0, 1\}\}$. We simply write $\mathcal{A}_{\mathbb{G}}$ if $S_1 = \cdots = S_n = \mathbb{G}$.

The class of abelian programs with limited input domains includes symmetric functions. A function $h : [d]^n \to \{0, 1\}$ is called symmetric if $h(x_{\pi(1)}, \ldots, x_{\pi(n)}) = h(x_1, \ldots, x_n)$ for all $(x_1, \ldots, x_n) \in [d]^n$ and $\pi \in \mathfrak{S}_n$. Following [3], let $\mathbb{G} = (\mathbb{Z}_{n+1})^d$ and $S_1 = \cdots = S_n = \{e_1, \ldots, e_d\} \subseteq \mathbb{G}$, where $e_i \in (\mathbb{Z}_{n+1})^d$ is the i-th unit vector. Then, we can see that $\mathcal{A}_{\mathbb{G}}^{S_1, \ldots, S_n}$ is equivalent to the class of all symmetric functions over $[d]^n$ identifying $x_i \in [d]$ with $e_{x_i} \in \mathbb{G}$ since the outputs $h(x_1, \ldots, x_n)$ of symmetric functions only depend on $\sum_{i \in [n]} e_{x_i}$.

Although assuming above that abelian programs output only one bit, it is possible to extend them to the ones outputting m bits by computing each output bit separately [3]. Specifically, given an NIMPC protocol Π for $\mathcal{A}_{\mathbb{G}}^{S_1, \ldots, S_n}$, we can construct a protocol Π_m for $\mathcal{H}_m := \{h : \mathcal{X} \to \{0, 1\}^m \mid h = (h_1, \ldots, h_m), h_i \in \mathcal{A}_{\mathbb{G}}^{S_1, \ldots, S_n}\}$ with m times higher communication complexity by running Π for each h_i separately.

We note that limiting players to inputs from smaller domains is not a straightforward task for NIMPC. For example, a t-robust NIMPC protocol for $\mathcal{A}_{\mathbb{G}}$ does not directly imply a t-robust protocol for $\mathcal{A}_{\mathbb{G}}^{S_1, \ldots, S_n}$. This is because in a 1-robust protocol for $h \in \mathcal{A}_{\mathbb{G}}$, any player P_i colluding with the evaluator learns the value of h on the honest inputs and every possible choice of x_i from $\mathbb{G}$ while in a protocol for $h \in \mathcal{A}_{\mathbb{G}}^{S_1, \ldots, S_n}$, P_i is allowed to evaluate the residual function only on x_i from S_i.

4 Efficient NIMPC Protocols for Abelian Programs

4.1 The Design of Our Protocol

First, we design an efficient fully robust NIMPC protocol for the class $\mathcal{A}_{\mathbb{G}}$ of abelian programs in which inputs take any value of $\mathbb{G}$. We have already explained a high-level idea of our construction in Sect. 2.1.

Construction Based on the Regular Representation. Recall that via the regular representation of $\mathbb{G}$, we identify every element $g \in \mathbb{G}$ with the linear map from $\mathbb{F}_2^N$ to itself translating every basis $e_x \in \mathbb{F}_2^N$ to $e_{x+g} \in \mathbb{F}_2^N$ for $x \in \mathbb{G}$. Here, $N = |\mathbb{G}|$ and we assume that $\mathbb{G}$ is the index set for N-dimensional vectors and for the rows and columns of N-by-N matrices. The linear map is in turn expressed as the permutation matrix $A_g := U_{\sigma_g} \in \mathrm{GL}_N(\mathbb{F}_2)$, where $\sigma_g : \mathbb{G} \ni x \mapsto x + g \in \mathbb{G}$. The summation of inputs x_i is now reduced to the multiplication of the A_{x_i}'s. To evaluate a function $f : \mathbb{G} \to \{0,1\}$ on the sum $s = \sum_{i \in [n]} x_i$, we associate f with the vector $v_f := \sum_{x \in f^{-1}(1)} e_x \in \mathbb{F}_2^N$. Then, we can translate the evaluation of f into the matrix-vector product $e_{0_{\mathbb{G}}}^\top A_s v_f = f(s)$, where $0_{\mathbb{G}}$ is the identity of $\mathbb{G}$. We use the randomization technique [14] to securely perform these linear algebra operations. Note that all the permutation matrices can be represented by $O(N \log N)$ bits.

To obtain a concrete protocol, suppose that we compute an abelian program h_f associated with $f : \mathbb{G} \to \{0,1\}$. We first randomly select $n-1$ permutations $\pi_1, \ldots, \pi_{n-1}$ over $\mathbb{G}$. Then, we give U_{π_1} to the player P_1, $(U_{\pi_{i-1}}^{-1} A_g U_{\pi_i})_{g \in \mathbb{G}}$ to P_i $(1 < i < n)$, and $(U_{\pi_{n-1}}^{-1} A_g v_f)_{g \in \mathbb{G}}$ to P_n. If P_1 sends $e_{0_{\mathbb{G}}}^\top A_{x_1} U_{\pi_1}$ and the other players send the matrices corresponding to their inputs, the evaluator can compute $f(\sum_{i \in [n]} x_i) = e_{0_{\mathbb{G}}}^\top (\prod_{i \in [n]} A_{x_i}) v_f$. However, there remain the following two problems: (1) the communication complexity of this protocol is $O(N^2 \log N)$ since it needs to communicate at most N permutation matrices and (2) it only works for the class $\{h_f\}$ consisting only of the specific abelian program associated with the fixed function f, not for $\mathcal{A}_{\mathbb{G}}$, since the randomness of P_n reveals partial information on the truth table of h_f, i.e., the value of $|f^{-1}(1)|$.

Reducing Communication Complexity and Hiding the Truth Table. To cut down the number of permutation matrices to communicate, we recall the fundamental theorem of finite abelian groups, e.g., [16, Theorem 6.44]. For any abelian group $\mathbb{G}$ of size N, there exists a generating set $\{s_j \mid j \in [m]\}$ of size $m = O(\log N)$. For each $x \in \mathbb{G}$, we fix m integers $\ell_j(x)$ $(j \in [m])$ such that $x = \sum_{j \in [m]} \ell_j(x) s_j$ in $\mathbb{G}$.

We now give $U_{\pi_{i-1}}^{-1} U_{\pi_i}$ and $(U_{\pi_{i-1}}^{-1} A_{s_j} U_{\pi_i})_{j \in [m]}$ to the player P_i with $1 < i < n$. Then, P_i can compute $U_{\pi_{i-1}}^{-1} A_{s_j} U_{\pi_{i-1}}$ for every $j \in [m]$. For an input $x_i \in \mathbb{G}$, he computes $\prod_{j \in [m]} (U_{\pi_{i-1}}^{-1} A_{s_j} U_{\pi_{i-1}})^{\ell_j(x_i)} = U_{\pi_{i-1}}^{-1} A_{x_i} U_{\pi_{i-1}}$. Finally, he obtains $U_{\pi_{i-1}}^{-1} A_{x_i} U_{\pi_i}$ by multiplying $U_{\pi_{i-1}}^{-1} U_{\pi_i}$. Similarly, we give P_n the randomness $U_{\pi_{n-1}}^{-1} U_{\pi_n}$, $(U_{\pi_{n-1}}^{-1} A_{s_j} U_{\pi_n})_{j \in [m]}$, and $U_{\pi_n}^{-1} v_f$, where $\pi_n \leftarrow_{\$} \mathfrak{S}_{\mathbb{G}}$. This protocol only communicates $O(m) = O(\log N)$ permutation matrices and hence achieves the communication complexity $O(N(\log N)^2)$.

Next, to hide the value of $|f^{-1}(1)|$, we augment the vector $\boldsymbol{v}_f$ of Hamming weight $|f^{-1}(1)|$ by a vector of weight $N - |f^{-1}(1)|$ to ensure that the number of ones in the augmented vector is N regardless of f. Specifically, we consider the group extension $\mathbb{H} := \mathbb{G} \times \mathbb{F}_2 = \{(x, b) \mid x \in \mathbb{G},\ b \in \mathbb{F}_2\}$ of $\mathbb{G}$ and replace the $|\mathbb{G}|$-dimensional vectors and matrices introduced above by some $|\mathbb{H}|$-dimensional ones. Since $|\mathbb{H}| = 2N$, the communication complexity is still $O(N(\log N)^2)$.

4.2   Abelian Programs with the Extended Input Domain

Now, we present the formal description of our protocol for $\mathcal{A}_\mathbb{G}$. Let $\mathbb{H} = \mathbb{G} \times \mathbb{F}_2$ be the direct product of $\mathbb{G}$ and $\mathbb{F}_2$. Instead of $\boldsymbol{v}_f$, we redefine the vector $\boldsymbol{w}_f \in \mathbb{F}_2^{|\mathbb{H}|}$ representing a function f as $\boldsymbol{w}_f = \sum_{x \in f^{-1}(1)} \boldsymbol{e}_{(x,0)} + \sum_{x \in f^{-1}(0)} \boldsymbol{e}_{(x,1)}$, where $\boldsymbol{e}_{(x,b)} \in \mathbb{F}_2^{|\mathbb{H}|}$ is the unit vector such that the entry indexed by (x, b) is 1. Here, $\mathbb{H}$ is the index set for $2N$-dimensional vectors and for the rows and columns of $2N$-by-$2N$ matrices. It can be seen that the Hamming weight of $\boldsymbol{w}_f$ is now N regardless of f.

According to that modification, we sample each permutation at random from $\mathfrak{S}_\mathbb{H}$ rather than $\mathfrak{S}_\mathbb{G}$. We also replace the permutation $\sigma_x \in \mathfrak{S}_\mathbb{G}$ representing $x \in \mathbb{G}$ with $\tau_x \in \mathfrak{S}_\mathbb{H}$ defined as $\tau_x(g, b) = (g + x, b)$ for $(g, b) \in \mathbb{H}$. We define $\boldsymbol{B}_x = \boldsymbol{U}_{\tau_x} \in \mathbb{F}_2^{2N \times 2N}$ instead of $\boldsymbol{A}_x$. Note that the $\boldsymbol{B}_x$'s also satisfy the following homomorphic property: $\boldsymbol{B}_x^{-1} = \boldsymbol{B}_{-x}$ and $\boldsymbol{B}_x \boldsymbol{B}_y = \boldsymbol{B}_y \boldsymbol{B}_x = \boldsymbol{B}_{x+y}$ for $x, y \in \mathbb{G}$.

Protocol Π_1 for $\mathcal{A}_\mathbb{G}$

$\mathsf{Gen}(h_f)$:
   1. Choose $\pi_1, \ldots, \pi_n \xleftarrow{\$} \mathfrak{S}_\mathbb{H}$.
   2. Output $R_0 = \bot$, $R_1 = \boldsymbol{U}_{\pi_1}$, $R_i = (\boldsymbol{U}_{\pi_{i-1}}^{-1}\boldsymbol{U}_{\pi_i}, (\boldsymbol{U}_{\pi_{i-1}}^{-1}\boldsymbol{B}_{s_j}\boldsymbol{U}_{\pi_i})_{j \in [m]})$ for $1 < i < n$, and $R_n = (\boldsymbol{U}_{\pi_{n-1}}^{-1}\boldsymbol{U}_{\pi_n}, (\boldsymbol{U}_{\pi_{n-1}}^{-1}\boldsymbol{B}_{s_j}\boldsymbol{U}_{\pi_n})_{j \in [m]}, \boldsymbol{U}_{\pi_n}^{-1}\boldsymbol{w}_f)$.
$\mathsf{Enc}_i(x_i, R_i)$:
   − $i = 1$:
      1. Output $M_1 = \boldsymbol{e}_{(0_\mathbb{G}, 0)}^\top \boldsymbol{B}_{x_1}\boldsymbol{U}_{\pi_1}$.
   − $1 < i < n$:
      1. Parse R_i as $(\boldsymbol{L}_0, (\boldsymbol{L}_j)_{j \in [m]})$, where $\boldsymbol{L}_j \in \mathbb{F}_2^{|\mathbb{H}| \times |\mathbb{H}|}$.
      2. Output $M_i = (\prod_{j \in [m]}(\boldsymbol{L}_j\boldsymbol{L}_0^{-1})^{\ell_j(x_i)})\boldsymbol{L}_0$.
   − $i = n$:
      1. Parse R_n as $(\boldsymbol{L}_0, (\boldsymbol{L}_j)_{j \in [m]}, \boldsymbol{r})$, where $\boldsymbol{L}_j \in \mathbb{F}_2^{|\mathbb{H}| \times |\mathbb{H}|}$ and $\boldsymbol{r} \in \mathbb{F}_2^{|\mathbb{H}|}$.
      2. Output $M_n = (\prod_{j \in [m]}(\boldsymbol{L}_j\boldsymbol{L}_0^{-1})^{\ell_j(x_n)})\boldsymbol{L}_0\boldsymbol{r}$.
$\mathsf{Dec}(M_1, \ldots, M_n)$:
   1. Output $\prod_{i \in [n]} M_i$.

Fig. 1. The NIMPC protocol Π_1 for the class of abelian programs $\mathcal{A}_\mathbb{G}$.

Theorem 1. *Let $\mathbb{G}$ be a finite abelian group. Let $S \subseteq \mathbb{G}$ be a generating set of $\mathbb{G}$. Let $\mathcal{X}_1 = \cdots = \mathcal{X}_n = \mathbb{G}$ and $\mathcal{X} = \mathcal{X}_1 \times \cdots \times \mathcal{X}_n$. Then, the protocol Π_1 described in Fig. 1 is a fully robust NIMPC protocol for $\mathcal{A}_{\mathbb{G}}$ such that*

$$\mathsf{CC}_{\mathsf{on}}(\Pi_1) = 2|\mathbb{G}| \cdot \lceil \log |\mathbb{G}| + 1 \rceil$$
$$\text{and } \mathsf{CC}_{\mathsf{off}}(\Pi_1) = 2|\mathbb{G}| \cdot \lceil \log |\mathbb{G}| + 1 \rceil \cdot (|S| + 1) + 2|\mathbb{G}|.$$

In particular, it holds that $\mathsf{CC}(\Pi_1) = O(|\mathbb{G}|(\log |\mathbb{G}|)^2)$.

Simulator $\mathsf{Sim}^{h|_{\overline{C}, x_{\overline{C}}}}(C)$ for Π_1

Input. A set of colluding players C.

Oracle access. The residual function $h|_{\overline{C}, x_{\overline{C}}}$ for the inputs $x_{\overline{C}}$ of honest players.

Output. Correlated randomness R_0 and $(R_i)_{i \in C}$ of the colluding players and messages $(M_i)_{i \in \overline{C}}$ of the honest players.

Algorithm.

- If $C = \emptyset$:
    1. Define $f' : \mathbb{G} \to \{0, 1\}$ as $f'(a) = h(x_1, \ldots, x_n)$ for all $a \in \mathbb{G}$ using the oracle.
    2. Define $h' : \mathbb{G}^n \to \{0, 1\}$ as $h'(a_1, \ldots, a_n) = f'(\sum_{i \in [n]} a_i)$ for all $a_1, \ldots, a_n \in \mathbb{G}$.
    3. Let $(R_0 = \perp, R_1, \ldots, R_n) \leftarrow \mathsf{Gen}(h')$.
    4. Set $M_i = \mathsf{Enc}_i(0_{\mathbb{G}}, R_i)$ for $i \in [n]$.
    5. Output $R_0 = \perp$ and $(M_1, \ldots, M_n)$.
- If $C \neq \emptyset$:
    1. Fix $i_0 \in C$.
    2. Define $f' : \mathbb{G} \to \{0, 1\}$ as follows. For every $a \in \mathbb{G}$:
        (a) Define x_C as $x_{i_0} = a$ and $x_i = 0_{\mathbb{G}}$ for $i \in C \setminus \{i_0\}$.
        (b) Let $f'(a) = h|_{\overline{C}, x_{\overline{C}}}(x_C)$ using the oracle $h|_{\overline{C}, x_{\overline{C}}}$.
    3. Define $h' : \mathbb{G}^n \to \{0, 1\}$ as $h'(a_1, \ldots, a_n) = f'(\sum_{i \in [n]} a_i)$ for all $a_1, \ldots, a_n \in \mathbb{G}$.
    4. Let $(R_0 = \perp, R_1, \ldots, R_n) \leftarrow \mathsf{Gen}(h')$.
    5. Set $M_i = \mathsf{Enc}_i(0_{\mathbb{G}}, R_i)$ for $i \in [n]$.
    6. Output $R_0 = \perp$, R_i for $i \in C$, and M_i for $i \in \overline{C}$.

Fig. 2. The simulator for the NIMPC protocol Π_1 for the class of abelian programs $\mathcal{A}_{\mathbb{G}}$.

Proof. **Correctness.** The message of P_1 is $e_{(0_{\mathbb{G}}, 0)}^{\top} B_{x_1} U_{\pi_1}$. The message of P_i with $1 < i < n$ is

$$M_i = \left(\prod_{j \in [m]} (U_{\pi_{i-1}}^{-1} B_{s_j} U_{\pi_{i-1}})^{\ell_j(x_i)} \right)(U_{\pi_{i-1}}^{-1} U_{\pi_i}) = U_{\pi_{i-1}}^{-1} B_{x_i} U_{\pi_i}.$$

The message of P_n is

$$M_i = (\prod_{j \in [m]} (U_{\pi_{n-1}}^{-1} B_{s_j} U_{\pi_{n-1}})^{\ell_j(x_n)})(U_{\pi_{n-1}}^{-1} U_{\pi_n})(U_{\pi_n}^{-1} \boldsymbol{w}_f) = U_{\pi_{n-1}}^{-1} B_{x_i} \boldsymbol{w}_f.$$

Therefore, letting $a = \sum_{i \in [n]} x_i$, we have

$$\prod_{i \in [n]} M_i = \boldsymbol{e}_{(0_{\mathbb{G}},0)}^{\top} \boldsymbol{B}_a \boldsymbol{w}_f$$

$$= \boldsymbol{e}_{(0_{\mathbb{G}},0)}^{\top} \boldsymbol{B}_a (\sum_{g \in \mathbb{G}} \boldsymbol{e}_{(g,1-f(g))})$$

$$= \boldsymbol{e}_{(0_{\mathbb{G}},0)}^{\top} (\sum_{g \in \mathbb{G}} \boldsymbol{e}_{(g-a,1-f(g))})$$

$$= \boldsymbol{e}_{(0_{\mathbb{G}},0)}^{\top} \boldsymbol{e}_{(0_{\mathbb{G}},1-f(a))}$$

$$= f(a).$$

Robustness. Let $C \subseteq [n]$. In the following, we show that for functions $f, f' : \mathbb{G} \to \{0,1\}$ and inputs $x_{\overline{C}}, x'_{\overline{C}}$ such that $h_f|_{\overline{C},x_{\overline{C}}} = h_{f'}|_{\overline{C},x'_{\overline{C}}}$, the messages of $\overline{C}$ and the correlated randomness of C are equally distributed in the protocol Π_1. Based on that observation, we can construct the simulator with oracle access to $h_f|_{\overline{C},x_{\overline{C}}}$ as follows: the simulator finds f' and $x'_{\overline{C}}$ giving the same residual function as $h_f|_{\overline{C},x_{\overline{C}}}$ and then executes Π_1 on $h_{f'}$ and $x'_{\overline{C}}$. Since $h_{f'}|_{\overline{C},x'_{\overline{C}}} = h_{f''}|_{\overline{C},0_{\overline{C}}}$ where $f''(x) = f'(x + \sum_{i \in \overline{C}} x'_i)$ and $0_{\overline{C}} = (0_{\mathbb{G}})_{i \in \overline{C}}$, the actual simulator $\mathrm{Sim}^{h|_{\overline{C},x_{\overline{C}}}}(C)$ described in Fig. 2 sets $x'_{\overline{C}} = 0_{\overline{C}}$ for simplicity.

We denote by $(R_C, M_{\overline{C}})(r)$ the joint distribution of the correlated randomness of C and the messages of $\overline{C}$ when Π_1 is executed on f and $x_{\overline{C}}$, where we specify the randomness $r \leftarrow_{\$} \mathfrak{S}_{\mathbb{H}}^n$ used by the protocol. Similarly, we define $(R'_C, M'_{\overline{C}})(r)$ for $r \leftarrow_{\$} \mathfrak{S}_{\mathbb{H}}^n$ as the joint distribution when Π_1 is executed on f' and $x'_{\overline{C}}$. It is sufficient to prove that there is a bijection $\phi : \mathfrak{S}_{\mathbb{H}}^n \to \mathfrak{S}_{\mathbb{H}}^n$ such that $(R_C, M_{\overline{C}})(r) = (R'_C, M'_{\overline{C}})(\phi(r))$ for all $r \in \mathfrak{S}_{\mathbb{H}}^n$.

The case of $C = \emptyset$. Let $a = \sum_{i \in [n]} x_i$ and $a' = \sum_{i \in [n]} x'_i$. Let $d_i = \sum_{j > i} x_j$ and $d'_i = \sum_{j > i} x'_j$ for $i \in [n]$, where we define $d_n = d'_n = 0_{\mathbb{G}}$. Let $S_f = \{(g, 1 - f(g)) \in \mathbb{H} \mid g \in \mathbb{G}\}$ and $S_{f'} = \{(g, 1 - f'(g)) \in \mathbb{H} \mid g \in \mathbb{G}\}$. From the definition, we have that $|S_f| = |S_{f'}| = |\mathbb{G}|$. It also follows from $h_f(x_1, \ldots, x_n) = h_{f'}(x'_1, \ldots, x'_n)$ that $(a, 0) \in S_f$ if and only if $(a', 0) \in S_{f'}$. Therefore, there is a permutation $\rho \in \mathfrak{S}_{\mathbb{H}}$ such that $\rho(a', 0) = (a, 0)$ and $\rho(S_{f'}) = S_f$. Define $\phi : \mathfrak{S}_{\mathbb{H}}^n \to \mathfrak{S}_{\mathbb{H}}^n$ as $\phi(\pi_1, \ldots, \pi_n) = (\pi'_1, \ldots, \pi'_n)$, where $\pi'_i = \pi_i \circ \tau_{-d_i} \circ \rho \circ \tau_{d'_i}$ for $i \in [n-1]$ and $\pi'_n = \pi_n$. Recall that τ_x is defined as $\tau_x(g, b) = (g + x, b)$ for $(g, b) \in \mathbb{H}$. From the definition of B_x's and permutation matrices, we have that $U_{\pi'_i} = B_{d'_i} U_\rho B_{-d_i} U_{\pi_i}$. We fix $r = (\pi_1, \ldots, \pi_n) \in \mathfrak{S}_{\mathbb{H}}^n$ and simply write $M_i = M_i(r)$ and $M'_i = M'_i(\phi(r))$.

Then, we have $M_i = M'_i$ for all $i \in [n]$ from the following:

- $i = n$: From the definition of ρ, we have

$$\sum_{s \in S_f} e_s = \sum_{s' \in S_{f'}} e_{\rho(s')} \iff w_f = U_\rho^{-1} w_{f'}$$

$$\iff B_{x_n} w_f = (B_{x_n} U_\rho^{-1} B_{-x'_n}) B_{x'_n} w_{f'}$$

$$\iff U_{\pi_{n-1}}^{-1} B_{x_n} w_f = U_{\pi'_{n-1}}^{-1} B_{x'_n} w_{f'}.$$

- $1 < i < n$: We have

$$U_{\pi'_{i-1}}^{-1} B_{x'_i} U_{\pi'_i} = U_{\pi_{i-1}}^{-1} B_{d_{i-1}} U_\rho^{-1} B_{-d'_{i-1}} B_{x'_i} B_{d'_i} U_\rho B_{-d_i} U_{\pi_i}$$

$$= U_{\pi_{i-1}}^{-1} B_{d_{i-1}-d_i} U_{\pi_i}$$

$$= U_{\pi_{i-1}}^{-1} B_{x_i} U_{\pi_i}.$$

- $i = 1$: From the definition of ρ, we have

$$(a,0) = \rho(a',0) \iff e_{(a,0)}^\top = e_{(a',0)}^\top U_\rho$$

$$\iff e_{(x_1,0)}^\top B_{d_1} = e_{(x'_1,0)}^\top B_{d'_1} U_\rho$$

$$\iff e_{(x_1,0)}^\top = e_{(x'_1,0)}^\top U_{\pi'_1} U_{\pi_1}^{-1}$$

$$\iff e_{(0_G,0)}^\top B_{x_1} U_{\pi_1} = e_{(0_G,0)}^\top B_{x'_1} U_{\pi'_1}$$

The case of $C \neq \emptyset$. Let $a = \sum_{j \in \overline{C}}(x_j - x'_j) \in G$, $d_i = \sum_{j>i, j \in \overline{C}}(x'_j - x_j) + a \in G$ for $i \in [n]$, where we define $d_n = a$. Since the residual functions $h_f|_{\overline{C}, x_{\overline{C}}}, h_{f'}|_{\overline{C}, x'_{\overline{C}}}$ are identical to each other, we have

$$f\left(g' + \sum_{j \in \overline{C}} x_j\right) = f'\left(g' + \sum_{j \in \overline{C}} x'_j\right) (\forall g' \in \mathbb{G})$$

$$\iff f(g) = f'(g - a) (\forall g \in \mathbb{G}).$$

Define $\phi : \mathfrak{S}_{\mathbb{H}}^n \to \mathfrak{S}_{\mathbb{H}}^n$ as $\phi(\pi_1, \ldots, \pi_n) = (\pi'_1, \ldots, \pi'_n)$, where $\pi'_i = \pi_i \circ \tau_{d_i}$ for $i \in [n]$. Then, from the above observation we have that $B_a w_f = w_{f'}$ since

$$B_a w_f = w_{f'} \iff \sum_{g \in G} e_{(g-a, 1-f(g))} = \sum_{g' \in G} e_{(g', 1-f'(g'))}$$

$$\iff \sum_{g' \in G} \left(e_{(g', 1-f(g'+a))} - e_{(g', 1-f'(g'))} \right) = 0$$

$$\iff f(g) = f'(g - a) (\forall g \in \mathbb{G}).$$

Observe that for any $1 < i \leq n$ and any $x \in G$,

$$U_{\pi'_{i-1}}^{-1} B_x U_{\pi'_i} = U_{\pi_{i-1}}^{-1} B_{-d_{i-1}} B_x B_{d_i} U_{\pi_i} = U_{\pi_{i-1}}^{-1} B_{x+(d_i-d_{i-1})} U_{\pi_i}. \tag{1}$$

We also have that

$$d_i - d_{i-1} = \begin{cases} x_i - x'_i, & \text{if } i \in \overline{C}, \\ 0_{\mathbb{G}}, & \text{otherwise.} \end{cases}$$

We fix $r = (\pi_1, \dots, \pi_n) \in \mathfrak{S}_{\mathbb{H}}^n$ and simply write $R_i = R_i(r), R'_i = R'_i(\phi(r))$ for $i \in C$ and $M_i = M_i(r), M'_i = M'_i(\phi(r))$ for $i \in \overline{C}$. Now, we have $R_i = R'_i$ for $i \in C$ and $M_i = M'_i$ for $i \in \overline{C}$ from the following:

- $i = n$:
  - If $n \in C$, then $d_n = d_{n-1}$. Therefore, substituting $x = 0_{\mathbb{G}}$ and $x = s_j$ into (1), we have $U_{\pi'_{n-1}}^{-1} U_{\pi'_n} = U_{\pi_{n-1}}^{-1} U_{\pi_n}$ and $U_{\pi'_{n-1}}^{-1} B_{s_j} U_{\pi'_n} = U_{\pi_{n-1}}^{-1} B_{s_j} U_{\pi_n}$ for $j \in [m]$, respectively. Furthermore, since $d_n = a$, we also have

    $$U_{\pi'_n}^{-1} \boldsymbol{w}_{f'} = U_{\pi_n}^{-1} B_{-d_n} \boldsymbol{w}_{f'} = U_{\pi_n}^{-1} \boldsymbol{w}_f.$$

  - If $n \in \overline{C}$, then $d_n - d_{n-1} = x_n - x'_n$, i.e., $x'_n - d_{n-1} = x_n - a$. Therefore,

    $$U_{\pi'_{n-1}}^{-1} B_{x'_n} \boldsymbol{w}_{f'} = U_{\pi_{n-1}}^{-1} B_{x'_n - d_{n-1}} B_a \boldsymbol{w}_f = U_{\pi_{n-1}}^{-1} B_{x_n} \boldsymbol{w}_f.$$

- $1 < i < n$:
  - If $i \in C$, then $d_i = d_{i-1}$. Therefore, substituting $x = 0_{\mathbb{G}}$ and $x = s_j$ into (1), we have $U_{\pi'_{i-1}}^{-1} U_{\pi'_i} = U_{\pi_{i-1}}^{-1} U_{\pi_i}$ and $U_{\pi'_{i-1}}^{-1} B_{s_j} U_{\pi'_i} = U_{\pi_{i-1}}^{-1} B_{s_j} U_{\pi_i}$ for $j \in [m]$, respectively.
  - If $i \in \overline{C}$, then $d_i - d_{i-1} = x_i - x'_i$. Therefore, substituting $x = x'_i$ into (1), we have $U_{\pi'_{i-1}}^{-1} B_{x'_i} U_{\pi'_i} = U_{\pi_{i-1}}^{-1} B_{x_i} U_{\pi_i}$.

- $i = 1$:
  - If $1 \in C$, then $d_1 = 0_{\mathbb{G}}$ and hence $U_{\pi'_1} = U_{\pi_1}$.
  - If $1 \in \overline{C}$, then $d_1 = x_1 - x'_1$ and hence

    $$\boldsymbol{e}_{(0_{\mathbb{G}},0)}^\top B_{x'_1} U_{\pi'_1} = \boldsymbol{e}_{(0_{\mathbb{G}},0)}^\top B_{x'_1} B_{x_1 - x'_1} U_{\pi_1} = \boldsymbol{e}_{(0_{\mathbb{G}},0)}^\top B_{x_1} U_{\pi_1}.$$

Communication complexity. The maximum component of on-line communication is the messages M_i of the players i with $1 < i < n$, each of which consists of one permutation matrix over $\mathbb{F}_2$ of size $|\mathbb{H}|$. The maximum component of off-line communication is the randomness R_n of the player n, which consists of $|S| + 1$ permutation matrices over $\mathbb{F}_2$ of size $|\mathbb{H}|$ and a vector over $\mathbb{F}_2$ of dimension $|\mathbb{H}|$. Note that every permutation matrix can be expressed by $|\mathbb{H}| \lceil \log |\mathbb{H}| \rceil$ bits. Since $|\mathbb{H}| = 2|\mathbb{G}|$, the protocol achieves the communication complexity in the statement. $\qquad \square$

4.3 Abelian Programs with Limited Input Domains

Next, we present a t-robust protocol for the class $\mathcal{A}_{\mathbb{G}}^{S_1, \dots, S_n}$ of abelian programs with limited input domains. As mentioned in Sect. 3.2, NIMPC protocols for $\mathcal{A}_{\mathbb{G}}$ is not directly applicable to $\mathcal{A}_{\mathbb{G}}^{S_1, \dots, S_n}$. Nevertheless, it is possible to obtain protocols for $\mathcal{A}_{\mathbb{G}}^{S_1, \dots, S_n}$ from the ones for $\mathcal{A}_{\mathbb{G}}$ with the help of the BKR transformation [6]. Note that we will show in Sect. 6 that their NIMPC protocol for outputting-message functions used in the transformation does not satisfy the desired security. Therefore, it is necessary to replace their protocol with our modified protocol given also in Sect. 6 when actually applying the BKR transformation.

Proposition 1 ([6]). *If there is a 0-robust NIMPC protocol for a class of functions $\mathcal{H}$ with communication complexity α, then for any t, there is a t-robust NIMPC protocol for $\mathcal{H}$ with communication complexity $p^{t+O(1)}\alpha$, where d is the maximum size of the input domains of functions in $\mathcal{H}$ and p is the smallest prime power such that $p \geq \max\{n, d\}$.*

Clearly, the protocol in Theorem 1 satisfies 0-robustness for $\mathcal{A}_{\mathbb{G}}$. Since the simulator to prove 0-robustness only receives the output of the function rather than a residual function, the simulation works regardless of whether the input domains are limited or not. Consequently, the 0-robust protocol also satisfies 0-robustness even for $\mathcal{A}_{\mathbb{G}}^{S_1,\ldots,S_n}$. By applying the BKR transformation to it, we obtain a t-robust protocol for $\mathcal{A}_{\mathbb{G}}^{S_1,\ldots,S_n}$ with some overhead in communication complexity.

Corollary 1. *Let $\mathbb{G}$ be a finite abelian group and $S_1,\ldots,S_n$ be subsets of $\mathbb{G}$. Then, there exists a t-robust NIMPC protocol Π for $\mathcal{A}_{\mathbb{G}}^{S_1,\ldots,S_n}$ such that $\mathsf{CC}(\Pi) = |\mathbb{G}|(\log|\mathbb{G}|)^2 p^{t+O(1)}$, where p is a prime power with $p \geq \max\{n, |S_1|,\ldots,|S_n|\}$.*

The authors of [3] present another method to limit the inputs of players while it only works for abelian programs. However, this method applied to Theorem 1 only provides us with a protocol with communication complexity $|\mathbb{G}|^2(\log|\mathbb{G}|)^2(nd)^{t+O(1)}$ and hence the protocol in Corollary 1 is more efficient.

Example 1. We apply our protocol for $\mathcal{A}_{\mathbb{G}}^{S_1,\ldots,S_n}$ to symmetric functions. We have noted in Sect. 3.2 that the class of all symmetric functions over $[d]^n$ is equivalent to $\mathcal{A}_{\mathbb{G}}^{S_1,\ldots,S_n}$ for $\mathbb{G} = (\mathbb{Z}_{n+1})^d$ and $S_1 = \cdots = S_n = \{e_1,\ldots,e_d\} \subseteq \mathbb{G}$, where $e_i \in (\mathbb{Z}_{n+1})^d$ is the i-th unit vector. Note that $\mathbb{G}$ can be generated by at most d elements. Therefore, we obtain a t-robust NIMPC protocol Π for the class of all symmetric functions over $[d]^n$ such that

$$\mathsf{CC}(\Pi) = p^{t+O(1)} \times O((n+1)^d d^2 (\log n)) = (\max\{n, d\})^{(1+o(1))t} n^{(1+o(1))d}.$$

Here, p is the smallest prime power such that $p \geq \max\{n, d\}$, which is chosen as $p = O(\max\{n, d\})$. This result is better than $(nd)^{(1+o(1))t} n^{(3+o(1))d}$ [3] and also improves $n^{(\log n+O(1))d}$ [6] if $t = o(\log n)$. In the case of boolean symmetric functions, i.e., $d = 2$, our protocol is more efficient than another t-robust protocol with communication complexity $n^{\log\log n+\log t+O(1)}$ [6] if $t = o(\log\log n)$.

5   New NIMPC Protocols for Linear Classifiers

5.1   Formalization of Linear Classifiers

Let $\mathbb{F}_q$ be a finite field and $S_1,\ldots,S_n$ be subsets of $\mathbb{F}_q$. Let $\mathcal{X}_i = S_i$ for $i \in [n]$ and $\mathcal{X} = \mathcal{X}_1 \times \cdots \times \mathcal{X}_n$. We say that a function $f : \mathbb{F}_q \to \{0,1\}$ is proper if

$|f^{-1}(1)| \notin \{0, q\}$. Define the linear classifier $h_{f,w} : \mathcal{X} \to \{0,1\}$ associated with $f : \mathbb{F}_q \to \{0,1\}$ and $w = (w_i)_{i \in [n]} \in \mathbb{F}_q^n$ as $h_{f,w}(x_1, \ldots, x_n) = f(\sum_{i \in [n]} w_i x_i)$. We then define $\mathcal{L}_{\mathbb{F}_q}^{S_1, \ldots, S_n}$ be the class of all the linear classifiers, that is,

$$\mathcal{L}_{\mathbb{F}_q}^{S_1, \ldots, S_n} = \{h_{f,w} \mid f : \mathbb{F}_q \to \{0,1\} \text{ is proper and } w \in \mathbb{F}_q^n\}.$$

We simply write $\mathcal{L}_{\mathbb{F}_q}$ if $S_1 = \cdots = S_n = \mathbb{F}_q$.

We note that focusing on proper functions does not limit the expressive power of linear classifiers. If $|f^{-1}(1)| = 0$, i.e., $f(x) = 0$ for all $x \in \mathbb{F}_q$, then the linear classifier $h_{f,w}$ for any $w \in \mathbb{F}_q^n$ is equivalent to $h_{f_0,0}$, where $f_0(x)$ outputs 0 if and only if $x = 0$. Similarly, any linear classifier $h_{f,w}$ with $|f^{-1}(1)| = q$ is equivalent to a linear classifier associated with some proper function.

In the same manner as abelian programs, we can extend linear classifiers to the ones outputting more than one bits by computing each output bit separately. Specifically, we first extend the definition of proper functions as follows. A function $f : \mathbb{F}_q \to \{0,1\}^m$ is said to be proper if $p_i \circ f : \mathbb{F}_q \to \{0,1\}$ is proper (in the above sense) for every $i \in [m]$, where $p_i : \{0,1\}^m \ni (b_j)_{j \in [m]} \mapsto b_i \in \{0,1\}$ is the i-th projection. Now, for $S_1, \ldots, S_n \subseteq \mathbb{F}_q$, we define the class of linear classifiers outputting m bits as

$$\mathcal{H}_m := \{h_{f,w}^m : \mathcal{X} \to \{0,1\}^m \mid f : \mathbb{F}_q \to \{0,1\}^m \text{ is proper and } w \in \mathbb{F}_q^n\},$$

where $\mathcal{X} = \prod_{i \in [n]} S_i$ and $h_{f,w}^m(x_1, \ldots, x_n) = f(\sum_{i \in [n]} w_i x_i)$. From the definition of proper functions, we have $\mathcal{H}_m = \{h : \mathcal{X} \to \{0,1\}^m \mid h = (h_1, \ldots, h_m), \; h_i \in \mathcal{L}_{\mathbb{F}_q}^{S_1, \ldots, S_n}\}$ for $\mathcal{L}_{\mathbb{F}_q}^{S_1, \ldots, S_n}$. Hence, given an NIMPC protocol Π for $\mathcal{L}_{\mathbb{F}_q}^{S_1, \ldots, S_n}$, we can construct a protocol Π_m for $\mathcal{H}_m$ with m times higher communication complexity by running Π for each $h_i \in \mathcal{L}_{\mathbb{F}_q}^{S_1, \ldots, S_n}$.

We assume in the above that all the arithmetic operations are performed in a finite field. For real-world applications, it is necessary to deal with weights and inputs expressed as real numbers. We can still use the above linear classifiers by embedding these values into a sufficiently large prime field using a fixed-point number representation.

5.2   NIMPC Protocols for Linear Classifiers

We first propose a fully robust protocol for $\mathcal{L}_{\mathbb{F}_q}$ (Theorem 2) and then construct a protocol for $\mathcal{L}_{\mathbb{F}_q}^{S_1, \ldots, S_n}$ by applying the BKR transformation (Corollary 2).

Let $f : \mathbb{F}_q \to \{0,1\}$ be a proper function and $w \in \mathbb{F}_q^n$ be a vector of weights. In Sect. 2.2, we have already shown a construction of a fully robust protocol for the class consisting only of the specific linear classifier $\{h_{f,w}\} \subseteq \mathcal{L}_{\mathbb{F}_q}$. In that protocol, if $f^{-1}(1) = \{u_1, \ldots, u_k\}$, the evaluator outputs $f(\sum_{i \in [n]} w_i x_i)$ according to the number of zeros of $u_0 = u - \sum_{i \in [n]} \mathbf{1}_k w_i x_i$, where $u = [u_1, \ldots, u_k]^\top \in \mathbb{F}_q^k$ and $\mathbf{1}_N$ denotes the vector of dimension N whose entries are all one. It can be seen that the technique for randomizing u_0 is equivalent to multiplying u_0 by

$T = \mathrm{diag}(r_1, \ldots, r_k) U_\pi \in \mathbb{F}_q^{k \times k}$ for $r_i \leftarrow_\$ \mathbb{F}_q \setminus \{0\}$ $(i \in [k])$ and $\pi \leftarrow_\$ \mathfrak{S}_{[k]}$. However, there remains the problem that the dimension $k = |f^{-1}(1)|$ is assumed to be constant, which is why it does not work for the class of all the linear classifiers.

A simple solution to hide k is *padding* the vector $\boldsymbol{u}$ with some $q - k$ elements $u_j \in \mathbb{F}_q$ $(k < j \leq q)$ to ensure that its dimension should be q. Accordingly, we redefine $\boldsymbol{u}_0$ as $\boldsymbol{u}_0 = \boldsymbol{u} - \sum_{i \in [n]} 1_q w_i x_i$. In this solution, however, there would exist some inputs x_i such that $\sum_{i \in [n]} w_i x_i \notin f^{-1}(1)$ but $u_{k+1} = \sum_{i \in [n]} w_i x_i$ and then the protocol incorrectly outputs 1. To overcome it, we consider an extension field $\mathbb{K}$ of $\mathbb{F}_q$ and randomly choose u_j $(k < j \leq q)$ from $\mathbb{K} \setminus \mathbb{F}_q$. Since $\sum_{i \in [n]} w_i x_i \in \mathbb{F}_q$, the above error never happens. Accordingly, we now uniformly select a permutation π and elements r_i $(i \in [q])$ from $\mathfrak{S}_{[q]}$ and $\mathbb{K} \setminus \{0\}$, respectively, and set $T = \mathrm{diag}(r_1, \ldots, r_q) U_\pi$. We also sample $\boldsymbol{s}_i$ $(i \in [n])$ from $\mathbb{K}^q$. The important point is that regardless of whether $x \in \mathbb{F}_q \setminus \{0\}$ or $x \in \mathbb{K} \setminus \mathbb{F}_q$, the product rx is uniformly distributed over $\mathbb{K} \setminus \{0\}$ if $r \leftarrow_\$ \mathbb{K} \setminus \{0\}$. This is why we consider an extension *field* of $\mathbb{F}_q$ rather than an extension *ring*. The above modified protocol communicates at most two vectors over $\mathbb{K}$ of dimension q. Since we can choose $\mathbb{K}$ as any extension field of $\mathbb{F}_q$, we may assume that $|\mathbb{K}| = q^2$. Therefore, the communication complexity is at most $O(q \log q)$.

Protocol Π_2 for $\mathcal{L}_{\mathbb{F}_q}$

$\mathsf{Gen}(h_{f,w})$:
1. Set $S = f^{-1}(1) = \{u_1, \ldots, u_k\} \subseteq \mathbb{F}_q$ and choose $u_j \leftarrow_\$ \mathbb{K} \setminus \mathbb{F}_q$ $(k < j \leq q)$.
2. Set $\boldsymbol{u} = [u_1, \ldots, u_q]^\top \in \mathbb{K}^q$.
3. Choose $r_i \leftarrow_\$ \mathbb{K} \setminus \{0\}$ $(i \in [q])$, $\pi \leftarrow_\$ \mathfrak{S}_{[q]}$, and $\boldsymbol{s}_i \leftarrow_\$ \mathbb{K}^q$ $(i \in [n])$.
4. Set $T = \mathrm{diag}(r_1, \ldots, r_q) U_\pi \in \mathbb{K}^{q \times q}$.
5. Output $R_0 = T\boldsymbol{u} + \sum_{i \in [n]} \boldsymbol{s}_i$ and $R_i = (T 1_q w_i, \boldsymbol{s}_i)$ for $i \in [n]$.

$\mathsf{Enc}_i(x_i, R_i)$:
1. Parse R_i as $(\boldsymbol{\rho}_{i1}, \boldsymbol{\rho}_{i2})$, where $\boldsymbol{\rho}_{i1}, \boldsymbol{\rho}_{i2} \in \mathbb{K}^q$.
2. Output $M_i = \boldsymbol{\rho}_{i1} x_i + \boldsymbol{\rho}_{i2}$.

$\mathsf{Dec}(R_0, M_1, \ldots, M_n)$:
1. If at least one entry of $R_0 - \sum_{i \in [n]} M_i$ is zero, then output 1 and otherwise output 0.

Fig. 3. The NIMPC protocol Π_2 for the class of linear classifiers $\mathcal{L}_{\mathbb{F}_q}$.

Theorem 2. *Let $\mathbb{F}_q$ be a finite field. Let $\mathcal{X}_1 = \cdots = \mathcal{X}_n = \mathbb{F}_q$ and $\mathcal{X} = \mathcal{X}_1 \times \cdots \times \mathcal{X}_n$. Then, the protocol Π_2 described in Fig. 3 is a fully robust NIMPC protocol for $\mathcal{L}_{\mathbb{F}_q}$ such that $\mathsf{CC}_{\mathrm{on}}(\Pi_2) = 2q\lceil 2 \log q \rceil$ and $\mathsf{CC}_{\mathrm{off}}(\Pi_2) = q\lceil 2 \log q \rceil$.*

Proof. **Correctness.** Let $h = h_{f,w}$ be a function to compute. Let $S = f^{-1}(1) = \{u_1, \ldots, u_k\}$, where $k = |S|$ and $u_i \in \mathbb{F}_q$ for $i \in [k]$. Correctness follows from the following observation: $h(x_1, \ldots, x_n) = 1$ if and only if the number of 0's in

---

Simulator $\mathrm{Sim}^{h|_{\overline{C}, x_{\overline{C}}}}(C)$ for Π_2

Input. A set of colluding players C.

Oracle access. The residual function $h|_{\overline{C}, x_{\overline{C}}}$ for the inputs $x_{\overline{C}}$ of honest players.

Output. Correlated randomness R_0 and $(R_i)_{i \in C}$ of the colluding players and messages $(M_i)_{i \in \overline{C}}$ of the honest players.

Algorithm.

- If $C = \emptyset$:
    1. Choose $(\tilde{v}_j)_{j \in [q]} \in \mathbb{K}^q$ uniformly at random from $(\mathbb{K} \setminus \{0\})^q$ if $h(x_1, \ldots, x_n) = 0$ and otherwise from $\{0\} \times (\mathbb{K} \setminus \{0\})^{q-1}$.
    2. Choose $\pi \leftarrow_{\$} \mathfrak{S}_q$ and set $\tilde{v} = (\tilde{v}_{\pi(j)})_{j \in [q]}$.
    3. Choose $\tilde{s}_i \leftarrow_{\$} \mathbb{K}^q$ $(i \in [n])$.
    4. Output $R_0 = \tilde{v} + \sum_{i \in [n]} \tilde{s}_i$ and $M_i = \tilde{s}_i$ for $i \in [n]$.

- If $C \neq \emptyset$:
    1. For $x_C = (x_i)_{i \in C} \in \mathbb{F}_q^{|C|}$, construct a set Δ_{x_C} using the oracle $h|_{\overline{C}, x_{\overline{C}}}$ as

$$\Delta_{x_C} = \{\alpha \in \mathbb{F}_q \mid h|_{\overline{C}, x_{\overline{C}}}(x_C \alpha) = 1\}.$$

    2. Construct a set Γ as $\Gamma = \{x_C \in \mathbb{F}_q^{|C|} \mid |\Delta_{x_C}| \in \{0, q\}\}$.
    3. Do the following.
        - If $|\Gamma| = q^{|C|}$:
          (a) Set $\tilde{w}_C = \mathbf{0}$.
          (b) Choose $(\tilde{v}_j)_{j \in [q]} \in \mathbb{K}^q$ uniformly at random from $(\mathbb{K} \setminus \{0\})^q$ if $|\Delta_{x_C}| = 0$ for all x_C and otherwise from $\{0\} \times (\mathbb{K} \setminus \{0\})^{q-1}$.
          (c) Choose $\pi \leftarrow_{\$} \mathfrak{S}_q$ and set $\tilde{v} = (\tilde{v}_{\pi(j)})_{j \in [q]}$.
          (d) Choose $\tilde{s}_i \leftarrow_{\$} \mathbb{K}^q$ $(i \in [n])$.
          (e) Output $R_0 = \tilde{v} + \sum_{i \in [n]} \tilde{s}_i$, $R_i = (0_q, \tilde{s}_i)$ for $i \in C$, and $M_i = \tilde{s}_i$ for $i \in \overline{C}$.
        - If $|\Gamma| \neq q^{|C|}$:
          (a) Fix $\tilde{w}_C = (\tilde{w}_i) \in \Gamma^{\perp} \setminus \{\mathbf{0}\}$.
          (b) Fix $x_C = (x_i)_{i \in C} \in \mathbb{F}_q^{|C|} \setminus \Gamma$ and write $\Delta_{x_C} = \{\alpha_1, \ldots, \alpha_k\}$, where $k = |\Delta_{x_C}|$.
          (c) Set $\tilde{v}_j = \alpha_j (\sum_{i \in C} \tilde{w}_i x_i)$ $(j \in [k])$, choose $\tilde{v}_j \leftarrow_{\$} \mathbb{K} \setminus \mathbb{F}_q$ $(k < j \leq q)$, and set $\tilde{v} = (\tilde{v}_j)_{j \in [q]}$.
          (d) Choose $\tilde{r}_j \leftarrow_{\$} \mathbb{K} \setminus \{0\}$ $(j \in [q])$, $\tilde{\pi} \leftarrow_{\$} \mathfrak{S}_{[q]}$, and $\tilde{s}_i \leftarrow_{\$} \mathbb{K}^q$ $(i \in [n])$ and set $\tilde{T} = \mathrm{diag}(\tilde{r}_1, \ldots, \tilde{r}_q)U_{\tilde{\pi}}$.
          (e) Output $R_0 = \tilde{T}\tilde{v} + \sum_{i \in [n]} \tilde{s}_i$, $R_i = (\tilde{T} 1_q \tilde{w}_i, \tilde{s}_i)$ for $i \in C$, and $M_i = \tilde{s}_i$ for $i \in \overline{C}$.

Fig. 4. The simulator for the NIMPC protocol Π_2 for the class of linear classifiers $\mathcal{L}_{\mathbb{F}_q}$.

$u - \sum_{i \in [n]} 1_q w_i x_i$ is at least one, which is in turn equivalent to the condition that the number of 0's in $R_0 - \sum_{i \in [n]} M_i = T(u - \sum_{i \in [n]} 1_q w_i x_i)$ is at least one.

Robustness. Let $C \subseteq [n]$. The adversary's view is

$$(\boldsymbol{Tu} + \sum_{i \in [n]} \boldsymbol{s}_i; (\boldsymbol{T1}_q w_i)_{i \in C}, (\boldsymbol{s}_i)_{i \in C}; (\boldsymbol{T1}_q w_i x_i + \boldsymbol{s}_i)_{i \in \overline{C}}),$$

where $\boldsymbol{T} = \mathrm{diag}(r_1, \dots, r_q)\boldsymbol{P}_\pi$, $r_i \leftarrow_{\$} \mathbb{K}\backslash\{0\}$ ($i \in [q]$), $\pi \leftarrow_{\$} \mathfrak{S}_q$, $\boldsymbol{u} = [u_1, \dots, u_q]^\top$, $u_j \leftarrow_{\$} \mathbb{K}\backslash\mathbb{F}_q$ ($k < j \leq q$), and $\boldsymbol{s}_i \leftarrow_{\$} \mathbb{K}^q$ ($i \in [n]$). It is sufficient to show that the following distribution can be perfectly simulated:

$$(\boldsymbol{Tv}; (\boldsymbol{T1}_q w_i)_{i \in C}, (\boldsymbol{s}_i)_{i \in C}; (\boldsymbol{T1}_q w_i x_i + \boldsymbol{s}_i)_{i \in \overline{C}}), \tag{2}$$

where we set $\overline{\gamma} = \boldsymbol{w}_{\overline{C}}^\top \boldsymbol{x}_{\overline{C}} = \sum_{i \in \overline{C}} w_i x_i$ and $\boldsymbol{v} = \boldsymbol{u} - \boldsymbol{1}_q \overline{\gamma}$. This is because the original view can be obtained by computing $\boldsymbol{Tu} + \sum_{i \in [n]} \boldsymbol{s}_i = \boldsymbol{Tv} + \sum_{i \in C} \boldsymbol{s}_i + \sum_{i \in \overline{C}}(\boldsymbol{T1}_q w_i x_i + \boldsymbol{s}_i)$.

<u>The case of $C = \emptyset$.</u> We can see below that the distribution of (2) is simulated by the simulator described in Fig. 4:

- If $h(x_1, \dots, x_n) = 0$, then $u_j \neq \overline{\gamma}$ for all $j \in [k]$. In addition, $u_j \neq \overline{\gamma}$ for all $k < j \leq q$ since the u_j's are selected from $\mathbb{K}\backslash\mathbb{F}_q$ and $\overline{\gamma}$ is an element of $\mathbb{F}_q$. Therefore, $\boldsymbol{v} \in (\mathbb{K}\backslash\{0\})^q$ and hence $\boldsymbol{Tv}$ is uniformly distributed over $(\mathbb{K}\backslash\{0\})^q$. Since the $\boldsymbol{s}_i$'s are chosen independent of $\boldsymbol{T}$, we have that $(\boldsymbol{Tv}; (\boldsymbol{T1}_q w_i x_i + \boldsymbol{s}_i)_{i \in [n]}) \equiv (\tilde{\boldsymbol{v}}; (\tilde{\boldsymbol{s}}_i)_{i \in [n]})$ for vectors $\tilde{\boldsymbol{v}}$ and $\tilde{\boldsymbol{s}}_i$ ($i \in [n]$) sampled by the simulator.
- If $h(x_1, \dots, x_n) = 1$, then there is the unique index $j \in [k]$ such that $u_j = \overline{\gamma}$. Again, it holds that $u_j \neq \overline{\gamma}$ for all $k < j \leq q$. Therefore, the number of 0's in $\boldsymbol{v}$ is exactly one and $\boldsymbol{Tv}$ is uniformly distributed over the set of all the vectors of $\mathbb{K}^q$ of Hamming weight $q - 1$. Since the $\boldsymbol{s}_i$'s are chosen independent of $\boldsymbol{T}$, we have that $(\boldsymbol{Tv}; (\boldsymbol{T1}_q w_i x_i + \boldsymbol{s}_i)_{i \in [n]}) \equiv (\tilde{\boldsymbol{v}}; (\tilde{\boldsymbol{s}}_i)_{i \in [n]})$ for vectors $\tilde{\boldsymbol{v}}$ and $\tilde{\boldsymbol{s}}_i$ ($i \in [n]$) sampled by the simulator.

<u>The case of $C \neq \emptyset$.</u> To begin with, observe that $\Delta_{\boldsymbol{x}_C}$ constructed by the simulator described in Fig. 4 satisfies $|\Delta_{\boldsymbol{x}_C}| \in \{0, q\}$ if and only if $\sum_{i \in C} w_i x_i = 0$ for any $\boldsymbol{x}_C = (x_i)_{i \in C}$. Indeed, if $\sum_{i \in C} w_i x_i = 0$, then for every $\alpha \in \mathbb{F}_q$, we have that

$$h|_{\overline{C}, \boldsymbol{x}_{\overline{C}}}(\boldsymbol{x}_C \alpha) = 1 \iff \sum_{i \in C} w_i x_i \alpha = u_j - \overline{\gamma} \ (\exists j \in [k])$$

$$\iff 0 = u_j - \overline{\gamma} \ (\exists j \in [k])$$

$$\iff h|_{\overline{C}, \boldsymbol{x}_{\overline{C}}}(\boldsymbol{0}) = 1.$$

Therefore, $h|_{\overline{C}, \boldsymbol{x}_{\overline{C}}}(\boldsymbol{x}_C \alpha) = h|_{\overline{C}, \boldsymbol{x}_{\overline{C}}}(\boldsymbol{0})$ for all $\alpha \in \mathbb{F}_q$ and hence $|\Delta_{\boldsymbol{x}_C}|$ is either q or 0 depending on whether $h|_{\overline{C}, \boldsymbol{x}_{\overline{C}}}(\boldsymbol{0}) = 1$ or not. Conversely, if $\sum_{i \in C} w_i x_i = \delta \neq 0$, then for every $\alpha \in \mathbb{F}_q$, we have that

$$h|_{\overline{C}, \boldsymbol{x}_{\overline{C}}}(\boldsymbol{x}_C \alpha) = 1 \iff \sum_{i \in C} w_i x_i \alpha = u_j - \overline{\gamma} \ (\exists j \in [k])$$

$$\iff \alpha = \delta^{-1}(u_j - \overline{\gamma}) \ (\exists j \in [k]).$$

Therefore, $|\Delta_{\boldsymbol{x}_C}| = k = |S| = |f^{-1}(1)| \notin \{0, q\}$.

It is then possible to determine $\boldsymbol{w}_C$ up to a scalar multiple from the size of the set Γ. Indeed, if $\boldsymbol{w}_C = \boldsymbol{0}$, then $|\Delta_{\boldsymbol{x}_C}| \in \{0, q\}$ for all $\boldsymbol{x}_C$ and hence $|\Gamma| = q^{|C|}$. If $\boldsymbol{w}_C \neq \boldsymbol{0}$, then a vector $\boldsymbol{x}_C$ satisfies $|\Delta_{\boldsymbol{x}_C}| \in \{0, q\}$ if and only if it is orthogonal to $\boldsymbol{w}_C$ and hence $|\Gamma| = q^{|C|-1}$. In the latter case, we have that $\Gamma^\perp = \boldsymbol{w}_C \cdot \mathbb{F}_q := \{\boldsymbol{w}_C\beta \mid \beta \in \mathbb{F}_q\}$ and so any non-zero vector in $\Gamma^\perp$ is a salar multiple of $\boldsymbol{w}_C$.

Now, we can see that the simulator in Fig. 4 simulates the distribution of (2):

- If $\Gamma = q^{|C|}$, we surely know that $\boldsymbol{w}_C = \boldsymbol{0}$ and particularly, $\widetilde{\boldsymbol{w}}_C = \boldsymbol{w}_C$. In this case, we should have either $|\Delta_{\boldsymbol{x}_C}| = 0$ for all $\boldsymbol{x}_C$ or $|\Delta_{\boldsymbol{x}_C}| = q$ for all $\boldsymbol{x}_C$ since $|\Delta_{\boldsymbol{x}_C}|$ only depends on $h|_{\overline{C}, \boldsymbol{x}_{\overline{C}}}(0)$ regardless of $\boldsymbol{x}_C$. If $|\Delta_{\boldsymbol{x}_C}| = 0$ for all $\boldsymbol{x}_C$, then it should hold that $h|_{\overline{C}, \boldsymbol{x}_{\overline{C}}}(0) = 0$ and $\overline{\gamma} \notin S$. Then, $\boldsymbol{v} \in (\mathbb{K}\backslash\{0\})^q$ and hence $\boldsymbol{Tv}$ is uniformly distributed over $(\mathbb{K}\backslash\{0\})^q$. Otherwise, it should hold that $h|_{\overline{C}, \boldsymbol{x}_{\overline{C}}}(0) = 1$ and $\overline{\gamma} \in S$. Then, the number of 0's in $\boldsymbol{v}$ is exactly one and $\boldsymbol{Tv}$ is uniformly distributed over the set of all the vectors of $\mathbb{K}^q$ of Hamming weight $q - 1$. Since the $\boldsymbol{s}_i$'s are chosen independent of $\boldsymbol{T}$, the distribution of (2) is simulated by $(\widetilde{\boldsymbol{v}}; (\boldsymbol{0}_q)_{i\in C}, (\widetilde{\boldsymbol{s}}_i)_{i\in C}; (\widetilde{\boldsymbol{s}}_i)_{i\in \overline{C}})$ for $\widetilde{\boldsymbol{v}}$ and $\widetilde{\boldsymbol{s}}_i$ ($i \in [n]$) sampled by the simulator.

- If $\Gamma \neq q^{|C|}$, we surely know that $\Gamma^\perp = \boldsymbol{w}_C \cdot \mathbb{F}_q$. The vector $\widetilde{\boldsymbol{w}}_C$ sampled by the simulator can be expressed as $\widetilde{\boldsymbol{w}}_C = \boldsymbol{w}_C \cdot \beta$ for some $\beta \in \mathbb{F}_q\backslash\{0\}$. Let $v_j = u_j - \overline{\gamma}$ for $j \in [k]$. Let $\boldsymbol{x}_C$ be inputs chosen by the simulator such that $\boldsymbol{x}_C \notin \Gamma$ and write $\Delta_{\boldsymbol{x}_C} = \{\alpha_1, \ldots, \alpha_k\}$ for the inputs $\boldsymbol{x}_C$. Let $\gamma = \sum_{i\in C} \widetilde{w}_i x_i \neq 0$ and $\delta = \sum_{i\in C} w_i x_i$. It holds that $\gamma = \delta\beta$. Note that the simulator knows $k = |S|$, $\widetilde{\boldsymbol{w}}_C$, α_j ($j \in [k]$), and γ.

We have that the values $\widetilde{v}_j := \alpha_j \gamma$ set by the simulator determine the v_j's up to a scalar and a permutation. Specifically, there exists $\tau \in \mathfrak{S}_{[k]} \subseteq \mathfrak{S}_{[q]}$ such that $\widetilde{v}_j = \beta v_{\tau(j)}$ for all $j \in [k]$ since for every $\alpha \in \Delta_{\boldsymbol{x}_C} = \{\alpha_1, \ldots, \alpha_k\}$, it holds that

$$\alpha \in \Delta_{\boldsymbol{x}_C} \iff \delta\alpha = v_j \ (\exists j \in [k])$$
$$\iff \alpha = \delta^{-1} v_j = \beta\gamma^{-1} v_j \ (\exists j \in [k])$$
$$\iff \alpha\gamma = \beta v_j \ (\exists j \in [k])$$

Since $\widetilde{v}_j$ and v_j for $k < j \leq q$ are both uniformly distributed over $\mathbb{K}\backslash\mathbb{F}_q$, we have $(v_j)_{j\in[q]} \equiv (\beta^{-1} \widetilde{v}_{\tau^{-1}(j)})_{j\in[q]}$. We also have $1_q w_i = 1_q \widetilde{w}_i \beta^{-1}$ for all $i \in C$. Since the $\boldsymbol{s}_i$'s are chosen independent of $\boldsymbol{T}$, we have the following:

$$(\boldsymbol{Tv}; (\boldsymbol{T}1_q w_i)_{i\in C}, (\boldsymbol{s}_i)_{i\in C}; (\boldsymbol{T}1_q w_i x_i + \boldsymbol{s}_i)_{i\in\overline{C}})$$
$$\equiv ((r_j v_{\pi(j)})_{j\in[q]}; ((r_j w_i)_{j\in[q]})_{i\in C}, (\widetilde{\boldsymbol{s}}_i)_{i\in C}; (\widetilde{\boldsymbol{s}}_i)_{i\in\overline{C}})$$
$$\equiv ((r_j \beta^{-1} \widetilde{v}_{(\tau^{-1}\circ\pi)(j)})_{j\in[q]}; ((r_j \beta^{-1} \widetilde{w}_i)_{j\in[q]})_{i\in C}, (\widetilde{\boldsymbol{s}}_i)_{i\in C}; (\widetilde{\boldsymbol{s}}_i)_{i\in\overline{C}})$$
$$\equiv ((\widetilde{r}_j \widetilde{v}_{\widetilde{\pi}(j)})_{j\in[q]}; ((\widetilde{r}_j \widetilde{w}_i)_{j\in[q]})_{i\in C}, (\widetilde{\boldsymbol{s}}_i)_{i\in C}; (\widetilde{\boldsymbol{s}}_i)_{i\in\overline{C}})$$
$$\equiv (\widetilde{\boldsymbol{T}}\widetilde{\boldsymbol{v}}; (\widetilde{\boldsymbol{T}}1_q \widetilde{w}_i)_{i\in C}, (\widetilde{\boldsymbol{s}}_i)_{i\in C}; (\widetilde{\boldsymbol{s}}_i)_{i\in\overline{C}}),$$

where $\widetilde{r}_j$ ($j \in [q]$), $\widetilde{\pi}$, $\widetilde{\boldsymbol{T}} = \mathrm{diag}(\widetilde{r}_1, \ldots, \widetilde{r}_q)\boldsymbol{U}_{\widetilde{\pi}}$, and $\widetilde{\boldsymbol{s}}_i$ ($i \in [n]$) are elements sampled by the simulator.

Communication complexity. The maximum component of on-line and off-line communication is the randomness R_i for $i \in [n]$, which consists of two vectors over $\mathbb{K}$ of dimension q. Since $\mathbb{K}$ can chosen as any extension field of $\mathbb{F}_q$, the protocol achieves the communication complexity in the statement. □

As in the case of abelian programs, NIMPC protocols for $\mathcal{L}_{\mathbb{F}_q}$ is not directly applicable to $\mathcal{L}_{\mathbb{F}_q}^{S_1,\dots,S_n}$. Nevertheless, from the same reason presented in Corollary 1, it is possible to obtain a protocol for $\mathcal{L}_{\mathbb{F}_q}^{S_1,\dots,S_n}$ by applying the BKR transformation to the protocol for $\mathcal{L}_{\mathbb{F}_q}$.

Corollary 2. *Let $\mathbb{F}_q$ be a finite field and $S_1,\dots,S_n$ be subsets of $\mathbb{F}_q$. Then, there exists a t-robust NIMPC protocol Π for $\mathcal{L}_{\mathbb{F}_q}^{S_1,\dots,S_n}$ such that $\mathsf{CC}(\Pi) = p^{t+O(1)} q \log q$, where p is a prime power with $p \geq \max\{n, |S_1|, \dots, |S_n|\}$.*

6   Revisiting the BKR Transformation

6.1   Analyzing and Fixing the NIMPC Protocol of [6] for Outputting-Message Functions

To realize the BKR transformation, the authors of [6] introduce the class of outputting-message functions. Let $\mathcal{M}$ be a finite set and let $\bot$ be the special symbol not in $\mathcal{M}$. Let $\mathcal{X}_1 = \cdots = \mathcal{X}_n = \mathbb{F}_q$ and $\mathcal{X} = \mathcal{X}_1 \times \cdots \times \mathcal{X}_n$. Let $\boldsymbol{A} = [\boldsymbol{a}_1,\dots,\boldsymbol{a}_n] \in \mathbb{F}_q^{k \times n}$ be a fixed matrix. Define the outputting-message function $h_{\boldsymbol{u},m} : \mathcal{X} \to \mathcal{M} \cup \{\bot\}$ associated with $\boldsymbol{u} \in \mathbb{F}_q^k$ and $m \in \mathcal{M}$ as

$$h_{\boldsymbol{u},m}(x_1,\dots,x_n) = \begin{cases} m, & \text{if } \boldsymbol{u} = \boldsymbol{A}[x_1,\dots,x_n]^\top, \\ \bot, & \text{otherwise.} \end{cases}$$

Define $\mathcal{O}_{\mathcal{M},\boldsymbol{A}}$ be the class of all the outputting-message functions, that is, $\mathcal{O}_{\mathcal{M},\boldsymbol{A}} = \{h_{\boldsymbol{u},m} \mid \boldsymbol{u} \in \mathbb{F}_q^k, m \in \mathcal{M}\}$.

The authors of [6] propose a fully robust NIMPC protocol for $\mathcal{O}_{\mathcal{M},\boldsymbol{A}}$ with communication complexity $O(k(\log q)(\log |\mathcal{M}|))$ and use it as a building block for the BKR transformation. However, we show that their protocol does not satisfy even 1-robustness if the matrix $\boldsymbol{A}$ satisfies a certain condition. We first recall their protocol for $\mathcal{O}_{\mathcal{M},\boldsymbol{A}}$. We denote by $\boldsymbol{a}_i \in \mathbb{F}_q^k$ the i-th column vector of $\boldsymbol{A} \in \mathbb{F}_q^{k \times n}$. We may assume $\mathcal{M} = \mathbb{F}_q$ since a protocol for an arbitrary message space $\mathcal{M}$ is obtained by expressing an element of $\mathcal{M}$ as a vector over $\mathbb{F}_q$ of dimension $\lceil \log_q |\mathcal{M}| \rceil$.

Proposition 2. *Let $C \subseteq [n]$. If there exists $j \in \overline{C}$ such that $\boldsymbol{a}_j \neq \boldsymbol{0}$ and $\{\boldsymbol{a}_i \mid i \in C \cup \{j\}\}$ does not span $\mathbb{F}_q^k$, then the protocol Π_{BKR} described in Fig. 5 is not C-robust.*

Proof. Let $\boldsymbol{u} \in \mathbb{F}_q^k$ be a vector that is not in the space spanned by $\{\boldsymbol{a}_i \mid i \in C \cup \{j\}\}$. Fix any $m \in \mathbb{F}_q$ and set $h = h_{\boldsymbol{u},m} \in \mathcal{O}_{\mathcal{M},\boldsymbol{A}}$. Let $\boldsymbol{x}_{\overline{C}}, \boldsymbol{y}_{\overline{C}}$ be two

---

Protocol Π_{BKR} for $\mathcal{O}_{\mathcal{M},A}$

$\mathsf{Gen}(h_{\boldsymbol{u},m})$:
1. Choose $\boldsymbol{s} \leftarrow_{\$} \mathbb{F}_q^k$, $r_i \leftarrow_{\$} \mathbb{F}_q$ ($i \in [n]$) and set $\mu_0 = m - \boldsymbol{s}^\top \boldsymbol{u} - \sum_{i \in [n]} r_i$.
2. Choose $\boldsymbol{s}_i \leftarrow_{\$} \mathbb{F}_q^k$ ($i \in [n]$) and set $\boldsymbol{\nu}_0 = \boldsymbol{u} + \sum_{i \in [n]} \boldsymbol{s}_i$.
3. Output $R_0 = (\mu_0, \boldsymbol{\nu}_0)$ and $R_i = (\boldsymbol{s}^\top \boldsymbol{a}_i, r_i, \boldsymbol{s}_i)$ for $i \in [n]$.

$\mathsf{Enc}_i(x_i, R_i)$:
1. Parse R_i as $(\mu_{i1}, \mu_{i2}, \boldsymbol{\rho}_i)$, where $\mu_{i1}, \mu_{i2} \in \mathbb{F}_q$ and $\boldsymbol{\rho}_i \in \mathbb{F}_q^k$.
2. Output $M_i = (\mu_{i1} x_i + \mu_{i2}, \boldsymbol{a}_i x_i + \boldsymbol{\rho}_i)$.

$\mathsf{Dec}(R_0, M_1, \ldots, M_n)$:
1. Parse R_0 as $(\mu_0, \boldsymbol{\nu}_0)$ and M_i as $(\mu_i, \boldsymbol{\nu}_i)$, where $\mu_i \in \mathbb{F}_q$ and $\boldsymbol{\nu}_i \in \mathbb{F}_q^k$.
2. If $\boldsymbol{\nu}_0 = \sum_{i \in [n]} \boldsymbol{\nu}_i$, then output $\mu_0 + \sum_{i \in [n]} \mu_i$ and otherwise output $\bot$.

Fig. 5. The NIMPC protocol Π_{BKR} of [6] for the class of outputting-message functions $\mathcal{O}_{\mathcal{M},A}$.

inputs such that $x_j \neq y_j$ and $x_i = y_i = 0$ for all $i \in \overline{C} \backslash \{j\}$. Then, it holds that $h|_{\overline{C}, x_{\overline{C}}}(z_{\overline{C}}) = h|_{\overline{C}, y_{\overline{C}}}(z_{\overline{C}}) = \bot$ for any $z_{\overline{C}} \in \mathcal{X}_C$. Assume that Π_{BKR} is C-robust and that there is a simulator Sim satisfying Definition 2. Since Sim simulates the adversary's view with oracle access to the same residual function $h|_{\overline{C}, x_{\overline{C}}} = h|_{\overline{C}, y_{\overline{C}}}$, the views of the execution of Π_{BKR} on $x_{\overline{C}}$ and $y_{\overline{C}}$ should be identical to each other.

On the other hand, the adversary can compute $\boldsymbol{d} := \boldsymbol{\nu}_0 - \sum_{i \in \overline{C}} \boldsymbol{\nu}_i - \sum_{i \in C} \boldsymbol{s}_i$ from his view. If $x_{\overline{C}}$ is inputted to Π_{BKR}, then $\boldsymbol{d} = \boldsymbol{u} - \boldsymbol{a}_j x_j$. If $y_{\overline{C}}$ is inputted, then $\boldsymbol{d} = \boldsymbol{u} - \boldsymbol{a}_j y_j \neq \boldsymbol{u} - \boldsymbol{a}_j x_j$, from which it follows that the two views are different. This is a contradiction. □

We note that the condition of Proposition 2 holds even for the matrix A used in the BKR transformation. Indeed, to transform a 0-robust NIMPC protocol into a t-robust one, it is necessary to choose $k = t + 1$ and $A = [H^\top, e_i]^\top$, where $H \in \mathbb{F}_q^{t \times n}$ is a matrix such that every t column vectors is linearly independent. For any set C of size at most $t - 1$ and any $j \in \overline{C}$, the column vectors of A indexed by $C \cup \{j\}$ span a subspace of $\mathbb{F}_q^k$ of dimension t, which therefore implies that the condition of Proposition 2 holds.

Next, we fix their protocol Π_{BKR}. The main issue is that the adversary is able to compute $\boldsymbol{d} = \boldsymbol{\nu}_0 - \sum_{i \in \overline{C}} \boldsymbol{\nu}_i - \sum_{i \in C} \boldsymbol{s}_i = \boldsymbol{u} - \sum_{i \in \overline{C}} \boldsymbol{a}_i x_i$ while the only information on $\boldsymbol{d}$ revealed by the residual function is whether it is in the space spanned by $\{\boldsymbol{a}_i \mid i \in C\}$. We therefore randomize the vectors $\boldsymbol{d}$ and $\boldsymbol{a}_i$ ($i \in C$) to ensure for the adversary not to learn more than their linear independence relation. Specifically, we choose a matrix T uniformly at random from $\mathrm{GL}_k(\mathbb{F}_q)$ and redefine $\boldsymbol{\nu}_0 = T\boldsymbol{u} + \sum_{i \in [n]} \boldsymbol{s}_i$. We additionally give $T\boldsymbol{a}_i$ to each P_i as randomness. Then, the adversary only learns $\boldsymbol{\nu}_0 - \sum_{i \in \overline{C}} \boldsymbol{\nu}_i - \sum_{i \in C} \boldsymbol{s}_i = T(\boldsymbol{u} - \sum_{i \in \overline{C}} \boldsymbol{a}_i x_i)$, which leaks the linear independence relation among $\boldsymbol{d}$ and $\boldsymbol{a}_i$ ($i \in C$) and nothing more. Note that our modification increases the communication complexity of Π_{BKR} only by a constant factor and hence the statements of [6] still hold true.

Protocol $\Pi^*_{\mathbf{BKR}}$ for $\mathcal{O}_{\mathcal{M},\mathbf{A}}$

$\mathsf{Gen}(h_{\boldsymbol{u},m})$:
1. Choose $\boldsymbol{s} \leftarrow_\$ \mathbb{F}^k_q$, $r_i \leftarrow_\$ \mathbb{F}_q$ ($i \in [n]$) and set $\mu_0 = m - \boldsymbol{s}^\top \boldsymbol{u} - \sum_{i \in [n]} r_i$.
2. Choose $\boldsymbol{T} \leftarrow_\$ \mathrm{GL}_k(\mathbb{F}_q)$, $\boldsymbol{s}_i \leftarrow_\$ \mathbb{F}^k_q$ ($i \in [n]$) and set $\boldsymbol{\nu}_0 = \boldsymbol{T}\boldsymbol{u} + \sum_{i \in [n]} \boldsymbol{s}_i$.
3. Output $R_0 = (\mu_0, \boldsymbol{\nu}_0)$ and $R_i = (\boldsymbol{s}^\top \boldsymbol{a}_i, r_i, \boldsymbol{T}\boldsymbol{a}_i, \boldsymbol{s}_i)$ for $i \in [n]$.

$\mathsf{Enc}_i(x_i, R_i)$:
1. Parse R_i as $(\mu_{i1}, \mu_{i2}, \boldsymbol{\rho}_{i1}, \boldsymbol{\rho}_{i2})$, where $\mu_{i1}, \mu_{i2} \in \mathbb{F}_q$ and $\boldsymbol{\rho}_{i1}, \boldsymbol{\rho}_{i2} \in \mathbb{F}^k_q$.
2. Output $M_i = (\mu_{i1}x_i + \mu_{i2}, \boldsymbol{\rho}_{i1}x_i + \boldsymbol{\rho}_{i2})$.

$\mathsf{Dec}(R_0, M_1, \ldots, M_n)$:
1. Parse R_0 as $(\mu_0, \boldsymbol{\nu}_0)$ and M_i as $(\mu_i, \boldsymbol{\nu}_i)$, where $\mu_i \in \mathbb{F}_q$ and $\boldsymbol{\nu}_i \in \mathbb{F}^k_q$.
2. If $\boldsymbol{\nu}_0 = \sum_{i \in [n]} \boldsymbol{\nu}_i$, then output $\mu_0 + \sum_{i \in [n]} \mu_i$ and otherwise output $\perp$.

Fig. 6. The NIMPC protocol Π^*_{BKR} for the class of outputting-message functions $\mathcal{O}_{\mathcal{M},\mathbf{A}}$.

Theorem 3. *Let $\mathcal{M}$ be a finite set and $\boldsymbol{A} \in \mathbb{F}^{k \times n}_q$ be a matrix. Let $\mathcal{X}_1 = \cdots = \mathcal{X}_n = \mathbb{F}_q$ and $\mathcal{X} = \mathcal{X}_1 \times \cdots \times \mathcal{X}_n$. Then, the protocol Π^*_{BKR} described in Fig. 6 is a fully robust NIMPC protocol for $\mathcal{O}_{\mathcal{M},\mathbf{A}}$ such that*

$$\mathsf{CC}_{\mathsf{on}}(\Pi^*_{BKR}) = (k + \lceil \log_q |\mathcal{M}| \rceil) \cdot \lceil \log q \rceil$$

and $\mathsf{CC}_{\mathsf{off}}(\Pi^*_{BKR}) = (2k + 2\lceil \log_q |\mathcal{M}| \rceil) \cdot \lceil \log q \rceil.$

To begin with, we show a lemma used in the proof of Theorem 3.

Lemma 1. *Let $\boldsymbol{A} = (\boldsymbol{a}_i)_{i \in [\ell]}$ be a tuple of ℓ vectors, where $\boldsymbol{a}_i \in \mathbb{F}^k_q$. Let $\Gamma = \mathrm{Ker}(\boldsymbol{A})$. Then, the distribution of $(\boldsymbol{T}\boldsymbol{a}_i)_{i \in [\ell]}$ induced by $\boldsymbol{T} \leftarrow_\$ \mathrm{GL}_k(\mathbb{F}_q)$ is the uniform distribution over $\mathcal{F}_\Gamma = \{(\boldsymbol{v}_i)_{i \in [\ell]} \mid \mathrm{Ker}((\boldsymbol{v}_i)_{i \in [\ell]}) = \Gamma\}$.*

Proof. Fix $\boldsymbol{W}_j = [\boldsymbol{w}_{j1}, \ldots, \boldsymbol{w}_{j\ell}] \in \mathcal{F}_\Gamma$ for $j = 1, 2$. Note that $\boldsymbol{T}\boldsymbol{A} \in \mathcal{F}_\Gamma$ for any $\boldsymbol{T} \in \mathrm{GL}_k(\mathbb{F}_q)$. It is sufficient to show that the probabilities of $\boldsymbol{T}\boldsymbol{A}$ being $\boldsymbol{W}_j$ are equal to each other.

Let $I_1 \subseteq [\ell]$ be such that $\{\boldsymbol{w}_{1i} \mid i \in I_1\}$ is a basis of $\boldsymbol{W}_1$, that is, $\{\boldsymbol{w}_{1i} \mid i \in I_1\}$ is linearly independent and for every $j \in [\ell] \setminus I_1$, there exist $c_{ij} \in \mathbb{F}_q$ such that $\boldsymbol{w}_{1j} = \sum_{i \in I_1} \boldsymbol{w}_{1i}c_{ij}$. Then, $\{\boldsymbol{w}_{2i} \mid i \in I_1\}$ is a basis of $\boldsymbol{W}_2$. Indeed, if $\sum_{i \in I_1} \boldsymbol{w}_{2i}d_i = \boldsymbol{0}$ for some $d_i \in \mathbb{F}_q$, then $(d_i)_{i \in I_1} \in \Gamma$. Hence $\sum_{i \in I_1} \boldsymbol{w}_{1i}d_i = \boldsymbol{0}$ and $d_i = 0$ for every $i \in I_1$. If $\{\boldsymbol{w}_{2i} \mid i \in I_2\}$ is linearly independent for some $I_2 \supseteq I_1$, then there is no non-zero $\boldsymbol{d} \in \Gamma$ such that $\mathrm{supp}(\boldsymbol{d}) \subseteq I_2$. Then, $\{\boldsymbol{w}_{1i} \mid i \in I_2\}$ is linearly independent and hence $I_2 = I_1$. Note that $\boldsymbol{w}_{2j} = \sum_{i \in I_1} \boldsymbol{w}_{2i}c_{ij}$.

Due to the linear independence, there exists $\boldsymbol{S} \in \mathrm{GL}_k(\mathbb{F}_q)$ such that $\boldsymbol{S}\boldsymbol{w}_{1i} = \boldsymbol{w}_{2i}$ for every $i \in I_1$. Then, $\boldsymbol{S}\boldsymbol{w}_{1j} = \sum_{i \in I_1} \boldsymbol{S}\boldsymbol{w}_{1i}c_{ij} = \sum_{i \in I_1} \boldsymbol{S}\boldsymbol{w}_{2i}c_{ij} = \boldsymbol{w}_{2j}$ for every $j \in [\ell] \setminus I_1$. Therefore,

$$
\Pr[\boldsymbol{T} \leftarrow_\$ \mathrm{GL}_k(\mathbb{F}_q) : \boldsymbol{T}\boldsymbol{A} = \boldsymbol{W}_1] = \Pr[\boldsymbol{T} \leftarrow_\$ \mathrm{GL}_k(\mathbb{F}_q) : \boldsymbol{S}\boldsymbol{T}\boldsymbol{A} = \boldsymbol{W}_2]
$$
$$
= \Pr[\boldsymbol{T} \leftarrow_\$ \mathrm{GL}_k(\mathbb{F}_q) : \boldsymbol{T}\boldsymbol{A} = \boldsymbol{W}_2].
$$

$\square$

Proof (of Theorem 3). We assume that $\mathcal{M} = \mathbb{F}_q$. It is possible to construct a protocol for any message space $\mathcal{M}$ in the same manner as [6].

Correctness. Let $h = h_{\boldsymbol{u},m}$ be a function to compute. Correctness follows from the following observation: the protocol outputs a message other than $\bot$ if and only if $\nu_0 - \sum_{i \in [n]} \nu_i = \boldsymbol{T}(\boldsymbol{u} - \sum_{i \in [n]} \boldsymbol{a}_i x_i) = \boldsymbol{0}$, which in turn occurs if and only if $\boldsymbol{u} = \sum_{i \in [n]} \boldsymbol{a}_i x_i$ since $\boldsymbol{T} \in \mathrm{GL}_k(\mathbb{F}_q)$. Then, the output is $\mu_0 + \sum_{i \in [n]} \mu_i = m - \boldsymbol{s}^\top(\boldsymbol{u} - \sum_{i \in [n]} \boldsymbol{a}_i x_i) = m$.

Robustness. Let $C \subseteq [n]$ and $C_0 = C \cup \{0\}$. The adversary's view can be decomposed into the following two parts:

$$
(\boldsymbol{T}\boldsymbol{u} + \sum_{i \in [n]} \boldsymbol{s}_i; (\boldsymbol{T}\boldsymbol{a}_i)_{i \in C}, (\boldsymbol{s}_i)_{i \in C}; (\boldsymbol{T}\boldsymbol{a}_i x_i + \boldsymbol{s}_i)_{i \in \overline{C}}),
$$

where $\boldsymbol{T} \leftarrow_\$ \mathrm{GL}_k(\mathbb{F}_q)$ and $\boldsymbol{s}_i \leftarrow_\$ \mathbb{F}_q^k$ $(i \in [n])$, and

$$
(m - \boldsymbol{s}^\top\boldsymbol{u} - \sum_{i \in [n]} r_i; (\boldsymbol{s}^\top\boldsymbol{a}_i)_{i \in C}, (r_i)_{i \in C}; (\boldsymbol{s}^\top\boldsymbol{a}_i x_i + r_i)_{i \in \overline{C}}),
$$

where $\boldsymbol{s} \leftarrow_\$ \mathbb{F}_q^k$ and $r_i \leftarrow_\$ \mathbb{F}_q$ $(i \in [n])$. We separately show that each of the two distributions is perfectly simulated by the simulator described in Fig. 7.

As for the first part, it is sufficient to show that the distribution of

$$
(\boldsymbol{T}\boldsymbol{a}_0; (\boldsymbol{T}\boldsymbol{a}_i)_{i \in C}, (\boldsymbol{s}_i)_{i \in C}; (\boldsymbol{T}\boldsymbol{a}_i x_i + \boldsymbol{s}_i)_{i \in \overline{C}}) \tag{3}
$$

is perfectly simulated, where $\boldsymbol{a}_0 = \sum_{i \in \overline{C}} \boldsymbol{a}_i x_i - \boldsymbol{u}$. This is because the original view can be obtained by computing $\nu_0 = -\boldsymbol{T}\boldsymbol{a}_0 + \sum_{i \in C} \boldsymbol{s}_i + \sum_{i \in \overline{C}}(\boldsymbol{T}\boldsymbol{a}_i x_i + \boldsymbol{s}_i)$.

The case of $C = \emptyset$. We have the following:

- If $h(x_1, \ldots, x_n) = \bot$, then $\boldsymbol{a}_0 \neq \boldsymbol{0}$ and $\boldsymbol{T}\boldsymbol{a}_0$ is uniformly distributed over $\mathbb{F}_q^k \setminus \{\boldsymbol{0}\}$. Since the $\boldsymbol{s}_i$'s are chosen independent of $\boldsymbol{T}$, letting $\boldsymbol{\Delta}_0 \leftarrow_\$ \mathbb{F}_q^k \setminus \{\boldsymbol{0}\}$ and $\widetilde{\boldsymbol{s}}_i \leftarrow_\$ \mathbb{F}_q^k$ $(i \in [n])$, we have $(\boldsymbol{T}\boldsymbol{a}_0; (\boldsymbol{T}\boldsymbol{a}_i x_i + \boldsymbol{s}_i)_{i \in [n]}) \equiv (\boldsymbol{\Delta}_0; (\widetilde{\boldsymbol{s}}_i)_{i \in [n]})$.
- If $h(x_1, \ldots, x_n) = m \neq \bot$, then $\boldsymbol{a}_0 = \boldsymbol{0}$ and $\boldsymbol{T}\boldsymbol{a}_0 = \boldsymbol{0}$. Since the $\boldsymbol{s}_i$'s are chosen independent of $\boldsymbol{T}$, letting $\boldsymbol{\Delta}_0 = \boldsymbol{0}$ and $\widetilde{\boldsymbol{s}}_i \leftarrow_\$ \mathbb{F}_q^k$ $(i \in [n])$, we have $(\boldsymbol{T}\boldsymbol{a}_0; (\boldsymbol{T}\boldsymbol{a}_i x_i + \boldsymbol{s}_i)_{i \in [n]}) \equiv (\boldsymbol{\Delta}_0; (\widetilde{\boldsymbol{s}}_i)_{i \in [n]})$.

Simulator $\mathrm{Sim}^{h|_{\overline{C}, x_{\overline{C}}}}(C)$ for Π^*_{BKR}

Input. A set of colluding players C.
Oracle access. The residual function $h|_{\overline{C}, x_{\overline{C}}}$ for the inputs $x_{\overline{C}}$ of honest players.
Output. Correlated randomness R_0 and $(R_i)_{i \in C}$ of the colluding players and messages $(M_i)_{i \in \overline{C}}$ of the honest players.
Algorithm.

- If $C = \emptyset$:
  1. Set $\delta_0 = m$ and $\boldsymbol{\Delta}_0 = \mathbf{0}$ if $h(x_1, \ldots, x_n) = m \neq \perp$ and otherwise choose $\delta_0 \leftarrow_{\$} \mathbb{F}_q$, $\boldsymbol{\Delta}_0 \leftarrow_{\$} \mathbb{F}_q^k \setminus \{\mathbf{0}\}$.
  2. Choose $\widetilde{r}_i \leftarrow_{\$} \mathbb{F}_q$ $(i \in [n])$, $\widetilde{\boldsymbol{s}}_i \leftarrow_{\$} \mathbb{F}_q^k$ $(i \in [n])$.
  3. Output $R_0 = (\delta_0 - \sum_{i \in [n]} \widetilde{r}_i, \boldsymbol{\Delta}_0 + \sum_{i \in [n]} \widetilde{\boldsymbol{s}}_i)$ and $M_i = (\widetilde{r}_i, \widetilde{\boldsymbol{s}}_i)$ for $i \in [n]$.
- If $C \neq \emptyset$:
  1. Construct Γ_0 and Γ_0' as

  $$\Gamma_0 = \{\boldsymbol{x}_C \in \mathbb{F}_q^{|C|} \mid \sum_{i \in C} a_i x_i = 0\} \text{ and } \Gamma_0' = \{(0, \boldsymbol{x}_C) \in \mathbb{F}_q^{|C|+1} \mid \boldsymbol{x}_C \in \Gamma_0\}.$$

  2. Construct Γ_1 and Γ_1' using the oracle $h|_{\overline{C}, x_{\overline{C}}}$ as

  $$\Gamma_1 = \{\boldsymbol{x}_C \in \mathbb{F}_q^{|C|} \mid h|_{\overline{C}, x_{\overline{C}}}(\boldsymbol{x}_C) \neq \perp\}$$
  $$\text{and } \Gamma_1' = \{(x_0, \boldsymbol{x}_C x_0) \in \mathbb{F}_q^{|C|+1} \mid x_0 \in \mathbb{F}_q \setminus \{0\}, \ \boldsymbol{x}_C \in \Gamma_1\}.$$

  3. Set $\Gamma' = \Gamma_0' \cup \Gamma_1'$ and define

  $$\mathcal{F}_{\Gamma'} = \{(\boldsymbol{\Delta}_i)_{i \in C \cup \{0\}} \in (\mathbb{F}_q^k)^{|C|+1} \mid \mathrm{Ker}((\boldsymbol{\Delta}_i)_{i \in C \cup \{0\}}) = \Gamma'\}.$$

  4. Choose $(\delta_i)_{i \in C \cup \{0\}} \leftarrow_{\$} (\Gamma')^{\perp}$, $(\boldsymbol{\Delta}_i)_{i \in C \cup \{0\}} \leftarrow_{\$} \mathcal{F}_{\Gamma'}$, $\widetilde{r}_i \leftarrow_{\$} \mathbb{F}_q$ $(i \in [n])$, and $\widetilde{\boldsymbol{s}}_i \leftarrow_{\$} \mathbb{F}_q^k$ $(i \in [n])$.
  5. If $\Gamma_1 = \emptyset$, output

  $$R_0 = (\delta_0 - \sum_{i \in [n]} \widetilde{r}_i, \sum_{i \in [n]} \widetilde{\boldsymbol{s}}_i - \boldsymbol{\Delta}_0), R_i = (\delta_i, \widetilde{r}_i, \boldsymbol{\Delta}_i, \widetilde{\boldsymbol{s}}_i) \text{ for } i \in C,$$
  and $M_i = (\widetilde{r}_i, \widetilde{\boldsymbol{s}}_i)$ for $i \in \overline{C}$.

  Otherwise, fix $\boldsymbol{x}_C \in \Gamma_1$ and set $m = h|_{\overline{C}, x_{\overline{C}}}(\boldsymbol{x}_C)$. Then, output

  $$R_0 = (\delta_0 + m - \sum_{i \in [n]} \widetilde{r}_i, \sum_{i \in [n]} \widetilde{\boldsymbol{s}}_i - \boldsymbol{\Delta}_0), R_i = (\delta_i, \widetilde{r}_i, \boldsymbol{\Delta}_i, \widetilde{\boldsymbol{s}}_i) \text{ for } i \in C,$$
  and $M_i = (\widetilde{r}_i, \widetilde{\boldsymbol{s}}_i)$ for $i \in \overline{C}$.

Fig. 7. The simulator for the NIMPC protocol Π^*_{BKR} for the class of outputting-message functions $\mathcal{O}_{\mathcal{M}, A}$.

The case of $C \neq \emptyset$. Let $\boldsymbol{B} = (\boldsymbol{a}_i)_{i \in C_0}$ and $\Gamma = \mathrm{Ker}(\boldsymbol{B})$. We show that Γ'_0 and $\overline{\Gamma'_1}$ constructed by the simulator satisfy $\Gamma'_0 \cup \Gamma'_1 = \Gamma$. Indeed, let $\boldsymbol{x}_{C_0} = (x_0, \boldsymbol{x}_C) \in \Gamma$. If $x_0 = 0$, then $\sum_{i \in C} \boldsymbol{a}_i x_i = \boldsymbol{0}$ and hence $\boldsymbol{x}_{C_0} = (0, \boldsymbol{x}_C) \in \Gamma'_0$. If $x_0 \neq 0$, then $\sum_{i \in \overline{C}} \boldsymbol{a}_i x_i + \sum_{i \in C} \boldsymbol{a}_i (x_i x_0^{-1}) = \boldsymbol{u}$ and $h|_{\overline{C}, \boldsymbol{x}_{\overline{C}}}(\boldsymbol{x}_C x_0^{-1}) = m \neq \bot$. Hence, $\boldsymbol{x}_{C_0} = (x_0, (\boldsymbol{x}_C x_0^{-1}) x_0) \in \Gamma'_1$. Conversely, any $(0, \boldsymbol{x}_C) \in \Gamma'_0$ is clearly an element of Γ. Any element of Γ'_1 can be expressed as $(x_0, \boldsymbol{x}_C x_0)$ for some $x_0 \neq 0$ and $\boldsymbol{x}_C = (x_i)_{i \in C}$ with $h|_{\overline{C}, \boldsymbol{x}_{\overline{C}}}(\boldsymbol{x}_C) \neq \bot$, i.e., $\sum_{i \in \overline{C}} \boldsymbol{a}_i x_i + \sum_{i \in C} \boldsymbol{a}_i x_i = \boldsymbol{u}$. Therefore, it holds that $\boldsymbol{a}_0 x_0 + \sum_{i \in C} \boldsymbol{a}_i (x_i x_0) = \boldsymbol{0}$ and hence $(x_0, \boldsymbol{x}_C x_0) \in \Gamma$.

It follows from Lemma 1 that $(\boldsymbol{T}\boldsymbol{a}_i)_{i \in C_0}$ is uniformly distributed over $\mathcal{F}_\Gamma = \{(\boldsymbol{\Delta}_i)_{i \in C_0} \mid \mathrm{Ker}((\boldsymbol{\Delta}_i)_{i \in C_0}) = \Gamma\}$ when $\boldsymbol{T} \leftarrow_\$ \mathrm{GL}_k(\mathbb{F}_q)$. Note that the $\boldsymbol{s}_i$'s are chosen independent of $\boldsymbol{T}$. Therefore, letting $(\boldsymbol{\Delta}_i)_{i \in C_0} \leftarrow_\$ \mathcal{F}_{\Gamma'} = \mathcal{F}_\Gamma$ and $\widetilde{\boldsymbol{s}}_i \leftarrow_\$ \mathbb{F}_q^k$ $(i \in [n])$, we have

$$(\boldsymbol{T}\boldsymbol{a}_0, (\boldsymbol{T}\boldsymbol{a}_i)_{i \in C}, (\boldsymbol{s}_i)_{i \in C}; (\boldsymbol{T}\boldsymbol{a}_i x_i + \boldsymbol{s}_i)_{i \in \overline{C}}) \equiv (\boldsymbol{\Delta}_0; (\boldsymbol{\Delta}_i)_{i \in C}, (\widetilde{\boldsymbol{s}}_i)_{i \in C}; (\widetilde{\boldsymbol{s}}_i)_{i \in \overline{C}}).$$

As for the second part, it is sufficient to show that the distribution of

$$(m + \boldsymbol{s}^\top \boldsymbol{a}_0; (\boldsymbol{s}^\top \boldsymbol{a}_i)_{i \in C}, (r_i)_{i \in C}; (\boldsymbol{s}^\top \boldsymbol{a}_i x_i + r_i)_{i \in \overline{C}}) \tag{4}$$

is perfectly simulated, where $\boldsymbol{a}_0 = \sum_{i \in \overline{C}} \boldsymbol{a}_i x_i - \boldsymbol{u}$. This is because the original view can be obtained by computing $\mu_0 = (m + \boldsymbol{s}^\top \boldsymbol{a}_0) - \sum_{i \in C} r_i - \sum_{i \in \overline{C}} (\boldsymbol{s}^\top \boldsymbol{a}_i x_i + r_i)$.

The case of $C = \emptyset$. We have the following:

- If $h(x_1, \ldots, x_n) = \bot$, then $\boldsymbol{a}_0 \neq \boldsymbol{0}$. It follows that $\boldsymbol{s}^\top \boldsymbol{a}_0$ and hence $m + \boldsymbol{s}\boldsymbol{a}_0$ are uniformly distributed over $\mathbb{F}_q$. Since the r_i's are chosen independent of $\boldsymbol{s}$, letting $\delta_0 \leftarrow_\$ \mathbb{F}_q$ and $\widetilde{r}_i \leftarrow_\$ \mathbb{F}_q$ $(i \in [n])$, we have $(m + \boldsymbol{s}^\top \boldsymbol{a}_0; (\boldsymbol{s}^\top \boldsymbol{a}_i x_i + r_i)_{i \in [n]}) \equiv (\delta_0; (\widetilde{r}_i)_{i \in [n]})$.
- If $h(x_1, \ldots, x_n) = m \neq \bot$, then $\boldsymbol{a}_0 = \boldsymbol{0}$ and $\boldsymbol{s}^\top \boldsymbol{a}_0 = 0$ for all $\boldsymbol{s} \in \mathbb{F}_q^k$. Since the r_i's are chosen independent of $\boldsymbol{s}$, letting $\delta_0 = m$ and $\widetilde{r}_i \leftarrow_\$ \mathbb{F}_q$ $(i \in [n])$, we have $(m + \boldsymbol{s}^\top \boldsymbol{a}_0; (\boldsymbol{s}^\top \boldsymbol{a}_i x_i + r_i)_{i \in [n]}) \equiv (\delta_0; (\widetilde{r}_i)_{i \in [n]})$.

The case of $C \neq \emptyset$. For $\boldsymbol{s} \leftarrow_\$ \mathbb{F}_q^k$, we have that $(m + \boldsymbol{s}^\top \boldsymbol{a}_0, (\boldsymbol{s}^\top \boldsymbol{a}_i)_{i \in C}) \equiv \boldsymbol{s}^\top \boldsymbol{B} + m\boldsymbol{e}_1$. Define $\mathrm{row}(\boldsymbol{B}) = \{\boldsymbol{s}^\top \boldsymbol{B} = (\boldsymbol{s}^\top \boldsymbol{a}_i)_{i \in C_0} \mid \boldsymbol{s} \in \mathbb{F}_q^k\}$. It then holds that $(\Gamma')^\perp = \Gamma^\perp = \mathrm{row}(\boldsymbol{B})$ since $\Gamma' = \Gamma = \mathrm{Ker}(\boldsymbol{B})$.

Now, we can see below that the distribution of (4) is perfectly simulated:

- If $h|_{\overline{C}, \boldsymbol{x}_{\overline{C}}}(\boldsymbol{x}_C) = \bot$ for all $\boldsymbol{x}_C$, then $\boldsymbol{a}_0$ is not in the space spanned by $\{\boldsymbol{a}_i \mid i \in C\}$. In particular, there exists a vector $\boldsymbol{s}_0 \in \mathbb{F}_q^k$ such that $\boldsymbol{s}_0^\top \boldsymbol{B} = \boldsymbol{e}_1^\top = [1, 0, \ldots, 0]$. Therefore, $\boldsymbol{s}^\top \boldsymbol{B} + m\boldsymbol{e}_1^\top = (\boldsymbol{s} + \boldsymbol{s}_0 m)^\top \boldsymbol{B}$ is uniformly distributed over $\mathrm{row}(\boldsymbol{B})$ if $\boldsymbol{s} \leftarrow_\$ \mathbb{F}_q^k$. Since the r_i's are chosen independent of $\boldsymbol{s}$, the distribution of (4) is identical to $(\delta_0; (\delta_i)_{i \in C}, (\widetilde{r}_i)_{i \in C}; (\widetilde{r}_i)_{i \in \overline{C}})$, where $(\delta_i)_{i \in C_0} \leftarrow_\$ (\Gamma')^\perp$ and $\widetilde{r}_i \leftarrow_\$ \mathbb{F}_q$ $(i \in [n])$ are sampled by the simulator.
- If $h|_{\overline{C}, \boldsymbol{x}_{\overline{C}}}(\boldsymbol{x}_C) \neq \bot$ for some $\boldsymbol{x}_C$, then the simulator actually gets the message $m \in \mathbb{F}_q$. We know that $(\boldsymbol{s}^\top \boldsymbol{a}_i)_{i \in C_0}$ is uniformly distributed over $\mathrm{row}(\boldsymbol{B})$ if

$s \leftarrow_\$ \mathbb{F}_q^k$. Therefore, since the r_i's are chosen independent of s, the distribution of (4) is identical to $(\delta_0 + m; (\delta_i)_{i\in C}, (\widetilde{r}_i)_{i\in C}; (\widetilde{r}_i)_{i\in \overline{C}})$, where $(\delta_i)_{i\in C_0} \leftarrow_\$ (\Gamma')^\perp$ and $\widetilde{r}_i \leftarrow_\$ \mathbb{F}_q$ $(i \in [n])$ are sampled by the simulator.

Communication complexity. The maximum component of on-line and off-line communication is the randomness R_i for $i \in [n]$, which consists of two scalars of $\mathbb{F}_q$ for outputting messages and two vectors over $\mathbb{F}_q$ of dimension k for checking the equality $u = Ax$. If elements of $\mathcal{M}$ are expressed as vectors over $\mathbb{F}_q$ of dimension ℓ, the communication complexity of the first two entries of R_i increases ℓ times. Therefore, the protocol achieves the communication complexity in the statement. $\qquad \square$

6.2   An Asymptotically Optimal NIMPC Protocol for Indicator Functions

As a byproduct of our modified protocol Π_{BKR}^*, we obtain a fully robust NIMPC protocol for indicator functions with asymptotically optimal communication complexity with respect to the input length.

We recall the definition of indicator functions [3]. Let $\mathcal{X}_i$ $(i \in [n])$ be finite sets and $\mathcal{X} = \mathcal{X}_1 \times \cdots \times \mathcal{X}_n$. Define the indicator function $h_a : \mathcal{X} \to \{0, 1\}$ for $a \in \mathcal{X}$ as $h_a(x) = 1$ if and only if $x = a$ for $x \in \mathcal{X}$. In addition, we define $\text{id}_0 : \mathcal{X} \to \{0, 1\}$ as $\text{id}_0(x) = 0$ for any $x \in \mathcal{X}$. Define $\mathcal{I}_\mathcal{X}$ be the class of all the indicator functions together with id_0, that is, $\mathcal{I}_\mathcal{X} = \{h_a \mid a \in \mathcal{X}\} \cup \{\text{id}_0\}$. Indicator functions are fundamental building blocks to realize NIMPC for an arbitrary class of functions. Actually, based on the fact that any function $h : \mathcal{X} \to \{0, 1\}$ is expressed as $h(x) = \sum_{a \in \mathcal{X}: h(a)=1} h_a(x)$, it is shown that an NIMPC protocol for any given class $\mathcal{H}$ can be obtained from any protocol for $\mathcal{I}_\mathcal{X}$ with a multiplicative overhead of $\max_{h \in \mathcal{H}} |h^{-1}(1)|$ [3]. The reason why we incorporate id_0 in $\mathcal{I}_\mathcal{X}$ is to prevent the equality $h = \sum_{a \in \mathcal{X}: h(a)=1} h_a$ from revealing $|h^{-1}(1)|$.

We show that the protocol Π_{BKR}^* can be used as a protocol for $\mathcal{I}_\mathcal{X}$ with a slight modification. Let q be a prime power such that $q > \max_{i \in [n]} |\mathcal{X}_i|$. We identify each $\mathcal{X}_i$ with a subset of $\mathbb{F}_q \backslash \{0\}$. Let $A = [e_1, \ldots, e_n]$ be the identity matrix of size n. Note that computing h_a for $a = (a_i)_{i \in [n]} \in \mathcal{X}$ is reduced to testing the equality $u = Ax$, where $u = [a_1, \ldots, a_n]^\top$. We also see that testing $Ax = 0$ is equivalent to computing id_0 since the inputs are represented as non-zero field elements. Therefore, we can realize NIMPC for $\mathcal{I}_\mathcal{X}$ by running the protocol Π_{BKR}^* for $\mathcal{O}_{\mathcal{M}, A}$ except that we skip the procedures to reveal messages.

Corollary 3. *Let $\mathcal{X}_1, \ldots, \mathcal{X}_n$ be finite sets and $\mathcal{X} = \mathcal{X}_1 \times \cdots \times \mathcal{X}_n$. Let q be a prime power such that $q > \max_{i \in [n]} |\mathcal{X}_i|$. Then, the protocol Π_3 described in Fig. 8 is a fully robust NIMPC protocol for $\mathcal{I}_\mathcal{X}$ such that $\mathsf{CC}_{\text{on}}(\Pi) = n \lceil \log q \rceil$ and $\mathsf{CC}_{\text{off}}(\Pi) = 2n \lceil \log q \rceil$.*

According to the lower bound [17], any NIMPC protocol for $\mathcal{I}_\mathcal{X}$ has communication complexity at least $n^{-1} \sum_{i \in [n]} \log |\mathcal{X}_i|$. Therefore, if the input domains all have the same size, i.e., $|\mathcal{X}_1| = \cdots = |\mathcal{X}_n|$, our protocol is asymptotically optimal with respect to the input length.

Protocol Π_3 for $\mathcal{I}_\mathcal{X}$

$\mathsf{Gen}(h)$:
- $h = \mathrm{id}_0$:
  1. Choose $\boldsymbol{T} \leftarrow_\$ \mathrm{GL}_n(\mathbb{F}_q), \boldsymbol{s}_i \leftarrow_\$ \mathbb{F}_q^n$ ($i \in [n]$) and set $\boldsymbol{\nu}_0 = \sum_{i \in [n]} \boldsymbol{s}_i$.
  2. Output $R_0 = \boldsymbol{\nu}_0$ and $R_i = (\boldsymbol{T}\boldsymbol{e}_i, \boldsymbol{s}_i)$ for $i \in [n]$.
- $h = h_a$ for $a = (a_1, \ldots, a_n)$:
  1. Set $\boldsymbol{u} = [a_1, \ldots, a_n]^\top \in \mathbb{F}_q^n$.
  2. Choose $\boldsymbol{T} \leftarrow_\$ \mathrm{GL}_n(\mathbb{F}_q), \boldsymbol{s}_i \leftarrow_\$ \mathbb{F}_q^n$ ($i \in [n]$) and set $\boldsymbol{\nu}_0 = \boldsymbol{T}\boldsymbol{u} + \sum_{i \in [n]} \boldsymbol{s}_i$.
  3. Output $R_0 = \boldsymbol{\nu}_0$ and $R_i = (\boldsymbol{T}\boldsymbol{e}_i, \boldsymbol{s}_i)$ for $i \in [n]$.

$\mathsf{Enc}_i(x_i, R_i)$:
  1. Parse R_i as $(\boldsymbol{\rho}_{i1}, \boldsymbol{\rho}_{i2})$, where $\boldsymbol{\rho}_{i1}, \boldsymbol{\rho}_{i2} \in \mathbb{F}_q^n$.
  2. Output $M_i = \boldsymbol{\rho}_{i1} x_i + \boldsymbol{\rho}_{i2}$.

$\mathsf{Dec}(R_0, M_1, \ldots, M_n)$:
  1. If $R_0 = \sum_{i \in [n]} M_i$, then output 1 and otherwise output 0.

Fig. 8. The NIMPC protocol Π_3 for the class of indicator functions $\mathcal{I}_\mathcal{X}$.

Acknowledgements. This research was partially supported by JSPS KAKENHI Grant Numbers JP20J20797 and 19H01109 and JST CREST JPMJCR19F6 and JPMJCR14D6.

References

1. Agarwal, N., Anand, S., Prabhakaran, M.: Uncovering algebraic structures in the MPC landscape. In: Ishai, Y., Rijmen, V. (eds.) EUROCRYPT 2019, Part II. LNCS, vol. 11477, pp. 381–406. Springer, Cham (2019). https://doi.org/10.1007/978-3-030-17656-3_14
2. Beimel, A., Gabizon, A., Ishai, Y., Kushilevitz, E., Meldgaard, S., Paskin-Cherniavsky, A.: Non-interactive secure multiparty computation. In: Garay, J.A., Gennaro, R. (eds.) CRYPTO 2014, Part II. LNCS, vol. 8617, pp. 387–404. Springer, Heidelberg (2014). https://doi.org/10.1007/978-3-662-44381-1_22
3. Beimel, A., Gabizon, A., Ishai, Y., Kushilevitz, E., Meldgaard, S., Paskin-Cherniavsky, A.: Non-interactive secure multiparty computation. Cryptology ePrint Archive, Report 2014/960 (2014). full version of [2]
4. Beimel, A., Ishai, Y., Kushilevitz, E.: Ad hoc PSM protocols: secure computation without coordination. In: Coron, J.-S., Nielsen, J.B. (eds.) EUROCRYPT 2017, Part III. LNCS, vol. 10212, pp. 580–608. Springer, Cham (2017). https://doi.org/10.1007/978-3-319-56617-7_20
5. Beimel, A., Kushilevitz, E., Nissim, P.: The complexity of multiparty PSM protocols and related models. In: Nielsen, J.B., Rijmen, V. (eds.) EUROCRYPT 2018, Part II. LNCS, vol. 10821, pp. 287–318. Springer, Cham (2018). https://doi.org/10.1007/978-3-319-78375-8_10
6. Benhamouda, F., Krawczyk, H., Rabin, T.: Robust non-interactive multiparty computation against constant-size collusion. In: Katz, J., Shacham, H. (eds.) CRYPTO 2017, Part I. LNCS, vol. 10401, pp. 391–419. Springer, Cham (2017). https://doi.org/10.1007/978-3-319-63688-7_13

7. Boser, B.E., Guyon, I.M., Vapnik, V.N.: A training algorithm for optimal margin classifiers. In: Proceedings of the Fifth Annual Workshop on Computational Learning Theory, COLT 1992, pp. 144–152 (1992)
8. Cortes, C., Vapnik, V.: Support-vector networks. Mach. Learn. **20**(3), 273–297 (1995)
9. Feige, U., Kilian, J., Naor, M.: A minimal model for secure computation (extended abstract). In: Proceedings of the Twenty-Sixth Annual ACM Symposium on Theory of Computing, STOC 1994, pp. 554–563 (1994)
10. Halevi, S., Ishai, Y., Jain, A., Kushilevitz, E., Rabin, T.: Secure multiparty computation with general interaction patterns. In: Proceedings of the 2016 ACM Conference on Innovations in Theoretical Computer Science, ITCS 2016, pp. 157–168 (2016)
11. Halevi, S., Ishai, Y., Kushilevitz, E., Rabin, T.: Best possible information-theoretic MPC. In: Beimel, A., Dziembowski, S. (eds.) TCC 2018, Part II. LNCS, vol. 11240, pp. 255–281. Springer, Cham (2018). https://doi.org/10.1007/978-3-030-03810-6_10
12. Halevi, S., Lindell, Y., Pinkas, B.: Secure computation on the web: computing without simultaneous interaction. In: Rogaway, P. (ed.) CRYPTO 2011. LNCS, vol. 6841, pp. 132–150. Springer, Heidelberg (2011). https://doi.org/10.1007/978-3-642-22792-9_8
13. Ishai, Y., Kushilevitz, E.: Private simultaneous messages protocols with applications. In: Proceedings of the Fifth Israeli Symposium on Theory of Computing and Systems, pp. 174–183 (1997)
14. Kilian, J.: Founding crytpography on oblivious transfer. In: Proceedings of the Twentieth Annual ACM Symposium on Theory of Computing, STOC 1988, pp. 20–31 (1988)
15. Obana, S., Yoshida, M.: An efficient construction of non-interactive secure multiparty computation. In: Foresti, S., Persiano, G. (eds.) CANS 2016. LNCS, vol. 10052, pp. 604–614. Springer, Cham (2016). https://doi.org/10.1007/978-3-319-48965-0_39
16. Shoup, V.: A Computational Introduction to Number Theory and Algebra. Cambridge University Press, Cambridge (2009)
17. Yoshida, M., Obana, S.: On the (in)efficiency of non-interactive secure multiparty computation. Des. Codes Cryptogr. **86**(8), 1793–1805 (2018)

Efficient Information-Theoretic Multi-party Computation over Non-commutative Rings

Daniel Escudero[1]($\boxtimes$) and Eduardo Soria-Vazquez[2]($\boxtimes$)

[1] Department of Computer Science, Aarhus University, Aarhus, Denmark
escudero@cs.au.dk
[2] Cryptography Research Centre, Technology Innovation Institute, Abu Dhabi, UAE
eduardo.soria-vazquez@tii.ae

Abstract. We construct the first efficient, unconditionally secure MPC protocol that only requires black-box access to a non-commutative ring R. Previous results in the same setting were efficient only either for a constant number of corruptions or when computing branching programs and formulas. Our techniques are based on a generalization of Shamir's secret sharing to non-commutative rings, which we derive from the work on Reed Solomon codes by Quintin, Barbier and Chabot (*IEEE Transactions on Information Theory, 2013*). When the center of the ring contains a set $A = \{\alpha_0, \ldots, \alpha_n\}$ such that $\forall i \neq j, \alpha_i - \alpha_j \in R^*$, the resulting secret sharing scheme is strongly multiplicative and we can generalize existing constructions over finite fields without much trouble.

Most of our work is devoted to the case where the elements of A do not commute with all of R, but they just commute with each other. For such rings, the secret sharing scheme cannot be linear "on both sides" and furthermore it is not multiplicative. Nevertheless, we are still able to build MPC protocols with a concretely efficient online phase and black-box access to R. As an example we consider the ring $\mathcal{M}_{m \times m}(\mathbb{Z}/2^k\mathbb{Z})$, for which when $m > \log(n+1)$, we obtain protocols that require around $\lceil \log(n+1) \rceil / 2$ less communication and $2\lceil \log(n+1) \rceil$ less computation than the state of the art protocol based on Circuit Amortization Friendly Encodings (Dalskov, Lee and Soria-Vazquez, *ASIACRYPT 2020*).

In this setting with a "less commutative" A, our black-box preprocessing phase has a less practical complexity of $\mathsf{poly}(n)$. We fix this by additionally providing specialized, concretely efficient preprocessing protocols for $\mathcal{M}_{m \times m}(\mathbb{Z}/2^k\mathbb{Z})$ that exploit the structure of the matrix ring.

1 Introduction

Multiparty Computation, or MPC for short, is a collection of techniques that enable a set of mutually distrustful parties $P_1, \ldots, P_n$ to securely compute a given function f on private inputs $x_1, \ldots, x_n$, while revealing only the output

---

E. Soria-Vazquez—Work partially done while at Aarhus University, Denmark.

T. Malkin and C. Peikert (Eds.): CRYPTO 2021, LNCS 12826, pp. 335–364, 2021.
https://doi.org/10.1007/978-3-030-84245-1_12

of the computation. Security is formalized by considering an adversary that corrupts t of the parties, and aims at learning as much as possible from the honest parties' inputs either by only seeing the messages corrupt parties send/receive without changing their behavior (passive adversary), or by arbitrarily deviating from the protocol specification (active adversary). Security requires that the adversary does not learn anything about the honest parties' inputs beyond what is possibly leaked by the output of the computation. MPC protocols exist in a wide variety of settings, and some very interesting ones are the settings in which $t < n/2$ and the stronger one in which $t < n/3$. It is well known that in these scenarios, MPC protocols whose security is completely independent of the hardness of any computational problem can be devised, and with the lack of these computational problems typically more efficiency is gained. These protocols are called information-theoretic protocols.

Many information-theoretic protocols exist in the $t < n/2$ and $t < n/3$ regimes, for which computation is primarily represented as an arithmetic circuit whose gates involve additions and multiplications over a finite ring. Traditionally, this ring has been restricted to be a finite field, since the lack of zero divisors simplifies protocol design and opens for a vast literature of algebraic tricks which can ensure that an active adversary does not cheat during the protocol. A recent line of work [ACD+19, DLS20, CRX19, ED20] designs protocols that operate over non-field rings, namely $\mathbb{Z}_{2^k}$ (integers modulo 2^k), and Galois ring extensions $GR(2^k, d)$ of these. The use of these rings is well motivated in practice due to their direct compatibility with hardware and their natural affinity with binary-based protocols like binary decomposition, secure comparison or secure truncation for fixed-point arithmetic. It is not hard to generalize the techniques presented in [ACD+19] to more general *commutative* rings, as long as the so-called Lenstra constant[1] of the ring is large enough. However, in spite of the recent progress in the design of MPC protocols over non-field rings, *non-commutative* rings have been mostly overlooked in the literature.

Studying non-commutative rings is a well motivated theoretical question, since it explores what are the minimal assumptions required on an algebraic structure so that MPC protocols can be naturally defined over it. Furthermore, there are some non-commutative rings that are very suitable for practical applications. For instance, matrix rings are very useful for applications based on linear algebra, which include statistics as well as the training and evaluation of different kinds of machine learning models. Another example are quaternion rings, which are particularly advantageous for describing rotations in a three-dimensional space. Due to this feature, quaternions are a useful tool in the domains of computer graphics, robotics and aerospace, including satellite navigation.

Motivated by the above, in this work we attack the question of designing *efficient* information-theoretic MPC protocols which work *directly* over not-necessarily-commutative finite rings.

---

[1] An exceptional set is a subset of ring elements whose non-zero pairwise differences are invertible. The Lenstra constant of a ring is the size of the largest exceptional set.

1.1 Theoretical Contributions

First, we observe that feasibility results for MPC have been established already since the 80s (e.g. [BGW88]), so in principle we could make use of any existing MPC protocol that allows computing *any* function in order to emulate arithmetic over any given ring R. However, we notice that this requires white-box access to the representation of elements in R, and moreover, it is unlikely to lead to efficient protocols if there is no certain "compatibility" between the ring R and the domain used for the underlying MPC protocol. For example, if R is a matrix ring over the integers modulo a prime, and the domain of computation of the given protocol is $\mathbb{Z}_2$, then there is a large overhead incurred in emulating each single addition and multiplication modulo a prime using binary circuits.

Given the above, we propose *efficient* unconditionally secure MPC protocols over rings containing big enough exceptional sets A which satisfy some additional commutativity properties. Our most general results only requires *black-box* access to the ring, which we start by precisely defining.

Definition 1. *We say that a protocol has* black-box access *to a ring R, or simply that it is* black-box, *if it only requires black-box access to the ring operations and the elements of a particular exceptional set A. Furthermore, we assume that it is efficient both to sample elements from R and to invert elements from R^*.*

Our protocols are based on a generalization of Shamir's linear secret sharing scheme to non-commutative rings. Prior to our work, Quintin, Barbier and Chabot [QBC13] showed how to construct Reed Solomon codes over rings that do not need to be commutative. By reinterpreting their results under the lenses of linear secret-sharing schemes (LSSS's), we first obtain the following result.

Theorem 1 ([Theorem 4, restated]). *Let R be a ring such that $Z(R)$ contains an exceptional set of size at least $n + 1$ and let $t < n/3$. Then, we can define a Shamir-style strongly multiplicative linear secret sharing scheme over R.*

This is discussed in Sect. 3. Given a ring satisfying the hypothesis of the previous theorem, we can adapt the perfectly secure protocol by Beerliova and Hirt [BTH08].

Corollary 1 (Corollary 2, restated). *Let R be a ring such that $Z(R)$ contains an exceptional set of size at least $2n$. Let $\mathcal{A}$ be an active adversary corrupting $t < n/3$ parties. There exists a perfectly secure, black-box MPC protocol with an amortized communication complexity of $O(n)$ ring elements per gate.*

While interesting, the previous result leaves out of the picture several non-commutative rings. For example, the centre of the ring of matrices over $\mathbb{Z}_{2^k}$, which is widely used in applications involving linear algebra, like machine learning, has a Lenstra constant of 2, which is not large enough to apply the results highlighted above. We fix this by relaxing the commutativity requirements for the elements of the exceptional set: instead of requiring this exceptional set to be a subset of the centre of the ring, we only ask the elements of the exceptional set to commute with each other. It is in this setting that the previous results on

Reed-Solomon codes [QBC13] do not help us as much. The resulting code (i.e. secret sharing scheme) is not linear "on both sides", but rather only when multiplied by scalars either on the left or on the right. Even more disastrously, the left-or-right LSSS that we obtain is not multiplicative, which rules out standard techniques to achieve unconditionally secure MPC. Considering all of this, most of our work relates to proving the following Theorem:

Theorem 2 (Informal). *Let R be a ring and $A = \{\alpha_0, \ldots, \alpha_n\} \subseteq R$ an exceptional set such that $\forall \alpha_i, \alpha_j \in A, \alpha_i \cdot \alpha_j = \alpha_j \cdot \alpha_i$. Let $\mathcal{A}$ be an active adversary corrupting t parties. For $t < n/2$ and $t < n/3$, there exist efficient, information-theoretically secure, black-box MPC protocols over R. The amortized communication complexity of their online phase is $O(n)$ ring elements per gate.*

The black-box online phase of our protocol is described in Sect. 4, while the black-box offline phase is presented in Sect. 5.1.

1.2 Concretely Efficient Protocols for $\mathcal{M}_{m \times m}(\mathbb{Z}_{2^k})$

Beyond their theoretical interest, our techniques also have relevance in the context of concretely efficient MPC. As an example for this, we provide constructions for the important ring $R = \mathcal{M}_{m \times m}(\mathbb{Z}_{2^k})$, the ring of m × m matrices with entries modulo 2^k, which improve upon the concrete efficiency of the online phase of the state of the art protocols in the same setting but without black-box access to R. As mentioned before, the centre of this ring does not have a large enough exceptional set, so the MPC techniques based on the multiplicativity of Shamir secret sharing (which are quite efficient) cannot be applied.

Given this, our approach is to make use of the black-box protocol from Theorem 2. First, we show that, whenever $m \geq \log(n+1)$, the hypothesis of this theorem is satisfied. This is due to the fact that $\mathsf{GR}(2^k, m)$ is a (commutative) subring of R and the Lenstra constant of $\mathsf{GR}(2^k, m)$ is precisely 2^m. Second, we show how to replace the black-box preprocessing from Theorem 2, which achieves only $\mathsf{poly}(n)$ communication complexity, by a more tailored preprocessing protocol for $R = \mathcal{M}_{m \times m}(\mathbb{Z}_{2^k})$. This is done in Sect. 5.2. Finally, we also show in the full version of this work how to do efficient error-correction of Shamir shares in this setting.

By following Theorem 2 we obtain a very efficient online phase, as described by the (generic) protocols we provide in Sect. 4. For this part of the protocol execution, the fact of having a secret sharing scheme directly over R is a significant efficiency advantage: each share of a secret is a single element of R, and arithmetic happens at the level of R. However, the price to pay for such an efficient online phase, which overcomes the issues of lacking multiplicativity, is that the offline phase becomes much more complex.

In Sect. 5.2 we show how to compute the required preprocessing material for $R = \mathcal{M}_{m \times m}(\mathbb{Z}_{2^k})$ by, intuitively, secret-sharing each entry of a matrix and then leveraging existing works on MPC over $\mathbb{Z}_{2^k}$ [ACD+19, DLS20]. As we need to compute the product between secret-shared matrices and retain information-theoretic security, this is our best approach for concrete efficiency. Secret-sharing each entry of a matrix in $\mathcal{M}_{m \times m}(\mathbb{Z}_{2^k})$ individually would require us to move to a Galois extension of $\mathbb{Z}_{2^k}$ of degree $d \simeq \log(n+1)$, which would add such overhead in terms of communication and a worse one for computation. Instead of naively secret-sharing each entry, we amortize the asymptotic communication cost of working over such Galois extension by using the Circuit Amortization Friendly Encodings (CAFEs) introduced in [DLS20]. Intuitively, what this means is that chunks of every row/column of each matrix will be secret-shared as a single Galois Ring element.

At this point, one could ask why not work with this type of secret-sharing for the whole protocol execution, rather than just the preprocessing phase. The CAFE for inner products that we use in our preprocessing phase allows to "pack" approximately $d/2$ elements from $\mathbb{Z}_{2^k}$ into $\mathsf{GR}(2^k, d)$, so that seems to be a small overhead. Some arguments for not following this route are as follows. First of all, the protocol from [DLS20] is only fully detailed for double sharings and in the case of security with abort. Our online protocol, on the other hand, has guaranteed output delivery (if $t < n/3$) and uses multiplication triples. Furthermore, it is most efficient when using a function-dependent preprocessing in the style of [BNO19, ED20]. These differences make a fair comparison more difficult, but even assuming an adaptation of [DLS20] to the function-dependent techniques of [BNO19, ED20], our online phase remains more efficient in the following aspects.

- Secret sharing input values: For the adapted [DLS20], when parties provide inputs to the computation, it would be important to check that they are rightly encoded. This issue is not specific to CAFEs, but merely to the fact of having to work over an extension ($\mathsf{GR}(2^k, d)$) of the ring one is actually interested in ($\mathbb{Z}_{2^k}$). The check can be performed by using preprocessing material, but it increases the communication and round complexity of the protocol. Our online phase does not need to perform any such check, as it works directly over $\mathcal{M}_{m \times m}(\mathbb{Z}_{2^k})$.
- Computing the product of two secret-shared matrices, communication: In our work, this requires to reconstruct two secrets in $\mathcal{M}_{m \times m}(\mathbb{Z}_{2^k})$. An adapted [DLS20], would need to reconstruct one element of $\mathsf{GR}(2^k, d)$ per entry of the matrix. Hence, in terms of communication we are around $d/2$ times better in our work.
- Computing the product of two secret-shared matrices, computation: Our work benefits from the fact that the shares each party holds, as well as the operations they perform on them, are in $\mathcal{M}_{m \times m}(\mathbb{Z}_{2^k})$. This has the advantage that an implementation of our protocol can fully exploit existing libraries for matrix arithmetic, which is quite efficient due to its relevance in multiple practical settings. On the other hand, using a potential extension of the techniques of [DLS20] in the online phase would require computation on Galois ring elements, which is way less studied than matrix arithmetic and it is also more inefficient. Each multiplications of two Galois ring elements costs d^2 operations in $\mathbb{Z}_{2^k}$, or potentially $d \log(d)$ using FFT-based techniques. This is not very concretely efficient, as explored experimentally in [DEK21], for example.

Instead of using CAFEs, Reverse Multiplication Friendly Embeddings (RMFEs) [CCXY18] could have been chosen. A generalization of the interpolation-based RMFE from [CCXY18] was presented in [DLS20] and the constructions based on algebraic geometric codes were also lifted to rings in [CRX19]. Whereas RMFEs are much computationally heavier than CAFEs, they can provide a slightly better communication complexity. More concretely, if δ is the amount of elements from the base ring that the RMFE can "pack", RMFEs incur in a communication complexity for the product of secret shared matrices that would be only d/δ, rather than $d/2$, worse than ours. On the other hand, using RMFEs require two sequential openings per matrix multiplication, rather than a single one as CAFEs do. This is due to a resharing operation to compute $\psi(\phi(\boldsymbol{a}) \cdot \phi(\boldsymbol{b}))$ in RMFEs.

In a nutshell, by using our seemingly theoretical tools, we are able to build MPC protocols which have a more efficient online phase than the state of the art protocols, while retaining a comparable preprocessing.

1.3 Related Work

There are a few works on MPC over non-abelian *groups*, rather than rings. Hence, we are not interested in those. These include [DPS+12] and [CDI+13]. Note that [CDI+13] additionally provides constructions for *commutative* rings.

MPC over non-commutative rings has been discussed in [CFIK03], but their results related to MPC from (multiplicative) Monotone Span Programs are restricted to (algebras over) commutative rings. They only seem to take care of the non-commutative case in Sects. 4.2 and 4.3, which deal only with branching programs and formulas, rather than circuits.

Although not mentioned explicitly in [BBY20], the basic building blocks (secure addition and multiplication) presented in that work for MPC based on replicated secret-sharing also work over a non-commutative ring. However, these techniques differ from ours in several ways. First, they use computational assumptions (PRFs) in order to improve their overall efficiency. Second, as it is inherent for MPC based on replicated secret-sharing, the communication complexity does not scale well as the number of parties increases. More precisely, each share consists of $\binom{n}{t}$ ring elements, which is exponential in n whenever $t = n/c$ for some $c > 1$, since $\binom{n}{n/c} \geq (c^{1/c})^n$.[2]

2   Preliminaries

Notation. Sometimes, we use $[n]$, where $n \in \mathbb{N}$, to represent $\{1, 2, \ldots, n\}$. We write $x \xleftarrow{\$} \mathcal{X}$ to denote sampling a value x uniformly from the set $\mathcal{X}$. We write $\mathbb{Z}_{p^k}$ to denote the ring of integers modulo p^k and $\mathcal{M}_{r \times c}(R)$ to refer to the ring of $r \times c$ matrices over R.

---

[2] Here we use the well known inequality $\binom{a}{b} \geq (a/b)^b$.

2.1   Multiparty Computation

We consider secure evaluation of functions $(y_1, \ldots, y_n) = f(x_1, \ldots, x_n)$ given by arithmetic circuits with addition and multiplication gates defined over a finite ring R, where party P_i is supposed to learn y_i.

The security of our protocols is proven in the UC framework by Cannetti [Can01]. We assume secure, synchronous channels, and we deal with active, static adversaries. In a nutshell, the adversary corrupts a subset of t parties actively, arbitrarily changing their behavior during the execution of the protocol. The adversary, also known as an *environment*, additionally provides the inputs for all the parties. A given protocol Π instantiates a given functionality $\mathcal{F}$, if there exists a simulator $\mathcal{S}$ who, by interacting with the adversary and with the functionality $\mathcal{F}$, creates an execution (called the *ideal* execution) that is indistinguishable to the adversary from the real execution in which the actual honest parties are running the protocol Π.

If the distributions in the two executions are exactly the same, then we say that Π instantiates $\mathcal{F}$ with perfect security. In contrast, if the distributions are only negligibly apart (in some security parameter κ), then we say that Π instantiates $\mathcal{F}$ with statistical security. Finally, sometimes we consider *hybrid* models in which a protocol Π instantiates a functionality $\mathcal{F}$, assuming access to another functionality $\mathcal{F}'$. In this case we say that Π instantiates $\mathcal{F}$ in the $\mathcal{F}'$-hybrid model. See [Can01] for details.

In this work we consider a broadcast functionality $\mathcal{F}_{\mathrm{BC}}$ that receives an input from a designated sender and relays this exact same value to all the parties.

We will take into account two functionalities for MPC. One is $\mathcal{F}_{\mathrm{MPC-GOD}}$, which receives inputs $x_1, \ldots, x_n$ from the parties, computes the given function $(y_1, \ldots, y_n) = f(x_1, \ldots, x_n)$, which is represented as an arithmetic circuit over a ring R composed of addition and multiplication gates, and returns the output y_i to each party P_i. The second functionality is $\mathcal{F}_{\mathrm{MPC-abort}}$, which is defined as $\mathcal{F}_{\mathrm{MPC-GOD}}$, except that, before delivering output to the parties, it waits for a message from the adversary. If the message is abort, then the functionality sends abort to all the parties. Else, if the message if ok, then the functionality sends the output y_i to each party P_i. In a real execution, when we say that an honest party "aborts", it means that this party sends an abort signal to all the parties using $\mathcal{F}_{\mathrm{BC}}$ and then outputs abort. A party aborts upon receiving an abort signal through the broadcast channel.

2.2   Background in Ring Theory

We turn to recall some useful results from ring theory. Outside of this section, whenever we talk about a ring R, we mean a finite ring with identity $1 \neq 0$ for which we do *not* assume commutativity. During this specific section we do not assume finiteness, so that it is clear which results require such hypothesis.

Working over these general rings hides subtleties which do not appear in the field case. Besides the lack of commutativity, one has to be careful about the fact that the rings we consider contain zero divisors. Moreover, it is important to reconsider what it means to be a unit. We recap some basic definitions and results in this area of algebra. These are standard results, and some of their proofs are provided in the full version of this work.

Definition 2. *Let R be a ring. An element $a \in R$ is a unit if there exists $b \in R$ such that $a \cdot b = b \cdot a = 1$. The set of all units is denoted by R^*.*

An element $a \in R \backslash \{0\}$ is a left (resp. right) zero divisor if $\exists\, b \in R \backslash \{0\}$ such that $a \cdot b = 0$ (resp. $b \cdot a = 0$). In this work, whenever we say that $a \in R \backslash \{0\}$ is a zero divisor we mean that a is both a left and right zero divisor.

Lemma 1. *1. $a \in R^*$ if and only if a is both left-invertible and right-invertible.*
2. If a has a right inverse, then a is not a right zero divisor.
3. If R is finite, then every element which has a right inverse is a unit.

Lemma 2. *Let R be a finite ring. Then all non-zero elements of R are either a unit or a zero divisor.*

Some elements of a non-commutative ring have better commutative properties than other. The two following definitions allow us to name them.

Definition 3. *The center of a ring R, denoted by $Z(R)$ consists of the elements $a \in Z(R)$ such that $\forall b \in R$, $ab = ba$.*

Definition 4 ([QBC13]). *Let $A = \{a_1, \ldots, a_n\} \subset R$. We say that A is a commutative set if $\forall a_i, a_j \in A, a_i \cdot a_j = a_j \cdot a_i$.*

Exceptional sets. Elements which satisfy that their pairwise differences are invertible will be fundamental in our constructions. These have received different names in the literature: 'subtractive sets' in [QBC13], 'exceptional sequences' in [ACD+19] and 'exceptional sets' in [DLS20]. We will stick with the latter denomination.

Definition 5. *Let $A = \{a_1, \ldots, a_n\} \subset R$. We say that A is an exceptional set if $\forall i \neq j, a_i - a_j \in R^*$. We define the Lenstra constant of R to be the maximum size of an exceptional set in R.*

2.3   Polynomials over Non-commutative Rings

Definition 6 (Polynomial Ring). *Let R be a ring and $A \subseteq R$. The set of polynomials over A of degree at most d is given by $A[\mathtt{X}]_{\leq d} = \{f(\mathtt{X}) = \sum_{i=0}^{d} a_i \cdot \mathtt{X}^i \mid a_i \in A\}$. The set of polynomials over A is $A[\mathtt{X}] = \cup_{d \geq 0} A[\mathtt{X}]$. Given two polynomials $a(\mathtt{X}) = \left(\sum_{i=0}^{d} a_i \cdot \mathtt{X}^i\right)$, $b(\mathtt{X}) = \left(\sum_{j=0}^{d'} b_j \cdot \mathtt{X}^j\right)$, the ring R induces the following operations:*

1. $c(\mathtt{X}) = a(\mathtt{X}) + b(\mathtt{X}) = \sum_{k=0}^{\max\{d,d'\}} (a_k + b_k) \cdot \mathtt{X}^k$, where $a_k = 0$ for $k > d$ and $b_k = 0$ for $k > d'$.

2. $c(X) = a(X) \cdot b(X) = \sum_{k=0}^{d+d'} c_k \cdot X^k$, *where*

$$c_k = \sum_{\substack{i+j=k \\ 0 \leq i \leq d,\ 0 \leq j \leq d'}} a_i b_j.$$

Furthermore, when A is a ring, so is $A[X]$.

Our definition of the product in a polynomial ring imposes that "the indeterminate X commutes with the coefficients". Otherwise, when formally multiplying two polynomials we would encounter terms of the form $a_i X^i b_j X^j$, which could not be turned into $a_i b_j X^{i+j}$. Allowing the indeterminate to commute with coefficients, rather than keeping everything non-commutative, allows us to prove a series of results leading to the existence and uniqueness of interpolating polynomials. On the other hand, granting this small commutativity property to polynomials requires to consider their evaluation more carefully, as we will see next.

Definition 7 (Evaluation Maps). *Let $f = \sum_{i=0}^{d} f_i X^i \in R[X]$ and $a \in R$. We define the evaluation at a on the right (resp. left) map $f^R(a)$ (resp. $f^L(a)$) as follows:*

$$\cdot^R(a) : R[X] \to R \qquad\qquad \cdot^L(a) : R[X] \to R$$

$$f \mapsto f^R(a) = \sum_{i=0}^{d} f_i a^i \qquad\qquad f \mapsto f^L(a) = \sum_{i=0}^{d} a^i f_i$$

We say that a is a right (rep. left) root whenever $f^R(a) = 0$ (resp. $f^L(a) = 0$). We use $f(a)$ to denote $f^R(a)$.

The evaluation maps above are additive homomorphisms but, in general, they are not ring homomorphisms. This is because, as mentioned above, in polynomial multiplication the indeterminate X commutes with the coefficients. It is important to keep in mind that we are dealing with *polynomials* as formal objects of their own, rather than confusing them with *polynomial functions* (where a "variable" X is "instantiated" with $a \in R$ when evaluating the polynomial) as one usually does in commutative rings. Fortunately, there are some cases in which some notion of multiplicative homomorphism holds for the evaluation maps, as described in the following lemma.

Lemma 3. *Let $f \in R[X]$.*

1. *Let A be a commutative set. If $g \in (A \cup Z(R))[X]$ and $a \in A$, then $(f \cdot g)^R(a) = f^R(a) \cdot g^R(a)$ and $(g \cdot f)^L(a) = g^L(a) \cdot f^L(a)$.*
2. *Let $g \in R[X]$. If $a \in Z(R)$, for all $h \in R[X]$, $h^R(a) = h^L(a)$. Furthermore, $(f \cdot g)^R(a) = f^R(a) \cdot g^R(a)$.*

Proof. We only prove the first part of the first statement, as the same reasoning applies for the rest of the claims. Let $a \in A$ and let $f(X) = \left(\sum_{i=0}^{d} f_i \cdot X^i \right) \in R[X]$ and $g(X) = \left(\sum_{j=0}^{d'} g_j \cdot X^j \right) \in (A \cup Z(R))[X]$ be our polynomials.

$$f^R(a) \cdot g^R(a) = \left(\sum_{i=0}^{d} f_i \cdot a^i\right) \cdot \left(\sum_{j=0}^{d'} g_j \cdot a^j\right) = \sum_{i=0}^{d} \sum_{j=0}^{d'} f_i \cdot a^i \cdot g_j \cdot a^j =$$

$$= \sum_{i=0}^{d} \sum_{j=0}^{d'} f_i \cdot a^{i-1} \cdot g_j \cdot a^{j+1} = \sum_{i=0}^{d} \sum_{j=0}^{d'} f_i \cdot g_j \cdot a^{i+j} = (f \cdot g)^R(a). \quad \blacksquare$$

Theorem 3 (Euclidean Algorithm over Rings). *Let $f(X) \in R[X]$ be a non-zero polynomial and let $g(X) \in R[X]$ be a monic polynomial. There exist unique $q_\ell(X), r_\ell(X)$ (resp. $q_r(X), r_r(X)$) such that $f(X) = q_\ell(X) \cdot g(X) + r_\ell(X)$ (resp. $f(X) = g(X) \cdot q_r(X) + r_r(X)$), where $\deg(r_\ell) < \deg(g)$ (resp. $\deg(r_r) < \deg(g)$).*

Given the two previous results, we can bound the number of roots of a polynomial as it is described in the next Lemma.

Lemma 4. *Let $f \in R[X]_{\leq n}$ be a non-zero polynomial. Then f has at most n distinct left (resp. right) roots in the same commutative exceptional set $A \subset R$. In other words, if f has at least $n+1$ left (resp. right) roots in A, then it is the zero polynomial.*

Proof. We focus on right roots for the result, and we reason by induction on the degree d of the non-zero polynomial f. The statement is clear when $d = 0$. Assuming the result for $d-1$, we now look at a degree-d polynomial f. If f does not have any roots, or if it only has one root, then the result clearly holds. Else, let $a, b \in A$ be two different roots of $f(X)$. As $g(X) = X - a$ is a monic polynomial, by Theorem 3 there exists $q(X) \in R[X]$ and $c \in R$ such that $f(X) = q(X) \cdot g(X) + c$. Observe that $\deg(q) < \deg(f)$.

Now, since $g(X) \in A[X]$, by Lemma 3 we have that $f^R(a) = q^R(a)g^R(a) + c$, so $0 = q^R(a) \cdot (a-a) + c = c$. From this, it follows that $0 = f^R(b) = q^R(b)g^R(b) = q^R(b) \cdot (b-a)$. Since $(b-a) \in R^*$, then it has to be that $q^R(b) = 0$.

By the induction hypothesis, $q(X)$ has at most $d-1$ distinct right roots in A, so we can conclude that $f(X)$ has at most d distinct right roots in A. $\quad \blacksquare$

Lagrange interpolation for sets of points $(x_i, y_i) \in R^2$ can be computed, as long as all the x_i are part of the same commutative exceptional set $A \subset R$. The following result was proven in [QBC13], but it only considered evaluation on the right. We reformulate and extend their result here for completeness and additional precision.

Proposition 1. *Let $A = \{x_1, \ldots, x_{n+1}\} \subset R$ be a commutative exceptional set and let $B = \{y_1, \ldots, y_{n+1}\} \subset R$. Then there exists a unique polynomial $f \in R[X]$ (resp. $g \in R[X]$) of degree at most d such that $f^R(x_i) = y_i$ (resp. $g^L(x_i) = y_i$) for $i = 1, \ldots, d+1$. Furthermore, if $A \cup B$ constitutes a commutative set, or if $A \subset Z(R)$, $f(X) = g(X)$.*

Proof. Let $L_i(X) = \prod_{j \neq i}(X - x_j) \in A[X]$. Observe that for all $j = 1, \ldots, d+1$ it holds that $L_i(x_j) \in R^*$, since $(x_i - x_j) \in R^*$.

It is easy to verify, with the help of Lemma 3, that the two following polynomials show the existence of solutions:

$$f(X) = \sum_{i=1}^{d+1} y_i L_i(x_i)^{-1} L_i(X); \qquad g(X) = \sum_{i=1}^{d+1} L_i(X) L_i(x_i)^{-1} y_i$$

The uniqueness of f (resp. g) is a consequence of Lemma 4. The fact that $f(X) = g(X)$ when $A \cup B$ constitutes a commutative set or $A \subset Z(R)$ follows from inspection. ∎

2.4 Galois Rings

Galois Rings relate to integers modulo a prime power p^k in the same way a Galois Field relates to integers modulo a prime p. They are a fundamental object of study among finite commutative rings.

Definition 8. *A Galois Ring* $GR(p^k, d)$ *is a ring of the form* $R = \mathbb{Z}_{p^k}[X]/(h(X))$, *where p is a prime, k a positive integer and $h(X) \in \mathbb{Z}_{p^k}[X]$ a monic polynomial of degree $d \geq 1$ such that its reduction modulo p is an irreducible polynomial in* $\mathbb{F}_p[X]$.

Given a base ring $\mathbb{Z}_{p^k}$, there is a unique degree d Galois extension of $\mathbb{Z}_{p^k}$, which is precisely the Galois Ring provided on the previous definition. Note that Galois Rings reconcile the study of finite fields $\mathbb{F}_{p^d} = GR(p, d)$ and finite rings of the form $\mathbb{Z}_{p^k} = GR(p^k, 1)$. Every Galois Ring $R = GR(p^k, d)$ is a local ring and its unique maximal ideal is (p). Hence, all the zero divisors of R are furthermore nilpotent, and they constitute the maximal ideal (p). Furthermore, we have that $R/(p) \cong \mathbb{F}_{p^d}$.

Proposition 2 ([ACD+19]). *The Lenstra constant of $R = GR(p^k, d)$ is p^d.*

Whenever we need to explicitly represent elements $a \in R$, we will consider two options. The first one, which we will denote the *additive representation*, follows from Definition 8 and consists of the residue classes

$$a \equiv a_0 + a_1 \cdot X + \cdots + a_{d-1} \cdot X^{d-1} \mod h(X), \quad a_i \in \mathbb{Z}_{p^k}. \tag{1}$$

The second option is what we shall call the *matrix representation*, which uses the embedding $\iota : GR(p^k, d) \hookrightarrow \mathcal{M}_{d \times d}(\mathbb{Z}_{p^k})$ and represents a as $\iota(a)$. It will be instructive to discuss this embedding more explicitly for other parts of this work. Let us look at how the product between $a, b \in GR(p^k, d)$ is computed. If we express a in its additive representation, $a = \sum_{\ell \in [d]} a_\ell \cdot X^\ell$, multiplication by b can be seen as the homomorphism of free $\mathbb{Z}_{p^k}$-modules $\phi_b : \mathbb{Z}_{p^k}^d \to \mathbb{Z}_{p^k}^d$, which maps the coefficients of a's additive representation to those of $c = \phi_b(a)$.

Notice that since $\mathsf{Im}(\iota) \simeq GR(p^k, d)$, we have that $\iota(a) \cdot \iota(b) = \iota(b) \cdot \iota(a)$. In other words, the matrices in $\mathsf{Im}(\iota)$ constitute a commutative subset of $\mathcal{M}_{d \times d}(\mathbb{Z}_{p^k})$.

3 Shamir's Secret Sharing over Non-commutative Rings

Secret sharing schemes (SSS) are one of the most fundamental building blocks in secure computation. There are three properties which we usually want from SSS in MPC. The first one is t-privacy, meaning that no set of at most t shares reveals any information about the secret. The second one is $t+1$-reconstruction, which allows to reconstruct the secret from any subset of $t+1$ correct shares. The third one is *linearity*, which requires talking about specific algebraic structures. In our work, as we will be working over rings for which we do not assume commutativity, we need to distinguish between *left* and *right* linearity.

Definition 9. *Let $C = \{(s, s_1, \ldots, s_n)\} \subseteq R^{n+1}$ be a SSS, where s is a secret and $s_1, \ldots, s_n$ are its shares. We say that C is a left (resp. right) linear secret sharing scheme if it is a left (resp. right) submodule of R^{n+1}. We will respectively denote the secret sharing of s by $[s], \langle s \rangle$. If C is a bisubmodule of R^{n+1}, then we simply call it a linear secret sharing scheme, which we denote as $[\![s]\!]$.*

In Shamir's secret sharing scheme, which was originally restricted to finite fields [Sha79], the submodule C is a Reed-Solomon code, i.e. $[\![s]\!]_t$ would be sampled from $C = \{(s, f(\alpha_1), \ldots, f(\alpha_n)) : f \in \mathbb{F}[X]_{\leq t} \wedge s = f(\alpha_0)\}$. This was later on generalized to commutative rings containing big enough exceptional sets [ACD+19]. In this work, we observe that Reed-Solomon codes have been constructed even over non-commutative rings [QBC13]. Throughout this section we translate the relevant parts of [QBC13] to the LSSS language. Moreover, we fill some gaps about error correction left by the authors of [QBC13], we generalize standard secret reconstruction procedures from [DN07] and we show where do matrix rings fit in these results.

Beyond linearity, another desirable property for a SSS to have is that of *(strong) multiplicativity*. Briefly, such notion guarantees that (even in the presence of active adversaries) the product of two secrets a, b can be reconstructed as a function of the coordinate-wise product of their shares, $a_i \cdot b_i$. For a formal definition see [CDM00].

Theorem 4. *Let R be a ring such that $Z(R)$ contains an exceptional set $A = \{\alpha_0, \ldots, \alpha_n\}$ and let $t < n/3$. Then, we can define a Shamir-style strongly multiplicative linear secret sharing scheme over R. In more detail, a degree-t sharing $[\![s]\!]_t$ is sampled from:*

$$\{(s, f^R(\alpha_1), \ldots, f^R(\alpha_n)) : f \in \mathbb{F}[X]_{\leq t} \wedge s = f^R(\alpha_0)\}$$

Strong multiplicativity in the previous result woks as usual in Shamir's LSSS. In more detail, given two shared values, $[\![a]\!]_t = (a, a_1, \ldots, a_n)$ using a polynomial $f \in R[X]_{\leq t}$ and $[\![b]\!]_t = (b, b_1, \ldots, b_n)$ using a polynomial $g \in R[X]_{\leq t}$, it holds that $[\![a \cdot b]\!]_{2t} = (ab, a_1 b_1, \ldots, a_n b_n)$. This is due to the fact that the points α_i where f and g are evaluated at are contained in $Z(R)$, and hence by Lemma 3 it holds that $(f \cdot g)^R(\alpha_i) = f^R(\alpha_i) \cdot g^R(\alpha_i)$, which is not generally the case for non-commutative polynomials.

Given the previous theorem, we can adapt the results of [BTH08, ACD+19] to work over non-commutative rings as the ones of the hypothesis without too much effort. This gives us the following result, for which a bit more details are given in the full version of this work. The increase on the size of the exceptional set is due to the use of so-called hyper-invertible matrices.

Corollary 2. *Let R be a ring such that $Z(R)$ contains an exceptional set of size at least $2n$. Let $\mathcal{A}$ be an active adversary corrupting $t < n/3$ parties. There exists a perfectly secure, black-box MPC protocol with an amortized communication complexity of $O(n)$ ring elements per gate.*

If we relax the hypothesis of Theorem 4, so that we only ask from the elements of the exceptional set to commute with each other, rather than being in the centre of the ring, we can still build Shamir-style secret sharing schemes.

Theorem 5. *Let R be a ring containing a commutative, exceptional set $A = \{\alpha_0, \ldots, \alpha_n\}$. Then, we can define a Shamir-style left-LSSS $[\cdot]$ and a Shamir-style right-LSSS $\langle \cdot \rangle$ over R. These secret sharing schemes are not multiplicative.*

We do not provide an explicit proof of the previous Theorem, but in Fig. 1 we show how to share a secret for the left-linear scheme $[\cdot]$. The right-linear scheme $\langle \cdot \rangle$ would produce shares in an analogous way, setting instead $s_i = f^{\mathsf{L}}(\alpha_i)$. The t-privacy and $t+1$-reconstruction properties are a consequence of Proposition 1. To see why these schemes are not multiplicative, remember that the evaluation maps are not ring homomorphisms in general, i.e. given $f, g \in R[\mathsf{X}]$, generally $f^{\mathsf{R}}(\alpha_i) \cdot g^{\mathsf{R}}(\alpha_i) \neq (f \cdot g)^{\mathsf{R}}(\alpha_i)$. Hence, in contrast with Theorem 4, given $[a]_t = (a, f^{\mathsf{R}}(\alpha_1), \ldots, f^{\mathsf{R}}(\alpha_n))$ and $[b]_t = (b, g^{\mathsf{R}}(\alpha_1), \ldots, g^{\mathsf{R}}(\alpha_n))$, Lemma 3 is of no help now, since the α_i values are not in the centre any more. Note that we cannot simply impose for the sampled polynomial f in Fig. 1 to be in $A[\mathsf{X}]_{\leq d}$. As an example, imagine the case when A is furthermore a subring of R. We would then have that $f^{\mathsf{R}}(\alpha_0) \in A$, effectively restricting the values that can be secret shared to those in the subring A itself.

Protocol $\Pi_{[\cdot]-\mathrm{Share}}(s, d)$

Input: A secret $s \in R$ held by a dealer P_D. A commutative exceptional set $A = \{\alpha_0, \ldots, \alpha_n\}$.
Output: Sharing $[s]_d$.
Protocol: The parties proceed as follows

1. P_D samples a polynomial $f \overset{\$}{\leftarrow} R[\mathsf{X}]_{\leq d}$ such that $f^{\mathsf{R}}(\alpha_0) = s$. Define the shares to be $s_i = f^{\mathsf{R}}(\alpha_i)$ for $i \in [n]$.
2. For $i \in [n] \setminus \{D\}$, P_D sends s_i to P_i.

Fig. 1. Sharing a secret using $[\cdot]$.

3.1   Secret Sharing over Matrix Rings

As our more practical results are related to the ring $\mathcal{M}_{m \times m}(\mathbb{Z}_{2^k})$, it will be useful to give already a more concrete analysis of how it fits with respect to Theorems 4 and 5, before returning to generic rings. We start by reminding the following basic result.

Lemma 5. *The centre of* $\mathcal{M}_{m \times m}(R)$, *where* R *is a commutative ring, is the* R-*multiples of the identity matrix.*

Besides which elements are in the centre of the ring, it is important that we identify exceptional sets in the ring. As we discussed in Sect. 2.4, there exists an embedding $\iota : \mathsf{GR}(p^k, m) \hookrightarrow \mathcal{M}_{m \times m}(\mathbb{Z}_{p^k})$. Hence, as the Lenstra constant of the former ring is p^m, that of $\mathcal{M}_{m \times m}(\mathbb{Z}_{p^k})$ has to be at least p^m. Furthermore, it can be proved that this is exactly the Lenstra constant of $\mathcal{M}_{m \times m}(\mathbb{Z}_{p^k})$, a result shown in the full version of this work.

Proposition 3. *The Lenstra constant of* $\mathcal{M}_{m \times m}(\mathbb{Z}_{p^k})$ *is* p^m.

Let us focus on the ring $R = \mathcal{M}_{m \times m}(\mathbb{Z}_{2^k})$. We know that $Z(R)$ cannot contain exceptional sets of size bigger than two, so Theorem 4 is ruled out. The good news are that, since $\mathsf{GR}(2^k, m)$ (more precisely, $\mathsf{Im}(\iota)$) is a *commutative subring* of R, we can easily identify within R a commutative exceptional set of size 2^m and construct the secret sharing schemes described in Theorem 5 whenever $m > \log(n + 1)$.

3.2   Error Correction and Robust Reconstruction

Let R be a finite ring and let $A = \{\alpha_0, \alpha_1, \ldots, \alpha_n\} \subseteq R$ be an exceptional commutative set. Let $[s]_d = (s_1, \ldots, s_n)$ be a secret-shared value $s \in R$ using a polynomial of degree at most d. For $i = 1, \ldots, n$, let $s_i' = s_i + \delta_i$, where at most e of the $\delta_i \in R$ are non-zero, with $n > d + 2e$. Our goal is to recover $(s_1, \ldots, s_n)$ from $(s_1', \ldots, s_n')$. This is an essential primitive when designing MPC protocols based on Shamir secret-sharing, as it corresponds to reconstructing a secret-shared value from a given set of announced shares among which some of them could be incorrect due to adversarial behavior. This is achieved by a generalization of the Berlekamp-Welch decoding algorithm for Reed-Solomon codes to the non-commutative setting. Such result was exhibited in [QBC13], although many holes were left due to the general approach taken by the authors. For instance, a crucial step in the decoding algorithm lies in solving a system of linear equations over a non-commutative ring, which as we discuss later on is not a very well studied area and concrete algorithms should be developed for each particular instantiation. Motivated by this, and also for the sake of clarity and self-containment, we present below our own version of the generalization of the Berlekamp-Welch algorithm, filling in the holes left in [QBC13]. Below, we let $n' = d + 2e + 1$.

Generalization of the Berlekamp-Welch algorithm. Below we let F denote the subring of R made of finite sums of terms of the form $\alpha_{i_1} \cdot \alpha_{i_2} \cdots \alpha_{i_\ell}$. We say that two polynomials $p(X), q(X) \in R[X]$ satisfy the BW-conditions if:

1. $\deg(p) \leq e$;
2. $\deg(q) \leq d + e$;
3. $p(X)$ is monic;
4. $p(X) \in F[X]$;
5. For all $i = 1, \ldots, n'$, it holds that $s_i' \cdot p(\alpha_i) = q(\alpha_i)$.

We begin with the following claim.

Claim. There exists a pair $p(X), q(X) \in R[X]$ that satisfies the BW-conditions above.

Proof. Let $f(X) = \sum_{i=0}^d c_i X^i \in R_{\leq d}[X]$ such that $f(\alpha_i) = s_i$ for $i = 1, \ldots, n'$, guaranteed by Proposition 1, and define $p(X) = \prod_{e_i \neq 0}(X - \alpha_i)$ and $q(X) = f(X)p(X)$. It can be easily verified, with the help of Lemma 3, that this choice of $p(X)$ and $q(X)$ satisfies the BW-conditions. ∎

The next claim shows that any other pair satisfying the BW-conditions is as good as the one guaranteed from the previous claim for the purpose of recovering $f(X)$.

Claim. Let $p(X), q(X)$ be defined as in the proof of the previous claim, and suppose that $\hat{p}(X), \hat{q}(X)$ satisfy the BW-conditions. Then $\hat{p}(X)$ divides $\hat{q}(X)$ and $\hat{q}(X)/\hat{p}(X) = f(X)$.[3]

Proof. Consider the polynomial $r(X) = \hat{q}(X)p(X) - q(X)\hat{p}(X)$. In light of Lemma 3, taking into account that $p(X) \in F[X]$, we have that for every $i = 1, \ldots, n'$:

$$r(\alpha_i) = \hat{q}(\alpha_i)p(\alpha_i) - q(\alpha_i)\hat{p}(\alpha_i) = s_i'\hat{p}(\alpha_i)p(\alpha_i) - s_i'p(\alpha_i)\hat{p}(\alpha_i) = 0.$$

Observe that in the last equality we have used the fact that $\hat{p}(\alpha_i)p(\alpha_i) = p(\alpha_i)\hat{p}(\alpha_i)$. Since $\deg(r) \leq d + 2e < n'$, it follows from Lemma 4 that $r(X) \equiv 0$, which shows that $\hat{q}(X)p(X) = q(X)\hat{p}(X)$. Given that $q(X) = f(X)p(X)$, we have that $\hat{q}(X)p(X) = f(X)p(X)\hat{p}(X)$, which implies $(\hat{q}(X) - f(X)\hat{p}(X)) \cdot p(X) = 0$.

We claim that $\hat{q}(X) - f(X)\hat{p}(X) = 0$, which can be shown by proving that this polynomial evaluates to 0 in at least $d + e + 1$ points on an exceptional set in light of Lemma 4. To see this, consider the evaluation of this polynomial at α_i for all i such that $e_i = 0$. Observe that there are at least $n' - e = d + e + 1$ such evaluation points. It is easy to see that in this case $p(\alpha_i)$ is invertible, so $(\hat{q}(\alpha_i) - f(\alpha_i)\hat{p}(\alpha_i)) \cdot p(\alpha_i) = 0$ implies that $\hat{q}(\alpha_i) - f(\alpha_i)\hat{p}(\alpha_i) = 0$, as required. At this point we see that $\hat{q}(X) = f(X)\hat{p}(X)$, which concludes the proof of the main claim. ∎

---

[3] $b(X)$ (right-)divides $a(X)$, if, after dividing a by b using Theorem 3 obtaining $q(X)$ and $r(X)$ such that $a(X) = q(X) \cdot b(X) + r(X)$ with $\deg(r) < \deg(b)$, it holds that $r(X) = 0$. The quotient $a(X)/b(X)$ is defined as $q(X)$.

Error Detection. Finally, if $n > d + e$ the parties may not be able to perform error correction, but they can still do error detection by checking if all the received shares $(s'_1, \ldots, s'_n)$ are consistent with a polynomial of degree at most d (e.g. by using the first $d + 1$ shares to interpolate such polynomial and checking that the remaining shares are consistent with it). If this is the case, since this polynomial is determined by any set of $d + 1$ shares, it is in particular determined by the $n - e \geq d + 1$ shares without errors.

Solving for the BW-conditions. In order to have an efficient decoder it remains to show how to find at least one pair $p(X), q(X)$ that satisfies the BW-conditions. First, notice that by treating the coefficients of the unknown polynomials $p(X), q(X)$ as unknowns, the BW-conditions transform into a system of $n' = d + 2e + 1$ linear equations on $d + 2e + 1$ variables over R.[4] Unfortunately, to the best of our knowledge the theory of linear equations over *general* non-commutative rings is not very well understood, with only a few works considering concrete instantiations of some types of rings (e.g. [Ore31, Son75, DKH+12]). Since it is of particular interest to us, we develop in the full version of this work efficient algorithms to solve systems of linear equations for the matrix ring case $R = \mathcal{M}_{m \times m}(\mathbb{Z}_{p^k})$.

3.3   Efficient Protocols for Secret Reconstruction

Protocol $\Pi_{\text{PrivOpen}}([s]_d, P_r)$

Input: Sharing $[s]_d$, a receiver party P_r.
Output: P_r learns s.
Protocol: The parties proceed as follows

1. Each party P_j for $j \in \{1, \ldots, n\} \setminus \{r\}$ sends its share of s to P_r.
2. Upon receiving all the shares of $[s]$, P_r defines $s_i = 0$ for every missing share s_i and proceeds as follows.
   - If $0 < n - d \leq t$: Interpolate the unique polynomial $f \in R[X]_{\leq d}$ such that $f^L(\alpha_i) = s_i$ for $i = 1, \ldots, d + 1$. Output $s' = f(\alpha_0)$.
   - If $t < n - d \leq 2t$: Interpolate the unique polynomial $f \in R[X]_{\leq d}$ such that $f^L(\alpha_i) = s_i$ for $i = 1, \ldots, d + 1$. Check if $f^L(\alpha_i) = s_i$ for $i = d + 2, \ldots, d + t + 1$. If this is the case, output $s = f(\alpha_0)$. Else abort.
   - If $2t < n - d$: Apply error correction (Section 3.2) on the shares $(s_1, \ldots, s_{d+2t+1})$ to recover a polynomial $f \in R[X]_{\leq d}$ such that $f^L(\alpha_i) = s_i$ for at least $d + t + 1$ points, and output $s = f(\alpha_0)$.

Fig. 2. Reconstructing secret-shared values efficiently to a single party.

---

[4] It is worth noting that some of the unknowns will have coefficients multiplying from both left and right.

Given the above, a party that receives n shares of degree $\leq d$, among which at most t can be corrupted by an adversary, can perform error detection if $t < n - d \leq 2t$, and it can perform error correction if $2t < n - d$. We denote by $\Pi_{\text{PrivOpen}}([s]_d, P_r)$ the protocol in which all parties send their share of $[s]_d$ to P_r. If all parties are intended to learn the secret s, we make use of a protocol $\Pi_{\text{PublicOpen}}([s_0]_d, \ldots, [s_d]_d)$ that opens a batch of secrets towards all the parties with an amortized communication complexity that is linear in n. This protocol is achieved by a natural generalization of the equivalent protocol in [DN07], except that great care must be taken when handling the different multiplications and polynomial evaluations when the ring is not commutative. This is described in detail in the full version of this work.

Finally, notice that the protocols $\Pi_{\text{PrivOpen}}, \Pi_{\text{PubOpen}}$ are currently described for $[\cdot]$-sharings, but they can be naturally adapted to $\langle \cdot \rangle$-sharings by evaluating the polynomial $f(\mathbf{X})$ on the right and computing $\langle f^{\mathsf{R}}(\alpha_i) \rangle = \sum_{j=0}^{t} \langle s_j \rangle \alpha_i^j$.

4   MPC in the Preprocessing Model

The goal of this section is to leverage the adaptations of Shamir's secret sharing described in Sect. 3 to build an MPC protocol that operates directly over R, in a black-box way. We assume an active adversary corrupting t out of n parties, where it could hold either that $t < n/3$ or $t < n/2$. In the first case we can obtain guaranteed output delivery with perfect security, and in the second case we achieve perfect security with abort (both in the preprocessing model).

Multiparty computation can be obtained from any linear secret sharing scheme satisfying certain multiplicative properties, as shown in [CDM00]. As we proved in Corollary 2, even more modern and efficient techniques for MPC over commutative rings can be adapted to the non-commutative setting, assuming that there is a large enough exceptional set in the centre of the ring. The challenge in this section is, however, that we only assume the existence of a big enough *commutative* exceptional set, i.e. the conditions of Theorem 2.

Losing multiplicativity leads to most existing techniques for secret-sharing based MPC to fail. A clever solution when multilpicativity is lost is to resort to properties of the *dual* of the error-correcting code underlying the secret-sharing scheme [CDM00]. However, although as shown in [QBC13] the usual properties of the dual code of Reed-Solomon codes do carry over to non-commutative rings, this requires that the evaluation points constitute not only an exceptional set, but that they are also contained in $Z(R)$. Unfortunately, this is precisely the assumption we do not want to make (and in fact, as said above, such assumption would yield a multiplicative LSSS *directly*).

Given the hurdles highlighted above, this work takes a different route. Our protocols are set in the offline/online paradigm, in which a set of input-independent correlated information is generated in a preprocessing phase, which is then used in an online phase once the inputs are known. By preprocessing the so-called Beaver triples, the online phase can be executed without relying on any multiplicativity property of the underlying secret-sharing scheme. However, due to non-commutativity, the usual approach to secure multiplication using Beaver triples does not directly work, as we will explain shortly. The rest of this section is then devoted to overcoming these issues and obtain a secure computation protocol in the preprocessing model, where we assume that the input-independent correlated data is given "for free". Our protocols for instantiating such preprocessing phase will be discussed in Sect. 5.

4.1 A First Approach

We begin by considering the typical approach to Beaver-based multiplication, and discuss why it fails in our setting. Assume for a moment that R is commutative. A Beaver triple is a set of shared values $(\llbracket a \rrbracket, \llbracket b \rrbracket, \llbracket c \rrbracket)$ such that $a, b \in R$ are uniformly random and $c = a \cdot b$. Given two shared values $\llbracket x \rrbracket, \llbracket y \rrbracket$, these can be multiplied by means of the following protocol:

1. Parties call $d = \Pi_{\mathsf{PubOpen}}(\llbracket x \rrbracket - \llbracket a \rrbracket)$ and $e = \Pi_{\mathsf{PubOpen}}(\llbracket y \rrbracket - \llbracket b \rrbracket)$.
2. Parties compute locally $\llbracket xy \rrbracket = \llbracket a \rrbracket e + d \llbracket b \rrbracket + \llbracket c \rrbracket + de$.

Privacy follows from the fact that the sensitive values x and y are being masked by uniformly random values a and b that are unknown to the adversary. Correctness follows from the fact that $xy = (d + a)(e + b) = ae + db + ab + de$, a relation that also holds even if R is non-commutative. Here we use the fact that, since $t < n/2$, the calls to Π_{PubOpen} result in the parties learning the correct underlying secret or aborting (and in the stronger case that $t < n/3$ then Π_{PubOpen} does not result in abort).

The issue with a non-commutative R is that, unless $Z(R)$ contains a big enough exceptional set, the secret sharing scheme $[\cdot]$ (resp. $\langle \cdot \rangle$) we can define is just a left (resp. right) submodule of R^n. In particular, the local operation $d \cdot [b]$ can be carried out, but $[a] \cdot e$ does not result in a $[\cdot]$-shared value[5]. To address this complication, let $([a], [b], [c])$ be a triple. Assume the existence of "sextuples", which are just triples of the form $([a], [b], [c])$ enhanced with shares of the form $(\langle a \rangle, [r], \langle r \rangle)$. These are produced by a functionality $\mathcal{F}_{\mathsf{Tuples}}$.[6] These tuples can be used to multiply $[x]$ and $[y]$ as follows:

1. Parties call $d = \Pi_{\mathsf{PubOpen}}([x]_t - [a]_t)$, $e = \Pi_{\mathsf{PubOpen}}([y]_t - [b]_t)$.
2. Parties call $f = \Pi_{\mathsf{PubOpen}}(\langle a \rangle_t \cdot e + \langle r \rangle_t)$.
3. Parties compute locally $[xy]_t = d \cdot e + d \cdot [b]_t + f - [r]_t + [c]_t$

Privacy follows from the fact that sensitive data x and y is masked by the uniformly random values a and b before opening and also because, before reconstructing $a \cdot e$ (which could potentially leak information about a), the uniformly random mask r is applied. In terms of correctness, we observe that the final

---

[5] More concretely, if we had $[a]_t$, multiplication by e on the right will *not* result on $[ae]_t$ in general.

[6] This functionality, together with some others used in this work, are formalized in the full version.

expression defining $[xy]_t$ is well defined given that only additions and multiplications *on the left* are used. Furthermore, the computation of f uses multiplication on the right on the sharings $\langle \cdot \rangle$, which admit such multiplications. The rest is simply a matter of using the definition of d, e, c and f in the final computation:
$$d \cdot e + d \cdot b + f - r + c = (x - a) \cdot (y - b) + (x - a) \cdot b + a \cdot (y - b) + r - r + a \cdot b = x \cdot y.$$

4.2 Improving Round-Complexity

The protocol sketched in the previous section suffers from the issue that its round complexity is quite high, requiring 4 rounds per multiplication (two sequential calls to Π_{PubOpen}, each requiring 2 rounds). In MPC protocols networking is usually the most scarce resource, and it can be argued that round-count is even more sensitive than communication complexity, specially in wide area networks that have high latency. Therefore, the rest of this section is devoted to lowering the round count of each secure multiplication.

In order to achieve secure multiplication with no sequential calls to Π_{PubOpen} in the non-commutative case, we modify the way multiplications are handled. First, each intermediate value of the computation x will not be represented by $[x]$, but rather by a pair $([\lambda_x], \mu_x)$, where $\lambda_x \in R$ is uniformly random and unknown to any party, and $\mu_x = x - \lambda_x$. Notice that this still maintains the privacy of x since the only public value is μ_x, which perfectly hides x as it is being masked by λ_x, that is random and unknown to any party.

Suppose the parties have two shared values $([\lambda_x], \mu_x = x - \lambda_x)$ and $([\lambda_y], \mu_y = y - \lambda_y)$. To obtain a shared representation of their sum, the parties simply locally compute $([\lambda_x + \lambda_y], \mu_x + \mu_y)$. On the other hand, to securely multiply these shared values, the process is as follows. Let $[\lambda_z]$ be the random mask associated to the output of the multiplication. To obtain $([\lambda_z], \mu_z)$, the parties need to get the value $\mu_z = x \cdot y - \lambda_z$ in the clear. This is achieved by noticing that, since $x = \mu_x + \lambda_x$ and $y = \mu_y + \lambda_y$, it holds that $\mu_z = \mu_x \mu_y + \mu_x \lambda_y + \lambda_x \mu_y + \lambda_x \lambda_y - \lambda_z$. Assume that the parties have $[\lambda_x \lambda_y]$, which can be preprocessed as λ_x and λ_y are simply random values. If R was commutative, then the parties could compute

$$[\mu_z] = \mu_x \mu_y + \mu_x [\lambda_y] + [\lambda_x] \mu_y + [\lambda_x \lambda_y] - [\lambda_z],$$

followed by opening μ_z. This approach was followed in [BNO19] in order to improve the communication complexity of secure multiplication in the dishonest majority setting. It was also used in the context of honest majority in [ED20], both to minimize online communication complexity and in order to avoid selective failure attacks.

Unfortunately, when R is non-commutative, this approach cannot be carried out as we find the exact same issue we had in the previous section, namely that $[\lambda_x] \mu_y$ is not well defined as the secret-sharing scheme $[\cdot]$ does not allow multiplication on the right. However, our crucial observation is that, unlike the traditional use of triples from Sect. 4.1, in this case the task is not to take a combination of sharings in order to obtain a *new shared value* but rather take a linear combination of sharings in order to *open* the result μ_z. This difference turns out to be essential in order to devise a protocol for the non-commutative case that does not require sequential openings, which we describe in detail below. The overall idea of our protocol is that the parties do not really need to convert $\langle \lambda_x \rangle \mu_y$ to $[\lambda_x \mu_y]$ as in Sect. 4.1, which adds an extra opening round, but rather it is enough to *open* this part separately from the other part that uses the $[\cdot]$-sharing, and then add the two opened values to obtain μ_z. Some masking is necessary to ensure that each separate piece does not leak anything, but this is easily achievable, as we will describe next.

Preprocessing functionality. Unfortunately, resorting to this new approach does not allow us to use the functionality $\mathcal{F}_{\text{Tuples}}$ directly. Instead, we must resort to a similar but different type of preprocessing, which is captured by functionality for function-dependent preprocessing $\mathcal{F}_{\text{F.D.Prep}}$, which is formalized in detail in the full version. In a nutshell, this functionality also distributes tuples $([\lambda_x]_t, [\lambda_y]_t, [\lambda_x \cdot \lambda_y]_t, \langle \lambda_x \rangle_t, [r]_t, \langle r \rangle_t)$, except that, if λ_x (resp. λ_y) is used to mask a value x (resp. y) for a given multiplication, then the same λ_x (resp. λ_y) must be used for all multiplications involving x (resp. y) as a left (resp. right) input. Since the structure of the tuples returned depend on the way multiplications are arranged in the circuit, we refer to this type of preprocessing as *function-dependent preprocessing*. This is in contrast to the preprocessing from $\mathcal{F}_{\text{Tuples}}$ which only depends on (an upper bound on) the *number* of multiplications in the circuit and not on the way these are arranged.

Protocols for MPC in the $(\mathcal{F}_{\text{F.D.Prep}}, \mathcal{F}_{\text{BC}})$-hybrid model. Now we finally describe our protocol for MPC in the $(\mathcal{F}_{\text{F.D.Prep}}, \mathcal{F}_{\text{BC}})$-hybrid model. The protocol Π_{Online}, described in Fig. 3 achieves guaranteed output delivery with perfect security against an active adversary corrupting $t < n/3$ parties, and it achieves perfect security with abort against an active adversary corrupting $t < n/2$ parties. The following makes use of a standard simulation-based proof which is provided in the full version of this work.

Theorem 6. *Assume that $t < n/3$. Then protocol Π_{Online} implements functionality $\mathcal{F}_{\text{MPC-GOD}}$ in the $(\mathcal{F}_{\text{F.D.Prep}}, \mathcal{F}_{\text{BC}})$-hybrid model with perfect security.*

We recall that the functionality $\mathcal{F}_{\text{BC}}$ can be instantiated with perfect security if $t < n/3$ [LSP82], which, together with Theorem 6, implies that there exists a protocol that instantiates $\mathcal{F}_{\text{MPC-GOD}}$ with perfect security in the $\mathcal{F}_{\text{F.D.Prep}}$-hybrid model.

Finally, in a similar way as the theorem above, the following is proved. The main difference lies in the fact that the simulator may send abort signals to the functionality $\mathcal{F}_{\text{MPC-abort}}$ if it detects that the adversary is sending inconsistent shares. This works since error detection in the $t < n/2$ case is possible.

Theorem 7. *Assume that $t < n/2$. Then protocol Π_{Online} implements functionality $\mathcal{F}_{\text{MPC-abort}}$ in the $(\mathcal{F}_{\text{F.D.Prep}}, \mathcal{F}_{\text{BC}})$-hybrid model with statistical security.*

Protocols Π_{Online}

PREPROCESSING PHASE

The parties call $\mathcal{F}_{\text{F.D.Prep}}$ to get the following.

- For every wire in the circuit x the parties have $[\lambda_x]$.
- Party P_i knows λ_x for every input gate x corresponding to P_i.
- For every multiplication gate with inputs x, y and output z, the parties have $[\lambda_x \lambda_y]$.

ONLINE PHASE

Input Gates. For every input gate x owned by party P_i, the parties do the following:
    1. P_i uses $\mathcal{F}_{\text{BC}}$ to send $\mu_x = x - \lambda_x$ to all parties.
    2. Upon receiving this value, the parties set the sharing $([\lambda_x], \mu_x)$
Addition Gates. For every addition gate with inputs $([\lambda_x], \mu_x)$ and $([\lambda_y], \mu_y)$, the parties locally get shares of the sum as $([\lambda_x] + [\lambda_y], \mu_x + \mu_y)$.
Multiplication Gates. For every multiplication gate with inputs $([\lambda_x], \mu_x)$ and $([\lambda_y], \mu_y)$, the parties proceed as follows:
    1. The parties call $\gamma \leftarrow \Pi_{\text{PubOpen}}(\mu_x \mu_y + \mu_x[\lambda_y] + [\lambda_x \lambda_y] - [\lambda_z] + [r])$ and $\rho \leftarrow \Pi_{\text{PubOpen}}(\langle \lambda_x \rangle \mu_y - \langle r \rangle)$,[a] and, if there was no abort, set $\mu_z = \gamma + \rho$.
    2. Output $([\lambda_z], \mu_z)$ as shares of the product.
Output Gates. If the parties did not abort above, then for every output gate $([\lambda_x], \mu_x)$ that is supposed to be learned by P_i, the parties do the following:
    1. The parties call $\Pi_{\text{PubOpen}}([\lambda_x], P_i)$.
    2. If this call does not result in abort, P_i outputs $\mu_x + \lambda_x$.

---

[a] Since Π_{PubOpen} takes as inputs *batches* of shares to be opened, this is called for all the multiplication gates on the given layer of the circuit in parallel, doing multiple calls if necessary.

Fig. 3. Online phase of our MPC protocol.

5 Preprocessing

In this section we provide different protocols to realize the $\mathcal{F}_{\text{Tuples}}$ functionality when $Z(R)$ does not contain a big enough exceptional set. Our presentation focuses in this simpler functionality, since $\mathcal{F}_{\text{F.D.Prep}}$ can be easily realized either in the $\mathcal{F}_{\text{Tuples}}$-hybrid or by slightly tweaking the protocols that implement $\mathcal{F}_{\text{Tuples}}$. In Sect. 5.1 we provide a generic protocol that only requires *black-box* access to the ring operations and the ability to sample random ring elements. On the downside, this theoretical result has a complexity of $\text{poly}(n)$, in contrast with the more specialized protocol for matrices over commutative rings we provide in Sect. 5.2. By additionally getting black-box access to the commutative ring operations, this optimized protocol has $O(n)$ communication complexity and $O(n \log n)$ computational complexity.

5.1   Generic, Black-Box Construction

Representing non-commutative ring arithmetic as operations in $\mathbb{G} = \mathbf{GL_3(R)}$. We quickly recap the work of Ben-Or and Cleve [BC92]. Let $a \in R$, where R is a possibly non commutative ring. We will keep the invariant of representing such elements within the group of 3×3 invertible matrices over R, $\mathbb{G} = \mathsf{GL}_3(R)$, as follows:

$$M(a) = \begin{pmatrix} 1 & 0 & a \\ 0 & 1 & 0 \\ 0 & 0 & 1 \end{pmatrix}$$

This allows us to compute additions as $M(a + b) = M(a) \cdot M(b)$. Multiplication is a bit more complicated. We can compute $M(a \cdot b) = J_1 \cdot M(b) \cdot J_2 \cdot M(a) \cdot J_3 \cdot M(b) \cdot J_4 \cdot M(a) \cdot J_5$, where the J_i matrices are the following:

$$J_1 = \begin{pmatrix} 0 & 1 & 0 \\ -1 & 0 & 0 \\ 0 & 0 & 1 \end{pmatrix} \quad J_2 = \begin{pmatrix} 0 & 0 & -1 \\ 1 & 0 & 0 \\ 0 & 1 & 0 \end{pmatrix} \quad J_3 = \begin{pmatrix} 0 & 1 & 0 \\ 0 & 0 & 1 \\ 1 & 0 & 0 \end{pmatrix} \quad J_4 = \begin{pmatrix} 0 & 0 & 1 \\ -1 & 0 & 0 \\ 0 & 1 & 0 \end{pmatrix} \quad J_5 = \begin{pmatrix} -1 & 0 & 0 \\ 0 & 0 & 1 \\ 0 & 1 & 0 \end{pmatrix}$$

Preprocessing for MPC over non-commutative rings. Given the previous representation, we can use existing results for efficient MPC over non-abelian groups [DPS+12, CDI+13] in order to implement the $\mathcal{F}_{\mathsf{Prep}}$ functionality required for the online phase in Sect. 4. In more detail, this can be computed as a constant-depth arithmetic circuit over R which we will represent as a series of products in the group $\mathbb{G} = \mathsf{GL}_3(R)$.

Note that the shares in the group-based protocol are according to the group law (i.e., they are "multiplicative shares"), whereas the protocols from Sect. 4 use Shamir's secret sharing. One option would be to compute something like $[M(a)]_\mathbb{G} = \prod_{i=1}^{t+1} [M(a_i)]_\mathbb{G}$, $[M(b)]_\mathbb{G} = \prod_{i=1}^{t+1} [M(b_i)]_\mathbb{G}$ and $[M(c)]_\mathbb{G} = J_1 \cdot [M(b)]_\mathbb{G} \cdot J_2 \cdot [M(a)]_\mathbb{G} \cdot J_3 \cdot [M(b)]_\mathbb{G} \cdot J_4 \cdot [M(a)]_\mathbb{G} \cdot J_5$, as well as generating "double shares" of the form $[M(r)]_\mathbb{G}, [r]$ to e.g. extract $(c + r)$ from $\mathsf{PublicOpen}([M(c)]_\mathbb{G} \cdot [M(r)]_\mathbb{G})$ and then compute $[c] = (c + r) - [r]$.

Alternatively, we can employ the following, more direct approach. Let $A = \{0, \alpha_1, \ldots, \alpha_n\}$ be the commutative exceptional set defining the non-commutative sharing scheme $[\cdot]$. Parties compute the following circuit, where each P_i inputs random $f_j^i, g_j^i, h_j^i \in R$ and receives as output their corresponding shares of $([a], [b], [c])$, that is, $(f(\alpha_i), g(\alpha_i), h(\alpha_i))$.

$$a = \sum_{i=1}^{t+1} f_0^i, \quad b = \sum_{i=1}^{t+1} g_0^i, \quad c = a \cdot b$$

$$f_j = \sum_{i=1}^{t+1} f_j^i, \quad g_j = \sum_{i=1}^{t+1} g_j^i \quad h_j = \sum_{i=1}^{t+1} h_j^i, \quad j \in [t]$$

$$f(\alpha_\ell) = a + \sum_{j=1}^{t} f_j \alpha_\ell^j, \quad g(\alpha_\ell) = b + \sum_{j=1}^{t} g_j \alpha_\ell^j, \quad h(\alpha_\ell) = c + \sum_{j=1}^{t} h_j \alpha_\ell^j, \quad \ell \in [n]$$

The downside of these two generic approaches is that their respective protocols inherit the $\mathsf{poly}(n)$ complexity of [CDI+13]. On the upside, any improvement to MPC over non-abelian groups would directly translate to our blackbox constructions.

5.2 Concretely Efficient Preprocessing for Matrix Rings

For our more practical construction, which works over the ring $R = \mathcal{M}_{m \times m}(\mathbb{Z}_{2^k})$, we describe how to implement $\mathcal{F}_{\text{Tuples}}$ using non-black-box protocols which are more efficient than the one from the previous section. Even though we specialize to matrices over $\mathbb{Z}_{2^k}$, our analysis and techniques can be generalized to matrices over other commutative rings.

Remember from Sect. 3.1 that $\mathcal{M}_{m \times m}(\mathbb{Z}_{2^k})$ contains a commutative exceptional set of size 2^m, which is why can only use the non-multiplicative secret sharing schemes from Theorem 5 that are linear only on one side.

In order to overcome the lack of multiplicativity, as $\mathcal{F}_{\text{Tuples}}$ requires to produce values $([A], [B], [C])$ such that $C = A \cdot B$, we use an existing MPC protocol for computation over $\mathbb{Z}_{2^k}$. Given such an entry-wise protocol, we can trivially emulate the whole arithmetic of R. The issue is that, by doing this, we need to work over a big enough Galois extension of $\mathbb{Z}_{2^k}$, so that we can define a multiplicative, Shamir-style linear secret sharing scheme $[\![\cdot]\!]$[7]. Once we have computed this matrix product from the entry-wise shares of the matrices A and B, we need to convert $[\![\cdot]\!]$ sharings of the entries of A, B, C to sharings $[\cdot]$ and $\langle \cdot \rangle$ over $\mathcal{M}_{m \times m}(\mathbb{Z}_{2^k})$, so that parties obtain the tuple $[A], \langle A \rangle, [B], [C], [r], \langle r \rangle$ required for the online protocols in Sect. 4.

In particular, we will use the InnerProd CAFE from [DLS20], which can compute inner products of length $\delta \simeq d/2$ over $R = \mathsf{GR}(2^k, d)$ at the cost of just 2 sharings and a single opening in R. If one wants to calculate an inner product of length $rd/2$, the cost would be $2r$ sharings and a single opening in R. The following proposition captures the properties of InnerProd we are interested in, without getting into details about the specific construction.

---

[7] This was described in [ACD+19], but it is also a consequence of Theorem 5. This is why we will use the $[\![\cdot]\!]$ notation to refer to the LSSS over the Galois Ring in this section. It should not be confused with $[\cdot]$ and $\langle \cdot \rangle$, which work over $\mathcal{M}_{m \times m}(\mathbb{Z}_{2^k})$.

Proposition 4 ([DLS20]). *Let $R = \mathsf{GR}(2^k, d)$ be a Galois Ring defined as $\mathbb{Z}_{2^k}[\mathsf{X}]/(h(\mathsf{X}))$. Let $\tilde{d}$ denote the degree of the second-highest degree monomial in $h(\mathsf{X})$. Let $\delta \in \mathbb{N}$ be such that $\delta < (d+1)/2$, $\delta < d - \tilde{d} + 1$. There exist three $\mathbb{Z}_{2^k}$-linear homomorphisms $\mathsf{E}_L : (\mathbb{Z}_{2^k})^\delta \to R$, $\mathsf{E}_R : (\mathbb{Z}_{2^k})^\delta \to R$ and $\mathsf{E}_{out} : \mathbb{Z}_{2^k} \to R$ satisfying:*

$$\mathsf{E}_L(a_1, \ldots, a_\delta) \cdot \mathsf{E}_R(b_1, \ldots, b_\delta) + \mathsf{E}_{out}(c) = \mathsf{E}_{out}\left(c + \sum_{\ell=1}^{\delta} a_\ell \cdot b_\ell\right)$$

Furthermore, the value $\mathsf{E}_{out}(c + \sum_{\ell=1}^{\delta} a_\ell \cdot b_\ell) \in R$ does not reveal any information beyond $c + \sum_{\ell=1}^{\delta} a_\ell \cdot b_\ell \in \mathbb{Z}_{2^k}$.

Since the maps $\mathsf{E}_L, \mathsf{E}_R$ and E_{out} are homomorphisms of $\mathbb{Z}_{2^k}$-modules, the image of each of them can be seen as a $\mathbb{Z}_{2^k}$-submodule of $\mathsf{GR}(2^k, d)$. We will indistinctively refer to either these homomorphisms, or the $\mathbb{Z}_{2^k}$-modules they define as *encodings*.

By extension, we define how these encodings can be applied to matrices. Given $A' \in \mathcal{M}_{1 \times \delta}(\mathbb{Z}_{2^k})$, $B' \in \mathcal{M}_{\delta \times 1}(\mathbb{Z}_{2^k})$, for which we want to compute $C' = A' \cdot B'$, where $C' \in \mathbb{Z}_{2^k}$, we simply view the entries of A', B' as elements of $(\mathbb{Z}_{2^k})^\delta$, to which we apply E_L and E_R, respectively. In order to compute the product of $A, B \in \mathcal{M}_{m \times m}(\mathbb{Z}_{2^k})$, we need to introduce some additional notation. Let $\Delta = \lceil m/\delta \rceil$. Let $\mathcal{A} \in \mathcal{M}_{m \times \delta\Delta}(\mathbb{Z}_{2^k})$ (resp. $\mathcal{B} \in \mathcal{M}_{\delta\Delta \times m}(\mathbb{Z}_{2^k})$) denote the matrix A padded with $\delta\Delta - m$ columns of zeroes (resp. the matrix B padded with $\delta\Delta - m$ rows of zeroes). For $\ell \in [m\Delta]$, let $A^{(\ell)} \in \mathcal{M}_{1 \times \delta}(\mathbb{Z}_{2^k})$, $B^{(\ell)} \in \mathcal{M}_{\delta \times 1}(\mathbb{Z}_{2^k})$ be submatrices such that

$$\mathcal{A} = \begin{pmatrix} A^{(1)} & A^{(2)} & \ldots & A^{(\Delta)} \\ A^{(\Delta+1)} & A^{(\Delta+2)} & \ldots & A^{(2\cdot\Delta)} \\ \vdots & \vdots & \ddots & \vdots \\ A^{((m-1)\cdot\Delta+1)} & A^{((m-1)\cdot\Delta+2)} & \ldots & A^{(m\cdot\Delta)} \end{pmatrix} \quad \mathcal{B} = \begin{pmatrix} B^{(1)} & B^{(\Delta+1)} & \ldots & B^{((m-1)\cdot\Delta+1)} \\ B^{(2)} & B^{(\Delta+2)} & \ldots & B^{((m-1)\cdot\Delta+2)} \\ \vdots & \vdots & \ddots & \vdots \\ B^{(\Delta)} & B^{(2\cdot\Delta)} & \ldots & B^{(m\cdot\Delta)} \end{pmatrix},$$

where $A^{(\Delta)}, A^{(2\cdot\Delta)}, \ldots, A^{(m\cdot\Delta)}$ and $B^{(\Delta)}, B^{(2\cdot\Delta)}, \ldots, B^{(m\cdot\Delta)}$ are the submatrices including the zero-padding. Let $\gamma \in \mathcal{M}_{m \times m}(\mathbb{Z}_{2^k})$ be a matrix that we will use to mask the result of $C = A \cdot B$ and let us denote the entries of $\gamma, C \in \mathcal{M}_{m \times m}(\mathbb{Z}_{2^k})$ as $C^{(\alpha,\beta)}, \gamma^{(\alpha,\beta)} \in \mathbb{Z}_{2^k}$, where $\alpha, \beta \in \{1, \ldots, m\}$. Taking into account Definition 4, we can compute:

$$\mathsf{E}_{out}(C^{(\alpha,\beta)} + \gamma^{(\alpha,\beta)}) = \mathsf{E}_{out}(\gamma^{(\alpha,\beta)}) + \sum_{\ell=1}^{\Delta} \mathsf{E}_L(A^{((\alpha-1)\Delta+\ell)}) \cdot \mathsf{E}_R(B^{((\beta-1)\Delta+\ell)})$$

Hyperinvertible matrices acting on commutative and non-commutative LSSS. Hyper-Invertible Matrices were introduced in [BTH08] as a tool for generating and checking linearly correlated randomness in the context of perfectly secure MPC over fields. We recall their properties in the full version of this work.

Let $R = \mathcal{M}_{m \times m}(\mathbb{Z}_{2^k})$, $d = 1 + \log n$, $S = \mathcal{M}_{n \times n}(\mathsf{GR}(2^k, d))$ and $M \in S$ be a hyper-invertible matrix. Let N be a $\mathbb{Z}_{2^k}$-module, such as those defined by commutative sharings of E_L, E_R or E_{out} encodings. Let N_L (resp. N_R) be the left (resp. right) R-module defined by $[\cdot]$ (resp. $\langle \cdot \rangle$). We want to define the action of multiplying by M on the left on those modules. We will refer to the morphisms they define as $\phi_M : N^{d \cdot n} \to N^{d \cdot n}$, $\psi_M^L : N_L^{d \cdot n} \to N_L^{d \cdot n}$ and $\psi_M^R : N_R^{d \cdot n} \to N_R^{d \cdot n}$.

Let us first look at the $\mathbb{Z}_{2^k}$-linear action of multiplying elements $\boldsymbol{a} \in N^d$ by $b \in \mathsf{GR}(2^k, d)$. As N^d is a $\mathbb{Z}_{2^k}$-module, we know how to multiply its elements with scalars from $\mathbb{Z}_{2^k}$, but how can we multiply them with scalars from $\mathsf{GR}(2^k, d)$? The formal answer is tensor products: N^d is isomorphic to $\mathsf{GR}(2^k, d) \otimes_{\mathbb{Z}_{2^k}} N$ as a $\mathbb{Z}_{2^k}$-module, but $\mathsf{GR}(2^k, d) \otimes_{\mathbb{Z}_{2^k}} N$ can also be seen as an $\mathsf{GR}(2^k, d)$-module compatible with the $\mathbb{Z}_{2^k}$-module structure N^d. Informally, one just needs to represent $b \in \mathsf{GR}(2^k, d)$ on its *matrix representation* $\iota(b)$ (see Sect. 2.4) and compute the matrix-vector product $\iota(b) \cdot \boldsymbol{a}$. We refer the reader interested in a more systematic exposition of the tensoring technique to the discussion on *interleaved generalized secret sharing schemes* in [CCXY18], which is restricted to fields but can be generalized to commutative rings [CRX19]. For those who want a more computational description, we recommend [DLS20, Section 4.1].

Given the description of the $\mathbb{Z}_{2^k}$-linear action of multiplying elements $\boldsymbol{a} \in N^d$ by $b \in \mathsf{GR}(2^k, d)$, we can deduce the $\mathbb{Z}_{2^k}$-linear action of multiplying elements in $(N^d)^n$ by the matrix M with entries in $\mathsf{GR}(2^k, d)$, giving result to the $\mathbb{Z}_{2^k}$-module homomorphism $\phi_M : (N^d)^n \to (N^d)^n$. We were talking about multiplying by the matrix $M \in S$ "on the left", so whereas one could easily imagine how everything works fine when defining $\psi_M^L : N_L^{d \cdot n} \to N_L^{d \cdot n}$, what happens with $\psi_M^R : N_R^{d \cdot n} \to N_R^{d \cdot n}$? The important remark here is that N_R is a right R-module, but it also a $\mathbb{Z}_{2^k}$-bimodule, so we can meaningfully "multiply by M on the left", as we are interested in the $\mathbb{Z}_{2^k}$-linear action of multiplication by M. Moreover, the $\mathbb{Z}_{2^k}$-bimodule structure of N_R is compatible with the right R-module structure, since $Z(R)$ consists of the $\mathbb{Z}_{2^k}$-multiples of the identity matrix and hence $\forall a \in \mathbb{Z}_{2^k}, \langle b \rangle \in N_R$, we have that $a \cdot \langle b \rangle = \langle b \rangle \cdot a = \langle b \cdot a \rangle = \langle a \cdot b \rangle$. This leads us to the observation that:

$$\psi_M^L([\tilde{r}_{1,1}]_t, \ldots, [\tilde{r}_{1,d}]_t; \ldots; [\tilde{r}_{n,1}]_t, \ldots, [\tilde{r}_{n,d}]_t)$$
$$= \psi_M^R(\langle \tilde{r}_{1,1} \rangle_t, \ldots, \langle \tilde{r}_{1,d} \rangle_t; \ldots; \langle \tilde{r}_{n,1} \rangle_t, \ldots, \langle \tilde{r}_{n,d} \rangle_t) \quad (2)$$

What is more, ψ_M^L and ψ_M^R will also be compatible with ϕ_M, as they are all defined by the unique $\mathbb{Z}_{2^k}$-linear action that is defined by multiplying by M on the left that we describe above, where M is basically interpreted as a block matrix over $\mathbb{Z}_{2^k}$ taking the matrix representation of its entries in $\mathsf{GR}(2^k, d)$. The following Lemma is stated for ψ_M^L, but it can be naturally adapted to ψ_M^R and ϕ_M.

Lemma 6. *Let $R = \mathcal{M}_{m \times m}(\mathbb{Z}_{2^k})$ and let N_L denote the R-module defined by $[\cdot]$. Let $M \in \mathcal{M}_{n \times n}(\mathsf{GR}(2^k, d))$ be a hyper-invertible matrix. Then, for all $A, B \subseteq [n]$ with $|A| + |B| = n$, there exists an isomorphism of R-modules $\psi_M^L : N_L^{nd} \to N_L^{nd}$,*

$\psi_M^L(\boldsymbol{x}) = \boldsymbol{y}$, *defined by the* $\mathbb{Z}_{2^k}$-*linear action of "multiplying* $\boldsymbol{x}$ *by* M *on the left"*, *such that* $\psi_M^L(\boldsymbol{x}_A, \boldsymbol{y}_B) = (\boldsymbol{x}_{\bar{A}}, \boldsymbol{y}_{\bar{B}})$, *where* $\bar{A} = [n] \backslash A$ *and* $\bar{B} = [n] \backslash B$.[8]

See protocol Π_{Tuples} on Fig. 4, Protocol $\Pi_{\text{Tuples-NC-Shares}}$ on Fig. 5 and $\Pi_{\text{TuplesCheck}}$ on Fig. 6. We provide a standard simulation-based proof of the following result in the full version of this work.

Protocol Π_{Tuples}

Let $T = n - 2t$. Let $R = \mathcal{M}_{m \times m}(\mathbb{Z}_{2^k})$ and $S = \mathcal{M}_{n \times n}(\mathsf{GR}(2^k, d))$. Let $M \in S$ be a hyper-invertible matrix. Let N be a $\mathbb{Z}_{2^k}$-module (such as those defined by $\mathsf{E}_L, \mathsf{E}_R$ or E_{out}) and let $\phi_M : N^{d \cdot n} \to N^{d \cdot n}$ and $\psi_M : R^{d \cdot n} \to R^{d \cdot n}$ be the morphisms defined by the $\mathbb{Z}_{2^k}$-linear action of M described in Section 5.2.

I. Commutative Shares. Parties generate commutative shares of the entries of the matrices A, B, so that they can compute the product $C = A \cdot B$.

For $i \in [n], j \in [d]$, each P_i samples at random $\tilde{A}_{i,j}, \tilde{B}_{i,j}, \tilde{\gamma}_{i,j} \in R$, extracts representations $\tilde{A}_{i,j}^{(\ell)}, \tilde{B}_{i,j}^{(\ell)}, \tilde{\gamma}_{i,j}^{(\alpha,\beta)}$ as described in Section 5.2 and calls $\Pi_{[\![\cdot]\!]}$ to distribute shares of $[\![\mathsf{E}_L(\tilde{A}_{i,j}^{(\ell)})]\!]_t, [\![\mathsf{E}_R(\tilde{B}_{i,j}^{(\ell)})]\!]_t$ and $[\![\mathsf{E}_{out}(\tilde{\gamma}_{i,j}^{(\alpha,\beta)})]\!]_{2t}$ to all parties.

  1. Parties locally compute:

$$([\![\mathsf{E}_L(A_{1,1}^{(\ell)})]\!]_t, \ldots, [\![\mathsf{E}_L(A_{1,d}^{(\ell)})]\!]_t; \ldots; [\![\mathsf{E}_L(A_{n,1}^{(\ell)})]\!]_t, \ldots, [\![\mathsf{E}_L(A_{n,d}^{(\ell)})]\!]_t)$$
$$= \phi_M([\![\mathsf{E}_L(\tilde{A}_{1,1}^{(\ell)})]\!]_t, \ldots, [\![\mathsf{E}_L(\tilde{A}_{1,d}^{(\ell)})]\!]_t; \ldots; [\![\mathsf{E}_L(\tilde{A}_{n,1}^{(\ell)})]\!]_t, \ldots, [\![\mathsf{E}_L(\tilde{A}_{n,d}^{(\ell)})]\!]_t)$$

$$([\![\mathsf{E}_R(B_{1,1}^{(\ell)})]\!]_t, \ldots, [\![\mathsf{E}_R(B_{1,d}^{(\ell)})]\!]_t; \ldots; [\![\mathsf{E}_R(B_{n,1}^{(\ell)})]\!]_t, \ldots, [\![\mathsf{E}_R(B_{n,d}^{(\ell)})]\!]_t)$$
$$= \phi_M([\![\mathsf{E}_R(\tilde{B}_{1,1}^{(\ell)})]\!]_t, \ldots, [\![\mathsf{E}_R(\tilde{B}_{1,d}^{(\ell)})]\!]_t; \ldots; [\![\mathsf{E}_R(\tilde{B}_{n,1}^{(\ell)})]\!]_t, \ldots, [\![\mathsf{E}_R(\tilde{B}_{n,d}^{(\ell)})]\!]_t)$$

$$([\![\mathsf{E}_{out}(\gamma_{1,1}^{(\alpha,\beta)})]\!]_{2t}, \ldots, [\![\mathsf{E}_{out}(\gamma_{1,d}^{(\alpha,\beta)})]\!]_{2t}; \ldots; [\![\mathsf{E}_{out}(\gamma_{n,1}^{(\alpha,\beta)})]\!]_{2t}, \ldots, [\![\mathsf{E}_{out}(\gamma_{n,d}^{(\alpha,\beta)})]\!]_{2t})$$
$$= \phi_M([\![\mathsf{E}_{out}(\tilde{\gamma}_{1,1}^{(\alpha,\beta)})]\!]_{2t}, \ldots, [\![\mathsf{E}_{out}(\tilde{\gamma}_{1,d}^{(\alpha,\beta)})]\!]_{2t}; \ldots; [\![\mathsf{E}_{out}(\tilde{\gamma}_{n,1}^{(\alpha,\beta)})]\!]_{2t}, \ldots, [\![\mathsf{E}_{out}(\tilde{\gamma}_{n,d}^{(\alpha,\beta)})]\!]_{2t})$$

  2. For $i = 1, \ldots, T; j = 1, \ldots, d; \alpha, \beta \in \{1, \ldots, m\}$ they additionally compute:

$$[\![\mathsf{E}_{out}(C_{i,j}^{(\alpha,\beta)} + \gamma_{i,j}^{(\alpha,\beta)})]\!]_{2t} = [\![\mathsf{E}_{out}(\gamma_{i,j}^{(\alpha,\beta)}))]\!]_{2t} + \sum_{\ell=1}^{\Delta} [\![\mathsf{E}_L(A_{i,j}^{((\alpha-1)\Delta+\ell)})]\!]_t \cdot [\![\mathsf{E}_R(B_{i,j}^{((\beta-1)\Delta+\ell)})]\!]_t$$

II. Non-Commutative Shares. Parties run the subprotocol $\Pi_{\text{Tuples-NC-Shares}}$ in Figure 5 to generate shares of the form $[A], \langle A \rangle, [B], [r], \langle r \rangle, [C]$.

III. Consistency Checks. Parties run the subprotocol $\Pi_{\text{TuplesCheck}}$ in Figure 6. If all the checks pass, they accept the output.

Fig. 4. Preprocessing phase for MPC over $R = \mathcal{M}_{m \times m}(\mathbb{Z}_{2^k})$.

---

[8] With the notation $\boldsymbol{x}_{\bar{A}}$, we refer to viewing $\boldsymbol{x}$ as an element of $(N^d)^n$ and taking, among the n "entries" in N^d, the ones indexed by A. These correspond to parties in our protocols.

Protocol $\Pi_{\text{Tuples-NC-Shares}}$

This is a subprotocol of Π_{Tuples} (Figure 4). Assume same conditions and notation.

II. Non-Commutative Shares. Parties generate non-commutative shares of the form $[A], \langle A \rangle, [B], [r], \langle r \rangle, [\gamma]$. The latter value will allow them to convert from $[\![\mathsf{E}_{out}(C + \gamma)]\!]_{2t}$ to $[C]_t$.

1. For $i \in [n], j \in [d]$, each P_i calls $\Pi_{[\cdot]}$ and $\Pi_{\langle \cdot \rangle}$ to distribute to all parties non-commutative shares of the values they sampled in Step I.

$$([A_{1,1}]_t, \ldots, [A_{1,d}]_t; \ldots; [A_{n,1}]_t, \ldots, [A_{n,d}]_t)$$
$$= \psi_M^L([\tilde{A}_{1,1}]_t, \ldots, [\tilde{A}_{1,d}]_t; \ldots; [\tilde{A}_{n,1}]_t, \ldots, [\tilde{A}_{n,d}]_t)$$

$$(\langle A_{1,1} \rangle_t, \ldots, \langle A_{1,d} \rangle_t; \ldots; \langle A_{n,1} \rangle_t, \ldots, \langle A_{n,d} \rangle_t)$$
$$= \psi_M^R(\langle \tilde{A}_{1,1} \rangle_t, \ldots, \langle \tilde{A}_{1,d} \rangle_t; \ldots; \langle \tilde{A}_{n,1} \rangle_t, \ldots, \langle \tilde{A}_{n,d} \rangle_t)$$

$$([B_{1,1}]_t, \ldots, [B_{1,d}]_t; \ldots; [B_{n,1}]_t, \ldots, [B_{n,d}]_t)$$
$$= \psi_M^L([\tilde{B}_{1,1}]_t, \ldots, [\tilde{B}_{1,d}]_t; \ldots; [\tilde{B}_{n,1}]_t, \ldots, [\tilde{B}_{n,d}]_t)$$

$$([\gamma_{1,1}]_t, \ldots, [\gamma_{1,d}]_t; \ldots; [\gamma_{n,1}]_t, \ldots, [\gamma_{n,d}]_t)$$
$$= \psi_M^L([\tilde{\gamma}_{1,1}]_t, \ldots, [\tilde{\gamma}_{1,d}]_t; \ldots; [\tilde{\gamma}_{n,1}]_t, \ldots, [\tilde{\gamma}_{n,d}]_t)$$

$$([r_{1,1}]_t, \ldots, [r_{1,d}]_t; \ldots; [r_{n,1}]_t, \ldots, [r_{n,d}]_t)$$
$$= \psi_M^L([\tilde{r}_{1,1}]_t, \ldots, [\tilde{r}_{1,d}]_t; \ldots; [\tilde{r}_{n,1}]_t, \ldots, [\tilde{r}_{n,d}]_t)$$

$$(\langle r_{1,1} \rangle_t, \ldots, \langle r_{1,d} \rangle_t; \ldots; \langle r_{n,1} \rangle_t, \ldots, \langle r_{n,d} \rangle_t)$$
$$= \psi_M^R(\langle \tilde{r}_{1,1} \rangle_t, \ldots, \langle \tilde{r}_{1,d} \rangle_t; \ldots; \langle \tilde{r}_{n,1} \rangle_t, \ldots, \langle \tilde{r}_{n,d} \rangle_t)$$

2. Parties use the double shares of $\gamma \in R$ in order to convert $[\![\mathsf{E}_{out}(C + \gamma)]\!]_{2t}$, where $\mathsf{E}_{out}(C + \gamma) \in S$, to $[C]$, where $C \in R$.
   (a) For $i \in \{1, \ldots, T\}, j \in \{1, \ldots, d\}, \alpha, \beta \in \{1, \ldots, m\}$ parties call Π_{PubOpen} with the values $[\![\mathsf{E}_{out}(C_{i,j}^{(\alpha,\beta)} + \gamma_{i,j}^{(\alpha,\beta)})]\!]_{2t}$, so that everyone obtains $C_{i,j} + \gamma_{i,j} \in \mathcal{M}_{m \times m}(\mathbb{Z}_{2^k})$, or abort.
   (b) Parties compute
   $$[C_{i,j}]_t = C_{i,j} + \gamma_{i,j} - [\gamma_{i,j}]_t$$

Fig. 5. Preprocessing phase for MPC over $\mathcal{M}_{m \times m}(\mathbb{Z}_{2^k})$: Non-Commutative Shares.

Theorem 8. *Assume that $t < n/3$. Then protocol Π_{Tuples} on Fig. 4 implements functionality $\mathcal{F}_{\text{Tuples}}^{\text{abort}}$ in the $\mathcal{F}_{\text{BC}}$-hybrid model with perfect security.*

The case of $n/3 \leq t < n/2$ is discussed in the full version of this work.

Consistency check subprotocol of Π_{Tuples} – Protocol $\Pi_{\text{TuplesCheck}}$

This is a subprotocol of Π_{Tuples} (Figure 4). Assume same conditions and notation.

III. Consistency Checks. For $i \in \{T+1, \ldots, n\}, j \in [d]$ every party sends their shares of $\{[\![\mathsf{E}_L(A_{i,j}^{(\ell)})]\!], [\![\mathsf{E}_R(B_{i,j}^{(\ell)})]\!]\}_{\ell \in [m\Delta]}, \{[\![\mathsf{E}_{out}(\gamma_{i,j}^{(\alpha,\beta)})]\!]_{2t}\}_{\alpha,\beta \in [m]}, [A_{i,j}], \langle A_{i,j} \rangle,$ $[B_{i,j}], [\gamma_{i,j}], [r_{i,j}], \langle r_{i,j} \rangle$ to P_i, who first checks that all the shares of any received secret lie on a polynomial of degree t (or $2t$ for $[\![\mathsf{E}_{out}(\gamma_{i,j}^{(\alpha,\beta)})]\!]_{2t}$). Furthermore, it performs the following checks:

1. Correct E_L and E_R encodings of $A_{i,j}^{(\ell)}, B_{i,j}^{(\ell)}$.[a]
2. Consistency between the alleged secrets $[\![\mathsf{E}_{out}(\gamma_{i,j}^{(\alpha,\beta)})]\!]_{2t}$ and $[\gamma_{i,j}]$.
3. Consistency between the alleged secrets $[r_{i,j}]$ and $\langle r_{i,j} \rangle$.
4. Consistency between the alleged secrets $[B_{i,j}]$ and $[\![\mathsf{E}_R(B_{i,j}^{(\ell)})]\!]$.
5. Consistency between the alleged secrets $[A_{i,j}], \langle A_{i,j} \rangle$ and $[\![\mathsf{E}_L(A_{i,j}^{(\ell)})]\!]$.

P_i uses $\mathcal{F}_{\text{BC}}$ to broadcast a bit which signals whether all the checks pass or not. If they do so for every $P_{T+1}, \ldots, P_n$, parties accept the tuples $[A_{\ell,j}], \langle A_{\ell,j} \rangle, [B_{\ell,j}], [C_{\ell,j}], [r_{\ell,j}], \langle r_{\ell,j} \rangle$ for $\ell \in [T]$.

---
[a] Note there is no need to check the E_{out} encoding of $\gamma_{i,j}^{(\alpha,\beta)}$.

Fig. 6. Consistency check of the preprocessing phase for MPC over $R = \mathcal{M}_{m \times m}(\mathbb{Z}_{2^k})$.

Acknowledgements. During his time at Aarhus University, Eduardo Soria-Vazquez was supported by the Carlsberg Foundation under the Semper Ardens Research Project CF18-112 (BCM). Daniel Escudero was supported by the European Research Council (ERC) under the European Union's Horizon 2020 research and innovation programme under grant agreement No. 669255 (MPCPRO).

References

[ACD+19] Abspoel, M., Cramer, R., Damgård, I., Escudero, D., Yuan, C.: Efficient information-theoretic secure multiparty computation over $\mathbb{Z}/p^k\mathbb{Z}$ via Galois rings. In: Hofheinz, D., Rosen, A. (eds.) TCC 2019, Part I. LNCS, vol. 11891, pp. 471–501. Springer, Cham (2019). https://doi.org/10.1007/978-3-030-36030-6_19

[BBY20] Baccarini, A., Blanton, M., Yuan, C.: Multi-party replicated secret sharing over a ring with applications to privacy-preserving machine learning. Cryptology ePrint Archive, Report 2020/1577 (2020). https://eprint.iacr.org/2020/1577

[BC92] Ben-Or, M., Cleve, R.: Computing algebraic formulas using a constant number of registers. SIAM J. Comput. **21**(1), 54–58 (1992)

[BGW88] Ben-Or, M., Goldwasser, S., Wigderson, A.: Completeness theorems for non-cryptographic fault-tolerant distributed computation (extended abstract). In: 20th ACM STOC, pp. 1–10. ACM Press (May 1988)

[BNO19]   Ben-Efraim, A., Nielsen, M., Omri, E.: Turbospeedz: double your online SPDZ! improving SPDZ using function dependent preprocessing. In: Deng, R.H., Gauthier-Umaña, V., Ochoa, M., Yung, M. (eds.) ACNS 2019. LNCS, vol. 11464, pp. 530–549. Springer, Cham (2019). https://doi.org/10.1007/978-3-030-21568-2_26

[BTH08]   Beerliová-Trubíniová, Z., Hirt, M.: Perfectly-secure MPC with linear communication complexity. In: Canetti, R. (ed.) TCC 2008. LNCS, vol. 4948, pp. 213–230. Springer, Heidelberg (2008). https://doi.org/10.1007/978-3-540-78524-8_13

[Can01]   Canetti, R., Universally composable security: a new paradigm for cryptographic protocols. In: 42nd FOCS, pp. 136–145. IEEE Computer Society Press, October 2001

[CCXY18] Cascudo, I., Cramer, R., Xing, C., Yuan, C.: Amortized complexity of information-theoretically secure MPC revisited. In: Shacham, H., Boldyreva, A. (eds.) CRYPTO 2018, Part III. LNCS, vol. 10993, pp. 395–426. Springer, Cham (2018). https://doi.org/10.1007/978-3-319-96878-0_14

[CDI+13] Cohen, G., et al.: Efficient multiparty protocols via log-depth threshold formulae. In: Canetti, R., Garay, J.A. (eds.) CRYPTO 2013, Part II. LNCS, vol. 8043, pp. 185–202. Springer, Heidelberg (2013). https://doi.org/10.1007/978-3-642-40084-1_11

[CDM00]   Cramer, R., Damgård, I., Maurer, U.M.: General secure multi-party computation from any linear secret-sharing scheme. In: Preneel, B. (ed.) EUROCRYPT 2000. LNCS, vol. 1807, pp. 316–334. Springer, Heidelberg (2000). https://doi.org/10.1007/3-540-45539-6_22

[CFIK03] Cramer, R., Fehr, S., Ishai, Y., Kushilevitz, E.: Efficient multi-party computation over rings. In: Biham, E. (ed.) EUROCRYPT 2003. LNCS, vol. 2656, pp. 596–613. Springer, Heidelberg (2003). https://doi.org/10.1007/3-540-39200-9_37

[CRX19]   Cramer, R., Rambaud, M., Xing, C.: Asymptotically-good arithmetic secret sharing over $\mathbb{Z}/p^\ell\mathbb{Z}$ with strong multiplication and its applications to efficient MPC. Cryptology ePrint Archive, Report 2019/832 (2019). https://eprint.iacr.org/2019/832

[DEK21]   Dalskov, A., Escudero, D., Keller, M.: Fantastic four: honest-majority four-party secure computation with malicious security. In: USENIX 2021 (2021)

[DKH+12] Dawar, A., Kopczynski, E., Holm, B., Grädel, E., Pakusa, W.: Definability of linear equation systems over groups and rings. arXiv preprint arXiv:1204.3022 (2012)

[DLS20]   Dalskov, A.P.K., Lee, E., Soria-Vazquez, E.: Circuit amortization friendly encodings and their application to statistically secure multiparty computation. In: Moriai, S., Wang, H. (eds.) ASIACRYPT 2020, Part III. LNCS, vol. 12493, pp. 213–243. Springer, Cham (2020). https://doi.org/10.1007/978-3-030-64840-4_8

[DN07]   Damgård, I., Nielsen, J.B.: Scalable and unconditionally secure multiparty computation. In: Menezes, A. (ed.) CRYPTO 2007. LNCS, vol. 4622, pp. 572–590. Springer, Heidelberg (2007). https://doi.org/10.1007/978-3-540-74143-5_32

[DPS+12] Desmedt, Y., et al.: Graph coloring applied to secure computation in non-abelian groups. J. Cryptol. 25(4), 557–600 (2012)

[ED20] Escudero, D., Dalskov, A.: Honest majority MPC with abort with minimal online communication. Cryptology ePrint Archive, Report 2020/1556 (2020). https://eprint.iacr.org/2020/1556

[LSP82] Lamport, L., Shostak, R., Pease, M.: The byzantine generals problem. ACM Trans. Program. Lang. Syst. **4**(3), 382–401 (1982)

[Ore31] Ore, O.: Linear equations in non-commutative fields. Ann. Math. **32**, 463–477 (1931)

[QBC13] Quintin, G., Barbier, M., Chabot, C.: On generalized Reed-Solomon codes over commutative and noncommutative rings. IEEE Trans. Inf. Theory **59**(9), 5882–5897 (2013)

[Sha79] Shamir, A.: How to share a secret. Commun. Assoc. Comput. Mach. **22**(11), 612–613 (1979)

[Son75] Sontag, E.D.: On linear systems and noncommutative rings. Math. Syst. Theory **9**(4), 327–344 (1975)

Pushing the Limits of Valiant's Universal Circuits: Simpler, Tighter and More Compact

Hanlin Liu[1], Yu Yu[1,2,3(✉)], Shuoyao Zhao[1], Jiang Zhang[4], Wenling Liu[1], and Zhenkai Hu[1]

[1] Department of Computer Science and Engineering, Shanghai Jiao Tong University, 800 Dongchuan Road, Shanghai 200240, China
{hans1024,yyuu}@sjtu.edu.cn
[2] Shanghai Qi Zhi Institute, 701 Yunjin Road, Shanghai 200232, China
[3] Shanghai Key Laboratory of Privacy-Preserving Computation, 701 Yunjin Road, Shanghai 200232, China
[4] State Key Laboratory of Cryptology, P.O. Box 5159, Beijing 100878, China

Abstract. A universal circuit (UC) is a general-purpose circuit that can simulate arbitrary circuits (up to a certain size n). Valiant provides a k-way recursive construction of UCs (STOC 1976), where k tunes the complexity of the recursion. More concretely, Valiant gives theoretical constructions of 2-way and 4-way UCs of asymptotic (multiplicative) sizes $5n \log n$ and $4.75n \log n$ respectively, which matches the asymptotic lower bound $\Omega(n \log n)$ up to some constant factor.

Motivated by various privacy-preserving cryptographic applications, Kiss et al. (Eurocrypt 2016) validated the practicality of 2-way universal circuits by giving example implementations for private function evaluation. Günther et al. (Asiacrypt 2017) and Alhassan et al. (J. Cryptology 2020) implemented the 2-way/4-way hybrid UCs with various optimizations in place towards making universal circuits more practical. Zhao et al. (Asiacrypt 2019) optimized Valiant's 4-way UC to asymptotic size $4.5n \log n$ and proved a lower bound $3.64n \log n$ for UCs under Valiant's framework. As the scale of computation goes beyond 10-million-gate ($n = 10^7$) or even billion-gate level ($n = 10^9$), the constant factor in UC's size plays an increasingly important role in application performance. In this work, we investigate Valiant's universal circuits and present an improved framework for constructing universal circuits with the following advantages.

Simplicity. Parameterization is no longer needed. In contrast to those previous implementations that resorted to a hybrid construction combining $k = 2$ and $k = 4$ for a tradeoff between fine granularity and asymptotic size-efficiency, our construction gets the best of both worlds when configured at the lowest complexity (i.e., $k = 2$).

Compactness. Our universal circuits have asymptotic size $3n \log n$, improving upon the best previously known $4.5n \log n$ by 33% and beating the $3.64n \log n$ lower bound for UCs constructed under Valiant's framework (Zhao et al., Asiacrypt 2019).

© International Association for Cryptologic Research 2021
T. Malkin and C. Peikert (Eds.): CRYPTO 2021, LNCS 12826, pp. 365–394, 2021.
https://doi.org/10.1007/978-3-030-84245-1_13

Tightness. We show that under our new framework the UC's size is lower bounded by $2.95n \log n$, which almost matches the $3n \log n$ circuit size of our 2-way construction.

We implement the 2-way universal circuit and evaluate its performance with other implementations, which confirms our theoretical analysis.

Keywords: Universal circuits · Private function evaluation · Multiparty computation

1 Introduction

A universal circuit (UC) is a programmable circuit capable of simulating arbitrary circuits (up to a certain scale), which is analogous to that a universal Turing machine is configured to simulate an arbitrary Turing machine or that a central processing unit (CPU) carries out computations specified by a sequence of instructions. More specifically, a universal circuit refers to a sequence of circuits, i.e., $\mathsf{UC} = \{\mathsf{UC}_n\}_{n \in \mathbb{N}}$, such that every circuit C of size n can be (efficiently) encoded into a string of control bits p_C to fulfill the simulation, i.e., for every valid input x: $\mathsf{C}(x) = \mathsf{UC}_n(p_\mathsf{C}, x)$. An explicit construction is an efficient algorithm that (on the input n) produces output UC_n in time polynomial in n.

Universal Model of Computation. Valiant's universal circuits [53] gave inspiration to universal parallel computers [22,45]. Cook and Hoover [15] proposed depth-optimal universal circuits, i.e., for any circuit of size n and depth d, they constructed a universal circuit $\mathsf{UC}(n, d)$ of size $O(n^3 d / \log n)$ and depth $O(d)$ that can simulate this circuit. Bera et al. [10] used the frameworks of universal circuits from [15,53] in their design of universal quantum circuits.

1.1 Cryptographic Applications

We sketch some cryptographic applications of universal circuits. The performance of most applications crucially relies on the size efficiency of universal circuits. We refer the readers to the cited publications for full details.

Private function evaluation. A major cryptographic application of universal circuits is private function evaluation (PFE)[1] [1,11,32,35,39], which can be based on the protocols for secure two-party/multiparty computation (2PC/MPC) [28,55,56]. Take the two-party setting as an example: a 2PC protocol enables two parties, Alice and Bob, to securely compute a publicly known function f on their respective private inputs x and y without revealing anything substantially more than the output of the computation $f(x,y)$, whereas

---

[1] Let us mention that there are other alternatives to PFE without using universal circuits, of which the most efficient one to date is the work by Katz and Malka [36].

in a PFE scenario Alice (with private input x) and Bob (with private function f) engage in a protocol such that at the end Alice (resp., Bob) learns nothing about f (resp., x) beyond what can be revealed from the output $f(x)$. A PFE reduces to a 2PC with the aid of a universal circuit: Alice and Bob invoke a 2PC to securely compute a publicly known universal circuit UC on Alice's private input x and Bob's private input p_f (a string that encodes f), which yields $\mathsf{UC}(p_f, x) = f(x)$. It is easy to see that the PFE protocol is as secure as the underlying 2PC/MPC protocol against the same type (semi-honest, covert or malicious) of adversaries, and the time/space efficiency of the PFE mainly depends on the size/depth of the UC. The takeaway is that one simply plugs a UC into an MPC framework (without changes to the underlying infrastructure) to enjoy the corresponding benefits and additional features, such as non-interactive PFE [41] and outsourced PFE [35] that are generalized from non-interactive and outsourced secure computation protocols [2] respectively. As its name suggests, PFE [1] can be applied to scenarios where some party wants to keep his function private but still hopes to evaluate it on others' inputs. Depending on the concrete instantiations of the private function, applications include privacy-preserving checking of loanee's credit-worthiness [20], protection of the code privacy of an autonomous mobile agent [14], oblivious filtering of remote streaming data [49], medical diagnostics [8], remote software fault diagnosis [13], blinded policy evaluation protocols [19,21], query-hiding database management systems (DBMSs) [18,50], private evaluation of branching programs [31,34,47] and privacy-preserving intrusion detection [47,48].

Applications beyond PFE. Universal circuits can be applied to various other cryptographic scenarios. UCs were used to hide the functions in verifiable computation [17] and multi-hop homomorphic encryption [27], to reduce the verifier's preprocessing costs in the NIZK argument [26], and to build the attribute-based encryption (ABE) scheme in [25]. Attrapadung [6] used UCs to transform the ABE schemes for any polynomial-size circuits [24,29] into ciphertext-policy ABE. Garg et al. [12,23] used UCs to construct universal branching programs, which were in turn used to build a candidate indistinguishability obfuscation (iO). The iO scheme [23] was implemented in [7], whose efficiency is closely related to the size of UCs. Zimmerman [59] proposed a new scheme to obfuscate programs by viewing UC as a keyed program for circuit families. Lipmaa et al. [41] suggested that UC can be used for efficient batch execution of secure two-party computation. The batch execution techniques [33,40] were originally intended for amortizing the cost of maliciously secure garbled circuits for the same function, and UCs can now enable batched execution for circuits of different functions (realized by the same UC). This protocol was made round-optimal in [46].

1.2   Valiant's Universal Circuits and Subsequent Works

Valiant [53] took a graph-theoretic approach to constructing universal circuits that were followed by almost all size-efficient universal circuits [3,30,37,41,57].

One may represent an arbitrary circuit by a direct acyclic graph (DAG) and then see a universal circuit as a special DAG called edge universal graph (EUG). The construction is recursive and parameterized by $k \geq 2$, which is the number of sub-problems (of scale $1/k$ of the original problem) it reduces to during each recursion. We typically refer to it as a k-way construction or a k-way UC. In more details, to construct a UC, we need to construct the corresponding EUG in a recursive manner: "an EUG simulating any DAG of size n", denoted by $\mathsf{EUG}(n)$, can be constructed based on k instances of $\mathsf{EUG}(\frac{n}{k})$, and the recursion repeats many times until a sufficiently small EUG to be built by hand. Moreover, during each recursion, k instances of $\mathsf{EUG}(\frac{n}{k})$ are connected to form a $\mathsf{EUG}(n)$ using a matching algorithm, whose complexity increases with respect to k. In the most desirable case $k = 2$, the matching algorithm is simply bipartite matching. Valiant provided 2-way and 4-way (i.e., $k = 2$ and $k = 4$) theoretical constructions of universal circuits of multiplicative sizes[2] $5n \log n$ and $4.75n \log n$ respectively (omitting smaller terms), which match the lower bound $\Omega(n \log n)$ up to constant factors [53,54]. Therefore, as a theoretical problem, explicit construction of size-efficient universal circuits was mostly solved by Valiant [53] more than forty years ago.

Valiant's universal circuit had long been recognized more as a feasibility result than a practical application. Kolesnikov and Schneider [39] turned to (and implemented for the first time) a modular design of universal circuits of size $1.5n \log^2 n + 2.5n \log n$. Despite not asymptotically size optimal, the UC [39] enables efficient simulation of small-scale circuits (e.g., for $n < 10^6$), thanks to the smaller constant factor in circuit size. Further, they gave the first implementation of UC-based PFE under the Fairplay secure computation framework [44]. More recently, Kiss et al. [37] implemented a hybrid UC combining Valiant's 2-way UC [53] and the UC of Kolesnikov and Schneider [39] integrated with various optimizations for many typical PFE applications. Günther et al. [30] gave a generic edge embedding algorithm for Valiant's k-way construction and implemented a hybrid of Valiant's 2-way and 4-way UCs. Concurrently, Lipmaa et al. [41,51] gave a generic construction of the k-way supernode (an important building block of Valiant's k-way universal circuit) and based on the method they estimated that the k's optimal value for minimizing the size of UC was $k = 3.147$ (i.e., $k \in \{3,4\}$ as an integer). In addition, Lipmaa et al. [41] brought down the size of 4-way UC from $19n \log n$ to $18n \log n$ by optimizing out some XOR gates. However, the number of AND gates remained the same as Valiant's 4-way UC [53] (i.e., $4.75n \log n$), and thus the improvement offers limited help to PFE or other applications with free XOR optimizations [38]. Zhao et al. [57] gave a more efficient 4-way UC of multiplicative circuit size $4.5n \log n$ (and circuit size $17.75n \log n$), which was the best size-efficient construction prior to our work. Alhassan et al. [3] designed an efficient and scalable algorithm for UC generation

---

[2] It is typically assumed that a circuit C consists of AND gates and XOR gates. The size of C refers to the number of gates in C, and its multiplicative size is the number of AND gates. As a major performance indicator for Valiant's (and our optimized) framework, the multiplicative size of a UC is roughly a quarter of its total size.

and programming, and implemented a hybrid construction of Valiant's 2-way UC and the 4-way UC by Zhao et al. [57]. We refer to Table 1 for asymptotic sizes of existing theoretical constructions.

1.3   Our Work

Outstanding issues. For efficiency and granularity of the construction[3], k is desired to be the smallest possible, i.e., $k = 2$, but 2-way universal circuits are less size-efficient than UC tuned at other values, e.g., $k = 4$. Therefore, the state-of-the-art implementations [3,30] resort to a hybrid construction of 2-way and 4-way UCs for a tradeoff between granularity and size efficiency. Further, there remains a significant gap between the $4.5n \log n$ achieved by the best size-efficient UC and the $3.64n \log n$ lower bound under Valiant's framework. With the growing trend of secure computation exceeding 10-million-gate or even billion-gate scale (e.g., [5,58]), the constant factor in asymptotic universal circuit size becomes increasingly important and practically relevant. To summarize, it is natural to raise the following question:

Can we build a UC with low(est) complexity and small(est) circuit size at the same time, ideally matching (or even beating) the $3.64n \log n$ lower bound?

Paper organization and our contributions. Section 2 gives the notations, definitions, and graph-theoretic preliminaries about universal circuits. Section 3.1 carries out an in-depth review of Valiant's construction (see Theorem 2). Section 3.2 then introduces an intermediate tweaked valiant of Valiant's construction that is not even acyclic (i.e., contains cycles). Despite the cyclicity, we argue in Corollary 1 that the intermediate construction preserves the "universal edge-embedding" function, which is referred to as a weak EUG ($\approx$EUG without acyclicity, see Definition 3). Section 3.3 observes that the weak EUG contains many redundant control nodes whose control options are predetermined, so they can be removed while preserving the universal edge-embedding capability. The removal of redundant nodes not only eliminates the cycles (brings back the EUG) but also results in a compact design of the EUG, where the $1/3$ size improvement benefits from the removal of redundant control nodes. Section 3.4 proves a $2.95n \log n$ lower bound on the size of UCs under our optimized framework, which tightly complements our construction of size $3n \log n$. Section 4 implements, optimizes and evaluates (the performance of) our universal circuit, which confirms our theoretical analysis and validates its practicality. In summary, compared with previous works (see Table 1), our construction has the following advantages:

---

[3] The edge embedding algorithm for constructing 2-way UC is simply a bipartite matching algorithm, while in contrast, a generic algorithm for k-way UC is much more complex and less efficient. Moreover, Valiant's construction only explicitly handles the case $n = Bk^j$ for arbitrary $j \in \mathbb{N}^+$ (i.e., the number of recursions) and small $B \in \mathbb{N}^+$ (i.e., EUG(B) is the initial EUG built from scratch). Optimization techniques [3,30] are helpful in adapting to arbitrary n, especially for $k = 2$.

Simplicity. Our approach inherits Valiant's framework but removes the need for parameter k. That is, always set $k = 2$ to obtain UCs that are most efficient to construct and offer good size efficiency simultaneously.

Compactness. Our universal circuits have asymptotic size $3n \log n$, improving upon the previous state-of-the-art $4.5n \log n$ by 33% and beating the $3.64n \log n$ lower bound in Valiant's framework [57].

Tightness. Our new framework bridges the gap between theory and practice of universal circuits: the universal circuit size $3n \log n$ achieved almost tightly matches the $2.95n \log n$ lower bound.

Note that the $2.95n \log n$ lower bound we proved is incomparable to (and thus not implied by) the $3.64n \log n$ bound [57] obtained under Valiant's framework, and it thus creates more room for efficiency improvement.

Table 1. The sizes, multiplicative sizes and lower bounds for previous universal circuits and ours, keeping only dominant terms.

Universal Circuit	MUL size (# of AND gates)	Lower Bound on MUL size	Total Size
Kolesnikov et al.'s UC [39]	$0.25n \log^2 n$	N/A	$n \log^2 n$
Valiant's 2-way UC [53]	$5n \log n$	$\geq 3.64n \log n$	$20n \log n$
Valiant's 3-way UC [30,53]	$5.05n \log n$	———"———	$20.19n \log n$
Valiant's 4-way UC [53]	$4.75n \log n$	———"———	$19n \log n$
Lipmaa et al.'s 4-way UC [41]	$4.75n \log n$	———"———	$18n \log n$
Zhao et al.'s 4-way UC [57]	$4.5n \log n$	———"———	$17.75n \log n$
Our 2-way UC	$3n \log n$	$\geq 2.95n \log n$	$12n \log n$

On the presentation strategy. A straightforward presentation is to describe and prove our main construction in Sect. 3.3 from scratch, which may take more effort and confidence to verify the correctness. Instead, we choose the following somewhat hybrid argument

$$\underbrace{\text{"Valiant's EUG"}}_{\text{Section 3.1}} \mapsto \underbrace{\text{"intermediate weak EUG"}}_{\text{Section 3.2}} \mapsto \underbrace{\text{"final EUG"}}_{\text{Section 3.3}}$$

from the known-to-be-correct Valiant's construction, to the intermediate one, and then to the final construction, where we highlight the (minor) difference between neighboring hybrids. Thus, the proof reduces to verifying that the minor changes do not affect the correctness. Essentially, the weak EUG can be viewed as a special variant of Valiant's EUG with quite some redundant control nodes, which are thus removed to yield the final construction. This way of presentation reproduces the process we discovered the construction, and helps to understand how our improvement benefits from the redundancy of Valiant's original design.

2   Preliminaries

Notations. We use $[n]$ to denote the set of the first n positive integers, i.e., $\{1, ..., n\}$. $|G|$ (resp., $|C|$) refers to the size of a graph G (resp., circuit C), namely, the number of nodes (resp., inputs and gates) in G (resp., C). More specifically, $C_{s,t}^g$ denotes a circuit of s inputs, t outputs and g gates of fan-in and fan-out 2, where circuit size $n = s + t$ by definition. $\mathsf{DAG}_2(n)$ refers to a Directed Acyclic Graph (DAG) of fan-in and fan-out 2, and size n, and UC_n denotes a UC of fan-in and fan-out 2 that can simulate any $C_{s,t}^g$ of size $s + g \leq n$.

Definition 1 (Universal Circuits [41,54,57]). *A circuit UC_n is a universal circuit, if for any circuit $C_{s,t}^g$ with $s + g \leq n$, there exists a bit-string $p_C \in \{0,1\}^m$ that configures UC_n to simulate $C_{s,t}^g$, i.e., $\forall x \in \{0,1\}^s, \mathsf{UC}(n)(p_C, x) = C_{s,t}^g(x)$.*

Universality refers to the ability to simulate arbitrary circuits (up to a certain scale), and the correctness of simulation requires that for every eligible circuit $C_{s,t}^g$ there exists a configuration p_C such that $\mathsf{UC}_n(p_C, \cdot)$ is functionally equivalent to $C_{s,t}^g(\cdot)$. Following previous works, we consider circuits with fan-in and fan-out bounded by 2 without loss of generality [3,30,41,53,57].

Graph representation. A circuit $C_{s,t}^g$ of fan-in and fan-out 2 can be represented by a $\mathsf{DAG}_2(n)$ for $n = s + g$ and vice versa, where circuit wires correspond to graph edges, and inputs and gates become nodes on the corresponding graph. As illustrated in Fig. 1, Valiant introduced a special DAG, referred to as edge-universal graph (EUG), such that "a universal circuit simulates arbitrary circuits" can be compared to that "an $\mathsf{EUG}_2(n)$ edge-embeds arbitrary $\mathsf{DAG}_2(n)$", where subscript 2 indicates fan-in and fan-out of the DAG and n is the size of the DAG. We provide an example of edge embedding for $n = 4$ in Fig. 2. Informally, the $\mathsf{DAG}_2(4)$ on the left-hand edge embeds into the $\mathsf{EUG}_2(4)$ on the right-hand in the sense that all nodes (i.e., the inputs x, y and the gates $\oplus$, $\wedge$) in $\mathsf{DAG}_2(4)$ one-to-one map to the counterparts in $\mathsf{EUG}_2(4)$ and all edges in $\mathsf{DAG}_2(4)$ find their respective edge-disjoint paths in $\mathsf{EUG}_2(4)$, e.g., the edge e corresponds to the path (e_1, e_2, e_3) and the edge f maps to the path (f_1, f_2). The edge universality of $\mathsf{EUG}_2(4)$ refers to that for every $\mathsf{DAG}_2(4)$ such an edge embedding always exists (and can be efficiently identified). We refer to Definition 2 and Definition 3 for formal statements about edge embedding and edge universal graphs.

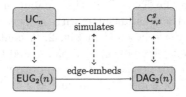

Fig. 1. "UC_n simulates $C_{s,t}^g$" is equivalent to "$\mathsf{EUG}_2(n)$ edge-embeds $\mathsf{DAG}_2(n)$".

Definition 2 (Edge-Embedding [3,41,53]**).** *Edge-embedding is a mapping from graph* $G = (V, E)$ *into* $G' = (V', E')$, *denoted by* $G \rightsquigarrow G'$, *such that*

1. V *maps to* V' *one-to-one, but not necessarily surjective (i.e.,* $|V| \leq |V'|$*).*
2. *Every edge* $e \in E$ *maps to a directed path in* E' *in an edge-disjoint manner, i.e., any edge* $e' \in E'$ *is found at most once (in the paths that are mapped from the edges in* E*).*

Definition 3 (Edge-Universal Graph [3,41,53]**).** *A directed graph* G' *is an Edge-Universal Graph for* $\mathsf{DAG}_d(n)$, *denoted by* $\mathsf{EUG}_d(n)$, *if it satisfies the following conditions:*

1. *(acyclicity).* G' *is a DAG.*
2. *(universality).* *Every* $G \in \mathsf{DAG}_d(n)$ *can be edge-embedded into* G'.
3. *(bounded fan-in/fan-out).* G' *has bounded fan-in/fan-out, typically bounded by 2.*

Further, G' *is a weak Edge-Universal Graph for* $\mathsf{DAG}_d(n)$, *denoted by* $\mathsf{wEUG}_d(n)$, *if it satisfies conditions 2 and 3 above.*

Remark 1. In the above definition, the condition that "G' is a DAG of bounded fan-in/fan-out" is decoupled into "acyclicity" (condition 1) and "bounded fan-in/fan-out" (condition 3). This facilitates the definition of weak EUG. In general, weak EUG is not a useful notion since it doesn't guarantee acyclicity, and thus does not give rise to a universal circuit (not even a circuit). However, looking ahead, we find the weak EUG notion simplifying our presentation when introducing our intermediate construction. Condition 3 is not strictly necessary for universal circuits, but it was respected by almost all previous works of universal circuits, and satisfying this condition makes comparison easy since the multiplicative size (resp., total size) of the resulting UC is roughly equal to (resp., four times) the size of the EUG.

Configuring EUG. Still using Fig. 2, we explain how edge embedding translates to the simulation of circuits. First, input nodes (e.g., x and y) simply map to the corresponding input poles in the EUG, and the gates (e.g., $\oplus$ and $\wedge$) are implemented by the universal gates in the EUG. As the name suggests, a universal gate can be configured to simulate any binary gate (see the full version of our paper [42, Appendix A] for more details). In addition to poles, there are also control nodes in the EUG (i.e., the smaller ones in the right-hand of Fig. 2), which can be further instantiated with X-switching gates, Y-switching gates, and splitters. They are labelled in Fig. 2. A control node (with a single incoming edge and two outgoing edges) is implemented by a splitter, where only two wires (i.e., no gates) are needed as the two outputs simply copy the value from the input. The control nodes with in-degree 2 and out-degree 2 (resp., 1) are implemented by X-switching (resp., Y-switching) gates, which can be configured in two different ways (see Fig. 3). In summary, the universal gates simulate

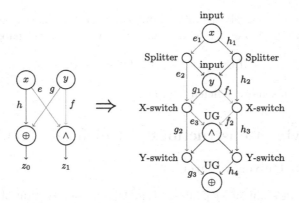

Fig. 2. An example of edge-embedding, where the nodes and edges of the left-hand DAG is mapped to corresponding poles and paths of the right-hand EUG respectively.

the corresponding gates in the original circuit, and the X/Y-switching gates are configured such that every intermediate value is carried from the origin to the destination (by following the route of edge embedding). For example in Fig. 2, the input x goes all the way, following the path (e_1, e_2, e_3), to the universal gate that computes $\wedge$, with a correct configuration of the X/Y- switching gates along the way. We refer to the full version [42, Appendix A] for details about universal gates and switching gates and their implementations. Finally, the control bits of universal gates and switching gates make up the program bits p_C for the universal circuits.

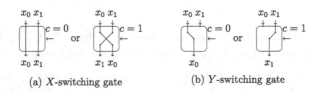

(a) X-switching gate   (b) Y-switching gate

Fig. 3. The configurations of X-switching and Y-switching gates.

Therefore, Valiant reduces the problem of constructing universal circuits to that of constructing edge-universal graphs. The size efficiency of the universal circuit mainly concerns total size and multiplicative size (the number of AND gates), both of which are proportional to the size of the EUG.

$$|\mathsf{UC}_n| = 4n_X + 3n_Y + 9n \le 4(n_X + n_Y + n) + 5n = 4|\mathsf{EUG}_2(n)| + 5n \quad,$$

$$\#(\text{AND}) = n_X + n_Y + 3n = (n_X + n_Y + n) + 2n = |\mathsf{EUG}_2(n)| + 2n \quad,$$

where n_X, n_Y and n are the numbers of X-switching gates, Y-switching gates and universal gates respectively. $4n_X$, $3n_Y$ and $9n$ further account for the numbers of basic gates needed to construct X-switching gates, Y-switching gates and universal gates respectively. Details about the implementations are provided in the full version [42, Appendix A]. Recall that $|\mathsf{EUG}_2(n)| = \Omega(n \log n)$ and thus

$$|\mathsf{EUG}_2(n)| \approx \#(\mathrm{AND}) \approx |\mathsf{UC}_n|/4$$

will be used as the major efficiency indicator.

3   Simplifying Constructions of Universal Circuits

3.1   Valiant's Universal Circuits

Following Valiant's blueprint [53] (see Fig. 4), the construction of universal circuits consists of the following steps:

1. Construct a UC_n based on an $\mathsf{EUG}_2(n)$;
2. Construct an $\mathsf{EUG}_2(n)$ by merging two instances of $\mathsf{EUG}_1(n)$;
3. Construct an $\mathsf{EUG}_1(n)$ based on $\mathsf{EUG}_1(\lceil n/k \rceil - 1)$, where the reduction is enabled with a special graph referred to as a k-way supernode, abbreviated as $\mathsf{SN}(k)$, for some small k (typically $k \in \{2, 3, 4\}$);
4. Repeat Step 3 recursively until EUG_1 is small enough to build by hand.

Fig. 4. A high-level view of Valiant's framework for contructing universal circuits.

The construction of the universal circuit UC_n from $\mathsf{EUG}_2(n)$ was already explained in the previous section. We proceed to the next steps.

Construct $\mathsf{EUG}_2(n)$ from $\mathsf{EUG}_1(n)$. We introduce Lemma 1 and Lemma 2 to show that the $\mathsf{EUG}_2(n)$ can be based on two instances of the $\mathsf{EUG}_1(n)$.

Theorem 1 (König's theorem [16,43]). *If $\mathbf{G}$ is bipartite and its nodes have at most k incoming and k outgoing edges, then the number of colors necessary to color $\mathbf{G}$ is k.*

Lemma 1 (Lemma 2.1 from [53]). *For any $\mathsf{DAG}_d(n) = (V, E)$, there exist d disjoint sets $E_1, E_2, \ldots, E_d$ such that $E = \cup_{i=1}^{d} E_i$ and each (V, E_i) (for $1 \leq i \leq d$) constitutes a $\mathsf{DAG}_1(n)$.*

Lemma 2 ([53]). *For any $n \in \mathbb{N}^+$ and any $\mathsf{EUG}_1(n)$ of size T, there exists an $\mathsf{EUG}_2(n)$ of size $2T - n$.*

We only sketch the proofs for completeness and to avoid redundancy. As exemplified in Fig. 5, we simply construct an $\mathsf{EUG}_2(n)$ based on two instances of $\mathsf{EUG}_1(n)$ by merging the corresponding poles and thus the size of the resulting $\mathsf{EUG}_2(n)$ is twice that of $\mathsf{EUG}_1(n)$ minus n. We now argue that the merged graph must be an $\mathsf{EUG}_2(n)$. Any $G = (V, E) \in \mathsf{DAG}_2(n)$ can be decomposed into $G_1 = (V, E_1), G_2 = (V, E_2) \in \mathsf{DAG}_1(n)$ by Lemma 1, for which there exist edge embeddings ρ_1 and ρ_2 that map G_1 and G_2 into the two instances of $\mathsf{EUG}_1(n)$ respectively. It is not hard to see that $\rho_1 \cup \rho_2$ is also an edge embedding (since edge-disjointness is preserved) that maps this (arbitrarily chosen) $G \in \mathsf{DAG}_2(n)$ into the candidate $\mathsf{EUG}_2(n)$, which is a merge of the two $\mathsf{EUG}_1(n)$ instances.

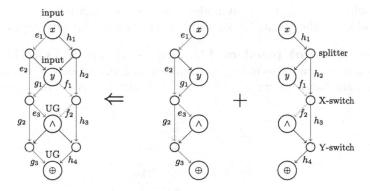

Fig. 5. An $\mathsf{EUG}_2(n)$ based on two instances of $\mathsf{EUG}_1(n)$.

DAG Augmentation. We introduce the notion of augmentation, as specified in Definition 4. Informally, a $\mathsf{DAG}_1(k)$ is augmented by adding k input nodes and k output nodes, and connecting every source (resp., sink) with a single edge from (resp., to) an input (resp., output) node. Each input/output node is connected by at most one edge and thus the resulting augmented DAG remains of fan-in/fan-out 1, namely, an augmented $\mathsf{DAG}_1(k)$ is a $\mathsf{DAG}_1(3k)$. Notice that inputs/outputs always suffice for augmentation since they are as many as the nodes in the original DAG. We also define k-way supernode, denoted by $\mathsf{SN}(k)$, in Definition 5 as a special $\mathsf{EUG}_1(3k)$ that edge embeds any augmented $\mathsf{DAG}_1(k)$, much as that an $\mathsf{EUG}_1(k)$ edge embeds any $\mathsf{DAG}_1(k)$. We refer to Fig. 6 for an example, where a $\mathsf{DAG}_1(4)$ is augmented and then edge embedded into an $\mathsf{SN}(4)$.

Definition 4 (Augmented DAG). *For any $k \in \mathbb{N}^+$ and any $G = (V, E) \in \mathsf{DAG}_1(k)$, we say that $G' = (V', E') \in \mathsf{DAG}_1(3k)$ is an augmented DAG for G if*

$$V' = \left(I = \{in^1, \ldots, in^k\} \right) \cup \left(V = (P_1, \ldots, P_k) \right) \cup \left(O = \{out^1, \ldots, out^k\} \right)$$

and $E' = E \cup E_{aux}$ satisfy

1. *(Soundness). Every $e \in E_{aux}$ satisfies either $e = (in_i, P_j)$ or $e = (P_j, out_i)$;*
2. *(Completeness). For every source (resp., sink) $P_j \in V$, there exists exactly one $i \in [k]$ such that $(in_i, P_j) \in E_{aux}$ (resp., $(P_j, out_i) \in E_{aux}$).*

Definition 5 (Supernode [41,57]). *A k-way supernode, denoted by $SN(k)$, is a DAG that can edge embed any augmented $DAG_1(k)$.*

Remark 2. To be in line with the augmented $DAG_1(k)$, an $SN(k)$ needs k inputs, k poles, k outputs and potentially more, say m, control nodes. We define the size of $SN(k)$, denoted by $|SN(k)|$, to be $m + k$ rather than $m + 3k$, i.e., excluding inputs and outputs. This seems a slight abuse of the definition of graph size, but it comes in handy when counting the size of Valiant's EUG construction (see Fig. 7), where the input/output nodes coincide with the poles in the smaller EUG (and hence their contribution to the graph size has already been counted).

Construct $EUG_1(n)$ based on $EUG_1(\lceil \frac{n}{k} \rceil - 1)$ and $SN(k)$. The core of Valiant's construction is to reduce the problem of EUG_1 to itself of a smaller size (by a constant factor k), with the aid of the special gadget called supernode.

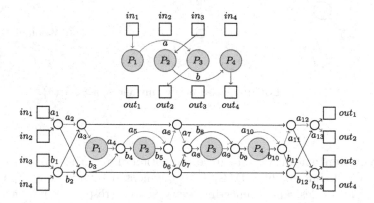

Fig. 6. A $DAG_1(4)$ with edges a, b is augmented and then edge embedded to an $SN(4)$.

Theorem 2 (Valiant's reduction [53]). *There exists an explicit construction of $EUG_1(n)$ based on k instances of $EUG_1(\lceil \frac{n}{k} \rceil - 1)$ and $\lceil \frac{n}{k} \rceil$ instances of k-way supernodes $SN(k)$ such that*

$$EUG_1(n) = k \cdot |EUG_1(\lceil \frac{n}{k} \rceil - 1)| + \lceil \frac{n}{k} \rceil \cdot |SN(k)| .$$

As visualized in Fig. 7, the n poles of the candidate $EUG_1(n)$ come from the poles of $\frac{n}{k}$ instances of $SN(k)$, i.e., $n = \frac{n}{k} \cdot k$. Merge the corresponding output and input nodes of neighboring $SN(k)$ (e.g., out_1^1 and in_2^1 in Fig. 7), which results in the merged nodes of in-degree and out-degree 1. Further, let the merged nodes coincide with the poles[4] of $\mathsf{EUG}_1(\lceil\frac{n}{k}\rceil - 1)$ that are also of in-degree and out-degree 1. Then, the eventually merged nodes are of in-degree/out-degree 2 and are thus instantiated with X-switching nodes. The fact below states that as long as one starts with an initial EUG_1 and an $\mathsf{SN}(k)$ that are DAG_2[5] with all poles of in-degree/out-degree 1, then the condition will be preserved for the recursively constructed EUG_1 of arbitrary size. Note that G's all poles are of in-degree/out-degree 1 doesn't conflict $G \in \mathsf{DAG}_2$ since the control nodes have in-degree/out-degree 2.

Fact 1 (degree preserving). *Consider the recursive construction in Fig. 7 (or Fig. 8). As long as the building block $\mathsf{SN}(k)$ and the initial EUG_1 satisfy*

1. *Each graph is of fan-in/fan-out 2;*
2. *The poles of each graph are of in-degree and out-degree 1.*

Then, the resulting EUG_1 (or wEUG_1) candidate satisfies the two conditions as well.

Proof. The proof goes by an induction. During each iteration, the poles of $\mathsf{EUG}_1(\lceil\frac{n}{k}\rceil - 1)$ are of in-degree and out-degree 1, and thus after merging with $\mathsf{SN}(k)$'s input/output nodes, it yields nodes of in-degree and out-degree 2 (i.e., not violating condition 1). Further, the poles of the $\mathsf{SN}(k)$'s now become the poles of the new $\mathsf{EUG}_1(n)$ candidate, and thus the "all poles are of in-degree and out-degree 1" condition is preserved for $\mathsf{EUG}_1(n)$ candidate.

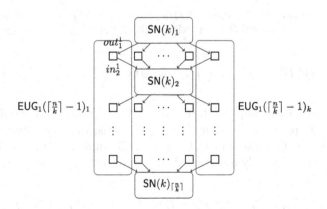

Fig. 7. Valiant's construction of $\mathsf{EUG}_1(n)$ based on k instances of $\mathsf{EUG}_1(\lceil\frac{n}{k}\rceil - 1)$ and $\lceil\frac{n}{k}\rceil$ instances of $\mathsf{SN}(k)$.

---

[4] Note that the poles of $\mathsf{EUG}_1(\lceil\frac{n}{k}\rceil - 1)$ do not constitute the poles of the $\mathsf{EUG}_1(n)$, but become X-switching nodes after merging with input/output nodes.

[5] Recall that subscript 1 in $\mathsf{EUG}_1(n)$ refers to its capability of edge embedding arbitrary $\mathsf{DAG}_1(n)$, instead of that $\mathsf{EUG}_1(n)$ is of fan-in/fan-out 1. In fact, an EUG_1 needs fan-in/fan-out 2 to cater for control nodes such as X/Y switching nodes.

Proof sketch of Theorem 2. It suffices to show any $G = (V, E) \in \mathsf{DAG}_1(n)$ can be edge embedded into the candidate $\mathsf{EUG}_1(n)$. For concreteness we give a working example (for $n = 30$ and $k = 6$) of how an arbitrary $G \in \mathsf{DAG}_1(30)$ is edge embedded into a candidate $\mathsf{EUG}_1(30)$ in the full version [42, Appendix D]. Denote the topologically sorted nodes in G by $V = \{p_1, p_2, \ldots, p_n\}$, and group them such that every k successive nodes make up a set, i.e., for each $i \in [[\lceil \frac{n}{k} \rceil]]$

$$V_i \stackrel{\text{def}}{=} \{p_{(i-1)k+1}, p_{(i-1)k+2}, \ldots, p_{(i-1)k+k}\} \, ,$$

let E_i be the set of edges connecting the nodes in V_i

$$E_i \stackrel{\text{def}}{=} \{(p_u, p_v) \in E, \mid p_u, p_v \in V_i\}$$

and let $E_\backslash$ be the rest edges (connecting nodes from different sets)

$$E_\backslash \stackrel{\text{def}}{=} E \setminus (E_1 \cup \ldots \cup E_{\lceil \frac{n}{k} \rceil}) \, .$$

First, augment (as per Definition 4) each $(V_i, E_i) \in \mathsf{DAG}_1(k)$ to a $(V_i', E_i') \in \mathsf{DAG}_1(3k)$ by adding input (resp., output) nodes, and connecting them to sources (resp., from sinks) in (V_i, E_i). There are also edges connecting nodes between different V_i, i.e., $(p_u, p_v) \in E_\backslash$ with $p_u \in V_i$ and $p_v \in V_j$ ($i < j$), where p_u (resp., p_v) must be a sink (resp., source) within (V_i, E_i) (resp., (V_j, E_j)) because any additional $e \in E$ other than (p_u, p_v) from p_u (resp., to p_v) would contradict that G is a DAG_1. Therefore, p_u will be connected to out_i^t and $in_j^{t'}$ will be linked to p_v when augmenting (V_i, E_i) and (V_j, E_j) respectively. In order to edge embed (p_u, p_v) to the augmented graph, we connect out_i^t to $in_j^{t'}$, and add $(out_i^t, in_j^{t'})$ to E_{vert}. Thus, we have the following edge embedding

$$G = (V, E) \rightsquigarrow G' = \left(\bigcup_{i=1}^{\lceil \frac{n}{k} \rceil} (I_i \cup V_i \cup O_i), \left(\bigcup_{i=1}^{\lceil \frac{n}{k} \rceil} E_i' \right) \cup E_{vert} \right) \, ,$$

where every node in V maps to itself, every edge in E_i maps to itself, and every $(p_u, p_v) \in E_\backslash$ maps to path $(p_u, out_i^t, in_j^{t'}, p_v)$. Thus, the edge embedding is not unique but up to the choices of (t, t'). Lemma 3 below guarantees (V_1, E_1), ..., $(V_{\lceil \frac{n}{k} \rceil}, E_{\lceil \frac{n}{k} \rceil})$ can be jointly augmented such that every pair $(out_i^t, in_j^{t'})$ is aligned vertically (i.e., $t = t'$).

Lemma 3. *For every $G = (V, E) \in \mathsf{DAG}_1(n)$ divided into (V_i, E_i) and $E_\backslash$ as aforementioned, one can augment (V_1, E_1), ..., $(V_{\lceil \frac{n}{k} \rceil}, E_{\lceil \frac{n}{k} \rceil}) \in \mathsf{DAG}_1(k)$ to the respective*

$$\left(I_1 \cup V_1 \cup O_1, \ E_1' \right), \ldots, \left(I_{\lceil \frac{n}{k} \rceil} \cup V_{\lceil \frac{n}{k} \rceil} \cup O_{\lceil \frac{n}{k} \rceil}, \ E_{\lceil \frac{n}{k} \rceil}' \right) \in \mathsf{DAG}_1(3k)$$

where $I_i = \{in_i^t\}_{t \in [k]}$ and $O_i = \{out_i^t\}_{t \in [k]}$, such that for every $(p_u, p_v) \in E_\backslash$ with $p_u \in V_i$ and $p_v \in V_j$ ($i < j$), the corresponding added edges $(p_u, out_i^t) \in E_i'$ and $(in_j^{t'}, p_v) \in E_j'$ satisfy $t = t'$.

Lemma 3 falls into a corollary of Theorem 1. To see this, view each I_i/O_i as a node (instead of a set of nodes) and consider the bipartite graph $(O \cup I, E_{bp})$ with disjoint node sets $O = \{O_1, \ldots, O_{\lceil \frac{n}{k} \rceil}\}$ and $I = \{I_1, \ldots, I_{\lceil \frac{n}{k} \rceil}\}$, where $(O_i, I_j) \in E_{bp}$ if and only if there exists $(p_u, p_v) \in E_\backslash$ with $p_u \in V_i$, $p_v \in V_j$ and $i < j$.[6] By Theorem 1, the bipartite graph is of fan-in/fan-out k and thus can be k-colored say with colors C-1 to C-k. Therefore, Lemma 3 follows by translating the coloring to graph augmentation, i.e., for every $(O_i, I_j) \in E_{bp}$ colored with C-t we add edges (p_u, out_i^t) and (in_j^t, p_v) to E_i' and E_j' respectively (and add (out_i^t, in_j^t) to E_{vert}). $\qquad \square$

G can be edge embedded to G', but G' cannot be edge embedded into the candidate $\mathsf{EUG}_1(n)$ because after adding the input/output nodes G' does not even look like (a subgraph of) the candidate $\mathsf{EUG}_1(n)$. To be compatible, we merge every output-input pair from the neighboring O_i and I_{i+1}, i.e., merge out_i^t and in_{i+1}^t for every $i \in [\lceil \frac{n}{k} \rceil - 1]$ and $t \in [k]$, and rename the merged node from out_i^t/in_{i+1}^t to oi_i^t. Let $OI_i \stackrel{\text{def}}{=} \{oi_i^t\}_{t \in [k]}$, let E_i'' and E_{vert}' be the counterparts of E_i' and E_{vert} respectively (by renaming out_i^t/in_{i+1}^t to oi_i^t) and eliminating self loops[7]. We denote the merged version of G' by

$$G'' = \left(I_1 \cup \bigcup_{i=1}^{\lceil \frac{n}{k} \rceil - 1} (V_i \cup OI_i) \cup O_{\lceil \frac{n}{k} \rceil}, \; \left(\bigcup_{i=1}^{\lceil \frac{n}{k} \rceil} E_i'' \right) \cup E_{vert}' \right),$$

and it remains to edge embed G'' to the candidate $\mathsf{EUG}_1(n)$. To achieve this, we edge embed every $(OI_{i-1} \cup V_i \cup OI_i, E_i'')$ into $\mathsf{SN}(k)_i$, where $OI_0 = I_1$ and $OI_{\lceil \frac{n}{k} \rceil} = O_{\lceil \frac{n}{k} \rceil}$. The task then reduces to

$$\left(\bigcup_{i=1}^{\lceil \frac{n}{k} \rceil - 1} OI_i = \bigcup_{t=1}^{k} \{oi_i^t\}_{i \in [\lceil \frac{n}{k} \rceil - 1]}, E_{vert}' \right) \rightsquigarrow \bigcup_{t=1}^{k} \mathsf{EUG}_1(\lceil \frac{n}{k} \rceil - 1)_t .$$

Thanks to Lemma 3, every $(oi_i^t, oi_j^{t'}) \in E_{vert}'$ satisfies $t = t'$, and thus the job furthers reduces to do edge embedding independently, i.e., for every $t \in [k]$

$$\left(V_t^{oi} \stackrel{\text{def}}{=} \{oi_i^t\}_{i \in [\lceil \frac{n}{k} \rceil - 1]}, E_t^{oi} \stackrel{\text{def}}{=} \{(oi_i^t, oi_j^t) \in E_{vert}'\} \right) \rightsquigarrow \mathsf{EUG}_1(\lceil \frac{n}{k} \rceil - 1)_t ,$$

where $\cup_{t=1}^k E_t^{oi} = E_{vert}'$. This is trivial since any $\mathsf{DAG}_1(\lceil \frac{n}{k} \rceil - 1)$ such as (V_t^{oi}, E_t^{oi}) can be edge embedded into an $\mathsf{EUG}_1(\lceil \frac{n}{k} \rceil - 1)$.

Theorem 3 (Valiant's universal circuits [53]). *For any integer $k \geq 2$, there exist explicit k-way constructions of $\mathsf{EUG}_2(n)$ and UC_n with*

$$|\mathsf{EUG}_2(n)| = \frac{2|\mathsf{SN}(k)|}{k \log k} n \log n - \Omega(n) \quad and \quad |\mathsf{UC}_n| \leq 4|\mathsf{EUG}_2(n)| + O(n) .$$

---

[6] No edge $(p_u, p_v) \in E_i$ (i.e., $i = j$) is considered, and the case for $i > j$ is not possible as nodes are topologically sorted in the first place. Further, if there are multiple edges from a node in V_i to one in V_j, then equally many copies of (O_i, I_j) are added.

[7] After merging, edge (out_i^t, in_{i+1}^t) becomes a self-loop which is not included in E_{vert}'.

The construction of $\mathsf{EUG}_2(n)$ eventually reduces to that of $\mathsf{EUG}_1(B)$ for small B, whose optimal sizes were known for $B \in \{2,\dots,8\}$ [30,41,53] (see Table 2). The size of $\mathsf{EUG}_2(n)$ follows from Lemma 2 and Theorem 2, i.e.,

$$|\mathsf{EUG}_2(n)| = 2|\mathsf{EUG}_1(n)| - n \ , \tag{1}$$

$$|\mathsf{EUG}_1(n)| = k|\mathsf{EUG}_1(\lceil\tfrac{n}{k}\rceil - 1)| + \lceil\tfrac{n}{k}\rceil|\mathsf{SN}(k)| \ , \tag{2}$$

where $|\mathsf{EUG}_1(B)|$ is irrelevant to the dominant term of $|\mathsf{EUG}_2(n)|$ but is reflected in (and absorbed by) the term $\Omega(n)$. Similarly, we get

$$|\mathsf{UC}_n| = \frac{2|\mathsf{CircuitSN}(k)|}{k\log k}n\log n - \Omega(n) \leq \frac{8|\mathsf{SN}(k)|}{k\log k}n\log n - \Omega(n) \ , \tag{3}$$

where $\mathsf{CircuitSN}(k)$ denotes the circuit counterpart of $\mathsf{SN}(k)$. Clearly, the size of universal circuits monotonically depends on the k-way supernode size, and thus constructing size-optimal universal circuits can be reduced to the search for optimal size-efficient supernodes. We know from the literature [30,53,57] the minimum of $|\mathsf{SN}(k)|$ for practical values $k = 2,3,4$ along with the corresponding sizes of edge universal graphs and universal circuits, as shown in the full version [42, Appendix C] and Table 3.

Table 2. The concrete sizes of size-optimal $\mathsf{EUG}_1(n)$ for $n \in \{2,\cdots,8\}$ [30,41,53].

n	2	3	4	5	6	7	8
$|\mathsf{EUG}_1(n)|$	2	4	6	10	13	19	23

Table 3. Size-efficient universal circuits for $k \in \{2,3,4\}$ under Valiant' framework, where graph and circuit sizes keep only dominant terms.

Construction	k	$|\mathsf{SN}(k)|$	$|\mathsf{EUG}_2(n)|$	$|\mathsf{UC}_n|$
Valiant's 2-way [53]	2	5	$5n\log n$	$20n\log n$
Günther et al.'s 3-way [30]	3	12	$5.05n\log n$	$20.19n\log n$
Valiant's 4-way [53]	4	19	$4.75n\log n$	$19n\log n$
Zhao et al.'s 4-way [57]	4	18	$4.5n\log n$	$17.75n\log n$

The supernode sizes in Table 3, i.e., $|\mathsf{SN}(k)| = 5, 12$ and 18 for $k \in \{2,3,4\}$ respectively, were shown optimal by an exhaustive search that no candidate graph of smaller sizes can constitute a k-way supernode [57]. However, size-optimal supernodes, for $k \geq 5$, are not known and even if they are found, the corresponding universal circuits are not practical because the time/memory complexity of the compiler (that involves EUG configuration, edge embedding, etc.) blows up dramatically with respect to k. Further, Zhao et al. [57] showed that under Valiant's framework, the $|\mathsf{EUG}_2(n)|$ is lower bounded by $3.64n\log n$ with minimum achieved at $k = 69$ (and thus unattainable in practice). Therefore, it is necessary to break the Valiant's framework to beat the $3.64n\log n$ lower bound.

3.2 An Intermediate wEUG$_1(n)$ Construction

As concluded, improvement to Valiant's universal circuits seemingly relies on better constructions of EUG$_1(n)$. As shown in Fig. 8, we give an intermediate construction of a candidate wEUG$_1(n)$: for every row i (i.e., SN$(k)_i$) we horizontally (i.e., for $t \in [k]$) merge every input-output pair (in_i^t, out_i^t) to the node io_i^t of in-degree and out-degree 1, and we further merge the nodes vertically, for every column t, let $(io_1^t, io_2^t, \ldots, io_{\lceil \frac{n}{k} \rceil}^t)$ merge with the poles of the wEUG$_1(\lceil \frac{n}{k} \rceil)_t$ component-wise. Prior to merging the poles of wEUG$_1(\lceil \frac{n}{k} \rceil)$ are of in-degree and out-degree 1 (see Fact 1), and therefore the merged nodes are X-switching nodes of in-degree and out-degree 2. This construction seems to be a variant of Valiant's construction in Fig. 7. The difference is that, instead of merging every pair of out_i^t and in_{i+1}^t ($1 \le t \le k$) from the neighboring SN$(k)_i$ and SN$(k)_{i+1}$, one merges in_i^t and out_i^t for the same SN$(k)_i$, for every $i \in [[\frac{n}{k}]]$ and $t \in [k]$. This introduces cycles to the graph and thus the best hope is to prove it to be a wEUG$_1(n)$.

Corollary 1 (The intermediate wEUG$_1(n)$). *The graph constructed from k instances of* wEUG$_1(\lceil \frac{n}{k} \rceil)$ *and* $\lceil \frac{n}{k} \rceil$ *instances of* SN(k), *as in Fig. 8, is a* wEUG$_1(n)$.

We sketch how the proof of Theorem 2 can be adapted to prove the above corollary. Consider an arbitrary $G = (V, E) \in$ DAG$_1(n)$ with topologically sorted nodes $V = \{p_1, p_2, \ldots, p_n\}$, and let V_i, E_i and $E_\backslash$ be defined the same way (as in proof of Theorem 2). After augmenting every $(V_i, E_i) \in$ DAG$_1(k)$ to a $(V_i', E_i') \in$ DAG$_1(3k)$, we can (efficiently) obtain such an edge embedding

$$G = (V, E) \rightsquigarrow G' = \left(\bigcup_{i=1}^{\lceil \frac{n}{k} \rceil} (I_i \cup V_i \cup O_i), \; \left(\bigcup_{i=1}^{\lceil \frac{n}{k} \rceil} E_i' \right) \cup E_{vert} \right),$$

where by Lemma 3 for every $(p_u, p_v) \in E_\backslash$ (i.e., $p_u \in V_i$, $p_v \in V_j$, $i < j$) there exists $t \in [k]$ such that edge (p_u, p_v) maps to path $(p_u, out_i^t, in_j^t, p_v)$ in the edge embedding. Notice that up till now the proof is exactly the same as that of Theorem 2. Next, instead of merging every pair of out_i^t and in_{i+1}^t ($t \in [k]$) from the neighboring O_i and I_{i+1} ($i \in [[\frac{n}{k}] - 1]$), we merge in_i^t and out_i^t for the same i, and for every $i \in [[\frac{n}{k}]]$ and $t \in [k]$, as shown in Fig. 8. Rename the merged node in_i^t / out_i^t to io_i^t, let $IO_i \stackrel{\text{def}}{=} \{io_i^t\}_{t \in [k]}$, and let E_i'' and E_{vert}' be the counterparts of E_i' and E_{vert} respectively by renaming the nodes (from in_i^t / out_i^t to io_i^t). This simplifies G' to

$$G'' = \left(\bigcup_{i=1}^{\lceil \frac{n}{k} \rceil} (IO_i \cup V_i), \; \left(\bigcup_{i=1}^{\lceil \frac{n}{k} \rceil} E_i'' \right) \cup E_{vert}' \right),$$

and it remains to show G'' can be edge embedded into the candidate weak EUG. Every $(I_i \cup V_i \cup O_i, E_i')$ can be edge embedded into $\mathsf{SN}(k)_i$ and so can do it when the corresponding in_i^t and out_i^t are merged, which ensures that every edge in E_i maps to a path in the candidate $\mathsf{wEUG}_1(n)$. Further, by the definition of weak EUG we have for every $t \in [k]$

$$\left(V_t^{io} \overset{\text{def}}{=} \{io_i^t\}_{i \in [\lceil \frac{n}{k} \rceil]}, \ E_t^{io} \overset{\text{def}}{=} \left\{ (io_i^t, io_j^t) \in E_{vert}' \right\} \right) \rightsquigarrow \mathsf{wEUG}_1(\lceil \tfrac{n}{k} \rceil)_t \ ,$$

which ensures that every $(p_u, p_v) \in E_\setminus$ maps to a path in the candidate $\mathsf{wEUG}_1(n)$. Finally, it is important to note that the aforementioned mappings of edges in E to the corresponding paths in the candidate $\mathsf{wEUG}_1(n)$ are edge disjoint.   □

Note that wEUG_1 is cyclic, and there are cycles that first leave a block and eventually returns to the same block. However, it is interesting to observe that such self-feedback paths will never appear in the edge-disjoint paths for edge-embedding any $\mathsf{DAG}_1(n)$. This is because for any topologically sorted $\mathsf{DAG}_1(n)$ and any edge $(u,v) \in \mathsf{DAG}_1(n)$ that belong to the same block we have $1 + (i-1)k \le u < v \le k + (i-1)k$, and by the definition of supernode $\mathsf{SN}(k)_i$ edge embeds (u,v) with a path that never leaves the block. Otherwise said, the X-switching nodes resulting from merging input/output nodes for every $\mathsf{SN}(k)_i$ (see node a in Fig. 8) are actually redundant, e.g., the self-feedback option $(4,2)/(1,3)$ for node a is never used. This motivates further optimizations in our final construction, and thanks to the removal of the redundant nodes, the end construction results in a DAG and we get an EUG in the end.

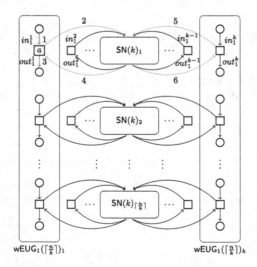

Fig. 8. The intermediate $\mathsf{wEUG}_1(n)$ based on k instances of $\mathsf{wEUG}_1(\lceil \frac{n}{k} \rceil)$ and $\lceil \frac{n}{k} \rceil$ instances of $\mathsf{SN}(k)$.

3.3 The Final Constructions of $\mathsf{EUG}_1(n)$ and Universal Circuits

On optimizing the intermediate construction. At first glance, this construction is nothing more than a weak version of Valiant's EUG, with roughly the same (actually slightly worse) circuit size. However, it serves to exhibit the redundancy of Valiant's construction. Our universal circuits use the EUG_1 construction in Fig. 9, which optimizes (differs from) Fig. 8 by avoiding merging the nodes (and save X-switching nodes). That is, for every $t \in [k]$ and $i \in [\lceil \frac{n}{k} \rceil]$, let (in_i^t, out_i^t) be the input-output pair from $\mathsf{SN}(k)_i$ and let p_i^t be the i-th pole of $\mathsf{wEUG}_1(\lceil \frac{n}{k} \rceil)_t$, we remove in_i^t, out_i^t and p_i^t (their associated edges) and add an edge connecting p_i^t's precursor node to in_i^t's successor node and another one linking out_i^t's precursor to p_i^t's successor. Here in_i^t's successor and out_i^t's precursor refer to the respective successor/precursor in $\mathsf{SN}(k)_i$ and p_i^t's precursor/successor is with respect to $\mathsf{wEUG}_1(\lceil \frac{n}{k} \rceil)_t$. These precursors/successors are all guaranteed to be unique by the definition of augmentation and Fact 1. It is important to note that after removing the nodes (and their associated edges, and making necessary adjustments), the candidate EUG_1 in Fig. 9 now becomes a DAG_2. We can prove that it is an EUG_1 by showing that the universality is preserved from the wEUG_1 in Fig. 8 (i.e., not affected by the optimization).

Table 4. Our k-way universal circuits from Theorem 4 for $k \in \{2, 3, 4\}$.

Our k-way UC	$\mathsf{SN}(k)$	$|\mathsf{EUG}_2(n)|$	$|\mathsf{UC}_n|$
2-way	5	$3n \log n$	$12n \log n$
3-way	12	$3.79n \log n$	$15.14n \log n$
4-way	18	$3.5n \log n$	$14n \log n$

Theorem 4 (Universal circuits). *For any integer $k \geq 2$, there exists explicit k-way constructions of $\mathsf{EUG}_2(n)$ and UC_n with*

$$|\mathsf{EUG}_2(n)| = \frac{2(|\mathsf{SN}(k)| - k)}{k \log k} n \log n - \Omega(n) \quad and \quad |\mathsf{UC}_n| \leq 4|\mathsf{EUG}_2(n)| + O(n) \ .$$

In particular, for $k = 2$ we have $|\mathsf{EUG}_2(n)| = 3n \log n - \Omega(n)$.

Proof. Now that Fig. 8 presents a correct wEUG_1 construction by Corollary 1, we further argue that Fig. 9 gives rise to an EUG_1 as well. By comparing Fig. 9 with Fig. 8, the difference is all X-switching nodes io_i^t, that merges (in_i^t, out_i^t) from $\mathsf{SN}(k)_i$ and pole p_i^t from $\mathsf{wEUG}_1(\lceil \frac{n}{k} \rceil)_t$, are now bypassed in Fig. 9. By right the X-switch node io_i^t offers two switching options:

$$\text{option 0: } (p_i^{t,pre}, io_i^t, in_i^{t,suc}) \ \& \ (out_i^{t,pre}, io_i^t, p_i^{t,suc})$$
$$\text{option 1: } (p_i^{t,pre}, io_i^t, p_i^{t,suc}) \ \& \ (out_i^{t,pre}, io_i^t, in_i^{t,suc})$$

where $p_i^{t,pre}$ and $p_i^{t,suc}$ denote the precursor and successor of p_i^t within the $\mathsf{wEUG}_1(\lceil \frac{n}{k} \rceil)$ respectively, and $in_i^{t,suc}$ (resp., $out_i^{t,pre}$) denotes the successor (resp., precursor) of in_i^t (resp., out_i^t) within the $\mathsf{SN}(k)$. In contrast, Fig. 9 simply hardwires the option-0 configuration and short-circuits every node io_i^t as follows:

$$(p_i^{t,pre}, in_i^{t,suc}) \ \& \ (out_i^{t,pre}, p_i^{t,suc}) \ .$$

It suffices to show that option 1 is redundant and is thus not needed. Recall the main idea of the $\mathsf{wEUG}_1(n)$ construction is that $\mathsf{wEUG}_1(\lceil \frac{n}{k} \rceil)$ edge-embeds inter-group edges, i.e., (p_u, p_v) for $p_u \in V_{i_1}$, $p_v \in V_{i_2}$ and $i_1 < i_2$, and $\mathsf{SN}(k)$ takes care of intra-group edges, i.e., (p_u, p_v) for $p_u, p_v \in V_i$. In the former case, edges $(p_u, out_{i_1}^t)$ and $(in_{i_2}^t, p_v)$ will be added during augmentation, where two option-0 configurations are needed: for $i = i_1$ we need $(out_i^{t,pre}, io_i^t, p_i^{t,suc})$ to make a path that originates from p_u's corresponding pole; and for $i = i_2$ it is necessary to have $(p_i^{t,pre}, io_i^t, in_i^{t,suc})$ for a path ending at p_v's pole. Note that edge $(out_{i_1}^t, in_{i_2}^t)$ will be mapped to a path in $\mathsf{wEUG}_1(\lceil \frac{n}{k} \rceil)_t$. In the latter case, the edge embedding of (p_u, p_v) is handled by $\mathsf{SN}(k)_i$ internally and thus no switching configurations are needed. Therefore, the wEUG_1 after optimization (by removing the cycles) becomes a DAG_1 (and is therefore an EUG_1). The optimized EUG_1 construction yields

$$|\mathsf{EUG}_1(n)| = k \cdot |\mathsf{EUG}_1(\lceil \tfrac{n}{k} \rceil)| + \lceil \tfrac{n}{k} \rceil \cdot |\mathsf{SN}(k)| - n \ ,$$

where n accounts for the number of X-switching node io_i^t saved (cf. Eq. 2). Based on this optimized EUG_1 construction, we follow Valiant's blueprint (see Fig. 4) to get an $\mathsf{EUG}_2(n)$ of size

$$|\mathsf{EUG}_2(n)| = 2|\mathsf{EUG}_1(n)| - n = \frac{2(|\mathsf{SN}(k)| - k)}{k \log k} n \log n - \Omega(n) \ ,$$

where choosing $k = 2$, $\mathsf{SN}(2) = 5$ yields efficient 2-way construction of size $3n \log n - \Omega(n)$.

Remark 3 (Why not optimizing Valiant's EUG_1?). One might ask why not directly optimize the Valiant's original construction in Fig. 7 and instead introduce the intermediate one in Fig. 8. This is because the merged nodes in Fig. 7 are actually necessary and cannot be saved for free. To see this, for every $i \in [\lceil \frac{n}{k} \rceil - 1]$ and $t \in [k]$, merge out_i^t, in_{i+1}^t and the i-th pole p_i^t of $\mathsf{EUG}_1(\lceil \frac{n}{k} \rceil - 1)_t$ to an X-switching node oi_i^t, where the switching options are as follows

$$\text{option 0: } (p_i^{t,pre}, oi_i^t, in_{i+1}^{t,suc}) \ \& \ (out_i^{t,pre}, oi_i^t, p_i^{t,suc}) \ ,$$
$$\text{option 1: } (p_i^{t,pre}, oi_i^t, p_i^{t,suc}) \ \& \ (out_i^{t,pre}, oi_i^t, in_{i+1}^{t,suc}) \ .$$

We mention that both options are necessary. Option 0 is needed for edge embedding (p_u, p_v) with either $p_u \in V_j$, $p_v \in V_{i+1}$ $(j < i)$ or $p_u \in V_i$, $p_v \in V_{j+1}$ $(j > i)$, whereas option 1 is required for the case that $p_u \in V_i$ and $p_v \in V_{i+1}$. Hence, we cannot save XOR switching node oi_i^t by hardwiring either options. In retrospect, the latter configuration is only needed for handling edges connecting neighboring node sets, which motivates us to use the variant in Fig. 8 to eliminate the need for option 1.

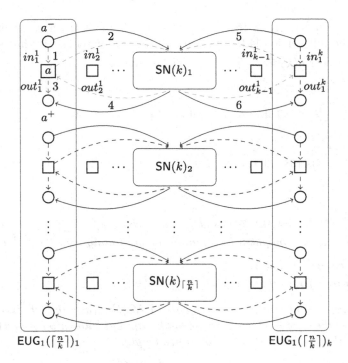

Fig. 9. The end $\mathsf{EUG}_1(n)$ based on k instances of $\mathsf{EUG}_1(\lceil\frac{n}{k}\rceil)$ and $\lceil\frac{n}{k}\rceil$ instances of k-way supernodes $\mathsf{SN}(k)$, where a^- and a^+ are the precursor and successor of pole a within $\mathsf{EUG}_2(\lceil\frac{n}{k}\rceil)_1$ respectively, and dashed edges do not exist (cf. Fig. 8).

As explicitly stated in Theorem 4, our 2-way universal circuits already improve upon the best previously known by reducing a third in circuit size. Curiously, one may wonder if the advantage can be further increased by using a large k. We list out the results in Table 4 for k up to 4 based on the corresponding optimal-size k-way supernodes.

3.4   A Lower Bound on Circuit Size in Our Framework

We lower bound the size of the k-way $\mathsf{EUG}_2(n)$ (and UC) in our framework based on the techniques introduced in [57].

Theorem 5 (A lower bound on $|\mathsf{EUG}_2(n)|$). *For any integer $k \geq 2$, any k-way $\mathsf{EUG}_2(n)$ constructed via the following two steps*

1. Recursively construct an $\mathsf{EUG}_1(n)$ as in Fig. 9;
2. Use Valiant's EUG_1-to-EUG_2 transform (see Lemma 2) to get an $\mathsf{EUG}_2(n)$.

must satisfy $|\mathsf{EUG}_2(n)| \geq 2.95n \log n$ for all sufficiently large n's.

Proof. Recall that by Theorem 3 we have

$$|\mathsf{EUG}_2(n)| = \frac{2(|\mathsf{SN}(k)| - k)}{k \log k} n \log n - \Omega(n) \geq \frac{2\lceil\log(F_k)\rceil}{k \log k} n \log n - \Omega(n)$$

where the inequality comes from [57], stated as Lemma 4, whose proof is reproduced in the full version [42, Appendix B] for completeness. It thus suffices to bound the factor $g(k) \overset{\text{def}}{=} \frac{2\lceil \log(F_k) \rceil}{k \log k}$ using Lemma 5.

Table 5. The values of $g(k)$ for $k \leq 30$.

k	2	3	4	...	8	9	10	...	29	30
$g(k)$	3	3.0158	2.9943	...	2.9547	2.9547	2.9565	...	3.0419	3.0449

Lemma 4 ([57]). $|SN(k)| \geq \lceil \log(F_k) + k \rceil$, where $F_k = \sum_{i=1}^{k} (\frac{k!}{(k-i)!})^2 A_{i,k}$ and $A_{i,k}$ in turn can be computed by dynamic programming with the following:

1. **(Base case).** $A_{1,k} = 1, \forall k \in \mathbb{N}^+$;
2. **(Recursive formula).** $A_{i,k} = \sum_{j=0}^{k-i} \binom{k-1}{j} A_{i-1,k-j-1}$.

F_k is defined as the number of augmented $\mathsf{DAG}_1(k)$ (as per Definition 4), and $A_{i,k}$ denotes the number of ways to spread k different balls into i ($i \leq k$) identical boxes with the condition that no boxes are empty.

Lemma 5. For any integer $k \geq 2$, $g(k) \overset{\text{def}}{=} \frac{2\lceil \log(F_k) \rceil}{k \log k} > 2.95$.

Proof. As a general closed-form expression for F_k seems difficult, we use dynamic programming to compute the values of $A_{i,k}$ F_k and $g(k)$ for k up to a few hundred, and list only partial results (up to $k = 30$) in Table 5 due to lack of space. Note that $g(8)$ and $g(9)$ are roughly the same and seemingly reach the minimum in terms of the values we computed. It remains to show that "$g(k)$ is monotonically increasing for $k \geq 9$" to complete the proof. We have

$$F_k = \sum_{i=1}^{k} (\frac{k!}{(k-i)!})^2 A_{i,k} \geq \sum_{i=k-1}^{k} (\frac{k!}{(k-i)!})^2 A_{i,k} = (A_{k-1,k} + A_{k,k})(k!)^2 ,$$

and $A_{k,k} = 1, A_{k-1,k} = \binom{k}{2} = \frac{(k-1)k}{2}$. Thus, $F_k \geq (\frac{(k-1)k}{2} + 1)(k!)^2$. It follows from Stirling's formula $\forall k \in \mathbb{N}^+$ $k! \geq \sqrt{2\pi k}(\frac{k}{e})^k$

$$F_k \geq (2\pi k)\left(\frac{(k-1)k}{2} + 1\right)\left(\frac{k}{e}\right)^{2k} ,$$

and therefore

$$g(k) \geq \frac{2\log(F_k)}{k \log k} \geq \frac{2\log(\pi k((k-1)k+2)(\frac{k}{e})^{2k})}{k \log k} \overset{\text{def}}{=} h(k) ,$$

where by taking the derivative we know that $h(k)$ in the right-hand is monotonically increasing for $k \geq 2$, and thus $g(k) \geq h(k) \geq h(9) \approx 2.95$ for all $k \geq 9$, which completes the proof.

On the (un)tightness of the $2.95n \log n$ bound. The bound is obtained by applying Lemma 4 and Lemma 5. The latter is tight as equality holds for $k = 9$ while the former is not. We observe that $\log(F_k) + k$ equals 5, 10.17 and 15.98 for $k = 2, 3, 4$ respectively, so $|\mathsf{SN}(k)|$, as an integer, is no less than 5, 11, and 16 for the respective $k = 2, 3, 4$. However, as shown in Table 4, the minimum of $|\mathsf{SN}(k)|$ equals 5, 12, 18 for $k = 2, 3, 4$ respectively. That is, the equality holds only at $k = 2$ and the gap seems to increase over k, where the untightness is attributed to the proof technique, i.e., that the number of possible configurations is no less than that of the augmented k-way DAG_1 is a loose argument due to the existence of redundant configurations (not all control nodes are needed to edge embed a specific DAG). To conclude, the lower bound $2.95n \log n$ is very close to $3n \log n$ achieved by our efficient construction, and the loose steps for deriving the lower bound suggests that the construction might already be optimal under the framework we introduced.

4 Implementation and Performance Evaluation

In this section, we give more details about the implementation and optimization of the universal circuits, and a performance comparison with the previous works. The source code of our implementation and optimization is available at [4].

4.1 Implementing and Optimizing the 2-Way Universal Circuits

We briefly describe how to implement and optimize our 2-way UC. Following previous implementations [3,30,37], we use the Fairplay compiler [9,44] with the Fairplay extension [39] to transform any functionality described in a high-level language into the standard circuit description written in SHDL (Secure Hardware Definition Language). The produced circuit description has fan-in 2, but has no limit on its fan-out. As required by Valiant's universal circuits, the fan-out of the circuit to be simulated must be bounded by 2 as well. Hence, the next step is to convert the circuit to a functionality equivalent one with fan-in/fan-out 2, which is achieved by using copying gates for those gates with out-degree more than 2. We refer to [37] for implementation details and how the conversion affects the size of practical circuits. Following the works [3,30,37], the circuit description format of the generated UC numbers the wires in sequential order and specifies universal, X-switching and Y-switching gates as follows:

$$U \ in_1 \ in_2 \ out_1$$
$$X \ in_1 \ in_2 \ out_1 \ out_2$$
$$Y \ in_1 \ in_2 \ out_1$$

where a gate with type (U, X or Y) and input wires in_1 and in_2 produces as output(s) wire out_1 (and possibly wire out_2), and control bits for the gates are not present in the above description but stored in the programming file of UC.

Our 2-way UC should be more efficient to generate than the hybrid counterparts in [3,30,37,57] due to the simplicity. However, a straightforward implementation of 2-way construction in Fig. 9 requires that n is a two's power and therefore optimization is needed to adapt to arbitrary n. Similar to [30], we define in Fig. 10 sub-components of $SN(2)$ called head block and tail blocks by removing the respective input and output nodes (and their associated edges and control nodes). This enables a more fine-grained recursive construction of $EUG_1(n)$ for arbitrary $n \in \mathbb{N}^+$ as follows:

1. If n is even, construct $EUG_1(n)$ as in Fig. 11(a) and invoke the two instances of $EUG_1(\frac{n}{2})$;
2. Otherwise (n is odd), construct $EUG_1(n)$ as in Fig. 11(b), and invoke $EUG_1(\frac{n+1}{2})$ and $EUG_1(\frac{n-1}{2})$.
3. Repeat until n is sufficiently small to build $EUG_1(n)$ by hand.

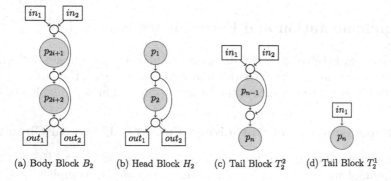

(a) Body Block B_2 (b) Head Block H_2 (c) Tail Block T_2^2 (d) Tail Block T_2^1

Fig. 10. (a) is Valiant's 2-way supernode, (b) is the head block that excludes input nodes, (c) and (d) are the tail blocks for two poles and a single pole respectively.

The construction gives the recursive relation on the size of $EUG_1(n)$ as follows:

$$|EUG_1(n)| = |\text{head}| + (\lceil \tfrac{n}{2} \rceil - 2) \cdot |\text{body}| + |\text{tail}(p_n)|$$
$$+ |EUG_1(\lceil \tfrac{n}{2} \rceil)| + |EUG_1(\lfloor \tfrac{n}{2} \rfloor)| - n \ , \tag{4}$$

where $p_n = 2$ if n is even, or $p_n = 1$ otherwise, $|\text{head}| = 4$ and $|\text{body}| = 5$ are the sizes of the head and standard body blocks respectively, and $|\text{tail}(1)| = 1$ and $|\text{tail}(2)| = 4$ are the sizes of different tail blocks determined by the parity of n as shown in Fig. 10. The above relation is more precise but it yields the same asymptotic sizes about $EUG_2(n)$ and UC_n as stated in Theorem 4, which are obtained in the simplified scenario $n = 2^j \cdot B$.

4.2   Performance Evaluation

We evaluate the multiplicative circuit sizes of our UC in simulating a set of typical circuits such as AES-128 with key expansion, MD5 and SHA-256 from [52]

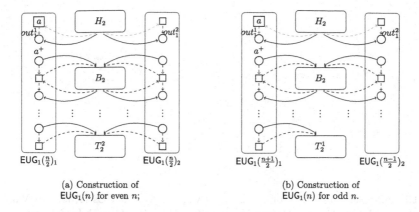

(a) Construction of
EUG₁(n) for even n;

(b) Construction of
EUG₁(n) for odd n.

Fig. 11. A more fine-grained construction of $\mathsf{EUG}_1(n)$ for arbitrary n (cf. Fig. 9), which starts with a head block, followed by $\lceil \frac{n}{2} - 2 \rceil$ standard blocks of $\mathsf{SN}(2)$, and ends with a tail block with one or two poles depending on the parity of n.

and compare the results with those from previous ones [3,30,37,57] in Table 6. We also run the experiments for a wider range of (fan-in/fan-out 2) circuits of size $15 \leq n \leq 10^8$, in particular, for every range $n \in \{10^i, \ldots, 10^{i+1}\}$ pick 100 equidistant points for n (or evaluate all if the number of points is less than 100). The comparison with previous implementations is visualized in Fig. 12. Both comparisons confirm that our 2-way universal circuits achieve roughly 33%, 37% and 40% reductions in circuit size over Zhao et al.'s UC, Valiant's 2-way and 4-way UCs respectively.

Table 6. A comparison (in terms of the sizes) of the Valiant's 2-way UCs [37], two hybrid UCs [3,30], Zhao et al.'s 4-way [57] and our 2-way UC implementations to simulate sample circuits from [52].

Functionality	n	Valiant's 2-way UC [3,53]	Valiant's 2-way & 4-way hybrid UC [30]	Zhao et al.'s 4-way UC [57]	Valiant's 2-way & Zhao et al.'s 4-way hybrid UC [3]	Our 2-way UC
Credit Checking	82	$1.50 \cdot 10^3$	$1.49 \cdot 10^3$	$1.43 \cdot 10^3$	$1.43 \cdot 10^3$	$1.16 \cdot 10^3$
Mobile Code	160	$3.65 \cdot 10^3$	$3.61 \cdot 10^3$	$3.58 \cdot 10^3$	$3.46 \cdot 10^3$	$2.73 \cdot 10^3$
ADD-32	342	$9.58 \cdot 10^3$	$9.44 \cdot 10^3$	$9.00 \cdot 10^3$	$9.00 \cdot 10^3$	$6.93 \cdot 10^3$
ADD-64	674	$2.21 \cdot 10^4$	$2.17 \cdot 10^4$	$2.14 \cdot 10^4$	$2.07 \cdot 10^4$	$1.57 \cdot 10^4$
MULT-32×32	12202	$6.54 \cdot 10^5$	$6.35 \cdot 10^5$	$6.12 \cdot 10^5$	$6.02 \cdot 10^5$	$4.39 \cdot 10^5$
AES-exp	38518	$2.39 \cdot 10^6$	$2.31 \cdot 10^6$	$2.19 \cdot 10^6$	$2.19 \cdot 10^6$	$1.58 \cdot 10^6$
MD5	66497	$4.42 \cdot 10^6$	$4.26 \cdot 10^6$	$4.05 \cdot 10^6$	$4.02 \cdot 10^6$	$2.90 \cdot 10^6$
SHA-256	201206	$1.49 \cdot 10^7$	$1.44 \cdot 10^7$	$1.38 \cdot 10^7$	$1.36 \cdot 10^7$	$9.65 \cdot 10^6$

Admittedly, our implementation only verifies the correctness of the construction and its size advantages over previous constructions. Further engineering

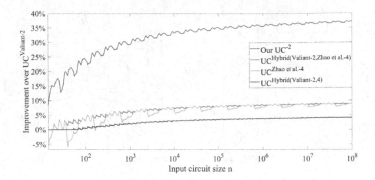

Fig. 12. Improvement in size of our 2-way UCs, two hybrid UCs [3,30] and Valiant's 4-way UCs [57] over Valiant's 2-way UCs [30] for $15 \leq n \leq 10^8$ with logarithmic x axis.

efforts are needed to optimize UC generation and programming process for practical use, and in this respect the scalable UC generation algorithm from [3] that reduces memory consumption from $O(n \log n)$ to $O(n)$ serves as a good reference. We also refer to [32, Appendix B] for a recent performance evaluation of universal circuits in the context of linear-complexity private function evaluation, where our UC exhibits a roughly 1/3 improvement over [3] in terms of the communication and runtime of the PFE protocols, and is thus recognized as the current state-of-the-art of universal circuits (e.g., [31,32]).

Acknowledgments. We are grateful to the authors of [3] for pointing out the issue in a previous version that our intermediate construction yields only a weak EUG, and for many helpful suggestions. Yu Yu, the corresponding author, was supported by the National Key Research and Development Program of China (Grant Nos. 2020YFA0309705 and 2018YFA0704701) and the National Natural Science Foundation of China (Grant Nos. 61872236 and 61971192). Jiang Zhang is supported by the National Natural Science Foundation of China (Grant Nos. 62022018, 61932019), the National Key Research and Development Program of China (Grant No. 2018YFB0804105). This work is also supported by Shandong Provincial Key Research and Development Program (Major Scientific and Technological Innovation Project, Grant No. 2019JZZY010133), Shandong Key Research and Development Program (Grant No. 2020ZLYS09).

References

1. Abadi, M., Feigenbaum, J.: Secure circuit evaluation. J. Cryptol. **2**(1), 1–12 (1990). https://doi.org/10.1007/BF02252866
2. Afshar, A., Mohassel, P., Pinkas, B., Riva, B.: Non-interactive secure computation based on cut-and-choose. In: Nguyen, P.Q., Oswald, E. (eds.) EUROCRYPT 2014. LNCS, vol. 8441, pp. 387–404. Springer, Heidelberg (2014). https://doi.org/10.1007/978-3-642-55220-5_22

3. Alhassan, M.Y., Günther, D., Kiss, Á., Schneider, T.: Efficient and scalable universal circuits. J. Cryptol. **33**(3), 1216–1271 (2020)
4. Anonymous: The C++ source code of our 2-way UC implementation (2020). https://github.com/Cryptogroup/universalcircuit
5. Araki, T., et al.: Optimized honest-majority MPC for malicious adversaries - breaking the 1 billion-gate per second barrier. In: 2017 IEEE Symposium on Security and Privacy, pp. 843–862. IEEE Computer Society Press, San Jose (May 2017). https://doi.org/10.1109/SP.2017.15
6. Attrapadung, N.: Fully secure and succinct attribute based encryption for circuits from multi-linear maps. Cryptology ePrint Archive, Report 2014/772 (2014). http://eprint.iacr.org/2014/772
7. Banescu, S., Ochoa, M., Kunze, N., Pretschner, A.: Idea: benchmarking indistinguishability obfuscation – a candidate implementation. In: Piessens, F., Caballero, J., Bielova, N. (eds.) ESSoS 2015. LNCS, vol. 8978, pp. 149–156. Springer, Cham (2015). https://doi.org/10.1007/978-3-319-15618-7_12
8. Barni, M., Failla, P., Kolesnikov, V., Lazzeretti, R., Sadeghi, A.R., Schneider, T.: Secure evaluation of private linear branching programs with medical applications. In: Backes, M., Ning, P. (eds.) ESORICS 2009. LNCS, vol. 5789, pp. 424–439. Springer, Heidelberg (2009). https://doi.org/10.1007/978-3-642-04444-1_26
9. Ben-David, A., Nisan, N., Pinkas, B.: FairplayMP: a system for secure multi-party computation. In: Ning, P., Syverson, P.F., Jha, S. (eds.) ACM CCS 2008, pp. 257–266. ACM Press, Alexandria (October 2008). https://doi.org/10.1145/1455770.1455804
10. Bera, D., Fenner, S.A., Green, F., Homer, S.: Efficient universal quantum circuits. Quantum Inf. Comput. **10**(1&2), 16–27 (2010). http://www.rintonpress.com/xxqic10/qic-10-12/0016-0027.pdf
11. Bicer, O., Bingol, M.A., Kiraz, M.S., Levi, A.: Towards practical PFE: an efficient 2-party private function evaluation protocol based on half gates. Cryptology ePrint Archive, Report 2017/415 (2017). http://eprint.iacr.org/2017/415
12. Bitansky, N., Vaikuntanathan, V.: Indistinguishability obfuscation from functional encryption. In: Guruswami, V. (ed.) 56th FOCS, pp. 171–190. IEEE Computer Society Press, Berkeley (October 2015). https://doi.org/10.1109/FOCS.2015.20
13. Brickell, J., Porter, D.E., Shmatikov, V., Witchel, E.: Privacy-preserving remote diagnostics. In: Ning, P., De Capitani di Vimercati, S., Syverson, P.F. (eds.) ACM CCS 2007, pp. 498–507. ACM Press, Alexandria (October 2007). https://doi.org/10.1145/1315245.1315307
14. Cachin, C., Camenisch, J., Kilian, J., Müller, J.: One-round secure computation and secure autonomous mobile agents. In: Montanari, U., Rolim, J.D.P., Welzl, E. (eds.) ICALP 2000. LNCS, vol. 1853, pp. 512–523. Springer, Heidelberg (2000). https://doi.org/10.1007/3-540-45022-X_43
15. Cook, S.A., Hoover, H.J.: A depth-universal circuit. SIAM J. Comput. **14**(4), 833–839 (1985)
16. Dénes, K.: Gráfok és mátrixok. Matematikai és Fizikai Lapok **38**, 116–119 (1931)
17. Fiore, D., Gennaro, R., Pastro, V.: Efficiently verifiable computation on encrypted data. In: Ahn, G.J., Yung, M., Li, N. (eds.) ACM CCS 2014, pp. 844–855. ACM Press, Scottsdale (November 2014). https://doi.org/10.1145/2660267.2660366
18. Fisch, B.A., et al.: Malicious-client security in blind seer: a scalable private DBMS. In: 2015 IEEE Symposium on Security and Privacy, pp. 395–410. IEEE Computer Society Press, San Jose (May 2015). https://doi.org/10.1109/SP.2015.31
19. Frikken, K., Atallah, M., Li, J.: Attribute-based access control with hidden policies and hidden credentials. IEEE Trans. Comput. **55**(10), 1259–1270 (2006)

20. Frikken, K., Atallah, M., Zhang, C.: Privacy-preserving credit checking. In: Proceedings of the 6th ACM Conference on Electronic Commerce, pp. 147–154 (2005)
21. Frikken, K.B., Li, J., Atallah, M.J.: Trust negotiation with hidden credentials, hidden policies, and policy cycles. In: NDSS 2006. The Internet Society, San Diego (February 2006)
22. Galil, Z., Paul, W.J.: An efficient general purpose parallel computer. In: 13th ACM STOC, pp. 247–262. ACM Press, Milwaukee (May 1981). https://doi.org/10.1145/800076.802478
23. Garg, S., Gentry, C., Halevi, S., Raykova, M., Sahai, A., Waters, B.: Candidate indistinguishability obfuscation and functional encryption for all circuits. In: 54th FOCS, pp. 40–49. IEEE Computer Society Press, Berkeley (October 2013). https://doi.org/10.1109/FOCS.2013.13
24. Garg, S., Gentry, C., Halevi, S., Sahai, A., Waters, B.: Attribute-based encryption for circuits from multilinear maps. In: Canetti, R., Garay, J.A. (eds.) CRYPTO 2013, Part II. LNCS, vol. 8043, pp. 479–499. Springer, Heidelberg (2013). https://doi.org/10.1007/978-3-642-40084-1_27
25. Garg, S., Gentry, C., Halevi, S., Zhandry, M.: Fully secure attribute based encryption from multilinear maps. Cryptology ePrint Archive, Report 2014/622 (2014). http://eprint.iacr.org/2014/622
26. Gennaro, R., Gentry, C., Parno, B., Raykova, M.: Quadratic span programs and succinct NIZKs without PCPs. In: Johansson, T., Nguyen, P.Q. (eds.) EUROCRYPT 2013. LNCS, vol. 7881, pp. 626–645. Springer, Heidelberg (2013). https://doi.org/10.1007/978-3-642-38348-9_37
27. Gentry, C., Halevi, S., Vaikuntanathan, V.: i-hop homomorphic encryption and rerandomizable Yao circuits. In: Rabin, T. (ed.) CRYPTO 2010. LNCS, vol. 6223, pp. 155–172. Springer, Heidelberg (2010). https://doi.org/10.1007/978-3-642-14623-7_9
28. Goldreich, O., Micali, S., Wigderson, A.: How to play any mental game or a completeness theorem for protocols with honest majority. In: Aho, A. (ed.) 19th ACM STOC, pp. 218–229. ACM Press, New York City (May 1987). https://doi.org/10.1145/28395.28420
29. Gorbunov, S., Vaikuntanathan, V., Wee, H.: Attribute-based encryption for circuits. In: Boneh, D., Roughgarden, T., Feigenbaum, J. (eds.) 45th ACM STOC, pp. 545–554. ACM Press, Palo Alto (June 2013). https://doi.org/10.1145/2488608.2488677
30. Günther, D., Kiss, Á., Schneider, T.: More efficient universal circuit constructions. In: Takagi, T., Peyrin, T. (eds.) ASIACRYPT 2017, Part II. LNCS, vol. 10625, pp. 443–470. Springer, Cham (2017). https://doi.org/10.1007/978-3-319-70697-9_16
31. Heath, D., Kolesnikov, V., Peceny, S.: MOTIF: (almost) free branching in GMW. In: Moriai, S., Wang, H. (eds.) ASIACRYPT 2020, Part III. LNCS, vol. 12493, pp. 3–30. Springer, Cham (2020). https://doi.org/10.1007/978-3-030-64840-4_1
32. Holz, M., Kiss, Á., Rathee, D., Schneider, T.: Linear-complexity private function evaluation is practical. In: Chen, L., Li, N., Liang, K., Schneider, S. (eds.) ESORICS 2020, Part II. LNCS, vol. 12309, pp. 401–420. Springer, Cham (2020). https://doi.org/10.1007/978-3-030-59013-0_20
33. Huang, Y., Katz, J., Kolesnikov, V., Kumaresan, R., Malozemoff, A.J.: Amortizing garbled circuits. In: Garay, J.A., Gennaro, R. (eds.) CRYPTO 2014, Part II. LNCS, vol. 8617, pp. 458–475. Springer, Heidelberg (2014). https://doi.org/10.1007/978-3-662-44381-1_26

34. Ishai, Y., Paskin, A.: Evaluating branching programs on encrypted data. In: Vadhan, S.P. (ed.) TCC 2007. LNCS, vol. 4392, pp. 575–594. Springer, Heidelberg (2007). https://doi.org/10.1007/978-3-540-70936-7_31

35. Kamara, S., Raykova, M.: Secure outsourced computation in a multi-tenant cloud. In: IBM Workshop on Cryptography and Security in Clouds, pp. 15–16 (2011)

36. Katz, J., Malka, L.: Constant-round private function evaluation with linear complexity. In: Lee, D.H., Wang, X. (eds.) ASIACRYPT 2011. LNCS, vol. 7073, pp. 556–571. Springer, Heidelberg (2011). https://doi.org/10.1007/978-3-642-25385-0_30

37. Kiss, Á., Schneider, T.: Valiant's universal circuit is practical. In: Fischlin, M., Coron, J.S. (eds.) EUROCRYPT 2016, Part I. LNCS, vol. 9665, pp. 699–728. Springer, Heidelberg (2016). https://doi.org/10.1007/978-3-662-49890-3_27

38. Kolesnikov, V., Schneider, T.: Improved garbled circuit: free XOR gates and applications. In: Aceto, L., Damgård, I., Goldberg, L.A., Halldórsson, M.M., Ingólfsdóttir, A., Walukiewicz, I. (eds.) ICALP 2008, Part II. LNCS, vol. 5126, pp. 486–498. Springer, Heidelberg (2008). https://doi.org/10.1007/978-3-540-70583-3_40

39. Kolesnikov, V., Schneider, T.: A practical universal circuit construction and secure evaluation of private functions. In: Tsudik, G. (ed.) FC 2008. LNCS, vol. 5143, pp. 83–97. Springer, Heidelberg (2008). https://doi.org/10.1007/978-3-540-85230-8_7

40. Lindell, Y., Riva, B.: Blazing fast 2PC in the offline/online setting with security for malicious adversaries. In: Ray, I., Li, N., Kruegel, C. (eds.) ACM CCS 2015, pp. 579–590. ACM Press, Denver (October 2015). https://doi.org/10.1145/2810103.2813666

41. Lipmaa, H., Mohassel, P., Sadeghian, S.: Valiant's universal circuit: improvements, implementation, and applications. Cryptology ePrint Archive, Report 2016/017 (2016). http://eprint.iacr.org/2016/017

42. Liu, H., Yu, Y., Zhao, S., Zhang, J., Liu, W., Hu, Z.: Pushing the limits of Valiant's universal circuits: simpler, tighter and more compact. Cryptology ePrint Archive, Report 2020/161 (2020). https://eprint.iacr.org/2020/161

43. Lovász, L., Plummer, M.D.: Matching Theory, vol. 367. American Mathematical Society, Providence (2009)

44. Malkhi, D., Nisan, N., Pinkas, B., Sella, Y.: Fairplay - secure two-party computation system. In: Blaze, M. (ed.) USENIX Security 2004, pp. 287–302. USENIX Association, San Diego (August 2004)

45. Meyer auf der Heide, F.: Efficiency of universal parallel computers. In: Cremers, A.B., Kriegel, H.-P. (eds.) GI-TCS 1983. LNCS, vol. 145, pp. 221–229. Springer, Heidelberg (1982). https://doi.org/10.1007/BFb0036483

46. Mohassel, P., Rosulek, M.: Non-interactive secure 2PC in the offline/online and batch settings. In: Coron, J., Nielsen, J.B. (eds.) EUROCRYPT 2017, Part III. LNCS, vol. 10212, pp. 425–455. Springer, Cham (2017). https://doi.org/10.1007/978-3-319-56617-7_15

47. Mohassel, P., Sadeghian, S.S.: How to hide circuits in MPC an efficient framework for private function evaluation. In: Johansson, T., Nguyen, P.Q. (eds.) EUROCRYPT 2013. LNCS, vol. 7881, pp. 557–574. Springer, Heidelberg (2013). https://doi.org/10.1007/978-3-642-38348-9_33

48. Niksefat, S., Sadeghiyan, B., Mohassel, P., Sadeghian, S.: Zids: a privacy-preserving intrusion detection system using secure two-party computation protocols. Comput. J. **57**(4), 494–509 (2014)

49. Ostrovsky, R., Skeith III, W.E.: Private searching on streaming data. In: Shoup, V. (ed.) CRYPTO 2005. LNCS, vol. 3621, pp. 223–240. Springer, Heidelberg (2005). https://doi.org/10.1007/11535218_14

50. Pappas, V., et al.: Blind seer: a scalable private DBMS. In: 2014 IEEE Symposium on Security and Privacy, pp. 359–374. IEEE Computer Society Press, Berkeley (May 2014). https://doi.org/10.1109/SP.2014.30

51. Sadeghian, S.S.: New techniques for private function evaluation. Ph.D. thesis (2015)

52. Tillich, S., Smart, N.: Circuits of basic functions suitable for MPC and FHE (2015). https://homes.esat.kuleuven.be/~nsmart/MPC/

53. Valiant, L.G.: Universal circuits (preliminary report). In: 8th ACM STOC, pp. 196–203 (1976)

54. Wegener, I.: The Complexity of Boolean Functions. Wiley, Hoboken (1987)

55. Yao, A.C.C.: Protocols for secure computations (extended abstract). In: 23rd FOCS, pp. 160–164. IEEE Computer Society Press, Chicago (November 1982). https://doi.org/10.1109/SFCS.1982.38

56. Yao, A.C.C.: How to generate and exchange secrets (extended abstract). In: 27th FOCS, pp. 162–167. IEEE Computer Society Press, Toronto (October 1986). https://doi.org/10.1109/SFCS.1986.25

57. Zhao, S., Yu, Yu., Zhang, J., Liu, H.: Valiant's universal circuits revisited: an overall improvement and a lower bound. In: Galbraith, S.D., Moriai, S. (eds.) ASIACRYPT 2019, Part I. LNCS, vol. 11921, pp. 401–425. Springer, Cham (2019). https://doi.org/10.1007/978-3-030-34578-5_15

58. Zhu, R., Cassel, D., Sabry, A., Huang, Y.: NANOPI: extreme-scale actively-secure multi-party computation. In: Lie, D., Mannan, M., Backes, M., Wang, X. (eds.) ACM CCS 2018, pp. 862–879. ACM Press, Toronto (October 2018). https://doi.org/10.1145/3243734.3243850

59. Zimmerman, J.: How to obfuscate programs directly. In: Oswald, E., Fischlin, M. (eds.) EUROCRYPT 2015, Part II. LNCS, vol. 9057, pp. 439–467. Springer, Heidelberg (2015). https://doi.org/10.1007/978-3-662-46803-6_15

Oblivious Key-Value Stores
and Amplification for Private Set
Intersection

Gayathri Garimella[1]($\boxtimes$), Benny Pinkas[2], Mike Rosulek[1], Ni Trieu[3],
and Avishay Yanai[4]

[1] Oregon State University, Corvallis, Oregon, USA
garimelg@oregonstate.edu
[2] Bar-Ilan University, Ramat Gan, Israel
[3] Arizona State University, Tempe, Arizona, USA
[4] VMware Research, Palo Alto, USA

Abstract. Many recent private set intersection (PSI) protocols encode input sets as polynomials. We consider the more general notion of an oblivious key-value store (OKVS), which is a data structure that compactly represents a desired mapping $k_i \mapsto v_i$. When the v_i values are random, the OKVS data structure hides the k_i values that were used to generate it. The simplest (and size-optimal) OKVS is a polynomial p that is chosen using interpolation such that $p(k_i) = v_i$.

We initiate the formal study of oblivious key-value stores, and show new constructions resulting in the fastest OKVS to date.

Similarly to cuckoo hashing, current analysis techniques are insufficient for finding *concrete* parameters to guarantee a small failure probability for our OKVS constructions. Moreover, it would cost too much to run experiments to validate a small upperbound on the failure probability. We therefore show novel techniques to amplify an OKVS construction which has a failure probability p, to an OKVS with a similar overhead and failure probability p^c. Setting p to be moderately small enables to validate it by running a relatively small number of $O(1/p)$ experiments. This validates a p^c failure probability for the amplified OKVS.

Finally, we describe how OKVS can significantly improve the state of the art of essentially all variants of PSI. This leads to the fastest two-party PSI protocols to date, for both the semi-honest and the malicious settings. Specifically, in networks with moderate bandwidth (e.g., 30–300 Mbps) our malicious two-party PSI protocol has 40% less communication and is 20–40% faster than the previous state of the art protocol, even though the latter only has heuristic confidence.

1 Introduction

Private set intersection (PSI) allows parties to learn the intersection of sets that they each hold, without revealing anything else about the individual sets. One common technique that has emerged in several PSI protocols (and protocols

© International Association for Cryptologic Research 2021
T. Malkin and C. Peikert (Eds.): CRYPTO 2021, LNCS 12826, pp. 395–425, 2021.
https://doi.org/10.1007/978-3-030-84245-1_14

for closely related tasks) is to encode data into a polynomial. More precisely, a party interpolates a polynomial P so that $P(x_i) = y_i$, where the x_i's are their PSI input set and y_i are some values that are relevant in the protocol. The polynomial P compactly encodes a chosen mapping from x_i's to y_i's, but it has the additional benefit that it hides the x_i's, when the y_i's are random. This property is critical since the x_i's coincide with some party's private input set, which must be hidden.

We present two major contributions. First, we abstract the properties of polynomials that are needed in these applications, and define "oblivious key-value stores" (OKVS) as objects satisfying these properties. We show how to construct a substantially more efficient OKVS that has linear size, similar to polynomials, and replaces the task of polynomial interpolation with an efficient linear time computation. Second, we observe that current analysis techniques are insufficient for setting concrete parameters to ensure a concrete upper bound (say, 2^{-40}) for the failure probability of our OKVS construction. (This is also true for many other randomized constructions, such as cuckoo hashing, used in PSI and in other cryptographic algorithms.) Furthermore, running experiments in order to validate this upper bound for a specific choice of parameters is extremely resource-intensive. Most previous work used heuristic techniques for setting the parameters for similar constructions. We overcome this issue by introducing new techniques for *amplifying* a randomized OKVS construction with a failure probability p, to an OKVS with a similar overhead and a failure probability p^c. Since p can be rather moderate, it is relatively easy to empirically validate that the failure probability of a specific choice of parameters is indeed bounded by p.

1.1 Polynomial Encodings for PSI

Cryptographic protocols which use polynomial encodings to hide input values date back to at least the work of Manulis, Pinkas, and Poettering [26], in the context of "secret handshake" protocols (closely related to covert MPC and to PSI). Other examples that we are aware of include:[1]

- Cho, Dachman-Soled, and Jarecki [9] achieve 2-party PSI using a polynomial whose outputs (y_i values) are protocol messages from a suitable string-equality test protocol.
- Kolesnikov et al. [24] introduce a primitive called oblivious *programmable* PRF (OPPRF), which acts like an oblivious PRF with a twist. A sender selects (or learns) a PRF seed k and a receiver learns $PRF(k, a)$ for one or more values a of his/her choosing. But additionally, the sender gets to "program" the PRF on values of its choice as $PRF(k, x_i) = z_i$, where the

---

[1] We note that there are also PSI constructions which use arithmetic manipulations of polynomials. These constructions encode input values as roots of polynomials [12,13,22] or into separate monomials of a polynomial [14], and manipulate the polynomials in order to compute set operations. Our focus is on encodings, which is the more efficient versions of PSI, and do not require arithmetic manipulation of polynomials in order to compute the intersection.

special x_i points remain secret. This is achieved by combining a standard oblivious PRF $F(k, x_i)$ with a polynomial which encodes "output corrections" that the receiver applies in order to make the output match the sender's $x_i \mapsto z_i$ mappings.

They use this OPPRF to construct a multi-party PSI protocol. Later, Pinkas *et al.* [34] also use an OPPRF to construct a protocol for computing arbitrary functions of the intersection (of two sets). Recently, OPPRFs were used by Chandran *et al.* for constructing circuit-PSI and multi-party PSI [5,6].

- Pinkas *et al.* [32] construct a low-communication PSI protocol using a polynomial whose outputs are values from the IKNP OT extension protocol [19].
- Kolesnikov *et al.* [25] construct a private set *union* protocol, using a variant of the OPPRF technique.

One downside to polynomials is that interpolating and evaluating them is not cheap. To interpolate a polynomial through n (unstructured) points, or to evaluate such a polynomial at n points, requires $O(n \log^2 n)$ field operations, using the FFT algorithms of [28]. This cost becomes substantial for larger values of n, and raises the following natural question:

Is there a data structure that is better than a polynomial, for use in these PSI (and related) protocols?

In addition to these applications of polynomials, Pinkas *et al.* [33] used a related technique to construct the fastest *malicious-secure* 2-party PSI protocol to date. They introduced a data structure called a PaXoS (probe and XOR of strings) which, similar to a polynomial, encodes a mapping from keys to values while hiding the keys. PaXoS took a significant step toward the abstraction of an OKVS, however, it is not sufficiently general. In particular, PaXoS is a specific, binary type of OKVS, whereas other types exist (like a linear OKVS, which is applicable in Oblivious Polynomial Evaluation [30]). The PaXoS data structure is the starting point for our constructions.

1.2   Correctness Amplification

One of the most challenging aspects of designing efficient PSI and OKVS constructions, is obtaining concrete bounds on extremal properties of randomized data structures. For example, exactly how many bins are required for cuckoo hashing with 3 hash functions, to ensure that the induced "cuckoo graph" avoids a certain structure with probability at least $1 - 2^{-40}$? This problem is crucial for PSI, since most PSI constructions are based on randomized data structures such as cuckoo hashing. Any failure in these constructions (e.g., too many collisions) leads to a violation of privacy. An implementation of PSI needs to be instantiated with specific parameters that will ensure a sufficiently small failure probability, but the available literature describing and analyzing the randomized constructions only describes asymptotic bounds, and it seems highly non-trivial to translate them to concrete numbers.

Prior PSI work which used such constructions, in particular variants of cuckoo hashing, either ran a small number of experiments in order to heuristically set the parameters, or, as in [36], invested significant efforts (*e.g.*, millions of core hours) to empirically measure the failure probability of these data structures. (This is needed since validating an upper bound of p on the failure probability requires running more than $1/p$ experiments.) But even after expending such efforts, it was not possible to validate the desired failure probabilities (*e.g.*, 2^{-40}), since they were too small. So ultimately in [36] and in other constructions which are based on the same set of experiments, the failure probabilities of the final constructions were only **extrapolated** from these empirical trials.

The lack of a concrete analysis for the failure probabilities of different randomized constructions, and the extreme cost of experimentally verifying small upper bounds on these probabilities, raise the following question:

> *Is is possible to start with a construction that has a moderately high failure probability, and which can therefore be validated through efficient experiments, and amplify it to obtain a construction which has a much smaller failure probability?*

For example, we can validate on a laptop an upper bound of 2^{-25} or 2^{-13}, whereas validating a 2^{-40} failure probability might require using a large cluster.

1.3   Our Results

In this work, we initiate the study of OKVS data structures and their properties.

- We introduce the abstraction of an **oblivious key-value store (OKVS)**. An OKVS consists of algorithms Encode and Decode. Encode takes a list of key-value pairs (k_i, v_i) as input and returns an abstract data structure S. Decode takes such a data structure and a key k as input, and gives some output. Decode can be called on any key, but if it is called on some k_i that was used to generate S, then the result is the corresponding v_i. The most basic property of an OKVS echoes the important property of polynomials; namely, S hides the k_i's, when the v_i's are random. We identify and formalize important properties that allow OKVS to be plugged into different protocols.
- We catalog existing OKVS constructions and introduce several new and improved ones.
- We describe **amplification techniques** that can be used to bootstrap strong OKVS out of weaker ones. Amplification only requires to validate a relatively high upper bound on the failure probability of the corresponding randomized construction, a task that can be accomplished through efficient experiments. As an example, we can construct an OKVS with *provable* error probability 2^{-40}, from an OKVS with error probability 2^{-25}. The latter probability is high enough that it can be empirically and efficiently verified with very high statistical confidence.
- Besides having more manageable error analysis, our new OKVS constructions improve considerably over the state of the art in terms of size and speed.

- We show that many existing PSI protocols can be written abstractly in terms of a generic OKVS. These PSI protocols are therefore automatically improved by instantiating with our improved OKVS constructions. As a flagship example, we demonstrate the improvement on the so-called "PaXoS-PSI" protocol of [33], which is the state of the art protocol with malicious security. Specifically, our protocol has 40% less communication and is 20% and 40% faster over medium and slow networks[2], respectively, for sets of a million items (over a fast network it is only 5% slower). In addition, on slow networks, our *malicious* protocol is even faster than the state of the art *semi-honest* protocol [32] (and is only about 10% and 20% slower than the best semi-honest protocols over fast [23] and medium [7] networks, respectively).

  We also note that the covert MPC protocols of [9, 26] can be expressed using our OKVS constructions to exhibit a higher level of abstraction and to achieve a better runtime.

- Finally, we show two improvements to existing PSI protocols, beyond replacing their underlying OKVS with a better one.

  First, we observe that the leading state-of-the-art PaXoS PSI protocol of [33] can be generalized to be built from vector-OLE rather than 1-out-of-N OT extension. Since vector-OLE enjoys more algebraic structure, the generalized PSI protocol can take advantage of a more general class of OKVS, and also avoid one source of overhead in the construction.

  Second, we show that one of the multi-party PSI constructions of Kolesnikov et al. [24], which is the most efficient of the constructions presented in that paper but only has "augmented semi-honest security" rather than semi-honest security, actually enjoys *malicious security*. Hence, we obtain the most efficient malicious, multi-party PSI protocol to date.

2 Oblivious Key-Value Stores

2.1 Definitions

Definition 1. *A **key-value store** is parameterized by a set $\mathcal{K}$ of keys, a set $\mathcal{V}$ of values, and a set of functions H, and consists of two algorithms:*

- Encode$_H$ *takes as input a set of (k_i, v_i) key-value pairs and outputs an object S (or, with statistically small probability, an error indicator $\perp$).*
- Decode$_H$ *takes as input an object S, a key k, and outputs a value v.*

A KVS is **correct** *if, for all $A \subseteq \mathcal{K} \times \mathcal{V}$ with distinct keys:*

$$(k, v) \in A \text{ and } \perp \neq S \leftarrow \text{Encode}_H(A) \implies \text{Decode}_H(S, k) = v$$

In the rest of the exposition we choose to omit the underlying parameter H as long as the text remains unambiguous.

---

[2] The slow network (33 Mib/s); medium network (260 Mib/s); fast network (4.6 Gib/s).

In all the algorithms that we describe, the decision whether Encode outputs $\perp$ depends on the functions H and the keys k_i and is independent of the values v_i. If the data is encoded as a polynomial then Encode always succeeds.

To be clear, one may invoke $\mathsf{Decode}(S, k)$ on *any* key k, and indeed it is our goal that one cannot tell whether k was used to generate S or not. This is stated in the next definition.

Definition 2. *A KVS is an **oblivious KVS (OKVS)** if, for all distinct $\{k_1^0, \ldots, k_n^0\}$ and all distinct $\{k_1^1, \ldots, k_n^1\}$, if Encode does not output $\perp$ for $(k_1^0, \ldots, k_n^0)$ or $(k_1^1, \ldots, k_n^1)$, then the output of $\mathcal{R}(k_1^0, \ldots, k_n^0)$ is computationally indistinguishable to that of $\mathcal{R}(k_1^1, \ldots, k_n^1)$, where:*

$$
\begin{array}{l}
\mathcal{R}(k_1, \ldots, k_n): \\
\hline
\quad \text{for } i \in [n]: \text{do } v_i \leftarrow \mathcal{V} \\
\quad \text{return } \mathsf{Encode}(\{(k_1, v_1), \ldots, (k_n, v_n)\})
\end{array}
$$

In other words, if the OKVS encodes random values (as it does in our applications), then for any two sets of keys K^0, K^1 it is infeasible to distinguish between an OKVS encoding of the keys of K^0 from an OKVS encoding of the keys of K^1. In fact, all our constructions satisfy the property that if the values encoded in the OKVS are random (as in the experiment R), then the two distributions are perfectly indistinguishable.

2.2   Linear OKVS

Some applications of an OKVS use it to encode data that is processed in some kind of homomorphic cryptographic primitive. In that case, it is convenient for $\mathsf{Decode}(\cdot, k)$ to be a **linear function** for all k.

Definition 3. *An OKVS is **linear** (over a field $\mathbb{F}$) if $\mathcal{V} = \mathbb{F}$ ("values" are elements of $\mathbb{F}$), the output of Encode is a vector S in $\mathbb{F}^m$, and the Decode function is defined as:*

$$
\mathsf{Decode}(S, k) = \langle \mathsf{d}(k), S \rangle \overset{\text{def}}{=} \sum_{j=1}^{m} \mathsf{d}(k)_j S_j
$$

for some function $\mathsf{d} : \mathcal{K} \to \mathbb{F}^m$. Hence $\mathsf{Decode}(\cdot, k)$ is a linear map from $\mathbb{F}^m$ to $\mathbb{F}$.

The mapping $\mathsf{d} : \mathcal{K} \to \mathbb{F}^m$ are typically defined by the hash function H.

For a linear OKVS, one can view the Encode function as generating a solution to the linear system of equations:

$$
\begin{bmatrix}
- \mathsf{d}(k_1) - \\
- \mathsf{d}(k_2) - \\
\vdots \\
- \mathsf{d}(k_n) -
\end{bmatrix}
S^\top =
\begin{bmatrix}
v_1 \\
v_2 \\
\vdots \\
v_n
\end{bmatrix}
$$

Hence, it is necessary that for all distinct $k_1, \ldots, k_n$, the set $\{\mathsf{d}(k_1), \ldots, \mathsf{d}(k_n)\}$ is linearly independent, with overwhelming probability. However, we also consider *how efficiently* Encode finds such a solution, since solving systems of linear equations is expensive in general. It is often convenient to characterize a linear OKVS by its d function alone.

Note that when Encode chooses *uniformly* from the set of solutions to the linear system, and the v_i values are uniform, the output S is uniformly distributed (and hence distributed independently of the k_i values). In other words, a linear OKVS satisfies the obliviousness property.

2.3   Binary OKVS

A **binary OKVS** over a field $\mathbb{F}$ is a special case of a linear OKVS, where the $\mathsf{d}(k)$ vectors are restricted to $\{0,1\}^m \subseteq \mathbb{F}^m$. Then $\mathsf{Decode}(S, k)$ is simply the sum of some positions in S.

We generally restrict our attention to $\mathbb{F} = GF(2^\ell) \cong \{0,1\}^\ell$, in which case the addition operation over $\mathbb{F}$ is XOR of strings. In [33], a binary OKVS is called a **probe and XOR of strings (PaXoS)** data structure.

In a binary OKVS we have (in addition to the usual properties of a linear OKVS) the property that:

$$\mathsf{Decode}\Big((S_1 \wedge x, \ldots, S_m \wedge x), k\Big) = \mathsf{Decode}\Big((S_1, \ldots, S_m), k\Big) \wedge x$$

where "$\wedge$" is bitwise-AND of strings, and $x \in \{0,1\}^\ell$. This additional property is used in one of the important applications of OKVS.

2.4   OKVS Overfitting

Often in malicious protocols, the simulator obtains an OKVS from a corrupt party and must "extract" the items that are encoded in that OKVS. Generally this is done by requiring an OKVS to include mappings $(k_i, v_i) \mapsto H(k_i)$ where H is a random oracle.[3] The simulator can observe the adversary's queries to H, and then later test which of those k satisfy $\mathsf{Decode}(S, k) = H(k)$.

An OKVS whose parameters are chosen to encode n items can often hold even more than n items, especially when generated by an adversary. In the context of PSI, this leads to an adversary holding more items than advertised. It is therefore important to be able to bound the number of items that an adversary can "overfit" into an OKVS. In order to define this property we define a "game" which lets the adversary choose an arbitrary data structure S, of a size which can normally encode n (key,value) pairs. The adversary wins the game if it can find an S which encodes much more than n pairs of the form $(k_i, H(k_i))$. More formally, we use the following definition.

---

[3] We abuse notation herein and use H to denote a random oracle rather than the underlying OKVS parameter, which remains implicit.

Definition 4. *The* (n, n')-***OKVS*** *overfitting game is as follows. Let* Encode, Decode *be an OKVS with parameters chosen to support* n *items, and let* $\mathcal{A}$ *be an arbitrary PPT adversary. Run* $S \leftarrow \mathcal{A}^H(1^\kappa)$. *Define*

$$X = \{k \mid \mathcal{A} \text{ queried } H \text{ at } k \text{ and } \mathsf{Decode}(S, k) = H(k)\}$$

If $|X| > n'$ *then the adversary wins.*

We say the (n, n')-*OKVS overfitting problem is* **hard** *for an OKVS construction if no PPT adversary wins this game except with negligible probability.*

The work in [33] gives an unconditional bound on the success probability in the overfitting game. They prove the bound for binary OKVS ("PaXoS", in their terminology), but the only property of OKVS they use is its correctness; hence it applies to any KVS:

Lemma 5 ([33]). *Let* H *be a random oracle with output length* ℓ, *and let* Encode, Decode *be an OKVS scheme supporting* n *key-value pairs, where the output of* Encode *is a bit string of length* ℓ'. *Then the probability that an adversary who makes* q *queries to* H *wins the* (n, n')-*OKVS overfitting game is* $\leq \binom{q}{n'} 2^{\ell' - n'\ell}$.

The nature of this bound is to argue that an OKVS that encodes n' items simply can't exist; for if it did exist, then it could be used to construct a compressed representation of the random oracle. One may further conjecture that an OKVS construction has a hard overfitting problem (for some relationship between n and n') against polynomial-time adversaries. For example, perhaps it may be hard to find a single polynomial of degree n that matches the random oracle on $n' = n + 100$ points, even in the case that such a polynomial exists.

Better cryptanalysis of these kinds of overfitting problems would lead to a tighter security analysis of our malicious-secure PSI protocols: the protocols would be proven to more strongly enforce the size of corrupt party's input sets.

2.5 Efficiency of OKVS

We can measure the efficiency of an OKVS based on the following measures: (1) The **rate** of an OKVS which encodes n elements from $\mathbb{F}$ is the ratio between the size of the OKVS and $n \cdot |\mathbb{F}|$, which is the minimal size required for this encoding. (2) The **encoding time** is the time which is required for encoding n items in the OKVS. (3) The **decoding time** is the time required for decoding (querying) a single element, while the **batch decoding time** is the time required for decoding n elements.

3 Existing OKVS Constructions

In this section we list existing constructions that fit to the OKVS definition. These are summarized in Fig. 1.

OKVS	type	rate	encoding cost	(batch) decoding cost
polynomial	linear	1	$O(n \log^2 n)$	$O(n \log^2 n)$
random matrix	linear	1	$O(n^3)$	$O(n^2)$
random matrix	binary	$1/(1+\lambda)$	$O(n^3)$	$O(n^2)$
garbled Bloom filter [11]	binary	$O(1/\lambda)$	$O(n\lambda)$	$O(n\lambda)$
PaXoS [33]	binary	$0.4 - o(1)$	$O(n\lambda)$	$O(n\lambda)$
Ours: 3H-GCT (§4.1)	binary linear	$0.81 - o(1)$	$O(n\lambda)$	$O(n\lambda)$

Fig. 1. Different OKVS constructions and their properties, for error probability $2^{-\lambda}$. (The rate of the 3H-GCT construction can be improved to 0.91 by using the hypergraph construction of [43], but this improvement takes effect only for very large values of n.)

Polynomials. A simple and natural OKVS is a polynomial P satisfying $P(k_i) = v_i$. The coefficients of the polynomial are the OKVS data structure, and decoding amounts to evaluating the polynomial at a point k. This OKVS has optimal rate 1, and is **linear** since $P(k)$ is the inner product of $(1, k, k^2, \ldots)$ and the vector of coefficients. Encoding n items takes $O(n \log^2 n)$ field operations using the FFT interpolating algorithms of [28]. Batch decoding of n items likewise takes $O(n \log^2 n)$ operations, while decoding a single items takes $O(n)$ operations.

Dense matrix. Another simple OKVS sets $\mathsf{d}(k)$ to be a random vector in $\mathbb{F}^m$ for each k. This means that the encoding matrix is a random matrix. It is well-known that a random matrix with n rows and $m \geq n$ columns has linearly *dependent* rows with probability at most

$$\sum_{j=1}^{n} \Pr[\text{row } j \in \text{ span of first } j-1 \text{ rows} \mid \text{first } j-1 \text{ rows linearly ind.}] \quad (1)$$

$$= \sum_{i=0}^{n-1} \frac{|\mathbb{F}|^i}{|\mathbb{F}|^m} = \frac{1}{|\mathbb{F}|^m} \cdot \frac{|\mathbb{F}|^n - 1}{|\mathbb{F}| - 1} < |\mathbb{F}|^{n-m-1} \quad (2)$$

For an exponentially large field $\mathbb{F}$, we can have $m = n$ and hence achieve rate 1. If we desire a binary OKVS, then $\mathsf{d}(k)$ are $\{0,1\}$-vectors and we must have $m \geq n + \lambda - 1$ for error probability $2^{-\lambda}$.

While achieving a good rate, the encoding and decoding procedures are expensive. Encoding n items corresponds to solving a linear system of n random equations, which requires $O(n^3)$ operations using Gaussian elimination. Decoding each item costs $O(n)$. A random matrix OKVS has worse performance than a polynomial-based OKVS. The main reason for using a random matrix OKVS is if the underlying field $\mathbb{F}$ is smaller than n, for example, is a binary field, in which case it is impossible to define an n-degree polynomial over $\mathbb{F}$.

Garbled Bloom filter (GBF). In a garbled Bloom filter [11], n items are encoded into a vector of length $m = O(\lambda n)$, i.e. it has a rate of $O(1/\lambda)$. The scheme is parameterized by λ random functions $H = \{h_1, \ldots, h_\lambda\}$ with range $[m]$. We have $\mathsf{d}(k)$ zero everywhere except in the positions $h_1(k), \ldots, h_\lambda(k)$, where it is 1. Hence a garbled Bloom filter is a binary OKVS.

Encoding is done in an online manner, one item at a time. Encoding fails with probability $1/2^\lambda$, and the specific error probability is exactly the same as the false-positive probability for a standard Bloom filter with the same parameters (namely, using λ hash functions and a vector of size $m = 1.44\lambda n$ result in a failure probability of $1/2^\lambda$ [27]).

Encoding n items costs $O(n\lambda)$, and decoding each item likewise costs $O(\lambda)$, since only λ positions in $\mathsf{d}(k)$ are nonzero.

GBFs were used in multiple PSI papers, beginning in [11], and including the multi-party protocols of [1,18,44]. A major drawback of the usage of GBFs is the larger communication overhead of sending a GBF of length $O(\lambda n)$, instead of sending an object of size $O(n)$, and computing $O(\lambda n)$ oblivious transfers.

PaXoS [33]. In a probe-and-xor of strings (PaXoS), n items are encoded into a vector S of length $m = (2 + \varepsilon)n + \log(n) + \lambda$.

Let us describe a simplified version of PaXos for which S is of size $m = (2+\varepsilon)n$. This scheme is parameterized by 2 random hash functions $H = \{h_1, h_2\}$ with a range $[(2+\varepsilon)n]$. Decoding of a key x sums the vector entries at $h_1(x)$ and $h_2(x)$. Encoding is done by generating the "cuckoo graph" implied by the n keys and the functions h_1, h_2. In that graph, there are m vertices $u_1, \ldots, u_m$ such that each k_i implies an edge $(u_{h_1(k_i)}, u_{h_2(k_i)})$. The encoding then *peels* that graph, by recursively removing each edge $(u_{h_1(k_i)}, u_{h_2(k_i)})$ for which the degree of either $u_{h_1(k_i)}$ or $u_{h_2(k_i)}$ is 1, and pushing that k_i to a stack. That process ends when the graph is empty of edges. Then, the *unpeeling* process iteratively pops an item k_j from the stack and uses it to fill the vector's entries: If both $S[u_{h_1(k_j)}]$ and $S[u_{h_2(k_j)}]$ are unassigned yet, then they are assigned random values such that $S[u_{h_1(k_j)}] + S[u_{h_2(k_j)}] = v_j$. Otherwise, if only $S[u_{h_2(k_j)}]$ is unassigned (w.l.o.g) then assign $S[u_{h_2(k_j)}] = v_j - S[u_{h_1(k_j)}]$. This process succeeds as long as the peeling indeed removes all edges. However, there is a high probability for the peeling process to end with a non-empty graph where none of the vertices is of degree 1. The size of the remaining graph is known to be with at most $O(\log n)$ vertices. This is solved by extending the vector S with extra $O(\log n) + \lambda$ entries.

In a concrete instantiation of PaXoS [33] the authors set $\varepsilon = 0.4$, which becomes standard in Cuckoo hashing based constructions. However, that assignment is heuristic, and no failure probability was proven. Encoding is linear in the number of items and decoding takes $2 + \frac{c \cdot \log n + \lambda}{2}$ time, for some constant c ([33] used $c = 5$).

4   New OKVS Constructions

The main issue that the new OKVS constructions aim to improve over the existing polynomial-based or random matrix OKVS constructions, is improving the run time to be linear in the number of key-value pairs. This comes at the cost of slightly increasing the size of the OKVS.

4.1 OKVS Based on a 3-Hash Garbled Cuckoo Table (3H-GCT)

The PaXoS construction of [33] uses cuckoo hashing with two hash functions. It is well-known that the efficiency of cuckoo hashing improves significantly when using three rather than two hash functions (see orientability analysis, with $\ell = 1$ and $k \in \{2, 3\}$ in [43, Table 1]). Hence, in this section we suggest generalizing the OKVS construction to three hash functions. (It is crucial that the construction uses not more than three hash functions. We describe in Footnote[4] that using more functions will result in better memory and network utilization, but will not support an efficient linear time peeling algorithm for finding the right assignment of values to memory locations. Therefore, with current techniques it seems that using three hash functions is optimal.)

Peeling. The construction follows a basic peeling based approach. The OKVS data structure S is a hypergraph $\mathcal{G}_{3,n,m}$, with m nodes and n hyperedges, each touching 3 nodes. The construction uses three hash functions h_1, h_2, h_3, and maps each key k to the hyperedge $(h_1(k), h_2(k), h_3(k))$.[5] The simplest OKVS construction is binary, and encodes a pair (k, v) into the graph to satisfy the property that $v = S(h_1(k)) \oplus S(h_2(k)) \oplus S(h_3(k))$. Namely, the value associated with a key k is encoded as the exclusive-or of the three nodes of the hyperedge to which it is mapped. The number of nodes m must be at least the number of values n, and our aim is to make it as close as possible to n.

This mapping is possible if the binary $n \times m$ matrix in which each row represents a key and has 1 entry corresponding to the three nodes to which the key is mapped, is of rank n, and can be therefore be found in time $O(n^3)$. However, our goal is to compute a mapping in time which is close to linear. This is done by a peeling based algorithm: Suppose that there is a key k with a

---

[4] For uniformly random d-regular hypergraphs (we use $d = 3$), increasing d improves the threshold of memory utilization that enables mapping values to hyperedges. Namely, increasing d enables to use a graph of fewer nodes in order to successfully orient the same number of hyperedges towards different nodes. Successfully orienting the nodes implies that it is possible to assign values to nodes to enable the recovery all values associated with hyperedges. However, this does not imply that mapping values to nodes can be efficiently found in linear time, such as by running by a peeling process. Unfortunately, increasing the degree d also makes it harder to succeed in peeling, and requires a substantially higher ratio between the number of nodes and the number of hyperedges in order for peeling to succeed (see first row of Table 1 in [43].) Our construction is based on peeling, and therefore our usage of hyperedges of size $d = 3$ is optimal.

[5] The hyperedge is sampled uniformly at random from all subsets of 3 *different* nodes in the graph. We simplify the notation by referring to hash functions h_1, h_2, h_3, but these functions are invoked together under the constraint that the outputs of the three hash functions are distinct from each other.

corresponding hyperedge $(h_1(k), h_2(k), h_3(k))$, and that, say, $h_2(k)$ is a node to which no other key is mapped. Then we can set values to all other nodes in the graph, including nodes $h_1(k)$ and $h_3(k)$, and afterwards set the value of node $h_2(k)$ so that the equality $v = S(h_1(k)) \oplus S(h_2(k)) \oplus S(h_3(k))$ holds. To denote this property we can orient the hyperedge towards $h_2(k)$. This property also means that we can remove this hyperedge from the graph, solve the mapping for all other keys, and then set the value of node $h_2(k)$ so that the mapping of k is correct. This can of course be done for all hyperedges that touch nodes of degree 1. Moreover, removing these hyperedges might reduce the degrees of other nodes, and this enables removing additional hyperedges from the graph.

The peeling process that we described essentially works by repeatedly choosing a node of degree 0 or 1 and removing it (and the incident edge if present) from the hypergraph. The removed edge is oriented towards the node. If this process can be repeated until all nodes are removed then the graph is said to be "peelable". Otherwise, the process ends with a 2-core of the hypergraph (the largest sub-hypergraph where all nodes have a degree of at least 2). We first discuss the expected number of nodes that is required to ensure that the peeling process can remove all edges. We then discuss how to handle the case that the peeling process ends with a non-empty 2-core.

Peelability threshold. It is well known that for random 3-hypergraphs, peelability asymptotically succeeds with high probability when the number of nodes is at least $1.23n$. (See [2,29] for an analysis, and [15] for implementation and measurements.) A recent result in [43] shows that choosing hyperedges based on a specific different distribution reduces the number of nodes to be as low as $1.1n$, but based on experiments in [43] and on our experiments these results seem to be applicable only to very large graphs of tens of millions of nodes.)(See footnote 5) Of course, we also wish to ensure that the OKVS construction fails with only *negligible* probability, or with a sufficiently small *concrete* probability ($2^{-\lambda}$, for $\lambda = 40$). The known analysis methods do not provide concrete parameters for guaranteeing a $2^{-\lambda}$ failure probability. We will describe in Sect. 5 how to amplify OKVS constructions in order to verify experimentally that failures happen with sufficiently small probability.

Handling the 2-core in binary 3-hash OKVS. Let $\chi(G)$ be the number of hyperedges in the 2-core of a hypergraph G with n edges, and let $d(n)$ be an upper bound on $\chi(G)$ which holds with overwhelming probability ($d(n)$ will typically be very small). The peeling stops working when reaching the 2-core. We follow [33] in using a datastructure of the form $S = L||R$, where L consists of the nodes of the hypergraph, and R includes additional $d(n) + \lambda$ nodes, where $2^{-\lambda}$ is the allowed statistical failure probability. The hypergraph construction maps each key k to 3 nodes in L. Denote these nodes using a binary vector $l(k)$ of length L, which has 3 bits set to 1. In addition, we use another hash function to map k to a random binary string $r(k)$ of length $d(n) + \lambda$, where the bits which are set to 1 indicate a subset of the nodes in R. The value of a key k from the OKVS is retrieved as the exclusive-or of the values of the 3 nodes to which it is mapped in L and the values of the nodes to which it is mapped in R, namely it is $(l(k)\|r(k)) \cdot S$. Therefore the encoding process must set the values in S to satisfy these requirements.

After running the peeling process, we are left with $\chi(G) \leq d(n)$ hyperedges in a 2-core of G. We solve the system of linear equations $(l(k_i)\|r(k_i)) \cdot S$ for all keys k_i whose corresponding hyperedges are in the 2-core.[6] Solving this system of equations sets values to the nodes in R, and to the nodes in L to which the edges in the 2-core are mapped. This can be done in $O((d + \lambda)^3)$ time. We can then run the peeling process in reverse: take the peeled hyperedges in reversed order and set values to the nodes in L to which they are oriented, to satisfy the decoding property for all other hyperedges in the graph. The entire algorithm is defined in Fig. 2. The proof of Lemma 6 below is in the full version.

Lemma 6. *Let $d(n)$ be a parameter such that $\Pr[\mathcal{G}_{3,n,m}$ has 2-core $> d(n)] \leq \varepsilon_1$. Then the construction with $|R| = d(n) + \lambda$ is an OKVS with error $\varepsilon_1 + 2^{-\lambda}$.*

4.2   OKVS Based on Simple Hashing and Dense Matrices

Another possible approach for constructing an OKVS is to randomly map the key-value pairs into many bins, and implement an independent OKVS per bin (using the polynomial-based or the random matrix approaches). The computation cost of these smaller OKVS instances is much smaller, and the space utilization only needs to take into account the maximum number of items that might be mapped into a bin.

Suppose we hash n pairs into m bins, where key-value pair (k, v) is placed into bin $h(k)$ based on a random function $h : \{0,1\}^* \to [m]$. Encode each bin's set of key-value pairs into its own OKVS using any "inner OKVS" construction. The overall result is also an OKVS. More formally, if (Encode, Decode) is the inner OKVS, then given $(D_1, \ldots, D_m) \leftarrow \mathsf{Encode}(\{k_i, v_i\})$ the new OKVS is

$$\mathsf{Decode}^*\Big((D_1, \ldots, D_m), k\Big) \overset{\text{def}}{=} \mathsf{Decode}(D_{h(k)}, k)$$

The corresponding Encode^* is defined as explained above.

---

[6] An alternative approach is to use a graph without an R component, and try to solve the system of equations for the $l(k_i)$ nodes of the 2-core alone. However, experiments that we ran show that in many cases where the 2-core is small but not empty, the 2-core includes only two hyperedges. This means that these two hyperedges are mapped to exactly the same set of 3 nodes, and therefore the two associated linear equations are identical and cannot be solved.

We additionally note that PSI applications require using a Binary linear combination of the OKVS values. Other applications might allow using linear combinations with larger coefficients. In these cases there will likely be no need for adding the R nodes to the graph.

Encode($\{k_i, v_i\}$):
Parameters:

- The algorithm is parameterized with the functions $H = \{h_1, h_2, h_3\}$, each has a range $[m]$.
- In addition the algorithm uses the functions $l(\cdot)$ and $r(\cdot)$ where $l(x)$ outputs a bit-vector of length m with zero at all entries except of entries $h_1(x), h_2(x)$ and $h_3(x)$. The function $r(x)$ outputs a random bit-vector of length r.

Algorithm:

1. Initialize empty vectors $L \in \mathbb{F}^m$ and $R \in \mathbb{F}^r$.
2. Initialize stack P.
3. (Identify nodes which are touched by only a single hyperedge, and push them to P.) While there is a node $j \in [m]$ such that the set $\{k_i \notin P \mid j \in \{h_1(k_i), h_2(k_i), h_3(k_i)\}\}$ is a singleton: Let k_i be the element of that singleton, and push k_i onto P.
4. Solve the system of equations $\langle l(k_i) \| r(k_i), L \| R \rangle = v_i$ for $k_i \notin P$, and assign the solutions to the corresponding locations in S.
5. While P not empty:
   (a) pop k_i from P.
   (b) L is undefined in at least one of the positions $h_1(k_i), h_2(k_i), h_3(k_i)$. Set the undefined position(s) so that $\langle l(k_i) \| r(k_i), L \| R \rangle = v_i$.
6. Set any empty position in L or R with a random value from $\mathbb{F}$.

Fig. 2. 3-Hash Garbled Cuckoo Table, fitting n key-value pairs (k_i, v_i) to a data structure $S \in \mathbb{F}^{m+r}$.

In choosing parameters for the inner OKVS, the naïve error analysis would proceed as follows. First compute a bound β such that all bins have at most β items except with the target ε probability. Choose parameters such that each bin's OKVS fails on β items with probability bounded by ε/m. Then by a union bound the entire encoding procedure fails with probability at most $m \cdot \varepsilon/m = \varepsilon$.

We can do better when the inner OKVS is a polynomial OKVS. If the field is small, we can use a random dense-matrix OKVS. For this OKVS the error probability within each bin drops off gradually with the number of items (rather than having a sharp threshold). Suppose we have n items into m bins, and each bin is a dense-matrix OKVS with w slots (so that the entire data structure is mw in size). If exactly t items happen to be assigned to a particular bin, then that bin's OKVS fails with probability bounded by $|\mathbb{F}|^{w-t}$. Using the union bound, we bound the probability of the *overall* OKVS failing as:

$$m \cdot \Pr[\text{bin \#1 OKVS fails}] \leq m \sum_t \underbrace{\binom{n}{t} \left(\frac{1}{m}\right)^t \left(\frac{m-1}{m}\right)^{n-t}}_{\Pr[\text{bin \#1 holds exactly } t \text{ items}]} \min\left\{1, \frac{1}{|\mathbb{F}|^{w-t}}\right\}$$

It is straightforward to calculate this probability exactly, and it leads to better bounds on OKVS size.

Example. Consider the case of $|\mathbb{F}| = \{0,1\}$, hashing $n = 1000$ items into $m = 100$ bins. How wide must each bin's dense-matrix OKVS be for an overall error probability of 2^{-40}? The naïve analysis proceeds as follows. With probability $1 - 2^{-40}$ all bins have at most 42 items. We must ensure Pr[inner OKVS fails on 42 items] $< 2^{-47}$, so that the union bound over $m = 100$ bins bounds the overall failure probability by 2^{-40}. Hence, each bin must have $w = 42 + 47 = 89$ slots. In contrast, the more specialized analysis above shows that only $w = 61$ slots suffice per bin, for error probability 2^{-40} (a 31% improvement).

5   Amplifying OKVS Correctness

Premise: Empirically Measuring Failure Probabilities. The most efficient OKVS constructions are likely to be based on randomized constructions. Unfortunately, we lack techniques for finding tight concrete bounds of the relevant failure probabilities for constructions of this type, such as cuckoo hashing, and for choosing appropriate concrete parameters (e.g., how many bins are needed to hash a concrete number of n items with k hash functions so that the 2-core of the cuckoo graph has size bounded by $2\log_2 n$ with probability $1 - 2^{-\lambda}$?[7,8]

The best we can currently hope for is to empirically measure failure probabilities. Since we seek data structures where the failure probabilities are extremely small (e.g., 2^{-40}) empirical measurement is extremely costly. One would have to perform trillions of trials before expecting to see any failures at all. Alternatively, one must typically perform many trials with higher error probabilities, and extrapolate to the lower probabilities. This approach was used in, e.g., [8,36].

In this section we show methods for **amplifying** the probabilistic guarantees of an OKVS. For example, we show how to use an OKVS with failure probability ε to build an OKVS with failure probability $c \cdot \varepsilon^d$ (for explicit constants c, d). Think of ε as being moderately small, e.g., $\varepsilon = 2^{-15}$, and therefore sufficiently large to enable running efficient empirical experiments to obtain 99.99% certainty about whether ε bounds the failure event. Using an OKVS with such an empirically-validated failure probability, we can construct a new OKVS with the desired failure probability (e.g., 2^{-40}).

Since our amplification algorithms may instantiate two or more OKVS structures for the same set of keys and values, in this section we make the set of hash

---

[7] For cuckoo hashing, the relation between the number of items n, number of hash functions k, number of bins $m = (1 + \beta)n$ for $\beta \in (0, 1)$, stash size s, and the insertion failure probability ε, is proven in [21]: for any $k \geq 2(1 + \beta) \ln \frac{1}{\beta}$ and $s > 0$, mapping n items to $(1 + \beta)n$ bins fails with probability $O(n^{1-c(s+1)})$ for a constant c and $n \to \infty$. However, the constants in the big "O" notation are unclear and therefore we do not know which concrete parameters are needed in order to instantiate such constructions.

[8] We stress that the failure events in Cuckoo hashing and in OKVS are slightly different. Specifically, an OKVS fails if the size of the 2-core is too large whereas CH can handle a large 2-core, as long as there are not too many intersecting cycles.

functions used in each instantiation explicit. That is, an OKVS scheme is a pair of algorithms $(\mathsf{Encode}_H, \mathsf{Decode}_H)$ as defined in Sect. 2.

In the following, we describe three amplification architectures for constructing a new OKVS scheme $(\mathsf{Encode}_H^*, \mathsf{Decode}_H^*)$ using an underlying OKVS scheme $(\mathsf{Encode}_H, \mathsf{Decode}_H)$. We assume that the OVKS is over a finite field and that randomly sampling a vector of appropriate length from that field samples a random OVKS. For the underlying scheme, we denote by $\mathsf{size}(n)$ the size of the resulting OKVS for encoding n items. (Recall that by the obliviousness property, it follows that the OKVS size depends only on the size of the key-value set and not on the keys themselves.) We note that the amplification constructions sometimes invoke Encode_H with a set of key-value pairs only to check whether encoding succeeds or fails, and do not necessarily use the outcome of that encoding. Recall that even though the input to Encode_H consists of key-value pairs, success or failure depend only on the keys.

5.1 Replication Architecture

The following construction is mainly described as a warmup towards more involved constructions, since it substantially increases the space requirements. The idea is to amplify the success probability by doubling the size and computation, by using two OKVS constructions and retrieving values as the sum of the retrieved values from both constructions. The encoding procedure checks if any of two random hash functions results in a successful OKVS for the given set of keys. The encoding fails only if both hash functions result in a failure. Its main disadvantage is the double space usage.

Formally:

- $\mathsf{Encode}_H^*(\{(k_i, v_i)\})$ views H as two sets of hash functions H_1 and H_2. It outputs two dictionaries S_1 and S_2 as follows:
  - Compute $S' \leftarrow \mathsf{Encode}_{H_1}(\{(k_i, v_i)\})$.
  - If $S' \neq \bot$: set $S_2 \leftarrow \mathbb{F}^{\mathsf{size}(n)}$ randomly, i.e. S_2 is a random OKVS independent of $\{(k_i, v_i)\}$. Then, define the set $\{(k_i, v_i')\}$ where $v_i' = v_i - \mathsf{Decode}_{H_2}(S_2, k_i)$. Finally, compute $S_1 \leftarrow \mathsf{Encode}_{H_1}(\{(k_i, v_i')\})$. We know that $S_1 \neq \bot$ (since $S' \neq \bot$ and S_1 uses the same set of keys as S') and therefore output $S = (S_1, S_2)$.
  - Otherwise $(S' = \bot)$: set $S_1 \leftarrow \mathbb{F}^{\mathsf{size}(n)}$. Then, define the set $\{(k_i, v_i')\}$ where $v_i' = v_i - \mathsf{Decode}_{H_1}(S_1, k_i)$ and compute $S_2 \leftarrow \mathsf{Encode}_{H_2}(\{(k_i, v_i')\})$. If $S_2 \neq \bot$ then output $S = (S_1, S_2)$, otherwise, output $\bot$.
- $\mathsf{Decode}_H^*(S, x)$: Interpret $H = (H_1, H_2)$ and $S = (S_1, S_2)$. Output $y = \mathsf{Decode}_{H_1}(S_1, x) + \mathsf{Decode}_{H_2}(S_2, x)$.

Clearly, this construction only fails if both encodings fail. Therefore, if $(\mathsf{Encode}, \mathsf{Decode})$ fails with probability ε then $(\mathsf{Encode}^*, \mathsf{Decode}^*)$ fails with probability ε^2.

Generalization. The above construction uses two 'replicas'. It could be generalized to $c > 2$ replicas, resulting in an OKVS of size $c \cdot \mathsf{size}(n)$, failure probability ε^c and overall encode/decode time that is c times greater than the underlying scheme. Denote an OKVS scheme with c replicas by $(\mathsf{Encode}^{*c}, \mathsf{Decode}^{*c})$. We use such a scheme in the generalized construction described below (Sect. 5.3).

The obvious undesirable property of this construction is that the size of the OKVS increases by a factor of c. (This is also true for the encoding and decoding times, but these performance parameters are typically less critical since they are small for hashing-based OKVS.) In the rest of this section we describe how to amplify the failure probability from ε to ε^c while keeping the size of the resulting OKVS not much larger than the underlying OKVS (certainly not larger by a factor of c).

5.2 Star Architecture

We next show how to reduce the error probability while keeping the OKVS size to be almost $\mathsf{size}(n)$. In our concrete instantiation (presented in Sect. 8) we are able to almost square the failure probability while increasing the OKVS size by less than 10% for $n = 2^{20}$ items.

At the high-level idea, imagine a star-shaped graph consisting of $q + 1$ nodes, one central node and q leaves. Each node, including the central node, is associated with an OKVS data structure and should be large enough to store about n/q items. Each item is retrieved from one leaf node and from the root node, and the returned value is the sum of the two retrieved values. More precisely, to probe for an item x, probe for x in the central OKVS and probe for x in the OKVS of leaf $\tilde{h}(x)$ (where $\tilde{h}$ is a random function), and add the results. The construction is robust to a hashing failure of a single node since we can set that node to have random values and can still set the values of all the other nodes to ensure that the correct sums are returned (this is true for either a leaf node or the root node). Therefore the system fails only if at least two nodes fail. Security holds since one node is set to be random, while the other nodes store random OKVS values.

Formally, the new OKVS scheme is defined in the following way: Let n' be an upper bound on the maximum load of a bin when mapping n balls into q bins, except with probability $2^{-\lambda}$. In the following description we treat the first OKVS (indexed by 0) as the center node, and the following q OKVS's, indexed 1 to q, as the leaf nodes.

- $\mathsf{Encode}^*_H(\{(k_i, v_i)\})$: Interpret $H = (\tilde{h}, H_0, \ldots, H_q)$.
  - Map the set $\{(k_i, v_i)\}$ to q subsets: $A_1, \ldots, A_q$ where $A_j = \{(k_i, v_i) \mid \tilde{h}(k_i) = j\}$.
  - For $j = 1, \ldots, q$ compute $S_j \leftarrow \mathsf{Encode}_{H_j}(A_j)$
  - **No failure.** ($\forall_{j \in [q]} : S_j \neq \perp$) In this case, set random values to the central node and adjust the values of other nodes accordingly.
    * Sample a random S_0 from $\mathbb{F}^{\mathsf{size}(n')}$.

     * For $j \in [q]$ compute the new set $A'_j = \{(k, v') \mid (k, v) \in A_j\}$ where $v' = v - \mathsf{Decode}_{H_0}(S_0, k)$; then, compute $S_j \leftarrow \mathsf{Encode}_{H_j}(A')$.

- **One failure.** $(\exists_{j*} : S_{j*} = \bot \wedge \forall_{j \in [q]\setminus\{j*\}} : S_j \neq \bot)$ In this case, set the central node to ensure the correct decoding of the values mapped to the failed node, and adjust the values of other nodes accordingly.

     * Sample a random S_{j*} from $\mathbb{F}^{\mathsf{size}(n')}$.

     * Compute a new set $A'_0 = \{(k, v') \mid (k, v) \in A_{j*}\}$ where $v' = v - \mathsf{Decode}_{H_{j*}}(S_{j*}, k)$ and then $S_0 \leftarrow \mathsf{Encode}_{H_0}(A'_0)$. If $S_0 = \bot$ then output $S = \bot$ and halt.

     * For $j \in [q]\setminus\{j^*\}$ compute the new set $A'_j = \{(k, v') \mid (k, v) \in A_j\}$ where $v' = v - \mathsf{Decode}_{H_0}(S_0, k)$; then, compute $S_j \leftarrow \mathsf{Encode}_{H_j}(A')$.

- **Two or more failures.** If $S_j = \bot$ for more than one OKVS j then output $S = \bot$ and halt.

- Output $S_0, \ldots, S_q$.

- $\mathsf{Decode}^*_H(S, x)$: Interpret $H = (\tilde{h}, H_0, \ldots, H_q)$ and $S = (S_0, \ldots, S_q)$. Compute $j = \tilde{h}(x)$ and output $y = \mathsf{Decode}_{H_j}(S_j, x) + \mathsf{Decode}_{H_0}(S_0, x)$.

Failure probability. The construction can tolerate a failure in any one of the $q + 1$ components (either a leaf or the center node). In other words, the new construction fails only when *two* of the $q + 1$ components fail. So if each of the underlying OKVS instances fails with probability ε, then the new construction fails with probability

$$\Pr[S = \bot] = \sum_{i=2}^{q+1} \binom{q+1}{i} \varepsilon^i (1 - \varepsilon)^{q+1-i} \tag{3}$$

$$= 1 - (1 - \varepsilon)^{q+1} - (q+1)\varepsilon(1-\varepsilon)^q \tag{4}$$

Looking at Eq. 3 and ignoring high order terms, we observe that if the failure probability of the underlying OKVS scheme is $\varepsilon = 2^{-\rho}$ then the failure probability of the star architecture is $\approx \binom{q+1}{2}\varepsilon^2 = 2^{\log\binom{q+1}{2}-2\rho}$. Thus, in order for the star architecture to fail with probability $2^{-\lambda}$ we need $\log\binom{q+1}{2} - 2\rho = -\lambda$ and thus $\rho = \frac{\lambda + \log\binom{q+1}{2}}{2} \approx \frac{\lambda + 2\log(q) - \log 2}{2} \approx \lambda/2 + \log(q)$.

OKVS size and encoding/decoding time. The size of the new OKVS is $(q + 1) \times \mathsf{size}(n')$ where n' is the upper bound on the maximum load when mapping n balls to q bins, that is,

$$n' = \min_{\tilde{n}} : \Pr[\text{"there exists bin with} \geq \tilde{n} \text{ elements"}] \leq 2^{-\lambda} \tag{5}$$

where

$$\Pr[\text{"there exists bin with} \geq \tilde{n} \text{ elements"}] \leq \sum_{i=1}^{q} \Pr[\text{"bin } i \text{ has} \geq \tilde{n} \text{ elements"}]$$

$$= q \cdot \sum_{i=\tilde{n}}^{n} \binom{n}{i} \left(\frac{1}{q}\right)^i \left(1 - \frac{1}{q}\right)^{n-i}$$

These equations enable to easily compute the maximal size $\tilde{n}$ of the bins. Note that since the number of bins q is typically very small compared to n, then $\tilde{n}$ is not much greater than the expected size of a bin which is n/q. Section 5.4 shows a concrete size analysis for a specific choice of parameters.

The new encoding requires at most $2q + 1$ invocations of the underlying encoding algorithm. Decoding works exactly as in the replication architecture, with 2 calls to the underlying decoding algorithm.

5.3   Generalized Star Architecture

In this section we improve the amplification method to achieve a failure probability of $O(\varepsilon^d)$ for an arbitrary d. This enables to weaken the requirement from the underlying scheme, and only require that it fails with probability of at most $\varepsilon = O(2^{-\lambda/d})$ instead of $\varepsilon = O(2^{-\lambda/2})$. This is an important step if we wish to use an underlying OKVS scheme for which the failure probability is *empirically* proven, like our 3-hash garbled cuckoo table scheme presented in Sect. 4.1. The larger d is, the less experiments we have to conduct in order to empirically prove a failure probability of ε for the overall scheme.

The generalized idea is exactly the same as the star architecture, except that the center OKVS can tolerate up to $d - 1$ failures of the OKVS instances in the leaves. The new OKVS is composed of two components: (1) q leaf nodes as before, each of size $\mathsf{size}(n')$, and (2) a center node of size $d \cdot \mathsf{size}(n')$ (whereas in the simple star architecture the center is of size only $\mathsf{size}(n')$). The center node uses the replicated scheme $(\mathsf{Encode}^{*d}, \mathsf{Decode}^{*d})$ described in Sect. 5.1. We require that both components fail with negligible probability in λ. Specifically, in order for the entire scheme to fail with probability $2^{-\lambda}$ each component has to fail with probability $2^{-(\lambda+1)}$.

The formal description of the new OKVS scheme is as follows:

- $\mathsf{Encode}^*_H(\{(k_i, v_i)\})$: Interpret $H = (\tilde{h}, \hat{H}, H_1, \ldots, H_q)$, then,
  - Map the set $\{(k_i, v_i)\}$ to q subsets: $A_1, \ldots, A_q$ where $A_j = \{(k_i, v_i) \mid \tilde{h}(k_i) = j\}$.
  - For $j = 1, \ldots, q$ compute $S_j \leftarrow \mathsf{Encode}_{H_j}(A_j)$ and record the set $F = \{j \mid S_j = \bot\}$ (the indices of leaf nodes for which encoding failed).
  - **Too many failures.** If $|F| \geq d$: output $S = \bot$ and halt.
  - **Otherwise.** If $|F| < d$:
    * For all $j \in F$ sample a random S_j from $\mathbb{F}^{\mathsf{size}(n')}$. (This procedure sets random values for all failed OKVS nodes.)
    * Define the set $\hat{A} = \bigcup_{j \in F} A_j$ of all items in the failed OKVS nodes. Compute a new set $A'_0 = \{(k, v')\}$ which contains for each $k \in \hat{A}$ the pair (k, v') where $v' = v - \mathsf{Decode}_{H_j}(S_j, k)$ where $j = \tilde{h}(k)$. (This ensures that the central node corrects the value assigned for the key in the node OKVS.)
      Set $\hat{S} \leftarrow \mathsf{Encode}_{\hat{H}}(A')$. If $\hat{S} = \bot$ then output $S = \bot$ and halt.

* For $j \in [q]\backslash F$, define the set $A'_j = \{(k, v') \mid (k, v) \in A_j\}$ where $v' = v - \mathsf{Decode}_{\hat{H}}(\hat{S}, k)$ and compute $S_j \leftarrow \mathsf{Encode}_{H_j}(A'_j)$.
* Output $S = (S_1, \ldots, S_q, \hat{S})$.
- $\mathsf{Decode}^*_H(S, x)$: Interpret $H = (\tilde{h}, H_1, \ldots, H_q, \hat{H})$ and $S = (S_1, \ldots, S_q, \hat{S})$. Compute $j = \tilde{h}(x)$ and output $y = \mathsf{Decode}_{H_j}(S_j, x) + \mathsf{Decode}^{*d}_{\hat{H}}(\hat{S}, x)$.

In the description used above we denoted the central node's OKVS by $\hat{S}$ instead of S_0 as in the simple star architecture, to emphasize the fact that the central node is encoded using a stronger OKVS, namely a replicated OKVS scheme ($\mathsf{Encode}^{*d}, \mathsf{Decode}^{*d}$).

Failure probability. The generalized star architecture fails if either the leaf nodes OKVS constructions or the central OKVS fail. Thus, we require that each component fails with probability $2^{-(\lambda+1)}$.

Let ε be the failure probability of the underlying OKVS scheme ($\mathsf{Encode}, \mathsf{Decode}$). The first component, with q leaf nodes, fails when $|F| \geq d$, which happens with probability $\sum_{i=d}^q \binom{q}{i} \varepsilon^i (1-\varepsilon)^{q-i} = O(\varepsilon^d)$. The second component, which is a scheme with d replicas, fails with probability ε^d, corresponding to the event where all replicas fail.

OKVS size and encoding/decoding time. The size of the new OKVS is $q \cdot \mathsf{size}(n') + \mathsf{size}^{*d}(n')$ where $\mathsf{size}(n')$ and $\mathsf{size}^{*d}(n')$ are the sizes of the resulting OKVS for the ($\mathsf{Encode}, \mathsf{Decode}$) and ($\mathsf{Encode}^{*d}, \mathsf{Decode}^{*d}$) schemes, respectively. The value n' is the upper bound on the maximum load when mapping n balls to q bins, as presented in Eq. (5).

The new encoding requires $2q$ invocations of Encode algorithm for the leaf nodes and a single invocation of Encode^{*d}. The new decoding requires one invocation of Decode and one invocation of Decode^{*d}.

5.4   A Concrete Instantiation

The underlying scheme ($\mathsf{Encode}_H, \mathsf{Decode}_H$) is instantiated using the scheme of Sect. 4.1 where the resulting OKVS, when encoded using n' items, is $S = L\|R$ where $|L| = 1.3n$ and $|R| = \lambda + 0.5 \log n$ (i.e. $\mathsf{size}(n') = 1.3n' + \lambda + 0.5 \log n'$). In this scheme an encoding 'failure' happens when the 2-core which remains after peeling is of size larger than $0.5 \log n'$.

We conducted 2^{33} runs of such a scheme with $n' = 6600$, using different sets of hash functions in each run. There was only a single run in which the 2-core was greater than $0.5 \log n'$. By the Clopper-Pearson method [10], we get that for a random set of hash function H

$$\varepsilon = \Pr[\mathsf{Encode}_H(\{(k_i, v_i)\}) = \bot] = 2^{-29.355}$$

with confidence level of 0.9999.

We can use that result in order to construct a new scheme (Encode_H^*, Decode_H^*) using the star architecture (Sect. 5.2, replication factor is $d = 1$, i.e., no replication):

- $n = 2^{16}$. We use $q = 10$ bins. Then, the maximum load according to Eq. (5) is $n' = 7117$, for which the above experiment applies[9]. Thus, the failure probability of the new scheme, according to Eq. (3), is $2^{-52.9}$.
- $n = 2^{20}$. We use $q = 160$ bins. Then, the maximum load according to Eq. (5) is $n' = 7163$. Thus, the failure probability of the new scheme, according to Eq. (3), is $2^{-45.05}$.

In both cases, the space usage is $(q + 1) \cdot (1.3n/q + \lambda + 0.5 \log(n/q)) \approx 1.3n$.

6   Applications of OKVS

In this section we discuss how OKVS can be used as a drop-in replacement for polynomials in many protocols.

6.1   Sparse OT Extension

Pinkas *et al.* (SpOT-light [32]) proposed a semi-honest PSI protocol with very low communication, based on oblivious transfer techniques. Suppose the PSI input sets are of size n, and hold items from the universe $[N]$. There is a natural protocol for PSI that uses N OTs, where the receiver uses choice bit 1 in only n of them and choice bit 0 in the rest. This protocol will have cost proportional to N because communication is required for each OT, making it unsuitable for exponential N. The work in [32] introduces a technique called *sparse OT extension*, which reduces this cost.

Suppose the N OTs are generated with IKNP OT extension [19]. In IKNP, the receiver sends a large matrix with N rows. The parties perform the ith OT by referencing only the ith row of this matrix. Consider the mapping $i \mapsto [i$th row of IKNP matrix]. In the PSI protocol, the receiver only cares about n out of the N values of this mapping. So instead of sending the entire mapping (*i.e.*, the entire IKNP matrix), the receiver sends a polynomial P that satisfies $P(i) = [i$th row of matrix], for the i-values of interest. Crucially, the communication has been reduced from N rows' worth of information to only n.

When the IKNP matrix is encoded in this way, the result is the spot-low PSI protocol of [32]. Any OKVS may replace the use of a polynomial in spot-low.[10]

---

[9] We assume that if $\Pr[\mathsf{Encode}_H(\{(k_i, v_i)\}) = \bot] = \varepsilon$ for encoding n' items then the same probability ε applies also to $n'' > n'$.

[10] [32] describe another protocol, spot-fast, which also uses polynomials. Instead of using one polynomial of large degree n, spot-fast uses many polynomials of very small degree (and by this incurs a larger communication overhead). Due to the low degree, replacing these polynomials with an OKVS would have minimal effect.

6.2   Oblivious Programmable PRF and its Applications

Kolesnikov *et al.* [24] introduced a primitive called **oblivious programmable PRF (OPPRF)**. In an OPPRF, the sender has a collection of n pairs of the form $x_i \mapsto y_i$, and the receiver has a list of x_i' values. The functionality chooses a pseudo-random function R, conditioned on $R(x_i) = y_i$ for all i. It gives (a description of) R to the sender and it gives $R(x_i')$ to the receiver, for each i. In [24] a natural OPPRF protocol is described, based on polynomials. The parties invoke a (plain) oblivious PRF protocol, where the sender learns a PRF seed s and the receiver learns $PRF(s, x_i')$ for each i. Then the sender interpolates a polynomial P containing "corrections" of the form $P(x_i) = PRF(s, x_i) \oplus y_i$, and sends it to the receiver. Now both parties define the function $R(x) \stackrel{\text{def}}{=} PRF(s, x) \oplus P(x)$, which indeed agrees with the $x_i \mapsto y_i$ mappings of the receiver but is otherwise pseudo-random. In this application it is of course crucial that P hides the points which were used for interpolating it. Naturally, any OKVS can replace the polynomial in the OPPRF construction.[11]

Applications. [24] used an OPPRF to construct the first concretely efficient multi-party PSI. They described two protocols: The first protocol is fully secure against semi-honest adversaries. The second is more efficient but proven secure in a weaker *augmented semi-honest* model, where the corrupt parties are assumed to run the protocol honestly, but the simulator in the ideal world is allowed to change the inputs of corrupt parties. Intuitively, the protocol leaks no more to a semi-honest party than what can be learned by using *some input* (not necessarily the one they executed the protocol on) in the ideal model. We discuss this latter protocol in more detail in Sect. 7.2, where we show that, surprisingly, the protocol is secure against malicious adversaries despite not being secure in the semi-honest model.

OPPRF is also used in the PSI protocol in [34] for circuit PSI – computing arbitrary functions of the intersection rather than the intersection itself. It is also used in the recent multi-party PSI protocols of Chandran *et al.* [5,6].

In a private set union protocol [25], a variant of OPPRF is used to perform a functionality of reverse private membership test. The functionality allows a party holding the set X to learn whether an input y of another party is in X, and nothing else. [25] also rely on simple hashing to improve the computation of the polynomial-based OKVS.

Finally, [41] proposes a new OPRF-based PSI protocol. Their construction combines a vector OLE with the PaXoS construction. We observe that it is

---

[11] Besides encoding these "corrections" as a polynomial, [24] actually propose two other methods. One method is a garbled Bloom filter [11], which is indeed an OKVS (with expansion λ). Another method that they refer to as the "table" construction is not a true OKVS, as it only is oblivious when the mapping $k_i \mapsto v_i$ is such that all of the k_i (not just the v_i) are uniformly distributed except possibly one k_i which can be known to the distinguisher. As such, this "table" construction is suitable only when the receiver learns one output from the underling OPRF/OPPRF.

possible to replace their use of PaXoS with any abstract OKVS, and with our new OKVS constructions in particular.

6.3   PaXoS PSI

The leading malicious 2-party PSI protocol is due to [33], and is known as PaXoS-PSI. The underlying data structure, a **probe and XOR of strings (PaXoS)**, is what we call a *binary OKVS* in this work. Their protocol and proofs are written in terms of an arbitrary PaXoS data structure, with definitions that are identical to the ones we require of a binary OKVS. Hence, the improved constructions of binary OKVS that we present in this work automatically give an improvement to the PaXoS-PSI protocol. We have implemented these improvements to PaXoS-PSI, and report on their concrete performance in Sect. 8.2.

In Sect. 7 we discuss more details of the PaXoS PSI protocol, and also introduce a new generalization that can take advantage of a non-binary OKVS.

6.4   Covert Computation

Covert computation is an enhanced form of MPC (not to be confused with the definition of covert security) which ensures that participating parties cannot distinguish protocol execution from a random noise, until the protocol ends with a desired output. The constructions in [9,26] enable two parties to run multiple such computations in linear time, while keeping the covertness property. The challenge is identifying the correspondence between the protocol invocation sets of both parties. This is solved using a primitive called Index-Hiding Message Encoding (IHME). The constructions in [9,26] convert a protocol for single-input functionality into a secure protocol for multi-input functionality, by encoding as value $P(x)$ of a polynomial P the protocol message for input x. (Here, the polynomial P implements the IHME primitive.) The usage of a polynomial can be replaced by any OKVS, to result in improved performance.

7   Other PSI Improvements

We present several improvements to leading PSI schemes which use OKVS.

7.1   Generalizing PaXoS-PSI to Linear OKVS

The PaXoS-PSI protocol [33] uses any *binary* OKVS data structure. We now present a generalization that can support any *linear* (not necessarily binary) OKVS. First, we review the protocol to understand its restriction to binary OKVS: The PaXoS-PSI protocol starts with the parties invoking the malicious OT-extension protocol of Orrú, Orsini and Scholl [31]. The receiver chooses a vector of strings $D = (d_1, \ldots, d_m)$, and learns an output vector $R = (r_1, \ldots, r_m)$.

The sender chooses a random string s and learns output $Q = (q_1, \ldots, q_m)$. The important correlation among these values is:

$$r_i = q_i \oplus C(d_i) \wedge s \tag{6}$$

where C is a binary, linear error correcting code with minimum distance κ, and $\wedge$ denotes bitwise-AND.

If we view D, R, and Q as OKVS data structures, we will see that Eq. (6) is compatible with the homomorphic properties of a binary OKVS (see Sect. 2.3). Hence:

$$\mathsf{Decode}(R, k) = \mathsf{Decode}(Q, k) \oplus C\big(\mathsf{Decode}(D, k)\big) \wedge s$$

Now, suppose the receiver has chosen their input D (an OKVS) so that $\mathsf{Decode}(D, y) = H(y)$, for each y in their PSI input set, where H is a random oracle. Suppose that for each x in their set, the sender computes

$$m_x = H'\Big(\mathsf{Decode}(Q, x) \oplus C(\mathsf{Decode}(D, x)) \wedge s\Big),$$

where H' is a random oracle. If that x is in the intersection, then the receiver can also compute/recognize m_x, since it is equal to $H'(\mathsf{Decode}(R, x))$. If x is not in the intersection, then $\mathsf{Decode}(D, x) = H(x) \oplus \delta$ for some nonzero string δ. Then through some simple substitutions, we get $m_x = H'(\mathsf{Decode}(R, k) \oplus C(\delta) \wedge s)$.

When H' is a correlation-robust hash function, values of the form $H'(a_i \oplus b_i \wedge s)$ are indistinguishable from random, when each b_i has hamming weight at least κ (as is guaranteed by the code) and s is uniform. In other words, when the sender has an item x and computes m_x, this value looks random to the receiver.

Binary OKVS and the generalization. Revisiting Eq. (6), we see that the relation $r_i = q_i \oplus C(d_i) \wedge s$ is homomorphic with respect to xor:

$$r_i \oplus r_j = (q_i \oplus q_j) \oplus C(d_i \oplus d_j) \wedge s.$$

This is what makes these correlated values compatible with a binary OKVS. However, if we view all strings as elements of a binary field, we see that more general linear combinations of r_i's do not work because the $\wedge$ operation is *bitwise*, i.e. it is not compatible with the field operation.

The fact that $\wedge$ is not a field operation is also the reason for the error-correcting code C in the expression $r_i = q_i \oplus C(d_i) \wedge s$. For any nonzero d_i, we use the fact that $C(d_i) \wedge s$ is an expression with at least κ bits of uncertainty (*i.e.*, we are bitmasking at least κ bits of s).

Now suppose that the parties had values that were not correlated according to Eq. (6), but instead used a field operation $\cdot$ in place of $\wedge$:

$$r_i = q_i \oplus d_i \cdot s \tag{7}$$

Then we could view D, R, and Q each as OKVS data structures, and if they were linear OKVS we would have:

$$\mathsf{Decode}(R, k) = \mathsf{Decode}(Q, k) \oplus \mathsf{Decode}(D, k) \cdot s.$$

Additionally, for any a_i, b_i pairs with nonzero b_i, a value of the form $H(a_i \oplus b_i \cdot s)$ would look random to the receiver.

Indeed, replacing the correlation of Eq. (6) with that of (7) and using any *linear* (not necessarily binary) OKVS will lead to a secure PSI protocol whose proof follows closely to PaXoS-PSI. Additionally, since an error-correcting code is not needed, communication is reduced relative to PaXoS-PSI. A protocol that generates correlations that follow Eq. (7) is called a **vector oblivious linear evaluation (vOLE)** protocol [3,4,42]. Our protocol would require a malicious-secure vOLE protocol, but to date no such vOLE has been implemented. We leave it to future work to determine whether a vOLE-based approach will be competitive with the original PaXoS (OT-extension) approach.

Parameters:

- Computational and statistical security parameters κ and λ
- Sender with set $X \subseteq \{0,1\}^*$ of size n
- Receiver with set $Y \subseteq \{0,1\}^*$ of size n
- Linear OKVS scheme (Encode, Decode) mapping n items to m slots
- Random oracles $H_1 : \{0,1\}^* \to \{0,1\}^{\ell_1}$ and $H_2 : \{0,1\}^* \to \{0,1\}^{\ell_2}$

Protocol:

1. The parties invoke the vOLE functionality where the sender's input is random string $s \leftarrow \{0,1\}^{\ell_1}$ and the receiver's input is:

$$D = (d_1, \ldots, d_m) = \mathsf{Encode}(\{(y, H_1(y)) \mid y \in Y\}).$$

   As a result, the sender obtains output $Q = (q_1, \ldots, q_m)$ and the receiver obtains output $R = (r_1, \ldots, r_m)$ satisfying $q_i = r_i \oplus d_i \cdot s$, with $\cdot$ denoting the field operation in $GF(2^{\ell_1})$.
2. The sender computes and sends a random permutation of the set

$$M = \left\{ H_2\Big(x, \mathsf{Decode}(Q, x) \oplus H_1(x) \cdot s\Big) \;\Big|\; x \in X \right\}.$$

3. The receiver coutputs $\{y \in Y \mid H_2(y, \mathsf{Decode}(R, y)) \in M\}$.

Fig. 3. Our generalized PaXoS-PSI protocol, adapted from [33]

Theorem 7. *If* (Encode, Decode) *is a linear OKVS, and other parameters* ℓ_1, ℓ_2 *are as in [33], then the protocol in Fig. 3 securely realizes 2-party PSI against malicious adversaries.*

7.2   Malicious Multi-party PSI

Multi-party Private Set Intersection($\mathcal{F}_{\text{m-psi}}$) allows a set of parties, each with a private set of items (P_i owns a set X_i), to learn the intersection of their sets $X_0 \cap X_1 \cap \cdots \cap X_n$ and nothing beyond that. The work of Kolesnikov *et al.* in [24] presents generic transformations from any 2-party oblivious PRF to a multi-party PSI protocol. One of these transformations is secure in the semi-honest model, and a more efficient transformation is secure in the weaker "augmented semi-honest" model, in which the ideal-world simulator is allowed to change the inputs of the corrupt parties. Here we observe that this more efficient protocol can actually be made secure in the **malicious model** with only a minor modification (post-processing of the OPRF outputs with a random oracle).

Malicious-secure but not Semi-honest secure? Here, we briefly address this apparent paradoxical situation of a protocol being malicious-secure but not semi-honest secure. For a semi-honest secure protocol the simulator cannot change the inputs of the corrupt parties; that is, it should be able to explain any well-defined input provided by the environment on behalf of the corrupt parties. We can interpret the "augmented semi-honest" secure protocol as "the protocol is semi-honest secure apart from the issue of simulators changing inputs". In contrast, simulators changing a corrupt party's inputs is no issue while proving malicious-security. It just so happens, that without the issue of "simulators changing inputs" the protocol in [24] is malicious-secure.

We discuss the protocol in detail in the full version, as well as its cost analysis, proof of security and possible extensions. We also discuss there the interesting interaction between semi-honest and malicious security.

To the best of our knowledge, [1,44] are the only other works that study concretely efficient malicious multi-party PSI. Their constructions rely heavily on BF/GBF, which is the most communication-expensive construction amongst the three PSI constructions presented in [24]. While our protocol achieves almost the same cost as that of the most efficient construction in [24], with only a minor (inexpensive) modification, the protocols of [44] and [1] are about 10× and 2× slower than [24]. We present a more detailed qualitative comparison with the recent work of [1] in the full version.

8   Concrete Performance

We now benchmark different OKVS constructions and our PSI schemes. We also present a comparison based on implementations of state-of-the-art semi-honest and malicious PSI protocols. We used the implementation of semi-honest protocols (KKRT [23], SpOT-low and SpOT-fast [32], CM [7]) and malicious protocols (RR [40], PaXos [33]) from the open source-code provided by the authors, and perform a series of benchmarks on the range of set size $n = \{2^{12}, 2^{16}, 2^{20}\}$. All cuckoo hash functions are public parameters of the protocols, and can be simply implemented as one party chooses the hash functions and broadcasts them to other parties.

We assume there is an authenticated secure channel between each pair of participants (e.g., with TLS). We evaluated the PSI protocols over three different network settings (so-called fast, medium, slow networks). The LAN setting (i.e., fast network) has two machines in the same region (N.Virginia) with bandwidth 4.6 Gib/s; The WAN1 (i.e., medium network) has one machine in Ohio and the other in Oregon with bandwidth 260 Mib/s; and the WAN2 (i.e., slow network) has one machine in Sao Paolo and the other in Sydney with bandwidth 33 Mib/s. While our protocol can be parallelized at the level of bins, all experiments, however, are performed with a single thread (with an additional thread used for communication). In all tables and figures of this section, "SH" and "M" stand for semi-honest and malicious, respectively. We describe detailed *microbenchmarking* results for OKVS in the full version.

8.1   Parameters for OKVS and PSI

Some OKVS schemes rely on a simple hashing which maps n pairs into m bins. The number of items assigned of any bin leaks a distribution about input set. Therefore, all bins must be padded to some maximum possible size. Using a standard ball-and-bin analysis based on the input size and number of bins, one can deduce an upper bound bin size m such that no bin contains more than m items with high probability $1-2^{-\lambda}$. When n balls are mapped at random to m bins, the probability that the most occupied bin has μ or more balls is $m\binom{n}{\mu}\frac{1}{m^{\mu}}$ [35,37]. We provide our choices of μ

n			2^{12}	2^{16}	2^{20}
Simple	#bins (m)		10	100	2000
hashing	bin size (μ)		555	854	714
GBF	# hash functions			40	
	table size			$60n$	
2hf Cuckoo expansion				$2.4n$	
3hf Cuckoo expansion				$1.3n$	
codeword length (SH)			448	473	495
codeword length (M)			627	616	605
ℓ_2 (SH) (see [33])			64	72	80
ℓ_2 (M) (see [33])				256	
λ				40	

Fig. 4. Parameters for OKVS and PSI.

for which the probability of a bin overflow is most $1 - 2^{-\lambda}$, as well as other relevant parameters for the OKVS schemes and PSI protocols in Fig. 4.

A garbled Bloom filter (GBF) [11] fails if a false-positive even occurs. Using λ hash functions and a vector of size $1.44\lambda n$ results in a failure probability of $1/2^{\lambda}$ [27]. Therefore, we use λ hash functions and an OKVS table size of $60n$. We use $m = 2.4n$ and $m = 1.3n$ bins as the acceptable heuristic for the PaXoS and 3H-GCT OKVS constructions, respectively, and the PSI protocols that use them. We use the concrete parameters for the star architecture based OKVS that are described in Sect. 5.4.

8.2   Improving PSI Protocols

A detailed benchmark and comparison of different PSI protocols is given in Table 1. Note that the SpOT-low [33] and RR [40] protocols run out of memory for set size $n = 2^{20}$, and are not included in the comparison for this case.

Communication improvement. The overall communication of our 3H-GCT and star-arch. based malicious PSI is 1.61× and 1.43×, respectively, less than the

Table 1. Communication in MB and run time in milliseconds. All protocols run with inputs of length $\sigma = 128$ except RR (SM) that supports 64 bits at most. The upper part of the table refers to semi-honest (SH) protocols whereas the lower part refers to malicious (M) protocols. Missing entries refer to experiments that failed due to lack of memory or took too much time. Reported results are by running over AWS c5d.2xlarge. *Note that we found an issue with the implementation of* [7,23,32,40], *which use network connection library* [38]. *Specifically, over a real network their protocols take more time than over a simulated network with similar bandwidth and latency. The difference is noticeable in CM* [7].

Protocol	Sett.	comm (MB)			4.6 Gbits/sec			260 Mbits/sec			33 Mbits/sec		
		2^{12}	2^{16}	2^{20}	2^{12}	2^{16}	2^{20}	2^{12}	2^{16}	2^{20}	2^{12}	2^{16}	2^{20}
KKRT [23]	SH	0.48	7.73	128.49	201	**368**	**4512**	665	2390	12568	4352	10220	146067
SpOT-low [32]		**0.25**	**3.9**	**63.18**	495	10035	220525	894	11154	—	3406	20337.7	—
SpOT-fast [32]		0.3	4.61	76.46	**173**	1795	24676	678	7455	26050	4364	17923	38737
PaXoS-2hf (2-core) [33]		0.59	9.9	169.67	217	410	4680	443	1395	11935	1974	8448	60159
CM* [7]		0.36	5.34	87.6	149	518	7251	807	2816	**7966**	4395	10303	85476
Ours: 3H-GCT (§4.1)		0.34	5.63	96.71	216	416	5831	**300**	1890	10604	**1264**	**7248**	38349
Ours: Star arch. (§5.4)		0.39	6.09	104.04	227	483	4938	355	**1343**	9504	1373	9491	**34870**
RR (EC-ROM variant) [40]	M	4.54	75.52	1260.82	122	951	16240	3505	9127	45962	19220	24867	271442
RR (SM variant, $\sigma = 64$) [40]		48.66	815.43	—	534	7694	—	4506	33236	—	35959	187801	—
PaXoS (2-core) [33]		0.92	14.23	223.89	221	**418**	**4779**	392	2119	12042	2531	8152	60771
Ours: 3H-GCT (§4.1+§6.3)		**0.57**	**8.68**	**136.66**	219	420	5855	**300**	2929	10417	**1365**	**6981**	37695
Ours: Star arch. (§5.4+§6.3)		0.64	9.27	145.42	227	496	4987	308	**1350**	**9631**	1375	7654	**36871**

previous state of the art, PaXoS. This is greatly due to the fact that our protocols invoke $1.3n$ and $1.41n$ OTs, respectively, compared to $2.4n$ in PaXoS.

Computation improvement. Over fast networks (4.6 Gbits/s) and $n = 2^{20}$, our protocol is only 1.05×–1.1× slower than the fastest PSI protocols (KKRT and PaXoS), where the running time is dominated by computation. Over slower networks our protocols are almost always the fastest in the semi-honest setting and always fastest in the malicious setting. For example, over a 33 Mbits/s network, our malicious star architecture-based construction is almost 2× faster than PaXoS.

Acknowledgements. We would like to thank Dan Boneh and Laliv Tauber, as well as the anonymous referees, for their valuable comments on earlier drafts of this paper. The first and third authors are partially supported by a Facebook research award. The second author is supported by the BIU Center for Research in Applied Cryptography and Cyber Security in conjunction with the Israel National Cyber Bureau in the Prime Minister's Office, and by a grant from the Alter family. The fourth author is partially supported by NSF awards #2031799, #2115075.

References

1. Ben-Efraim, A., Nissenbaum, O., Omri, E., Paskin-Cherniavsky, A.: PSImple: practical multiparty maliciously-secure private set intersection. ePrint, 2021/122 (2021)
2. Botelho, F.C., Pagh, R., Ziviani, N.: Practical perfect hashing in nearly optimal space. Inf. Syst. **38**(1), 108–131 (2013)

3. Boyle, E., Couteau, G., Gilboa, N., Ishai, Y.: Compressing vector OLE. In: ACM Conference on Computer and Communications Security, pp. 896–912. ACM (2018)
4. E. Boyle, G. Couteau, N. Gilboa, Y. Ishai, L. Kohl, and P. Scholl. Efficient pseudorandom correlation generators: Silent OT extension and more. In CRYPTO (3), volume 11694 of LNCS, pages 489–518. Springer, 2019
5. Chandran, N., Dasgupta, N., Gupta, D., Obbattu, S.L.B., Sekar, S., Shah, A.: Efficient linear multiparty PSI and extensions to circuit/quorum psi. ePrint 2021/172 (2021)
6. Chandran, N., Gupta, D., Shah, A.: Circuit-PSI with linear complexity via relaxed batch OPPRF. Cryptology ePrint Archive, Report 2021/034 (2021)
7. Chase, M., Miao, P.: Private set intersection in the internet setting from lightweight oblivious PRF. CRYPTO 2020. Part III, volume 12172 of LNCS, pp. 34–63. Springer, Heidelberg (2020)
8. Chen, H., Laine, K., Rindal, P.: Fast private set intersection from homomorphic encryption. In: Thuraisingham, B.M., Evans, D., Malkin, T., Xu, D. (eds.) ACM CCS 2017, pp. 1243–1255. ACM Press, October/November 2017
9. Cho, C., Dachman-Soled, D., Jarecki, S.: Efficient concurrent covert computation of string equality and set intersection. In: Sako, K. (ed.) CT-RSA 2016, volume 9610 of LNCS, pp. 164–179. Springer, Heidelberg, Feb. / (2016)
10. C. J. Clopper and E. S. Pearson. The use of confidence or fiducial limits illustrated in the case of the binomial. Biometrika, 26(4), pp. 404–413, 1934
11. Dong, C., Chen, L., Wen, Z.: When private set intersection meets big data: an efficient and scalable protocol. In: Sadeghi, A.-R., Gligor, V.D., Yung, M. (eds.) ACM CCS 2013, pp. 789–800. ACM Press, November 2013
12. Freedman, M.J., Nissim, K., Pinkas, B.: Efficient private matching and set intersection. In: Cachin, C., Camenisch, J.L. (eds.) EUROCRYPT 2004. LNCS, vol. 3027, pp. 1–19. Springer, Heidelberg (2004). https://doi.org/10.1007/978-3-540-24676-3_1
13. Ghosh, S., Nilges, T.: An algebraic approach to maliciously secure private set intersection. In: Ishai, Y., Rijmen, V. (eds.) EUROCRYPT 2019. Part III, volume 11478 of LNCS, pp. 154–185. Springer, Heidelberg (2019)
14. S. Ghosh and M. Simkin. The communication complexity of threshold private set intersection. In CRYPTO (2), volume 11693 of LNCS, pages 3–29, 2019
15. Graf, T.M., Lemire, D.: XOR filters: faster and smaller than bloom and cuckoo filters. CoRR, abs/1912.08258 (2019)
16. Hazay, C., Lindell, Y.: A note on the relation between the definitions of security for semi-honest and malicious adversaries. Cryptology ePrint Archive, Report 2010/551 (2010). http://eprint.iacr.org/2010/551
17. C. Hazay and M. Venkitasubramaniam. Scalable multi-party private set-intersection. In PKC 2017, Part I, volume 10174 of LNCS, pages 175–203, 2017
18. R. Inbar, E. Omri, and B. Pinkas. Efficient scalable multiparty private set-intersection via garbled bloom filters. In SCN, pages 235–252, 2018
19. Ishai, Y., Kilian, J., Nissim, K., Petrank, E.: Extending oblivious transfers efficiently. In: Boneh, D. (ed.) CRYPTO 2003. LNCS, vol. 2729, pp. 145–161. Springer, Heidelberg (2003)
20. Kilian, J.: More general completeness theorems for secure two-party computation. In: 32nd ACM STOC, pp. 316–324. ACM Press, May 2000
21. Kirsch, A., Mitzenmacher, M., Wieder, U.: More robust hashing: Cuckoo hashing with a stash. SIAM J. Comput. 39(4), 1543–1561 (2009)

22. Kissner, L., Song, D.X.: Privacy-preserving set operations. In: Shoup, V. (ed.) CRYPTO 2005. LNCS, vol. 3621, pp. 241–257. Springer, Heidelberg (2005). https://doi.org/10.1007/11535218_15

23. Kolesnikov, V., Kumaresan, R., Rosulek, M., Trieu, N.: Efficient batched oblivious PRF with applications to private set intersection. In: ACM CCS 2016, pp. 818–829 (2016)

24. Kolesnikov, V., Matania, N., Pinkas, B., Rosulek, M., Trieu, N.: Practical multi-party private set intersection from symmetric-key techniques. In: ACM CCS 2017, pp. 1257–1272. ACM Press, October/November 2017

25. V. Kolesnikov, M. Rosulek, N. Trieu, and X. Wang. Scalable private set union from symmetric-key techniques. In *ASIACRYPT 2019, Part II*, volume 11922 of *LNCS*, pages 636–666. Springer, Heidelberg, 2019

26. M. Manulis, B. Pinkas, and B. Poettering. Privacy-preserving group discovery with linear complexity. In ACNS 10, volume 6123 of LNCS, pages 420–437, 2010

27. Mitzenmacher, M., Upfal, E.: Probability and Computing: Randomized Algorithms and Probabilistic Analysis. Cambridge University Press, Cambridge (2005)

28. Moenck, R., Borodin, A.: Fast modular transforms via division. In: Switching and Automata Theory, pp. 90–96 (1972)

29. Molloy, M.: The pure literal rule threshold and cores in random hypergraphs. In: SODA, pp. 672–681. SIAM (2004)

30. Naor, M., Pinkas, B.: Oblivious transfer and polynomial evaluation. In: 31st ACM STOC, pp. 245–254. ACM Press, May 1999

31. Orrù, M., Orsini, E., Scholl, P.: Actively secure 1-out-of-N OT extension with application to private set intersection. In: Handschuh, H. (ed.) CT-RSA 2017. LNCS, vol. 10159, pp. 381–396. Springer, Heidelberg (2017)

32. Pinkas, B., Rosulek, M., Trieu, N., Yanai, A.: SpOT-light: Lightweight private set intersection from sparse OT extension. CRYPTO 2019. Part III, volume 11694 of LNCS, pp. 401–431. Springer, Heidelberg (2019)

33. Pinkas, B., Rosulek, M., Trieu, N., Yanai, A.: PSI from PaXoS: Fast, malicious private set intersection. EUROCRYPT 2020. Part II, volume 12106 of LNCS, pp. 739–767. Springer, Heidelberg (2020)

34. Pinkas, B., Schneider, T., Tkachenko, O., Yanai, A.: Efficient circuit-based PSI with linear communication. In: Ishai, Y., Rijmen, V. (eds.) EUROCRYPT 2019. Part III, volume 11478 of LNCS, pp. 122–153. Springer, Heidelberg (2019)

35. Pinkas, B., Schneider, T., Zohner, M.: Faster private set intersection based on OT extension. In: Fu, K., Jung, J. (eds.) USENIX Security 2014, pp. 797–812. USENIX Association, August 2014

36. Pinkas, B., Schneider, T., Zohner, M.: Scalable private set intersection based on OT extension. ACM Trans. Priv. Secur. 21(2), 7:1–7:35 (2018)

37. M. Raab and A. Steger. "balls into bins" - a simple and tight analysis. In Workshop on Randomization and Approximation Techniques in Computer Science, RANDOM '98, page 159–170. Springer-Verlag, 1998

38. Rindal, P.: Cryptotools. https://github.com/ladnir/cryptoTools

39. P. Rindal and M. Rosulek. Improved private set intersection against malicious adversaries. In EUROCRYPT 2017, Part I, volume 10210, pages 235–259, 2017

40. Rindal, P., Rosulek, M.: Malicious-secure private set intersection via dual execution. In: ACM CCS 2017, pp. 1229–1242. ACM Press, October/November 2017

41. Rindal, P., Schoppmann, P.: VOLE-PSI: fast OPRF and circuit-psi from vector-ole. IACR Cryptol. ePrint Arch. **2021**, 266 (2021)

42. Schoppmann, P., Gascón, A., Reichert, L., Raykova, M.: Distributed vector-OLE: improved constructions and implementation. In: ACM Conference on Computer and Communications Security, pp. 1055–1072. ACM (2019)
43. Walzer, S.: Peeling close to the orientability threshold - spatial coupling in hashing-based data structures. In: Marx, D. (ed.) SODA, pp. 2194–2211. SIAM (2021)
44. Zhang, E., Liu, F.-H., Lai, Q., Jin, G., Li, Y.: Efficient multi-party private set intersection against malicious adversaries. In: ACM SIGSAC Conference on Cloud Computing Security Workshop, CCSW 2019, pp. 93–104 (2019)

MHz2k: MPC from HE over $\mathbb{Z}_{2^k}$ with New Packing, Simpler Reshare, and Better ZKP

Jung Hee Cheon[1,3], Dongwoo Kim[2(✉)], and Keewoo Lee[1(✉)]

[1] Seoul National University, Seoul, Republic of Korea
{jhcheon,activecondor}@snu.ac.kr
[2] Western Digital Research, Milpitas, USA
Dongwoo.Kim@wdc.com
[3] Crypto Lab Inc., Seoul, Republic of Korea

Abstract. We propose a multi-party computation (MPC) protocol over $\mathbb{Z}_{2^k}$ secure against actively corrupted majority from somewhat homomorphic encryption. The main technical contributions are: (i) a new efficient packing method for $\mathbb{Z}_{2^k}$-messages in lattice-based somewhat homomorphic encryption schemes, (ii) a simpler reshare protocol for level-dependent packings, (iii) a more efficient zero-knowledge proof of plaintext knowledge on cyclotomic rings $\mathbb{Z}[X]/\Phi_M(X)$ with M being a prime. Integrating them, our protocol shows from 2.2x upto 4.8x improvements in amortized communication costs compared to the previous best results. Our techniques not only improve the efficiency of MPC over $\mathbb{Z}_{2^k}$ considerably, but also provide a toolkit that can be leveraged when designing other cryptographic primitives over $\mathbb{Z}_{2^k}$.

Keywords: Multi-party computation · Dishonest majority · Homomorphic encryption · Packing method · Zero-knowledge proof · $\mathbb{Z}_{2^k}$

1 Introduction

Secure Multi-Party Computation (MPC) aims to jointly compute a function f on input $(x_1, \cdots, x_n)$ each held by n parties $(P_1, \cdots, P_n)$, without revealing any information other than the desired output to each other. Through steady development from the feasibility results in 1980s (e.g., [18]), MPC research is now at the stage of improving practicality and developing applications to diverse use-cases: auction [7], secure statistical analysis [6], privacy-preserving machine learning [15], etc.

Among various settings of MPC, the most important setting in practice is the actively corrupted dishonest majority case: corrupted majority is the only meaningful goal in two-party computation (2PC), and modeling the security threat as passive (honest-but-curious) adversaries is often unsatisfactory in real-life applications. At the same time, however, it is notoriously difficult to handle

D. Kim—Work done while at Seoul National University.

T. Malkin and C. Peikert (Eds.): CRYPTO 2021, LNCS 12826, pp. 426–456, 2021.
https://doi.org/10.1007/978-3-030-84245-1_15

actively corrupted majority efficiently. It is a well-known fact that lightweight information-theoretically secure primitives are not sufficient in this setting and we need rather heavier primitives [12].

A seminal work BeDOZa [4] observed that one can push the use of heavy public key machinery into a preprocessing phase, without knowing input values and functions to compute. Meanwhile in an online phase, one can securely compute a function using only lightweight primitives. This paradigm, so-called *preprocessing model*, spotlighted the possibility of designing an efficient MPC protocol even in actively corrupted dishonest majority setting. From then, there have been active and steady research on improving efficiency of MPC protocol in this setting: [2,16,17,21,22].

All previously mentioned works consider MPC only over finite fields where arithmetic message authentication code (MAC), the main ingredients of the protocols, is easily defined. Recently, SPDZ$_{2^k}$ [14] initiated a study of efficient MPC over $\mathbb{Z}_{2^k}$ in actively corrupted dishonest majority setting by introducing an arithmetic MAC for $\mathbb{Z}_{2^k}$-messages. This is to leverage the fact that integer arithmetic on modern CPUs is done modulo 2^k, e.g. $k = 32, 64, 128$; using MPC over $\mathbb{Z}_{2^k}$, one can naturally deal with such arithmetic. Also, there is no need to emulate modulo prime P operations on CPUs, simplifying the online phase implementation. The authors of SPDZ$_{2^k}$ claimed that these advantages are much beneficial than the loss from the modified MAC for $\mathbb{Z}_{2^k}$. The claim was convinced by the recent implementation and experimental results [15].

In regard to the cost of the preprocessing phase, however, there still remains a substantial gap between the finite field case and the $\mathbb{Z}_{2^k}$ case. Particularly, the authors of SPDZ$_{2^k}$, which is based on oblivious transfer (OT), left an open problem to design an efficient preprocessing phase for MPC over $\mathbb{Z}_{2^k}$ from lattice-based homomorphic encryption (HE). The motivation here is that the HE-based approach has proved the best performance in the finite field case.

The main difficulty is that the conventional message packing method using the isomorphism of cyclotomic ring $\mathbb{Z}_t[X]/\Phi_M(X) \cong \mathbb{Z}_t^{\varphi(M)}$ does not work when t is not prime, especially when $t = 2^k$. In fact, cyclotomic polynomials $\Phi_M(X)$ never fully split in $\mathbb{Z}_{2^k}[X]$. This makes it hard to fully leverage the batching technique of HE and causes inefficiency compared to the finite field case. Followup works, Overdrive2k [23] and MonZ$_{2^k}$a [10], proposed more efficient preprocessing phases for MPC over $\mathbb{Z}_{2^k}$, yet they do not give a satisfactory solution to this problem.

1.1 Our Contribution

MHz2k—MPC from HE over $\mathbb{Z}_{2^k}$. We propose MHz2k, an MPC over $\mathbb{Z}_{2^k}$ from Somewhat HE (SHE) in actively corrupted dishonest majority setting. It is based on our new solution to the aforementioned problem (of developing high-parallelism in SHE with $\mathbb{Z}_{2^k}$-messages) and non-trivial adaptations of techniques used in the finite field case to the $\mathbb{Z}_{2^k}$ case.

Note that the core of an SHE-based MPC preprocessing phase is the triple (or *authenticated* Beaver's triple [3]) generation protocol which consists of the following building blocks (see Sect. 2.5):

- a *packing* method for SHE which enables parallelism of the protocol and enhances amortized performance;
- the *reshare* protocol which re-encrypts a *level-0* ciphertext to a *fresh* ciphertext allowing two-level SHE to be sufficient for the generation of authenticated triples;
- and *ZKPoPK* (zero-knowledge proof of plaintext knowledge) which guarantees that ciphertexts are validly generated from a plaintext and restricts adversaries from submitting maliciously generated ciphertexts.

We present improvements on all of these building blocks for $\mathbb{Z}_{2^k}$-messages and integrate them into our new preprocessing phase, which is compatible with the online phase of SPD$\mathbb{Z}_{2^k}$.

New Packing Method for $\mathbb{Z}_{2^k}$-messages. We suggest a new efficient $\mathbb{Z}_{2^k}$-message packing method for SHE which can be applied to a preprocessing phase over $\mathbb{Z}_{2^k}$ (Sect. 3). Under the plaintext ring of degree N, our packing method achieves near $N/2$-fold parallelism while providing depth-1 homomorphic correspondence which is enough for the preprocessing phase. Previously, the best solution over $\mathbb{Z}_{2^k}$ of Overdrive2k [23] only achieved roughly $N/5$-fold parallelism. Thus, our packing method directly offers 2.5x improvement in the overall (amortized) performance of the preprocessing phase.

When constructing our packing method, to remedy the impossibility[1] of interpolation on $\mathbb{Z}_{2^k}$, we devise a *tweaked* interpolation, in which we lift the target points of $\mathbb{Z}_{2^k}$ to a larger ring $\mathbb{Z}_{2^{k+\delta}}$ (Lemma 1).

Reshare Protocol for Level-Dependent Packings. A seeming problem is that it is difficult to design a *level-consistent* packing method for $\mathbb{Z}_{2^k}$-messages with high parallelism, while the previous reshare protocol for messages in finite fields (with *level-consistent* packing) should be modified to be utilized in this setting. To this end, in the reshare protocol of Overdrive2k [23], an extra masking ciphertext with ZKPoPK, which is the most costly part, is provided. We propose a new reshare protocol for *level-dependent* packings, which resolves this problem and closes the gap between the field case and the $\mathbb{Z}_{2^k}$ case (Sect. 4). Concretely, in our triple generation, the total number of ZKPoPK is *five* as using the original reshare, whereas Overdrive2k requires *seven*. From this aspect, we gain an additional 1.4x efficiency improvement in total communication cost.

TopGear2k—Better ZKPoPKs over $\mathbb{Z}[X]/\Phi_p(X)$. When the messages are in $\mathbb{Z}_{2^k}$, using power-of-two cyclotomic rings $\mathbb{Z}[X]/\Phi_{2^m}(X)$ introduces a huge inefficiency in packing, since $\Phi_{2^m}(X)$ has only one irreducible factor in $\mathbb{Z}_{2^k}[X]$. Thus, it is common to use *odd* cyclotomic rings for $\mathbb{Z}_{2^k}$-messages. In this case, however,

---

[1] For example, over $\mathbb{Z}_{2^k}$, a polynomial $f(X)$ of degree 2 such that $f(0) = f(1) = 0$ and $f(2) = 1$ does not exist.

we cannot leverage known efficient ZKPoPKs over the ciphertexts regarding $\mathbb{Z}[X]/\Phi_{2^m}(X)$, such as TopGear [2][2].

To this end, we develop an efficient ZKPoPK over $\mathbb{Z}[X]/\Phi_p(X)$ where p is a prime (Sect. 5). This new protocol named TopGear2k is an adaptation of TopGear to the $\mathbb{Z}_{2^k}$ case. The essence of TopGear2k is that the core properties of power-of-two cyclotomic rings, which was observed in [5], hold similarly also in prime cyclotomic rings (Lemma 4). This fact not only improves the amortized communication cost, latency, and memory consumption of our ZKPoPK, but can also has ramifications on works derived from [5].

ZKP of Message Knowledge. For the MPC preprocessing for messages from a finite field $\mathbb{Z}_P$, where SHE has the plaintext space $\mathbb{Z}_P[X]/\Phi_{2^m}(X)$ *isomorphic* to the message space $\mathbb{Z}_P^{\varphi(2^m)}$, ZKPoPK is sufficient. In the $\mathbb{Z}_{2^k}$ case, however, packing methods are not *surjective*. In other words, there exist invalidly encoded plaintexts which do not correspond to any messages. Thus, we must also make sure that malicious adversaries had not deviated from the packing method when generating the ciphertext. To this end, we propose a Zero-Knowledge Proof of *Message* Knowledge (ZKPoMK) which guarantees that the given ciphertext is generated with a plaintext which is a *valid encoding* with respect to our new packing method (Sect. 6).

Performance. MHz2k achieves the best efficiency in amortized communication cost among all state-of-the-art MPC protocols over $\mathbb{Z}_{2^k}$ in the actively corrupted dishonest majority setting. Concretely, in our preprocessing phase, the amortized communication costs for triple generation[3] (in kbit) over $\mathbb{Z}_{2^{32}}$ and $\mathbb{Z}_{2^{64}}$, respectively, are 27.4 and 43.3 which outperforms the current best results, 59.1 of MonZ$_{2^k}$a [10] and 153.3 of Overdrive2k [23], respectively showing 2.2x and 3.5x improvements. Comparing our protocol with TopGear2k optimization (MHz2k-TG2k) and without it (MHz2k-Plain), our ZKPoPK together with our ZKPoMK improves memory requirement over 5.6x.

1.2 Roadmap

In Sect. 2, we define notations and recall some known ideas which we frequently refer to in our paper. In Sect. 3, 4, 5, and 6, we present our results on packing, reshare, ZKPoPK, and ZKPoMK, respectively. In Sect. 7, we present a performance analysis of our protocols: MHz2k-plain (which exploits our new packing and reshare protocol) and MHz2k-TG2k (which additionally exploits our ZKPoPK and ZKPoMK).

Figure 1 describes dependencies of this paper. Arrows denote dependencies, and the dashed arrow denote rather weak dependency. Sect. 4 refers to Sect. 3

---

[2] It is the recent refinement with the most efficient ZKPoPK among the line of works [2,17,22] exploiting (S)HE to MPC over a finite field.

[3] We assume a two-party case, and similar improvements occur in multi-party cases.

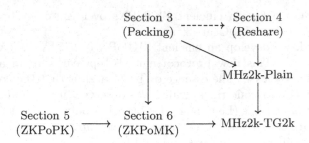

Fig. 1. Dependencies of This Paper

only in Sect. 4.2 to note that our new packing method is compatible with the new reshare process. Sect. 3, 4, and 5 can be read (except Sect. 4.2) and employed independently.

1.3   Related Work

We present the previous works achieving the same goal as ours: MPC over the ring $\mathbb{Z}_{2^k}$ secure against actively corrupted dishonest majority. All of the works (including ours) share the same online phase proposed by $SPD\mathbb{Z}_{2^k}$ [14], whereas the preprocessing phases are all different.

$SPD\mathbb{Z}_{2^k}$ [14] is the first MPC protocol over $\mathbb{Z}_{2^k}$ secure against actively corrupted dishonest majority. Their main technical contribution is the online phase with an efficient MAC for $\mathbb{Z}_{2^k}$ (see Sect. 2.5). Their preprocessing phase resembles that of MASCOT [21] which is based on oblivious transfers. The authors of $SPD\mathbb{Z}_{2^k}$ left an open problem to design an efficient HE-based protocol over $\mathbb{Z}_{2^k}$ since, in the finite field setting, it is the approach with the best performance.

Overdrive2k [23] is an HE-based MPC protocol over $\mathbb{Z}_{2^k}$, partially solving the open problem given in $SPD\mathbb{Z}_{2^k}$. The protocol mainly follows the approach of SPDZ [17] with the BGV SHE scheme [8]. Their main idea is a new HE-packing method for $\mathbb{Z}_{2^k}$ messages supporting one homomorphic multiplication only (See Sect. 2.4). Using their method, however, packing density for their parameters stay below 0.25. Moreover, to remedy their *level-dependent* packing, they provide extra masking ciphertexts with ZKPoPKs, substantially increasing the cost of the preprocessing phase.

$Mon\mathbb{Z}_{2^k}a$ [10] is a 2PC protocol over $\mathbb{Z}_{2^k}$ which mainly follows the linear-HE-based approach of BDOZ [4] and Overdrive [22], but with a different HE scheme by Joye-Libert [20]. Note that the Joye-Libert scheme does not provide packing for batched computations, whereas major and fastest approaches of MPC over finite fields leverage packing. Also note that $Mon\mathbb{Z}_{2^k}a$ provides only 2PC and does not provide general MPC.

2 Preliminaries

2.1 Notations

The ring $\mathbb{Z}_q := \mathbb{Z}/q\mathbb{Z}$ is identified with the set of integers in $(-q/2, q/2]$. We denote the set $\{1, 2, \cdots, d\}$ by $[d]$ and the set $\{0, 1, \cdots, d\}$ by $[0, d]$. The additive share of i-th party is denoted as $[\cdot]_i$. For a positive integer a, let $\nu_2(a)$ be the exponent of the largest power of two that divides a. All logarithms $\log(\cdot)$ are of base 2. On homomorphic encryption, ciphertext additions, subtractions, and multiplications are denoted as $\boxplus$, $\boxminus$, and $\boxtimes$, respectively. We denote the Mth cyclotomic polynomial as $\Phi_M(X)$ and reserve N for its degree, i.e., $N = \varphi(M)$ where $\varphi(\cdot)$ denotes Euler's totient function. Each elements of $\mathbb{Z}[X]/f(X)$ is identified with its representative of minimal degree. For an element $a \in \mathbb{Z}[X]/f(X)$, we measure the size of a by $||a||_\infty$, the largest absolute value of its coefficients.

2.2 The BGV Homomorphic Encryption Scheme

Following the approach of SPDZ [17], our preprocessing only requires secure computations of multiplicative depth one. Hence, it is enough to initiate the BGV [8] homomorphic encryption scheme supporting only two levels. Here, we only give a brief description of the scheme, focusing on the necessary parts for our proposal.

Two-Level BGV Scheme with Power-of-Two Plaintext Modulus. Let $R := \mathbb{Z}[X]/\Phi_M(X)$. The scheme consists of six algorithms (KeyGen, Enc, ModSwitch, Dec, Add, Mult), has a ring $R_{2^t} := R/2^t R = \mathbb{Z}_{2^t}[X]/\Phi_M(X)$ as a plaintext space, and each ciphertext has a level $\ell \in \{0, 1\}$.

For a given security parameter λ, the public parameter pp_λ fixes a cyclotomic polynomial $\Phi_M(X)$ with a sufficiently large degree; ciphertext moduli $q_1 = p_1 \cdot p_0$ and $q_0 = p_0$ for some prime p_0, p_1. Now, the algorithms are as follows:

- KeyGen(pp_λ): Given a public parameter pp_λ, outputs a secret key $\mathfrak{st} \in R$, a public key $\mathfrak{pk} = (a, b) \in R_{q_1}^2$, and relinearization data [8] for the ciphertext multiplication.
- Enc($m, r; \mathfrak{pk}$): For given plaintext $m \in R_{2^t}$, samples randomnesses $r = (e_0, e_1, v) \in R^3$ as $e_0, e_1 \leftarrow \mathsf{DG}(3.16^2)$ and $v \leftarrow \mathsf{ZO}(0.5)$,[4] then sets,

$$c_0 = b \cdot v + 2^t \cdot e_0 + m \pmod{q_1}, \quad c_1 = a \cdot v + 2^t \cdot e_1 \pmod{q_1}.$$

Then, outputs a level-one ciphertext $\mathfrak{ct}^{(1)} = (c_0, c_1) \in R_{q_1}^2$.
- ModSwitch($\mathfrak{ct}^{(1)} = (c_0, c_1)$): Given a level-one ciphertext $\mathfrak{ct}^{(1)}$, outputs a level-zero ciphertext $\mathfrak{ct}^{(0)} = (c_0', c_1') \in R_{q_0}^2$ having the *same* message as $\mathfrak{ct}^{(1)}$. We call this a modulus-switching operation.

---

[4] $\mathsf{DG}(\sigma^2)$ samples each coefficient from discrete Gaussian distribution, $\mathsf{ZO}(\rho)$ samples from $\{-1, 0, 1\}$ with probability $\rho/2$ for each of -1 and 1, probability $1 - \rho$ for 0.

- Dec($\mathfrak{ct}^{(\ell)} = (c_0, c_1); \mathfrak{sk}$): If $\ell \neq 0$, it gets a level-zero ciphertext $\mathfrak{ct}^{(0)} = (c'_0, c'_1)$ via ModSwitch. Then, it decrypts as

$$(c'_0 - \mathfrak{sk} \cdot c'_1 \pmod{q_0}) \pmod{2^t},$$

and outputs an element of R_{2^t}.
- Homomorphic Operations: Ciphertexts at the same level can be added ($\boxplus$) or multiplied ($\boxtimes$) with each other, resulting in a ciphertext encrypting the sum or the product of the plaintexts in R_{2^t}. Only level-*one* ciphertexts can be multiplied (with each other) to result in a ciphertext of level-*zero*.

2.3 Cyclotomic Rings and CRT Isomorphism in $\mathbb{Z}_{2^T}[X]$

For an odd M, the cyclotomic polynomial $\Phi_M(X)$ of degree N is factorized as $\prod_{i=1}^r f_i(X)$ in $\mathbb{Z}_2[X]$ where each irreducible $f_i(X)$ has the same degree $d = \mathrm{ord}_M(2)$, the order of 2 modulo M. Hence, $N = r \cdot d$ holds. The factorization induces the following ring isomorphism by the CRT, for any power of two 2^T:

$$\mathbb{Z}_{2^T}[X]/\Phi_M(X) \cong (\mathbb{Z}_{2^T}[X]/F_1(X)) \times \cdots \times (\mathbb{Z}_{2^T}[X]/F_r(X)), \tag{1}$$

where each $F_i(X) \in \mathbb{Z}_{2^T}[X]$ is the Hensel lifting of $f_i(X)$ with degree d. Each $\mathbb{Z}_{2^T}[X]/F_i(X)$ is often referred to as a *slot* of $\mathbb{Z}_{2^T}[X]/\Phi_M(X)$. In this paper, we frequently refer to the isomorphism Eq. (1) and the notation $\varphi(M) = N = r \cdot d$.

2.4 Packing Methods for SHE Schemes

Message, Plaintext, and Packing. This paper carefully distinguishes between the use of the terms *message* and *plaintext*. Messages are those we want to compute with using HE. On the other hand, plaintexts are defined by the HE scheme we are using. In this paper, messages are in $\mathbb{Z}_t$ and plaintexts are in $\mathbb{Z}_t[X]/\Phi_M(X)$, for possibly different t's.

Packing is the process of encoding multiple messages into a plaintext while satisfying (somewhat) homomorphic correspondence. Then, when performing homomorphic computations on a ciphertext packed with multiple messages, one can have the effect of *batching*. The idea of packing [24] is very useful in most cases, since plaintext space $\mathbb{Z}_t[X]/\Phi_M(X)$ of practical lattice-based HE schemes is usually not the space we want to compute in.

Basic Packing Methods. In lattice-based SHE schemes, including BGV [8], it is common to choose the plaintext modulus as a prime P such that $\Phi_M(X)$ fully splits in $\mathbb{Z}_P[X]$. Then, we can pack N messages of $\mathbb{Z}_P$ into one plaintext in $\mathbb{Z}_P[X]/\Phi_M(X)$ by the CRT ring isomorphism $\mathbb{Z}_P[X]/\Phi_M(X) \cong \mathbb{Z}_P^N$.

Above method, however, does not work for the case of $\mathbb{Z}_{2^k}$-messages, since $\Phi_M(X)$ never fully splits in $\mathbb{Z}_{2^k}[X]$. A common way [19] to detour this problem is to identify each $\mathbb{Z}_{2^k}$-message with each constant term of $\mathbb{Z}_{2^k}[X]/F_i(X)$ in Eq. (1). It provides fully homomorphic correspondence between r messages of $\mathbb{Z}_{2^k}$ and one element of $\mathbb{Z}_{2^k}[X]/\Phi_M(X)$, but with extremely low packing density $1/d$, following the notations of Sect. 2.3.

Overdrive2k Packing. Overdrive2k [23] observed that what we actually need for MPC protocol is a packing method which provides *somewhat* homomorphic correspondence supporting one multiplication (See Sect. 2.5). For a given degree $d = \deg F_1(X)$, they consider a subset $A = \{a_i\}_{i=1}^w$ of $[0, d-1]$ such that $2a_i \neq a_{j_1} + a_{j_2}$ for all $(i, i) \neq (j_1, j_2)$ and $a_i + a_j < d$ for all i, j. They pack w messages in $\mathbb{Z}_{2^k}$ as the a_i-th coefficients ($a_i \in A$) of a polynomial in $\mathbb{Z}_{2^k}[X]/F_1(X)$, putting zeroes in the other coefficients. Repeating this r times for each slot in Eq. (1), we can pack $r \cdot w$ messages into one plaintext achieving the packing density of w/d. Since the set A is carefully chosen, if we multiply two packed plaintexts, the $(2a_i)$-th coefficient of the result equals to the product of a_i-th coefficients of the original plaintexts, providing depth-1 homomorphic correspondence. Note that the Overdrive2k packing is *level-dependent*: messages are at a_i-th coefficients for level one plaintexts, and $(2a_i)$-th coefficients for level zero plaintexts. The authors of Overdrive2k note that the packing density of their method with an optimal subset A seems to follow the trend of $d^{0.6}/d$, approximately.

2.5 Preprocessing Phase—Generation of Authenticated Triples

Since our MPC protocol follows the online phase of SPDZ$_{2^k}$ [14], the goal of our preprocessing phases is to generate *authenticated triples* with respect to SPDZ$_{2^k}$-MAC. That is, n parties together securely generate secret shares $[a]_i, [b]_i, [c]_i$ and $[\alpha a]_i, [\alpha b]_i, [\alpha c]_i$ in $\mathbb{Z}_{2^{\tilde{k}}}$ such that $\sum_i [a]_i = a \pmod{2^k}$, $\sum_i [\alpha a]_i = \alpha a \pmod{2^{\tilde{k}}}$, and similar for the others, satisfying $c = ab \pmod{2^k}$. Here, $\tilde{k} := k + s$ with s as a security parameter[5], and $\alpha \in \mathbb{Z}_{2^{\tilde{k}}}$ is a single global MAC key of which share $[\alpha]_i \in \mathbb{Z}_{2^s}$ is given to the i-th party. Then, in the online phase, the parties can securely compute any arithmetic circuit via Beaver's trick [3,14] with these authenticated triples.

Overview of Triple Generation. We give an overview of our preprocessing phase, focusing on the triple generation protocol, which follows the standard methods of SPDZ [17] (and Overdrive2k [23]) exploiting *two-level* SHE and zero-knowledge proofs (ZKP) on it. We remark that message packing of SHE enable the parties to generate multiple authenticated triples (represented by vectors) in one execution of the triple generation protocol, significantly reducing the amortized costs.

First, each party P_i generates and broadcasts ciphertexts $\mathfrak{ct}_{a_i}$ and $\mathfrak{ct}_{b_i}$ each encrypting the *vectors* $[a]_i$ and $[b]_i$ of random shares from $\mathbb{Z}_{2^k}$; we omit the superscript[(1)] for level-one ciphertexts. Then, all parties run ZKPs (ZKPoPK and ZKPoMK in Sect. 5 and 6) on $\mathfrak{ct}_a = \sum_i \mathfrak{ct}_{a_i}$ and $\mathfrak{ct}_b = \sum_i \mathfrak{ct}_{b_i}$ to guarantee that each ciphertext is generated correctly. Next, all parties compute a ciphertext $\mathfrak{ct}_c^{(0)} := \mathfrak{ct}_a \boxtimes \mathfrak{ct}_b$ whose underlying message is the Hadamard product $c = a \odot b$. Similarly, given ciphertexts $\mathfrak{ct}_{\alpha_i}$, all parties can also compute $\mathfrak{ct}_{\alpha a}^{(0)}$ and $\mathfrak{ct}_{\alpha b}^{(0)}$ with homomorphic operations on the ciphertexts. The parties, however, cannot

---

[5] SPDZ$_{2^k}$-MAC provides $\mathsf{sec} = s - \log(s+1)$-bit statistical security ([14, Theorem 1]).

directly compute $\mathfrak{ct}_{\alpha c}$ from ciphertext multiplication between $\mathfrak{ct}_c^{(0)}$ and $\mathfrak{ct}_\alpha$ since the former is of level-zero.

Thus, the parties perform so-called *reshare* protocol [17] which, given $\mathfrak{ct}_c^{(0)}$ as the input, outputs a *level-one* ciphertext $\mathfrak{ct}_c$ having the same message as the input and/or the random shares $[c]_i$ of the message to each party. Roughly, it proceeds by decrypting the masked input $\mathsf{ModSwitch}(\mathfrak{ct}_f) \boxplus \mathfrak{ct}_c^{(0)}$ to get a (masked) message $f + c$, then subtracting the mask $\mathfrak{ct}_f$ from the fresh encryption $\mathfrak{ct}_{f+c}$ of the message, resulting in $\mathfrak{ct}_c = \mathfrak{ct}_{f+c} \boxminus \mathfrak{ct}_f$. Then, parties can compute $\mathfrak{ct}_{\alpha c}^{(0)} := \mathfrak{ct}_c \boxtimes \mathfrak{ct}_\alpha$. Here, ZKPs for the masking ciphertext $\mathfrak{ct}_f$ is also required.

Finally, parties jointly perform *distributed decryption* on the ciphertexts $\mathfrak{ct}_{\alpha a}$, $\mathfrak{ct}_{\alpha b}$, and $\mathfrak{ct}_{\alpha c}$ to get random shares of the underlying messages: $[\alpha a]_i$, $[\alpha b]_i$, and $[\alpha c]_i$. The parties already have the other components of the triple ($[a]_i$, $[b]_i$, and $[c]_i$), so the authenticated triple is generated.

3   New Packing Method for $\mathbb{Z}_{2^k}$-Messages

In this section, we present a new and efficient $\mathbb{Z}_{2^k}$-message packing method for contemporary SHE schemes, e.g. BGV [8]. Since the conventional plaintext packing method of using the isomorphism $\mathbb{Z}_t[X]/\Phi_M(X) \cong \mathbb{Z}_t^{\varphi(M)}$ does not work when $t = 2^k$, an alternative method is required to provide high parallelism.

To tackle this problem, unlike previous approaches which packed messages in coefficients of a polynomial (Sect. 2.4), we pack messages in evaluation points of a polynomial. Here, we detour the impossibility[6] of interpolation on $\mathbb{Z}_{2^k}$ by introducing a *tweaked* interpolation on $\mathbb{Z}_{2^k}$.

3.1   Tweaked Interpolation

The crux of our packing method is the following lemma: we can perform interpolation on $\mathbb{Z}_{2^k}$ if we lift the target points of $\mathbb{Z}_{2^k}$ upto a larger ring $\mathbb{Z}_{2^{k+\delta}}$, multiplying an appropriate power of two to eliminate the effect of non-invertible elements.

Lemma 1 (Tweaked Interpolation on $\mathbb{Z}_{2^k}$). *Let $\mu_0, \mu_1, \ldots, \mu_n$ be elements in $\mathbb{Z}_{2^k}$. Assume that an integer δ is not smaller than $\nu_2(n!)$, the multiplicity of 2 in the factorization of $n!$. Then, there exists a polynomial $\Lambda(X) \in \mathbb{Z}_{2^{k+\delta}}[X]$ of degree at most n such that*

$$\Lambda(i) = \mu_i \cdot 2^\delta \qquad \forall i \in [0, n].$$

Proof. Recall that, for $i \in [0, n]$, an i-th Lagrange polynomial on $[0, n]$ is defined as $\lambda_i(X) := \prod_{j \in [0,n] \setminus \{i\}} \frac{X-j}{i-j} \in \mathbb{Q}[X]$. Lagrange polynomial satisfies

$$\lambda_i(X) = \begin{cases} 0 & \text{if } X \in [0, n] \text{ and } X \neq i, \\ 1 & \text{if } X = i. \end{cases}$$

---

[6] For example, over $\mathbb{Z}_{2^k}$, a polynomial $f(X)$ of degree 2 such that $f(0) = f(1) = 0$ and $f(2) = 1$ does not exist.

Note that $2^\delta \lambda_i(X)$ has no multiples of 2 in denominators of its coefficients since $\delta \geq \nu_2(n!)$. Then, we can identify $2^\delta \lambda_i(X)$ as a polynomial over $\mathbb{Z}_{2^{k+\delta}}$ of degree at most n, since the denominator of each coefficient is now invertible in $\mathbb{Z}_{2^{k+\delta}}$. Let $\tilde{\lambda}_i(X) \in \mathbb{Z}_{2^{k+\delta}}[X]$ denote the polynomial. Then,

$$\tilde{\lambda}_i(X) = \begin{cases} 0 & \text{if } X \in [0, n] \text{ and } X \neq i, \\ 2^\delta & \text{if } X = i. \end{cases}$$

Now, $\Lambda(X) := \sum_{i=0}^n \mu_i \cdot \tilde{\lambda}_i(X) \in \mathbb{Z}_{2^{k+\delta}}[X]$ satisfies the claimed property.   □

3.2   New Packing Method from Tweaked Interpolation

Our tweaked interpolation on $\mathbb{Z}_{2^k}$ gives an efficient $\mathbb{Z}_{2^k}$-message packing into $\mathbb{Z}_{2^{k+2\delta}}[X]/\Phi_M(X)$, while providing *depth-1 homomorphic correspondence*. Notice the extra δ added to preserve packed messages: after multiplying two polynomials constructed from tweaked interpolation, the resulting polynomial carries a factor of $2^{2\delta}$. In bird's eye view, our new packing method applies tweaked interpolation on each CRT slots (Eq. (1), Sect. 2.3), while preventing degree overflow and modulus overflow when multiplying two packed polynomials. Recall the isomorphism Eq. (1) and the notation $\varphi(M) = r \cdot d$ of $\Phi_M(X)$ (Sect. 2.3).

Theorem 1 (Tweaked Interpolation Packing). *Let $\{\mu_{ij}\}_{i,j}$ be $\mathbb{Z}_{2^k}$-messages for $i \in [r]$ and $j \in [0, \lfloor \frac{d-1}{2} \rfloor]$. For integers δ, t satisfying $\delta \geq \nu_2(\lfloor \frac{d-1}{2} \rfloor!)$ and $t \geq k + \delta$, there exists $L(X) \in \mathbb{Z}_{2^t}[X]/\Phi_M(X)$ satisfying the following properties:*

Let $L_i(X)$ be the projection of $L(X)$ onto the i-th slot $\mathbb{Z}_{2^t}[X]/F_i(X)$. Then, for each i and j,

(i) $\deg(L_i(X)) \leq \lfloor \frac{d-1}{2} \rfloor$,
(ii) $L_i(j) = \mu_{ij} \cdot 2^\delta \mod 2^{k+\delta}$.

We call such $L(X)$ a tweaked interpolation packing of $\{\mu_{ij}\}$.

Proof. By Lemma 1, the condition on δ guarantees that there exists $L_i(X) \in \mathbb{Z}_{2^{k+\delta}}[X] \subset \mathbb{Z}_{2^t}[X]$ of degree not greater than $\lfloor \frac{d-1}{2} \rfloor$ such that $L_i(j) = \mu_{ij} \cdot 2^\delta \mod 2^{k+\delta}$ for all $j \in [0, \lfloor \frac{d-1}{2} \rfloor]$. Now, we can define $L(X) \in \mathbb{Z}_{2^t}[X]/\Phi_M(X)$ as the isomorphic image of $(L_1(X), \cdots, L_r(X)) \in \prod_{i=1}^r \mathbb{Z}_{2^t}[X]/F_i(X)$ from the CRT isomorphism; $L(X)$ satisfies the property.   □

The next theorem suggests that the tweaked interpolation packing (Theorem 1) homomorphically preserves the messages under (multiplicative) depth-1 arithmetic circuits. This property implies that we can naturally plug our packing method into the two-level BGV scheme (Sect. 2.2) with a plaintext space $\mathbb{Z}_{2^{k+2\delta}}[X]/\Phi_M(X)$ and exploit it for MPC preprocessing phase.

Theorem 2 (Depth-1 Homomorphic Correspondence[7]). *Let $L(X)$ and $R(X)$ be polynomials in $\mathbb{Z}_{2^{k+2\delta}}[X]/\Phi_M(X)$ which are tweaked interpolation packings (Theorem 1, $t = k + 2\delta$) of $\mathbb{Z}_{2^k}$-messages $\{\mu_{ij}^L\}$ and $\{\mu_{ij}^R\}$, respectively. For $\alpha \in \mathbb{Z}_{2^k}$, let $\tilde{\alpha}$ denote an element of $\mathbb{Z}_{2^{k+2\delta}}$ such that $\tilde{\alpha} = \alpha \pmod{2^k}$. Then,*

(a) $L(X) + R(X)$ is a tweaked interpolation packing of $\{\mu_{ij}^L + \mu_{ij}^R\}$.
(b) $\tilde{\alpha} \cdot L(X)$ is a tweaked interpolation packing of $\{\alpha \cdot \mu_{ij}^L\}$.
(c) From $LR(X) := L(X) \cdot R(X)$, one can decode homomorphically multiplied $\mathbb{Z}_{2^k}$-messages $\{\mu_{ij}^L \cdot \mu_{ij}^R\}$.

Proof. Properties (a) and (b) are straightforward from the linearity of projection map and evaluation map, together with the fact that additions and scalar multiplications preserves the degree of polynomial.

To prove (c), let $L_i(X)$, $R_i(X)$, and $LR_i(X)$ respectively be the projection of $L(X)$, $R(X)$, and $LR(X)$ onto the i-th slot $\mathbb{Z}_{2^{k+2\delta}}[X]/F_i(X)$. Then,

$$LR_i(X) = L_i(X) \cdot R_i(X) \qquad \text{in } \mathbb{Z}_{2^{k+2\delta}}[X]/F_i(X).$$

Note that the above equation holds also in $\mathbb{Z}_{2^{k+2\delta}}[X]$: Since the degree of $L_i(X)$ and $R_i(X)$ are at most $\lfloor \frac{d-1}{2} \rfloor$, the sum of their degree is less than the degree d of $F_i(X)$. Therefore,

$$LR_i(j) = L_i(j) \cdot R_i(j) = \mu_{ij}^L \cdot \mu_{ij}^R \cdot 2^{2\delta} \pmod{2^{k+2\delta}},$$

from which one can decode the desired values. $\square$

Remark 1. We call the packing structure of $LR(X)$ in Theorem 2(c) the *level-zero* tweaked interpolation packing, whereas the original packing in Theorem 1 is called *level-one* packing. We omit the level when the packing is of level-one.

3.3   Performance Analysis

Efficiency (Packing Density). As a measure of the efficiency of packing methods, we define *packing density* as the ratio of the total (bit)-size of points packed in a polynomial to the (bit)-size of the polynomial. For example, in the case of finite field $\mathbb{F}$, we can pack N points (of $\mathbb{F}$) to one polynomial (over $\mathbb{F}$) of degree $N - 1$ (having N coefficients), which gives the perfect packing density of 1.

Now, let $\kappa_k(d)$ denote the packing density of tweaked interpolation packing method for $\mathbb{Z}_{2^k}$-messages when the cyclotomic polynomial $\Phi_M(X)$ splits into irreducible factors of degree d. Then,

$$\kappa_k(d) = \frac{k \cdot \lfloor \frac{d+1}{2} \rfloor}{(k + 2\nu_2(\lfloor \frac{d-1}{2} \rfloor!)) \, d} \approx \frac{k}{2(k+d)},$$

where the approximation follows from $\nu_2(\lfloor \frac{d-1}{2} \rfloor!) \approx \frac{d}{2}$ and $\lfloor \frac{d+1}{2} \rfloor \approx \frac{d}{2}$.

---

[7] Our packing $(\mathbb{Z}_{2^k}^n \hookrightarrow \mathbb{Z}_{2^{k+2\delta}}[X]/F_i(X))$ can be interpreted as an analogue of *reverse multiplication-friendly embeddings* $(\mathbb{F}_q^n \hookrightarrow \mathbb{F}_{q^d})$ [9]. The *composition* lemma holds similarly in $\mathbb{Z}_{2^k}$ case, since a Galois extension of a Galois ring is again a Galois ring.

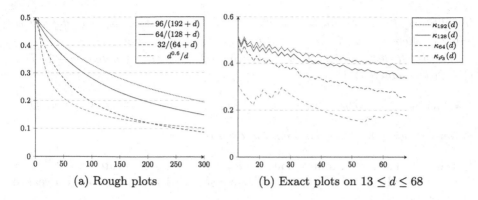

(a) Rough plots   (b) Exact plots on $13 \leq d \leq 68$

Fig. 2. Comparison of packing densities on each method according to d

Remark 2. For a fixed $\mathbb{Z}_{2^k}$, the packing density of our method (Theorem 1) depends only on d: it is better to use $\Phi_M(X)$ with smaller d. When d is sufficiently smaller than k, the packing density of our method approaches $\frac{1}{2}$.

Comparison with Overdrive2k. Let $\kappa_{\tilde{\rho}_3}(d)$ denote the packing density of Overdrive2k packing [23] for given d (Sect. 2.4). In Fig. 2a, the rough plots of packing densities according to d are presented: the lowest one is the plot of $d^{0.6}/d$ which was mentioned as a rough estimate of $\kappa_{\tilde{\rho}_3}(d)$ in [23]. The graph suggests that our method has higher packing density than theirs when k is not too small compared to d. For practical parameters, this is always the case: in Fig. 2b, the exact plots of packing densities on $13 \leq d \leq 68$ demonstrates that the density of our method is higher than that of Overdrive2k.

3.4 Predicates for Valid Packing

In this subsection, we define some predicates $\mathsf{P} : R \rightarrow \{\mathsf{true}, \mathsf{false}\}$ over a cyclotomic ring $R = \mathbb{Z}[X]/\Phi_M(X)$, with which we can formally describe the state of a plaintext in regards to our new packing method. We will use these predicates when describing our Reshare protocol (in Sect. 4) and our ZKP of Message Knowledge (ZKPoMK) (in Sect. 6). Readers may skip this subsection and consult it when succeeding sections refer to the definitions.

Definition 1 (Predicates). *The predicates* $\mathsf{Deg}_T^{(D)}$, $\mathsf{Div}_T^{(D,\Delta)}$, *and* $\mathsf{Pack}_T^{(D,\Delta)}$, *each mapping R to* $\{\mathsf{true}, \mathsf{false}\}$, *are defined as follows:*

For an element $a \in R$, let $\tilde{a} \in R_{2^T}$ be defined by $\tilde{a} \equiv a \pmod{2^T}$, and let $(\tilde{a}_i)_{i=1}^r$ be the CRT projections (Eq. (1)) of $\tilde{a}$.

- $\mathsf{Deg}_T^{(D)}(a) = true \qquad \Longleftrightarrow \qquad \deg \tilde{a}_i \leq D \quad \forall i \in [r]$
- $\mathsf{Div}_T^{(D,\Delta)}(a) = true \qquad \Longleftrightarrow \qquad 2^\Delta \ divides \ \tilde{a}_i(j) \quad \forall i \in [r] \ \& \ j \in [0, D]$
- $\mathsf{Pack}_T^{(D,\Delta)}(a) = true \qquad \Longleftrightarrow \qquad \mathsf{Deg}_T^{(D)}(a) = true \quad \wedge \quad \mathsf{Div}_T^{(D,\Delta)}(a) = true.$

In addition, the predicate $\mathsf{DivCheck}_T^{(D,\Delta)} : R \times \hat{R} \to \{\mathit{true}, \mathit{false}\}$ *is defined as follows, where* $\hat{R} = \mathbb{Z}[X]/\Phi_{\hat{M}}(X)$ *is another cyclotomic ring:*

For $b \in \hat{R}$, *let* $\tilde{b}_{ij} \in \mathbb{Z}_{2^T}$ *be* $\tilde{b}_{ij} \equiv b_{ij} \pmod{2^T}$, *where* b_{ij} *is the* $((i-1)(D+1)+j)$-*th coefficient of* b.[8]

- $\mathsf{DivCheck}_T^{(D,\Delta)}(a, b) = \mathit{true} \iff \tilde{a}_i(j) = 2^\Delta \cdot \tilde{b}_{ij} \quad \forall i \in [r] \ \& \ j \in [0, D]$

We omit T *when it is obvious from the context.*

Example 1. Theorem 1 states that, for $\nu = \lfloor \frac{d-1}{2} \rfloor$, the predicate $\mathsf{Pack}_t^{(\nu,\delta)}(a) = \mathit{true}$ if and only if $a \in R$ contains $\mathbb{Z}_{2^k}$-messages with respect to the tweaked interpolation packing.

Example 2. The essence of Theorem 2(c) is the following fact:
If $\mathsf{Pack}_{k+2\delta}^{(\nu,\delta)}(a) \wedge \mathsf{Pack}_{k+2\delta}^{(\nu,\delta)}(b) = \mathit{true}$, then $\mathsf{Deg}_{k+2\delta}^{(2\nu)}(a \cdot b) \wedge \mathsf{Div}_{k+2\delta}^{(\nu,2\delta)}(a \cdot b) = \mathit{true}$.

3.5   Sampling Zero Polynomials in $\mathbb{Z}_{2^k}[X]$

We propose *efficient* random sampling algorithms from the sets of elements satisfying the *predicates* defined in Sect. 3.4. These play important roles when we construct our **Reshare** protocol (in Sect. 4) and our ZKP of Message Knowledge (ZKPoMK) (in Sect. 6). Readers may skip this subsection and consult it when succeeding sections refer to the definitions.

Due to the unique feature of $\mathbb{Z}_{2^k}$, sampling process is not trivial and has a deep connection with zero polynomials[9] in $\mathbb{Z}_{2^k}[X]$. Our result possibly has ramifications on cryptographic works regarding polynomial evaluation (or interpolation) over $\mathbb{Z}_{2^k}$, outside of our protocols.

Definition 2 (Distribution with Predicate). *Let* $\mathcal{U}(B)$ *be the uniform distribution over* $\{a \in R : ||a||_\infty \leq B\}$. *For a predicate* $\mathsf{P} \in \{\mathsf{Deg}, \mathsf{Div}\}$ *(we omit the superscripts) over* $R = \mathbb{Z}[X]/\Phi_M(X)$, *the distribution* $\mathcal{U}_\mathsf{P}(B)$ *is the uniform distribution over the following set:*

$$\{a \in R : \quad ||a||_\infty \leq B \wedge \mathsf{P}(a) = \mathit{true}\}.$$

To show that one can efficiently sample elements from $\mathcal{U}_\mathsf{P}(B)$ with $\mathsf{P} = \mathsf{Div}$, we first identify all zero polynomials in $\mathbb{Z}_{2^k}[X]$ as follows.

Lemma 2. *For* $\chi_0(X) := 1$ *and* $\chi_i(X) := \prod_{\ell=0}^{i-1}(X - \ell) \in \mathbb{Z}_{2^k}[X]$, *let* $f(X) = \sum_{i=0}^d c_i \chi_i(X)$. *Then,* $f(j) = 0 \pmod{2^k}$ *for all* $j \in [0, n]$ *if and only if* $c_i \cdot i! = 0 \pmod{2^k}$ *for all* $i \in [0, n]$.

Proof. Assume $f(j) = 0 \pmod{2^k}$ for all $j \in [0, n]$. We proceed by mathematical induction on i. First, since $f(0) = 0 \pmod{2^k}$, $c_0 \cdot 0! = c_0 = 0 \pmod{2^k}$. Assume

---

[8] Such tricky definition is useful when describing our ZKPoMK (Sect. 6.1).

[9] A zero polynomial is a polynomial whose evaluations at certain points are all zero.

$c_i \cdot i! = 0 \pmod{2^k}$ holds for all $0 \le i < s \le n$. Then, from the fact that $\chi_i(s) = 0$ for $i > s$ and that $i!$ divides $\chi_i(s)$, along with the induction hypothesis, the following equations hold.

$$0 = f(s) = \sum_{i=0}^{n} c_i \chi_i(s) = \sum_{i=0}^{s} c_i \chi_i(s) = c_s \chi_s(s) = c_s \cdot s! \pmod{2^k}$$

For the other direction, assume $c_i \cdot i! = 0 \pmod{2^k}$ holds for all $i \in [0, n]$. Since $i!$ always divides $\chi_i(j)$ for any $j \in \mathbb{Z}$, $c_i \chi_i(j) = 0 \pmod{2^k}$ holds. Then, $f(j) = \sum_{i=0}^{n} c_i \chi_i(j) = 0 \pmod{2^k}$ for all $j \in [0, n]$. $\quad \square$

Corollary 1 (Zero Polynomials over $\mathbb{Z}_{2^k}$). *Let $f(X)$ be a polynomial in $\mathbb{Z}_{2^k}[X]$. Then, for a positive integer n, $f(j) = 0 \pmod{2^k}$ for all $j \in [0, n]$ if and only if $f(X)$ is of the form $\chi_{n+1}(X) \cdot q(X) + \sum_{i=0}^{n} c_i \chi_i(X)$ where c_i's are such that $c_i \cdot i! = 0 \pmod{2^k}$ for all $i \in [0, n]$.*

Proof. Note that $\{\chi_i(X)\}_{i=0}^{n}$ form a basis of the polynomials of degree at most n and $\chi_{n+1}(j) = 0$ for all $j \in [0, n]$. Then, the claim follows from Lemma 2. $\quad \square$

With the identification of zero polynomials from Corollary 1, we can efficiently sample an element from the distribution $\mathcal{U}_{\mathsf{P}}(B)$ as follows.

Corollary 2 (Efficient Sampling from $\mathcal{U}_{\mathsf{P}}(B)$). *Let $\mathsf{P} \in \{\mathsf{Deg}_T^{(D)}, \mathsf{Div}_T^{(D,\Delta)},$ $\mathsf{Pack}_T^{(D,\Delta)}\}$ be a predicate over $R = \mathbb{Z}[X]/\Phi_M(X)$. Then, one can efficiently sample an element from the distribution $\mathcal{U}_{\mathsf{P}}(B)$, given that $T \ge \Delta \ge \nu_2(D!)$.*

Proof. In both cases, it suffices to sample an element satisfying the predicate from $\mathbb{Z}_{2^T}[X]/\Phi_M(X)$ first with CRT isomorphism (Eq. (1)), then add an element from the distribution $\mathcal{U}(B)$ conditioned on multiples of 2^T.

The case of $\mathsf{P} = \mathsf{Deg}$ is straightforward, since one can sample a polynomial of bounded degree on each CRT slot. For the cases of $\mathsf{P} = \mathsf{Div}$ and $\mathsf{P} = \mathsf{Pack}$, first note that differences of tweaked interpolations with same messages are zero polynomials. Fixing representatives for tweaked interpolations with same messages, each CRT slot of an element satisfying P can be uniquely represented modulo 2^T by the sum of a tweaked interpolation and a zero polynomial. Thus, to randomly sample from each CRT slot of $\mathbb{Z}_{2^T}[X]/\Phi_M(X)$, first compute a tweaked interpolation (Lemma 1 with $\delta = \Delta, n = D$) with uniform random points from $\mathbb{Z}_{2^{T-\Delta}}$. Then, for $\mathsf{Div}_T^{(D,\Delta)}$, add a random zero polynomial of degree at most d (Eq. (1)) using Corollary 1 with $n = D$. For $\mathsf{Pack}_T^{(D,\Delta)}$, add a random zero polynomial of degree at most D. $\quad \square$

Finally, for the construction of ZKPoMK (Sect. 6), we present the adaptation of usual statistical masking method to our case with the predicates.

Lemma 3 (Statistical Masking). *For a positive integer $B < B_\infty$ and a predicate $\mathsf{P} \in \{\mathsf{Deg}, \mathsf{Div}, \mathsf{Pack}\}$, let $a \in R = \mathbb{Z}[X]/\Phi_M(X)$ be an element such that $||a||_\infty \le B$ and $\mathsf{P}(a) = \mathsf{true}$. Then, the statistical distance between $a + \mathcal{U}_{\mathsf{P}}(B_\infty)$ and $\mathcal{U}_{\mathsf{P}}(B_\infty)$ is bounded by $\frac{NB}{B_\infty}$ where $N = \varphi(M)$. The similar holds for $\mathcal{U}$.*

Proof. The case of $N = 1$ directly follows from the definition of statistical distance, and the claim is a generalization with $(B_\infty - B)^N > B_\infty^N - NB_\infty^{N-1}B$. $\quad \square$

4   Reshare Protocol for Level-Dependent Packings

When designing a packing method for $\mathbb{Z}_{2^k}$-messages with high parallelism, it is inevitable to design a *level-dependent* packing, e.g., the Overdrive2k [23] packing (Sect. 2.4) and our tweaked interpolation packing (Sect. 3, Remark 1). However, this leads to a complication in the reshare protocol for $\mathbb{Z}_{2^k}$-messages, which does not occur in the case of a finite field $\mathbb{Z}_P$ with *level-consistent* packing from the isomorphism $\mathbb{Z}_P[X]/\Phi_{2^m}(X) \cong \mathbb{Z}_P^{\varphi(2^m)}$. In particular, the reshare protocol of Overdrive2k [23] exploits an extra masking ciphertext with ZKPoPK on it, which is the most costly part, to remedy the issue.

In this section, we propose a new reshare protocol for *level-dependent* packings, which resolves this complication: our protocol extends the previous reshare protocol of the finite field case to operate also with level-dependent packings *without any extra cost*. Our result closes the gap between the finite field and the $\mathbb{Z}_{2^k}$ cases which originates from the level-dependency.

4.1   Improved Reshare Protocol for Level-Dependent Packings

The Problem of Level-Dependent Packings. Recall that the goal of the reshare protocols is, for an input level-zero ciphertext, to output shares of the underlying message along with a *level-one* ciphertext having the same message as the input (Sect. 2.5). The complication, with a level-dependent packing, is that we have to manage not only the *ciphertext level* but also the *packing level*.

Recall that one masking ciphertext $\mathfrak{ct}_f$ is used twice in the reshare protocol for the finite field case: once to mask the input ciphertext of level-zero and once to reconstruct the fresh ciphertext of level-one by subtracting it (Sect. 2.5). While the difference of ciphertext levels can be managed easily with modulus-switching, that of the packing levels seems to be problematic.

Solution of Overdrive2k. To resolve this problem, Overdrive2k [23] provides two masking ciphertexts having the *same messages* but in *different packing*: one with level-zero packing and the other with level-one packing. This approach requires an extra ZKPoPK with the additional broadcast of the masking ciphertext, doubling the cost of the reshare protocol. It results in substantial increase of cost in the whole preprocessing protocol. In the triple generation protocol, the number of ZKPoPK with broadcasts of ciphertexts is *five* using the original reshare protocol in the field case, whereas Overdrive2k requires *seven* due to their reshare protocol, resulting roughly a 1.4x reduction in efficiency.[10]

Our Solution. The crux of our reshare protocol for level-dependent packings is the idea of generating the ciphertext $\mathfrak{ct}_\alpha$ of the MAC key $\alpha \in \mathbb{Z}_{2^s}$ by treating α as a constant in the cyclotomic ring $\mathbb{Z}_{2^t}/\Phi_M(X)$, i.e. $\mathfrak{ct}_\alpha = \mathsf{Enc}(\alpha)$ for $\alpha \in \mathbb{Z}_{2^t}/\Phi_M(X)$ *without* any packing structure. Then, we actually do *not* need

---

[10] The number of ZKPoPK is counted regarding the *correlated* sacrifice technique [21].

the fresh ciphertext to be of packing level-one: it is okay to be of packing level-zero. This is because, whereas multiplying $\mathfrak{ct}_\alpha$ to a ciphertext consumes a ciphertext level, multiplying α to a plaintext does not consumes a packing level, i.e. multiplying α is a linear operation in the aspect of packing (Theorem 2(b)).

Our reshare protocol itself is more or less verbatim of the previous reshare protocol for the finite field cases [17]. Thus, we omit the formal description and proof of our reshare protocol for general level-dependent packings. Instead, we present an instantiation of our reshare protocol with our tweaked interpolation packing in the next subsection.

4.2   Compatibility with Our Packing Method

We present our reshare protocol instantiated with our tweaked interpolation packing (Sect. 3). While our protocol resembles the Reshare protocol of [17] with $\mathbb{Z}_p$ messages, it is slightly more involved due to the nontrivial task of masking the $\mathbb{Z}_{2^k}$ messages encoded with our tweaked interpolation (we will borrow the results from Sect. 3.5). We give an overview focusing on our modification and correctness of the protocol, and refer to the full version for the formal description.

Our reshare protocol Π_{Reshare} is presented in Fig. 3. The protocol exploits a zero-knowledge proof on a ciphertext, depicted as ZKPoPK and ZKPoMK, which will be described in Sect. 5, 6. For now, we simply assume that they guarantee that the messages are encoded correctly in the ciphertext with respect to our packing method.

A noticeable difference of our protocol from other reshare protocols of [17,23] is that each party samples the message f_i of a mask ciphertext from the distribution with predicate, $\mathcal{U}_{\mathsf{P}}(2^T)$ with $\mathsf{P} = \mathsf{Div}_T^{(D,\Delta)}$ (Definition 2, Corollary 2). It not only *preserves* the packing structure, but also *prevent* the information leakage from our packing method in the following distributed decryption (5.-7. in Fig. 3). If f_i was sampled from a random polynomial without any restriction, $\mathsf{Div}_T^{(D,\Delta)}(v) = \mathsf{false}$ (with high probability) and each party cannot retrieve $[m]_i$. On the other hand, if f_i was not added as a mask, each party can get additional information from the plaintext polynomial v which may contain more coefficients than the messages.

Since the mask r_i together with f_i can be seen as a statistical masking from $\mathcal{U}_{\mathsf{P}}(B_{\mathsf{DDec}})$ of Lemma 3, we can show that the protocol implements the $\mathcal{F}_{\mathsf{DistrDec}}$ functionality (see the full version) which is required in the SPDZ2k preprocessing phase (Sect. 2.5, or formally, Π_{Prep} in the full version).

Theorem 3 (Reshare Protocol). *On a cyclotomic ring $\mathbb{Z}[X]/\Phi_M(X)$, the protocol $\Pi_{Reshare}$ (Fig. 3) implements the functionality $\mathcal{F}_{DistrDec}.D2$ against any static, active adversary corrupting up to $n-1$ parties in the $(\mathcal{F}_{KeyGen}, \mathcal{F}_{Rand})$-hybrid model with statistical security $\varphi(M) \cdot 2^{-sec}$ if $B_{DDec} > 2^{sec} \cdot (B_{noise} + 2^T)$ and $(B_{noise} + n \cdot B_{DDec}) < q_0/2.$*

Proof. We refer to the full version.

Protocol Π_{Reshare}

Implicitly call $\mathcal{F}_{\text{Rand}}$ (full version) when it is required in ZKPoPK (or ZKPoMK).

PARAMETERS:
- B_{DDec}: a bound on the coefficients of the mask values.
- B_{noise}: a bound on the noise of input ciphertexts.
- n: the number of participating parties P_i.

COMMON INPUT:
- The parameter $\mathsf{pp} = (D, \Delta, T)$ for the predicate $\text{Div}_T^{(D,\Delta)}$ (Definition 1).
- $\mathfrak{ct}_m^{(0)}$: a level-zero ciphertext satisfying that $\text{Div}_T^{(D,\Delta)}(\text{Dec}(\mathfrak{ct}_m^{(0)}, \mathfrak{st})) = \text{true}$, having a message $\boldsymbol{m} \in \mathbb{Z}_{2^k}^\nu$ with our encoding method (Theorem 1, 2).

Initialize: Each party P_i calls $\mathcal{F}_{\text{KeyGen}}$ (full version) receiving $(\mathfrak{pt}, [\mathfrak{st}]_i)$.

D2: On input ciphertext $\mathfrak{ct}_m^{(0)}$ (see COMMON INPUT), parties do as follows.

1. Set $\mathsf{P} = \text{Div}_T^{(D,\Delta)}$. Each P_i samples a polynomial $f_i \leftarrow \mathcal{U}_\mathsf{P}(2^{T-1})$ and set $\boldsymbol{f}_i \in \mathbb{Z}_{2^k}^\nu$ as the uniform random points used in the sampling process, i.e., $\boldsymbol{f}_i$ are messages of f_i when regarded as a tweaked interpolation (see the proof of Corollary 2).

2. Each P_i generates level-one ciphertext $\mathfrak{ct}_{f_i}^{(1)}$ having the polynomial f_i as a message, then broadcasts this ciphertext.

3. All parties together run ZKPoPK (and ZKPoMK) as provers and verifiers on the summed ciphertext $\mathfrak{ct}_f^{(1)} = \sum_i \mathfrak{ct}_{f_i}^{(1)}$. If the proof of ZKPoPK is rejected, then abort.

4. All parties compute $\mathfrak{ct}_f^{(0)} = \text{ModSwitch}(\mathfrak{ct}_f^{(1)})$, then compute $\mathfrak{ct}_{m+f}^{(0)} = \mathfrak{ct}_m^{(0)} \boxplus \mathfrak{ct}_f^{(0)}$. Let $\mathfrak{ct}_{m+f}^{(0)}$ be (c_0, c_1).

5. Each P_i computes $w_i = \begin{cases} c_0 - [\mathfrak{st}]_1 \cdot c_1 & \text{if } i = 1 \\ -[\mathfrak{st}]_i \cdot c_1 & \text{if } i \neq 1 \end{cases}$.

6. Each P_i samples a mask $r_i \leftarrow \mathcal{U}(B_{\text{DDec}}/2^T)$ (Definition 2), then broadcasts $v_i = w_i + 2^T \cdot r_i \pmod{q_0}$.

7. All parties compute $v = \sum_i v_i \pmod{q_0}$, then check if $||v||_\infty < B_{\text{noise}} + n \cdot B_{\text{DDec}}$ and $\text{Div}_T^{(D,\Delta)}(v) = \text{true}$. If not, abort.

8. All parties retrieve $\boldsymbol{m} + \boldsymbol{f}$ from v by regarding v as a Tweaked Interpolation (Theorem 1) with $\delta = \Delta$, $\lfloor \frac{d-1}{2} \rfloor = D$, and $t = T$.

9. Each P_i sets $[\boldsymbol{m}]_i = \begin{cases} (\boldsymbol{m} + \boldsymbol{f}) - [\boldsymbol{f}]_1 & \text{if } i = 1 \\ -[\boldsymbol{f}]_i & \text{if } i \neq 1 \end{cases}$.

10. All parties compute, using default value (e.g., $\boldsymbol{0}$) for the randomness,

$$\bar{\mathfrak{ct}}_m^{(1)} = (\text{Enc}(m + f, \boldsymbol{0}; \mathfrak{pt})) \boxminus \mathfrak{ct}_f^{(1)},$$

where the polynomial $m + f \in \mathbb{Z}_{2^t}[X]/\Phi_M(X)$ is the Tweaked Interpolation (Theorem 1) for the message $\boldsymbol{m} + \boldsymbol{f} \in \mathbb{Z}_{2^k}^\nu$ with $\delta = \Delta$, $\lfloor \frac{d-1}{2} \rfloor = D$, and $t = T$.

Fig. 3. Our reshare protocol

5   Better ZKP for Lattice Encryption on $\mathbb{Z}[X]/\Phi_p(X)$

We present an improved ZKP of Plaintext Knowledge (ZKPoPK) for BGV [8] ciphertexts over *prime* cyclotomic rings $\mathbb{Z}[X]/\Phi_p(X)$, which proves that a ciphertext is generated with appropriate *sizes* of noises and a plaintext. ZKPoPK plays an important role in SHE-based MPC preprocessing phases [17, 22, 23] as it restricts adversaries from submitting maliciously generated ciphertexts.

Note that power-of-two cyclotomic polynomials $\Phi_{2^m}(X)$ are detrimental for $\mathbb{Z}_{2^k}$-messages.[11] Accordingly, Overdrive2k [23] proposed a ZKPoPK over *prime* cyclotomic rings, adapting the High Gear approach of Overdrive [22] which is over power-of-two cyclotomic rings. Likewise to Overdrive, the challenge space of Overdrive2k is restricted to a rather small set: $\{0, 1\}$.

Taking one step further, we propose a ZKPoPK named TopGear2k for prime cyclotomic rings, adapting the state-of-the-art ZKPoPK over power-of-two cyclotomic rings called TopGear [2]. Our ZKPoPK, similarly as TopGear, allows a *larger challenge space* $\{X^j\}_j \cup \{0\}$, resulting in a better efficiency. The essence is a new observation that the core properties of power-of-two cyclotomic rings (observed in [5]) also hold similarly in prime cyclotomic rings. Our result possibly has ramifications on works derived from [5], outside of our specific ZKPoPK.

5.1   A Technical Lemma on Cyclotomic Polynomials of Primes

We present a technical lemma on cyclotomic polynomials of primes, which is the essence of our ZKPoPK protocol. We first recall some facts on $R = \mathbb{Z}[X]/\Phi_M(X)$ when M is a power-of-two, which are the main ingredients of the TopGear protocol [2] and its forebear [5].

(a) For all $a(X) \in R$ and $i \in \mathbb{Z}$, it holds that $\|a(X) \cdot X^i\|_\infty = \|a(X)\|_\infty$.
(b) ([5, Lemma 4]) For all $1 \le j < i \le M$, there exists $h(X) \in R$ such that
 - $(X^i - X^j) \cdot h(X) \equiv 2 \pmod{\Phi_M(X)}$
 - and $\|h(X)\|_\infty = 1$.

Statement (a) indicates that the coefficients do not grow when multiplied by X^i, which is straightforward from the fact that multiplication by X^i acts as *skewed* coefficient shift in $\mathbb{Z}[X]/(X^{M/2} + 1)$. On the other hand, (b) says, roughly, that there is a *scaled* inverse of $(X^i - X^j)$ in R with small coefficients.

We now present an analogue of the above facts when M is a prime.

Lemma 4. *For a prime p and $R := \mathbb{Z}[X]/\Phi_p(X)$, the followings hold.*

(a) For all $a(X) \in R$ and $i \in \mathbb{Z}$, it holds that $\|a(X) \cdot X^i\|_\infty \le 2\|a(X)\|_\infty$.
(b) For all $1 \le j < i \le p$, there exists $h(X) \in R$ such that
 - *$(X^i - X^j) \cdot h(X) \equiv p \pmod{\Phi_p(X)}$*
 - *and $\|h(X)\|_\infty \le p - 1$.*

---

[11] For $k > 1$, the ring $\mathbb{Z}_{2^k}[X]/\Phi_{2^m}(X)$ never split into a product of smaller rings, resulting low packing density (see the full version).

Proof. (a) Let $\tilde{a}(X) \in \mathbb{Z}[X]$ be the representative of $a(X)$ with the minimal degree. When reduced modulo (X^p-1), every monomials of $\tilde{a}(X) \cdot X^i$ are reduced to distinct-degree monomials preserving the coefficients. Let us denote the ℓ-th coefficient of $(\tilde{a}(X) \cdot X^i \bmod (X^p - 1))$ as $\tilde{a}_\ell^{(i)}$. Applying modulo $\Phi_p(X)$ to $(\tilde{a}(X) \cdot X^i \bmod (X^p-1))$, the ℓ-th coefficients of $(\tilde{a}(X) \cdot X^i \bmod \Phi_p(X))$ equals $(\tilde{a}_\ell^{(i)} - \tilde{a}_{(p-1)}^{(i)})$, and the inequality $||a \cdot X^i||_\infty \le 2||a||_\infty$ follows.

(b) Consider the following polynomial in $\mathbb{Z}[X]$.

$$v(X) := \frac{\Phi_p(X) - p}{X - 1} = \sum_{k=0}^{p-1} (p - 1 - k) \cdot X^k$$

We claim that $\tilde{h}(X) := -X^{p-j} \cdot v(X^{i-j}) \in \mathbb{Z}[X]$ satisfies the conditions after being reduced by $\Phi_p(X)$. By definition, the first condition can be easily checked with the fact that $\Phi_p(X)$ divides $\Phi_p(X^{i-j})$ since p does not divide $(i - j)$.

Since p does not divide $(i-j)$, when reduced modulo (X^p-1), every monomials of $\tilde{h}(X)$ are reduced to distinct-degree monomials with coefficients remaining in the interval $[1-p, 0]$. Let us denote the ℓ-th coefficient of $(\tilde{h}(X) \;(\bmod\; (X^p-1)))$ as $\tilde{h}_\ell \in [1-p, 0]$. Applying modulo $\Phi_p(X)$ to $(\tilde{h}(X) \;(\bmod\; (X^p-1)))$, the ℓ-th coefficients of $(\tilde{h}(X) \;(\bmod\; \Phi_p(X)))$ equals $(\tilde{h}_\ell - \tilde{h}_{(p-1)})$. Certainly, $(\tilde{h}_\ell - \tilde{h}_{(p-1)})$ lies in the interval of $[1-p, p-1]$. Thus, the inequality $||\tilde{h}(X) \;(\bmod\; \Phi_p(X))||_\infty \le p-1$ holds. □

5.2   TopGear2k: Better ZKPoPK over $\mathbb{Z}[X]/\Phi_p(X)$

We describe our ZKPoPK protocol named TopGear2k for BGV ciphertexts with prime cyclotomic rings $\mathbb{Z}[X]/\Phi_p(X)$. In a high level, our ZKPoPK is a batched Schnorr-like protocol as those of SPDZ-family [17,22,23].

ZKPoPK Framewok—Schnorr-Like Protocol with Predicates. We first introduce the ZKPoPK framework of SPDZ-family which proceeds as the standard *batched* Schnorr-like protocols [13] to prove that the underlying plaintext satisfies a certain predicate. While our protocol (Fig. 4) follows the *global* proof style of Overdrive [22] for efficiency, we describe in *per-party* proof style of SPDZ [17] for simplicity.

To prove that a plaintext vector $\boldsymbol{a} = (a_i)_{i=1}^u, (a_i \in R := \mathbb{Z}[X]/\Phi_M(X))$ of input ciphertexts $\mathfrak{ct}_{\boldsymbol{a}} = (\mathsf{Enc}(a_i))_{i=1}^u$ satisfy a given predicate $\mathsf{P} : R \to \{\mathsf{true}, \mathsf{false}\}$[12], the prover publishes a vector of masking ciphertexts $\mathfrak{ct}_{\boldsymbol{y}}$ for a plaintext vector $\boldsymbol{y} \in R^v$ satisfying P. Then, after the verifier queries a challenge matrix $W \in R^{v \times u}$, the prover publishes a plaintext vector $\boldsymbol{z} \in R^v$ with which the verifier checks if $\mathsf{P}(\boldsymbol{z}) = \mathsf{true}$ and $\mathfrak{ct}_{\boldsymbol{y}} + W \cdot \mathfrak{ct}_{\boldsymbol{a}} = \mathfrak{ct}_{\boldsymbol{z}}$. The prover/verifier do similar proofs/checks on the randomnesses required in the encryptions.

---

[12] The predicate, for example, can capture the boundedness of the sizes of plaintext and randomnesses, or the correctness of packing (Definition 1).

Then, the usual rewinding argument guarantees that the elements of $\boldsymbol{a}$ also satisfy P as follows: by inverting the equation on plaintexts $(W - \overline{W}) \cdot \boldsymbol{a} = \boldsymbol{z} - \bar{\boldsymbol{z}}$ derived from the two accepting transcripts with different challenge matrices W and $\overline{W}$, we deduce that $\boldsymbol{a}$ also satisfies the predicate P given that $\mathsf{P}(\boldsymbol{z}) = \mathsf{P}(\bar{\boldsymbol{z}}) = \mathsf{true}$. Note, for this argument to work, two conditions are required: (a) the difference $(W - \overline{W})$ should satisfy some types of *invertibility*, so that one can derive, e.g., $\boldsymbol{a} = (W - \overline{W})^{-1} \cdot (\boldsymbol{z} - \bar{\boldsymbol{z}})$, (b) the predicate should be *homomorphic* under (additions and) multiplications by challenge matrices W (and also by *pseudo-inverses* of their differences), i.e. $\mathsf{P}(\boldsymbol{a}) = \mathsf{true} \implies \mathsf{P}(W \cdot \boldsymbol{a}) = \mathsf{true}$ (and similarly for the pseudo-inverse).

Here, the difficulty is to identify a *nice* challenge space, where the elements of W are sampled from, which meets all of the above conditions. In the previous works [17,22,23], the challenge space is restricted to the set $\{0, 1\}$ (and the form of W was also restricted) to satisfy the above conditions. In this case, however, v (the size of masking ciphertext vector) should be as large as the soundness security parameter, leading to substantial inefficiency.

TopGear Review. TopGear [2] offers the most efficient ZKPoPK among the line of works [17,22] exploiting (S)HE to MPC over finite fields with power-of-two cyclotomic rings. It is also a batched Schnorr-like protocol (described above) with global proof approach. The essence of their work is to use a *larger challenge space* $\mathsf{Chal} = \{X^j\}_{j=1}^{2^m} \cup \{0\}$ than $\{0, 1\}$ of the other previous works. This is an adaptation of the nice properties (Sect. 5.1) of power-of-two cyclotomic ring $\mathbb{Z}[X]/\Phi_{2^m}(X)$ from [5] to the ZKPoPK framework, and is desirable in communication cost, latency, and memory consumption.

Extending the result of TopGear to other cyclotomic polynomials, however, was an open problem, e.g., Overdrive2k [23] exploited a rather small challenge space of $\{0, 1\}$, mentioning that "TopGear improvements cannot be applied directly" to their work.

TopGear2k: Our ZKPoPK over $\mathbb{Z}[X]/\Phi_p(X)$. Following the above framework, we propose ZKPoPK named TopGear2k which is a batched Schnorr-like protocol with global proofs, working over prime cyclotomic rings $\mathbb{Z}[X]/\Phi_M(X)$ ($M = p$ is a prime[13]) with larger challenge space $\mathsf{Chal} = \{X^j\}_{j=1}^M \cup \{0\}$, adapting Lemma 4. Our ZKPoPK is a prime cyclotomic ring analogue of the ZKPoPK of TopGear [2] over power-of-two cyclotomic rings. The full description of our ZKPoPK protocol TopGear2k ($\Pi_{\mathsf{PoPK}}^{\mathsf{TG2k}}$) is given in Fig. 4.

Our TopGear2k aims to prove that the given ciphertexts are generated with appropriate sizes of a plaintext and randomnesses. If all parties run Sampling honestly, then the outputs satisfy the following relation:

---

[13] We denote p as the smallest prime factor of M. This is to consider the general case of $M = p^s$ and $M = p^s q^t$ in Sect. 5.4.

Protocol $\Pi_{\mathsf{PoPK}}^{\mathsf{TG2k}}$

PARAMETERS:
- ZK_sec: the zero-knowledge security parameter.
- 2^t: the plaintext modulus.
- u: the number of ciphertexts to be verified in one protocol execution.
- v: the number of masking ciphertexts (related to soundness probability).
- n: the number of participating parties P_i ($i \in [n]$).

Sampling$_i$ (Sampling phase for the ith party P_i)

1. For each $k \in [u]$ do
   (a) Choose a plaintext $a_k^i \in \mathbb{Z}_{2^t}[X]/\Phi_M(X)$ and proper randomness $(r_{a_k}^{(i)})$. [14]
   (b) Compute a ciphertext $\mathsf{ct}_{a_k}^i = \mathsf{Enc}(a_k^i, r_{a_k}^i; \mathfrak{pe})$.
2. Let $\mathsf{ct}_a^i = (\mathsf{ct}_{a_1}^i, \mathsf{ct}_{a_2}^i, \ldots, \mathsf{ct}_{a_u}^i)$, $a^i = (a_1^i, a_2^i, \ldots, a_u^i)$, and $r_a^i = (r_{a_1}^i, r_{a_2}^i, \ldots, r_{a_u}^i)$.
3. Output $(\mathsf{ct}_a^i, a^i, r_a^i)$.

Commit (Commitment phase)

1. To generate v masking ciphertexts, each party P_i do the followings, for each $l \in [v]$.
   (a) P_i samples $y_l^i \leftarrow \mathcal{U}(2^{\mathsf{ZK\_sec}} \cdot 2^{t-1})$ and $r_{y_l}^i = (r_{y_l}^{i,(\ell)} \leftarrow \mathcal{U}(2^{\mathsf{ZK\_sec}} \cdot \rho_\ell))_{\ell \in [3]}$.
   (b) P_i computes $\mathsf{ct}_{y_l}^i = \mathsf{Enc}(y_l^i, r_{y_l}^i; \mathfrak{pe})$.
2. Party P_i keeps $\mathsf{state}_i = (y^i, r_y^i)$ where $y^i = (y_l^i)_{l \in [v]}$ and $r_y^i = (r_{y_l}^i)_{l \in [v]}$.
3. Party P_i broadcasts $\mathsf{comm}_i = \mathsf{ct}_y^i$ where $\mathsf{ct}_y^i = (\mathsf{ct}_{y_l}^i)_{l \in [v]}$.

Challenge (Challenge phase)

1. Parties together randomly sample challenge matrix W of size $v \times u$, whose entries are sampled from the challenge space $\mathsf{Chal} = \{X^j\}_{j=1}^M \cup \{0\}$.

Response (Response phase)

1. Each party P_i computes $z^i = y^i + W \cdot a^i$ and $r_z^i = r_y^i + W \cdot r_a^i$. [15]
2. Party P_i sets $\mathsf{resp}_i = (z^i, r_z^i)$ and broadcasts resp_i.

Verify (Verification phase)

1. Each party P_i computes,
   (a) $\mathsf{ct}_z^i = (\mathsf{Enc}(z_l^i, r_{z_l}^i; \mathfrak{pe}))_{l \in [v]}$.
   (b) $\mathsf{ct}_a = \sum_{i=1}^n \mathsf{ct}_a^i$, $\mathsf{ct}_y = \sum_{i=1}^n \mathsf{ct}_y^i$, $\mathsf{ct}_z = \sum_{i=1}^n \mathsf{ct}_z^i$.
   (c) $z = \sum_{i=1}^n z^i$, $r_z = \sum_{i=1}^n r_z^i$.
2. Parties accept if all of the followings hold, otherwise they reject.
   (a) $\mathsf{ct}_z = \mathsf{ct}_y + W \cdot \mathsf{ct}_a$.
   (b) For $l \in [v]$,

   $$||z_l||_\infty \leq n \cdot 2^{\mathsf{ZK\_sec}} \cdot 2^t, \quad ||r_{z_l}^{(\ell)}||_\infty \leq n \cdot 2^{\mathsf{ZK\_sec}+1} \cdot \rho_\ell \text{ for } \ell \in [3]. \quad (2)$$

---

[14] Sample $(r^{(1)}, r^{(2)}, r^{(3)})$ where $r^{(1)}, r^{(2)} \leftarrow \mathsf{DG}(\sigma^2)$ and $r^{(3)} \leftarrow \mathsf{ZO}(\rho)$ (Section 2.2).
[15] This means that $r_z^{i,(\ell)} = r_y^{i,(\ell)} + W \cdot r_a^{i,(\ell)}$ for each $\ell \in [3]$.

Fig. 4. Protocol $\Pi_{\mathsf{PoPK}}^{\mathsf{TG2k}}$

$$\mathcal{R}_{\mathsf{PoPK}}^u := \left\{ \mathsf{input} \left(\left\{ \left(\mathsf{ct}_{a_k}^i \right)_{i=1}^n \right\}_{k \in [u]}, \mathfrak{pk} \right), \mathsf{witness} \left(\left\{ \left(a_k^i, r_k^i \right)_{i=1}^n \right\}_{k \in [u]} \right) : \right.$$

$$\text{For all } k \in [u], \quad \mathsf{ct}_{a_k} = \sum_{i=1}^n \mathsf{ct}_{a_k}^i, \ a_k = \sum_{i=1}^n a_k^i, \ r_k = \sum_{i=1}^n r_k^i,$$

$$\left. \mathsf{ct}_{a_k} = \mathsf{Enc}(a_k, r_k; \mathfrak{pk}), \|a_k\|_\infty \le n \cdot 2^{t-1}, \|r_k^{(j)}\|_\infty \le n\rho_j \ (\forall j \in [3]) \right\},$$

where $\rho_1 = \rho_2 = 20$, and $\rho_3 = 1$ are the bound of noises and randomnesses, while 2^t is the plaintext modulus.

However, our protocol only guarantees that the given ciphertexts $\{\mathsf{ct}_k\}_{k \in [u]}$ satisfies the following relation $\mathcal{R}_{\mathsf{PoPK}}^{S,u}$ which is relaxed from $\mathcal{R}_{\mathsf{PoPK}}^u$:

$$\mathcal{R}_{\mathsf{PoPK}}^{S,u} := \left\{ \text{the same input and witness as } \mathcal{R}_{\mathsf{PoPK}}^u : \right.$$

$$\text{For all } k \in [u], \quad \mathsf{ct}_{a_k}, a_k, r_k \text{ are defined the same as } \mathcal{R}_{\mathsf{PoPK}}^u, \tag{2}$$
$$\mathsf{ct}_{a_k} = \mathsf{Enc}(a_k, r_k; \mathfrak{pk}),$$

$$\left. \|a_k\|_\infty \le nS \cdot 2^{t-1}, \|r_k^{(j)}\|_\infty \le nS\rho_j \ (\forall j \in [3]) \right\},$$

where S is called a *soundness slack*. This soundness slack S comes from the rewinding process and appears also in the previous ZKPoPKs [2,17,22,23] for MPC and ZKPs for lattice encryptions [5]. Meanwhile, it is standard to design the (S)HE-based MPC preprocessing phase so that it runs correctly even with the soundness slack, e.g., by enlarging the ciphertext modulus.

5.3 Correctness, Zero-Knowledge, and Soundness

We show that $\Pi_{\mathsf{PoPK}}^{\mathsf{TG2k}}$ satisfies the correctness, soundness, and zero-knowledge properties. For correctness, it suffices to show that honest inputs pass the checks in line 2 of Verify algorithm, which can be done by setting the parameters considering Lemma 4(a).

Theorem 4 (Correctness). *The n-party ZKPoPK protocol $\Pi_{\mathsf{PoPK}}^{\mathsf{TG2k}}$ (Fig. 4) with $u \le 2^{\mathsf{ZK\_sec}-1}$ satisfies the following Correctness:*

- *If all parties P_i, with inputs sampled using Sampling algorithm, follow the protocol honestly, then Verify algorithm outputs accept with probability one.*

Proof. The correctness of the equality check (a) in line 2 of Verify is trivial. For the bound checks (b), let $(W)_l \cdot \boldsymbol{a}^i$ denotes the innerproduct between the l-th row of W and the vector $\boldsymbol{a}^i$. Then, by the equality $\boldsymbol{z}^i = \boldsymbol{y}^i + W \cdot \boldsymbol{a}^i$ and Lemma 4(a),

$$\|z_l\|_\infty = \|\sum_{i=1}^n z_l^i\|_\infty \le \sum_{i=1}^n \|y_l^i + (W)_l \cdot \boldsymbol{a}^i\|_\infty$$

$$\le n \cdot (2^{\mathsf{ZK\_sec}} \cdot \frac{2^t}{2} + u \cdot 2 \cdot \frac{2^t}{2}) \le n \cdot 2^{\mathsf{ZK\_sec}} \cdot 2^t,$$

where the final inequality follows from our assumption $u \leq 2^{\mathsf{ZK\_sec}-1}$. The bound on $r_{z_l}^{(\ell)}$ can be proved similarly. □

Zero-knowledgeness essentially follows from the fact that the $\boldsymbol{y}^i$'s in protocol $\Pi_{\mathsf{PoPK}}^{\mathsf{TG2k}}$ can statistically mask the responses with Lemma 3.

Theorem 5 (Zero-Knowledge). *The* n-party ZKPoPK *protocol* $\Pi_{\mathsf{PoPK}}^{\mathsf{TG2k}}$ *(Fig. 4) satisfies the following **Honest-verifier Zero-knowledge**:*

– *There exists a PPT algorithm* $S_{I'}$ *indexed by a (honest) set* $I' \subset [n]$, *which takes as input an element in* $\mathcal{R}_{\mathsf{PoPK}}^u$ *and a challenge* W, *and outputs tuples* $\{\mathsf{comm}_i, \mathsf{resp}_i\}_{i \in I'}$ *such that this output is statistically indistinguishable from a valid execution of the protocol (with statistical distance* $\leq 8Muv/2^{\mathsf{ZK\_sec}}$).

Proof. Let the simulator $S_{I'}$ output resp_i by sampling each component from the uniform distribution with sufficiently large bound, e.g., sample $\boldsymbol{z}^i = (z_l^i)_{l \in [v]}$ where $z_l^i \leftarrow \mathcal{U}(2^{\mathsf{ZK\_sec}} \cdot 2^{t-1})$. Then it outputs comm_i by computing each component from the challenge W and corresponding input ciphertexts, e.g., $\mathsf{ct}_y^i = \mathsf{Enc}(\boldsymbol{z}^i, r_z^i; \mathsf{pk}) - W \cdot \mathsf{ct}_a^i$.

Note that the statistical distance between the simulated and the real execution is determined by that between the distribution of resp_i in both executions (since each comm_i is computed in the same way from resp_i). In the real execution, $\boldsymbol{z}^i$ is computed by sampling $\boldsymbol{y}^i$ and adding $W \cdot \boldsymbol{a}^i$. Thus, Lemma 3 (without P) gives that the distance between $\boldsymbol{z}^i$ from both executions are bounded by $\varphi(M)\frac{\|(W)_l \cdot \boldsymbol{a}^i\|_\infty}{2^{\mathsf{ZK\_sec}} \cdot 2^{t-1}} \cdot \leq \frac{2Mu}{2^{\mathsf{ZK\_sec}}}$, and similar results hold for r_z^i. □

Finally, the soundness of $\Pi_{\mathsf{PoPK}}^{\mathsf{TG2k}}$ follows from the usual rewinding argument leveraging Lemma 4(b) on invertibility.

Theorem 6 (Soundness). *Assume that the* n-party ZKPoPK *protocol* $\Pi_{\mathsf{PoPK}}^{\mathsf{TG2k}}$ *(Fig. 4) is parameterized with* $v \geq (\mathsf{Snd\_sec} + 2)/\log(|\mathsf{Chal}|)$ *where* $\mathsf{Snd\_sec}$ *is the soundness security parameter and* $|\mathsf{Chal}|$ *is the size of the challenge space. Then, it satisfies the **Soundness** (see [2, Definition 1]) with soundness probability* $2^{-\mathsf{Snd\_sec}}$ *and slack* $S = 8\varphi(M) \cdot 2^{\mathsf{ZK\_sec}}$.

Proof. The proof mostly resembles that of [2, Theorem 1], and we give detailed description focusing on the unique aspects of our protocol. With a usual rewinding argument (we refer to [2, Theorem 1] for formal description of an extractor), an extractor can output $(W, \{\boldsymbol{z}^i, r_z^i\}_{i=1}^n)$ and $(\overline{W}, \{\bar{\boldsymbol{z}}^i, \bar{r}_z^i\}_{i=1}^n)$, which are two accepting transcripts corresponding to ct_a and ct_y such that W and $\overline{W}$ are identical except k-th column. Let $\boldsymbol{z} := \sum_{i=1}^n \boldsymbol{z}^i$ and similarly for r_z, $\bar{\boldsymbol{z}}$, $\bar{r}_z$. Then, since these values satisfy the equation at line 2(a) of Verify algorithm (Fig. 4) and ciphertexts have homomorphic property, we get $\boldsymbol{z} = \boldsymbol{y} + W \cdot \boldsymbol{a}$ and $\bar{\boldsymbol{z}} = \boldsymbol{y} + \overline{W} \cdot \boldsymbol{a}$. With subtraction, since W and $\overline{W}$ are identical except k-th column, we get,

$$z_l - \bar{z}_l = (w_{l,k} - \bar{w}_{l,k}) \cdot a_k \text{ for some } l \in [v],$$

where $w_{l,k}$ and $\bar{w}_{l,k}$ are entries of W and $\overline{W}$ and are from $\{X^j\}_{j=1}^M$. Thus, multiplying $h(X)$ (of Lemma 4 (b)) according to $(w_{l,k} - \bar{w}_{l,k})$ on both sides, we get

$$\|p \cdot a_k\|_\infty = \|h(X) \cdot (z_{1,l} - \bar{z}_{1,l})\|_\infty \leq 2 \cdot \varphi(M) \cdot \|h(X)\|_\infty \cdot \|z_{1,l} - \bar{z}_{1,l}\|_\infty$$
$$\leq 2 \cdot \varphi(M) \cdot (p-1) \cdot \|z_{1,l} - \bar{z}_{1,l}\|_\infty$$
$$\leq 2 \cdot \varphi(M) \cdot (p-1) \cdot 2 \left(n \cdot 2^{\mathsf{ZK\_sec}} \cdot 2^t \right).$$

The first inequality follows by regarding $h(X)$ as sum of monomials then applying Lemma 4 (a). The second inequality is obtained by the definition of $h(X)$ (Lemma 4 (b)). The last inequality follows from Eq. (2) (Fig. 4). Hence, $\|a_k\|_\infty \leq nS \cdot 2^{t-1}$ with the desired soundness slack $S = 8\varphi(M) \cdot 2^{\mathsf{ZK\_sec}}$. Similarly, one can derive the bound and slackness on the r_{a_k} from $r_z, \bar{r}_z$ in the transcripts.   □

5.4   Extension to $\Phi_{p^s}(X)$ and $\Phi_{p^s q^t}(X)$

In fact, we can extend our ZKPoPK to work over cyclotomic polynomials $\Phi_M(X)$ with $M = p^s$ or $M = p^s q^t$ where p, q are primes satisfying $p < q$ and s, t are positive integers. Then, we can increase the packing density of our packing by taking cyclotomic polynomials of composites into consideration, which allow parameters with smaller $d = \mathrm{ord}_M(2)$ (see Sect. 3.3).

These follow from the results of [11] which are generalization of Lemma 4 to the cases with $M = p^s$ or $M = p^s q^t$. Then, in both cases of $\Phi_{p^s}(X)$ and $\Phi_{p^s q^t}(X)$, the protocol $\Pi_{\mathsf{PoPK}}^{\mathsf{TG2k}}$ is exactly the same with the prime case. In the case of p^s, the statements and the proofs of Theorem 4, 5, 6 also stay exactly the same. (We carefully distinguished the role of M and p for this.) In the case of $p^s q^t$, the major changes are the followings: the condition on u in Theorem 4 is $u \leq 2^{\mathsf{ZK\_sec}-1}/p$, the statistical distance in Theorem 5 is bounded by $8pMuv/2^{\mathsf{ZK\_sec}}$, and the soundness slack in Theorem 6 is $S = 8p^2 M \cdot 2^{\mathsf{ZK\_sec}}$.

6   Zero-Knowledge Proof of Message Knowledge

In SHE with messages from a finite field $\mathbb{Z}_P$, the plaintext space $\mathbb{Z}_P[X]/\Phi_{2^m}(X)$ can be taken to be *isomorphic* to $\mathbb{Z}_P^{\varphi(2^m)}$, a product of message spaces. When we deal with messages from $\mathbb{Z}_{2^k}$, however, the plaintext space $\mathbb{Z}_{2^t}[X]/\Phi_M(X)$ is never isomorphic to a product of $\mathbb{Z}_{2^k}$'s. It is inevitable that some plaintexts do not correspond to any packing of messages. Thus, we must be guaranteed, in MPC preprocessings for $\mathbb{Z}_{2^k}$-messages, that each party encrypted a *valid* plaintext according to a specific packing method, in addition to the guarantee of valid encryption. This is an intricacy of the $\mathbb{Z}_{2^k}$-case that differs from the $\mathbb{Z}_P$-case where ZKPoPK (for the guarantee of valid encryption) is sufficient [2,17,22].

Therefore, we propose, in addition to ZKPoPK, a Zero-Knowledge Proof of Message Knowledge (ZKPoMK) which guarantees that the given ciphertext is generated with a plaintext which is a *valid encoding* with respect to our tweaked interpolation packing (Sect. 3).[16]

6.1   ZKPoMK for Tweaked Interpolation Packing

As our ZKPoPK, our ZKPoMK is a batched Schnorr-like protocol with predicates, and it proceeds similarly but with appropriate challenge spaces for the predicates which capture the valid plaintexts of our packing method. Since most parts of our ZKPoMK are similar to the ZKPoPK, here we only give an overview and refer to the full version for the detailed description.

Overview of Our ZKPoMK. Recall the predicates (Definition 1) presented in Sect. 3.4 and that $a \in R$ is a valid plaintext, i.e. a tweaked interpolation of Theorem 1, if and only if, for $D = \lfloor \frac{d-1}{2} \rfloor$, $\Delta = \delta$, and $T = t$,

$$\mathsf{Pack}_T^{(D,\Delta)}(a) \iff \mathsf{Deg}_T^{(D)}(a) \wedge \mathsf{Div}_T^{(D,\Delta)}(a).$$

Our ZKPoMK separately proves those two statements (i) $\mathsf{Deg}_T^{(D)}(a) = \mathsf{true}$ and (ii) $\mathsf{Div}_T^{(D,\Delta)}(a) = \mathsf{true}$ as follows.

For the statement (i), we run the same as our $\Pi_{\mathsf{PoPK}}^{\mathsf{TG2k}}$ (Fig. 4) but with two modifications: (1) set the predicate $\mathsf{P} = \mathsf{Pack}_T^{(D,\Delta)}$ then sample the masks y_l^i from $\mathcal{U}_{\mathsf{P}}(2^{\mathsf{ZK\_sec}} \cdot 2^{t-1})$ using Corollary 2 and check if $\mathsf{P}(z_l) = \mathsf{true}$, instead of the bound check on it; (2) set the challenge space $\mathsf{Chal} = [-2^E + 1, 2^E] \cap \mathbb{Z}$ for a positive integer E. Note that these *constants* from the challenge space *preserve* the degree of given element a when multiplied, giving the key equation for the rewinding argument (and the soundness), while *enlarging* the challenge space. We remark that this approach introduces a new type of *slackness* which will be described later in this section.

For the statement (ii), a prover provides a' such that $\mathsf{DivCheck}_T^{(D,\Delta)}(a, a') = \mathsf{true}$ (see Definition 1), or very roughly, $a' = a/2^\Delta$. For zero-knowledgeness, a' must be provided as a ciphertext $\hat{\mathfrak{ct}}_{a'}$ with the proof that $\hat{\mathfrak{ct}}_{a'}$ is generated correctly as well. Then, the parties (simultaneously) execute Schnorr-like protocol on $\mathfrak{ct}_{a'}$ with the same challenge matrix W from the above proof on $\mathfrak{ct}_a$ for the statement (i) and the masks $y_l'^i$ such that $\mathsf{DivCheck}_T^{(D,\Delta)}(y_l^i, y_l'^i) = \mathsf{true}$. Then verifiers check if $\mathsf{DivCheck}_T^{(D,\Delta)}(z, z') = \mathsf{true}$ from which one can derive $\mathsf{DivCheck}_T^{(D,\Delta)}(a, a') = \mathsf{true}$ with a rewinding argument (see the full version).

A caveat here is that we *cannot* use tweaked interpolation packing for $\hat{\mathfrak{ct}}_{a'}$: a factor of 2^T will also arise in the tweaked interpolation packing for $\hat{\mathfrak{ct}}_{a'}$; and we again need ZKPoMK on $\hat{\mathfrak{ct}}_{a'}$ to check that it is encoded correctly.

The key observation for our solution is that $\hat{\mathfrak{ct}}_{a'}$ (in contrasts to $\mathfrak{ct}_a$) does not need to satisfy multiplicative homomorphism (on message space) since it is only

---

[16] Overdrive2k [23] performs ZKPoMK implicitly in their ZKPoPK. If we set $\mathsf{Chal} = \{0, 1\}$ as their ZKPoPK, our ZKPoMK can also be integrated into ZKPoPK (by additionally checking if z is a valid encoding), resulting in our MHz2k-Plain protocol.

used in ZKPoMK for $\mathfrak{ct}_a$, which requires linear homomorphism only. Therefore, we exploit coefficient packing (i.e., each message is encoded as each coefficient of a') for $\hat{\mathfrak{ct}}_{a'}$,[17] which makes ZKPoPK $\Pi_{\mathsf{PoPK}}^{\mathsf{TG2k}}$ (without any ZKPoMK) suffices to guarantee that $\hat{\mathfrak{ct}}_{a'}$ is correctly encoded. As a bonus, we can use considerably smaller parameters for $\hat{\mathfrak{ct}}_{a'}$, providing almost perfect packing density and resulting better efficiency.

A New Type of Slackness. We now describe the new type of slackness arises from our ZKPoMK Π_{PoMK}. If all parties run Sampling honestly, then the outputs satisfy the following relation:

$$\mathcal{R}_{\mathsf{PoMK}}^{u,\mathsf{Pack}} := \big\{\text{the same input and witness as } \mathcal{R}_{\mathsf{PoPK}}^u :$$
$$\text{For all } k \in [u], \quad \mathsf{Pack}_T^{(D,\Delta)}(a_k) = \mathsf{true}\big\}$$

Note that, however, a verifier *cannot* be guaranteed that $\mathsf{Deg}_T^{(D)}(a_k) = \mathsf{true}$ with our ZKPoMK (for the statement (i) in above). This is because, in the rewinding argument, $\mathsf{Deg}_T^{(D)}((w_{l,k} - \bar{w}_{l,k}) \cdot a_k) = \mathsf{true}$ can occur even with $\mathsf{Deg}_T^{(D)}(a_k) = \mathsf{false}$, since there is a possibility of some non-zero coefficients of a_k becoming zero when multiplied by $(w_{l,k} - \bar{w}_{l,k})$. However, since the difference $w_{l,k} - \bar{w}_{l,k}$ of elements from the challenge space $\mathsf{Chal} = [-2^E + 1, 2^E] \cap \mathbb{Z}$ is at most divisible by 2^E, our ZKPoMK protocol can only guarantee that the given ciphertexts $\{\mathfrak{ct}_k\}_{k \in [u]}$ satisfies the following relation $\mathcal{R}_{\mathsf{PoMK}}^{u,\mathsf{Pack\_sl}}$ which is relaxed from $\mathcal{R}_{\mathsf{PoMK}}^{u,\mathsf{Pack}}$:

$$\mathcal{R}_{\mathsf{PoMK}}^{u,\mathsf{Pack\_sl}} := \{\text{the same input and witness as } \mathcal{R}_{\mathsf{PoPK}}^u :$$
$$\text{For all } k \in [u], \quad \mathsf{Pack\_sl}_T(a_k) = \mathsf{true}\},$$

where the predicate $\mathsf{Pack\_sl} : R \to \{\mathsf{true}, \mathsf{false}\}$ is defined as follows (see Sect. 3.4 for comparison with the original predicates). For $a \in R$, let $(\tilde{a}_i)_{i=1}^r$ denote the CRT projections (Eq. (1)) of $\tilde{a} = a \pmod{2^T}$.

- $\mathsf{Pack\_sl}_T^{(D,\Delta,E)}(a) = \mathsf{true} \iff \mathsf{Deg\_sl}_T^{(D,E)}(a) = \mathsf{true} \quad \wedge \quad \mathsf{Div}_T^{(D,\Delta)}(a) = \mathsf{true}.$
- $\mathsf{Deg\_sl}_T^{(D,E)}(a) = \mathsf{true} \iff$ All CRT projections $\tilde{a}_i$ of a satisfy that

  coefficients at $\deg > D$ are divisible by 2^{T-E}.

While the soundness slack S of ZKPoPK appeared also in the previous literature, above *slackness* represented by the predicate $\mathsf{Pack\_sl}$ is a unique feature of our ZKPoMK protocol.

6.2 Managing the Slackness in MPC Preprocessing

In this subsection, we clarify that the new type of slackness which arises in our ZKPoMK can be managed, i.e., that the guarantee of ZKPoMK is sufficient for the MPC preprocessing phase (Sect. 2.5).

---

[17] This is why we denoted it as $\hat{\mathfrak{ct}}_{a'}$ (not $\mathfrak{ct}_{a'}$) and DivCheck is defined in such a way.

The idea is to reserve an extra space in the plaintext modulus for the slackness E: for $\mathbb{Z}_{2^k}$-messages, we apply the tweaked interpolation packing (Theorem 1) with $t = E + k + 2\delta$ instead of $t = k + 2\delta$ (Theorem 2)[18].

Let $\mathfrak{ct}_a$ be a ciphertext encrypting $a(X)$, which passed the verification of our ZKPoMK parameterized by $D = \lfloor \frac{d-1}{2} \rfloor$, $\Delta = \delta$, $T = t$, and E. For simplicity, we assume that the plaintext space $\mathbb{Z}_{2^T}[X]/\Phi_M(X)$ does not split. Since $\mathsf{Pack\_sl}_T^{(D,\Delta,E)}(a) = \mathsf{true}$ and $T - E = k + 2\delta$, we can regard $a(X) \pmod{2^{T-E}}$ as a tweaked interpolation packing of $\mathbb{Z}_{2^k}$-messages in $\mathbb{Z}_{2^{k+2\delta}}[X]/\Phi_M(X)$ as before. The only thing we have to make sure is that, when performing the distributed decryption, the upper E bits do not leak any information about the plaintexts. This can be done trivially by masking the upper E bits in the distributed decryption.

7 Performance Analysis

In this section, we analyze the performance of our MHz2k with comparison to other works in the literature. We can summarize the improvements by our packing (Sect. 3) and reshare protocol (Sect. 4) as follows: (i) Our tweaked interpolation packing achieves near $1/2$ packing density, 2.5x compared to $1/5$ of Overdrive2k [23], (ii) Our reshare protocol requires only 5 ZKPoPKs which is 1.4x less than 7 ZKPoPKs of Overdrive2k. In total, we can expect that the amortized communication costs of MHz2k-Plain (without the Topgear2k optimization) will show 3.5x improvements from Overdrive2k.

On the other hand, how our ZKPoPK and ZKPoMK (Sect. 5, 6) affect the performance in MHz2k is a bit more involved. In the following subsection we provide a brief cost analysis on our ZKPs.

7.1   Cost Analysis on ZKPoPK and ZKPoMK

The communication cost of ZKPoPK and ZKPoMK *per party* can be estimated by the size of ciphertexts arise in protocols, which dominates the others. Excluding the u input ciphertexts $\mathfrak{ct}_a^i$, using our ZKPoPK and ZKPoMK, there arise additional u ciphertexts $\hat{\mathfrak{ct}}_{a'}^i$, $2v$ masking ciphertexts $\mathfrak{ct}_y^i$, and $2v$ masking ciphertexts $\hat{\mathfrak{ct}}_{y'}^i$. Assuming that $u = 2v$ (as in Topgear [2]) and that the size of $\hat{\mathfrak{ct}}$ is a half of that of $\mathfrak{ct}$, we can conclude that the total cost is roughly $2u \cdot |\mathfrak{ct}|$ in ZKPoPK and ZKPoMK on u input ciphertexts $\mathfrak{ct}_a^i$.

On the other hand, following the approach of Overdrive2k [23], MHz2k can also be initiated with the challenge space of $\{0,1\}$ without TopGear2k optimization, which we call MHz2k-Plain. In this case, while the challenge space is restricted to $\{0,1\}$, it requires only *one* Schnorr-like protocol (contrary to *four* in our case) but with $v = 2u - 1$. Hence, the size of masking ciphertexts $\mathfrak{ct}_y^i$ will be roughly $2u \cdot |\mathfrak{ct}|$, and in *amortized* sense, the communication cost does not differ

---

[18] Our ZKPoMK does not produce the slackness when $E = 0$. An appropriate $E > 0$ enlarges the challenge space in a cost of only a slight reduction in the packing density.

Table 1. Amortized communication (in kbit) of producing triples (2PC)

(k, s)	SPDZ$_{2^k}$	MonZ$_{2^k}$a	Overdrive2k	MHz2k Plain	MHz2k TG2k $(u = 2v)$	MHz2k TG2k $(u = 4v)$
(32,32)	79.9	59.1	101.8 (72.8)	27.2	26.4	**20.1**
(64,64)	319.5	175.5	171.4 (153.3)	46.2	43.3	**31.9**
(128,64)	557.1	176.6	190.4 (212.2)	56.6	55.0	**40.9**

seriously between the case with TopGear2k and without it. The main advantage of our TopGear2k with ZKPoMK (similarly as TopGear [2] to [17,22,23]) is that u can be chosen much smaller than that of ZKPoPK of [17,22,23] where u is forced to be as large as statistical security parameter at least. This contributes to the substantial reduction of latency and memory requirement (Table 2). Moreover, since there is a trade-off between amortized communication cost versus latency and memory requirement along the choice of u, we can shift the improvements to the amortized communication cost.

7.2 Comparison

For comparison, we present the communication costs of our schemes and previous works. Though we restrict our discussion to secure two-party computation (2PC), similar efficiency improvements occur in any multi-party case. We refer to the full version for the detailed description on the parameters for our schemes and others. All parameters are set to satisfy 128 bits computational security.

In Table 1, we compare the previous works [10,14,23] and ours with respect to (amortized) communication costs for triple generation. For lattice-based HE approaches (Overdrive2k, MHz2k-Plain, and MHz2k-TG2k), the results are computed from the parameters with more than 128 bits security according to LWE Estimator [1]. For reader's convenience, we also present communication costs of Overdrive2k which are listed in the paper [23] in parentheses[19]. Note that MonZ$_{2^k}$a only provides secure two-party computation, whereas other protocols can be used for general multi-party computation. MHz2k-Plain shows substantial improvements in communication costs from previous works. In particular, we can check that MHz2k-Plain shows roughly 3.5x improvement from Overdrive2k as we predicted in Sect. 7.1. As mentioned, applying TopGear2k technique to MHz2k-Plain does not significantly effect the communication costs, if we choose parameters as $u = 2v$. However, increasing the ratio between u and v, we can further reduce the communication costs utilizing more memory (still, less memory than Overdrive2k).

In Table 2, we compare the memory consumption of SHE-based approaches, which are computed as $(u + v) \cdot 2\varphi(M) \log q$. Applying TopGear2k optimization,

---

[19] Due to the lack of information, it was hard to reproduce the communication costs of Overdrive2k. In particular, their parameters does not seem to achieve 128 bits security if we consider key-switching modulus which is not noted.

Table 2. Memory usage (in MB) of producing triples (2PC)

(k, s)	Overdrive2k	MHz2k-Plain	MHz2k-TG2k $(u = 2v)$	MHz2k-TG2k $(u = 4v)$
(32,32)	272	503	**44**	74
(64,64)	1273	1392	**137**	229
(128,64)	2555	2237	**241**	402

we can significantly reduce the memory consumption. With Table 1, we can also check the trade-off between the amortized communication costs and the memory utilization along the choice of u.

Acknowledgement. In addition to the appreciation on constructive comments of the reviewers of Crypto 2021, the authors express gratitude to the reviewers of Eurocrypt 2021 who provided invaluable comments to improve the earlier version of this paper. The authors also thank Duhyeong Kim, Jiseung Kim, and Yongsoo Song for helpful discussions. This work was supported by Institute of Information & Communications Technology Planning & Evaluation (IITP) grant funded by the Korea government (MSIT) (No.2020-0-00840, Development and Library Implementation of Fully Homomorphic Machine Learning Algorithms supporting Neural Network Learning over Encrypted Data).

References

1. Albrecht, M.R., Player, R., Scott, S.: On the concrete hardness of learning with errors. J. Math. Cryptol. **9**(3), 169–203 (2015)
2. Baum, C., Cozzo, D., Smart, N.P.: Using topgear in overdrive: a more efficient ZKPoK for SPDZ. In: Paterson, K.G., Stebila, D. (eds.) SAC 2019. LNCS, vol. 11959, pp. 274–302. Springer, Cham (2020). https://doi.org/10.1007/978-3-030-38471-5_12
3. Beaver, D.: Efficient multiparty protocols using circuit randomization. In: Feigenbaum, J. (ed.) CRYPTO 1991. LNCS, vol. 576, pp. 420–432. Springer, Heidelberg (1992). https://doi.org/10.1007/3-540-46766-1_34
4. Bendlin, R., Damgård, I., Orlandi, C., Zakarias, S.: Semi-homomorphic encryption and multiparty computation. In: Paterson, K.G. (ed.) EUROCRYPT 2011. LNCS, vol. 6632, pp. 169–188. Springer, Heidelberg (2011). https://doi.org/10.1007/978-3-642-20465-4_11
5. Benhamouda, F., Camenisch, J., Krenn, S., Lyubashevsky, V., Neven, G.: Better zero-knowledge proofs for lattice encryption and their application to group signatures. In: Sarkar, P., Iwata, T. (eds.) ASIACRYPT 2014. LNCS, vol. 8873, pp. 551–572. Springer, Heidelberg (2014). https://doi.org/10.1007/978-3-662-45611-8_29
6. Bogdanov, D., Jõemets, M., Siim, S., Vaht, M.: How the estonian tax and customs board evaluated a tax fraud detection system based on secure multi-party computation. In: Böhme, R., Okamoto, T. (eds.) FC 2015. LNCS, vol. 8975, pp. 227–234. Springer, Heidelberg (2015). https://doi.org/10.1007/978-3-662-47854-7_14

7. Bogetoft, P., et al.: Secure multiparty computation goes live. In: Dingledine, R., Golle, P. (eds.) FC 2009. LNCS, vol. 5628, pp. 325–343. Springer, Heidelberg (2009). https://doi.org/10.1007/978-3-642-03549-4_20

8. Brakerski, Z., Gentry, C., Vaikuntanathan, V.: (Leveled) fully homomorphic encryption without bootstrapping. ACM Trans. Comput. Theory (TOCT) **6**(3), 1–36 (2014)

9. Cascudo, I., Cramer, R., Xing, C., Yuan, C.: Amortized complexity of information-theoretically secure MPC revisited. In: Shacham, H., Boldyreva, A. (eds.) CRYPTO 2018. LNCS, vol. 10993, pp. 395–426. Springer, Cham (2018). https://doi.org/10.1007/978-3-319-96878-0_14

10. Catalano, D., Di Raimondo, M., Fiore, D., Giacomelli, I.: MonZ$_{2^k}$a: fast maliciously secure two party computation on $\mathbb{Z}_{2^k}$. In: Kiayias, A., Kohlweiss, M., Wallden, P., Zikas, V. (eds.) PKC 2020. LNCS, vol. 12111, pp. 357–386. Springer, Cham (2020). https://doi.org/10.1007/978-3-030-45388-6_13

11. Cheon, J.H., Kim, D., Kim, D., Lee, K.: On the scaled inverse of $(x^i - x^j)$ modulo cyclotomic polynomial of the form $\phi_{p^s}(x)$ or $\phi_{p^s q^t}(x)$. arXiv preprint arXiv:2106.01742 (2021)

12. Chor, B., Kushilevitz, E.: A zero-one law for boolean privacy. In: Proceedings of the Twenty-first Annual ACM Symposium on Theory of Computing, pp. 62–72 (1989)

13. Cramer, R., Damgård, I.: On the amortized complexity of zero-knowledge protocols. In: Halevi, S. (ed.) CRYPTO 2009. LNCS, vol. 5677, pp. 177–191. Springer, Heidelberg (2009). https://doi.org/10.1007/978-3-642-03356-8_11

14. Cramer, R., Damgård, I., Escudero, D., Scholl, P., Xing, C.: SPDZ$_{2^k}$: efficient MPC mod 2^k for dishonest majority. In: Shacham, H., Boldyreva, A. (eds.) CRYPTO 2018. LNCS, vol. 10992, pp. 769–798. Springer, Cham (2018). https://doi.org/10.1007/978-3-319-96881-0_26

15. Damgård, I., Escudero, D., Frederiksen, T., Keller, M., Scholl, P., Volgushev, N.: New primitives for actively-secure MPC over rings with applications to private machine learning. In: 2019 IEEE Symposium on Security and Privacy (SP), pp. 1102–1120. IEEE (2019)

16. Damgård, I., Keller, M., Larraia, E., Pastro, V., Scholl, P., Smart, N.P.: Practical covertly secure MPC for dishonest majority–or: breaking the SPDZ limits. In: Crampton, J., Jajodia, S., Mayes, K. (eds.) ESORICS 2013. LNCS, vol. 8134, pp. 1–18. Springer, Heidelberg (2013). https://doi.org/10.1007/978-3-642-40203-6_1

17. Damgård, I., Pastro, V., Smart, N., Zakarias, S.: Multiparty computation from somewhat homomorphic encryption. In: Safavi-Naini, R., Canetti, R. (eds.) CRYPTO 2012. LNCS, vol. 7417, pp. 643–662. Springer, Heidelberg (2012). https://doi.org/10.1007/978-3-642-32009-5_38

18. Goldwasser, S., Ben-Or, M., Wigderson, A.: Completeness theorems for non-cryptographic fault-tolerant distributed computing. In: Proceedings of the 20th STOC, pp. 1–10 (1988)

19. Halevi, S., Shoup, V.: Bootstrapping for HElib. In: Oswald, E., Fischlin, M. (eds.) EUROCRYPT 2015. LNCS, vol. 9056, pp. 641–670. Springer, Heidelberg (2015). https://doi.org/10.1007/978-3-662-46800-5_25

20. Joye, M., Libert, B.: Efficient cryptosystems from 2^k-th power residue symbols. In: Johansson, T., Nguyen, P.Q. (eds.) EUROCRYPT 2013. LNCS, vol. 7881, pp. 76–92. Springer, Heidelberg (2013). https://doi.org/10.1007/978-3-642-38348-9_5

21. Keller, M., Orsini, E., Scholl, P.: Mascot: faster malicious arithmetic secure computation with oblivious transfer. In: Proceedings of the 2016 ACM SIGSAC Conference on Computer and Communications Security, pp. 830–842 (2016)

22. Keller, M., Pastro, V., Rotaru, D.: Overdrive: making SPDZ great again. In: Nielsen, J.B., Rijmen, V. (eds.) EUROCRYPT 2018. LNCS, vol. 10822, pp. 158–189. Springer, Cham (2018). https://doi.org/10.1007/978-3-319-78372-7_6
23. Orsini, E., Smart, N.P., Vercauteren, F.: Overdrive2k: efficient secure MPC over $\mathbb{Z}_{2^k}$ from somewhat homomorphic encryption. In: Jarecki, S. (ed.) CT-RSA 2020. LNCS, vol. 12006, pp. 254–283. Springer, Cham (2020). https://doi.org/10.1007/978-3-030-40186-3_12
24. Smart, N.P., Vercauteren, F.: Fully homomorphic simd operations. Des. Codes Crypt. **71**(1), 57–81 (2014)

Sublinear GMW-Style Compiler for MPC with Preprocessing

Elette Boyle[1(✉)], Niv Gilboa[2], Yuval Ishai[3], and Ariel Nof[3]

[1] IDC Herzliya, Herzliya, Israel
eboyle@alum.mit.edu
[2] Ben-Gurion University, Be'er Sheva, Israel
gilboan@bgu.ac.il
[3] Technion, Haifa, Israel
{yuvali,ariel.nof}@cs.technion.ac.il

Abstract. We consider the efficiency of protocols for secure multiparty computation (MPC) with a dishonest majority. A popular approach for the design of such protocols is to employ *preprocessing*. Before the inputs are known, the parties generate correlated secret randomness, which is consumed by a fast and possibly "information-theoretic" online protocol.

A powerful technique for securing such protocols against malicious parties uses *homomorphic MACs* to authenticate the values produced by the online protocol. Compared to a baseline protocol, which is only secure against semi-honest parties, this involves a significant increase in the size of the correlated randomness, by a factor of up to a statistical security parameter. Different approaches for partially mitigating this extra storage cost come at the expense of increasing the online communication.

In this work we propose a new technique for protecting MPC with preprocessing against malicious parties. We show that for circuit evaluation protocols that satisfy mild security and structural requirements, that are met by many standard protocols with semi-honest security, the extra *additive* storage and online communication costs are both *logarithmic* in the circuit size. This applies to Boolean circuits and to arithmetic circuits over fields or rings, and to both information-theoretic and computationally secure protocols. Our protocol can be viewed as a sublinear information-theoretic variant of the celebrated "GMW compiler" that applies to natural protocols for MPC with preprocessing.

Our compiler makes a novel use of the techniques of Boneh et al. (Crypto 2019) for sublinear distributed zero knowledge, which were previously only used in the setting of *honest-majority* MPC.

1 Introduction

Protocols for secure computation [3,14,23,30] enable a set of parties with private inputs to compute a joint function of their inputs while revealing nothing but the output. Secure computation protocols provide a general-purpose tool for computing on sensitive data while eliminating single points of failure, and their

© International Association for Cryptologic Research 2021
T. Malkin and C. Peikert (Eds.): CRYPTO 2021, LNCS 12826, pp. 457–485, 2021.
https://doi.org/10.1007/978-3-030-84245-1_16

asymptotic and concrete optimization has been the subject of a significant body of research.

A popular approach for the design of such protocols is to employ *preprocessing*. Before the inputs are known, the parties generate correlated secret randomness, which is consumed by a lightweight and typically "information-theoretic" online protocol. This model, known also as the offline/online model, is in particular appealing when no honest majority can be guaranteed, since it allows to push the heavy "cryptographic" part of the protocol to the offline phase, minimizing the cost of the online protocol. It also enables modular analysis, where security of the online protocol can be treated independently given access to an idealized "dealer" who delivers the correlated randomness from the offline phase. The dealer can then be emulated by the parties via a secure preprocessing protocol for generating the correlated randomness. Alternatively, the dealer can be directly realized by an external party or by trusted hardware, both of which are only used before the protocol's execution.

Originating from the work of Beaver [1], who showed how to use "multiplication triples" for secure arithmetic computation with no honest majority, many protocols for secure computation make extensive use of correlated randomness [4,9,15,16,18–20,25,28]. In particular, a powerful technique for securing such protocols against malicious parties uses *homomorphic MACs* to authenticate the values produced by the online protocol [4,19].

Efficiency of MPC protocols with security against malicious parties is typically measured with respect to the costs of the best known protocols with a "minimal" level of security, namely security against semi-honest parties, who act as prescribed by the protocol but try to learn additional information from messages they receive. In the case of MPC with preprocessing, two primary efficiency metrics are:

i. overhead to the *online communication* cost; and
ii. overhead to the *correlated randomness* consumed by the online protocol.

Indeed, communication and storage costs (as opposed to computation) typically dominate the online cost of concretely efficient MPC protocols in the preprocessing model. Minimizing both of these measures simultaneously is instrumental for achieving a fast and scalable online protocol.

However, current MPC with preprocessing protocols exhibit a trade-off between these two efficiency goals. For the case of evaluating an arithmetic circuit C with $|C|$ multiplication gates, some protocols [4,15,19,28] succeed to minimize the online communication cost, but with a large correlated randomness overhead of $O(|C|)$ field elements over large fields, or $O(|C| \cdot \kappa)$ for Boolean circuits or circuits over rings of any size, where κ is a statistical security parameter. Other protocols [13,20] manage to achieve $O(|C|)$ correlated randomness size for Boolean circuits (which asymptotically improves the storage cost), but at the expense of substantially increasing the online communication cost and relying on algebraic geometric codes that hurt concrete efficiency.

This raises the following question about MPC with preprocessing:

Can we achieve malicious security with sublinear (in $|C|$) additive overhead in
  <u>both</u> the online communication and amount of correlated randomness?

Further, *can this be done without introducing any new assumption?*

1.1   Our Contribution

In this work, we answer the above question in the affirmative. We present a compiler from any MPC with preprocessing protocol for arithmetic circuits that satisfies mild security and structural requirements (met by most standard protocols with semi-honest security), to one achieving standard security against malicious adversaries, where the extra *additive* storage and online communication costs are both *logarithmic* in the circuit size. This applies to Boolean circuits and to arithmetic circuits over fields or rings, and to both information-theoretic and computationally secure protocols. In particular, our compiler introduces no additional assumptions. Our compiler can be viewed as an information-theoretic variant of the "GMW compiler" [23] that applies to the setting of MPC with preprocessing.

The compiler requires two properties from the underlying semi-honest secure protocol. First, the protocol must be secure *up to additive attacks*. Such a protocol guarantees not only standard semi-honest security, but further that the actions of a malicious adversary reduce to the ability to inject additive errors to the circuit wires (independent of secret values). This notion was formulated by [21], who showed that many semi-honest protocols that are based on secret sharing (both in the honest- and the dishonest-majority setting), satisfy this requirement. This in particular is true for standard semi-honest protocols in the preprocessing model, which is what interests us in this work.

Our second requirement is a structural robustness property we refer to as *"star-compliance."* We observe that most natural semi-honest protocols with preprocessing exhibit the following structure. The correlated randomness includes additive shares of a random mask r_w for each wire w within the circuit being evaluated; then, in the online phase, the parties iteratively compute the *masked wire values* $(x_w - r_w)$.[1] Effectively, after an honest execution, each wire value x_w is held in a particular secret-shared form, which can be linearly reconstructed either by all parties together by adding to $(x_w - r_w)$ their shares of r_w, or by any individual party together with the dealer who knows r_w—thus forming a "star" structure.

Recall that the dealer is a physical or virtual entity that generates correlated randomness for the online protocol. One of the ideas of this work, as we will see later, is that the dealer itself can act as an additional honest party in the system, with the restriction that its actions must be fully done before the start of the online phase.

Our main result is summarized by the following theorem, which assumes only point-to-point communication except for a final broadcast (of one bit) to enable security with unanimous abort.

---

[1] Note that x_w may not be the *correct* wire value following an additive attack by the adversary. This is not an issue.

Theorem 1.1 (Sublinear GMW-style compiler, informal). *Let C be an arithmetic circuit of size $|C|$ (counting multiplication gates, inputs and outputs) over a ring R, where R is either a finite field $\mathbb{F}$ or the ring $\mathbb{Z}_{2^k}$. Then, every n-party MPC protocol Π in the preprocessing model that computes C with additive security and is star-compliant can be compiled into a protocol Π' that computes C with security against malicious parties and the following efficiency features.*

- CORRELATED RANDOMNESS: *Π' uses the correlated randomness of Π and additional $O(n \cdot \log|C| \cdot \kappa)$ elements of R per party for a statistical security parameter κ;*
- ONLINE COMMUNICATION: *In addition to the online communication of Π, each party in Π' communicates $O(\log|C| \cdot \kappa)$ elements of R.*

Furthermore, if Π has information-theoretic security then so does Π'.

We use this theorem to derive concretely efficient protocols with malicious security, by applying our compiler to semi-honest secure protocols based on multiplication triples [1]. Using circuit-dependent preprocessing (where the correlated randomness can depend on the choice of the circuit C), we obtain a protocol where each party sends $(2 - \frac{2}{n})$ elements per multiplication gate, and the correlated randomness includes $|C| + O(n \cdot \log|C| \cdot \kappa)$ ring elements given to one of the parties and $O(n \cdot \log|C| \cdot \kappa)$ elements given to the remaining $n - 1$ parties (in addition to seeds to a pseudorandom generator). Beginning with a semi-honest protocol with circuit-independent preprocessing (where the correlated randomness depends on the size of C, but not its topology), we obtain a protocol with the same amount of correlated randomness but with slightly higher communication, namely, $(4 - \frac{4}{n})$ elements per multiplication gate per party.

The (logarithmic size) extra correlated randomness introduced by our compiler *does* depend on the structure of the circuit, and thus the resulting protocols in both cases are in the circuit-dependent preprocessing model. However, we address both versions, as the semi-honest portion of the correlated randomness is a dominating cost that can be generated more efficiently in the circuit-independent case (including recent techniques for concretely efficient generation with sublinear communication via pseudorandom correlation generators (PCGs) [7]).[2]

Corollary 1.1 (Efficient MPC with preprocessing, informal). *Let C be an arithmetic circuit of size $|C|$ (counting multiplication gates, inputs and outputs) over ring R, where R is either a finite field or the ring $\mathbb{Z}_{2^k}$. Then there exist n-party MPC protocols in the preprocessing model with security against malicious parties and the following efficiency features.*

- CORRELATED RANDOMNESS: *$4 \cdot |C| + O(n \cdot \log|C| \cdot \kappa)$ R-elements per party, where κ is a statistical security parameter. Settling for computational security*

---

[2] We remark that efficient PCG constructions also exist for more complex correlations, including circuit-dependent multiplication triples, as well as authenticated multiplication triples [8]; however, these constructions rely on stronger tools and do not extend effectively beyond the 2-party setting.

and making a black-box use of a pseudorandom generator, this can be compressed to $|C| + O(n \cdot \log |C| \cdot \kappa)$ *R-elements to one party and* $O(n \cdot \log |C| \cdot \kappa)$ *to the other* $n - 1$ *parties.*

- ONLINE COMMUNICATION:
  - $(2 - \frac{2}{n})$ *R-elements per party per gate (circuit-dependent preprocessing);*
  - $(4 - \frac{4}{n})$ *R-elements per party per gate (circuit-independent preprocessing).*

More concretely, the correlated randomness in the above protocols consists of shared multiplication triples (i.e., additive shares of random $a, b \in R$, and $a \cdot b$, where the shares of random values are directly compressible via black-box use of a pseudorandom generator), together with additional $O(n \cdot \log |C| \cdot \kappa)$ R-elements resulting from our compiler.

Note that our improvement is particularly significant when the computation is carried out over small fields or rings. For example, for Boolean circuits we are able to eliminate the $O(|C| \cdot \kappa)$ additive storage overhead completely, without increasing online communication as done in previous works.

A PCG-based compression. As noted above, by using a PCG to compress the multiplication triples we can get the *total* storage complexity to be sublinear in $|C|$. In particular, for secure 2-party computation of Boolean circuits, each triple can be locally generated using 2 random OT correlations, where the latter can be efficiently compressed using fast PCGs for OT [6,7,29]. For concretely efficient PCG-based protocols for $n \geq 3$ parties, one can use a PCG for OLE [8] for arithmetic circuits over big fields or a PCG for OT for Boolean circuits, though the latter incurs an $O(n^2)$ multiplicative overhead to the online communication.

Distributing the dealer. In Sect. 4 we discuss the cost of emulating the dealer in our protocols by a secure preprocessing protocol involving the parties. Concretely, we show that given the multiplication triples required by the semi-honest protocol, generating the (sublinear) extra correlated randomness can be done using roughly $4|C| + 2n|C|$ secure multiplications.

1.2   Our Techniques

Fully linear proofs. The main technical building block in our compiler is a *fully linear proof system* [5], enabling information-theoretic zero-knowledge proofs with sublinear communication, on secret-shared input statements. In this setting, there is a prover who wishes to prove some statement over an input x to a verifier. In each round of the protocol, the prover produces a proof which can be queried by the verifier using linear queries only. Moreover, the verifier is allowed to also make linear queries to the input x (this is what makes the proof system *fully* linear). The main observation of [5] is that for low-degree languages (i.e., languages for which membership can be checked using a degree-d polynomial), there exist fully linear proof systems with communication which is only logarithmic in the size of the input.

A central motivating application of such proof systems is to proofs on input statements which are distributed or linearly secret-shared between two or more verifiers. If the prover also shares the proof in the same way, then the parties can query their shares of the proof and the input, and then reconstruct the answers. This is particularly useful for achieving malicious security in MPC protocols, since it allows the parties to prove honest behavior, given the data being shared across the parties. Indeed, this tool was used by [5,10,11] to compile semi-honest protocols to malicious security with sublinear communication cost in the honest majority setting, by observing that the statement to be proven in MPC protocols can be represented by a low-degree polynomial.

All of these works crucially relies on the fact that in the honest majority setting, the secret sharing is *robust*, meaning that the shares held by the honest parties determine all the other shares. This fact is what prevents the corrupted parties from cheating in the proof, since even if the prover colludes with some of the verifiers, they cannot change the answers to the queries without being caught by the honest verifiers.

Thus, at first glance, it seems that fully linear proof systems *cannot* be used in the setting where an honest majority is not guaranteed, without adding some kind of authentication to all sharings held by the parties during the execution, thereby increasing significantly the amount of correlated randomness. Our main observation towards overcoming this challenge is that, in the preprocessing model, we can view the star-sharing scheme discussed above, as a robust secret sharing, since any honest party together with the trusted dealer determine the shares held by the corrupted parties! Leveraging this property, we view the dealer as one of the verifiers in the fully linear proof.

Our main technical contribution is a novel protocol with sublinear communication to verify the correctness of a semi-honest computation, which builds upon the fully linear proof system. In each step of the protocol, we carefully make sure that each piece of information along the way is robustly shared across the parties and the dealer using the star-sharing scheme, which is what eventually guarantees that any cheating will be detected. Finally, we observe that all messages sent by the dealer during the verification protocol are a function of random data, and so we can let the dealer precompute all its messages and commit to them before the start of the computation. When distributing the role of the dealer, this amounts to having the parties securely compute the dealer's messages, and then output an authenticated secret sharing of each message, which can be later reconstructed by the parties. The main and final point here is that the proof size and the public randomness in the verification protocol are both *logarithmic* in the size of the computed circuit. This follows directly from the efficiency features of fully linear proof systems for simple languages [5]. Thus, the amount of correlated randomness the dealer needs to generate is also logarithmic in the size of the circuit, thereby achieving our main result.

We believe that our technique is quite broadly applicable and will open the door to new applications of fully linear proof systems in the dishonest majority setting, which is something that has not been done prior to this work.

1.3   Related Work

A long line of works have used an authenticated variant of Beaver's protocol [1] to achieve malicious security [4,15,16,19,26,27], without increasing the online communication cost beyond that of the semi-honest protocol. These protocols use *authenticated multiplication triples* of the form $(a \cdot \Delta, b \cdot \Delta, ab \cdot \Delta)$ for a random secret Δ. The parties receives additive shares of each value in the authenticated triple as well as shares of Δ (and of course shares of a, b and c, which are required for the semi-honest protocol). These are used to authenticate the opening of the actual values. Over a field $\mathbb{F}$, the cheating probability is $\frac{1}{|\mathbb{F}|}$. Thus, over a large field this method doubles the amount of correlated randomness compared to that of the semi-honest protocol. When working over a small field, the triples should be produced over a larger field, thus increasing the size of correlated randomness. The situation is worse for rings, where the cheating probability is $1/2$ regardless of the size of the ring. Naively, this implies an overhead of $|C| \cdot \kappa$ for some statistical parameter κ. This is indeed the case for the TinyOT protocol [28] for Boolean circuits.

However, some improvements were suggested over the years. The MiniMac protocol [20] (optimized and implemented in [17]) focuses on reducing overall computation costs for circuits over small fields (including preprocessing correlated randomness size) at the expense of greater online communication. Their idea is to batch the authentication via linear error-correcting codes (ECC). However, the ECC being used requires good minimal distance for security within multiplications of batched vectors. Achieving this requires smaller rate, translating to greater communication overhead. A recent work by [13] has suggested an alternative to linear ECC of MiniMAC, via "reverse multiplication friendly embeddings" for embedding $(\mathbb{F}_q)^k$-vector mults into a single $F_{q^{k'}}$ field mult. However, the gap between k and k' yields overheads. While this construction reduces the online work, it requires generating extra correlated randomness in the preprocessing phase. The MiniMac protocol and its followers offer a trade-off between the amount of correlated randomness and online communication for computation over Boolean circuits. Their batching ideas remove the κ multiplicative factor, but increase the online communication. In any way, both the correlated randomness and the online cost do not match those of the underlying semi-honest protocols, which we are able to achieve.

Over a large ring, the SPDZ-2k protocol [15] introduced a way to reduce the extra correlated randomness, without increasing communication. Specifically, they require *adding* κ bits to the size of the authenticated triples instead of multiplying the size by κ. For large rings, this amounts to doubling the size of the correlated randomness compared to fields.

Finally, a different approach for 2-party computation was suggested in the TinyTable protocol [18], based on generating a permuted version of its truth table. The overhead of this protocol is $O(|C|)$ for both communication and the correlated randomness.

As can be seen from the above, we are the first to achieve sublinear overhead for both the communication cost and the amount of correlated randomness.

2   Preliminaries

Notation. Let $P_1, \ldots, P_n$ be the parties participating in the protocol. We use $[n]$ to denote the set $\{1, \ldots, n\}$. Let R be a ring which is either a finite field $\mathbb{F}$ or the ring $\mathbb{Z}_{2^k}$ and let $|R|$ be its size. Finally, let κ be the security parameter.

2.1   MPC with Preprocessing

In our setting, there is a set of n parties who wish to jointly run some computation. We assume that all parties are connected via point-to-point channels, which enable them to send private messages to each other.

We begin with defining the meaning of an n-party protocol to compute any functionality in the preprocessing model.

Definition 2.1 (MPC with preprocessing). *Let $\mathcal{F}$ be a family on n-party functionalities and let $f \in \mathcal{F}$ be a function description. A protocol Π to compute $\mathcal{F}$ consists of the PPT algorithm* NextMsg, *which given $(1^\kappa, f, j, i, x_i, r_i, \boldsymbol{m})$ outputs a vector of messages sent by P_i in round j, based on its input x_i, randomness r_i and vector $\boldsymbol{m}$ of messages sent to P_i in previous rounds. If the output of* NextMsg *to P_i is of the form* (out, y), *then P_i outputs y and halts.*

We say that Π is a protocol with function-dependent preprocessing, *if in addition to* NextMsg, *it consists of a PPT algorithm $\mathcal{D}$ (called "the dealer"), which receives 1^κ and f as an input, and outputs correlated random strings $r_1, \ldots, r_n$. We say that Π is a* protocol with function-independent preprocessing, *if $\mathcal{D}$ receives only a bound 1^S on the size of f as an input instead of f.*

A protocol $\pi = (\mathsf{NextMsg}, \mathcal{D})$ computes any arithmetic circuit, when $\mathcal{F}$ is the class of arithmetic circuits and f is a description of a ring R and a circuit C over R, with the size S being a description of the ring and the number of output wires and multiplication gates in C.

To define what it means to securely compute a functionality, we follow the standard ideal-world vs. real-world paradigm of MPC [12,22]. Let $\mathcal{A}$ be an adversary who chooses a set of parties before the beginning of the execution and corrupts them. There are two main types of adversaries which are usually considered in the literature. A *semi-honest* adversary follow the protocol instructions, but sees the input and randomness of the corrupted parties, and all the messages they receive in the execution. A *malicious* adversary can also choose the messages sent by the corrupted parties. We assume that the adversary is *rushing*, meaning that it first receives the messages sent by the honest parties in each round, and only then determines the corrupted parties' messages in this round.

To formally define security, let $\mathrm{REAL}_{\Pi,\mathcal{A},T}(1^\kappa, f, \boldsymbol{v})$ be a random variable that consists of the view of the adversary A controlling a set of parties T, and the honest parties' outputs, following an execution of Π over a vector of inputs $\boldsymbol{v}$ to compute f with security parameter κ. Similarly, we define an ideal-world execution with an ideal-world adversary $\mathcal{S}$, where $\mathcal{S}$ and the honest parties interact with a trusted party who computes f for them. We consider secure computation *with selective abort*, meaning that $\mathcal{S}$ is allowed to send the trusted party computing f a special command abort. Specifically, $\mathcal{S}$ can send an abort command instead of handing the corrupted parties' inputs to the trusted party (causing all parties to abort the execution), or, hand the inputs and then, after receiving the corrupted parties' outputs from the trusted party, send abort_j for an honest party P_j, preventing it from receiving its outputs[3]. We denote by $\text{IDEAL}_{\mathcal{F},\mathcal{S},T}(1^\kappa, f, \boldsymbol{v})$, the random variable that consists of the output of $\mathcal{S}$'s and the honest parties in an ideal execution to compute f, over a vector of inputs $\boldsymbol{v}$, where $\mathcal{S}$ controls a set of parties T. The security definition states that a protocol Π securely computes f with statistical error ε, if for every real-world adversary there exists an ideal-world adversary, such that the statistical distance between the two random variables is less than ε.

Definition 2.2 (Statistically-secure MPC with preprocessing). *Let $\mathcal{F}$ be a family of n-party functionalities and $\varepsilon = \varepsilon(\kappa, f)$ be a statistical error bound. We say that a protocol $\Pi = (\text{NextMsg}, \mathcal{D})$ ε-securely computes $\mathcal{F}$ with abort in the preprocessing model, if for every real-world malicious adversary $\mathcal{A}$ controlling a set of parties T with $|T| \leq n - 1$, there exists an ideal-world adversary $\mathcal{S}$, such that for every $f \in \mathcal{F}$, every κ and every vector of inputs $\boldsymbol{v}$ it holds that*

$$SD\left(\text{REAL}_{\Pi,\mathcal{A},T}(f, \boldsymbol{v}), \text{IDEAL}_{\mathcal{F},\mathcal{S},T}(f, \boldsymbol{v})\right) \leq \varepsilon$$

where $SD(X, Y)$ is the statistical distance between X and Y.

Secure computation of circuits with additive attacks [21]. In this work, our protocol computes arithmetic circuits, which are defined in a natural way, using addition and multiplication gates. We next define a weaker notion of security for computing arithmetic circuits, called "security-up-to-additive-attack", which was introduced by Genkin et al. [21]. In this model, we also allow the ideal-world adversary $\mathcal{S}$ to add an error to the value on some of the wires of the circuit. Specifically, we allow additive attacks on *input wires to multiplication gates and on the circuit's output wires*. The trusted party then determines the output of the honest parties by computing the circuit over the parties' inputs and the additive errors. We denote by $\text{IDEAL}_{\mathcal{F},\mathcal{S},T}^{add}(1^\kappa, C, \boldsymbol{v})$ the random variable consists of $\mathcal{S}$'s and honest parties' outputs in such an execution. Given this new model of ideal-world execution, security is defined similarly to Definition 2.2.

Definition 2.3 (Secure MPC with additive security). *Let $\mathcal{F}$ be the class of n-party functionalities represented by an arithmetic circuit C and let $\varepsilon = \varepsilon(\kappa, C)$ be a statistical error bound. We say that a protocol $\Pi = (\text{NextMsg}, \mathcal{D})$ ε-securely computes $\mathcal{F}$ with abort and with additive security, in the pre-processing model, if for every real-world malicious adversary $\mathcal{A}$ controlling a set of parties T with $|T| \leq n - 1$, there exists an ideal-world adversary $\mathcal{S}$, such that for every circuit $C \in \mathcal{F}$, every κ, and every vector of inputs $\boldsymbol{v}$ it holds that $SD\left(\text{REAL}_{\Pi,\mathcal{A},T}(1^\kappa, C, \boldsymbol{v}), \text{IDEAL}_{\mathcal{F},\mathcal{S},T}^{add}(1^\kappa, C, \boldsymbol{v})\right) \leq \varepsilon$.*

---

[3] It easy to modify our protocol so that the honest parties unanimously abort by running a single Byzantine agreement at the end of the protocol. For simplicity, we omit the details from the description of our protocols.

The Hybrid Model. We use the hybrid model to prove security of our protocols. In this model, the parties run a protocol with real messages and also have access to a trusted party computing a subfunctionality for them. The modular sequential composition theorem of [12] states that it is possible to replace the trusted party computing the subfunctionality with a real secure protocol computing the subfunctionality. When the subfunctionality is g, we say that the protocol works in the g-hybrid model.

Instantiations. Many standard semi-honest protocols in the preprocessing model used in the literature are in fact, or can easily be converted into being additively-secure. Most notably, a semi-honest protocol which uses the well-known Beaver's method [1] to compute multiplication gates via random triples satisfies this definition. For completeness, in Appendix A.1 we present the version of this method which relies on circuit-dependent preprocessing (due to [9] and [2]), and in Appendix A.1, the standard circuit-independent version.

2.2 Fully Linear Proof Systems

A main technical building block in our protocols is a *fully linear* proof system [5], enabling information-theoretic sublinear-communication zero-knowledge proofs on secret-shared input statements. More concretely, we can use any (public-coin) *zero-knowledge fully linear interactive oracle proof* (zk-FLIOP), as defined in Definition 2.4. In a nutshell, a zk-FLIOP is an information-theoretic proof system in which a prover P wishes to prove that some statement about an input x to a verifier V. In each round of the protocol, P produces a proof which, together with x, can be queried by V using *linear queries* only. Then, a public random challenge is generated and the parties proceed to the next round. At the end, the verifier V accepts or rejects based on the answers it received to its queries.

Definition 2.4 (Public-coin zk-FLIOP [5]). *A public-coin fully linear interactive proof system over R with ρ-round and ℓ-query and message length $(u_1, \ldots, u_\rho) \in \mathbb{N}^t$, consists of a randomized prover algorithm P and a deterministic verifier algorithm V. Let the input to P be $x \in R^m$ and let $r_0 = \bot$. In each round $i \in [\rho]$:*

1. *P outputs a proof $\pi_i \in R^{u_1}$, computed as a function of x, $r_1, \ldots, r_{i-1}$ and $\pi_1, \ldots, \pi_{i-1}$.*
2. *A random public challenge r_i is chosen uniformly from a finite set S_i.*
3. *ℓ linear oracle queries $q_1^i, \ldots, q_\ell^i \in R^{m+u_i}$ are determined based on $r_1, \ldots, r_i$. Then, V receives ℓ answers $(\langle q_1^i, x||\pi_i \rangle, \ldots, \langle q_\ell^i, x||\pi_i \rangle)$.*

At the end of round ρ, V outputs accept *or* reject *based on the random challenges and all the answers to the queries.*

Let $\mathcal{L} \subseteq R^m$ be an efficiently recognizable language. We say that ρ-round ℓ-query interactive fully linear protocol $(\mathsf{P_{FLIOP}}, \mathsf{V_{FLIOP}})$ over R is zero-knowledge fully linear interactive oracle proof system for $\mathcal{L}$ with soundness error ϵ if it satisfies the following properties:

- COMPLETENESS: *If $x \in \mathcal{L}$, then* $\mathsf{V_{FLIOP}}$ *always outputs* accept
- SOUNDNESS: *If $x \notin \mathcal{L}$, then for all* P^**, the probability that* $\mathsf{V_{FLIOP}}$ *outputs* accept *is at most* $2^{-\epsilon}$.
- ZERO-KNOWLEDGE: *There exists a simulator* $\mathcal{S}_{\mathsf{FLIOP}}$ *such that for all* $x \in \mathcal{L}$ *it holds that* $\mathcal{S}_{\mathsf{FLIOP}} \equiv \mathsf{view}_{[\mathsf{P_{FLIOP}}(x),\mathsf{V_{FLIOP}}]}(\mathsf{V_{FLIOP}})$ *(where the verifier's view* $\mathsf{view}_{[\mathsf{P_{FLIOP}}(x),\mathsf{V_{FLIOP}}]}(\mathsf{V_{FLIOP}})$ *consists of* $\{r_i\}_{i \in [\rho]}$ *and* $\{(q_1^i, \ldots, q_\ell^i)\}_{i \in [\rho]}$*).*

In this paper, we will use this tool for degree-d languages. That is, languages for which membership can be checked using a degree-d polynomial. The following theorem, which will be used by us, states that for degree-d languages, there are zk-FLIOP protocols with sublinear communication and rounds in the size of the input and number of monomials.

Theorem 2.1 ([5]). *Let $q : R^m \to R$ be a polynomial of degree-d with M monomials, and let $\mathcal{L}_q = \{x \in R^m \mid q(x) = 0\}$. Let ϵ be the required soundess error. Then, there is a zk-FLIOP for $\mathcal{L}_q$ with the following properties:*

- CONSTANT ROUNDS, $d = 2$: *It has 1 round, proof length $O(\eta\sqrt{m})$, challenge length $O(\eta)$ and the number of queries is $O(\sqrt{m})$, where $\eta = \log_{|R|}\left(\frac{\sqrt{m}}{\epsilon}\right)$ when R is a finite field, and $\eta = \log_2\left(\frac{\sqrt{m}}{\epsilon}\right)$ when $R = \mathbb{Z}_{2^k}$. The computational complexity is $\tilde{O}(M)$.*
- LOGARITHMIC ROUNDS, $d \geq 2$: *It has $O(\log M)$ rounds, proof length $O(d\eta \log M)$, challenge length $O(\eta \log M)$and the number of queries is $O(d + \log M)$, where $\eta = \log_{|R|}\left(\frac{d\log m}{\epsilon}\right)$ when R is a finite field, and $\eta = \log_2\left(\frac{d\log m}{\epsilon}\right)$ when $R = \mathbb{Z}_{2^k}$. The computational complexity is $O(dM)$.*

2.3   Ideal Functionalities

We now describe two ideal functionalities that will be used in our construction. We stress that both of them are called sublinear number of times (in the size of the computed circuit), and so any way to implement them will suffice.

Honest dealer commitment with selective abort. We denote by $F_{\mathsf{com}}^{\mathsf{dealer}}$ an ideal functionality which allows an honest dealer to commit to a value which is revealed to parties at a later stage. Upon receiving a secret from the dealer, the functionality $F_{\mathsf{com}}^{\mathsf{dealer}}$ stores it. Then, upon receiving a request from the honest parties to reveal it to parties in a set J, it lets the adversary decide for each party in J, whether to send each party P_j in J the secret or the command abort$_j$.

To implement it with information-theoretic security we can use information-theoretic MACs as in [4,19]. Specifically, each party will hold an additive sharing of the secret x, and in addition, will hold an additive sharing of a information-theoretic MAC over x computed with each party's key. Then, when opening the secret towards a party P_i, all parties send it their additive shares of x and their additive shares of the MAC computed using P_i's key. Since P_i knows its own key, it can use it to check the correctness of x. If any party tries to cheat, then over a field $\mathbb{F}$, it will succeed without being caught with probability of $\frac{1}{|\mathbb{F}|}$. Over a small field or a ring, we can have the MAC over an extension field or ring, to achieve a sufficiently small error.

Broadcast with selective abort. Throughout the paper, when we say that a party broadcasts x to the other parties, it means that it uses an ideal functionality $\mathcal{F}_{bc}$ which allows sending a message to all parties, while, as before, giving the adversary the ability to cause any party to abort. This can be implemented by having each party sending x to all other parties and then having all parties echo-broadcast the message they received to the other parties. It is possible to batch the second-round check for many messages together, by taking a random linear combination of all received messages. The random coefficients can be derived from a single random element r, by taking $r, r^2 \ldots$ and so on. If the parties check m messages together, then the random linear combination yields a polynomial of degree m, which is evaluated on a random point r. Thus, the cheating probability in this case when working over a field $\mathbb{F}$ is, by the Schwartz-Zippel Lemma, $\frac{m}{|\mathbb{F}|}$. As before, to obtain a sufficiently small error over small fields or over rings, this check should be run over a suitable extension field or ring.

3   The General Framework

In this section, we present a protocol to compute any arithmetic circuit with malicious security and dishonest majority. Our protocol works by first computing the circuit using a secure-up-to-additive-attack protocol, and then running a light verification step, where the parties verify the correctness of the computation and abort if cheating was detected. Our protocol is statistically secure in the preprocessing model, i.e., it relies on a trusted dealer $\mathcal{D}$ which provides correlated randomness to the parties. We will discuss how to securely distribute the dealer in the next section.

Before proceeding, we define an additional property that will be required from our protocol. Specifically, we require the parties to maintain an invariant over wires which we call "star-sharing".

Definition 3.1 (Star-sharing). *We say that $x \in R$ is* star-shared *across a set of parties $\mathcal{P} = \{P_1, \ldots, P_n\}$ and a trusted dealer $\mathcal{D}$, if there exists $\hat{x}, (r_1, \ldots, r_n)$, such that each party P_i holds the pair $(\hat{x}, r_i)$, where $\hat{x} = x - r$, $r = \sum_{i=1}^{n} r_i$, and $\mathcal{D}$ holds $\{r_i\}_{i=1}^{n}$.*

The main feature of this sharing scheme is that it is *robust*, in the sense that an honest party and the dealer alone determine all the other values, and in particular the values held by the corrupted parties. In addition, as we will see later, given star-sharing of x and star-sharing of y, this scheme allows local conversion to an *additive* sharing of $x \cdot y$. These two features will play an important role in our constructions.

We next define what it means for a protocol to be "star-sharing compliant".

Definition 3.2 (Star-sharing compliance). *Let $\Pi = (\mathsf{NextMsg}, \mathcal{D})$ be a protocol with preprocessing to compute any arithmetic circuit C, and let W denote the set of output wires and input wires to multiplication gates in C. We say that Π is* star sharing compliant *if the following holds: if all parties follow the protocol's instructions, then the parties hold a star-sharing of the value on each wire $w \in W$.*

Note that if a protocol is both secure-up-to-additive-attack and star-sharing compliant, then it implies that the parties hold on each wire $w \in W$ a star-sharing of either the correct value or of a different value determined by the adversary's additive attack.

3.1   Verifying Correctness via zk-FLIOP

In this section, we present our protocol to verify the correctness of the values the parties hold on the circuit's wires. Recall that we allow the adversary to add errors to wires of the circuit. The protocol we describe in this section aims to detect such cheating. Let W be the set of the circuit's output wires and multiplication gates' input wires. For each wire $w \in W$, the parties need to verify that they hold a sharing of the correct value on w, given the sharings they hold on wires that feed w. Specifically, let G_w be the set of multiplication gates that feed w (i.e., that between their output wire and w there are no other multiplication gates). For each $g \in G_w$, let x_1^g, x_2^g be the two input wires to g. The parties wish thus to verify for each $w \in W$ that $\phi(x_w, \{x_1^g, x_2^g\}_{g \in G_w}) = x_w - \sum_{g \in G_w} x_1^g \cdot x_2^g = 0$. Recall that the parties hold $\hat{x}_w = x_w - r_w$, $\hat{x}_1^g = x_1^g - r_1^g$, $\hat{x}_2^g = x_2^g - r_2^g$ on each wire, as well as additive shares $r_{w,i}$, $r_{1,i}^g$ and $r_{2,i}^g$ for each party P_i. The trusted dealer $\mathcal{D}$ knows the additive shares of all parties and so knows the mask on each wire. Now, in the protocol, instead of checking equality to 0 for each equation separately, the parties will batch all the checks together, by taking a random linear combination of all $\phi(x_w, \{x_1^g, x_2^g\}_{g \in G_w})$ for each $w \in W$. That is, the parties will check that

$$p(W) = \sum_{w \in W} \alpha_w \cdot \phi\left(x_w, \{x_1^g, x_2^g\}_{g \in G_w}\right) = 0.$$

Next, for each multiplication gate g_ℓ, let W^{g_ℓ} be the set of wires w for which $g_\ell \in G_w$ (i.e., that g_ℓ's output feed these wires). Then, let $\gamma_\ell = \sum_{w \in W^{g_\ell}} \alpha_w$.

Letting mult be the set of all multiplication gates, we can thus write

$$p(W) = \sum_{w \in W} \alpha_w \cdot x_w - \sum_{g_\ell \in \text{mult}} \gamma_\ell \cdot (x_1^{g_\ell} \cdot x_2^{g_\ell})$$

$$= \sum_{w \in W} \alpha_w \cdot (\hat{x}_w + r_w) - \sum_{g_\ell \in \text{mult}} \gamma_\ell \cdot ((\hat{x}_1^{g_\ell} + r_1^{g_\ell}) \cdot (\hat{x}_2^{g_\ell} + r_2^{g_\ell}))$$

$$= \sum_{w \in W} \alpha_w \cdot \hat{x}_w + \sum_{w \in W} \alpha_w \cdot r_w - \sum_{g_\ell \in \text{mult}} \gamma_\ell \cdot (\hat{x}_1^{g_\ell} \cdot \hat{x}_2^{g_\ell})$$

$$- \sum_{g_\ell \in \text{mult}} \gamma_\ell \cdot (\hat{x}_1^{g_\ell} \cdot r_2^{g_\ell} + \hat{x}_2^{g_\ell} \cdot r_1^{g_\ell}) + \sum_{g_\ell \in \text{mult}} \gamma_\ell \cdot (r_1^{g_\ell} \cdot r_2^{g_\ell})$$

Now, letting

$$\Lambda = \sum_{w \in W} \alpha_w \cdot \hat{x}_w - \sum_{g_\ell \in \text{mult}} \gamma_\ell \cdot (\hat{x}_1^{g_\ell} \cdot \hat{x}_2^{g_\ell}),$$

$$\Gamma_i = \sum_{g_\ell \in \text{mult}} \gamma_\ell \cdot (\hat{x}_1^{g_\ell} \cdot r_{2,i}^{g_\ell} + \hat{x}_2^{g_\ell} \cdot r_{1,i}^{g_\ell}) \tag{1}$$

and

$$\Omega = \sum_{w \in W} \alpha_w \cdot r_w + \sum_{g_\ell \in \text{mult}} \gamma_\ell \cdot (r_1^{g_\ell} \cdot r_2^{g_\ell})$$

we have that checking that $p(W) = 0$ is equivalent to checking that

$$\Lambda - \sum_{i=1}^{n} \Gamma_i + \Omega = 0.$$

Observe that the parties can locally compute Λ, each party can locally compute Γ_i and the dealer can locally compute Ω. In our protocol, we will ask each P_i to compute Γ_i and share it to the other parties via our robust star-sharing scheme. This can be done by having the trusted dealer hand a random string s_i to P_i , which then broadcasts $\hat{\Gamma}_i = \Gamma_i - s_i$ to the parties. Similarly, the trusted dealer can compute Ω and share it to the parties. Since now Γ_i for each $i \in [n]$ and Ω are shared in a robust way across the parties, and Λ is known, the parties can locally compute a robust secret sharing of $p(W)$, open it by unmasking the secret with the help of the dealer, and check equality to 0. The only remaining problem is that a corrupt P_i may have cheated and share an incorrect Γ_i. Here is where the zk-FLIOP machinery becomes useful. Define the vector of inputs $\boldsymbol{y} \in \mathbb{F}^{|W|+4|\text{mult}|+2}$ as:

$$\boldsymbol{y} = (y_1, \ldots, y_{4|\text{mult}|+2})$$

$$= \left(\hat{\Gamma}_i, s_i, \{(\gamma_\ell \cdot \hat{x}_1^{g_\ell}), r_{2,i}^{g_\ell}, (\gamma_\ell \cdot \hat{x}_2^{g_\ell}), r_{1,i}^{g_\ell}\}_{g_\ell \in \text{mult}} \right) \tag{2}$$

and consider the 2-degree polynomial c defined by

$$c(\boldsymbol{y}) = y_1 + y_2 + \sum_{k=1}^{|\text{mult}|} \left(y_{[4(k-1)+|W|+3]} \cdot y_{[4(k-1)+|W|+4]} \right.$$

$$\left. + y_{[4(k-1)+|W|+5]} \cdot y_{[4(k-1)+|W|+6]} \right).$$

This polynomial checks that each party star-shared Γ_i correctly, by verifying that Eq. (1) holds. By Theorem 2.1, there exists a zk-FLIOP for proving the satisfiability of this polynomial with sublinear proof size. We thus let each party P_i prove that it shared the correct value, by proving that the output of the polynomial is 0. In particular, party P_i emulates the role of the prover in the zk-FLIOP protocol, whereas the other parties emulate together the role of the verifier. A crucial point that we rely upon in the protocol, is that each input to the circuit is known by either all parties *or* by P_i and the dealer. In addition, in the zk-FLIOP protocol, we ask the prover to star-share the proof that it generates in each step. This implies that each piece of information (inputs or the proof) is known by an honest participant (i.e., an honest party or the trusted dealer). This fact is what helps us to prevent a cheating prover from convincing the other parties that a false statement is correct. From the side of the verifiers, holding their star-shares of both the proof and the input, they can make the zk-FLIOP queries over their *shares*. Observe that here we crucially rely on the fact that in zk-FLIOP, all the queries are *linear*, and so querying the star-shares of the proof or the input, will yield a star-sharing of the answer. Then, the answers are revealed by having the trusted dealer send its star-share of the answers (these shares are eventually a random mask of the answer). Privacy is maintained in this process, since the parties see in each round, a masked proof which looks random, and answers to the linear queries, which by the zero-knowledge property of the zk-FLIOP, leak no information on the inputs and can be simulated. Formally, our protocol works as follows (we describe the protocol for *finite fields* and explain how to extend it to rings later):

Π_{vrfy}: Let $(\mathsf{P}_{\text{FLIOP}}, \mathsf{V}_{\text{FLIOP}})$ be a zk-FLIOP protocol with ρ rounds, ℓ-queries per round and message length $u_1, \ldots, u_\rho \in \mathbb{N}$.

1. The trusted dealer $\mathcal{D}$:
   (a) For each $i \in [n]$, it chooses a random $s_i \in \mathbb{F}$ and hands it to P_i.
   (b) chooses a random seed $\alpha \in \mathbb{F}$ and hands in to the parties.
   (c) For each $j \in [\rho]$ and $i \subset [n]$, it chooses a random $t_j^i \in \mathbb{F}^{u_j}$ and hands it to P_i.
   (d) computes Ω (after expanding all α_w from α), chooses a random $\mu \in \mathbb{F}$ and then hand $\hat{\Omega} = \Omega - \mu$ to the parties.
2. The parties set for each $w \in W$: $\alpha_w = \alpha^w$ (or use α as a seed to a PRG).
3. Each party P_i locally compute Λ and Γ_i. Then, each P_i broadcasts $\hat{\Gamma}_i = \Gamma_i - s_i$ to the other parties.
4. For each $i \in [n]$, party P_i proves that Γ_i was computed correctly:
   Let $\boldsymbol{y}_i$ be the vector of inputs for the proof of P_i (as defined in Eq. (2)). Let $\boldsymbol{y}_i^{\mathcal{P}}$ a vector of elements generated by replacing all elements in $\boldsymbol{y}_i$ which are *not* known to all parties by 0, and let $\boldsymbol{y}_i^{\mathcal{D}}$ be a vector of elements generated by replacing all elements in $\boldsymbol{y}_i$ *not* known to $\mathcal{D}$ by 0. Note that $\boldsymbol{y}_i = \boldsymbol{y}_i^{\mathcal{P}} + \boldsymbol{y}_i^{\mathcal{D}}$.
   (a) For each round j of the zk-FLIOP:
      i. If $j = 1$, party P_i lets $\pi_j^i = \mathsf{P}_{\text{FLIOP}}(\boldsymbol{y}_i, \perp)$. Otherwise, it lets $\pi_j^i = \mathsf{P}_{\text{FLIOP}}(\boldsymbol{y}_i, \pi_{j-1}^i, r_{j-1}^i)$.
      ii. P_i broadcasts $\hat{\pi}_j^i = \pi_j^i - t_j^i$ to the other parties.

iii. The dealer $\mathcal{D}$ chooses a random challenge r_j^i and hands it to the parties.

iv. The parties and the dealer let $q_{j,1}^i, \ldots, q_{j,\ell}^i$ be the query vector determined by $\mathsf{V}_{\mathsf{FLIOP}}$ based on r_j^i. Then, the parties compute the answers

$$\hat{a}_{j,1}^i, \ldots, \hat{a}_{j,\ell}^i \leftarrow \langle q_{j,1}^i, \boldsymbol{y}_i^{\mathcal{P}} \| \hat{\pi}_j^i \rangle, \ldots, \langle q_{j,\ell}^i, \boldsymbol{y}_i^{\mathcal{P}} \| \hat{\pi}_j^i \rangle.$$

Similarly, $\mathcal{D}$ computes his answers

$$\widetilde{a}_{j,1}^i, \ldots, \widetilde{a}_{j,\ell}^i \leftarrow \langle q_{j,1}^i, \boldsymbol{y}_i^{\mathcal{P}} \| t_j^i \rangle, \ldots, \langle q_{j,\ell}^i, \boldsymbol{y}_i^{\mathcal{P}} \| t_j^i \rangle.$$

v. The Dealer $\mathcal{D}$ sends $\widetilde{a}_{j,1}^i, \ldots, \widetilde{a}_{j,\ell}^i$ to the parties, who then compute

$$a_{j,1}^i, \ldots, a_{j,\ell}^i \leftarrow \hat{a}_{j,1}^i + \widetilde{a}_{j,1}^i, \ldots, \hat{a}_{j,\ell}^i + \widetilde{a}_{j,\ell}^i.$$

(b) The parties run the decision predicate of $\mathsf{V}_{\mathsf{FLIOP}}$ on all the queries' answers they received. If any party received reject, then it outputs reject. Otherwise, the parties proceed to the next step.

5. The parties locally compute $\hat{p}(W) = \Lambda - \sum_{i=1}^n \hat{\Gamma}_i + \hat{\Omega}$. Then, the dealer $\mathcal{D}$ hands $s = -\sum_{i=1}^n s_i + \mu$ to the parties.

6. The parties locally compute $p(W) = \hat{p}(W) + s$. If $p(W) = 0$, then the parties output accept. Otherwise, they output reject.

Proposition 3.1. *Let ϵ_w be additive error on each wire $w \in W$ (where W is the set of all output wires and inputs to multiplication gates), and let $(\mathsf{P}_{\mathsf{FLIOP}}, \mathsf{V}_{\mathsf{FLIOP}})$ be a ρ-rounds, ℓ-queries and ε-soundness error zk-FLIOP protocol. Then, Π_{vrfy} satisfies the following properties:*

1. CORRECTNESS: *If $\forall w \in W : \epsilon_w = 0$ and all parties follow the protocol's instructions, then the honest parties always output accept.*

2. SOUNDNESS: *If $\exists w \in W : \epsilon_w \neq 0$, then the honest parties output accept with probability of at most $\frac{|W|}{|\mathbb{F}|} + \varepsilon$.*

3. PRIVACY: *For every adversary $\mathcal{A}$ controlling a subset T of size $\leq n-1$, there exists a simulator $\mathcal{S}$, who receives $\{\epsilon_w, \hat{x}_w, \{r_{w,i}\}_{i \in T}\}_{w \in W}$ as an input, and outputs a transcript $\mathsf{view}_{\mathcal{S}}$, such that $\mathsf{view}_{\mathcal{S}} \equiv \mathsf{view}_{\mathcal{A}}^{\pi_{\mathsf{vrfy}}}$.*

Proof: CORRECTNESS. It is easy to see from the description of the protocol, that if no additive errors were introduced and all parties acted honestly in the protocol, then $p(W) = 0$. It remains to show that the parties will output accept in the zk-FLIOP protocol. Given a proof π_j^i, it holds that $\pi_j^i = \hat{\pi}_j^i + t_j^i$. Then, when the parties compute the answers to the linear queries, we have $\forall l \in [\ell]$:

$$a_{j,l}^i = \hat{a}_{j,l}^i + \widetilde{a}_{j,l}^i = \langle q_{j,l}^i, \boldsymbol{y}_i^{\mathcal{P}} \| (\pi_j^i - t_j^i) \rangle + \langle q_{j,l}^i, \boldsymbol{y}_i^{\mathcal{P}} \| t_j^i \rangle = \langle q_{j,l}^i, \boldsymbol{y}_i \| \pi_j^i \rangle$$

and so by the completeness of the zk-FLIOP protocol, they will hold the correct answer and output accept.

SOUNDNESS. If $\exists w \in W : \epsilon_w \neq 0$, then the parties will output accept if $p(W) = 0$. This can happen if one of two events occur: (i) the random linear combination yield 0. since $\alpha_w = \alpha^w$ for a random α, we have that $p(W) = \sum_{w \in W} \alpha_w \cdot \epsilon_w = \sum_{w \in W} \alpha^w \cdot \epsilon_w$ and so, fixing all ϵ_w, this is a polynomial of degree $|W|$ evaluated on a random point α. Thus, by the Schwartz-Zippel lemma, $p(W) = 0$ with probability $\frac{|W|}{|\mathbb{F}|}$. (ii) the parties output accept in the zk-FLIOP, even though a corrupted party P_i shared an incorrect Γ_i. By the soundness property of the zk-FLIOP protocol, this can happen with probability of at most ε. Hence, by the union bound, the overall cheating probability is $\frac{|W|}{|\mathbb{F}|} + \varepsilon$.

PRIVACY. We construct a simulator $\mathcal{S}$ for our protocol and show that the view it generates is distributed identically to the adversary $\mathcal{A}$'s view in a real execution. The simulator $\mathcal{S}$ receives $\{\epsilon_w, \hat{x}_w, \{r_{w,i}\}_{i \in T}\}_{w \in W}$ as an input, and then interacts with $\mathcal{A}$ playing the role of the honest parties and the trusted dealer $\mathcal{D}$. In particular, $\mathcal{S}$ works as follows:

1. Playing the role of $\mathcal{D}$, it hands $\mathcal{A}$ a random s_i for each $i \in T$, a random seed α and a random t_j^i for each $i \in T$ and $j \in [\rho]$. In addition, $\mathcal{S}$ chooses a random $\hat{\Omega}$ and hands it to $\mathcal{A}$.
2. For each honest party P_i, it chooses a random $\hat{\Gamma}_i$ and hands it to $\mathcal{A}$.
3. $\mathcal{S}$ computes all α_w and then, knowing all the corrupted parties' inputs, it computes Γ_i for each corrupted party P_i. In addition, knowing all $\hat{x}_w$, it computs Λ.
4. Upon receiving from $\mathcal{A}$ all $\{\hat{\Gamma}_i\}_{i \in T}$, the simulator $\mathcal{S}$ computes for each $i \in T$, $\Gamma_i' = \hat{\Gamma}_i + s_i$.
5. Simulating the zk-FLIOP execution:
   - The prover P_i is honest: In each round $j \in [\rho]$, $\mathcal{S}$ chooses a random $\hat{\pi}_j^i$ and sends it to $\mathcal{A}$. Then, playing the role of $\mathcal{D}$, it hands a random challenge r_j^i to $\mathcal{A}$. To simulate the opening of the query answers, $\mathcal{S}$ run $\mathcal{S}_{FLIOP}$ to receive $a_{j,1}^i, \ldots, a_{j,\ell}^i$. Then, for each $l \in [\ell]$, it computes $\hat{a}_{j,l}^i$ (since it knows all the corrupted parties' inputs and so all the values in $\boldsymbol{y}_i^{\mathcal{P}}$) and then sets $\tilde{a}_{j,l}^i = a_{j,l}^i - \hat{a}_{j,l}^i$ and hands the answers to $\mathcal{A}$.
   - The prover P_i is corrupted: In this case, $\mathcal{S}$ simply plays the role of the honest parties acting as verifiers in this proof, and the role of $\mathcal{D}$. Since it knows the corrupted parties' inputs, it knows the verifiers' inputs to this proof, and so it can perfectly simulate this execution.
6. $\mathcal{S}$ computes $p(W) = \sum_{w \in W} \alpha_w \cdot \epsilon_w + \sum_{i \in T}(\Gamma_i' - \Gamma_i)$ and $\hat{p}(W) = \Lambda - \sum_{i=1}^{n} \hat{\Gamma}_i + \hat{\Omega}$.
   Then it sets $s = p(W) - \hat{p}(W)$ and hands it to $\mathcal{A}$.

Observe that the view of $\mathcal{A}$ in a real execution consists of three types of values:(i) masked data which is distributed uniformly over $\mathbb{F}$; (ii) the answers to the zk-FLIOP linear queries; (iii) and the value of $p(W)$ which is determined by $\mathcal{A}$ (since it chooses the additive errors). In the simulation, values of type (i) are chosen uniformly from $\mathbb{F}$ and so are distributed the same as in the real execution. Type (ii) of data is distributed the same by the ZK property of the zk-FLIOP.

Finally, since S knows all the inputs held by A and the additive errors, it can compute the actual value of $p(W)$ and so perfectly simulate the opening of this value. We conclude that the view generated by the simulation is identically distributed to the view in the real execution. This concludes the proof. ∎

Working over small fields. The soundness error of our protocol depends on the size of the field $\mathbb{F}$. When we compute the circuit over small fields, it is possible to run Π_{vrfy} over an extension field to reduce the error. This is carried-out by lifting each input to the verification protocol into the extension field. Suppose that we want the error to be $2^{-\varepsilon}$. Then, one can choose an extension field $\tilde{\mathbb{F}}$ such that $\frac{|W|}{|\tilde{\mathbb{F}}|} + \varepsilon_1 \leq 2^{-\varepsilon}$, where ε_1 is the soundness error of the zk-FLOIP protocol over $\tilde{\mathbb{F}}$.

Working over the ring $\mathbb{Z}_{2^k}$. When the circuit is computed over the ring $\mathbb{Z}_{2^k}$, then by Theorem 2.1, we still have a zk-FLIOP with sublinear cost. However, the probability that $p(W) = 0$ when the random coefficients taken as $r, r^2, \ldots, r^{|W|}$ and so p is a polynomial of degree $|W|$ evaluated on a random point r, is constant regardless of the size of the ring. Nevertheless, since the cost of our verification protocol is small, we can afford an "expensive" solution here, and run Π_{vrfy} over the extension ring $\mathbb{Z}_{2^k}[x]/f(x)$, i.e., the ring of polynomials with coefficients from $\mathbb{Z}_{2^k}$ modulo a polynomial $f(x)$ which is of the right degree and is irreducible over $\mathbb{Z}_2$. As shown in [5,10], taking f of degree d, the number of roots of a polynomial of degree δ over $\mathbb{Z}_{2^k}[x]/f(x)$ is at most $2^{(k-1)d}\delta + 1$. Thus, the probability that $p(W) = 0$ when r is chosen at random, is at most $\frac{2^{(k-1)d}|W|+1}{2^{kd}} \approx \frac{|W|}{2^d}$. Hence, by choosing d appropriately, we can achieve a desired soundness error.

From an active dealer to an offline dealer. In the above description we treated the dealer as an active participant in the computation. Note however, that all the operations carried-out by the dealer in our protocol, can be done offline before the start of the computation, because they depend only on random data. These include operations over randomness it chooses for the execution of Π_{vrfy}, and operations over the prover's random shares of the masks, which were chosen by the dealer.

Now, there are two types of randomness that the dealer provides in the execution:

<u>Type I:</u> *randomness given to a single party.* This type of randomness can be handed to the intended party before the beginning of the execution. This includes: (i) random masks $s_i \in R$ and $\{t_j^i\}_{j \in [\rho]}$ where $t_j^i \in R^{u_j}$, given to each party P_i.

<u>Type II:</u> *randomness given to all parties during the protocol.* For each randomness of this type, the dealer can precompute it and send it to $F_{\mathsf{com}}^{\mathsf{dealer}}$ before the beginning of the computation. Then, whenever the parties reach the point where the randomness needs to be revealed, they can send a reveal command to $F_{\mathsf{com}}^{\mathsf{dealer}}$. This includes: (ii) a random seed $\alpha \in R$ given to all parties; (iii)

$\hat{\Omega} = \sum_{w \in W} \alpha_w \cdot r_w + \sum_{g_\ell \in \text{mult}} \gamma_\ell \cdot (r_1^{g_\ell} \cdot r_2^{g_\ell}) - \nu$ given to all parties, where each α_w and γ_ℓ is expanded from α and $\nu \in R$ is random; (iv) a challenge $r_j^i \in R$ for each $i \in [n]$ and $j \in [\rho]$; (v) the queries' answers $\tilde{a}_{j,1}^i, \ldots, \tilde{a}_{j,\ell}^i$, for each $j \in [\rho]$ and $i \in [n]$ (which are computed over the random challenges and prover's inputs which are known to the dealer); and (vi) the random mask s.

Summing the above and given that the extension degree used in the verification protocol is d, then the amount of correlated randomness is

$$\left(3 + n \cdot \left(\sum_{j=1}^{\rho} u_j + \rho(1 + \ell) \right) \right) \cdot d \text{ ring elements.}$$

The main observation is that the amount of correlated randomness is *logarithmic* in the size of the input to the verification subprotocol, i.e., logarithmic in $|W|$. This holds since by Theorem 2.1, there exists a zk-FLIOP protocol, where the proof, $\sum_{j=1}^{\rho} u_j$, the number of rounds ρ and the number of queries $\ell \cdot \rho$ are all of size $\log(M)$, with M being the number of distinct monomials in the polynomial for which the proof takes place. As can be seen from Eq. (1), in our case, M equals to $2|\text{mult}|$. It follows that the amount of required correlated randomness is $O(n \cdot \log|\text{mult}| \cdot d)$.

Communication cost. The interaction in Π_{vrfy} consists of having each party sending the proof to the other parties in each round, and interaction with $F_{\text{com}}^{\text{dealer}}$ to reveal the public randomness. Thus, the overall cost is $(n \cdot \sum_{j=1}^{\rho} u_j) \cdot d + (3 + n \cdot (\rho + \rho \cdot \ell)) \cdot d \cdot F_{\text{com}}^{\text{dealer}}$ ring elements, which by Theorem 2.1, for the same reasoning explained above for the correlated randomness, is of size $O(n \cdot \log|\text{mult}| \cdot d)$

Computation cost. In Π_{vrfy}, each party P_i first computes $\alpha_w = \alpha^w$ for each $w \in W$ and Λ and Γ_i. Each of these computations consists of $O(|W|)$ local multiplication operation. Then, the parties run the zk-FLIOP protocol to prove the correctness of Γ_i for each $i \in [n]$, where by Theorem 2.1, the computational complexity is $O(M)$, which means, as explained above, that the computation complexity is $O(n \cdot |W|)$.

Summing the above, we obtain:

Proposition 3.2. *Let ε be a statistical error bound. Then, Protocol Π_{vrfy} has communication cost $O(\log|\text{mult}| \cdot \kappa)$ per party, computational cost $O(n \cdot |W|)$ per party and the amount of correlated randomness required from the dealer is $O(n \cdot \log|\text{mult}| \cdot \kappa)$ per party, where $\kappa = \log_{|\mathbb{F}|}\left(\frac{|W|}{\varepsilon}\right)$ when R is finite field, and $\kappa = \log_2\left(\frac{|W|}{\varepsilon}\right)$ when $R = \mathbb{Z}_{2^k}$ (where W is the set of output wires and input wires to multiplication gate in the verified circuit).*

Concrete instantiation for the zk-FLIOP. Based on the general constructions from [5], we describe a concrete protocol in the full version for implementing the zk-FLIOP protocol in our setting with the following parameters:

- $\rho = \log(2|\text{mult}|) - 1$

- $u_j = 3$ for $j \in [\rho - 1]$ and $u_\rho = 8$
- $\ell = 1$

Furthermore, we show how to optimize the protocol such that the number of queries becomes constant instead of logarithmic. The concrete costs of the realization we obtain are:

- *communication cost:* $3(\log(2|\mathsf{mult}|) - 1) + 8$ elements broadcasted by the prover.
- *Correlated randomness:* the dealer needs to provide $5(\log(2|\mathsf{mult}|) - 1) + 9$ elements.
- *Computation:* each party performs approximately $2|\mathsf{mult}|$ local operations.

3.2 The Main Protocol

We are now ready to present the main protocol to compute any arithmetic circuits with malicious security. Informally, Our protocol takes any secure-up-to-additive attack and star-sharing compliant protocol, and compile it into malicious security, by adding a verification step, where the parties run the protocol Π_{vrfy} from Sect. 3.1. Formally:

Π_{MPC}: Let C be the circuit to compute, defined over a ring R, let W be the set of C's output wires and input to multiplication gates and let ε be a desired statistical security bound. Let $\Pi_{\mathsf{mpc}}^{\mathsf{add}}$ be a protocol to compute C which is secure-up-to-additive-attack with star-sharing compliance. Let $\tilde{R}$ be an extension ring of R defined as:

- If R is a finite field $\mathbb{F}$, then set $\tilde{R} = \mathbb{F}^\kappa$, such that κ is the smallest number for which $\frac{|W|}{|\mathbb{F}^\kappa|} \leq \varepsilon/2$.
- If $R = \mathbb{Z}_{2^k}$, then set $\tilde{R} = \mathbb{Z}_{2^k}[x]/f(x)$ where f is a polynomial of degree κ which is irreducible over $\mathbb{Z}_2$, such that κ is the smallest number for which $\frac{|W|}{|2^\kappa|} \leq \varepsilon/2$.
- **Preprocessing:** The dealer $\mathcal{D}$ hands the parties the following correlated randomness:
  - For input wire k held by party P_i, it hands a random mask $s_i^k \in R$ to P_i and a random $s_{i,j}^k$ to P_j such that $s_i^k = \sum_{j=1}^n s_{i,j}^k$.
  - It hands the parties the correlated randomness required by $\Pi_{\mathsf{mpc}}^{\mathsf{add}}$. This includes a random $r_{w,i}$ for each party P_i and wire w.
  - It hands the parties the correlated randomness required by Π_{vrfy} as defined is Sect. 3.1 over $\tilde{R}$.
  - For each output wire w, it sends the random mask r_w of this wire to $F_{\mathsf{com}}^{\mathsf{dealer}}$.
- **The online protocol:**
  - SHARING THE INPUTS: For each wire k, with input v_i^k held by P_i, it broadcasts $\hat{v}_i^k = v_i^k - s_i^k$ to the other parties.

- CIRCUIT EMULATION: The parties compute the circuit C gate-by-gate in some predetermined topological order, by running $\Pi_{\mathsf{mpc}}^{\mathsf{add}}$, using the correlated randomness received from the dealer, up to and not including the output reconstruction step.
- VERIFICATION STEP: Let $(\hat{x}_w, r_{w,i})$ be the pair held by each party P_i on each wire $w \in W$. The parties lift $\left(\hat{x}_w, \{r_{w,i}\}_{i \in [n]}\right)_{w \in W}$ into $\tilde{R}$. Then, they run Π_{vrfy} with a zk-FLIOP protocol with soundness error $\varepsilon/2$ on the lifted values and on the correlated randomness received from the dealer. If any party outputs reject, then it sends abort to the other parties and aborts the protocol. Otherwise, the parties proceed to the next step.
- OUTPUT RECONSTRUCTION: For each output wire w, with output intended to party P_i, let $\hat{x}_w$ be the value held by the parties on this wire. Then, the parties send (w, i) to $F_{\mathsf{com}}^{\mathsf{dealer}}$, who sends r_w to P_i. Finally, party P_i sets $x_w = \hat{x}_w + r_w$ as its output.

We thus obtain the following proposition:

Proposition 3.3. *Let f be a n-party functionality represented by an arithmetic circuit C over a ring R and let ε be a statistical security bound. Then, if $\Pi_{\mathsf{mpc}}^{\mathsf{add}}$ is star-sharing compliant and securely computes f with additive security as defined in Definition 2.3, and $(\mathsf{P}_{\mathsf{FLIOP}}, \mathsf{V}_{\mathsf{FLIOP}})$ is public-coin zk-FLIOP as defined in Definition 2.4, then Π_{MPC} (ε)-securely computes f in the $F_{\mathsf{com}}^{\mathsf{dealer}}$-hybrid model with abort in the preprocessing model.*

Proof: We describe a simulator $\mathcal{S}$ for our protocol. In the simulation, $\mathcal{S}$ plays the role of the honest parties and the dealer $\mathcal{D}$ when interacting with the real-world adversary $\mathcal{A}$, who controls a set of parties T with $|T| \leq n - 1$. The simulator $\mathcal{S}$ invokes $\mathcal{A}$ by handing it the correlated randomness for the honest parties as would $\mathcal{D}$ do. Then, in the online protocol it works as follows:

- Input sharing step: The simulator $\mathcal{S}$ sends random elements to $\mathcal{A}$ as the masked inputs of the honest parties. Upon receiving the masked inputs $\hat{x}_k$ of the corrupted parties for each input wire k from $\mathcal{A}$, it extracts the corrupted parties' inputs by computing $x_k = \hat{x}_k + r_k$.
- Circuit emulation: Let $\mathcal{S}_{add}$ be the simulator for $\Pi_{\mathsf{mpc}}^{\mathsf{add}}$. The simulator $\mathcal{S}$ follows the instructions of $\mathcal{S}_{add}$ while interacting with $\mathcal{A}$. Playing the role of $\mathcal{S}_{add}$, it extracts the additive attack ϵ_w for each wire $w \in W$.
- Verification: Let $\mathcal{S}_{vrfy}$ be the simulator for Π_{vrfy} from Theorem 3.1. The simulator $\mathcal{S}$ invokes $\mathcal{S}_{vrfy}$ on $\{\epsilon_w, \hat{x}_w, \{r_{w,i}\}_{i \in T}\}_{w \in W}$, and follows its instructions. Let out be the output held by the honest parties, played by $\mathcal{S}$, at the end of the execution. If out = reject, then $\mathcal{S}$ sends abort to the trusted party computing f and outputs whatever $\mathcal{A}$ outputs. Else, out = accept. If $\forall w \in W : \epsilon_w = 0$, then $\mathcal{S}$ proceeds to the next step. Otherwise, $\exists w \in W : \epsilon_w \neq 0$ and the output is accept. In this case, $\mathcal{S}$ outputs fail and halts.
- Output reconstruction: The simulator $\mathcal{S}$ sends the corrupted parties' inputs to the trusted party computing f, to receive back their outputs. For each output wire w with output x_w on it, $\mathcal{S}$ sends to $\mathcal{A}$ the random mask $r_w = x_w - \hat{x}_w$.

For each output intended to an honest party P_j, it waits for $\mathcal{A}$'s command to $F_{\mathsf{com}}^{\mathsf{dealer}}$. If $\mathcal{A}$ sends abort to $F_{\mathsf{com}}^{\mathsf{dealer}}$, then $\mathcal{S}$ sends abort$_j$ to the trusted party. Otherwise, it sends continue$_j$. Finally, $\mathcal{S}$ outputs whatever $\mathcal{A}$ outputs.

We show that $\mathcal{A}$'s view in the simulation is statistically close to its view in the real execution. First, observe that in the input sharing step, $\mathcal{A}$ sees random masked values in both executions. In the circuit emulation step, by the definition of $\Pi_{\mathsf{mpc}}^{\mathsf{add}}$, the simulation has at most statistical distance from the real execution. In the verification step, by the privacy property of Π_{vrfy}, the views are distributed identically, except for the case $\mathcal{S}$ outputs fail. Note however that this event occurs when the honest parties output accept even though $\exists \epsilon_w \neq 0$. From the soundness property of Π_{vrfy}, it thus follows that $\Pr[\mathsf{fail}] = \varepsilon/2 + \varepsilon/2 = \varepsilon$. To see why this holds, recall that $\tilde{R}$ was chosen such that $\frac{|W|}{|\mathbb{F}^\kappa|} \leq \varepsilon/2$ when $R = \mathbb{F}$ and $\frac{|W|}{|2^\kappa|} \leq \varepsilon/2$ when $R = \mathbb{Z}_{2^k}$, and that the parties called the zk-FLIOP protocol with parameter $\varepsilon/2$. By the soundness property of Π_{vrfy} (Proposition 3.1), the cheating probability is $\frac{|W|}{|\mathbb{F}^\kappa|} + \frac{\varepsilon}{2}$ when $R = \mathbb{F}$, and $\frac{|W|}{2^\kappa} + \frac{\varepsilon}{2}$ when $R = \mathbb{Z}_{2^k}$, implying that it is bounded by ε. Finally, given that the view until the reconstruction step are distributed similarly in both executions, then the same applies for this step as well, since $\mathcal{A}$ sees only random values. Overall, by a standard hybrid argument, we have that $\mathcal{A}$'s view is distributed the same with statistical error ε as allowed by the theorem. This concludes the proof. ∎

Combining Proposition 3.2 and Proposition 3.3, we obtain the following theorem, which summarize our main result in this work:

Theorem 3.1. *Let f be a n-party functionality represented by an arithmetic circuit C of size $|C|$ (number of multiplication gates and output wires) over a ring R which is either a finite field or the ring $\mathbb{Z}_{2^k}$ and let ε be a statistical security bound. Then, every protocol in the preprocessing model which securely computes f with additive security and is star-compliant, can be compiled into a ε-secure protocol, with additional $O(n \cdot \log |C| \cdot \kappa)$ correlated randomness and $O(\log |C| \cdot \kappa)$ communication per party, where $\kappa = \log_{|\mathbb{F}|}\left(\frac{|C|}{\varepsilon}\right)$ when R is finite field, and $\kappa = \log_2\left(\frac{|C|}{\varepsilon}\right)$ when $R = \mathbb{Z}_{2^k}$.*

From our main theorem we derive the following corollaries. We apply our construction on the well-known semi-honest protocol based on Beaver triples [1]. First, we obtain a protocol in the circuit-dependent preporocessing, where both the amortized communication cost and the amount of correlated randomness match the cost of the underlying semi-honest protocol, for rings of *any* size:

Corollary 3.1 (Circuit-dependent preprocessing). *Let C be a circuit with size $|C|$ (which is the number of multiplication gates, input and output wires in C) defined over a ring R which is either a finite field $\mathbb{F}$ or the ring $\mathbb{Z}_{2^k}$ and let ε be a statistical error bound. Then, there exists a protocol to ε-securely compute C with abort, with the following properties:*

- COMMUNICATION: *each party sends* $(2 - \frac{2}{n}) \cdot |C| + O(\log |C| \cdot \kappa)$ *ring elements.*
- CORRELATED RANDOMNESS: *the circuit-dependent preprocessing outputs* $4 \cdot |C| + O(n \cdot \log |C| \cdot \kappa)$ *ring elements to each party.*
  With PRG-based compression, this can be reduced to $|C| + O(n \cdot \log |C| \cdot \kappa)$ *elements to one party, and* $O(n \cdot \log |C| \cdot \kappa)$ *elements to the other parties.*

where κ is defined as in Theorem 3.1.

Proof: Consider the semi-honest protocol described in Appendix A.1, which is the circuit-dependent version of the well-known Beaver's [1] protocol, as described in [9]. In this protocol, the parties hold $\hat{x}_w = x_w - r_w$ for each wire w, which is a circuit's output wire or input wire to a multiplication gate. In addition, they hold for each multiplication gate g with input wires $w_{i_1}^g$ and $w_{i_2}^g$ and output wire w_o^g, an additive sharings of $r_{i_1}^g$, $r_{i_2}^g$, $r_{i_1}^g \cdot r_{i_2}^g$ and r_o^g. Then, they use these to locally compute an additive sharing of masked output (masked with r_o^g) and interact to reveal the masked output, by having each party sending $2 - \frac{2}{n}$ ring elements. The amount of correlated randomness in this protocol is 4 ring elements per multiplication gate without compression. Alternatively, the dealer can hand each party a PRG seed from which its shares of $r_{i_1}^g$, $r_{i_2}^g$ and r_o^g are derived, thereby removing completely $3 \cdot |C|$ elements of correlated randomness. For $r_{i_1}^g \cdot r_{i_2}^g$, the dealer can hand $n - 1$ parties a PRG seed from which their shares are expanded, and give the remaining party one share for each gate. We remark that for each input, each party needs to send one element (masked input) to all parties, while for each output wire, the dealer sends the mask to one party. Thus, *per party*, the communication cost for an input/output wire is bounded by the cost per multiplication.

The protocol is thus star-sharing compliant. In addition, as shown in Appendix A.1, the protocol satisfies the property of additive security. Hence, by applying Theorem 3.1 on this protocol the corollary follows. ∎

In the circuit-independent model, we have a similar result. Here the communication is slightly higher because the cost of the underlying semi-honest protocol is higher.

Corollary 3.2 (Circuit-independent preprocessing). *Let C be a circuit with size $|C|$ (number of multiplication gates, input and output wires in C) defined over a ring R which is either a finite field $\mathbb{F}$ or the ring $\mathbb{Z}_{2^k}$ and let ε be a statistical error bound. Then, there exists a protocol to ε-securely compute C with abort, with the following properties:*

- COMMUNICATION: *each party sends* $(4 - \frac{4}{n}) \cdot |C| + O(\log |C| \cdot \kappa)$ *ring elements.*
- CORRELATED RANDOMNESS: *the circuit-independent preprocessing outputs* $3 \cdot |C|$ *ring elements to each party, and there is an additional circuit-dependent preprocessing which outputs* $O(n \cdot \log |C| \cdot \kappa)$ *elements to each party.*
  With PRG-based compression, this can be reduced to $|C| + O(n \cdot \log |C| \cdot \kappa)$ *elements to one party, and* $O(n \cdot \log |C| \cdot \kappa)$ *elements to the other parties.*

where κ is defined as in Theorem 3.1.

Proof: The proof is identical to the proof of Corollary 3.1, with the only difference being the underlying protocol with additive security. Here we use the standard multplication with Beaver triples shown in Appendix A.2. The parties interact for each multiplication's input wire and thus communication is doubled. The correlated randomness consists of additive sharings of the input masks and their multiplication, and so the per gate each party stores 3 random ring elements. ∎

Remark 3.1 (multicast Vs. private channels). The communication cost presented in Corollaries 3.1 and 3.2 is achieved when only private channels between the parties exist. In case the parties have access to a multicast channel, where sending one message to n parties has the same cost as sending n private messages, then the communication cost is 1 ring element per multiplication gate per party in the circuit-dependent preprocesssing model, and 2 ring elements with circuit-independent preprocessing.

4   Distributing the Dealer

In this section, we show how the role of the trusted dealer can be emulated by the parties in a secure way. Our focus here is only on the correlated randomness required by our compiler, ignoring the correlated randomness for the underlying additively-secure protocol, which is usually easier to generate. To this end, we need to present a MPC protocol which outputs to each party the correlated randomness required by our verification protocol. Our approach to this task is to view the dealer's work as computing an arithmetic circuit, and then one can use any general MPC protocol to compute this circuit by the parties. This is motivated by the fact that, as shown in Sect. 3.1, the computational work of the dealer in the verification protocol, is $O(n \cdot |C|)$. This implies that the computational work is asymptotically proportional to the size of the circuit (times the number of parties). We now show that the hidden constants are actually very small, which means that the circuit computed by the dealer has almost the same size as the original circuit. We remind the reader that general MPC protocols require interaction only for multiplication operations and not for linear operations. Thus, we are only interested here in counting the number of multiplication operations carried-out by the dealer.

When looking into our verification protocol Π_{vrfy}, we identify three computations which require multiplications:

- Computing the random coefficients α_w for each output wire or multiplication gate's input wire w. This computation is done by taking $\alpha_w = \alpha^w$ for a random $\alpha \in R$. Thus, for $|W|$ wires, this requires $|W|$ multiplications. Assuming that the number of outputs is considerably smaller compared to the number of multiplication gates, this amount to $2|C|$ multiplications.
- Computing $\Omega = \sum_{w \in W} \alpha_w \cdot r_w + \sum_{g_\ell \in \mathsf{mult}} \gamma_\ell \cdot (r_1^{g_\ell} \cdot r_2^{g_\ell})$. Recall that the random coefficients γ_ℓ are computed as a summation of several α_w coefficients, and

so are computed without interaction. Thus, the cost here is 2 multiplications for each multiplication gate g_ℓ, and so $2 \cdot |C|$.

- Computing the queries answers $\tilde{a}^i_{j,1}, \ldots, \tilde{a}^i_{j,\ell} \leftarrow \langle q^i_{j,1}, \boldsymbol{y}^{\mathcal{P}}_i \| t^i_j \rangle, \ldots, \langle q^i_{j,\ell}, \boldsymbol{y}^{\mathcal{P}}_i \| t^i_j \rangle$ in each round of the zk-FLIOP. The cost here depends of course on the way the zk-FLIOP is realized. When using the logarithmic construction described in the full version, the parties need to compute approximately $2|\mathsf{mult}|$ multiplications overall, and so $2|C|$ multiplications for each of the n calls to the zk-FLIOP.

Summing the above, we conclude that the size of the dealer's circuit, measured by the number of multiplications, is $4|C| + n \cdot 2|C|$. For the popular setting of 2-party secure computation, for instance, this amount so $8 \cdot |C|$.

Thus, to securely compute this circuit, the parties can use any state-of-art general MPC protocols for computing arithmetic circuits, such as the recent results of [8, 15, 24, 27], depending on the type of underlying ring/field. Together with our light online protocol, this yields a protocol for computing arithmetic circuits with practical potential.

Remark 4.1 (Distributing the dealer for PRG-based protocols.). The approach above works also when the semi-honest correlated randomness is compressed using a PRG. In particular, distributing the dealer does not require securely evaluating the PRG. To illustrate this, consider PRG compression in protocols based on multiplication triples (as in Corollary 3.1 and 3.2). When the n parties emulate the dealer, each party chooses a PRG seed from which it derives its shares of vectors a and b. In addition, all but one party derive their share of $c = a \cdot b$ from their seed. Then, the parties run an MPC protocol to compute the share of c of the remaining party from the $3n - 1$ vectors, and finally the correlated randomness for sublinear ZK verification. The crucial point is that feeding the MPC with an incorrect PRG output does not hurt the security of the online protocol since the latter is secure even with the "corruptible" version of the multiplication triples correlation (this was also observed in the context of SPDZ-style protocols and pseudorandom correlation generators, see [7]).

Acknowledgements. E. Boyle supported by ISF grant 1861/16, AFOSR Award FA9550-17-1-0069 FA9550-21-1-0046, and ERC Project HSS (852952).

N. Gilboa supported by ISF grant 2951/20, ERC grant 876110, and a grant by the BGU Cyber Center.

Y. Ishai supported by ERC Project NTSC (742754), NSF-BSF grant 2015782, BSF grant 2018393, and ISF grant 2774/20.

A. Nof supported by ERC Project NTSC (742754).

A   Protocols which are Secure-up-to-Additive-Attack

In this section, we present two instatiations for a protocol to compute an arithmetic circuit, which is secure up to additive attack, as defined in Definition 2.3 and star-sharing compliant as defined in Defintion 3.2. Recall that the requirement is that for each multiplication gate or output wire of the circuit, the parties will hold a masked value on this wire, plus an error that the adversary added, which can be extracted by a simulator.

A.1   Multiplication in the Circuit-Dependent Preprocessing Model [9]

In this model, the structure of the circuit is known in advance. At the beginning of the protocol, the parties hold two masked inputs $\hat{x} = x - r_1$ and $\hat{y} = y - r_2$. The parties wish to obtain $\hat{z} = x \cdot y - r_3$. Observe that

$$\hat{z} = x \cdot y - r_3 = (\hat{x} + r_1)(\hat{y} + r_2) - r_3$$
$$= \hat{x} \cdot \hat{y} + r_1 \cdot \hat{y} + r_2 \cdot \hat{x} + r_1 \cdot r_2 - r_3 \qquad (3)$$

and so if the parties are given an additive sharing of $r_1, r_2, r_1 \cdot r_2$ and r_3, they can locally compute an additive sharing of $\hat{z}$. Note that in this approach, if a multiplication's output wire is entering multiple gates in the next layer, then we need to make sure that the same mask is used for the input wires of the following gates. This is why the correlated randomness for this protocol is circuit-dependent, i.e., depends on the structure of the circuit. The multiplication protocol thus works as follows:

- **Inputs**: Each party P_i holds: $\hat{x}, \hat{y}, r_1^i, r_2^i, (r_1 \cdot r_2)^i$ and r_3^i.
- **The protocol**:
  1. Each party P_i locally computes $z^i = r_1^i \cdot \hat{y} + r_2^i \cdot \hat{x} + (r_1 \cdot r_2)^i - r_3^i$ and sends z^i to P_1.
  2. Party P_1 computes $z' = \sum_{i=1}^{n} z^i$ and broadcasts z' to all the other parties.
  3. The parties compute $\hat{z} = \hat{x} \cdot \hat{y} + z'$ and store the result as the output.

Recall that when P_1 broadcasting z', this amounts to sending z' to all parties and then at the end run a batch check with constant cost for the entire circuit, to assert that the same z' was sent to all parties in each gate (see Section 2.3). Thus, the overall communication cost in this protocol is $2(n-1)$ elements, and so each party sends $2 - \frac{2}{n}$ elements per multiplication gate. Note that for 2-party computation, this comes down to sending just a *single element* per party per multiplication.

Security up to an additive error. The above protocol does not guarantee correctness; a corrupted party can send incorrect values and cause the output to be incorrect. However, the only attack that corrupted parties can carry-out is to add an error to the output. To see this, consider a simulator that holds $\hat{x}, \hat{y}$ and the randomness of the corrupted parties. Such a simulator can predict the messages sent by the corrupted parties. Thus, it can interact with the adversary, by sending him random values as the messages from the honest parties. Once it receives the messages from the corrutped parties, it can compute the error by comparing the received messages and the messages that should have been sent.

A.2 Multiplication in the Circuit-Independent Preprocessing Model [1]

When the structure of the circuit to be computed is yet to be known, we view the preprocessing as a service which produces random multiplication triples (i.e., Beaver triples). These triples are later consumed by the online computation. In this model, the parties interact to compute the masked input for each multiplication gate or a circuit's output wire. Then, they locally compute an additive sharing of the multiplication's output value. Addition gates which are between two multiplication gates are locally computed over the additive sharing of wire values. The protocol works as follows:

- **Inputs:** Each party P_i holds: x^i, y^i, r_1^i, r_2^i and $(r_1 \cdot r_2)^i$.
- **The protocol:**
  1. Each party computes $x^i - r_1^i$ and $y^i - r_2^i$ and sends it to P_1.
  2. Party P_1 computes $\hat{x} = x - r_1 = \sum_{i=1}^{n} (x^i - r_1^i)$ and $\hat{y} = y - r_2 = \sum_{i=1}^{n} (y^i - r_2^i)$. Then, it broadcasts $\hat{x}$ and $\hat{y}$ to all the other parties.
  3. Each party P_i computes $z^i = r_1^i \cdot \hat{y} + r_2^i \cdot \hat{x} + (r_1 \cdot r_2)^i$. Then, party P_1 defines $\hat{x} \cdot \hat{t} + z^1$ as its output share, where each P_i, with $i \neq 1$ defines z^i as its output share.

Observe that the communication cost here is doubled compared to the multiplication protocol in the circuit-dependent preprocessing model.

By the same reasoning which was used to compute the additive error for each multiplication gate *separately* in the circuit-dependent model presented above, we can compute the additive error on each *multiplication's input wire* or *circuit's output wire*, given the masked inputs to multiplication gates which feed these wires and the corrupted parties' randomness.

References

1. Beaver, D.: Efficient multiparty protocols using circuit randomization. In: Feigenbaum, J. (ed.) CRYPTO 1991. LNCS, vol. 576, pp. 420–432. Springer, Heidelberg (1992). https://doi.org/10.1007/3-540-46766-1_34
2. Ben-Efraim, A., Nielsen, M., Omri, E.: Turbospeedz: double your online SPDZ! improving SPDZ using function dependent preprocessing. In: Deng, R.H., Gauthier-Umaña, V., Ochoa, M., Yung, M. (eds.) ACNS 2019. LNCS, vol. 11464, pp. 530–549. Springer, Cham (2019). https://doi.org/10.1007/978-3-030-21568-2_26
3. Ben-Or, M., Goldwasser, S., Wigderson, A.: Completeness theorems for non-cryptographic fault-tolerant distributed computation (extended abstract). In: STOC (1988)
4. Bendlin, R., Damgård, I., Orlandi, C., Zakarias, S.: Semi-homomorphic encryption and multiparty computation. In: Paterson, K.G. (ed.) EUROCRYPT 2011. LNCS, vol. 6632, pp. 169–188. Springer, Heidelberg (2011). https://doi.org/10.1007/978-3-642-20465-4_11

5. Boneh, D., Boyle, E., Corrigan-Gibbs, H., Gilboa, N., Ishai, Y.: Zero-knowledge proofs on secret-shared data via fully linear PCPs. In: Boldyreva, A., Micciancio, D. (eds.) CRYPTO 2019. LNCS, vol. 11694, pp. 67–97. Springer, Cham (2019). https://doi.org/10.1007/978-3-030-26954-8_3

6. Boyle, E., et al.: Efficient two-round OT extension and silent non-interactive secure computation. In: ACM CCS (2019)

7. Boyle, E., Couteau, G., Gilboa, N., Ishai, Y., Kohl, L., Scholl, P.: Efficient pseudorandom correlation generators: silent OT extension and more. In: Boldyreva, A., Micciancio, D. (eds.) CRYPTO 2019, Part III. LNCS, vol. 11694, pp. 489–518. Springer, Cham (2019). https://doi.org/10.1007/978-3-030-26954-8_16

8. Boyle, E., Couteau, G., Gilboa, N., Ishai, Y., Kohl, L., Scholl, P.: Efficient pseudorandom correlation generators from ring-LPN. In: Micciancio, D., Ristenpart, T. (eds.) CRYPTO 2020. LNCS, vol. 12171, pp. 387–416. Springer, Cham (2020). https://doi.org/10.1007/978-3-030-56880-1_14

9. Boyle, E., Gilboa, N., Ishai, Y.: Secure computation with preprocessing via function secret sharing. In: Hofheinz, D., Rosen, A. (eds.) TCC 2019. LNCS, vol. 11891, pp. 341–371. Springer, Cham (2019). https://doi.org/10.1007/978-3-030-36030-6_14

10. Boyle, E., Gilboa, N., Ishai, Y., Nof, A.: Practical fully secure three-party computation via sublinear distributed zero-knowledge proofs. In: ACM CCS (2019)

11. Boyle, E., Gilboa, N., Ishai, Y., Nof, A.: Efficient fully secure computation via distributed zero-knowledge proofs. In: Moriai, S., Wang, H. (eds.) ASIACRYPT 2020. LNCS, vol. 12493, pp. 244–276. Springer, Cham (2020). https://doi.org/10.1007/978-3-030-64840-4_9

12. Canetti, R.: Security and composition of multiparty cryptographic protocols. J. Cryptol. 13(1), 143–202 (2000)

13. Cascudo, I., Gundersen, J.S.: A secret-sharing based MPC protocol for boolean circuits with good amortized complexity. In: Pass, R., Pietrzak, K. (eds.) TCC 2020. LNCS, vol. 12551, pp. 652–682. Springer, Cham (2020). https://doi.org/10.1007/978-3-030-64378-2_23

14. Chaum, D., Crépeau, C., Damgård, I.: Multiparty unconditionally secure protocols (extended abstract). In: STOC (1988)

15. Cramer, R., Damgård, I., Escudero, D., Scholl, P., Xing, C.: SPDZ$_{2^k}$: efficient MPC mod 2^k for dishonest majority. In: Shacham, H., Boldyreva, A. (eds.) CRYPTO 2018. LNCS, vol. 10992, pp. 769–798. Springer, Cham (2018). https://doi.org/10.1007/978-3-319-96881-0_26

16. Damgård, I., Keller, M., Larraia, E., Pastro, V., Scholl, P., Smart, N.P.: Practical covertly secure MPC for dishonest majority - or: Breaking the SPDZ limits. In: ESORICS (2013)

17. Damgård, I., Lauritsen, R., Toft, T.: An empirical study and some improvements of the MiniMac protocol for secure computation. In: Abdalla, M., De Prisco, R. (eds.) SCN 2014. LNCS, vol. 8642, pp. 398–415. Springer, Cham (2014). https://doi.org/10.1007/978-3-319-10879-7_23

18. Damgård, I., Nielsen, J.B., Nielsen, M., Ranellucci, S.: The tinytable protocol for 2-Party secure computation, or: gate-scrambling revisited. In: Katz, J., Shacham, H. (eds.) CRYPTO 2017. LNCS, vol. 10401, pp. 167–187. Springer, Cham (2017). https://doi.org/10.1007/978-3-319-63688-7_6

19. Damgård, I., Pastro, V., Smart, N., Zakarias, S.: Multiparty computation from somewhat homomorphic encryption. In: Safavi-Naini, R., Canetti, R. (eds.) CRYPTO 2012. LNCS, vol. 7417, pp. 643–662. Springer, Heidelberg (2012). https://doi.org/10.1007/978-3-642-32009-5_38

20. Damgård, I., Zakarias, S.: Constant-overhead secure computation of boolean circuits using preprocessing. In: Sahai, A. (ed.) TCC 2013. LNCS, vol. 7785, pp. 621–641. Springer, Heidelberg (2013). https://doi.org/10.1007/978-3-642-36594-2_35

21. Genkin, D., Ishai, Y., Prabhakaran, M., Sahai, A., Tromer, E.: Circuits resilient to additive attacks with applications to secure computation. In: STOC (2014)

22. Goldreich, O.: The Foundations of Cryptography -, vol. 2. Cambridge University Press, Basic Applications (2004)

23. Goldreich, O., Micali, S., Wigderson, A.: How to play any mental game or A completeness theorem for protocols with honest majority. In: STOC (1987)

24. Hazay, C., Ishai, Y., Marcedone, A., Venkitasubramaniam, M.: Leviosa: Lightweight secure arithmetic computation. In: ACM CCS (2019)

25. Ishai, Y., Kushilevitz, E., Meldgaard, S., Orlandi, C., Paskin-Cherniavsky, A.: On the power of correlated randomness in secure computation. In: Sahai, A. (ed.) TCC 2013. LNCS, vol. 7785, pp. 600–620. Springer, Heidelberg (2013). https://doi.org/10.1007/978-3-642-36594-2_34

26. Keller, M., Orsini, E., Scholl, P.: MASCOT: faster malicious arithmetic secure computation with oblivious transfer. In: ACM CCS (2016)

27. Keller, M., Pastro, V., Rotaru, D.: Overdrive: making SPDZ great again. In: Nielsen, J.B., Rijmen, V. (eds.) EUROCRYPT 2018. LNCS, vol. 10822, pp. 158–189. Springer, Cham (2018). https://doi.org/10.1007/978-3-319-78372-7_6

28. Nielsen, J.B., Nordholt, P.S., Orlandi, C., Burra, S.S.: A new approach to practical active-secure two-party computation. In: Safavi-Naini, R., Canetti, R. (eds.) CRYPTO 2012. LNCS, vol. 7417, pp. 681–700. Springer, Heidelberg (2012). https://doi.org/10.1007/978-3-642-32009-5_40

29. Yang, K., Weng, C., Lan, X., Zhang, J., Wang, X.: Ferret: Fast extension for correlated OT with small communication. In: ACM CCS (2020)

30. Yao, A.C.: How to generate and exchange secrets (extended abstract). In: FOCS (1986)

Limits on the Adaptive Security of Yao's Garbling

Chethan Kamath[1]([⊠]), Karen Klein[2], Krzysztof Pietrzak[2], and Daniel Wichs[3,4]

[1] Boston, USA
ckamath@protonmail.com
[2] IST Austria, Klosterneuburg, Austria
{kklein,pietrzak}@ist.ac.at
[3] Northeastern University, Boston, USA
wichs@northeastern.edu
[4] NTT Research, Tokyo, Japan

Abstract. Yao's garbling scheme is one of the most fundamental cryptographic constructions. Lindell and Pinkas (Journal of Cryptograhy 2009) gave a formal proof of security in the *selective* setting where the adversary chooses the challenge inputs before seeing the garbled circuit assuming secure symmetric-key encryption (and hence one-way functions). This was followed by results, both positive and negative, concerning its security in the, stronger, *adaptive* setting. Applebaum et al. (Crypto 2013) showed that it cannot satisfy adaptive security as is, due to a simple incompressibility argument. Jafargholi and Wichs (TCC 2017) considered a natural adaptation of Yao's scheme (where the output mapping is sent in the *online phase*, together with the garbled input) that circumvents this negative result, and proved that it is adaptively secure, at least for shallow circuits. In particular, they showed that for the class of circuits of depth δ, the loss in security is at most exponential in δ. The above results all concern the *simulation-based* notion of security.

In this work, we show that the upper bound of Jafargholi and Wichs is basically optimal in a strong sense. As our main result, we show that there exists a family of Boolean circuits, one for each depth $\delta \in \mathbb{N}$, such that *any* black-box reduction proving the adaptive *indistinguishability* of the natural adaptation of Yao's scheme from any symmetric-key encryption has to lose a factor that is exponential in $\sqrt{\delta}$. Since indistinguishability is a weaker notion than simulation, our bound also applies to adaptive simulation.

C. Kamath—Most of the work was done while the author was at Northeastern University, supported by the IARPA grant IARPA/2019-19-020700009, and Charles University, funded by project PRIMUS/17/SCI/9.

K. Klein and K. Pietrzak—Funded by the European Research Council (ERC) under the European Union's Horizon 2020 research and innovation programme (682815 - TOCNeT).

D. Wichs—Research supported by NSF grant CNS-1750795 and the Alfred P. Sloan Research Fellowship.

T. Malkin and C. Peikert (Eds.): CRYPTO 2021, LNCS 12826, pp. 486–515, 2021.
https://doi.org/10.1007/978-3-030-84245-1_17

To establish our results, we build on the recent approach of Kamath et al. (Eprint 2021), which uses pebbling lower bounds in conjunction with oracle separations to prove fine-grained lower bounds on loss in cryptographic security.

1   Introduction

A garbling scheme allows one to garble a circuit C and an input x such that only the output $C(x)$ can be learned while everything else – besides some leakage such as the size or topology of the circuit – remains hidden. It was originally used by Yao as a means to achieve secure function-evaluation [17,18]. Despite its huge impact on cryptography, it was formally defined as a stand-alone primitive only much later by Bellare, Hoang and Rogaway [6]. In addition to a syntactic definition, they propose two different security notions for garbling schemes: simulatability and indistinguishability. They show the equivalence of the two definitions[1] in the presence of a *selective* adversary, which sends the circuit and input to be garbled in one shot. In contrast, for the more general case in which the adversary first – in an *offline* phase – chooses a circuit C and then (after receiving its garbling) – in the *online* phase – *adaptively* chooses its input x, the notion of indistinguishability turns out to be strictly weaker than simulatability. Many applications require security in such an adaptive setting, and for the sake of efficiency the cost during the online phase is to be kept minimal.

Prior work on security. Whilst there exist several constructions of provably-secure (even in the adaptive sense) garbling schemes (see Sect. 1.3), a feature of Yao's scheme (and variants thereof) is that security can be proven under the minimal assumption of one-way functions. At the same time, this scheme offers almost-optimal online complexity, with the size of the garbled input being linear in the input-size, and independent of the output- as well as circuit-size. A formal security proof of Yao's scheme in the *selective* setting was given by Lindell and Pinkas [16]. There exists a generic approach to reduce adaptive security to selective security: the adaptive reduction simply guesses the input x and then runs the selective reduction on the adaptive adversary. This, unfortunately, leads to a loss in security that is exponential in $|x|$. Furthermore, Applebaum et al. [3] showed that the *online complexity* of any adaptively-simulatable garbling scheme must exceed the output-size of the circuit, thereby proving a first limitation of Yao's scheme.

All of this led Jafargholi and Wichs [14] to consider a natural adaptation of Yao's garbling scheme (described in Sect. 1.1), where the mapping of output labels to output bits is sent in the online phase as part of the garbled input (see below for the construction). The negative result by Applebaum et al. does

---

[1] In the security game for simulatability, the simulator has to simulate $\tilde{C}$ given only the output $y = C(x)$ and some *leakage* $\Phi(C)$. While equivalence of selective simulatability and selective indistinguishability holds for the most natural leakage functions (e.g. the size or topology of C), it *does not* hold for arbitrary leakage functions Φ.

not apply to this adaptation of Yao's garbling scheme since its online complexity exceeds the output size. Therefore, this adaptation is the natural version of Yao's garbling scheme for the case of adaptive security, and is the scheme that we consider in this work and will simply refer to as "Yao's garbling" from now on. Jafargholi and Wichs [14] were able to show that it satisfies adaptive security for a wide class of circuits, including $\mathbf{NC}^1$ circuits. More precisely, they prove adaptive security of Yao's garbling via a black-box reduction to the IND-CPA security of the underlying symmetric-key encryption (SKE) scheme with a loss in security that is exponential in the *depth* of the circuit. Their proof employs a specially tailored *pebble game* on graphs, and is an application of the *piecewise-guessing framework* of Jafargholi et al. [11]. Since our work concerns the optimality of this proof, let's look at it in a bit more detail.

1.1 Yao's Scheme and Adaptive Indistinguishability

Let's first informally recall Yao's garbling scheme. A circuit $C : \{0,1\}^n \to \{0,1\}^\ell$ is garbled in the offline phase as follows:

1. For each wire w in C, choose a pair of secret keys $k_w^0, k_w^1 \leftarrow \mathsf{Gen}(1^\lambda)$ for a SKE $(\mathsf{Gen}, \mathsf{Enc}, \mathsf{Dec})$.
2. For every gate $g : \{0,1\} \times \{0,1\} \to \{0,1\}$ with left input wire u, right input wire v, and output wire w, compute a garbling table $\tilde{g}$ consisting of the following four ciphertexts (in a random order).

$$
\begin{aligned}
c_1 &:= \mathsf{Enc}_{k_u^0}(\mathsf{Enc}_{k_v^0}(k_w^{g(0,0)})) & c_2 &:= \mathsf{Enc}_{k_u^1}(\mathsf{Enc}_{k_v^0}(k_w^{g(1,0)})) \\
c_3 &:= \mathsf{Enc}_{k_u^0}(\mathsf{Enc}_{k_v^1}(k_w^{g(0,1)})) & c_4 &:= \mathsf{Enc}_{k_u^1}(\mathsf{Enc}_{k_v^1}(k_w^{g(1,1)}))
\end{aligned}
\tag{1}
$$

3. If C has s wires and output wires denoted by $w_{s-\ell+1}, \ldots, w_s$, assemble the output mapping $\{k_w^b \to b\}_{i \in [s-\ell+1, s], \, b \in \{0,1\}}$.

The garbled circuit $\tilde{C}$ consists of all the garbling tables $\tilde{g}$ as well as the output mapping. To garble an input $x = (b_1, \ldots, b_n)$ in the online phase, simply set

$$
\tilde{x} := (k_{w_1}^{b_1}, \ldots, k_{w_n}^{b_n})
$$

where w_i denotes the ith input wire. The only difference in the variant from [14] is that the sending of the output mapping is moved to the online phase, which leads to an increase in the online complexity to linear in the input- *and* output-size.

To evaluate the garbled circuit on the garbled input, one requires the following *special property* of the SKE: For each ciphertext $c \leftarrow \mathsf{Enc}_k(m)$ there exists a unique key – namely k – such that decryption doesn't fail. Evaluation of the garbled circuit given the garbled input then works starting from the gates at the lowest level by simply trying which of the four ciphertexts can be decrypted using the two given input keys. This allows to recover exactly one of the two keys associated to the output wire of the respective gate and in the end the output mapping is used to map the sequence of revealed output keys to an output string $y \in \{0,1\}^\ell$.

Adaptive indistinguishability. A garbling scheme is adaptively indistinguishable if no efficient adversary can succeed in the following experiment[2] with non-negligible advantage:

1. The adversary submits a circuit C to the challenger, who responds with $\tilde{C}$.
2. The adversary then submits a pair of inputs (x_0, x_1).
3. The challenger flips a coin b and responds with $\tilde{x}_b$.
4. The adversary wins if it guesses the bit b correctly.

In the following, we will refer to the two games for $b = 0$ and $b = 1$ as the "left" and "right" games, respectively.

To prove adaptive indistinguishability[3] of Yao's scheme for an arbitrary SKE (satisfying the special property), Jafargholi and Wichs construct a black-box reduction from the IND-CPA security of the SKE. More precisely, they proceed by a hybrid argument, where they define a sequence of hybrid games interpolating between the left and the right game such that each pair of subsequent hybrid games only differs in a single ciphertext (in the garbling table) and can be proven indistinguishable by relying on the IND-CPA security of the SKE.

The loss in security incurred by such a reduction then depends on the length of the sequence and the amount of information required to simulate the hybrid games. To end up with a meaningful security guarantee, thus, the sequence of hybrid games must not be too long and it must be possible to simulate any of the hybrid games without relying on too much information, particularly the knowledge of the entire input. Jafargholi and Wichs design such a sequence of hybrid games by using an appropriate pebble game on the topology graph underlying the circuit. In that game, a pebble on a gate indicates that the gate is not honestly garbled (as in Eq. (1)) but is, instead, garbled in some *input-dependent* mode. The pebble rules, which dictate when a pebble can be placed on or removed from a vertex, guarantee that two subsequent hybrids can be proven indistinguishable, and the loss in security directly relates to the number of pebbles on the graph.

Keeping this proof technique in mind, the main idea of this work is to turn a pebble lower bound (w.r.t. an appropriate pebble game) into a lower bound on the security loss inherent to any black-box reduction of adaptive indistinguishability of Yao's scheme. Such an approach was recently adopted by Kamath et al. [15], also in the context of adaptive security but for primitives that are of a different flavour (e.g., multi-cast encryption). However, the case of garbled circuits turns out very different for several reasons we will highlight later (see Sect. 2.5).

---

[2] In fact, we define a *weaker* security notion than indistinguishability as defined in [6]; according to their definition the adversary can choose *two* circuits C_0, C_1 of the same topology and inputs x_0, x_1 such that $C_0(x_0) = C_1(x_1)$. Aiming at a lower bound on the gap between the security of Yao's scheme and the security of the underlying SKE, the additional restriction we put on our adversary only strengthens our results.

[3] To be precise, [14] prove the stronger security notion of simulatability, which implies indistinguishability.

1.2 Our Results

We prove a lower bound on the loss in security incurred by any black-box reduction proving adaptive indistinguishability of Yao's garbling scheme [14] from IND-CPA security of the SKE scheme. This immediately implies a similar lower bound with respect to the (stronger) more common security notion of adaptive simulatability. Our lower bound is subexponential in the depth d of the circuit, hence almost matches the best known upper bound from [14].

Theorem (main, Theorem 4.1). Any black-box reduction from adaptive indistinguishability (and thus also simulatability) of Yao's garbling scheme on the class of circuits with input length n and depth $\delta \leq 2n$ to the IND-CPA security of the underlying SKE loses at least a factor $\mathsf{loss} = \frac{1}{q} \cdot 2^{\sqrt{\delta}/61}$, where q denotes the number of times the reduction rewinds the adversary.

Two remarks concerning the theorem are in order. Firstly, we are proving a negation of the statement in [14], which upper bounds loss for *every* graph in a class. Therefore, when we say that the class of circuits above loses at least a factor loss, we mean that there *exists* some circuit G in that class such that any reduction loses by that factor (and not that every circuit in that class loses by that factor). The design of this circuit G is one of the main technical contributions of this work. The second remark concerns the design of this circuit G. In addition to some structural properties that we will come to later, we design G to output the constant bit 0. This implies that the output mapping can easily be guessed by a reduction, and therefore the difference, in this case, between Yao's original scheme and [14] is only marginal.

Comparison with Applebaum et al. [3]. The result in [3] rules out adaptively-simulatable randomised encodings with online complexity less than the output-size of the function it encodes. Since Yao's garbling is one instantiation of randomised encodings, their result immediately rules out its adaptive simulatability. However, [3] does not apply to our setting for three reasons. Firstly, their result only applies to the original construction of Yao's garbled circuits where the garbled input can be smaller than the output size. In this work we consider the adaptation of Yao's garbling scheme [14] where the output mapping is sent in the online phase, hence the online complexity always exceeds the output size. Secondly, their result applies to circuits with large output, while our result holds even for Boolean circuits with outputs of length 1. Finally, their result only applies to simulation security, while our result even holds for indistinguishability.

Comparison with Hemenway et al. [10]. We would like to emphasise that our lower bound only holds for the *specific* construction of Yao's garbled circuits, and it does not rule out other constructions, even potentially from one-way functions. In fact, the construction of Hemenway et al. already circumvents our result and it is instructive to see how. On a high level, their idea (similar to [5]) is to take Yao's garbling scheme and then encrypt all the resulting garbling tables with an additional layer of "somewhere equivocal" encryption on top. This change allows them to prove adaptive security with only a *polynomial* loss in security (at the cost of increased online complexity). The intuitive reason why our approach does not apply to this construction is that the additional layer of encryption somehow "blurs out" all the details about the individual garbling tables, on which our argument depends (see Sect. 2.4).

1.3 Further Related Work on Adaptive Security

Adaptive security for garbled circuits. The problem of constructing adaptively-secure garbling schemes was first raised by Bellare, Hoang and Rogaway in [5]; they gave a first adaptively-secure construction in the random oracle model, which bypasses the lower bound of Applebaum et al. [3]. Bellare, Hoang and Keelveedhi [4] then proved the previous scheme adaptively-secure in the standard model, but under non-standard assumptions on hash functions. Further constructions from various assumption followed: Boneh et al. [7] constructed an adaptively-secure scheme from the learning with errors (LWE) assumption, where the online complexity depends on the depth of the circuit family. Ananth and Sahai [2] constructed an optimal garbling scheme from iO. In [13], Jafargholi et al. relax the simulation-based security to *indistinguishability* and show how to construct adaptively-secure garbling schemes from the minimal assumption of one-way functions, where the online complexity only depends on the pebble complexity and the input-size, but is *independent* of the output-size. Later, Ananth and Lombardi [1] constructed succinct garbling schemes from functional encryption. A particularly strong result in this area was due to Garg and Srinivasan [9], who constructed adaptively-secure garbling with near optimal online complexity that can be based on standard assumptions such as the computational Diffie-Hellman (CDH), the factoring, or the LWE assumption. While this list is far from complete, we finally mention a recent work by Jafargholi and Oechsner [12] who analyze adaptive security of several practical garbling schemes. They give positive as well as negative results, and argue why the techniques from [14] cannot be applied to certain garbling schemes.

Adaptive security for other graph-based games. Jafargholi et al. gave a framework for proving adaptive security [11], also known as *piecewise guessing* technique. Beside several applications to other *graph-based* security games, this framework also comprises the reduction from [14] as a special case. Kamath et al. [15] considered optimality of this approach for certain graph-based games which arise in the context of e.g., multicast encryption, continuous group key agreement, and constrained PRF. They gave non-trivial fine-grained lower bounds on the loss in adaptive security incurred by (oblivious) reductions via *pebble lower bounds*.

2 Technical Overview

We aim to prove *fine-grained* lower bounds on loss in security incurred by black-box reductions in a setting where a primitive F is used in a protocol Π^F. In our case F is SKE and Π^F is Yao's garbling scheme using the SKE. In order to bound loss, the loss in security incurred by any efficient black-box reduction R that breaks F when given black-box access to an adversary that breaks Π^F (i.e., from F to Π^F), we must show that for *every* R, there exists

- an instance F (not necessarily efficiently-implementable) of F and
- an adversary A (not necessarily efficient) that breaks Π^F

such that loss in security incurred by R in breaking F is at least loss.[4] We next describe how the instance and the adversary are defined in our setting.

2.1   Our Oracles

We define two oracles $\mathcal{F}$ and $\mathcal{A}$ implementing an ideal SKE and an adversary, respectively, such that

- the SKE scheme $\mathcal{F} = (\mathsf{Gen}, \mathsf{Enc}, \mathsf{Dec})$ satisfies IND-CPA security *information-theoretically*,
- the (inefficient) adversary $\mathcal{A}$ breaks indistinguishability of the garbling scheme $\Pi^{\mathcal{F}}$, but is not helpful in breaking the IND-CPA security of $\mathcal{F}$.

Ideal encryption. We will define the ideal SKE oracle $\mathcal{F}$ such that Enc is defined through a random expanding function (which is injective with overwhelming probability). Since the security of $\mathcal{F}$ is information-theoretic, any advantage against IND-CPA which a reduction with oracle access to $\mathcal{F}$ and $\mathcal{A}$ obtains must stem (almost) entirely from the interaction with $\mathcal{A}$. This is true since the reduction can only make polynomially many queries and thus the probability that the answer to one of its oracle queries coincides with the IND-CPA challenge is negligible. On the other hand, a computationally unbounded adversary using an unlimited number of queries can break the scheme and (thanks to injectivity) perfectly recover messages and secret keys from any ciphertext.

The adversary. As for the (inefficient) adversary $\mathcal{A}$, we define a so-called *threshold* adversary which does the following in the indistinguishability game:

1. $\mathcal{A}$ chooses a particular circuit G (see Sect. 2.3) which has constant output (bit) 0 and sends G to the challenger.
2. After receiving the garbled circuit $\tilde{\mathsf{G}}$, $\mathcal{A}$ chooses garbling inputs x_0 and x_1 uniformly at random and sends them to the challenger. Note that $\mathsf{G}(x_0) = \mathsf{G}(x_1)$ trivially holds since G has constant output.
3. On receipt of the garbled input $\tilde{x}_b$ along with an output mapping, $\mathcal{A}$ first runs some initial checks on $(\tilde{\mathsf{G}}, \tilde{x}_b)$ to verify that the garbling has the correct syntax, and then *extracts a pebble configuration* $\mathcal{P}$ on G (see Sect. 2.4). That is, every gate in G is either assigned a pebble or not, depending on the content

---

[4] This is obtained by simply negating the definition of a black-box reduction: *there exists an efficient reduction R for every implementation (not necessarily efficient) F of F and for every (not necessarily efficient) adversary A that breaks Π^F such that the loss in security is at most loss.*

of its garbling table in $\tilde{\mathsf{G}}$ and the garbled input $\tilde{x}_b$. To compute this mapping, the inefficient adversary $\mathcal{A}$ simply breaks the underlying encryption by brute force. Finally, $\mathcal{A}$ outputs 0 (denoting 'left') if the extracted pebble configuration is *good* (defined later through some pebble game), and 1 (denoting 'right') otherwise.

By design, the left indistinguishability game (where $b = 0$) will correspond to a good configuration, whereas the right game will not. Therefore the above adversary is a valid distinguisher for the indistinguishability game (Lemma 4.5). Moreover, $\mathcal{A}$ concentrates all its distinguishing advantage at the *threshold* of good and bad configurations (hence the name). Therefore, intuitively speaking, for any reduction to exploit $\mathcal{A}$'s distinguishing advantage, it must somehow embed its own (IND-CPA) challenge at the threshold. All the technicality in proving our main theorem goes into formalising this intuition, which we summarise next in Sect. 2.2.

2.2   High-Level Idea

To prove a lower bound on loss (Theorem 4.1), we construct a *punctured* adversary $\mathcal{A}[c^*]$ (see Sect. 4.5) which behaves similar to $\mathcal{A}$ *except* when it comes to the hardcoded challenge ciphertext $c^* \leftarrow \mathsf{Enc}_{k^*}(m)$ (for some arbitrary message m). We aim to puncture $\mathcal{A}[c^*]$ such that it never decrypts c^* but instead just proceeds by assuming that c^* decrypts to the all-0 string, and hence cannot be of any help to a reduction that aims to break c^*. However, we have to be careful here since the reduction embedding c^* in $\tilde{\mathsf{G}}$ will also embed other ciphertexts under key k^* (which it can derive through querying its IND-CPA encryption oracle Enc_{k^*}), and hence $\mathcal{A}[c^*]$ would learn the key k^* when brute-force decrypting these ciphertexts. We solve this issue by endowing $\mathcal{A}[c^*]$ with a decryption oracle Dec_{k^*} that allows to find and decrypt those ciphertexts under k^*. Since our ideal encryption scheme actually satisfies the stronger notion of IND-CCA security, this decryption oracle is of no help to the reduction.

  The core of our lower bound is now to define the circuit G and the notion of *good* pebble configurations such that the following holds:

– Our threshold adversary $\mathcal{A}$ indeed breaks the garbling scheme.
– It is hard to distinguish $\mathcal{A}$ from $\mathcal{A}[c^*]$.

For the latter property, note that any efficient reduction R can only distinguish $\mathcal{A}$ from $\mathcal{A}[c^*]$ if their outputs differ, which only happens if they extract different pebbling configurations $\mathcal{P} \neq \mathcal{P}^*$ such that one of them is good and the other bad. Thus, to bound the success probability of R, it suffices to establish the following two properties:

1. The pebbling configurations $\mathcal{P}$ and $\mathcal{P}^*$ extracted by $\mathcal{A}$ and $\mathcal{A}[c^*]$ (in the same execution of the game, using the same randomness) differ by at most one valid pebbling move in some natural pebble game[5], where a pebble can be

---

[5] In Sect. 4.3 we actually consider a much more finegrained pebble game, where different types of pebbles represent different garbling modes of a gate. For this exposition, it suffices to focus on this simplified game.

placed on or removed from a gate if at least one of its parent gates carries a pebble.

2. It is hard for any reduction to produce $(\tilde{\mathsf{G}}, \tilde{x})$ such that $\mathcal{A}$ extracts a *threshold* configuration, i.e. a pebble configuration that is good but can be switched to a bad configuration within one valid pebbling move.

Intuitively, pebbles on gates in the circuit represent malformed gates, i.e., gates whose garbling table is different from the honest garbling table. When considering circuits consisting only of non-constant gates, the pebbling rule in Property 1 captures the fact that a reduction cannot produce ciphertexts encrypting the key k^* under which its challenge ciphertext $c^* \leftarrow \mathsf{Enc}_{k^*}(m)$ (for some arbitrary m) was encrypted. Hence, in order to embed c^* at a gate, the reduction has to first output a malformed garbling (not encoding k^*) for its predecessor gate. Now, to see why Property 1 holds – i.e., the pebbling configurations $\mathcal{P}$ and $\mathcal{P}^*$ extracted by $\mathcal{A}$ and $\mathcal{A}[c^*]$ follow the same dynamics – note that the behaviour of $\mathcal{A}$ and $\mathcal{A}[c^*]$ can only differ if k^* is not encrypted in any ciphertext.

The tricky part of our proof is to establish Property 2 which, on a high level, works as follows. For a reduction R to simulate a threshold configuration we first force it to maul – and hence pebble – several gates. Then, for this mauling to go 'undetected' we force R to correctly guess the value of these gates when G is evaluated at x_0. This, intuitively, will be the source of its loss. To this end, we design our circuit G to consist of two blocks[6], $\mathsf{G}^\oplus$ and $\mathsf{G}^\wedge$. Looking ahead, whether there is a pebble on a gate in $\mathsf{G}^\oplus$ will be *independent* of the input and correspond to R's attempt at guessing x_0 (this relies on the properties of XOR gates). The pebbles on $\mathsf{G}^\wedge$, in contrast, will be extractable with respect to the input garbling $\tilde{x}_b$ and indicate whether or not the guesses on x_0 in the $\mathsf{G}^\oplus$ block were correct (this relies on the properties of AND gates). Moreover, by definition:

- In case of a proper garbling of (G, x_0) (i.e., the left game), the adversary $\mathcal{A}$ will not extract any pebble on $\mathsf{G}^\oplus$ or $\mathsf{G}^\wedge$.
- In case of a proper garbling of (G, x_1) (i.e., the right game), on the other hand, the adversary $\mathcal{A}$ will not extract any pebbles on $\mathsf{G}^\oplus$, but will extract some pebbles on $\mathsf{G}^\wedge$ (since $x_1 \neq x_0$).

Accordingly, we define the *good* predicate such that the empty configuration is good, whereas any configuration containing a pebble on $\mathsf{G}^\wedge$ is bad, and therefore the above ensures that $\mathcal{A}$ breaks the security of the garbling scheme. Furthermore, the threshold configurations contain many pebbles on $\mathsf{G}^\oplus$, but no pebbles on $\mathsf{G}^\wedge$. In other words, threshold configurations require R to make many guesses about x_0 and all of them need to be correct, which is unlikely to occur. This establishes Property 2.

2.3 The Circuit G and the Good Predicate

The design of topology of the circuit $\mathsf{G}^\oplus$ is such that it has high pebbling complexity with respect to our pebble game: i.e., every valid pebbling sequence

---

[6] For this high-level overview, we ignore the third block G^0 consisting of a binary tree of AND gates, whose sole purpose is to guarantee constant 0 (bit) output.

starting from the *initial* empty configuration and reaching a *final* configuration that has a pebble on an output gate of $G^{\oplus}$, must contain a "heavy" configuration with many, say d, pebbles. To guarantee that threshold configurations contain many pebbles, we define the good configurations as those that are reachable with $d - 1$ pebbles following valid pebbling moves. Since $G^{\wedge}$ will (topologically) succeed $G^{\oplus}$ in G, any configuration with a pebble on $G^{\wedge}$ is in particular bad (since an output gate of $G^{\oplus}$ must have been pebbled first). At the same time, to allow for our "control mechanism", we construct G so that each gate g in $G^{\oplus}$ has a 'companion' successor gate in $G^{\wedge}$ that helps check correctness of g's output. Thus for each AND gate in $G^{\wedge}$, one of the inputs comes from the output of $G^{\oplus}$ and the other from the output of its companion gate (see Fig. 1). This fixes the topology of G and we choose the type of gate as to enforce Property 2, as explained below.

- The $G^{\oplus}$ circuit is composed only of XOR gates, since these gates allow us to maintain *high entropy* (of the input), and hence guarantee that it is hard to guess the outputs of the pebbled gates in $G^{\oplus}$ (see Sect. 4.2). Furthermore, XOR gates are *symmetric* with respect to their input in the sense that from the garbling table alone even an inefficient adversary cannot distinguish which keys are associated with which bits. This property allows $\mathcal{A}$ to extract the pebbling configuration of $G^{\oplus}$ just from $\tilde{G}$, independently of the input (see next section).
- The $G^{\wedge}$ circuit, on the other hand, is composed of AND gates. Since AND gates are *asymmetric* (since only $(1,1)$ maps to 1, while all three other input pairs map to 0), we can use them to detect errors in the $G^{\oplus}$ circuit: i.e., looking at a garbling table of an AND gate our adversary $\mathcal{A}$ can exploit this asymmetry to easily associate keys to bits. Thus, whenever during evaluation of $\tilde{G}$ on input $\tilde{x}$ the adversary $\mathcal{A}$ receives wrong input keys for a (properly garbled) AND gate, $\mathcal{A}$ considers this gate as malformed and associates it with a pebble. (The case of AND gates which are not properly garbled is rather technical and we refer the reader to Sect. 4.4.)

2.4 Extracting the Pebble Configuration

Since it is central to the working of our adversary $\mathcal{A}$ (and is a somewhat subtle matter), here we provide a high-level description of the extraction mechanism.[7] First of all, recall that pebbles on $G^{\oplus}$ and $G^{\wedge}$ have different meanings: a pebbled XOR gate indicates that its garbling table is *malformed* whereas a pebbled AND gate indicates that R's guess for the companion XOR gate is *wrong*. This, coupled

---

[7] In Sect. 4.4 we consider a more general extraction mechanism that can be extended to arbitrary gates and assigns different types of pebbles, representing the "distance" of a garbling table $\tilde{g}'$ for a gate g from an honest garbling table $\tilde{g}$. For ease of exposition, here we consider a simplified pebble game and only discuss how to extract pebbles for XOR and AND gates, where a pebble in this simplified game would correspond to different sets of pebbles for XOR and AND gates in the more fine-grained pebble game.

with the fact that the gates have differently-structured gate tables (i.e., symmetric vs. asymmetric) means that the extraction mechanism for the two gates (and hence the blocks) is also different. In particular, as we will see, the pebble status of an XOR gate is something that can inferred solely from the garbled circuit $\tilde{\mathsf{G}}$ (and thus can be done in the offline phase) whereas the pebble status of an AND gate is something that also depends on the garbled input $\tilde{x}$ and is necessarily done in the online phase. Let's look at how the respective extraction is carried out. First, given $\tilde{\mathsf{G}}$, $\mathcal{A}$ extracts a key pair for each wire in G from the encryptions associated with its *successor* gates, or the output mapping; if this cannot be done uniquely, $\mathcal{A}$ aborts and outputs 1 (we refer to Sect. 4.4 for more details). In the following, for a gate g, let u and v denote the input wires, w the output wire, and k_u, k_u', k_v, k_v', k_w, k_w' the corresponding keys associated with these wires.

- If g is an XOR gate, then the honest garbling table of g can be derived from Eq. (1) as

$$\mathsf{Enc}_{k_u}(\mathsf{Enc}_{k_v}(k_w)) \qquad \mathsf{Enc}_{k_u'}(\mathsf{Enc}_{k_v}(k_w'))$$
$$\mathsf{Enc}_{k_u}(\mathsf{Enc}_{k_v'}(k_w')) \qquad \mathsf{Enc}_{k_u'}(\mathsf{Enc}_{k_v'}(k_w)).$$

Whenever a garbling table $\tilde{g}$ differs from this representation (i.e., not symmetric), $\mathcal{A}$ assigns g a pebble and this assignment is *independent* of the bits running over the wires u, v, w and the keys revealed during evaluation. Thus, $\mathcal{A}$ can extract pebbles on $\mathsf{G}^{\oplus}$ already *before* it chose the inputs x_0, x_1, in particular independently of $\tilde{x}$.

- For an AND gate g, on the other hand, the garbling table of g consists of four ciphertexts derived from Eq. (1) as

$$\mathsf{Enc}_{k_u}(\mathsf{Enc}_{k_v}(k_w)) \qquad \mathsf{Enc}_{k_u'}(\mathsf{Enc}_{k_v}(k_w))$$
$$\mathsf{Enc}_{k_u}(\mathsf{Enc}_{k_v'}(k_w)) \qquad \mathsf{Enc}_{k_u'}(\mathsf{Enc}_{k_v'}(k_w')).$$

Since the roles of the keys are *asymmetric*, the pebble extraction will depend on the bits b_u, b_v, b_w running over the wires and the keys k_u^r, k_v^r, k_w^r revealed during evaluation. A first attempt would be to simply map keys to bits as $k_u, k_v, k_w \to 0$ and $k_u', k_v', k_w' \to 1$, and assign g a pebble if $k_\eta^r \not\to b_\eta$ for some $\eta \in \{u, v, w\}$. Unfortunately, this simple idea does not work since a reduction R might embed its challenge ciphertext $c^* \leftarrow \mathsf{Enc}_{k^*}(m)$ in the garbling of an AND gate (recall from Sect. 2.3 that the gates in $\mathsf{G}^{\wedge}$ receive one input from an output gate of $\mathsf{G}^{\oplus}$ and the other input from their companion gate *within* the circuit $\mathsf{G}^{\oplus}$). Now, if R embeds the challenge key k^* at an output wire of $\mathsf{G}^{\oplus}$, it must pebble an output gate in $\mathsf{G}^{\oplus}$, hence end up with a bad pebbling configuration independently of c^*. However, this is not true if R embeds k^* at the other input wire of the AND gate. Thus, $\mathcal{A}$ must not extract a pebble for a garbling table that can be derived from an honest garbling table by embedding a challenge key at this wire. We show in Sect. 4.4 that such malformed garblings of AND gates either involve guessing the input bits or they can still be used for our "control mechanism".

2.5   Comparison with [15]

While both, [15] and our work, model choices made by a reduction by putting pebbles on a graph structure, the analogy basically ends there. In [15] an interactive game between a "builder" and a "pebbler" is considered in which the builder chooses edges and the pebbler decides adaptively whether to pebble them. The goal of the pebbler is to get into a "good" configuration, and the difficulty for the reduction (playing the role of the pebbler) there lies in the fact that the graph is only revealed edge-by-edge. In contrast, in this work the graph structure is initially known and the game has just two rounds. The difficulty for the reduction here comes from having to guess the bits running over a subset of wires during evaluation of the circuit. None of the main ideas from [15] seem applicable in this setting and vice versa. For example, most of the results in [15] are restricted to the limited class of so-called oblivious reductions, while our setting doesn't share the difficulties encountered in [15]; in particular, our result holds for arbitrary black-box reductions.

3   Preliminaries

Notation and Definitions. For integers $m, n \in \mathbb{N}$ with $m < n$, let $[n] := \{1, 2, \ldots, n\}$, $[n]_0 := \{0, 1, \ldots, n\}$, and $[m, n] := \{m, m+1, \ldots, n\}$. For two sets $\mathcal{S}, \mathcal{S}'$ we write $\mathcal{S} \subset \mathcal{S}'$ if $\mathcal{S}$ is a (not necessarily strict) subset of $\mathcal{S}'$. Furthermore, let log be always base 2. For the classical definitions of IND-CPA and IND-CCA security of symmetric-key encryption (SKE) we refer the reder to the full version of this paper.

Garbling Schemes. The definitions are taken mostly from [13]; more details can be found in [6].

Definition 3.1. *A garbling scheme* **GC** *is a tuple of PPT algorithms* (GCircuit, GInput, GEval) *with syntax and semantics defined as follows.*

$(\tilde{\mathsf{C}}, K) \leftarrow$ GCircuit$(1^\lambda, \mathsf{C})$. *On inputs a security parameter λ and a circuit $\mathsf{C} : \{0,1\}^n \rightarrow \{0,1\}^\ell$, the garble-circuit algorithm* GCircuit *outputs the garbled circuit $\tilde{\mathsf{C}}$ and key K.*

$\tilde{x} \leftarrow$ GInput(K, x). *On input an input $x \in \{0,1\}^n$ and key K, the garble-input algorithm* GInput *outputs $\tilde{x}$.*

$y =$ GEval$(\tilde{\mathsf{C}}, \tilde{x})$. *On input a garbled circuit $\tilde{\mathsf{C}}$ and a garbled input $\tilde{x}$, the evaluate algorithm* GEval *outputs $y \in \{0,1\}^\ell$.*

Correctness. There is a negligible function $\epsilon = \epsilon(\lambda)$ such that for any $\lambda \in \mathbb{N}$, any circuit C and input x it holds that

$$\Pr\left[\mathsf{C}(x) = \mathsf{GEval}(\tilde{\mathsf{C}}, \tilde{x})\right] = 1 - \epsilon(\lambda),$$

where $(\tilde{\mathsf{C}}, K) \leftarrow \mathsf{GCircuit}(1^\lambda, \mathsf{C})$, $\tilde{x} \leftarrow \mathsf{GInput}(K, x)$.

In this work we only consider the security notion of adaptive indistinguishability. For reference we provide the definition of the strictly stronger notion of adaptive simulatability in the full version of this paper.

Definition 3.2 (Adaptive Indistinguishability). *A garbling scheme* **GC** *is* (ϵ, T)-*adaptively-indistinguishable for a class of circuits* $\mathcal{C}$, *if for any probabilistic adversary* A *of size* $T = T(\lambda)$,

$$\left| \Pr\left[\mathsf{Game}_{\mathsf{A},\mathbf{GC}}(1^\lambda, 0) = 1 \right] - \Pr\left[\mathsf{Game}_{\mathsf{A},\mathbf{GC}}(1^\lambda, 1) = 1 \right] \right| \le \epsilon(\lambda).$$

where the experiment $\mathsf{Game}_{\mathsf{A},\mathbf{GC},\mathsf{S}}(1^\lambda, b)$ *is defined as follows:*

1. A *selects a circuits* $\mathsf{C} \in \mathcal{C}$ *and receives* $\tilde{\mathsf{C}}$, *where* $(\tilde{\mathsf{C}}, K) \leftarrow \mathsf{GCircuit}(1^\lambda, \mathsf{C})$.
2. A *specifies* x_0, x_1 *such that* $\mathsf{C}(x_0) = \mathsf{C}(x_1)$ *and receives* $\tilde{x}_b \leftarrow \mathsf{GInput}(x_b, K)$.
3. *Finally,* A *outputs a bit* b', *which is the output of the experiment.*

In the indistinguishability game as defined in [6] the adversary can select *two* circuits $\mathsf{C}_0, \mathsf{C}_1$ of the same topology and receives a garbling $\tilde{\mathsf{C}}_b$ of one of them. The choice of input x_0, x_1 is then restricted to satisfy $\mathsf{C}_0(x_0) = \mathsf{C}_1(x_1)$. Our notion of indistinguishability is clearly weaker, which strengthens our lower bound.

Yao's garbled circuit. In the full version of this paper we describe the variant [14] of Yao's garbling scheme $\Pi^{\mathcal{F}}$ based on a symmetric encryption scheme $\mathcal{F}$ with the special property defined below. Recall that in contrast to the original scheme, here the output map is sent along with the garbled input in the online phase.

Definition 3.3 (Special Property of Encryption). *We say an encryption scheme* $\mathcal{F} = (\mathsf{Gen}, \mathsf{Enc}, \mathsf{Dec})$ *satisfies the special property if for every security parameter* λ, *every key* $k \leftarrow \mathsf{Gen}(1^\lambda)$, *every message* $m \in \mathcal{M}$, *and encryption* $c \leftarrow \mathsf{Enc}_k(m)$ *it holds* $\mathsf{Dec}_{k'}(c) = \bot$ *for all* $k' \ne k$.

4   Lower Bound for Yao's Garbling Scheme

Let Π denote the variant of Yao's garbling scheme as analysed in [14]. As explained in the introduction, we follow the approach in [15] and define two oracles $\mathcal{F}$ and $\mathcal{A}$ implementing an ideal SKE scheme and an adversary, respectively, such that $\mathcal{A}$ is not helpful in breaking IND-CPA security of $\mathcal{F}$. For the precise description of $\mathcal{F}$ we refer to Sect. 4.5. The (inefficient) threshold adversary $\mathcal{A}$ we define as follows:

1. On input the security parameter in unary, 1^λ, the adversary $\mathcal{A}$ chooses a circuit G with input size $n = \Theta(\lambda)$, constant output, and depth $\delta(d) \in O(n)$ for a parameter d. The circuit G consists of three parts, i.e., $\mathsf{G} = \mathsf{G}^0 \circ \mathsf{G}^\wedge \circ \mathsf{G}^\oplus$; see introduction. $\mathcal{A}$ sends G to the challenger.

2. After receiving $\tilde{\mathsf{G}}$, the adversary $\mathcal{A}$ chooses $x_0, x_1 \leftarrow \{0,1\}^n$ uniformly at random. Note that $\mathsf{G}(x_0) = \mathsf{G}(x_1)$ trivially holds since G has constant output. $\mathcal{A}$ sends x_0, x_1 to the challenger.

3. On receipt of $\tilde{x}_b = (k_1, \dots, k_n)$ along with an output mapping, $\mathcal{A}$ extracts a *pebbling configuration* on the graph $G \setminus G^0$ corresponding to $\mathsf{G}^\wedge \circ \mathsf{G}^\oplus$ as described in Sect. 4.4. $\mathcal{A}$ outputs $b' = 0$ if the pebbling configuration is *good* as per Definition 4.2, and $b' = 1$ otherwise.

4.1   The Circuit

We construct a family of circuits $\mathsf{G} := \{\mathsf{G}_d\}_{d \in \mathbb{N}}$ and show that the loss in security for G_d is sub-exponential in d. The circuit is designed keeping our high-level idea in mind. The circuit $\mathsf{G}_d := \mathsf{G}_d^0 \circ \mathsf{G}_d^\wedge \circ \mathsf{G}_d^\oplus$ consists of the three blocks $\mathsf{G}_d^\oplus$, $\mathsf{G}_d^\wedge$ and G_d^0, with underlying graphs denoted by $G_d^\oplus$, $G_d^\wedge$ and G_d^0, respectively. The graph $G_d^\oplus$ (see Fig. 2.(b)) is a so-called *tower graph* [8], and is obtained from so-called pyramid graphs of depth d (see Fig. 2.(a)).

- $G_d^\oplus$ is obtained from $G_d^\oplus$ by substituting each vertex with an XOR gate as shown in Fig. 2. On a high level, the pyramid structure ensures high pebbling complexity whereas the XOR gates preserve (most) entropy in the input , which makes it hard for a reduction to obtain correct evaluation of pebbled gates.
- G_d^0 consists of a binary tree of AND gates and its sole role is to set the output of the circuit G to constant 0.[8]
- $G_d^\wedge$ sits in between the $\mathsf{G}_d^\oplus$ and G_d^0 blocks (see Fig. 1), and consists of one AND gate serving as "control" gate for each XOR gate in $\mathsf{G}_d^\oplus$ and each input gate. Each AND gate g in $G_d^\wedge$ receives its inputs from (i) the output of its companion XOR gate in $G_d^\oplus$ (resp. input gate) and (ii) the XOR gate in the last layer of $G_d^\oplus$ in (vertical) alignment with g (see Fig. 1, formal definition in the full version of this paper). As mentioned previously, intuitively, this block will act as an "error detection" mechanism for the $\mathsf{G}_d^\oplus$ block in the sense that it helps detect if (malformed) garblings of XOR gates evaluate wrongly.

For a precise description of the circuit and a proof that G is indeed constant, we refer to the appendix.

4.2   Vulnerability of the Circuit $\mathsf{G}^\oplus$

In Sect. 4.5 we will prove that any black-box reduction R that aims to use $\mathcal{A}$ to gain advantage in breaking the IND-CPA security of encryption scheme $\mathcal{F}$ has to simulate $(\tilde{\mathsf{G}}, \tilde{x})$ such that the extracted pebbling configuration on $\mathsf{G}^\oplus$ contains $d - 1$ or d gray or black pebbles. Each of these pebbles implies that at least one of the ciphertexts associated to that gate must be malformed and modify

---

[8] In principle we could have used constant-0 gates in place of the AND gates, or simply a single constant-0 gate of high fan-in (which would considerably simplify the description). But we prefer to stick to the standard Boolean basis.

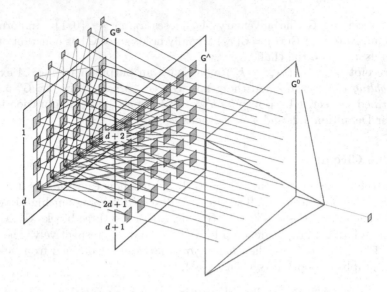

Fig. 1. Schematic diagram for the candidate circuit of width 5 and depth 4. The input and output wires are coloured green. The layer number is indicated on the left. The first two blocks are the XOR and AND layers respectively; the final pyramid denotes the binary tree. (Color figure online)

the output of some input key pair. In the case that all AND gates are properly garbled, all keys can be mapped to bits and hence such a switch of the output can be detected (cf. Lemma 4.6). Thus, we consider the following game.

- On input a circuit C and a parameter d, R chooses a circuit C' of the same topology as C such that all except exactly d (non-input) gates coincide with the corresponding gates in C. R sends C' to $\mathcal{A}$.
- On receipt of C', $\mathcal{A}$ samples $x \leftarrow \{0,1\}^n$ uniformly at random.
- R wins if for all gates in C' the output during evaluation on input x coincides with the corresponding output bit when evaluating C.

We now prove that for $\mathsf{C} = \mathsf{G}^\oplus$, no algorithm R wins the above game with non-negligible (in d) probability.

Lemma 4.1. *Let $d \in [1, n]$. For $\mathsf{G} = \mathsf{G}^\oplus$ and any R, the probability that R wins the above game is at most $(\frac{3}{4})^{\sqrt{d}/4}$.*

First, note that all except d gates in G' are XOR gates, and in particular a linear function over $\mathbb{Z}_2$. For each of the remaining d malformed gates, on the other hand, at least one input pair is mapped to a different output bit than it would be in an XOR operation. We call the corresponding gates in the original circuit $\mathsf{G}^\oplus$ *pebbled*. To prove Lemma 4.1, we will show that there exists a subset of at least $\sqrt{d}/4$ of those d pebbled gates such that their input is determined by independent linear functions. This implies that instead of choosing $x \leftarrow \{0,1\}^n$,

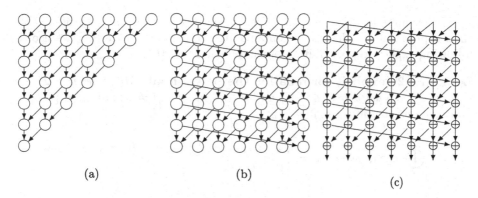

(a)   (b)   (c)

Fig. 2. The graphs and the circuit for parameter $d = 6$: (a) A pyramid graph of depth d, (b) Extending the pyramid graph to get a tower graph $G_d^\oplus$ of depth d and (c) Circuit $G_d^\oplus$ obtained replacing the vertices in $G_d^\oplus$ with XOR gates.

$\mathcal{A}$ can equivalently choose the $\sqrt{d}/2$ input bits uniformly at random, and then choose x uniformly under the constraint that the values running over these wires during evaluation of $G^\oplus$ must be consistent with the predetermined bits. Clearly, x chosen this way is still uniformly random in $\{0,1\}^n$. By definition of the game, R only wins the game if for all gates in G' the output during evaluation on input x coincides with the corresponding output bit when evaluating G, and this must in particular also hold for the pebbled gates. Since each of the malformed gates in G' flips the output of at least one of the four possible input pairs, and the input bits of $\sqrt{d}/4$ of the pebbled gates were chosen independently and uniformly at random, the probability that R wins is at most $(\frac{3}{4})^{\sqrt{d}/4}$.

Towards proving Lemma 4.1, let M denote the linear mapping corresponding to one layer of gates in the circuit $G^\oplus$, i.e., written in matrix notation,

$$M = \begin{pmatrix} 1\,1\,0 & \cdots & 0\,0\,0 \\ 0\,1\,1 & \cdots & 0\,0\,0 \\ \vdots & \ddots & \vdots \\ 0\,0\,0 & \cdots & 0\,1\,1 \\ 1\,0\,0 & \cdots & 0\,0\,1 \end{pmatrix}.$$

The output of the μth layer of $G^\oplus$ on input $x \in \{0,1\}^n$ is given by $M^\mu \cdot x$, hence we denote the degree-1 polynomial in $\mathbb{Z}_2[x_1,\ldots,x_n]$ which determines its ν-th bit by M_ν^μ (for $\mu \in [0,n]$ and $\nu \in [1,n]$). Denoting by $\overline{\nu+1}$ the representation of the residue class $\nu+1 \mod n$ in $[n]$, we have e.g.,

$$M_\nu^0 = x_\nu, \quad M_\nu^1 = x_\nu \oplus x_{\overline{\nu+1}}, \quad M_\nu^2 = x_\nu \oplus x_{\overline{\nu+2}}, \quad M_\nu^3 = x_\nu \oplus x_{\overline{\nu+1}} \oplus x_{\overline{\nu+2}} \oplus x_{\overline{\nu+3}}$$

and in general it holds

$$M_\nu^\mu = M_\nu^{\mu-1} \oplus M_{\overline{\nu+1}}^{\mu-1} \tag{2}$$

for all $\mu \in \mathbb{N}, \nu \in [1,n]$. In the following we will associate gates with the corresponding polynomials that determine their outputs.

If the input length n is odd – for convenience we assume n to be one less than a power of 2 – then $\mathsf{G}^\oplus$ maintains high entropy; to prove this, we use the following explicit representation of the polynomials M_ν^μ.

Lemma 4.2 (explicit formula for the polynomials M_ν^μ). *Let* $n = 2^\kappa - 1$, $\kappa \in \mathbb{N}$, M *defined above*, $\mu \in \mathbb{N}$, *and* $\nu \in [1, n]$. *For* $\overline{\mu} \neq n$ *and* $\beta_k \in \{0, 1\}$ *its binary decomposition, i.e.* $\overline{\mu} = \sum_{k \in [0, \kappa - 1]} \beta_k 2^k$, *it holds:*

$$
M_\nu^\mu = \bigoplus_{i \in [1, n]} \alpha_i x_i, \text{ where } \alpha_i = \begin{cases} 1 & \text{if } i \in \nu + \sum_{k \in [0, \kappa-1]} \{0, \beta_k\} \cdot 2^k \mod n, \\ 0 & \text{else.} \end{cases}
$$

$$(3)$$

Note, M_ν^μ *only depends on* $\overline{\mu}$, *not on* μ. *For* $\overline{\mu} = n = 2^\kappa - 1$, *it holds:*

$$
M_\nu^\mu = \bigoplus_{i \in [1, n]} \alpha_i x_i, \text{ where } \alpha_i = \begin{cases} 1 & \text{if } i \neq \nu, \\ 0 & \text{else.} \end{cases}
$$

$$(4)$$

A proof of Lemma 4.2 can be found in the full version of this paper. Lemma 4.2 directly implies several useful properties, which we summarize in the following corollary.

Corollary 4.1 (Properties of M and $\mathsf{G}^\oplus$). *For M defined as above, $n = 2^\kappa - 1$, $\kappa \in \mathbb{N}$, it holds*

1. $M^{2^\kappa} = M$, *which implies* $\mathrm{rank}(M^k) = n - 1$ *for all* $k \geq 1$, *i.e.,* $\mathsf{G}^\oplus = M^d$ *is 2-to-1 for any d.*
2. *Any $n - 1$ output bits of M^k ($k \geq 1$) are determined by linearly independent degree-1 polynomials.*
3. $\mathsf{Image}(\mathsf{G}^\oplus) = \{x = (x_1, \ldots, x_n) \in \{0, 1\}^n \mid \bigoplus_{i \in [1, n]} x_i = 0\}$, *i.e., all vectors in the image of $\mathsf{G}^\oplus$ contain an even number of 1s.*

The first property immediately follows from Lemma 4.2 since for $\mu = 2^\kappa$ we have $\overline{\mu} = 1$. The second property then follows from $\mathrm{rank}(M^k) = n - 1$. For the last property, note that the set $\nu + \sum_{k \in [0, \kappa-1]} \{0, \beta_k\} \cdot 2^k \mod n$ is even whenever a single bit β_k is nonzero (which is true for all $\overline{\mu} > 0$), and also the set $\{i \in [n] \mid i \neq \nu\}$ is even since n is odd.

The following Lemma immediately implies Lemma 4.1, a proof can be found in the full version of this paper.

Lemma 4.3. *Any subset* $S \subset \{M_\nu^\mu\}_{\mu \in [0, n], \nu \in [1, n]}$ *of polynomials in $\mathbb{Z}_2[x_1, \ldots, x_n]$ with $s := |S|$ contains a subset S' of size $\sqrt{s}/4$ such that $|\mathsf{parents}(S')| = \sqrt{s}/2$ and $\mathsf{parents}(S')$ is linearly independent, where $\mathsf{parents}(M_\nu^\mu) := \{M_\nu^{\mu-1}, M_{\nu+1}^{\mu-1}\}$.*

Lemma 4.1 now follows, since for any set of d pebbled gates, by Lemma 4.3 there exists a subset S' of $\sqrt{d}/4$ pebbled gates such that their parents are distinct and form a linearly independent set.

4.3 Pebbling Game and Threshold

Recall that in Yao's garbling scheme, each gate g is associated with a (honest) garbling table $\tilde{g}$, which consists of four double encryptions that encode g's gate table. However, a reduction is free to alter the contents of the honest garbling table in any way. In fact, the upper bounds in [14,16] crucially rely on the ability to do this in an indistinguishable manner: in the real game the garbling tables are all honest, whereas in the simulated game the garbling tables all encode the constant-0 gate, and the hybrids involve replacing the honest garbling tables one by one with that of the constant-0 gate.[9] We introduce a pebble game to precisely model such different simulations of the garbled circuit $\tilde{\mathsf{G}}$ (by the reduction). Loosely speaking, the extracted pebble configuration is an abstract representation of the simulation $(\tilde{\mathsf{G}}, \tilde{x}_b)$, and the pebbling rules model the reduction's ability to maul garbling tables in $\tilde{\mathsf{G}}$ without being noticed (indistinguishability).

The pebbles. Intuitively, the pebble on a gate g encodes how "different" the garbling table $\tilde{g}'$ which $\mathcal{A}$ receives is from an honest garbling $\tilde{g}$. To this end, we employ three different pebbles: white, gray and black.

- A white pebble on g indicates that $\tilde{g}'$ and $\tilde{g}$ are at "distance" 0 (defined below), i.e., $\tilde{g}$ is (distributed identically to) an honest garbling table of g.
- A gray or black pebble on g indicates that $\tilde{g}'$ is malformed. What differentiates gray from black is the degree of malformation: loosely speaking, a gray pebble indicates that $\tilde{g}'$ is at a distance 1 from $\tilde{g}$, whereas a black pebble indicates that $\tilde{g}'$ is at a distance 2 (or more).

To understand what we mean by distance, we need to take a closer look at the structure of a garbling table. An honest garbling table $\tilde{g}$ consists of the four double encryptions shown in Table 1.(a). We assign a gray pebble to a gate g if the garbling table of g in $\tilde{\mathsf{G}}$ can be proven indistinguishable from $\tilde{g}$ by embedding a *single* IND-CPA challenge key (among k_u^0, k_u^1, k_v^0 and k_v^1). For example, let's consider an AND gate and its honest garbling table (Table 1.(b)): a malformed table that is at distance one (via the key k_u^1 or k_v^1) from it is, e.g., a garbling table that encodes the constant-0 gate (Table 1.(d)). A garbling of an XOR gate, in contrast, is at distance 2 from a garbling of a constant gate: If k_u^a and k_v^b are the keys revealed during evaluation, then the garbling of an XOR gate can be proven indistinguishable from the constant-$(a \oplus b)$ gate only by first embedding a challenge key at k_u^{1-a} and then a second challenge key at k_v^{1-b}, or vice versa; i.e. the reduction needs to embed challenges at each input wire.

---

[9] Note, this simulation crucially relies on the fact that keys can be *equivocated*: While the output keys are all associated to 0, when altering the output mapping accordingly evaluation will still succeed. Note that in the selective setting for Yao's original scheme as well as in the adaptive setting for the modified scheme [14] the input is known before the output mapping is sent.

Table 1. Garbling tables for (a) general gate g, (b) AND gate, (c) XOR gate, and (d) constant-0 gate. u and v denote the two input wires, whereas w denotes the output wire.

$\mathsf{E}_{k_u^0}(\mathsf{E}_{k_v^0}(k_w^{g(0,0)}))$	$\mathsf{E}_{k_u^0}(\mathsf{E}_{k_v^0}(k_w^0))$	$\mathsf{E}_{k_u^0}(\mathsf{E}_{k_v^0}(k_w^0))$	$\mathsf{E}_{k_u^0}(\mathsf{E}_{k_v^0}(k_w^0))$
$\mathsf{E}_{k_u^1}(\mathsf{E}_{k_v^0}(k_w^{g(1,0)}))$	$\mathsf{E}_{k_u^1}(\mathsf{E}_{k_v^0}(k_w^0))$	$\mathsf{E}_{k_u^1}(\mathsf{E}_{k_v^0}(k_w^1))$	$\mathsf{E}_{k_u^1}(\mathsf{E}_{k_v^0}(k_w^0))$
$\mathsf{E}_{k_u^0}(\mathsf{E}_{k_v^1}(k_w^{g(0,1)}))$	$\mathsf{E}_{k_u^0}(\mathsf{E}_{k_v^1}(k_w^0))$	$\mathsf{E}_{k_u^0}(\mathsf{E}_{k_v^1}(k_w^1))$	$\mathsf{E}_{k_u^0}(\mathsf{E}_{k_v^1}(k_w^0))$
$\mathsf{E}_{k_u^1}(\mathsf{E}_{k_v^1}(k_w^{g(1,1)}))$	$\mathsf{E}_{k_u^1}(\mathsf{E}_{k_v^1}(k_w^1))$	$\mathsf{E}_{k_u^1}(\mathsf{E}_{k_v^1}(k_w^0))$	$\mathsf{E}_{k_u^1}(\mathsf{E}_{k_v^1}(k_w^0))$
(a)	(b)	(c)	(d)

Pebbling rules. To complete the description of a pebble game, we need to describe the pebbling rules. These rules essentially capture the following observation: a reduction (with overwhelming probability) cannot possess encryptions of its (IND-CPA) challenge key. Therefore, whenever the garbling table $\tilde{g}$ of a gate g has been switched to a malformed garbling $\tilde{g}'$ (say) at distance one, (at least) one of the garbling tables associated to its predecessor gates, say g_u, *must* have been first switched to a garbling that encodes only one of g_u's output keys. This is required to "free up" one of g_u's output keys (so that it can now be set as the challenge key). Looking ahead, we will be interested in pebbling the circuit $\mathsf{G}^\oplus$ which consists of XOR gates only. Hence, the pebbling rules are designed to capture the structure of XOR gates. Recall that an XOR gate is at distance 2 from a constant gate, thus, we end up with the following rules (where g_u and g_v denote the two predecessors of g):

1. a gray pebble can be placed on or removed from a gate g only if (at least) one of its predecessor gates (say g_u) carries a black pebble; and
2. a gray pebble on a gate g can be swapped with a black pebble if the *other* predecessor gate (i.e., g_v) carries a black pebble.

The actual game. The above white-gray-black (WGB) pebble game is a simplified version of the (WG³B) pebble game we end up using, but it is sufficient to convey the essential ideas that we use. The actual game, defined in Definition 4.1 (Sect. 4.3), is more fine-grained: in order to keep track of the inner and outer encryptions, we introduce three types of gray pebbles (gray-left, gray-right and gray-free), and the pebbling rules are also modified accordingly.

Definition 4.1 (Reversible WG³B pebbling game for indegree-2 graphs). *Consider a directed acyclic graph $G = (\mathcal{V}, \mathcal{E})$ with $\mathcal{V} = [1, S]$ and let $\mathcal{X} = \{W, G_*, G_L, G_R, B\}$ denote the set of colours of the pebbles. Consider a sequence $\mathcal{P} := (\mathcal{P}_0, \ldots, \mathcal{P}_\tau)$ of pebbling configurations for G, where $\mathcal{P}_i \in \mathcal{X}^{\mathcal{V}}$ for all $i \in [0, \tau]$. We call such a sequence a WG³B pebbling strategy for G if the following two criteria are satisfied:*

1. *In the initial configuration all the vertices are pebbled white (i.e., $\mathcal{P}_0 = (W, \ldots, W)$) and in the final configuration at least one sink of G is pebbled gray (i.e., $\mathcal{P}_\tau = (\ldots, G_\cdot, \ldots)$), where $G_\cdot$ denotes an arbitrary type of gray, i.e. $G_\cdot \in \{G_*, G_L, G_R\}$.*

2. *Two subsequent configurations differ only in one vertex and the following rules are respected in each move:*

   (a) $W \leftrightarrow G_*$: *a white pebble can be replaced by a G_* pebble (and vice versa) if one of its parents is black-pebbled*

   (b) $W/G_* \leftrightarrow G_L$: *a white or G_* pebble can be replaced by a G_L pebble (and vice versa) if its* left *parent is black-pebbled*

   (c) $W/G_* \leftrightarrow G_R$: *a white or G_* pebble can be replaced by a G_R pebble (and vice versa) if its* right *parent is black-pebbled*

   (d) $G_L \leftrightarrow B$: *a G_L pebble can be replaced by a black pebble (and vice versa) if its* right *parent is black-pebbled*

   (e) $G_R \leftrightarrow B$: *a G_R pebble can be replaced by a black pebble (and vice versa) if its* left *parent is black-pebbled*

The space-complexity of a WG^3B pebbling strategy $\mathcal{P} = (\mathcal{P}_0, \ldots, \mathcal{P}_\tau)$ for a DAG G is defined as

$$\sigma_G(\mathcal{P}) := \max_{i \in [0,\tau]} |\{j \in [1,S] : \mathcal{P}_i(j) \in \{G_*, G_L, G_R, B\}\}|.$$

For a subgraph G' induced on vertex set $\mathcal{V}' \subset \mathcal{V}$, the space-complexity of $\mathcal{P}$ restricted to G' is defined as

$$\sigma_{|G'}(\mathcal{P}) := \max_{i \in [0,\tau]} |\{j \in \mathcal{V}' : \mathcal{P}_i(j) \in \{G_*, G_L, G_R, B\}\}|.$$

The space-complexity of a DAG G is the minimum space-complexity over all of its strategies $\mathcal{P}^G$:

$$\sigma(G) := \min_{\mathcal{P} \in \mathcal{P}^G} \sigma_G(\mathcal{P}). \tag{5}$$

The following lemma gives a lower bound on the WG^3B pebbling complexity of the graph $G \setminus G^0$ underlying the first two blocks $G^\wedge \circ G^\oplus$ of our candidate circuit G. A proof can be found in the full version of this paper.

Lemma 4.4 (Pebbling lower bound on $G \setminus G^0$). *Let $G \setminus G^0$ be the graph underlying the circuit $G^\wedge \circ G^\oplus$. To gray-pebble a gate on layer $d' \in [1, d+1]$ following the reversible WG^3B pebbling rules from Definition 4.1, one requires space-complexity at least $d' - 1$. Furthermore, to G_L- or B-pebble a gate on layer $d' \geq d+1$, one requires at least d gray or black pebbles simultaneously on the first d layers.*

The following definition now gives a *cut in the configuration graph*; our adversary $\mathcal{A}$ will be a *threshold* adversary with respect to this cut.

Definition 4.2 (Good pebbling configurations). *A pebbling configuration $\mathcal{P}$ on DAG $G \setminus G^0$ is called* good *if it is reachable by reversible WG^3B pebbling moves using less than d gray or black pebbles on the first d layers simultaneously, i.e., there exists a WG^3B pebbling strategy $\mathcal{P} := (\mathcal{P}_0, \ldots, \mathcal{P})$ for G such that $\sigma_{|G^\oplus}(\mathcal{P}) \leq d - 1$.*

In particular, by Lemma 4.4, any pebbling configuration $\mathcal{P}$ with a G_L or B pebble on a gate in $G^\wedge$ is bad.

4.4   Extraction of Pebbling Configuration on $G \setminus G^0$

In this section we will discuss how to extract such a pebbling configuration. Note, that $\mathcal{A}$ is computationally unbounded, hence can extract messages and keys from ciphertexts by brute-force search.

1. First, check whether $(\tilde{\mathsf{G}}, \tilde{x})$ *evaluates correctly*, i.e., $\mathsf{GEval}(\tilde{\mathsf{G}}, \tilde{x}) = \mathsf{G}(x_0)$.

   If the evaluation check passes, check whether $\tilde{\mathsf{G}}, \tilde{x}$ have the *correct syntax*: Check whether $\tilde{\mathsf{G}}$ consists of four ciphertexts for each gate, which have the following form

   $$c_1 = \mathsf{Enc}_{k_1}(\mathsf{Enc}_{k_3}(k_5)), \ c_2 = \mathsf{Enc}_{k_1}(\mathsf{Enc}_{k_4}(m_2)), \tag{6}$$
   $$\{c_3, c_4\} = \{\mathsf{Enc}_{k_2}(m_3), \mathsf{Enc}_{k_2}(m_4)\},$$

   for distinct keys k_1, k_2, k_3, k_4, k_5 and arbitrary (not necessarily distinct) messages m_2, m_3, m_4, where keys k_1 and k_3 are revealed during evaluation $\mathsf{GEval}(\tilde{\mathsf{G}}, \tilde{x})$. I.e., two of the four ciphertexts are encryptions under the same left secret keys k_1 and k_2, respectively, one of them is a double encryption $\mathsf{Enc}_{k_1}(\mathsf{Enc}_{k_3}(k_5))$ under left key k_1 and some right key k_3 of an output key k_5 (all these being revealed throughout evaluation), and the second encryption under k_1 encrypts an encryption under a second right key k_4 (of an arbitrary message m_2).

   Finally, check *consistency of keys*: For each gate, extract key pairs (k_1, k_2) and (k_3, k_4) corresponding to left and right input wires, and check whether they are consistent with the keys extracted from sibling gates: If gate g is the left sibling of g', then g's right input key pair must coincide with the left key pair extracted from g', i.e., $(k_3, k_4) = (k_1', k_2')$. Note, if this check passes, then all wires in the circuit can be uniquely associated with a key pair. Finally, check that all extracted keys are distinct.

   If any of these checks fails, map $(\tilde{\mathsf{G}}, \tilde{x})$ to a bad pebbling configuration, e.g., to the pebbling configuration on G where all gates at levels $[d + 1, 2d + 1]$ are black pebbled[10] and quit.

Remark 4.1. Note, syntax and consistency checks allow a reduction to distinguish

- a ciphertext from a non-ciphertext,
- a ciphertext under key k from a ciphertext under key $k' \neq k$.

We will argue in Sect. 4.5 that this is of no help to the reduction for breaking IND-CPA security of the information-theoretic encryption scheme $\mathcal{F}$.

For all garblings $(\tilde{\mathsf{G}}, \tilde{x})$ that pass correctness, syntax, and consistency checks, $\mathcal{A}$ will extract a pebbling configuration on $G \setminus G^0$ by mapping each gate to a color in $\{\mathsf{W}, \mathsf{G}_*, \mathsf{G}_L, \mathsf{G}_R, \mathsf{B}\}$.

---

[10] This choice was made for convenience (see Lemmas 4.6 to 4.8), but in principle could be an arbitrary bad configuration, and should simply guarantee that no reduction can gain any advantage by departing from the protocol in an obvious way.

2. For each XOR gate g_j ($j \in [1, d] \cdot n + [0, n]$): Check whether g_j is garbled correctly with respect to input x_0. To this aim, let b_l, b_r, and $b_o = g_j(b_l, b_r) = b_l \oplus b_r$ denote the left/right input and the output bit of g_j, respectively, when evaluating G on x_0. We use the same notation as in Eq. 6 above; furthermore, let k_6 be the second key associated with the output wire (which was extracted from the garbling tables of the successor gates).

   - If g_j is garbled similar to the case of an honest garbling of (G, x_0), i.e., $m_2 = k_6$, $m_3 = \mathsf{Enc}_{k_3}(k_6)$, and $m_4 = \mathsf{Enc}_{k_4}(k_5)$ (or the roles of m_3, m_4 permuted), then associate g_j with a W pebble.
   - If m_2 and m_3 are as in the previous case, but $m_4 = \mathsf{Enc}_{k_4}(m)$ for some message $m \neq k_5$, then associate g_j with a G_* pebble. Similarly for the case where the roles of m_3, m_4 are permuted.
   - If m_3 is as in the first case, $m_4 = \mathsf{Enc}_{k_4}(m)$ for an arbitrary message m, but $m_2 \neq k_6$, then associate g_j with a G_R pebble. Similarly for the case where the roles of m_3, m_4 are permuted.
   - If $m_2 = k_6$ is as in the first case, but $\{m_3, m_4\}$ differs from the previous cases, then associate g_j with a G_L pebble.
   - For all other cases, associate g_j with a B pebble.

Remark 4.2. Due to symmetry of the XOR operation, whether a gate is considered properly garbled (i.e. mapped to a white pebble) or not (i.e. mapped to gray or black) does *not* depend on the input keys. Thus, the set of black and gray pebbles on $G^\oplus$ can be extracted *independently* of x_0 and $\tilde{x}$.

3. For each AND gate g_j ($j \in [d+1, 2d+1] \cdot n + [0, n]$): Similar to the case of XOR gates, check whether the gate is correctly garbled with respect to x_0. Using the same notation as above, associate g_j with a pebble as follows:
   - If g_j is garbled similar to the case of an honest garbling of (G, x_0), i.e., for

     $(b_l, b_r) = (0, 0)$, we have $m_2 = k_5$, $m_3 = \mathsf{Enc}_{k_3}(k_5)$, and $m_4 = \mathsf{Enc}_{k_4}(k_6)$,

     $(b_l, b_r) = (0, 1)$, we have $m_2 = k_5$, $m_3 = \mathsf{Enc}_{k_3}(k_6)$, and $m_4 = \mathsf{Enc}_{k_4}(k_5)$,

     $(b_l, b_r) = (1, 0)$, we have $m_2 = k_6$, $m_3 = \mathsf{Enc}_{k_3}(k_5)$, and $m_4 = \mathsf{Enc}_{k_4}(k_5)$,

     $(b_l, b_r) = (1, 1)$, we have $m_2 = k_6$, $m_3 = \mathsf{Enc}_{k_3}(k_6)$, and $m_4 = \mathsf{Enc}_{k_4}(k_6)$,

     (or the roles of m_3, m_4 permuted) then associate g_j with a W pebble.
   - If m_2 and m_3 are as in the previous case, but $m_4 = \mathsf{Enc}_{k_4}(m)$ for some message m that differs from above, then associate g_j with a G_* pebble. (Similarly for the case where the roles of m_3, m_4 are permuted.)
   - If m_3 is as in the first case, $m_4 = \mathsf{Enc}_{k_4}(m)$ for an arbitrary message m, but m_2 differs from the previous case, then associate g_j with a G_R pebble. (Similarly for the case where the roles of m_3, m_4 are permuted.)
   - If m_2 is as in the first case, but $\{m_3, m_4\}$ differs from the previous cases, then associate g_j with a G_L pebble.
   - For all other cases, associate g_j with a B pebble.

Remark 4.3. At first sight, it might seem counterintuitive that the mapping from gates to colours not only depends on the associated ciphertexts, but also on the input x_0. This however is unavoidable since the adversary $\mathcal{A}$ cannot simply map keys to bits, but can only *relate* them to the keys it learned from $\tilde{x}$, which might be properly garbled or not.

In the following lemma, we prove that the adversary $\mathcal{A}$ using the above pebbling extraction indeed breaks indistinguishability of Yao's garbling scheme. A proof can be found in the full version of this paper.

Lemma 4.5. $\mathcal{A}$ *breaks indistinguishability of the garbling scheme with probability* $1 - 1/2^{n-1}$.

Since $\mathcal{A}$ extracts the pebble mode of a gate with regard to the garbled input (i.e., the keys it learns through evaluation), the reduction can still change the mode of a gate *after* it output $\tilde{\mathsf{G}}$ by choosing different input keys for $\tilde{x}$. In the following lemmas we prove that this flexibility of choosing the input keys is of not much help to a reduction aiming at a good pebbling configuration, where in particular all gates at layers $[d+1, 2d+1]$ are mapped to W, G_*, or G_R pebbles.

First, we consider the case of a properly garbled AND gates. In this case, due to the asymmetry of the AND operation, input keys can be associated with bits and hence a properly garbled layer of AND gates has a similar function as an output mapping. A proof can be found in the full version of this paper.

Lemma 4.6. *For any garbling of an AND gate on layer* $[d+1, 2d+1]$, *and any input bits* b_l, b_r, *there exists at most one input key pair* (k_1, k_3) *such that the gate will be mapped to a* W *pebble.*

The situation becomes a bit more involved if AND gates are not properly garbled, since in this case asymmetry might be broken. However, if the left input keys can be mapped to bits, then we can still obtain some meaningful guarantees. We first consider the case that an AND gate is garbled in G_* mode, i.e. one ciphertext is malformed and there exist some input bits (b_l, b_r) such that it will be mapped to a G_* pebble. In the following Lemma we prove that for a different right input bit $1 - b_r$ the gate will be mapped to a G_L pebble instead. A proof can be found in the full version of this paper.

Lemma 4.7. *For any garbling of an AND gate, any left input bit* b_l, *and fixed left input key, there exists at most one* $b_r \in \{0, 1\}$ *such that there exists a (not necessarily unique) right input key such that the gate will be mapped to a* G_* *pebble. If such a right input bit* b_r *exists, then for right input bit* $1 - b_r$ *the gate will be mapped to a* G_L *pebble.*

Next we consider the case of an AND gate that is garbled in G_R mode w.r.t. some input bits (b_l, b_r). In this case we have to distinguish two different ways to garble a gate such that it will be mapped to a G_R pebble. For one type of G_R pebble we can map keys to bits, just as in the case of properly garbled gates. For the second type of G_R pebble we obtain a similar guarantee as for G_* pebbles. A proof can be found in the full version of this paper.

Lemma 4.8. *For any garbling of an AND gate on layer* $[d + 1, 2d + 1]$, *any left input bit* b_l, *and fixed left input key, one of the following is true:*

1. *For any right input bit* $b_r \in \{0, 1\}$ *there exists at most one right input key such that the gate will be mapped to a* G_R *pebble. If such a key exists, then for any other right input key the gate will be mapped to a* B *pebble.*
2. *There exists at most one input bit* $b_r \in \{0, 1\}$ *such that there exists a right input key* k_r *such that the gate will be mapped to a* G_R *pebble. If such a bit exists, then for right input bit* $1 - b_r$ *and any right input key the gate will be mapped to a* B *pebble.*

These two cases characterize two different types of G_R *pebbled gates, where we denote a gate as* G_R-*type-1 if case 1 is true, and* G_R-*type-2 if only case 2 is true.*

4.5 Lower Bound on Security Loss for Any Reduction

In this section we will combine all previous results to prove a lower bound on adaptive security of Yao's garbling scheme. More precisely, we will prove that any black-box reduction which aims to exploit $\mathcal{A}$'s distinguishing advantage to break IND-CPA security of the underlying encryption scheme loses a factor subexponential in the depth of the circuit.

Let R be an arbitrary PPT reduction which has black-box access to an adversary $\mathcal{A}$ that breaks indistinguishability of Yao's garbling scheme, and attempts to solve an IND-CPA challenge with respect to an encryption scheme (Gen, Enc, Dec). Following the approach of Kamath et al. [15], we define an *information-theoretically* secure encryption scheme $\mathcal{F} = $ (Gen, Enc, Dec) as follows: For $l \in \{1, 6\}$, let $E_l : \{0, 1\}^{(l+2)\lambda} \rightarrow \{0, 1\}^{2(l+2)\lambda}$ be a random expanding function (which is injective with overwhelming probability).

- Key generation $\mathsf{Gen}(1^\lambda)$: On input a security parameter λ in unary, output a key $k \leftarrow \{0, 1\}^{1=*}$ uniformly at random.
- Encryption $\mathsf{Enc}(k, m)$: On input a key $k \in \{0, 1\}^\lambda$ and a message $m \in \{0, 1\}^{l \cdot \lambda}$ with $l \in \{1, 6\}$, sample randomness $r \leftarrow \{0, 1\}^\lambda$, and output $E_l(k, m; r)$.
- Decryption $\mathsf{Dec}(k, c)$ is simulated to be consistent with Enc: On input a key $k \in \{0, 1\}^\lambda$ and a ciphertext $c \in \{0, 1\}^{2(l+2)\lambda}$ with $l \in \{1, 6\}$, check whether c lies in the image of $E_l(k, \cdot; \cdot)$, if so extract $m \in \{0, 1\}^{l \cdot \lambda}$, $r \in \{0, 1\}^\lambda$ such that $c = E_l(k, m; r)$ and output m, otherwise output $\perp$.

Choosing E_l ($l \in \{1, 6\}$) to be random functions implies that $\mathcal{F}$ is information-theoretically IND-CCA secure. Thus, since R only makes polynomially many queries, the only non-negligible advantage R has in breaking the IND-CPA security of $\mathcal{F}$ must stem from its interaction with $\mathcal{A}$. Furthermore, with all but negligible (in λ) probability $\mathcal{F}$ satisfies the special property (Definition 3.3), hence can be used in Yao's garbling scheme.

We first argue that neither checking correctness, syntax, nor consistency (cf. Sect. 4.4) is of any help to R. Obviously, this is true for the correctness check, since R can efficiently evaluate $\mathsf{GEval}(\tilde{\mathsf{G}}, \tilde{x})$. However, we have to argue a bit more to prove that also syntax and consistency checks are of no help to R. To this aim, we construct an oracle $\mathcal{O}$ that allows to distinguish

- a ciphertext from an arbitrary string in $\{0,1\}^{2(l+2)\lambda}$ for $l \in \{1,6\}$,
- a ciphertext under key $k \in \{0,1\}^{\lambda}$ from a ciphertext under key $k' \neq k$.

More precisely, $\mathcal{O}$ takes as input two strings $s \in \{0,1\}^{2(l+2)\lambda}$ and $s' \in \{0,1\}^{2(l'+2)\lambda}$ ($l, l' \in \{1,6\}$) and checks whether s, s' lie in the image of $\mathsf{E}_l, \mathsf{E}_{l'}$, respectively. If this check fails for one of the strings, then $\mathcal{O}$ outputs $\perp$. Otherwise, it extracts preimages $(k, m, r) \in \{0,1\}^{(l+2)\lambda}$ under E_l and $(k', m', r') \in \{0,1\}^{(l'+2)\lambda}$ under $\mathsf{E}_{l'}$. If $k = k'$, $\mathcal{O}$ outputs 1, otherwise 0.

In the full version of this paper we first show that access to oracle $\mathcal{O}$ allows R to efficiently carry out syntax and consistency checks, and then prove that $\mathcal{F}$ remains information-theoretically IND-CPA secure even against adversaries that have access to $\mathcal{O}$.

Now, to prove that any black-box reduction from indistinguishability of Yao's garbling scheme to IND-CPA security of the underlying encryption scheme suffers from a loss that is subexponential in the depth δ of the circuit, we construct an adversary $\mathcal{A}[c^*]$ that behaves just like $\mathcal{A}$ but doesn't decrypt challenge ciphertext c^*. More precisely, $\mathcal{A}[c^*]$ with input a ciphertext c^*, has oracle access to $\mathcal{O}$, $\mathcal{F}$, as well as an IND-CCA decryption oracle Dec_{k^*} that it can query on any ciphertext $c \neq c^*$. We construct $\mathcal{A}[c^*]$ such that it never decrypts c^* unless it already knows the encryption key k^* from other keys and ciphertexts in $\tilde{\mathsf{G}}, \tilde{x}$:

- First $\mathcal{A}[c^*]$ runs evaluation, syntax, and consistency checks using oracle $\mathcal{O}$. If these checks pass, similar to $\mathcal{A}$, the algorithm $\mathcal{A}[c^*]$ uses brute-force search to decrypt all ciphertexts *except* for those encrypted under k^* (to check whether a ciphertext is encrypted under k^* it uses $\mathcal{O}$ and c^*). Ciphertexts $c \neq c^*$ encrypted under k^* it decrypts using oracle Dec_{k^*}. For c^*, there are two cases:
  - If the key k^* was learned from previous decryptions (this can be checked by decrypting c^* under all known keys), $\mathcal{A}[c^*]$ simply decrypts c^* using k^*.
  - If the k^* is not known to $\mathcal{A}[c^*]$, then it simply *assumes* $c^* \in \{0,1\}^{2(l+2)\lambda}$ with $l \in \{1,6\}$ would decrypt to $0^{l\cdot\lambda}$.
  $\mathcal{A}[c^*]$ then continues analogous to $\mathcal{A}$ by mapping $(\tilde{\mathsf{G}}, \tilde{x})$ to a pebbling configuration and outputting 0 whenever the pebbling configuration is good per Definition 4.2, and 1 otherwise.

Clearly, since $\mathcal{A}[c^*]$ never decrypts c^* except if k^* is known, there is no chance for R to use $\mathcal{A}[c^*]$ to break IND-CPA security of $\mathcal{F}$.[11] It remains to bound the success probability of any PPT distinguisher D to distinguish $\mathcal{A}[c^*]$ from $\mathcal{A}$.[12]

---

[11] Recall that our ideal encryption scheme $\mathcal{F}$ is IND-CCA secure, hence access to the oracle Dec_{k^*} used by $\mathcal{A}[c^*]$ is of no help to R.

[12] Note, we assume that $\mathcal{A}[c^*]$ has *private* access to its oracles and D cannot observe its oracle queries to distinguish it from $\mathcal{A}$.

To this aim, we will first show how the $\mathtt{WG}^3\mathtt{B}$ pebbling game relates to this issue. A proof of the following Lemma can be found in the full version of this paper.

Lemma 4.9. *Let $c^* \leftarrow \mathsf{Enc}_{k^*}(m)$ be an arbitrary ciphertext and let $\mathcal{P}$, $\mathcal{P}^*$ be the two pebbling configurations extracted by $\mathcal{A}$ and $\mathcal{A}[c^*]$, respectively, in the same execution of the game, i.e. using the same randomness. Then $\mathcal{P}^*$ differs from $\mathcal{P}$ by at most one valid $\mathtt{WG}^3 B$ pebbling move.*

We will now bound the distinguishing advantage of $\mathsf{D}^{\mathcal{F}}$. Recall that a pebbling configuration on $G \setminus G^0$ is good per Definition 4.2 if it can be reached by $\mathtt{WG}^3\mathtt{B}$ pebbling moves using at most $d - 1$ pebbles on the first d layers. Thus, by Lemma 4.9, any successful distinguisher D has to simulate $\tilde{\mathsf{G}}$ and $\tilde{x}$ such that the pebbling configurations $\mathcal{P}, \mathcal{P}^*$ on G extracted by $\mathcal{A}$ and $\mathcal{A}[c^*]$, respectively, contain exactly $d-1$ or d black and gray pebbles on the first d layers (depending on the IND-CPA challenge bit b^*), contain only $\mathtt{W}$, $\mathtt{G}_*$, and $\mathtt{G}_R$ pebbles on higher layers, and differ by a valid $\mathtt{WG}^3\mathtt{B}$ pebbling move within layers $[1, d+1]$.

In the following we will first restrict our analysis to *non-rewinding* distinguishers and assume x_0, x_1 were chosen uniformly at random by $\mathcal{A}$ *after* it sees G. Finally we will discuss how to slightly modify our adversary $\mathcal{A}$ to also cover the case that D chooses $\mathcal{A}$'s randomness and rewinds $\mathcal{A}$.

To bound the success probability of D, let r be arbitrary random coins and consider two cases:

(1) there exists s such that the output of $\mathcal{A}(s)$ and $\mathcal{A}[c^*](s)$ after interaction with $\mathsf{D}(r, c^*)$ differs and in $\mathcal{P}$ and $\mathcal{P}^*$ there are *more than* $\bar{d}$ $\mathtt{G}_*$ and $\mathtt{G}_R$-type-2 (as defined in Lemma 4.8) pebbles in layers $[d + 2, 2d + 1]$,
(2) there exists s such that the output of $\mathcal{A}(s)$ and $\mathcal{A}[c^*](s)$ after interaction with $\mathsf{D}(r, c^*)$ differs and in $\mathcal{P}$ and $\mathcal{P}^*$ there are *at most* $\bar{d}$ $\mathtt{G}_*$ and $\mathtt{G}_R$-type-2 pebbles in layers $[d + 2, 2d + 1]$.

We leave the parameter $\bar{d} < d/3$ undefined for now and optimize it later. In Lemmas 4.10 and 4.11, we will argue that, intuitively, in both cases the distinguisher D must have correctly guessed many of the input bits in x_0.

Lemma 4.10. *Let r be arbitrary coins such that case (1) is true. Then the probability (over uniformly random coins s) that the output of $\mathcal{A}(s)$ and $\mathcal{A}[c^*](s)$ differs after interaction with $\mathsf{D}(r, c^*)$ is at most $(3/4)^{\sqrt{\bar{d}}/7}$.*

Proof. To prove this lemma, we will use Lemmas 4.6 to 4.8. First, note that D can only succeed if at most one of the gates at layer $d + 1$ is not mapped to a $\mathtt{W}$ pebble, since the adversary $\mathcal{A}$ outputs 1 whenever any gate at layer $d+1$ is not $\mathtt{W}$ pebbled. Now, by Lemma 4.6, there is at most one pair of input keys to an AND gate that leads to this gate being mapped to a $\mathtt{W}$ pebble. As the input to all but one gate at layer $d + 1$ comprises *all* input to layer $d + 1$, this implies that D can only succeed, if it properly garbles all gates at layer $d + 1$ and the input keys which are revealed through $\mathsf{GEval}(\tilde{\mathsf{G}}, \tilde{x})$ are associated with the corresponding bits in $\mathsf{G}^{\oplus}(x_0)$.

Next, consider the AND gates at layers $[d+2, 2d+1]$. For D to succeed, these gates must *not* end up G_L or B pebbled. Since all these gates have their left input from layer d and by the previous argument all these keys are fixed, we can apply Lemmas 4.7 and 4.8: Let $\mathcal{S}$ denote the set of $\bar{d}$ gates in layers $[d+2, 2d+1]$ that are mapped to G_* or G_R-type-2 pebbles (for some random coins s such that (1) is true). Then by Lemma 4.3 there exists a subset $\mathcal{S}' \subseteq \mathcal{S}$ of size $\sqrt{\bar{d}}/4$ such that the set of right parents $\mathcal{S}_R$ of $\mathcal{S}'$ is linearly independent over $\mathbb{Z}_2$; and for each gate $g \in \mathcal{S}'$ left and right parent are linearly independent. To see that the latter is true, note that any subset smaller than n of gates within one layer or within one column is linearly independent (cf. Lemma 4.2). It directly follows that left and right parents of any gate $g \in \mathcal{S}'$ since they lie in the same column. Furthermore, the set of left parents $\mathcal{S}_L$ to $\mathcal{S}'$ is linearly independent since it is a subset of $\leq \bar{d} < n$ gates at layer d.

To argue that D must have guessed many of the right input bits to $S^\wedge$ correctly, we use the following simple result from linear algebra. A proof can be found in the full version of this paper.

Claim. Let $m \in [1, n]$ and $\mathcal{S}_1 = \{u_i\}_{i \in [1,m]}$ a subset of $\{0,1\}^n$ that is linearly independent over $\mathbb{Z}_2$. Let $\mathcal{S}_2 = \{v_i\}_{i \in [1,m]}$ be a multiset of elements in $\{0,1\}^n$ such that $\mathcal{S}_2$ as a set is linearly independent over $\mathbb{Z}_2$. Furthermore, assume $\{u_i, v_i\}$ is linearly independent for all $i \in [1, m]$. Then there exists an index set $\mathcal{I} \subset [1, m]$ of size $|\mathcal{I}| = \lfloor m/4 \rfloor$ such that $\bigcup_{i \in \mathcal{I}} \{u_i\} \cup \{v_i\}$ is linearly independent.

Since the multiset $\mathcal{S}_L$ and the set $\mathcal{S}_R$ of left and right parents of $\mathcal{S}'$ are linearly independent (as sets), respectively, and for any $g \in \mathcal{S}'$ left and right input to G are linearly independent, we can apply the claim to obtain a subset $\mathcal{S}'' \subset \mathcal{S}'$ of size $|\mathcal{S}'|/4$ such that the union of the parents of $\mathcal{S}''$ is linearly independent. For $\mathcal{S}''$, we can now use Lemmas 4.7 and 4.8 to see that any successful D must have correctly guessed all right input bits to $\mathcal{S}''$; i.e., for s sampled uniformly at random, the probability that D succeeds is at most $(1/2)^{|\mathcal{S}''|}$. As $|\mathcal{S}'| \geq \sqrt{\bar{d}}/4$, the probability that D succeeds can be upper-bounded by $(1/2)^{\sqrt{\bar{d}}/16} < (3/4)^{\sqrt{\bar{d}}/7}$.

$\square$

Lemma 4.11. *Let r be arbitrary coins such that case (2) is true. Then the probability (over uniformly random coins s) that the output of $\mathcal{A}(s)$ and $\mathcal{A}[c^*](s)$ differs after interaction with $D(r, c^*)$ is at most $(3/4)^{\sqrt{d-3\bar{d}/4}}$.*

Proof. Recall that whenever the consistency check passes, each wire in $\tilde{G}$ can be uniquely associated with two keys. Now, in case (2), for all but $\bar{d}$ wires in $G \setminus G^0$ the following holds: By Lemmas 4.6 and 4.8, for each bit running over the wire w in G, there exists at most one key associated with w in $\tilde{G}^\oplus$ such that the AND gates with right input wire w is mapped to a "good" (W or G_R-type-1) pebble, while for the other key associated to w it would be mapped to a "bad" pebble (G_L or B). Note that in the latter case D immediately fails.

This allows us to map keys associated with wires in $\tilde{G}^\oplus$ to bits, hence implies a mapping from $(\tilde{G}, \tilde{x})$ to a circuit $\hat{G}$ and input $\hat{x}$, where $\hat{G}$ contains at most $3\bar{d}$

"undefined" gates (note, each internal wire effects 3 gates in $G^{\oplus}$). Now, for D to succeed, it has to simulate $(\tilde{G}, \tilde{x})$ such that at least $d' := d - 3\bar{d}$ "well-defined" gates in the circuit $\hat{G}$ differ from XOR gates and $\hat{x} = x_0$. At the same time, all input and output wires of the well-defined gates have to carry the correct bits during evaluation (for "evaluation" of $\hat{G}$ on $\hat{x}$ we apply the mapping from keys to bits to $\mathsf{Eval}(\tilde{G}, \tilde{x})$ to extract a bit for all wires connected to well-defined gates).

Ignoring the undefined gates in $\hat{G}$, this exactly corresponds to the game introduced in Sect. 4.2: D simulates a circuit such that all but d' gates are garbled correctly as XOR gates, and D succeeds, if for all gates the (input and) output bits correspond to the respective bits during evaluation of $G^{\oplus}$ on input x_0. Lemma 4.1 now implies an upper bound on D's success probability in case (2):

$\Pr[\text{D succeeds in case (2)}] \leq (3/4)^{\sqrt{d'}/4} = (3/4)^{\sqrt{d-3\bar{d}}/4}$. □

Thus, Lemmas 4.10 and 4.11 imply the following bound on any non-rewinding PPT distinguisher D (choose $\bar{d} = d/4$):

Corollary 4.2. *No non-rewinding PPT distinguisher $\mathsf{D}^{\mathcal{F}}$ can distinguish $\mathcal{A}[c^*]$ from $\mathcal{A}$ with probability larger than $(3/4)^{\sqrt{d}/14}$.*

To handle arbitrary – potentially rewinding – distinguishers D, we modify $\mathcal{A}$ as follows: Instead of sampling x_0, x_1 using random coins s, we assume a pseudorandom function f_k with uniformly random key k was hardcoded in $\mathcal{A}$, which takes as input a garbled circuit $\tilde{G}$ and coins s, and outputs a tuple (x_0, x_1). Since D only has *black-box* access to $\mathcal{A}/\mathcal{A}[c^*]$, the secret key k is hidden from D, thus for two different inputs $(\tilde{G}, s), (\tilde{G}', s')$ to $\mathcal{A}/\mathcal{A}[c^*]$ the input pairs $(x_0, x_1), (x_0', x_1')$ look like independently sampled uniformly random strings.

With this modification in place, we finally arrive at the following lower bound on the security loss of any *black-box reduction* R (where we used $\delta < 3d$, hence $\sqrt{d}/14 > \sqrt{\delta}/25$). Note that our bounds naturally only apply to $d \leq n$, hence we assume $\delta < 2n$ in our theorem statement.

Theorem 4.1. *Any black-box reduction from the indistinguishability of Yao's garbling scheme (or its variant from [14]) on the class of circuits with input length n and depth $\delta \leq 2n$ to the IND-CPA security of the underlying encryption scheme loses at least a factor $\frac{1}{q} \cdot (\frac{4}{3})^{\sqrt{\delta}/25} > \frac{1}{q} \cdot 2^{\sqrt{\delta}/61}$, where q denotes the number of times the reduction rewinds the adversary.*

5 Discussion and Open Problems

In this work we prove that any black-box reduction from indistinguishability of (the modification [14] of) Yao's garbling scheme to IND-CPA security of the underlying encryption scheme must involve a loss in security that is subexponential in the depth of the circuit. This clearly also implies limitations to the stronger and more common simulation-based security and shows that the approach of [14] is essentially optimal. However, we leave it to future work if our fine-grained separation can be turned into an actual attack against Yao's garbling scheme.

Beside this most exciting open problem, one can also consider if our approach can be optimized. It might be possible to push our lower bound to an exponential loss, which would exactly match the upper bound from [14]. Following our approach, this requires a more sophisticated pebbling lower bound. Another interesting question would be if an even stronger bound can be found for the original construction of Yao, where the output mapping is sent in the offline phase, and certain limitations are already known from [3].

Acknowledgements. We would like to thank the anonymous reviewers of Crypto'21 whose detailed comments helped us considerably improve the presentation of the paper.

References

1. Ananth, P., Lombardi, A.: Succinct garbling schemes from functional encryption through a local simulation paradigm. In: Beimel, A., Dziembowski, S. (eds.) TCC 2018, Part II. LNCS, vol. 11240, pp. 455–472. Springer, Cham (2018). https://doi. org/10.1007/978-3-030-03810-6_17
2. Ananth, P., Sahai, A.: Functional encryption for turing machines. In: Kushilevitz, E., Malkin, T. (eds.) TCC 2016, Part I. LNCS, vol. 9562, pp. 125–153. Springer, Heidelberg (2016). https://doi.org/10.1007/978-3-662-49096-9_6
3. Applebaum, B., Ishai, Y., Kushilevitz, E., Waters, B.: Encoding functions with constant online rate or how to compress garbled circuits keys. In: Canetti, R., Garay, J.A. (eds.) CRYPTO 2013, Part II. LNCS, vol. 8043, pp. 166–184. Springer, Heidelberg (2013). https://doi.org/10.1007/978-3-642-40084-1_10
4. Bellare, M., Hoang, V.T., Keelveedhi, S.: Instantiating random oracles via UCEs. In: Canetti, R., Garay, J.A. (eds.) CRYPTO 2013, Part II. LNCS, vol. 8043, pp. 398–415. Springer, Heidelberg (2013). https://doi.org/10.1007/978-3-642-40084-1_23
5. Bellare, M., Hoang, V.T., Rogaway, P.: Adaptively secure garbling with applications to one-time programs and secure outsourcing. In: Wang, X., Sako, K. (eds.) ASIACRYPT 2012. LNCS, vol. 7658, pp. 134–153. Springer, Heidelberg (2012). https://doi.org/10.1007/978-3-642-34961-4_10
6. Bellare, M., Hoang, V.T., Rogaway, P.: Foundations of garbled circuits. In: Yu, T., Danezis, G., Gligor, V.D. (eds.) ACM CCS 2012, pp. 784–796. ACM Press, October 2012
7. Boneh, D., et al.: Fully key-homomorphic encryption, arithmetic circuit ABE and compact garbled circuits. In: Nguyen, P.Q., Oswald, E. (eds.) EUROCRYPT 2014. LNCS, vol. 8441, pp. 533–556. Springer, Heidelberg (2014). https://doi.org/10. 1007/978-3-642-55220-5_30
8. Dziembowski, S., Kazana, T., Wichs, D.: Key-evolution schemes resilient to space-bounded leakage. In: Rogaway, P. (ed.) CRYPTO 2011. LNCS, vol. 6841, pp. 335–353. Springer, Heidelberg (2011). https://doi.org/10.1007/978-3-642-22792-9_19
9. Garg, S., Srinivasan, A.: Adaptively secure garbling with near optimal online complexity. In: Nielsen, J.B., Rijmen, V. (eds.) EUROCRYPT 2018, Part II. LNCS, vol. 10821, pp. 535–565. Springer, Cham (2018). https://doi.org/10.1007/978-3-319-78375-8_18

10. Hemenway, B., Jafargholi, Z., Ostrovsky, R., Scafuro, A., Wichs, D.: Adaptively secure garbled circuits from one-way functions. In: Robshaw, M., Katz, J. (eds.) CRYPTO 2016, Part III. LNCS, vol. 9816, pp. 149–178. Springer, Heidelberg (2016). https://doi.org/10.1007/978-3-662-53015-3_6

11. Jafargholi, Z., Kamath, C., Klein, K., Komargodski, I., Pietrzak, K., Wichs, D.: Be adaptive, avoid overcommitting. In: Katz, J., Shacham, H. (eds.) CRYPTO 2017, Part I. LNCS, vol. 10401, pp. 133–163. Springer, Cham (2017). https://doi.org/10.1007/978-3-319-63688-7_5

12. Jafargholi, Z., Oechsner, S.: Adaptive security of practical garbling schemes. In: Bhargavan, K., Oswald, E., Prabhakaran, M. (eds.) INDOCRYPT 2020. LNCS, vol. 12578, pp. 741–762. Springer, Cham (2020). https://doi.org/10.1007/978-3-030-65277-7_33

13. Jafargholi, Z., Scafuro, A., Wichs, D.: Adaptively indistinguishable garbled circuits. In: Kalai, Y., Reyzin, L. (eds.) TCC 2017, Part II. LNCS, vol. 10678, pp. 40–71. Springer, Cham (2017). https://doi.org/10.1007/978-3-319-70503-3_2

14. Jafargholi, Z., Wichs, D.: Adaptive security of Yao's garbled circuits. In: Hirt, M., Smith, A. (eds.) TCC 2016, Part I. LNCS, vol. 9985, pp. 433–458. Springer, Heidelberg (2016). https://doi.org/10.1007/978-3-662-53641-4_17

15. Kamath, C., Klein, K., Pietrzak, K., Walter, M.: On the cost of adaptivity in graph-based games. Cryptology ePrint Archive, Report 2021/059 (2021). https://eprint.iacr.org/2021/059

16. Lindell, Y., Pinkas, B.: A proof of security of Yao's protocol for two-party computation. J. Cryptol. **22**(2), 161–188 (2009). https://doi.org/10.1007/s00145-008-9036-8

17. Yao, A.C.-C.: Protocols for secure computations (extended abstract). In: 23rd FOCS, pp. 160–164. IEEE Computer Society Press, November 1982

18. Yao, A.C.-C.: How to generate and exchange secrets (extended abstract). In: 27th FOCS, pp. 162–167. IEEE Computer Society Press, October 1986

Lattice Cryptography

Subtractive Sets over Cyclotomic Rings
Limits of Schnorr-Like Arguments over Lattices

Martin R. Albrecht[1](✉) and Russell W. F. Lai[2](✉)

[1] Information Security Group, Royal Holloway, University of London, Egham, UK
martin.albrecht@royalholloway.ac.uk
[2] Chair of Applied Cryptography, Friedrich-Alexander-Universität
Erlangen-Nürnberg, Nürnberg, Germany
russell.lai@cs.fau.de

Abstract. We study when (dual) Vandermonde systems of the form $\mathbf{V}_T^{(\mathsf{T})} \cdot \mathbf{z} = s \cdot \mathbf{w}$ admit a solution $\mathbf{z}$ over a ring $\mathcal{R}$, where $\mathbf{V}_T$ is the Vandermonde matrix defined by a set T and where the "slack" s is a measure of the quality of solutions. To this end, we propose the notion of (s,t)-subtractive sets over a ring $\mathcal{R}$, with the property that if S is (s,t)-subtractive then the above (dual) Vandermonde systems defined by any t-subset $T \subseteq S$ are solvable over $\mathcal{R}$. The challenge is then to find large sets S while minimising (the norm of) s when given a ring $\mathcal{R}$.

By constructing families of (s,t)-subtractive sets S of size $n = \mathsf{poly}(\lambda)$ over cyclotomic rings $\mathcal{R} = \mathbb{Z}[\zeta_{p^\ell}]$ for prime p, we construct Schnorr-like lattice-based proofs of knowledge for the SIS relation $\mathbf{A} \cdot \mathbf{x} = s \cdot \mathbf{y} \bmod q$ with $O(1/n)$ knowledge error, and $s = 1$ in case $p = \mathsf{poly}(\lambda)$. Our technique slots naturally into the lattice Bulletproof framework from Crypto'20, producing lattice-based succinct arguments for NP with better parameters.

We then give matching impossibility results constraining n relative to s, which suggest that our Bulletproof-compatible protocols are optimal unless fundamentally new techniques are discovered. Noting that the knowledge error of lattice Bulletproofs is $\Omega(\log k/n)$ for witnesses in $\mathcal{R}^k$ and subtractive set size n, our result represents a barrier to practically efficient lattice-based succinct arguments in the Bulletproof framework.

Beyond these main results, the concept of (s,t)-subtractive sets bridges group-based threshold cryptography to lattice settings, which we demonstrate by relating it to distributed pseudorandom functions.

1 Introduction

Proving knowledge of a short integral vector $\mathbf{x}$ satisfying a system of linear equations of the form $\mathbf{A} \cdot \mathbf{x} = \mathbf{y} \bmod q$ defined over some ring $\mathcal{R}$, i.e. an answer to a

The research of MA was supported by EPSRC grants EP/S020330/1, EP/S02087X/1, by the European Union Horizon 2020 Research and Innovation Program Grant 780701 and Innovate UK grant AQuaSec.

Russell W. F. Lai is supported by the State of Bavaria at the Nuremberg Campus of Technology (NCT). NCT is a research cooperation between the Friedrich-Alexander-Universität Erlangen-Nürnberg (FAU) and the Technische Hochschule Nürnberg Georg Simon Ohm (THN).

T. Malkin and C. Peikert (Eds.): CRYPTO 2021, LNCS 12826, pp. 519–548, 2021.
https://doi.org/10.1007/978-3-030-84245-1_18

short integer solution (SIS) problem and its generalisations, is a central task in lattice-based cryptography. Indeed, zero-knowledge variants of such proofs catalyse constructions of lattice-based privacy-preserving protocols such as group and ring signatures (e.g. [18,28,38]). These proofs are often also required for proving the well-formedness of the inputs of basic lattice building blocks. This is because random elements in $\mathcal{R}$ are easily trapdoored [23] such that using them in computations touching secret values risks their exposure. Furthermore, when $\mathbf{y}$ is a commitment of $\mathbf{x}$ encoding the witness to an NP statement, such a proof of knowledge can be compiled into a (succinct) argument of knowledge for NP [3,11]. The practical performance of such proofs has thus far-reaching consequences.

Prior to 2019 plausibly post-quantum secure proof systems for the SIS problem could be categorised into three classes: probabilistically-checkable proofs (PCP), "Stern-like" or "Schnorr-like".[1]

PCP-based systems [27] offer succinct proofs for arithmetic circuits from symmetric primitives only (e.g. [5]).

Stern-like systems [26,29,36] rely on the combinatorial cut-and-choose technique, and come with a knowledge extractor which is able to extract a solution $\tilde{\mathbf{x}}$ with $\|\mathbf{x}\| = \|\tilde{\mathbf{x}}\|$ satisfying $\mathbf{A} \cdot \tilde{\mathbf{x}} = \mathbf{y} \bmod q$. Due to their combinatorial nature, however, Stern-like systems only achieve constant knowledge error and have to be repeated $O(\lambda)$ times to make that negligible.

Schnorr-like systems (e.g. [30]) are algebraic and can achieve inverse polynomial or even negligible error, hence only $O(\lambda/\log \lambda)$ repetitions are needed in the former case and none in the latter. However, the knowledge extractors for Schnorr-like proofs are only able to extract a solution $\tilde{\mathbf{x}}$ to a relaxed statement $\mathbf{A} \cdot \tilde{\mathbf{x}} = s \cdot \mathbf{y} \bmod q$ with a "slack" $s \neq 1$ and "stretch" $\|\tilde{\mathbf{x}}\|/\|\mathbf{x}\| > 1$, which ultimately force the systems to be instantiated with larger moduli q. These relaxations may be acceptable in some applications, such as digital signatures, but can be prohibitive for others, e.g. when the system is recursively composed.

In the discrete logarithm setting, Bünz *et al.* [13] discovered that the linearity of Schnorr-like proofs can be exploited for recursive composition. This "Bulletproof" template was adapted to the lattice setting by Bootle *et al.* [11], where the task of proving $\mathbf{A} \cdot \mathbf{x} = \mathbf{y} \bmod q$, with $\mathbf{A} = (\mathbf{A}_0, \mathbf{A}_1)$, is reduced to that of proving $\tilde{\mathbf{A}} \cdot \tilde{\mathbf{x}} = \tilde{\mathbf{y}} \bmod q$ with $\tilde{\mathbf{A}} = c\mathbf{A}_0 + \mathbf{A}_1$ and $\tilde{\mathbf{y}}$ dependent on some random challenge c, and the dimension of $\tilde{\mathbf{x}}$ halved compared to $\mathbf{x}$. By recursively composing the above protocol $\log k$ times, where k is the dimension of $\mathbf{x}$, Bootle *et al.* [11] obtained a protocol with poly-logarithmic communication for proving $\mathbf{A}\mathbf{x} = \mathbf{y} \bmod q$, which implies [3] the first lattice-based zero-knowledge arguments for NP with poly-logarithmic communication that deviates from the PCP-based framework.

Since 2019 several works [7,12,20,38] managed to give (almost) the best of both the Stern and Schnorr worlds: neither slack nor stretch as in Stern-like protocols and inverse-polynomial (but not negligible) soundness error as in Schnorr-like

---

[1] Without counting highly generic constructions requiring Karp reductions.

protocols. All these works prove $\mathbf{A} \cdot \mathbf{x} = \mathbf{y} \bmod q$ exactly, i.e. $\mathbf{A} \cdot \tilde{\mathbf{x}} = s \cdot \mathbf{y} \bmod q$ with $s = 1$ and $\|\tilde{\mathbf{x}}\| = \|\mathbf{x}\|$. The work of Beullens [7] generalises the "MPC in the head with preprocessing" idea of [25] to give a variant of Stern's protocol with inverse-polynomial soundness error.[2] The works [12,20,38] augment a Schnorr-like protocol with non-linear constraints fixing $\mathbf{x}$ to be, say, ternary.

While these works resolve the question of proving $\mathbf{A} \cdot \mathbf{x} = \mathbf{y} \bmod q$ without slack or stretch, they all share the properties of introducing non-linear constraints and producing linear-size proofs.[3] Indeed, unless new techniques are developed, it is unclear how the non-linear constraints used in these systems can be integrated into the Bulletproof framework of "folding down" the problem to polylogarithmic size, exploiting linearity. Thus, it is natural to ask if the approaches taken in these prior works are necessary, or whether Schnorr-like constructions that reduce or eliminate stretch and slack while achieving inverse-(super-)polynomial soundness error have yet to be found.

Knowledge extraction in Schnorr-like proofs for the SIS problem classically proceeds roughly as follows. Let $S = \{c_0, \ldots, c_{n-1}\}$ be a set of challenges. Given a convincing prover, the extractor $\mathcal{E}$ runs the prover multiple times to extract t solutions $\tilde{\mathbf{x}}_i$ satisfying $\mathbf{A} \cdot \tilde{\mathbf{x}}_i = \tilde{\mathbf{y}}_0 + c_i \mathbf{y} + c_i^2 \tilde{\mathbf{y}}_2 + \cdots + c_i^{t-1} \tilde{\mathbf{y}}_{t-1} \bmod q$ for distinct $c_i \in S$. In the simple $t = 2$ case which captures linear-size proofs, $\mathcal{E}$ subtracts the two relations and obtains $\mathbf{A} \cdot (\tilde{\mathbf{x}}_{i_0} - \tilde{\mathbf{x}}_{i_1}) = (c_{i_0} - c_{i_1}) \cdot \mathbf{y} \bmod q$. If $c_{i_0} - c_{i_1}$ is invertible, e.g. when the c_i's are field elements, and we do not care about the length of the extracted solution, then $\mathcal{E}$ could simply divide both sides by $c_{i_0} - c_{i_1}$ and obtain an exact solution. The issue in the lattice settings is that the relation $\mathbf{A} \cdot \mathbf{x} = \mathbf{y} \bmod q$ is defined over e.g. a cyclotomic ring $\mathcal{R} = \mathbb{Z}[\zeta]$, where not all elements are invertible. Even if $c_{i_0} - c_{i_1}$ is invertible (mod q), its inverse and hence the extracted solution might not be short (relative to q).

A workaround is to accept a slack of s which is divisible by $c_i - c_j$ over $\mathcal{R}$ for all possible $c_i, c_j \in S$. Then by choosing a large enough modulus $q \in \mathbb{N}$, $\mathcal{E}$ can extract a short (relative to q) solution $\tilde{\mathbf{x}}$ to $\mathbf{A} \cdot \tilde{\mathbf{x}} = s \cdot \mathbf{y} \bmod q$. In matrix form, it means that the extractor $\mathcal{E}$ solves a linear system of the form $\mathbf{V}_T^\mathsf{T} \cdot \mathbf{z} = s \cdot \mathbf{w}$ where $\mathbf{V}_T$ is the Vandermonde matrix (Eq. (3)) defined by $T = \{c_{i_0}, c_{i_1}\}$ and $\mathbf{w} = (0, 1)^\mathsf{T}$. In the $t = 3$ case which captures one level of the lattice Bulletproof protocol [11], $\mathcal{E}$ solves a linear system of the same form except that $T = \{c_{i_0}, c_{i_1}, c_{i_2}\}$ and $\mathbf{w} = (0, 1, 0)^\mathsf{T}$. In both cases $\mathcal{E}$ extracts $\tilde{\mathbf{x}} = \sum_{i \in \mathbb{Z}_t} z_i \cdot \tilde{\mathbf{x}}_i$ as a solution to $\mathbf{A} \cdot \tilde{\mathbf{x}} = s \cdot \mathbf{y} \bmod q$ with stretch dependent on $\|\mathbf{z}\|$.

From this discussion we can reduce the task of finding Schnorr-like protocols (especially Bulletproof-compatible ones) with small soundness error to the task of finding a large set S and a small slack s, so that for any t-subset $T \subseteq S$ for some desired threshold t, the dual Vandermonde systems of linear equations of the form $V_T^\mathsf{T} \cdot \mathbf{z} = s \cdot \mathbf{w}$ have a short solution $\mathbf{z}$ over $\mathcal{R}$.

---

[2] A similar approach is taken in [4] but for proofs from symmetric primitives.

[3] Proof effort can be amortised, though [10].

Contribution. In this work, we give both positive and negative resolutions to the above problem. Our main results are summarised below.

(s,t)-*subtractive sets.* In Sect. 3 we define the notion of (s,t)-subtractive sets of size n over a ring $\mathcal{R}$. If $S \subseteq \mathcal{R}$ is (s,t)-subtractive, then for any t-subset $T \subseteq S$, (dual) Vandermonde systems defined by T are solvable over $\mathcal{R}$. If S is $(1,t)$-subtractive (without slack) then we simply call S subtractive.

(s,t)-*subtractive sets over power-of-2 rings.* In Sect. 3.1 we construct a family of (s,t)-subtractive sets, with different tradeoffs between the set size n, slack s, and threshold t, over any power-of-2 cyclotomic ring $\mathcal{R} = \mathbb{Z}[\zeta_m]$ where $m = 2^{\ell}$. This can be seen as a generalisation of [6] who essentially constructed a $(2,2)$-subtractive set of size m. Our family includes a $(2,3)$-subtractive set of size $n = m/2 + 1$, which implies a lattice Bulletproof protocol with slack k and stretch $\tilde{O}(k^{2\log m + 0.58})$. In comparison, the protocol of Bootle *et al.* [11] had slack k^3 and stretch $\tilde{O}(k^{3\log m + 4.5})$.[4]

Subtractive sets over prime-power rings. In Sect. 3.2 we construct a subtractive set S of prime size p over any prime-power cyclotomic ring $\mathcal{R} = \mathbb{Z}[\zeta_{p^{\ell}}]$. For $p = \mathsf{poly}(\lambda)$ it implies a Schnorr-like proof of knowledge for lattice statements over $\mathcal{R}$ without slack with knowledge error $O(1/\mathsf{poly}(\lambda))$, which in turn implies a lattice Bulletproof protocol with no slack and stretch $\tilde{O}(k^{3\log m + 4.58})$.

No large (s,t)-subtractive sets. In Sect. 3.3 we prove that if $\mathcal{R}$ has an ideal $\mathfrak{q}$ of algebraic norm q, then for any (s,t)-subtractive set S over $\mathcal{R}$ of size $n > q$, we necessarily have $s \in \mathfrak{q}$. Consequently, there is no family of $(2,t)$-subtractive sets of size $n > m + 1$ over power-of-2 cyclotomic rings, meaning that our $(2,3)$-subtractive set of size $n = m/2 + 1$ is within a factor of 2 of being optimal. There is also no subtractive set of size $n > p$ over prime-power cyclotomic rings, meaning that our subtractive sets of size $n = p$ are optimal.

Soundness of lattice Bulletproofs. In Sect. 4 we construct a slight generalisation of the Bulletproof protocol from [11] and instantiate it with our subtractive sets. We prove both completeness and soundness for each level. For the recursive composition, we note that unfortunately the knowledge error of $O(1/n)$ given in [11] turns out to be too optimistic: it does not account for the freedom of the prover to choose for which level(s) to cheat. As we discuss in Sect. 4.2, we can hope for $O(\log k/n)$ by applying a union bound. Indeed, applying [19, Lemma 3.2], we obtain a knowledge error of $8.16 \log k/n$. We consider our more careful analysis of the knowledge error in [11] an independent contribution.

Small slack and negligible knowledge error is unlikely. Based on the technique for proving the impossibility of large (s,t)-subtractive sets we prove that, for a natural class of "algebraic" knowledge extractors for Schnorr-like protocols, it is impossible to achieve knowledge error $\kappa < q^{-1}$ if $\mathcal{R}$ has an ideal $\mathfrak{q}$ of algebraic norm q unless we accept a slack $s \in \mathfrak{q}$. For a natural generalisation of Schnorr-like protocols, where the verifier sends two challenges chosen from sets S_0 and S_1 instead of one, it is still impossible[5] for algebraic knowledge

---

[4] Their stretch analysis appears to be generous, though. We discuss the tightness of our analysis in Sect. 4.3.

[5] Under mild additional assumptions.

extractors to achieve knowledge error $\kappa < q^{-2}$ unless $s \in \mathfrak{q}$. For concreteness, we note that a prime-power cyclotomic ring $\mathcal{R} = \mathbb{Z}[\zeta_{p^\ell}]$ always has an ideal $\langle 1 - \zeta_{p^\ell} \rangle$ of norm p. Therefore our instantiations over prime-power rings are optimal assuming algebraic extractors. We interpret this as a limit to achieving negligible knowledge error in Schnorr-like (Bulletproof-compatible) proofs for the SIS problem with small slack without introducing non-linear relations.

Application to homomorphic secret sharing over rings. Apart from its applications in constructing Schnorr-like protocols, in the full version of this work we demonstrate how (s, t)-subtractive sets can be used as a tool to bridge group-based threshold cryptography techniques to the lattice setting by relating them to the construction of homomorphic secret sharing schemes over rings. Roughly, in matrix form, the recovery procedure in such a scheme is equivalent to finding the first term z_0 of the solution $\mathbf{z}$ to a linear system of the form $\mathbf{V}_T \cdot \mathbf{z} = s \cdot \mathbf{w}$ where $\mathbf{V}_T$ is the Vandermonde matrix defined by T (as above). As a concrete example, we generalise the construction of distributed pseudorandom functions from (almost) key-homomorphic pseudorandom functions and Shamir secret sharing by Boneh *et al.* [8] using (s, t)-subtractive sets.

2   Preliminaries

Let $\lambda \in \mathbb{N}$ be the security parameter. For $n \in \mathbb{N}$, write $[n] := \{1, 2, \ldots, n\}$, $\mathbb{Z}_n := \{0, 1, \ldots, n - 1\}$ denotes the ring of integers modulo n, $\mathbb{Z}_n^*$ denotes the multiplicative group of integers modulo n, and the Euler totient function $\varphi(n)$ denotes the number of positive integers at most and coprime with n. If $T \subseteq S$ are sets and T has t elements, we write $T \subseteq_t S$. If S is a finite set then $\leftarrow_\$ S$ denotes the sampling of a uniformly random element from S.

2.1   Cyclotomic Rings

For $m \in \mathbb{N}$, let $\zeta_m \in \mathbb{C}$ be any fixed primitive m-th root of unity. Denote by $K = \mathbb{Q}(\zeta_m)$ the cyclotomic field of order $m \geq 2$ and degree $\varphi(m)$, and by $\mathcal{R} = \mathbb{Z}[\zeta_m]$ its ring of integers, called a cyclotomic ring for short. We have $\mathcal{R} \cong \mathbb{Z}[x]/\langle \Phi_m(x) \rangle$, where $\Phi_m(x)$ is the m-th cyclotomic polynomial. We write $\sigma_i(x)$ for $0 \leq i < \varphi(m)$ be the $\varphi(m)$ different embeddings of $x \in \mathbb{Q}[\zeta_m]$ into $\mathbb{C}$. Cyclotomic fields $\mathbb{Q}[\zeta_m]$ are Galois extensions of $\mathbb{Q}$ [37, Thm 2.5], i.e. for all embeddings $\sigma_i(\cdot)$ of the field to $\mathbb{C}$ we have $\sigma_i(\mathbb{Q}[\zeta_m]) = \mathbb{Q}[\zeta_m]$. If $f_1, \ldots, f_k \in \mathcal{R}$, we write $\langle f_1, \ldots, f_k \rangle \subseteq \mathcal{R}$ for the ideal generated by $f_1, \ldots, f_k$. If $T \subseteq \mathcal{R}$, we also write $\langle T \rangle$ for the ideal generated by the elements in T. For $T_0, T_1 \subseteq \mathcal{R}$, we write $T_0 - T_1 := \{t_0 - t_1 : t_i \in T_i\}$. Similarly, we write $T_0 \cdot T_1 - T_2 \cdot T_3 := \{t_0 \cdot t_1 - t_2 \cdot t_3 : t_i \in T_i\}$ and so on. When m is clear from the context, we omit the subscript m and write $\zeta = \zeta_m$. We will focus primarily on $m \geq 2$ which is a prime-power. Using the "powerful" basis $\{\zeta^i\}_{i \in \mathbb{Z}_{\varphi(m)}}$, we can view $\mathcal{R}$ as a $\mathbb{Z}$-module of dimension $\varphi(m)$.

2.2 Norms and Ring Expansion Factors

For elements $x \in \mathcal{R}$ we denote the infinity norm of its coefficient vector (with the powerful basis) as $\|x\|$. If $\mathbf{x} \in \mathcal{R}^k$ we write $\|\mathbf{x}\|$ for the infinity norm of $\mathbf{x}$. We denote the algebraic norm of elements $x \in \mathcal{R}$ by $N(x) := \prod_{0 \le i < n} \sigma_i(x)$. It holds that $N(x) = |\mathcal{R}/\langle x \rangle|$. We define the degree-$d$ expansion factor of a ring $\mathcal{R}$.

Definition 1. *Let $\mathcal{R}$ be a ring. The degree-d expansion factor of $\mathcal{R}$, denoted by $\gamma_{\mathcal{R},d}$, is defined as $\gamma_{\mathcal{R},d} := \max_{S \subseteq_d \mathcal{R}} \left\| \prod_{a \in S} a \right\| / \prod_{a \in S} \|a\|$. If $d = 2$ we simply write $\gamma_{\mathcal{R}} = \gamma_{\mathcal{R},2}$.*

To upper bound $\gamma_{\mathcal{R},d}$ for a cyclotomic ring $\mathcal{R}$, we prove the following technical lemma which can be seen as a generalisation of [31, Theorem 3.3] to prime-power cyclotomic rings together with Proposition 1 given below.

Lemma 1. *Let $\zeta = \zeta_m$ where $m = p^\ell$ for some prime p. Let $d \in \mathbb{N}$. Then the expression $a = \sum_{i \in \mathbb{Z}_{dm}} a_i \cdot \zeta^i$ where $\max_{i \in \mathbb{Z}_{dm}} \|a_i\| \le \alpha$ can be reduced to $a = \sum_{i \in \mathbb{Z}_{\varphi(m)}} a'_i \cdot \zeta^i$ with $\max_{i \in \mathbb{Z}_{\varphi(m)}} \|a'_i\| \le 2\, d \cdot \alpha$. Assume further that $a_i \ge 0$ for all $i \in \mathbb{Z}_{dm}$, then we have $\max_{i \in \mathbb{Z}_{\varphi(m)}} \|a'_i\| \le d \cdot \alpha$.*

Proof. Recall that ζ is a root of $\Phi_m(x) = \sum_{i=0}^{p-1} x^{ip^{\ell-1}}$. We thus have the identities $\zeta^{m-k} = -\sum_{i=1}^{p-1} \zeta^{ip^{\ell-1}-k}$ for $k \in [p^{\ell-1}]$. Suppose that the monomials $\{\zeta^{ip^{\ell-1}-k} : i \in [p-1]\}$ of ζ^{m-k} overlap with those of $\zeta^{m-k'}$, we then have $ip^{\ell-1} - k = i'p^{\ell-1} - k'$ for some $i, i' \in [p-1]$ and $k, k' \in [p^{\ell-1}]$. We have $|i' - i|p^{\ell-1} = |k' - k| < p^{\ell-1}$ which forces $i = i'$ and hence $k = k'$. In other words, the sets of monomials of ζ^{m-k} are non-overlapping for distinct $k \in [p^{\ell-1}]$. For $i \in \mathbb{Z}_{dm}$, write $i = jm + k$ for $j \in \mathbb{Z}_d$ and $k \in \mathbb{Z}_m$, and rename a_i to $a_{j,k}$. Then $a = \sum_{i \in \mathbb{Z}_{dm}} a_i \cdot \zeta^i = \sum_{j \in \mathbb{Z}_d} \zeta^{jm} \cdot \sum_{k \in \mathbb{Z}_m} a_{j,k} \cdot \zeta^k = \sum_{j \in \mathbb{Z}_d} \sum_{k \in \mathbb{Z}_m} a_{j,k} \cdot \zeta^k := \sum_{j \in \mathbb{Z}_d} \bar{a}_j$. We observe that each term $\bar{a}_j = \sum_{k \in \mathbb{Z}_m} a_{j,k} \cdot \zeta^k$ where $\max_{i \in \mathbb{Z}_{dm}} \|a_i\| \le \alpha$ can be reduced using the above identities to $\bar{a}_j = \sum_{k \in \mathbb{Z}_{\varphi(m)}} a'_{j,k} \cdot \zeta^k$ with $\max_{k \in \mathbb{Z}_{\varphi(m)}} \left\| a'_{j,k} \right\| \le 2\alpha$. If $a_i \ge 0$ for all $i \in \mathbb{Z}_{dm}$, then we have $\max_{k \in \mathbb{Z}_{\varphi(m)}} \left\| a'_{j,k} \right\| \le \alpha$. The claim then follows. $\square$

Proposition 1. *Let $i \in \mathbb{N}$, $m = p^\ell$ for some prime p, $\zeta = \zeta_m$ and $a \in \mathcal{R}$, then $\|\zeta_m^i \cdot a\| \le 2\|a\|$. When $p = 2$ then $\|\zeta_m^i \cdot a\| = \|a\|$.*

Proof. Since the power-of-two case is well known to just be a rotation, we treat the general case. Let $j = i \bmod m$ then $\zeta^i \cdot a = \zeta^j \cdot a$. Write $a = \sum_{k \in \mathbb{Z}_m} a_k \zeta^k$ ($a_k = 0$ for $k \ge \varphi(m)$), then

$$\zeta^j \cdot a = \sum_{k \in \mathbb{Z}_m} a_k \cdot \zeta^{j+k}$$

$$= \sum_{k:\ j+k < m} a_k \cdot \zeta^{j+k} + \zeta^m \cdot \sum_{k:\ m \le j+k < 2m-1} a_k \cdot \zeta^{j+k-m}$$

$$= \sum_{k' \in \mathbb{Z}_m} a_{k'-j} \cdot \zeta^{k'} + \sum_{k'' \in \mathbb{Z}_m} a_{k''+m-j} \cdot \zeta^{k''} = b + c.$$

By Lemma 1, b and c can each be expressed in the powerful basis with ternary coefficients. Therefore $\|\zeta^i \cdot a\| = \|b + c\| \leq \|b\| + \|c\| \leq 2 \cdot \|a\|$.   □

Combining the above we arrive at bounds for $\gamma_{\mathcal{R},d}$.

Proposition 2. *If $\mathcal{R}$ is a prime-power cyclotomic ring, then $\gamma_{\mathcal{R},d} \leq \min(2d, 2^{d-1}) \cdot \varphi(m)^{d-1}$. If $\mathcal{R}$ is a power-of-2 cyclotomic ring, then $\gamma_{\mathcal{R},d} \leq \varphi(m)^{d-1}$.*

Proof. For the power-of-2 case and $a, b \in \mathcal{R}$, write $a \cdot b$ as $\varphi(m)$ multiplications of the form $a_i \zeta^i \cdot b$, where the a_i are the coefficients of a. By Proposition 1, we obtain $\gamma_{\mathcal{R}} \leq \varphi(m)$. Recursively composing gives the claimed bound.

For the general prime-power case, the same argument gives $\gamma_{\mathcal{R},d} \leq 2^{d-1} \cdot \varphi(m)^{d-1}$. For the other bound, consider the product $r = a_{(0)} \cdots a_{(d-1)}$ for $a_{(i)} \in \mathcal{R}$. Write $r = a_{(0)} \cdots a_{(d-1)} = \sum_{i \in \mathbb{Z}_{dm}} r_i \cdot \zeta^i$ without modular reduction. Then for each coefficient r_i of r we have $\|r_i\| \leq \varphi(m)^{d-1} \cdot \prod_{j \in \mathbb{Z}_d} \|a_{(j)}\|$. By Lemma 1, after reduction we have $\|r\| \leq 2d \cdot \varphi(m)^{d-1} \cdot \prod_{j \in \mathbb{Z}_d} \|a_{(j)}\|$.   □

We finish this subsection by giving some propositions that will be useful when we construct (s,t)-subtractive sets in Sects. 3.1 and 3.2.

Proposition 3. *For any $m \geq 2$, $\sum_{i \in \mathbb{Z}_m} \zeta_m^i = 0$.*

Proof. We realise $\zeta_m^m - 1 = (\zeta_m - 1) \cdot (\sum_{i \in \mathbb{Z}_m} \zeta_m^i) = 0$ but $\zeta_m \neq 1$.   □

Proposition 4. *Let $m = p^\ell \in \mathbb{N}$ for some prime p, then $\|(1 - \zeta^n)/(1 - \zeta^f)\| \leq 1$ for $n, f \in \mathbb{Z}_m^*$.*

Proof. Let $g = f^{-1} \mod m$ and $k = g \cdot n \mod m$. Then

$$(1 - \zeta^n)/(1 - \zeta^f) = (1 - \zeta^{fgn})/(1 - \zeta^f) = \sum_{i \in \mathbb{Z}_k} \zeta^{f \cdot i}.$$

Note that for any $i \in \mathbb{Z}_k \setminus \{0\}$, we have $i \in \mathbb{Z}_m^*$. Therefore, observing that $f\mathbb{Z}_m = \mathbb{Z}_m$ since $f \in \mathbb{Z}_m^*$, we note that the sum $1 + \sum_{i \in \mathbb{Z}_k \setminus \{0\}} \zeta^{f \cdot i}$ can be expressed as $a = \sum_{i \in \mathbb{Z}_m} a_i \zeta^i$ with binary coefficients a_i. Then by Lemma 1 we conclude that a can be expressed in the powerful basis as a ternary vector.   □

2.3   Ideals in Cyclotomic Rings

Our results critically rely on the presence and absence of ideals in $\mathcal{R}$. We recall some basic facts. In the ring of integers $\mathcal{R}$ of any number field, any ideal $\mathcal{I} \in \mathcal{R}$ can written in a unique way as $\mathcal{I} = \prod_{\mathfrak{P}} \mathfrak{P}^{v_{\mathfrak{P}}(\mathcal{I})}$, the product being over a finite set of prime ideals, and the exponent $v_{\mathfrak{P}}(\mathcal{I})$ being in $\mathbb{Z}$. When $\mathcal{I}$ is an integral ideal then all $v_{\mathfrak{P}}(\mathcal{I}) \geq 0$ [15, Thm 4.6.14]. Otherwise it is fractional. We mostly deal with integral ideals in this work. The norm $N(\mathcal{I})$ of the ideal $\mathcal{I}$, i.e. $|\mathcal{R}/\mathcal{I}|$, is $N(\mathcal{I}) = \prod_{\mathfrak{P}} N(\mathfrak{P}^{v_{\mathfrak{P}}(\mathcal{I})}) = \prod_{\mathfrak{P}} N(\mathfrak{P})^{v_{\mathfrak{P}}(\mathcal{I})}$ [15, p.187]. For any prime ideal

$\mathfrak{P} \subset \mathcal{R}$ we have $\mathfrak{P} \cap \mathbb{Z} = p\mathbb{Z}$ for some rational prime $p \in \mathbb{Z}$ and we write that $\mathfrak{P}$ "is above" p [15, Prop. 4.8.1]. Moreover, for any prime $p \in \mathbb{Z}$ there exist positive integers e_i such that $p\mathcal{R} = \prod_{i=1}^{g} \mathfrak{P}_i^{e_i}$ [15, Thm. 4.8.3], the integer e_i is called the "ramification index" of p at $\mathfrak{P}_i$. The degree f_i of the field extension defined by $f_i = [\mathcal{R}/\mathfrak{P}_i : \mathbb{Z}_p]$ is the "residual degree" of p. We have $N(\mathfrak{P}_i) = p^{f_i}$ and $\sum_{i=1}^{g} e_i f_i = \varphi(m)$ [15, Thm. 4.8.5]. Since $\mathbb{Q}[\zeta_m]$ is a Galois extension, all $e_i = e$ for some fixed e and $f_i = f$ for some fixed f and $\varphi(m) = efg$ [15, Thm. 4.8.6]. A prime $p \in \mathbb{Z}$ ramifies, i.e. has some $e_i > 1$, if and only if it divides the discriminant of $\mathbb{Q}[\zeta_m]$ [15, Thm. 4.8.8]. The discriminant of a prime-power cyclotomic field of order q^k is given by $\pm q^{q^{n-1}((q-1)\cdot n-1)}$, i.e. a power of q [37, Prop. 2.1]. Thus, on the one hand, q ramifies completely in $\mathbb{Z}[\zeta_{q^k}]$ and $\langle q \rangle = \langle 1 - \zeta_{q^k} \rangle^{\varphi(m)}$ [37, Lem. 1.4, Prop. 2.3, p.15]. On the other hand, for all $p \neq q$ we have $e = 1$ and obtain $\varphi(m) = fg$. For any prime $p \in \mathbb{Z}$ that does not divide m, let f be the smallest positive integer s.t. $p^f \equiv 1 \bmod m$. Then p splits into $g = \varphi(m)/f$ distinct prime ideals in $\mathcal{R}$ [37, Thm. 2.13]. Note that this implies $p^f > m$. Combining these results, we obtain:

Proposition 5. *Let $\mathcal{R} = \mathbb{Z}[\zeta_m]$ with $m = p^k$ a prime power. Then there exists no ideal of norm $\leq m$ in $\mathcal{R}$ except for the ideals above p, i.e. powers of $\langle 1 - \zeta_m \rangle$. The proper ideal of smallest norm is $\langle 1 - \zeta_m \rangle$ of norm $N(\langle 1 - \zeta_m \rangle) = p$.*

Remark 1. The bound in Proposition 5 is tight. For example, in $\mathbb{Z}[\zeta_{256}]$, the ideal $\langle 257, \zeta_{256} + 3 \rangle$ is of norm $m + 1$ not above 2. There are, however, $\mathbb{Z}[\zeta_m]$ where no ideal of norm $m + 1$ exists. For example, no such ideal exists in $\mathbb{Z}[\zeta_{1024}]$: the ideal with smallest norm not above 2 has norm 12289 (found by brute force search).

2.4   Proof of Knowledge

Let $R(\mathsf{stmt}, \mathsf{wit})$ be a binary relation. The language L associated to the relation R is a set $L := \{\mathsf{stmt} : \exists \ \mathsf{wit} \ s.t. \ R(\mathsf{stmt}, \mathsf{wit}) = 1\}$.

Definition 2 (Proof Systems). *A proof system Π is an interactive protocol $\langle \mathcal{P}(\mathsf{stmt}, \mathsf{wit}), \mathcal{V}(\mathsf{stmt}) \rangle$ between a PPT prover $\mathcal{P}$ and a PPT verifier $\mathcal{V}$, both input a statement stmt. The prover $\mathcal{P}$ additionally inputs a witness wit. Upon termination the verifier $\mathcal{V}$ should decide to accept or reject stmt by outputing a bit b, while the prover $\mathcal{P}$ outputs nothing. For convenience we write $b \leftarrow \langle \mathcal{P}(\mathsf{stmt}, \mathsf{wit}), \mathcal{V}(\mathsf{stmt}) \rangle$.*

A wide class of proof systems, including the so-called sigma protocols, conform to the following pattern.

Definition 3 (Challenges, Moves, Public Coin). *A proof system Π is said to be f-challenge, $(2g + 1)$-move, and public-coin with challenge sets $S_{i,j}$ for $i \in [f]$ and $j \in [g]$, if the protocol $\langle \mathcal{P}, \mathcal{V} \rangle$ conforms to the following pattern:*

- *$2g + 1$-Move: There are in total $2g + 1$ messages being communicated, where $\mathcal{P}$ sends the first, $\mathcal{V}$ sends the second, $\mathcal{P}$ sends the third, and so on. The prover $\mathcal{P}$ sends the last, i.e. $(2g + 1)$-th message and after which the verifier $\mathcal{V}$ outputs a bit b.*

- *f-Challenge and Public-Coin:* For $j \in [g]$, the j-th message sent by $\mathcal{V}$ is a tuple $(c_{i,j})_{i \in [f]}$ where $c_{i,j} \leftarrow_\$ S_{i,j}$ for all $i \in [f]$.

A proof system Π should satisfy completeness and knowledge soundness. We omit the zero-knowledge property as it is not needed for our purpose.

Definition 4 (ϵ-Completeness). *Π is ϵ-complete relative to L if*

$$\Pr\left[\langle \mathcal{P}(\mathsf{stmt}, \mathsf{wit}), \mathcal{V}(\mathsf{stmt})\rangle\right] \geq \epsilon$$

whenever $\mathsf{stmt} \in L$ *and* $R(\mathsf{stmt}, \mathsf{wit}) = 1$. *If $\epsilon = 1$, Π is perfectly complete.*

Definition 5 (κ-Knowledge Soundness). *Let $\mathcal{E}$ be a* PPT *knowledge extractor. Π is said to have κ-knowledge soundness relative to $(\mathcal{E}, L')$, if for any* stmt *and for any (unbounded) adversary $\mathcal{A}$ such that $\langle \mathcal{A}, \mathcal{V}(\mathsf{stmt})\rangle = 1$ with probability $\rho > \kappa$ (over the randomness of $\mathcal{A}$ and $\mathcal{V}$), $\mathcal{E}^{\mathcal{A}}$ outputs* wit *such that $R'(\mathsf{stmt}, \mathsf{wit}) = 1$ with probability at least $\rho - \kappa$, where R' is the relation associated to L'.*

If the above holds, we call Π a proof of knowledge, κ the knowledge error of Π, $\mathcal{E}$ an extractor for L'. If $\kappa = 0$ we say Π has perfect knowledge soundness. If the above only holds for PPT *adversaries $\mathcal{A}$, we say that Π has computational κ-knowledge soundness. Π is then called an argument of knowledge by convention.*

We remark that a proof system Π could be complete relative to L while having knowledge soundness relative to L', where $L \subset L'$ are not necessarily equal. In this case we say that Π is a proof system for the languages (L, L'). This is common in lattice-based proof systems where the knowledge extractor is only able to extract a relaxed witness of the statement being proven.

3 Subtractive Sets over Cyclotomic Rings

As the central tool for our results, we construct (generalised) subtractive sets over cyclotomic rings. Let $S := \{c_0, \ldots, c_{n-1}\} \subseteq_n \mathcal{R}$. Borrowing the terminology from [32,34], we say that S is *subtractive* if $c_i - c_j$ is invertible over $\mathcal{R}$ for any distinct i and j. Since (the products of) $c_i - c_j$ might be not quite invertible, but divide some element $s \in \mathcal{R}$, we generalise the notion of subtractiveness as follows.

Definition 6 ((s,t)-Subtractive Sets[6]). *For $s \in \mathcal{R}$ and $1 < t \leq n \in \mathbb{N}$, we say that $S \subseteq_n \mathcal{R}$ is (s,t)-subtractive if for any $T = \{c_0, \ldots, c_{t-1}\} \subseteq_t S$, and for all $i \in \mathbb{Z}_t$, it holds that $s \in \left\langle \prod_{j \in \mathbb{Z}_t \setminus \{i\}} (c_i - c_j) \right\rangle$. The element s is called the slack of S. If S is $(1,n)$-subtractive, meaning that $c_i - c_j$ is invertible in $\mathcal{R}$ for any distinct $i, j \in \mathbb{Z}_n$, we simply say that S is subtractive.*

---

[6] Special cases of (s,t)-subtractive sets are studied in the literature under different names. For example, $(1,2)$-subtractive sets are called exceptional sets [16,21] and sequences [1], while $(s,2)$-subtractive sets are called s-exceptional sets [2]. We choose the name "subtractive" since it appears to be the earliest [32] and the most informative.

The expansion factor $\gamma_S^{(s,t)}$ of S (as an (s,t)-subtractive set) is defined as $\gamma_S^{(s,t)} := \max_{T \subseteq_t S, i \in \mathbb{Z}_t} \left\| s / \prod_{j \in \mathbb{Z}_t \setminus \{i\}} (c_i - c_j) \right\|$ where the maximum is over all t-subsets $T \subseteq_t S$ and all $i \in \mathbb{Z}_t$.

The above definition of (s,t)-subtractive sets is motivated by the problem of solving (dual) Vandermonde systems of linear equations of the form

$$\mathbf{V}_T \cdot \mathbf{z} = s \cdot \mathbf{w} \quad (1) \qquad \text{and} \qquad \mathbf{V}_T^\mathsf{T} \cdot \mathbf{z} = s \cdot \mathbf{w} \quad (2)$$

respectively in the variable $\mathbf{z}$ where $\mathbf{V}_T$ is the Vandermonde matrix

$$\mathbf{V}_T = \begin{pmatrix} 1 & c_0 & \cdots & c_0^{t-1} \\ 1 & c_1 & \cdots & c_1^{t-1} \\ \vdots & \vdots & \ddots & \vdots \\ 1 & c_{t-1} & \cdots & c_{t-1}^{t-1} \end{pmatrix} \tag{3}$$

defined by the elements in $T = \{c_0, \ldots, c_{t-1}\}$ and $\mathbf{t} \in \mathcal{R}^t$ is some vector over $\mathcal{R}$. If S is (s,t)-subtractive, then for any $T \subseteq_t S$, Eqs. (1) and (2) each admits a solution $\mathbf{z}$ over $\mathcal{R}$.

Since fully expanded formulae for the solutions to Eqs. (1) and (2) (instead of, e.g. those in terms of determinants or matrix inverses) do not seem to be widely available in the literature, we give them explicitly.

Proposition 6. Fix $T = \{c_0, \ldots, c_{t-1}\}$. Let $\mathbf{V}_T$ be the Vandermonde matrix for T, i.e. $(\mathbf{V}_T)_{i,j} = c_i^j$ for $i, j \in \mathbb{Z}_t$. For $i \in \mathbb{Z}_t$, let $T_i := T \setminus \{c_i\}$ and $\binom{T_i}{j} := \sum_{J \subseteq_j T_i} \prod_{c \in J} c \in \mathcal{R}$, the latter denoting the sum of products of j elements in T_i where the sum is over all possible j-subsets of T_i. Further, let $d_i := \prod_{j \in \mathbb{Z}_t \setminus \{i\}} (c_i - c_j) \in \mathcal{R}$ and $\mathbf{w} = (w_0, \ldots, w_{t-1})$.

Then, the solution to $\mathbf{V}_T \cdot \mathbf{z} = s \cdot \mathbf{w}$ is given by $\mathbf{z} = (z_0, \ldots, z_{t-1})$ where

$$z_i = \sum_{j \in \mathbb{Z}_t} (-1)^{t-i-1} \frac{s}{d_j} \binom{T_j}{t-i-1} w_j.$$

The solution to $\mathbf{V}_T^\mathsf{T} \cdot \mathbf{z} = s \cdot \mathbf{w}$ is given by $\mathbf{z} = (z_0, \ldots, z_{t-1})$ where

$$z_i = \sum_{j \in \mathbb{Z}_t} (-1)^{t-j-1} \frac{s}{d_i} \binom{T_i}{t-j-1} w_j.$$

Furthermore, if S is (s,t)-subtractive then for any $T \subseteq_t S$, we have s/d_i and $s/d_j \in \mathcal{R}$ for all $i, j \in \mathbb{Z}_t$, and therefore $z_i \in \mathcal{R}$ for all $i \in \mathbb{Z}_t$.

In the context of cryptography, problems in the form $\mathbf{V}_T \cdot \mathbf{z} = s \cdot \mathbf{w}$ arise naturally, e.g. when recovering secrets shared using Shamir secret sharing. On the other hand, problems in the form $\mathbf{V}_T^\mathsf{T} \cdot \mathbf{z} = s \cdot \mathbf{w}$ arise, e.g. when constructing knowledge extractors for Schnorr-like proof systems.

We first prove a simple property that, if S is (s,t)-subtractive, then it is also $(s, t-1)$-subtractive.

Proposition 7. If S is (s,t)-subtractive, then S is (s,t')-subtractive for $t' \leq t$.

Proof. Fix any $t' \in \{2, \ldots, t\}$ and any $T' = \{c_0, \ldots, c_{t'-1}\} \subseteq_{t'} S$. Let T be such that $T' \subseteq_{t'} T \subseteq_t S$. Write $T = \{c_0, \ldots, c_{t'-1}, \ldots, c_{t-1}\}$. Since S is (s,t)-subtractive, it holds that $s \in \left\langle \prod_{j \in \mathbb{Z}_t \setminus \{i\}} (c_i - c_j) \right\rangle$ for all $j \in \mathbb{Z}_t$. However, for all $i \in \mathbb{Z}_{t'}$, it holds that $\left\langle \prod_{j \in \mathbb{Z}_t \setminus \{i\}} (c_i - c_j) \right\rangle \subseteq \left\langle \prod_{j \in \mathbb{Z}_{t'} \setminus \{i\}} (c_i - c_j) \right\rangle$. We therefore have $s \in \left\langle \prod_{j \in \mathbb{Z}_{t'} \setminus \{i\}} (c_i - c_j) \right\rangle$ which means S is (s,t')-subtractive. $\square$

To prepare for our impossibility results, we generalise the notion of subtractive sets to weak subtractive sets which permit arbitrary ring operations on differences.

Definition 7 (Weak (s,t)-Subtractive Sets). *For $s \in \mathcal{R}$ and $1 < t \leq n \in \mathbb{N}$, $S \subseteq_n \mathcal{R}$ is weakly (s,t)-subtractive if for any $T \subseteq_t S$, it holds that $s \in \langle T - T \rangle$.*

Since subtractive sets are defined by products of differences, they are weakly $(s,2)$-subtractive.

Proposition 8. *If S is (s,t)-subtractive, then S is weakly $(s,2)$-subtractive.*

Proof. Fix any $T = \{c_0, \ldots, c_{t-1}\} \subseteq_t S$. Since S is (s,t)-subtractive,

$$s \in \left\langle (c_0 - c_1) \cdot \prod_{j \in \mathbb{Z}_t \setminus \{0,1\}} (c_0 - c_j) \right\rangle \in \langle c_0 - c_1 \rangle.$$

$\square$

The following proposition is immediate by realising that for any $T' \supseteq T$ we have $\langle T' - T' \rangle \supseteq \langle T - T \rangle$.

Proposition 9. *If $S \subseteq_n \mathcal{R}$ is weakly (s,t) subtractive then S is weakly (s,t') subtractive for any $t < t' \leq n$.*

Remark 2. Note that t behaves differently between (s,t)-subtractive sets and weakly (s,t)-subtractive sets. On the one hand, S being (s,t)-subtractive implies S being (s,t')-subtractive for *smaller* t'. On the other hand, S being weakly (s,t)-subtractive implies S being weakly (s,t')-subtractive for *larger* t'.

3.1 Power-of-2 Cyclotomic Rings

Power-of-2 cyclotomic rings $\mathcal{R} = \mathbb{Z}[\zeta_m]$, where $m = 2^\ell$ for some $\ell \in \mathbb{N}$, are popular among lattice-based constructions due to implementation convenience such as fast multiplication via a number theoretic transform (NTT). We construct families of (s,t)-subtractive sets over $\mathcal{R}$ with different tradeoffs between n, t, and s.

Theorem 1. *Let $\mathcal{R} = \mathbb{Z}[\zeta_m]$ with $m = 2^\ell \geq 4$. Then for $i = 0, \ldots, \ell$, the set*

$$S_i := \{0, 1, \zeta, \ldots, \zeta^{2^i - 1}\} \subseteq_{n_i} \mathcal{R}$$

is $(s_{i,t}, t)$-subtractive for any $s_{i,t} \in \langle 1 - \zeta \rangle^{\lceil \log t \rceil (n_i - 1)/2}$, where $n_i = 2^i + 1$.

Let j_t be the smallest such that $\lceil \log t \rceil \leq 2^{j_t}$. If $i + j_t \leq \ell$, then we can pick $s_{i,t} = 1 - \zeta^{2^{i+j_t-1}}$ such that $\gamma_{S_i}^{(s_{i,2},2)} = 1$ and $\gamma_{S_i}^{(s_{i,3},3)} \leq \varphi(m)$ for all $i = 0, \ldots, \ell$. Empirically, for $4 \leq m \leq 2048$, we have $\gamma_{S_{\ell-1}}^{(2,3)} = m/8$ and $\gamma_{S_{\ell-2}}^{(1-\zeta^{m/4}, 3)} = m/16$.

Proof. If $i = 0$, then $S_i = \{0, 1\}$ is subtractive. In the following we assume $i \in [\ell]$.

For $k \in \mathbb{Z}$, let $\mathrm{Ev}(k)$ be the even part of k, i.e. the largest power of 2 which divides k. It suffices to consider the case $0 \notin T \subseteq_t S_i$, since in the case where $0 \in T$, the difference between any other element in T and 0 is a unit. To handle both cases together, let $T' = T \setminus \{0\}$ so that $t' = |T'| = t$ if $0 \notin T$ and $t' = t - 1$ otherwise. In any case, we have $t' \leq 2^i$ and $t' \leq t$. Write $T' = \{\zeta^{j_0}, \dots, \zeta^{j_{t'-1}}\}$. We consider the ideal

$$\left\langle \prod_{k \in \mathbb{Z}_{t'} \setminus \{0\}} (\zeta^{j_0} - \zeta^{j_k}) \right\rangle = \left\langle \prod_{k \in \mathbb{Z}_{t'} \setminus \{0\}} (1 - \zeta^{j_0 - j_k}) \right\rangle$$

$$= \left\langle \prod_{k \in \mathbb{Z}_{t'} \setminus \{0\}} (1 - \zeta^{\mathrm{Ev}(j_0 - j_k)}) \right\rangle \qquad (4)$$

$$= \prod_{k \in \mathbb{Z}_{t'} \setminus \{0\}} \langle 1 - \zeta \rangle^{\mathrm{Ev}(j_0 - j_k)} \qquad (5)$$

$$= \langle 1 - \zeta \rangle^{\sum_{k \in \mathbb{Z}_{t'} \setminus \{0\}} \mathrm{Ev}(j_0 - j_k)}.$$

For Equality (4) we use that if $k = ef$ with e a power of 2 and f odd, then $1 - \zeta^{ef}$ and $1 - \zeta^e$ are divisible by each other in $\mathcal{R}$. First, note that $(1 - \zeta^{ef})/(1 - \zeta^e) = 1 + \zeta^e + \cdots + \zeta^{e(f-1)}$. Second, since $\gcd(f, m) = 1$, let $g = f^{-1} \bmod m$ and observe $(1 - \zeta^e)/(1 - \zeta^{ef}) = (1 - \zeta^{efg})/(1 - \zeta^{ef}) = 1 + \zeta^{ef} + \cdots + \zeta^{ef(g-1)}$. For Equality (5) we use $1 - \zeta^2 = -(1 - \zeta)^2 + 2(1 - \zeta)$, $2 \in \langle (1 - \zeta)^2 \rangle$, and $2 \in \langle 1 - \zeta^2 \rangle$.

Note that since $0 \leq j_0, j_k < 2^i$, we have $\mathrm{Ev}(j_0 - j_k) \leq 2^{i-1}$. Furthermore, for any fixed j_0, there is at most one j_k such that $\mathrm{Ev}(j_0 - j_k) = 2^{i-1}$. Beside such k, there are then at most $2 = 2^1$ other j_k's such that $\mathrm{Ev}(j_0 - j_k) = 2^{i-2}$. Beside these k's, there are at most $4 = 2^2$ other j_k's such that $\mathrm{Ev}(j_0 - j_k) = 2^{i-3}$. Continue this way, we have

$$\sum_{k \in \mathbb{Z}_{t'} \setminus \{0\}} \mathrm{Ev}(j_0 - j_k) \leq 1 \cdot 2^{i-1} + 2 \cdot 2^{i-2} + \cdots + 2^{\tau-1} \cdot 2^{i-\tau-2} + (t' - 2^\tau) \cdot 2^{i-\tau-1}$$

$$< 1 \cdot 2^{i-1} + 2 \cdot 2^{i-2} + \cdots + 2^{\tau-1} \cdot 2^{i-\tau-2} + 2^\tau \cdot 2^{i-\tau-1}$$

$$= (\tau + 1) \cdot 2^{i-1} \leq \lceil \log t' \rceil 2^{i-1} \leq \lceil \log t \rceil 2^{i-1}$$

where τ is the maximum non-negative integer such that $1 + 2 + 4 + \cdots + 2^{\tau-1} \leq t' - 2$ or equivalently $2^\tau < t' \leq 2^{\tau+1}$. Note that $2^\tau < t' \leq 2^i$ and hence $\tau < i$. Therefore $i - \tau - 1 \geq 0$ and hence $2^{i-\tau-1} \geq 1$.

Since $\sum_{k \in \mathbb{Z}_{t'} \setminus \{0\}} \mathrm{Ev}(j_0 - j_k) \leq \lceil \log t \rceil 2^{i-1}$, we have

$$\langle 1 - \zeta \rangle^{\lceil \log t \rceil 2^{i-1}} \subseteq \langle 1 - \zeta \rangle^{\sum_{k \in \mathbb{Z}_{t'} \setminus \{0\}} \mathrm{Ev}(j_0 - j_k)} = \left\langle \prod_{k \in \mathbb{Z}_{t'} \setminus \{0\}} (\zeta^{j_0} - \zeta^{j_k}) \right\rangle$$

for all $k \in \mathbb{Z}_{t'}$. Therefore, for any $s_{i,t} \in \langle 1 - \zeta \rangle^{\lceil \log t \rceil 2^{i-1}}$, we have

$$s_{i,t} \in \left\langle \prod_{k \in \mathbb{Z}_{t'} \backslash \{0\}} (\zeta^{j_0} - \zeta^{j_k}) \right\rangle$$

for all $k \in \mathbb{Z}_{t'}$. Thus S_i is $(s_{i,t}, t)$-subtractive.

Let j_t be the smallest such that $\lceil \log t \rceil \leq 2^{j_t}$. Let $s_{i,t} = 1 - \zeta^{2^{e_{i,t}}}$ where $e_{i,t} := i + j_t - 1$. Suppose $i + j_t \leq \ell$, then $\lceil \log t \rceil 2^{i-1} \leq 2^{i+j_t-1} \leq 2^{\ell-1} = m/2$. Therefore $\langle s_{i,t} \rangle = \langle 1 - \zeta \rangle^{2^{e_{i,t}}} \subseteq \langle 1 - \zeta \rangle^{\lceil \log t \rceil 2^{i-1}}$ and hence $s_{i,t} \in \langle 1 - \zeta \rangle^{\lceil \log t \rceil 2^{i-1}}$.

We now establish $\gamma_{S_i}^{(s,t)}$ as claimed above, starting with $t = 2$. Hence, we have $j_t = \lceil \log \lceil \log t \rceil \rceil = 0$, $s_{i,2} = 1 - \zeta^{2^{i-1}}$ and

$$\gamma_{S_i}^{(s_{i,2},2)} = \max_{\alpha,\beta \in \mathbb{Z}_{2^i}} \left\| \frac{s_{i,2}}{\zeta^\alpha - \zeta^\beta} \right\| = \max_{\alpha,\beta \in \mathbb{Z}_{2^i}} \left\| \frac{1 - \zeta^{2^{i-1}}}{\zeta^\alpha(1 - \zeta^{\beta-\alpha})} \right\| = \max_{\alpha,\beta \in \mathbb{Z}_{2^i}} \left\| \frac{1 - \zeta^{2^{i-1}}}{1 - \zeta^{2^\eta \mu}} \right\| \leq 1$$

where $2^\eta = \mathrm{Ev}(\beta - \alpha)$ with $\eta \in \mathbb{Z}_i$, μ is the odd part of $\beta - \alpha$ satisfying $\beta - \alpha = 2^\eta \mu$, and the last equality can be derived through a routine calculation. For $t = 3$, hence $j_t = \lceil \log \lceil \log t \rceil \rceil = 1$ and $s_{i,2} = 1 - \zeta^{2^i}$, we have

$$\gamma_{S_i}^{(s_{i,3},3)} = \max_{\alpha,\beta,\gamma \in \mathbb{Z}_i} \left\| \frac{s_{i,3}}{(\zeta^\alpha - \zeta^\beta)(\zeta^\alpha - \zeta^\gamma)} \right\|$$

$$= \max_{\alpha,\beta,\gamma \in \mathbb{Z}_i} \left\| \frac{1 - \zeta^{2^i}}{(1 - \zeta^{\beta-\alpha})(1 - \zeta^{\gamma-\alpha})} \right\| = \max_{\alpha,\beta,\gamma \in \mathbb{Z}_i} \left\| \frac{1 - \zeta^{2^{i-1}}}{1 - \zeta^{\beta-\alpha}} \cdot \frac{1 + \zeta^{2^{i-1}}}{1 - \zeta^{\gamma-\alpha}} \right\|$$

$$\leq \gamma_{\mathcal{R}} \cdot \left(\gamma_{S_i}^{(s_{i,2},2)} \right)^2 = \gamma_{\mathcal{R}} = \varphi(m).$$

The empirical results are verified by direct computation. □

We highlight some notable settings of (s, t) in Theorem 1. The case $t = 2$ is useful for constructing knowledge extractors of Schnorr-like proof systems. In this setting, $S_\ell \subseteq_{m+1} \mathcal{R}$ chosen in prior works [6] is $(2, 2)$-subtractive, while $S_{\ell-1} \subseteq_{m/2+1}$ is $(1 - \zeta^{m/4}, 2)$-subtractive. Note that although $\|1 - \zeta^{m/4}\| = 1$, multiplying $(1 - \zeta^{m/4})$ to an element $f \in \mathcal{R}$ results in an element of length $\|(1 - \zeta^{m/4})f\| \leq 2\|f\|$ if we consider the infinity norm as prior works did [11], and hence $S_{\ell-1}$ appears to be not better than S_ℓ in terms of slack. However, for the Euclidean norm $\|\cdot\|_2$, we have $\|(1 - \zeta^{m/4})f\|_2 < \sqrt{2}\|f\|_2 \leq 2\|f\|_2 = \|2f\|_2$.

The case $t = 3$ is useful for lattice Bulletproofs, as we will see in Sect. 4.1. Bootle et al. [11] chose $S_\ell \backslash \{0\} \subseteq_m \mathcal{R}$ as the challenge set for their instantiation of lattice Bulletproof, and essentially proved that $S_\ell \backslash \{0\}$ is $(8, 3)$-subtractive. The above tighter analysis shows that S_ℓ is in fact $(4, 3)$-subtractive. Similar to the $t = 2$ case, we notice that $S_{\ell-1} \subseteq_{m/2+1} \mathcal{R}$ is $(2, 3)$-subtractive and $S_{\ell-2} \subseteq_{m/4+1} \mathcal{R}$ is $(1 - \zeta^{m/4}, 3)$-subtractive. As discussed in the $t = 2$ case, the slack $1 - \zeta^{m/4}$ is better than 2 if we consider the Euclidean norm.

For general n_i and t useful in t-out-of-n_i secret sharing, assuming $m = 2^\ell$ is (polynomially) large enough so that $\ell > i + t_j$, then $\|s_{i,t}\| = 1$, which is more manageable than the $(n!, t)$-subtractive set $\mathbb{Z}_n$ chosen by Boneh et al. [8].

We observe that among all sets S_i constructed in Theorem 1, only $S_0 \subseteq_2 \mathcal{R}$ is subtractive, while the others are $(s_{i,t}, t)$-subtractive for some $s_{i,t} \neq 1$. As we will see in Sect. 3.3, this is not a shortcoming of the construction but rather a fundamental limit in power-of-2 cyclotomic rings. Indeed, in Proposition 12 and Lemma 2 we show that over power-of-2 cyclotomic rings no subtractive set of size greater than 2 exists.

We finish this section with a technical proposition, giving a bound for $\|c_i z_i\|$ that is tighter than the generic bound $2 \cdot \gamma_R \cdot \gamma_S^{(2,3)}$.

Proposition 10. *Let* $S = S_{\ell-1}$, $(s, t) = (2, 3)$, $\{c_0, c_1, c_2\} \subset_t S$ *and* z_i *as defined in Proposition 6, then* $\|c_i \cdot z_i\| \leq \varphi(m)$. *Empirically, for all* $8 \leq m = 2^\ell \leq 512$ *we have* $\max(\|c_i \cdot z_i\|) = \varphi(m) - 2$.

Proof. We write $c_0 = \zeta^i, c_1 = \zeta^j, c_2 = \zeta^k$. Wlog, we consider

$$c_0 \cdot z_0 = \frac{-s \cdot c_0 \cdot (c_1 + c_2)}{(c_0 - c_1) \cdot (c_0 - c_2)} = \frac{2 \cdot \zeta^i(\zeta^j + \zeta^k)}{(\zeta^i - \zeta^j) \cdot (\zeta^j - \zeta^k)} = \frac{2 \cdot \zeta^{i-j} \cdot (\zeta^{j-k} + 1)}{(\zeta^{i-j} - 1) \cdot (\zeta^{i-k} - 1)}.$$

Multiplying by ζ^{i-j} does not change the norm so we can consider

$$\|g\| = \left\| \frac{2 \cdot (\zeta^{j-k} + 1)}{(\zeta^{i-j} - 1) \cdot (\zeta^{i-k} - 1)} \right\|$$

$$\|2g\| = \left\| (\zeta^{j-k} + 1) \cdot \frac{2}{\zeta^{i-j} - 1} \cdot \frac{2}{\zeta^{i-k} - 1} \right\| \leq 2 \cdot \gamma_R \cdot \left(\gamma_S^{(2,2)} \right)^2.$$

Since $\|c_0 \cdot z_0\| = \|g\| = \|2g\|/2$, we obtain $\|c_0 \cdot z_0\| \leq \varphi(m)$. The empirical results are verified by direct computation. $\quad\square$

3.2   Prime-Power Cyclotomic Rings

We turn to prime-power cyclotomic rings $\mathcal{R} := \mathbb{Z}[\zeta_m]$ where m is a power of a prime p. Although we are interested mostly in the case $p > 2$, the following results also hold for $p = 2$. To construct subtractive sets over prime-power cyclotomic rings, we recall the well-known fact that $\mu_k := (\zeta^k - 1)/(\zeta - 1)$ is invertible over $\mathcal{R}$ when $\gcd(k, p) = \gcd(k, m) = 1$. Indeed its inverse is given by $\nu_k := \sum_{i \in \mathbb{Z}_h} \zeta^{ik \bmod m}$ where $h = k^{-1} \bmod m$. Our subtractive set of size over prime-power cyclotomic rings of order consist precisely of these invertible elements with an additional zero.

Theorem 2 (Prime-Power). *Let* $\mathcal{R} = \mathbb{Z}[\zeta_m]$ *with* $m = p^\ell$ *for some prime* p. *Then the set*

$$S := \{\mu_0, \dots, \mu_{p-1}\} \subseteq_p \mathcal{R}$$

is subtractive, where $\mu_i = (\zeta^i - 1)/(\zeta - 1)$ *for* $i \in \mathbb{Z}_p$. *Furthermore,* $\gamma_S^{(1,2)} = 1$, $\gamma_S^{(1,3)} \leq 4\varphi(m)$ *and* $4(t-1) \cdot \varphi(m)^{t-2}$ *for* $3 < t \leq p$. *Empirically,* $\gamma_S^{(1,3)} = \varphi(m)/2$ *for all primes* $3 \leq m \leq 277$.

Proof. For any $0 \leq i < j < p$, it holds that[7]

$$\mu_j - \mu_i = \frac{\zeta^j - 1}{\zeta - 1} - \frac{\zeta^i - 1}{\zeta - 1} = \sum_{k=0}^{j-1} \zeta^k - \sum_{k=0}^{i-1} \zeta^k = \zeta^i + \zeta^{i+1} + \cdots + \zeta^{j-1}$$

$$= \zeta^i \cdot (1 + \zeta + \cdots + \zeta^{j-i+1}) = \zeta^i \cdot \mu_{j-i}$$

which is a unit in $\mathcal{R}$ since $j - i \in \mathbb{Z}_p^*$. Consequently $\mu_i - \mu_j = (-1) \cdot (\mu_j - \mu_i)$ is also a unit in $\mathcal{R}$. Therefore S is subtractive.

We next upper bound $\gamma_S^{(1,t)}$. In the case $t = 2$, we have

$$\gamma_S^{(1,2)} = \max_{i,j \in \mathbb{Z}_p} \left\| \frac{1}{\mu_j - \mu_i} \right\| = \max_{i,j \in \mathbb{Z}_p} \left\| \frac{1}{\mu_{j-i}} \right\| \leq 1$$

where the inequality is due to Proposition 4.

For $2 < t \leq p$, let $T = \{\mu_{i_0}, \ldots, \mu_{i_{t-1}}\} \subseteq_t S$. We examine the norm of r^{-1} where $r := \prod_{j \in [t-1]} (\mu_{i_0} - \mu_{i_j})$. By the above analysis, we know that $\mu_{i_0} - \mu_{i_j}$ equals some power of ζ multiplied by $\mu_{i_0 - i_j}$. Therefore r can be written as $r = \zeta^{j_0} \mu_{j_1} \cdots \mu_{j_{t-1}}$ for some $j_0 \in \mathbb{Z}$ and $j_1, \ldots, j_{t-1} \in \mathbb{Z}_p^*$. Note that multiplication by ζ^{j_0} increases the norm at most by a factor of two. Let $\nu_j = \mu_j^{-1}$ for $j \in \{j_1, \ldots, j_{t-1}\}$. Then $\nu_j = \sum_{i=0}^{k-1} \zeta^{ij \bmod m}$ where $k = j^{-1} \bmod m$. By Lemma 1, we have $\|\nu_j\| \leq 1$ for all $j \in \mathbb{Z}_p^*$. Summarising the above, we can upper bound $\gamma_S^{(1,t)}$ as

$$\gamma_S^{(1,t)} \leq 2 \gamma_{\mathcal{R},t-1} \|\nu_{j_1}\| \cdots \|\nu_{j_{t-1}}\| \leq 4 (t - 1) \cdot \varphi(m)^{t-2}$$

where in the second inquality we used Proposition 2. When $t = 3$, we can use $\gamma_{\mathcal{R},2} \leq 2\varphi(m)$. The empirical results are verified by direct computation. □

Remark 3. Theorem 2 can be generalised to give a size $\varphi(\mathrm{rad}(m))+1$ subtractive set over the cyclotomic ring of any order m with prime-power factorisation $m = \prod_i p_i^{\ell_i}$, where the radical $\mathrm{rad}(m) = \prod_i p_i$ of m is the product of distinct prime divisors of m, by viewing the m-th cyclotomic ring as a tensor product of the $p_i^{\ell_i}$-th cyclotomic rings.

Proposition 11. *Let S be as defined in Theorem 2, $(s,t) = (1,3)$, $\{c_0, c_1, c_2\} \subset_t$ S and z_i as defined in Proposition 6, $c_i \cdot z_i = \zeta^j \cdot a$ for some a with $\|a\| \leq 4\,\varphi(m)$ and thus $\|c_i \cdot z_i\| \leq 8\,\varphi(m)$. Empirically, for all prime $3 \leq m \leq 229$ we have $\max(\|c_i \cdot z_i\|) = \varphi(m) - 1$.*

Proof. We write $c_0 = (\zeta^i - 1)/(\zeta - 1), c_1 = (\zeta^j - 1)/(\zeta - 1), c_2 = (\zeta^k - 1)/(\zeta - 1)$. Wlog, we consider

$$c_0 \cdot z_0 = \frac{-s \cdot c_0 \cdot (c_1 + c_2)}{(c_0 - c_1) \cdot (c_0 - c_2)} = \frac{-(\zeta^i - 1) \cdot (\zeta^j + \zeta^k - 2)}{((\zeta^i - \zeta^j) \cdot (\zeta^i - \zeta^k))}$$

$$= -\zeta^{-j-k} \cdot \left[\frac{\zeta^i - 1}{\zeta^{i-j} - 1} \cdot \frac{\zeta^j - 1}{\zeta^{i-k} - 1} + \frac{\zeta^i - 1}{\zeta^{i-j} - 1} \cdot \frac{\zeta^k - 1}{\zeta^{i-k} - 1} \right]$$

---

[7] We adopt the convention that the empty sum is 0.

Multiplication by $-\zeta^{-j-k}$ at most doubles the norm (Proposition 1) and we have $\left\|(\zeta^i - 1)/(\zeta^j - 1)\right\| = 1$ for $j \neq 0$ (Proposition 4). Thus, $\|c_0 \cdot z_0\| \leq 4 \cdot \gamma_R \leq 8\varphi(m)$. The empirical results are verified by direct computation. $\qquad\square$

3.3 Impossibility of Large Subtractive Sets

In this section we prove two flavours of impossibility results concerning subtractive sets. The first kind of results state that if S is an (s,t)-subtractive set of sufficient size, then s belongs to the ideal $\langle 1 - \zeta \rangle^e$ for some e lower bounded from 0. The second kind of results state that if $\mathcal{R}$ contains an ideal of small algebraic norm, then either S cannot be too large, or S is weakly (s,t)-subtractive with s belonging to that ideal. The key observation in all our proofs is that if we consider $N(\mathcal{I}) + 1$ elements $c_i \in \mathcal{R}$ then there must be two elements, say, c_i, c_j s.t. $c_i \equiv c_j \bmod \mathcal{I}$ and thus $c_i - c_j \in \mathcal{I}$.

We first prove that $S \subseteq_n \mathcal{R}$ cannot be (s,t)-subtractive unless

$$s \in \mathcal{I} = \langle 1 - \zeta \rangle^{\min\{\lceil n/p \rceil, t\} - 1}.$$

The size of $\mathcal{I}$ in a sense shrinks when t and n grow, since $|\mathcal{R}/\mathcal{I}| = p^{\min\{\lceil n/p \rceil, t\} - 1}$. The result thus rules out all S that are too "large" relative to s, in the sense that $\mathcal{I}$ becomes so "small" that the choice of $s \in \mathcal{I}$ is highly restrictive.

Proposition 12. *Let $\mathcal{R}$ be a prime-power cyclotomic ring of order m a power of p, and $n > p$. If $S \subseteq_n \mathcal{R}$ is (s,t)-subtractive, then $s \in \langle 1 - \zeta \rangle^e$ where*

$$e \geq \min\{\lceil n/p \rceil, t\} - 1 > 0.$$

Proof. Proposition 5 shows that $N(\langle 1 - \zeta \rangle) = |\mathcal{R}/\langle 1 - \zeta \rangle| = p$. The ideal $\langle 1 - \zeta \rangle$ therefore partitions $\mathcal{R}$ into p cosets. Let $n = \sum_{k \in \mathbb{Z}_p} n_k$ such that n_k elements in S belong to the k-th coset. Let $\bar{n} := \max_{k \in \mathbb{Z}_p} n_k \geq \lceil n/p \rceil$ be attained when $k = \bar{k}$. Let $T = \{c_0, \ldots, c_{t-1}\} \subseteq_t S$ be such that T contains $\min\{\bar{n}, t\} \geq \min\{\lceil n/p \rceil, t\} > 0$ elements in the $\bar{k}$-th coset. Let j be such that v_j belongs to the $\bar{k}$-th coset. The product $r = \prod_{i \in \mathbb{Z}_t \setminus \{\bar{j}\}} (c_i - c_j)$ has a factor $1 - \zeta$ with multiplicity at least $\min\{\lceil n/p \rceil, t\} - 1$. Since S is (s,t)-subtractive, s has a factor $1 - \zeta$ with multiplicity at least $\min\{\lceil n/p \rceil, t\} - 1$. In other words, $s \in \langle 1 - \zeta \rangle^{\min\{\lceil n/p \rceil, t\} - 1}$. $\qquad\square$

Remark 4. An interesting observation is that, when $m = 2$ hence $\zeta = -1$ and $\mathcal{R} = \mathbb{Z}$, the above lower bound implies that an (s,t)-subtractive set $S \subseteq_n \mathbb{Z}$ for $t \geq \lceil n/2 \rceil$ must have $|s| \geq 2^{\lceil n/2 \rceil - 1} = 2^{\Omega(n)}$. On the other hand, the trivial choice of $S = \mathbb{Z}_n$ (chosen by, e.g. Boneh *et al.* [8] for higher m) has a slack of $n! = 2^{O(n \lg n)}$ which almost reaches the lower bound. When m is a higher power of 2, there are however much better choices of S, such as the ones constructed in Theorem 1 rather than $S = \mathbb{Z}_n$.

Through a more careful analysis, we can prove a strengthened lower bound.

Lemma 2. *Let $\mathcal{R}$ be a prime-power cyclotomic ring of order m a power of p. Let $n > p^\ell$ for some $\ell \in \mathbb{N}$. If $S \subseteq_n \mathcal{R}$ is (s, t)-subtractive, then $s \in \langle 1 - \zeta \rangle^e$ where*

$$e \geq \sum_{i=1}^{\ell} \min\{\lceil n/p^i \rceil - 1, t - 1\} > 0.$$

Proof. Let $\mathfrak{P} = \langle 1 - \zeta \rangle$. Recall from Proposition 5 that $N(\mathfrak{P}) = |\mathcal{R}/\mathfrak{P}| = p$. Since $|S| = n > p^\ell$, by the pigeonhole principle there exists $S_1 \subseteq_{\lceil n/p \rceil} S$ such that all elements of S_1 belong to the same equivalence class $\mathfrak{C}_1$ modulo $\mathfrak{P}$. Similarly, there exists $S_2 \subseteq_{\lceil n/p^2 \rceil} S_1$ such that all elements of S_1 belong to the same equivalence class $\mathfrak{C}_2$ modulo $\mathfrak{P}^2$. Continue analogously, for $j \in [\ell]$, there exists $S_j \subseteq_{\lceil n/p^j \rceil} S_{j-1}$ such that all elements of S_j belong to the same equivalence class $\mathfrak{C}_j$ modulo $\mathfrak{P}^j$.

Consider a binary matrix H of ℓ rows and n columns, where the first $\lceil n/p^j \rceil$ columns are labeled by the elements of S_j for $j \in [\ell]$. The remaining columns are labeled by the elements of $S \setminus S_1$. The (i, v)-th entry is 1 if v belongs to the equivalence class $\mathfrak{C}_i$ modulo $\mathfrak{P}^i$, i.e. the first $\lceil n/p^i \rceil$ entries of row i are 1.

Pick $T \subseteq_t S$ such that $S_\ell \subseteq \ldots \subseteq S_k \subseteq T \subseteq S_{k-1} \subseteq S$ for some $k \in [\ell]$, where $S_0 := S$. Note that T labels the first t columns of H.

Let $v^* \in S_\ell \subseteq T$ be the element that labels the first column of H, and $\bar{T} = T \setminus \{v^*\}$ labels the second to the t-th column. Consider the product $r = \prod_{v \in \bar{T}} (v - v^*)$. Note that for $v \in \bar{T}$, if v belongs to the equivalence class $\mathfrak{C}_i$ modulo $\mathfrak{P}^i$, then $(v - v^*)$ contributes a factor $(1 - \zeta)^i$ of r. The multiplicity of the factor $(1 - \zeta)$ of r is at least the number of 1's in the first t columns of H minus that of the first column. By collecting the columns of interest, let H_t be the submatrix of H formed by the second to the t-th column. Observe that the i-th row of H_t contains $\min\{\lceil n/p^i \rceil, t\} - 1$ many 1's. Therefore the number of 1's in H_t is given by $\sum_{i=1}^{\ell} \min\{\lceil n/p^i \rceil - 1, t - 1\}$. $\qquad\square$

Concretely, for power-of-2 cyclotomic rings we obtain:

Corollary 1. *Let $\mathcal{R}$ be a power-of-2 cyclotomic ring of order $m \geq 8$ and $n \geq \varphi(m)$. If $S \subseteq_n \mathcal{R}$ is $(s, 3)$-subtractive, then $s \in \langle 1 - \zeta \rangle^e$ where $e \geq 2 \log_2 m - 3$.*

Proof. Let $m = 2^{\ell+2}$ for some $\ell \in \mathbb{N}$. Then $n \geq \varphi(m) = 2^{\ell+1}$. By Lemma 2 we have $e + \ell \geq \sum_{i=1}^{\ell} \min\{\lceil n/2^i \rceil, 3\}$. Note that since $n \geq 2^{\ell+1}$ we have $n/2^{\ell-1} \geq 4$ and hence $n/2^i \geq 3$ for $i = 1, \ldots, \ell - 1$. When $i = \ell$, we have $n/2^\ell \geq 2$ and therefore $\min\{\lceil n/2^\ell \rceil, 3\} \geq 2$. Therefore $e + \ell \geq 3(\ell - 1) + 2 = 3\ell - 1$, or in other words $e \geq 2\ell - 1 = 2 \log_2 m - 3$. $\qquad\square$

Next, we upper bound the size n of weakly (s, t)-subtractive sets.

Lemma 3. *Let $\mathcal{I} \subset \mathcal{R}$ be an ideal of norm $N(\mathcal{I})$. There exists no weakly (s, t)-subtractive set of size $(t - 1) \cdot N(\mathcal{I}) + 1$ for $s \notin \mathcal{I}$.*

Proof. Assume S is such a weakly (s, t) subtractive set of size $(t - 1) \cdot N(\mathcal{I}) + 1$. There are $N(\mathcal{I})$ cosets of $\mathcal{I}$. Sort the elements of S into buckets depending on which coset of mod $\mathcal{I}$ they land in. By the pigeonhole principle, there must exist at least one bucket containing t elements. Let $T = \{c_i\}_{i \in \mathbb{Z}_t}$ be a such a set of challenges of size t s.t. all $c_i \equiv c_j \mod \mathcal{I}$ for $i, j \in \mathbb{Z}_t \Leftrightarrow c_i - c_j \in \mathcal{I}$. Thus, $\langle T - T \rangle \subset \mathcal{I}$ and $s \in \mathcal{I}$. $\qquad \square$

Finally, deploying Proposition 12 and Lemmas 2 and 3 we arrive at our central impossibility results for power-of-two cyclotomic rings and prime cyclotomic rings.

First, since $(2, t)$-subtractive sets are weakly $(2, 2)$-subtractive and there are power-of-two cyclotomic rings that contain an ideal of norm $m + 1$, we arrive at the theorem below. We state the result for $s = 2$ as opposed to, say, $s = 1 - \zeta$ as the former is more general than the latter: the existence $(1 - \zeta, t)$-subtractive sets implies the existence of $(2, t)$-subtractive sets.

Theorem 3. *There is no family of $(2, t)$-subtractive sets of size $n > m + 1$ in the power of two cyclotomic ring $\mathbb{Z}[\zeta_m]$ where $m = 2^\ell$ for some $\ell \in \mathbb{N}$.*

Putting Theorems 1 and 3 together, we see that our $(2, 3)$-subtractive set construction achieves size $m/2 + 1$ compared to the limit of $m + 1$. This construction is thus within a factor of 2 of being optimal. However, we note that Theorem 3 does not rule out the existence of $(2, t)$-subtractive sets of size $n > m + 1$ for specific choices of m, e.g. $m = 2^{10} = 1024$ is a good candidate, cf. Remark 1.

Second, since $(1, t)$-subtractive sets are weakly $(1, 2)$-subtractive and prime-power cyclotomic rings contain an ideal of norm p, Lemma 3 rules out larger subtractive sets. An alternative route to the same statement is by noting that $e \geq 1$ in Proposition 12 and that $1 \notin \langle 1 - \zeta \rangle$. Therefore the subtractive sets for prime-power cyclotomic rings in Theorem 2 are in a sense optimal. On the flip side it means that over a power-of-2 cyclotomic ring the only subtractive sets are of size 2, such as $S = \{0, 1\}$.

Theorem 4. *There is no subtractive set of size $n > p$ in any prime-power cyclotomic ring $\mathbb{Z}[\zeta_{p^\ell}]$ for any prime $p \in \mathbb{N}$ and any $\ell \in \mathbb{N}$.*

Finally, Lemma 3 rules out many natural algebraic strategies of constructing knowledge extractors for Schnorr-like proof systems that go beyond some generalised form of matrix inversion. For example, an algebraic extractor could attempt to compute s by running an extended Euclidean algorithm on pairs $c_0 - c_1, c_2 - c_3$, i.e. attempt to find (small) r_0, r_1 s.t. $s = r_0 \cdot (c_0 - c_1) + r_1 \cdot (c_2 - c_3)$, cf. [22, 33, 35] for the application of the Euclidean algorithm for finding small elements of this form in number rings. By Lemma 3 such extensions do not significantly improve the bounds. We will make use of this implicitly in Sect. 4 below.

4   Proof of Knowledge of Lattice Statements

In this section we give positive and negative results on using subtractive sets over cyclotomic rings to construct proof systems for lattice statements of the form

$$L_{s,\beta} := \{(\mathbf{A}, \mathbf{y}) \in \mathcal{R}_q^{h \times k} \times \mathcal{R}_q^h : \exists \mathbf{x} \in \mathcal{R}^k \text{ s.t. } \mathbf{A}\mathbf{x} = s\mathbf{y} \wedge \|\mathbf{x}\| \leq \beta\}.$$

$\Pi_r.\langle \mathcal{P}((\mathbf{A},\mathbf{y}),\mathbf{x})|\mathcal{V}(\mathbf{A},\mathbf{y})\rangle$ where $(\mathbf{A},\mathbf{y}) \in \mathcal{R}_q^{h \times k_r} \times \mathcal{R}_q^h$, $\mathbf{x} \in \mathcal{R}^{k_r}$, $r \in \mathbb{Z}_{\log k}$

$\mathbf{l} := \mathbf{A}_1\mathbf{x}_0,\ \mathbf{r} := \mathbf{A}_0\mathbf{x}_1$ $\qquad \xrightarrow{\quad \mathbf{l},\mathbf{r} \in \mathcal{R}^h \quad} \qquad$ $c \leftarrow_\$ S_0,\ d \leftarrow_\$ S_1$

$\qquad \xleftarrow{\quad c \in \mathcal{R}, d \in \mathcal{R} \quad}$ $\qquad \tilde{\mathbf{A}} := (c\mathbf{A}_0 + d\mathbf{A}_1)$

$\qquad\qquad\qquad\qquad\qquad\qquad\qquad \tilde{\mathbf{y}} := d^2\mathbf{l} + cd\mathbf{y} + c^2\mathbf{r}$

$\tilde{\mathbf{x}} := d\mathbf{x}_0 + c\mathbf{x}_1$ $\qquad \xrightarrow{\quad \tilde{\mathbf{x}} \in \mathcal{R}^{k_{r+1}} \quad}$ $\qquad \tilde{\mathbf{A}} \cdot \tilde{\mathbf{x}} \overset{?}{=} \tilde{\mathbf{y}}$

$\qquad\qquad\qquad\qquad\qquad\qquad\qquad\qquad \|\tilde{\mathbf{x}}\| \overset{?}{\leq} \gamma_r$

$\Pi_{\log k}.\langle \mathcal{P}((\mathbf{A},\mathbf{y}),\mathbf{x})|\mathcal{V}(\mathbf{A},\mathbf{y})\rangle$ where $(\mathbf{A},\mathbf{y}) \in \mathcal{R}_q^{h \times 1} \times \mathcal{R}_q^h$, $\mathbf{x} \in \mathcal{R}$, $r = \log k$

$\qquad \xrightarrow{\quad \mathbf{x} \in \mathcal{R} \quad}$ $\qquad \mathbf{A}\mathbf{x} \overset{?}{=} \mathbf{y}$

$\qquad\qquad\qquad\qquad\qquad\qquad \|\mathbf{x}\| \overset{?}{\leq} \gamma_{\log k}$

Fig. 1. Lattice Bulletproof protocol Π_r for round $r \in \{0, \ldots, \log k\}$ generalised from [11].

4.1 Generalised Lattice Bulletproof

Let k be a power of 2, $k_r := k/2^r$ and $\gamma_r > 0$ for $r \in \{0, \ldots, \log k\}$, and $S_0, S_1 \subseteq \mathcal{R}$. In Fig. 1 we write down a slight generalisation of the lattice Bulletproof protocol in [11], who considered $h = 1$, $\mathcal{R}$ being a power-of-2 cyclotomic ring, and $S_1 = \{1\}$. Given a matrix $\mathbf{A} \in \mathcal{R}^{h \times k_r}$, we can parse it as $\mathbf{A} = (\mathbf{A}_0, \mathbf{A}_1)$ with $\mathbf{A}_i \in \mathcal{R}^{h \times k_{r+1}}$. Similarly, given a vector $\mathbf{x} \in \mathcal{R}^{k_r}$ we can parse it as $\mathbf{x} = (\mathbf{x}_0, \mathbf{x}_1)$ with $\mathbf{x}_i \in \mathcal{R}^{k_{r+1}}$.

Lemma 4. *Suppose that $\|c\| \leq 1$ for all $c \in S_0$ and $\|d\| \leq 1$ for all $d \in S_1$ (which is the case for S constructed in Theorems 1 and 2). Let $\gamma_r = 2^{r+1} \cdot \gamma_{\mathcal{R},r+2} \cdot \beta$ for $r \in \mathbb{Z}_{\log k}$ and $\gamma_{\log k} = \gamma_{\log k-1} = k \cdot \gamma_{\mathcal{R}, \log k+1} \cdot \beta$. In Π_0, if the prover's input $\mathbf{x}^{(0)}$ satisfies $\|\mathbf{x}\| \leq \beta$, then the verifier accepts with certainty. For $r \in [\log k]$, if for all $r' \in [r]$, the prover's input $\mathbf{x}^{(r')}$ is equal to the prover's second message sent in an honest execution of $\Pi_{r'-1}$, then the verifier in Π_r accepts with certainty. Consequently, the recursive composition of $\Pi_0, \ldots, \Pi_{\log k}$ yields a proof system Π which is perfectly complete relative to $L_{1,\beta}$.*

In case $\mathcal{R} = \mathbb{Z}[\zeta_{2^\ell}]$, S_0 is constructed from Theorem 1, and $S_1 = \{1\}$, then we can set $\gamma_r := 2^{r+1} \cdot \beta$ and $\gamma_{\log k} = k \cdot \beta$ instead.

Proof. For all $r \in \mathbb{Z}_{\log k}$, suppose that $\mathbf{A} \cdot \mathbf{x} = \mathbf{y}$, then

$$(c\mathbf{A}_0 + d\mathbf{A}_1) \cdot \mathbf{z} = (c\mathbf{A}_0 + d\mathbf{A}_1) \cdot (d\mathbf{x}_0 + c\mathbf{x}_1)$$
$$= d^2\mathbf{A}_1 \cdot \mathbf{x}_0 + c \cdot d \cdot (\mathbf{A}_0 \cdot \mathbf{x}_0 + \mathbf{A}_1 \cdot \mathbf{x}_1) + c^2 \mathbf{A}_0 \cdot \mathbf{x}_1$$
$$= d^2\mathbf{l} + cd\mathbf{y} + c^2\mathbf{r}.$$

In Π_0, if $\|\mathbf{x}\| \leq \beta$, then observe that $\|d\,\mathbf{x}_0 + c\,\mathbf{x}_1\| \leq 2\,\gamma_{\mathcal{R}}\,\beta$. Fix $r \in [\log k]$. Since for all $r' \in [r]$, the prover's input $\mathbf{x}^{(r')}$ is equal to the prover's second message sent in an honest execution of $\Pi_{r'-1}$, we have that the prover's input $\mathbf{x}^{(r)}$ is equal to a sum of 2^r terms, each term being a product of r challenges and a subvector of $\mathbf{x}^{(0)}$. If $r = \log k$, then the input $\mathbf{x}^{(\log k)}$ is sent directly to the verifier, which has norm upper bounded by $k \cdot \gamma_{\mathcal{R},\log k+1} \cdot \beta = \gamma_{\log k}$. If $r < \log k$, then the prover's second message in Π_r is a sum of 2^{r+1} terms, each term being a product of $r+1$ challenges and a subvector of $\mathbf{x}^{(0)}$. The norm of this message is thus upper bounded by $2^{r+1} \cdot \gamma_{\mathcal{R},r+2} \cdot \beta = \gamma_r$.

The strengthened claim regarding power-of-2 cyclotomic rings follows from realising that each element in S_0 is either zero or a power of ζ, and that multiplication by ζ does not increase norm. $\square$

Theorem 5. *Let $\mathcal{R}$ be a prime-power cyclotomic ring of order m being a power of a prime p. Let $S_0 \subseteq_n \mathcal{R}$ be an $(s,3)$-subtractive set of size $n = \mathsf{poly}(\lambda)$ and $S_1 = \{1\}$. For $r \in \{0,\ldots,\log k\}$, let γ_r be defined as in Lemma 4. Suppose that S_0 is constructed from Theorem 1 or Theorem 2, then $\Pi_{\log k}$ has perfect knowledge soundness relative to $L_{s,\gamma'_{\log k}}$, and Π_r has $\frac{2(r+1)}{n}$-knowledge soundness relative to L_{s,γ'_r} for $r \in \mathbb{Z}_{\log k}$, where $\gamma'_{\log k} = \gamma'_{\log k-1}$, and*

$$\gamma'_r = \begin{cases} 24 \cdot \varphi(m) \cdot \gamma_{\mathcal{R}} \cdot \gamma_r & p > 2 \\ 3 \cdot \varphi(m) \cdot \gamma_{\mathcal{R}} \cdot \gamma_r & p = 2. \end{cases}$$

Proof. For $r = \log k$, there exists a trivial $(\log k)$-th extractor $\mathcal{E}_{\log k}$ which simply outputs the prover's message. If a prover $\mathcal{A}$ successfully convinces the verifier $\mathcal{V}$, then the prover's message is exactly the witness.

For $r \in \mathbb{Z}_{\log k}$, let $\mathcal{A}$ be a prover who successfully convinces the verifier $\mathcal{V}$ in Π_r to accept a statement $(\mathbf{A}, \mathbf{y})$ with probability $\rho > 2(r+1)/n$. Consider a binary matrix H with rows indexed by the random coins χ of $\mathcal{A}$, columns indexed by $c \in S_0$, and the (χ, c)-th entry is $\langle \mathcal{A}(\chi), \mathcal{V}(\mathsf{stmt}; c) \rangle$, i.e. whether $\mathcal{V}$ accepts of rejects when $\mathcal{A}$ runs on the randomness χ and $\mathcal{V}$ chooses $c \in S_0$ as the challenge. By our assumption on $\mathcal{A}$, a ρ-fraction of the entries of H are 1. Adopting the terminologies in [17], a row of H is semi-heavy if it contains at least three 1's. Since $\rho > 2(r+1)/n \geq 2/n$, write $\rho = (2+\delta)/n$ for some $\delta > 2r$. Suppose there are in total R rows in H, so that $\rho R n = (2 + \delta)R$ entries are 1. At most $2R$ of them can be located in non-semi-heavy rows, while at least δR of them are in semi-heavy rows. Therefore the fraction of 1's in semi-heavy rows among all 1's is at least $\delta/(2+\delta)$.

With the above observation, we construct the r-th knowledge extractor $\mathcal{E} = \mathcal{E}_r$ as follows. $\mathcal{E}$ runs $\langle \mathcal{A}(\chi), \mathcal{V}(\mathsf{stmt}; c_0) \rangle$ for some uniformly chosen χ and $c_0 \leftarrow_{\$} S_0$. If $\langle \mathcal{A}(\chi), \mathcal{V}(\mathsf{stmt}; c_0) \rangle = 0$, $\mathcal{E}$ aborts. Otherwise, we have $\langle \mathcal{A}(\chi), \mathcal{V}(\mathsf{stmt}; c_0) \rangle = 1$, which happens with probability ρ. Then, $\mathcal{E}$ runs $\langle \mathcal{A}(\chi), \mathcal{V}(\mathsf{stmt}; c) \rangle$ for all $c \in S_0 \setminus \{c_0\}$. Note that this can be done in polynomial time since $n = \mathsf{poly}(\lambda)$. By the above observation about semi-heavy rows, since the (χ, c_0)-th entry of H is 1, with probability at least $\delta/(2 + \delta)$, the row in H indexed by χ is a semi-heavy row, and in this case there are at least 2 more

1's in this row. Denote the indices of two of these entries by (χ, c_1) and (χ, c_2) respectivly. To summarise, with probability $\rho\delta/(2+\delta) = \delta/n > 2r/n \geq 0$, we have $\langle \mathcal{A}(\chi), \mathcal{V}(\text{stmt}; c) \rangle = 1$ for $c \in \{c_0, c_1, c_2\}$.

Suppose the above event happens, $\mathcal{E}$ reads from the communication transcripts the responses $\tilde{\mathbf{x}}_i$ which satisfy

$$(c_i \mathbf{A}_0 + \mathbf{A}_1) \cdot \tilde{\mathbf{x}}_i = 1 + c_i \mathbf{y} + c_i^2 \mathbf{r} \text{ and } \|\tilde{\mathbf{x}}_i\| \leq \gamma_r$$

for all $i \in \mathbb{Z}_3$. In matrix form, we can write

$$\mathbf{A} \cdot \begin{pmatrix} c_0 \tilde{\mathbf{x}}_0 & c_1 \tilde{\mathbf{x}}_1 & c_2 \tilde{\mathbf{x}}_2 \\ \tilde{\mathbf{x}}_0 & \tilde{\mathbf{x}}_1 & \tilde{\mathbf{x}}_2 \end{pmatrix} = (\mathbf{1} \ \mathbf{y} \ \mathbf{r}) \cdot V_{\{c_0, c_1, c_2\}}^{\mathsf{T}}$$

Let $\mathbf{w} = (0, 1, 0) \in \mathcal{R}^3$. By Proposition 6, the solution $\mathbf{z} = (z_0, z_1, z_2)$ to the equation $V_{\{c_0, c_1, c_2\}}^{\mathsf{T}} \cdot \mathbf{z} = s \cdot \mathbf{w}$ is given by

$$z_i = -\frac{s}{d_i} \sum_{j \in \mathbb{Z}_3 \setminus \{i\}} c_j$$

for $i \in \mathbb{Z}_3$. Define $\mathbf{x} = (\sum_{i=0}^{2} c_i z_i \cdot \tilde{\mathbf{x}}_i, \sum_{i=0}^{2} z_i \cdot \tilde{\mathbf{x}}_i)$. We have

$$\mathbf{A} \cdot \mathbf{x} = \mathbf{A} \cdot \begin{pmatrix} c_0 \tilde{\mathbf{x}}_0 & c_1 \tilde{\mathbf{x}}_1 & c_2 \tilde{\mathbf{x}}_2 \\ \tilde{\mathbf{x}}_0 & \tilde{\mathbf{x}}_1 & \tilde{\mathbf{x}}_2 \end{pmatrix} \cdot \mathbf{z} = (\mathbf{1} \ \mathbf{y} \ \mathbf{r}) \cdot V_{\{c_0, c_1, c_2\}}^{\mathsf{T}} \cdot \mathbf{z} = s \cdot \mathbf{y}.$$

Furthermore, we notice that $\mathbf{x}$ is a sum of 3 terms, each being a product of $c_i z_i$ and $\tilde{\mathbf{x}}_i$. Using Propositions 10 and 11 we have $\|c_i z_i\| \leq \varphi(m)$ and $8\varphi(m)$ respectively, and $\tilde{\mathbf{x}}_i$ of norm at most γ_r. The norm $\|\mathbf{x}\|$ therefore satisfies

$$\|\mathbf{x}\| \leq \begin{cases} 24 \cdot \varphi(m) \cdot \gamma_{\mathcal{R}} \cdot \gamma_r & p > 2 \\ 3 \cdot \varphi(m) \cdot \gamma_{\mathcal{R}} \cdot \gamma_r & p = 2 \end{cases} = \gamma_r'$$

Our r-th extractor $\mathcal{E}$ therefore outputs $\mathbf{x}$ as a witness of $(\mathbf{A}, \mathbf{y}) \in L_{s, \gamma_r'}$ with probability at least $\delta/n > 2r/n$. $\qquad \square$

4.2 On the Knowledge Soundness of Recursive Composition

Knowledge error is at least $\Omega(\log k/n)$. In their original analysis, Bootle *et al.* [11] optimistically claimed without proof that the protocol Π obtained from the recursive composition of $\Pi_0, \ldots, \Pi_{\log k}$ has knowledge error $O(1/n)$. We disprove this by constructing a cheating prover who can convince the verifier in Π_r with probability at least $1/n$ for any statement $(\mathbf{A}, \mathbf{y})$. Consequently we obtain a cheating prover who can convince the verifier in Π with probability at least $1 - (1 - 1/n)^{\log k} \geq \frac{\log k}{2n} = \omega(1/n)$ assuming $n \geq \log k = \omega(1)$.

Our cheating prover $\mathcal{A}_r$ for Π_r is essentially a "zero-knowledge simulator" which does the following. Guess the challenge to be sent by the verifier as c^* uniformly at random. Sample an arbitrary vector $\tilde{\mathbf{x}} \in \mathcal{R}^{kr+1}$ of norm at most γ_r. Compute $(\tilde{\mathbf{A}}, \tilde{\mathbf{y}})$ as an honest prover would. Pick an arbitrary vector $\mathbf{r} \in \mathcal{R}^h$. Compute $\mathbf{l} = \tilde{\mathbf{A}}\tilde{\mathbf{x}} - c\tilde{\mathbf{y}} - c^2\mathbf{r}$. Send $(\mathbf{l}, \mathbf{r})$ as the first message and receive a challenge c.

If $c \neq c^*$ then abort. Otherwise send $\tilde{\mathbf{x}}$ as the second message. Clearly $\mathcal{A}_r$ succeeds whenever $c = c^*$, which happens with probability at least $1/n$.

Now consider an adversary $\mathcal{A}$ against the verifier in Π. To cheat, it suffices for $\mathcal{A}$ to cheat in at least one round $r \in \mathbb{Z}_{\log k}$. The success probability of $\mathcal{A}$ is then at least $1 - (1 - 1/n)^{\log k} \geq 1 - \frac{1}{1 + \log k/n} = \frac{\log k}{n + \log k} \geq \frac{\log k}{2n} = \omega(1/n)$, where we assumed $n \geq \log k = \omega(1)$. In general, if Π is obtained by recursively composing $\Pi_0, \ldots, \Pi_\ell$ for some $\ell \geq 0$, where in Π_ℓ the prover simply sends the witness, then $\mathcal{A}$ succeeds with probability at least $\Omega(\ell/n)$ which is $\omega(1/n)$ if the number of rounds ℓ is super-constant.

On achieving knowledge error $O(\log k/n)$. In the proof of Theorem 5, we showed that for $r \in \mathbb{Z}_{\log k}$ if $\mathcal{A}_r$ is a cheating prover in Π_r with success probability greater than $2(r + 1)/n$, then our extractor $\mathcal{E}_r$ succeeds with probability greater than $2r/n$. This intuitively suggests that if $\mathcal{A}$ is a cheating prover in Π obtained by recursively composing $\Pi_0, \ldots, \Pi_{\log k}$ with success probability greater than $2 \log k/n$, then by recursively running the extractors $\mathcal{E}_{\log k}, \ldots, \mathcal{E}_0$ one should construct an extractor $\mathcal{E}$ which succeeds with positive probability. In other words, the knowledge error of Π is intuitively at most $2 \log k/n$. This does not contradict with the existence of the attacker $\mathcal{A}$ with success probability $1 - (1 - 1/n)^{\log k}$ constructed above, since by the union bound we have $1 - (1 - 1/n)^{\log k} \leq \sum_{r \in \mathbb{Z}_{\log k}} 1/n = \log k/n$. If the knowledge error is indeed at most $2 \log k/n$, then repeating the protocol $\lambda/(\log n - \log \log k - 1)$ times (instead of $\lambda/\log n$ times suggested in [11]) suffices to achieve knowledge error $2^{-\lambda}$.

Formalising the above intuition requires a very strong "forking lemma" which extracts a full depth-$(\log k)$ ternary tree of accepting transcripts in expected polynomial time when given any cheating prover for Π with success probability greater than $2 \log k/n$. Unfortunately, such a formalisation appears to be out of reach with the current proof techniques. Indeed, the forking lemma in [9, Lemma 1] (and its variants) used in subsequent works (e.g. [13,14]) implies a knowledge error of $n^{-1/3}k^{1.58}$. The concrete analysis in [24] implies a knowledge error of $5n^{-1/2}k^{1.58} \log k$. A common problem in these analyses is that the extractor being constructed runs the cheating prover with uniformly random challenges every time, without insisting that the challenges in each round are distinct. This incurs a substantial loss in extraction probability.

At the time of writing, the tightest bound that we are aware of is given in [19, Lemma 3.2], which implies a knowledge error of $\frac{\alpha^{\log k}}{\alpha - 1} \frac{3}{n}$ for any $\alpha > \left(\frac{n}{n-3}\right)^2$. The minimum of the factor $\frac{\alpha^{\log k}}{\alpha - 1}$ is $\left(1 + \frac{1}{\log k - 1}\right)^{\log k} / \frac{1}{\log k - 1} \leq e \log k$ attained when $\alpha = 1 + \frac{1}{\log k - 1}$ and e is Euler's number. Let $n \geq 9 \log k$.[8] We can check that the requirement $\alpha > \left(\frac{n}{n-3}\right)^2$ is fulfilled. We therefore obtain a knowledge error of $\frac{8.16 \log k}{n}$ whenever $n \geq 9 \log k$, which requires $\lambda/(\log n - \log \log k - 4)$ parallel repetitions to achieve a knowledge error of $2^{-\lambda}$.

---

[8] The requirement $n \geq 9 \log k$ is realistic. Typically, we have $n \approx 1000$ and $\log k \ll 100$.

For a concrete feeling of the number of repetitions required, suppose we aim for around 2^{-80} knowledge error, choose a ring $\mathcal{R}$ of degree $\varphi(m) \approx 1024$, an $(s, 3)$-subtractive set of size $n \approx 2^{10}$, and $k = 2^{20}$, which encodes the assignment of the internal wires an arithmetic circuit of size 2^{30}. Then if we can achieve the (near optimal) knowledge error of $2 \log k / n$, only 20 repetitions are needed.[9] With the provable knowledge error of $8.16 \log k / n$ however, we need 50 repetitions.

4.3   On the Quality of the Extracted Witness

Suppose we are able to construct an extractor by using one of the forking lemmas, then due to the additional structural guarantee of the extracted solution, we can obtain a tighter upper bound of the norm of the extracted solution $\mathbf{x}$. Specifically, observe that by construction $\mathbf{x}$ is a sum of $3^{\log k}$ terms, each term being a product of $\log k$ terms of the form $c_i z_i$ and one more term of norm at most $\gamma'_{\log k}$.

For the prime-power case, recall that $\gamma'_{\log k} = k \cdot \gamma_{\mathcal{R}, \log k + 1} \cdot \beta$. From Proposition 11 we have $\|c_i z_i\| \leq 8m$ and a naive application would yield a factor of $(8m)^{\log k}$ in the bound of $\|\mathbf{x}\|$. We can obtain a slightly better bound by observing that a factor 2 in $8m$ is contributed by a multiplication by a power of ζ (cf. Proposition 11). If we collect all the $\log k$ powers of ζ and only multiply them in one shot, then $(8m)^{\log k}$ can be replaced by $2 \cdot (4m)^{\log k}$. We therefore obtain

$$\|\mathbf{x}\| \leq 3^{\log k} \cdot \gamma_{\mathcal{R}, \log k + 1} \cdot \left(2 \cdot (4m)^{\log k}\right) \cdot (k \cdot \gamma_{\mathcal{R}, \log k + 1} \cdot \beta)$$

$$= 3^{\log k} \cdot \left(2 \left(\log k + 1\right) \cdot \varphi(m)^{\log k}\right)^2 \cdot 2 \cdot (4m)^{\log k} \cdot k \cdot \beta$$

$$= \tilde{O}(k^{3 \log m + 4.58}) \cdot \beta.$$

When when $p = \mathsf{poly}(\lambda)$, we can set $s = 1$ and choose a modulus

$$q = \tilde{O}(k^{3 \log m + 4.58}) \cdot \beta.$$

We remark that even with the more careful analysis, the factor $2 \cdot (4m)^{\log k}$ is still somewhat loose. If we instead use the empirical estimation in Proposition 11 that $\|c_i \cdot z_i\| \leq m$, we can set

$$q = O(\|\mathbf{x}\|) = \tilde{O}(k^{3 \log m + 2.58}) \cdot \beta.$$

For the power-of-2 case we recall that $\gamma'_{\log k} = k \cdot \beta$ and thus

$$\|\mathbf{x}\| \leq 3^{\log k} \cdot \gamma_{\mathcal{R}, \log k + 1} \cdot \varphi(m)^{\log k} \cdot (k \cdot \beta)$$

$$= 3^{\log k} \cdot \varphi(m)^{2 \log k} \cdot k \cdot \beta$$

$$= \tilde{O}(k^{2 \log m + 0.58}) \cdot \beta.$$

Since $s = 2$ for the power-of-2 case, we have a total slack of k after recursive composition. Therefore we can choose a modulus $q = \tilde{O}(k^{2 \log m + 1.58}) \cdot \beta$. For comparison, [11] give a bound of $\tilde{O}(k^{3 \log m + 4.5}) \cdot \beta$ which is larger by a factor of $\tilde{O}(k^{\log m + 3})$.

---

[9] A concurrent work [2] proves that the knowledge error of $\frac{2 \log k}{n}$ can be achieved.

Remark 5. We may ask if another factor of $\log k$ can be shaved off the exponent by a more careful analysis of products of the form $\prod_{0 \leq j < \log k} c_{i_j} \cdot z_{i_j}$. Experimenting with random products of this form in the power-of-2 case suggests the norm grows as $(m/4)^{2(\log k - 1)}$ in the worst case (over the choice of $c_{i_j} \cdot z_{i_j}$) which is comparable to our analytical bound. The same bound is also approached from above in the prime case as m grows. Using that these products are over randomness of the extractor, we may also consider the average case which empirically grows as $(m/4)^{\log k + o(\log k)}$. Based on this data, we speculate that $q = \tilde{O}(k^{\log m + O(1)}) \cdot \beta$ is attainable.

4.4   Impossibility

A wide class of proof systems has knowledge soundness relative to $(\mathcal{E}, L_{s,\beta})$, where $\mathcal{E}$ is a knowledge extractor conforming to the following pattern.

Definition 8 (Algebraic Extractors). *Let Π be a proof system conforming to Definition 3 with $g = 1$ (3-move). Let $\mathcal{E}$ be an extractor for $L_{s,\beta}$. We say $\mathcal{E}$ is 3-move degree-d algebraic if $\mathcal{E}^{\mathcal{P}}$ conforms to the following pattern:*

1. *$\mathcal{E}$ specifies a special monomial $M^* \in \mathcal{M}$, where $\mathcal{M}$ is the set of all f-variate degree-d homogenous monomials.*
2. *$\mathcal{E}$ runs $\mathcal{P}$ some number of times to generate t accepting transcripts for some $t \in \mathbb{N}$. In the k-th transcript, let the verifier challenges be $(c_{i,k})_{i \in \mathbb{Z}_f}$.*
3. *$\mathcal{E}$ finds coefficients $a_k \in \mathcal{R}$ for $k \in \mathbb{Z}_t$ such that*

$$\sum_{k \in \mathbb{Z}_t} a_k \cdot M(\mathbf{c}_k) = 0 \qquad \forall\, M \in \mathcal{M} \setminus \{M^*\},$$

$$\sum_{k \in \mathbb{Z}_t} a_k \cdot M^*(\mathbf{c}_k) = s.$$

4. *If $\mathcal{E}$ fails to find the coefficients a_k in the above step, it aborts.*

We justify the definition of algebraic extractors, focusing on 3-move 2-challenge protocols. One challenge protocols can be captured by setting $S_1 := \{1\}$.

We first consider a linear-size Schnorr-like proof system which is complete for $L_{1,\beta}$. Classically a knowledge extractor $\mathcal{E}$ for $L_{s,\beta'}$ for some (s, β') is of degree $d = 1$ and proceeds as follows: Suppose $\mathcal{P}$ is a convincing prover for the statement $(\mathbf{A}, \mathbf{y})$. The extractor $\mathcal{E}^{\mathcal{P}}$ collects from $t = 2$ correlated accepting transcripts an image $\tilde{\mathbf{y}}$ and two preimages $\hat{\mathbf{x}}_0$ and $\hat{\mathbf{x}}_1$, such that $\mathbf{A} \cdot \hat{\mathbf{x}}_0 = c_{1,0}\tilde{\mathbf{y}} + c_{0,0}\mathbf{y}$ and $\mathbf{A} \cdot \hat{\mathbf{x}}_1 = c_{1,1}\tilde{\mathbf{y}} + c_{0,1}\mathbf{y}$. Subtracting the two equations yields $\mathbf{A} \cdot (\hat{\mathbf{x}}_0 - \hat{\mathbf{x}}_1) = (c_{1,0} - c_{1,1}) \cdot \tilde{\mathbf{y}} + (c_{0,0} - c_{0,1}) \cdot \mathbf{y}$. The extractor $\mathcal{E}$ then attempts to solve the following system of linear equations

$$\begin{pmatrix} c_{1,0} & c_{1,1} \\ c_{0,0} & c_{0,1} \end{pmatrix} \mathbf{z} = s \begin{pmatrix} 0 \\ 1 \end{pmatrix}$$

for $\mathbf{z} = (z_0, z_1)$, and return $\mathbf{x} = z_0\hat{\mathbf{x}}_0 + z_1\hat{\mathbf{x}}_1$. The special monomial here is $M^*(\{(X_0, X_1)\}) = X_0$ for some formal variables X_i.

Next we observe that in the proof of knowledge soundness of the lattice Bulletproof protocol constructed in Sect. 4.1, the degree-2 knowledge extractor solves the following system of linear equations

$$\begin{pmatrix} c_{1,0}^2 & c_{1,1}^2 & c_{1,2}^2 \\ c_{0,0} \cdot c_{1,0} & c_{0,1} \cdot c_{1,1} & c_{0,2} \cdot c_{1,2} \\ c_{0,0}^2 & c_{0,1}^2 & c_{0,2}^2 \end{pmatrix} \mathbf{z} = s \begin{pmatrix} 0 \\ 1 \\ 0 \end{pmatrix}$$

for $\mathbf{z} = (z_0, z_1, z_2)$. The special monomial here is $M^*(\{(X_0, X_1)\}) = X_0 X_1$.

A degree-$2d$ example can be obtained by modifying the lattice Bulletproof protocol in Sect. 4.1, such that instead of "folding" $\mathbf{A}$ and $\mathbf{x}$ in halves when given challenges (c_0, c_1), we compute

$$\tilde{\mathbf{A}} := \sum_{k=0}^{d} c_0^{d-k} \cdot c_1^k \cdot \mathbf{A}_k \quad \text{and} \quad \tilde{\mathbf{x}} := \sum_{k=0}^{d} c_0^k \cdot c_1^{d-k} \cdot \mathbf{x}_k.$$

Let $M^*(\{(X_0, X_1)\}) = X_0^d \cdot X_1^d$ and notice that

$$\tilde{\mathbf{A}} \cdot \tilde{\mathbf{x}} \in M^*(\{(c_0, c_1)\}) \cdot \mathbf{y} + \langle \{M(\{(c_0, c_1)\}) : M \in \mathcal{M} \setminus \{M^*\}\}\rangle.$$

Remark 6. Both Definition 8 and our results below can be generalised to $g > 1$. However, we found no good candidate construction with more than three moves. Thus, to avoid preempting future generalisations we do not formalise it here.

The next technical lemma shows that the above extraction strategy forces $s \in \langle M^*(\mathbf{S}^*) - M^*(\mathbf{S}^*)\rangle \cdot \mathcal{I}^{-1}$ (a fractional ideal) for some ideal $\mathcal{I}$ and for $\mathbf{S}^* = \{(c_{0,k}, \ldots, c_{f-1,k})\}_{k \in \mathbb{Z}_t}$. Here and in what follows we extend the notation of $M^*(\cdot)$ to sets in the natural way, e.g. $M^*(X_0, X_1) = X_0 \cdot X_1$ is extended to $M^*(\{(X_0, X_1), (Y_0, Y_1)\}) = \{X_0 \cdot X_1, Y_0 \cdot Y_1\}$. To illustrate the lemma, consider the linear-size Schnorr proof with $S_1 = \{1\}$ as an example. Here the lemma states that $s \in \langle c_{0,0} - c_{0,1}\rangle$. Similarly, for the lattice Bulletproof the lemma states that $s \in \left\langle \{c_{i,0} \cdot c_{i,1} - c_{j,0} \cdot c_{j,1}\}_{i \neq j} \right\rangle$ when $\langle \{c_{i,0}^2\}, \{c_{j,0}^2\}\rangle = \mathcal{R}$ for $i, j \in \mathbb{Z}_3$.

Lemma 5. *Let $d, f, t \in \mathbb{N}$, $a_k, c_{i,k} \in \mathcal{R}$ for $i \in \mathbb{Z}_f$ and $k \in \mathbb{Z}_t$. For $i \in \mathbb{Z}_f$, write $S_i^* := \{c_{i,k} : k \in \mathbb{Z}_t\}$, $\mathbf{S}^* = \prod_{i \in \mathbb{Z}_f} S_i^*$. For $k \in \mathbb{Z}_t$, write $\mathbf{c}_k = (c_{0,k}, \ldots, c_{f-1,k}) \in \mathbf{S}^*$. Let $\mathcal{M}$ be the set of f-variate degree-d homogeneous monomials. Fix $M^* \in \mathcal{M}$. For $M \in \mathcal{M} \setminus \{M^*\}$, let $\bar{M} := M/\gcd(M, M^*)$. Suppose*

$$U := \{(M, j) : M \in \mathcal{M} \setminus \{M^*\}, M(\mathbf{c}_j) \neq 0, j \in \mathbb{Z}_t\} \neq \emptyset.$$

Let $\mathcal{I} := \bigcap_{(M,j) \in U} \langle \bar{M}(\mathbf{c}_j)\rangle$. If $\sum_{k \in \mathbb{Z}_t} a_k \cdot M(\mathbf{c}_k) = 0$ for all $M \in \mathcal{M} \setminus \{M^*\}$ then

$$s := \sum_{k \in \mathbb{Z}_t} a_k \cdot M^*(\mathbf{c}_k) \in \langle M^*(\mathbf{S}^*) - M^*(\mathbf{S}^*)\rangle \cdot \mathcal{I}^{-1}$$

the latter being a fractional ideal in the field of fractions K of $\mathcal{R}$.

Proof. For any $(M, j) \in U$, we have $a_j = -\sum_{k \in \mathbb{Z}_t \setminus \{j\}} a_k \frac{M(\mathbf{c}_k)}{M(\mathbf{c}_j)} \in K$. Extending the given notation, let $\hat{M}^* = M^*/\gcd(M, M^*)$ (dependent on M). We obtain

$$
\begin{aligned}
s = \sum_{k \in \mathbb{Z}_t} a_k M^*(\mathbf{c}_k) &= \sum_{k \in \mathbb{Z}_t \setminus \{j\}} a_k M^*(\mathbf{c}_k) + a_j M^*(\mathbf{c}_j) \\
&= \sum_{k \in \mathbb{Z}_t \setminus \{j\}} a_k M^*(\mathbf{c}_k) - \left(\sum_{k \in \mathbb{Z}_t \setminus \{j\}} a_k \frac{M(\mathbf{c}_k)}{M(\mathbf{c}_j)} \right) M^*(\mathbf{c}_j) \\
&= \sum_{k \in \mathbb{Z}_t \setminus \{j\}} a_k \left(M^*(\mathbf{c}_k) M(\mathbf{c}_j) - M(\mathbf{c}_k) M^*(\mathbf{c}_j) \right) / M(\mathbf{c}_j) \\
&= \sum_{k \in \mathbb{Z}_t \setminus \{j\}} a_k \left(M^*(\mathbf{c}_k) \bar{M}(\mathbf{c}_j) - M(\mathbf{c}_k) \hat{M}^*(\mathbf{c}_j) \right) / \bar{M}(\mathbf{c}_j) \\
&\in \frac{1}{\bar{M}(\mathbf{c}_j)} \left\langle M(\mathbf{S}^*) \hat{M}^*(\mathbf{S}^*) - M^*(\mathbf{S}^*) \bar{M}(\mathbf{S}^*) \right\rangle \\
&= \frac{1}{\bar{M}(\mathbf{c}_j)} \left\langle \bar{M}(\mathbf{S}^*) M^*(\mathbf{S}^*) - \bar{M}(\mathbf{S}^*) M^*(\mathbf{S}^*) \right\rangle \\
&\subseteq \frac{1}{\bar{M}(\mathbf{c}_j)} \left\langle M^*(\mathbf{S}^*) - M^*(\mathbf{S}^*) \right\rangle .
\end{aligned}
$$

We conclude that

$$
s \in \bigcap_{(M,j) \in U} \frac{1}{\bar{M}(\mathbf{c}_j)} \left\langle M^*(\mathbf{S}^*) - M^*(\mathbf{S}^*) \right\rangle = \left\langle M^*(\mathbf{S}^*) - M^*(\mathbf{S}^*) \right\rangle \cdot \mathcal{I}^{-1}.
$$

$\square$

We can now state the main result of this section which rules out algebraic extractors achieving inverse polynomial soundness error and small slack. We state our impossibility for 3-move protocols for simplicity. However, as mentioned above, the ideas in the proof generalise to arbitrary moves. At a high level, our proof strategy is to construct an adversary that only answers challenges such that all accepting transcripts land in the same coset $\mathfrak{c}$ of some ideal $\mathfrak{q}$ chosen by the adversary, i.e. $\mathfrak{c} \equiv c_{i,k} \bmod \mathfrak{q}$. Then, e.g. for linear-size Schnorr proofs $c_{0,0} - c_{0,1} \in \mathfrak{q}$ which implies $s \in \mathfrak{q}$ by Lemma 5.

Theorem 6. *Let $\mathcal{R}$ be a cyclotomic ring. Let $\mathfrak{q} \subseteq \mathcal{R}$ be a prime ideal of norm $N(\mathfrak{q}) = |\mathcal{R}/\mathfrak{q}| = q$. Let Π be an f-challenge 3-move public-coin proof system, where $S_i \setminus \{0\} \neq \emptyset$ for $i \in \mathbb{Z}_f$, and $\prod_{i \in \mathbb{Z}_f} |S_i| = \prod_{i \in \mathbb{Z}_f} n_i \geq q^f$. Let $\mathcal{E}$ be a degree-d algebraic extractor for $L_{s,\beta}$. Let $\kappa < q^{-f}/2$. Suppose Π has κ-knowledge soundness relative to $(\mathcal{E}, L_{s,\beta})$ for some $\beta \in \mathcal{R}$, then $s \in \mathfrak{q}^{d-1}$.*

Proof. Let $\kappa = q^{-f}/2 - \epsilon$ for some $\epsilon > 0$. Suppose the claim is false, then $s \notin \mathfrak{q}^{d-1}$.

Let M^* be the special monomial specified by $\mathcal{E}$. Pick any $i^* \in \mathbb{Z}_f$ such that $M^*(\mathbf{C}) \neq C_{i^*}^d$. Let $S_{i^*}^* \subseteq S_{i^*} \setminus \{0\}$ be a largest subset so that all elements belong to the same coset modulo $\mathfrak{q}$. For each $i \in \mathbb{Z}_f \setminus \{i^*\}$, let $S_i^* \subseteq S_i$ be a largest subset so that all elements belong to the same coset modulo $\mathfrak{q}$. We note that by construction S_i^* has the property that $S_i^* - S_i^* \subseteq \mathfrak{q}$ for all $i \in \mathbb{Z}_f$, and $S_{i^*}^*$ contains only non-zero elements. Since $\mathfrak{q}$ has q cosets, by the pigeonhole principle, $|S_i^*| \geq \lceil n_i/q \rceil$ for all $i \in \mathbb{Z}_f \setminus \{i^*\}$. For $i = i^*$, if S_{i^*} contains only non-zero elements, then $|S_{i^*}^*| \geq \lceil n_{i^*}/q \rceil$. Otherwise $|S_{i^*}^*| \geq \lceil (n_{i^*} - 1)/q \rceil$.

We construct an adversary $\mathcal{A}$. This adversary $\mathcal{A}$ behaves almost exactly like the honest prover $\mathcal{P}$, except that it insists on answering only those challenges coming from $\mathbf{S}^* := \prod_{i \in \mathbb{Z}_f} S_i^*$. If $\mathcal{A}$ is challenged with any other values, it aborts. If S_{i^*} contains only non-zero elements, then $\mathcal{A}$ successfully convinces the honest verifier $\mathcal{V}$ with probability $\rho = \prod_{i \in \mathbb{Z}_f} \lceil n_i/q \rceil / n_i \geq q^{-f} > q^{-f}/2 - \epsilon = \kappa$. Otherwise, by noting that $n_{i^*} > 1$ since S_{i^*} contains at least one non-zero element, we have $\rho = (\lceil (n_{i^*} - 1)/q \rceil / n_{i^*}) \prod_{i \in \mathbb{Z}_f \setminus \{i^*\}} (\lceil n_i/q \rceil / n_i) \geq q^{-1}(1 - 1/n_{i^*})q^{-(f-1)} \geq q^{-f}/2 > q^{-f}/2 - \epsilon = \kappa$.

On the other hand, we see that for any algebraic extractor $\mathcal{E}$, $\mathcal{E}^{\mathcal{A}}$ fails to find algebraic combinations of differences of challenges to produce s. To see why, suppose that $\mathcal{E}$ does not abort according to Definition 8. Since $S_{i^*}^*$ is constructed such that $0 \notin S_{i^*}^*$ and $M^*(\mathbf{C}) \neq C_{i^*}^d$, the set U defined in the statement of Lemma 5 is non-empty. By Lemma 5, we have $s \in \langle M^*(\mathbf{C}) - M^*(\mathbf{C}) \rangle \cdot \mathcal{I}^{-1} \subseteq \mathfrak{q}^d \cdot \mathcal{I}^{-1}$. Since $\mathfrak{q}$ is prime, we either have $\mathfrak{q} = \mathcal{I}$, or $\mathfrak{q}$ and $\mathcal{I}$ are coprime. In the former case we have $s \in \mathfrak{q}^{d-1}$, and in the latter we have $s \in \mathfrak{q}^d \subseteq \mathfrak{q}^{d-1}$ since s is integral.

To conclude, $\mathcal{E}^{\mathcal{A}}$ always fails, which contradicts to the claim that Π has κ-knowledge soundness relative to $(\mathcal{E}, L_{s,\beta})$ for some $\beta \in \mathbb{R}$. $\square$

Remarks about the tightness of Theorem 6. The assumption that $\mathfrak{q}$ is prime is made without loss of generality: if $\mathfrak{q}$ is not prime then we can pick a prime factor of $\mathfrak{q}$. The assumption $\prod_{i \in \mathbb{Z}_f} |S_i| \geq q^f$ can typically be dropped if Π admits a "zero-knowledge simulator" which simulates the prover's messages by guessing the challenge to be sent by the verifier, which can be done with probability at least q^{-f} if $\prod_{i \in \mathbb{Z}_f} |S_i| < q^f$.[10] The assumption $\kappa < q^{-f}/2$ (instead of $\kappa < q^{-f}$) is made to account for the unlikely scenario that the extractor $\mathcal{E}$ manages to collect challenge tuples which contain too many zeros. The conclusion $s \in \mathfrak{q}^{d-1}$ (instead of $s \in \mathfrak{q}^d$) is to account for the unlikely event that $\mathcal{I} \neq \mathcal{R}$.

For example, if there exists $i^* \in \mathbb{Z}_f$ such that $M^*(\mathbf{C}) \neq C_{i^*}^d$, $0 \notin S_{i^*}$, and $\mu \in S_{i^*}$ for some invertible element $\mu \in \mathcal{R}$ (e.g. $\mu = 1$), then we can assume $\kappa < q^{-f}$ instead and conclude that $s \in \mathfrak{q}^d$ using the same proof. In particular, with this additional (natural) assumption, if $s = 1$ and $\mathfrak{q} = \langle 1 - \zeta \rangle$ which has norm p, then Π does not have κ-knowledge soundness relative to $(\mathcal{E}, L_{s,\beta})$ for any algebraic extractor $\mathcal{E}$, any $\beta \in \mathbb{R}$, any $\kappa < q^{-f}$, and any $f \in \mathbb{N}$.

By repeating f times a 1-challenge 3-move public-coin proof system with knowledge error p^{-1}, which can be constructed from a subtractive set of size p, such as the one constructed in Theorem 2, one can reduce the knowledge error to p^{-f} relative to an algebraic extractor. Therefore the bound $\kappa < p^{-f}$ in Theorem 6 is in a sense tight, assuming algebraic extractors.

---

[10] Although such a simulator usually exists naturally, it seems difficult to argue about its existence generically.

Acknowledgments. We thank Jonathan Bootle for comments on an earlier version of this work.

References

1. Abspoel, M., Cramer, R., Damgård, I., Escudero, D., Yuan, C.: Efficient information-theoretic secure multiparty computation over $\mathbb{Z}/p^k\mathbb{Z}$ via Galois rings. In: Hofheinz, D., Rosen, A. (eds.) TCC 2019. LNCS, vol. 11891, pp. 471–501. Springer, Cham (2019). https://doi.org/10.1007/978-3-030-36030-6_19
2. Attema, T., Cramer, R., Kohl, L.: A compressed σ-protocol theory for lattices. Cryptology ePrint Archive, Report 2021/307 (2021). https://eprint.iacr.org/2021/307
3. Baum, C., Bootle, J., Cerulli, A., del Pino, R., Groth, J., Lyubashevsky, V.: Sublinear lattice-based zero-knowledge arguments for arithmetic circuits. In: Shacham, H., Boldyreva, A. (eds.) CRYPTO 2018, Part II. LNCS, vol. 10992, pp. 669–699. Springer, Cham (2018). https://doi.org/10.1007/978-3-319-96881-0_23
4. Baum, C., Nof, A.: Concretely-efficient zero-knowledge arguments for arithmetic circuits and their application to lattice-based cryptography. In: Kiayias, A., Kohlweiss, M., Wallden, P., Zikas, V. (eds.) PKC 2020, Part I. LNCS, vol. 12110, pp. 495–526. Springer, Cham (2020). https://doi.org/10.1007/978-3-030-45374-9_17
5. Ben-Sasson, E., Chiesa, A., Riabzev, M., Spooner, N., Virza, M., Ward, N.P.: Aurora: transparent succinct arguments for R1CS. In: Ishai, Y., Rijmen, V. (eds.) EUROCRYPT 2019, Part I. LNCS, vol. 11476, pp. 103–128. Springer, Cham (2019). https://doi.org/10.1007/978-3-030-17653-2_4
6. Benhamouda, F., Camenisch, J., Krenn, S., Lyubashevsky, V., Neven, G.: Better zero-knowledge proofs for lattice encryption and their application to group signatures. In: Sarkar, P., Iwata, T. (eds.) ASIACRYPT 2014, Part I. LNCS, vol. 8873, pp. 551–572. Springer, Heidelberg (2014). https://doi.org/10.1007/978-3-662-45611-8_29
7. Beullens, W.: Sigma protocols for MQ, PKP and SIS, and Fishy signature schemes. In: Canteaut, A., Ishai, Y. (eds.) EUROCRYPT 2020, Part III. LNCS, vol. 12107, pp. 183–211. Springer, Cham (2020). https://doi.org/10.1007/978-3-030-45727-3_7
8. Boneh, D., Lewi, K., Montgomery, H., Raghunathan, A.: Key homomorphic PRFs and their applications. In: Canetti, R., Garay, J.A. (eds.) CRYPTO 2013, Part I. LNCS, vol. 8042, pp. 410–428. Springer, Heidelberg (2013). https://doi.org/10.1007/978-3-642-40041-4_23
9. Bootle, J., Cerulli, A., Chaidos, P., Groth, J., Petit, C.: Efficient zero-knowledge arguments for arithmetic circuits in the discrete log setting. In: Fischlin, M., Coron, J.-S. (eds.) EUROCRYPT 2016, Part II. LNCS, vol. 9666, pp. 327–357. Springer, Heidelberg (2016). https://doi.org/10.1007/978-3-662-49896-5_12
10. Bootle, J., Lyubashevsky, V., Nguyen, N.K., Seiler, G.: More efficient amortization of exact zero-knowledge proofs for LWE. Cryptology ePrint Archive, Report 2020/1449 (2020). https://eprint.iacr.org/2020/1449
11. Bootle, J., Lyubashevsky, V., Nguyen, N.K., Seiler, G.: A non-PCP approach to succinct quantum-safe zero-knowledge. In: Micciancio, D., Ristenpart, T. (eds.) CRYPTO 2020, Part II. LNCS, vol. 12171, pp. 441–469. Springer, Cham (2020). https://doi.org/10.1007/978-3-030-56880-1_16

12. Bootle, J., Lyubashevsky, V., Seiler, G.: Algebraic techniques for short(er) exact lattice-based zero-knowledge proofs. In: Boldyreva, A., Micciancio, D. (eds.) CRYPTO 2019, Part I. LNCS, vol. 11692, pp. 176–202. Springer, Cham (2019). https://doi.org/10.1007/978-3-030-26948-7_7

13. Bünz, B., Bootle, J., Boneh, D., Poelstra, A., Wuille, P., Maxwell, G.: Bulletproofs: short proofs for confidential transactions and more. In: 2018 IEEE Symposium on Security and Privacy, pp. 315–334. IEEE Computer Society Press, May 2018. https://doi.org/10.1109/SP.2018.00020

14. Bünz, B., Fisch, B., Szepieniec, A.: Transparent SNARKs from DARK compilers. In: Canteaut, A., Ishai, Y. (eds.) EUROCRYPT 2020, Part I. LNCS, vol. 12105, pp. 677–706. Springer, Cham (2020). https://doi.org/10.1007/978-3-030-45721-1_24

15. Cohen, H.: A Course in Computational Algebraic Number Theory. Graduate Texts in Mathematics, vol. 138. Springer, Heidelberg (2013). https://doi.org/10.1007/978-3-662-02945-9

16. Dalskov, A., Lee, E., Soria-Vazquez, E.: Circuit amortization friendly encodings and their application to statistically secure multiparty computation. In: Moriai, S., Wang, H. (eds.) ASIACRYPT 2020, Part III. LNCS, vol. 12493, pp. 213–243. Springer, Cham (2020). https://doi.org/10.1007/978-3-030-64840-4_8

17. Damgård, I.: On σ-protocols (2010). https://www.cs.au.dk/~ivan/Sigma.pdf

18. del Pino, R., Lyubashevsky, V., Seiler, G.: Lattice-based group signatures and zero-knowledge proofs of automorphism stability. In: Lie, D., Mannan, M., Backes, M., Wang, X. (eds.) ACM CCS 2018, pp. 574–591. ACM Press, October 2018. https://doi.org/10.1145/3243734.3243852

19. del Pino, R., Lyubashevsky, V., Seiler, G.: Short discrete log proofs for FHE and ring-LWE ciphertexts. In: Lin, D., Sako, K. (eds.) PKC 2019, Part I. LNCS, vol. 11442, pp. 344–373. Springer, Cham (2019). https://doi.org/10.1007/978-3-030-17253-4_12

20. Esgin, M.F., Nguyen, N.K., Seiler, G.: Practical exact proofs from lattices: new techniques to exploit fully-splitting rings. In: Moriai, S., Wang, H. (eds.) ASIACRYPT 2020, Part II. LNCS, vol. 12492, pp. 259–288. Springer, Cham (2020). https://doi.org/10.1007/978-3-030-64834-3_9

21. Ganesh, C., Nitulescu, A., Soria-Vazquez, E.: Rinocchio: snarks for ring arithmetic. Cryptology ePrint Archive, Report 2021/322 (2021). https://eprint.iacr.org/2021/322

22. Hoffstein, J., Howgrave-Graham, N., Pipher, J., Silverman, J.H., Whyte, W.: NTRUSign: digital signatures using the NTRU lattice. In: Joye, M. (ed.) CT-RSA 2003. LNCS, vol. 2612, pp. 122–140. Springer, Heidelberg (2003). https://doi.org/10.1007/3-540-36563-X_9

23. Hoffstein, J., Pipher, J., Silverman, J.H.: NTRU: a ring-based public key cryptosystem. In: ANTS, pp. 267–288 (1998)

24. Jaeger, J., Tessaro, S.: Expected-time cryptography: generic techniques and applications to concrete soundness. In: Pass, R., Pietrzak, K. (eds.) TCC 2020, Part III. LNCS, vol. 12552, pp. 414–443. Springer, Cham (2020). https://doi.org/10.1007/978-3-030-64381-2_15

25. Katz, J., Kolesnikov, V., Wang, X.: Improved non-interactive zero knowledge with applications to post-quantum signatures. In: Lie, D., Mannan, M., Backes, M., Wang, X. (eds.) ACM CCS 2018, pp. 525–537. ACM Press, October 2018. https://doi.org/10.1145/3243734.3243805

26. Kawachi, A., Tanaka, K., Xagawa, K.: Concurrently secure identification schemes based on the worst-case hardness of lattice problems. In: Pieprzyk, J. (ed.) ASIACRYPT 2008. LNCS, vol. 5350, pp. 372–389. Springer, Heidelberg (2008). https://doi.org/10.1007/978-3-540-89255-7_23

27. Kilian, J.: A note on efficient zero-knowledge proofs and arguments (extended abstract). In: 24th ACM STOC, pp. 723–732. ACM Press, May 1992. https://doi.org/10.1145/129712.129782

28. Libert, B., Ling, S., Nguyen, K., Wang, H.: Zero-knowledge arguments for lattice-based accumulators: logarithmic-size ring signatures and group signatures without trapdoors. In: Fischlin, M., Coron, J.-S. (eds.) EUROCRYPT 2016, Part II. LNCS, vol. 9666, pp. 1–31. Springer, Heidelberg (2016). https://doi.org/10.1007/978-3-662-49896-5_1

29. Ling, S., Nguyen, K., Stehlé, D., Wang, H.: Improved zero-knowledge proofs of knowledge for the ISIS problem, and applications. In: Kurosawa, K., Hanaoka, G. (eds.) PKC 2013. LNCS, vol. 7778, pp. 107–124. Springer, Heidelberg (2013). https://doi.org/10.1007/978-3-642-36362-7_8

30. Lyubashevsky, V.: Lattice signatures without trapdoors. In: Pointcheval, D., Johansson, T. (eds.) EUROCRYPT 2012. LNCS, vol. 7237, pp. 738–755. Springer, Heidelberg (2012). https://doi.org/10.1007/978-3-642-29011-4_43

31. Lyubashevsky, V., Micciancio, D.: Generalized compact knapsacks are collision resistant. In: Bugliesi, M., Preneel, B., Sassone, V., Wegener, I. (eds.) ICALP 2006, Part II. LNCS, vol. 4052, pp. 144–155. Springer, Heidelberg (2006). https://doi.org/10.1007/11787006_13

32. Norton, G.H., Salagean-Mandache, A.: On the key equation over a commutative ring. Des. Codes Cryptogr. **20**(2), 125–141 (2000)

33. Pornin, T., Prest, T.: More efficient algorithms for the NTRU key generation using the field norm. In: Lin, D., Sako, K. (eds.) PKC 2019, Part II. LNCS, vol. 11443, pp. 504–533. Springer, Cham (2019). https://doi.org/10.1007/978-3-030-17259-6_17

34. Quintin, G., Barbier, M., Chabot, C.: On generalized Reed-Solomon codes over commutative and noncommutative rings. IEEE Trans. Inf. Theory **59**(9), 5882–5897 (2013). https://doi.org/10.1109/TIT.2013.2264797

35. Stehlé, D., Steinfeld, R.: Making NTRUEncrypt and NTRUSign as secure as standard worst-case problems over ideal lattices. Cryptology ePrint Archive, Report 2013/004 (2013). https://eprint.iacr.org/2013/004

36. Stern, J.: A new identification scheme based on syndrome decoding. In: Stinson, D.R. (ed.) CRYPTO 1993. LNCS, vol. 773, pp. 13–21. Springer, Heidelberg (1994). https://doi.org/10.1007/3-540-48329-2_2

37. Washington, L.C.: Introduction to Cyclotomic Fields, vol. 83. Springer, New York (1997). https://doi.org/10.1007/978-1-4612-1934-7

38. Yang, R., Au, M.H., Zhang, Z., Xu, Q., Yu, Z., Whyte, W.: Efficient lattice-based zero-knowledge arguments with standard soundness: construction and applications. In: Boldyreva, A., Micciancio, D. (eds.) CRYPTO 2019, Part I. LNCS, vol. 11692, pp. 147–175. Springer, Cham (2019). https://doi.org/10.1007/978-3-030-26948-7_6

A Compressed Σ-Protocol Theory
for Lattices

Thomas Attema[1,2,3]([✉]), Ronald Cramer[1,2], and Lisa Kohl[1]

[1] Cryptology Group, CWI, Amsterdam, The Netherlands
{cramer,lisa.kohl}@cwi.nl
[2] Mathematical Institute, Leiden University, Leiden, The Netherlands
cramer@math.leidenuniv.nl
[3] Cyber Security and Robustness, TNO, The Hague, The Netherlands
thomas.attema@tno.nl

Abstract. We show a *lattice-based* solution for commit-and-prove transparent circuit zero-knowledge (ZK) with *polylog-communication*, the *first* not depending on PCPs.

We start from *compressed Σ-protocol theory* (CRYPTO 2020), which is built around basic Σ-protocols for opening an arbitrary linear form on a long secret vector that is compactly committed to. These protocols are first compressed using a recursive "folding-technique" adapted from Bulletproofs, at the expense of logarithmic rounds. Proving in ZK that the secret vector satisfies a given constraint – captured by a circuit – is then by (blackbox) reduction to the linear case, via arithmetic secret-sharing techniques adapted from MPC. Commit-and-prove is also facilitated, i.e., when commitment(s) to the secret vector are created ahead of any circuit-ZK proof. On several platforms (incl. DL) this leads to logarithmic communication. Non-interactive versions follow from Fiat-Shamir.

This abstract modular theory strongly suggests that it should somehow be supported by a lattice-platform *as well*. However, when going through the motions and trying to establish low communication (on a SIS-platform), a certain significant lack in current understanding of multiround protocols is exposed.

Namely, as opposed to the DL-case, the basic Σ-protocol in question typically has *poly-small challenge* space. Taking into account the compression-step – which yields *non-constant* rounds – and the necessity for parallelization to reduce error, there is no known tight result that the compound protocol admits an efficient knowledge extractor. We resolve the state of affairs here by a combination of two novel results which are fully general and of independent interest. The first gives a tight analysis of efficient knowledge extraction in case of non-constant rounds combined with poly-small challenge space, whereas the second shows that parallel repetition indeed forces rapid decrease of knowledge error.

Moreover, in our present context, arithmetic secret sharing is not defined over a large finite field but over a quotient of a number ring and this forces our careful adaptation of how the linearization techniques are deployed.

We develop our protocols in an abstract framework that is conceptually simple and can be flexibly instantiated. In particular, the framework applies to arbitrary rings and norms.

© International Association for Cryptologic Research 2021
T. Malkin and C. Peikert (Eds.): CRYPTO 2021, LNCS 12826, pp. 549–579, 2021.
https://doi.org/10.1007/978-3-030-84245-1_19

1   Introduction

Compressed Σ-Protocol Theory [6] is built around basic Σ-protocols for opening an arbitrary linear form on a long secret vector that is compactly committed to. More precisely, these Σ-protocols allow a prover to prove that a committed vector $\mathbf{x}$ satisfies a constraint $L(\mathbf{x}) = y$ captured by a linear form L. They are first compressed using a recursive "folding-technique" adapted from Bulletproofs [14,16]. Compression reduces the communication complexity from linear down to logarithmic in the dimension of the secret vector $\mathbf{x}$, at the expense of a logarithmic number of rounds. Proving in ZK that the secret vector satisfies an arbitrary (non-linear) constraint – captured by an arithmetic circuit – is then by (blackbox) reduction to the linear case, via arithmetic secret-sharing techniques adapted from MPC. It was shown how to instantiate this theory from different hardness assumptions, i.e., the Discrete Logarithm (DL), Strong-RSA and Knowledge-of-Exponent (KEA) assumption. The latter assumption even results in *constant* communication, instead of logarithmic. Non-interactive versions follow from the Fiat-Shamir transform [26].

The starting point is always a compact and homomorphic vector commitment scheme, i.e., commitments should have size constant (or logarithmic) in the dimension of the committed vector. After instantiating such a commitment scheme from any of the aforementioned hardness assumption, compressed Σ-protocol theory can be described in an abstract and modular manner. This strongly suggests that the theory should also be supported by a lattice platform. This belief was further strengthened by the recent lattice-based Bulletproof instantiation for proving knowledge of a SIS preimage [15].

However, when going through the motions and trying to establish low communication (on a SIS-platform), a certain significant lack in current understanding of multi-round protocols and several challenges are exposed.

1.1   Challenges for Lattice Instantiations

As opposed to the DL-case, the lattice-based Σ-protocol typically has polynomially small challenge space. Taking into account the compression-step – which yields non-constant rounds – there is no known result from which a tight knowledge soundness property can be derived. In prior works, this lack in understanding was handled by an alternative non-tight security analysis [14]. Recent works, while remaining non-tight, have improved the tightness [3,21,30,31,41].

The situation is further complicated by the necessity for parallelization to reduce the knowledge error. While parallel repetition of interactive proofs has been studied extensively in the context of decreasing the *soundness error* [18,19, 28], to the best of our knowledge there does not exist a general parallel repetition theorem for decreasing the *knowledge error*.

Setting aside the knowledge error issues addressed previously, the main difference between the lattice setting and the other settings is a norm bound. Instead of proving knowledge of a preimage for some homomorphism Ψ, we aim to prove knowledge of a *short* pre-image. More precisely, for some homomorphism Ψ, we aim to construct a protocol for the following relation

$$R_{\Psi,\alpha} = \{(P;x) : P = \Psi(x), \|x\| \leq \alpha\}$$

where $(P;x) \in R_{\Psi,\alpha}$ is a pair of a public statement P and a secret witness x. The DL-based protocols are designed for exactly the same abstract relation, but without the norm-bound. This minor difference introduces a number of challenges that have been dealt with in the context of plain Σ-protocols for some time now. For example, given a preimage x with $\|x\| \leq \beta$, a prover is typically only capable of proving knowledge of a preimage y with $\|y\| \leq \alpha\beta$. The factor $\alpha \geq 1$ is referred to as the *soundness slack*. In multi-round protocols the soundness slack accumulates and a more careful analysis is warranted.

Finally, in our present lattice context, committed vectors typically have coefficients in the quotient of a number ring $\mathcal{R} = \mathbb{Z}[X]/(f(X))$ by a rational prime (p). However, the structure of the ring $\mathcal{R}_p$ may not readily allow for the large sets with invertible pairwise differences required for Shamir secret sharing.

1.2   Contributions

We show a lattice-based solution for commit-and-prove transparent circuit ZK with polylogarithmic communication, the first not depending on PCPs.

To this end, we resolve the lack in understanding regarding knowledge soundness by a combination of two novel results which are fully general and of independent interest. The first gives a tight analysis of efficient knowledge extraction in case of non-constant rounds, whereas the second shows that parallel repetition indeed forces rapid decrease of knowledge error.

By our extractor analysis, we *tightly* prove that $(k_1, \ldots, k_\mu)$-special soundness implies knowledge soundness, without imposing any restrictions on the size of the challenge sets. In a concurrent and independent work this result was deemed out of reach with current techniques [3]. More concretely, they apply the non-tight analysis of [21] and derive a knowledge error $\kappa \leq 8.16 \log n/|\mathcal{C}|$, where n is the size of the input. By contrast, we provide a tight bound and show that $\kappa \leq 2 \log n/|\mathcal{C}|$. This inequality contains a simplified expression and is therefore non-tight, for the tight bound we refer to Theorem 1. Furthermore, our result answers an open question regarding knowledge extractors, recently made explicit [30, Question D.4.], in the affirmative. It is generally applicable to all aforementioned platforms and therefore improves upon the analysis of [3, 14, 21, 30, 31, 41], directly yielding better parameters for multi-round protocols such as Bulletproofs. Towards showing that $(k_1, \ldots, k_\mu)$-special soundness tightly implies knowledge soundness, we observe that for the special case of 2-special soundness (where this implication is well-known) we can give a very simple proof that we have not encountered in the literature before. In contrast to standard proof techniques, our extractor can be modeled by a negative hyper geometric distribution. This simplification turns out to be generalizable to the multi-round scenario. Even though the general proof is building on this simplification, its analysis turns out to be quite involved.

By the second result, we show that parallel repetition indeed forces a rapid decrease of knowledge error, explicitly proving a result that is often taken for granted whereas it actually requires a careful analysis. More precisely, it is known that parallel repetition decreases the *soundness* error. However, *knowledge soundness* is a strictly stronger notion than soundness. Nevertheless, by a careful analysis, we prove that prior results also apply to knowledge sound protocols and allow for a rapid decrease of knowledge error. The $(2, 2)$-special sound signature scheme MQDSS was already presented with a tight knowledge error analysis [17]. However, their analysis crucially depends on the fact that this signature scheme has a *constant* number of rounds and therefore does not apply to our setting. Our techniques are generic and also apply to this protocol, indeed yielding exactly the same knowledge error.

Furthermore, we describe a careful adaptation of the arithmetic secret sharing based linearization strategy from [6]. First, the evaluation points of Shamir's secret sharing scheme have to be chosen from an *exceptional*, instead of an arbitrary, subset of the ring $\mathcal{R}_p$, i.e., a subset with invertible differences. In many practical scenarios this minor adaptation suffices. However, some rings do not contain "large enough" exceptional subsets. For this reason, we extend the linearization technique to work for small rings $\mathcal{R}_p$ by defining the secret sharing scheme over an appropriately chosen ring extension. Some care is warranted to prevent dishonest provers from choosing secret elements in the extension ring.

Subsequently, we note that working in a lattice-platform is considerably more tedious. Traditionally the security analysis depends strongly on various protocol design choices. Our approach is less sensitive to these choices. This is very convenient when considering variations. More precisely, we develop our protocols in an abstract framework that is conceptually simple and can be flexibly instantiated. In particular, the framework applies to arbitrary rings, challenge sets and norms. Our framework captures general rejection sampling strategies, gives precise bounds on the introduced soundness slack and generalizes beyond factor-2 per-round compression.

The communication complexity of our protocols, when instantiated from the Module Short Integer Solution (MSIS) assumption and appropriately chosen rings, is polylogarithmic in the input size. Due to the soundness slack it does not achieve the logarithmic communication of a DL-based instantiation. Our protocols are transparent, i.e., no trusted setup, and easily ported to the commit-and-prove paradigm, where commitment(s) to the secret vector have been created ahead of any circuit-ZK proof. Moreover, various efficiency improvements, developed for DL-based (compressed) Σ-protocol theory, almost directly carry over to the lattice-setting.

1.3 Related Work

Circuit ZK with Polylogarithmic Complexity from PCPs. A generic class of (zero-knowledge) proof systems is based on *Probabilistically Checkable Proofs* (PCPs). The security of these protocols only relies on the existence of collision-resistant hash functions and they achieve polylogarithmic communication complexity.

However, large concrete costs have long prevented PCP-based protocols from being deployed in practice. Recent advances have rendered PCP-based protocols practical [5,11,12]. Still, for small problem instances, PCP-based protocols are often outperformed by other approaches relying on more structured hardness assumptions. In particular, PCP approaches rely on Merkle-tree commitments and therefore have an implicit lower bound in the order of a hundred kilobytes, whereas protocols relying on the compression mechanism such as Bulletproofs can go down to as much as a few kilobytes. Even though the soundness slack introduced by the compression mechanism is currently somewhat limiting in terms of concrete efficiency, we expect that on the long run the non-PCP lattice-based approach will lead to more succinct proofs.

Circuit ZK with Sublinear Complexity from Lattice Assumptions. The first protocol of this form achieving a sub-linear communication complexity $\widetilde{\mathcal{O}}(\sqrt{\lambda n})$, where n is the input size and λ the security parameter, was presented in [9]. A key component of their protocol is a compact commitment scheme. In our lattice instantiation we use exactly the same compact commitment scheme. While their approach is inherently limited to communication complexity in the order of $\widetilde{\mathcal{O}}(\sqrt{\lambda n})$, our approach yields the first lattice-based (non-PCP) protocol that achieves polylogarithmic complexity in the input length. On the other hand, our approach requires a larger number of rounds. Getting a similar communication-complexity/round trade-off as [9] by using a larger per-round compression seems currently out of reach, due to the large soundness slack introduced (which scales exponentially in the compression factor).

Lattice-based proof of knowledge of SIS preimages. The lattice-based Bulletproof instantiation of [15] is most similar to our compressed Σ-protocol. However, in this work the aforementioned knowledge error issues were overlooked. Moreover, their work only considers proving knowledge of a SIS preimage, i.e., it does not consider generic arithmetic circuit relations. Furthermore, it is not zero-knowledge and it is tailored to a specific lattice-instantiation. By contrast, our protocol is a circuit ZK protocol that can be instantiated from a wide variety of lattices. For the specific scenario of proving knowledge of a SIS preimage, we obtain a comparable communication complexity.

1.4   Roadmap

We start by presenting the general result that $(k_1, \ldots, k_\mu)$-special soundness tightly implies knowledge soundness in Sect. 3. We first outline a very simple proof for the special case of 2-special soundness, which is novel to the best of our knowledge. Subsequently, we show how this proof can be generalized to the multi-round setting. Using results from [19], we prove that parallel repetition of multi-round public-coin protocols not only reduces the soundness error, but also the knowledge error (see Sect. 4). In Sect. 5, we give an abstract theory for lattice-based compressed Σ-protocols. In Sect. 6, we show how to instantiate our abstract framework from the Module Short Integer Solution (MSIS) problem.

We further provide an asymptotic parameter analysis for our instantiation and comparison with [15]. In Sect. 7, we briefly explain how to handle non-linear relations and refer to the full version of this paper [1] for a detailed description of our techniques. Moreover, in the full version, we discuss a number of extensions for amortization over many linear forms, reducing the communication complexity and for obtaining commit-and-prove protocols directly.

2   Preliminaries

We say a function is *negligible*, if it vanishes faster than any inverse polynomial. If a function vanishes slower than some inverse polynomial, we say it is *noticeable*. For formal definitions and definitions of *statistical distance* and *statistically close distributions* we refer to the full version of this paper [1].

2.1   Interactive Proofs

Let $R \subset \{0,1\}^* \times \{0,1\}^*$ be a binary relation. If $(x;w) \in R$, we say x is a *statement* and w is a *witness* for x. We only consider NP relations, i.e., relations R for which a witness w can be verified in time poly($|x|$) for all $(x;w) \in R$. In particular it follows that $|w| = \text{poly}(|x|)$. The set of statements x that admit a witness w is denoted by L_R, i.e., $L_R = \{x : \exists w \text{ s.t. } (x;w) \in R\}$. The set of witnesses for a statement x is denoted by $R(x)$, i.e., $R(x) = \{w : (x;w) \in R\}$.

In the following we give a brief overview of interactive proof systems. For a more thorough treatment, we refer to the full version of this paper [1].

An *interactive proof* $\Pi = (\mathcal{P}, \mathcal{V})$ for relation R is an interactive protocol between two probabilistic polynomial time machines, a prover $\mathcal{P}$ and a verifier $\mathcal{V}$. Both $\mathcal{P}$ and $\mathcal{V}$ take as public input a statement x and, additionally, $\mathcal{P}$ takes as private input a witness $w \in R(x)$, which is written as $\Pi(x;w)$ or $\text{INPUT}(x;w)$. If all of the verifier's random coins are made public, Π is said to be *public-coin*.

We say an interactive proof is *complete* if $\mathcal{V}$ accepts after every honest execution that takes as input a public-private pair $(x;w) \in R$.

An interactive proof is said to be *knowledge sound* with knowledge error κ, if from every (potentially dishonest) efficient prover P^* that convinces the verifier with probability $\epsilon(x) > \kappa(|x|)$, one can efficiently extract a witness w with $(x;w) \in R$ with probability at least $\epsilon(x) - \kappa(|x|)$.

An interactive proof that is both complete with completeness error $\gamma \colon \mathbb{N} \to [0,1)$ and knowledge sound with knowledge error $\kappa < 1 - \gamma$ is said to be a *Proof or Knowledge* (PoK). PoKs for which knowledge soundness only holds under computational assumptions are also referred to as *Arguments of Knowledge*.

An interactive protocol Π is said to be *special honest verifier zero-knowledge* (SHVZK) if given the challenge by the verifier, one can efficiently simulate accepting transcripts. If simulation is restricted to non-aborting executions of Π, we refer to the protocol as *non-abort special honest verifier zero knowledge*.

A 3-move public-coin protocol is said to be *special sound* if there exists a polynomial time algorithm that on input a statement x and two accepting transcripts (a, c, z) and (a, c', z'), with $c \neq c'$ and common first message a, outputs a witness $w \in R(x)$. If the algorithm takes as input k transcripts, with pairwise distinct challenges and a common first message, the protocol is k-*special sound*.

A 3-move protocol that is public-coin, complete, k-special sound and SHVZK is said to be Σ-*protocol*.

A $(k_1, \ldots, k_\mu)$-*tree of transcripts* for a $(2\mu+1)$-move protocol is a set of $K = \prod_{i=1}^{\mu} k_i$ transcripts arranged in a tree structure, such that the nodes in this tree correspond to the prover's messages and the edges correspond to the verifier's challenges, and that further every node at depth i has precisely k_i children corresponding to k_i pairwise distinct challenges. For a graphic representation we refer to Figure 1 of the full version of this paper [1].

A $(2\mu+1)$-move public-coin protocol is $(k_1, \ldots, k_\mu)$-special sound if there exists an efficient algorithm that on input a $(k_1, \ldots, k_\mu)$-tree of accepting transcripts outputs a witness $w \in R(x)$.

2.2 Lattices

A lattice Λ is a discrete additive subgroup of $\mathbb{R}^m$. The lattice Λ is said to be q-ary if $q\mathbb{Z}^m \subset \Lambda \subset \mathbb{Z}^m$. Let $A \in \mathbb{Z}_q^{k \times m}$, then $\Lambda_q^{\perp}(A) = \{\mathbf{x} \in \mathbb{Z}^m : A\mathbf{x} = 0 \mod q\}$ defines a q-ary lattice in $\mathbb{Z}^m$.

We also consider lattices defined over a ring $\mathcal{R} = \mathbb{Z}[X]/f(X)$, where $f(X)$ is a monic irreducible polynomial of degree d. Via the coefficient embedding norms on $\mathbb{C}$-vector spaces extend to vectors of ring elements, i.e., for $\mathbf{x} = (x_1, \ldots, x_m) \in \mathcal{R}^m$ with $x_i = \sum_{j=1}^{d} a_{i,j} X^{j-1} \in \mathcal{R}$ we define

$$\|\mathbf{x}\|_2 = \|(a_{1,1}, \ldots, a_{m,d})\|_2, \quad \text{and} \quad \|\mathbf{x}\|_\infty = \max_{i,j} |a_{i,j}|.$$

For a prime $q \in \mathbb{N}$, we write $\mathcal{R}_q = \mathbb{Z}[X]/(q, f(X)) = \mathbb{Z}_q[X]/(f(X))$. Let $A \in \mathcal{R}^{k \times m}$, then $\Lambda_q^{\perp}(A) = \{\mathbf{x} \in \mathcal{R}^m : A\mathbf{x} = 0 \mod q\}$ defines a q-ary lattice in $\mathbb{Z}^{dm}$. Finding a non-zero and short element in a lattice $\Lambda_q^{\perp}(A)$ is referred to as the Module Short Integer Solution (MSIS) problem [33]. The MSIS problem is assumed to be a computationally hard problem.

Definition 1 (MSIS$_{k,m,\beta}$ **Problem**). *Let $\mathcal{R} = \mathbb{Z}[X]/f(X)$ for a monic and irreducible polynomial $f(X)$ and let $q \in \mathbb{N}$ be a prime. The* MSIS$_{k,m,\beta}$ *problem over $\mathcal{R}_q$ is defined as follows. Given a matrix $A \leftarrow_R \mathcal{R}_q^{k \times m}$ sampled uniformly at random, find a non-zero vector $\mathbf{s} \in \mathcal{R}^m$ such that $A\mathbf{s} = 0 \mod q$ and $\|\mathbf{s}\|_2 \leq \beta$.*

Micciancio and Regev [38] showed that a MSIS-algorithm is expected to output a MSIS solution with norm

$$\|\mathbf{s}\|_2 \geq \min\left(q, 2^{2\sqrt{dk \log \delta \log q}}\right), \tag{1}$$

where δ is the root Hermite factor of the lattice reduction algorithm that is used. In particular, smaller values of δ require better lattice reduction algorithms. In general, $\delta \approx 1.0045$ is assumed to achieve 128-bit computational security [4,25].

In this work, we will be interested in vectors that are short with respect to the ℓ_∞-norm. For this reason we also consider the following variant of the MSIS problem, where "shortness" is defined in terms of the ℓ_∞-norm. Clearly, the hardness of $\mathrm{MSIS}^\infty_{k,m,\beta}$ is implied by the hardness of $\mathrm{MSIS}_{k,m,\sqrt{dm}\beta}$.

Definition 2 ($\mathrm{MSIS}^\infty_{k,m,\beta}$ Problem over $\mathcal{R}_q$). *Let $\mathcal{R} = \mathbb{Z}[X]/f(X)$ for a monic and irreducible polynomial $f(X)$ and let $q \in \mathbb{N}$ be a prime. The $\mathrm{MSIS}^\infty_{k,m,\beta}$ problem over $\mathcal{R}_q$ is defined as follows. Given a matrix $A \leftarrow_R \mathcal{R}_q^{k \times m}$ sampled uniformly at random, find a non-zero vector $\mathbf{s} \in \mathcal{R}^m$ such that $A\mathbf{s} = 0 \mod q$ and $\|\mathbf{s}\|_\infty \leq \beta$.*

2.3 Commitment Schemes

A commitment scheme allows a prover to create a commitment P to an element x such that the prover can later open P to the committed element x. Informally, a commitment scheme is required to be *binding*, i.e., a prover cannot open a commitment P to two different elements $x \neq y$, and *hiding*, i.e., the commitment P does not reveal any information about the committed vector x. A commitment scheme consists of a setup algorithm, generating the scheme's public parameters, and a commitment function COM. The commitment function takes as input an element x and randomness γ (and public parameters pp) and outputs a commitment P, i.e., $\mathrm{COM}(x, \gamma) = P$. To open a commitment a prover reveals (x, γ) such that a verifier can verify that $\mathrm{COM}(x, \gamma) = P$. The commitment scheme is said to be *homomorphic* if the commitment function COM (considered respective to fixed public parameters) is a group homomorphism.

The primary commitment scheme of interest to us, described in Definition 3, was already implicit in Ajtai's seminal work [2]. It allows a prover to commit to a *short* vector $\mathbf{x} \in S^n_\eta = \{\mathbf{y} \in \mathcal{R}^n : \|\mathbf{y}\|_\infty \leq \eta\}$ by sampling $\gamma \leftarrow_R S^r_\eta$ uniformly at random and evaluating the commitment function $P = \mathrm{COM}(x, \gamma)$. Note that, we consider this commitment scheme for secrets and randomness bounded in the ℓ_∞-norm. We will typically instantiate this commitment scheme with norm bound $\eta = \lceil (p-1)/2 \rceil$ for some prime $p < q$. This allows a prover to commit to arbitrary vectors in $\mathcal{R}^n_p$. The properties of this commitment scheme are summarized in Lemma 1 and Lemma 2. Note in particular that by Eq. 1 it follows that the hardness does not depend on the rank n. It follows that the size of a commitment is constant in the rank $m = n+r$; we say that this commitment scheme is *compact*.

Definition 3 (Compact Lattice-Based Commitment Scheme [2]). *Let $\mathcal{R} = \mathbb{Z}[X]/f(X)$ for a monic and irreducible polynomial $f(x) \in \mathbb{Z}[X]$ of degree d and let $q \in \mathbb{N}$ be a prime. Let $\eta \in \mathbb{N}$ and let $S_\eta = \{x \in \mathcal{R} : \|x\|_\infty \leq \eta\}$. Then, the following setup and commitment algorithms define a commitment scheme:*

- *Setup: $A_1 \leftarrow_R \mathcal{R}_q^{k \times r}$, $A_2 \leftarrow_R \mathcal{R}_q^{k \times n}$.*
- *Commit: $\mathrm{COM} : S^n_\eta \times S^r_\eta \to \mathcal{R}^k_q$, $(\mathbf{x}, \gamma) \mapsto A_1\gamma + A_2\mathbf{x} \mod q$.*

Lemma 1 (Hiding). *The commitment scheme of Definition 3 is statistically hiding with statistical security parameter λ, where $\lambda \in \mathbb{N}$ is such that $r \geq \frac{dk \log q + 2\lambda}{d \log(2\eta + 1)}$.*

Lemma 2 (Binding). *The commitment scheme of Definition 3 is binding, conditioned on the hardness of the $\mathrm{MSIS}^{\infty}_{k,n+r,2\eta}$-problem over $\mathcal{R}_q$.*

It is generally hard to construct efficient protocols for proving knowledge of an opening $(\mathbf{x}, \gamma)$ for a commitment P, i.e., $(\mathbf{x}, \gamma)$ such that $\mathrm{COM}(\mathbf{x}, \gamma) = P$ and $\|(\mathbf{x}, \gamma)\|_{\infty} \leq \eta$. For this reason, we introduce the notion of relaxed openings.

Definition 4 ((β, ζ)-Relaxed Commitment Opening). *Let $\beta \in \mathbb{N}$ and $\zeta \in \mathcal{R}$. A (β, ζ)-relaxed opening of a commitment P is a tuple $(\mathbf{x}, \gamma) \in \mathcal{R}^{n+r}$, such that $\mathrm{COM}(\mathbf{x}, \gamma) = \zeta P$ and $\|(\mathbf{x}, \gamma)\|_{\infty} \leq \beta$.*

Hence, a relaxed opening differs in two ways from a standard commitment opening. First, a relaxed opening for P contains an approximation factor ζ, such that the opening gives a short preimage for ζP instead of the commitment P. Second, the norm-bound β of relaxed openings can be different from the norm bound η on honestly committed vectors (typically $\beta > \eta$).

As long as it is infeasible to find two distinct relaxed openings $(\mathbf{x}, \gamma)$ and $(\mathbf{x}', \gamma')$ of a commitment P with $(\mathbf{x}, \gamma) \neq (\mathbf{x}', \gamma')$, proving knowledge of relaxed opening is sufficient in most practical scenarios. In this case, we say the commitment scheme is binding with respect to relaxed openings.

Lemma 3 (Binding with respect to (β, ζ)-Relaxed Openings). *Let $\beta \in \mathbb{N}$ and $\zeta \in \mathcal{R}$. The commitment scheme of Definition 3 is binding with respect to (β, ζ)-relaxed openings, conditioned on the hardness of the $\mathrm{MSIS}^{\infty}_{k,n+r,2\beta}$-problem over $\mathcal{R}_q$.*

3 Multi-round Special Soundness Tightly Implies Knowledge Soundness

In this section we prove that a $(k_1, \ldots, k_{\mu})$-special sound protocol is *knowledge sound* and give a concrete and tight knowledge error. More precisely, we show the existence of an efficient knowledge extractor. From this it follows that Bulletproofs [14,16] and Compressed Σ-Protocols [6] are *Proofs/Arguments of Knowledge* (PoKs). We are the first to prove a *tight* bound on the knowledge error. Prior works mainly relied on the asymptotic extractor analysis of [14]. This asymptotic analysis results in conservative concrete security estimates. Moreover, the analysis of [14] is restricted to protocols with exponentially large challenge sets. When the challenge sets are small, such as in lattice based protocols, a refined analysis is required. Our result solves both problems. It gives tight security guarantees resulting in optimal concrete parameters for $(k_1, \ldots, k_{\mu})$-special sound protocols and it is applicable to protocols with small challenge sets. The main result of this section is summarized in Theorem 1.

Theorem 1 ($(k_1, \ldots, k_\mu)$-Special Soundness implies Knowledge Soundness). *Let $\mu, k_1, \ldots, k_\mu \in \mathbb{N}$ be such that $K = \prod_{i=1}^{\mu} k_i$ can be upper bounded by a polynomial. Let $(\mathcal{P}, \mathcal{V})$ be a $(k_1, \ldots, k_\mu)$-special sound $(2\mu + 1)$-move interactive protocol for relation R, where $\mathcal{V}$ samples each challenge uniformly at random from a challenge set of size $N \geq \max_i(k_i)$. Then $(\mathcal{P}, \mathcal{V})$ is knowledge sound with knowledge error*

$$\kappa = \frac{N^\mu - \prod_{i=1}^{\mu}(N - k_i + 1)}{N^\mu} \leq \frac{\sum_{i=1}^{\mu}(k_i - 1)}{N}. \tag{2}$$

First, in Sect. 3.1, we considers the special case of 2-special soundness (for which the above implication is well-known). We give a very simple proof that we have not encountered in literature before. In contrast to standard proof techniques, this simplification turns out to be generalizable to the multi-round scenario. Second, in Sect. 3.2, we prove Theorem 1 in its full generality.

3.1   2-Special Soundness

This section is a warm up in which we present a novel proof for the well-known result that 2-special soundness implies knowledge soundness. Later we show that our techniques generalize to prove a similar result for $2\mu + 1$-move protocols that are $(k_1, \ldots, k_\mu)$-special sound. We make a minor modification to the "collision-game" defined in [20]. The knowledge extractor essentially plays this game in order to extract a collision of two accepting transcripts (a, c, z) and (a, c', z') with common first message a. By the special soundness property a witness can be computed efficiently given this collision. Our modification increases the success probability of the knowledge extractor of [20] from $(\epsilon(x) - \kappa(|x|))^2$ to $\epsilon(x) - \kappa(|x|)$, where $\kappa(|x|)$ is the knowledge error and $\epsilon(x)$ the success probability of the prover for a statement x. In contrast to the extractor of [20], which runs in *strict* polynomial time, our extractor runs in *expected* polynomial time. However, this is sufficient for proving knowledge soundness.

If the input x is clear from context, we simply write ϵ to denote $\epsilon(x)$. All other parameters will implicitly depend on $|x|$ (e.g., we denote $\kappa(|x|)$ by κ).

A similar result can be found in [29]. However, our approach significantly simplifies the knowledge extractor and its analysis. For instance, the extractor of [29] is composed of two algorithms considering different scenarios, whereas this case distinction is not required in our knowledge extractor. This simplification will allow for a generalization to the $(k_1, \ldots, k_\mu)$-special sound case.

The collision game. Let us now describe the game. We consider a binary matrix $H \in \{0, 1\}^{R \times N}$. The R rows correspond to the prover's randomness and the N columns correspond to the verifier's randomness, i.e., the verifier samples a challenge uniformly at random from a challenge set of size N. An entry of H equals 1 if and only if the corresponding protocol transcript is accepting.

The idea of the knowledge extractor is to sample elements from H until two 1-entries in the same row are found. The ij-th entry of H can be obtained by executing the prover with fixed randomness corresponding to the i-th row and verifier's challenge corresponding to the j-th column, and checking if the resulting transcript would be accepted. As the prover's randomness is fixed along one row, finding two 1-entries in the same row corresponds to two finding two accepting transcripts (a, c, e) and (a, c', e'), which by the 2-special soundness allows to extract a witness. The difference to the knowledge extractor of [29] is the following:

1. Our knowledge extractor checks one entry of H (for position ij sampled at random), *and aborts if this is not a 1-entry*.
2. If the first entry was a 1-entry, our knowledge extractor then samples along row i *without replacement*.

More precisely, the knowledge extractor will play the following collision-game. An entry of H is selected uniformly at random. If this entry equals 1, continue sampling different elements from this row (without replacement) until a second 1-entry is found or until the row has been exhausted. If the first entry does not equal 1, the game aborts. The collision game outputs success if and only if two 1-entries in the same row have been found.

In contrast the above collision-game, the collision-game of [20] simply checks 2 random entries of H and outputs success if both of them are 1-entries.

Lemma 4 (Collision-Game). *Let $H \in \{0, 1\}^{R \times N}$ and let ϵ denote the fraction of 1-entries in H. The expected number of H-entries queried in the collision-game defined above is at most 2. Moreover, the success probability of the collision-game is greater than or equal to $\epsilon - 1/N$.*

Proof. **Expected Number of Queries.** Let ϵ_i be the fraction of 1-entries in row i. Assuming that the first entry lies in row i and equals 1, the remainder of the collision game can be modeled by a negative hypergeometric distribution. Elements from a population of size $N - 1$, containing $\epsilon_i N - 1$ 1-entries, are drawn (without replacement) until a second 1-entry has been found. The expected number of draws equals $(N - 1 + 1)/(\epsilon_i N - 1 + 1) = 1/\epsilon_i$ if $\epsilon_i > 1/N$ (see the full version of this paper [1]). If there is no second 1-entry in the row, then the number of draws is always equal to $N - 1$. Hence, the expected number of draws can be upper bounded by $1/\epsilon_i$. The expected number of H-entries queried is therefore at most

$$\frac{1}{R} \sum_{i=1}^{R} \left(1 + \epsilon_i \frac{1}{\epsilon_i}\right) = 2.$$

Success Probability. The collision-game succeeds if the first entry is a 1 that lies in a row containing at least two 1-entries. For $0 \leq k \leq N$, let δ_k be the fraction of rows with exactly k 1-entries. Then the success probability equals

$$\sum_{k=2}^{N} \frac{k}{N} \delta_k = \left(\sum_{k=0}^{N} \frac{k}{N} \delta_k\right) - \frac{\delta_1}{N} \geq \epsilon - 1/N,$$

which proves the second part of the lemma. $\square$

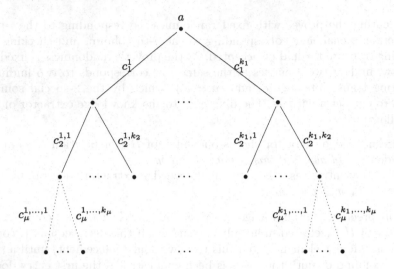

Fig. 1. We say a $(k_1, \ldots, k_\mu)$-tree as depicted above is a $(k_1, \ldots, k_\mu)$-tree of 1-entries in H, if $H(a, c_1^1, c_2^{1,1}, \ldots, c_\mu^{1,\ldots,1}) = H(a, c_1^1, c_2^{1,1}, \ldots, c_\mu^{1,\ldots,2}) = \cdots = H(a, c_1^{k_1}, c_2^{k_1,k_2}, \ldots, c_\mu^{k_1,\ldots,k_\mu}) = 1$.

From Lemma 4 it immediately follows that 2-special soundness implies knowledge soundness with knowledge error $1/N$.

Corollary 1. *Let $(\mathcal{P}, \mathcal{V})$ be a special sound 3-move interactive protocol for relation R, where $\mathcal{V}$ samples each challenge uniformly at random from a challenge set of size $N \geq k$. Then $(\mathcal{P}, \mathcal{V})$ is knowledge sound with knowledge error $\kappa = 1/N$.*

Remark 1. Lemma 4 has a straightforward generalization to the k-special soundness scenario. In this generalization the collision game draws until it has obtained k, instead of 2, 1-entries in the same row. Hence, it again involves a negative hypergeometric distribution, but now with different parameters. In this case, the expected number of queries is at most k and the success probability is greater than or equal to $\epsilon - (k-1)/N$.

3.2 $(k_1, \ldots, k_\mu)$-Special Soundness

In this section, we generalize the collision-game of Sect. 3.1 to the $(k_1, \ldots, k_\mu)$-special soundness scenario.

The $(k_1, \ldots, k_\mu)$-collision game. To define the $(k_1, \ldots, k_\mu)$-collision-game, let $H \in \{0,1\}^{R \times N \times \cdots \times N}$ be a $(\mu+1)$-dimensional binary matrix. For $a \in \{1, \ldots, R\}$ and $c_1, \ldots, c_i \in \{1, \ldots, N\}$, we let $H(a, c_1, \ldots, c_i) \in \{0,1\}^{N \times \cdots \times N}$ be the $(\mu - i)$ dimensional submatrix of H that contains all entries of H for which the first $i + 1$ coordinates are equal to $(a, c_1, \ldots, c_i)$. The first dimension corresponds to the prover's randomness and the other dimensions correspond to the verifier's random choices, i.e., we consider protocols in which the verifier samples all μ challenges uniformly at random from a challenge set of size N. For a fixed public input x, we define the matrix H such that $H(a, c_1, \ldots, c_\mu) = 1$ if and only if a transcript with prover's randomness a and verifier's challenges $c_1, \ldots, c_\mu$ will lead to an accepting transcript.

In Sect. 2, we have defined $(k_1, \ldots, k_\mu)$-trees of accepting transcripts for $(2\mu + 1)$-move protocols. Similarly, we define $(k_1, \ldots, k_\mu)$-trees of 1-entries in matrix H (Fig. 1). Such trees can be defined recursively as follows. For $\mu = 0$, a tree of 1-entries is simply a 1-entry in H. For arbitrary μ, a $(k_1, \ldots, k_\mu)$-tree is the union of k_1 $(k_2, \ldots, k_\mu)$-trees in $H(a, c_1), \ldots, H(a, c_{k_1})$, respectively, for a fixed a and pairwise distinct c_i. Hence, a $(k_1, \ldots, k_\mu)$-tree of 1-entries in matrix H is a set of $K = \prod_{i=1}^{\mu} k_i$ 1-entries that are in a $(k_1, \ldots, k_\mu)$-tree structure.

We define TREE to be the algorithm playing the $(k_1, \ldots, k_\mu)$-collision-game. By playing this game TREE aims to find a $(k_1, \ldots, k_\mu)$-tree of 1-entries in matrix H. The algorithm TREE is defined recursively as follows. On input $a \in \{1, \ldots, R\}$ and $c_1, \ldots, c_\mu \in \{1, \ldots, N\}$, $\text{TREE}_\mu(a, c_1, \ldots, c_\mu)$ successfully outputs $H(a, c_1, \ldots, c_\mu)$ if this entry equals 1 and it aborts otherwise. For $0 \le i \le \mu - 1$ and on input $a \in \{1, \ldots, R\}$ and $c_1, \ldots, c_i \in \{1, \ldots, N\}$, $\text{TREE}_i(a, c_1, \ldots, c_i)$ aims to find a $(k_{i+1}, \ldots, k_\mu)$-tree of 1-entries in matrix $H(a, c_1, \ldots, c_i)$. The algorithm $\text{TREE}_i(a, c_1, \ldots, c_i)$ proceeds by sampling $c_{i+1} \in \{1, \ldots N\}$ uniformly at random and running $\text{TREE}_{i+1}(a, c_1, \ldots, c_{i+1})$. If this instantiation of TREE_{i+1} aborts the algorithm $\text{TREE}_i(a, c_1, \ldots, c_i)$ aborts. Otherwise it continues sampling different c_{i+1}'s (i.e., without replacement) until it has found k_{i+1} $(k_{i+2}, \ldots, k_\mu)$-trees of 1-entries or until it has exhausted all possible c_{i+1}'s. In the latter case $\text{TREE}_i(a, c_1, \ldots, c_i)$ aborts, in the former case $\text{TREE}_i(a, c_1, \ldots, c_i)$ outputs a $(k_{i+1}, \ldots, k_\mu)$-tree of 1-entries in matrix $H(a, c_1, \ldots, c_i)$.

The $(k_1, \ldots, k_\mu)$-collision-game samples $a \in \{1, \ldots, R\}$ uniformly at random and runs $\text{TREE}_0(a)$. If $\text{TREE}_0(a) = \bot$ it aborts and otherwise it outputs a $(k_1, \ldots, k_\mu)$-tree of 1-entries in $H(a)$. The following lemma gives the expected run-time and success probability of the tree finding algorithm TREE. For a proof of the following lemma, we refer to the full version of this paper [1].

Lemma 5 $((k_1, \ldots, k_\mu)$-Tree Finding Algorithm). *Let* $H \in \{0,1\}^{R \times N \times \cdots \times N}$ *be a* $(\mu + 1)$*-dimensional matrix and let* ϵ *denote the fraction of 1-entries in* H*. The expected number of entries queried by the* $(k_1, \ldots, k_\mu)$*-tree finding algorithm* TREE *defined above is at most* $K = \prod_{i=1}^{\mu} k_i$*. Moreover,* TREE *successfully outputs a* $(k_1, \ldots, k_\mu)$*-tree of 1-entries in* H *with probability at least*

$$\epsilon - \frac{N^\mu - \prod_{i=1}^{\mu}(N - k_i + 1)}{N^\mu} \ge \epsilon - \frac{\sum_{i=1}^{\mu}(k_i - 1)}{N}.$$

A knowledge extractor, with rewindable black-box access to a possible dishonest prover $\mathcal{P}^*$, essentially runs this tree finding algorithm to obtain a $(k_1, \ldots, k_\mu)$-tree of accepting transcripts. It evaluates one protocol interaction with $\mathcal{P}^*$ and recursively rewinds $\mathcal{P}^*$, fixing its internal randomness and following the tree finding strategy of TREE. By the $(k_1, \ldots, k_\mu)$-special soundness property a witness can then be extracted efficiently from the obtained $(k_1, \ldots, k_\mu)$-tree of accepting transcripts. Hence, from Lemma 5 it immediately follows that a $(k_1, \ldots, k_\mu)$-special sound protocol is knowledge sound with knowledge error κ, where

$$\kappa = \frac{N^\mu - \prod_{i=1}^{\mu}(N - k_i + 1)}{N^\mu} \leq \frac{\sum_{i=1}^{\mu}(k_i - 1)}{N}.$$

The latter inequality follows since we have $N \geq \max_i(k_i)$ and thus $\prod_{i=1}^{\mu}(N - k_i + 1) \leq N^\mu - N^{\mu-1}\sum_{i=1}^{\mu}(k_i - 1)$. This proves Theorem 1.

3.3   Tightness of Our Extraction Analysis

The knowledge error κ of Theorem 1 is optimal, i.e., there exists a dishonest prover that succeeds in cheating with probability κ. Typically a dishonest prover can cheat in a k-special sound protocol by guessing a set of $k - 1$ challenges and hoping that the verifier selects one of these challenges. The success probability of this attack is equal to $(k - 1)/N$, where N is the size of the challenge set. More generally, a cheating strategy for a $(k_1, \ldots, k_\mu)$-special sound $(2\mu + 1)$-move protocol goes as follows. For every round i, the cheating prover guesses a set of $k_i - 1$ challenges. The cheating prover succeeds if there exists a round i for which the verifier chooses one of the $k_i - 1$ challenges guessed by the prover. The success probability of this attack is easily seen to be equal to the knowledge error κ. Hence, this knowledge error is optimal. Alternatively, we observe that there exist matrices H with $\epsilon = \kappa$, i.e., for which the fraction of 1-entries equals κ, that do not contain a $(k_1, \ldots, k_\mu)$-tree of 1-entries.

Moreover, the tree finding algorithm is optimal in the following sense. The expected number of H-entries that are queried is exactly equal to the number of entries in a tree. Hence, we can not hope to find a tree faster than this. Moreover, taking a closer look at the proof of Lemma 5 shows that the success probability actually has the following lower bound

$$f(\epsilon) = \left(\prod_{j=1}^{\mu} \frac{N}{N - k_j + 1} \right)(\epsilon - \kappa).$$

Hence, if $\epsilon = 1$ the success probability of TREE is at least $f(1) = 1$, which is what we would expect.

3.4   A Note on Witness Extended Emulation

Lindell showed that a technical issue arises when using Proofs of Knowledge as subprotocols in larger cryptographic protocols [34]. To prove security of the compound protocol, a simulator is typically required to run the extractor of the PoK. However, the naive simulation approach does not necessarily run in polynomial time. To this end, Lindell defined the notion of *witness-extended emulation* (WEE), capturing precisely the properties required when using PoKs as subprotocols. Moreover, he showed that any PoK has WEE, thereby solving this technical issue for all PoKs at once. Hence, from our extraction analysis it follows that any $(k_1, \ldots, k_\mu)$-special sound protocol has WEE.

Previously, there was no proof showing that a $(k_1, \ldots, k_\mu)$-special sound protocol is knowledge sound. For this reason prior works (e.g., [14]) resorted to proving witness-extended emulation directly. However, these results are non-tight and only apply to protocols with exponentially large challenge sets.

4 Decreasing the Knowledge Error of Public-Coin Interactive Protocols

In this section, we establish a novel parallel repetition theorem showing that the knowledge error can be decreased by repeating the protocol in parallel.

We want the knowledge error of a PoK to be negligible in the security parameter. If this is not the case the protocol is typically repeated, say t times. The verifier of the composed protocol only accepts if all t instances of the basic protocol are accepted. Ideally, and perhaps intuitively, this approach reduces the knowledge error from κ down to κ^t. This is indeed the case if the repetitions are executed sequentially [27]. However, sequential repetition increases the round complexity. Since the security loss due to the Fiat-Shamir transformation increases exponentially in the number of rounds [23], this is unacceptable when considering the non-interactive instantiations of our protocols (see the full version of this paper [1]). Further, also in the interactive setting we would like to avoid the additional round complexity introduced by sequential composition.

For this reason, we aim to repeat the protocol in parallel. We write $(\mathcal{P}^t, \mathcal{V}^t)$ for the t-fold parallel repetition of an interactive argument $(\mathcal{P}, \mathcal{V})$. However, it is not true in general that parallel repetition decreases the knowledge error exponentially. There even exist interactive protocols for which parallel repetition does not decrease the success probability of a dishonest prover at all [10, 39]. Analyzing parallel repetitions is significantly more complicated than analyzing sequential repetitions, because a dishonest prover does not have to treat all t parallel instances independently, i.e., a message corresponding to a specific instance may depend on the messages and challenges of the other parallel instances.

If $(\mathcal{P}, \mathcal{V})$ is a 2-special sound 3-move protocol, then $(\mathcal{P}^t, \mathcal{V}^t)$ is 2-special sound too. It therefore follows that the knowledge error of a 2-special sound protocol decreases exponentially in the number of parallel repetitions. However, a similar result does not hold in general, i.e., in general special-soundness is not preserved by parallel repetition. For example, it is easily seen that the parallel repetition of a k-special sound protocol for $k \neq 2$ is not k-special-sound.

Several parallel repetition results, considering multi-round public-coin interactive arguments, have been established [18, 19, 28], showing that parallel repetition reduces the soundness error. However, "soundness" is a weaker notion than "knowledge soundness". Informally the soundness error is the success probability of a cheating prover and soundness does not require the existence of a knowledge extractor.

To the best of our knowledge a parallel repetition result for decreasing the *knowledge error* has not been established yet, even though the lattice-based Bulletproof protocols of [15] implicitly rely on such a parallel repetition result. In Theorem 3, we show that the knowledge error of a public-coin argument decreases close to exponentially in the number of parallel repetitions. Our proof uses the following result from [19]. This theorem shows that, given oracle access to a (possibly dishonest) prover $\mathcal{P}^*$ that, for statements x, succeeds in convincing $\mathcal{V}^t$ with probability $\epsilon(x)$, a prover $\mathfrak{P}^{(\mathcal{P}^*)}$ that succeeds in convincing $\mathcal{V}$ with probability $\approx \epsilon(x)^{1/t}$ can be constructed.

Theorem 2 (Theorem 2 of [19]). *Let $(\mathcal{P}, \mathcal{V})$ be a public-coin interactive argument for a language L. Let $t \colon \mathbb{N} \to \mathbb{N}$, and let $(\mathcal{P}^t, \mathcal{V}^t)$ be the t-fold parallel repetition of $(\mathcal{P}, \mathcal{V})$. There exists an oracle machine $\mathfrak{P}^{(\cdot)}$ such that for every $\xi \colon \mathbb{N} \to (0,1)$, every $\delta \colon \{0,1\}^* \to (0,1)$, every $x \in \{0,1\}^*$, and every PPT prover $\mathcal{P}^*$, it holds that if*

$$\Pr\left((\mathcal{P}^*, \mathcal{V}^t)(x) = 1\right) \geq \underbrace{(1 + \xi(|x|))\delta(x)^{t(|x|)}}_{\epsilon(x):=},$$

then

$$\Pr\left((\mathfrak{P}^{(\mathcal{P}^*)}, \mathcal{V})(x) = 1\right) \geq \delta(x).$$

Furthermore, $\mathfrak{P}^{(\mathcal{P}^*)}$ runs in time $\mathrm{poly}(|x|, t(|x|), \xi(|x|)^{-1}, \epsilon(x)^{-1}, (1 - \delta(x))^{-1})$.

Theorem 3 now shows that the t-fold parallel repetition of knowledge sound interactive argument is knowledge sound and that the knowledge error decreases close to exponential in t. More precisely, the theorem shows that if $(\mathcal{P}, \mathcal{V})$ has knowledge error κ, then $(\mathcal{P}^t, \mathcal{V}^t)$ has knowledge error $\kappa^t + \nu$, for arbitrary noticeable ν. Therefore, by choosing t large enough, we can show that $(\mathcal{P}^t, \mathcal{V}^t)$ has knowledge error $1/|x|^c$ for *any* $c \in \mathbb{N}$. Note though that we cannot show that $(\mathcal{P}^t, \mathcal{V}^t)$ has negligible knowledge error $\mathrm{negl}(\lambda)$, because the running time of $\mathfrak{P}^{(\mathcal{P}^*)}$ scales with the inverse success probability of $\mathcal{P}^*$.

While it might seem that this barrier is rather an artifact of the proof technique of [19] on which we build, it was shown by [22] that Theorem 2 is tight when considering soundness amplification of protocols in general. More precisely, based on some cryptographic assumptions they showed that parallel repetition does not amplify security beyond negligible, meaning that for any negligible function negl one can find an instantiation that when starting with non-negligible soundness error, the protocol can always be broken with probability $\mathrm{negl}(|x|)$, no matter how many parallel repetitions one runs.

For a proof of the theorem we refer to the full version of this paper [1].

Theorem 3. *Let $(\mathcal{P}, \mathcal{V})$ be a public-coin interactive argument for a relation R that is knowledge sound with knowledge error $\kappa \colon \mathbb{N} \to (0,1)$. Let $t \colon \mathbb{N} \to \mathbb{N}$ be upper bounded by a polynomial. Let $\nu \colon \mathbb{N} \to (0,1)$ be an arbitrary noticeable function. Then, $(\mathcal{P}^t, \mathcal{V}^t)$ is knowledge sound with knowledge error $\kappa' = \kappa^t + \nu$.*

Remark 2. The properties *completeness* and *special honest verifier zero-knowledge* are easily seen to be preserved by parallel repetition, although the completeness error increases in the number parallel repetitions.

5 A General Framework for Compressed Σ-Protocols over Lattices

The main pivot of compressed Σ-protocol theory [6] is a basic Σ-protocol for proving that a committed vector satisfies some linear constraint. Subsequently, a compression mechanism is applied (recursively) to reduce the communication complexity from linear down to polylogarithmic in the input size. The composition of these protocols is referred to as a compressed Σ-protocol. In this section we present a natural abstraction similar to the one presented in [7, Appendix A] extended to the lattice setting. This requires a number of non-trivial adaptations that are explained in the following. Subsequently, we show how to instantiate this abstraction from a concrete lattice assumption.

In the following we first give an abstraction of the standard Σ-protocol to the lattice setting and then explain how the compression mechanism extends to this setting. Note that we give both protocols in a very abstract fashion, with the goal of allowing to instantiate them from a broad variety of lattice-based assumptions. Note that our abstraction is not restricted to instantiations based on lattices, but is tailored to this setting.

5.1 Standard Σ-Protocol

In this section we recall what we will refer to as *standard Σ-protocol* for proving knowledge of a preimage of some given module homomorphism Ψ.[1] This protocol can be viewed as the abstraction of the protocol of Schnorr [40] to arbitrary module homomorphisms, where we have to build in several relaxations in order to make it compatible with the lattice setting.

First, in the lattice setting the witness is required to be small, we therefore define a pair $(Y; y)$ to be in the target relation if $Y = \Psi(y)$ *and* $\|y\| \leq \alpha$, for some $\alpha \in \mathbb{N}$. Note that this requires to define a norm in the preimage space, we therefore in the following restrict to modules with norm. If the preimage is not required to be small (as, e.g., is the case in the discrete log setting), one does not have to require a norm on the module and can simply ignore the corresponding requirements in the protocols. The requirement of the witness y to have small norm is also where the main difficulty stems from, because one now has to transform a witness y into a witness x, such that

1. the norm of x is not much larger than y (as otherwise the statement becomes meaningless), but
2. x still hides y.

---

[1] For an introduction into modules and module homomorphisms we refer to [32].

In order to ensure the second without a too large knowledge error, the relation that one can prove knowledge of does not correspond to the target relation R, but some relaxed relation R'. In this case, we say the protocol is a protocol for the pair of relations (R, R'), i.e., an honest prover knows a witness for R but can only prove knowledge of a witness for R'.

In fact, there are two sources introducing "soundness slack": First, x itself will in general already have larger norm than y (in order to ensure hiding). Second, even worse, extracting a witness $\tilde{y}$ from two accepting transcripts, introduces additional slack. This slack is more difficult to control, as it depends on the inverse of challenge differences. As challenge differences will not necessarily be invertible over the underlying ring, we introduce an additional relaxation on the relation. Namely, for some fixed element ζ (in our examples, we will typically have that ζ is a power of two) we will consider relations R', such that $(X; x) \in R'$ if $\Psi(x) = \zeta \cdot X$ and $\|x\| \leq \beta$. We refer to ζ as an approximation factor.

More formally, let $\mathcal{R} = \{\mathcal{R}_\lambda\}_{\lambda \in \mathbb{N}}$ be an ensemble of rings, let $M = \{M_\lambda\}_{\lambda \in \mathbb{N}}, N = \{N_\lambda\}_{\lambda \in \mathbb{N}}$ be ensembles of $\mathcal{R}$-modules, let $\Psi = \{\Psi_\lambda \colon M_\lambda \to N_\lambda\}_{\lambda \in \mathbb{N}}$ be an ensemble of efficiently computable $\mathcal{R}$-module homomorphisms and let $\zeta = \{\zeta_\lambda\}_{\lambda \in \mathbb{N}}$ be an ensemble of approximation factors (i.e., $\zeta_\lambda \in \mathcal{R}_\lambda$ for all λ). Let further $\|\cdot\|$ be a norm on M, let $\alpha, \beta \colon \mathbb{N} \to \mathbb{N}$ with $\alpha \leq \beta$. Then, we define the relations $R(\Psi, \alpha) = \{R_\lambda(\Psi, \alpha)\}_{\lambda \in \mathbb{N}}$ and $R(\Psi, \beta, \zeta) = \{R_\lambda(\Psi, \beta, \zeta)\}_{\lambda \in \mathbb{N}}$ via

$$R_\lambda(\Psi, \alpha) = \left\{ (Y; y) : y \in M_\lambda, Y = \Psi_\lambda(y), \|y\| \leq \alpha(\lambda) \right\},$$

$$R_\lambda(\Psi, \beta, \zeta) = \left\{ (Y; y) : y \in M_\lambda, \zeta_\lambda \cdot Y = \Psi_\lambda(y), \|y\| \leq \beta(\lambda) \right\}.$$

In the following we abstract the notion of *rejection sampling* [35,36], which is used in lattice based cryptography to sample a value, such that

1. the sample algorithm is somewhat norm-preserving, i.e., the norm of the sampled value is not too much larger than the norm of the witness,
2. adding this value to the witness statistically hides the witness or the rejection sampling strategy aborts, and, finally,
3. the abort probability is essentially independent of the witness.

Definition 5 (V-Hiding and β-Bounded Sampling). *Let $\mathcal{R} = \{\mathcal{R}_\lambda\}_{\lambda \in \mathbb{N}}$ be an ensemble of rings and let $M = \{M_\lambda\}_{\lambda \in \mathbb{N}}$ be an ensemble of $\mathcal{R}$-modules. Let $V = \{V_\lambda\}_{\lambda \in \mathbb{N}}$ be an ensemble of sets with $V_\lambda \subseteq M_\lambda$ for all λ. Let $(\mathcal{D}, \mathcal{F})$ such that $\mathcal{D}$ is an ensemble of efficiently sampleable distributions $\mathcal{D} = \{\mathcal{D}_\lambda\}_{\lambda \in \mathbb{N}}$ over M, and $\mathcal{F}$ a PPT algorithm. We say $(\mathcal{D}, \mathcal{F})$-is V-hiding, if there exists a PPT algorithm $\mathcal{F}'$ such that for each $\lambda \in \mathbb{N}$:*

- *$\mathcal{F}$ on input $r \in M_\lambda$ and $v \in V_\lambda$, outputs $r + v$ or $\perp$,*
- *$\mathcal{F}'$ on input 1^λ, outputs an element $z \in M_\lambda$ or $\perp$,*

such that the output distributions of $(\mathcal{D}, \mathcal{F})$ and $\mathcal{F}'$ are statistically close. More precisely, there exists a negligible function $\mathrm{negl} \colon \mathbb{N} \to \mathbb{N}$ such that for all $\lambda \in \mathbb{N}$ and for all $v \in V_\lambda$ we have

$$\Delta\left(\{\mathcal{F}(r, v) \mid r \leftarrow \mathcal{D}_\lambda\}, \{\mathcal{F}'(1^\lambda)\}\right) \leq \mathrm{negl}(\lambda),$$

where the probability is taken over the randomness of $\mathcal{D}_\lambda$ and the random coins of $\mathcal{F}, \mathcal{F}'$. If the distribution of $(\mathcal{D}, \mathcal{F})$ and $\mathcal{F}'$ are equal, we say $(\mathcal{D}, \mathcal{F})$-is perfectly V-hiding.

Note that by the above considerations we can upper bound the abort probability of $(\mathcal{D}, \mathcal{F})$ by

$$\delta(\lambda) = \Pr[\mathcal{F}'(1^\lambda) = \perp] + \text{negl}(\lambda),$$

for all $\lambda \in \mathbb{N}$.

Let further $\beta: \mathbb{N} \to \mathbb{N}$. We say that $(\mathcal{D}, \mathcal{F})$ is β-bounded if for all $\lambda \in \mathbb{N}$, $v \in V_\lambda$ and r in the support of $\mathcal{D}_\lambda$ it holds $\|\mathcal{F}(r, v)\| \leq \beta(\lambda)$ whenever $\mathcal{F}(r, v) \neq \perp$.

To improve readability, we will in the following omit the security parameter, and, e.g., simply say "Let $\mathcal{R}$ be a ring...", or "Let $\alpha \in \mathbb{N}$...", even though we assume all variables to be parametrized by the security parameter.

Before stating the Σ-protocol, we introduce the notion of an ζ-*exceptional subset*, which will ensure that the protocol satisfies special soundness.

Definition 6 (ζ-Exceptional Subset). *Let $\mathcal{R}$ be a ring, $\zeta \in \mathcal{R}$ and $\mathcal{C} \subseteq \mathcal{R}$ be a set. We say $\mathcal{C}$ is an ζ-exceptional subset of $\mathcal{R}$, if for all pairs of distinct elements $c, c' \in \mathcal{C}$ there exists a non-zero element $a \in \mathcal{R}$ such that $a(c - c') = \zeta$. If $\mathcal{C}$ is a 1-exceptional subset of $\mathcal{R}$, we simply say that $\mathcal{C}$ is an exceptional subset.*

We further need to give bounds on the soundness slack introduced by extraction. To this end, for ζ-exceptional subsets $\mathcal{C} \subset \mathcal{R}$ we define $w(\mathcal{C})$ and $\bar{w}(\mathcal{C}, \zeta)$:

$$w(\mathcal{C}) = \max_{c \in \mathcal{C}, x \in \mathcal{R} \setminus \{0\}} \frac{\|cx\|}{\|x\|},$$

$$\bar{w}(\mathcal{C}, \zeta) = \max_{c \neq c' \in \mathcal{C}, x \in \mathcal{R} \setminus \{0\}} \max_{a \in \mathcal{R}: a(c-c') = \zeta} \frac{\|ax\|}{\|x\|}. \tag{3}$$

The value $w(\mathcal{C})$ gives an upper bound on how much the norm of an element in $\mathcal{R}$ increases when multiplied by an element in $\mathcal{C}$, i.e., $w(\mathcal{C})$ is such that $\|cx\| \leq w(\mathcal{C})\|x\|$ for all $c \in \mathcal{C}$ and $x \in \mathcal{R}$. Note that if $\mathcal{R} = \mathbb{Z}$ and with absolute value $|\cdot|$, we simply have $w(\mathcal{C}) = \max\{|c|: c \in \mathcal{C}\}$.

The value $\bar{w}(\mathcal{C}, 1)$ gives an upper bound on how much the norm of an element in $\mathcal{R}$ increases when multiplied with the inverse of challenge differences, i.e., $\bar{w}(\mathcal{C}, 1)$ is such that $\|(c-c')^{-1}x\| \leq \bar{w}(\mathcal{C}, 1)\|x\|$ for all $x \in \mathcal{R}$ and distinct $c, c' \in \mathcal{C}$. In general, the value $\bar{w}(\mathcal{C}, \zeta)$ gives an upper bound on how much the norm of an element in $\mathcal{R}$ increases when multiplied with an a such that $a(c - c') = \zeta$ for challenges $c \neq c'$. Note that $\bar{w}(\mathcal{C}, \zeta)$ is only well-defined if $\mathcal{C}$ is ζ-exceptional.

The maximum over $a \in \mathcal{R}$ in Eq. 3 can be replaced by a minimum, potentially resulting in tighter norm bounds. More precisely, the extractor can choose the element a that minimizes $\|ax\|/\|x\|$. However, this requires the minimum to be efficiently computable. To avoid this additional assumption we take the maximum over all a. Moreover, in most practical applications $\mathcal{R}$ does not have zero-divisors and $a \in R$ is uniquely defined.

For a module M over $\mathcal{R}$ with norm $\|\cdot\|$, similarly we define

$$w_M(\mathcal{C}) = \max_{c \in \mathcal{C}, x \in M \setminus \{0\}} \frac{\|cx\|}{\|x\|} \quad \text{and} \quad \bar{w}_M(\mathcal{C}, \zeta) = \max_{c \neq c' \in \mathcal{C}, x \in M \setminus \{0\}} \max_{a \in \mathcal{R}: a(c-c')=\zeta} \frac{\|ax\|}{\|x\|}.$$

Note that for $M = \mathcal{R}^n$ and $\|\cdot\|$ over M defined as ℓ_p-norm (for $p \in \mathbb{N} \cup \{\infty\}$), we have $w_M(\mathcal{C}) = w(\mathcal{C})$ and $\bar{w}_M(\mathcal{C}, \zeta) = \bar{w}(\mathcal{C}, \zeta)$.

We now state the standard Σ-protocol Π_0 for the pair of relations $(R(\Psi, \alpha), R(\Psi, 2\beta, \zeta))$ in Protocol 1. Further, we summarize its properties in Theorem 4. For a proof we refer to the full version of this paper [1].

Protocol 1 Standard Σ-Protocol Π_0 for the pair of relations $(R(\Psi, \alpha), R(\Psi, 2\beta\sigma, \zeta))$, where $\sigma = \bar{w}_M(\mathcal{C}, \zeta)$. Here, $(\mathcal{D}, \mathcal{F})$ is V-hiding and β-bounded, where $V = \{cy \mid y \in M, \|y\| \leq \alpha, c \in \mathcal{C}\}$.

INPUT$(Y; y)$
$Y = \Psi(y)$

Prover   Verifier

$w \leftarrow_R \mathcal{D}, W = \Psi(w)$ $\xrightarrow{\quad W \quad}$

$c_0 \leftarrow_R \mathcal{C} \subset \mathcal{R}$

$\xleftarrow{\quad c_0 \quad}$

If $\mathcal{F}(w, c_0 y) = \bot$:
    Abort
Else: $x = w + c_0 y$

$\xrightarrow{\quad x \quad}$ $\|x\| \overset{?}{\leq} \beta, \Psi(x) \overset{?}{=} W + c_0 Y$

Theorem 4 (Standard Σ-Protocol). *Let $\mathcal{R}$ be a ring, let M, N be $\mathcal{R}$-modules and let $\Psi \colon M \to N$ be an efficiently computable $\mathcal{R}$-module homomorphism.*

Further, let $\zeta \in \mathcal{R}$ and $\mathcal{C} \subset \mathcal{R}$ be a finite ζ-exceptional subset of $\mathcal{R}$, let $\alpha, \beta \in \mathbb{N}$ and $\delta \in [0, 1)$, let $V = \{cy \mid y \in M, \|y\| \leq \alpha, c \in \mathcal{C}\}$ and let $(\mathcal{D}, \mathcal{F})$ be a β-bounded V-hiding distribution with abort probability δ.

Then, the protocol Π_0 (as defined in Protocol 1) is a 3-move protocol for relations $(R(\Psi, \alpha), R(\Psi, 2\beta\sigma, \zeta))$ defined via

$$R(\Psi, \alpha) = \Big\{ (Y; y) : y \in M, Y = \Psi(y), \|y\| \leq \alpha \Big\},$$

$$R(\Psi, 2\beta\sigma, \zeta) = \Big\{ (Y; y) : y \in M, \zeta \cdot Y = \Psi(y), \|y\| \leq 2\beta\sigma \Big\},$$

where $\sigma = \bar{w}_M(\mathcal{C}, \zeta)$.

It is complete with completeness error δ, unconditionally 2-special sound and statistical non-abort special honest verifier zero-knowledge.

Remark 3. In some settings it is beneficial to introduce another relaxation. For example, if $\zeta = 1$ (i.e., if challenge difference are invertible), the aforementioned approach requires *inverses* of challenge differences to be of small norm. The following relaxed relation only requires challenge differences, and not necessarily their inverses, to be of small norm. It introduces an adapted approximation factor $\bar{c} \in \bar{\mathcal{C}} = \{c - c'; c, c' \in \mathcal{C}, \ c \neq c'\}$ and is defined as follows

$$R(\Psi, \beta, \bar{\mathcal{C}}) = \Big\{ (Y; y, \bar{c}) : y \in M, \bar{c} \cdot Y = \Psi(y), \|y\| \leq \beta, \bar{c} \in \bar{\mathcal{C}} \Big\}.$$

The approximation factor $\bar{c}$ is not fixed and part of the secret witness. This relaxation allows for more efficient Σ-protocols. However, when composed with other protocols the fact that the approximation factors are not fixed introduces additional difficulties. These can be handled, but in most settings the required adjustments negate the benefits of this relaxed relation, we therefore do not consider it further.

For a generic transformation from non-abort SHVZK to SHVZK (or even standard zero-knowledge) we refer to the full version of this paper [1].

5.2   Compression Mechanism

Observe that the final message x of protocol Π_0 is a witness for statement $X := W + c_0 Y$, i.e., the final message can be viewed as a trivial proof of knowledge for $X \in L_{R(\Psi, \beta)}$. In the following, we will present a general view on the compression mechanism that allows to replace this trivial PoK by a more efficient one, using Bulletproof's folding mechanism [14,16]. This protocol does not need to be SHVZK, since it is a replacement for the trivial PoK.

Compression function. The Bulletproof folding mechanism relies on an compression function that allows to compress the witness iteratively. In the following, we outline the properties the compression function has to satisfy. The main purpose of giving this abstraction is to improve readability of the protocols. In the full version of this paper [1], we further give an abstraction generalizing to larger compression rate and the corresponding compression mechanism.

Definition 7 (Extractable compression function). *Let M, M' be $\mathcal{R}$-modules, such that M is of even rank n and M' of rank $n/2$. Let $\mathcal{C} \subset \mathcal{R}$ be an exceptional subset of $\mathcal{R}$. Let $\mathsf{Comp} = \{\mathsf{Comp}_c \colon M \to M' : c \in \mathcal{C}\}$ and $\Phi = \{\Phi_c \colon M' \to M : c \in \mathcal{C}\}$, where Φ_c is an $\mathcal{R}$-module homomorphism for each $c \in \mathcal{C}$. Then, we say (Comp, Φ) is an extractable compression function for $\mathcal{C}$, if the following holds: There exist maps $\pi_L, \pi_R \colon M \to M$, such that for all $c \in \mathcal{C}$:*

$$\Phi_c(\mathsf{Comp}_c(x)) = \pi_L(x) + c \cdot x + c^2 \cdot \pi_R(x).$$

We further say that (Comp, Φ) is (τ, τ')-norm preserving, if for all $c \in \mathcal{C}, x \in M, z \in M'$:

$$\|\mathsf{Comp}_c(x)\| \leq \tau \cdot \|x\| \ \text{ and } \ \|\Phi_c(z)\| \leq \tau' \cdot \|z\|.$$

The reason why $\Phi_c \circ \mathsf{Comp}_c$ has to be of this specific form is to allow *extractability* even if the maps π_L, π_R are not evaluated honestly. More precisely, let $\Psi\colon M \to N$. Then, given pairwise distinct $c_1, c_2, c_3 \in \mathcal{C}$ and $z_1, z_2, z_3 \in M'$ such that $\Psi \circ \Phi_{c_i}(z_i) = A + c_i X + c_i^2 B$ for $i \in [3]$ (for arbitrary $A, B \in N$), it is possible to extract an $x \in M$ with $\Psi(x) = X$ (resulting in 3-special soundness of the compression mechanism). In the lattice setting it is further crucial that we can give a meaningful bound on the norm of the extracted x. In the proof of Theorem 5 we will show that this is indeed the case.

Example 1 (Bulletproof compression function [14,16]). Let $M = \mathcal{R}^n$ and $M' = \mathcal{R}^{n/2}$. Then, the Bulletproof compression function is obtained as

$$\mathsf{Comp}_c((x_L, x_R)) = x_L + c \cdot x_R,$$
$$\Phi_c(z) = (cz, z),$$

and

$$\pi_L((x_L, x_R)) = (0, x_L),$$
$$\pi_R((x_L, x_R)) = (x_R, 0).$$

Recall that $w(\mathcal{C}) = \max_{c \in \mathcal{C}, x \in \mathcal{R}\setminus\{0\}} \|cx\|_\infty / \|x\|_\infty$. The Bulletproof compression function is $(1 + w(\mathcal{C}), w(\mathcal{C}))$-norm preserving, as for all $c \in \mathcal{C}, x \in M$

$$\|x_L + c \cdot x_R\|_\infty \le \|x\|_\infty + w(\mathcal{C})\|x\|_\infty,$$
$$\|(cz, z)\|_\infty \le w(\mathcal{C})\|z\|_\infty,$$

whenever $w(\mathcal{C}) \ge 1$ (which will be the case for our instantiations).

Using the Bulletproof compression function with the p-norm $\|\cdot\|_p$ for arbitrary $p \in \mathbb{N} \cup \{\infty\}$ instead of restricting to the infinity norm, we obtain that the Bulletproof compression function is $(1 + w_p(\mathcal{C}), 1 + w_p(\mathcal{C}))$-norm preserving, because in general we can only guarantee

$$\|(cz, z)\|_p \le w_p(\mathcal{C})\|z\|_p + \|z\|_p,$$

where now $w_p(\mathcal{C}) = \max_{c \in \mathcal{C}, x \in \mathcal{R}\setminus\{0\}} \|cx\|_p / \|x\|_p$.

The idea of the compression mechanism is as follows: First the prover commits to $A = \Psi(\pi_L(x))$ and $B = \Psi(\pi_R(x))$. Next, the verifier sends a challenge $c \in \mathcal{C}$. Using the compression mechanism, the prover then compresses x as $z = \mathsf{Comp}_c(x)$. Now, the verifier can check if indeed $\Psi(\Phi_c(z)) = A + cX + c^2 B$. As $\mathsf{Comp}_c(x)$ is 2-compressing, this strategy reduces communication complexity by roughly a factor 2. Note that this factor 2 reduction comes at the cost of sending two elements $A, B \in N$. Hence, in practice the reduction of the communication cost depends on the size of the $\mathcal{R}$-module N. Finally, by extrability it follows that the compression mechanism is 3-special sound.

The compression mechanism is graphically displayed in Protocol 2 and its properties are summarized in Theorem 5. For a formal proof we refer to the full version of this paper [1].

Protocol 2 Generic Compression Mechanism Π_1 for relations $(R(\Psi, \beta),$ $R(\Psi, \beta\sigma, \zeta^3))$, where $\sigma = 6\tau\tau' w_M(\mathcal{C})^2 \bar{w}_M(\mathcal{C}, \zeta)^3$. Recall that $(\mathsf{Comp}, \varPhi)$ is a (τ, τ')-norm preserving extractable compression map, i.e. for all $c \in \mathcal{C}$:

$$\varPhi_c(\mathsf{Comp}_c(x)) = \pi_L(x) + cx + c^2\pi_R(x).$$

$\mathrm{INPUT}(X; x)$
$X = \Psi(x) \in N$

Prover   Verifier

$A = \Psi(\pi_L(x))$

$B = \Psi(\pi_R(x))$ $\xrightarrow{\quad A, B \quad}$

$c \leftarrow_R \mathcal{C} \subset \mathcal{R}$

$\xleftarrow{\quad c \quad}$

$z = \mathsf{Comp}_c(x)$

$\xrightarrow{\quad z \quad}$

$$\|z\| \overset{?}{\leq} \beta \cdot \tau,$$
$$\Psi(\varPhi_c(z)) \overset{?}{=} A + cX + c^2 B$$

Theorem 5 (Compression Mechanism). *Let M, M', N be $\mathcal{R}$-modules, such that M has even rank n and M' has rank $n/2$ over $\mathcal{R}$, and let $\Psi: M \to N$ be an $\mathcal{R}$-module homomorphism. Further, let $\zeta \in \mathcal{R}$ and let $\mathcal{C}$ be a finite ζ-exceptional subset of $\mathcal{R}$, let $(\mathsf{Comp}, \varPhi)$ be a (τ, τ')-norm preserving extractable compression function for $\mathcal{C}$ with projection maps π_L, π_R, and let $\sigma = 6\tau\tau' w_M(\mathcal{C})^2 \bar{w}_M(\mathcal{C}, \zeta)^3$. Then, Π_1 as given in Protocol 2 is a 3-move protocol for relations $(R(\Psi, \beta), R(\Psi, \beta\sigma, \zeta^3))$ which satisfies perfect completeness and unconditional 3-special soundness.*

5.3 Compressed Σ-Protocol

In this setting we build on the previous sections in order to present the compressed Σ-Protocol Π_{comp}, allowing to reduce complexity to polylogarithmic in the input length (when choosing a suitable instantiation).

The introduced soundness slack makes concatenating protocols a bit more involved than in the plain setting. For more details and a formal treatment of this issue we refer to the full version of this paper [1]. Informally

$$\Pi_{\mathrm{comp}} = \Pi_1 \diamond \cdots \diamond \Pi_1 \diamond \Pi_0,$$

for the appropriate instantiations of Π_0 and Π_1. Recall, that in the composition $\Pi_b \diamond \Pi_a$, the final message of protocol Π_a is replaced by an execution of Π_b.

Building on the composition theorem and the results of the previous sections, where the compression function is instantiated with the Bulletproof compression function, we obtain the following corollary.

Corollary 2 (Generic Compressed Σ-Protocol). *Let $\mu \in \mathbb{N}$. Let $M = \mathcal{R}^{2^\mu}$ and $\|\cdot\|_\infty$ the infinity norm on M (for some underlying norm on $\mathcal{R}$). Let $\Psi \colon M \to N$ be an $\mathcal{R}$-module homomorphism, let $\zeta \in \mathcal{R}$ and let $\mathcal{C}$ be a finite ζ-exceptional subset of $\mathcal{R}$. Let $\alpha, \beta \in \mathbb{N}$ and $\delta \in [0,1)$, let $V = \{cy \mid y \in M, \|y\|_\infty \le \alpha, c \in \mathcal{C}\}$ and let $(\mathcal{D}, \mathcal{F})$ be a β-bounded V-hiding distribution with abort probability δ. Then, there exists a $(2\mu + 3)$-move public-coin protocol Π_{comp} for the pair of relations*

$$\left(R(\Psi, \alpha), R(\Psi, 2\beta \cdot \bar{w}(\mathcal{C}, \zeta) \cdot \sigma^\mu, \zeta^{3\mu+1}) \right),$$

where $\sigma = 6 \cdot w(\mathcal{C})^3 \cdot (1 + w(\mathcal{C})) \cdot \bar{w}(\mathcal{C}, \zeta)^3$.

It is complete with completeness error δ, unconditionally $(2, 3, \ldots, 3)$-special sound and non-abort special honest-verifier zero-knowledge. Moreover, the communication costs are:

- *$\mathcal{P} \to \mathcal{V}$: $2\mu + 1$ elements of N and 1 element of $\mathcal{R}$.*
- *$\mathcal{V} \to \mathcal{P}$: $\mu + 1$ elements of $\mathcal{C}$.*

In the full version of this paper [1], we outline how the abstract Σ-protocol theory yields a proof of knowledge with knowledge error $\kappa \le (2\mu + 1)/|\mathcal{C}|$, which can be decreased to $1/\lambda^d$ for arbitrary constant $d \in \mathbb{N}$ by applying the parallel repetition theorem (Theorem 3). Moreover, there we discuss the issues that arise when applying the Fiat-Shamir transform to our protocol in order to transform it into a non-interactive PoK. We further give details on how to use our compressed Σ-protocols non-interactively via the Fiat-Shamir transform.

6   Compressed Σ-Protocols from the MSIS Assumption

The compressed Σ-protocol Π_{comp} of Corollary 2 is typically instantiated with $\Psi(\mathbf{x}, \gamma) = (\mathrm{COM}(\mathbf{x}, \gamma), L(\mathbf{x}))$ for a commitment scheme COM and a linear form L, where γ is the commitment randomness. This allows a prover to show that a committed vector $\mathbf{x}$ satisfies a *linear* constraint. When instantiated with a compact or compressing commitment scheme, for which the size of a commitment is at most polylogarithmic in the size of the secret vector, protocol Π_{comp} achieves communication complexity polylogarithmic in the input size. In the full version of this paper [1], we show how to linearize non-linear constraints and thereby prove that committed vectors satisfy arbitrary *non-linear* constraints. Therefore compressed Σ-protocol Π_{comp} is only required to handle linear instances.

The generalizations of Sect. 5 were introduced to handle *lattice-based* commitment schemes. In this section, we instantiate compressed Σ-protocol Π_{comp} for the following lattice-based commitment function (Definition 3)

$$\mathrm{COM} \colon \mathcal{R}^n \times \mathcal{R}^r \to \mathcal{R}_q^k, \quad (\mathbf{x}, \gamma) \mapsto A_1\gamma + A_2\mathbf{x} \mod q.$$

Recall that, $\mathcal{R} = \mathbb{Z}[X]/f(X)$ for a monic irreducible polynomial $f(X)$, $\mathcal{R}_q = \mathcal{R}/(q)$ for a rational prime q, and $A_1 \in \mathcal{R}_q^{k \times r}$ and $A_2 \in \mathcal{R}_q^{k \times n}$ are sampled uniformly at random in the setup phase. This commitment scheme allows a prover to commit to "short" ring elements. We use it to commit to secret vectors of

$\mathcal{R}_p^n$ via their unique representation in $\{x \in \mathcal{R} : \|x\|_\infty \leq \lceil (p-1)/2 \rceil\}$. Subsequently, we aim to prove that a committed vector $\mathbf{x} \in \mathcal{R}_p^n$ satisfies an $\mathcal{R}_p$-linear constraint $L(\mathbf{x}) = y$ for a linear form $L : \mathcal{R}_p^n \to \mathcal{R}_p$. To this end, we instantiate protocol Π_{comp} with $\alpha = \lceil (p-1)/2 \rceil$ for the $\mathcal{R}$-module homomorphism

$$\Psi : \mathcal{R}^n \times \mathcal{R}^r \to \mathcal{R}_q^k \times \mathcal{R}_p, \quad (\mathbf{x}, \gamma) \mapsto (\mathrm{COM}(\mathbf{x}, \gamma), L(\mathbf{x}) \mod p).$$

Note that the protocol of Corollary 2 contains an approximation factor $\zeta^{3\mu+1}$. This means that, in the instantiation of this section, a prover claims to know an exact opening $(\mathbf{x}, \gamma)$ of a commitment P satisfying $L(\mathbf{x}) = y$, but is only capable of proving knowledge of a relaxed opening $(\mathbf{x}', \gamma')$ such that $\mathrm{COM}(\mathbf{x}', \gamma') = \zeta^{3\mu+1}$. P and $L(\mathbf{x}) = \zeta^{3\mu+1} \cdot y \in \mathcal{R}_p$. For this reason, we require the approximation factor ζ to be invertible in $\mathcal{R}_p$. In this case, a commitment to a vector $\mathbf{x}' \in \mathcal{R}_p^n$ is also a commitment to the vector $\tilde{\mathbf{x}} = \zeta^{-3\mu-1}\mathbf{x}' \in \mathcal{R}_p^n$ satisfying the linear constraint $L(\tilde{\mathbf{x}}) = y$. Hence, if $\zeta \in \mathcal{R}_p^*$, we derive precisely the desired functionality of proving that a committed vector satisfies a linear constraint.

The lattice instantiation requires a distribution-algorithm pair $(\mathcal{D}, \mathcal{F})$ that is V-hiding, for $V = \{cy \mid y \in M, \|y\|_\infty \leq \alpha, c \in \mathcal{C}\}$, and β-bounded for some reasonably small $\beta \in \mathbb{N}$. We let $\mathcal{D}$ be a uniform distribution over an appropriate subset of $\mathcal{R}^{n+r}$. The following lemma shows that this approach gives the required properties. The smallest lattice-based signatures take $\mathcal{D}$ to be a Gaussian distribution. Namely, when the secrets have a bounded ℓ_2-norm, the Gaussian distribution results in better protocol parameters. In our scenario this is not the case; our secrets are bounded in the ℓ_∞-norm. Additionally, uniform sampling is less prone to side-channel attacks. For this reason, the digital signature scheme Dilithium also deploys a uniform rejection sampling approach [24].

Lemma 6 (Uniform Rejection Sampling). *Let* $\mathcal{R} = \mathbb{Z}[X]/f(X)$ *for a monic and irreducible polynomial* $f(X) \in \mathbb{Z}[X]$ *of degree* d, $\mathcal{C} \subset \mathcal{R}$ *and* $m, \eta \in \mathbb{N}$. *Let* $\|z\|_\infty$ *be the* ℓ_∞-*norm of the coefficient vector of* $z \in \mathcal{R}^m$ *and let* $w(\mathcal{C}) = \max_{c \in \mathcal{R}, x \in \mathcal{R} \setminus \{0\}} \|cx\|_\infty / \|x\|_\infty$. *Let* $V = \{cx \in \mathcal{R}^m : c \in \mathcal{C} \subset \mathcal{R}, \|x\|_\infty \leq \lceil (p-1)/2 \rceil\}$. *Let* $\mathcal{D}$ *be the uniform distribution over* $\{x \in \mathcal{R}^m : \|x\|_\infty \leq \eta\}$ *and let*

$$\mathcal{F}(r,v) = \begin{cases} \bot, & \text{if } \|v + r\|_\infty > \eta - w(\mathcal{C}) \lceil (p-1)/2 \rceil, \\ v + r, & \text{otherwise.} \end{cases}$$

Then $(\mathcal{D}, \mathcal{F})$ *is perfectly* V-*hiding and* $(\eta - w(\mathcal{C}) \lceil (p-1)/2 \rceil)$-*bounded, with abort probability* $\delta \leq 1 - e^{-\frac{w(\mathcal{C})pmd}{2\eta+1}}$.

Proof. Note that, for all $v \in V$, it holds that $\|v\|_\infty \leq w(\mathcal{C}) \lceil (p-1)/2 \rceil$. Hence, the abort probability of the probabilistic algorithm $\{\mathcal{F}(r,v) \mid r \leftarrow \mathcal{D}\}$ equals

$$\delta = 1 - \left(1 - \frac{2w(\mathcal{C}) \lceil (p-1)/2 \rceil}{2\eta + 1}\right)^{md},$$

$$\leq 1 - e^{md \log\left(1 - \frac{w(\mathcal{C})p}{2\eta+1}\right)} \leq 1 - e^{-\frac{w(\mathcal{C})pmd}{2\eta+1}}.$$

Now let $\mathcal{F}'$ be the algorithm that aborts with probability δ and otherwise outputs a $z \in \{x \in \mathcal{R}^m : \|x\|_\infty \le \eta - w(\mathcal{C})\lceil(p-1)/2\rceil\}$ sampled uniformly at random. Then it is easily seen that $\{\mathcal{F}(r,v) \mid r \leftarrow \mathcal{D}\}$ and $\{\mathcal{F}'\}$ have exactly the same output distributions, i.e., $(\mathcal{D}, \mathcal{F})$ is V-hiding.

Finally, $(\mathcal{D}, \mathcal{F})$ is clearly $(\eta - w(\mathcal{C})\lceil(p-1)/2\rceil)$-bounded. $\qquad \square$

The resulting instantiation of Π_{comp}, denoted by $\Lambda_{\text{comp}}(\eta)$, is parameterized by $\eta \in \mathbb{N}$ allowing for a trade-off between the abort probability and communication complexity of the protocol. Its properties are summarized in Corollary 3.

Corollary 3 (Lattice-Based Compressed Σ-Protocol). *Let $n, r, \mu, \eta \in \mathbb{N}$ such that $n + r = 2^\mu$ and let $p, q \in \mathbb{N}$ be primes. Let $\mathcal{R} = \mathbb{Z}[X]/f(X)$ for a monic and irreducible polynomial $f(X) \in \mathbb{Z}[X]$ of degree d. Let $\zeta \in \mathcal{R}$ such that $\zeta \in \mathcal{R}_p^*$ and let $\mathcal{C}$ be a ζ-exceptional subset of $\mathcal{R}$. Let $A_1 \in \mathcal{R}_q^{k \times r}$, $A_2 \in \mathcal{R}_q^{k \times n}$ and*

$$\Psi: \mathcal{R}^n \times \mathcal{R}^r \to \mathcal{R}_q^k \times \mathcal{R}_p, \quad (\mathbf{x}, \gamma) \mapsto (A_1\gamma + A_2\mathbf{x} \mod q, L(\mathbf{x}) \mod p).$$

Then, there exists a $(2\mu + 3)$-move public-coin protocol $\Lambda_{comp}(\eta)$ for the pair of relations

$$R = \Big\{ (P; x) : P = \Psi(x), \|x\|_\infty \le \lceil(p-1)/2\rceil \Big\},$$

$$R' = \Big\{ (P; x) : \zeta^{3\mu+1} \cdot P = \Psi(x), \|x\|_\infty \le 2\sigma^\mu \bar{w}(\mathcal{C}, \zeta)(\eta - w(\mathcal{C})\lceil(p-1)/2\rceil) \Big\},$$

where $\sigma = 6 \cdot w(\mathcal{C})^3 \cdot (1 + w(\mathcal{C})) \cdot \bar{w}(\mathcal{C}, \zeta)^3$ with $w(\cdot)$ and $\bar{w}(\cdot)$ defined as in Eq. 3.

It is unconditionally $(2, 3, \ldots, 3)$-special sound, non-abort special honest-verifier zero-knowledge and complete with completeness error

$$\delta \le 1 - e^{-\frac{w(\mathcal{C})p(n+r)d}{2\eta+1}}.$$

Moreover, the communication costs are:

- *$\mathcal{P} \to \mathcal{V}$: $2\mu + 1$ elements of $\mathcal{R}_q^k$, $2\mu + 1$ elements of $\mathcal{R}_p$ and 1 element of $\mathcal{R}$.*
- *$\mathcal{V} \to \mathcal{P}$: $\mu + 1$ elements of $\mathcal{C}$.*

Remark 4. Corollary 3 does not require ζ to be invertible in $\mathcal{R}_p$. In particular, this result is still valid for $\zeta = 0$. However, in this case 0 is a witness for all statements $P \in L_{R'}$ and thereby the claim that is being proven becomes vacuous. For this reason, in most practical scenarios we assume that $\zeta \in \mathcal{R}_p^*$.

6.1 Parameters

In this section, we consider compressed Σ-protocol $\Lambda_{\text{comp}}(\eta)$ defined over the cyclotomic number ring $\mathcal{R} = \mathbb{Z}[X]/(X^d + 1)$ with d a power of two and with challenge set $\mathcal{C} = \{0, \pm 1, \pm X, \ldots, \pm X^{d-1}\}$. We show that this protocol has communication complexity *polylogarithmic* in the input size. We only consider the simplified scenario of proving knowledge of a commitment opening.

Power-of-two cyclotomic number rings $\mathcal{R}$ and their monomial challenge set $\mathcal{C}$ have certain convenient properties. In particular, $w(\mathcal{C}) = 1$ and $\mathcal{C}$ is a 2-exceptional subset of $\mathcal{R}$. More precisely, $2/(c - c') \in \mathcal{R}$ is a polynomial with coefficients in $\{-1, 0, 1\}$ for all distinct $c, c' \in \mathcal{C}$ [13]. From this it follows that $\bar{w}(\mathcal{C}, 2) \le d$. For a more detailed discussion on optimal challenge sets see [8,37].

Let us now determine the asymptotic communication complexity. First note that, by Theorem 1, $\Lambda_{\mathrm{comp}}(\eta)$ has knowledge error $\kappa \le (2\log(n + r) + 1)/(2d + 1) \le \log(n + r)/d$ (assuming that $\log(n + r) < d$). For this reason $t = \Theta\left(\lambda/(\log d - \log\log(n + r))\right)$ parallel repetitions are required, where λ is the security parameter. Note that, in the analysis of the lattice-based Bulletproof folding technique it is incorrectly claimed that their protocol achieves $\mathcal{O}(1/d)$ knowledge error [15, p. 20].[2] However, similar to our protocol, it achieves a $\mathcal{O}(\log(n + r)/d)$ knowledge error.

Moreover, we assume $\eta = \Theta(tdp(n + r))$, which by Corollary 3 is enough to achieve a constant completeness error. From Corollary 3 it now follows that the extractor outputs a $(B, 2^{3\mu+1})$-relaxed commitment opening, where

$$
B = 2d \cdot (12d^3)^\mu \left(\eta - \left\lceil \frac{p-1}{2} \right\rceil\right) = \Theta(d^2 tp(n + r)^{3 + \log 3 + 3\log d}).
$$

Hence, the commitment scheme must be instantiated to be binding with respect to $(B, 2^{3\mu+1})$-relaxed commitment openings, i.e., the $\mathrm{MSIS}^\infty_{k,n+r,2B}$ problem over $\mathcal{R}_q$ must be computationally infeasible (Lemma 3). Recall that commitments are vectors in $\mathcal{R}_q^k$. From the Micciancio-Regev bound (Eq. 1) it follows that this problem is hard if

$$
dk \log q \ge \frac{\log^2(2B\sqrt{n+r})}{4\log\delta} = \Theta\left(\frac{\log^2 d \log^2 tdp(n+r)}{\log\delta}\right), \tag{4}
$$

where δ is the root Hermite factor. Note that we derive an additional $\sqrt{n+r}$ factor because we reduce the MSIS-problem from the ℓ_∞-norm to the ℓ_2-norm. When these commitments are considered stand-alone their size is independent of the input rank n, i.e., they are compact. However, the soundness slack of our protocols depends (polynomially) on n. Hence, the commitment scheme must be instantiated such that the bit size $dk \log q$ of commitments is polylogarithmic.

By Lemma 1 it now follows that r is polylogarithmic in the input size. Together with Corollary 3 and the fact that $t = \Theta\left(\lambda/(\log d - \log\log(n + r))\right)$, this shows that the prover has to send

$$
\mathcal{O}\left(\frac{\lambda \log^2 d \log n \log^2 \lambda dpn}{\log\delta(\log d - \log\log n)}\right)
$$

bits of information to the verifier. Hence, this instantiation of $\Lambda_{\mathrm{comp}}(\alpha, \eta)$ indeed achieves communication complexity polylogarithmic in the input size.

---

[2] This was confirmed to us by the authors in personal communication and also observed in [3].

Remark 5. The lattice based Bulletproof instantiation of [15] considers the case $k = 1$ and they derive a communication complexity of $\mathcal{O}(d\lambda \log n \log pn / \log \delta)$ (using our notation) under the assumption that $\log q = \Theta(\log d \log pn)$. However, to ensure that the underlying commitment scheme is binding they must choose $d = \Theta(\log q)$. Moreover, they incorrectly estimate their knowledge error to be $\mathcal{O}(1/d)$ instead of $\mathcal{O}(\log n/d)$. Taking these two issues into account gives their protocol a communication complexity of

$$\mathcal{O}\left(\frac{\lambda \log^2 d \log n \log^2 pn}{\log \delta (\log d - \log \log n)} \right).$$

The additional factor λd inside the logarithm of our communication complexity can be explained by the fact that, in contrast to [15], our protocol is zero-knowledge. Besides this factor, our communication complexity is the same.

Remark 6. Because the security loss of the Fiat-Shamir transform is exponential in the number of rounds, the non-interactive variant of the t-fold parallel repetition of protocol $\Lambda_{\text{comp}}(\eta)$ requires a factor $\mathcal{O}(\mu) = \mathcal{O}(\log n)$ more parallel repetitions than the interactive variant. Therefore, the communication complexity of the non-interactive variant is a factor $\mathcal{O}(\log n)$ larger. This issue has been overlooked in prior works.

7   Proving Non-linear Relations

Thus far, we have shown how to prove that committed vectors satisfy *linear* constraints. To handle non-linear constraints, we deploy an adaptation of the strategy from [6] that uses secret sharing to linearize non-linearities.

The techniques from [6] are not directly applicable to the lattice setting, since their relations and arithmetic secret sharing are defined over a large field. In our adaptation the arithmetic secret sharing is not defined over a field but over a quotient of a number ring. This introduces two challenges: (1) the ring may be small and (2) not all ring elements have a multiplicative inverse. In our adaptation, these challenges are handled by defining the secret sharing scheme over an appropriately chosen ring extension. For more details we refer to the full version of this paper [1].

Acknowledgements. We thank Jelle Don, Serge Fehr, Michael Klooß, Vadim Lyuba-shevsky and Gregor Seiler for the helpful and insightful discussions. Furthermore, we thank Andrej Bogdanov for pointing out an oversight regarding the composition theorem in the first version of this work.

Thomas Attema has been supported by EU H2020 project No 780701 (PROMETHEUS). Ronald Cramer has been supported by ERC ADG project No 74079 (ALGSTRONGCRYPTO) and by the NWO Gravitation project QSC. Lisa Kohl has been supported by the NWO Gravitation project QSC.

References

1. Full version of this paper. IACR ePrint 2021/307
2. Ajtai, M.: Generating hard instances of lattice problems (extended abstract). In: STOC, pp. 99–108. ACM (1996)
3. Albrecht, M.R., Lai, R.W.: Subtractive sets over cyclotomic rings: limits of Schnorr-like arguments over lattices. In: Malkin, T., Peikert, C. (eds.) CRYPTO 2021. LNCS, vol. 12826, pp. 519–548 (2021, to appear)
4. Albrecht, M.R., Player, R., Scott, S.: On the concrete hardness of learning with errors. J. Math. Cryptol. **9**, 169–203 (2015)
5. Ames, S., Hazay, C., Ishai, Y., Venkitasubramaniam, M.: Ligero: lightweight sublinear arguments without a trusted setup. In: CCS, pp. 2087–2104 (2017)
6. Attema, T., Cramer, R.: Compressed Σ-protocol theory and practical application to plug & play secure algorithmics. In: Micciancio, D., Ristenpart, T. (eds.) CRYPTO 2020. LNCS, vol. 12172, pp. 513–543. Springer, Cham (2020). https://doi.org/10.1007/978-3-030-56877-1_18
7. Attema, T., Cramer, R., Fehr, S.: Compressing proofs of k-out-of-n partial knowledge. In: Malkin, T., Peikert, C. (eds.) CRYPTO 2021. LNCS, vol. 12828, pp. 65–91 (2021, to appear)
8. Attema, T., Cramer, R., Xing, C.: A note on short invertible ring elements and applications to cyclotomic and trinomials number fields. Math. Cryptol. **1**, 45–70 (2021)
9. Baum, C., Bootle, J., Cerulli, A., del Pino, R., Groth, J., Lyubashevsky, V.: Sublinear lattice-based zero-knowledge arguments for arithmetic circuits. In: Shacham, H., Boldyreva, A. (eds.) CRYPTO 2018. LNCS, vol. 10992, pp. 669–699. Springer, Cham (2018). https://doi.org/10.1007/978-3-319-96881-0_23
10. Bellare, M., Impagliazzo, R., Naor, M.: Does parallel repetition lower the error in computationally sound protocols? In: FOCS, pp. 374–383 (1997)
11. Ben-Sasson, E., et al.: Computational integrity with a public random string from quasi-linear PCPs. In: Coron, J.-S., Nielsen, J.B. (eds.) EUROCRYPT 2017. LNCS, vol. 10212, pp. 551–579. Springer, Cham (2017). https://doi.org/10.1007/978-3-319-56617-7_19
12. Ben-Sasson, E., Chiesa, A., Riabzev, M., Spooner, N., Virza, M., Ward, N.P.: Aurora: transparent succinct arguments for R1CS. In: Ishai, Y., Rijmen, V. (eds.) EUROCRYPT 2019. LNCS, vol. 11476, pp. 103–128. Springer, Cham (2019). https://doi.org/10.1007/978-3-030-17653-2_4
13. Benhamouda, F., Camenisch, J., Krenn, S., Lyubashevsky, V., Neven, G.: Better zero-knowledge proofs for lattice encryption and their application to group signatures. In: Sarkar, P., Iwata, T. (eds.) ASIACRYPT 2014. LNCS, vol. 8873, pp. 551–572. Springer, Heidelberg (2014). https://doi.org/10.1007/978-3-662-45611-8_29
14. Bootle, J., Cerulli, A., Chaidos, P., Groth, J., Petit, C.: Efficient zero-knowledge arguments for arithmetic circuits in the discrete log setting. In: Fischlin, M., Coron, J.-S. (eds.) EUROCRYPT 2016. LNCS, vol. 9666, pp. 327–357. Springer, Heidelberg (2016). https://doi.org/10.1007/978-3-662-49896-5_12
15. Bootle, J., Lyubashevsky, V., Nguyen, N.K., Seiler, G.: A non-PCP approach to succinct quantum-safe zero-knowledge. In: Micciancio, D., Ristenpart, T. (eds.) CRYPTO 2020. LNCS, vol. 12171, pp. 441–469. Springer, Cham (2020). https://doi.org/10.1007/978-3-030-56880-1_16

16. Bünz, B., Bootle, J., Boneh, D., Poelstra, A., Wuille, P., Maxwell, G.: Bulletproofs: short proofs for confidential transactions and more. In: IEEE S&P, pp. 315–334 (2018)
17. Chen, M.-S., Hülsing, A., Rijneveld, J., Samardjiska, S., Schwabe, P.: From 5-Pass $\mathcal{MQ}$-based identification to $\mathcal{MQ}$-based signatures. In: Cheon, J.H., Takagi, T. (eds.) ASIACRYPT 2016. LNCS, vol. 10032, pp. 135–165. Springer, Heidelberg (2016). https://doi.org/10.1007/978-3-662-53890-6_5
18. Chung, K.-M., Liu, F.-H.: Parallel repetition theorems for interactive arguments. In: Micciancio, D. (ed.) TCC 2010. LNCS, vol. 5978, pp. 19–36. Springer, Heidelberg (2010). https://doi.org/10.1007/978-3-642-11799-2_2
19. Chung, K.-M., Pass, R.: Tight parallel repetition theorems for public-coin arguments using KL-divergence. In: Dodis, Y., Nielsen, J.B. (eds.) TCC 2015. LNCS, vol. 9015, pp. 229–246. Springer, Heidelberg (2015). https://doi.org/10.1007/978-3-662-46497-7_9
20. Cramer, R.: Modular design of secure yet practical cryptographic protocols. Ph.D. thesis, CWI and University of Amsterdam (1996)
21. del Pino, R., Lyubashevsky, V., Seiler, G.: Short discrete log proofs for FHE and ring-LWE ciphertexts. In: Lin, D., Sako, K. (eds.) PKC 2019. LNCS, vol. 11442, pp. 344–373. Springer, Cham (2019). https://doi.org/10.1007/978-3-030-17253-4_12
22. Dodis, Y., Jain, A., Moran, T., Wichs, D.: Counterexamples to hardness amplification beyond negligible. In: Cramer, R. (ed.) TCC 2012. LNCS, vol. 7194, pp. 476–493. Springer, Heidelberg (2012). https://doi.org/10.1007/978-3-642-28914-9_27
23. Don, J., Fehr, S., Majenz, C.: The measure-and-reprogram technique 2.0: multi-round Fiat-Shamir and more. In: Micciancio, D., Ristenpart, T. (eds.) CRYPTO 2020. LNCS, vol. 12172, pp. 602–631. Springer, Cham (2020). https://doi.org/10.1007/978-3-030-56877-1_21
24. Ducas, L., et al.: CRYSTALS-Dilithium: A lattice-based digital signature scheme. TCHES pp. 238–268 (2018)
25. Esgin, M.F., Steinfeld, R., Sakzad, A., Liu, J.K., Liu, D.: Short lattice-based one-out-of-many proofs and applications to ring signatures. In: Deng, R.H., Gauthier-Umaña, V., Ochoa, M., Yung, M. (eds.) ACNS 2019. LNCS, vol. 11464, pp. 67–88. Springer, Cham (2019). https://doi.org/10.1007/978-3-030-21568-2_4
26. Fiat, A., Shamir, A.: How to prove yourself: practical solutions to identification and signature problems. In: Odlyzko, A.M. (ed.) CRYPTO 1986. LNCS, vol. 263, pp. 186–194. Springer, Heidelberg (1987). https://doi.org/10.1007/3-540-47721-7_12
27. Goldreich, O.: Foundations of Cryptography: Basic Tools, vol. 1. Cambridge University Press, Cambridge (2001)
28. Håstad, J., Pass, R., Wikström, D., Pietrzak, K.: An efficient parallel repetition theorem. In: Micciancio, D. (ed.) TCC 2010. LNCS, vol. 5978, pp. 1–18. Springer, Heidelberg (2010). https://doi.org/10.1007/978-3-642-11799-2_1
29. Hazay, C., Lindell, Y.: Efficient Secure Two-Party Protocols - Techniques and Constructions. Springer, Information Security and Cryptography (2010)
30. Hoffmann, M., Klooß, M., Rupp, A.: Efficient zero-knowledge arguments in the discrete log setting, revisited. In: CCS, pp. 2093–2110 (2019)
31. Jaeger, J., Tessaro, S.: Expected-time cryptography: generic techniques and applications to concrete soundness. In: Pass, R., Pietrzak, K. (eds.) TCC 2020. LNCS, vol. 12552, pp. 414–443. Springer, Cham (2020). https://doi.org/10.1007/978-3-030-64381-2_15
32. Lang, S.: Algebra, Graduate Texts in Mathematics, vol. 211, 3rd edn. Springer, New York (2002). https://doi.org/10.1007/978-1-4613-0041-0

33. Langlois, A., Stehlé, D.: Worst-case to average-case reductions for module lattices. Des. Codes Cryptogr. **75**, 565–599 (2015)
34. Lindell, Y.: Parallel coin-tossing and constant-round secure two-party computation. J. Cyrptol. **16**, 143–184 (2003). https://doi.org/10.1007/s00145-002-0143-7
35. Lyubashevsky, V.: Fiat-Shamir with aborts: applications to lattice and factoring-based signatures. In: Matsui, M. (ed.) ASIACRYPT 2009. LNCS, vol. 5912, pp. 598–616. Springer, Heidelberg (2009). https://doi.org/10.1007/978-3-642-10366-7_35
36. Lyubashevsky, V.: Lattice signatures without trapdoors. In: Pointcheval, D., Johansson, T. (eds.) EUROCRYPT 2012. LNCS, vol. 7237, pp. 738–755. Springer, Heidelberg (2012). https://doi.org/10.1007/978-3-642-29011-4_43
37. Lyubashevsky, V., Seiler, G.: Short, invertible elements in partially splitting cyclotomic rings and applications to lattice-based zero-knowledge proofs. In: Nielsen, J.B., Rijmen, V. (eds.) EUROCRYPT 2018. LNCS, vol. 10820, pp. 204–224. Springer, Cham (2018). https://doi.org/10.1007/978-3-319-78381-9_8
38. Micciancio, D., Regev, O.: Lattice-based cryptography. In: Bernstein, D.J., Buchmann, J., Dahmen, E. (eds.) Post-Quantum Cryptography, pp. 147–191. Springer, Heidelberg (2009). https://doi.org/10.1007/978-3-540-88702-7_5
39. Pietrzak, K., Wikström, D.: Parallel repetition of computationally sound protocols revisited. In: Vadhan, S.P. (ed.) TCC 2007. LNCS, vol. 4392, pp. 86–102. Springer, Heidelberg (2007). https://doi.org/10.1007/978-3-540-70936-7_5
40. Schnorr, C.P.: Efficient identification and signatures for smart cards. In: Brassard, G. (ed.) CRYPTO 1989. LNCS, vol. 435, pp. 239–252. Springer, New York (1990). https://doi.org/10.1007/0-387-34805-0_22
41. Wikström, D.: Special soundness revisited. IACR ePrint 2018/1157

A New Simple Technique to Bootstrap Various Lattice Zero-Knowledge Proofs to QROM Secure NIZKs

Shuichi Katsumata[✉]

AIST, Tokyo, Japan
shuichi.katsumata@aist.go.jp

Abstract. Many of the recent advanced lattice-based Σ-/public-coin honest verifier (HVZK) interactive protocols based on the techniques developed by Lyubashevsky (Asiacrypt'09, Eurocrypt'12) can be transformed into a non-interactive zero-knowledge (NIZK) proof in the random oracle model (ROM) using the Fiat-Shamir transform. Unfortunately, although they are known to be secure in the *classical* ROM, existing proof techniques are incapable of proving them secure in the *quantum* ROM (QROM). Alternatively, while we could instead rely on the Unruh transform (Eurocrypt'15), the resulting QROM secure NIZK will incur a large overhead compared to the underlying interactive protocol.

In this paper, we present a new simple semi-generic transform that compiles many existing lattice-based Σ-/public-coin HVZK interactive protocols into QROM secure NIZKs. Our transform builds on a new primitive called *extractable linear homomorphic commitment* protocol. The resulting NIZK has several appealing features: it is not only a proof of knowledge but also straight-line extractable; the proof overhead is smaller compared to the Unruh transform; it enjoys a relatively small reduction loss; and it requires minimal background on quantum computation. To illustrate the generality of our technique, we show how to transform the recent Bootle et al.'s 5-round protocol with an exact sound proof (Crypto'19) into a QROM secure NIZK by increasing the proof size by a factor of 2.6. This compares favorably to the Unruh transform that requires a factor of more than 50.

1 Introduction

The Fiat-Shamir transform [17] is one of the most popular methods to construct non-interactive zero-knowledge (NIZK) proofs[1] in the random oracle model (ROM) based on a Σ-protocol (or more generally a public-coin honest-verifier zero-knowledge (HVZK) interactive protocol). Due to the ever-growing risk of quantum computers, understanding the *quantum* security of NIZKs in the *quantum* ROM [6] based on the Fiat-Shamir transform (or related transforms) have been considered to be an important research topic both in theory and practice.

---

[1] We may simply refer to NIZK proofs or NIZK proofs of knowledge as NIZKs when the distinction is not relevant.

© International Association for Cryptologic Research 2021
T. Malkin and C. Peikert (Eds.): CRYPTO 2021, LNCS 12826, pp. 580–610, 2021.
https://doi.org/10.1007/978-3-030-84245-1_20

However, although many techniques in the QROM have accumulated in the last decade, including but not limited to [6,7,13,14,23,25,32–34,37,38], our understanding of NIZKs in the QROM is still not as clear as those in the classical ROM. Notably, many of the recent lattice-based Σ-/public-coin HVZK interactive protocols, such as [1–3,8,15,35], based on the techniques developed by Lyubashevsky [27,28] fall into the following situations:

- they are not known to be (in)secure when applied the Fiat-Shamir transform in the QROM, and/or
- they can be transformed into a QROM secure NIZK using the Unruh transform [33] but incurs a large overhead, say at least ×50, compared to the underlying interactive protocol.

Considering that we can securely apply the Fiat-Shamir transform to these protocols in the classical ROM to obtain efficient NIZKs, the current state-of-the-affair is unsatisfactory. Below, we briefly recall NIZKs in the QROM.

QROM secure NIZKs. Broadly speaking, there are two breeds of transformation to obtain QROM secure NIZKs (that are a proof *of knowledge*) from a Σ-/public-coin HVZK interactive protocol. One is the Fiat-Shamir transform [17] and the other is the Unruh transform [33].

Recently, Don et al. [14] and Liu and Zhandry [25] showed how to argue security of the Fiat-Shamir transform in the QROM in two steps: they first showed that the Fiat-Shamir transform converts a standard Σ-protocol that is additionally a *quantum proof of knowledge* into an NIZK secure in the QROM, and then additionally showed how to construct a Σ-protocol that is a quantum proof of knowledge. Let us call such a Σ-protocol as a *quantum secure Σ-protocol*. It was shown in [25] (and partially in [14]) that Lyubashevsky's Σ-protocol for proving possession of a short vector $\mathbf{e}$ such that $\mathbf{Ae} = \mathbf{u}$ is quantum secure for appropriate parameters. Concretely, by increasing the parameters compared to those required by the classically secure protocol, they showed that Lyubashevsky's Σ-protocol has a "collapsing" property. However, such techniques for proving that a Σ-protocol is quantum secure are still limited and it seems non-trivial to generalize them to work for the recent more advanced lattice-based protocols. Moreover, these techniques that require rewinding quantum adversaries so far incur a large reduction loss of at least a factor Q^{4t-2}, where Q is the number of adversarial random oracle queries and t is the number of valid transcripts required to invoke special soundness of the underlying Σ-protocol. Since setting the parameters without taking these huge reduction losses into consideration sometimes lead to concrete attacks [22,24], having a tighter reduction is desirable.

On the other hand, Unruh [33] showed an elegant transform that converts any standard Σ-protocol into a QROM secure NIZK. The benefit of the Unruh transform is that it works for any Σ-protocol, the reduction loss is tight, and it is also *straight-line extractable*.[2] The last strong property guarantees that the witness from a proof can be extracted without rewinding the adversary and is

---

[2] This notion is also called *online* extractable in the literature.

especially suitable for applications requiring multiple concurrent executions of NIZKs such as group signatures [4] and anonymous attestations [9]. On the other hand, one of the main downsides is that it may incur a noticeable overhead in the proof size compared to the Fiat-Shamir transform since the transformation crucially relies on the challenge set being small. While the overhead can be reasonable when the underlying Σ-protocol already has a small challenge set, e.g., [10], it becomes prohibitively large as the challenge set grows. Recently, Chen et al. [11] extended the Unruh transform to work against a 5-round public-coin HVZK interactive protocol when restricting the second challenge to be *binary*.

Coming back to lattice-based ZK proofs. There are two main approaches in the current literature to construct lattice-based NIZKs. One builds on the Fiat-Shamir with abort paradigm developed by Lyubashevsky [27,28] and the other builds on Stern's protocol [21,31]. While the QROM security of the latter approach is well understood since it has a simple combinatorial "commit-and-open" structure [13,14], the QROM security of the former approach remains elusive. Notably, for the recent lattice-based protocols such as [1–3,8,15,35], we either still do not know how to apply the Fiat-Shamir transform and/or require to pay a huge overhead when adopting the Unruh transform to argue QROM security. Therefore, a natural question is:

> *Can we generically and more efficiently transform lattice-based Σ-/public-coin HVZKinteractive protocols based on the Fiat-Shamir with abort paradigm into QROM secure NIZKs?*

Ultimately, we would like the transform to achieve the best of the two known transforms: to maintain similar proof size and soundness error of the underlying Σ-protocol like the Fiat-Shamir transform [17], while also providing a tight reduction along with a straight-line extractor like the Unruh transform [33].

1.1   Our Contribution

In this work, we provide partial affirmative answers to the above problem. We present a new simple semi-generic transform that compiles many existing lattice-based Σ-/public-coin HVZK interactive protocols such as [1,3,8,15,35] into a QROM secure NIZK that is also straight-line (simulation) extractable [16]. The proof overhead is smaller compared to the Unruh transform and enjoys a relatively small reduction loss. In many cases, the reduction loss only scales linearly with t (i.e., number of valid transcripts to invoke special soundness), rather than exponentially (e.g., Q^{4t-2}) required by the Fiat-Shamir transform explained above. This is quite desirable since t can get quite large in recent advanced protocols; for instance [1] requires $t = 32$ in one of their settings, making the reduction loss as large as 2^{638} for a modest $Q = 2^{20}$.

As a concrete example, we show how to transform the recent Bootle et al.'s 5-round protocol with an exact sound proof [8] into a QROM secure NIZK by only increasing the proof size by a factor of 2.6.[3] This is in contrast to using the recent extended Unruh transform [11] [4], which increases the proof size by a larger factor of 51.8. Note that we are not aware of any method to securely apply the Fiat-Shamir transform to Bootle et al.'s protocol in the QROM. Finally, we highlight that not only our transform is very simple but the security proofs are also quite simple and involves a minimal amount of discussion regarding quantum computation.

Our contribution can be divided into the following steps. We only provide a high-level explanation of each step below and refer to Sect. 1.2 for a more detailed overview.

1. We first propose a new 3-round public-coin interactive protocol called *extractable linear-homomorphic commitment* (LinHC) protocol. (See Sect. 3)
2. We then show how to bootstrap a broad class of Σ-protocols into a Σ-protocol that is also a *quantum straight-line proof of knowledge* by using an extractable LinHC protocol. Here, we consider the class of Σ-protocols where the response (i.e., the prover's third message) is of the form $\mathbf{z} = \beta \cdot \mathbf{e} + \mathbf{r}$, where $\mathbf{e} \in \mathbb{Z}_q^m$ is the witness, β is the challenge sampled by the verifier, and $\mathbf{r} \in \mathbb{Z}_q^m$ is the masking term committed in the prover's first message.[5] (See Sect. 4.1)
3. We further show that we can apply the Fiat-Shamir transform to Σ-protocols with a quantum straight-line proof of knowledge to construct a QROM secure NIZK that is also straight-line extractable. (See Sect. 4.2)
4. We provide two simple constructions of lattice-based extractable LinHC protocols: one based on the module learning with errors (MLWE) problem, and the other based on the MLWE *and* the decisional small matrix ratio (DSMR) problem, where the latter is more efficient. Here the DSMR problem is a generalization of the decisional small polynomial ratio problem [26,30] defined over a module NTRU lattice [12]. (See Sect. 3.4)
5. Finally, we discuss how to apply extractable LinHC protocols to more advanced lattice-based public-coin HVZK interactive protocols. As a concrete example, we provide the details on how to make Bootle et al.'s 5-round protocol with an exact sound proof [8] into a QROM secure NIZK with concrete parameters. We chose this protocol since it is one of the more complex protocols that have appeared in the literature while still being relatively simple enough to fit in our framework. We show how the ideas can be used to obtain similar results for other protocols such as [1,3,15,35]. (See Sect. 5)

One notable difference between our transform and prior transforms that achieve straight-line extractable NIZKs either in the classical or post-quantum

---

[3] As a point of reference, the signature scheme Dilithium, a finalist to the NIST post-quantum standardization process based on the simple Lyubashevsky's Σ-protocol, requires to increase the sum of public key and signature size by a factor 3.2 to achieve QROM security [23].

[4] Since Bootle et al.'s protocol requires slightly more transcripts for special soundness compared to those considered in [11], the security proof of [11] may need to be modified to apply the transform to Bootle et al.'s protocol.

[5] Although we consider a slightly broader type of Σ-protocols in the main body, we keep the presentation simple here as the main idea generalizes easily.

setting (i.e., Fischlin [18] and Unruh [33]) is that ours do not put any restriction on the size of the challenge set of the underlying Σ-protocol. Therefore, if the underlying Σ-protocol has an exponentially large challenge set, we can use it directly to obtain an NIZK, thus circumventing an inefficient soundness amplification required by prior transforms. We note that our result does not contradict the impossibility result of Fischlin [18] who (roughly) showed that an NIZK in the ROM with a straight-line extractor that cannot program the random oracle requires a prover to query the random oracle on at least $\omega(\log \kappa)$ points to produce a proof, where κ is the security parameter. The main reason is that our NIZK requires the extractor to program the (Q)RO similar to the proof in the Fiat-Shamir transform. The difference between the Fiat-Shamir transform is that our extractor reprograms the (Q)RO in a way that it does not require to rewind the adversary to extract the witness.

Related works on Σ-protocols, NIZKs, and lattice-based ZK proofs and QROM secure signatures are provided in the full version.

1.2   Technical Overview

We provide an overview of each step explained in the above contribution.

Items 1 and 2: Extractable LinHCprotocols and integrating it to Σ-protocols. We use Lyubashevsky's Σ-protocol [27,28], which we denote by Σ_{Lyu}-protocol, as a leading example. It forms the basis of lattice-based zero-knowledge proofs based on the Fiat-Shamir with abort paradigm and the ideas presented below extend naturally to more advanced protocols.

Let $\mathbf{A} \in R_q^{n \times m}$ and $\mathbf{u} \in R_q^n$ be public, where R and R_q denote the rings $\mathbb{Z}[X]/(X^d+1)$ and $\mathbb{Z}_q[X]/(X^d+1)$. Then, the Σ_{Lyu}-protocol allows one to prove knowledge of a short vector $\mathbf{e} \in R^m$ satisfying $\mathbf{Ae} = \mathbf{u}$.[6] The prover first sends $\mathbf{w} = \mathbf{Ar}$ to the verifier where $\mathbf{r} \in R^m$ is a random short vector sampled from some specific distribution. The verifier returns a randomly sampled challenge $\beta \leftarrow \{0,1\}^d$, where β is viewed as an element over R by the standard coefficient embedding. Finally, the prover sends $\mathbf{z} = \beta \cdot \mathbf{e} + \mathbf{r}$ to the verifier. Here, it is standard to perform a rejection sampling step to make $\mathbf{z}$ statistically independent from $\mathbf{e}$. However, we ignore this subtle issue in the overview. Finally, the verifier accepts if $\mathbf{z}$ is short and $\mathbf{Az} = \beta \cdot \mathbf{u} + \mathbf{w}$ holds. It is known that the Σ_{Lyu}-protocol satisfies *relaxed* (rather than *exact*) special soundness: Given two valid transcripts of the form $(\mathbf{w}, \beta, \mathbf{z})$ and $(\mathbf{w}, \beta', \mathbf{z}')$ with $\beta \neq \beta'$, an extractor $\mathsf{Extract}_{\mathsf{ss}}$ outputs a witness $\mathbf{z}^* = \mathbf{z} - \mathbf{z}'$ such that $\mathbf{Az}^* = (\beta - \beta') \cdot \mathbf{u}$. Here, although $\mathbf{z}^*$ does not lie in the original relation, such proof of knowledge for a *relaxed* relation has proven to suffice in many applications.

Modifying the Σ_{Lyu}-protocol. Our idea to turn the Σ_{Lyu}-protocol to be a straight-line proof of knowledge is simple. Here, recall that to show a Σ-protocol is straight-line proof of knowledge, informally we need to construct an extractor SL-Extract that on input a single valid transcript (and some private information),

---

[6] All operations with elements over R_q are understood to be performed over mod q.

outputs a witness $\mathbf{z}^*$. As a first step, we let the prover commit to its witness $\mathbf{e}$ and randomness $\mathbf{r}$ by a *linear homomorphic* commitment scheme. The prover outputs $\mathbf{w} = \mathbf{A}\mathbf{r}$ as in the original protocol along with two commitments $\mathsf{com}_{\mathbf{e}} = \mathsf{Com}_{\mathsf{pk}}(\mathbf{e})[\delta_{\mathbf{e}}]$ and $\mathsf{com}_{\mathbf{r}} = \mathsf{Com}_{\mathsf{pk}}(\mathbf{r})[\delta_{\mathbf{r}}]$, where pk is a commitment key, and $\delta_{\mathbf{e}}$ and $\delta_{\mathbf{r}}$ are commitment randomness.[7] Then, given a random challenge β from the verifier, the prover returns $\mathbf{z} = \beta \cdot \mathbf{e} + \mathbf{r}$ *and* the commitment randomness $\delta_{\mathbf{z}} := \beta \cdot \delta_{\mathbf{e}} + \delta_{\mathbf{r}}$ as the third message. The verifier accepts if $\mathbf{z}$ is short; $\mathbf{A}\mathbf{z} = \beta \cdot \mathbf{u} + \mathbf{w}$ holds; *and* $\mathsf{Com}_{\mathsf{pk}}(\mathbf{z})[\delta_{\mathbf{z}}] = \beta \cdot \mathsf{com}_{\mathbf{e}} + \mathsf{com}_{\mathbf{r}}$ holds. Here, for correctness to hold, we require the commitment scheme to satisfy linear homomorphism also over the randomness, i.e., $\beta \cdot \mathsf{com}_{\mathbf{e}} + \mathsf{com}_{\mathbf{r}} = \mathsf{Com}_{\mathsf{pk}}(\beta \cdot \mathbf{e} + \mathbf{r})[\beta \cdot \delta_{\mathbf{e}} + \delta_{\mathbf{r}}]$ for any $\beta \in \{0,1\}^d \subset R$.

We first check our modified Σ_{Lyu}-protocol remains secure in the standard sense. Special soundness follows since two valid transcripts of the modified Σ_{Lyu}-protocol include two valid transcripts of the original Σ_{Lyu}-protocol. Next, assume $\delta_{\mathbf{z}}$ does not leak any information on the original commitment randomness $\delta_{\mathbf{e}}$ and $\delta_{\mathbf{r}}$. Then, (roughly) we can invoke the hiding property of the commitment scheme to argue that $\delta_{\mathbf{z}}$, $\mathsf{com}_{\mathbf{e}}$, and $\mathsf{com}_{\mathbf{r}}$ leak no information on $\mathbf{e}$ and $\mathbf{r}$ expect that they satisfy $\mathbf{z} = \beta \cdot \mathbf{e} + \mathbf{r}$. Therefore, since the Σ_{Lyu}-protocol is HVZK, so is our modified Σ_{Lyu}-protocol.

How to extract a witness. To show that it is a straight-line proof of knowledge, we enhance the linearly homomorphic commitment scheme to be *extractable*. Namely, we assume there exists an alternative key generation algorithm $\mathsf{SimKeyGen}$ that outputs a simulated commitment key pk^* with an associated trapdoor τ with the following properties: pk^* is indistinguishable from pk output by the honest key generation algorithm KeyGen, and there exists a commitment extractor $\mathsf{Extract}_{\mathsf{Com}}$ such that on input the trapdoor τ and an honestly generated commitment $\mathsf{com}_{\mathbf{x}} = \mathsf{Com}_{\mathsf{pk}^*}(\mathbf{x})[\delta_{\mathbf{x}}]$, outputs $\mathbf{x}$. Intuitively, it seems such an extractor $\mathsf{Extract}_{\mathsf{Com}}$ immediately implies a straight-line extractor $\mathsf{SL\text{-}Extract}$. On input a valid transcript $((\mathbf{w}, \mathsf{com}_{\mathbf{e}}, \mathsf{com}_{\mathbf{r}}), \beta, (\mathbf{z}, \delta_{\mathbf{z}}))$, $\mathsf{SL\text{-}Extract}$ just runs $\mathbf{e} \leftarrow \mathsf{Extract}_{\mathsf{Com}}(\tau, \mathsf{com}_{\mathbf{e}})$ to extract the witness $\mathbf{e}$. However, this intuition is clearly wrong since an adversary might have constructed a *malformed* commitment $\mathsf{com}_{\mathbf{e}}$ and $\mathsf{com}_{\mathbf{r}}$ that satisfies $\mathsf{Com}_{\mathsf{pk}^*}(\mathbf{z})[\delta_{\mathbf{z}}] = \beta \cdot \mathsf{com}_{\mathbf{e}} + \mathsf{com}_{\mathbf{r}}$. Notably, the only commitment $\mathsf{SL\text{-}Extract}$ sees that is guaranteed to be valid is $\beta \cdot \mathsf{com}_{\mathbf{e}} + \mathsf{com}_{\mathbf{r}}$ due to correctness. However, since $\mathsf{SL\text{-}Extract}$ already knows that this opens to $\mathbf{z}$, there seems to be no point using the trapdoor τ.

The main observation here is that since the adversary must prepare $\mathsf{com}_{\mathbf{e}}$ and $\mathsf{com}_{\mathbf{r}}$ *before* seeing the challenge β, there should be several other β's in $\{0,1\}^d$ that it would have been able to produce valid openings to. To make the discussion simple, we first assume the case where the challenge space of the Σ_{Lyu}-protocol is only of polynomial size and the existence of another valid commitment $\beta' \cdot \mathsf{com}_{\mathbf{e}} + \mathsf{com}_{\mathbf{r}}$ with $\beta' \neq \beta$ is guaranteed. Then, $\mathsf{SL\text{-}Extract}$ runs through all $\beta \in \{0,1\}^d$ and executes $\mathsf{Extract}_{\mathsf{Com}}(\tau, \beta \cdot \mathsf{com}_{\mathbf{e}} + \mathsf{com}_{\mathbf{r}})$ in polynomial time. Since $\beta' \cdot \mathsf{com}_{\mathbf{e}} + \mathsf{com}_{\mathbf{r}}$ is guaranteed to be a valid commitment, $\mathsf{Extract}_{\mathsf{Com}}$

---

[7] For any probabilistic algorithm $\mathcal{A}$, $\mathcal{A}(x)[\rho]$ denotes running $\mathcal{A}$ on input x with randomness ρ.

outputs the corresponding message $\mathbf{z}'$ committed to $\beta' \cdot \mathsf{com_e} + \mathsf{com_r}$. After finding such $\mathbf{z}'$, SL-Extract can invoke the special soundness extractor $\mathsf{Extract_{ss}}$ on input $(\mathbf{w}, \beta, \beta', \mathbf{z}, \mathbf{z}')$ to obtain a witness $\mathbf{z}^*$ for the (relaxed) relation. We can turn this rough idea into a formal proof by performing parallel repetition of the Σ_{Lyu}-protocol to amplify the soundness error to be negligible while noticing that SL-Extract still only needs to invoke $\mathsf{Extract_{Com}}$ a polynomial time. However, recall the goal was to extract without having to restrict the challenge space of the Σ_{Lyu}-protocol to be polynomial size as required by the Fischlin and Unruh transforms [18,33].[8]

Making the challenge set exponentially large. By slightly refining the above argument, we can make sure the above idea works even when the challenge set is exponentially large. Assume an adversary has a non-negligible probability ϵ in completing the Σ_{Lyu}-protocol with an honest verifier. Then conditioning on the adversary succeeding, a standard statistical argument shows that with probability at least $1/2$, the adversary must have been able to output a valid response for at least ϵ-fraction of the challenges. That is, there exists $2^d \cdot \epsilon$ other β's in $\{0,1\}^d$ that the adversary was able to output a valid third message $(\mathbf{z}, \delta_{\mathbf{z}})$. Therefore, we define the SL-Extract to execute $\mathsf{Extract_{Com}}(\tau, \beta \cdot \mathsf{com_e} + \mathsf{com_r})$ on roughly (κ/ϵ)-randomly chosen β's. Then, with probability at least $1 - 2^{-\kappa}$, SL-Extract finds the desired $\mathbf{z}'$ and the rest follows the same argument made above.

Since the above argument is purely statistical and agnostic to whether the adversary is classical or quantum, the resulting modified Σ_{Lyu}-protocol is by default a *quantum* straight-line proof of knowledge. In Sect. 3, we formalize the properties required by the underling commitment scheme and define it as a new interactive protocol called the *extractable linear homomorphic commitment* (LinHC) protocol. We note that the extractable LinHC protocol can be naturally plugged into multi-round public-coin HVZK interactive protocols with similar structures. Finally, an acute reader may have noticed that our resulting Σ-protocol is in the common reference string (CRS) model since it requires a commitment key pk. Although this is true in general, for our specific extractable LinHC protocol, the pk can be the output of the (Q)RO on any input of the prover's choice so the resulting Σ-protocol will *not* require any CRS.

Item 3: Applying the Fiat-Shamir transform in the QROM. A quantum straight-line extractable Σ-protocol is particularly quantum secure so we can appeal to recent techniques [14,25] to transform it into a QROM secure NIZK or a QROM secure signature. However, we can take advantage of the straight-line extractability of the Σ-protocol to provide simpler and tighter proofs. Recall one of the main reasons that made the proof of Fiat-Shamir transform in the QROM difficult when basing on standard Σ-protocols was that there was no easy way to extract a witness from a forged proof output by the adversary. Therefore, by using the straight-line extractor SL-Extract to extract from the forged proof, it seems we

---

[8] To be precise, [18] can use any Σ-protocol with an exponential challenge set size. Nevertheless, it still needs to rely on parallel repetition to amplify soundness since it can only use polynomially of the challenges in a meaningful way.

can overcome one of the most difficult obstacles. We outline the proof and explain some of the pitfalls. As commonly done in the literature, below we consider the proof for the deterministic signature scheme based on the Fiat-Shamir transform (which captures the essence of a simulation sound/extractable NIZK).[9]

Proof overview. The proof consists of two parts: first show that if the signature scheme is unforgeable against no-message attack (UF-NMA) secure, then it is secure in the standard sense, i.e., unforgeable against chosen message attack (UF-CMA) secure; next, show that if the relation used by the Σ-protocol is hard, then the signature scheme is UF-NMA secure. Here, recall UF-NMA considers the setting where an adversary is not allowed to make any signing queries.

Part 1: UF-NMA *to* UF-CMA. The first part of the proof follows closely to those given by Kiltz et al. [23] (which themselves follow [33,34]) who showed quantum security of a Fiat-Shamir transformed signature scheme basing on a special type of Σ-protocol (or more specifically a lossy identification protocol). The main observation is that by using the HVZK simulator of the Σ-protocol, we can make the proof *history-free* [6]. In particular, for each message M, we *deterministically* generate a transcript $(\mathbf{w}_M, \beta_M, \mathbf{z}_M)$ of the Σ-protocol using the HVZK simulator run on message-dependent randomness. Since the simulated transcript is determined uniquely by the message, we can program the random oracle H at the beginning of the game *before* invoking the adversary so that $H(\mathbf{w}\|M)$ outputs β_M if and only if $\mathbf{w} = \mathbf{w}_M$. Then, to answer a signature query, the simulator can output the already programmed simulated proof as the signature.

This high-level approach works for Kiltz et al. [23] without complications, however, we encountered a slight issue in our setting. The main difference is that while the Σ-protocol of Kiltz et al. satisfied statistical HVZK, ours is only computational HVZK. Concretely, for our specific instantiation of the extractable LinHC protocol based on the MLWE assumption, we informally need to argue that a superposition of the MLWE samples of the form $\sum_{\mathbf{s}_M, \mathbf{s}'_M} |\mathbf{B}\rangle |\mathbf{B} \cdot \mathbf{s}_M + \mathbf{s}'_M\rangle$, where $\mathbf{s}_M, \mathbf{s}'_M$ are random MLWE secrets, is indistinguishable from $\sum_{\mathbf{s}_M, \mathbf{s}'_M} |\mathbf{B}\rangle |\mathbf{b}_{\mathbf{s}_M, \mathbf{s}'_M}\rangle$, where $\mathbf{b}_{\mathbf{s}_M, \mathbf{s}'_M}$ is a random vector. Unfortunately, we were not able to reduce the standard MLWE assumption to such an assumption. Here, roughly, $\mathbf{B}$ corresponds to the commitment key of the extractable LinHC protocol and each $\mathbf{B} \cdot \mathbf{s}_M + \mathbf{s}'_M$ corresponds to the commitment.

To resolve this issue, we tweak the extractable LinHC protocol to use fresh commitment keys $\mathbf{B}_M$ for each message M and provide a slightly more general definition than what we laid out above. In particular, the extractable LinHC protocol we require to construct a QROM secure NIZK/signature needs to have a more general structure compared to those required to construct a Σ-protocol with a quantum proof of knowledge. In Sect. 3, the latter is referred to as the "simplified" definition. Here, if we only care about the classical setting, then this issue does not appear so we can always rely on the simplified definition for both cases.

---

[9] Note that considering deterministic signature schemes is w.l.o.g since we can always derandomize the signing algorithm using pseudorandom functions.

Part 2: Straight-line extractable Σ-protocol to UF-NMA. The remaining piece is to show that we can extract a witness from the forgery output by the adversary. The reduction is the same as before: provided a forgery, the extractor probes many challenges β randomly until $\mathsf{Extract_{Com}}(\tau, \beta \cdot \mathsf{com_e} + \mathsf{com_r})$ outputs a valid $\mathbf{z}$, where $\mathsf{com_e}$ and $\mathsf{com_r}$ are the commitments of the extractable LinHC protocol included in the adversary's forgery. The main difference is in the analysis of the success probability of such a procedure. Since β is generated as $\mathsf{H}(\cdots \|\mathsf{com_e}\|\mathsf{com_r})$ when applying the Fiat-Shamir transform, the adversary has some control over the β it uses. To make matters worse, it can make quantum queries to H to obtain a superposition of challenges $\sum_\beta \alpha_\beta |\beta\rangle$. Therefore, we can no longer rely on the simple statistical argument that relied on β being uniformly random. We will show how to upper bound the number of random sampling the extractor must perform before finding a "good" challenge β by using bounds on the generic quantum search problem [20,23,36].

Item 4: Constructing extractable LinHC protocols. It remains to show how to construct an extractable LinHC protocol based on lattices. The construction is a simple variant of the (dual) Regev public-key encryption scheme [19,29] that is known to be linearly homomorphic. The commitment key is two random matrices $\mathsf{pk} = (\mathbf{A}, \mathbf{B}) \in R_q^{m \times n} \times R_q^{m \times n}$ and commitments to the short vectors $(\mathbf{e}, \mathbf{r}) \in R_q^m \times R_q^m$ are defined as follows for $X \in \{\mathbf{e}, \mathbf{r}\}$:

$$\mathsf{com}_X := \big(p \cdot (\mathbf{A}\mathbf{s}_{X,1} + \mathbf{s}_{X,2}),\ p \cdot (\mathbf{B}\mathbf{s}_{X,1} + \mathbf{s}_{X,3}) + X\big),$$

where p is some odd integer coprime to q and the $\mathbf{s}$'s are commitment randomness sampled from an appropriate domain. Then, for any challenge $\beta \in \{0,1\}^d \subset R$, we can construct a commitment to $\mathbf{z} = \beta \cdot \mathbf{e} + \mathbf{r}$ by computing $\mathsf{com_z} = \beta \cdot \mathsf{com_e} + \mathsf{com_r}$, which is again of the form $\mathsf{com_z} = \big(p \cdot (\mathbf{A}\mathbf{s}_{\mathbf{z},1} + \mathbf{s}_{\mathbf{z},2}),\ p \cdot (\mathbf{B}\mathbf{s}_{\mathbf{z},1} + \mathbf{s}_{\mathbf{z},3}) + \mathbf{z}\big)$, where $\mathbf{s}_{\mathbf{z},i} = \beta \cdot \mathbf{s}_{\mathbf{e},i} + \mathbf{s}_{\mathbf{r},i}$ for $i \in [3]$. However, we cannot simply output the tuple $(\mathbf{s}_{\mathbf{z},i})_{i \in [3]}$ as the opening of $\mathsf{com_z}$ to the message $\mathbf{z}$ since $\mathbf{s}_{\mathbf{z},i}$ may leak information of $\mathbf{s}_{\mathbf{e},i}$ and $\mathbf{s}_{\mathbf{r},i}$. Instead, we use the rejection sampling technique [27,28] and sample each $\mathbf{s}_{\mathbf{r},i}$ for $i \in [3]$ from a slightly wider distribution compared to those of the $\mathbf{s}_{\mathbf{e},i}$'s and only output the tuple $(\mathbf{s}_{\mathbf{z},i})_{i \in [3]}$ with some fixed probability.[10] Effectively, the opening $(\mathbf{s}_{\mathbf{z},i})_{i \in [3]}$ are independent of the $\mathbf{s}_{\mathbf{e},i}$'s. At this point, we can argue $\mathsf{com_e}$ is indistinguishable from random by invoking the MLWE assumption. Moreover, since $\mathsf{com_r} = \mathsf{com_z} - \beta \cdot \mathsf{com_e}$, we conclude that we can simulate $\mathsf{com_r}$, $\mathsf{com_e}$, and $(\mathbf{s}_{\mathbf{z},i})_{i \in [3]}$ only using $\mathbf{z} = \beta \cdot \mathbf{e} + \mathbf{r}$. Finally, extractability follows by switching the commitment key pk to be the real public-key of the encryption scheme. We set $\mathsf{pk}^* = (\mathbf{A}, \mathbf{B})$, where $\mathbf{B} = \mathbf{D}_1 \mathbf{A} + \mathbf{D}_2$ for two matrices $\mathbf{D}_1$ and $\mathbf{D}_2$ with small entries. Then, for an appropriate set of parameters, given $\mathsf{com_z} = (\mathbf{t}_1, \mathbf{t}_2)$, we can decrypt it by $(\mathbf{t}_2 - \mathbf{D}_1 \mathbf{t}_1) \mod p = \mathbf{z}$.

Item 5: A concrete example. Finally, we provide a more interesting use-case for our extractable LinHC protocol other than the Lyubashevsky's Σ-protocol explained above. We consider the 5-round public-coin HVZK interactive protocol by Bootle et al. [8] that achieves *exact* special soundness. So far, we do not know

---

[10] We ignore in the overview the fact that our extractable LinHC protocol has non-negligible correctness error as it is standard in lattice-based Σ-protocols.

how to apply the Fiat-Shamir transform securely in the QROM to this protocol since unlike the Lyubashevsky's Σ-protocol, there is no natural notion of "collapsingness" [14, 25]. We can instead try applying the recent Unruh transform extended to 5-round protocols by Chen et al. [11] by limiting the second challenge used by the verifier to be binary. For completeness, we show in the full version that assuming the extended Unruh transform applies to Bootle et al.'s protocol, we incur a factor 51.8 blowup in the proof size. In Sect. 5, we show that our extractable LinHC works simply as a wrapper and bootstraps the original protocol of Bootle et al. to be quantum secure with an overhead of only a factor 2.6. We also discuss how the same ideas are applicable to other lattice-based protocols such as [1, 3, 15, 35]. As the main focus of this study is to introduce new theoretical tools and ideas to transform Σ-protocols into QROM secure NIZKs, we leave optimization and assessment of the concrete security of other lattice-based protocols as future work. Finally, we note that applying our extractable LinHC on Lyubashevsky's Σ-protocol does not result in a more efficient QROM secure signature scheme compared to the QROM secure Dilithium proposed in [23]. Roughly, this is because when viewed as an NIZK, ours achieve a stronger property: while [23] only achieves soundness, we also achieve (straight-line) proof of knowledge.

2 Preliminary

The notations we use in this paper and a minimal set of tools on quantum computation in provided in the full version.

2.1 Σ-Protocol

We use the standard notion of Σ-protocol in the *common reference string* model.[11] We note that it is standard in lattice-based protocols to consider *non-abort* honest-verifier zero-knowledge (naHVZK), where the ZK simulator is only required to simulate non-aborting transcripts. Due to page limitation, we refer the basic definitions to the full version and only provide the definition of *straight-line proof of knowledge* below.

Definition 2.1 (Straight-line proof of knowledge). *A Σ-protocol has a (quantum) ϵ_{IndO}-straight-line proof of knowledge (SL-PoK) if there exists a PPT simulator SimSetup and a PPT straight-line extractor SL-Extract with the following properties:*

- *For any QPT $\mathcal{A}$, the advantage $\mathsf{Adv}^{\mathsf{IndCRS}}(\mathcal{A})$ defined below is less than $\epsilon_{\mathsf{IndCRS}}$:*
  $\mathsf{Adv}^{\mathsf{IndCRS}}(\mathcal{A}) := |\Pr[\mathsf{crs} \leftarrow \mathsf{Setup}(1^\kappa) : \mathcal{A}(1^\kappa, \mathsf{crs}) \to 1] - \Pr[(\widetilde{\mathsf{crs}}, \tau) \leftarrow \mathsf{SimSetup}(1^\kappa) : \mathcal{A}(1^\kappa, \widetilde{\mathsf{crs}}) \to 1]|.$
- *For any QPT $\mathcal{A}$ and any $\mathsf{X} \in \mathcal{L}$ satisfying*

$$\Pr\left[\begin{array}{l} \mathsf{crs} \leftarrow \mathsf{Setup}(1^\kappa),\ (\alpha, \mathsf{st}) \leftarrow \mathcal{A}(\mathsf{crs}, \mathsf{X}) \\ \beta \leftarrow \mathsf{ChSet},\ \gamma \leftarrow \mathcal{A}(\mathsf{crs}, \mathsf{X}, \alpha, \beta, \mathsf{st}) \end{array} : \mathsf{Verify}(\mathsf{crs}, \mathsf{X}, (\alpha, \beta, \gamma)) = \top \right] \geq \epsilon,$$

---

[11] We define Σ-protocols in the CRS model for generality but emphasize that our concrete resulting Σ-protocols do not require them.

we have

$$\Pr \left[\begin{array}{cc} (\widetilde{\mathsf{crs}}, \tau) \leftarrow \mathsf{SimSetup}(1^\kappa) & \\ (\alpha, \mathsf{st}) \leftarrow \mathcal{A}(\widetilde{\mathsf{crs}}, \mathsf{X}), & \mathsf{Verify}(\widetilde{\mathsf{crs}}, \mathsf{X}, (\alpha, \beta, \gamma)) = \top \\ \beta \leftarrow \mathsf{ChSet} & : \mathsf{W} \leftarrow \mathsf{SL\text{-}Extract}(\tau, (\alpha, \beta, \gamma)) \\ \gamma \leftarrow \mathcal{A}(\widetilde{\mathsf{crs}}, \mathsf{X}, \alpha, \beta, \mathsf{st}) & (\mathsf{X}, \mathsf{W}) \in \mathcal{R}' \end{array} \right] \geq \frac{\epsilon - \nu_1}{p_1},$$

for some polynomial p_1 and negligible function ν_1. Moreover, the runtime of SL-Extract *is upper bounded by* $p_2 \cdot \left(\frac{\epsilon - \nu_2}{p_3} - \frac{1}{|\mathsf{ChSet}|} \right)^{-1}$ *for some polynomials p_2, p_3 and negligible function ν_2.[12] Concretely, if ϵ is non-negligible and* |ChSet| *is super-polynomially large, then* SL-Extract *runs in polynomial time.*

2.2   Lattices

Basic notations and well known tools for lattices are provided in the full version. We let S_η denote the set of all elements in $a \in R_q$ such that $\|w\|_\infty \leq \eta$. As with all Σ-protocols that rely on the Fiat-Shamir with abort technique, we use the rejection sampling technique [27, 28]. We denote the rejection sampling algorithm as Rej. To construct extractable LinHC protocols, we rely on a variant of the standard module learning with errors MLWE assumption, where the adversary is allowed to obtain a superposition of *independent* MLWE samples (which remains as hard as the standard MLWE assumption). We also consider the quantum accessible decisional small *matrix* ratio (DSMR) assumption, which is essentially the underlying hardness assumption of (module) NTRU.

3   Extractable Linear Homomorphic Commitment Protocol

In this section, we introduce a new interactive protocol called the *extractable linear homomorphic commitment* (LinHC) protocol. We first provide the definition of an extractable LinHC protocol and then give two instantiations: one from the MLWE assumption and the other from the MLWE *and* the DSMR assumption. Below whenever we say Σ-protocols, the readers may safely replace them by public-coin HVZK non-interactive protocols.

We first define extractable LinHC protocol in its most general form and provide a simplified variant in the subsequent section. As explained in the introduction, the general definition, which is defined in the QROM, is useful when directly constructing (straight-line simulation extractable) NIZKs[13] in the QROM from a possibly non-quantum secure Σ-protocol (see Sect. 4.2). In contrast, the simplified definition, which is defined in the standard model, is useful when constructing a quantum straight-line proof of knowledge Σ-protocol from a non-quantum secure Σ-protocol (see Sect. 4.1).

---

[12] In case the term inside $(\cdot)^{-1}$ is a non-positive, it is understood that SL-Extract simply outputs $\perp$ on invocation.

[13] Roughly, this is type of NIZK that, even after seeing many simulated proofs, whenever an adversary outputs a valid proof, we can straight-line extract a witness from the proof [16].

3.1   Definition

An illustration of the extractable LinHC protocol is provided in Fig. 1. Looking ahead, in the context of Σ-protocols, the $\mathbf{e}_i$'s and $\mathbf{r}$ correspond to the witness and commitment randomness (or masking term), respectively.

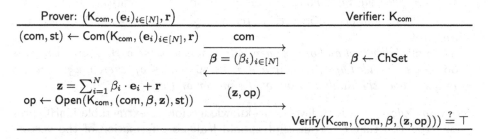

Fig. 1. An extractable linear homomorphic commitment protocol. $\mathsf{K}_{\mathsf{com}}$ is a commitment key generated by $\mathsf{KeyGen}^{\mathsf{H}}(1^\kappa)$, where H is modeled as a random oracle.

Definition 3.1 (Extractable linear homomorphic commitment protocol in QROM). *An* extractable linear homomorphic commitment *(LinHC) protocol is a three-round public-coin interactive protocol run between two parties (prover and verifier), and is defined by a tuple of PPT algorithms* $\Pi_{\mathsf{LinHC}} = (\mathsf{KeyGen}, \mathsf{Com}, \mathsf{Open}, \mathsf{Verify})$ *and a challenge set* $\mathsf{ChSet} \subseteq (R_q)^N$*. The protocol procedure is as follows:*

1. *A random oracle* H *is chosen and the* key generation *algorithm is executed* $\mathsf{K}_{\mathsf{com}} \leftarrow \mathsf{KeyGen}^{\mathsf{H}}(1^\kappa)$*. Here, let* $\{0,1\}^\nu$ *be the randomness space used by* KeyGen*;*
2. *The prover on input vectors* $((\mathbf{e}_i)_{i \in [N]}, \mathbf{r}) \in (R_q^m)^N \times R_q^m$*, runs the commitment algorithm* $(\mathsf{com}, \mathsf{st}) \leftarrow \mathsf{Com}(\mathsf{K}_{\mathsf{com}}, (\mathbf{e}_i)_{i \in [N]}, \mathbf{r})$*, and sends the first message* com *to the verifier;*
3. *The verifier samples a random challenge* $\boldsymbol{\beta} \leftarrow \mathsf{ChSet}$ *and sends the second message* $\boldsymbol{\beta}$ *to the prover;*
4. *The prover computes* $\mathbf{z} \leftarrow \sum_{i=1}^{N} \beta_i \cdot \mathbf{e}_i + \mathbf{r}^{14}$*, runs the opening algorithm* $\mathsf{op} \leftarrow \mathsf{Open}(\mathsf{K}_{\mathsf{com}}, (\mathsf{com}, \boldsymbol{\beta}, \mathbf{z}), \mathsf{st})$*, and sends the third message* $(\mathbf{z}, \mathsf{op})$ *to the verifier. We allow* $\mathsf{op} = \bot$ *for a special symbol* $\bot$ *to indicate failure;*
5. *The verifier returns the output of the* deterministic *verification algorithm* $\mathsf{Verify}(\mathsf{K}_{\mathsf{com}}, (\mathsf{com}, \boldsymbol{\beta}, (\mathbf{z}, \mathsf{op})))$*, where* $\top$ *indicates accept and* $\bot$ *indicates reject. We call* $(\mathsf{com}, \boldsymbol{\beta}, (\mathbf{z}, \mathsf{op}))$ *the transcript and call* $(\mathsf{com}, \boldsymbol{\beta}, \mathsf{op})$ *a valid opening for* $\mathbf{z}$ *if the verifier accepts.*

We require the following properties to hold.

---

[14] Although it suffices to consider $\mathbf{z} = \boldsymbol{\beta} \cdot \mathbf{e} + \mathbf{r}$ in many cases, there are recent protocols that require this extra level of generality, e.g., [15].

Definition 3.2 (Correctness). *An extractable linear homomorphic commitment protocol Π_{LinHC} has correctness error (δ_0, δ_1) if for any choice of random oracle H, $\mathsf{K_{com}} \in \mathsf{KeyGen}^\mathsf{H}(1^\kappa)$, and $((\mathbf{e}_i)_{i \in [N]}, \mathbf{r}) \in (R_q^m)^N \times R_q^m$ the following holds:*

- *We have $\Pr[\mathsf{Verify}(\mathsf{K_{com}}, (\mathsf{com}, \boldsymbol{\beta}, (\mathbf{z}, \mathsf{op}))) = \top] \geq 1 - \delta_1$, where the probability is taken over the randomness to sample $(\mathsf{com}, \mathsf{st}) \leftarrow \mathsf{Com}(\mathsf{K_{com}}, (\mathbf{e}_i)_{i \in [N]}, \mathbf{r})$, $\boldsymbol{\beta} \leftarrow \mathsf{ChSet}$, and $\mathsf{op} \leftarrow \mathsf{Open}(\mathsf{K_{com}}, (\mathsf{com}, \boldsymbol{\beta}, \sum_{i=1}^N \beta_i \cdot \mathbf{e}_i + \mathbf{r}), \mathsf{st})$ conditioned on $\mathsf{op} \neq \bot$.*
- *The probability that an honestly generated transcript $(\mathsf{com}, \boldsymbol{\beta}, (\mathbf{z}, \mathsf{op}))$ contains $\mathsf{op} = \bot$ is bounded by δ_1. In particular, $\Pr[\mathsf{op} = \bot] \leq \delta_1$ where the probability is taken over the random coins of the prover and verifier.*

Zero-knowledge. At a high level, zero-knowledge for an extractable LinHC protocol stipulates that the transcript should leak no information of the vectors $(\mathbf{e}_i)_{i \in [N]}$ and $\mathbf{r}$ other than the fact that it adds up to $\mathbf{z}$. Below, we provide a definition of zero-knowledge where an adversary can obtain superpositions of simulated proofs. Since $(\mathbf{e}_i)_{i \in [N]}$ corresponds to the witness of the underlying Σ-protocol, it will be reused many times. On the other hand, $\mathbf{r}$ is the commitment randomness that is freshly sampled for each transcript. This is reflected in the following definition by fixing $(\mathbf{e}_i)_{i \in [N]}$ and sampling fresh $\mathbf{r}$ (and challenge $\boldsymbol{\beta}$) using the distribution $D_{\boldsymbol{\beta}, \mathbf{r}}$. Also, one can think of each ρ in the definition as a specific tag to distinguish each transcripts. Below, we say it is "semi"-honest-verifier since $\boldsymbol{\beta}$ does not necessarily need to be uniformly distributed over ChSet.

Definition 3.3 (Quantum accessible no-abort (semi-)honest-verifier zero-knowledge). *Let $D_{\boldsymbol{\beta}, \mathbf{r}}$ be any distribution over $\mathsf{ChSet} \times R_q^m$. For an oracle H and algorithm ZKSim, define the following algorithms:*

- *$D_{\mathsf{trans}}^{\not{\cdot}}(\rho, (\mathbf{e}_i)_{i \in [N]})$: On input $\rho \in \{0,1\}^\nu$ and $(\mathbf{e}_i)_{i \in [N]} \in (R_q^m)^N$, generate $\mathsf{K_{com}} \leftarrow \mathsf{KeyGen}^\mathsf{H}(1^\kappa)[\rho]$ and sample $(\boldsymbol{\beta}, \mathbf{r}) \leftarrow D_{\boldsymbol{\beta}, \mathbf{r}}$. Then run an honest protocol with prover input $(\mathsf{K_{com}}, ((\mathbf{e}_i)_{i \in [N]}, \mathbf{r}))$ conditioned on the verifier message being $\boldsymbol{\beta}$ and $\mathsf{op} \neq \bot$ (i.e., a non-aborting protocol). Finally, output $\mathbf{r}$ along with the valid transcript $(\mathbf{r}, \mathsf{trans} = (\mathsf{com}, \boldsymbol{\beta}, (\mathbf{z}, \mathsf{op})))$.*
- *$D_{\mathsf{sim}}(\rho, (\mathbf{e}_i)_{i \in [N]})$: On input $\rho \in \{0,1\}^\nu$ and $(\mathbf{e}_i)_{i \in [N]} \in (R_q^m)^N$, generate $\mathsf{K_{com}} \leftarrow \mathsf{KeyGen}^\mathsf{H}(1^\kappa)[\rho]$, sample $(\boldsymbol{\beta}, \mathbf{r}) \leftarrow D_{\boldsymbol{\beta}, \mathbf{r}}$, and compute $\mathbf{z} \leftarrow \sum_{i=1}^N \beta_i \cdot \mathbf{e}_i + \mathbf{r}$. Then, run $(\mathsf{com}, \mathsf{op}) \leftarrow \mathsf{ZKSim}(\mathsf{K_{com}}, \boldsymbol{\beta}, \mathbf{z})$ and output $(\mathbf{r}, \mathsf{trans} = (\mathsf{com}, \boldsymbol{\beta}, (\mathbf{z}, \mathsf{op})))$.*

In above, we assume $D_{\mathsf{trans}}^{\not{\cdot}}$ and D_{sim} run on a uniform and independent randomness for each input $\rho \in \{0,1\}^\nu$ and reuse the same randomness when run again on the same ρ.

    Then, we say an extractable linear homomorphic commitment protocol Π_{LinHC} has ϵ_{zk}-quantum accessible no-abort (semi-)honest-verifier zero-knowledge, if there exists a PPT algorithm ZKSim such that for any $(\mathbf{e}_i)_{i \in [N]} \in (R_q^m)^N$, distribution $D_{\boldsymbol{\beta}, \mathbf{r}}$, and QPT $\mathcal{A}$, the advantage $\mathsf{Adv}^{\mathsf{QAnaHVZK}}(\mathcal{A})$ defined below is less than ϵ_{zk}:

$$\left| \Pr\left[\mathcal{A}^{|\mathsf{H}\rangle, |D_{\mathsf{trans}}^{\mathcal{L}}(\cdot, (\mathbf{e}_i)_{i \in [N]})\rangle}(1^\kappa) \to 1 \right] - \Pr\left[\mathcal{A}^{|\mathsf{H}\rangle, |D_{\mathsf{sim}}(\cdot, (\mathbf{e}_i)_{i \in [N]})\rangle}(1^\kappa) \to 1 \right] \right|,$$

where the probability is also taken over the random choice of the random oracle H.

Extractability. When considering extractable LinHC protocol as a tool to be integrated into a preexisting Σ-protocol, the third message $\mathbf{z}$ corresponds to the third message (usually referred to as the "response") of the Σ-protocol. See Fig. 4 for an illustrative example. In particular, the verifier will always perform an additional check $f(\boldsymbol{\beta}, \mathbf{z}) \stackrel{?}{=} \top$, where f is some function defined by the verifier algorithm of the underlying Σ-protocol. Therefore, for an extractable LinHC to be useful in the context of Σ protocols, we want it to be able to extract valid tuples $\{(\boldsymbol{\beta}_i, \mathbf{z}_i)\}_{i \in [k]}$ such that $f(\boldsymbol{\beta}_i, \mathbf{z}_i) = \top$ *without* rewinding the adversary only given an accepting transcript. After such k tuples are collected, we can invoke the k-special soundness extractor of the underlying Σ-protocol to extract a witness. More formally, we require the following.

Definition 3.4 ($\mathcal{F}$-Almost straight-line extractable). *Let $\mathcal{X}$ and $\mathcal{Y}$ be the input and output space required by the random oracle* H. *An extractable linear homomorphic commitment protocol* Π_{LinHC} *is* ϵ_{IndO}-$\mathcal{F}$-*almost straight-line extractable for a function family* $\mathcal{F}$ *if there exists PPT algorithms* SimOracle *and* LinCExtract *with the following properties:*

1. *For any QPT* $\mathcal{A}$, *the advantage* $\mathsf{Adv}^{\mathsf{IndO}}(\mathcal{A})$ *defined below is less than* ϵ_{IndO}:

$$\left| \Pr[\mathsf{H} \leftarrow \mathsf{Func}(\mathcal{X}, \mathcal{Y}) : \mathcal{A}^{|\mathsf{H}\rangle}(1^\kappa) \to 1] - \Pr[(\widetilde{\mathsf{H}}, \tau) \leftarrow \mathsf{SimOracle}(1^\kappa) : \mathcal{A}^{|\widetilde{\mathsf{H}}\rangle}(1^\kappa) \to 1] \right|.$$

2. *For any* $(\widetilde{\mathsf{H}}, \tau) \in \mathsf{SimOracle}(1^\kappa)$, *randomness* $\rho \in \{0,1\}^\nu$, *first message* com, *and any efficiently computable function* $f \in \mathcal{F}$ *with binary output* $\{\top, \bot\}$, *define the set* $S_f(\rho, \mathsf{com})$ *as*

$$\{\boldsymbol{\beta} \mid \exists (\mathbf{z}, \mathsf{op}) \ s.t. \ \mathsf{Verify}(\mathsf{K}_{\mathsf{com}}, (\mathsf{com}, \boldsymbol{\beta}, (\mathbf{z}, \mathsf{op}))) = \top \ \wedge \ f(\boldsymbol{\beta}, \mathbf{z}) = \top\},$$

where $\mathsf{K}_{\mathsf{com}} = \mathsf{KeyGen}^{\widetilde{\mathsf{H}}}(1^\kappa)[\rho]$. *Let* δ, k *be any positive integers such that* $k < |S_f(\rho, \mathsf{com})|$, *and denote* $T^* = \frac{k \cdot \delta \cdot |\mathsf{ChSet}|}{|S_f(\rho, \mathsf{com})| - k}$. *Then, on input a valid transcript* $\mathsf{trans} = (\mathsf{com}, \boldsymbol{\beta}, (\mathbf{z}, \mathsf{op}))$, *the linear commitment extractor* $\mathsf{LinCExtract}(\tau, \rho, \mathsf{trans})$ *outputs either a set* $L = \{(\boldsymbol{\beta}_j, \mathbf{z}_j)\}_{j \in [k]}$ *or* $\bot$ *in time* $T^* \cdot \mathsf{poly}(\kappa)$ *for some fixed polynomial* $\mathsf{poly}(\kappa)$, *where all the* $\boldsymbol{\beta}_j$'s *in* L *are pairwise distinct and satisfies* $f(\boldsymbol{\beta}_j, \mathbf{z}_j) = \top$. *Moreover, the probability that it outputs* L *is at least* $1 - k \cdot 2^{-\delta}$. *Concretely, when* k *is a constant,* $\delta = \kappa$, *and* $|S_f(\rho, \mathsf{com})| = |\mathsf{ChSet}| \cdot \epsilon$ *for a non-negligible* ϵ, *then* $\mathsf{LinCExtract}$ *outputs* L *in polynomial time with overwhelming probability.*

In general we cannot efficiently check if the extracted $\boldsymbol{\beta}_j$ satisfies $\boldsymbol{\beta}_j \in S_f(\rho, \mathsf{com})$ since we cannot extract op_j corresponding to $(\boldsymbol{\beta}_j, \mathbf{z}_j)$, hence the term "almost" straight-line extractable. This implies that the set L may include an invalid $(\beta_j, \mathbf{z}_j)$ for which there does not exist a valid op_j. However, this will not be an issue for most of our application where f defines the entire verification algorithm of the underlying Σ-protocol. In these cases, we only need $f(\beta_j, \mathbf{z}_j) = \top$ for k-tuples to hold to invoke the k-special soundness extractor. We also point out that in many cases we are not able to efficiently compute the cardinality of the set $S_f(\rho, \mathsf{com})$ so we do not know if $\mathsf{LinCExtract}$ runs in polynomial time. However, in typical applications, we can deduce that $S_f(\rho, \mathsf{com})$ must be of size $|\mathsf{ChSet}| \cdot \epsilon$ for a non-negligible ϵ unless the adversary breaks some other intractable problem.

Optional. Finally, we consider two optional properties for $\mathcal{F}$-almost straight-line extractability that help simplify the proofs in some cases. The first property is useful when the underlying public-coin HVZK interactive protocol already uses a small (i.e., poly-large) challenge set. These shows up in multi-round protocols where the verifier may sample randomness from different challenge sets in each round. (See Sect. 5 for an example.) The second property allows to argue that for each challenge $\beta \in \mathsf{ChSet}$, there exist at most one response $\mathbf{z}$ that passes the verification. Due to page limitation, we omit the details to the full version.

3.2 Simplified Definition of Extractable LinHC

In case the goal is to construct quantum secure Σ-protocols (and not a QROM secure simulation extractable NIZK or a signature), we can use a simplified definition of extractable LinHC protocols in the standard model. One of the main simplification comes from the fact that since all of the security notions are decoupled from the QRO, the proofs follow much like the classical counterparts. For example, zero-knowledge of a simplified extractable LinHC protocol is defined similarly to standard naHVZK of a Σ-protocol. We omit the details to the full version.

3.3 Interlude: Extractable LinHC Specialized for Lattices

In most, if not all, lattice-based Σ-protocols, the witness being proven is a "short" vector. Therefore, throughout this work, we assume such shortness condition holds by default and integrate it into the definition of the extractable LinHC protocol. Effectively, we are able to construct a more efficient extractable LinHC protocol by taking advantage of these bounds.

Norm bound on $(\mathbf{e}_i)_{i \in [N]}$ and $\mathbf{r}$. In the following, we assume the size of the vectors $(\mathbf{e}_i)_{i \in [N]}$ and $\mathbf{r}$ in R_q^m have an upper bound. That is, for all $i \in [N]$, there exist positive integers $B_{\infty,\mathbf{e}}, B_{2,\mathbf{e}}, B_{\infty,\mathbf{r}}$, and $B_{2,\mathbf{r}}$ such that $\|\mathbf{e}_i\|_\infty \leq B_{\infty,\mathbf{e}_i}$, $\|\mathbf{e}_i\|_2 \leq B_{2,\mathbf{e}_i}$, $\|\mathbf{r}\|_\infty \leq B_{\infty,\mathbf{r}}$ and $\|\mathbf{r}\|_2 \leq B_{2,\mathbf{r}}$. In particular, we only guarantee correctness and naHVZK for such $\mathbf{e}_i$'s and $\mathbf{r}$.

Restricting the function class $\mathcal{F}$ to check norm bound. As explained in the previous section, the function class $\mathcal{F}$ of $\mathcal{F}$-almost straight-line extractability (Definition 3.4) corresponds to the the check performed by the verifier of the underlying Σ-protocol, which we are trying to make secure in the (Q)ROM via extractable LinHC. Namely, the verifier of the Σ-protocol receives $\mathbf{z}$ from the prover and then checks whether some condition $f \in \mathcal{F}$ holds with respect to the challenge $\boldsymbol{\beta}$ it sampled, i.e., $f(\boldsymbol{\beta}, \mathbf{z}) \overset{?}{=} \top$. In any lattice-based Σ-protocol, one of the conditions that is always checked by the verifier is whether $\mathbf{z}$ is "small" (see Sect. 4.1 for a concrete example). We therefore restrict the function class $\mathcal{F}$ to be a family of functions $\mathcal{F}_B$ such that for any $f \in \mathcal{F}_B$, f includes the check $\|\mathbf{z}\|_2 \leq B$. [15] In many lattice-based Σ-protocols, we have $B \approx B_{\infty,\mathbf{r}}$ or $B_{2,\mathbf{r}}$, where recall $\mathbf{r}$ is the "masking" term to hide $(\mathbf{e}_i)_{i \in [N]}$.

3.4 Construction of Extractable LinHC

We propose two constructions of extractable LinHC protocols: one based only on MLWE and the other based on MLWE *and* DSMR. Since the two constructions are almost identical, we explain the former and refer the details on the latter to the full version. The latter has proof size half of the former while relying on the extra DSMR assumption. The construction of our first extractable LinHC protocol based on MLWE is provided in Fig. 2.

$\text{KeyGen}^{\text{H}}(1^\kappa)$

1: $\rho \leftarrow \{0,1\}^\nu$
2: $(\mathbf{A}, \mathbf{B}) \leftarrow \mathsf{H}(\rho)$
3: **return** $\mathsf{K}_{\text{com}} := (\mathbf{A}, \mathbf{B}) \in R_q^{m \times n} \times R_q^{m \times n}$

$\text{Com}(\mathsf{K}_{\text{com}}, (\mathbf{e}_i)_{i \in [N]}, \mathbf{r})$

1: **for** $i \in [N]$ **do**
2: $\quad (\mathbf{s}_{i,1}, \mathbf{s}_{i,2}, \mathbf{s}_{i,3}) \leftarrow S_\eta^n \times S_\eta^m \times S_\eta^m$
3: $\quad \mathbf{t}_{i,1} \leftarrow p \cdot (\mathbf{A}\mathbf{s}_{i,1} + \mathbf{s}_{i,2})$
4: $\quad \mathbf{t}_{i,2} \leftarrow p \cdot (\mathbf{B}\mathbf{s}_{i,1} + \mathbf{s}_{i,3}) + \mathbf{e}_i$
5: $(\mathbf{y}_1, \mathbf{y}_2, \mathbf{y}_3) \leftarrow D_{\phi \cdot T}^n \times D_{\phi \cdot T}^m \times D_{\phi \cdot T}^m$
6: $\mathbf{w}_1 \leftarrow p \cdot (\mathbf{A}\mathbf{y}_1 + \mathbf{y}_2)$
7: $\mathbf{w}_2 \leftarrow p \cdot (\mathbf{B}\mathbf{y}_1 + \mathbf{y}_3) + \mathbf{r}$
8: $\text{com} := \left((\mathbf{t}_{i,1}, \mathbf{t}_{i,2})_{i \in [N]}, \mathbf{w}_1, \mathbf{w}_2 \right)$
9: $\text{st} := \left((\mathbf{s}_{i,1}.\mathbf{s}_{i,2}, \mathbf{s}_{i,3})_{i \in [N]}, \mathbf{y}_1, \mathbf{y}_2, \mathbf{y}_3 \right)$
10: **return** (com, st)

$\text{Open}(\mathsf{K}_{\text{com}}, (\text{com}, \boldsymbol{\beta}, \mathbf{z}), \text{st}))$

1: $(\beta_1, \cdots, \beta_N) \leftarrow \boldsymbol{\beta}$
2: **for** $\ell \in \{1, 2, 3\}$ **do**
3: $\quad \bar{\mathbf{s}}_\ell \leftarrow \sum_{i=1}^N \beta_i \cdot \mathbf{s}_{i,\ell}$
4: $\quad \mathbf{z}_\ell \leftarrow \bar{\mathbf{s}}_\ell + \mathbf{y}_\ell$
5: $b \leftarrow \text{Rej}([\mathbf{z}_1\|\mathbf{z}_2\|\mathbf{z}_3], [\bar{\mathbf{s}}_1\|\bar{\mathbf{s}}_2\|\bar{\mathbf{s}}_3], \phi, T, \text{err})$
6: **if** $b = \bot$ **then return** $\text{op} := \bot$
7: **else return** $\text{op} := [\mathbf{z}_1\|\mathbf{z}_2\|\mathbf{z}_3]$

$\text{Verify}(\mathsf{K}_{\text{com}}, (\text{com}, \boldsymbol{\beta}, (\mathbf{z}, \text{op} \neq \bot)))$

1: $(\beta_1, \cdots, \beta_N) \leftarrow \boldsymbol{\beta}$
2: $\left(\mathbf{z}_{\mathbf{r}}, (\mathbf{t}_{i,1}.\mathbf{t}_{i,2})_{i \in [N]}, \mathbf{w}_1, \mathbf{w}_2 \right) \leftarrow \text{com}$
3: $[\mathbf{z}_1\|\mathbf{z}_2\|\mathbf{z}_3] \leftarrow \text{op}$
4: **for** $\ell \in \{1, 2, 3\}$ **do**
5: $\quad$ **if** $\|\mathbf{z}_\ell\|_2 > \sqrt{2nd} \cdot \phi \cdot T$ **then re-**
$\quad$ turn $\bot$
6: $\mathbf{z}_{\mathbf{A}} \leftarrow \sum_{i=1}^N \beta_i \cdot \mathbf{t}_{i,1} + \mathbf{w}_1 - p \cdot (\mathbf{A}\mathbf{z}_1 + \mathbf{z}_2)$
7: $\mathbf{z}_{\mathbf{B}} \leftarrow \sum_{i=1}^N \beta_i \cdot \mathbf{t}_{i,2} + \mathbf{w}_2 - p \cdot (\mathbf{B}\mathbf{z}_1 + \mathbf{z}_3)$
8: **if** $\mathbf{z}_{\mathbf{A}} \neq \mathbf{0} \vee \mathbf{z} \neq \mathbf{z}_{\mathbf{B}}$ **then return** $\bot$
9: **else return** $\top$

Fig. 2. An extractable LinHC protocol based on MLWE.

---

[15] The choice of the Euclidean norm is arbitral and we can also chose the infinity norm (or include both norms).

Parameters and asymptotic size. Let the dimension d of the ring R_q be larger than 256 and n, m be positive integers such that $n \leq m$,[16] $p < q$ be coprime odd integers, η a positive real, and H be a random oracle with domain $\{0,1\}^\nu$ and range $R_q^{m \times n} \times R_q^{m \times n}$. The concrete value of ν is specific to the underlying Σ-protocol being used. Let T, ϕ, and err be parameters required by the rejection sampling algorithm, where we set $T = \eta \cdot \sum_{i=1}^{N} \|\beta_i\|_\infty \cdot \sqrt{(n+2m)d}$.

The size of the first message com is $2md(N+1)\log q$ and the third message op is $(n+2m)d \cdot \log(10\phi T)$. Looking ahead, when we make the protocol non-interactive via the Fiat-Shamir transform, we can send the challenge β instead of $(\mathbf{w}_1, \mathbf{w}_2)$ since the latter can be recovered from the other components and β. Then, the total size becomes $2mdN \log q + (n+2m)d \cdot \log(10\phi T) + |\mathsf{ChSet}|$.

Properties. Due to page limitation, we omit the details of the proof of correctness and the quantum accessible non-abort HVZK (QAnaHVZK) to the full version. We note that for QAnaHVZK, we rely on the *quantum accessible* MLWE assumption.

$\widetilde{\mathsf{H}}(\rho)$
1: $(\rho_1, \rho_2, \rho_3) \leftarrow \mathsf{PRF}(\mathsf{K}, \rho)$
2: $\mathbf{A} \leftarrow R_q^{m \times n}[\rho_1]$
3: $(\mathbf{D}_1, \mathbf{D}_2) \leftarrow S_\eta^{m \times m}[\rho_2] \times S_\eta^{m \times n}[\rho_3]$
4: $\mathbf{B} \leftarrow \mathbf{D}_1 \mathbf{A} + \mathbf{D}_2$
5: **return** $(\mathbf{A}, \mathbf{B})$

$\mathsf{SimOracle}(1^\kappa)$
1: $\mathsf{K} \leftarrow \mathcal{K}$ ▷ Sample PRF key
2: **return** $(\widetilde{\mathsf{H}}, \tau := \mathsf{K})$

$\mathsf{LinCExtract}(\tau = \mathsf{K}, \rho, \mathsf{trans} = (\mathsf{com}, \beta, (\mathbf{z}, \mathsf{op})))$
1: $(\rho_1, \rho_2, \rho_3) \leftarrow \mathsf{PRF}(\mathsf{K}, \rho)$
2: $\mathbf{D}_1 \leftarrow S_\eta^{m \times m}[\rho_2]$
3: $\left((\mathbf{t}_{i,1}.\mathbf{t}_{i,2})_{i \in [N]}, \mathbf{w}_1, \mathbf{w}_2\right) \leftarrow \mathsf{com}$
4: $(\beta_1, \cdots, \beta_N) \leftarrow \beta$
5: $(c, L) \leftarrow (0, (\beta, \mathbf{z}))$
6: **while** $|L| \leq k \vee c \leq T^*$ **do**
7:     $\widetilde{\beta} = (\widetilde{\beta}_1, \cdots, \widetilde{\beta}_N) \leftarrow \mathsf{ChSet} \setminus L_\beta$
8:     $\widetilde{\mathbf{z}} \leftarrow \left(\sum_{i=1}^{N} \widetilde{\beta}_i \cdot \mathbf{t}_{i,2} + \mathbf{w}_2\right)$
            $-\mathbf{D}_1\left(\sum_{i=1}^{N} \widetilde{\beta}_i \cdot \mathbf{t}_{i,1} + \mathbf{w}_1\right) \mod p$
10:     **if** $f(\widetilde{\beta}, \widetilde{\mathbf{z}}) = \top$ **then** $L \leftarrow L \cup \{(\widetilde{\beta}, \widetilde{\mathbf{z}})\}$
11:     $c \leftarrow c+1$
12: **if** $|L| < k$ **then return** $\perp$
13: **else return** L

Fig. 3. Description of SimOracle, $\widetilde{\mathsf{H}}$, and LinCExtract for the extractable LinHC protocol in Fig. 2. Here the PRF key K is assumed to be hardwired to $\widetilde{\mathsf{H}}$ and denote L_β as the set $\{\beta \mid (\beta, \mathbf{z}) \in L\}$.

Lemma 3.1 ($\mathcal{F}_B$-Almost straight-line extractable). *Assume* $B \geq \sqrt{2nd} \cdot \phi \cdot T$, $2\sqrt{2}p(nd\eta + \sqrt{nm}d\eta + \sqrt{nd})\phi T + 2B < q/2$, *and* $B \leq (p-1)/4$. *Define the oracle simulator* SimOracle *and linear commitment extractor* LinCExtract *as in Fig. 3, where* T^* *in Line 6 of algorithm* LinCExtract *is* $T^* = \frac{k \cdot \delta \cdot |\mathsf{ChSet}|}{|S_f(\rho, \mathsf{com})| - k}$. *Then,*

---

[16] d could be set arbitrarily as long as the underling hardness assumptions (MLWE and DSMR) hold. We consider a lower bound of 256 to make it easier to provide concrete bounds on the properties of extractable LinHC.

the extractable LinHC *protocol in Fig. 2 is* $\mathcal{F}_B$*-almost straight-line extractable.*
Moreover, for any QPT adversary $\mathcal{A}$ *that distinguishes between a random* H *and*
$\widetilde{H}$ *output by* SimOracle *making at most* Q *queries, there exists a QPT adversary*
$\mathcal{B}_1$ *against the quantum accessible* MLWE$_{m,n,2^\nu,Q,\eta}$ *problem and a QPT adversary*
$\mathcal{B}_2$ *against the quantum accessible* PRF *such that*

$$\mathsf{Adv}^{\mathsf{IndO}}(\mathcal{A}) \le m \cdot \mathsf{Adv}^{\mathsf{qaMLWE}_{m,n,2^\nu,Q,\eta}}(\mathcal{B}_1) + \mathsf{Adv}^{\mathsf{qaPRF}}(\mathcal{B}_2),$$

where $\mathsf{Time}(\mathcal{A}) = \mathsf{Time}(\mathcal{B}_1) \approx \mathsf{Time}(\mathcal{B}_2)$.

Proof We only prove Item 2 below and refer the others to the full version.

Item 2. Fix any $(\widetilde{H}, \tau = K)$, randomness $\rho \in \{0,1\}^\nu$, first message com $=$
$((\mathbf{t}_{i,1}, \mathbf{t}_{i,2})_{i \in [N]}, \mathbf{w}_1, \mathbf{w}_2)$, and any function $f \in \mathcal{F}_B$. Moreover, let trans $=$
$(\mathsf{com}, \beta, (\mathbf{z}, \mathsf{op}))$ be a valid transcript. We first show that conditioned on $\widetilde{\beta} \in$
$S_f(\rho, \mathsf{com}) \backslash \{\beta\} \subset \mathsf{ChSet}$ being sampled in Line 7, LinCExtract$(\tau, \rho, \mathsf{trans})$ always
succeeds in outputting a valid $\widetilde{\mathbf{z}}$ such that $f(\widetilde{\beta}, \widetilde{\mathbf{z}}) = \top$. By definition of the
set $S_f(\rho, \mathsf{com})$, existence of $(\widetilde{\mathbf{z}}, \widetilde{\mathsf{op}})$ such that Verify$(\mathsf{K_{com}}, (\mathsf{com}, \widetilde{\beta}, (\widetilde{\mathbf{z}}, \widetilde{\mathsf{op}}))) = \top$
and $f(\widetilde{\beta}, \widetilde{\mathbf{z}}) = \top$ is guaranteed. Therefore, denoting $\widetilde{\mathsf{op}} = [\widetilde{\mathbf{z}}_1 \| \widetilde{\mathbf{z}}_2 \| \widetilde{\mathbf{z}}_3]$, we
have $\|\widetilde{\mathbf{z}}_\ell\|_2 \le \sqrt{2nd} \cdot \phi \cdot T$ for all $\ell \in \{1,2,3\}$, and $p \cdot (\mathbf{A}\widetilde{\mathbf{z}}_1 + \widetilde{\mathbf{z}}_2) =$
$\sum_{i=1}^N \widetilde{\beta}_i \cdot \mathbf{t}_{i,1} + \mathbf{w}_1$, $p \cdot (\mathbf{B}\widetilde{\mathbf{z}}_3) + \widetilde{\mathbf{z}} = \sum_{i=1}^N \widetilde{\beta}_i \cdot \mathbf{t}_{i,2} + \mathbf{w}_2$, where $\mathbf{A}$ and
$\mathbf{B} = \mathbf{D}_1\mathbf{A} + \mathbf{D}_2$ are uniquely defined by $\widetilde{H}(\rho)$ and $\tau = K$ as in Fig. 3. Therefore,
since $\mathbf{v} := (\sum_{i=1}^N \widetilde{\beta}_i \cdot \mathbf{t}_{i,2} + \mathbf{w}_2) - \mathbf{D}_1(\sum_{i=1}^N \widetilde{\beta}_i \cdot \mathbf{t}_{i,1} + \mathbf{w}_1) = p \cdot (\mathbf{D}_2\widetilde{\mathbf{z}}_1 - \mathbf{D}_1\widetilde{\mathbf{z}}_2 + \widetilde{\mathbf{z}}_3) + \widetilde{\mathbf{z}}$,
we have

$$\|\mathbf{v}\|_\infty \le p \cdot (\sqrt{nd}\|\mathbf{D}_2\|_\infty \cdot \|\widetilde{\mathbf{z}}_1\|_2 + \sqrt{md}\|\mathbf{D}_1\|_\infty \cdot \|\widetilde{\mathbf{z}}_2\|_2 + \|\widetilde{\mathbf{z}}_3\|_\infty) + \|\widetilde{\mathbf{z}}\|_\infty$$
$$\le \sqrt{2}p(nd\eta + \sqrt{nmd}\eta + \sqrt{nd})\phi T + 2B < q/2,$$

where we have $\|\widetilde{\mathbf{z}}\|_2 \le B$ by definition of $\mathcal{F}_B$ (see Sect. 3.3), $\|\mathbf{D}_1\|_\infty, \|\mathbf{D}_2\|_\infty \le \eta$,
and the last equation holds from the assumption in the statement. Moreover, we
use the fact that for two vectors $\mathbf{a}, \mathbf{b} \in \mathbb{Z}^n$, we have $\|\mathbf{a}^\top\mathbf{b}\|_\infty \le \sqrt{n}\|\mathbf{a}\|_\infty\|\mathbf{b}\|_2$.
This implies that the equality holds over R, and in particular, when $\|\widetilde{\mathbf{z}}\|_\infty \le$
$B \le (p-1)/2$, $(\sum_{i=1}^N \widetilde{\beta}_i \cdot \mathbf{t}_{i,2} + \mathbf{w}_2) - \mathbf{D}_1(\sum_{i=1}^N \widetilde{\beta}_i \cdot \mathbf{t}_{i,1} + \mathbf{w}_1) \mod p$ is identical
to $\widetilde{\mathbf{z}}$. Hence, we are able to extract $\widetilde{\mathbf{z}}$ such that $f(\widetilde{\beta}, \widetilde{\mathbf{z}}) = \top$.

Next, we check that LinCExtract succeeds in outputting a set $L =$
$\{(\widetilde{\beta}_j, \widetilde{\mathbf{z}}_j)\}_{j \in [k]}$ such that $f(\widetilde{\beta}_j, \widetilde{\mathbf{z}}_j) = \top$ for all $j \in [k]$, where by construction
all the $\widetilde{\beta}_j$'s are pairwise distinct. Since $\widetilde{\beta}$ is sampled uniformly random from
$\mathsf{ChSet} \backslash L_\beta$, the probability of sampling $\widetilde{\beta} \in S_f(\rho, \mathsf{com}) \backslash L_\beta$ in one loop is at least
$\frac{|S_f(\rho, \mathsf{com})| - k}{|\mathsf{ChSet}|}$. Therefore, given any L, if we sample $\widetilde{\beta}$ $\frac{\delta \cdot |\mathsf{ChSet}|}{|S_f(\rho, \mathsf{com})| - k}$-times from the
set $\mathsf{ChSet} \backslash L_\beta$, then the probability of sampling $\widetilde{\beta} \in S_f(\rho, \mathsf{com}) \backslash L_\beta$ is at least
$1 - 2^{-\delta}$. Since each loop is independent from each other, after $T^* = \frac{k \cdot \delta \cdot |\mathsf{ChSet}|}{|S_f(\rho, \mathsf{com})| - k}$-
loops, we obtain the desired set L with probability at least $1 - k \cdot 2^{-\delta}$, where
the bound follows from the union bound. Finally, since each loop takes a fixed
polynomial time, the running time of LinCExtract is $T^* \cdot \mathsf{poly}(\kappa)$ as desired. We
note that there could exist $\widetilde{\beta} \notin S_f(\rho, \mathsf{com})$ for which LinCExtract succeeds in

extracting $\widetilde{\mathbf{z}}$ such that $f(\widetilde{\beta}, \widetilde{\mathbf{z}}) = \top$. However, this will not be a problem since such $\widetilde{\beta}$ can only increase the success probability and lower the running time of LinCExtract.

This completes the proof of Item 2.   □

We note that we can get an asymptotically more efficient extractor by allowing algorithm LinCExtract to be QPT and perform Grover's search. Finally, we also discuss how to "downgrade" the above extractable LinHC protocol to only satisfy the properties of a simplified/classical extractable LinHC protocol. The benefit of doing this is that it provides tighter reductions since we no longer need to work with QROs. The details are provide in the full version.

4   How to Use Extractable LinHC

In this section, we provide a basic example of bootstrapping the ROM secure Lyubashevsky's Σ-protocol [27,28] to be QROM secure using an extractable LinHC protocol. The aim of this section is to provide a guide on how to prove QROM security using an extractable LinHC protocol. In Sect. 5, we see how these ideas can be used to prove QROM security of more complex protocols.

As explained in the beginning of Sect. 3, we can either construct a (1) quantum straight-line extractable Σ-protocol using the simplified extractable LinHC protocol (see Sect. 3.2) or a (2) quantum secure simulation straight-line extractable NIZK (or a signature scheme) using the standard extractable LinHC protocol. We explain both items. The former is easier to prove and makes it simpler to understand the essence of the extractable LinHC protocol, while the latter provides a stronger and more useful result.

4.1   Lyubashevsky's Σ-Protocol $\Rightarrow$ Quantum Secure Σ-Protocol via Simplified Extractable LinHC

We show how to make the classical lattice-based Σ-protocol of Lyubashevsky into a Σ-protocol that is quantum straight-line proof of knowledge in the CRS model by integrating it with a simplified extractable LinHC in the standard model. Below, we denote Lyubashevsky's Σ-protocol as Σ_{Lyu}-protocol.

Preparation. Let ChSet $\subset \{0,1\}^{\kappa}$ be a set such that all $\beta \in$ ChSet satisfies $\|\beta\|_1 \leq \ell$. Here, ℓ is chosen in such a way to guarantee $\binom{n}{\ell} \geq 2^{256}$. Let ϕ and err be parameters specified by the rejection sampling algorithm. Let $B_{\mathbf{e}}$, $B_{\mathbf{r}}$, and $B_{\mathbf{z}}$ be positive reals such that $B_{\mathbf{r}} \geq \sqrt{2md} \cdot \ell \cdot B_{\mathbf{e}}$ and $B_{\mathbf{z}} \geq \sqrt{2nd} \cdot \phi \cdot B_{\mathbf{r}}$. Define the MSIS relation as $\mathcal{R}_{\mathsf{MSIS}} = \{(\mathsf{X} := (\mathbf{A}, \mathbf{u}), \mathsf{W} := \mathbf{e}) \mid \mathbf{A}\mathbf{e} = \mathbf{u} \ \wedge \ \|\mathbf{e}\|_2 \leq B_{\mathbf{e}}\}$, where $\mathbf{A} \in R_q^{n \times m}$, $\mathbf{u} \in R_q^n$, and $\mathbf{e} \in R_q^m$. We also define the "relaxed" relation $\mathcal{R}'_{\mathsf{MSIS}}$ where the only difference between $\mathcal{R}_{\mathsf{MSIS}}$ is that $\mathbf{e}$ now only satisfies $\mathbf{A}\mathbf{e} = (\beta - \widetilde{\beta}) \cdot \mathbf{u}$ for some $\beta, \widetilde{\beta} \in$ ChSet and $\|\mathbf{e}\|_2 \leq B'_{\mathbf{e}}$ for a slightly larger bound $B'_{\mathbf{e}} > B_{\mathbf{e}}$. It is known that the Σ_{Lyu}-protocol is naHVZK and satisfies relaxed 2-special soundness.

Quantum secure Σ-protocol. The construction is depicted in Fig. 4. Setup of the Σ protocol runs KeyGen of the extractable LinHC protocol. Below, we show correctness, naHVZK, and SL-PoK of our Σ-protocol in Fig. 4. Since the first two properties follows almost immediately from the underlying Σ_{Lyu}-protocol and the simplified extractable LinHC protocol, we omit them to the full version.

Prover: $\mathsf{X} = (\mathbf{A}, \mathbf{u}) \in R_q^{n \times m} \times R_q^n$ $W = \mathbf{e} \in R_q^m$		crs $= \mathsf{K}_{\mathsf{com}}$ Verifier: $\mathsf{X} = (\mathbf{A}, \mathbf{u})$
$\mathbf{r} \leftarrow D_{\phi \cdot B_r}^m$		
$\mathbf{w} \leftarrow \mathbf{Ar}$	$\mathbf{w}, \mathsf{com}$	
$(\mathsf{com}, \mathsf{st}) \leftarrow \mathsf{Com}(\mathsf{K}_{\mathsf{com}}, (\mathbf{e}, \mathbf{r}))$	$\xrightarrow{\hspace{2cm}}$	
	β	$\beta \leftarrow \mathsf{ChSet}$
	$\xleftarrow{\hspace{2cm}}$	
$\mathbf{z} \leftarrow \beta \cdot \mathbf{e} + \mathbf{r}$		$\mathsf{Verify}(\mathsf{K}_{\mathsf{com}}, (\mathsf{com}, \beta, (\mathbf{z}, \mathsf{op}))) \overset{?}{=} \top$
$\mathsf{op} \leftarrow \mathsf{Open}(\mathsf{K}_{\mathsf{com}}, (\mathsf{com}, \beta, \mathbf{z}), \mathsf{st}))$	$\mathbf{z}, \mathsf{op}$	
If $\mathsf{op} = \bot$, abort	$\xrightarrow{\hspace{2cm}}$	$\|\mathbf{z}\|_2 \overset{?}{\leq} B_z$
If $\mathsf{Rej}(\mathbf{z}, \beta \cdot \mathbf{e}, \phi, B_r, \mathsf{err}) = \bot$, abort		$\mathbf{Az} \overset{?}{=} \beta \cdot \mathbf{u} + \mathbf{w}$

Fig. 4. Quantum secure Σ-protocol in the CRS model for the lattice relation $\mathbf{Ae} = \mathbf{u}$, where crs is $\mathsf{K}_{\mathsf{com}} \leftarrow \mathsf{KeyGen}(1^\kappa)$. The witness $\mathbf{e}$ satisfies $\|\mathbf{e}\|_2 \leq B_e$. The gray indicates the components that are used in the Σ_{Lyu}-protocol.

$\underline{\mathsf{SimSetup}(1^\kappa)}$

1: $(\widetilde{\mathsf{K}}_{\mathsf{com}}, \tau) \leftarrow \mathsf{SimKeyGen}(1^\kappa)$
2: **return** $(\widetilde{\mathsf{crs}} := \widetilde{\mathsf{K}}_{\mathsf{com}}, \tau)$

$\underline{\mathsf{SL\text{-}Extract}(\tau, ((\mathbf{w}, \mathsf{com}), \beta, (\mathbf{z}, \mathsf{op})))}$

1: Run $L \leftarrow \mathsf{LinCExtract}(\tau, (\mathsf{com}, \beta, (\mathbf{z}, \mathsf{op})))$
 and **return** $\bot$ if it does not terminate in
 time $T^* \cdot \mathsf{poly}(\kappa)$.
2: **if** $L = \bot$ **then return** $\bot$
3: $\{(\beta, \mathbf{z}), (\widetilde{\beta}, \widetilde{\mathbf{z}})\} \leftarrow L$
4: $\mathbf{z}^* \leftarrow \mathsf{Extract}_{\mathsf{ss}}(\mathbf{w}, (\beta, \mathbf{z}), (\widetilde{\beta}, \widetilde{\mathbf{z}}))$
5: **return** $W := \mathbf{z}^*$

Fig. 5. Description of $\mathsf{SimSetup}$ and $\mathsf{SL\text{-}Extract}$ for the Σ-protocol in Fig. 4.

Lemma 4.1 (SL-PoK). *Let the Σ_{Lyu}-protocol for the relations $(\mathcal{R}_{\mathsf{MSIS}}, \mathcal{R}'_{\mathsf{MSIS}})$ be relax 2-special sound with extractor $\mathsf{Extract}_{\mathsf{ss}}$. Let the simplified extractable LinHC protocol be $\epsilon_{\mathsf{IndCom}}$-$\mathcal{F}_{B_z}$-almost straight-line extractable with simulator $\mathsf{SimKeyGen}$ and linear commitment extractor $\mathsf{LinCExtract}$, where $\mathcal{F}_{B_z}$ is the family of functions of the form $f_{\mathbf{A}, \mathbf{u}, \mathbf{w}}(\beta, \mathbf{z}) = \top$ if and only if $\|\mathbf{z}\|_2 \leq B_z$ and $\mathbf{Az} = \beta \cdot \mathbf{u} + \mathbf{w}$. Finally, let $T^* = ((\epsilon - \nu_2)/2 - 1/|\mathsf{ChSet}|)^{-1}$ where ϵ is the advantage of the adversary $\mathcal{A}$ and ν_2 is a negligible function as in the statement of Definition 2.1, and $\mathsf{poly}(\kappa)$ is some fixed polynomial independent of $\mathcal{A}$.*

Then our Σ-protocol in the CRS model for the relations $(\mathcal{R}_{\mathsf{MSIS}}, \mathcal{R}'_{\mathsf{MSIS}})$ in Fig. 4 is a straight-line PoK *with simulator* SimSetup *and straight-line extractor* SL-Extract *described in Fig. 5.*

Proof. Fix any $X = (\mathbf{A}, \mathbf{u})$. Let $\mathcal{A}$ be a QPT algorithm that outputs a valid transcript with probability ϵ as in the statement of Definition 2.1. Then, we have

$$\Pr\left[\begin{array}{c} (\widetilde{\mathsf{crs}} = \widetilde{\mathsf{K}}_{\mathsf{com}}, \tau) \leftarrow \mathsf{SimSetup}(1^\kappa) \\ (\alpha, \mathsf{st}) \leftarrow \mathcal{A}(\widetilde{\mathsf{crs}}, X) \\ \beta \leftarrow \mathsf{ChSet} \\ \gamma \leftarrow \mathcal{A}(\widetilde{\mathsf{crs}}, X, \alpha, \beta, \mathsf{st}) \end{array} : \mathsf{Verify}(\widetilde{\mathsf{crs}}, X, (\alpha, \beta, \gamma)) = \top \right] \geq \epsilon - \epsilon_{\mathsf{IndCom}}, \quad (1)$$

where $\alpha = (\mathbf{w}, \mathsf{com})$ and $\gamma = (\mathbf{z}, \mathsf{op})$. Let $\Gamma = |\mathsf{ChSet}| \cdot \frac{\epsilon - \epsilon_{\mathsf{IndCom}}}{2}$ which we assume to be a positive integer larger than 2 without loss of generality. Omitting the randomness for better readability, we can rewrite the l.h.s of Eq. (1) as

$$\Pr\left[\mathsf{Verify}(\widetilde{\mathsf{crs}}, X, (\alpha, \beta, \gamma)) = \top \;\wedge\; |S_f(\widetilde{\mathsf{K}}_{\mathsf{com}}, \mathsf{com})| \geq \Gamma\right]$$
$$+ \Pr\left[\mathsf{Verify}(\widetilde{\mathsf{crs}}, X, (\alpha, \beta, \gamma)) = \top \;\wedge\; |S_f(\widetilde{\mathsf{K}}_{\mathsf{com}}, \mathsf{com})| < \Gamma\right]. \quad (2)$$

Here, $f \in \mathcal{F}_{B_{\mathbf{z}}}$ is the function that on input $(\beta, \mathbf{z})$, outputs $\top$ if and only if $\|\mathbf{z}\|_2 \leq B_{\mathbf{z}}$ and $\mathbf{A}\mathbf{z} = \beta \cdot \mathbf{u} + \mathbf{w}$, where $\mathbf{w}$ is the vector included in α output by $\mathcal{A}$. Since β is sampled uniformly random from ChSet and independently of com output by $\mathcal{A}$, and $S_f(\widetilde{\mathsf{K}}_{\mathsf{com}}, \mathsf{com})$ is the set of β's that permit a valid $(\mathbf{z}, \mathsf{op})$ we have $\Pr[\mathsf{Verify}(\widetilde{\mathsf{crs}}, X, (\alpha, \beta, \gamma)) = \top \;\wedge\; |S_f(\widetilde{\mathsf{K}}_{\mathsf{com}}, \mathsf{com})| < \Gamma] < \frac{\Gamma}{|\mathsf{ChSet}|} = \frac{\epsilon - \epsilon_{\mathsf{IndCom}}}{2}$. Combining this with Eq. (1) and (2), we have $\Pr[\mathsf{Verify}(\widetilde{\mathsf{crs}}, X, (\alpha, \beta, \gamma)) = \top \;\wedge\; |S_f(\widetilde{\mathsf{K}}_{\mathsf{com}}, \mathsf{com})| \geq \Gamma] \geq \frac{\epsilon - \epsilon_{\mathsf{IndCom}}}{2}$. Specifically, with probability at least $\frac{\epsilon - \epsilon_{\mathsf{IndCom}}}{2}$, we have $|S_f(\widetilde{\mathsf{K}}_{\mathsf{com}}, \mathsf{com})| \geq \Gamma$. Conditioning on such an event, we have that $\mathsf{LinCExtract}(\tau, (\mathsf{com}, \beta, (\mathbf{z}, \mathsf{op})))$ outputs a tuple $L = \{(\beta, \mathbf{z}), (\widetilde{\beta}, \widetilde{\mathbf{z}})\}$ such that $\beta \neq \widetilde{\beta}$ and $f(\widetilde{\beta}, \widetilde{\mathbf{z}}) = \top$ in time at most $\left(\frac{|\mathsf{ChSet}|}{\Gamma - 1}\right) \cdot \mathsf{poly}_{\mathsf{LinHC}}(\kappa)$ with probability at least $1 - 2^{-\kappa}$, where we set $\delta = \kappa$. By setting $T^* = \frac{|\mathsf{ChSet}|}{\Gamma - 1}$ and $\mathsf{poly}(\kappa) = \mathsf{poly}_{\mathsf{LinHC}}(\kappa)$ in Fig. 5, with probability at least $\frac{\epsilon - \epsilon_{\mathsf{IndCom}}}{2} \cdot (1 - 2^{-\kappa})$, SL-Extract moves on to Line 3. By definition of $f \in \mathcal{F}_{B_{\mathbf{z}}}$, $(\mathbf{w}, \beta, \mathbf{z})$ and $(\mathbf{w}, \widetilde{\beta}, \widetilde{\mathbf{z}})$ are two valid transcripts for the underlying classical Σ-protocol. Hence, we obtain $\mathbf{z}^* \leftarrow \mathsf{Extract}_{\mathsf{ss}}(\mathbf{w}, (\beta, \mathbf{z}), (\widetilde{\beta}, \widetilde{\mathbf{z}}))$ such that $(X, W = \mathbf{z}^*) \in \mathcal{R}'_{\mathsf{MSIS}}$ as desired. This completes the proof. $\qquad\square$

4.2 Lyubashevsky's Σ-Protocol $\Rightarrow$ QROM Secure Signature via Extractable LinHC and Fiat-Shamir

We show how to directly compile the Σ_{Lyu}-protocol into an eu-cma secure signature scheme using the Fiat-Shamir transform The main technicality of this section is to show that even if an adversary gets to observe polynomially many simulated proofs (i.e., signatures), we are still able to extract a witness from a valid proof (i.e., extract the secret key from a signature forgery) output by the adversary *without* rewinding.

QROM secure signature scheme. The construction of our (deterministic) signature scheme in the QROM is provided in Fig. 6.[17] The algorithms are provided oracle access to the random oracle H, and we use appropriate domain separation to simulate two independent random oracles with different domains and ranges: H_{LHC} for the extractable LinHC protocol and H_{FS} for applying the Fiat-Shamir transform The output space of H_{FS} is $\mathsf{ChSet} := \{\beta \in \{0,1\}^\kappa \mid \|\beta\|_1 \leq \ell\}$. Let all the parameters be defined identically to those of the Σ-protocol. We assume that each first message ($\mathbf{w} = \mathbf{A}\mathbf{r}$) of the underlying Σ_{Lyu}-protocol has ζ-min-entropy and further assume with overwhelming probability that there exists at least two short vectors $\mathbf{e}, \mathbf{e}' \in S_{B_e}^m$ such that $\mathbf{A}\mathbf{e} = \mathbf{A}\mathbf{e}' = \mathbf{u}$. Both of these assumptions are standard in prior works.

$\underline{\mathsf{S.KeyGen}^H(1^\kappa)}$
1: $(\mathbf{A}, \mathbf{e}) \leftarrow R_q^{n \times m} \times S_{B_e}^m$
2: $\mathbf{u} = \mathbf{A}\mathbf{e}$
3: $\mathsf{K} \leftarrow \mathcal{K}$
4: $\mathsf{vk} := (\mathbf{A}, \mathbf{u})$
5: $\mathsf{sk} := (\mathbf{e}, \mathsf{K})$
6: **return** $(\mathsf{vk}, \mathsf{sk})$

$\underline{\mathsf{S.Verify}^H(\mathsf{vk}, \sigma, M)}$
1: $(\beta, \mathbf{z}, \mathsf{com}, \mathsf{op}) \leftarrow \sigma$
2: $\mathsf{K_{com}} \leftarrow \mathsf{KeyGen}^{H_{LHC}}(1^\kappa)[M]$
3: $b \leftarrow \mathsf{Verify}(\mathsf{K_{com}}, (\mathsf{com}, \beta, (\mathbf{z}, \mathsf{op})))$
4: **if** $b = \perp$ **then return** $\perp$
5: $\mathbf{w} \leftarrow \mathbf{A}\mathbf{z} - \beta \cdot \mathbf{u}$
6: **if** $\|\mathbf{z}\|_2 > B_\mathbf{z}$ or $\beta \neq H_{FS}(\mathbf{w}\|\mathsf{com}\|M)$ **then return** $\perp$
7: **else return** $\top$

$\underline{\mathsf{S.Sign}^H(\mathsf{vk}, \mathsf{sk}, M)}$
1: $\mathsf{K_{com}} \leftarrow \mathsf{KeyGen}^{H_{LHC}}(1^\kappa)[M]$
2: $(b, \mathsf{op}, c) \leftarrow (\perp, \perp, 0)$
3: **while** $b = \perp \vee \mathsf{op} = \perp$ **do**
4: $\quad \rho_\mathbf{r}\|\rho_{Rej}\|\rho_{Com}\|\rho_{Open} \leftarrow \mathsf{PRF}(\mathsf{K}, M\|c)$
5: $\quad \mathbf{r} \leftarrow D_{\phi \cdot B_\mathbf{r}}^m[\rho_\mathbf{r}]$
6: $\quad \mathbf{w} \leftarrow \mathbf{A}\mathbf{r}$
7: $\quad (\mathsf{com}, \mathsf{st}) \leftarrow \mathsf{Com}(\mathsf{K_{com}}, (\mathbf{e}, \mathbf{r}))[\rho_{Com}]$
8: $\quad \beta \leftarrow H_{FS}(\mathbf{w}\|\mathsf{com}\|M)$
9: $\quad \mathbf{z} \leftarrow \beta \cdot \mathbf{e} + \mathbf{r}$
10: $\quad b \leftarrow \mathsf{Rej}(\mathbf{z}, \beta \cdot \mathbf{e}, \phi, B_\mathbf{r}, \mathsf{err})[\rho_{Rej}]$
11: $\quad \mathsf{op} \leftarrow \mathsf{Open}(\mathsf{K_{com}}, (\mathsf{com}, \beta, \mathbf{z}), \mathsf{st})[\rho_{Open}]$
12: $\quad c \leftarrow c + 1$
13: **return** $\sigma := (\beta, \mathbf{z}, \mathsf{com}, \mathsf{op})$

Fig. 6. QROM secure signature scheme by applying the Fiat-Shamir transform to our Σ-protocol in Fig. 4. Oracles H_{LHC} and H_{FS} are implemented using H.

Properties. Due to page limitation, we provide the proof of eu-cma security in the full version. For an overview of the proof, we refer the readers to the technical overview in Sect. 1.2. The main technicality of the proof is showing that with high probability, there must have been another challenge the adversary was able

---

[17] Strictly speaking, we require an upper bound on the number of loops we perform in the **while** clause to make the signature algorithm terminate in strict polynomial time. However, since our main focus is to showcase how to use the extractable LinHC protocol and this issue can be handled in a straightforward manner (see [23] for example), we ignore this unrelated subtlety for better readability.

to forge on even though it had some control over which challenge it used through quantumly accessing the random oracle H_{FS}.

5   Application: Quantum Secure 5-Round Public-Coin Exact Sound Proof and NIZK

In this section, to showcase the generality of the extractable LinHC protocol, we show how to integrate it to the recent 5-round public-coin HVZK interactive *exact sound* proof of Bootle et al. [8]. The main motivation for choosing [8] as the case study is because the ideas presented in this section can be directly applied to other recent works [1,3,15,35]. We can convert the protocol of [8] into either (1) a quantum secure straight-line extractable *interactive* proof using the simplified extractable LinHC protocol (as in Sect. 4.1) or (2) into a quantum secure simulation straight-line extractable NIZK (or a signature scheme) using the extractable LinHC protocol (as in Sect. 4.2).

5.1   Quantum Secure Exact Sound Interactive Proof via Simplified Extractable LinHC

We first show how to apply the simplified extractable LinHC protocol to Bootle et al.'s protocol [8] to obtain a 5-round public-coin interactive proof that is quantum secure, straight-line extractable, and exact sound. In brief, Bootle et al. constructs an interactive protocol that allows the prover to prove knowledge of a vector $s \in \{0, 1, 2\}^d$ satisfying $\mathbf{A}s = \mathbf{u}$, where the main difference between Lyubashevsky's protocol is that it *exact* sound. That is, a knowledge extractor extracts a witness that satisfies the original relation used by the prover (and not a "relaxed" relation). While zero-knowledge of our protocol is a direct consequence of that of Bootle et al.'s protocol, soundness needs slightly more work.

Parameters. Following Bootle et al., we chose the dimension d and modulus q so that R_q completely splits into d linear factors modulo q, e.g., d is a power of 2 and $q \equiv 1 \mod 2d$. For a ring element $s \in R_q$, we denote $\hat{s} \in \mathbb{Z}_q^d$ as the NTT representation of s. Then, for a matrix-vector pair $(\mathbf{A}, \mathbf{u}) \in \mathbb{Z}_q^{m \times d} \times \mathbb{Z}_q^m$, we consider the relation $\mathcal{R}_{ES} = \{s \in R_q \mid \mathbf{A}\hat{s} = \mathbf{u} \ \wedge \ \hat{s} \in \{0, 1, 2\}^d\}$. Let C denote the set $\{0, X^i \mid 0 \le i < 2d\} \subset R_q$, and ϕ and err be parameters specified by the rejection sampling algorithm. Let B_e, B_r, and B_z be positive reals such that $B_r \ge \sqrt{6d} \cdot B_e$ and $B_z \ge \sqrt{12d} \cdot \phi \cdot B_r$, where the size of B_e dictates the hardness of the MLWE assumption.

Quantum secure exact sound protocol. The protocol is depicted in Fig. 7. It can be seen that the way we apply the extractable LinHC protocol is very similar to what was done for Lyubashevsky's protocol (see Fig. 4). Correctness and naHVZK are straightforward to prove and we omit them to the full version.

The high level idea of the proof for straight-line proof of knowledge is similar to those provided by Bootle et al. [8, Theorem 3.1]. The main difference is how we extract a witness from *partial* valid transcripts. Recall Bootle et al. first

Prover: $X = (\mathbf{A}, \mathbf{u}) \in \mathbb{Z}_q^{m \times d} \times \mathbb{Z}_q^m$
$W = s \in R_q$ · crs $= (\mathbf{B}, \mathsf{K_{com}})$ Verifier: $X = (\mathbf{A}, \mathbf{u})$

$y \leftarrow R_q$

$\mathbf{e} \leftarrow S_{B_e}^6$

$\mathbf{t} \leftarrow \begin{pmatrix} \mathbf{b}_1^\top \\ \mathbf{b}_2^\top \\ \mathbf{b}_3^\top \\ \mathbf{b}_4^\top \\ \mathbf{b}_5^\top \end{pmatrix} \mathbf{e} + \begin{pmatrix} 0 \\ y \\ s \\ y(2s-3) \\ y^2(s-3) \end{pmatrix} \in R_q^5$

$\mathbf{w} \leftarrow \mathbf{A}\hat{y} \in \mathbb{Z}_q^m$

$\mathbf{r} \leftarrow D_{\phi \cdot B_r}^6$

$(\mathsf{com}, \mathsf{st}) \leftarrow \mathsf{Com}(\mathsf{K_{com}}, (\mathbf{e}, \mathbf{r}))$

$\xrightarrow{\quad (\mathbf{t}, \mathbf{w}, \mathsf{com}) \quad}$

$\xleftarrow{\quad c \quad}$ $c \leftarrow \mathbb{Z}_q$

$z_0 \leftarrow c \cdot s + y$

$x_0 \leftarrow \mathbf{b}_1^\top \mathbf{r}$

$x_1 \leftarrow (\mathbf{b}_2^\top + c \cdot \mathbf{b}_3^\top)\mathbf{r}$

$x_2 \leftarrow ((z_0 - c)(z_0 - 2c) \cdot \mathbf{b}_3^\top$
$\qquad -z_0 \cdot \mathbf{b}_4^\top + \mathbf{b}_5^\top)\mathbf{r}$

$\xrightarrow{\quad (z_0, x_0, x_1, x_2) \quad}$

$\xleftarrow{\quad \beta \quad}$ $\beta \leftarrow C$

$\mathsf{Verify}(\mathsf{K_{com}}, (\mathsf{com}, \beta, (\mathbf{z}, \mathsf{op}))) \overset{?}{=} \top$

$\|\mathbf{z}\|_2 \overset{?}{<} B_z$

$\mathbf{A}\hat{\mathbf{z}}_0 \overset{?}{=} c \cdot \mathbf{u} + \mathbf{w}$

$\mathbf{b}_1^\top \mathbf{z} \overset{?}{=} \beta \cdot t_1 + x_0$

$\mathbf{z} \leftarrow \beta \cdot \mathbf{e} + \mathbf{r}$

$\mathsf{op} \leftarrow \mathsf{Open}(\mathsf{K_{com}}, (\mathsf{com}, \beta, \mathbf{z}), \mathsf{st})$

If $\mathsf{op} = \bot$, abort

If $\mathsf{Rej}(\mathbf{z}, \beta \cdot \mathbf{e}, \phi, B_r, \mathsf{err}) = \bot$, abort

$\xrightarrow{\quad (\mathbf{z}, \mathsf{op}) \quad}$

$(\mathbf{b}_2^\top + c \cdot \mathbf{b}_3^\top)\mathbf{z} + \beta \cdot z_0$
$\qquad \overset{?}{=} \beta \cdot (c \cdot t_3 + t_2) + x_1$

$((z_0 - c)(z_0 - 2c) \cdot \mathbf{b}_3^\top$
$\qquad -z_0 \cdot \mathbf{b}_4^\top + \mathbf{b}_5^\top)\mathbf{z}$

$\qquad \overset{?}{=} \beta \cdot ((z_0 - c)(z_0 - 2c) \cdot t_3$
$\qquad -z_0 \cdot t_4 + t_5) + x_2$

Fig. 7. Quantum secure exact sound public-coin interactive protocol in the CRS model for the relation $\mathcal{R}_{\mathsf{ES}}$. $\mathbf{B} \in R_q^{5 \times 6}$ is the public parameter of the (implicit) commitment scheme Π_{Com} Π_{Com}, and $\mathbf{b}_i^\top$ denotes its i-th row vector. The gray indicates the components that are used in the protocol of Bootle et al. [8].

rewinds the adversary to obtain six valid transcripts with a specific form and then shows how to extract a witness from such transcripts. In our proof, we are only able to extract a small portion of the six valid transcripts so we need to rely on a different argument compared to Bootle et al.

Lemma 5.1 (SL-PoK). *Let the simplified extractable* LinHC *protocol be* $\epsilon_{\mathsf{IndCom}}$-$\mathcal{F}_{B_z}$-*almost straight-line extractable with simulator* SimKeyGen *and linear commitment extractor* LinCExtract, *where* $\mathcal{F}_{B_z}$ *is the singleton set* $\{f\}$ *for a* f *such that* $f(\beta, \mathbf{z}) = \top$ *if and only if* $\|\mathbf{z}\|_2 \leq B_z$.

Then, there exists a PPT simulator SimSetup *and a straight-line extractor* SL-Extract *with the following property: Let* $\mathcal{A}$ *be an adversary that outputs a valid transcript with probability* $\epsilon > 3/q + 2/d^{18}$ *Then, on input a valid transcript output by* $\mathcal{A}$ *executed on a simulated* crs *output by* SimSetup, SL-Extract *outputs either a witness* $s \in R_q$ *in the relation* $\mathcal{R}_{ES}$ *or a* $\mathsf{MSIS}_{n,6n,8B_z}$ *solution for* $\mathbf{b}_1^\top$ *with probability* $(\epsilon - \nu)/3$ *for a negligible function* ν. *Moreover, the runtime of* SL-Extract *is independent of the runtime of* $\mathcal{A}$ *and depends only polynomially on* d *and* $\log q$.

Proof. Assume $\mathcal{A}$ successfully fools the honest verifier with advantage $\epsilon > 3/q + 2/d$ and the resulting transcript is $\mathsf{trans}^* = ((\mathbf{t}, \mathbf{w}, \mathsf{com}), c^{(1)}, (z_0^{(1)}, x_0^{(1)}, x_1^{(1)}, x_2^{(1)}), \beta^{(1,1)}, (\mathbf{z}^{(1,1)}, \mathsf{op}^{(1,1)}))$. Firstly, since $\mathcal{A}$ has advantage greater than $3/q + 2/d$, using the same statistical argument made in the proof of Lemma 4.1, with probability at least $1/3$, the transcript trans^* output by $\mathcal{A}$ satisfies the following property: there exists at least three distinct first challenges $c^{(1)}, c^{(2)}, c^{(3)} \in \mathbb{Z}_q$ and two distinct second challenges $\beta^{(k,1)}, \beta^{(k,2)} \in C$ for each $k \in [3]$ such that there exists some third message $(z_0^{(k)}, x_0^{(k)}, x_1^{(k)}, x_2^{(k)})$ and fifth message $(\mathbf{z}^{(k,j)}, \mathsf{op}^{(k,j)})$ where $\mathsf{trans}^{(k,j)} = ((\mathbf{t}, \mathbf{w}, \mathsf{com}), c^{(k)}, (z_0^{(k)}, x_0^{(k)}, x_1^{(k)}, x_2^{(k)}), \beta^{(k,j)}, (\mathbf{z}^{(k,j)}, \mathsf{op}^{(k,j)}))$ is a valid transcript for all $(k, j) \in [3] \times [2]$. Below, we first show how SL-Extract obtains a list that contains all $((\beta^{(k,j)}, \mathbf{z}^{(k,j)}))_{(k,j) \in [3] \times [2]}$ using the straight-line extractability of the simplified extractable LinHC protocol.

We define SimSetup to run $(\widetilde{\mathsf{K}}_{\mathsf{com}}, \tau) \leftarrow \mathsf{SimKeyGen}(1^\kappa)$ and output $\mathsf{crs} = (\mathbf{B}, \widetilde{\mathsf{K}}_{\mathsf{com}})$. Due to the simplified $\epsilon_{\mathsf{IndCom}}\text{-}\mathcal{F}_{B_z}$-almost straight-line extractability, $\mathcal{A}$ still has advantage $(\epsilon - \epsilon_{\mathsf{IndCom}})/3$ in outputting a valid transcript trans^* with the above property run on this modified crs. Next, SL-Extract can use the extractor of the simplified extractable LinHC protocol $\mathsf{LinCExtract}(\tau, \mathsf{trans}^*)$ to obtain a set $L = ((\beta_j, \mathbf{z}_j))_{j \in [d]}$ in time polynomial in $|C| = d^{19}$, where we are guaranteed to extract all $\beta \in C$ that has a corresponding $(\mathbf{z}', \mathsf{op}')$ such that $\mathsf{Verify}(\mathsf{K}_{\mathsf{com}}, (\mathsf{com}, \beta, (\mathbf{z}', \mathsf{op}'))) = \top$ and $\|\mathbf{z}'\|_2 \le B_z$. That is, all the extracted β satisfies $\beta \in S_f(\mathsf{K}_{\mathsf{com}}, \mathsf{com})$. Moreover, once com is fixed, there exists at most one $\mathbf{z}'$ satisfying $\mathsf{Verify}(\mathsf{K}_{\mathsf{com}}, (\mathsf{com}, \beta, (\mathbf{z}', \mathsf{op}'))) = \top$ for each $\beta \in C$ and any op' regardless of the choice of the second and third messages (i.e., $c \in \mathbb{Z}_q$ and (z, w, x_1, x_2)).[20] Therefore, the extracted $\mathbf{z}$ must be the unique $\mathbf{z}'$. Combining the argument so far, we have established $((\beta^{(k,j)}, \mathbf{z}^{(k,j)}))_{(k,j) \in [3] \times [2]} \subseteq L$. Here, note $\beta^{(k,j)}$ and $\beta^{(k',j')}$ may be the same when $k \ne k'$. In the following, we show how SL-Extract determines which two tuples $(\beta, \mathbf{z})$ and $(\beta', \mathbf{z}') \in L$ correspond to the tuples $(\beta^{(k,1)}, \mathbf{z}^{(k,1)})$ and $(\beta^{(k,2)}, \mathbf{z}^{(k,2)})$.

Assume we knew which elements in the set L corresponded to $(\beta^{(k,1)}, \mathbf{z}^{(k,1)})$ and $(\beta^{(k,2)}, \mathbf{z}^{(k,2)})$ for each $k \in [3]$. Then, since $(\mathsf{trans}^{(k,j)})_{(k,j) \in [3] \times [2]}$ are valid transcripts, we have $\mathbf{b}_1^\top \mathbf{z}^{(k)} = \beta^{(k,j)} \cdot t_1 + x_0^{(k)}$ for an unknown $x_0^{(k)}$. By subtracting

---

[18] Bootle et al. [8, Theorem 3.1] only requires $\epsilon > 2/q + 2/d$. However, this slight modification makes our proof slightly easier to state and has minimal impact on the concrete efficiency of the scheme.

[19] Since d is the dimension of the lattice, we can assume that it is polynomial in the security parameter κ.

[20] This argument relies on a natural yet extra property of the LinHC. The detail is provided in the full version.

$j = 1, 2$ for each $k \in [3]$, we can remove $x_0^{(k)}$ to obtain $\mathbf{b}_1^\top \mathbf{z}^{(k)} - \beta^{(k,1)} \cdot t_1 = \mathbf{b}_1^\top \mathbf{z}^{(k)} - \beta^{(k,2)} \cdot t_1$. Notice that we can check this equality with only knowledge of $\mathbf{B}$ in the crs and $\mathbf{t}$ in the first message, which is shared among all the transcripts. With this observation in mind, SL-Extract performs the following:

1. Prepare an empty list S and counter $t = 1$.
2. For each pair $(\beta, \mathbf{z}), (\beta', \mathbf{z}') \in L$, check if $\mathbf{b}_1^\top \mathbf{z} - \beta \cdot t_1 = \mathbf{b}_1^\top \mathbf{z}' - \beta' \cdot t_1$. If not move on to the next pair. Otherwise, add $(t, (\beta.\mathbf{z}), (\beta', \mathbf{z}'))$ to the list S, update $t = t + 1$, and move on to the next pair.

For each $(t, (\beta, \mathbf{z}), (\beta', \mathbf{z}')) \in S$, denote $\overline{\beta}_t = \beta - \beta'$ and $\overline{\mathbf{z}}_t = \mathbf{z} - \mathbf{z}'$. Then, we have $\mathbf{b}_1^\top \overline{\mathbf{z}}_t = \overline{\beta}_t \cdot t_1$, which is an approximate solution to the first equation of the commitment $\mathbf{t}$. Therefore, we can compute openings $\mathsf{M}_{t,2}$, $\mathsf{M}_{t,3}$ and $\mathsf{M}_{t,4}$ and $\mathsf{M}_{t,5}$ of $\mathbf{t}$ by setting $\mathsf{M}_{t,\ell} = t_\ell - \overline{\beta}_t^{-1} \cdot (\mathbf{b}_\ell^\top \overline{\mathbf{z}}_t) \in R_q$ for each $\ell \in \{2, 3, 4, 5\}$. Here, note that these openings are valid relaxed openings for the commitment scheme with $\|\overline{\mathbf{z}}_t\|_2 \le 2B_\mathbf{z}$. Hence, unless $\mathcal{A}$ breaks the binding property of the commitment, we are guaranteed that $\mathsf{M}_{t,2}$, $\mathsf{M}_{t,3}$, $\mathsf{M}_{t,4}$, and $\mathsf{M}_{t,5}$ are the same value for all $t \in |S|$. Conditioning on $\mathcal{A}$ not breaking the $\mathsf{MSIS}_{n,6n,8B_\mathbf{z}}$ problem, SL-Extract outputs $s^* := \mathsf{M}_{1,3} = \cdots = \mathsf{M}_{|S|,3}$ as the witness. Here, observe that the runtime of SL-Extract is only polynomially related to $|C| = d$: it takes time $d \cdot \mathsf{poly}(\kappa)$ to prepare the list L and takes time at most $d^2 \cdot \mathsf{poly}(\kappa)$ to prepare the list S. Therefore, it remains to show that $s^* \in R_q$ output by SL-Extract indeed satisfies $\mathbf{A}\hat{\mathbf{s}}^* = \mathbf{u}$ and $\hat{\mathbf{s}}^* \in \{0, 1, 2\}$, where $\hat{\mathbf{s}}^* \in \mathbb{Z}_q^d$ is the NTT representation of s^*. In the following, since all the messages are the same unless $\mathcal{A}$ breaks the $\mathsf{MSIS}_{n,6n,8B_\mathbf{z}}$ problem, we drop the subscript t from the messages M and further denote $y^* = \mathsf{M}_2$.

Although we do not know $(c^{(k)}, (z_0^{(k)}, x_0^{(k)}, x_1^{(k)}, x_2^{(k)}))_{k \in [3]}$, we have L that is guaranteed to contain $(\beta^{(k,j)}, \mathbf{z}^{(k,j)})_{(k,j) \in [3] \times [2]}$ included in $(\mathsf{trans}^{(k,j)})_{(k,j) \in [3] \times [2]}$. For each $(k, j) \in [3] \times [2]$ consider the following verification equation

$$(\mathbf{b}_2^\top + c^{(k)} \cdot \mathbf{b}_3^\top)\mathbf{z}^{(k,j)} + \beta^{(k,j)} \cdot z_0^{(k)} = \beta^{(k,j)} \cdot (c^{(k)} \cdot t_3 + t_2) + x_1^{(k)},$$

where recall that $z_0^{(k)}$ and $x_1^{(k)}$ are unknown but guaranteed to exist. Subtracting the equations for the same k and $j = 1, 2$, we obtain $(\mathbf{b}_2^\top + c^{(k)} \cdot \mathbf{b}_3^\top)\overline{\mathbf{z}}^{(k)} + \overline{\beta}^{(k)} \cdot z_0^{(k)} = \overline{\beta}^{(k)} \cdot (c^{(k)} \cdot t_3 + t_2)$, where $\overline{\beta}^{(k)} = \beta^{(k,1)} - \beta^{(k,2)}$ and $\overline{\mathbf{z}}^{(k)} = \mathbf{z}^{(k,1)} - \mathbf{z}^{(k,2)}$. Further substituting the commitment openings for t_2 and t_3 to the above equation and making routine calculation shows $z_0^{(k)} = y^* + c^{(k)} \cdot s^*$. By performing the same argument on the final verification equation and substituting the commitment openings for t_4 and t_5, we obtain

$$((y^*)^2 s^* - y^* \mathsf{M}_4 + \mathsf{M}_5) + ((y^*(2s^* - 3) - \mathsf{M}_4)s^*) \cdot c^{(k)} + (s^*(s^* - 1)(s^* - 2)) \cdot (c^{(k)})^2 = 0.$$

Since this equation holds for all $k \in [3]$ and $c^{(1)} \ne c^{(2)} \ne c^{(3)} \in \mathbb{Z}_q$, we must have $s^*(s^* - 1)(s^* - 2) = 0$ over R_q. Applying the NTT transform, this equation implies that $\hat{\mathbf{s}}^* \in \{0, 1, 2\}^d$. Finally, by subtracting the second verification equation from one another, we get $\mathbf{A}(\hat{\mathbf{z}}_0^{(1)} - \hat{\mathbf{z}}_0^{(2)}) = (c^{(1)} - c^{(2)}) \cdot \mathbf{u}$. Since $c^{(1)} \neq c^{(2)}$ and we established $z_0^{(k)} = y^* + c^{(k)} \cdot s^*$ for each $k \in [3]$, this implies $\mathbf{A}\hat{\mathbf{s}}^* = \mathbf{u}$ as desired.

To summarize, with probability $1/3$, L contains $((\beta^{(k,j)}, \mathbf{z}^{(k,j)}))_{(k,j) \in [3] \times [2]}$. Conditioned on this fact, SL-Extract outputs a valid witness $s^* \in \mathcal{R}_{\mathsf{ES}}$ unless it finds a solution to the $\mathsf{MSIS}_{n,6n,8B_z}$ problem. Note that SL-Extract performs all the steps without explicitly knowing $(c^{(k)}, (z_0^{(k)}, x_0^{(k)}, x_1^{(k)}, x_2^{(k)}))_{k \in [3]}$.   □

5.2 QROM Secure Exact Sound NIZK via Extractable LinHC and Fiat-Shamir

Bootle et al. [8] transformed their interactive protocol into a classical NIZK in the ROM using the Fiat-Shamir transform. Noticing that the two challenge sets $\mathbb{Z}_q$ and C have different size, they provided a more optimized soundness amplification technique. We explain in detail how we can incorporate such optimization technique when we instantiate the extractable LinHC protocol with the two constructions provided in Sect. 3.4. Since most of the argument is identical to those of the previous section, we refer the details to the full version.

5.3 Comparison

We compare Bootle et al.'s ROM secure NIZK and our QROM secure NIZK. We consider the application of proving knowledge of the ternary secret in LWE samples over $\mathbb{Z}_q$, which is commonly used in the literature to provide a basic benchmark, e.g., [5,8]. Such relation captures the setting of FHE schemes and group signatures. Aiming at the 128-bit quantum security level, our provably quantum secure NIZK has a proof size of 2071 KB while Bootle et al.'s (heuristically quantum secure) NIZK has proof size of 812 KB.[21] The overhead is around a factor of 2.6. The full detail on how we arrive at these values is provided in the full version. In contrast, if assume we were able to make Bootle et al.'s NIZK secure in the QROM using the extended Unruh transform [11] (see Footnote 4), the proof size becomes 44.9 MB, where the overhead is a larger factor of 51.8. For completeness, we provide the details in the full version. Finally, note that it is unclear whether the Fiat-Shamir transform in the QROM can be securely applied to Bootle et al.'s NIZK.

5.4 Further Applications of Extractable LinHC

We show that other recent Σ-/public-coin HVZK interactive protocols are compatible with our extractable LinHC protocol. Due to page limitation, below we only remark on one of the recent lattice-based protocols. We provide further discussion in the full version for the rest of the protocols: proof of opening of

---

[21] Bootle et al. [8] provides a proof size of 384 KB. Ours is around two times larger since we require $t = 8$, unlike $t = 4$, to achieve a minimal level of post-quantum security. Moreover, we do not reuse the commitment $t_{3,i}$ for all $i \in [t]$ as in [8] since it would harm zero-knowledge.

commitments [3], one-out-of-many proofs [15], exact sound proofs for quadratic relations [35], and product proofs for commitments [1].

[15]: **Range proofs.** Range proof allows one to prove that a committed value resides in a specific range and is used in applications such as confidential transactions in cryptocurrencies. Recently, Esgin et al. [15] provided an efficient range proof by using new ideas on CRT-packing supporting "inter-slot" operations and NTT-friendly tools that permit the use of fully-splitting rings. It can be checked that the Σ-protocol for the range relation provided in [15, Theorem 1] is compatible with extractable LinHC protocols. Although it was not necessary for their scheme, we can modify the verifier in [15, Protocol 2] (without affecting any parameters) to further check the bound on f_{crt} to perfectly fit the description of the extractable LinHC protocol. Concretely, we can view $(a_j^i)_{(i,j)\in[\psi,k_i-1]}, r_a, r_d$, and r_e in their Protocol 2 as $\mathbf{r}$, and $(b_j^i)_{(i,j)\in[\psi,k_i-1]}, r_b, r_c$, and r in their Protocol 2 as $\mathbf{e}$ of the extractable LinHC protocol in our Fig. 1.

Finally, we elucidate an inconvenient feature of some of the recent advanced lattice-based protocols. While conventional protocols only require 2 to 3 valid transcripts for special soundness, as much as 32 valid transcripts is required in the recent protocols [1]. Therefore, even if the protocols came with a compatible lossy function as in the definition of [25], the Fiat-Shamir transform incurs an extremely large reduction loss. Combining [14, Lemma 29] and [25, Theorem 1], a knowledge extractor (for the underlying protocol) given black-box access to a quantum adversary outputting a valid NIZK proof with probability ϵ after making Q hash queries, is only guaranteed in extracting a witness with probability $(\epsilon/Q^2)^{2\times32-1} = \epsilon^{63}/Q^{126}$. In such cases, extractable LinHC protocols may provide a much tighter proof and a smaller set of provably secure parameters.

Acknowledgement. Shuichi Katsumata was supported by JST CREST Grant Number JPMJCR19F6. We thank Thomas Prest, Alexandre Wallet, and Thomas Espitau for helpful inputs on NTRU. We also want to thank Patrick Hough for helpful discussions about this work while he visited AIST in 2020.

References

1. Attema, T., Lyubashevsky, V., Seiler, G.: Practical product proofs for lattice commitments. In: Micciancio, D., Ristenpart, T. (eds.) CRYPTO 2020. LNCS, vol. 12171, pp. 470–499. Springer, Cham (2020). https://doi.org/10.1007/978-3-030-56880-1_17

2. Baum, C., Bootle, J., Cerulli, A., del Pino, R., Groth, J., Lyubashevsky, V.: Sublinear lattice-based zero-knowledge arguments for arithmetic circuits. In: Shacham, H., Boldyreva, A. (eds.) CRYPTO 2018. LNCS, vol. 10992, pp. 669–699. Springer, Cham (2018). https://doi.org/10.1007/978-3-319-96881-0_23

3. Baum, C., Damgård, I., Lyubashevsky, V., Oechsner, S., Peikert, C.: More efficient commitments from structured lattice assumptions. In: Catalano, D., De Prisco, R. (eds.) SCN 2018. LNCS, vol. 11035, pp. 368–385. Springer, Cham (2018). https://doi.org/10.1007/978-3-319-98113-0_20

4. Bellare, M., Micciancio, D., Warinschi, B.: Foundations of group signatures: formal definitions, simplified requirements, and a construction based on general assumptions. In: Biham, E. (ed.) EUROCRYPT 2003. LNCS, vol. 2656, pp. 614–629. Springer, Heidelberg (2003). https://doi.org/10.1007/3-540-39200-9_38

5. Beullens, W.: Sigma protocols for MQ, PKP and SIS, and fishy signature schemes. In: Canteaut, A., Ishai, Y. (eds.) EUROCRYPT 2020. LNCS, vol. 12107, pp. 183–211. Springer, Cham (2020). https://doi.org/10.1007/978-3-030-45727-3_7

6. Boneh, D., Dagdelen, Ö., Fischlin, M., Lehmann, A., Schaffner, C., Zhandry, M.: Random oracles in a quantum world. In: Lee, D.H., Wang, X. (eds.) ASIACRYPT 2011. LNCS, vol. 7073, pp. 41–69. Springer, Heidelberg (2011). https://doi.org/10.1007/978-3-642-25385-0_3

7. Boneh, D., Zhandry, M.: Secure signatures and chosen ciphertext security in a quantum computing world. In: Canetti, R., Garay, J.A. (eds.) CRYPTO 2013. LNCS, vol. 8043, pp. 361–379. Springer, Heidelberg (2013). https://doi.org/10.1007/978-3-642-40084-1_21

8. Bootle, J., Lyubashevsky, V., Seiler, G.: Algebraic techniques for short(er) exact lattice-based zero-knowledge proofs. In: Boldyreva, A., Micciancio, D. (eds.) CRYPTO 2019. LNCS, vol. 11692, pp. 176–202. Springer, Cham (2019). https://doi.org/10.1007/978-3-030-26948-7_7

9. Brickell, E.F., Camenisch, J., Chen, L.: Direct anonymous attestation. In: ACM CCS (2004)

10. Chase, M., et al.: Post-quantum zero-knowledge and signatures from symmetric-key primitives. In: ACM CCS (2017)

11. Chen, M.-S., Hülsing, A., Rijneveld, J., Samardjiska, S., Schwabe, P.: SOFIA: $\mathcal{MQ}$-based signatures in the QROM. In: Abdalla, M., Dahab, R. (eds.) PKC 2018. LNCS, vol. 10770, pp. 3–33. Springer, Cham (2018). https://doi.org/10.1007/978-3-319-76581-5_1

12. Chuengsatiansup, C., Prest, T., Stehlé, D., Wallet, A., Xagawa, K.: ModFalcon: compact signatures based on module NTRU lattices. Cryptology ePrint Archive, Report 2019/1456

13. Don, J., Fehr, S., Majenz, C.: The measure-and-reprogram technique 2.0: multiround Fiat-Shamir and more. In: Micciancio, D., Ristenpart, T. (eds.) CRYPTO 2020. LNCS, vol. 12172, pp. 602–631. Springer, Cham (2020). https://doi.org/10.1007/978-3-030-56877-1_21

14. Don, J., Fehr, S., Majenz, C., Schaffner, C.: Security of the Fiat-Shamir transformation in the quantum random-oracle model. In: Boldyreva, A., Micciancio, D. (eds.) CRYPTO 2019. LNCS, vol. 11693, pp. 356–383. Springer, Cham (2019). https://doi.org/10.1007/978-3-030-26951-7_13

15. Esgin, M.F., Steinfeld, R., Liu, J.K., Liu, D.: Lattice-based zero-knowledge proofs: new techniques for shorter and faster constructions and applications. In: Boldyreva, A., Micciancio, D. (eds.) CRYPTO 2019. LNCS, vol. 11692, pp. 115–146. Springer, Cham (2019). https://doi.org/10.1007/978-3-030-26948-7_5

16. Faust, S., Kohlweiss, M., Marson, G.A., Venturi, D.: On the non-malleability of the Fiat-Shamir transform. In: Galbraith, S., Nandi, M. (eds.) INDOCRYPT 2012. LNCS, vol. 7668, pp. 60–79. Springer, Heidelberg (2012). https://doi.org/10.1007/978-3-642-34931-7_5

17. Fiat, A., Shamir, A.: How to prove yourself: practical solutions to identification and signature problems. In: Odlyzko, A.M. (ed.) CRYPTO 1986. LNCS, vol. 263, pp. 186–194. Springer, Heidelberg (1987). https://doi.org/10.1007/3-540-47721-7_12

18. Fischlin, M.: Communication-efficient non-interactive proofs of knowledge with online extractors. In: Shoup, V. (ed.) CRYPTO 2005. LNCS, vol. 3621, pp. 152–168. Springer, Heidelberg (2005). https://doi.org/10.1007/11535218_10

19. Gentry, C., Peikert, C., Vaikuntanathan, V.: Trapdoors for hard lattices and new cryptographic constructions. In: 40th ACM STOC (2008)

20. Hülsing, A., Rijneveld, J., Song, F.: Mitigating multi-target attacks in hash-based signatures. In: Cheng, C.-M., Chung, K.-M., Persiano, G., Yang, B.-Y. (eds.) PKC 2016. LNCS, vol. 9614, pp. 387–416. Springer, Heidelberg (2016). https://doi.org/10.1007/978-3-662-49384-7_15

21. Kawachi, A., Tanaka, K., Xagawa, K.: Concurrently secure identification schemes based on the worst-case hardness of lattice problems. In: Pieprzyk, J. (ed.) ASIACRYPT 2008. LNCS, vol. 5350, pp. 372–389. Springer, Heidelberg (2008). https://doi.org/10.1007/978-3-540-89255-7_23

22. Kales, D., Zaverucha, G.: An attack on some signature schemes constructed from five-pass identification schemes. In: Krenn, S., Shulman, H., Vaudenay, S. (eds.) CANS 2020. LNCS, vol. 12579, pp. 3–22. Springer, Cham (2020). https://doi.org/10.1007/978-3-030-65411-5_1

23. Kiltz, E., Lyubashevsky, V., Schaffner, C.: A concrete treatment of Fiat-Shamir signatures in the quantum random-oracle model. In: Nielsen, J.B., Rijmen, V. (eds.) EUROCRYPT 2018. LNCS, vol. 10822, pp. 552–586. Springer, Cham (2018). https://doi.org/10.1007/978-3-319-78372-7_18

24. Koblitz, N., Menezes, A.J.: Another look at "provable security". J. Cryptol. **20**(1), 3–37 (2005). https://doi.org/10.1007/s00145-005-0432-z

25. Liu, Q., Zhandry, M.: Revisiting post-quantum Fiat-Shamir. In: Boldyreva, A., Micciancio, D. (eds.) CRYPTO 2019. LNCS, vol. 11693, pp. 326–355. Springer, Cham (2019). https://doi.org/10.1007/978-3-030-26951-7_12

26. López-Alt, A., Tromer, E., Vaikuntanathan, V.: On-the-fly multiparty computation on the cloud via multikey fully homomorphic encryption. In: 44th ACM STOC (2012)

27. Lyubashevsky, V.: Fiat-Shamir with aborts: applications to lattice and factoring-based signatures. In: Matsui, M. (ed.) ASIACRYPT 2009. LNCS, vol. 5912, pp. 598–616. Springer, Heidelberg (2009). https://doi.org/10.1007/978-3-642-10366-7_35

28. Lyubashevsky, V.: Lattice signatures without trapdoors. In: Pointcheval, D., Johansson, T. (eds.) EUROCRYPT 2012. LNCS, vol. 7237, pp. 738–755. Springer, Heidelberg (2012). https://doi.org/10.1007/978-3-642-29011-4_43

29. Regev, O.: On lattices, learning with errors, random linear codes, and cryptography. In: 37th ACM STOC

30. Saito, T., Xagawa, K., Yamakawa, T.: Tightly-secure key-encapsulation mechanism in the quantum random oracle model. In: Nielsen, J.B., Rijmen, V. (eds.) EUROCRYPT 2018. LNCS, vol. 10822, pp. 520–551. Springer, Cham (2018). https://doi.org/10.1007/978-3-319-78372-7_17

31. Stern, J.: A new identification scheme based on syndrome decoding. In: Stinson, D.R. (ed.) CRYPTO 1993. LNCS, vol. 773, pp. 13–21. Springer, Heidelberg (1994). https://doi.org/10.1007/3-540-48329-2_2

32. Unruh, D.: Quantum proofs of knowledge. In: Pointcheval, D., Johansson, T. (eds.) EUROCRYPT 2012. LNCS, vol. 7237, pp. 135–152. Springer, Heidelberg (2012). https://doi.org/10.1007/978-3-642-29011-4_10

33. Unruh, D.: Non-interactive zero-knowledge proofs in the quantum random oracle model. In: Oswald, E., Fischlin, M. (eds.) EUROCRYPT 2015. LNCS, vol. 9057, pp. 755–784. Springer, Heidelberg (2015). https://doi.org/10.1007/978-3-662-46803-6_25
34. Unruh, D.: Post-quantum security of Fiat-Shamir. In: Takagi, T., Peyrin, T. (eds.) ASIACRYPT 2017. LNCS, vol. 10624, pp. 65–95. Springer, Cham (2017). https://doi.org/10.1007/978-3-319-70694-8_3
35. Yang, R., Au, M.H., Zhang, Z., Xu, Q., Yu, Z., Whyte, W.: Efficient lattice-based zero-knowledge arguments with standard soundness: construction and applications. In: Boldyreva, A., Micciancio, D. (eds.) CRYPTO 2019. LNCS, vol. 11692, pp. 147–175. Springer, Cham (2019). https://doi.org/10.1007/978-3-030-26948-7_6
36. Zhandry, M.: How to construct quantum random functions. In: 53rd FOCS (2012)
37. Zhandry, M.: Secure identity-based encryption in the quantum random oracle model. In: Safavi-Naini, R., Canetti, R. (eds.) CRYPTO 2012. LNCS, vol. 7417, pp. 758–775. Springer, Heidelberg (2012). https://doi.org/10.1007/978-3-642-32009-5_44
38. Zhandry, M.: How to record quantum queries, and applications to quantum indifferentiability. In: Boldyreva, A., Micciancio, D. (eds.) CRYPTO 2019. LNCS, vol. 11693, pp. 239–268. Springer, Cham (2019). https://doi.org/10.1007/978-3-030-26951-7_9

SMILE: Set Membership from Ideal Lattices with Applications to Ring Signatures and Confidential Transactions

Vadim Lyubashevsky[1]([✉]), Ngoc Khanh Nguyen[1,2], and Gregor Seiler[1,2]

[1] IBM Research Europe, Zurich, Switzerland
[2] ETH Zurich, Zurich, Switzerland

Abstract. In a set membership proof, the public information consists of a set of elements and a commitment. The prover then produces a zero-knowledge proof showing that the commitment is indeed to some element from the set. This primitive is closely related to concepts like ring signatures and "one-out-of-many" proofs that underlie many anonymity and privacy protocols. The main result of this work is a new succinct lattice-based set membership proof whose size is logarithmic in the size of the set.

We also give a transformation of our set membership proof to a ring signature scheme. The ring signature size is also logarithmic in the size of the public key set and has size 16 KB for a set of 2^5 elements, and 22 KB for a set of size 2^{25}. At an approximately 128-bit security level, these outputs are between 1.5× and 7× smaller than the current state of the art succinct ring signatures of Beullens et al. (Asiacrypt 2020) and Esgin et al. (CCS 2019).

We then show that our ring signature, combined with a few other techniques and optimizations, can be turned into a fairly efficient Monero-like confidential transaction system based on the MatRiCT framework of Esgin et al. (CCS 2019). With our new techniques, we are able to reduce the transaction proof size by factors of about 4X - 10X over the aforementioned work. For example, a transaction with two inputs and two outputs, where each input is hidden among 2^{15} other accounts, requires approximately 30KB in our protocol.

1 Introduction

Privacy-based transaction systems are steadily gaining in popularity to the point that central banks of the US and the EU are exploring an eventual shift to digital currency. Transaction systems can be equipped with various degrees of privacy, possibilities for auditability, and permission types for joining the transaction network. The common element at the heart of most of these schemes is a zero-knowledge proof which can be adapted to endow the scheme with the desired features. The most efficient zero-knowledge proofs which allow for proving a rich set of statements are generally based on the hardness of the discrete logarithm problem over elliptic curves. This poses a problem for the eventual use of digital

© International Association for Cryptologic Research 2021
T. Malkin and C. Peikert (Eds.): CRYPTO 2021, LNCS 12826, pp. 611–640, 2021.
https://doi.org/10.1007/978-3-030-84245-1_21

currency because the timeline for widescale deployment of these transaction systems could very well coincide with the advent of a quantum computer that is able to break them. It is therefore important to begin considering schemes which are based on assumptions that are believed to be resistant to quantum attacks.

The currently most efficient, in terms of size and speed, quantum-safe basic primitives are based on the hardness of lattice problems with algebraic structure. Lattice-based constructions are therefore natural candidates for more advanced cryptographic tools like zero-knowledge proofs. Over the last few years, there has indeed been rapid progress in the field of lattice-based zero knowledge (e.g. [1,2,6,7,10–13,18,25]). There now exist fairly practical protocols for proving knowledge of pre-images of lattice-based 1-way functions, arithmetic sums and products of committed values, as well as various primitives such as ring signatures and group signatures. In virtually all of these cases, the lattice-based solutions result in the most efficient (potentially) quantum-safe option.

As far as a relatively complete quantum-safe transaction system, the recent work of Esgin et al. [13], also based on the hardness of lattice problems, appears to be the most efficient solution. Their work adapts the RingCT protocol [22], which serves as the foundation of the digital currency Monero, and provides formal definitions upon which they construct their MatRiCT protocol. While certainly not as efficient as discrete logarithm based schemes, this work showed that a lattice-based confidential transaction system is something that may eventually be a very reasonable solution.

Our Results and Related Work. At the core of many privacy-based protocols (including the one from [13]) is a set membership proof in which the prover shows, in zero-knowledge, that a commitment is to a value from a public set. This concept is very closely related to "one-out-of-many" proofs [14] and ring signatures [24]. The main result of this work is a new set membership proof which is logarithmic in the size of the set and leads to a ring signature scheme with outputs noticeably smaller than the currently shortest schemes from [4,13].[1] We point out that "one-out-of many" proofs [14], in which the prover shows that one of the commitments in a set is a commitment to 0, are actually equivalent to the ring signatures that we construct. This is because lattice-based public keys can be thought of as commitments to 0. We then show how to use our ring signature scheme/"one-out-of-many" proof, together with a few other optimizations of prior work, to create a more efficient confidential transaction system based upon the MatRiCT definitions.

We now give a brief overview of where the efficiency advantage comes from. The shorter proofs in our scheme are partly a result of the fact that the modulus in our underlying polynomial ring stays the same for all practical set sizes. On the

---

[1] One can also obtain ring signatures which are linear (rather than logarithmic) in the size of the public key set by plugging in a lattice-based signature scheme based on a trapdoor function, such as [23], into the generic framework of [24]. Even though for small set sizes (around a dozen), this may be smaller than our solution, it quickly becomes much larger (see Fig. 2).

other hand, if the size of the set is $n = 32^m$, then the exponent of the modulus in the ring used in [13] increases linearly in m. The reason for this difference is that [13] use "Ajtai-type" commitments which compress the input, but only allow for commitments of "short" messages. In our construction, however, we use BDLOP commitments [3] which allow commitments to arbitrary-size elements, at the expense of a slightly larger commitment size. But because the number of commitments we need is logarithmic in the size of the set, this does not pose a problem with the commitment size becoming too big.

An additional advantage of BDLOP commitments that we extensively use is that if one plans ahead by choosing a long-enough randomness vector in the beginning of the protocol, then one can adjoin a new commitment at any time and the size of the commitment only increases by the size of the committed message. In particular, the increase in size does not depend on the security parameter, which is what one would need if creating a new commitment. We use this property when combining our new techniques along with the framework for proving various relations committed to in BDLOP commitments from [1, 10,18]. Thus our constructions essentially have just one BDLOP commitment for the entire protocol. We further reduce the transaction size by employing an amortization technique so that the proof contains just two elements whose size depends on the security parameter.

In the rest of the introduction, we give rather detailed high-level descriptions of our constructions. The reason for this level of detail is that the protocols in the body of the paper use optimizations that combine the new ideas together with prior work in a non-black box manner, which tends to somewhat obfuscate the high level picture. In the introduction, we instead give slightly less efficient constructions that try to highlight the separate parts making up the complete protocols. We would then hope that with the high-level intuition in hand, the interested reader can better follow the complete protocols in the body.

1.1   The Polynomial Ring and BDLOP Commitments

Throughout this paper, we will be working over the polynomial ring $\mathcal{R}_q = \mathbb{Z}_q[X]/(X^{128}+1)$ where q is set such that $X^{128}+1 = \prod_{i=1}^{32}(X^4 - r_i)$ and $X^4 - r_i$ are irreducible modulo q (c.f. [21] for how to set q to obtain such a factorization). We will be exclusively using BDLOP commitments [3], where a commitment to a polynomial vector $\vec{m} \in \mathcal{R}_q^k$ is of the form

$$\begin{bmatrix} B_0 \\ B_1 \end{bmatrix} \vec{r} + \begin{bmatrix} \vec{0} \\ \vec{m} \end{bmatrix} = \begin{bmatrix} \vec{t}_0 \\ \vec{t}_1 \end{bmatrix}, \tag{1}$$

where B_i are uniform[2] public random matrices and $\vec{r}$ is a random low-norm vector which serves as the commitment randomness. To open the commitment

---

[2] For efficiency, a large portion of B_i can be the identity matrix (c.f. [3]), but we ignore the form of the public randomness in this paper, as it does not affect any output sizes.

without revealing it, one would ideally want to give a zero-knowledge proof of a low-norm $\vec{r}$ satisfying $B_0\vec{r} = \vec{t}_0$. Unfortunately, there is no particularly efficient zero-knowledge proof for this statement, and so a relaxed opening is defined which consists of a vector $\vec{v}$ and a polynomial c satisfying $B_0\vec{v} = \vec{t}_0$ such that $\|c\|$ and $\|c\vec{v}\|$ are small (but $\vec{v}$ is not necessarily small itself). The committed message is then implicitly

$$\vec{m} = \vec{t}_1 - B_1\vec{v}. \tag{2}$$

An efficient zero-knowledge proof for the above opening was given in [3]. That work also showed how to prove linear (over $\mathcal{R}_q$) relations of $\vec{m}$ without increasing the proof size. For this, it's in fact enough to just be able to prove that the commitment is to $\vec{0}$. The reason is that a commitment of $\vec{m}$ can be easily converted to a commitment of $\vec{m} + \vec{m}'$ by adding $\vec{m}'$ to $\vec{t}_1$. Similarly, for any matrix L over $\mathcal{R}_q$, one can convert a commitment of $\vec{m}$ to one of $L\vec{m}$ by multiplying the bottom part by L to obtain $\begin{bmatrix} B_0 \\ LB_1 \end{bmatrix} \cdot \vec{r} + \begin{bmatrix} \vec{0} \\ L\vec{m} \end{bmatrix} = \begin{bmatrix} \vec{t}_0 \\ L\vec{t}_1 \end{bmatrix}$. Thus proving that the message $\vec{m}$ in (1) satisfies $L\vec{m} = \vec{u}$, involves proving that the commitment $\begin{bmatrix} \vec{t}_0 \\ L\vec{t}_1 - \vec{u} \end{bmatrix}$ with public key $\begin{bmatrix} B_0 \\ LB_1 \end{bmatrix}$ is a commitment to $\vec{0}$.

Later works (e.g. [1,10,18]) showed how to prove more complicated relations between the committed messages in BDLOP commitments. These include proving multiplicative relations among the polynomials comprising $\vec{m}$ and proving linear relations over $\mathbb{Z}_q$ (rather than $\mathcal{R}_q$) of the integer coefficients comprising $\vec{m}$. An important feature of these aforementioned proofs is that the proof size does not grow with the number of relations that one needs to prove about one commitment. So the cost, in terms of proof size, of proving multiple relations about one commitment is the cost of proving the most expensive one.

1.2   The New Set Membership Proof

In this work we extend the toolbox of what can be proved about $\vec{m}$ in BDLOP commitments by showing how to do set membership proofs. Given a collection of polynomial vectors $\vec{p}_i$, and a commitment to one on them, we would like to prove that the committed $\vec{w}$ is indeed one of the $\vec{p}_i$.

More specifically, the public information consists of $P = [\vec{p}_1 \mid \dots \mid \vec{p}_n]$, where $n = l^m = 32^m$, and a commitment ω. The prover gives a zero knowledge proof that a commitment ω opens to $(\vec{v}_1, \dots, \vec{v}_m, \vec{w})$ where

$$P \cdot (\vec{v}_1 \otimes \dots \otimes \vec{v}_m) = \vec{w} \tag{3}$$

$$\forall i, \vec{v}_i \in \{0, 1\}^l \text{ and } \|\vec{v}_i\|_1 = 1. \tag{4}$$

Notice that by definition of the $\vec{v}_i$, their tensor product will be a vector of length n consisting of all zeros and one 1 (this decomposition observation was originally used in [14]). If each vector $\vec{v}_i$ will be committed as a polynomial m_i in the BDLOP commitment,[3] then (4) can already be proved using the aforementioned techniques from [1,10]. Our main result in this work is an efficient proof of (3) whose size is linear in m, and thus logarithmic in the number of elements in $\boldsymbol{P}$. We also prove a more generic k-dimensional version of this problem. In this version, there are k public lists

$$\boldsymbol{P}^{(1)} = \left[\vec{\boldsymbol{p}}_1^{(1)} \mid \cdots \mid \vec{\boldsymbol{p}}_n^{(1)}\right], \ldots, \boldsymbol{P}^{(k)} = \left[\vec{\boldsymbol{p}}_1^{(k)} \mid \cdots \mid \vec{\boldsymbol{p}}_n^{(k)}\right]$$

and $\vec{w}$ is a sum of k elements, one taken from each set. The prover gives a zero knowledge proof that the commitment ω opens to

$$(\vec{v}_1^{(1)}, \ldots, \vec{v}_m^{(1)}, \ldots, \vec{v}_1^{(k)}, \ldots, \vec{v}_m^{(k)}, \boldsymbol{w})$$

where

$$\sum_{j=1}^{k} \boldsymbol{P}^{(j)} \cdot (\vec{v}_1^{(j)} \otimes \ldots \otimes \vec{v}_m^{(j)}) = \vec{w} \tag{5}$$

$$\forall i, j, \ \vec{v}_i^{(j)} \in \{0,1\}^l \text{ and } \|\vec{v}_i^{(j)}\|_1 = 1 \tag{6}$$

This proof is of size $O(mk)$, so there is no amortization happening. But being able to prove the above will allow us to amortize away many of the other parts of the anonymous transaction protocol.

1.3 Set Membership Proof Sketch

We now give a sketch of how to prove (3) and (4). Let us first define the set $\mathcal{M}_q = \mathbb{Z}_q + \mathbb{Z}_q X + \mathbb{Z}_q X^2 + \mathbb{Z}_q X^3$. Because of the way we defined $\mathcal{R}_q$, the NTT and inverse NTT functions are bijective functions $\mathsf{NTT}\,(\boldsymbol{w}) : \mathcal{R}_q \to \mathcal{M}_q^{32}$ and $\mathsf{NTT}^{-1}\,(\vec{w}) : \mathcal{M}_q^{32} \to \mathcal{R}_q$ where

$$\mathsf{NTT}\,(\boldsymbol{w}) = (\boldsymbol{w} \bmod X^4 - r_1, \ldots, \boldsymbol{w} \bmod X^4 - r_{32}).$$

These functions extend to polynomial vectors in the natural way by being applied to each polynomial separately.

We will also need to overload the inner product operator. For a polynomial $\boldsymbol{w}$ such that $\mathsf{NTT}\,(\boldsymbol{w}) = \vec{w} = (w_1, \ldots, w_{32}) \in \mathcal{M}_q^{32}$, define the function $g(\boldsymbol{w}) = \sum_{i=1}^{32} w_i$. In other words, it's just the sum of the NTT coefficients as polynomials in $\mathcal{M}_q$. For two vectors $\vec{w}, \vec{w}' \in \mathcal{M}_q^{32}$, we define $\langle \vec{w}, \vec{w}' \rangle = g(\mathsf{NTT}^{-1}\,(w)\,\mathsf{NTT}^{-1}\,(w'))$. It resembles an inner product because we can equivalently write it as

$$\langle \vec{w}, \vec{w}' \rangle = \sum_{i=1}^{32} w_i w_i' \bmod (X^4 - r_i).$$

---

[3] Actually the inverse NTT of the vector $\vec{v}_i$, which is an element of $\mathcal{R}_q$, will be committed – see Sect. 1.3.

The multiplication is performed modulo different polynomials, amd so this function is not an inner product. But it is commutative and satisfies $\langle \vec{w} + \vec{w}', \vec{w}'' \rangle = \langle \vec{w}, \vec{w}'' \rangle + \langle \vec{w}', \vec{w}'' \rangle$. Similarly, for $\vec{w} = (\vec{w}_1, \dots, \vec{w}_k), \vec{w}' = (\vec{w}'_1, \dots, \vec{w}'_k)$, where each $\vec{w}_i, \vec{w}'_i \in \mathcal{M}_q^{32}$, one defines $\langle \vec{w}, \vec{w}' \rangle = \sum_{i=1}^{k} \langle \vec{w}_i, \vec{w}'_i \rangle$.

For convenience, we will now rewrite the set membership problem to be over $\mathcal{M}_q$. In particular, the public information consists of vectors $P = [\vec{p}_1 \mid \dots \mid \vec{p}_n]$ where each $\vec{p}_i \in \mathcal{M}_q^{32k}$, for some arbitrary k. And we also have a commitment to a vector $\vec{w} \in \mathcal{M}_q^{32k}$ such that $\vec{w} = \vec{p}_i$ for some i. Notice that the $\vec{p}_i$ and $\vec{w}$ are the NTT of the $\vec{p}_i, \vec{w}$ from (3). To commit to the vector $\vec{w}$, we define the polynomial vector $\vec{w} = \mathsf{NTT}^{-1}(\vec{w}) \in \mathcal{R}_q^k$ and then use the BDLOP commitment from (1) to commit to $\vec{w}$. Later rows of this BDLOP commitment will also include commitments to the vectors $\vec{v}_1, \dots, \vec{v}_m \in \mathcal{M}_q^{32}$ (defined as in (4)). We will define the polynomials $v_j = \mathsf{NTT}^{-1}(\vec{v}_j)$ and commit to them in the BDLOP commitment. Note that we can already prove (4) using the techniques from [1,10] by proving that $\vec{v} \cdot (\vec{1} - \vec{v}) = \vec{0}$ and that the NTT coefficients of each polynomial in $\vec{v}$ sum to 1.

We now describe how to prove (3) – in other words, that $P \cdot (\vec{v}_1 \otimes \dots \otimes \vec{v}_m) - \vec{w} = \vec{0}$. We will prove this by showing that for a random challenge $\vec{\gamma} \in \mathcal{M}_q^{32k}$, the "inner product" $\langle P \cdot (\vec{v}_1 \otimes \dots \otimes \vec{v}_m) - \vec{w}, \vec{\gamma} \rangle = 0$. Because $\mathbb{Z}_q[X]/(X^4 - r_i)$ are fields and of size q^4, it's not hard to see that if the left term in the inner product is not $\vec{0}$, then the probability of the inner product being 0 is exactly q^{-4}. Because we will be working with a $q \approx 2^{32}$, this probability is approximately 2^{-128}, so no repetitions are required.

We now get to the main technical part of the protocol. Let's break up P into 32 parts as $P = [P_1 \mid \dots, \mid P_{32}]$ and define $P' := \begin{bmatrix} \gamma^T P_1 \\ \vdots \\ \gamma^T P_{32} \end{bmatrix} \in \mathcal{M}_q^{32 \times 32^{m-1}}$.

Then using the property that $\vec{v}_i$ are vectors over $\mathcal{M}_q$ with just constant coefficients,[4] with some algebraic manipulation (see (18)), it can be shown that

$$\langle P(\vec{v}_1 \otimes \dots \otimes \vec{v}_m) - \vec{w}, \vec{\gamma} \rangle = \langle \vec{v}_1, P'(\vec{v}_2 \otimes \dots \otimes \vec{v}_m) \rangle - \langle \vec{w}, \vec{\gamma} \rangle. \tag{7}$$

To prove that the left-hand side is 0, it is therefore equivalent to prove that the right-hand side is 0. The crucial part is that the right-hand side contains an expression which selects one element from a set P' – but this set is 32 times smaller than P. If we define $\vec{x} = P'(\vec{v}_2 \otimes \dots \otimes \vec{v}_m)$ and send a commitment to $\vec{x}$, then proving the original set membership involves proving a new set membership proof in which the set is 32 times smaller, as well as the equation $\langle \vec{v}_1, \vec{x} \rangle = \langle \vec{w}, \vec{\gamma} \rangle$.

---

[4] Intuitively, if the coefficients of $\vec{v}_i$ were polynomials of degree > 0, then the term $\langle \vec{v}_1, P'(\vec{v}_2 \otimes \dots \otimes \vec{v}_m) \rangle$ in (7) would make very little algebraic sense because there is a multiplication on one side of P' which involves reduction modulo $X^4 - r_j$, and then there would be a multiplication on the other side which would get reduced modulo different $X^4 - r_{j'}$. But since vectors $\vec{v}_i$ only have constant terms, the "inner product" with $\vec{v}_i$ does not involve any modular reduction.

If this latter equation can be proved with a constant number of commitments (in our case, it will essentially be one), then continuing the proof recursively would mean that the whole proof requires approximately $2m$ commitments for sets P containing $n = 32^m$ elements.

Both $\vec{w}$ and $\vec{\gamma}$ are vectors in $\mathcal{M}_q^{32k}$, so let us write them as $\vec{w} = (\vec{w}_1, \dots, \vec{w}_k)$ and $\vec{\gamma} = (\vec{\gamma}_1, \dots, \vec{\gamma}_k)$ where $\vec{w}_i, \vec{\gamma}_i \in \mathcal{M}_q^{32}$. Then

$$\langle \vec{v}_1, \vec{x} \rangle = \langle \vec{w}, \vec{\gamma} \rangle \Leftrightarrow g(\boldsymbol{v}_1 \boldsymbol{x}) = g\left(\sum_{i=1}^{k} \boldsymbol{w}_i \boldsymbol{\gamma}_i\right),$$

where the bold letters correspond to the inverse NTTs and the function g is the sum of the NTT's of the polynomial. Because we have BDLOP commitments to $\boldsymbol{x}$ and $\boldsymbol{w}_i$, we can compute a commitment to $\boldsymbol{y} = \boldsymbol{v}_1 \boldsymbol{x} - \sum_{i=1}^{k} \boldsymbol{w}_i \boldsymbol{\gamma}_i$, and then we just have to prove that the sum of the NTT coefficients of this polynomial is 0. For this, we employ a lemma used in [10], which states that for the ring $\mathcal{R}_q$ as defined in this section and a polynomial $\boldsymbol{y} \in \mathcal{R}_q = \sum_{i=0}^{127} y_i X^i$, we have $g(\boldsymbol{y}) = 32(y_0 + y_1 X + y_2 X^2 + y_3 X^3)$. In other words, the sum of the NTT coefficients is 0 if and only if the first four coefficients of the polynomial representation are 0. To prove this in zero knowledge, we can first commit to a masking polynomial $\boldsymbol{z}$ whose first 4 coefficients are 0 and the rest uniform in $\mathbb{Z}_q$, and then output $\boldsymbol{y} + \boldsymbol{z}$ and prove that this is indeed the right sum. The verifier can then check that the first four coefficients are 0. We don't need to multiply $\boldsymbol{y}$ by a challenge because in our case, it already contains a challenge $\vec{\gamma}$. In the body of the paper, we present an efficient way to do this proof which does not require committing to $\boldsymbol{y}$ and so we just need an extra commitment to $\vec{x} \in \mathcal{M}_q^{32}$ at each level of the recursion.

1.4   From Set Membership to Ring Signatures

A ring signature scheme allows a signer to sign in a way that hides the public key that he is using. More specifically, the signer creates a set comprised of his public key and other public keys for which he may not know the secret key. He then creates a signature with the property that the verifier can check that the message was signed by an entity who knows the secret key to one of the public keys in the list. We now sketch how one can convert a "Schnorr-like" lattice-based signature scheme into a ring signature by using a set membership proof.

The basic signature scheme underlying the ring signature follows the usual "Fiat-Shamir with Aborts" approach for constructing lattice-based digital signatures (e.g. [9,16,17]). In particular, the secret key is a low-norm vector $\vec{s}$, while the public key consists of a random matrix $\boldsymbol{A}$ and a vector $\vec{t} = \boldsymbol{A}\vec{s}$. The signature is then a "relaxed" zero-knowledge proof of knowledge (made non-interactive using the Fiat-Shamir transform) of a vector $\vec{s}'$ and a polynomial c', both with small norms, satisfying $c'\vec{t} = \boldsymbol{A}\vec{s}'$.

The ring signature public information consists of the matrix A and vectors $\vec{t}_1, \ldots, \vec{t}_n$. A signer who knows an $\vec{s}_i$ satisfying $A\vec{s}_i = \vec{t}_i$ will want to give a zero-knowledge proof knowledge of $\vec{s}'$, c', and $i \in [0, n)$ satisfying $c'\vec{t}_i = A\vec{s}'$. An interactive version of this proof is presented in Fig. 1 and it is then made non-interactive using the Fiat-Shamir transform and inserting the message to be signed into the random oracle which is used to produce the challenge.

Private information: $\vec{v}_1, \ldots, \vec{v}_m \in \{0, 1\}^l$ as in (4), and $\vec{s}$ with a small norm
Public information: A, $T = [\ \vec{t}_1\ |\ \ldots\ |\ \vec{t}_n]$, where $n = l^m$ s.t. $T \cdot (\vec{v}_1 \otimes \ldots \otimes \vec{v}_m) = A\vec{s}$

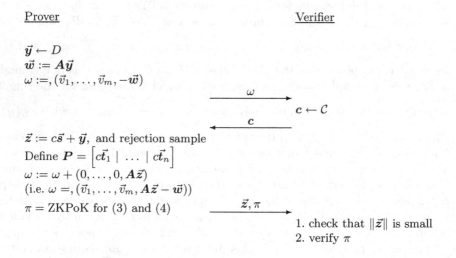

Fig. 1. A lattice-based ring signature using the set membership proof. , is a BDLOP commitment, while D is a distribution that outputs polynomial vectors with small coefficients. As in Sect. 1.3, a BDLOP commitment to v_i is a commitment to the polynomial $\mathsf{NTT}^{-1}(v_i) \in \mathcal{R}_q$.

To see that this proof is complete (assuming that all the norm-checks pass), notice that $A\vec{z} - c\vec{t}_i = A\vec{y} = \vec{w}$. And this is exactly what π proves. The zero-knowledge property follows from the fact that π is a zero-knowledge proof and that $\vec{z}$ is independent of $\vec{s}$ and c due to the employed rejection sampling. To see that the protocol is a proof of knowledge, note that verifying π implies that $A\vec{z} - c\vec{t}_i = \vec{w}$. Because the $\vec{v}_i$ and $\vec{w}$ in the commitment are fixed, if we rewind the prover with a different challenge c', we will obtain $A\vec{z}' - c'\vec{t}_i = \vec{w}$. Eliminating $\vec{w}$ by subtracting the two equations results in the statement that we would like to extract.

1.5   Bimodal Gaussians (almost) for Free

The goal of the rejection sampling in the signing algorithm is to remove the dependence of the secret key $\vec{s}$ from the output $\vec{z}$. If the distribution D in

Ring Size	2^3	2^5	2^6	2^{10}	2^{12}	2^{15}	2^{21}	2^{25}
Falafl [4]	30		32		35		39	
Esgin et al. [13]	19		31		59		148	
Raptor [15] / [24]+[23]	10		81		5161			
This Work		16		18		19		22

Fig. 2. Sizes, in KB, of the different lattice-based ring signature schemes with approximately 128 bits of security. The sizes for [4,13,15] are taken from [4, Table 1].

Fig. 1 is a zero-centered discrete Gaussian, then the distribution of $\vec{z} = c\vec{s} + \vec{y}$ before rejection sampling is performed is a discrete Gaussian centered at $c\vec{s}$. In order for the rejection probability to not be too large (e.g. $< 1 - 1/e$), one needs the standard deviation of the $\vec{z}$ after the rejection sampling to be around $12 \cdot \|c\vec{s}\|$ [17]. In [8], it was shown that if one can get the distribution of $\vec{z}$ before rejection sampling to follow a *bimodal* Gaussian distribution with the two centers being $\pm c\vec{s}$, then one only needs the standard deviation of the $\vec{z}$ after rejection sampling to be $\|c\vec{s}\|/\sqrt{2}$ for the same repetition rate. Such a reduction has a direct consequence on reducing the output length and increasing the SIS-hardness of the underlying problem.

The way to create a bimodal gaussian with the two centers being $\pm c\vec{s}$ is for the prover to choose a $y \leftarrow D$ and also a $b \leftarrow \{-1, 1\}$ and then create $\vec{z} = bc\vec{s} + \vec{y}$. It is crucial for security that b remains hidden and so the verifier is not allowed to know b or use it during verification. This could be an issue in regular signature schemes because the verifier would need to directly check that

$$A\vec{z} = c\vec{t} + \vec{w}. \tag{8}$$

Since $A\vec{z} = A(bc\vec{s} + \vec{y})$, we would need $A\vec{s} = -A\vec{s}$ to always hold. In our case, this does not hold, but it will not pose a problem because the verifier does not directly verify (8) because, for privacy, the prover cannot send $\vec{w}$ in the clear anyway. Instead, the verifier gets , $(\vec{w})$ and a ZK proof that this commitment opens to a $\vec{w}$ satisfying (8). Since the prover already sends a commitment to $\vec{w}$ along with the ones for $\vec{v}_i$ (and eventually all the "garbage terms" required in π), he can just increase the commitment size by one (128-degree) polynomial and also commit to b. Then the proof π would need to be modified to prove that

$$[bc\vec{t}_1 \mid \ldots \mid bc\vec{t}_n] \cdot (\vec{v}_1 \otimes \ldots \otimes \vec{v}_m) = \vec{w} - A\vec{z}.$$

Notice that because $b \in \{-1, 1\}$ and all the $\vec{v}_i$ consist of all 0's and one 1, this can be rewritten as

$$[c\vec{t}_1 \mid \ldots \mid c\vec{t}_n] \cdot (b\vec{v}_1 \otimes \vec{v}_2 \otimes \ldots \otimes \vec{v}_m) = \vec{w} - A\vec{z},$$

and so the only thing that changes is that instead of committing to $\vec{v}_1$, the prover commits to $b\vec{v}_1$. He then just has to show that the coefficients of $b\vec{v}_1$ are in $\{0, b\}$ rather than $\{0, 1\}$ – but this proof is exactly the same if we already have a commitment to b (which we proved to be in $\{-1, 1\}$).

1.6   Application to Confidential Transactions

We now show how to construct a confidential transaction system in the model of [13]. The setup is the following: at any given moment, the state (which is managed by the blockchain, and is outside the scope of this work) consists of a set of accounts $\mathsf{act} = (\mathsf{pk}, \mathsf{cn})$, each of which contains a public key and a coin. The state also contains a set of serial numbers which implicitly correspond to the accounts that were already spent (to prevent double-spending). The secret account key associated to each account is $\mathsf{ask} = (\mathsf{sk}, \mathsf{ck}, \mathsf{amt})$, which consists of the secret key corresponding to pk and the commitment key ck, which is the randomness used to create the BDLOP commitment cn to the amount amt in the account. As in [13], we will assume that amt takes values between 0 and $2^{64} - 1$. Since we are working over rings with 32 NTT slots, we will represent the values in base 4. The basic operation has the sender choosing M input accounts for which he knows the secret keys associated to $\mathsf{pk}^{(1)}, \ldots, \mathsf{pk}^{(M)}$, and then creating S new output accounts with given public keys for which he does not need to know the associated secret keys. There are three correctness constraints. The first is that the spender knows the associated secret keys for the M input accounts. The second is that the sum of the values of the input coins (i.e. the sum of the amt) equals to the sum of the values of the output coins. And the third is that none of the M input accounts were used as inputs in any previous transaction.

In addition to correctness, there are also secrecy and anonymity requirements. The secrecy requirement states that nothing about the amounts amt is known except that the sum of the input and output coins is equal. The spender's anonymity is defined by hiding the spenders account among N other accounts. In particular, rather than stating which M accounts the spender is using, he will instead choose M sets of N accounts each, and then choose one account from each set in a way that hides which of the N accounts has been chosen. How the spender chooses the $N - 1$ other accounts is a policy issue that is outside the scope of this work.

The public information for the system consists of a polynomial matrix $\boldsymbol{B}$ which forms the "top part" of the BDLOP commitment. The polynomial vectors $\vec{\boldsymbol{b}}_c$ (which will be used to commit to amt) and $\vec{\boldsymbol{b}}_s$ (which will be used to "commit" to zero, with the commitment being the serial number) form the "bottom part" of the commitments. In particular, sk is a low-norm vector $\vec{\boldsymbol{s}}$ where

$$\begin{bmatrix} \boldsymbol{B} \\ \vec{\boldsymbol{b}}_s \end{bmatrix} \vec{\boldsymbol{s}} = \begin{bmatrix} \mathsf{pk} \\ \mathsf{sn} \end{bmatrix}. \tag{9}$$

And ck is another low-norm vector $\vec{\boldsymbol{r}}$ such that

$$\begin{bmatrix} \boldsymbol{B} \\ \vec{\boldsymbol{b}}_c \end{bmatrix} \vec{\boldsymbol{r}} + \begin{bmatrix} 0 \\ \mathsf{amt} \end{bmatrix} = \mathsf{cn}. \tag{10}$$

Correctness. Let's ignore anonymity for a moment, and just briefly discuss how the correctness of the protocol could be handled. If the spender wants to spend accounts $\mathsf{act}^{(1)}, \ldots, \mathsf{act}^{(M)}$, then he outputs the values $\mathsf{sn}^{(j)}, \vec{s}^{(j)}, \vec{r}^{(j)}, \mathsf{amt}^{(j)}$ for the input accounts, and the verifier can check that (9) and (10) are satisfied. Furthermore, the verifier checks that none of the $\mathsf{sn}^{(j)}$ are in the set of used serial numbers, and adds these $\mathsf{sn}^{(j)}$ to the set. Note that because the value of $\vec{s}^{(j)}$ is uniquely determined by B and pk (unless SIS is easy), the value of sn is uniquely tied to pk; and so it is not possible to spend a coin more than once. The spender then creates valid output tokens with the values of pk that he is given and creates the output coins with by picking small vectors $\vec{r}$ and using them to create BDLOP commitments to amt as in (10). He then outputs these $\vec{r}$ and amt so that everyone can check that the sum of the input amounts is equal to the sum of the output amounts.

Anonymity and Secrecy. We now sketch how anonymity and secrecy is achieved in our confidential transactions protocol. The spender chooses the M accounts $\mathsf{act}^{(j)} = (\mathsf{pk}^{(j)}, \mathsf{cn}^{(j)})$ that he wants to spend. He puts each of the right hand sides of (10) (i.e. the coin commitments) from these accounts into M lists $T^{(j)}$, one coin per list. The rest of the lists are filled with N coins from accounts among which the spender wants to hide his. He then creates S output accounts $\mathsf{act}^{(j)} = (\mathsf{pk}^{(j)}, \mathsf{cn}^{(j)})$ using the given public keys. He does not need to hide these accounts and so he just creates S lists of size 1 for the output coins. He then wants to create one BDLOP commitment that includes all the coin values (i.e. the amt) from the input and output tokens. This protocol is described in Fig. 6. Once the spender has one BDLOP commitment, he can prove that the sum of the input and output tokens matches, which can be done using techniques similar to those in [13, 18].

The prover also needs to show that he knows $\vec{s}$ that satisfy (9) for the input accounts. He does this by creating M lists $U^{(j)}$ that are derived from $T^{(j)}$. If the spender's coin is in position i in the list $T^{(j)}$, then he puts $\begin{bmatrix} \mathsf{pk}_i^{(j)} \\ \mathsf{sn}^{(j)} \end{bmatrix}$ into position i. He then fills the list with the public keys from the accounts corresponding to the coins in $T^{(j)}$. For the serial numbers, he attaches the same one (i.e. the one corresponding to his public key) to all the public keys. In particular, if the spender wants to hide the jth account that he will be using in position i among $N - 1$ other accounts $\mathsf{act}_1, \ldots, \mathsf{act}_{i-1}, \mathsf{act}_{i+1}, \ldots, \mathsf{act}_N$, then the lists $T^{(j)}$ and $U^{(j)}$ are

$$T^{(j)} = \left[\mathsf{cn}_1^{(j)}, \ldots, \mathsf{cn}_N^{(j)} \right]$$

$$U^{(j)} = \left[\begin{bmatrix} \mathsf{pk}_1^{(j)} \\ \mathsf{sn}^{(j)} \end{bmatrix}, \ldots, \begin{bmatrix} \mathsf{pk}_{i-1}^{(j)} \\ \mathsf{sn}^{(j)} \end{bmatrix}, \begin{bmatrix} \mathsf{pk}_i^{(j)} \\ \mathsf{sn}^{(j)} \end{bmatrix}, \begin{bmatrix} \mathsf{pk}_{i+1}^{(j)} \\ \mathsf{sn}^{(j)} \end{bmatrix}, \ldots, \begin{bmatrix} \mathsf{pk}_N^{(j)} \\ \mathsf{sn}^{(j)} \end{bmatrix} \right]$$

For the lists $U^{(j)}$, the spender simply wants to prove that he knows the secret keys $\vec{s}^{(j)}$ for the elements in the same position as those in $T^{(j)}$. Since the positions are already committed to, the proof of knowledge of the $\vec{s}^{(j)}$ does not require any extra BDLOP commitments and the proof of knowledge of the $\vec{s}^{(j)}$ can be amortized into the output vector $\vec{z}$ in Fig. 6. The verifier will need to check that the serial numbers $\mathsf{sn}^{(j)}$ have never been used (i.e. don't appear in the

(M, S)	ring size N				
	2^5	2^{10}	2^{15}	2^{20}	2^{25}
$(1, 2)$ This Work	22 KB	24 KB	25 KB	27 KB	28 KB
$(1, 2)$ Esgin et al. [13]	100 KB	160 KB	250 KB	375 KB	520 KB
$(2, 2)$ This Work	24 KB	27 KB	30 KB	33 KB	36 KB
$(2, 2)$ Esgin et al. [13]	110 KB	190 KB	300 KB	440 KB	660 KB

Fig. 3. Transaction proof sizes depending on ring size (anonymity set size) N, number M of input accounts, and number S of output accounts. The sizes for [13] are taken from [13, Figure 1].

M	25	50	75	100
size (This Work $N = 1024$)	100 KB	180 KB	262 KB	345 KB
size (Esgin et al. [13] $N = 100$)	370 KB	610 KB	900 KB	1170 KB

Fig. 4. Transaction proof sizes with M input accounts and $S = 2$ output accounts. The anonymity set N is 100 in [13] and $32^2 = 1024$ in our work. The sizes for [13] are taken from [13, Figure 2].

"used" pile) and that the lists $\boldsymbol{T}^{(j)}, \boldsymbol{m}^{(j)}$ are valid (i.e. the positions $\mathsf{pk}_i^{(j)}$ in list $\boldsymbol{T}^{(j)}$ and $\mathsf{cn}_i^{(j)}$ in list $\boldsymbol{U}^{(j)}$ correspond to some account $\mathsf{act} = \left(\mathsf{pk}_i^{(j)}, \mathsf{cn}_i^{(j)}\right)$). The verifier also has to verify the proof from Fig. 6 and the addition proof confirming that the amounts in the input and output accounts match.

The protocol in Fig. 6, which is at the center of the confidential transaction protocol, creates a new BDLOP commitment and proves that it is committing to the same values as the M input and S output accounts. It additionally proves that the spender knows the secret keys of the M input accounts. This involves using the protocol for the k-dimensional version of the set membership problem as well as an amortization technique which will allow us to only send one "masked value" for all the randomness used in the $M+S$ accounts.

Aggregating BDLOP Commitments. Before describing the protocol in Fig. 6, we ignore the part where each of the M input accounts are hidden among N others, and give a simpler protocol in Fig. 5 that takes k BDLOP commitments with distinct randomnesses, and creates one BDLOP commitment to the same messages. The improvement in this protocol over the trivial one is in the fact that only one output $\vec{z}$ is enough to prove knowledge that all k commitments are valid. The norm of this vector $\vec{z}$ is larger by a factor of k (or $\sqrt{k}$ in the asymptote), so its representation grows only logarithmically in k.

Private information: For $1 \le i \le k$, polynomials m_i, low-norm vectors $\vec{s}_i$

Public information: Uniformly random $B, \vec{b}, A, \vec{a}_w, \vec{a}_i, \begin{bmatrix} t_i \\ u_i \end{bmatrix} = \begin{bmatrix} B \\ \vec{b} \end{bmatrix} \vec{s}_i + \begin{bmatrix} \vec{0} \\ m_i \end{bmatrix}$

<u>Prover</u>   <u>Verifier</u>

$(\vec{y}, \vec{r}) \leftarrow D_y \times D_r$

$\vec{w} := B\vec{y}; \ \tilde{w} := \vec{b} \cdot \vec{y}$

$\begin{bmatrix} A \\ \vec{a}_1 \\ \dots \\ \vec{a}_k \\ \vec{a}_w \end{bmatrix} \vec{r} + \begin{bmatrix} \vec{0} \\ m_1 \\ \dots \\ m_k \\ \tilde{w} \end{bmatrix} = \begin{bmatrix} \vec{f} \\ g_1 \\ \dots \\ g_k \\ \tilde{g}_w \end{bmatrix} = \omega$ $\xrightarrow{\ \vec{w}, \omega\ }$

$\xleftarrow{\ c_1, \dots, c_k\ }$ $c_1, \dots, c_k \leftarrow C$

$\vec{z} := \vec{y} + \sum c_i \vec{s}_i$, and rejection sample

$\vec{a}^* := \sum_{i=1}^{k} c_i \vec{a}_i - \vec{a}_w$

$g^* := \sum_{i=1}^{k} c_i g_i - \vec{g}_w + \vec{b} \cdot \vec{z}$

$\pi = \text{ZKPoK that } \begin{bmatrix} \vec{f} \\ g^* \end{bmatrix} \text{ under public key}$

$\begin{bmatrix} A \\ \vec{a}^* \end{bmatrix}$ is a commitment to $\sum_{i=1}^{k} c_i u_i$

$\xrightarrow{\ \vec{z}, \pi\ }$

1. check that $\|\vec{z}\|$ is small

2. check that $\sum_{i=1}^{k} c_i \vec{t}_i = B\vec{z} - \vec{w}$

3. Compute $\vec{a}^*, g^*$ and verify π

Fig. 5. A protocol which takes commitments $\begin{bmatrix} t_i \\ u_i \end{bmatrix} = \begin{bmatrix} B \\ \vec{b} \end{bmatrix} \vec{s}_i + \begin{bmatrix} \vec{0} \\ m_i \end{bmatrix}$ to m_i under distinct randomnesses $\vec{s}_i$, and outputs one BDLOP commitment ω to all the m_i (and some auxiliary garage term(s)) under one common randomness $\vec{r}$. Along with outputting the commitment, the protocol also proves that $\begin{bmatrix} t_i \\ u_i \end{bmatrix}$ are valid commitments and that the new commitment is to the same m_i.

The protocol in Fig. 5 takes as input k BDLOP commitments under randomness $\vec{s}_i$ and produces one BDLOP commitment ω under randomness $\vec{r}$. The commitment includes all the m_i and one additional "garbage polynomial" $\tilde{w}$. When the prover computes and outputs $\vec{z}$, he proves that all the k commitments under $\vec{s}_i$ are valid. The rest of the steps are needed to show that the commitment under $\vec{r}$ is to the same m_i. We discuss this in more detail below.

The proof that the k commitments are valid follows from the ideas in [2] where one does rewinding by keeping most of the challenge fixed. As long as the new challenge still has κ bits of entropy conditioned on the prior challenge, the soundness error will still be $\approx 2^{-\kappa}$. Without loss of generality, suppose that we would like to prove that the new commitment is a commitment to $\boldsymbol{m}_1$ (in the row that contains $\boldsymbol{g}_1$). Let $(\vec{\boldsymbol{w}}, \omega, \boldsymbol{c}_1, \boldsymbol{c}_2 \ldots, \boldsymbol{c}_k, \vec{\boldsymbol{z}}, \pi)$ be the transcript of one run and $(\vec{\boldsymbol{w}}, \omega, \boldsymbol{c}_1', \boldsymbol{c}_2 \ldots, \boldsymbol{c}_k, \vec{\boldsymbol{z}}', \pi')$ be the view of the second run when we rewind while keeping all the challenges, except for $\boldsymbol{c}_1$ fixed.

Rewinding on the second verification equation, we obtain $(\boldsymbol{c}_1 - \boldsymbol{c}_1')\vec{\boldsymbol{t}}_1 = \boldsymbol{A}(\vec{\boldsymbol{z}} - \vec{\boldsymbol{z}}')$. By (2), this implies that the message $\boldsymbol{m}_i$ committed to by $\begin{bmatrix} \vec{\boldsymbol{t}}_1 \\ \boldsymbol{u}_1 \end{bmatrix}$ satisfies

$$(\boldsymbol{c}_1 - \boldsymbol{c}_1')\boldsymbol{m}_1 = (\boldsymbol{c} - \boldsymbol{c}')\boldsymbol{u}_1 - \vec{\boldsymbol{b}} \cdot (\vec{\boldsymbol{z}} - \vec{\boldsymbol{z}}'). \tag{11}$$

Notice that repeating this for all i, we can prove that all the commitments $\begin{bmatrix} \vec{\boldsymbol{t}}_i \\ \boldsymbol{u}_i \end{bmatrix}$ are valid. The intuition for proving that ω is a commitment to the same messages is to prove that the messages in the commitment of ω (call them $\bar{\boldsymbol{m}}_i$ and $\bar{\boldsymbol{w}}$) satisfy the linear equation

$$\sum_i \boldsymbol{c}_i \bar{\boldsymbol{m}}_i = \sum_i \boldsymbol{c}_i \boldsymbol{u}_i + \bar{\boldsymbol{w}} - \vec{\boldsymbol{b}} \cdot \vec{\boldsymbol{z}}. \tag{12}$$

Rewinding in the same way as above, we would obtain

$$(\boldsymbol{c}_1 - \boldsymbol{c}_1')\bar{\boldsymbol{m}}_1 = (\boldsymbol{c}_1 - \boldsymbol{c}_1')\boldsymbol{u}_1 - \vec{\boldsymbol{b}} \cdot (\vec{\boldsymbol{z}} - \vec{\boldsymbol{z}}').$$

Substituting $\vec{\boldsymbol{b}} \cdot (\vec{\boldsymbol{z}} - \vec{\boldsymbol{z}}')$ from (11), we get $(\boldsymbol{c}_1 - \boldsymbol{c}_1')\bar{\boldsymbol{m}}_1 = (\boldsymbol{c}_1 - \boldsymbol{c}_1')\boldsymbol{m}_1$. And since $\boldsymbol{c}_1 - \boldsymbol{c}_1'$ is invertible, we have $\boldsymbol{m}_1 = \bar{\boldsymbol{m}}_1$ as desired.

We now observe that we exactly prove (12). The proof π proves that ω is a valid commitment and therefore there is a unique $\vec{\boldsymbol{v}}$ (and a short polynomial d s.t. $d\vec{\boldsymbol{v}}$ has small norm) satisfying $g_i - \vec{\boldsymbol{a}}_i \cdot \vec{\boldsymbol{v}} = \bar{\boldsymbol{m}}_i$ and $g_w - \vec{\boldsymbol{a}}_w \cdot \vec{\boldsymbol{v}} = \bar{w}$. Because we also prove that $\sum \boldsymbol{c}_i \boldsymbol{u}_i$ is a valid commitment, it implies that $\langle \vec{\boldsymbol{a}}^*, \vec{\boldsymbol{v}} \rangle + \sum \boldsymbol{c}_i v_i = g^*$. If we expand out the definitions of $\vec{\boldsymbol{a}}^*$ and g^*, and then plug it in, along with the expressions for $(\boldsymbol{c}_i - \boldsymbol{c}_i')g_i$ and $(\boldsymbol{c}_i - \boldsymbol{c}_i')g_w$, into the previous equation, we will exactly end up with (12).

We now sketch the zero-knowledge proof. By assumption, π can be simulated and $\vec{\boldsymbol{z}}$ is independent of $\vec{\boldsymbol{s}}_i$ and $\boldsymbol{c}_i$ by rejection sampling. The BDLOP commitment ω is indistinguishable from uniform by the LWE assumption, and $\vec{\boldsymbol{w}}$ is unique once $\vec{\boldsymbol{z}}$ and $\boldsymbol{c}_i$ are chosen. Something worth noting is that while $\vec{\boldsymbol{w}} = \boldsymbol{B}\vec{\boldsymbol{y}}$ can be sent in the clear, the value $\tilde{\boldsymbol{w}} = \boldsymbol{b} \cdot \vec{\boldsymbol{y}}$ needs to be sent as part of a commitment because revealing it in the clear would end up revealing some function of the $\boldsymbol{m}_i$.

Private information: For $1 \leq j \leq k$, $V^{(j)} = (\vec{v}_1^{(j)}, \ldots, \vec{v}_m^{(j)}) \in \{0,1\}^{l \times m}$ s.t.
$\|\vec{v}_i^{(j)}\|_1 = 1$, $\vec{s}^{(j)}$ with a small norm, and message polynomials $m^{(j)}$

Public information: $\boldsymbol{B}$, $\vec{b}$, $\boldsymbol{T}^{(j)} = \left[\begin{bmatrix} \vec{t}_1^{(j)} \\ \boldsymbol{u}_1^{(j)} \end{bmatrix} \mid \ldots \mid \begin{bmatrix} \vec{t}_n^{(j)} \\ \boldsymbol{u}_n^{(j)} \end{bmatrix} \right]$, where $n = l^m$, s.t

$$\boldsymbol{T}^{(j)} \cdot (\vec{v}_1^{(j)} \otimes \ldots \otimes \vec{v}_m^{(j)}) = \begin{bmatrix} \boldsymbol{B} \\ \vec{b} \end{bmatrix} \vec{s}^{(j)} + \begin{bmatrix} \vec{0} \\ m^{(j)} \end{bmatrix}$$

<u>Prover</u>   <u>Verifier</u>

$\vec{y} \leftarrow D$
$\vec{w} := \boldsymbol{B}\vec{y}$
$\tilde{w} := \vec{b} \cdot \vec{y}$
$\omega = \mathsf{Com}(m^{(1)}, \ldots, m^{(k)}, V^{(1)}, \ldots, V^{(k)}, \tilde{w}, -\vec{w})$

$\xrightarrow{\quad \omega \quad}$

$\xleftarrow{\quad c^{(1)}, \ldots, c^{(k)} \quad}$ $c^{(1)}, \ldots, c^{(k)} \leftarrow \mathcal{C}$

$\vec{z} := \vec{y} + \sum c^{(j)} \vec{s}^{(j)}$, and rejection sample
Define $\boldsymbol{P}^{(i)} = c^{(i)} \boldsymbol{T}^{(i)}$

Define $g^* := \sum_{j=1}^{k} c^{(j)} g^{(j)} - \tilde{g}^{(w)} + \vec{b} \cdot \vec{z}$

$\pi = \mathsf{ZKPoK}$ that $\begin{bmatrix} \boldsymbol{B}\vec{z} - \vec{w} \\ g^* \end{bmatrix}$ is a

commitment to $\sum_{j=1}^{k} \boldsymbol{P}^{(j)} \cdot (\vec{v}_1^{(j)} \otimes \ldots \otimes \vec{v}_m^{(j)})$ $\xrightarrow{\quad \vec{z}, \pi \quad}$

1. check that $\|\vec{z}\|$ is small
2. verify π

Fig. 6. Given $\boldsymbol{T}^{(j)} \cdot (\vec{v}_1^{(j)} \otimes \ldots \otimes \vec{v}_m^{(j)}) = \begin{bmatrix} \boldsymbol{B} \\ \vec{b} \end{bmatrix} \vec{s}^{(j)} + \begin{bmatrix} \vec{0} \\ m^{(j)} \end{bmatrix}$, the prover creates a BDLOP commitment to all the k $m^{(j)}$ and proves its correctness. The new commitment , uses public matrices (e.g. $\boldsymbol{A}$, etc. as in Fig. 5) which we do not explicitly state in this sketch. The terms comprising g^* are parts of ω, and are described in detail in the protocol in Fig. 5 (except with subscripts instead of superscripts).

Aggregation and Set Membership. Converting the protocol from Fig. 5 into the one in Fig. 6 uses very similar intuition as when converting a signature scheme into a ring signature scheme in Fig. 1.

We will now proceed to briefly explain the transition from the protocol in Fig. 5 to the one in Fig. 6. First, the second verifier check in Fig. 5 cannot be done in the clear – that is the verifier cannot know $\vec{w}$. If he knows $\vec{w}$, then he can compute the weighted sum of the committed values $\sum c_i \vec{t}_i$, which would leak information about which commitments were chosen. The prover therefore must commit to $\vec{w}$. So the commitment ω in Fig. 6 creates commitments to $m^{(j)}, \tilde{w}$ exactly like to $m_i, \tilde{w}$ in Fig. 5, and also commits to $\vec{w}$ and to $V^{(j)}$, which are needed for the set membership proof.

The prover then sets up the $\vec{a}^*$ and g^* exactly as in Fig. 5. Therefore g^* is a commitment to the bottom part of $\sum_{j=1}^{k} c^{(j)} T^{(j)} \cdot (\vec{v}_1^{(j)} \otimes \cdots \otimes \vec{v}_m^{(j)})$. From the second verification equation in Fig. 5, we know that the top part of the preceding is $B\vec{z} - \vec{w}$, and we can create a commitment to this value by adding $B\vec{z}$ to the commitment of $-\vec{w}$ that we already have. We therefore have a commitment to $\sum_{j=1}^{k} c^{(j)} T^{(j)} \cdot (\vec{v}_1^{(j)} \otimes \cdots \otimes \vec{v}_m^{(j)})$ and creating the proof π is therefore equivalent to creating a proof for (5) and (6). Showing that this protocol is sound is done the same way as the one in Fig. 5 because $\vec{z}$ and π in Fig. 6 satisfy the three verification parts in Fig. 5.

2 Preliminaries

2.1 Notation

Let $N \in \mathbb{N}$ be a security parameter and q be an odd prime. We write $x \leftarrow S$ when $x \in S$ is sampled uniformly at random from the finite set S and similarly $x \leftarrow D$ when x is sampled according to the distribution D. For $a < b$ and $n \in \mathbb{N}$, we define $[a, b] := \{a, a + 1 \ldots, b\}$ and $[n] := [1, n]$. Given two functions $f, g : \mathbb{N} \rightarrow [0, 1]$, we write $f(\mu) \approx g(\mu)$ if $|f(\mu) - g(\mu)| < \mu^{-\omega(1)}$. A function f is negligible if $f \approx 0$. We write $\mathsf{negl}(n)$ to denote an unspecified negligible function in n.

For a power of two d, denote $\mathcal{R}$ and $\mathcal{R}_q$ respectively to be the rings $\mathbb{Z}[X]/(X^d + 1)$ and $\mathbb{Z}_q[X]/(X^d + 1)$. Bold lower-case letters denote elements in $\mathcal{R}$ or $\mathcal{R}_q$ and bold lower-case letters with arrows represent column vectors with coefficients in $\mathcal{R}$ or $\mathcal{R}_q$. We also write bold upper-case letters for matrices in $\mathcal{R}$ or $\mathcal{R}_q$. By default, for a polynomial denoted as a bold letter, we write its i-th coefficient as its corresponding regular font letter subscript i, e.g. $f_0 \in \mathbb{Z}_q$ is a constant coefficient of $f \in \mathcal{R}_q$.

2.2 Cyclotomic Rings

Suppose q splits into l prime ideals of degree d/l in $\mathcal{R}$. This means $X^d + 1 \equiv \varphi_1 \ldots \varphi_l \pmod{q}$ with irreducible polynomials φ_j of degree d/l modulo q. We assume that $\mathbb{Z}_q$ contains a primitive $2l$-th root of unity $\zeta \in \mathbb{Z}_q$ but no elements whose order is a higher power of two, i.e. $q - 1 \equiv 2l \pmod{4l}$. Therefore, we have

$$X^d + 1 \equiv \prod_{j \in \mathbb{Z}_l} \left(X^{\frac{d}{l}} - \zeta^{2j+1} \right) \pmod{q}. \tag{13}$$

Let $\mathcal{M}_q := \{p \in \mathbb{Z}_q[X] : \deg(p) < d/l\}$ be the $\mathbb{Z}_q$-module of polynomials of degree less than d/l. We define the Number Theoretic Transform (NTT) of a polynomial $p \in \mathcal{R}_q$ as follows:

$$\mathsf{NTT}\,(p) := \begin{bmatrix} \hat{p}_0 \\ \vdots \\ \hat{p}_{l-1} \end{bmatrix} \in \mathcal{M}_q^l \text{ where } \mathsf{NTT}\,(p)_j = \hat{p}_j = p \bmod (X^{\frac{d}{l}} - \zeta^{2j+1}).$$

Furthermore, we expand the definition of NTT to vectors of polynomials $\vec{p} \in \mathcal{R}_q^k$, where the NTT operation is applied to each coefficient of $\vec{p}$, resulting in a vector in $\mathcal{M}_q^{kl}$.

We also define the inverse NTT operation. Namely, for a vector $\vec{v} \in \mathcal{M}_q^l$, $\mathsf{NTT}^{-1}(\vec{v})$ is the polynomial $p \in \mathcal{R}_q$ such that $\mathsf{NTT}(p) = \vec{v}$.

Let $\vec{v} = (v_0, \ldots, v_{l-1}), \vec{w} = (w_0, \ldots, w_{l-1}) \in \mathcal{M}_q^l$. Then, we define the component-wise product $\vec{v} \circ \vec{w}$ to be the vector $\vec{u} = (u_0, \ldots, u_{l-1}) \in \mathcal{M}_q^l$ such that

$$u_j = v_j w_j \bmod (X^{\frac{d}{l}} - \zeta^{2j+1})$$

for $j \in \mathbb{Z}_l$. By definition, we have the following property of the inverse NTT operation:

$$\mathsf{NTT}^{-1}(\vec{v}) \cdot \mathsf{NTT}^{-1}(\vec{w}) = \mathsf{NTT}^{-1}(\vec{v} \circ \vec{w}).$$

Similarly, we define the *inner product*:

$$\langle \vec{v}, \vec{w} \rangle = \sum_{j=0}^{l-1} \left(v_j w_j \bmod (X^{\frac{d}{l}} - \zeta^{2j+1}) \right).$$

We remark that this operation is not an inner product in the strictly mathematical sense (e.g. it is not linear). However, it has a few properties which are characteristic for an inner product. For instance, given arbitrary vectors $\vec{x}, \vec{y}, \vec{z} \in \mathcal{M}_q^l$ and scalar $c \in \mathbb{Z}_q$ we have: $\langle \vec{x}, \vec{y} \rangle = \langle \vec{y}, \vec{x} \rangle$ (symmetry), $\langle \vec{x} + \vec{y}, \vec{z} \rangle = \langle \vec{x}, \vec{z} \rangle + \langle \vec{y}, \vec{z} \rangle$ (distributive law) and $\langle c\vec{x}, y \rangle = c \langle \vec{x}, \vec{z} \rangle$. We also highlight that the definition of $\langle \cdot, \cdot \rangle$ depends on the factors of $X^d + 1$ modulo q.

We generalise the newly introduced operations to work for vectors $\vec{v} = (\vec{v}_1, \ldots, \vec{v}_k)$ and $\vec{w} = (\vec{w}_1, \ldots, \vec{w}_k) \in \mathcal{M}_q^{kl}$ of length being a multiple of l in the usual way. In particular $\langle \vec{v}, \vec{w} \rangle = \sum_{i=1}^{k} \langle \vec{v}_i, \vec{w}_i \rangle$.

Eventually, for a matrix $A \in \mathcal{M}_q^{n \times kl}$ with rows $\vec{a}_1, \ldots, \vec{a}_n \in \mathcal{M}_q^{kl}$ and a vector $\vec{v} \in \mathcal{M}_q^{kl}$, we define the matrix-vector operation:

$$A\vec{v} = \begin{pmatrix} \langle \vec{a}_1, \vec{v} \rangle \\ \vdots \\ \langle \vec{a}_n, \vec{v} \rangle \end{pmatrix} \in \mathcal{M}_q^n.$$

In proving linear relations, we will need the following simple lemma.

Lemma 2.1. *Let $n, k \in \mathbb{N}$. Then, for any $A \in \mathcal{M}_q^{nl \times kl}, \vec{v} \in \mathcal{M}_q^{nl}$ and $\vec{s} \in \mathbb{Z}_q^{kl}$ we have*

$$\langle A\vec{s}, \vec{v} \rangle = \langle \vec{s}, A^T \vec{v} \rangle.$$

Proof. We prove the statement for $k = n = 1$. The proof can then be easily using the definition of an inner product. Let $\vec{a}_i$ be the $(i + 1)$-th row of A and $a_{i,j} \in M_q$ be its $(j + 1)$-th coefficient. Similarly, we define s_i and v_i to be the $(i + 1)$-th coefficient of $\vec{s}$ and $\vec{v}$ respectively. Then, by definition we have:

$$\langle A\vec{s}, \vec{v} \rangle = \sum_{i=0}^{l-1} \langle \vec{a}_i, \vec{s} \rangle v_i \bmod (X^{\frac{d}{l}} - \zeta^{2i+1})$$

$$= \sum_{i=0}^{l-1} \left(\sum_{j=0}^{l-1} a_{i,j} s_j \bmod (X^{\frac{d}{l}} - \zeta^{2j+1}) \right) v_i \bmod (X^{\frac{d}{l}} - \zeta^{2i+1})$$

$$= \sum_{i=0}^{l-1} \sum_{j=0}^{l-1} a_{i,j} s_j v_i \bmod (X^{\frac{d}{l}} - \zeta^{2i+1}) \tag{14}$$

$$= \sum_{j=0}^{l-1} s_j \left(\sum_{i=0}^{l-1} a_{i,j} v_i \bmod (X^{\frac{d}{l}} - \zeta^{2i+1}) \right)$$

$$= \langle \vec{s}, A^T \vec{v} \rangle.$$

Here, the crucial step was the observation that for $\vec{s} \in \mathbb{Z}_q^l$ and any $i, j \in \mathbb{Z}_l$ we have:

$$a_{i,j} s_j \bmod (X^{\frac{d}{l}} - \zeta^{2j+1}) = a_{i,j} s_j,$$

i.e. there is no reduction modulo the polynomial when multiplying by a scalar. □

Last but not least, we recall the following lemma from [10].

Lemma 2.2. *Let* $p = p_0 + p_1 X + \ldots + p_{d-1} X^{d-1} \in \mathcal{R}_q$. *Then,*

$$\frac{1}{l} \sum_{i=0}^{l} \mathsf{NTT}\,(p)_i = \sum_{i=0}^{d/l-1} p_i X^i.$$

For our constructions in this work, the practical hardness of either of the problems against known attacks is not affected by the parameter m. Therefore, we sometimes simply write M-SIS$_{\kappa,B}$ or M-LWE$_{\lambda,\chi}$. The parameters κ and λ denote the *module ranks* for M-SIS and M-LWE, respectively. Also, when χ is a uniform distribution for the set $[-\mu, \mu]$, we simply denote M-LWE$_{\lambda,\mu}$.

2.3   Probability Distributions

In this paper we sample the coefficients of the random polynomials in the commitment scheme using the distribution χ on $\{-1, 0, 1\}$ where ± 1 both have probability $5/16$ and 0 has probability $6/16$ identically as in [1,6,10].

Discrete Gaussian distribution. We now define the discrete Gaussian distribution used for the rejection sampling.

Definition 2.3. *The* discrete Gaussian distribution *on* $\mathcal{R}^\ell$ *centered around* $\vec{v} \in \mathcal{R}^\ell$ *with standard deviation* $\mathfrak{s} > 0$ *is given by*

$$D_{v,\mathfrak{s}}^{\ell d}(\vec{z}) = \frac{e^{-\|\vec{z}-\vec{v}\|^2/2\mathfrak{s}^2}}{\sum_{\vec{z}' \in \mathcal{R}^\ell} e^{-\|\vec{z}'\|^2/2\mathfrak{s}^2}}.$$

When it is centered around $\vec{0} \in \mathcal{R}^\ell$ *we write* $D_{\mathfrak{s}}^{\ell d} = D_{\vec{0},\mathfrak{s}}^{\ell d}$

2.4 BDLOP Commitment Scheme

We recall the BDLOP commitment scheme from [3]. Suppose that we want to commit to a message vector $\vec{m} = (m_1, \ldots, m_n) \in \mathcal{R}_q^n$ for $n \geq 1$ and that module ranks of κ and λ are required for M-SIS and M-LWE security, respectively. Then, in the key generation, a matrix $\boldsymbol{B}_0 \leftarrow \mathcal{R}_q^{\kappa \times (\kappa+\lambda+n)}$ and vectors $\vec{b}_1, \ldots, \vec{b}_n \leftarrow \mathcal{R}_q^{\kappa+\lambda+n}$ are generated and output as public parameters. Note that one could choose to generate $\boldsymbol{B}_0, \vec{b}_1, \ldots, \vec{b}_n$ in a more structured way as in [3] since it saves some computation. However, for readability, we write the commitment matrices in the "Knapsack" form as above. In our case, the hiding property of the commitment scheme is established via the duality between the Knapsack and M-LWE problems. We refer to [13, Appendix C] for a more detailed discussion.

To commit to the message $\vec{m}$, we first sample $\vec{r} \leftarrow \chi^{d \cdot (\kappa+\lambda+n)}$. Now, there are two parts of the commitment scheme: the binding part and the message encoding part. In particular, we compute

$$\vec{t}_0 = \boldsymbol{B}_0 \vec{r} \bmod q,$$

$$t_i = \langle \vec{b}_i, \vec{r} \rangle + m_i \bmod q,$$

for $i \in [n]$, where $\vec{t}_0$ forms the binding part and each t_i encodes a message polynomial m_i. In this paper, when we write that we compute a BDLOP commitment to a vector $\vec{m} = (\vec{m}_1, \ldots, \vec{m}_n) \in \mathcal{M}_q^{nl}$, we mean that we commit to the vector of polynomials $\vec{m} = (\mathsf{NTT}^{-1}(\vec{m}_1), \ldots, \mathsf{NTT}^{-1}(\vec{m}_n)) \in \mathcal{R}_q^n$ as above.

Next, we define the notion of a weak opening of the commitment [1].

Definition 2.4. *A* weak opening *for the commitment* $\vec{t} = \vec{t}_0 \| t_1 \| \cdots \| t_n$ *consists of a polynomial* $\bar{c} \in \mathcal{R}_q$, *a randomness vector* $\vec{r}^*$ *over* $\mathcal{R}_q$ *and messages* $m_1^*, \ldots, m_n^* \in \mathcal{R}_q$ *such that*

$$\|\bar{c}\|_1 \leq 2d \text{ and } \bar{c} \text{ is invertible over } \mathcal{R}_q$$
$$\|\bar{c}\vec{r}^*\|_2 \leq 2\beta,$$
$$\boldsymbol{B}_0 \vec{r}^* = \vec{t}_0,$$
$$\langle \vec{b}_i, \vec{r}^* \rangle + m_i^* = t_i \text{ for } i \in [n].$$

Attema et al. [1] show that the commitment scheme is still binding with respect to weak openings if M-SIS$_{\kappa, 8d\beta}$ is hard.

3   Efficient Lattice-Based Set Membership Proof

In this section we construct an efficient logarithmic-size ring signature protocol using recent results [1,10,18,19] as the building blocks. Security analysis of the interactive protocol as well as ring signature instantiation are described in the full version of the paper [20].

3.1   Overview

In order to showcase our main techniques, let us consider the following set membership problem. Namely, suppose we would like to prove knowledge of a secret element $\vec{w}_i \in \mathcal{M}_q^{kl}$, for some $k \in \mathbb{N}$, such that $\vec{w} \in S$, where S is a public set $S = \{\vec{p}_1, \ldots, \vec{p}_n\} \subseteq \mathcal{M}_q^{kl}$ of size $n = l^m$ which is a power of l.

We now use the observation from [5,12,14] that $\vec{w} \in S$ if and only if there exists a binary vector $\vec{v} \in \{0,1\}^n$ with exactly one 1 such that $P\vec{v} = \vec{w}$ where $P \in \mathcal{M}_q^{kl \times n}$ is the matrix with i-th column being $\vec{p}_i$. One could then directly prove knowledge of $\vec{w}$ and $\vec{v}$ which satisfy conditions above using e.g. the protocol from [10,18]. However, the proof size grows significantly when n gets bigger. In order to overcome this limitation, [5,14] observe that vector $\vec{v}$ can be uniquely decomposed into smaller vectors $\vec{v}_1, \ldots, \vec{v}_m \in \{0,1\}^l$ which have exactly one 1 each and

$$\vec{v} = \vec{v}_1 \otimes \vec{v}_2 \otimes \cdots \otimes \vec{v}_m. \tag{15}$$

In the end, we want to commit to $\vec{w}$ and smaller vectors $\vec{v}_1, \ldots, \vec{v}_m$ and prove

$$P(\vec{v}_1 \otimes \cdots \otimes \vec{v}_m) = \vec{w} \tag{16}$$

along with

$$\vec{v}_i \circ (\vec{v}_i - \vec{1}) = \vec{0} \text{ and } \langle \vec{1}, \vec{v}_i \rangle = 1 \text{ for } i \in [m] \tag{17}$$

where for an integer $a \in \mathbb{Z}_q$, $\vec{a} := (a, \ldots, a) \in \mathbb{Z}_q^l$. We highlight that Eq. 16 is over the $\mathbb{Z}_q$-module $\mathcal{M}_q$ (see Sect. 2.2).

We now present a new recursive approach to prove (16) and (17) efficiently. For readability, we first introduce the following notation:

$$\vec{u}_j := \vec{v}_j \otimes \cdots \otimes \vec{v}_m \text{ for } j \in [m],$$
$$P_1 := P \text{ and } \vec{x}_1 = (\vec{x}_{1,1}, \ldots, \vec{x}_{1,k}) := \vec{w}.$$

We start by sending the BDLOP commitments (as described in Sects. 1.1 and 2.4) to $\vec{v}_1, \ldots, \vec{v}_m, \vec{w}_1, \ldots, \vec{w}_k$ to the verifier:

$$\vec{t}_0 = \boldsymbol{B}_0 \vec{r} \bmod q,$$
$$t_i = \langle \vec{b}_i, \vec{r} \rangle + \mathsf{NTT}^{-1}(\vec{v}_i) \bmod q \text{ for } i \in [m]$$
$$t_{m+i} = \langle \vec{b}_{m+i}, \vec{r} \rangle + \mathsf{NTT}^{-1}(\vec{x}_i) \bmod q \text{ for } i \in [k].$$

Then, a verifier $\mathcal{V}$ sends a challenge $\vec{\gamma}_1 = (\vec{\gamma}_{1,1}, \ldots, \vec{\gamma}_{1,k}) \leftarrow \mathcal{M}_q^{kl}$. Clearly, if (16) holds then we have

$$\langle P_1(\vec{v}_1 \otimes \vec{u}_2) - \vec{x}_1, \vec{\gamma}_1 \rangle = 0.$$

Otherwise, the probability that the inner product above is equal to zero is exactly $q^{-d/l}$ which is negligible.

Now, by Lemma 2.1 and using the fact that each $\vec{v}_i \in \mathbb{Z}_q^l$, we have:

$$
\begin{aligned}
\langle P_1(\vec{v}_1 \otimes \vec{u}_2) - \vec{x}_1, \vec{\gamma}_1 \rangle &= \langle \vec{v}_1 \otimes \vec{u}_2, P_1^T \vec{\gamma}_1 \rangle - \langle \vec{x}_1, \vec{\gamma}_1 \rangle \\
&= \sum_{i=1}^{l} v_{1,i} \langle \vec{u}_2, P_{1,i}^T \vec{\gamma}_1 \rangle - \langle \vec{x}_1, \vec{\gamma}_1 \rangle \\
&= \sum_{i=1}^{l} v_{1,i} \gamma_1^T P_{1,i} \vec{u}_2 - \langle \vec{x}_1, \vec{\gamma}_1 \rangle \\
&= \vec{v}_1^T P_2 \vec{u}_2 - \langle \vec{x}_1, \vec{\gamma}_1 \rangle = \langle \vec{v}_1, P_2 \vec{u}_2 \rangle - \langle \vec{x}_1, \vec{\gamma}_1 \rangle
\end{aligned}
\tag{18}
$$

where we denote

$$
P_1 = (P_{1,1}\ P_{1,2}\ \cdots\ P_{1,l}) \in \mathcal{M}_q^{l \times l^m}
$$

and the matrix P_2 is defined as

$$
P_2 := \begin{pmatrix} \gamma_1^T P_{1,1} \\ \vdots \\ \gamma_1^T P_{1,l} \end{pmatrix} \in \mathcal{M}_q^{l \times l^{m-1}}.
\tag{19}
$$

Let us define the following vectors:

$$
\vec{x}_2 := P_2 \vec{u}_2 \in \mathcal{M}_q^l \text{ and } \vec{y}_1 := \vec{v}_1 \circ \vec{x}_2 - \sum_{i=1}^{k} \vec{x}_{1,i} \circ \vec{\gamma}_{1,i}.
\tag{20}
$$

First, we prove that $\vec{x}_2$ is constructed correctly. Note that by definition of $\vec{u}_2$ we have

$$
\vec{x}_2 = P_2(\vec{v}_2 \otimes \cdots \otimes \vec{v}_m)
$$

which is of the form (16) but with one less tensor. Hence, in order to prove this equation, we recursively follow the argument above. Then, assuming one can prove (20) for $\vec{x}_2$, by Lemma 2.2 we know that $\langle P_1(\vec{v}_1 \otimes \cdots \otimes \vec{v}_m) - \vec{x}_1, \vec{\gamma}_1 \rangle = 0$ if and only if $y_1 := \mathsf{NTT}^{-1}(\vec{y}_1)$ has the first d/l coefficients equal to zero. We present how to prove this property for y_1 below.

Let us fix $j = 2$. Suppose that $j < m$. Then, in order to show that $\vec{x}_2$ from (20) is well-formed, we apply the exact strategy as before. Namely, we send a commitment to $\vec{x}_j$:

$$
t_{m+k+j-1} = \langle \vec{b}_{m+k+j-1}, \vec{r} \rangle + \mathsf{NTT}^{-1}(\vec{x}_j).
$$

Then, given a challenge $\vec{\gamma}_j \leftarrow \mathcal{M}_q^l$, we deduce as in Eq. 18 that

$$
\langle P_j(\vec{v}_j \otimes \vec{u}_{j+1}) - \vec{x}_j, \vec{\gamma} \rangle = \langle \vec{v}_j, P_{j+1} \vec{u}_{j+1} \rangle - \langle \vec{x}_j, \vec{\gamma}_j \rangle
$$

where

$$
P_j = (P_{j,1}\ P_{j,2}\ \cdots\ P_{j,l}) \in \mathcal{M}_q^{l \times l^{m-j+1}}
$$

and the matrix P_{j+1} is defined as

$$P_{j+1} := \begin{pmatrix} \gamma_j^T P_{j,1} \\ \vdots \\ \gamma_j^T P_{j,l} \end{pmatrix} \in \mathcal{M}_q^{l \times l^{m-j}}. \tag{21}$$

Next, we define vectors $\vec{x}_{j+1}, \vec{y}_j \in \mathcal{M}_q^l$:

$$\vec{x}_{j+1} := P_{j+1}\vec{u}_{j+1} \text{ and } \vec{y}_j := \vec{v}_j \circ \vec{x}_{j+1} - \vec{x}_j \circ \vec{\gamma}_j. \tag{22}$$

Now, in order to prove well-formedness of $\vec{x}_{j+1}$ we simply run the argument from this paragraph for $j := j + 1$. Assuming that $\vec{x}_{j+1}$ is constructed correctly, we also need to prove that the coefficients of $\vec{y}_j$ sum up to 0, i.e. the first d/l coefficients of $y_j = \mathsf{NTT}^{-1}(\vec{y}_j)$ are all zeroes. Below we describe how it can be done for all the y_j's simultaneously.

Eventually, for $j = m$ we want to prove that $\vec{x}_m = P_m\vec{u}_m = P_m\vec{v}_m$ which is a simple linear proof from [10]. We also want to show $\langle \vec{1}, \vec{v}_i \rangle = 1$ for $i \in [m]$. All these relations can be combined into one linear equation:

$$\begin{pmatrix} 0 & 0 & \cdots & 0 & P_m \\ B & 0 & \cdots & 0 & 0 \\ 0 & B & \cdots & 0 & 0 \\ \vdots & \vdots & \vdots & \vdots & \vdots \\ 0 & 0 & \cdots & B & 0 \end{pmatrix} \begin{pmatrix} \vec{v}_1 \\ \vdots \\ \vec{v}_m \end{pmatrix} = \begin{pmatrix} \vec{x}_m \\ \vec{e}_1 \\ \vdots \\ \vec{e}_1 \end{pmatrix} \tag{23}$$

where

$$B = \begin{pmatrix} 1 & \cdots & 1 \\ 0 & \cdots & 0 \\ \vdots & \vdots & \vdots \\ 0 & \cdots & 0 \end{pmatrix} \in \mathbb{Z}_q^{l \times l} \text{ and } \vec{e}_1 = \begin{pmatrix} 1 \\ 0 \\ \vdots \\ 0 \end{pmatrix} \in \mathbb{Z}_q^l.$$

Let us denote $\tilde{P}_m \in \mathcal{M}_q^{(m+1)l \times ml}$ to be the matrix on the left-hand side of Eq. 23.

We proceed to proving (23). First, we get a challenge vector

$$\vec{\gamma}_m = (\vec{\gamma}_{m,1}, \ldots, \vec{\gamma}_{m,m+1}) \leftarrow \mathcal{M}_q^{(m+1)l}$$

from $\mathcal{V}$ and deduce that:

$$\left\langle \tilde{P}_m \begin{pmatrix} \vec{v}_1 \\ \vdots \\ \vec{v}_m \end{pmatrix} - \begin{pmatrix} \vec{x}_m \\ \vec{e}_1 \\ \vdots \\ \vec{e}_1 \end{pmatrix}, \vec{\gamma}_m \right\rangle = \left\langle \begin{pmatrix} \vec{v}_1 \\ \vdots \\ \vec{v}_m \end{pmatrix}, \tilde{P}_m^T \vec{\gamma}_m \right\rangle - \langle \vec{x}_m, \vec{\gamma}_{m,1} \rangle - \sum_{i=1}^m \langle \vec{e}_1, \vec{\gamma}_{m,i+1} \rangle.$$

Let $\vec{x}_{m+1} = (\vec{x}_{m+1,1}, \ldots, \vec{x}_{m+1,m}) := \tilde{P}_m^T \vec{\gamma}_m \in \mathcal{M}_q^{ml}$ and

$$\vec{y}_m := \left(\sum_{i=1}^m \vec{v}_i \circ \vec{x}_{m+1,i} \right) - \vec{x}_m \circ \vec{\gamma}_{m,1} - \vec{e}_1 \circ \sum_{i=1}^m \vec{\gamma}_{m,i}. \tag{24}$$

Note that in this case $\vec{x}_{m+1}$ is public (as opposed to $\vec{x}_1, \ldots, \vec{x}_m$). Then, as before we get that $\boldsymbol{y}_m = y_{m,0} + y_{m,1}X + \ldots + y_{m,d-1}X^{d-1} = \mathsf{NTT}^{-1}(\vec{y}_m)$ satisfies:

$$
y_{m,0} + \ldots + y_{m,d/l-1}X^{d/l-1} = \frac{1}{l}\left\langle \tilde{P}_m \begin{pmatrix} \vec{v}_1 \\ \vdots \\ \vec{v}_m \end{pmatrix} - \begin{pmatrix} \vec{x}_m \\ \vec{e}_1 \\ \vdots \\ \vec{e}_1 \end{pmatrix}, \vec{\gamma}_m \right\rangle.
$$

Therefore, we need to argue that $\boldsymbol{y}_m$ has the first d/l polynomial coefficients equal to 0.

Finally, what have left to prove is that (i) polynomials $\boldsymbol{y}_1, \ldots, \boldsymbol{y}_m$ have the first d/l coefficients equal to zero and (ii) vectors $\vec{v}_i$ are binary. We first focus on (i) and adapt the strategy shown in [10]. At the beginning, we will commit to a uniformly random polynomial $\boldsymbol{g}$ which has the first d/l coefficients equal to zero:

$$
t_{k+2m} = \langle \vec{b}_{k+2m}, \vec{r} \rangle + \boldsymbol{g}.
$$

Then, we will reveal the polynomial

$$
\boldsymbol{h} = \boldsymbol{g} + \boldsymbol{y}_1 + \ldots + \boldsymbol{y}_m. \tag{25}
$$

Hence, the verifier manually checks the the first d/l coefficients of $\boldsymbol{h}$ are indeed zeroes. On the other hand, to prove (25) we follow the approach for proving multiplicative relations from [1].

Let $\vec{y} \leftarrow D^{(\kappa+\lambda+k+2m)}$ be the masking vector. That is, given a challenge polynomial $\boldsymbol{c} \leftarrow C$ from a challenge distribution C (defined in Sect. 3.2), the prover will output a masked opening $\vec{z}$ of the randomness $\vec{r}$ defined as: $\vec{z} = \vec{y} + \boldsymbol{c}\vec{r}$. Then, define polynomials $\boldsymbol{f}_\eta$ as:

$$
\boldsymbol{f}_\eta = \begin{cases} \langle \vec{b}_\eta, \vec{y} \rangle - \boldsymbol{c}v_\eta & \text{if } \eta \in [m] \\ \langle \vec{b}_{m+i}, \vec{y} \rangle - \boldsymbol{c}x_{1,i} & \text{for } \eta = m+i; i \in [k] \\ \langle \vec{b}_{m+k+j}, \vec{y} \rangle - \boldsymbol{c}x_{j+1} & \text{for } \eta = m+k+j; j \in [m-1] \\ \langle \vec{b}_{k+2m}, \vec{y} \rangle - \boldsymbol{c}\boldsymbol{g} & \text{if } \eta = k+2m \end{cases}
$$

where $x_j = \mathsf{NTT}^{-1}(\vec{x}_j)$ and similarly for v_i and γ_j. Note that $\boldsymbol{f}_\eta = \langle \vec{b}_\eta, \vec{z} \rangle - \boldsymbol{c}\vec{t}_\eta$ for all η and thus can be calculated by the verifier.

First, let us focus on $\boldsymbol{y}_1$. By definition we have (see (20)):

$$
F_1 := \boldsymbol{f}_1 \boldsymbol{f}_{m+k+1} + \boldsymbol{c} \sum_{i=1}^{k} \gamma_{1,i} \boldsymbol{f}_{m+i} = \omega_1 + \psi_1 \boldsymbol{c} + \boldsymbol{y}_1 \boldsymbol{c}^2
$$

where polynomials ω_1, ψ_1 are defined as follows

$$
\omega_1 := \langle \vec{b}_1, \vec{y} \rangle \langle \vec{b}_{m+k+1}, \vec{y} \rangle
$$

$$
\psi_1 := \sum_{i=1}^{k} \gamma_{1,i} \langle \vec{b}_{m+i}, \vec{y} \rangle - \langle \vec{b}_1, \vec{y} \rangle x_2 - \langle \vec{b}_{m+k+1}, \vec{y} \rangle v_1
$$

Now, by Definition of y_j (see (22)), for fixed $j \in [2, m-1]$ we have:

$$F_j := f_j f_{m+k+j} + c\gamma_j f_{m+k+j-1} = \omega_j + \psi_j c + y_j c^2$$

where

$$\omega_j := \langle \vec{b}_j, \vec{y} \rangle \langle \vec{b}_{m+k+j}, \vec{y} \rangle \tag{26}$$
$$\psi_j := \gamma_j \langle \vec{b}_{m+k+j-1}, \vec{y} \rangle - \langle \vec{b}_j, \vec{y} \rangle x_{j+1} - \langle \vec{b}_{m+k+j}, \vec{y} \rangle v_j.$$

In case of $j = m$, we transform Eq. 24 into:

$$F_m := c \left(-\sum_{i=1}^{m} x_{m+1,i} f_i + \gamma_{m,1} f_{k+2m-1} - e_1 \sum_{i=1}^{m} \gamma_{m,i} \right) = \psi_m c + y_m c^2$$

where

$$\psi_m := -\sum_{i=1}^{m} x_{m+1,i} \langle \vec{b}_{i\cdot}, \vec{y} \rangle + \gamma_{m,1} \langle \vec{b}_{k+2m-1}, \vec{y} \rangle - e_1 \sum_{i=1}^{m} \gamma_{m,i}. \tag{27}$$

Clearly, all F_j can be computed by the verifier. Therefore, if we denote

$$\omega_{\mathsf{sm}} := \sum_{i=1}^{m-1} \omega_i \text{ and } \psi_{\mathsf{sm}} := \sum_{i=1}^{m} \psi_i - \langle \vec{b}_{k+2m}, \vec{y} \rangle \tag{28}$$

then we obtain:

$$\sum_{j=1}^{m} F_j - cf_{k+2m} - c^2 h = \omega_{\mathsf{sm}} + \psi_{\mathsf{sm}} c + (y_1 + \ldots + y_m + g - h)c^2.$$

Hence, we want to prove that the coefficient corresponding to the quadratic term of $\sum_{j=1}^{m} F_j - cf_{k+2m} - c^2 h$ vanishes.

Recall that we still need to prove (ii), i.e. all $\vec{v}_i$'s are binary. We first get challenges $\alpha_0, \ldots, \alpha_m \leftarrow \mathcal{R}_q$ from the verifier. Then, we observe that

$$\sum_{i=1}^{m} \alpha_i (f_i^2 + cf_i) = \omega_{\mathsf{bin}} + \psi_{\mathsf{bin}} c + \left(\sum_{i=1}^{m} \alpha_i v_i (v_i - 1) \right) c^2$$

where

$$\omega_{\mathsf{bin}} := \sum_{i=1}^{m} \alpha_i \langle \vec{b}_i, \vec{y} \rangle^2 \text{ and } \psi_{\mathsf{bin}} := \sum_{i=1}^{m} \alpha_i \langle \vec{b}_i, \vec{y} \rangle (1 - 2v_i). \tag{29}$$

Therefore, we combine (i) and (ii) by proving that the quadratic term in

$$\alpha_0 \left(\sum_{j=1}^{m} F_j - cf_{k+2m} - c^2 h \right) + \sum_{i=1}^{m} \alpha_i (f_i^2 + cf_i) \tag{30}$$

is equal to zero. In order to do so, we commit to the garbage polynomial

$$t_{k+2m+1} = \langle \vec{b}_{k+2m+1}, \vec{r} \rangle + \psi_{\mathsf{bin}} + \alpha_0 \psi_{\mathsf{sm}}$$

and additionally send $\omega := \langle \vec{b}_{k+2m+1}, \vec{y} \rangle + \omega_{\mathsf{bin}} + \alpha_0 \omega_{\mathsf{sm}}$. Then, the verifier computes $f_{k+2m+1} = \langle \vec{b}_{k+2m+1}, \vec{z} \rangle - c t_{k+2m+1}$ and checks whether:

$$\alpha_0 \left(\sum_{j=1}^m F_j - c f_{k+2m} - c^2 h \right) + \sum_{i=1}^m \alpha_i (f_i^2 + c f_i) + f_{k+2m+1} \overset{?}{=} \omega.$$

3.2 Main Protocol

We present our main lattice-based one-out-of-many proof using the techniques from Sect. 3.1 and show how it can be turned into an efficient, logarithmic-sized ring signature.

Similarly as in the previous works [12,13], the secret key of a user is a vector $\vec{s} \leftarrow [-\mu, \mu]^{\ell d}$ of short polynomials over $\mathcal{R}_q$ and the corresponding public key $\vec{pk} \in \mathcal{R}_q^k$ is defined as $\vec{pk} := A\vec{s}$ for a public matrix $A \in \mathcal{R}_q^{k \times \ell}$. Suppose there are $n = l^m$ users in the ring[5] and for $\iota \in [n]$, let $\vec{pk}_\iota$ be the public key corresponding to the ι-th user. Then, during the signing process, user ι wants to prove knowledge of a short vector $\vec{s}$ such that

$$A\vec{s} \in \{\vec{pk}_1, \ldots, \vec{pk}_n\}$$

without revealing any information about its index ι.

We present the main protocol in Fig. 7 with verification equations in Fig. 9. User $\iota \in [n]$, which acts as a prover $\mathcal{P}$, starts by decomposing the index vector $\vec{v} = (0, \ldots, 0, 1, 0, \ldots, 0) \in \{0,1\}^n$, where the ι-th coefficient is equal to 1, into m smaller vectors of length l as in (15). Note that each $\vec{v}_i \in \mathbb{Z}_q^l$ satisfies (17). At the same time, $\mathcal{P}$ samples a masking $\vec{y}' \leftarrow D_{\vec{s}'}^{\ell d}$ and computes $\vec{w}' = (w_1', \ldots, w_k') = A\vec{y}' \in \mathcal{R}_q^k$. Furthermore, for the linear proof $\mathcal{P}$ generates a random $g \in \mathcal{R}_q$ such that $g_0 = \ldots = g_{d/l-1} = 0$. Now, the prover sends the BDLOP commitments to $\vec{v}_i$ as well as to $\vec{w}'$ and g. Namely, it generates a randomness vector $\vec{r} \leftarrow \chi^{(\lambda+\kappa+2m+1)d}$ and sends:

$$\vec{t}_0 = B_0 \vec{r} \bmod q,$$

$$t_i = \langle \vec{b}_i, \vec{r} \rangle + \mathsf{NTT}^{-1}(\vec{v}_i) \text{ for } i \in [m]$$

$$t_{m+i} = \langle \vec{b}_{m+i}, \vec{r} \rangle + w_i' \text{ for } i \in [k].$$

$$t_{k+2m} = \langle \vec{b}_{k+2m}, \vec{r} \rangle + g$$

---

[5] If there are less than l^m users then we simply add the zero vectors as public keys so that the ring has exactly l^m elements. Then the proof that the prover knows a short preimage to one of the columns implies that they must know a preimage to one of the actual public keys because knowing a preimage for one of the zero columns would constitute a SIS solution.

Prover $\mathcal{P}$ Verifier $\mathcal{V}$

Inputs:

$\boldsymbol{B}_0 \in \mathcal{R}_q^{\kappa \times (\lambda + \kappa + k + 2m + 1)}, \vec{\boldsymbol{b}}_1, \ldots, \vec{\boldsymbol{b}}_{k+2m+1} \in \mathcal{R}_q^{\lambda + \kappa + k + 2m + 1}$ $\boldsymbol{B}_0, \vec{\boldsymbol{b}}_1, \ldots, \vec{\boldsymbol{b}}_{k+2m+1}$

$\vec{v} = \vec{v}_1 \otimes \cdots \otimes \vec{v}_m$ where $\forall j \neq \iota, v_j = 0$ and $v_\iota = 1$ $\boldsymbol{A}, \{\vec{pk}_1, \ldots, \vec{pk}_n\}$

$\boldsymbol{A} \in \mathcal{R}_q^{k \times \ell}, \vec{\boldsymbol{s}} \in [-\mu, \mu]^{\ell d}$ such that $\boldsymbol{A}\vec{\boldsymbol{s}} = \vec{pk}_\iota$

$\vec{\boldsymbol{r}} \leftarrow \chi^{(\lambda + \kappa + k + 2m + 1)d}$

$g \leftarrow \{p \in \mathcal{R}_q : p_0 = \ldots = p_{d/l-1} = 0\}$

$\vec{\boldsymbol{y}} \leftarrow D_s^{(\lambda + \kappa + k + 2m + 1)d}, \vec{\boldsymbol{y}}' \leftarrow D_{s'}^{\ell}$

$\vec{\boldsymbol{w}} = \boldsymbol{B}_0 \vec{\boldsymbol{y}}, \vec{\boldsymbol{w}}' = \boldsymbol{A}\vec{\boldsymbol{y}}'$

$\vec{w}_i' = \mathsf{NTT}(\boldsymbol{w}_i')$ for $i \in [k]$

$t_i = \langle \vec{\boldsymbol{b}}_i, \vec{\boldsymbol{r}} \rangle + \mathsf{NTT}^{-1}(\vec{v}_i)$ for $i \in [m]$

$t_{m+i} = \langle \vec{\boldsymbol{b}}_{m+i}, \vec{\boldsymbol{r}} \rangle + w_i'$ for $i \in [k]$

$\vec{t} = (\vec{t}_0, t_1, \ldots, t_{m+k})$

$t_{k+2m} = \langle \vec{\boldsymbol{b}}_{k+2m}, \vec{\boldsymbol{r}} \rangle + g$

            $\xrightarrow{\quad \vec{t}, t_{k+2m}, \vec{\boldsymbol{w}} \quad}$

            $\xleftarrow{\quad c' \quad}$ $c' \leftarrow C$

$\vec{\boldsymbol{z}}' = \vec{\boldsymbol{y}}' + c' \vec{\boldsymbol{s}}$

If $\mathsf{Rej}_0(\vec{\boldsymbol{z}}', c'\vec{\boldsymbol{s}}, \mathfrak{s}') = 1$, abort $\xrightarrow{\quad \vec{\boldsymbol{z}}' \quad}$

Define $P_1 \in \mathcal{M}_q^{kl \times n}$ as in (31)

$\vec{x}_1 = \mathsf{NTT}(\vec{\boldsymbol{w}}' - \boldsymbol{A}\vec{\boldsymbol{z}}')$

For $j = 1, 2, \ldots, m - 1$:

    $(P_{j+1}, \vec{x}_{j+1}, \vec{y}_j) \leftarrow \mathsf{SM}_j(P_j, (\vec{v}_j, \ldots, \vec{v}_m), \vec{x}_j)$

            $\xleftarrow{\quad \vec{\gamma}_m \quad}$ $\vec{\gamma}_m \leftarrow \mathcal{M}_q^{(m+1)l}$

Define $\tilde{P}_m$ as the matrix in Equation 23

$(\vec{x}_{m+1,1}, \ldots, \vec{x}_{m+1,m}) = \tilde{P}_m^T \vec{\gamma}_m$

$\vec{y}_m := \left(\sum_{i=1}^m \vec{v}_i \circ \vec{x}_{m+1,i} \right) - \vec{x}_m \circ \vec{\gamma}_{m,1} - \vec{e}_1 \circ \sum_{i=1}^m \vec{\gamma}_{m,i}$

$\boldsymbol{y}_i = \mathsf{NTT}^{-1}(\vec{y}_i)$ for $i \in [m]$

$h = g + \boldsymbol{y}_1 + \ldots + \boldsymbol{y}_m$

            $\xrightarrow{\quad h \quad}$

            $\xleftarrow{\quad \alpha_0, \ldots, \alpha_m \quad}$ $\alpha_0, \ldots, \alpha_m \leftarrow \mathcal{R}_q$

Compute $\psi_{\mathsf{sm}}, \omega_{\mathsf{sm}}, \psi_{\mathsf{bin}}, \omega_{\mathsf{bin}}$ as in (28) and (29)

$t_{k+2m+1} = \langle \vec{\boldsymbol{b}}_{k+2m+1}, \vec{\boldsymbol{r}} \rangle + \alpha_0 \psi_{\mathsf{sm}} + \psi_{\mathsf{bin}}$

$\omega = \langle \vec{\boldsymbol{b}}_{k+2m+1}, \vec{\boldsymbol{y}} \rangle + \alpha_0 \omega_{\mathsf{sm}} + \omega_{\mathsf{bin}}$

            $\xrightarrow{\quad t_{k+2m+1}, \omega \quad}$

            $\xleftarrow{\quad c \quad}$ $c \leftarrow C$

$\vec{\boldsymbol{z}} = \vec{\boldsymbol{y}} + c\vec{\boldsymbol{r}}$

If $\mathsf{Rej}_1(\vec{\boldsymbol{z}}, c\vec{\boldsymbol{r}}, \mathfrak{s}) = 1$, abort $\xrightarrow{\quad \vec{\boldsymbol{z}} \quad}$

            $\mathsf{Ver}(\vec{t}_0, t_i, h, \omega, c, c'$
                        $, \vec{\boldsymbol{z}}, \vec{\boldsymbol{z}}', \vec{\gamma}_j, \vec{\alpha}_j)$

Fig. 7. Interactive protocol for our ring signature construction. Verifications equations Ver and the sub-protocol $\mathsf{SM}_j(P_j, (\boldsymbol{v}_j, \ldots, \boldsymbol{v}_m), \boldsymbol{x}_j)$ are defined in Fig. 9 and 8 respectively. We note that Rej_i, for $i = 0, 1$, are the rejection sampling algorithms from [17] and [19] respectively. See [20, Appendix A.3] for more details.

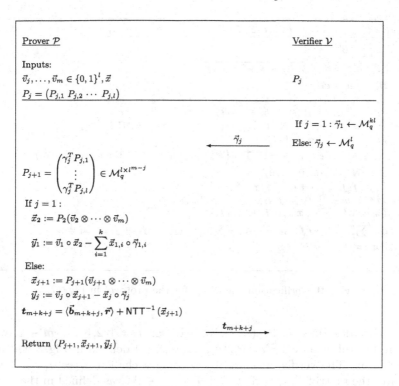

Fig. 8. The sub-protocol $\mathsf{SM}_j(P_j, (\vec{v}_j, \ldots, \vec{v}_m), \vec{x}_j)$ used in Fig. 7.

Additionally, $\mathcal{P}$ computes $\vec{w} = B_0\vec{y}$ for $\vec{y}$ sampled from $D_s^{(\kappa+k+2m+1)d}$. Then, $\mathcal{P}$ sends

$$(\vec{t}_0, t_1, \ldots, t_{m+k}, t_{k+2m}, \vec{w})$$

to the verifier.

The verifier $\mathcal{V}$ outputs a challenge polynomial $c' \leftarrow C$. Next, $\mathcal{P}$ computes $\vec{z}' = \vec{y}' + c'\vec{s}$ and applies the rejection sampling algorithm. If it does not abort, $\mathcal{P}$ returns $\vec{z}'$.

Let $P \in \mathcal{M}_q^{kl \times n}$ be the matrix defined as

$$P = \left(\mathsf{NTT}\left(-c' \cdot \vec{pk}_1\right) \mid \cdots \mid \mathsf{NTT}\left(-c' \cdot \vec{pk}_n\right)\right), \tag{31}$$

i.e. the i-th column of P is equal to $\mathsf{NTT}\left(-c' \cdot \vec{pk}_i\right) \in \mathcal{M}_q^{kl}$. Clearly, it can be computed by the verifier. Also, define

$$\vec{w} = \mathsf{NTT}\left(w' - A\vec{z}'\right) \in \mathcal{M}_q^{kl}.$$

Then, user ι wants to prove that $P(\vec{v}_1 \otimes \cdots \otimes \vec{v}_m) = \vec{w}$. Obviously, the verifier can manually construct a commitment to $\vec{w}$ by subtracting $(t_{m+1}, \ldots, t_{m+k})$ by $A\vec{z}'$. One observes that this is the equation of type (16) and it is where we apply

$$\boxed{\begin{array}{ll}
\multicolumn{2}{l}{\mathsf{Ver}(\vec{t}_0, t_1, \ldots, t_{k+2m+1}, h, \omega, c, c', \vec{z}, \vec{z}', \vec{\gamma}_1, \ldots, \vec{\gamma}_m, \alpha_0, \ldots, \alpha_m)} \\
01 & \|\vec{z}'\|_2 \overset{?}{<} \beta' = \mathfrak{s}'\sqrt{2\ell d} \\
02 & \|\vec{z}\|_2 \overset{?}{<} \beta = \mathfrak{s}\sqrt{2(\lambda + \kappa + k + 2m + 1)d} \\
03 & B_0 \vec{z} \overset{?}{=} \vec{w} + c\vec{t}_0 \\
04 & (t_{m+1}, \ldots, t_{m+k}) = (t_{m+1}, \ldots, t_{m+k}) - A\vec{z}' \in \mathcal{R}_q^k \\
05 & \forall j \in [k+2m+1], f_j = \langle \vec{b}_j, \vec{z} \rangle - ct_j \\
06 & \forall i \in [m+1], \gamma_{m,i} := \mathsf{NTT}^{-1}(\vec{\gamma}_{1,i}); \forall j \in [1,k], \gamma_{1,j} := \mathsf{NTT}^{-1}(\vec{\gamma}_{1,j}) \\
07 & \forall j \in [2, m-1], \gamma_j = \mathsf{NTT}^{-1}(\vec{\gamma}_j) \\
08 & (x_{m+1,1}, \ldots, x_{m+1,m}) := \mathsf{NTT}^{-1}\left(\tilde{P}_m^T \vec{\gamma}_m\right) \text{ where } \tilde{P}_m \text{ is the matrix in (23)} \\
09 & e_1 := \mathsf{NTT}^{-1}((1, 0, \ldots, 0)) \\
10 & F_1 := f_1 f_{m+k+1} + c \sum_{i=1}^{k} \gamma_{1,i} f_{m+i} \\
11 & \forall j \in [2, m-1], F_j := f_j f_{m+k+j} + c\gamma_j f_{m+k+j-1} \\
12 & F_m := c\left(-\sum_{i=1}^{m} x_{m+1,i} f_i + \gamma_{m,1} f_{k+2m-1} - e_1 \sum_{i=1}^{m} \gamma_{m,i}\right) \\
13 & \alpha_0 \left(\sum_{j=1}^{m} F_j - cf_{k+2m} - c^2 h\right) + \sum_{i=1}^{m} \alpha_i (f_i^2 + cf_i) + f_{k+2m+1} \overset{?}{=} \omega \\
14 & \text{For } i = 0, \ldots, d/l - 1 : \\
15 & \quad h_i \overset{?}{=} 0
\end{array}}$$

Fig. 9. Verification equations for the protocol in Fig. 7.

the strategy described in Sect. 3.1. Namely, for $j = 1, 2, 3, \ldots, m - 1$, we run a two-round sub-protocol $\mathsf{SM}_j(P_j, (\vec{v}_j, \ldots, \vec{v}_m), \vec{x}_j)$ defined in Fig. 8 which does the following. The verifier $\mathcal{V}$ starts by sending a challenge vector $\vec{\gamma}_j$. Then, $\mathcal{P}$ computes the matrix P_{j+1} and vectors $\vec{x}_{j+1}, \vec{y}_j \in \mathcal{M}_q^l$ as defined in the previous section. Eventually, it outputs the commitment to $\vec{x}_{j+1}$:

$$t_{m+k+j} = \langle \vec{b}_{m+k+j}, \vec{r} \rangle + \mathsf{NTT}^{-1}(\vec{x}_{j+1}).$$

In the end, the sub-protocol returns

$$(P_{j+1}, \vec{x}_{j+1}, \vec{y}_j) \leftarrow \mathsf{SM}_j(P_j, (\vec{v}_j, \ldots, \vec{v}_m), \vec{x}_j).$$

After executing the SM sub-protocol $m - 1$ times, the verifier sends $\vec{\gamma}_m \leftarrow \mathcal{M}_q^{(m+1)l}$. Then, in order to prove Eq. 23, $\mathcal{P}$ first computes $\vec{y}_m$ as in Eq. 24 and outputs the polynomial $h = g + y_1 + \ldots + y_m$, where $y_i = \mathsf{NTT}^{-1}(\vec{y}_i)$ for $i \in [m]$.

Next, $\mathcal{V}$ sends uniform polynomials $\alpha_0, \ldots, \alpha_m \leftarrow \mathcal{R}_q$. Then, $\mathcal{P}$ returns a commitment

$$t_{k+2m+1} = \langle \vec{b}_{k+2m+1}, \vec{y} \rangle + \psi$$

to the garbage polynomial $\psi = \psi_{\mathsf{bin}} + \alpha_0 \psi_{\mathsf{sm}}$ along with $\omega := \langle \vec{b}_{k+2m+1}, \vec{y} \rangle + \omega_{\mathsf{bin}} + \alpha_0 \omega_{\mathsf{sm}}$ (where their components are defined in (28) and (29)).

Finally, the verifier picks a challenge $c \leftarrow C$ and outputs c. Here, the coefficients of a challenge $c \leftarrow C$ are independently identically distributed with $P(0) = 1/2$ and $\Pr(1) = \Pr(-1) = 1/4$[6]. Then, prover $\mathcal{P}$ computes $\vec{z} = \vec{y} + c\vec{r}$ and applies rejection sampling. If it does not abort, $\mathcal{P}$ returns $\vec{z}$.

---

[6] We will make use of the properties of C described in [1]. We refer to [20, Appendix A.1] for more details.

Acknowledgements. We would like to thank anonymous reviews for useful feedback. This work was supported by the SNSF ERC Transfer Grant CRETP2-166734 FELICITY.

References

1. Attema, T., Lyubashevsky, V., Seiler, G.: Practical product proofs for lattice commitments. In: Micciancio, D., Ristenpart, T. (eds.) CRYPTO 2020. LNCS, vol. 12171, pp. 470–499. Springer, Cham (2020). https://doi.org/10.1007/978-3-030-56880-1_17
2. Baum, C., Bootle, J., Cerulli, A., del Pino, R., Groth, J., Lyubashevsky, V.: Sublinear lattice-based zero-knowledge arguments for arithmetic circuits. In: Shacham, H., Boldyreva, A. (eds.) CRYPTO 2018. LNCS, vol. 10992, pp. 669–699. Springer, Cham (2018). https://doi.org/10.1007/978-3-319-96881-0_23
3. Baum, C., Damgård, I., Lyubashevsky, V., Oechsner, S., Peikert, C.: More efficient commitments from structured lattice assumptions. In: Catalano, D., De Prisco, R. (eds.) SCN 2018. LNCS, vol. 11035, pp. 368–385. Springer, Cham (2018). https://doi.org/10.1007/978-3-319-98113-0_20
4. Beullens, W., Katsumata, S., Pintore, F.: Calamari and Falafl: logarithmic (linkable) ring signatures from isogenies and lattices. In: Moriai, S., Wang, H. (eds.) ASIACRYPT 2020. LNCS, vol. 12492, pp. 464–492. Springer, Cham (2020). https://doi.org/10.1007/978-3-030-64834-3_16
5. Bootle, J., Cerulli, A., Chaidos, P., Ghadafi, E., Groth, J., Petit, C.: Short accountable ring signatures based on DDH. In: Pernul, G., Ryan, P.Y.A., Weippl, E. (eds.) ESORICS 2015. LNCS, vol. 9326, pp. 243–265. Springer, Cham (2015). https://doi.org/10.1007/978-3-319-24174-6_13
6. Bootle, J., Lyubashevsky, V., Seiler, G.: Algebraic techniques for short(er) exact lattice-based zero-knowledge proofs. In: Boldyreva, A., Micciancio, D. (eds.) CRYPTO 2019. LNCS, vol. 11692, pp. 176–202. Springer, Cham (2019). https://doi.org/10.1007/978-3-030-26948-7_7
7. del Pino, R., Lyubashevsky, V., Seiler, G.: Lattice-based group signatures and zero-knowledge proofs of automorphism stability. In: ACM Conference on Computer and Communications Security, pp. 574–591. ACM (2018)
8. Ducas, L., Durmus, A., Lepoint, T., Lyubashevsky, V.: Lattice signatures and bimodal gaussians. In: Canetti, R., Garay, J.A. (eds.) CRYPTO 2013. LNCS, vol. 8042, pp. 40–56. Springer, Heidelberg (2013). https://doi.org/10.1007/978-3-642-40041-4_3
9. Ducas, L., et al.: Crystals-dilithium: a lattice-based digital signature scheme. IACR Trans. Cryptogr. Hardw. Embed. Syst. **2018**(1), 238–268 (2018)
10. Esgin, M.F., Nguyen, N.K., Seiler, G.: Practical exact proofs from lattices: new techniques to exploit fully-splitting rings. In: Moriai, S., Wang, H. (eds.) ASIACRYPT 2020. LNCS, vol. 12492, pp. 259–288. Springer, Cham (2020). https://doi.org/10.1007/978-3-030-64834-3_9
11. Esgin, M.F., Steinfeld, R., Liu, J.K., Liu, D.: Lattice-based zero-knowledge proofs: new techniques for shorter and faster constructions and applications. In: Boldyreva, A., Micciancio, D. (eds.) CRYPTO 2019. LNCS, vol. 11692, pp. 115–146. Springer, Cham (2019). https://doi.org/10.1007/978-3-030-26948-7_5

12. Esgin, M.F., Steinfeld, R., Sakzad, A., Liu, J.K., Liu, D.: Short lattice-based one-out-of-many proofs and applications to ring signatures. In: Deng, R.H., Gauthier-Umaña, V., Ochoa, M., Yung, M. (eds.) ACNS 2019. LNCS, vol. 11464, pp. 67–88. Springer, Cham (2019). https://doi.org/10.1007/978-3-030-21568-2_4

13. Esgin, M.F., Zhao, R.K., Steinfeld, R., Liu, J.K., Liu, D.: MatRiCT: efficient, scalable and post-quantum blockchain confidential transactions protocol. In: CCS, pp. 567–584. ACM (2019)

14. Groth, J., Kohlweiss, M.: One-out-of-many proofs: or how to leak a secret and spend a coin. In: Oswald, E., Fischlin, M. (eds.) EUROCRYPT 2015. LNCS, vol. 9057, pp. 253–280. Springer, Heidelberg (2015). https://doi.org/10.1007/978-3-662-46803-6_9

15. Lu, X., Au, M.H., Zhang, Z.: Raptor: a practical lattice-based (linkable) ring signature. In: Deng, R.H., Gauthier-Umaña, V., Ochoa, M., Yung, M. (eds.) ACNS 2019. LNCS, vol. 11464, pp. 110–130. Springer, Cham (2019). https://doi.org/10.1007/978-3-030-21568-2_6

16. Lyubashevsky, V.: Fiat-Shamir with aborts: applications to lattice and factoring-based signatures. In: Matsui, M. (ed.) ASIACRYPT 2009. LNCS, vol. 5912, pp. 598–616. Springer, Heidelberg (2009). https://doi.org/10.1007/978-3-642-10366-7_35

17. Lyubashevsky, V.: Lattice signatures without trapdoors. In: Pointcheval, D., Johansson, T. (eds.) EUROCRYPT 2012. LNCS, vol. 7237, pp. 738–755. Springer, Heidelberg (2012). https://doi.org/10.1007/978-3-642-29011-4_43

18. Lyubashevsky, V., Nguyen, N.K., Seiler, G.: Practical lattice-based zero-knowledge proofs for integer relations. In: CCS, pp. 1051–1070. ACM (2020)

19. Lyubashevsky, V., Nguyen, N.K., Seiler, G.: Shorter lattice-based zero-knowledge proofs via one-time commitments. In: Garay, J.A. (ed.) PKC 2021. LNCS, vol. 12710, pp. 215–241. Springer, Cham (2021). https://doi.org/10.1007/978-3-030-75245-3_9

20. Lyubashevsky, V., Nguyen, N.K., Seiler, G.: SMILE: set membership from ideal lattices with applications to ring signatures and confidential transactions. Cryptology ePrint Archive, Report 2021/564 (2021). https://eprint.iacr.org/2021/564

21. Lyubashevsky, V., Seiler, G.: Short, invertible elements in partially splitting cyclotomic rings and applications to lattice-based zero-knowledge proofs. In: Nielsen, J.B., Rijmen, V. (eds.) EUROCRYPT 2018. LNCS, vol. 10820, pp. 204–224. Springer, Cham (2018). https://doi.org/10.1007/978-3-319-78381-9_8

22. Noether, S.: Ring signature confidential transactions for Monero. IACR Cryptol. ePrint Arch. **2015**, 1098 (2015)

23. Prest, T., et al.: FALCON. Technical report, National Institute of Standards and Technology (2017) https://csrc.nist.gov/projects/post-quantum-cryptography/round-1-submissions

24. Rivest, R.L., Shamir, A., Tauman, Y.: How to leak a secret. In: Boyd, C. (ed.) ASIACRYPT 2001. LNCS, vol. 2248, pp. 552–565. Springer, Heidelberg (2001). https://doi.org/10.1007/3-540-45682-1_32

25. Yang, R., Au, M.H., Zhang, Z., Xu, Q., Yu, Z., Whyte, W.: Efficient lattice-based zero-knowledge arguments with standard soundness: construction and applications. In: Boldyreva, A., Micciancio, D. (eds.) CRYPTO 2019. LNCS, vol. 11692, pp. 147–175. Springer, Cham (2019). https://doi.org/10.1007/978-3-030-26948-7_6

Deniable Fully Homomorphic Encryption from Learning with Errors

Shweta Agrawal[1($\boxtimes$)], Shafi Goldwasser[2], and Saleet Mossel[3]

[1] IIT Madras, Chennai, India
shweta.a@cse.iitm.ac.in
[2] Simons Institute of TOC at UC Berkeley, Berkeley, CA, USA
[3] MIT, Cambridge, MA, USA
saleet@mit.edu

Abstract. We define and construct *Deniable Fully Homomorphic Encryption* based on the Learning With Errors (LWE) polynomial hardness assumption. Deniable FHE enables storing encrypted data in the cloud to be processed securely without decryption, maintaining deniability of the encrypted data, as well the prevention of vote-buying in electronic voting schemes where encrypted votes can be tallied without decryption.

Our constructions achieve *compactness* independently of the level of deniability- both the size of the public key and the size of the ciphertexts are bounded by a fixed polynomial, independent of the detection probability achieved by the scheme. This is in contrast to all previous constructions of deniable encryption schemes (even without requiring homomorphisms) which are based on polynomial hardness assumptions, originating with the seminal work of Canetti, Dwork, Naor and Ostrovsky (CRYPTO 1997) in which the ciphertext size grows with the inverse of the detection probability. Canetti *et al.* argued that this dependence "seems inherent", but our constructions illustrate this is not the case. We note that the Sahai-Waters (STOC 2014) construction of deniable encryption from indistinguishability obfuscation achieves compactness and can be easily modified to achieve deniable FHE as well, but it requires multiple, stronger sub-exponential hardness assumptions, which are furthermore not post-quantum secure. In contrast, our constructions rely only on the LWE polynomial hardness assumption, as currently required for FHE even without deniability.

The running time of our encryption algorithm depends on the inverse of the detection probability, thus the scheme falls short of achieving simultaneously compactness, negligible deniability probability *and* polynomial encryption time. Yet, we believe that achieving compactness is a fundamental step on the way to achieving all properties simultaneously as has been the historical journey for other primitives such as functional encryption. Our constructions support large message spaces, whereas previous constructions were bit by bit, and can be run in online-offline model of encryption, where the bulk of computation is independent of the message and may be performed in an offline pre-processing phase.

© International Association for Cryptologic Research 2021
T. Malkin and C. Peikert (Eds.): CRYPTO 2021, LNCS 12826, pp. 641–670, 2021.
https://doi.org/10.1007/978-3-030-84245-1_22

This results in an efficient online phase whose running time is independent of the detection probability. At the heart of our constructions is a new way to use bootstrapping to obliviously generate FHE ciphertexts so that it supports faking under coercion.

1   Introduction

Deniable (public-key) encryption, which was introduced in a seminal work by Canetti, Dwork, Naor and Ostrovsky (CRYPTO 1997) [13], is a seemingly paradoxical primitive that enables a user, who may be coerced to reveal the plaintexts corresponding to her public ciphertexts, to successfully lie about which messages she encrypted.

In particular, suppose Alice encrypted a message m with ciphertext ct which she deposits in the cloud for the purpose of cloud computing, and is later forced by the government to reveal the randomness she used and the message encrypted. Deniable encryption allows her to chose a different message m' at coercion time and reveal *fake* random coins, which convincingly explain ct as the encryption of m'. Clearly, deniability is a property which may be highly desirable when one uses a public resource such as cloud computing which expose him to possible coercion. Another use case is preventing vote buying in electronic elections: if the voter encrypts her vote using deniable encryption, then she can claim she encrypted an alternate message when forced to reveal her vote, deeming vote selling ineffective and encouraging honest voting since the voter cannot be forced to reveal her choice.

In this work, we introduce the notion of deniable *fully homomorphic encryption* (FHE) and provide the first constructions based on the Learning With Errors polynomial hardness assumption. In deniable FHE, the encryptor can produce ciphertexts that can be opened to fake messages under coercion, and additionally support fully homomorphic computations and achieve security as in (by now) classical FHE. We emphasize that for all the applications of deniable public key encryption mentioned above, the capability of homomorphism is an important implicit requirement – indeed, several modern e-voting protocols use FHE [15,27], and present-day encrypted data is often stored on a cloud server which assists the data owner with computing "blind-folded" via FHE [21].

We proceed to describe important prior work before we proceeding to describe our results in detail.

1.1   Prior Work on Deniability

Canetti et al. (CDNO) [13] provided elegant constructions of deniable encryption based on the construct of so called "translucent sets", which in turn can be constructed from trapdoor permutations. A major disadvantage of the CDNO construction was lack of compactness – the ciphertext size grows with the inverse of the detection probability achieved by the scheme. Furthermore, it encodes large messages bit by bit, where the ciphertext for each bit grows inversely with the detection probability. CDNO provided a lower bound that shows that their construction is in some sense optimal. They identified a structural property of encryption, which they term as *separability* and argued that as long as a construction is separable, the dependence of the ciphertext size with the inverse of the detection probability "seems inherent" [13].

A significant step forward in our understanding of deniable encryption and compactness was achieved via the work of Sahai and Waters in 2014 [29] which provided the first construction achieving negligible deniability assuming indistinguishability obfuscation (iO) and one way functions. However, iO seems to be an inherently sub-exponential assumption [19,20], and while exciting as a feasibility result, does not provide a satisfying solution to the question of deniable encryption from standard polynomial hardness assumptions.

CDNO also suggested the notion of *weak* deniability where the encryptor can lie not only about the random coins used to generate the ciphertext, but also the *algorithm* used to encrypt the message and the notion of *receiver* deniability, where the receiver can also produce a fake secret key that decrypts the message to an alternate one. In the weak model, [13] showed that compact public key and ciphertext as well as negligible deniability are possible. However, whether the weak model is meaningful for practical applications has been the subject of some debate – as discussed in [28], a common objection to the weak model is "since there are alternative deniable algorithms that are strictly more powerful than the normal ones, why would anyone ever run the normal algorithms? And given this situation, why would a coercer ever accept a transcript corresponding to the normal algorithms?". We refer the reader to [28] for a detailed discussion.

Other extensions to deniable encryption were also explored – O'Neill, Peikert and Waters [28] provided the first constructions of non-interactive *bi*-deniable encryption schemes where both the sender and the receiver can fake simultaneously as well as the first construction of identity based bi-deniable encryption. Apon, Fan and Liu [4] extended their results to provide the first construction deniable *attribute based encryption*. However, in the full model, both works [4,28] inherit the detection probability of CDNO, which is inverse polynomial. Additional prior work not directly related to the current work is discussed in Sect. 1.5.

Summarizing, barring the iO based construction which seems to require a sub-exponential hardness assumption, all proposals for (fully) sender deniable encryption schemes from standard assumptions suffer from ciphertext size that is inversely proportional to the detection probability. This implies a prohibitively large blow on efficiency. For a primitive as fundamental and interesting as deniable encryption, this state of affairs is very dissatisfying.

1.2   Our Results

In this work, we introduce the notion of deniable *fully homomorphic encryption* (FHE) and provide the first constructions of deniable FHE based on the Learning With Errors (LWE) assumption. Our constructions enjoy deniability compactness - the public key as well as the ciphertext of our schemes have size that can be bounded by a fixed polynomial, and are, in particular, independent of the level of deniability (or detection probability) achieved by the scheme. Our constructions support large messages paces, whereas all prior constructions encoded large messages bit by bit. On the down side, our encryption time depends on the inverse of the detection probability, thus the scheme falls short of achieving simultaneously compactness, negligible deniability and polynomial encryption time. Luckily, the scheme can be run in online-offline model of encryption, where the bulk of computation, which grows with the inverse of the detection probability, is independent of the message and may be performed in an offline pre-processing phase. The running time of the online phase, is independent of the detection probability.

We believe that achieving compact ciphertext even at the price of large encryption time is a fundamental step forward – indeed, note that for the related primitive of functional encryption (FE), compact ciphertext was later found to imply compact running time [26] by additionally assuming LWE via the "succinct" FE of Goldwasser et al. [24]. While this implication does not hold true for our work at present, it is a tantalizing possibility for future work.

We now proceed to on expound on the particulars of our results.

Deniable FHE. A (public key, sender) *deniable fully homomorphic encryption* consists of a tuple of algorithms $\mathsf{DFhe} = (\mathsf{Gen}, \mathsf{Enc}, \mathsf{Eval}, \mathsf{Dec}, \mathsf{Fake})$ where Gen, Enc and Dec are the standard key-generation, encryption and decryption algorithms, Eval is an algorithm that takes as input the public key, a circuit $\mathcal{C}$ and a tuple of ciphertexts $\mathsf{ct}_1, \ldots, \mathsf{ct}_n$ encrypting $x_1, \ldots, x_n$ respectively, and outputs a ciphertext ct^* which encrypts $\mathcal{C}(x_1, \ldots, x_n)$, and Fake is a faking algorithm, which takes as input the public key, an original message m, randomness r, and a fake message m^* and outputs a fake randomness r^* so that the encryption of message m using randomness r produces the same ciphertext as the encryption of message m^* using randomness r^*, i.e. $\mathsf{Enc}(\mathsf{pk}, m; r) = \mathsf{Enc}(\mathsf{pk}, m^*; r^*)$. The detection probability is the probability with which an adversary can distinguish r from r^*, and we denote it by $1/\delta = 1/\delta(\lambda)$ where λ is the security parameter. Our notion of deniable FHE is formalized in Definition 2.8.

We naturally extend this definition to the *weak* model (Definition 2.11) – a weakly deniable FHE is defined as $\mathsf{wDFhe} = (\mathsf{Gen}, \mathsf{DEnc}, \mathsf{Enc}, \mathsf{Eval}, \mathsf{Dec}, \mathsf{Fake})$ which is distinct from "fully" deniable FHE in that there are two distinct algorithms for encryption, namely Enc and DEnc. Here, as in [13], leveraging the additional secret "deniable" encryption algorithm DEnc, allows for better constructions as discussed below (in particular, those that achieve negligible deniability in polynomial time).

In more detail, Enc is an "honest" encryption algorithm and is used by the encryptor when it does *not* wish to fake a ciphertext, and DEnc is a "deniable" encryption algorithm, which is used when the encryptor wishes to retain the ability of faking a ciphertext in the future. Let us say the encryptor wishes to compute an encryption of m which it may later want to explain differently. Then it produces a ciphertext ct^* by running the algorithm DEnc with message m using randomness r. To explain ct^* as encrypting an arbitrary fake message m^* at a later time, the encryptor produces random coins r^* using the Fake algorithm, so that the ciphertext output by the *honest* encryption algorithm Enc on m^* using r^* equals the ciphertext ct* which was produced using the deniable encryption algorithm DEnc, i.e. DEnc(pk, $m; r$) = Enc(pk, $m^*; r^*$).

Next, we describe our constructions. We provide:

1. A *weakly* deniable FHE scheme for bits with negligible detection probability (Sect. 4.1). We extend this scheme to support larger (polynomial sized) message spaces (Sect. 5).
2. A *fully* deniable FHE scheme for bits with inverse polynomial detection probability (Sect. 4.2). We also extend this scheme to support larger (polynomial sized) message spaces (see the full version [1]). Both our fully deniable FHE schemes have compact public key and ciphertext, i.e. with size independent of the detection probability, but with encryption running time that grows with the inverse of the detection probability.
3. *Plan-ahead* deniable FHE schemes which support exponentially large message spaces (see the full version [1]). Plan-ahead deniable encryption [13] requires the encryptor to choose all (polynomially many) possible fake messages at the time of encryption. Later, when the encryptor desires to explain a ciphertext, it can only provide convincing fake randomness for one of the fake messages chosen during encryption.

Fake Evaluation. We note that our notions of deniable FHE also allow, in some cases, to explain *evaluated* ciphertexts as encoding a fake message. For instance, in the case that Eval is a deterministic algorithm, suppose that ct* was computed by homomorphically evaluating a polynomial sized circuit C on ciphertexts ct$_1, \ldots,$ ct$_n$ which encode messages $x_1, \ldots, x_n$ respectively. Suppose an encryptor wishes to explain ct* as an encryption of an arbitrary message $m^* \neq C(x_1, \ldots, x_n)$, and C supports inversion, i.e. given a value m^*, it is possible to efficiently sample $x'_1, \ldots x'_n$ such that $C(x'_1, \ldots, x'_n) = m^*$. Then, the encryptor may simply explain ct$_i$ as an encryption of x'_i for $i \in [n]$ and exhibit that the homomorphic evaluation procedure for C results in ct*. This convinces the adversary that ct* encodes m^*, as desired. We note that for several applications of interest, the circuit C can indeed be invertible – for instance, C may represent the vote counting circuit, which is simply addition and hence easily invertible.

On the Underlying Assumptions. We remark that the Sahai-Waters construction of public key deniable encryption from indistinguishability obfuscation (iO) [29] can be modified in a natural way to construct deniable fully homomorphic encryption. This provides an appealing feasibility result for deniable fully homomorphic encryption with negligible deniability, but rely on the strong hammer of indistinguishability obfuscation. While (concurrent) exciting recent work [25] has based indistinguishability obfuscation on well-founded assumptions, this construction relies on the subexponential hardness of four different assumptions, including assumptions on bilinear maps which are known to be insecure in the post-quantum regime. It is also well known that existing reductions to indistinguishability obfuscation [29] run into subexponential barrier due to the number of hybrids used in the security reductions – this results a subexponential assumption, please see [20] for a discussion.

The focus of our work is to rely on *minimal* assumptions. The primitive of levelled (respectively, pure) fully homomorphic encryption may be based on the polynomial hardness of the Learning With Errors (respectively, with circular security) assumption, with polynomial approximation factors [12]. Our constructions show that we can achieve (polynomially) deniable FHE without making any additional assumptions.

Compact Deniable PKE from FHE. Homomorphism aside, as discussed above, our construction implies, as a special case, a *compact* deniable public key encryption scheme, where the size of the public key and ciphertext are independent of the detection probability, which can be made an arbitrarily small inverse polynomial. However, as discussed above, the running time of our encryption algorithm *does* grow linearly with the inverse of the detection probability. This dependence again seems inherent, since our constructions can be shown to be separable in the sense of CDNO and hence subject to the lower bound (see the full version [1]). We discuss in Sect. 1.4 the technical barriers in circumventing this lower bound from non-obfuscation assumptions.

Online-Offline Encryption. Our constructions of deniable FHE also enjoy a desirable *online-offline* property, which allows the encryptor to do the bulk of the work in an offline phase that is independent of the message to be encrypted. In more detail, our encryption algorithm can be divided into two parts – an offline, message independent part which runs in time $O(\delta)$ (recall that $\frac{1}{\delta}$ is the detection probability), and an online phase which is efficient and independent of δ. We believe this feature makes these schemes especially attractive for practice since it mitigates the disadvantage of the large running time of encryption.

1.3 Our Techniques

The primary technical challenge in (full) deniable encryption is satisfying the many constraints imposed by the faking algorithm: the adversary knows the encryption algorithm and must be shown correctly distributed randomness that explains a given challenge ciphertext to a fake message. Excepting the construction based on obfuscation [29], all prior work addressed this challenge by setting the ciphertext to be a long sequence of elements that are either random or pseudorandom, and encoding the message bit in the parity of the number of pseudorandom elements. To fake, the encryptor pretends that one of the pseudorandom elements is in fact random, thus flipping the parity of the number of pseudorandom elements, and hence the encoded message. To construct a deniable fully homomorphic encryption scheme, the first challenge that arises is that an FHE ciphertext is highly structured, and this is necessary if it has to support homomorphic evaluation. Moreover, valid FHE ciphertexts are sparse in the ciphertext space, so randomly sampled elements are unlikely to be well-formed ciphertexts. Hence, if the encryptor for deniable FHE constructs all components of the ciphertext by running the FHE encryption algorithm i.e. Fhe.Enc(pk, $m; r$), then it is forced to open the FHE ciphertexts to provide r honestly – the structure of ciphertexts does not support lying about any of the encoded bits. The encryptor is thus faced with the incongruous task of producing highly structured ciphertexts without running the FHE encryption algorithm.

The Magic of Bootstrapping. To overcome this hurdle, we leverage the clever idea of "bootstrapping" proposed by Gentry [21]. At a high level, bootstrapping is the procedure of homomorphically computing the decryption circuit of a given scheme, say Fhe, on a ciphertext of the same scheme, using an encryption of the scheme's secret key, denoted by ct_{sk}. This procedure assumes circular security, namely that semantic security of Fhe holds even when the adversary is provided an encryption of the scheme's own secret key. The original motivation for bootstrapping was to reduce the "noise" level in FHE ciphertext – since the decryption circuit of an FHE scheme is quite shallow, running the decryption circuit homomorphically on some FHE ciphertext ct using the encryption of the FHE secret key ct_{sk}, removes the noise contained in ct via decryption, and the noise in output ciphertext ct' can be bound depending on the depth of the decryption circuit and the noise in ct_{sk}. To date, all constructions of "pure" FHE, namely, FHE that supports unbounded depth circuits, must assume circular security of the underlying "somewhat homomomorphic" encryption scheme, and hence of the underlying Learning With Errors (LWE) assumption. Since circular security is required anyway for the construction of pure FHE, we assume it in our construction of deniable (pure) FHE, and in the exposition below for simplicity. For the case of "levelled" FHE, which assumes a bound on the depth of supported circuits, and which can be built from standard LWE, this requirement can be removed as discussed in the full version [1].

Aside from noise reduction, an additional attractive feature of bootstrapping is that it suggests a way to *obliviously* generate FHE ciphertexts. Suppose our FHE scheme's decryption algorithm always outputs a valid message regardless of whether the ciphertext is well-formed or not. Then, by running the bootstrapping procedure on a random element from the ciphertext space, we obtain a well formed, valid FHE ciphertext for an unknown bit, by correctness of FHE evaluation. Moreover, if we run the bootstrapping procedure on a valid FHE ciphertext of any bit, the ciphertext output by bootstrapping still encodes the same bit, by correctness of FHE decryption and evaluation. If FHE ciphertexts are indistinguishable from random (which they usually are), then the encryptor may cheat about which of the two types of inputs was provided to the bootstrapping procedure and thereby lie about the encoded bit in the bootstrapped ciphertext.

While this feels like progress, it is still unclear how to encrypt a single bit of one's choosing using obliviously generated ciphertexts of unknown bits and honestly generated ciphertexts of known bits.

Deniable FHE in the Weak Model. As a warm-up, let us consider the weak model of deniability, where the encryptor can lie not only about the randomness used in encryption but also the algorithm used. Let us suppose for the moment that we may engineer the bootstrapping procedure so that an obliviously generated FHE ciphertext is biased and encodes the bit 0 with overwhelming probability (we will weaken this assumption later). Then, an approach to encrypt in the weak model is as follows.

Let the bootstrapping procedure be denoted by boot. In the honest mode, the encryptor encrypts bit 0 by choosing R_1 and R_2 randomly from the ciphertext space, converting these to well formed FHE ciphertexts via the bootstrapping procedure, and finally computing the homomorphic XOR operation (denoted by $\oplus_2$) on these FHE ciphertexts. Thus, we have:

$$\mathsf{ct}_0 = \mathsf{boot}(R_1) \oplus_2 \mathsf{boot}(R_2)$$

Since we assumed that random elements are bootstrapped to encode 0 with overwhelming probability, the ciphertext ct_0 encodes 0 due to correctness of the FHE evaluation procedure. To encrypt bit 1, the encryptor chooses R_3 randomly from the ciphertext space, and computes R_4 as an honest encryption of 1 using the FHE encryption algorithm. It then sets:

$$\mathsf{ct}_1 = \mathsf{boot}(R_3) \oplus_2 \mathsf{boot}(R_4)$$

It is easy to see that correctness is preserved by the same arguments as above.

In the deniable or fake encryption algorithm, the sender changes the way it encrypts 0. Instead of choosing R_1 and R_2 uniformly at random, it now computes both R_1 and R_2 as well formed FHE ciphertexts of 1. Bootstrapping preserves the message bit and homomorphic evaluation of addition modulo 2 ensures that ct_0 is a valid encryption of 0. The bit 1 is encrypted as before. However, if asked to explain, the encryptor can pretend that ct_0 is in fact an encryption of 1 by claiming that R_1 is chosen uniformly and by explaining R_2 as an encryption of 1. Since R_1 is an FHE ciphertext, the adversary cannot tell the difference as long as FHE ciphertext is pseudorandom. Similarly, if asked to explain ct_1 as an encryption of 0, she explains R_4 as a randomly chosen element in the ciphertext space. Thus, we obtain a construction of weakly deniable FHE for bits which achieves negligible detection probability. For more details, please see Sect. 4.1.

Deniable FHE in the Full Model. In the full model, the encryptor is not allowed to cheat about the algorithm it used for encryption, hence we may not take advantage of different ways of sampling randomness in the real and deniable encryption algorithms – there is only one encryption algorithm. In this model, we obtain FHE with polynomial deniability but with compact public key and ciphertext, that is, the size of the public key and ciphertext are independent of the detection probability. We proceed to describe the main ideas in the construction.

Let δ be the inverse of the desired detection probability. To encrypt a bit b, the encryptor samples uniform random bits $x_1, \ldots, x_\delta$ such that $\sum_{i \in [\delta]} x_i = b$ (mod 2). It then computes δ elements $R_1, \ldots, R_\delta$ of which, R_i is computed as an FHE encryption of 1 when $x_i = 1$, and R_i is sampled uniformly at random when $x_i = 0$. Finally, it outputs

$$\mathsf{ct} = \mathsf{boot}(R_1) \oplus_2 \mathsf{boot}(R_2) \oplus_2 \ldots \oplus_2 \mathsf{boot}(R_\delta)$$

To fake, it samples a random $j \in [\delta]$ such that $x_j = 1$, sets $x_j^* = 0$, and $x_i^* = x_i$ for every $i \neq j, i \in [\delta]$. It pretends that R_j is chosen uniformly at random, implying that $\mathsf{boot}(R_j)$ encodes 0 with overwhelming probability. It is easy to see that this flips the message bit that was chosen during encryption. Moreover, the statistical distance between honest randomness and fake randomness is $O(\frac{1}{\delta})$ and we achieve polynomial deniability, so long as the encryption time is polynomial. Please see Sect. 4.2 for more details.

Special FHE. The above informal description brushes several important details under the rug. For instance, we assumed various properties about the underlying FHE scheme which are not true in general. The most problematic assumption we made is that the FHE bootstrapping procedure can be engineered so that it outputs an encryption of 0 for a random input with overwhelming probability.

Some thought reveals that existing FHE schemes do not satisfy this property. Fortunately however, we show that some constructions can be modified to do so. For concreteness, we describe how to modify the FHE scheme by Brakerski, Gentry and Vaikuntanathan [10] to get the "special FHE" that we require. At a high level, decryption in the BGV cryptosystem is a two step procedure, where the first step computes the inner product of the ciphertext and the secret key over the ambient ring, and the second step computes the least significant bit of the result, which is then output. One can check that for any well formed ciphertext in this scheme, regardless of whether it encodes 0 or 1, the first step of the decryption procedure always yields a "small" element. On the other hand, for a random element in the ciphertext space, the first step of decryption yields a random element, i.e. it is small with low probability. Thus, we may modify the BGV decryption algorithm so that after computing the inner product in the first step, it checks whether the output is small, and outputs 0 if not. This does not change decryption for well formed ciphertexts but by a suitable setting of parameters, it biases the output of decryption to 0 for random inputs. In fact, we can make do with a weaker requirement on bias, namely that the bootstrapping procedure outputs an encryption of 0 for a random input with only non-negligible (not overwhelming) probability. However this makes the scheme more complicated, so we do not discuss it here. Please see the full version [1] for details. We also require some additional properties from our special FHE, which we define and establish in Sect. 3.

Large Messages. In all prior constructions of deniable encryption, larger messages were encoded bit by bit, where the ciphertext for a single bit is itself quite substantial $(O(\delta))$ as discussed above. To further improve efficiency, we again leverage the power of FHE. This enables our schemes to support large message spaces natively, thereby inheriting the significant advances in FHE schemes with large information rate [9,10,22,30], and bringing deniable FHE closer to practice.

Let $\mathcal{M}$ be the message space of an FHE scheme Fhe such that $|\mathcal{M}| = \text{poly}(\lambda)$. Further, let us assume that Fhe satisfies the special properties discussed above (formalized in Sect. 3). Then, to compute a ciphertext for a message $m_k \in \mathcal{M}$, we express m_k as the output of a "selector" function which computes the inner product of the kth unit vector with a vector of all messages in $\mathcal{M}$. In more detail, we express

$$m_k = 1 \cdot m_k + \sum_{m_i \in \mathcal{M}, i \neq k} 0 \cdot m_i$$

Here, the bits 0 or 1 are referred to as "selector" bits for obvious reasons. Our main observation is that the deniable encryption scheme for bits can now be used to add deniability to ciphertexts of selector bits and thereby to the overall ciphertext.

In more detail, assume that the sender selects message m_k at the time of encryption. To compute a ciphertext of m_k, she computes FHE ciphertexts ct_i for all $m_i \in \mathcal{M}$ and selector bit ciphertexts $\mathsf{ct}_i^{\mathsf{sel}}$ for $i \in [|\mathcal{M}|]$ where $\mathsf{ct}_i^{\mathsf{sel}}$ encodes 0 if $i \neq k$ and 1 otherwise. We use deniable encryption to compute the ciphertexts of selector bits as described above; thus, each selector bit is computed using multiple elements $\{R_i\}$ where $i \in [\delta]$. She then homomorphically computes the selector function described above to obtain a ciphertext ct^* encoding m_k. Under coercion, she may explain ct^* as encoding of any message m_i, even for $i \neq k$, by explaining the corresponding selector bits differently, i.e. by explaining $\mathsf{ct}_i^{\mathsf{sel}}$ as an encryption of 1 and $\mathsf{ct}_k^{\mathsf{sel}}$ as an encryption of 0.

We note that the above description is oversimplified and glosses over many technical details – for instance, the deniable FHE scheme for bits assumes that decryption of a random element in the ciphertext space is biased to 0 with overwhelming probability, which is no longer the case for FHE with large message spaces. However, this and other issues can be addressed, and we get schemes in both the weak and full models – please see Sect. 5 and the full version [1] for details.

Plan-Ahead Deniability. Plan-ahead deniable encryption [13] requires the sender to choose all possible fake messages at the time of encryption itself. For plan-ahead fully homomorphic encryption, it becomes possible to instantiate the underlying FHE to have super-polynomial message space. Intuitively, without the plan-ahead restriction, the construction discussed above fails for exponentially large message spaces, since it is not possible to "select" between exponentially many options in polynomial time. However, if the number of possible fake messages is fixed to some polynomial in advance, as is the case for plan-ahead deniability, then the same construction as above works, as long as we can establish the "special" properties of the FHE. We discuss how this can be achieved, please see the full version [1] for details.

Online-Offline Encryption. We now describe how our encryption algorithms lend themselves naturally to the online-offline model, where a bulk of the computation required for encryption is performed before the message is available. Consider the encryption algorithm for bits in the full model. Observe that sampling δ

random bits $x_1, \ldots, x_\delta$ such that $\sum_{i \in [\delta]} x_i = b \pmod 2$ is the same as sampling $\delta - 1$ random bits $x_1, \ldots, x_{\delta-1}$ and setting $x_\delta = b + \sum_{i \in [\delta-1]} x_i \pmod 2$. In the offline phase, we may select $\delta - 1$ bits $x_1, \ldots, x_{\delta-1}$ at random as well as the corresponding $\delta - 1$ elements R_i based on the bit x_i as specified in the encryption algorithm. Next, we homomorphically evaluate the bootstrapping circuit on the $\delta - 1$ random elements, i.e. $\mathsf{boot}(R_i)$ for $i \in [\delta - 1]$ and then compute:

$$\mathsf{ct_{offline}} = \mathsf{boot}(R_1) \oplus_2 \mathsf{boot}(R_2) \oplus_2 \ldots \oplus_2 \mathsf{boot}(R_{\delta-1}).$$

Now, in the online phase we can simply select the last bit and corresponding randomness R_δ according to the message b being encrypted, compute the homomorphic bootstrapping algorithm on R_δ, and evaluate the homomorphic addition mod 2 as: $\mathsf{ct} = \mathsf{ct_{offline}} \oplus_2 \mathsf{boot}(R_\delta)$. Thus, the online encryption time is independent of δ.

Next, consider the encryption scheme for large message spaces. Even here, note that the dependence of the encryption running time on the detection probability comes from the construction of selector bits. Since the construction of any ciphertext involves $|\mathcal{M}| - 1$ encryptions of 0 and a single encryption of 1, the encryptions of these selector bits can be computed in an offline pre-processing phase. The encryptions of all possible messages in the message space can also be performed offline. Then, in the online phase, given message m_k, the encryptor needs only to perform the homomorphic evaluation of the selector function to compute the final ciphertext. This leads to an online encryption time which grows with $|\mathcal{M}|$ but not with the inverse of the detection probability.

The online processing time may be optimized further as follows – now, additionally in the offline phase, let the encryptor perform the homomorphic evaluation of the selector function with *all* the selector bits set to 0, i.e. $\sum_{m_i \in \mathcal{M}} 0 \cdot m_i$. It stores the ciphertexts for all possible messages $m \in \mathcal{M}$, the ciphertexts of the computed selector bits which are set to 0 as well as a ciphertext ct^1 for an extra selector bit which is set to 1. In the online phase, when m_k is known, it subtracts the "wrong" term $\mathsf{ct}_k^0 \cdot \mathsf{ct}_k$ and adds the term $\mathsf{ct}^1 \cdot \mathsf{ct}_k$ to the evaluated ciphertext to obtain the correct ciphertext. Thus, the online phase can be performed in time independent of both $|\mathcal{M}|$ as well as δ.

Removing the Circularity Assumption for Levelled FHE. Above, our usage of the bootstrapping procedure implies the assumption of circular secure homomorphic encryption, hence circular secure LWE. Since circular security is required anyway for all known constructions of pure FHE (we refer the reader to [8] for a discussion), this assumption currently comes "for free" in the construction of deniable pure FHE. However, for levelled FHE, which only supports circuits of bounded depth and can be constructed from standard LWE [10, 11, 23], the assumption of circularity is not implied. In this setting, our construction can be easily adapted to make do without the circularity assumption, as observed by [3]. The idea is simple – instead of assuming that the encryption of a scheme's secret key under it's own public key is secure, we can instead rely on two encryption schemes and assume that the secret key of first scheme sk_1 can be securely encrypted using the public key of the second scheme pk_2. Let us denote this ciphertext by ct_{sk_1}. Now, the obliviously sampled ciphertexts can be seen as encrypted under pk_1 and the ciphertext ct_{sk_1} may be used to translate these to valid ciphertexts under pk_2 via a variant of the bootstrapping procedure discussed above. In more detail, the modified bootstrapping procedure computes the homomomorphic evaluation procedure of the second scheme using as inputs the ciphertext ct_{sk_1} and the decryption circuit of the first scheme to produce valid ciphertexts under the second scheme. We refer the reader to the full version [1] for more details.

1.4   Perspective: FHE as a Tool

As discussed above, bootstrapping enables us to obliviously sample FHE ciphertexts, and homomorphic evaluation enables us to "compactify" the final ciphertext – this makes FHE a useful tool even in the context of deniable *public key encryption* (PKE). One of the main insights of our work is that *evaluation* compactness in FHE can be leveraged to achieve *deniability* compactness in PKE. All constructions of non-interactive sender deniable encryption in the full model known from 1997 to date (excepting the one based on iO [29]), must provide multiple elements in the ciphertext, both pseudorandom and random, and encode the message bit in the parity of the number of pseudorandom elements leading to ciphertext size that grows inversely with detection probability. We can avoid this dependence using FHE.

Can FHE also help achieve compact runtime of encryption? If so, this would lead to negligibly deniable PKE from LWE, resolving the long-standing open problem of deniable PKE from a standard, polynomial hardness assumption, with the post-quantum advantage as the "icing on the cake". While this exciting possibility cannot be ruled out, a thorny technical barrier that arises is the hardness of inverting the bootstrapping procedure. Intuitively, deniable encryption requires *invertible biased oblivious sampling* – the encryption procedure must obliviously sample a ciphertext (biased to encoding 0, say) and the faking procedure must invert a given ciphertext, encoding either 0 or 1, to produce a well distributed randomness. In hindsight, even the iO based construction of Sahai and Waters [29] can be viewed as a construction of invertible oblivious sampling – indeed, similar techniques have been used to construct invertible sampling [17].

Using our current techniques, bootstrapping enables us to perform oblivious sampling, but not inversion. Due to this limitation, we are restricted to cheating only in one direction – we can pretend that a ciphertext of 1 encodes 0 but not the other way around. This leads to the attack discussed in the full version [1], which curtails the scheme to polynomial deniability. However if, given $y = \mathsf{boot}(R)$, we could compute well-distributed R' such that $\mathsf{boot}(R') = y \oplus_2 1$, where $\oplus_2 1$ denotes homomorphic XOR of the bit 1, then we would gain the ability to cheat in both directions and obtain negligibly deniable PKE. We remark that while boot is a one way function, infeasibility of inversion does not apply since we have potentially useful side information about the preimage – we must find the preimage of $y \oplus_2 1$ and know the preimage to y. Unfortunately, we currently do not know how to leverage this information. Nevertheless, we view ciphertext compactness as a useful stepping stone to full runtime compactness from LWE, and hope it can lead to progress towards a full solution. Please see the full version [1] for a more in-depth discussion on the barriers in achieving negligible deniability.

In the full version [1], we discuss the notion of receiver deniable FHE.

1.5   Other Related Work

De Caro, Iovino and O'Neill [18] studied the notion of *receiver deniable functional encryption*, but instantiating these constructions requires the assumption of full fledged functional encryption, which in turn is known to imply indistinguishability obfuscation (iO) [2,6].

Aside from work extending the functionality of deniable encryption, there was also progress in lower bounds – for receiver deniability, [5] showed that a non-interactive public-key scheme having key size δ can be fully receiver-deniable only with non-negligible $\Omega(\frac{1}{\delta})$ detection probability while for sender deniability, Dachman-Soled [16] showed that there is no black-box construction of sender-deniable public key encryption with super-polynomial deniability from simulatable public key encryption. There has also been work on *interactive* deniable encryption where the sender and receiver are allowed to participate in an interactive protocol – in this setting, negligible bi-deniability in the full model has been achieved based on subexponentially secure indistinguishability obfuscation and one-way functions [14]. Our focus in this work is the non-interactive setting.

2   Preliminaries

In this section, we define the notation and preliminaries that we require in this work. Some standard notions are moved to the full version [1] due to space constraints.

2.1   Fully Homomorphic Encryption

Definition 2.1 (Fully Homomorphic Encryption). *A public-key fully homomorphic encryption scheme for a message space* $\mathcal{M}$ *consists of PPT algorithms* Fhe = (Gen, Enc, Eval, Dec) *with the following syntax:*

- Gen$(1^\lambda) \to$ (pk, sk)*: on input the unary representation of the security parameter* λ*, generates a public-key* pk *and a secret-key* sk*.*
- Enc$($pk$, m) \to$ ct*: on input a public-key* pk *and a message* $m \in \mathcal{M}$*, outputs a ciphertext* ct*.*
- Eval$($pk$, \mathcal{C},$ct$_1, \ldots,$ ct$_k) \to$ ct*: on input a public-key* pk*, a circuit* $\mathcal{C} : \mathcal{M}^k \to \mathcal{M}$*, and a tuple of ciphertexts* ct$_1, \ldots,$ ct$_k$*, outputs a ciphertext* ct*.*
- Dec$($sk$,$ ct$) \to m$*: on input a secret-key* sk *and a ciphertext* ct*, outputs a message* $m \in \mathcal{M}$*.*

The scheme should satisfies the following properties:

Correctness. *A scheme* Fhe *is correct if for every security parameter* λ, *polynomial-time circuit* $\mathcal{C} : \mathcal{M}^k \to \mathcal{M}$, *and messages* $m_i \in \mathcal{M}$ *for* $i \in [k]$:

$$\Pr[\mathsf{Dec}(\mathsf{sk}, \mathsf{Eval}(\mathsf{pk}, \mathcal{C}, \mathsf{ct}_1, \ldots, \mathsf{ct}_k)) = \mathcal{C}(m_1, \ldots, m_k)] = 1 - \mathsf{negl}(\lambda)$$

where $(\mathsf{pk}, \mathsf{sk}) \leftarrow \mathsf{Gen}(1^\lambda)$, *and* $\mathsf{ct}_i \leftarrow \mathsf{Enc}(\mathsf{pk}, m_i)$ *for* $i \in [k]$.

Compactness. *A scheme* Fhe *is compact if there exists a polynomial* $\mathrm{poly}(\cdot)$ *such that for all security parameter* λ, *polynomial-time circuit* $\mathcal{C} : \mathcal{M}^k \to \mathcal{M}$, *and messages* $m_i \in \mathcal{M}$ *for* $i \in [k]$:

$$\Pr\left[|\mathsf{Eval}(\mathsf{pk}, \mathcal{C}, \mathsf{ct}_1, \ldots, \mathsf{ct}_k)| \leq \mathrm{poly}(\lambda)\right] = 1$$

where $(\mathsf{pk}, \mathsf{sk}) \leftarrow \mathsf{Gen}(1^\lambda)$, *and* $\mathsf{ct}_i \leftarrow \mathsf{Enc}(\mathsf{pk}, m_i)$ *for* $i \in [k]$.

CPA Security. *A scheme* Fhe *is IND-CPA secure if for all PPT adversary* $\mathcal{A}$:

$$\left|\Pr\left[\mathsf{FheGame}^0_{\mathcal{A}}(\lambda) = 1\right] - \Pr\left[\mathsf{FheGame}^1_{\mathcal{A}}(\lambda) = 1\right]\right| \leq \mathsf{negl}(\lambda)$$

where $\mathsf{FheGame}^b_{\mathcal{A}}(\lambda)$ *is a game between an adversary and a challenger with a challenge bit* b *defined as follows:*

– *Sample* $(\mathsf{pk}, \mathsf{sk}) \leftarrow \mathsf{Gen}(1^\lambda)$, *and send* pk *to* $\mathcal{A}$.
– *The adversary chooses* $m_0, m_1 \in \mathcal{M}$.
– *Compute* $\mathsf{ct} \leftarrow \mathsf{Enc}(\mathsf{pk}, m_b)$, *and send* ct *to* $\mathcal{A}$.
– *The adversary* $\mathcal{A}$ *outputs a bit* b' *which we define as the output of the game.*

Definition 2.2 (Circular Security). *A public-key encryption scheme with key generation algorithm* Gen *and encryption algorithm* Enc *is circular secure if for every PPT adversary* $\mathcal{A}$:

$$\left|\Pr\left[\mathsf{CircGame}^0_{\mathcal{A}}(\lambda) = 1\right] - \Pr\left[\mathsf{CircGame}^1_{\mathcal{A}}(\lambda) = 1\right]\right| \leq \mathsf{negl}(\lambda)$$

where $\mathsf{CircGame}^b_{\mathcal{A}}(\lambda)$ *is a game between an adversary and a challenger with a challenge bit* b *defined as follows:*

– *Sample* $(\mathsf{pk}, \mathsf{sk}) \leftarrow \mathsf{Gen}(1^\lambda)$, *compute* $\mathsf{ct}_{\mathsf{sk}} \leftarrow \mathsf{Enc}(\mathsf{pk}, \mathsf{sk})$, *and give* $(\mathsf{pk}, \mathsf{ct}_{\mathsf{sk}})$ *to* $\mathcal{A}$.
– *The adversary chooses* $m_0, m_1 \in \mathcal{M}$.
– *Compute* $\mathsf{ct} \leftarrow \mathsf{Enc}(\mathsf{pk}, m_b)$, *and give* ct *to* $\mathcal{A}$.
– *The adversary* $\mathcal{A}$ *outputs a bit* b' *which we define as the output of the game.*

Definition 2.3 (Bootstrapping Procedure). *[21] Let* Fhe $=$ (Gen, Enc, Eval, Dec) *be a public-key FHE scheme for a message space* $\mathcal{M}$ *with ciphertext space* $\mathcal{R}^{\ell_c}$. *We define the bootstrapping procedure, denoted by* $\mathsf{boot} : \mathcal{R}^{\ell_c} \to \mathcal{R}^{\ell_c}$, *as*

$$\mathsf{boot}(x) = \mathsf{Fhe.Eval}(\mathsf{pk}, \mathsf{Dec}_x, \mathsf{ct}_{\mathsf{sk}})$$

where $(\mathsf{pk}, \mathsf{sk}) \leftarrow \mathsf{Fhe.Gen}(1^\lambda)$, $\mathsf{ct}_{\mathsf{sk}} \leftarrow \mathsf{Fhe.Enc}(\mathsf{pk}, \mathsf{sk})$, *and* $\mathsf{Dec}_x(\mathsf{sk}) = \mathsf{Fhe.Dec}(\mathsf{sk}, x)$. *Above, when* $\mathsf{sk} \notin \mathcal{M}$, *we assume that* sk *may be represented as a vector of elements in* $\mathcal{M}$, *which would make* $\mathsf{ct}_{\mathsf{sk}}$ *a vector of ciphertexts.*

Definition 2.4 (Valid Ciphertext). *We say that an* Fhe *ciphertext* ct *is a valid ciphertext of* m, *if either*

$$ct \leftarrow \mathsf{Enc}(\mathsf{pk}, m),$$

or for any polynomial-sized circuit $\mathcal{C}$, *we have that:*

$$\Pr[\mathsf{Dec}(\mathsf{sk}, \mathsf{Eval}(\mathsf{pk}, \mathcal{C}, \mathsf{ct})) = \mathcal{C}(m)] = 1 - \mathsf{negl}(\lambda),$$

where $(\mathsf{pk}, \mathsf{sk}) \leftarrow \mathsf{Gen}(1^\lambda)$ *and* λ *is the security parameter.*

Some Useful Functions. In this paragraph, we define notation for some functions that will prove useful in our constructions.

Definition 2.5 (Addition Modulo 2). *We denote by* $\oplus_2$ *the homomorphic evaluation of addition modulo 2 circuit, that is for* $k \geq 2$, $\oplus_2(\mathsf{ct}_1, \ldots, \mathsf{ct}_k) = \mathsf{ct}$, ct *is a valid encryption of* $\sum_{i=1}^k x_i \pmod 2$ *where* $x_i \in \{0, 1\}$ *and* ct_i *is a valid encryption of* x_i *for* $i \in [k]$.

For ease of readability, we will often denote $\oplus_2(\mathsf{ct}_1, \ldots, \mathsf{ct}_k)$ by $\mathsf{ct}_1 \oplus_2 \mathsf{ct}_2 \ldots \oplus_2 \mathsf{ct}_k$.

Definition 2.6 (Selector). *Let* $b_i \in \{0, 1\}$ *such that for all* $i \in [k], i \neq j$, $b_i = 0$, *and* $b_j = 1$ *for some fixed* $j \in [k]$. *For all* $i \in [k]$, *let* $x_i \in \mathcal{M}$. *We define a selector function as* $\sum_{i \in [k]} b_i x_i = x_j$.
We denote the homomorphic evaluation of this function by

$$\sum_{i \in [k]} \mathsf{ct}_i^{\mathsf{sel}} \otimes \mathsf{ct}_i = \mathsf{ct},$$

where ct *is a valid encryption of the selected message* x_j, $\mathsf{ct}_i^{\mathsf{sel}}$ *is a valid encryption of* b_i *and* ct_i *is a valid encryption of* x_i *for all* $i \in [k]$.

Definition 2.7 (Indicator Function). *The indicator function for the set* $\mathcal{X}$, *denoted by* $\mathbf{1}_{\mathcal{X}}(\cdot)$, *defined as*

$$\mathbf{1}_{\mathcal{X}}(x) = \begin{cases} 1 & x \in \mathcal{X} \\ 0 & x \notin \mathcal{X} \end{cases}.$$

2.2   Deniable Homomorphic Encryption

Definition 2.8 (Compact Deniable FHE.). *A compact public-key deniable fully homomorphic encryption scheme for message space* $\mathcal{M}$ *consists of PPT algorithms* $\mathsf{DFhe} = (\mathsf{Gen}, \mathsf{Enc}, \mathsf{Eval}, \mathsf{Dec}, \mathsf{Fake})$ *with the following syntax:*

- $\mathsf{Gen}(1^\lambda) \rightarrow (\mathsf{dpk}, \mathsf{dsk})$: *on input the unary representation of the security parameter* λ, *generates a public-key* dpk *and a secret-key* dsk.
- $\mathsf{Enc}(\mathsf{dpk}, m; r) \rightarrow \mathsf{ct}$: *on input a public-key* dpk *and a message* $m \in \mathcal{M}$, *uses* ℓ-bit string randomness r, *outputs a ciphertexts* dct.

- Eval(dpk, $\mathcal{C}$, dct$_1$, ..., dct$_k$) → dct: *on input a public-key* dpk, *a circuit* $\mathcal{C}$: $\mathcal{M}^k \to \mathcal{M}$, *and a tuple of ciphertexts* dct$_1$, ..., dct$_k$, *outputs a ciphertext* dct.
- Dec(dsk, dct) → m: *on input a secret-key* dsk *and a ciphertext* dct, *outputs a message* $m \in \mathcal{M}$.
- Fake(dpk, m, r, m^*) → r^*: *on input a public-key* dpk, *an original message* $m \in \mathcal{M}$, *an ℓ-bit string randomness* r, *and a fake message* $m^* \in \mathcal{M}$, *output an ℓ-bit string randomness* r^*.

The scheme should satisfies the following properties:

Correctness, Compactness & CPA Security. *A scheme* DFhe *is correct, compact and secure if the scheme* (Gen, Enc, Eval, Dec) *satisfies the standard notions of correctness, compactness and IND-CPA security properties of fully homomorphic encryption, as in Definition 2.1. We remark that a scheme cannot simultaneously satisfy perfect correctness and deniability, so negligible decryption error in correctness is inherent.*

Deniability. *A scheme* DFhe *is $\delta(\lambda)$-deniable if for all PPT adversary $\mathcal{A}$:*

$$\left| \Pr\left[\mathsf{DnblGame}_{\mathcal{A}}^0(\lambda) = 1 \right] - \Pr\left[\mathsf{DnblGame}_{\mathcal{A}}^1(\lambda) = 1 \right] \right| \leq \delta(\lambda)$$

where $\mathsf{DnblGame}_{\mathcal{A}}^b(\lambda)$ *is a game between an adversary and a challenger with a challenge bit b defined as follows:*

- *Sample* (dpk, dsk) ← Gen(1^λ), *and send* dpk *to $\mathcal{A}$.*
- *The adversary chooses $m, m^* \in \mathcal{M}$.*
- *Sample* $r \leftarrow \{0,1\}^\ell$, *and* $r^* \leftarrow$ Fake(dpk, m, r, m^*); *if $b = 0$ give* $(m^*, r, \mathsf{Enc}(\mathsf{dpk}, m^*; r))$ *to $\mathcal{A}$, else if $b = 1$, give* $(m^*, r^*, \mathsf{Enc}(\mathsf{dpk}, m; r))$ *to $\mathcal{A}$.*
- *The adversary $\mathcal{A}$ outputs a bit b' which we define as the output of the game.*

Remark 2.9. We note that in our constructions, the length of randomness used during encryption may depend on the message being encrypted. This does not affect deniability, because the length of the randomness is only revealed together with the encrypted message. For ease of exposition, we do not introduce additional notation to capture this nuance.

Deniability Compactness. *A $\delta(\lambda)$-deniable scheme* DFhe *is deniability compact if there exists a a polynomial* poly($\cdot$) *such that for all security parameters λ, and message $m \in \mathcal{M}$:*

$$\Pr[|\mathsf{Enc}(\mathsf{dpk}, m)| \leq \mathrm{poly}(\lambda)] = 1$$

where (dpk, dsk) ← Gen(1^λ), *regardless of the encryption running time.*

Remark 2.10. The above definition can be modified to capture a compact deniable public key encryption scheme by removing the evaluation algorithm required by FHE.

Definition 2.11 (Weak Deniable FHE). *A public-key weak deniable fully homomorphic encryption scheme for message space $\mathcal{M}$ consists of PPT algorithms* wDFhe $=$ (Gen, DEnc, Enc, Eval, Dec, Fake) *where* Gen, Eval, *and* Dec *have the same syntax as in Definition 2.8, and* DEnc, Enc *and* Fake *have the following syntax:*

- DEnc(dpk, $m; r$) $\to$ ct: *on input a public-key* dpk *and a message* $m \in \mathcal{M}$, *uses ℓ-bit string randomness r, outputs a ciphertexts* dct.
- Enc(dpk, $m; r$) $\to$ ct: *on input a public-key* dpk *and a message* $m \in \mathcal{M}$, *uses ℓ^*-bit string randomness r, outputs a ciphertexts* dct.
- Fake(dpk, m, r, m^*) $\to r^*$: *on input a public-key* dpk, *an original message $m \in \mathcal{M}$, an ℓ-bit string randomness r, and a faking message $m^* \in \mathcal{M}$, output an ℓ^*-bit string randomness r^*.*

The scheme should satisfies the following properties:

Correctness, Compactness & CPA Security. *A scheme* wDFhe *is correct, compact and secure if both schemes* (Gen, Enc, Eval, Dec), *and* (Gen, DEnc, Eval, Dec) *satisfy the standard notions of correctness, compactness and IND-CPA security properties of fully homomorphic encryption, as in Definition 2.1.*

Weak Deniability. *A scheme* wDFhe *is weakly-deniable if for all PPT adversaries $\mathcal{A}$:*

$$\left| \Pr\left[\mathsf{wDnblGame}^0_{\mathcal{A}}(\lambda) = 1\right] - \Pr\left[\mathsf{wDnblGame}^1_{\mathcal{A}}(\lambda) = 1\right] \right| \le \mathsf{negl}(\lambda)$$

where $\mathsf{wDnblGame}^b_{\mathcal{A}}(\lambda)$ *is a game between an adversary and a challenger with a challenge bit b defined as follows:*
- *Sample* (dpk, dsk) $\gets$ Gen(1^λ), *and send* dpk *to $\mathcal{A}$.*
- *The adversary $\mathcal{A}$ chooses* $m, m^* \in \mathcal{M}$.
- *Sample* $r \gets \{0,1\}^{\ell^*}$, $r' \gets \{0,1\}^\ell$, *and* $r^* \gets$ Fake(dpk, m, r', m^*); *if $b = 0$ return* $(m^*, r, \mathsf{Enc}(\mathsf{dpk}, m^*; r))$ *else if $b = 1$ return* $(m^*, r^*, \mathsf{DEnc}(\mathsf{dpk}, m; r'))$ *to $\mathcal{A}$.*
- *The adversary $\mathcal{A}$ outputs a bit b' which we define as the output of the game.*

3 Special Homomorphic Encryption

Our constructions rely on a fully homomorphic encryption scheme which satisfies some special properties. We define these and instantiate it below.

Definition 3.1 (Special FHE). *A special public-key FHE scheme for a message space $\mathcal{M}$ with ciphertext space $\mathcal{R}^{\ell_c}$ is a public-key FHE scheme,* Fhe $=$ (Gen, Enc, Eval, Dec), *with the following additional properties:*

1. *Deterministic Algorithms. The evaluation and decryption algorithms,* Eval *and* Dec *respectively, are deterministic. In particular, this implies the bootstrapping procedure* boot, *defined in 2.3, is deterministic.*

2. *Pseudorandom Ciphertext.* The distribution $\mathsf{Fhe.Enc}(\mathsf{pk}, m; U^\ell)$ is computationally indistinguishable from $\mathcal{R}^{\ell_c}$, where U^ℓ is the uniform distribution over ℓ-bit strings, $(\mathsf{pk}, \mathsf{sk}) \leftarrow \mathsf{Fhe.Gen}(1^\lambda)$, and $m \in \mathcal{M}$. Moreover, the distribution $\mathsf{boot}(\mathcal{R}^{\ell_c})$ is computationally indistinguishable from $\mathcal{R}^{\ell_c}$, where boot is the bootstrapping procedure as in Definition 2.3.

3. *Decryption Outputs Valid Message.* The decryption algorithm, $\mathsf{Fhe.Dec}$, always outputs a message from the message space $\mathcal{M}$. Namely, for any $x \in \mathcal{R}^{\ell_c}$, $\mathsf{Fhe.Dec}(\mathsf{sk}, x) \in \mathcal{M}$ where $(\mathsf{pk}, \mathsf{sk}) \leftarrow \mathsf{Fhe.Gen}(1^\lambda)$. In particular, this implies that the output of the bootstrapping procedure boot is always a valid ciphertext (Definition 2.4).

4. *Biased Decryption on Random Input (Strong Version).* The decryption algorithm $\mathsf{Fhe.Dec}$, when invoked with a random element in the ciphertext space $x \leftarrow \mathcal{R}^{\ell_c}$, outputs a message from a fixed (strict) subset of the message space $\mathcal{S} \subset \mathcal{M}$ with overwhelming probability.

   Formally, we require that there exists a strict subset of the message space, $\mathcal{S} \subset \mathcal{M}$, such that

$$P(\mathcal{S}) := \sum_{m \in \mathcal{S}} P(m) \geq 1 - \mathsf{negl}(\lambda)$$

   where $P : \mathcal{M} \to \mathbb{R}$ is defined as $P(m) := \Pr\left[\mathsf{Fhe.Dec}\,(\mathsf{sk}, x) = m\right]$ where $x \leftarrow \mathcal{R}^{\ell_c}$ and $(\mathsf{pk}, \mathsf{sk}) \leftarrow \mathsf{Fhe.Gen}(1^\lambda)$. Moreover, we require that $0 \in \mathcal{S}$. Thus, if the message space is binary, then $\mathcal{S} = \{0\}$.

   We remark that the above property, while sufficient, is not strictly necessary for our constructions. However, for ease of exposition, our constructions assume the "strong version" stated above. In the full version [1] we describe how to modify our constructions to instead use the weaker version below. Biased Decryption on Random Input (Weak Version). This version weakens overwhelming to noticeable in the above definition, i.e. using the notation above, we require:

$$P(\mathcal{S}) := \sum_{m \in \mathcal{S}} P(m) \geq 1/\mathsf{poly}(\lambda)$$

   As before, we require that $0 \in \mathcal{S}$.

5. *Circular Secure.* The scheme Fhe is circular secure as in Definition 2.2. As discussed in Sect. 1, this condition may be removed at the cost of making the construction more complicated, please see the full version [1] for details. Since this condition is anyway required for the construction of pure FHE, we assume it for ease of exposition.

3.1   Instantiation

For concreteness, we instantiate our special FHE scheme with (a modified version of) the scheme by Brakerski, Gentry and Vaikuntanathan [10] (henceforth BGV), which is based on the hardness of the learning with errors (LWE) problem. To begin, note that BGV already satisfies the property that the algorithms for evaluation and decryption are deterministic (property 1), the property that the ciphertext is pseudorandom (property 2) as well as the property that decryption always outputs valid message (property 3). The property of circular security (property 5) does not provably hold in BGV, or indeed any existing FHE scheme, but is widely *assumed* to hold for BGV. In particular, the authors already assume it for optimized versions of their main construction (which does not require this assumption)– please see [10, Section 5] for a discussion. We also remark that circular security is assumed by all "pure" FHE schemes, namely, schemes that can support homomorphic evaluation of circuits of arbitrary polynomial depth. We require circular security for a different reason – to support the bootstrapping operation, which allows us to obliviously sample FHE ciphertexts. Thus, it remains to establish the property that decryption of a (truly) random element from the ciphertext space outputs a biased message from the message space (property 4). Establishing this property requires slight modifications to the BGV scheme[1]. Next, we describe these modifications for the case when the $\mathcal{M}$ is binary, of polynomial size and of super-polynomial size.

Recap of BGV. Let us consider the BGV construction for binary messages [10, Section 4]. We begin by providing a brief recap of the features of BGV that we require. We use the same notation as in their paper for ease of verification. Let $\mathcal{R}$ be a ring and $|\mathcal{R}| = q$. Recall that the key generation algorithm of BGV samples a vector $\mathbf{s}' \in \mathcal{R}^n$ such that all the entries of $\mathbf{s}'$ are "small" with high probability (details of the distribution are not relevant here) and outputs $\mathsf{sk} = \mathbf{s} = (1, \mathbf{s}')$. The public key is constructed by sampling a uniform random matrix $\mathbf{A}' \leftarrow \mathcal{R}^{N \times n}$, an error vector $\mathbf{e} \in \mathcal{R}^N$ from a special "error" distribution, and setting $\mathbf{b} = \mathbf{A}'\mathbf{s}' + 2 \cdot \mathbf{e}$. Denote by $\mathbf{A}$ the $(n+1)$ column matrix consisting of $\mathbf{b}$ followed by the n columns of $-\mathbf{A}'$. Observe that $\mathbf{A} \cdot \mathbf{s} = 2\mathbf{e}$. The public key contains $\mathbf{A}$ in addition to some other elements which are not relevant for our discussion[2]. To encrypt a message bit m, set $\mathbf{m} = (m, 0, 0, \ldots, 0) \in \{0,1\}^{n+1}$, sample $\mathbf{r} \leftarrow \{0,1\}^N$ and output $\mathsf{ct} = \mathbf{m} + \mathbf{A}^\top \mathbf{r}$. To decrypt, compute and output $[[\langle \mathsf{ct}, \mathsf{sk} \rangle]_q]_2$, where $\langle \cdot, \cdot \rangle$ denotes inner product over the ring, and $[\cdot]_p$ denotes reduction modulo p. The above construction can be adapted to support larger message spaces. A simple extension is to choose the message from $\mathbb{Z}_p$ for a polynomial sized prime p and multiply the error with p instead of 2. This, and other extensions are discussed in detail in [10, Section 5].

Creating a Bias. Observe that the decryption algorithm, given a ciphertext ct and secret sk, outputs the decrypted message bit as $[[\langle \mathsf{ct}, \mathsf{sk} \rangle]_q]_2$ regardless of the distribution of ct. Thus, even if ct is a random element from the ciphertext space $\mathcal{R}^{n+1}$ which may not be well formed, it still outputs a valid message from the message space. However, it is easy to see that for a random element $R \leftarrow \mathcal{R}^{n+1}$, the output of $[[\langle R, \mathsf{sk} \rangle]_q]_2$ is a uniformly distributed random bit, whereas we require the decryption algorithm to output a biased bit to satisfy property 4. Below, we will describe the modification to BGV to achieve the strong version

---

[1] We note that these properties are also satisfied by several other FHE schemes, for instance [7,11,23].

[2] Since we assume circular security which BGV do not, we can simplify their scheme – in particular, we not need fresh keys for each level of the circuit as they do.

of property 4. In the full version [1], we describe how we can instead rely on the weak version of the property, which is satisfied by BGV unmodified.

To create a bias, an idea is to build in an additional step in the decryption algorithm, which first checks whether the input ciphertext ct is well-formed. If so, it proceeds with legitimate decryption, i.e. computes $[[\langle \mathsf{ct},\ \mathsf{sk}\rangle]_q]_2$. If not, it simply outputs 0. Since well-formed ciphertexts in the BGV FHE are sparse in the ciphertext space $\mathcal{R}^{n+1}$, this ensures that a randomly chosen element from the ciphertext space is decrypted to 0 with high probability.

It remains to identify an efficient check for the well-formedness of the ciphertext. Towards this, we observe that for any valid ciphertext (Definition 2.4), the inner product $[\langle \mathsf{ct},\ \mathsf{sk}\rangle]_q = m + 2e$ where m is the encrypted bit and e is some error whose norm may be bounded using bounds on the norms of the secret key $\mathbf{s}$, the randomness $\mathbf{r}$, the error term in the public key $\mathbf{e}$ and the depth of the circuit – of which the norms of all aforementioned elements were chosen to be sufficiently "small" and the depth of the circuit can be bounded by the depth of the bootstrapping circuit [21].

Let us assume that the decryption error is bounded above by $B - 1$, for some $B = \mathsf{poly}(\lambda)$. We note that this bound holds true for the current setting of parameters in [10]. Then, it follows that the output of step 1 of decryption can be bounded from above by B (for any well formed ciphertext). On the other hand, the output of $[\langle R,\ \mathsf{sk}\rangle]_q$ for a random element R will also be uniformly distributed, and hence will have norm $\leq B$ only with probability $O(\frac{B}{q})$. If we set q to be super-polynomial in the security parameter, then this term is negligible. Thus, we may modify the BGV decryption algorithm so that after computing $[\langle \mathsf{ct},\ \mathsf{sk}\rangle]_q$, it checks whether the output is $\leq B$, and outputs 0 if not. This biases the output of decryption to 0 for random inputs – in more detail, decryption of a random element yields 0 with probability $1 - \mathsf{negl}(\lambda)$ as desired. With this modification, we ensured that BGV satisfies all the properties required by special FHE. We refer the reader to [10] for more details about the full construction of FHE.

In the above description, we chose the ring modulus q to be super-polynomial in the security parameter to obtain the desired bias. However, this large modulus is unnecessary and affects the efficiency of the scheme negatively. In the full version [1], we describe how to relax this requirement.

Next, we discuss how to modify the BGV scheme supporting larger (polynomial) message spaces, as discussed in [10, Section 5]. As in the case of binary messages (discussed above), we have that without performing any modifications, the BGV decryption algorithm, if executed on a random element in the ciphertext space, outputs a uniformly distributed message from the message space.

It remains to establish property 4 which requires that there exists a strict subset of the message space, $\mathcal{S} \subset \mathcal{M}$, such that

$$P(\mathcal{S}) := \sum_{m \in S} P(m) \geq 1 - \mathsf{negl}(\lambda)$$

where $P : \mathcal{M} \to \mathbb{R}$ is defined as $P(m) := \Pr[\mathsf{Fhe.Dec}(\mathsf{sk}, x) = m]$ where $x \leftarrow \mathcal{R}^{\ell_c}$ and $(\mathsf{pk}, \mathsf{sk}) \leftarrow \mathsf{Fhe.Gen}(1^\lambda)$.

Let $\mathcal{S}$ be an arbitrary subset of $\mathcal{M}$ that contains 0. For the binary message case above, we described a trick that ensures that random elements are decrypted to 0 with overwhelming probability. The same trick may be generalized to larger message spaces. If the modulus q is superpolynomial, and the message space is polynomial (say of size p), then the first step of decryption yields $[\langle \mathsf{ct}, \mathsf{sk} \rangle]_q = m + p \cdot e$ for well-formed ciphertexts, and a random element in $\mathcal{R}$ otherwise. Again, this term can be bounded by some polynomial B and the decryption procedure can be modified to output 0 (or any element from the set $\mathcal{S}$) if the output of step 1 is greater than B. By the same reasoning as above, this biases the output to $\mathcal{S}$ with overwhelming probability as long as q is super-polynomial. Please see the full version [1] to avoid the restriction of super-polynomial q.

Finally, we remark that BGV also includes variants where the message space is super-polynomial in size [10, Section 5.4]. In this case, biasing the output to a fixed set $\mathcal{S}$ is simple: we can just set $\mathcal{S} = \mathcal{M} \setminus \{1\}$. Moreover $\mathcal{S}$ has efficient representation since it can simply be represented by its complement, which is of small size and it is clear that the decryption output of a random element is biased to $\mathcal{S}$ with overwhelming probability.

4   Deniable Encryption for Bits

In this section, we provide our constructions for weak deniable FHE, as in Definition 2.11, and compact deniable FHE, as in Definition 2.8. Let $\mathsf{Fhe} = (\mathsf{Gen}, \mathsf{Enc}, \mathsf{Eval}, \mathsf{Dec})$ be a *special* public-key FHE scheme for the message space $\mathcal{M} = \{0, 1\}$ with ciphertext space $\mathcal{R}^{\ell_c}$, as in Definition 3.1. For reading convenience, we denote by lowercase r, the ℓ-bit string randomness that is input to an Fhe.Enc algorithm, and by uppercase R, the elements in $\mathcal{R}^{\ell_c}$, where $\mathcal{R}^{\ell_c}$ is the co-domain of the algorithm Fhe.Enc. We denote by ℓ'_c the bit length of elements in $\mathcal{R}^{\ell_c}$ (that is, $\ell'_c = \lceil \ell_c \log_2(|\mathcal{R}|) \rceil$). Recall that boot denotes the bootstrapping procedure described in Definition 2.3 and $\oplus_2$ denotes the homomorphic evaluation of addition mod 2 described in Definition 2.5.

4.1   Weakly Deniable FHE for Bits

Our public-key weak deniable fully homomorphic encryption scheme for message space $\mathcal{M} = \{0, 1\}$, wDFhe $= (\mathsf{Gen}, \mathsf{DEnc}, \mathsf{Enc}, \mathsf{Eval}, \mathsf{Dec}, \mathsf{Fake})$, is described as follows:

wDFhe.Gen(1^λ) : Upon input the unary representation of the security parameter λ, do the following:
  1. Sample $(\mathsf{pk}, \mathsf{sk}) \leftarrow \mathsf{Fhe.Gen}(1^\lambda)$, and $\mathsf{ct_{sk}} \leftarrow \mathsf{Fhe.Enc}(\mathsf{pk}, \mathsf{sk})$.
  2. Outputs $\mathsf{dpk} := (\mathsf{pk}, \mathsf{ct_{sk}}), \mathsf{dsk} := \mathsf{sk}$
wDFhe.DEnc$(\mathsf{dpk}, m; r)$: Upon input the public key dpk, a message bit m and $(3\ell + \ell'_c)$-bit string randomness r, do the following:
  1. Parse $\mathsf{dpk} := (\mathsf{pk}, \mathsf{ct_{sk}})$ and $r = (r_1, r_2, r_3, R_4)$, where $|r_i| = \ell$ for $i \in [3]$ and $|R_4| = \ell'_c$.
  2. For $i \in [3]$, set $R_i = \mathsf{Fhe.Enc}(\mathsf{pk}, 1; r_i)$.

3. Let $\mathsf{ct}_0 = \mathsf{boot}(R_1) \oplus_2 \mathsf{boot}(R_2)$ and $\mathsf{ct}_1 = \mathsf{boot}(R_4) \oplus_2 \mathsf{boot}(R_3)$.
4. Output $\mathsf{dct} = \mathsf{ct}_m$.

wDFhe.Enc(dpk, m; r) : Upon input the public-key dpk, the message bit m, and the $(\ell + 3\ell_c')$-bit string randomness r, do the following:

1. Parse dpk := (pk, $\mathsf{ct_{sk}}$) and r = (R_1, R_2, R_3, r_4), where $|R_i| = \ell_c'$ for $i \in [3]$ and $|r_4| = \ell$.
2. Set $R_4 = \mathsf{Fhe.Enc}(\mathsf{pk}, 1; r_4)$.
3. Let $\mathsf{ct}_0 = \mathsf{boot}(R_1) \oplus_2 \mathsf{boot}(R_2)$ and $\mathsf{ct}_1 = \mathsf{boot}(R_3) \oplus_2 \mathsf{boot}(R_4)$.
4. Output $\mathsf{dct} = \mathsf{ct}_m$.

wDFhe.Eval(dpk, $\mathcal{C}$, $\mathsf{dct}_1, \ldots, \mathsf{dct}_k$): Upon input the public key dpk = (pk, $\mathsf{ct_{sk}}$), the circuit $\mathcal{C}$ and the ciphertexts $\mathsf{dct}_1, \ldots, \mathsf{dct}_k$, interpret dct_i as Fhe ciphertext ct_i for $i \in [k]$, and output $\mathsf{dct} = \mathsf{Fhe.Eval}(\mathsf{pk}, \mathcal{C}, \mathsf{ct}_1, \ldots, \mathsf{ct}_k)$.

wDFhe.Dec(dsk, dct): Upon input the secret key dsk and the ciphertext dct, interpret dsk and dct as Fhe secret key sk and Fhe ciphertext ct and output Fhe.Dec(sk, ct).

wDFhe.Fake(dpk, m, r, m^*): Upon input the public key dpk, the original message bit m, $(3\ell + \ell_c')$-bit string randomness r, and the faking message bit m^*, do the following:

1. Parse dpk := (pk, $\mathsf{ct_{sk}}$) and r = (r_1, r_2, r_3, R_4), where $|r_i| = \ell$ for $i \in [3]$ and $|R_4| = \ell_c'$.
2. For $i \in [3]$, set $R_i = \mathsf{Fhe.Enc}(\mathsf{pk}, 1; r_i)$.
3. If $m = m^*$, then set $R_1^* = R_1$, $R_2^* = R_2$, $R_3^* = R_4$, and $r_4^* = r_3$.
4. Else if $m \neq m^*$, then set $R_1^* = R_4$, $R_2^* = R_3$, $R_3^* = R_1$, and $r_4^* = r_2$.
5. Output r$^* = (R_1^*, R_2^*, R_3^*, r_4^*)$

We now prove the scheme satisfies correctness, compactness, CPA security and weak deniability.

Compactness and Security. Observe that the output of both wDFhe.DEnc and wDFhe.Enc is a valid ciphertext of the underlying Fhe scheme. This is due to property 3 of the special FHE which states that the FHE decryption algorithm always outputs a valid bit, and due to the correctness of FHE evaluation which implies correctness of bootstrapping. Together, these two properties ensure that boot always outputs a valid ciphertext. Moreover, correctness of homomorphic evaluation implies that the addition mod 2 operation is performed correctly, so that the output of wDFhe.DEnc and wDFhe.Enc is a valid ciphertext of FHE.

Since the underlying FHE scheme satisfies compactness, it holds that the ciphertext output by wDFhe.DEnc and wDFhe.Enc is also compact. Similarly, due to property 5 which states that the scheme is circular secure, and since the ciphertext of the underlying FHE satisfies semantic security, so does the ciphertext output by wDFhe.DEnc and wDFhe.Enc. Thus, both schemes are compact and secure as the underlying FHE scheme is.

Correctness. We start by proving correctness of the deniable encryption algorithm wDFhe.DEnc. Parse r $\in \{0, 1\}^{3\ell + \ell_c'}$ as r = (r_1, r_2, r_3, R_4). Observe that:

1. Since $R_i = \mathsf{Fhe.Enc}(\mathsf{pk}, 1; r_i)$ for $i \in [3]$, we have by correctness of the underlying Fhe, that R_1, R_2 and R_3 are valid encryptions of 1.

2. By properties 3 and 4 which state that FHE decryption always outputs a bit and this bit is biased to 0 with overwhelming probability when decryption is invoked with a truly random input, we have that $\mathsf{boot}(R_4)$ is a valid encryption of 0 with overwhelming probability.

Now, by correctness of FHE evaluation, we have that $\mathsf{ct}_0 = \mathsf{boot}(R_1) \oplus_2 \mathsf{boot}(R_2)$ is a valid encryption of 0 and $\mathsf{ct}_1 = \mathsf{boot}(R_4) \oplus_2 \mathsf{boot}(R_3)$ is a valid encryption of 1.

Next we prove correctness of $\mathsf{wDFhe.Enc}$. Parse $\mathsf{r} \in \{0,1\}^{\ell + 3\ell'_c}$ as $\mathsf{r} = (R_1, R_2, R_3, r_4)$. Observe that:

1. Since $R_4 = \mathsf{Fhe.Enc}(\mathsf{pk}, 1; r_4)$, we have that R_4 is a valid encryption of 1.
2. As above, we have by properties 3 and 4 that $\mathsf{boot}(R_i)$ for $i \in [3]$ are valid encryptions of 0 with overwhelming probability.

Thus, again by correctness of FHE evaluation, we have that $\mathsf{ct}_0 = \mathsf{boot}(R_1) \oplus_2 \mathsf{boot}(R_2)$ is a valid encryption of 0 and $\mathsf{ct}_1 = \mathsf{boot}(R_3) \oplus_2 \mathsf{boot}(R_4)$ is a valid encryption of 1.

Weak-Deniability. Next, we prove weak deniability of the construction. Fix a security parameter λ, an original message $m \in \{0,1\}$, and a faking message $m^* \in \{0,1\}$. Let $(\mathsf{dpk}, \mathsf{dsk}) \leftarrow \mathsf{wDFhe.Gen}(1^\lambda)$, and parse $\mathsf{dpk} := (\mathsf{pk}, \mathsf{ct}_{\mathsf{sk}}), \mathsf{dsk} := \mathsf{sk}$.

Faking Case. First consider the distribution of $(\mathsf{dpk}, m^*, \mathsf{r}, \mathsf{DEnc}(\mathsf{dpk}, m; r'))$ in the case of faking.
1. Select uniformly at random $r' \leftarrow \{0,1\}^{3\ell} \times \mathcal{R}^{\ell_c}$.
2. Parse $r' := (r_1, r_2, r_3, R_4)$, where $|r_i| = \ell$ for $i \in [3]$ and $|R_4| = \ell'_c$.
3. For $i \in [3]$, set $R_i = \mathsf{Fhe.Enc}(\mathsf{pk}, 1; r_i)$.
4. Let $\mathsf{r}^* = \mathsf{wDFhe.Fake}(\mathsf{dpk}, m, r', m^*)$.
5. By the faking algorithm $\mathsf{r}^* = (R_1^*, R_2^*, R_3^*, r_4^*)$ which is computed as follows:
   (a) *Case $m = m^*$:*
$$R_1^* = R_1, \quad R_2^* = R_2, \quad R_3^* = R_4, \quad r_4^* = r_3.$$

   By property 2 which asserts that ciphertexts are pseudorandom, we can explain R_1^* and R_2^* as uniform from the ciphertexts space $\mathcal{R}^{\ell_c}$. Here, $R_3^* = R_4$ is already a uniform element in $\mathcal{R}^{\ell_c}$, and $r_4^* = r_3$ is a uniform ℓ bit string.
   (b) *Case $m \neq m^*$:*
$$R_1^* = R_4, \quad R_2^* = R_3, \quad R_3^* = R_1, \quad r_4^* = r_2.$$

   As above, we can explain R_2^* and R_3^* as uniform elements in $\mathcal{R}^{\ell_c}$, and $R_1^* = R_4$ and $r_4^* = r_2$ are already uniform.
6. The output of this hybrid is:
$$\left(\mathsf{dpk}, m^*, \mathsf{r}^* = (R_1^*, R_2^*, R_3^*, r_4^*), \mathsf{ct}^* = \mathsf{wDFhe.DEnc}(\mathsf{dpk}, m; r') \right)$$

where $\mathsf{ct}^* := \mathsf{ct}_m$, $\mathsf{ct}_0 = \mathsf{boot}(R_1) \oplus_2 \mathsf{boot}(R_2)$ and $\mathsf{ct}_1 = \mathsf{boot}(R_4) \oplus_2 \mathsf{boot}(R_3)$.

Observe that $\mathsf{ct}^* = \mathsf{wDFhe}.\mathsf{Enc}(\mathsf{dpk}, m^*; r^*)$. Thus, the output of this hybrid can be written as:

$$\left(\mathsf{dpk}, m^*, \mathsf{r}^* = (R_1^*, R_2^*, R_3^*, r_4^*), \mathsf{ct}^* = \mathsf{wDFhe}.\mathsf{Enc}(\mathsf{dpk}, m^*; r^*) \right)$$

where $\mathsf{ct}^* := \mathsf{ct}_{m^*}$, $\mathsf{ct}_0 = \mathsf{boot}(R_1^*) \oplus_2 \mathsf{boot}(R_2^*)$, $\mathsf{ct}_1 = \mathsf{boot}(R_3^*) \oplus_2 \mathsf{boot}(R_4^*)$ and R_1^*, R_2^*, R_3^* and r_4^* are explained as uniform in $\mathcal{R}^{3\ell_c} \times \{0,1\}^\ell$.

Honest Case. Next, note that in the honest case $\mathsf{r} \leftarrow \mathcal{R}^{3\ell_c} \times \{0,1\}^\ell$, so the output distribution is:

$$\left(\mathsf{dpk}, m^*, \mathsf{r} = (R_1, R_2, R_3, r_4), \mathsf{ct}^* = \mathsf{wDFhe}.\mathsf{Enc}(\mathsf{dpk}, m^*; r) \right)$$

where $\mathsf{ct}^* := \mathsf{ct}_{m^*}$, $\mathsf{ct}_0 = \mathsf{boot}(R_1) \oplus_2 \mathsf{boot}(R_2)$, $\mathsf{ct}_1 = \mathsf{boot}(R_3) \oplus_2 \mathsf{boot}(R_4)$ and R_1, R_2, R_3 and r_4 are sampled uniformly. Hence, the two distributions are indistinguishable.

4.2 Fully Deniable FHE for Bits

Our compact public-key $1/\delta$-deniable[3] fully homomorphic encryption scheme for message space $\mathcal{M} = \{0,1\}$, $\mathsf{DFhe} = (\mathsf{Gen}, \mathsf{DEnc}, \mathsf{Enc}, \mathsf{Eval}, \mathsf{Dec}, \mathsf{Fake})$, is described below. We also provide an alternate construction with slightly different parameters in the full version [1]. Recall that boot denotes the bootstrapping procedure described in Definition 2.3 and $\oplus_2$ denotes the homomorphic evaluation of addition mod 2 described in Definition 2.5). We let $n = \delta^2$.

$\mathsf{DFhe}.\mathsf{Gen}(1^\lambda)$: Upon input the unary representation of the security parameter λ, do the following:
1. Sample $(\mathsf{pk}, \mathsf{sk}) \leftarrow \mathsf{Fhe}.\mathsf{Gen}(1^\lambda)$, and $\mathsf{ct}_{\mathsf{sk}} \leftarrow \mathsf{Fhe}.\mathsf{Enc}(\mathsf{pk}, \mathsf{sk})$.
2. Outputs $\mathsf{dpk} := (\mathsf{pk}, \mathsf{ct}_{\mathsf{sk}})$, $\mathsf{dsk} := \mathsf{sk}$.

$\mathsf{DFhe}.\mathsf{Enc}(\mathsf{dpk}, m)$: Upon input the public-key dpk, the message bit m, do the following:
1. Parse $\mathsf{dpk} := (\mathsf{pk}, \mathsf{ct}_{\mathsf{sk}})$
2. Select r as follows:
    (a) Select uniformly $x_1, \ldots, x_n \in \{0,1\}$ such that $\sum_{i=1}^n x_i = m \pmod 2$.
    (b) For $i \in [n]$: if $x_i = 1$, then select $r_i \leftarrow \{0,1\}^\ell$; else if $x_i = 0$, select $R_i \leftarrow \mathcal{R}^{\ell_c}$.
3. For $i \in [n]$ such that $x_i = 1$, set $R_i = \mathsf{Fhe}.\mathsf{Enc}(\mathsf{pk}, 1; r_i)$.
4. Output $\mathsf{dct} = \oplus_2(\mathsf{boot}(R_1), \ldots, \mathsf{boot}(R_n))$

$\mathsf{DFhe}.\mathsf{Eval}(\mathsf{dpk}, \mathcal{C}, \mathsf{dct}_1, \ldots, \mathsf{dct}_k)$: Upon input the public key $\mathsf{dpk} = (\mathsf{pk}, \mathsf{ct}_{\mathsf{sk}})$, the circuit $\mathcal{C}$ and the ciphertexts $\mathsf{dct}_1, \ldots, \mathsf{dct}_k$, interpret dct_i as Fhe ciphertext ct_i for $i \in [k]$, and output $\mathsf{dct} = \mathsf{Fhe}.\mathsf{Eval}(\mathsf{pk}, \mathcal{C}, \mathsf{ct}_1, \ldots, \mathsf{ct}_k)$.

$\mathsf{DFhe}.\mathsf{Dec}(\mathsf{dsk}, \mathsf{dct})$: Upon input the secret key dsk and the ciphertext dct, interpret dsk and dct as Fhe secret key sk and Fhe ciphertext ct and output $\mathsf{Fhe}.\mathsf{Dec}(\mathsf{sk}, \mathsf{ct})$.

---

[3] We remind the reader that $\delta = \delta(\lambda)$, but we drop the λ for readability.

DFhe.Fake(dpk, m, r, m^*): Upon input the public key dpk, the original message bit m, randomness r, and the fake message m^* do the following:

1. If $m = m^*$, output $r^* = r$.
2. Parse dpk := (pk, ct_{sk}) and r = $(x_1, \ldots, x_n, \rho_1, \ldots, \rho_n)$, where $x_1, \ldots, x_n \in \{0, 1\}$, and for each $i \in [n]$, if $x_i = 1$, then $|\rho_i| = \ell$; else if $x_i = 0$, $|\rho_i| = \ell'_c$.
3. Select uniform $i^* \in [n]$ such that $x_{i^*} = 1$. If there is no such i^*, output "cheating impossible"; else:
   (a) Set $x_{i^*}^* = 0$ and $\rho_{i^*}^* = $ Fhe.Enc(pk, 1; ρ_{i^*});
   (b) For $i \in [n] \setminus \{i^*\}$, set $x_i^* = x_i$ and $\rho_i^* = \rho_i$.
4. Output $r^* = (x_1^*, \ldots, x_n^*, \rho_1^*, \ldots, \rho_n^*)$.

We now prove the scheme satisfies correctness, compactness, CPA security and poly deniability. Compactness and security follow exactly as in Sect. 4.1.

Correctness. To argue correctness, we note that:

1. Since $R_i = $ Fhe.Enc(pk, 1; r_i) for i such that $x_i = 1$, we have by correctness of the underlying Fhe that R_i, and hence boot(R_i) are valid encryptions of 1 for all $i \in [n]$ such that $x_i = 1$.
2. By properties 3 and 4 which state that FHE decryption always outputs a bit and this bit is biased to 0 with overwhelming probability when decryption is invoked with a truly random input, we have that boot(R_i) for i such that $x_i = 0$ is valid encryption of 0 with overwhelming probability.

Hence, since $\sum_{i=1}^n x_i = m \pmod 2$, the (FHE evaluation of) addition mod 2 of boot(R_i) for $i \in [n]$ yields an encryption of m. Hence, the scheme encodes the message bit correctly.

Deniability. Next, we prove $1/\delta$-deniability of the construction. Fix a security parameter λ, an original message $m \in \{0, 1\}$, and a faking message $m^* \in \{0, 1\}$. Let (dpk, dsk) $\leftarrow$ DFhe.Gen(1^λ), and parse dpk := (pk, ct_{sk}), dsk := sk. When the original message m and the fake message m^* are the same, the faked randomness r^* is equal to the original randomness r. Thus in this case, $m = m^*$, the distributions are identical:

$$(dpk, m^*, r, DFhe.Enc(dpk, m^*; r)) = (dpk, m^*, r^*, DFhe.Enc(dpk, m; r)).$$

When the original message m and the fake message m^* are not the same, observe that "cheating impossible" will be output only in case that $x_i = 0$ for all $i \in [n]$, which occurs with probability 2^{-n}. Assuming we are not in this case, the output distribution is:

Faking Case. First consider the distribution of (dpk, m^*, r^*, DFhe.Enc(dpk, m; r)) in the case of faking, where $r^* \leftarrow$ DFhe.Fake(dpk, m, r; m^*).

1. Select uniform r := $(x_1, \ldots, x_n, \rho_1, \ldots, \rho_n)$, by,
   (a) Select $x_i \leftarrow \{0, 1\}$ for $i \in [n]$ such that $\sum_{i \in [n]} x_i = m \pmod 2$
   (b) For $i \in [n]$, if $x_i = 1$, select $\rho_i \leftarrow \{0, 1\}^\ell$
   (c) For $i \in [n]$, if $x_i = 0$, select $\rho_i \leftarrow \mathcal{R}^{\ell_c}$

2. Let $r^* = \mathsf{DFhe.Fake(dpk}, m, r, m^*)$, that is $r^* = (x_1^*, \ldots, x_n^*, \rho_1^*, \ldots, \rho_n^*)$ which is computed as follows:

   (a) Select a uniform index $i^* \in [n]$ such that $x_{i^*} = 1$, i.e. $i^* \leftarrow \{i | x_i = 1\}$.

   (b) For $i \in [n], i \neq i^*$, set $x_i^* = x_i$ and $\rho_i^* = \rho_i$.

   (c) Set $x_{i^*} = 0$, and $\rho_{i^*}^* = \mathsf{Fhe.Enc(pk}, 1; \rho_{i^*})$.

Intermediate Case. By property 2 of the special FHE, which asserts that ciphertexts are pseudorandom, we can explain $\rho_{i^*}^* = \mathsf{Fhe.Enc(pk}, 1; \rho_{i^*})$ as uniform element from the ciphertexts space $\mathcal{R}^{\ell_c}$. The distribution of this hybrid is $(\mathsf{dpk}, m^*, r', \mathsf{DFhe.Enc(dpk}, m; r))$, where $r' = (x_1', \ldots, x_n', \rho_1', \ldots, \rho_n')$ is sampled as follows:

1. Select $x_i \leftarrow \{0,1\}$ for $i \in [n]$ such that $\sum_{i \in [n]} x_i = m \pmod 2$
2. Select a uniform index $i' \in [n]$ such that $x_{i'} = 1$ (i.e. $i' \leftarrow \{i | x_i = 1\}$), and set $x_{i'}' = 0$, and for all $i \in [n] \setminus \{i'\}$ set $x_i' = x_i$.
3. For $i \in [n]$, if $x_i' = 1$, select $\rho_i' \leftarrow \{0,1\}^\ell$
4. For $i \in [n]$, if $x_i' = 0$, select $\rho_i' \leftarrow \mathcal{R}^{\ell_c}$

Honest Case. Note that in the honest case the distribution is $(\mathsf{dpk}, m^*, r, \mathsf{DFhe.Enc(dpk}, m^*; r))$, where $r = (x_1, \ldots, x_n, \rho_1, \ldots, \rho_n)$ is sampled as follows:

1. Select $x_i \leftarrow \{0,1\}$ for $i \in [n]$ such that $\sum_{i \in [n]} x_i = m^* \pmod 2$.
2. For $i \in [n]$, if $x_i = 1$, select $\rho_i' \leftarrow \{0,1\}^\ell$
3. For $i \in [n]$, if $x_i = 0$, select $\rho_i' \leftarrow \mathcal{R}^{\ell_c}$

The statistical distance between the two distributions used to sample $(x_1, \ldots, x_n)$, in the honest case and in the intermediate/faking case, is $\frac{1}{\sqrt{n}}$. Hence, any PPT adversary $\mathcal{A}$ can win the $\mathsf{DnblGame}_\mathcal{A}^b(\lambda)$ game with probability at most $\frac{1}{\sqrt{n}}$, which is $\frac{1}{\delta}$ by our choice of n.

5 Weakly Deniable FHE with Large Message Space

In this section, we provide our construction for weak deniable FHE for polynomial size[4] message space $\mathcal{M}$, as in Definition 2.11. Let $\mathsf{Fhe} = (\mathsf{Gen}, \mathsf{Enc}, \mathsf{Eval}, \mathsf{Dec})$ be a *special* public-key fully homomorphic encryption for the message space $\mathcal{M}$ with ciphertext space $\mathcal{R}^{\ell_c}$, as in Definition 3.1, and $\mathsf{boot}(x)$ be the bootstrapping procedure, described in Definition 2.3. We denote by $\mathcal{S}$ a strict subset of the message space to which decryption of random elements is biased,[5] by $1_{\overline{\mathcal{S}}}$ the indicator function for the set $\overline{\mathcal{S}} = \mathcal{M} \setminus \mathcal{S}$, described in Definition 2.7, and by s a fixed element in $\overline{\mathcal{S}}$. Recall that $\oplus_2$ denotes the homomorphic evaluation of addition mod 2 described in Definition 2.5 and select denotes the selector circuit described in Definition 2.6.

For reading convenience, we denote by lowercase r, the ℓ-bit string randomness that is input to an $\mathsf{Fhe.Enc}$ algorithm, and by upper case R, the elements in $\mathcal{R}^{\ell_c}$, where $\mathcal{R}^{\ell_c}$ is the co-domain of the FHE encryption algorithm. We denote by ℓ_c' the bit length of elements in $\mathcal{R}^{\ell_c}$ (that is, $\ell_c' = \lceil \ell_c \log_2(|R|) \rceil$). We index the messages in the message space as $\mathcal{M} = \{m_0, \ldots, m_\mu\}$.

---

[4] Polynomial in the security parameter. That is $|\mathcal{M}| = \mathrm{poly}(\lambda)$.

[5] Note that this exists from property 4 of the special Fhe.

Our (public-key) weakly deniable fully homomorphic encryption scheme for message space $\mathcal{M}$ wDFhe = (Gen, DEnc, Enc, Eval, Dec, Fake) is described as follows:

wDFhe.Gen(1^λ) : Upon input the unary representation of the security parameter λ, do the following:
1. Sample (pk, sk) $\leftarrow$ Fhe.Gen(1^λ), and $\mathsf{ct_{sk}} \leftarrow$ Fhe.Enc(pk, sk).
2. Outputs dpk := (pk, $\mathsf{ct_{sk}}$), dsk := sk

wDFhe.DEnc(dpk, m_k; r): Upon input the public key dpk, a message $m_k \in \mathcal{M}$ and $((4\ell + \ell'_c)\mu)$-bit string randomness r, do the following:
1. Parse the input.
   dpk := (pk, $\mathsf{ct_{sk}}$), r = $(r_1, \dots, r_\mu, (r_{1,1}, r_{1,2}, r_{1,3}, \hat{R}_{1,4}), \dots, (r_{\mu,1}, r_{\mu,2}, r_{\mu,3},$ $\hat{R}_{\mu,4}))$ where $|r_i| = |r_{i,j}| = \ell$ and $|\hat{R}_{i,4}| = \ell'_c$ for $i \in [\mu], j \in [3]$.
2. Generate ciphertexts for every possible message.
   For $i \in [\mu]$, set ct_i = Fhe.Enc(pk, m_i; r_i).
3. Generate ciphertexts for "selector" bits.
   (a) For every $i \in [\mu], j \in [3]$, set $\hat{R}_{i,j}$ = Fhe.Enc(pk, s; $r_{i,j}$).
   (b) For every $i \in [\mu], j \in [4]$, set $R_{i,j}$ = Fhe.Eval(pk, $1_{\overline{s}}$, $\hat{R}_{i,j}$).
   (c) We compute ciphertexts for selector bits 0 and 1 for every index as follows. For $i \in [\mu]$, compute

$$\mathsf{ct}_0^i = \mathsf{boot}(R_{i,1}) \oplus_2 \mathsf{boot}(R_{i,2}), \quad \mathsf{ct}_1^i = \mathsf{boot}(R_{i,4}) \oplus_2 \mathsf{boot}(R_{i,3})$$

   (d) We let the kth message to be selected by setting it's selector bit to 1, and all others to 0 as follows. For every $i \in [\mu]$ if $i \neq k$, set $\mathsf{ct}_i^{\mathsf{sel}} = \mathsf{ct}_0^i$; else if $i = k$, set $\mathsf{ct}_i^{\mathsf{sel}} = \mathsf{ct}_1^i$.
4. Evaluate selector circuit on ciphertexts.
   Compute and output dct = select($\mathsf{ct}_1, \dots, \mathsf{ct}_\mu, \mathsf{ct}_1^{\mathsf{sel}}, \dots, \mathsf{ct}_\mu^{\mathsf{sel}}$), that is dct = $\sum_{i \in [\mu]} (\mathsf{ct}_i^{\mathsf{sel}} \otimes \mathsf{ct}_i)$.

wDFhe.Enc(dpk, m_k; r) : Upon input public-key dpk, a message $m_k \in \mathcal{M}$, and $((2\ell + 3\ell'_c)\mu)$-bit string randomness r, do the following:
1. Parse the input.
   dpk := (pk, $\mathsf{ct_{sk}}$), r = $(r_1, \dots, r_\mu, (\hat{R}_{1,1}, \hat{R}_{1,2}, \hat{R}_{1,3}, r_{1,4}), \dots, (\hat{R}_{\mu,1}, \hat{R}_{\mu,2},$ $\hat{R}_{\mu,3}, r_{\mu,4}))$ where $|r_i| = |r_{i,4}| = \ell$ and $|\hat{R}_{i,j}| = \ell'_c$ for $i \in [\mu], j \in [3]$.
2. Generate ciphertexts for every possible message.
   For $i \in [\mu]$, set ct_i = Fhe.Enc(pk, m_i; r_i).
3. Generate ciphertexts for "selector" bits.
   (a) For every $i \in [\mu]$, set $\hat{R}_{i,4}$ = Fhe.Enc(pk, s; $r_{i,4}$).
   (b) For every $i \in [\mu], j \in [4]$, set $R_{i,j}$ = Fhe.Eval(pk, $1_{\overline{s}}$, $\hat{R}_{i,j}$).
   (c) We compute ciphertexts for selector bits 0 and 1 for every index as follows.
      For $i \in [\mu]$, compute

$$\mathsf{ct}_0^i = \mathsf{boot}(R_{i,1}) \oplus_2 \mathsf{boot}(R_{i,2}), \quad \mathsf{ct}_1^i = \mathsf{boot}(R_{i,3}) \oplus_2 \mathsf{boot}(R_{i,4}).$$

   (d) We let the kth message to be selected by setting it's selector bit to 1, and all others to 0 as follows. For every $i \in [\mu]$ if $i \neq k$, set $\mathsf{ct}_i^{\mathsf{sel}} = \mathsf{ct}_0^i$; else if $i = k$, set $\mathsf{ct}_i^{\mathsf{sel}} = \mathsf{ct}_1^i$.

4. Evaluate selector circuit on ciphertexts.
   Compute and output $\mathsf{dct} = \mathsf{select}(\mathsf{ct}_1, \ldots, \mathsf{ct}_\mu, \mathsf{ct}_1^{\mathsf{sel}}, \ldots, \mathsf{ct}_\mu^{\mathsf{sel}})$, that is $\sum_{i \in [\mu]} (\mathsf{ct}_i^{\mathsf{sel}} \otimes \mathsf{ct}_i)$.

$\mathsf{wDFhe.Eval}(\mathsf{dpk}, \mathcal{C}, \mathsf{dct}_1, \ldots, \mathsf{dct}_k)$: Upon input the public key $\mathsf{dpk} = (\mathsf{pk}, \mathsf{ct}_{\mathsf{sk}})$, the circuit $\mathcal{C}$ and the ciphertexts $\mathsf{dct}_1, \ldots, \mathsf{dct}_k$, interpret dct_i as Fhe ciphertext ct_i for $i \in [k]$, and output $\mathsf{dct} = \mathsf{Fhe.Eval}(\mathsf{pk}, \mathcal{C}, \mathsf{ct}_1, \ldots, \mathsf{ct}_k)$.

$\mathsf{wDFhe.Dec}(\mathsf{dsk}, \mathsf{dct})$: Upon input the secret key dsk and the ciphertext dct, interpret dsk and dct as Fhe secret key sk and Fhe ciphertext ct and output $\mathsf{Fhe.Dec}(\mathsf{sk}, \mathsf{ct})$.

$\mathsf{wDFhe.Fake}(\mathsf{dpk}, m_k, \mathsf{r}, m_{k^*})$: Upon input the public key dpk, the original message $m_k \in \mathcal{M}$, $((4\ell + \ell_c)\mu)$-bit string randomness r and the fake message m_{k^*}, do the following:

1. Parse $\mathsf{dpk} := (\mathsf{pk}, \mathsf{ct}_{\mathsf{sk}})$, and
   $$\mathsf{r} := (r_1, \ldots, r_\mu, (r_{1,1}, r_{1,2}, r_{1,3}, \hat{R}_{1,4}), \ldots, (r_{\mu,1}, r_{\mu,2}, r_{\mu,3}, \hat{R}_{\mu,4})), \quad \text{where}$$
   $|r_i| = |r_{i,j}| = \ell$ and $|\hat{R}_{i,4}| = \ell'_c$ for $i \in [\mu], j \in [3]$.
2. For all $i \in [\mu]$, set $r_i^* = r_i$.
3. For every $i \in [\mu], j \in [3]$, set $\hat{R}_{i,j} = \mathsf{Fhe.Enc}(\mathsf{pk}, s; r_{i,j})$.
4. For every $i \in [\mu] \setminus \{k, k^*\}$ set
   $$\hat{R}_{i,1}^* = \hat{R}_{i,1}, \quad \hat{R}_{i,2}^* = \hat{R}_{i,2}, \quad \hat{R}_{i,3}^* = \hat{R}_{i,3}, \quad r_{i,4}^* = r_{i,4}.$$
5. If $k = k^*$, then set
   $$\hat{R}_{k,1}^* = \hat{R}_{k,1}, \quad \hat{R}_{k,2}^* = \hat{R}_{k,2}, \quad \hat{R}_{k,3}^* = \hat{R}_{k,4}, \quad r_{k,4}^* = r_{k,3};$$
   Else if $k \neq k^*$, for every $i \in \{k, k^*\}$ set
   $$\hat{R}_{i,1}^* = \hat{R}_{i,4}, \quad \hat{R}_{i,2}^* = \hat{R}_{i,3}, \quad \hat{R}_{i,3}^* = \hat{R}_{i,1}, \quad r_{i,4}^* = r_{i,2}.$$
6. Output
   $$\mathsf{r}^* = (r_1^*, \ldots, r_\mu^*, (\hat{R}_{1,1}^*, \hat{R}_{1,2}^*, \hat{R}_{1,3}^*, r_{1,4}^*), \ldots, (\hat{R}_{\mu,1}^*, \hat{R}_{\mu,2}^*, \hat{R}_{\mu,3}^*, r_{\mu,4}^*))$$

Remark 5.1. We observe that by using the circuit Mux instead of the circuit select, we can use smaller randomness – in particular, we can achieve $|\mathsf{r}| = \mu\ell + 2\log_2(\mu)\ell'_c$.

In the full version [1], we prove the scheme satisfies correctness, compactness, CPA security and weak deniability. Due to space constraints, we provide our construction of compact public-key $1/\delta$-deniable fully homomorphic encryption scheme for polynomial sized message space in the full model in the full version of this paper [1].

Acknowledgment. We are grateful to Daniele Micciancio for very insightful discussions about bootstrapping, and helpful comments that helped us improve the quality of this writeup. We thank Vinod Vaikuntanathan and Aayush Jain for suggesting the use of a key-chain rather than key-cycle to get rid of circular security for the case of levelled FHE. Research of the first author is supported by the DST "Swarnajayanti" fellowship, an Indo-French CEFIPRA project and the CCD Centre of Excellence. Part of the research corresponding to this work was conducted while visiting the Simons Institute for the Theory of Computing. Research of the second author is supported in part by DARPA under Agreement No. HR00112020023. Any opinions, findings and conclusions or recommendations expressed in this material are those of the author(s) and do not necessarily reflect the views of the United States Government or DARPA.

References

1. Agrawal, S., Goldwasser, S., Mossel, S.: Deniable fully homomorphic encryption from lwe. Cryptology ePrint Archive, Report 2020/1588 (2020). https://eprint. iacr.org/2020/1588
2. Ananth, P., Jain, A.: Indistinguishability obfuscation from compact functional encryption. In: Gennaro, R., Robshaw, M. (eds.) CRYPTO 2015. LNCS, vol. 9215, pp. 308–326. Springer, Heidelberg (2015). https://doi.org/10.1007/978-3-662-47989-6_15
3. Anonymous. Removing circularity for levelled fhe. Personal Communication (2020)
4. Apon, D., Fan, X., Liu, F.-H.: Deniable attribute based encryption for branching programs from LWE. In: Hirt, M., Smith, A. (eds.) TCC 2016. LNCS, vol. 9986, pp. 299–329. Springer, Heidelberg (2016). https://doi.org/10.1007/978-3-662-53644-5_12
5. Bendlin, R., Nielsen, J.B., Nordholt, P.S., Orlandi, C.: Lower and upper bounds for deniable public-key encryption. In: Lee, D.H., Wang, X. (eds.) ASIACRYPT 2011. LNCS, vol. 7073, pp. 125–142. Springer, Heidelberg (2011). https://doi.org/10.1007/978-3-642-25385-0_7
6. Bitansky, N., Vaikuntanathan, V.: Indistinguishability obfuscation from functional encryption. J. ACM (JACM) 65(6), 1–37 (2018)
7. Brakerski, Z.: Fully homomorphic encryption without modulus switching from classical GapSVP. In: Safavi-Naini, R., Canetti, R. (eds.) CRYPTO 2012. LNCS, vol. 7417, pp. 868–886. Springer, Heidelberg (2012). https://doi.org/10.1007/978-3-642-32009-5_50
8. Brakerski, Z.: Fundamentals of fully homomorphic encryption. On the Work of Shafi Goldwasser and Silvio Micali. In: Providing Sound Foundations for Cryptography (2019)
9. Brakerski, Z., Döttling, N., Garg, S., Malavolta, G.: Leveraging linear decryption: Rate-1 fully-homomorphic encryption and time-lock puzzles. In: Hofheinz, D., Rosen, A. (eds.) TCC 2019. LNCS, vol. 11892, pp. 407–437. Springer, Cham (2019). https://doi.org/10.1007/978-3-030-36033-7_16
10. Brakerski, Z., Gentry, C., Vaikuntanathan, V.: (Leveled) fully homomorphic encryption without bootstrapping. ACM Trans. Comput. Theor. (TOCT) 6(3), 1–36 (2014)
11. Brakerski, Z., Vaikuntanathan, V.: Efficient fully homomorphic encryption from (standard) LWE. SIAM J. Comput. 43(2), 831–871 (2014)
12. Brakerski, Z., Vaikuntanathan, V.: Lattice-based FHE as secure as PKE. In: ITCS (2014)
13. Canetti, R., Dwork, C., Naor, M., Ostrovsky, R.: Deniable encryption. In: Kaliski, B.S. (ed.) CRYPTO 1997. LNCS, vol. 1294, pp. 90–104. Springer, Heidelberg (1997). https://doi.org/10.1007/BFb0052229
14. Canetti, R., Park, S., Poburinnaya, O.: Fully deniable interactive encryption. In: Micciancio, D., Ristenpart, T. (eds.) CRYPTO 2020. LNCS, vol. 12170, pp. 807–835. Springer, Cham (2020). https://doi.org/10.1007/978-3-030-56784-2_27

15. Chillotti, I., Gama, N., Georgieva, M., Izabachène, M.: A homomorphic LWE based E-voting scheme. In: Takagi, T. (ed.) PQCrypto 2016. LNCS, vol. 9606, pp. 245–265. Springer, Cham (2016). https://doi.org/10.1007/978-3-319-29360-8_16

16. Dachman-Soled, D.: On minimal assumptions for sender-deniable public key encryption. In: Krawczyk, H. (ed.) PKC 2014. LNCS, vol. 8383, pp. 574–591. Springer, Heidelberg (2014). https://doi.org/10.1007/978-3-642-54631-0_33

17. Dachman-Soled, D., Katz, J., Rao, V.: Adaptively secure, universally composable, multiparty computation in constant rounds. In: Dodis, Y., Nielsen, J.B. (eds.) TCC 2015. LNCS, vol. 9015, pp. 586–613. Springer, Heidelberg (2015). https://doi.org/10.1007/978-3-662-46497-7_23

18. De Caro, A., Iovino, V., O'Neill, A.: Deniable functional encryption. In: Cheng, C.-M., Chung, K.-M., Persiano, G., Yang, B.-Y. (eds.) PKC 2016. LNCS, vol. 9614, pp. 196–222. Springer, Heidelberg (2016). https://doi.org/10.1007/978-3-662-49384-7_8

19. Garg, S., Gentry, C., Halevi, V., Raykova, M., Sahai, A., Waters, B.: Candidate indistinguishability obfuscation and functional encryption for all circuits. SIAM J. Comput. 45(3), 882–929 (2016)

20. Garg, S., Pandey, O., Srinivasan, A., Zhandry, M.: Breaking the sub-exponential barrier in obfustopia. In: Coron, J.-S., Nielsen, J.B. (eds.) EUROCRYPT 2017. LNCS, vol. 10212, pp. 156–181. Springer, Cham (2017). https://doi.org/10.1007/978-3-319-56617-7_6

21. Gentry, C.: A fully homomorphic encryption scheme. PhD thesis, Stanford University (2009). crypto.stanford.edu/craig

22. Gentry, C., Halevi, S.: Compressible FHE with applications to PIR. In: Hofheinz, D., Rosen, A. (eds.) TCC 2019. LNCS, vol. 11892, pp. 438–464. Springer, Cham (2019). https://doi.org/10.1007/978-3-030-36033-7_17

23. Gentry, C., Sahai, A., Waters, B.: Homomorphic encryption from learning with errors: conceptually-simpler, asymptotically-faster, attribute-based. In: Canetti, R., Garay, J.A. (eds.) CRYPTO 2013. LNCS, vol. 8042, pp. 75–92. Springer, Heidelberg (2013). https://doi.org/10.1007/978-3-642-40041-4_5

24. Goldwasser, S., Kalai, Y., Popa, R.A., Vaikuntanathan, V., Zeldovich, N.: Reusable garbled circuits and succinct functional encryption. In: STOC (2013)

25. Jain, A., Lin, H., Sahai, A.: Indistinguishability obfuscation from well-founded assumptions. In: STOC (2021)

26. Lin, H., Pass, R., Seth, K., Telang, S.: Indistinguishability obfuscation with non-trivial efficiency. In: Cheng, C.-M., Chung, K.-M., Persiano, G., Yang, B.-Y. (eds.) PKC 2016. LNCS, vol. 9615, pp. 447–462. Springer, Heidelberg (2016). https://doi.org/10.1007/978-3-662-49387-8_17

27. Meng, B.: A secure internet voting protocol based on non-interactive deniable authentication protocol and proof protocol that two ciphertexts are encryption of the same plaintext. J. Netw. 4(5), 370–377 (2009)

28. O'Neill, A., Peikert, C., Waters, B.: Bi-deniable public-key encryption. In: Rogaway, P. (ed.) CRYPTO 2011. LNCS, vol. 6841, pp. 525–542. Springer, Heidelberg (2011). https://doi.org/10.1007/978-3-642-22792-9_30

29. Sahai, A., Waters, B.: How to use indistinguishability obfuscation: deniable encryption, and more. In: STOC (2014)

30. Smart, N.P., Vercauteren, F.: Fully homomorphic encryption with relatively small key and ciphertext sizes. In: Nguyen, P.Q., Pointcheval, D. (eds.) PKC 2010. LNCS, vol. 6056, pp. 420–443. Springer, Heidelberg (2010). https://doi.org/10.1007/978-3-642-13013-7_25

Lattice Cryptanalysis

Counterexamples to New Circular Security Assumptions Underlying iO

Sam Hopkins[1(✉)], Aayush Jain[2], and Huijia Lin[3]

[1] UC Berkeley, Berkeley, USA
hopkins@berkeley.edu
[2] UCLA, Center for Encrypted Functionalities, and NTT Research,
Los Angeles, USA
aayushjain@cs.ucla.edu
[3] UW, Los Angeles, USA
rachel@cs.washington.edu

Abstract. We study several strengthening of classical circular security assumptions which were recently introduced in four new lattice-based constructions of indistinguishability obfuscation: Brakerski-Döttling-Garg-Malavolta (Eurocrypt 2020), Gay-Pass (STOC 2021), Brakerski-Döttling-Garg-Malavolta (Eprint 2020) and Wee-Wichs (Eprint 2020).

We provide explicit counterexamples to the *2-circular shielded randomness leakage* assumption w.r.t. the Gentry-Sahai-Waters fully homomorphic encryption scheme proposed by Gay-Pass, and the *homomorphic pseudorandom LWE samples* conjecture proposed by Wee-Wichs. Our work suggests a separation between classical circular security of the kind underlying un-levelled fully-homomorphic encryption from the strengthened versions underlying recent iO constructions, showing that they are not (yet) on the same footing.

Our counterexamples exploit the flexibility to choose specific implementations of circuits, which is explicitly allowed in the Gay-Pass assumption and unspecified in the Wee-Wichs assumption. Their indistinguishabilty obfuscation schemes are still unbroken. Our work shows that the assumptions, at least, need refinement. In particular, generic leakage-resilient circular security assumptions are delicate, and their security is sensitive to the specific structure of the leakages involved.

1 Introduction

Indistinguishability obfuscation ($i\mathcal{O}$) for general programs computable in polynomial time [7] enables turning programs into unintelligible ones while preserving their functionality. $i\mathcal{O}$ is a fundamental primitive and has found many applications in cryptography and beyond. As such, it is extremely important to base the feasibility of $i\mathcal{O}$ on simple and well-studied hardness assumptions, and to thoroughly understand the objects and assumptions that imply $i\mathcal{O}$. Current constructions of $i\mathcal{O}$ can be broadly categorized into two schools: those using multilinear or bilinear pairing, and those without pairing. Very recently, we have seen exciting advances on both fronts. Using pairing, Jain, Lin, and Sahai [31] constructed

© International Association for Cryptologic Research 2021
T. Malkin and C. Peikert (Eds.): CRYPTO 2021, LNCS 12826, pp. 673–700, 2021.
https://doi.org/10.1007/978-3-030-84245-1_23

$i\mathcal{O}$ from four well-studied assumptions: Learning With Errors (LWE) [40], Decisional Linear assumption (DLIN) [6] over bilinear maps, Learning Pairity with Noise over general fields [28], and Pseudo-Random Generators in NC_0 [24]. Without pairing, three works [11,20,42], following [10], based $i\mathcal{O}$ on new types of circular security assumptions on integer lattices.

In this work, we focus on these recent constructions [10,11,20,42] and the new circular security assumptions they are based on. These constructions are very interesting because of their novel approaches and distinctive features. First, they are built solely on integer lattices (instead of drawing hardness from multiple cryptosystems) and therefore are possibly secure against quantum attacks. Second, their security assumptions are similar in flavor to the classical circular security heuristic [9,15], which by now has been extensively studied and widely applied, most notably to un-leveled Fully Homomorphic Encryption (FHE) using Gentry's boostrapping mechanism [21].

At the same time, the new assumptions are stronger than classical circular security in non-trivial ways. Consider the Gay-Pass assumption. Classical circular security w.r.t. a public key encryption scheme postulates that it is Chosen-Message-Attack (CPA) secure, even in the presence of an encrypted key-cycle that possibly uses other encryption schemes. The Gay-Pass assumption generalizes this blueprint to consider *leakage-resilient CPA security*: it says that if an encryption scheme is CPA secure when the adversary has access to certain leakage on the randomness of encryption, then additionally publishing an encrypted key-cycle should not harm this leakage-resilient CPA security. Concretely, their $i\mathcal{O}$ scheme assumes *Shielded Randomness Leakage (SRL) resilience* in the presence of *2-circular encryption*, w.r.t. the Gentry-Sahai-Waters FHE scheme [23] and a Packed version of Regev's encryption [39,40][1]. The work [11] proposes a variant of the Gay-Pass assumption with a key-randomness cycle. Wee and Wichs [42] take a different approach and construct $i\mathcal{O}$ based on LWE and a new conjecture, *Homomorphic Pseudorandom LWE Samples* (HPLS). Though this conjecture does not directly follow the circular security blueprint, close examination reveals a circular security flavor, involving the dual-GSW homomorphic commitment [23,25] and a Pseudo-Random Function (PRF).

Although stronger and more complex than the classical circular security, these new assumptions were formulated in a principled way – indeed, on the surface, they seem to place $i\mathcal{O}$ on qualitatively similar footing as un-leveled FHE! While exciting and encouraging, when it comes to new assumptions, it is important to be cautious and imperative to conduct cryptanalysis to develop deeper understandings. That is the purpose of our work.

Our Results. We present counterexamples to the Gay-Pass and Wee-Wichs assumptions. In both cases, we consider the GSW FHE scheme and the dual-GSW homomorphic commitment scheme for evaluating *arithmetic circuits* consisting of arithmetic addition, multiplication, and multiplication by constant gates. We stress that both schemes natively support these arithmetic operations [23]. In particular, in our counterexample to the Wee-Wichs conjecture we

---

[1] Or alternatively, the Damgård-Jurik encryption [17,38].

will leverage multiplication by a large constant, $2^{-1} \bmod p$ (which is not needed for the counterexample to Gay-Pass assumption).

- First, we show that the Gay-Pass assumption is false when instantiated with the GSW FHE scheme by presenting a concrete attack.
- Second, Wee and Wichs's HPLS conjecture is parameterized with a sampling algorithm D that takes random coins τ and produces a random LWE secret $s \leftarrow \mathbb{Z}_p^n$ and an error vector e according to some error distribution. We show the conjecture is sensitive to the circuit implementation of D, namely, for every D, there is an arithmetic circuit C_D implementing it such that the HPLS conjecture instantiated with C_D is false. Again, we present a concrete attack.

Notably, classical circular security plausibly holds w.r.t. both the modified GSW and dual GSW schemes. Hence, our work gives the first examples that separate classical circular security and the strengthened versions of circular security underlying recent $i\mathcal{O}$ schemes, showing evidence that they are not (yet) on the same footing.

Our counterexamples exploit some flexibility in the implementation details of the Gay-Pass and Wee-Wichs assumptions. The choice of such implementation is explicitly given to the adversary in the Gay-Pass assumption and is left unspecified in the Wee-Wichs conjecture. It remains possible that other choices of implementation of circuits do result in an unbroken assumption. Nevertheless, our work shows that this will, at least, require refinement of the assumptions, and in particular that generic circular security assumptions/definitions are delicate, and their security is actually sensitive to the specific structure of the leakages involved.

Next, we describe the Gay-Pass and Wee-Wichs assumptions and our counterexamples in more detail.

Counterexample to the Gay-Pass assumption. As stated in Gay and Pass [20], the *2-circular assumption* w.r.t. two public key encryption schemes Enc^1 and Enc^2 that are Chosen-Plaintext-Attack (CPA) secure postulates that

- *Classical 2-circular security assumption w.r.t.* $\mathsf{Enc}^1, \mathsf{Enc}^2$: Enc^1 is (still) CPA secure – that is, honestly generated ciphertexts $\mathsf{Enc}^1_{\mathsf{pk}^1}(m^0)$ and $\mathsf{Enc}^1_{\mathsf{pk}^1}(m^1)$ for any two chosen messages m^0, m^1 are indistinguishable – when a length-two encrypted key cycle $\mathsf{Enc}^1_{\mathsf{pk}^1}(\mathsf{sk}^2), \mathsf{Enc}^2_{\mathsf{pk}^2}(\mathsf{sk}^1)$ is published.

Classical circular security has been extensively studied as encrypted key cycles of different lengths naturally arise in applications such as encrypted storage system, anonymous credentials [15], and un-leveled FHE [21]. So far, though counterexamples to 2-circular security or 1-circular security for bit encryption[2] (where the key cycle has length 1 $\{\mathsf{Enc}_{\mathsf{pk}}(\mathsf{sk}_i)\}_{i \in [|\mathsf{sk}|]}$) have been constructed (see e.g. [1,8,16,26,27,32,33,35,41,43]), no attacks have been shown against any "natural" encryption schemes. Therefore, classical circular security is still commonly assumed w.r.t. natural encryption schemes such as homomorphic encryption [12,14,23], Regev's encryption [40] etc.

---

[2] Crafting a counterexample for 1-circular security for string encryption is trivial.

Gay and Pass extend 2-circular security to consider CPA security in the presence of the so-called shielded randomness leakage (SRL). More specifically, shielded randomness leakage is only defined w.r.t. FHE schemes with certain properties including randomness homomorphism. The leakage is captured by an oracle $\mathcal{O}_{SRL}$ (described shortly below) and reveals certain information of the randomness of encryption. A public-key FHE scheme Enc^1 is *SRL-secure* if CPA security holds even if the adversary has access to $\mathcal{O}_{SRL}$. Then the 2-circular SRL security assumption w.r.t. $\mathsf{Enc}^1, \mathsf{Enc}^2$ where Enc^1 is SRL secure and Enc^2 is CPA secure, states that:

- *2-circular SRL security assumption w.r.t.* $\mathsf{Enc}^1, \mathsf{Enc}^2$: Enc^1 is (still) SRL secure – that is, honestly generated ciphertexts $\mathsf{Enc}^1_{\mathsf{pk}^1}(m^0)$ and $\mathsf{Enc}^1_{\mathsf{pk}^1}(m^1)$ for any two chosen messages m^0, m^1 are indistinguishable, even if the adversary has access to $\mathcal{O}_{SRL}$ – when a length two encrypted key cycle $\mathsf{Enc}^1_{\mathsf{pk}^1}(\mathsf{sk}^2)$, $\mathsf{Enc}^2_{\mathsf{pk}^2}(\mathsf{sk}^1)$ is published.

The Gay-Pass $i\mathcal{O}$ scheme relies on the above assumption w.r.t. the GSW FHE scheme as Enc^1 and the packed Regev encryption as Enc^2. Notably, they prove that the GSW scheme is SRL-secure based on LWE.

Let's now understand what shielded randomness leakage is. In the plain SRL security game (without encrypted key cycles), the adversary is given a collection of challenge ciphertexts $\{\mathsf{ct}_i = \mathsf{Enc}^1_{\mathsf{pk}^1}(m_i^b; \mathbf{R}_i)\}_i$ encrypting one of the two sets of chosen messages, $\{m_i^0\}_i$ or $\{m_i^1\}_i$, for a random b, using randomness $\{\mathbf{R}_i\}_i$. In addition, the adversary $\mathcal{A}$ can interact with the SRL oracle $\mathcal{O}_{SRL}$ as follows to help it distinguish.

- *The $\mathcal{O}_{SRL}$ Oracle (Simplified)* gives leakage on the message and randomness $\{m_i^b; \mathbf{R}_i\}_i$ underlying the challenge ciphertexts as follows:
  1. Upon invocation, $\mathcal{O}_{SRL}$ samples a fresh encryption $\mathsf{ct}^\star = \mathsf{Enc}^1_{\mathsf{pk}^1}(0; \mathbf{R}^\star)$ of zero using randomness $\mathbf{R}^\star$ and sends $\mathsf{ct}^\star$ to the adversary[3].
  2. $\mathcal{A}$ chooses a circuit C and an output y.
  3. $\mathcal{O}_{SRL}$ homomorphically evaluates C on $\mathsf{ct}^\star$ and the challenge ciphertexts $\{\mathsf{ct}_i\}_i$ to obtain an output ciphertext $\mathsf{ct}_C = \mathsf{HEval}(C, \mathsf{ct}^\star, \{\mathsf{ct}_i\})$ that encrypts y' with randomness $\mathbf{R}_C$ (computed by the randomness homomorphism property of HE from $\{m_i^b; \mathbf{R}_i\}_i$). It returns $\mathbf{R}^\star - \mathbf{R}_C$ if $y = y'$, or nothing if $y \neq y'$.

In the *2-circular* SRL-security game, the adversary is additionally given an encrypted key cycle $\mathsf{Enc}^1_{\mathsf{pk}^1}(\mathsf{sk}^2)$, $\mathsf{Enc}^2_{\mathsf{pk}^2}(\mathsf{sk}^1)$ along with the challenge ciphertexts $\{\mathsf{ct}_i\}$ at the beginning. We remark that for security of the ensuing Gay-Pass $i\mathcal{O}$ construction it is crucial that the adversary is allowed to choose C adaptively. This means in the plain SRL security game, C may depend on $\mathsf{ct}^\star, \{\mathsf{ct}_i\}$, and, in the 2-circular SRL security game, additionally on the encrypted cycle $\mathsf{Enc}^1_{\mathsf{pk}^1}(\mathsf{sk}^2)$, $\mathsf{Enc}^2_{\mathsf{pk}^2}(\mathsf{sk}^1)$. Indeed, the security reduction from $i\mathcal{O}$ to the 2-circular

---

[3] More concretely for the GSW scheme, this encryption of zero is extra noisy, meaning the magnitude of entries of $\mathbf{R}^\star$ is large enough to smudge entries of $\mathbf{R}_C$ below.

SRL security chooses such a "dependent" C. Looking ahead, our counterexample also crucially exploits this adaptivity.

   Our counterexample: We show that the 2-circular SRL security assumption is false w.r.t. the GSW FHE scheme in [23]. Let us now give more details.

   Our Ideas In a Nut shell: Given that (modified) GSW is both SRL-secure and plausibly circular secure, the attack must simultaneously leverage the shield-randomness leakage $\mathbf{R}^* - \mathbf{R}_C$ and the encrypted key cycle $\mathsf{Enc}^1_{\mathsf{pk}^1}(\mathsf{sk}^2)$, $\mathsf{Enc}^2_{\mathsf{pk}^2}(\mathsf{sk}^1)$. Recall that the attack can adaptively choose the circuit C depending on the key cycle, ct^*, and $\{\mathsf{ct}_i\}$, meaning they can be hardcoded in C. Observe also that the input to C is $(\{m_i^b\}, \mathsf{sk}^2)$, and hence C can compute as an intermediate value sk^1 and can also "access" $\mathbf{R}^*$ (by decrypting $\mathsf{Enc}^2_{\mathsf{pk}^2}(\mathsf{sk}^1)$ and ct^*). Since C can "access" both $\mathbf{R}^*$ and $\{m_i^b\}$, our attack carefully engineers C so that homomorphic evaluation of C produces an output ciphertext ct_C with randomness $\mathbf{R}_C$ correlated with $(\mathbf{R}^*, \{m_i^b\})$, and then the shield randomness leakage $\mathbf{R}^* - \mathbf{R}_C$ reveals information of b. More specifically, the attack creates correlation between the *parity bit of noises and values* by carefully engineering C using the following correlation-inducing *gadget circuits*.

- *Correlation Gadget:* The gadget circuit $G(x, 0)$ multiplies x with 0 and produces a fixed output of 0. Homomorphically evaluating G on GSW ciphertexts ct of x and ct_0 of 0 produces a new ciphertext $\mathsf{ct}' = \mathbf{A}\mathbf{R}'$ of zero of the following form:

$$\mathsf{ct} = \mathbf{A}\mathbf{R} + x\mathbf{G}, \ \mathsf{ct}_0 = \mathbf{A}\mathbf{R}_0 \ \overset{\mathsf{HEval}, \ \times}{\longrightarrow} \ \mathsf{ct}' = \mathbf{A}\mathbf{R}', \ \mathbf{R}' = \mathbf{R} \cdot G^{-1}(\mathsf{ct}_0) + x\mathbf{R}_0$$

Consider an attack that chooses a circuit C which first computes $x = f(m_i^b, \mathsf{sk}^2)$ and then the above $G(x, 0)$ (f is specified shortly below). The attack receives from the SRL oracle leakage

$$\mathbf{R}^* + \mathbf{R} \cdot G^{-1}(\mathsf{ct}_0) + x\mathbf{R}_0 \ .$$

To learn the bit b, we want to *1)* correlate x with $\mathbf{R}^*$ and b, and *2)* eliminate the middle term $\mathbf{R} \cdot G^{-1}(\mathsf{ct}_0)$.

- We achieve the second by finding a vector $\boldsymbol{v} \in \{0, 1\}^m$ such that $G^{-1}(\mathsf{ct}_0) \cdot \boldsymbol{v} = 0 \bmod 2$. This is possible with probability close to $1/2$ as $G^{-1}(\mathsf{ct}_0)$ is a pseudorandom binary matrix and hence is non-singular mod 2 with probability close to $1/2$.
- We achieve the first by letting the function f compute $b \cdot e\mathbf{R}^*\boldsymbol{v} \bmod 2$. Observe that this is computable since homomorphically decrypting ct^* gives exactly $e\mathbf{R}^*$. One can then further multiply b and $\boldsymbol{v}$, followed by modulo 2.

This means the attack can learn

$$\boldsymbol{z} = \mathbf{R}^*\boldsymbol{v} + b \cdot (e\mathbf{R}^*\boldsymbol{v})\mathbf{R}_0\boldsymbol{v} \bmod 2 \ .$$

Let us observe the difference between the cases when $b = 0$ or 1. If $b = 0$, $\boldsymbol{z} = \mathbf{R}^*\boldsymbol{v} \bmod 2$ which is random since $\mathbf{R}^*$ is random and independent of $\boldsymbol{v}$. On the other hand, if $b = 0$, $z = \mathbf{R}^* v + (e\mathbf{R}^* v)\mathbf{R}_0 v \bmod 2$, which satisfies $e \cdot z = 0 \bmod 2$ if $e\mathbf{R}_0 v = 1$. The latter condition holds with probability $1/2$ over the random choice of $\mathbf{R}_0$. This difference is sufficient for creating a distinguishing attack: Repeat the above many times to collect different z_i w.r.t. to *different* $\mathrm{ct}_i^* = \mathbf{B}\mathbf{R}_i^*$, and the *same* $\mathrm{ct}_0 = \mathbf{B}\mathbf{R}_0$. If $b = 0$, all z_i's are random, whereas if $b = 1$, all z_i's satisfy $e \cdot z_i = 0 \bmod 2$ conditioned on the event $e\mathbf{R}_0 v = 1$ of probability $1/2$.

Please see Sect. 5.1 for how we construct the challenge circuit C and other details in the attack. We note that though our attack is described w.r.t. GSW FHE for arithmetic circuits, it can be easily translated into an attack w.r.t. GSW FHE for Boolean circuits. In particular, the correlation gadget circuit will compute homomorphic AND which translates to computing homomorphic multiplication in GSW and the rest of the attack is the same.

Counterexample to the Wee-Wichs assumption. Wee and Wichs [42] take a different approach, constructing $i\mathcal{O}$ assuming LWE and the ability to obliviously generate LWE samples without knowing the corresponding secrets. They then proposed a heuristic mechanism for *oblivious LWE sampling*, using the dual-GSW homomorphic commitment and any Pseudo-Random Function (PRF). They formulated a concrete conjecture, called the Homomorphic Pseudorandom LWE Samples conjecture, to capture the security of their mechanism. Let us now recall their conjecture.

The Dual GSW Homomorphic Commitment Scheme The scheme is a variant of the homomorphic encryption/commitment schemes of [23,25] with the feature that one can homomorphically evaluate a function with a vector output $f : \{0,1\}^\ell \to \mathbb{Z}_p^m$, and the decommitment to the output commitment to $f(x)$ is shorter than m. Given a public random matrix $\mathbf{A} \in \mathbb{Z}_p^{m \times n}$ where $m \gg n$, a commitment $\mathbf{C}$ to an input $x \in \{0,1\}^\ell$ is

$$\mathbf{C} = (\mathbf{A}\mathbf{R}_1 + x_1\mathbf{G} + \mathbf{E}_1, \cdots, \mathbf{A}\mathbf{R}_\ell + x_\ell\mathbf{G} + \mathbf{E}_\ell)$$

where $\mathbf{R}_i \leftarrow \mathbb{Z}_p^{n \times m \log q}$, $\mathbf{E}_i \leftarrow \chi^{m \times m \log q}$, and $\mathbf{G}$ is the gadget matrix.

The key difference from [23,25] are: *1)* the matrix $\mathbf{A}$ is a thin/tall matrix, whereas in GSW $\mathbf{A}$ is fat/short, *2)* $\mathbf{R}_i$ is fat/short and uniformly sampled, whereas in GSW, they are square matrices consisting of small entries, and *3)* because of the shapes of matrices $\mathbf{A}\mathbf{R}_i$ is far from (pseudo)random and hence additional noises $\mathbf{E}_i$ are added. On the other hand, the hiding property of the commitments still follows directly from LWE, and the same homomorphic evaluation procedure applies. For any Boolean function $f : \{0,1\}^\ell \to \{0,1\}$, one can homomorphically derive a commitment $\mathbf{C}_f = \mathbf{A}\mathbf{R}_f + f(x)\mathbf{G} + \mathbf{E}_f$. Additionally, using the same "packing" procedure, one can homomorphically evaluate $g : \{0,1\}^\ell \to \mathbb{Z}_p^m$ with a vector output to derive a commitment $\mathbf{C}_g = \mathbf{A}\mathbf{r}_g + g(x) + e_g$. Observe that the opening to this output commitment is r_g of length $n \log p \ll m$.

The Homomorphic Pseudorandom LWE Samples (HPLS) conjecture considers the following two distributions parameterized by a PRF PRF.

$$\forall \beta \in \{0,1\}, \quad \mathrm{DIST}(\beta) \to (\{d_i = \mathbf{A}\widehat{s}_i + \widehat{e}_i\}_{i \in [Q]}, \mathbf{A}, \mathbf{C}, \{s_i\}_{i \in [Q]})$$

where the random variables are sampled as follows: *1)* $\{d_i\}$ are fresh LWE samples with secret $\widehat{s}_i \leftarrow \mathbb{Z}_p^n$ and noise $\widehat{e}_i \leftarrow \chi^m$, *2)* $\mathbf{C}$ is a dual-GSW commitment to a randomly sampled PRF key k and the bit β, and *3)* each s_i is derived from homomorphically evaluating the following computation $g_i(k, \beta)$: the function g_i first evaluates PRF to obtain random bits τ_i, then uses them to sample random LWE secret s_i^{PRF} and noise $e_i^{\mathsf{PRF}} \leftarrow \chi_{\mathsf{PRF}}^m$ according to a sampling algorithm D, and finally outputs a vector $\mathbf{A}s_i^{\mathsf{PRF}} + e_i^{\mathsf{PRF}} + \beta d_i$.

$$g_i(k, \beta) : i) \text{ compute } \tau_i \leftarrow \mathsf{PRF}(k, i) \qquad ii) \text{ sample } (s_i^{\mathsf{PRF}}, e_i^{\mathsf{PRF}}) \leftarrow \mathsf{D}(\tau_i)$$

$$iii) \text{ compute and output } \mathbf{A}s_i^{\mathsf{PRF}} + e_i^{\mathsf{PRF}} + \beta d_i = \mathbf{A}(s_i^{\mathsf{PRF}} + \beta \widehat{s}_i) + (e_i^{\mathsf{PRF}} + \beta \widehat{e}_i)$$

$$\mathbf{C}_{g_i} = \mathsf{HEval}(g_i, \mathbf{C}) = \mathbf{A}r_i^{\mathsf{Eval}} + g_i(k, \beta) + e_i^{\mathsf{Eval}}$$

$$= \mathbf{A}\underbrace{(r_i^{\mathsf{Eval}} + s_i^{\mathsf{PRF}} + \beta \widehat{s}_i)}_{s_i} + \underbrace{(e_i^{\mathsf{PRF}} + \beta \widehat{e}_i + e_i^{\mathsf{Eval}})}_{e_i}$$

The HPLS conjecture states that for appropriate settings of parameters, in particular when the magnitude of the noises satisfy $e_i^{\mathsf{PRF}} \gg \widehat{e}_i \gg e_i^{\mathsf{Eval}}$, there is a choice of PRF such that DIST(0) and DIST(1) are indistinguishable.

Observe that given a sample from the distribution, one can easily compute the noise e_i in $\mathbf{C}_{g_i}$ by using the opened secret vectors s_i. Then, the circular security nature of the HPLS conjecture lies in that on one hand we rely on the PRF security to argue that e_i^{PRF} smudges $\beta \widehat{e}_i + e_i^{\mathsf{Eval}}$, otherwise dual-GSW security is broken, on the other hand, we rely on the dual-GSW security to argue that the PRF key k remains hidden.

Our Counterexample. Our counterexample states that when using dual-GSW for arithmetic computation, for every sampling algorithm D used in the second step of g_i's (that converts random bits τ to a random LWE secret vector s and an error vector e of some distribution χ_{PRF}) there is an arithmetic circuit C_{D} that implements D, such that, for every PRF PRF (and every circuit implementation of PRF), the distributions DIST(0) and DIST(1) are distinguishable. In short, the HPLS conjecture is false for every PRF and every sampling algorithm D, if the circuit implementation of D is allowed to be arbitrarily chosen.

Our Ideas In a Nutshell: Our counterexample attacks the noise $\{e_i = (e_i^{\mathsf{PRF}} + \beta \widehat{e}_i + e_i^{\mathsf{Eval}})\}$ that can be derived from a sample of the distribution. To distinguish between $\beta = 0$ or 1, our idea is to create correlation between the parity of $e_i^{\mathsf{PRF}}[1]$ and $e_i^{\mathsf{Eval}}[1]$, so that $e_i[1] \bmod 2$ reveals information about β. We do so by carefully crafting the circuit C_{D} using two gadget circuits described below.

– *Even Gadget:* $G_1(x)$ implements the identity function on a single element x. It first multiplies x by $1/2$, and then adds $x/2$ with itself to get back x (computation over $\mathbb{Z}_p$). Homomorphically evaluating G_1 on a dual-GSW commitment $\mathsf{ct} = \mathbf{A}\mathbf{R} + x\mathbf{G} + \mathbf{E}$ to x produces a commitment $\mathbf{C}' = \mathbf{A}\mathbf{R}' + x\mathbf{G} + \mathbf{E}'$ with even errors $\mathbf{E}'$.

$$\mathbf{C} = \mathbf{A}\mathbf{R} + x\mathbf{G} + \mathbf{E} \xrightarrow{\mathsf{HEval} \times \frac{1}{2}} \mathbf{C}'' = \mathbf{A}\mathbf{R}'' + \frac{x}{2}\mathbf{G} + \mathbf{E}''$$

$$\xrightarrow{\mathsf{HEval} +} \mathbf{C}' = \mathbf{A}\mathbf{R}' + x\mathbf{G} + \mathbf{E}', \quad \text{where } \mathbf{E}' = 2\mathbf{E}''$$

– *Correlation Gadget:* The second gadget circuit $G_2(x, 1)$ first computes $G_1(x)$ to get x, and then multiplies it with 1. Homomorphically evaluating G_2 on dual-GSW commitment $\mathbf{C}$ to x and $\mathbf{C}_1$ to 1 produces a new commitment $\mathbf{C}' = \mathbf{AR}' + x\mathbf{G} + \mathbf{E}'$ of x where the parity of $\mathbf{E}'[1, 1]$ is correlated with x if $\mathbf{E}_1[1, 1]$ is odd, where $\mathbf{E}_1$ is the noise in $\mathbf{C}_1$.

$$\mathsf{ct} = \mathbf{AR} + x\mathbf{G} + \mathbf{E} \quad \xrightarrow{\mathsf{HEval}\ G_1} \quad \mathsf{ct}'' = \mathbf{AR}' + x\mathbf{G} + (2\mathbf{E}'')$$

$$\xrightarrow{\mathsf{HEval}\ \times(\mathsf{ct}_1 = \mathbf{AR}_1 + \mathbf{G} + \mathbf{E}_1)} \quad \mathsf{ct}' = \mathbf{AR}' + x\mathbf{G} + \mathbf{E}', \ \mathbf{E}' = 2\mathbf{E}''G^{-1}(\mathsf{ct}_1) + x\mathbf{E}_1$$

Using them, we create correlation between $e_i^{\mathsf{PRF}}[1] \bmod 2$ and $e_i^{\mathsf{Eval}}[1] \bmod 2$.

Before we can declare success, we must resolve two other issues. First, the correlation created by the second gadget is probabilistic, depending on the parity of noise $\mathbf{E}_1[1, 1]$ embedded in commitment $\mathbf{C}_1$. This is not too much of a problem since $\mathbf{C}_1$ is reused for all index i and hence with probability $1/2$, we see an observable pattern in all e_i. Second, the homomorphic evaluation of βd_i is outside the control of C_D and its noise will be added to the final output of g_i. We overcome the issue by observing that noises resulting from this homomorphic evaluation induces an over-determined linear system over the noises $\mathbf{E}_\beta$ in the commitment to β. Thus, we can use linearity testing to help the attack distinguish.

Possible Extension. One natural follow-up question is whether our techniques can be extended to directly attack these recent $i\mathcal{O}$ constructions [10,11,20,42], beyond the circular security assumptions they rely on. On this front, we think that our attack ideas can be extended to break the security of the $i\mathcal{O}$ scheme of [10] (and possibly its followups [11,20]), if one is allowed to manipulate the implementation of the underlying FHE scheme (e.g., using odd noises to generate the public key of the GSW FHE scheme) and the implementation of circuits computed (e.g., the circuit for computing mod). However, in this work, we focus only on the assumptions, and leave direct attacks to the schemes as future work.

A Perspective. First, our attacks highlight the importance of building schemes from well-founded assumptions. However, in cases where existing techniques are far from reaching this goal, one way of making progress is through cycles of proposals and attacks, and a measure of progress is the simplicity of the proposed assumptions, and whether they are natural and connected to well-studied areas in computer science. For instance, the recent line of $i\mathcal{O}$ constructions [4,5,19,29,30,34] started with assuming new assumptions, and eventually led to the first $i\mathcal{O}$ construction [31] based on four well-founded assumptions – LWE, the decision linear assumption over symmetric key pairing, LPN over large fields, and PRG in NC^0.

At this moment, we still lack good understanding on the front of constructing $i\mathcal{O}$ solely from lattices (or constructing post-quantum secure $i\mathcal{O}$). The works of [10,11,20,42] proposed refreshing approaches and ideas. The purpose of our work, through counterexamples, is finding weak points in these new approaches, so that, they can be addressed and the assumptions can be refined in future works. In particular, a main lesson from our counterexamples is that when working with leakage of noises in LWE, it is important to examine the specific leakage carefully.

Other $i\mathcal{O}$Constructions. Our work focuses on the new types of circular security assumptions/hard problems underlying recent $i\mathcal{O}$ constructions of [10,11,20,42]. Prior to their work, Agrawal [2] gave an $i\mathcal{O}$ construction based on noisy linear functional encryption and proposed a candidate noisy linear functional encryption based on new types of NTRU assumptions. The work of [3] cryptanalyzed of the new NTRU assumptions and further refined them. There are many $i\mathcal{O}$ constructions based on multilinear maps, which can be instantiated from lattices (see references in [31]). Though all known multilinear map instantiation have been attacked, there are still $i\mathcal{O}$ candidates based on them that are unbroken, for instance [18]. Furthermore, Gentry, Jutla and Kane [22] proposed an $i\mathcal{O}$ candidate using tensor products. Finally, using bilinear pairing, a line of constructions [4,5,19,29,30,34] recently led to the first $i\mathcal{O}$ construction by [31] based on four well-founded assumptions – LWE, the decision linear assumption over symmetric key pairing, LPN over large fields, and PRG in NC^0.

2   Preliminaries

We start by recalling the security definitions that will be useful for the rest of the paper.

2.1   Security Definitions Introduced by Gay-Pass

We now recall the notion of $\mathcal{O}$-leakage resilience property of a public key encryption scheme, PKE. A PKE scheme satisfies $\mathcal{O}$-leakage resilience property if it is hard for a computationally efficient adversary to guess the challenge bit even in presence of valid oracle queries from the oracle $\mathcal{O}$, which may potentially leak information about the challenge message as well as the randomness.

Definition 1 ($\mathcal{O}$-leakage resilient security). *We say that a* PKE = (Setup, Enc, Dec) *scheme satisfies $\mathcal{O}$-leakage resilience security if for every stateful non-uniform ppt adversaries $\mathcal{A}$, there exists some negligible function* $\mathsf{negl}(\cdot)$ *such that for* $\lambda \in \mathbb{N}$, $\Pr[\mathsf{Expt}^{\mathsf{PKE}}_{\lambda,\mathcal{A}} = 1] \leq \frac{1}{2} + \mathsf{negl}$, *where the experiment* $\mathsf{Expt}^{\mathsf{PKE}}_{\lambda,\mathcal{A}}$ *is defined as follows*[4]:

$$\mathsf{Expt}^{\mathsf{PKE}}_{\lambda,\mathcal{A}} = \left\{ \begin{array}{c} (\mathsf{pk}, \mathsf{sk}) \leftarrow \mathsf{Setup}(1^\lambda) \\ (\boldsymbol{m}^0, \boldsymbol{m}^1) \leftarrow \mathcal{A}(\mathsf{pk}), \; b \leftarrow \{0,1\} \\ \boldsymbol{m}^* = \boldsymbol{m}^b, \; r \leftarrow \{0,1\}^* \\ \mathsf{ct} = \mathsf{Enc}(\mathsf{pk}, \boldsymbol{m}^*; r); b' \leftarrow \mathcal{A}^{\mathcal{O}(\mathsf{pk}, \boldsymbol{m}^*, r)}(\mathsf{ct}) \\ Return \; 1 \; if \; |\boldsymbol{m}^0| = |\boldsymbol{m}^1|, \; b' = b \; and \; \mathcal{O} \; did \; not \; return \perp; \; 0 \; otherwise \end{array} \right\}$$

We say that a PKE *scheme is secure if it is not given access to any oracle in the same experiment.*

---

[4] In the definition below and otherwise, we denote by shorthand $r \leftarrow \{0,1\}^*$ to mean that the randomness is sampled from the appropriate distribution.

We now define the notion $\mathcal{O}$-leakage resilient security in presence of encrypted key cycles. The notion is called $\mathcal{O}$-leakage resilient 2-circular security.

Definition 2 ($\mathcal{O}$-leakage resilient 2-circular security). *We say that the scheme* $\mathsf{PKE}_1 = (\mathsf{Setup}_1, \mathsf{Enc}_1, \mathsf{Dec}_1)$ *and the scheme* $\mathsf{PKE}_2 = (\mathsf{Setup}_2, \mathsf{Enc}_2, \mathsf{Dec}_2)$ *satisfies* $\mathcal{O}$-*leakage resilient 2- circular security if for every stateful non-uniform ppt adversaries* $\mathcal{A}$, *there exists some negligible function* $\mathsf{negl}(\cdot)$ *such that for* $\lambda \in \mathbb{N}$, $\Pr[\mathsf{Expt}_{\lambda,(\mathcal{A})}^{\mathsf{PKE}_1,\mathsf{PKE}_2} = 1] \leq \frac{1}{2} + \mathsf{negl}$, *where the experiment* $\mathsf{Expt}_{\lambda,\mathcal{A}}^{\mathsf{PKE}_1,\mathsf{PKE}_2}$ *is defined as follows:*

$$\mathsf{Expt}_{\lambda,\mathcal{A}}^{\mathsf{PKE}_1,\mathsf{PKE}_2} = \left\{ \begin{array}{c} (\mathsf{pk}_1,\mathsf{sk}_1) \leftarrow \mathsf{Setup}_1(1^\lambda), \ (\mathsf{pk}_2,\mathsf{sk}_2) \leftarrow \mathsf{Setup}_2(1^\lambda) \\ (m^0, m^1) \leftarrow \mathcal{A}(\mathsf{pk}_1, \mathsf{pk}_2), \ b \leftarrow \{0,1\} \\ m^* = \mathsf{sk}_2 \| m^b, \ r \leftarrow \{0,1\}^* \\ \mathsf{ct}_1 = \mathsf{Enc}_1(\mathsf{pk}_1, m^*; r); \ \mathsf{ct}_2 = \mathsf{Enc}_2(\mathsf{pk}_2, \mathsf{sk}_1); \ b' \leftarrow \mathcal{A}^{\mathcal{O}(\mathsf{pk}_1, m^*, r)}(\mathsf{ct}_1, \mathsf{ct}_2) \\ Return \ 1 \ if \ |m^0| = |m^1|, \ b' = b \ and \ \mathcal{O} \ did \ not \ return \ \bot; \ 0 \ otherwise \end{array} \right\}$$

We say that a PKE *scheme is 2-circular secure if it is not given access to any oracle in the same experiment.*

2.2 Fully-Homomorphic Encryption Scheme

We present the definition of a fully-homomorphic encryption scheme below with additional properties as defined by [20].

Definition 3 (FHE). *A fully homomorphic encryption scheme for the circuit class* $\mathcal{C} = \{\mathcal{C}_{\lambda,d}\}_{\lambda,d \in \mathbb{N}}$ *and randomness space* $\mathcal{R} = \{\mathcal{R}_{\lambda,d}\}_{\lambda.d \in \mathbb{N}}$ *is a tuple of PPT algorithms*

$$\mathsf{FHE} = (\mathsf{Setup}, \mathsf{Enc}, \mathsf{Eval}, \mathsf{Dec})$$

satisfying the following specifications:

$(\mathsf{pk}, \mathsf{sk}) \leftarrow \mathsf{Setup}(1^\lambda, 1^d)$: *The setup algorithm takes as input a security parameter* $\lambda \in \mathbb{N}$, *a circuit depth bound* $d \in \mathbb{N}$ *(which is a polynomial in the security parameter). It outputs a key pair* $(\mathsf{pk}, \mathsf{sk})$.

$\mathsf{ct} \leftarrow \mathsf{Enc}(\mathsf{pk}, m; r)$: *It takes as input a public key pk and a plaintext* $m \in \{0,1\}$ *and a randomness* $r \in \mathcal{R}_{\lambda,d}$ *and outputs a ciphertext* ct. *Here* $\mathcal{R}_{\lambda,d} \subseteq \{0,1\}^*$ *is some finite set. Encryption of multiple bits is done by encrypting each of them separately.*

$\widehat{\mathsf{ct}} \leftarrow \mathsf{Eval}(C, \mathsf{ct}_1, \ldots, \mathsf{ct}_\ell)$: *It takes as input a boolean circuit* $C: \{0,1\}^\ell \rightarrow \{0,1\} \in \mathcal{C}_{\lambda,d}$ *of depth* $\leq d$ *and ciphertexts* $\mathsf{ct}_1, \ldots, \mathsf{ct}_\ell$. *It outputs an evaluated ciphertext* $\widehat{\mathsf{ct}}$.

$\widehat{m} \leftarrow \mathsf{Dec}(\mathsf{sk}, \widehat{\mathsf{ct}})$: *The decryption algorithm takes in the secret key sk and a possibly evaluated ciphertext* $\widehat{\mathsf{ct}}$. *It outputs* $\widehat{m} \in \{0, 1, \bot\}$.

A fully-homomorphic encryption scheme satisfies correctness:

(Perfect) Correctness: *For every λ, any polynomial $d(\lambda) \in \mathbb{N}$ and $\ell \in \mathbb{N}$, every key-pair $(\mathsf{pk}, \mathsf{sk})$ in the support of $\mathsf{Setup}(1^\lambda, 1^d)$, every set of messages $m_1, \ldots, m_\ell \in \{0,1\}^\ell$, every ciphertext $\{\mathsf{ct}_i\}_{i \in [\ell]}$ in the support of $\{\mathsf{Enc}(\mathsf{pk}, m_i)\}_{i \in [\ell]}$ and every circuit $C : \{0,1\}^\ell \rightarrow \{0,1\}$ in $\mathcal{C}_{\lambda, d}$, $\mathsf{Dec}(\mathsf{sk}, \widehat{\mathsf{ct}}) = C(m_1, \ldots, m_\ell)$ where $\widehat{\mathsf{ct}} = \mathsf{Eval}(C, \mathsf{ct}_1, \ldots, \mathsf{ct}_\ell)$.*

Remark 1. For any polynomial $d(\cdot)$, We denote by FHE_d, an FHE scheme where the depth is hardwired to be $d(\lambda)$.

Above we omit the security definition which is identical to the definition of security for a public-key encryption scheme and the notion of (levelled) compactness which says that the size of a fresh as well as an evaluated ciphertext encrypting a single bit is bounded by $\mathsf{poly}(\lambda, d)$ for some fixed polynomial poly. We refer the reader to [12,23] for detailed definitions.

Now we define additional algorithms that were introduced by [20]. Any FHE scheme is not required to exhibit these, although, most of the known schemes do.

Definition 4 (Extra-Noisy Encryption). *We denote by Enc^* an extra-noisy encryption algorithm, which has the same syntax as the encryption algorithm Enc, except that the randomness it uses is sampled uniformly from another set $\mathcal{R}^* = \{\mathcal{R}^*_{\lambda, d}\}_{\lambda, d \in \mathbb{N}}$.*

We call $\mathcal{R}^*$ as the extra-noisy randomness space and any ciphertext encrypted using Enc^* as an "extra-noisy" encryption.

Randomness Homomorphism. Given $\ell \in \mathbb{N}$ ciphertexts, $\{\mathsf{ct}_i\}_{i \in [\ell]}$, underlying message $\{m_i\}_{i \in [\ell]}$ and randomness $\{r_i\}_{i \in [\ell]}$ where each $r_i \in \mathcal{R}_{\lambda, d}$, and any circuit $C \in \mathcal{C}_{\lambda, d}$, in most FHE schemes it is possible to efficiently recover randomness $r_C \in \mathcal{R}^*_{\lambda, d}$ such that $\mathsf{Eval}(\mathsf{pk}, C, \mathsf{ct}_1, \ldots, \mathsf{ct}_\ell) = \mathsf{Enc}^*(\mathsf{pk}, C(m_1, \ldots, m_\ell); r_C)$. This algorithm is denoted by $\mathsf{RandEval}$.

Definition 5 (Randomness Homomorphism). *An FHE scheme with extra noisy randomness space $\mathcal{R}^*$ satisfies randomness homomorphism property if there exists a probabilistic polynomial time algorithm $\mathsf{RandEval}$ with the following property.*
For any $\lambda \in \mathbb{N}$ and any polynomial $d(\lambda) \in \mathbb{N}$, $\mathsf{RandEval}(\mathsf{pk}, C, r, m)$ takes as input a public key pk in the support of $\mathsf{Setup}(1^\lambda, 1^d)$, a circuit $C : \{0,1\}^\ell \rightarrow \{0,1\} \in \mathcal{C}_{\lambda, d}$, randomness $r = (r_1, \ldots, r_\ell) \in \mathcal{R}^\ell_{\lambda, d}$ and messages $m = (m_1, \ldots, m_\ell) \in \{0,1\}^\ell$, and it outputs $r_C \in \mathcal{R}^*_{\lambda, d}$ such that:

$$\mathsf{Eval}(\mathsf{pk}, C, \mathsf{Enc}(\mathsf{pk}, m_1; r_1), \ldots, \mathsf{Enc}(\mathsf{pk}, m_\ell; r_\ell)) = \mathsf{Enc}^*(\mathsf{pk}, C(m_1, \ldots, m_\ell); r_C)$$

We now define the notion of SRL security for a fully-homomorphic encryption scheme with an extra-noisy encryption algorithm and randomness homomorphism property.

Definition 6. *A fully homomorphic encryption scheme with extra-noisy encryption and randomness homomorphism property for depth d, denoted as FHE_d is said to be SRL-secure if it is $\mathcal{O}_{\mathsf{SRL}}^{\mathsf{FHE}_d}$-leakage resilient secure for the following oracle.*

Oracle $\mathcal{O}_{\mathsf{SRL}}^{\mathsf{FHE}_d}(\mathsf{pk}, \boldsymbol{m}^*, \boldsymbol{r})$

$\boldsymbol{r}^* \leftarrow \mathcal{R}^*$, $\mathsf{ct}^* = \mathsf{Enc}^*(\mathsf{pk}, 0; \boldsymbol{r}^*)$
$(f, \alpha) \leftarrow \mathcal{A}(\mathsf{ct}^*)$
$\boldsymbol{r}_f = \mathsf{RandEval}(\mathsf{pk}, f, \boldsymbol{r}, \boldsymbol{m}^*)$
If $f \in \mathcal{C}_{\lambda,d}$ and $\alpha = f(\boldsymbol{m}^*)$, then set $\mathsf{leak} = \boldsymbol{r}^* - \boldsymbol{r}_f \in \mathcal{R}^*$
Otherwise set $\mathsf{leak} = \perp$. *Output* leak.

---

3 Homomorphic Encryption Schemes

Below we recall both GSW Encryption [23] and its Dual formulation [13]. In the sections, we also specify the exact modifications we need for our counterexample. We assume familiarity with some notations relevant in lattice based cryptography. For completeness, they are outlined in Appendix A.

3.1 Gentry-Sahai-Waters FHE Scheme

We now describe our scheme, and set parameters later when needed in the counterexample. Below is a list of symbols to be used in the scheme.

- λ is the security parameter,
- $d(\lambda)$ is the polynomial depth bound,
- p is the prime modulus used in the scheme,
- n, m, w are polynomials in λ, and are used as dimensions of the matrices involved,
- χ is an error distribution used for generating LWE samples,
- B_1, B_2 are $\mathsf{poly}(\lambda, d)$-bit positive integers that are used as bounds. B_1 is the bound on the infinity norm of the randomness in the evaluated ciphertext after evaluating a depth d circuit,
- Assuming $w = n \cdot \lceil \log_2 p \rceil$, let $\mathbf{G}$ be the gadget matrix of dimension $n \times w$,
- $\mathcal{C}_{\lambda,d}$ consists of all polynomial sized arithmetic circuits of depth d with Boolean inputs and outputs composed of multiplication, addition and multiplication by a constant in $\mathbb{Z}_p$, with the following special property: For any Boolean input, during the evaluation, all the multiplication gates are evaluated on Boolean inputs.

Remark 2. In the circuit class $\mathcal{C}_{\lambda,d}$, in particular, we allow multiplication by a potentially large field element, as long as all inputs to all multiplication gates are Boolean. Our counterexample for 2-Circ SRL security will only exploit boolean computations, whereas the counterexample for [42] will exploit such multiplication by constant gates.

Now we describe the scheme:

$\mathsf{Setup}(1^\lambda, 1^d) \to (\mathsf{pk}, \mathsf{sk})$: Perform the following steps.
- Sample $\mathbf{A} \leftarrow \mathbb{Z}_p^{(n-1) \times m}$.
- Sample $\boldsymbol{s} \leftarrow \mathbb{Z}_p^{1 \times (n-1)}$.
- Sample $\boldsymbol{e} \leftarrow \chi^{1 \times m}$. Set $\boldsymbol{b} = \boldsymbol{s} \cdot \mathbf{A} + \boldsymbol{e} \mod p$
- Set $\mathbf{U} = [\mathbf{A}^\top | \mathbf{b}^\top]^\top \in \mathbb{Z}_p^{n \times m}$.
- Output $\mathsf{pk} = \mathbf{U}$ and $\mathsf{sk} = \boldsymbol{s}$.

$\mathsf{Enc}(\mathsf{pk}, \mu) \to \mathsf{ct}$: To encrypt a bit $\mu \in \{0, 1\}$ perform the following steps.
- Sample $\mathbf{R} \leftarrow [-1, 1]^{m \times w}$.
- Compute and output $\mathsf{ct} = \mathbf{U} \cdot \mathbf{R} + \mu \cdot \mathbf{G}$ where $\mathbf{G}$ is the gadget matrix of dimension $n \times w$.

$\mathsf{Eval}(\mathsf{pk}, C, \mathsf{ct}_1, \ldots, \mathsf{ct}_\ell) \to \widehat{\mathsf{ct}}$: To evaluate an arithmetic circuit $C : \{0, 1\}^\ell \to \{0, 1\}$, perform the following operations gate by gate, as per the gate evaluation rules below and according to the topological ordering provided by the circuit.
- **Addition:** $\mathsf{Add}(\mathsf{ct}_1', \mathsf{ct}_2')$, Output $\mathsf{ct}_1' + \mathsf{ct}_2'$.
- **Multiplication:** $\mathsf{Mult}(\mathsf{ct}_1', \mathsf{ct}_2')$, Output $\mathsf{ct}_1' \cdot \mathbf{G}^{-1}(\mathsf{ct}_2')$.
- **Multiplication by a constant** $c \in \mathbb{Z}_q$: $\mathsf{ConstMult}(c, \mathsf{ct}_1')$, Output $\mathsf{ct}_1' \cdot \mathbf{G}^{-1}(c \cdot \mathbf{G})$.

$\mathsf{Dec}(\mathsf{sk}, \widehat{\mathsf{ct}})$: To decrypt, compute: $z = (-\boldsymbol{s}\|1) \cdot \widehat{\mathsf{ct}} \cdot \boldsymbol{v}$ where $\boldsymbol{v} \in \{0, 1\}^{w \times 1}$ with $\boldsymbol{v}_i = 1$ iff $i = w - 2$. Output 0 if $|z| \leq \frac{p}{16}$ and 1 otherwise.

We now observe that the GSW scheme above satisfies Randomness Homomorphism property.

Randomness Homomorphism: Below we define the algorithms that make up the the the randomness homomorphism property.

$\mathsf{Enc}^*(\mathsf{pk}, \mu)$: For an extra noisy encryption of a bit $\mu \in \{0, 1\}$ perform the following steps.
- Sample $\mathbf{R}^* \leftarrow [-B_2, B_2]^{m \times w}$.
- Compute and output $\mathsf{ct}^* = \mathbf{U} \cdot \mathbf{R}^* + \mu \cdot \mathbf{G}$ where $\mathbf{G}$ is the gadget matrix of dimension $n \times w$.

$\mathsf{RandEval}(\mathsf{pk}, C, \{\mathbf{R}_i\}_{i \in [\ell]}, \{m_i\}_{i \in [\ell]})$: Just as in evaluation of ciphertext, compute the randomness gate by gate. For gates with fan-in 2, let $\mathbf{R}_1'$ and $\mathbf{R}_2'$ be the input randomness, m_1', m_2' be the input messages and ct_1', ct_2' be the corresponding ciphertext. For the multiplication gate, let the input be the values with subscript "1". Below we describe the process to compute the randomness that is propagated. Messages can be computed by evaluating the circuit.
- For addition gate, output $\mathbf{R}_1' + \mathbf{R}_2'$.
- For multiplication gate, output $\mathbf{R}_1' \cdot \mathbf{G}^{-1}(\mathsf{ct}_2') + m_1' \cdot \mathbf{R}_2'$.
- For multiplication by the constant c, output $\mathbf{R}_1' \cdot \mathbf{G}^{-1}(c \cdot \mathbf{G})$.

[20] observed that GSW scheme satisfies plain SRL security.

3.2   Dual-GSW Homomomorphic Commitment Scheme

We now provide the Dual-GSW homomorphic commitment scheme [13] as described by [42]. We set parameters later when needed in the counterexample. Below is a list of symbols to be used in the scheme.

- λ is the security parameter,
- $d(\lambda)$ is the polynomial depth bound,
- p is the prime modulus used in the scheme,
- n, m, w are polynomials in λ, and are used as dimensions of the matrices involved,
- χ is an error distribution used for generating LWE samples,
- Assuming $w = m \cdot \lceil \log_2 p \rceil$, let $\mathbf{G}$ be the gadget matrix of dimension $m \times w$,
- $\mathcal{C}_{\lambda,d}$ consists of all polynomial sized arithmetic circuits of depth d with boolean inputs and outputs composed of multiplication, addition and multiplication by a constant in $\mathbb{Z}_p$, with the following special property: For any boolean input, during the evaluation, all the multiplication gates are evaluated on binary inputs.

Now we describe the scheme,

$\mathsf{Setup}(1^\lambda, 1^d) \to \mathsf{pk}$: Perform the following steps.
   - Sample $\mathbf{A} \leftarrow \mathbb{Z}_p^{m \times n}$.
   - Output $\mathsf{pk} = \mathbf{A}$.
$\mathsf{Enc}(\mathsf{pk}, \mu) \to \mathsf{ct}$: To compute a commitment ct to a bit $\mu \in \{0, 1\}$ perform the following steps.
   - Sample $\mathbf{R} \leftarrow \mathbb{Z}_p^{n \times w}$.
   - Sample $\mathbf{E} \leftarrow \chi^{m \times w}$.
   - Compute and output $\mathsf{ct} = \mathbf{A} \cdot \mathbf{R} + \mu \cdot \mathbf{G} + \mathbf{E}$ where $\mathbf{G}$ is the gadget matrix of dimension $m \times w$.
Evaluation We now define two evaluation algorithms, Eval_1 and Eval_2. Eval_1 takes as inputs $\mathsf{ct}_1, \ldots, \mathsf{ct}_\ell$ committing bits $\mu_1, \ldots, \mu_\ell$ and a function $C : \{0,1\}^\ell \to \mathbb{Z}_p$ in $\mathcal{C}_{\lambda,d}$ and computes a commitment of $C(\mu_1, \ldots, \mu_\ell)$. Eval_2 takes as input commitments $\widehat{\mathsf{ct}}_1, \ldots, \widehat{\mathsf{ct}}_m$ commiting elements $\widehat{\mu}_1, \ldots, \widehat{\mu}_m$ and outputs a packed commitment $\widehat{\mathsf{ct}}_{packed} \in \mathbb{Z}_p^{m \times 1}$ of the form $\mathbf{A}\widehat{\mathbf{r}} + \widehat{\mu} + \mathbf{e}$ where $\widehat{\mu} = (\widehat{\mu}_1, \ldots, \widehat{\mu}_m)^\top$. The evaluation algorithm for circuits of the form $g : \{0,1\}^\ell \to \mathbb{Z}_p^m \in \mathcal{C}_{\lambda,d}$ in [42] is a composition of these two evaluation algorithms (Eval_1 followed by Eval_2).
$\mathsf{Eval}_1(\mathsf{pk}, C, \mathsf{ct}_1, \ldots, \mathsf{ct}_\ell) \to \widehat{\mathsf{ct}}$: To evaluate an arithmetic circuit $C : \{0,1\}^\ell \to \mathbb{Z}_p$ in $\mathcal{C}_{\lambda,d}$, perform the following operations gate by gate, as per the gate evaluation rules below and according to the topological ordering provided by the circuit.
   - **Addition:** $\mathsf{Add}(\mathsf{ct}'_1, \mathsf{ct}'_2)$, Output $\mathsf{ct}'_1 + \mathsf{ct}'_2$.
   - **Multiplication:** $\mathsf{Mult}(\mathsf{ct}'_1, \mathsf{ct}'_2)$, Output $\mathsf{ct}'_1 \cdot \mathbf{G}^{-1}(\mathsf{ct}'_2)$.
   - **Multiplication by a constant** $c \in \mathbb{Z}_p$: $\mathsf{ConstMult}(c, \mathsf{ct}'_1)$, Output $\mathsf{ct}'_1 \cdot \mathbf{G}^{-1}(c \cdot \mathbf{G})$.
$\mathsf{Eval}_2(\mathsf{ct}_1, \ldots, \mathsf{ct}_m) \to \widehat{\mathsf{ct}}_{packed}$

- Output $\widehat{\mathsf{ct}}_{packed} = \sum_{i \in [m]} \mathsf{ct}_i \cdot \mathbf{G}^{-1}(\mathbf{1}_i)$ where $\mathbf{1}_i \in \{0,1\}^{1 \times m}$ is the indicator vector with 1 at the ith position. We refer to this output as a packed commitment.

$\mathsf{Eval}_{open,packed}(g, \mathbf{A}, \{\mathbf{R}_i\}_{i \in [\ell]}, \{x_i\}_{i \in [\ell]}, \{\mathbf{E}_i\}_{i \in [\ell]})$, the $\mathsf{Eval}_{open,packed}$ takes as input a circuit $g : \{0,1\}^\ell \to \mathbb{Z}_p^m \in \mathcal{C}_{\lambda,d}$, public key $\mathbf{A}$, and ℓ randomness-message tuples $(\mathbf{R}_i, \mathbf{E}_i, x_i)$, and it outputs the opening for $\widehat{\mathsf{ct}}_{packed} = \mathsf{Eval}(g, \mathsf{ct}_1, \ldots, \mathsf{ct}_\ell) = \mathbf{A}\widehat{\mathbf{r}} + \widehat{\mathbf{e}} + g(\boldsymbol{x})$ where $\mathsf{ct}_i = \mathbf{A}\mathbf{R}_i + \mathbf{E}_i + x_i\mathbf{G}$. This is done in two steps. First, it propagates openings for unpacked ciphertexts. Let g_i for $i \in [m]$, denote the circuit computing the ith component. It runs $\mathsf{Eval}_{open}(g_i, \mathbf{A}, \{\mathbf{R}_i\}_{i \in [\ell]}, \{x_i\}_{i \in [\ell]}, \{\mathbf{E}_i\}_{i \in [\ell]})$ for $i \in [m]$ below:

- $\mathsf{Eval}_{open}(g_i, \mathbf{A}, \{\mathbf{R}_i\}_{i \in [\ell]}, \{x_i\}_{i \in [\ell]}, \{\mathbf{E}_i\}_{i \in [\ell]})$, the Eval_{open} algorithm takes as input a circuit $g_i : \{0,1\}^\ell \to \mathbb{Z}_p \in \mathcal{C}_{\lambda,d}$, matrix $\mathbf{A}$, randomness and messages for commitments $\mathsf{ct}_i = \mathbf{A}\mathbf{R}_i + x_i\mathbf{G} + \mathbf{E}_i$ and it outputs randomness and messages of the evaluated commitment $\widehat{\mathsf{ct}}_i = \mathbf{A}\widehat{\mathbf{R}}_i + \widehat{\mathbf{E}}_i + g_i(x_1, \ldots, x_\ell)\mathbf{G}$. This is done by propagating gate by gate. Let $\mathbf{R}'_1, \mathbf{R}'_2, \mathbf{E}'_1$ and $\mathbf{E}'_2$ be the input randomness, and x'_1 and x'_2 be the inputs. For gates with a single input, let the subscript of the input be 1. Let $\mathsf{ct}'_b = \mathbf{A}\mathbf{R}'_b + x_b\mathbf{G} + \mathbf{E}'_b$ for $b \in \{1,2\}$.
  - For addition gate, output $\mathbf{R}'_1 + \mathbf{R}'_2$, $\mathbf{E}'_1 + \mathbf{E}'_2$ and $x'_1 + x'_2$.
  - For multiplication gate, output $\mathbf{R}'_1 \cdot \mathbf{G}^{-1}(\mathsf{ct}'_2) + x'_1 \cdot \mathbf{R}'_2$, $\mathbf{E}'_1 \cdot \mathbf{G}^{-1}(\mathsf{ct}'_2) + x'_1 \cdot \mathbf{E}'_2$ and $x'_1 \cdot x'_2$.
  - For multiplication by constant output $\mathbf{R}'_1 \cdot \mathbf{G}^{-1}(c \cdot \mathbf{G})$, $\mathbf{E}'_1 \cdot \mathbf{G}^{-1}(c \cdot \mathbf{G})$ and $c \cdot x'_1$.

Then, for the opening of the packed commitment it outputs $\widehat{\mathbf{r}} = \sum_{i \in [m]} \widehat{\mathbf{R}}_i \mathbf{G}^{-1}(\mathbf{1}_i)$, $\widehat{\mathbf{e}} = \sum_{i \in [m]} \widehat{\mathbf{E}}_i \mathbf{G}^{-1}(\mathbf{1}_i)$ and $\boldsymbol{y} = g(\boldsymbol{x})$.

4   Correlation-Inducing Gates

We turn to the conceptual heart of our attacks: two simple transformations on FHE ciphertexts which, put together, have the following effect. Given the ciphertext ct_x for a bit $x \in \{0,1\}$, we produce a new ciphertext ct'_x which still decrypts to x, such that the "noise part" of ct'_x is correlated with x. The exact meaning of "noise part" depends on the underlying FHE scheme – we show this for the dual version of [23] as described by [13].

Crucially, these transformations can be realized by standard homomorphic evaluation of multiplication and addition gates, as well as homomorphic evaluation of gates which multiply by constants $c \in \mathbb{Z}_p$. Therefore, we can package them into a special identity gate which can be appended to any circuit to produce a new circuit which computes the same function as the old one, but such that standard homomorphic evaluation of that circuit produces a ciphertext where the noise part and message part are correlated.

4.1   Correlation-Inducing Gate for Dual-GSW

In this subsection we adopt notation as in Sect. 3.2. In particular, we assume the presence of a public key $\mathbf{A} \in \mathbb{Z}_p^{m \times n}$.

The first half of our correlation-inducing gate for dual-GSW is captured in the following lemma.

Lemma 1 (Even-noise gate for dual-GSW). *Let* $\mathsf{ct}_x = \mathbf{AS} + x\mathbf{G} + \mathbf{E}$ *be a dual-GSW encryption of some* $x \in \mathbb{Z}_p$, *where each entry* $|\mathbf{E}[i,j]| \leq B$ *for some* $B \leq p/(100w)$ *and let* ct'_x *be the result of homomorphically evaluating the following two gates:*

1. $g_1(x) = \frac{1}{2}x$
2. $g_2(x) = x + x$.

That is, $\mathsf{ct}'_x = \mathsf{Eval}(g_2, \mathsf{Eval}(g_1, \mathsf{ct}_x))$ *(where we use the public key* $\mathbf{A}$*). Then* $\mathsf{ct}'_x = \mathbf{AS}' + x\mathbf{G} + \mathbf{E}'$ *for some* $\mathbf{S}' \in \mathbb{Z}_p^{n \times w}$ *and some matrix* $\mathbf{E}' \in \mathbb{Z}_p^{m \times w}$ *for which every entry satisfies* $\mathbf{E}'[i,j] = 2 \cdot e_{ij}$ *for some* $e_{ij} \in \mathbb{Z}_p$ *with* $|e_{i,j}| \leq O(Bw)$.

The proof is a simple calculation

Proof. Expanding,

$$\mathsf{Eval}(g_1, \mathsf{ct}_x) = (\mathbf{AS} + x\mathbf{G} + \mathbf{E}) \cdot \mathbf{G}^{-1}(\tfrac{1}{2} \cdot \mathbf{G})$$
$$= \mathbf{A}(\mathbf{S} \cdot \mathbf{G}^{-1}(\tfrac{1}{2} \cdot \mathbf{G})) + x \cdot \tfrac{1}{2} \cdot \mathbf{G} + \mathbf{E} \cdot \mathbf{G}^{-1}(\tfrac{1}{2} \cdot \mathbf{G})$$

So,

$$\mathsf{Eval}(g_2, \mathbf{A}(\mathbf{S} \cdot \mathbf{G}^{-1}(\tfrac{1}{2} \cdot \mathbf{G})) + x \cdot \tfrac{1}{2} \cdot \mathbf{G} + \mathbf{E} \cdot \mathbf{G}^{-1}(\tfrac{1}{2} \cdot \mathbf{G}))$$
$$= \mathbf{A}(2 \cdot \mathbf{S} \cdot \mathbf{G}^{-1}(\tfrac{1}{2} \cdot \mathbf{G})) + x \cdot \mathbf{G} + 2 \cdot \mathbf{E} \cdot \mathbf{G}^{-1}(\tfrac{1}{2} \cdot \mathbf{G})$$

Since $\mathbf{G}^{-1}(\tfrac{1}{2} \cdot \mathbf{G}) \in \{0,1\}^{w \times w}$, we have $|(\mathbf{E} \cdot \mathbf{G}^{-1}(\tfrac{1}{2} \cdot \mathbf{G}))[i,j]| \leq O(Bw)$.

We turn to the second half of the correlation-inducing gate.

Lemma 2 (Multiply-by-one gate for dual-GSW). *Let* $\mathsf{ct}^* = \mathbf{AS}^* + \mathbf{G} + \mathbf{E}^*$ *be a dual-GSW encryption of the constant* 1, *where* $|\mathbf{E}^*[i,j]| \leq p/10$. *Let* $x \in \{0,1\}$ *and let* $\mathsf{ct}_x = \mathbf{AS} + x \cdot \mathbf{G} + \mathbf{E}$ *be a dual-GSW encryption of* x *such each entry* $\mathbf{E}[i,j] = 2\mathbf{E}'[i,j]$ *where* $|\mathbf{E}'[i,j]| \leq p/(100w)$. *Let* $g(x,y) = x \cdot y$. *Then* $\mathsf{Eval}(g, \mathsf{ct}_x, \mathsf{ct}^*) = \mathbf{AS}' + x \cdot \mathbf{G} + \mathbf{E}'$, *where* $\mathbf{S}' \in \mathbb{Z}_p^{n \times w}$ *and* $\mathbf{E}'[1,1] = x \cdot \mathbf{E}^*[1,1]$ mod 2.[5]

Proof. We observe that

$$\mathsf{Eval}(g, \mathsf{ct}_x, \mathsf{ct}^*) = (\mathbf{AS} + x \cdot \mathbf{G} + \mathbf{E}) \cdot \mathbf{G}^{-1}(\mathbf{AS}^* + \mathbf{G} + \mathbf{E}^*)$$
$$= \mathbf{A}(\mathbf{SG}^{-1}(\mathbf{AS}^* + \mathbf{G} + \mathbf{E}^*) + x\mathbf{S}^*)$$
$$+ x \cdot \mathbf{G} + (x \cdot \mathbf{E}^* + \mathbf{EG}^{-1}(\mathbf{AS}^* + \mathbf{G} + \mathbf{E}^*)).$$

The entries of $\mathbf{EG}^{-1}(M)$ for any matrix M are at most $p/100$ in magnitude. The lemma follows.

---

[5] For two field elements $a, b \in \mathbb{Z}_q$, we write $a = b \mod 2$ if this holds in the embedding of $\mathbb{Z}_q$ into the integers $[-\lceil q/2 \rceil, \lfloor q/2 \rfloor]$.

From Lemmas 1 and 2 we have the following corollary, capturing the correlation-inducing gate for dual-GSW. The gate takes x, multiplies by the constant $1/2$, adds the result to itself, and multiplies by the constant 1. Homomorphically evaluated, this operation introduces correlation between x and the error part of the output ciphertext.

Corollary 1. *Let* $\mathsf{ct}^* = \mathbf{AS}^* + \mathbf{G} + \mathbf{E}^*$ *be a dual-GSW encryption of the constant* 1, *where* $|\mathbf{E}^*[i,j]| \leq p/10$ *for all* i,j. *Let* $x \in \{0,1\}$ *and let* $\mathsf{ct}_x = \mathbf{AS} + x\mathbf{G} + \mathbf{E}$ *be a dual-GSW encryption of* x *such that* $|\mathbf{E}[i,j]| \leq q/\mathsf{poly}(m, \log q)$ *for all* i,j. *Then, for* g_1, g_2 *as in Lemma 1 and* g *as in Lemma 2,*

$$\mathsf{Eval}(g, \mathsf{Eval}(g_2, \mathsf{Eval}(g_1, \mathsf{ct}_x)), \mathsf{ct}^*) = \mathbf{AS}' + x\mathbf{G} + \mathbf{E}'$$

where $\mathbf{E}'[1,1] = x\mathbf{E}^*[1,1] \mod 2$.

In both Lemma 2 and Corollary 1, we actually have the stronger conclusion that $\mathbf{E}' = x \cdot \mathbf{E}^* \mod 2$, rather than just the $[1,1]$ entry – however, we will only use the weaker conclusion for the $[1,1]$ entry.

4.2 Correlation-Inducing Gate for GSW

We now state the following fact as a lemma, which follows directly from the properties of homomorphic evaluation of the GSW ciphertexts.

Lemma 3 (Multiply-by-zero). *Let* $\mathsf{ct}^* = \mathbf{UR}^*$ *be a GSW encryption of the constant 0. Let* $\mathsf{ct}_x = \mathbf{UR} + x \cdot \mathbf{G}$ *be a GSW encryption of a bit* $x \in \{0,1\}$, *where* $|\mathbf{R}[i,j]|, |\mathbf{R}^*[i,j]| \leq B$, *for all* i,j. *Let* g *be the multiplication gate. Let* $\hat{\mathsf{ct}} = \mathsf{Eval}(g, \mathsf{ct}_x, \mathsf{ct}^*) = \mathbf{UR}'$. *Then* $\mathbf{R}' = \mathbf{RG}^{-1}(\mathsf{ct}^*) + x\mathbf{R}^*$. *Further, for all* i,j $|\mathbf{R}'[i,j]| = O(B \cdot w)$

We will use this structure of the multiplication by 0 operation to counterexample to 2-circ SRL security.

5   Counter Example to 2-Circular SRL Security

In this section we show that the GSW encryption scheme provided in the Sect. 3.1 serves as a counterexample to 2-Circ SRL security.

5.1   Counter Example Details

We prove the following theorem:

Theorem 1. *Let* PKE *be any encryption scheme where the depth of the decryption circuit is* $d'(\lambda)$ *for some polynomial* d'. *Let* FHE_d *be the GSW fully-homomorphic encryption scheme described in Sect. 3.1 for the circuit class* $\mathcal{C}_{\lambda,d}$ *where* $d > d' + \lambda$, *then,* $(\mathsf{FHE}_d, \mathsf{PKE})$ *are not* 2-Circ-SRL *secure.*

We show an explicit polynomial time adversary attacking the 2-Circ-SRL- secure scheme. Below, we write down the interaction between the challenger and adversary $\mathcal{A}$ in the security game and then we prove that the adversary wins with constant (better than $1/2$) probability.

1. The challenger runs PKE.Setup$(1^\lambda) \rightarrow$ (pk$_2$, sk$_2$) and FHE.Setup$(1^\lambda, 1^d) \rightarrow$ (pk$_1$, sk$_1$). Here pk$_1$ is a matrix $\mathbf{U}$ and the secret key sk$_1$ is a vector such that $(-\text{sk}_1, 1) \cdot \mathbf{U} = e$ where e was the errors sampled from $\chi^{1\times m}$. The ciphertexts live in $\mathbb{F}_p^{n\times w}$ and all dimensions n, m and w are polynomial in λ. As a consequence given the secret key, for any ciphertext $\mathbf{US}$ encrypting 0 with randomness $\mathbf{S}$, one can compute $e \cdot \mathbf{S}$ by multiplying with the secret key.
2. The adversary submits two messages $\boldsymbol{m}^0, \boldsymbol{m}^1 \in \{0,1\}^{\lambda+1}$. Here, $\boldsymbol{m}^\beta = (\beta, 0, \ldots, 0)$ for $\beta \in \{0,1\}$. The challenger samples $\beta \leftarrow \{0,1\}$ and lets $\boldsymbol{m}^* = (\boldsymbol{m}^\beta \| \text{sk}_2)$. Denote by ℓ the size of sk$_2$.
3. The challenger computes ct$_1$ = (ct$_{1,1}, \ldots,$ ct$_{1,\ell+2}$) and ct$_2$ as follows. For $j \in [2+\ell]$, compute ct$_{1,j}$ = FHE.Enc(pk$_1, \boldsymbol{m}_j^*; \mathbf{R}_{1,j}$) where $\mathbf{R}_{1,j}$ is chosen as in the scheme. It also computes ct$_2$ = PKE.Enc(pk$_2,$ sk$_1$). Both ct$_1$, ct$_2$ are given to the adversary $\mathcal{A}$. Each ct$_{1,j} \in \mathbb{F}_p^{n\times w}$ and $\mathbf{G}^{-1}(\text{ct}_{1,j}) \in \{0,1\}^{w\times w}$.
4. The adversary finds at random an index $j_v \in [2, \lambda+1]$ (which is an index for which ct$_{1,j_v}$ encrypts 0) such that there exists a vector $\boldsymbol{v} \in \{0,1\}^{w\times 1}$ such that $\mathbf{G}^{-1}(\text{ct}_{1,j_v})\boldsymbol{v} = \mathbf{0}^{w\times 1} \mod 2$. This can be done with overwhelming probability because each $\mathbf{G}^{-1}(\text{ct}_{1,j})$ for $j \in [2, \lambda+1]$ is rank deficient with probability at least $\frac{1}{2} - \text{negl}(\lambda)$.
5. Use ct$_1$ and ct$_2$ to compute ct$_{\text{sk}_1}$ which is an FHE encryption of sk$_1$.
6. The adversary now submits $q = \lambda \cdot m$ functions, value tuples $(f_i, 0)$ for $i \in [q]$. For query $i \in [q]$, the function f_i is described below. The function f_i is described in terms of the FHE$_d$ evaluation directly. The underlying boolean function can be inferred from the FHE$_d$ evaluation. The function description depends on ct$_1$, ct$_{\text{sk}_1}$, ct$_i^*$ = Enc*(pk$_1, 0; \mathbf{R}_i^*$) which is the ith sampled extra noisy ciphertext, the vector $\boldsymbol{v}$ and the index j_v. For every $i \in [q]$, the adversary receives leak$_i$ = $\mathbf{R}_i^* - \widehat{\mathbf{R}}_i$ where $\widehat{\mathbf{R}}_i$ is the randomness in the evaluated ciphertext computed for computing f_i.
7. The adversary simply finds the dimension of the space $W = \{\boldsymbol{y} \in \{0,1\}^{1\times w} | \boldsymbol{y} \cdot (\text{leak}_i \cdot \boldsymbol{v}) = 0 \mod 2 \ \forall \ i \in [q]\}$ over $\mathbb{F}_2^m$. If the dimension is 0, output the guess $\beta' = 0$, otherwise output $\beta' = 1$.

Function $\mathsf{FHE}_d.\mathsf{Eval}(f_i, \cdot)$

Input: ct_1
Hardwired: $\mathsf{ct}_{\mathsf{sk}_1}, \mathsf{ct}_i^*, \boldsymbol{v}$

1. Compute $\mathsf{ct}_i' = \mathbf{U}\mathbf{R}'_i + (\beta \cdot \langle \boldsymbol{e}, \mathbf{R}_i^* \cdot \boldsymbol{v} \rangle \mod 2)\mathbf{G}$. This is computable because given the secret key sk_1 of the FHE_d, one can compute $\boldsymbol{e}\mathbf{R}_i^*$ as pointed earlier, and we have encryption $\mathsf{ct}_{\mathsf{sk}_1}$ hardwired. Denote $\gamma_v = (\beta \cdot \langle \boldsymbol{e}, \mathbf{R}_i^* \cdot \boldsymbol{v} \rangle \mod 2)$

2. Multiply ct_i' with ct_{1,j_v} to get the following ciphertext (see Lemma 3).

$$\widehat{\mathsf{ct}}_i = \mathbf{U}\underbrace{(\mathbf{R}'_i\mathbf{G}^{-1}(\mathsf{ct}_{1,j_v}) + \gamma_v \mathbf{R}_{1,j_v})}_{\widehat{\mathbf{R}}_i}$$

3. Output $\widehat{\mathsf{ct}}_i$.

We now argue that the success probability of the adversary is almost $3/4$. First of all, note that the adversary is admissible because f_i on $\boldsymbol{m}^*$ always outputs 0. This is ensured because in the step 2 of the circuit, ct_i' which computes γ_v is multiplied by ct_{j_v} (which encrypts 0). Hence the output is always 0.

Let's now analyze the depth of the circuit f_i. Encryption of $\mathsf{ct}_{\mathsf{sk}_1}$ can be computed by a circuit that is computable in depth d' (which is the decryption circuit depth of PKE). The second step is in NC^1, because $((-1, \mathsf{sk}_1) \cdot \mathsf{ct}_{i^*}) \mod 2 = \boldsymbol{e}\mathbf{R}_i^* \mod 2$. Finally, the last step consists of taking the resulting vector's inner product with $\beta \cdot \boldsymbol{v} \mod 2$, which can also be done in NC^1. So, if $d > d' + \lambda$, the function f_i is computable in depth d.

Now we analyze the success probability of this attack. Observe that since $\mathbf{G}^{-1}(\mathsf{ct}_{1,j})$ for all $j \in [2, \lambda + 1]$ behave pseudorandomly, with probability at least $0.5 - \mathsf{negl}(\lambda)$, a given $\mathsf{ct}_{1,j}$ is going to have a vector in the nullspace (the determinant of a random matrix over $\mathbb{F}_2$ is random over $\mathbb{F}_2$). Thus, point 4) succeeds with probability at least $1 - \mathsf{negl}(\lambda)$. Now let us analyze the randomness of the evaluated ciphertext during each step of the evaluation.

1. $\mathsf{leak}_i = \mathbf{R}_i^* - \widehat{\mathbf{R}}_i$. Remember, $\widehat{\mathbf{R}}_i = \mathbf{R}'_i \cdot \mathbf{G}^{-1}(\mathsf{ct}_{1,j_v}) + \gamma_v \mathbf{R}_{1,j_v}$.
2. The last step computes $\mathsf{leak}_i \cdot \boldsymbol{v} \mod 2$ which produces:

$$\mathsf{leak}_i \cdot \boldsymbol{v} = \mathbf{R}_i^* \cdot \boldsymbol{v} - \gamma_v \mathbf{R}_{1,j_v} \boldsymbol{v} \mod 2.$$

This is because $\mathbf{G}^{-1}(\mathsf{ct}_{1,j_v})\boldsymbol{v} = \mathbf{0} \mod 2$.

3. If $\beta = 0$, $\gamma_v = 0$ and thus $\mathsf{leak}_i \cdot \boldsymbol{v} = \mathbf{R}_i^* \cdot \boldsymbol{v}$. Since $\boldsymbol{v}$ is independent of $\mathbf{R}_i^*$, $\mathbf{R}_i^* \cdot \boldsymbol{v} \mod 2$ is distributed identically like a random vector over $\mathbb{F}_2$. Since $q = m \cdot \lambda$, with probability $1 - \mathsf{negl}(\lambda)$, no non-zero vector $\boldsymbol{y} \mod 2 \in \mathbb{F}_2^{1 \times m}$, can satisfy $\boldsymbol{y} \cdot \mathbf{R}_i^* \boldsymbol{v} \mod 2 = 0$ for all i. This can be shown by computing the probability of a fixed $\boldsymbol{y}$ to satisfy all q independent equations, which is 2^{-q}, and then doing a union bound over all 2^m choices of $\boldsymbol{y}$.

4. If $\beta = 1$, $\gamma_v = \langle e, \mathbf{R}_i^* \cdot v \rangle \mod 2$ and thus $\mathsf{leak}_i \cdot v = \mathbf{R}_i^* \cdot v + \gamma_v \mathbf{R}_{1,j_v} v$. Since e is independent of $\mathbf{R}_{1,j_v}$ and v and further $\mathbf{R}_{1,j_v} \cdot v \neq 0$ (with probability $1 - \mathsf{negl}(\lambda)$ as ct_{1,j_v} is lossy for $\mathbf{R}_{1,j_v}$), it holds that with probability $0.5 - \mathsf{negl}(\lambda)$, $\langle e, \mathbf{R}_{1,j_v} v \rangle \mod 2 = 1$. In this case, we have that at least the vector $e \mod 2$ is a solution of:

$$0 = y \cdot \mathsf{leak}_i \cdot v = y\mathbf{R}_i^* \cdot v - (\langle e, \mathbf{R}_i^* \cdot v \rangle \mod 2) \, y \cdot \mathbf{R}_{1,j_v} v \mod 2,$$

for every $i \in [q]$. This can be seen by substituting e for y. Hence dimension of W is at least 1, with probability $0.5 - \mathsf{negl}(\lambda)$.

Thus the probability of guessing β correctly is:

$$\frac{1}{2}(\Pr[\mathsf{Dim}(W) = 0 | \beta = 0] + \Pr[\mathsf{Dim}(W) > 0 | \beta = 1])$$

$$\geq \frac{1}{2}(1 - \mathsf{negl}(\lambda) + 0.5 - \mathsf{negl}(\lambda))(\text{from the observations above})$$

$$\geq \frac{3}{4} - \mathsf{negl}(\lambda)$$

This concludes the proof.

6 Counter Example for the Conjecture by Wee-Wichs

Now we describe our counterexample to the conjecture of Wee and Wichs [42].

6.1 Homomorphic Pseudorandom LWE Samples Conjecture

The following presentation closely follows Sect. 6 of [42] – for additional context on the use of these definitions and conjecture to construct an oblivious LWE sampler and then iO, we refer the reader to [42].

For some parameters λ, n, m, p, Q, we will define two distributions over tuples of the form $(\{b_i\}_{i \in [Q]}, \mathbf{A}, \mathbf{C}, \{s_i\}_{i \in [Q]})$, where $b_i \in \mathbb{Z}_p^m$, $\mathbf{A} \in \mathbb{Z}_p^{m \times n}$, $\mathbf{C} = \mathbf{C}_1, \ldots, \mathbf{C}_{\lambda+1}$ with $\mathbf{C}_i \in \mathbb{Z}_p^{m \times m \log q}$, and $s_i \in \mathbb{Z}_p^n$. The conjecture will be that these distributions are computationally indistinguishable.

We first need some additional setup.

Setup for pseudorandom error distribution:

- Let χ_{PRF} be a distribution on $\mathbb{Z}_p$.
- Let D be an algorithm which takes v random coins in $\{0,1\}$ and outputs samples $s \leftarrow \mathbb{Z}_p^n$ and $e \leftarrow \chi_{\mathsf{PRF}}^m$.
- Let $\mathsf{PRF} : \{0,1\}^\lambda \times \{0,1\}^* \to \{0,1\}^v$ be a pseudo-random function.

Setup for pseudorandomly generating LWE samples:

- For $i \in [Q]$, $b \in \mathbb{Z}_p^m$, let $g_{i,b,\mathbf{A}}$ be a circuit with values $(i, b, \mathbf{A})$ hard-coded and which performs the following computation on input $(k, \beta) \in \{0,1\}^{\lambda+1}$:

$$\text{Let } (s_i^{\mathsf{PRF}}, e_i^{\mathsf{PRF}}) = \mathsf{D}(\mathsf{PRF}(k, i)). \text{ Output } \mathbf{A}s_i^{\mathsf{PRF}} + e_i^{\mathsf{PRF}} + \beta \cdot b$$

Following [42], we now define two distributions $\mathsf{DIST}(\beta)$ for $\beta \in \{0,1\}$ as follows. Let χ be a B-bounded distribution.

- For $i \in [Q]$, generate LWE samples $\boldsymbol{b}_i$. Concretely, $\mathbf{A} \leftarrow \mathbb{Z}_p^{m \times n}$, $\widehat{\boldsymbol{s}}_i \leftarrow \mathbb{Z}_p^n$, $\widehat{\boldsymbol{e}}_i \leftarrow \widehat{\chi}^m$.
- Let $k \leftarrow \{0,1\}^\lambda$ and sample dual-GSW commitments $\mathbf{C}_1, \ldots, \mathbf{C}_\lambda$ to $k_1, \ldots, k_\lambda$. That is, sample $\mathbf{R}_i \leftarrow \mathbb{Z}_p^{n \times w}$ and $\mathbf{E}_i \leftarrow \chi^{m \times w}$ and set $\mathbf{C}_i = \mathbf{A}\mathbf{R}_i + k_i \mathbf{G} + \mathbf{E}_i$.
- Let $\mathbf{C}_\beta = \mathbf{A}\mathbf{R}_\beta + \beta \mathbf{G} + \mathbf{E}_\beta$ be a dual-GSW commitment to β.
- For $i \in [Q]$, let $(\boldsymbol{s}_i^{\mathsf{PRF}}, \boldsymbol{e}_i^{\mathsf{PRF}}) = \mathsf{D}(\mathsf{PRF}(k,i))$.
- Let $(\boldsymbol{r}_i^{\mathsf{Eval}}, \boldsymbol{e}_i^{\mathsf{Eval}}) = \mathsf{Eval}_{open, packed}(g_{i, \mathbf{A}\widehat{\boldsymbol{s}}_i + \widehat{\boldsymbol{e}}_i, \mathbf{A}}, \mathbf{A}, (k, \beta), \mathbf{R}, \mathbf{E})$.
- Let $\boldsymbol{s}_i = \boldsymbol{r}_i^{\mathsf{Eval}} + \boldsymbol{s}_i^{\mathsf{PRF}} + \beta \widehat{\boldsymbol{s}}_i$.
- Output $(\{\mathbf{A}\widehat{\boldsymbol{s}}_i + \widehat{\boldsymbol{e}}_i\}_{i \in [Q]}, \mathbf{A}, \mathbf{C}_1, \ldots, \mathbf{C}_\lambda, \mathbf{C}_\beta, \{\boldsymbol{s}_i\}_{i \in [Q]})$.

Conjecture 1 (HPLS Conjecture, [42] Conjecture 6.4). Let λ be a security parameter and $n, m, q, \chi, \widehat{\chi}, \chi^{\mathsf{PRF}}$ be such that the LWE assumption holds with parameters (n, q, χ) and with $(n, q, \widehat{\chi})$. Furthermore, suppose that χ^{PRF} smudges out error of size $\widehat{B} + B \cdot m^{O(t)}$, where t is the depth of the circuit $g_{i,b,\mathbf{A}}$ (which is dominated by the depth of PRF). Then there is a choice of PRF such that $\mathsf{DIST}(0)$ and $\mathsf{DIST}(1)$ are computationally indistinguishable.

6.2   Counter Example Details

In our main theorem, we make the following assumption about implementation details of the circuit $g_{i,b,\mathbf{A}}$ which are left unspecified in [42]. We assume there is a Boolean circuit C_{PRF} computing the pseudorandom function and another Boolean circuit C_{D} implementing the sampling algorithm D, whose outputs are the binary expansion of $(\boldsymbol{s}_i^{\mathsf{PRF}}, \boldsymbol{e}_i^{\mathsf{PRF}})$. Then g is given by

1. composing the circuits $C_{\mathsf{PRF}}, C_{\mathsf{D}}$,
2. multiplying by field elements in $\mathbb{Z}_p$ and adding to compute each entry of the vector $\mathbf{A}\boldsymbol{s}_i^{\mathsf{PRF}} + \boldsymbol{e}_i^{\mathsf{PRF}}$,
3. multiplying the input β by the field element $\boldsymbol{b}[j]$ for $j \leq m$, and
4. adding (2) and (3) to obtain the final outputs. $(\mathbf{A}\boldsymbol{s}_i^{\mathsf{PRF}})[j] + \boldsymbol{e}_i[j] + \beta \cdot \boldsymbol{b}[j]$, for $j \in [m]$. These outputs are packed into a vector by Eval.

We prove the following theorem:

Theorem 2. *With $\lambda, n, m, q, \chi, \widehat{\chi}, \chi^{\mathsf{PRF}}$ as in Conjecture 1, for any sampling algorithm D as above there is an arithmetic circuit C_{D} over $\mathbb{Z}_p$ implementing D such that for any function $F : \{0,1\}^\lambda \times \{0,1\}^* \to \{0,1\}^v$, if $Q \gg m^2 \log q$ then the resulting distributions $\mathsf{DIST}(0)$ and $\mathsf{DIST}(1)$ are distinguishable with nontrivial probability in polynomial time.*

Remark 3. A somewhat easier argument than the below shows the same result if we allow ourselves nonstandard implementations of parts (2) and (3) of $g_{i,b,\mathbf{A}}$. A merit of our attack is that it allows any sampling algorithm D and any choice of PRF, and requires only a careful choice of circuit C_{D} to implement D.

The circuit C_D We start by describing the circuit C_D. Start with any circuit C for D, with output in binary, and modify it in the following way.

- Let C_0 be a circuit which takes the first bit x_1 of its input and performs the computation $x_1 + (1 + (q-1) \cdot x_1))$. (The output wire of C_0 therefore always carries the value 1.)
- To the output wire of C_0 corresponding to the lowest-order bit of $e_i^{\mathsf{PRF}}[1]$, attach a new gate which performs the correlation-inducing transformation described in Corollary 1, using the output wire of C_0 as the special "1" input.
- To all of the other output wires, attach a gate performing the "even-noise" transformation of Lemma 1. (As noted before, these gates can be implemented using only multiplication and addition of boolean values and multiplication by a field element.) The result is the new circuit C_D.

A Linear System Part (3) above of the circuit computing $g_{i,b,\mathbf{A}}$ induces a linear system in $m \times m \log q$ variables E_{ij}, in the following way. On input $C_\beta(E) = \mathbf{AS}_\beta + \beta\mathbf{G} + E$, part (3) of that circuit, evaluated homomorphically, produces outputs of the form $\mathbf{ASG}^{-1}(\boldsymbol{b}_i[j]) + \beta\boldsymbol{b}_i[j]\mathbf{G} + EG^{-1}(\boldsymbol{b}_i[j])$. Let $L_{\boldsymbol{b}_i[j]}(E)$ be the matrix of linear functions given in E given by $EG^{-1}(\boldsymbol{b}_i[j])$. Let $L_i(E)$ be the linear function in E given by the $L_{\boldsymbol{b}_i[j]}(E)[1,1]$.

Distinguishing algorithm Now we describe an algorithm to distinguish $\mathsf{DIST}(0)$ and $\mathsf{DIST}(1)$ with the above choice of F.

  Input: $(\{\boldsymbol{b}_i\}_{i\in[Q]}, \mathbf{A}, \mathbf{C}_1, \ldots, \mathbf{C}_\lambda, \mathbf{C}_\beta, \{\boldsymbol{s}_i\}_{i\in[Q]})$,

1. Using the commitments $\mathbf{C}_1, \ldots, \mathbf{C}_\lambda, \mathbf{C}_\beta$, homomorphically evaluate the circuits $g_{i,b_i,\mathbf{A}}$ to obtain (packed) ciphertexts $\mathsf{ct}_1, \ldots, \mathsf{ct}_Q \in \mathbb{Z}_p^m$.
2. Compute vectors $\boldsymbol{e}_i' = \mathsf{ct}_i - \mathbf{As}_i$. Let e_i be the first entry of $\boldsymbol{e}_i'$.
3. Check if the linear system in $m \times m \log q$ variables E given by the equations $L_i(E) = e_i$ has a solution over $\mathbb{F}_2$. If it does, output "$\beta = 0$". Otherwise, output a random $\beta \in \{0,1\}$.

Proof (Proof of Theorem 2). To prove the theorem it will be enough to show that the linear system $L_i(E) = e_i$ has a solution with probability $\Omega(1)$ when the underlying distribution is $\mathsf{DIST}(0)$, but has a solution only with probability $o(1)$ when the underlying distribution is $\mathsf{DIST}(1)$.

We start by examining the structure of e_i in both the $\beta = 0$ and $\beta = 1$ cases. We first expand ct_i.

$$\mathsf{ct}_i = \mathbf{A}r_i^{\mathsf{Eval}} + \mathbf{A}s_i^{\mathsf{PRF}} + e_i^{\mathsf{PRF}} + \beta \cdot (\mathbf{A}\widehat{s}_i + \widehat{e}_i) + e_i^{\mathsf{Eval}}.$$

Then

$$\boldsymbol{e}_i' = \mathsf{ct}_i - \mathbf{As}_i = e_i^{\mathsf{PRF}} + e_i^{\mathsf{Eval}} + \beta \cdot \widehat{e}_i.$$

Furthermore, e_i^{Eval} has two parts, coming from parts (2) and (3) of the circuit for g – let us call $e_i^{\mathsf{Eval}^2}$ the part coming from step (2) and $e_i^{\mathsf{Eval}^3}$ the part from step (3), so that $e_i^{\mathsf{Eval}} = e_i^{\mathsf{Eval}^2} + e_i^{\mathsf{Eval}^3}$ and

$$\boldsymbol{e}_i' = e_i^{\mathsf{PRF}} + e_i^{\mathsf{Eval}^2} + e_i^{\mathsf{Eval}^3} + \beta \cdot \widehat{e}_i$$

We claim that with probability $\Omega(1)$, all $i \in [Q]$ satisfy $\boldsymbol{e}_i^{\mathsf{PRF}}[1] = \boldsymbol{e}_i^{\mathsf{Eval}^2}[1]$ mod 2, as a result of our design of the circuit C_{D}. In fact, we claim that this occurs whenever the (random) commitment $\mathbf{C}_1$ to k_1 is such that homomorphically evaluating the circuit C_0 yields a ciphertext $\mathbf{AS}^* + k_1 \cdot \mathbf{G} + \mathbf{E}^*$ such that $\mathbf{E}^*[1,1]$ is odd, which occurs with probability $1/2$. This follows directly from Lemmas 1 and 2, Corollary 1, and our assumption about the structure of the circuit g. Together, these ensure that:

- the noise coming from homomorphically evaluating $\mathbf{A}\boldsymbol{s}^{\mathsf{PRF}}$ is all $0 \mod 2$, and
- the noise coming from homomorphically evaluating $\boldsymbol{e}_i^{\mathsf{PRF}}[1]$ has upper-left entry equal to $0 \mod 2$ (this entry is preserved by packing).

We conclude that, on the event above, $e_i = \boldsymbol{e}_i^{\mathsf{Eval}^3} + \beta \cdot \widehat{\boldsymbol{e}}_i \mod 2$. Now, if $\beta = 0$, observe that $\boldsymbol{e}_i^{\mathsf{Eval}_3} = L_i(E)$, the linear function described above in $m \times m \log q$ variables E. So the linear system has a solution. Finally, if $\beta = 1$, since $Q \gg m^2 \log q$ the linear system is whp overdetermined, and $e_i \mod 2$ is independent of the coefficients of L_i and independent of other e_i', because of the presence of the random vector $\widehat{e}_i$. So whp the linear system is unsatisfiable.

Acknowledgements. Sam Hopkins was supported by the Miller Institute, UC Berkeley.

Aayush Jain was supported by a Google PhD fellowship in the area of security and privacy (2018) and in part from DARPA SAFEWARE and SIEVE awards, NTT Research, NSF Frontier Award 1413955, and NSF grant 1619348, BSF grant 2012378, a Xerox Faculty Research Award, a Google Faculty Research Award, an equipment grant from Intel, and an Okawa Foundation Research Grant. This material is based upon work supported by the Defense Advanced Research Projects Agency through Award HR00112020024 and the ARL under Contract W911NF-15-C- 0205.

Huijia Lin was supported by NSF grants CNS-1528178, CNS-1929901, CNS-1936825 (CAREER), CNS-2026774, a Hellman Fellowship, a JP Morgan AI Research Award, a Simons Collaboration grant on the Theory of Algorithmic Fairness, the Defense Advanced Research Projects Agency (DARPA) and Army Research Office (ARO) under Contract No. W911NF-15-C-0236, and a subcontract No. 2017-002 through Galois.

A   Lattice Preliminaries

Lattices. An m-dimensional lattice $\mathcal{L}$ is a discrete additive subgroup of $\mathbb{R}^m$ (not contained in any subspace of strictly smaller dimension). Given positive integers n, m, q and a matrix $\mathbf{A} \in \mathbb{Z}_q^{n \times m}$, we let $\Lambda_q^{\perp}(\mathbf{A})$ denote the lattice $\{\boldsymbol{x} \in \mathbb{Z}^m \mid \mathbf{A}\boldsymbol{x} = \mathbf{0} \bmod q\}$.

Discrete Gaussians. Let σ be any positive real number. The Gaussian distribution $\mathcal{D}_\sigma$ with parameter σ is defined by the probability distribution function $\rho_\sigma(x) = \exp(-\pi\|x\|^2/\sigma^2)$. For any discrete set $\mathcal{L} \subseteq \mathbb{R}^m$, define $\rho_\sigma(\mathcal{L}) = \sum_{x\in\mathcal{L}} \rho_\sigma(x)$. The discrete Gaussian distribution $\mathcal{D}_{\mathcal{L},\sigma}$ over $\mathcal{L}$ with parameter σ is defined by the probability distribution function $\rho_{\mathcal{L},\sigma}(x) = \rho_\sigma(x)/\rho_\sigma(\mathcal{L})$.

The following lemma (e.g., [37, Lemma 4.4]) shows that if the parameter σ of a discrete Gaussian distribution is small, then any vector drawn from this distribution will be short (with high probability).

Lemma 4. *Let m, n, q be positive integers with $m > n$, $q > 2$. Let $\mathbf{A} \in \mathbb{Z}_q^{n\times m}$ be a matrix of dimensions $n \times m$, $\sigma \in \tilde{\Omega}(n)$, and $\mathcal{L} = \Lambda_q^\perp(\mathbf{A})$. Then, there is a negligible function $\mathsf{negl}(\cdot)$ such that*

$$\Pr_{x\leftarrow\mathcal{D}_{\mathcal{L},\sigma}}\left[\|x\| > \sqrt{m}\sigma\right] \leq \mathsf{negl}(n),$$

where $\|x\|$ denotes the ℓ_2 norm of x.

Truncated Discrete Gaussians. The truncated discrete Gaussian distribution over $\mathbb{Z}^m$ with parameter σ, denoted by $\tilde{\mathcal{D}}_{\mathbb{Z}^m,\sigma}$, is the same as the discrete Gaussian distribution $\mathcal{D}_{\mathbb{Z}^m,\sigma}$ except that it outputs 0 whenever the ℓ_∞ norm exceeds $\sqrt{m}\sigma$. By definition, we can say that $\tilde{\mathcal{D}}_{\mathbb{Z}^m,\sigma}$ is $\sqrt{m}\sigma$-bounded, where a family of distributions $\mathcal{D} = \{\mathcal{D}_\lambda\}_{\lambda\in\mathbb{N}}$ over the integers is B-*bounded* (for $B = B(\lambda) > 0$) if for every $\lambda \in \mathbb{N}$ it holds that $\Pr_{x\leftarrow\mathcal{D}_\lambda}[|x| \leq B(\lambda)] = 1$.

Also by 4, $\tilde{\mathcal{D}}_{\mathbb{Z}^m,\sigma}$ and $\mathcal{D}_{\mathbb{Z}^m,\sigma}$ are statistically indistinguishable. Therefore, in the preliminaries below, unless specified, the lemmata will apply in the setting where by sampling from discrete Gaussian we mean sampling from truncated discrete Gaussian distribution.

A.1   Learning With Errors

The learning with errors (LWE) problem was defined by Regev [40]. The $\mathsf{LWE}_{n,m,q,\chi}$ problem for parameters $n, m, q \in \mathbb{N}$ and for a distribution χ supported over $\mathbb{Z}$ is to distinguish between the following pair of distributions

$$(\mathbf{A}, s\mathbf{A} + e \bmod q) \quad \text{and} \quad (\mathbf{A}, u),$$

where $\mathbf{A} \leftarrow \mathbb{Z}_q^{n\times m}$, $s \leftarrow \mathbb{Z}_q^{1\times n}$, $e \leftarrow \chi^{1\times n}$ and $u \leftarrow \mathbb{Z}_q^{1\times m}$. Similarly, we can define the matrix version of the problem, which is known to be hard, if the version above is hard. Specifically, let $k \in \mathsf{poly}(n,m)$, then in the matrix the task is to distinguish between the following two distributions

$$(\mathbf{A}, \mathbf{S}\mathbf{A} + \mathbf{E} \bmod q) \quad \text{and} \quad (\mathbf{A}, \mathbf{U}),$$

where $\mathbf{A} \leftarrow \mathbb{Z}_q^{n\times m}$, $\mathbf{S} \leftarrow \mathbb{Z}_q^{k\times n}$, $\mathbf{E} \leftarrow \chi^{k\times n}$ and $\mathbf{U} \leftarrow \mathbb{Z}_q^{k\times m}$.

The gadget matrix [36]. Fix a dimension n and a modulus q. Define the gadget vector $\boldsymbol{g} = (1, 2, 4, \ldots, 2^{\lceil \log q \rceil - 1})$ and the gadget function $g^{-1} \colon \mathbb{Z}_q \to \{0, 1\}^{\lceil \log q \rceil}$ to be the function that computes the $(\log q)$th bit decomposition of an integer. For some integer z the function is defined as $g^{-1}(z) = \boldsymbol{v} = (v_1, \ldots, v_{\log q})$ where $v_i \in \{0, 1\}$ such that $z = \langle \boldsymbol{g}, \boldsymbol{v} \rangle$. By extension we define the augmented gadget function $G^{-1} \colon \mathbb{Z}_q^{n \times m} \to \{0, 1\}^{(n \cdot \lceil \log q \rceil) \times m}$ to be the function that computes the $(\log q)$th bit decomposition of every integer in a matrix $\mathbf{A} \in \mathbb{Z}_q^{n \times m}$, and arranges them as a binary matrix of dimension $(n \cdot \lceil \log q \rceil) \times m$ which we denote $G^{-1}(\mathbf{A})$. Hence, $\mathbf{G}_n \cdot G^{-1}(z) = \mathbf{Z}$, where the gadget matrix $\mathbf{G}_n$ is $\mathbf{G}_n = \boldsymbol{g} \otimes \mathbf{I}_n \in \mathbb{Z}_q^{n \times (n \cdot \lceil \log q \rceil)}$. When n is clear from context, we denote $\mathbf{G}_n$ simply by $\mathbf{G}$.

References

1. Acar, T., Belenkiy, M., Bellare, M., Cash, D.: Cryptographic agility and its relation to circular encryption. In: Gilbert, H. (ed.) EUROCRYPT 2010. LNCS, vol. 6110, pp. 403–422. Springer, Heidelberg (2010). https://doi.org/10.1007/978-3-642-13190-5_21

2. Agrawal, S.: Indistinguishability obfuscation without multilinear maps: new methods for bootstrapping and instantiation. In: Ishai, Y., Rijmen, V. (eds.) EUROCRYPT 2019, Part I. LNCS, vol. 11476, pp. 191–225. Springer, Cham (2019). https://doi.org/10.1007/978-3-030-17653-2_7

3. Agrawal, S., Pellet-Mary, A.: Indistinguishability obfuscation without maps: attacks and fixes for noisy linear FE. In: Canteaut, A., Ishai, Y. (eds.) EUROCRYPT 2020, Part I. LNCS, vol. 12105, pp. 110–140. Springer, Cham (2020). https://doi.org/10.1007/978-3-030-45721-1_5

4. Ananth, P., Jain, A., Lin, H., Matt, C., Sahai, A.: Indistinguishability obfuscation without multilinear maps: new paradigms via low degree weak pseudorandomness and security amplification. In: Boldyreva, A., Micciancio, D. (eds.) CRYPTO 2019, Part III. LNCS, vol. 11694, pp. 284–332. Springer, Cham (2019). https://doi.org/10.1007/978-3-030-26954-8_10

5. Ananth, P., Jain, A., Sahai, A.: Indistinguishability obfuscation without multilinear maps: IO from LWE, bilinear maps, and weak pseudorandomness. IACR Cryptology ePrint Archive 2018, 615 (2018)

6. Ballard, L., Green, M., de Medeiros, B., Monrose, F.: Correlation-resistant storage via keyword-searchable encryption. Cryptology ePrint Archive, Report 2005/417 (2005). http://eprint.iacr.org/2005/417

7. Barak, B., et al.: On the (im)possibility of obfuscating programs. In: Kilian, J. (ed.) CRYPTO 2001. LNCS, vol. 2139, pp. 1–18. Springer, Heidelberg (2001). https://doi.org/10.1007/3-540-44647-8_1

8. Bishop, A., Hohenberger, S., Waters, B.: New circular security counterexamples from decision linear and learning with errors. In: Iwata, T., Cheon, J.H. (eds.) ASIACRYPT 2015, Part II. LNCS, vol. 9453, pp. 776–800. Springer, Heidelberg (2015). https://doi.org/10.1007/978-3-662-48800-3_32

9. Black, J., Rogaway, P., Shrimpton, T.: Encryption-scheme security in the presence of key-dependent messages. IACR Cryptology ePrint Archive 2002, 100 (2002). http://eprint.iacr.org/2002/100

10. Brakerski, Z., Döttling, N., Garg, S., Malavolta, G.: Candidate iO from homomorphic encryption schemes. In: Canteaut, A., Ishai, Y. (eds.) EUROCRYPT 2020, Part I. LNCS, vol. 12105, pp. 79–109. Springer, Cham (2020). https://doi.org/10.1007/978-3-030-45721-1_4

11. Brakerski, Z., Döttling, N., Garg, S., Malavolta, G.: Factoring and pairings are not necessary for io: circular-secure LWE suffices. IACR Cryptology ePrint Archive 2020, 1024 (2020). https://eprint.iacr.org/2020/1024

12. Brakerski, Z., Gentry, C., Vaikuntanathan, V.: (Leveled) fully homomorphic encryption without bootstrapping. In: Goldwasser, S. (ed.) Innovations in Theoretical Computer Science 2012, ITCS 2012, Cambridge, MA, USA, 8–10 January 2012, pp. 309–325. ACM, January 2012. https://doi.org/10.1145/2090236.2090262

13. Brakerski, Z., Halevi, S., Polychroniadou, A.: Four round secure computation without setup. In: Kalai, Y., Reyzin, L. (eds.) TCC 2017, Part I. LNCS, vol. 10677, pp. 645–677. Springer, Cham (2017). https://doi.org/10.1007/978-3-319-70500-2_22

14. Brakerski, Z., Vaikuntanathan, V.: Efficient fully homomorphic encryption from (standard) LWE. In: Ostrovsky, R. (ed.) 52nd FOCS, pp. 97–106. IEEE Computer Society Press, October 2011. https://doi.org/10.1109/FOCS.2011.12

15. Camenisch, J., Lysyanskaya, A.: An Efficient System for Non-transferable Anonymous Credentials with Optional Anonymity Revocation. In: Pfitzmann, B. (ed.) EUROCRYPT 2001. LNCS, vol. 2045, pp. 93–118. Springer, Heidelberg (2001). https://doi.org/10.1007/3-540-44987-6_7

16. Cash, D., Green, M., Hohenberger, S.: New definitions and separations for circular security. In: Fischlin, M., Buchmann, J., Manulis, M. (eds.) PKC 2012. LNCS, vol. 7293, pp. 540–557. Springer, Heidelberg (2012). https://doi.org/10.1007/978-3-642-30057-8_32

17. Damgård, I., Jurik, M.: A generalisation, a simplification and some applications of Paillier's probabilistic public-key system. In: Kim, K. (ed.) PKC 2001. LNCS, vol. 1992, pp. 119–136. Springer, Heidelberg (2001). https://doi.org/10.1007/3-540-44586-2_9

18. Garg, S., Miles, E., Mukherjee, P., Sahai, A., Srinivasan, A., Zhandry, M.: Secure obfuscation in a weak multilinear map model. In: Hirt, M., Smith, A. (eds.) TCC 2016-B, Part II. LNCS, vol. 9986, pp. 241–268. Springer, Heidelberg (2016). https://doi.org/10.1007/978-3-662-53644-5_10

19. Gay, R., Jain, A., Lin, H., Sahai, A.: Indistinguishability obfuscation from simple-to-state hard problems: new assumptions, new techniques, and simplification. IACR Cryptology ePrint Archive 2020, 764 (2020)

20. Gay, R., Pass, R.: Indistinguishability obfuscation from circular security. In: Proceedings of the 41st Annual ACM Symposium on Theory of Computing, STOC 2021. ACM (2021)

21. Gentry, C.: Fully homomorphic encryption using ideal lattices. In: Mitzenmacher, M. (ed.) 41st ACM STOC, pp. 169–178. ACM Pres, May/Jun 2009. https://doi.org/10.1145/1536414.1536440

22. Gentry, C., Jutla, C.S., Kane, D.: Obfuscation using tensor products. Electron. Colloq. Comput. Complex. **ECCC) 25**, 149 (2018)

23. Gentry, C., Sahai, A., Waters, B.: Homomorphic encryption from learning with errors: conceptually-simpler, asymptotically-faster, attribute-based. In: Canetti, R., Garay, J.A. (eds.) CRYPTO 2013, Part I. LNCS, vol. 8042, pp. 75–92. Springer, Heidelberg (2013). https://doi.org/10.1007/978-3-642-40041-4_5

24. Goldreich, O.: Candidate one-way functions based on expander graphs. Electron. Colloq. Comput. Complex. (ECCC) **7**(90) (2000)

25. Gorbunov, S., Vaikuntanathan, V., Wichs, D.: Leveled fully homomorphic signatures from standard lattices. In: Servedio, R.A., Rubinfeld, R. (eds.) 47th ACM STOC, pp. 469–477. ACM Press, June 2015. https://doi.org/10.1145/2746539.2746576

26. Goyal, R., Koppula, V., Waters, B.: Separating semantic and circular security for symmetric-key bit encryption from the learning with errors assumption. In: Coron, J.-S., Nielsen, J.B. (eds.) EUROCRYPT 2017, Part II. LNCS, vol. 10211, pp. 528–557. Springer, Cham (2017). https://doi.org/10.1007/978-3-319-56614-6_18

27. Green, M., Hohenberger, S.: CPA and CCA-secure encryption systems that are not 2-circular secure. IACR Cryptology ePrint Archive 2010, 144 (2010)

28. Ishai, Y., Prabhakaran, M., Sahai, A.: Secure arithmetic computation with no honest majority. In: Reingold, O. (ed.) TCC 2009. LNCS, vol. 5444, pp. 294–314. Springer, Heidelberg (2009). https://doi.org/10.1007/978-3-642-00457-5_18

29. Jain, A., Lin, H., Matt, C., Sahai, A.: How to leverage hardness of constant-degree expanding polynomials over $\mathbb{R}$ to build $i\mathcal{O}$. In: Ishai, Y., Rijmen, V. (eds.) EUROCRYPT 2019, Part I. LNCS, vol. 11476, pp. 251–281. Springer, Cham (2019). https://doi.org/10.1007/978-3-030-17653-2_9

30. Jain, A., Lin, H., Sahai, A.: Simplifying constructions and assumptions for $i\mathcal{O}$. IACR Cryptology ePrint Archive 2019, 1252 (2019). https://eprint.iacr.org/2019/1252

31. Jain, A., Lin, H., Sahai, A.: Indistinguishability obfuscation from well-founded assumptions. In: Proceedings of the 41st Annual ACM Symposium on Theory of Computing, STOC 2021. ACM (2021)

32. Koppula, V., Ramchen, K., Waters, B.: Separations in circular security for arbitrary length key cycles. In: Dodis, Y., Nielsen, J.B. (eds.) TCC 2015, Part II. LNCS, vol. 9015, pp. 378–400. Springer, Heidelberg (2015). https://doi.org/10.1007/978-3-662-46497-7_15

33. Koppula, V., Waters, B.: Circular security separations for arbitrary length cycles from LWE. In: Robshaw, M., Katz, J. (eds.) CRYPTO 2016, Part II. LNCS, vol. 9815, pp. 681–700. Springer, Heidelberg (2016). https://doi.org/10.1007/978-3-662-53008-5_24

34. Lin, H., Matt, C.: Pseudo flawed-smudging generators and their application to indistinguishability obfuscation. IACR Cryptology ePrint Archive 2018, 646 (2018)

35. Marcedone, A., Orlandi, C.: Obfuscation $\Rightarrow$ (IND-CPA security $\not\Rightarrow$ circular security). In: Abdalla, M., De Prisco, R. (eds.) SCN 2014. LNCS, vol. 8642, pp. 77–90. Springer, Cham (2014). https://doi.org/10.1007/978-3-319-10879-7_5

36. Micciancio, D., Peikert, C.: Trapdoors for lattices: simpler, tighter, faster, smaller. In: Pointcheval, D., Johansson, T. (eds.) EUROCRYPT 2012. LNCS, vol. 7237, pp. 700–718. Springer, Heidelberg (2012). https://doi.org/10.1007/978-3-642-29011-4_41

37. Micciancio, D., Regev, O.: Worst-case to average-case reductions based on Gaussian measures. In: 45th FOCS, pp. 372–381. IEEE Computer Society Press, October 2004. https://doi.org/10.1109/FOCS.2004.72

38. Paillier, P.: Public-key cryptosystems based on composite degree residuosity classes. In: Stern, J. (ed.) EUROCRYPT 1999. LNCS, vol. 1592, pp. 223–238. Springer, Heidelberg (1999). https://doi.org/10.1007/3-540-48910-X_16

39. Peikert, C., Vaikuntanathan, V., Waters, B.: A framework for efficient and composable oblivious transfer. In: Wagner, D. (ed.) CRYPTO 2008. LNCS, vol. 5157, pp. 554–571. Springer, Heidelberg (2008). https://doi.org/10.1007/978-3-540-85174-5_31

40. Regev, O.: On lattices, learning with errors, random linear codes, and cryptography. In: Gabow, H.N., Fagin, R. (eds.) 37th ACM STOC, pp. 84–93. ACM Press, May 2005. https://doi.org/10.1145/1060590.1060603
41. Rothblum, R.D.: On the circular security of bit-encryption. In: Sahai, A. (ed.) TCC 2013. LNCS, vol. 7785, pp. 579–598. Springer, Heidelberg (2013). https://doi.org/10.1007/978-3-642-36594-2_32
42. Wee, H., Wichs, D.: Candidate obfuscation via oblivious LWE sampling. In: Canteaut, A., Standaert, F.-X. (eds.) EUROCRYPT 2021. LNCS, vol. 12698, pp. 127–156. Springer, Cham (2021). https://doi.org/10.1007/978-3-030-77883-5_5
43. Wichs, D., Zirdelis, G.: Obfuscating compute-and-compare programs under LWE. In: Umans, C. (ed.) 58th FOCS, pp. 600–611. IEEE Computer Society Press, October 2017. https://doi.org/10.1109/FOCS.2017.61

How to Meet Ternary LWE Keys

Alexander May[(✉)]

Ruhr-University Bochum, Bochum, Germany
`alex.may@rub.de`

Abstract. The LWE problem with its ring variants is today the most prominent candidate for building efficient public key cryptosystems resistant to quantum computers. NTRU-type cryptosystems use an LWE-type variant with small max-norm secrets, usually with ternary coefficients from the set $\{-1, 0, 1\}$. The presumably best attack on these schemes is a hybrid attack that combines lattice reduction techniques with Odlyzko's Meet-in-the-Middle approach. Odlyzko's algorithm is a classical combinatorial attack that for key space size S runs in time $S^{0.5}$. We substantially improve on this Meet-in-the-Middle approach, using the representation technique developed for subset sum algorithms. Asymptotically, our heuristic Meet-in-the-Middle attack runs in time roughly $S^{0.25}$, which also beats the $S^{\frac{1}{3}}$ complexity of the best known quantum algorithm.

For the round-3 NIST post-quantum encryptions NTRU and NTRU Prime we obtain non-asymptotic instantiations of our attack with complexity roughly $S^{0.3}$. As opposed to other combinatorial attacks, our attack benefits from larger LWE field sizes q, as they are often used in modern lattice-based signatures. For example, for BLISS and GLP signatures we obtain non-asymptotic combinatorial attacks around $S^{0.28}$.

Our attacks do not invalidate the security claims of the aforementioned schemes. However, they establish improved combinatorial upper bounds for their security. We leave it is an open question whether our new Meet-in-the-Middle attack in combination with lattice reduction can be used to speed up the hybrid attack.

Keywords: Meet in the middle · Representation technique · NTRU/BLISS/GLP

1 Introduction

In the LWE problem [Reg03], we are given a (random) matrix $A \in \mathbb{Z}_q^{m \times n}$ and a target vector $\mathbf{b} \in \mathbb{Z}_q^m$ with the promise that there exist small $\mathbf{s} \in \mathbb{Z}_q^n$ and $\mathbf{e} \in \mathbb{Z}_q^m$ such that $A\mathbf{s} = \mathbf{b} + \mathbf{e} \bmod q$. In this paper, we consider only the case $m = n$, i.e. m equals the LWE dimension n, which is the standard setting in modern lattice-based encryption and signature schemes. In the Ring-LWE case [LPR10],

A. May—Funded by DFG under Germany's Excellence Strategy - EXC 2092 CASA - 390781972.

T. Malkin and C. Peikert (Eds.): CRYPTO 2021, LNCS 12826, pp. 701–731, 2021.
https://doi.org/10.1007/978-3-030-84245-1_24

one uses the algebraic structure of rings to compactly represent A. All results in this work also apply to the ring setting, and in fact all of our applications are in the ring setting, but for the sake of LWE generality we do not exploit any ring properties in our analysis.

The LWE problem, and especially its ring variants, are an extremely versatile source for the construction of cryptographic primitives [Reg03, Gen09, GPV08, BDK+17]. Due to its beautiful connection to worst-case lattice problems, one usually calls the resulting schemes lattice-based, although the LWE problem is per se more a combinatorial problem that asks to find a small solution **s** to some erroneous—by error **e**—linear system of equations.

While asymptotically the worst-case connection of LWE to hard lattice problems guarantees security for sufficiently large dimension n, it is still a tricky business to instantiate LWE parameters (n, q) and the error distribution for **e** that lead to practical cryptographic schemes, which yet provide a concrete level of security. LWE security proofs usually utilize a discrete Gaussian distribution for **e** (and often also for **s**). However, certain schemes prove security with Gaussians, and then in turn define especially efficient parameters sets where **s**, **e** are binary or ternary vectors, such as BLISS [DDLL13] or GLP [GLP12]. The NTRU encryption scheme took the other way round, starting with an efficient scheme [HPS98], whose security was later proved for less efficient variants [SS11]. LWE with $\mathbf{s}, \mathbf{e} \in \{0, 1\}^n$ is also known as binary-LWE, and its security has been studied recently [BLP+13, MP13, BG14, BGPW16]. In this paper, we focus on ternary vectors $\mathbf{s}, \mathbf{e} \in \{-1, 0, 1\}^n$, as they are frequently used in modern NTRU-type schemes. Limiting the distribution to vectors of small max-norm 1 (or any small constant) has several advantages for cryptographic schemes.

Efficiency and simplicity. The implementation of discrete Gaussian sampling is quite involved, and costs a reasonable amount of random bits [DN12]. Proper randomness is in practice often a scarce source. Instead, sampling ternary vectors is comparably simple and much less error-prone to implement. Moreover, the resulting keys are especially compact.

Correctness of decryption. The use of ternary vectors allows to define encryption schemes that always decrypt correctly. Among the remaining lattice-based encryption schemes in NIST competition's third round there are only two schemes, both NTRU variants with ternary secrets, that do not have decryption failure. This property is particularly important, since even smallish decryption failures give rise to powerful attacks [HNP+03, DRV20].

As a consequence, designers of recent cryptosystems often replace Gaussian error distributions by small max-norm secrets (still guarding against lattice attacks), with the argument that despite of 25 years NTRU-type cryptanalysis there is no combinatorial algorithm better than Odlyzko's Meet-in-the-Middle (MitM) attack—mentioned in the original 1996 NTRU paper [HPS98]—that can directly take advantage of small max-norm keys, such as ternary keys. Our work invalidates this argument. Our new MitM attack for ternary secrets heavily uses the small max-norm property and significantly improves over Odlyzko's algorithm.

The development of more involved combinatorial LWE MitM search algorithms usually directly influences the parameter choice of NTRU-type cryptosystems, since the presumably best known attack on these schemes—Howgrave-Graham's *Hybrid* approach [How07]—is up to now a combination of Odlyzko's MitM attack on a projected sub-key and lattice reduction on a projected sub-lattice. The Hybrid attack balances the cost of MitM and lattice reduction by properly adjusting the dimensions of these projections.

On the one hand, there is a long line of research that decreased the complexity of lattice reduction [NV08, Laa15, BDGL16, HKL18], using involved techniques. On the other hand, for the combinatorial part there is still only the comparatively simple and costly Odlyzko MitM with square root complexity of the search space. The best quantum attack is a quantum version of Odlyzko's MitM that achieves third root complexity of the search space [WMM13, dBDJW18]. This complexity imbalance currently puts large emphasis on lattice reduction in the Hybrid attack.

On the theoretical side, we cannot expect to fully break LWE with ternary keys. In 2013, Brakerski, Langlois, Peikert, Regev, Stehlé [BLP+13] and Micciancio, Peikert [MP13] provide reductions showing that LWE with binary or ternary secrets is indeed still hard. However, these reductions require to increase the LWE dimension from n to approximately $n \log q$. Our new MitM approach gives cryptanalytic indication that small norm secrets are indeed significantly easier to recover.

We would like to point out that other known algebraic/combinatorial attacks [GJS15, KF15, ACF+14] do not work in our scenario due to the limited number of samples $m = n$, or because they require superpolynomial q.

Our Results. We give the first significant progress for MitM attacks on ternary LWE keys since Odlyzko's attack from 1996 [HPS98, HGSW03]. Let the LWE secret key $\mathbf{s} \in \mathbb{Z}_q^n$ be taken from an exponential (in n) search space size $\mathcal{S}$. Then Odlyzko's attack recovers $\mathbf{s}$ in time $\mathcal{S}^{0.5}$. E.g. random ternary secrets $\mathbf{s} \in \{-1, 0, 1\}^n$ have $\mathcal{S} = 3^n$ and Odlyzko's attack runs in time $3^{n/2} = 2^{\log_2(3)n/2}$. A quantum version of Odlyzko's attack runs in time $\mathcal{S}^{\frac{1}{3}}$ [WMM13, dBDJW18].

Other attacks [MS01, Ngu21] use the structure of the public LWE key A in the ring setting, but these speedups are polynomial in n and thus lead to run time $\mathcal{S}^{0.5-o(1)}$. We show that the exponent 0.5 can be significantly reduced for small max-norm keys $\mathbf{s}$ and $\mathbf{e}$ in the supposedly hard LWE case where q is polynomial in n. Notice that for larger q efficient attacks are known [ABD16].

In a nutshell, our algorithm guesses r coordinates of $\mathbf{e} \in \mathbb{Z}_q$, where $r = \mathcal{O}(\frac{n}{\log q}) = \mathcal{O}(\frac{n}{\log n})$ is slightly sub-linear in the LWE dimension n. This can be done in slightly subexponential time $2^{\mathcal{O}(\frac{n}{\log q})}$. We then solve a vectorial subset sum problem $A\mathbf{s} = \mathbf{b} + \mathbf{e}$ on the known r coordinates. This is done by generalizing search tree-based subset sum algorithms [HJ10, BCJ11, BBSS20] to our setting, where the columns of A define the subset sum instance with target vector $\mathbf{b}$, and the max-norm of $\mathbf{s}$ defines which linear combinations are allowed.

In the original subset sum setting, we are allowed to take $0/1$-combinations, whereas for ternary s we have to take $0/\pm 1$ combinations. Intuitively, although a larger digit set for the linear combinations increases the combinatorial complexity, it might at the time weaken subset sum instances, since it introduces symmetries. The latter effect can be seen in our results. Our subset sum instances on r coordinates can be solved more efficiently than the original $0/1$-instances from [HJ10, BCJ11, BBSS20], despite the fact that—as opposed to the subset sum setting—we also have to take the complexity of guessing r coordinates of e into account.

Eventually, our subset sum-type algorithm outputs two (sorted) lists of size $\mathcal{S}^c$, $c < 0.5$ from which the secret s can be recovered in time linear in the list size by using Odlyzko's algorithm on the remaining $n - r$ coordinates.

We give different instantiations of our algorithm using different representations of $s = s_1 + s_2$ as a sum of two vectors $s_1, s_2 \in \mathbb{Z}_q^n$. The more representations we have of s, the larger is the number r of guessed coordinates, and the smaller gets c. Intuitively, choosing larger r in this tradeoff pays off, since key guessing is slightly subexponential, whereas $\mathcal{S}$ is fully exponentially in n.

This bias in the tradeoff can be seen in the instantiations of our MitM. We choose three different instantiations—called REP-0, REP-1, REP-2—with an increasing number of representations. More representations yield smaller list sizes and therefore complexities $\mathcal{S}^c$ with smaller c. For REP-0, REP-1 and REP-2 we optimize the search trees in our subset sum-type list construction to find a minimal c, while using relatively small search tree depths 3 or 4.

We also show that, despite the key guessing, our MitM leads to significantly improved non-asymptotic combinatorial attacks. As running example, we consider the current NIST round-3 candidate encryption schemes NTRU [CDH+19] and NTRU Prime [BCLvV17, BCLvV], which both have ternary secrets s, e. As examples for signature schemes, we address the efficient GLP version [GLP12] of Lyubashevksy's scheme [Lyu12] and BLISS [DDLL13], both using ternary secrets. For BLISS we also analyze an instance with secret $s \in \{-2, -1, 0, 1, 2\}^n$.

For these schemes, we illustrate the effects of our new MitM LWE key search, instantiated with REP-0 to REP-2. We compute the list sizes and therefore complexities *non-asymptotically* exact, but for ease of exposition throughout the paper we ignore polynomial factors that stem from list operations like sorting or hashing. These polynomial factors usually increase the run time, but tricks like using rotations in ring-LWE might also decrease our complexities by other polynomial factors.

Our non-asymptotic analysis nicely illustrates the tradeoff between guessing r coordinates and decreasing the complexity of the subset sum-type list constructions. See Table 1 for a numerical example.

Table 1. Illustration of our non-asymptotic improvements.

(n, q, w)	Odlyzko[bit]	REP-0 [bit]	REP-1 [bit]	REP-2 [bit]
NTRU (821,4096,510)	643	**520** = 487+33	**393** = 334+59	**378** = 318+60

The largest of the three proposed NTRU parameter sets is $(n, q) = (821, 4096)$, where the ternary secret has exactly 255 1-coordinates and 255 (-1)-coordinates. This gives search space size $\mathcal{S} = \binom{821}{255,255,311} \approx 2^{1286}$. Thus, we obtain $\mathcal{S}^{0.5} \approx 2^{643}$, or 643 bit, complexity for Odlyzko's attack.

Using REP-0, we decrease to 520 bit, where we require 487 bit for the subset sum-type list construction and 33 bit for key guessing. Using REP-1, we further decrease to 393 bit, using 334 bit for list construction and 59 bit for guessing. Eventually using REP-2, we even further decrease to 378 bit, using only 318 bit for list construction and 60 bit for guessing.

In total, our new purely combinatorial MitM on parameter set $(821, 4096)$ has complexity $2^{378} \approx \mathcal{S}^{0.29}$—with list construction time $2^{318} \approx \mathcal{S}^{0.25}$—instead of Odlyzko's $2^{643} \approx \mathcal{S}^{\frac{1}{2}}$. For all six officially proposed instances of NTRU and NTRU Prime we obtain complexity roughly $\mathcal{S}^{0.3}$. For BLISS signatures we obtain complexities between $\mathcal{S}^{0.28}$ and $\mathcal{S}^{0.3}$, and for GLP signatures complexity $\mathcal{S}^{0.28}$. The reason for these improved complexities is that lattice-based signatures (as opposed to encryption schemes) typically use larger q, from which our LWE MitM key search algorithm benefits.

The memory requirement of our attack is roughly $\mathcal{S}^{0.25}$, asymptotically and non-asymptotically, as compared to $\mathcal{S}^{0.5}$ for Odlyzko's attack. However, we show that our techniques also lead to time-memory tradeoffs that improve over the best known time-memory tradeoff for Odlyzko's attack by van Vredendaal [vV16].

Table 2. Comparison of our MitM (non-asymptotic REP-2) with lattice estimate [APS15]

(n, q, w)	REP-2[bit]	lattice [bit]
NTRU-Encypt		
(509,2048,254)	227	123
(677,2048,254)	273	162
(821,4096,510)	378	196
NTRU Prime		
(653,4621,288)	272	145
(761,4591,286)	301	168
(857,5167,322)	338	189
NTRU ees659ep1		
(659,2048,98)	176	115
BLISS		
I+II:(512,12289,154)	187	103
IV:(512,12289,230,30)	246	104
GLP I		
(512,8383489,342)	225	58

Although our MitM performs much better than the best known combinatorial attack, our results do not invalidate the security claims of current LWE-type systems like NTRU, BLISS and GLP. In comparison to the current best lattice estimates ([APS15] using Core-SVP $2^{0.292\beta+16.4}$), our results so far cannot compete, see Table 2. For modern schemes like NTRU, NTRU Prime and BLISS our attack complexities are almost the square of the estimated lattice complexities. However, for the NTRU standard ees659ep1 [ntr08] with its small weight $w = 98$ we achieve a purely classical MitM using complexity only 2^{157} for list construction and additionally 2^{19} for key guessing. This is not too far off from the current 115-bit lattice estimate. Thus, our attack shows its strength in the small error regime, as one would expect from a combinatorial attack.

We also consider it important to establish new solid combinatorial upper bounds on the security of small key LWE-type schemes. Up to now, the LWE parameter selection is solely based on lattice reduction estimates which involve not only a good amount of heuristics like e.g. the Gaussian Heuristic and the Geometric Series Assumption, but also a variety of run time formulas for estimating BKZ lattice reduction. Our impression is that (for good reasons) the security of current LWE type schemes is rather underestimated by current lattice complexity estimates.

In contrast, our MitM uses only very mild heuristic assumptions from subset sum-type list constructions that have already been thoroughly experimentally verified in other settings [BCJ11,BJMM12], and our run time analysis can be considered quite accurate.

The major open problem that arises from our work is whether our MitM attack can be used to speed up the lattice hybrid attack by the amount that we improve over Odlyzko's MitM. We discuss potential directions in Sect. 10.

Organization of our paper. We recall known MitM attacks from Odlyzko (Sect. 3) and Howgrave-Graham (Sect. 4, not to be confused with Hybrid). These two MitMs are sometimes mixed in the literature, although they are algorithmically different. We show that Howgrave-Graham's method is strictly inferior, but it can be used as the basis for our improved LWE MitM key search algorithm MEET-LWE in Sect. 5. We instantiate MEET-LWE with different representations REP-0 (Sect. 6), REP-1 (Sect. 7) and REP-2 (Sect. 8). Some improved time-memory tradeoffs are given in Sect. 9. In Sect. 10, we discuss why MEET-LWE fails to be directly applicable to Howgrave-Graham's lattice Hybrid attack, and discuss possible work-arounds.

2   Preliminaries

2.1   LWE-Key and Max-Norm Key Search

Definition 1 (Small Max-Norm LWE Secret Key). *An LWE public key is a tuple* $(A, \mathbf{b}) \in \mathbb{Z}_q^{m \times n}$ *satisfying the identity*

$$A\mathbf{s} = \mathbf{b} + \mathbf{e} \bmod q$$

for some secret vectors $\mathbf{s} \in \mathbb{Z}_q^n$ *and* $\mathbf{e} \in \mathbb{Z}_q^m$. *We call* $\mathbf{s}, \mathbf{e}$ small max-norm LWE secret keys *if* $\|\mathbf{s}\|_\infty = \|\mathbf{e}\|_\infty = \mathcal{O}(1)$. *We call max-norm 1 vectors* ternary. *We denote the set of* n-*dimensional ternary vectors by* $\mathcal{T}^n = \mathbb{Z}_q^n \cap \{-1, 0, 1\}^n$.

All small max-norm LWE keys allow for simple checking of key guess correctness. Namely, with overwhelming probability (over the randomness of A) there is a unique $\mathbf{s}$ such that $A\mathbf{s} - \mathbf{b}$ has small max-norm. Throughout the paper, we use square $A \in \mathbb{Z}_q^{n \times n}$, and assume that A's entries are uniformly at random from $\mathbb{Z}_q$. For Ring-LWE type cryptosystems the entries are in fact dependent, but we do not make use of any ring structure.

If not specified otherwise we use **ternary LWE keys**, since almost all prominent running examples of NTRU-type cryptosystems in this paper—NTRU [CDH+19], NTRU Prime [BCLvV], BLISS [DDLL13] and GLP [GLP12]—use coefficients in $\{-1, 0, 1\}$. We also analyze a max-norm 2 BLISS example in Sect. 8.3. In principle, our technique applies to any max-norm, but we consider our algorithms most effective for very small max-norms like 1 and 2. Moreover, our technique is currently harder to analyze with increasing max-norm.

Most NTRU-type systems such as the above examples do not only use *small max-norm keys*, but they also restrict the number of non-zero entries.

Definition 2 (Weight). *Let* $\mathbf{s} = (s_1, \dots, s_n) \in \mathbb{F}_q^n$. *Then the* weight w *of* $\mathbf{s}$ *is defined as its Hamming weight* $w := \sum_{s_i \neq 0} 1$. *We often specify the weight relative to* n *as* $w = \omega n$ *for some* $0 \leq \omega \leq 1$. *We denote the set of* n-*dimensional ternary weight-*w *vectors that split their weight evenly in* $w/2$ (-1)-*entries and* 1-*entries by*

$$\mathcal{T}^n(w/2) = \{\mathbf{s} \in \mathcal{T}^n \mid \mathbf{s} \text{ has } w/2 \ (\pm 1) -\text{entries each.}\}$$

For notational convenience we omit any roundings. Asymptotically, roundings can be neglected. For real-world security estimates we round appropriately.

NTRU's security analysis so far yields an optimal relative weight in the range $\omega \in [\frac{1}{3}, \frac{2}{3}]$ [CDH+19, BCLvV]. A prominent choice is $\omega = \frac{3}{8}$, which is used in one (out of three) suggested NTRU parameter sets with dimension $n = 677$ and in two (out of three) suggested NTRU Prime parameter sets with $n = 761$ and $n = 857$. Throughout the paper when we speak of NTRU instances, we address parameter sets of the HPS variant, but in principle our attack also applies to HRSS, see [CDH+19]. Similar, with NTRU Prime we address the Streamlined NTRU variant, but our attack also works for NTRU LPRime, see [BCLvV].

2.2 Search Space, Entropy and Representations

Obviously, there are 3^n ternary vectors $\mathbf{s} \in \mathcal{T}^n$. When using asymptotics (and only in this case!), we frequently approximate sets of vectors with a fixed number of certain coefficients by the following well-known Shannon entropy formula that stems from Stirling's approximation [MU17].

Lemma 1 (Multinomial approximation). *Let* $D = \{d_1, \ldots, d_k\} \subset \mathbb{Z}_q$ *be a digit set of cardinality* k. *The number of vectors* $\mathbf{s} \in \mathbb{Z}_q^n \cap D^n$ *having exactly* $c_i n$ *many* d_i*-entries,* $\sum_{i=1}^n c_i = 1$, *is*

$$\binom{n}{c_1 n, \ldots, c_k n} \approx 2^{H(c_1, \ldots, c_k)n}, \text{ with entropy } H(c_1, \ldots, c_k) = \sum_{i=1}^k c_i \log_2\left(\frac{1}{c_i}\right).$$

Notice that Lemma 1 approximates the number of ternary vectors having exactly $n/3$ coefficients for each of $-1, 0, 1$ as

$$2^{H(\frac{1}{3}, \frac{1}{3}, \frac{1}{3})n} = 2^{3 \cdot \frac{1}{3} \log_2(3)n} = 3^n.$$

The straight-forward proof of Lemma 1 via Stirling approximation shows that the approximation suppresses for the above setting a $\frac{1}{n}$-factor, which implies that a $\frac{1}{n}$-fraction of all ternary vectors splits its coefficients evenly among the entries $-1, 0, 1$. In our notation, $\mathcal{T}^n(n/3)$ is up to a (small) polynomial factor as large as $\mathcal{T}^n$.

For ease of notation, in the following we always assume that we search for ternary keys with a predefined portion of entries. This is true e.g. for NTRU, GLP and BLISS. However, we can easily generalize our attack to systems with arbitrary portions of entries, such as NTRU Prime, by simply guessing each portion. Since we only consider constant max-norm, such a guessing costs only an $n^{\mathcal{O}(1)}$-factor.

2.3 Asymptotics and Real-World Applications

Although our NTRU-applications in mind require real-world security estimates, we usually start our analysis with asymptotic notion, before giving non-asymptotics for concrete instances. Asymptotics often allows for much cleaner results, clearly indicating the dependence on the involved LWE parameters (n, q, w). In the asymptotic setting, we suppress all polynomial factors. For exponential run times, we simply round the run time exponent upwards, e.g. $n^2 \cdot 2^{n/3}$ is upper bounded as $2^{0.334n}$.

All modern NTRU-type cryptosystems require $q = \Omega(n)$, encryption schemes have such a lower bound to eliminate decryption errors. E.g. NTRU Prime restricts the weight $w \geq \frac{1}{3}n$ and chooses $q \geq 16w + 1$, and NTRU recommends only parameter sets $q \in [\frac{8}{3}n, \frac{16}{3}n]$. Restricting $q = \mathcal{O}(n)$ is used to obtain small ciphertexts/signatures.

3 Odlyzko's Meet-in-the-Middle Algorithm

Odlyzko's attack was originally designed for binary vectors, but the following generalization to ternary (or even small max-norm) vectors is straight-forward.

In the following, we use the short-hand multinomial notion $\binom{n}{a_1, \ldots, a_k, \cdot}$, where $\cdot$ stands for the missing argument $n - a_1 - \ldots - a_k$. Analogous, we use the entropy notion $H(c_1, \ldots, c_k, \cdot)$, where $\cdot$ represents the missing arguments $1 - c_1 - \ldots - c_k$.

Let the search space consist of all ternary weight-w vectors $\mathbf{s} \in \mathcal{T}^n(w/2)$ with even number $w/2$ of ± 1. By Lemma 1, the search space size $\mathcal{S}$ can be approximated as

$$\mathcal{S} = \binom{n}{\frac{w}{2}, \frac{w}{2}, \cdot} \approx 2^{H(\frac{w}{2}, \frac{w}{2}, \cdot)n}.$$

We split $\mathbf{s} = (\mathbf{s}_1, \mathbf{s}_2) \in \mathcal{T}^{n/2}(w/4) \times \mathcal{T}^{n/2}(w/4)$ in ternary weight-$w/2$ vectors $\mathbf{s}_1, \mathbf{s}_2$ with again an even split of ± 1. Notice that we may rerandomize the positions of (± 1)-entries in $\mathbf{s}$ via permutation of A's columns. The probability that a rerandomized $\mathbf{s}$ has the desired weight distribution split can be estimated via Lemma 1 as

$$\frac{\left(\binom{\frac{n}{2}}{\frac{w}{4}, \frac{w}{4}, \cdot}\right)^2}{\binom{n}{\frac{w}{2}, \frac{w}{2}, \cdot}} \approx 2^{2H(\frac{w}{2}, \frac{w}{2}, \cdot)\frac{n}{2} - H(\frac{w}{2}, \frac{w}{2}, \cdot)n} = 1.$$

Since $\approx$ suppresses polynomial factors, our probability is more precisely $1/\text{poly}(n)$. Thus via permutation of A's columns we always achieve the desired distribution after $\text{poly}(n)$ iterations. Therefore, without loss of generality we always assume throughout this paper that we can evenly split all coefficients of our secrets (up to minor rounding issues).

Let $A = (A_1 | A_2) \in \mathbb{Z}_q^{n \times n}$, where A_1 (respectively A_2) denote the left (respectively right) $n/2$ columns of A. From Definition 1 we obtain the identity $A_1 \mathbf{s}_1 = \mathbf{b} - A_2 \mathbf{s}_2 + \mathbf{e} \bmod q$. Thus, the terms $A_1 \mathbf{s}_1$ and $\mathbf{b} - A_2 \mathbf{s}_2$ differ by at most ± 1. We may rewrite this as

$$A_1 \mathbf{s}_1 + \mathbf{e}_1 = \mathbf{b} - A_2 \mathbf{s}_2 + \mathbf{e}_2 \bmod q \text{ where } \mathbf{e}_1, \mathbf{e}_2 \in \{0, 1\}^n. \tag{1}$$

Since we do not know the error vectors $\mathbf{e}_1, \mathbf{e}_2$, Odlyzko proposed a simple locality sensitive hashing approach. We assign to each $\mathbf{x} = (x_1, \ldots, x_n) \in \mathbb{Z}_q^n$ coordinate-wise the following binary hash labels $\ell(\mathbf{x})_i$ that can be interpreted as most significant bits of the x_i

$$\ell : \mathbb{Z}_q^n \to \{0, 1\}^n \text{ with } \ell(\mathbf{x})_i = \begin{cases} 0 & \text{if } 0 \leq x_i < \lfloor q/2 \rfloor - 1 \\ 1 & \text{if } \lfloor q/2 \rfloor \leq x_i < q - 1 \end{cases}. \tag{2}$$

For any candidates $\mathbf{s}_1, \mathbf{s}_2$ we hash $A_1 \mathbf{s}_1$ and $\mathbf{b} - A_2 \mathbf{s}_2$. Notice that for the two *border values* $\lfloor q/2 \rfloor - 1$ and $q - 1$ the error vectors $\mathbf{e}_1, \mathbf{e}_2$ may result in a flip of the hash value. Therefore, we assign for these entries both labels 0 and 1.

Example: Let $q = 4096$. Then the vector $\mathbf{x} = (0, 2047, 3000, 4095)$ with border values $2047, 4095$ in positions $2, 4$ gets assigned all four labels from the set $\{0\} \times \{0, 1\} \times \{1\} \times \{0, 1\}$.

For all elements we store their labels (sorted). Let X be a random variable for the number of border values for each entry. Then every entry is stored in 2^X places. Since $\mathbb{E}[X] = \frac{2}{q}n = \Theta(1)$, every element occupies only linear space.

Odlyzko's MitM algorithm is given in Algorithm 1, complexities for our addressed cryptosystems can be found in Table 3.

3.1   Correctness

By definition of the hash function ℓ every candidate tuple $(\mathbf{s}_1, \mathbf{s}_2)$ that satisfies Eq. (1) for some binary $\mathbf{e}_1, \mathbf{e}_2 \in \{0,1\}^n$ leads to colliding labels $\ell(A_1 \mathbf{s}_1) = \ell(\mathbf{b} - A_2 \mathbf{s}_2)$.

Algorithm 1. Odlyzko's Meet-in-the-Middle

Require: LWE public key $(A, \mathbf{b}) \in \mathbb{Z}_q^{n \times n} \times \mathbb{Z}_q^m$, weight $w \in \mathbb{N}$
Ensure: $\mathbf{s} \in \mathcal{T}^n(w/2)$ satisfying $\mathbf{e} := A\mathbf{s} - \mathbf{b} \bmod q \in \mathcal{T}^n$
1: **for all** $\mathbf{s}_1 \in \mathcal{T}^{n/2}(w/4)$ **do**
2:     Store $(\mathbf{s}_1, \ell(A_1 \mathbf{s}_1))$ in list L_1.
3: **for all** $\mathbf{s}_2 \in \mathcal{T}^{n/2}(w/4)$ **do**
4:     Store $(\mathbf{s}_2, \ell(\mathbf{b} - A_2 \mathbf{s}_2))$ in list L_2.
5: **for all** matches of $(\mathbf{s}_1, \cdot)$ and $(\mathbf{s}_2, \cdot)$ in the second component of $L_1 \times L_2$ **do**
6:     **if** $A(\mathbf{s}_1, \mathbf{s}_2) - \mathbf{b} \bmod q \in \mathcal{T}^n$ **then return** $\mathbf{s} = (\mathbf{s}_1, \mathbf{s}_2)$

Table 3. Odlyzko's MitM complexity.

	(n, q, w)	$\mathcal{S}$	Odlyzko
NTRU	(509,2048,254)	754 bit	377 bit
	(677,2048,254)	891 bit	445 bit
	(821,4096,510)	1286 bit	643 bit
NTRU Prime	(653,4621,288)	925 bit	463 bit
	(761,4591,286)	1003 bit	502 bit
	(857,5167,322)	1131 bit	566 bit
BLISS I+II	(512,12289,154)	597 bit	299 bit
GLP I	(512,8383489,342)	802 bit	401 bit

Contrary, let $(\mathbf{s}_1, \mathbf{s}_2)$ be a candidate tuple that does not satisfy Eq. (1) for some binary $\mathbf{e}_1, \mathbf{e}_2 \in \{0,1\}^n$. By A's randomness we have colliding labels $\ell(A_1 \mathbf{s}_1) = \ell(\mathbf{b} - A_2 \mathbf{s}_2)$ with probability only (roughly) 2^{-n}.

Notice that Odlyzko's locality sensitive hashing makes use of a large field size q to separate wrong candidates $(\mathbf{s}_1, \mathbf{s}_2)$ from the unique correct solution.

3.2   Runtime

Runtime and memory consumption of Algorithm 1 is dominated by the list sizes

$$|L_1| = |L_2| = \binom{\frac{n}{2}}{\frac{w}{4}, \frac{w}{4}, \cdot} \approx 2^{H(\frac{w}{2}, \frac{w}{2}, \cdot)\frac{n}{2}} = \sqrt{\mathcal{S}}. \tag{3}$$

Notice that in line 5 of Algorithm 1 we expect $2^{-n} \cdot |L_1| \cdot |L_2|$ matches, which is larger than $|L_1|, |L_2|$, if $|L_1|, |L_2|$ are larger than 2^n. In this case, we may modify Odlyzko's hash function such that its range gets greater than the list sizes (by assigning more than two labels, see also Sect. 9).

4 Howgrave-Graham's MitM Algorithm

There is a second Meet-in-the-Middle attack that was first analyzed in [HGSW03]. Howgrave-Graham described it in [How07] as Odlyzko's MitM, which let people mix (and confuse) both approaches in the literature.

We briefly discuss this second MitM, which we attribute to Howgrave-Graham. We show that it performs worse than Odlyzko's MitM for ternary vectors for every weight w. However, Howgrave-Graham's method is a first step to our new MitM, since both approaches are based on ambiguous sum representations, also known as the *representation technique*.

Whereas Odlyzko splits $s = (s_1, s_2)$ *uniquely* as $n/2$-dimensional s_i, Howgrave-Graham represents $s \in \mathcal{T}^n(w/2)$ *ambiguously* as $s_1 + s_2$ with n-dimensional $s_i \in \mathcal{T}^n(w/4)$. As a consequence, the search space for the s_i is of increased size

$$\mathcal{S}^{(1)} = \binom{n}{\frac{w}{4}, \frac{w}{4}, \cdot}, \tag{4}$$

as compared to $\binom{\frac{n}{2}}{\frac{w}{4}, \frac{w}{4}, \cdot}$ from (3) in Odlyzko's MitM. But the ambiguity also introduces $R^{(1)} = \binom{w/2}{w/4} \cdot \binom{w/2}{w/4}$ representations of the desired solution s, since each of the $w/2$ 1-coordinates in s can be represented as $1 + 0$ or $0 + 1$, and analogous for the $w/2$ (-1)-coordinates.

Note that our MitM identity from Equation (1) now becomes $As_1 + e_1 = b - As_2 + e_2$. We describe Howgrave-Graham's approach in Algorithm 2. Its correctness follows analogous to Sect. 3.1.

Algorithm 2. Howgrave-Graham's Meet-in-the-Middle

Require: LWE public key $(A, b) \in \mathbb{Z}_q^{n \times n} \times \mathbb{Z}_q^m$, weight $w \in \mathbb{N}$
Ensure: $s \in \mathcal{T}^n(w/2)$ satisfying $e := As - b \bmod q \in \mathcal{T}^n$
1: **repeat**
2:    Sample some $s_1 \in \mathcal{T}^n(w/4)$. Store $(s_1, \ell(A_1 s_1))$ in list L_1.
3:    Sample some $s_2 \in \mathcal{T}^n(w/4)$. Store $(s_2, \ell(b - A_2 s_2))$ in list L_2.
4: **until** there exists a match $(s_1, \cdot)$, $(s_2, \cdot)$ in 2nd component of $L_1 \times L_2$ with $s_1 + s_2 \in \mathcal{T}^n$
5: **if** $A(s_1 + s_2) - b \bmod q \in \mathcal{T}^n$ **then return** $s = (s_1 + s_2)$

Run Time. In each iteration of the **repeat**-loop we hit a vector s_1 or s_2 that is part of a representation (s_1, s_2) of s with probability $p = \frac{R^{(1)}}{\mathcal{S}^{(1)}}$. After $\sqrt{R^{(1)}}$ hits, by the birthday paradox we expect to have both parts s_1, s_2 of a representation in L_1, L_2. Thus the expected number of iterations in Algorithm 2 is

$$p^{-1} \cdot \sqrt{R^{(1)}} = \frac{\mathcal{S}^{(1)}}{R^{(1)}} \cdot \sqrt{R^{(1)}} = \binom{n}{\frac{w}{4}, \frac{w}{4}, \cdot} \cdot \binom{\frac{w}{2}}{\frac{w}{4}}^{-1} \approx 2^{(H(\frac{w}{4}, \frac{w}{4}, \cdot) - \frac{w}{2})n}.$$

We see in Fig. 1 that the run time exponent $H(\frac{\omega}{4}, \frac{\omega}{4}, \cdot) - \frac{\omega}{2}$ is larger than Odlyzko's run time exponent $\frac{1}{2}H(\frac{\omega}{2}, \frac{\omega}{2}, \cdot)$ for every $\omega \in [\frac{1}{3}, \frac{2}{3}]$ (in fact this holds for all $0 \leq \omega \leq 1$). E.g. for the prominent NTRU setting $\omega = \frac{3}{8}$ we obtain exponents 0.697 versus 0.665. Hence, one should always prefer Odlyzko's algorithm for ternary secrets.

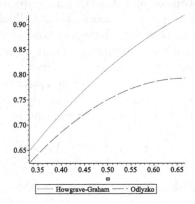

Fig. 1. Run Time Comparison Odlyzko vs Howgrave-Graham

Intuitively, in a subset sum-type approach of the representation technique as in [HJ10], one would try to construct two lists L_1, L_2 with entries $(\mathbf{s}_1, \ell(A\mathbf{s}_1))$, $(\mathbf{s}_2, \ell(\mathbf{b} - A\mathbf{s}_2))$ recursively such that on expectation $L_1 \times L_2$ contains a single representation. However, the non-linearity of Odlyzko's hash function ℓ hinders such a direct recursive application of the representation technique. We solve this technical issue in the following section.

5   Our New MitM Algorithm – High Level Idea

Let us first state our new LWE key search algorithm MEET-LWE in a high-level manner, for an illustration see Fig. 2. Moreover, we introduce some more scalable notation that will prove useful in subsequent sections. For ease of exposition, we again focus on ternary secret LWE keys $\mathbf{s}, \mathbf{e} \in T^n$.

As in Sect. 4, we represent a weight-w ternary $\mathbf{s} \in T^n$ as a sum $\mathbf{s}_1 + \mathbf{s}_2$ of n-dimensional $\mathbf{s}_1, \mathbf{s}_2$ in $R^{(1)}$ ways. Here, $\mathbf{s}_1, \mathbf{s}_2$ may be ternary weight-$w/2$ vectors (Sect. 6), ternary vectors with weight larger than $w/2$ (Sect. 7), or even non-ternary vectors (Sect. 8). As a rule of thumb, the larger the search space for $\mathbf{s}_1, \mathbf{s}_2$, the larger also the number of representations $R^{(1)}$.

Let us start with the LWE identity $A\mathbf{s}_1 = \mathbf{b} - A\mathbf{s}_2 + \mathbf{e}$ for some ternary $\mathbf{e} \in \{0, 1\}^n$. Define $\mathbf{e}_1 \in T^{n/2} \times 0^{n/2}$ and $\mathbf{e}_2 \in 0^{n/2} \times T^{n/2}$ such that $\mathbf{e} = \mathbf{e}_2 - \mathbf{e}_1$. Then we obtain

$$A\mathbf{s}_1 + \mathbf{e}_1 = \mathbf{b} - A\mathbf{s}_2 + \mathbf{e}_2 \text{ with } \mathbf{e}_1 \in T^{n/2} \times 0^{n/2}, \mathbf{e}_2 \in 0^{n/2} \times T^{n/2}. \quad (5)$$

Thus, we split $\mathbf{e}$ in a typical MitM fashion into $\mathbf{e}_1, \mathbf{e}_2$.

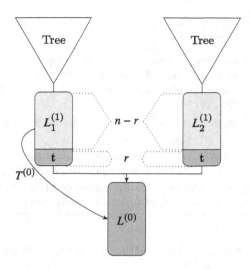

Fig. 2. MEET-LWE high level structure

Assume for a moment that we know the error vector $\mathbf{e}$, and thus $\mathbf{e}_1, \mathbf{e}_2$. Let $r = \lfloor \log_q R^{(1)} \rfloor$, and fix a randomly chosen target vector $\mathbf{t} \in \mathbb{Z}_q^r$. Moreover, let us define the projection π_r on the first r coordinates as

$$\pi_r : \mathbb{Z}_q^n \to \mathbb{Z}_q^r, \ \mathbf{x} = (x_1, \ldots, x_n) \mapsto (x_1, \ldots, x_r), \tag{6}$$

which is a ring homomorphism (as opposed to Odlyzko's hash function).

Notice that the range $\mathbb{Z}_q^r$ of π_r has size $q^r < q^{\log_q R^{(1)}} - R^{(1)}$. Therefore, we expect that for at least one out of the $R^{(1)}$ representations $(\mathbf{s}_1, \mathbf{s}_2)$ of $\mathbf{s}$ its projection via π_r matches the random target $\mathbf{t}$, i.e.

$$\pi_r(A\mathbf{s}_1 + \mathbf{e}_1) = \mathbf{t} \bmod q.$$

By Eq. (5) and π_r's ring homomorphism property, this automatically implies the second identity $\pi_r(\mathbf{b} - A\mathbf{s}_2 + \mathbf{e}_2) = \mathbf{t} \bmod q$, as well. Let us stress that for checking both identities it suffices to only know the first r coordinates $\pi_r(\mathbf{e})$ of $\mathbf{e}$. As in Eq. (5), we may split $\pi_r(\mathbf{e}) = \pi_r(\mathbf{e}_2) - \pi_r(\mathbf{e}_1)$.

Let $\ell : \mathbb{F}_q^n \to \{0, 1\}^n$ be Odlyzko's hash function from Eq. (2). Our goal is to construct lists $L_1^{(1)}, L_2^{(1)}$ (see also Fig. 2) satisfying

$$L_1^{(1)} = \{(\mathbf{s}_1, \ell(A\mathbf{s}_1)) \mid \pi_r(A\mathbf{s}_1 + \mathbf{e}_1) = \mathbf{t} \bmod q\},$$

$$L_2^{(1)} = \{(\mathbf{s}_2, \ell(\mathbf{b} - A\mathbf{s}_2)) \mid \pi_r(\mathbf{b} - A\mathbf{s}_2 + \mathbf{e}_2) = \mathbf{t} \bmod q\}. \tag{7}$$

Our resulting LWE MitM key search is given in Algorithm 3, called MEET-LWE.

5.1   Correctness

In a nutshell, MEET-LWE (Algorithm 3) constructs an $\mathbf{s}$ that fulfills $A\mathbf{s} = \mathbf{b} + \mathbf{e}$ on r coordinates exactly, and on the remaining $n - r$ coordinates approximately

---

Algorithm 3. LWE Key Search MEET-LWE (High-Level)

Require: LWE key $(A, \mathbf{b}) \in \mathbb{Z}_q^{n \times n} \times \mathbb{Z}_q^n$, weight $w \in \mathbb{N}$
Ensure: ternary weight-w $\mathbf{s}$ satisfying $\mathbf{e} = A\mathbf{s} - \mathbf{b} \bmod q \in \mathcal{T}^n$
  1: We represent $\mathbf{s} = \mathbf{s}_1 + \mathbf{s}_2$ using different vector sets for $\mathbf{s}_1, \mathbf{s}_2$ (see Sect. 6 and 8).
     Let $R^{(1)}$ be the resulting number of representations. Let $r = \lfloor \log_q(R^{(1)}) \rfloor$.
  2: **for all** $\pi_r(\mathbf{e}_1) \in \mathcal{T}^{r/2} \times 0^{r/2}$ **do**
  3:     Construct $L_1^{(1)}$ from Eq. (7), using some tree-based list construction.
  4: **for all** $\pi_r(\mathbf{e}_2) \in 0^{r/2} \times \mathcal{T}^{r/2}$ **do**
  5:     Construct $L_2^{(1)}$ from Eq. (7), using some tree-based list construction.
  6:                                    ▷ For both list constructions see Sect. 6 and 8.
  7: **for all** matches of $(\mathbf{s}_1, \cdot)$ and $(\mathbf{s}_2, \cdot)$ in the second component of $L_1 \times L_2$ **do**
  8:     **if** $(\mathbf{s} := \mathbf{s}_1 + \mathbf{s}_2 \in \mathcal{T}^n$ has weight w) and $(A\mathbf{s} - \mathbf{b} \bmod q \in \mathcal{T}^n)$ **then return** $\mathbf{s}$

---

via Odlyzko's hash function. Thus, MEET-LWE's correctness follows from the discussion in Sect. 3 and 4.

While Odlyzko's matching of $\mathbf{s}_1, \mathbf{s}_2$ guarantees that $A(\mathbf{s}_1 + \mathbf{s}_2) - \mathbf{b} \in \mathcal{T}^n$ (with high probability), it does not ensure that $\mathbf{s} = \mathbf{s}_1 + \mathbf{s}_2$ is a ternary weight-w vector. Therefore, we check for *consistency* of $\mathbf{s}$ in line 8 of Algorithm 3. Filtering out inconsistent solutions is called *Match-and-filter*, a standard technique for representations [BCJ11,BJMM12].

5.2 Runtime

Algorithm 3 has two outer **for**-loops that each guess $r/2$ coordinates of $\mathbf{e}$ with inner loops that are subset sum-type list construction steps.

Let us start with the outer loop's guessing complexity T_g. Assume $\mathbf{e}$ is a random ternary vector. Then the guessing complexity is

$$T_g = 3^{r/2} \le 3^{\frac{1}{2} \log_q R^{(1)}} = 2^{\frac{1}{2} \log_2(3) \frac{\log_2 R^{(1)}}{\log_2 q}}.$$

For low weight $\mathbf{e}$ we may further improve. This could be e.g. done for BLISS, but for simplicity we ignore such improvements in this paper. For all other cryptosystems that we address in our applications $\mathbf{e}$ is not low weight.

In our instantiations of MEET-LWE in the following sections, we have $\log_2 R^{(1)} = \mathcal{O}(n)$. Since $q = \Omega(n)$ (see Sect. 2), we obtain a guessing complexity of

$$T_g = 2^{\mathcal{O}\left(\frac{n}{\log q}\right)} = 2^{\mathcal{O}\left(\frac{n}{\log n}\right)}.$$

Since the inner loop has—as in Odlyzko's attack—list construction complexity $T_\ell = 2^{\mathcal{O}(n)}$, the overall *asymptotic* complexity $T = T_g \cdot T_\ell$ is fully determined by the inner loop's complexity T_ℓ, and guessing r coordinates of $\mathbf{e}$ just adds an $o(1)$-term to the inner loop's run time exponent!

In the following sections, we see that guessing $\pi_r(\mathbf{e}_1), \pi_r(\mathbf{e}_2)$ also leads to tolerable *non-asymptotic* overheads T_g for real-world parameters, for which we cannot simply neglect a $2^{\mathcal{O}\left(\frac{n}{\log n}\right)}$-term.

In Sect. 6–8, we instantiate Algorithm 3 with varying representations of ternary $\mathbf{s}$ with increasing $R^{(1)}$. As a warm-up, we start in Sect. 6 with Howgrave-Graham's representation from Sect. 4 as $\mathbf{s} = \mathbf{s}_1^{(1)} + \mathbf{s}_2^{(1)} \in \mathcal{T}^n(w/2)$ with ternary $\mathbf{s}_1^{(1)}, \mathbf{s}_2^{(1)} \in \mathcal{T}^n(w/4)$. This already leads to an (asymptotical) complexity improvement from $\frac{S^{(1)}}{\sqrt{R^{(1)}}}$ downto $\frac{S^{(1)}}{R^{(1)}}$, superior to Odlyzko's attack.

6   REP-0: First Instantiation of MEET-LWE

The reader is advised to compare Figs. 2 and 3. MEET-LWE's tree-based list construction from Fig. 2 is realized by a single additional tree layer in Fig. 3.

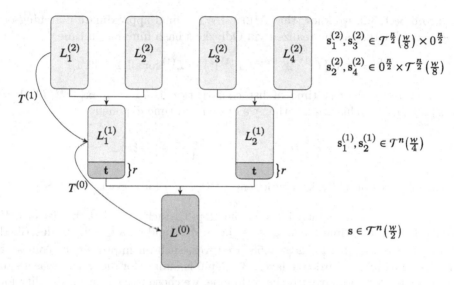

Fig. 3. REP-0 instantiation of MEET-LWE

Let $\mathbf{s} \in \mathcal{T}^n(w/2)$ be the weight-w ternary secret. We represent $\mathbf{s}$ as the sum of weight-$w/2$ ternary secrets $\mathbf{s}_1^{(1)}, \mathbf{s}_2^{(1)} \in \mathcal{T}^n(w/4)$.

Recall from Sect. 4, Eq. (4) that the search space for the $\mathbf{s}_i^{(1)}$ is of size $S^{(1)} = \binom{n}{\frac{w}{4}, \frac{w}{4}, \cdot} \approx 2^{H\left(\frac{w}{4}, \frac{w}{4}, \cdot\right)n}$ and we have $R^{(1)} = \binom{w/2}{w/4}^2 \approx 2^{\omega n}$ representations. Hence the lists $L_1^{(1)}, L_2^{(1)}$ in Algorithm 3 are both of size

$$L^{(1)} = \frac{S^{(1)}}{q^r} \approx \frac{S^{(1)}}{R^{(1)}} = \binom{n}{\frac{w}{4}, \frac{w}{4}, \cdot}\binom{\frac{w}{2}}{\frac{w}{4}}^{-2} \approx 2^{\left(H\left(\frac{w}{4}, \frac{w}{4}, \cdot\right) - \omega\right)n}.$$

Let us construct $L_1^{(1)}, L_2^{(1)}$ in a standard MitM manner. Namely, we enumerate $\mathbf{s}_1^{(1)} \in \mathcal{T}^n(w/4)$ as the sum of

$$\mathbf{s}_1^{(2)} \in \mathcal{T}^{\frac{n}{2}}(w/8) \times 0^{\frac{n}{2}} \text{ and } \mathbf{s}_2^{(2)} \in 0^{\frac{n}{2}} \times \mathcal{T}^{\frac{n}{2}}(w/8).$$

Analogous, we proceed with $\mathbf{s}_2^{(1)}$. All four $\mathbf{s}_i^{(2)}$ are from a search space of size $S^{(2)} = \sqrt{S^{(1)}}$. Thus, on level 2 of our complete binary search tree we obtain four lists $L_1^{(2)}, \ldots, L_4^{(2)}$ each of size

$$L^{(2)} = S^{(2)} = \binom{\frac{n}{2}}{\frac{w}{8}, \frac{w}{8}, \cdot} \approx 2^{\frac{1}{2} H(\frac{w}{4}, \frac{w}{4}, \cdot)n}.$$

The time $T^{(1)}$ to construct the level-1 lists $L_1^{(1)}$, respectively $L_2^{(1)}$, from the (sorted) level-2 lists $L_1^{(2)}, L_2^{(2)}$, respectively $L_3^{(2)}, L_4^{(2)}$, is

$$T^{(1)} = \max\{L^{(2)}, L^{(1)}\}.$$

From Sect. 3.2, we know that MEET-LWE's final approximate matching on $n - r$ coordinates can be realized via Odlyzko's hash function in time

$$T^{(0)} = \max\{L^{(1)}, 2^{-(n-r)}(L^{(1)})^2\} = L^{(1)} \text{ for all } \omega \in [0, 1].$$

Thus, the total run time of list construction is $T_\ell = \max\{T^{(1)}, T^{(0)}\} = \max\{L^{(2)}, L^{(1)}\}$. This implies that we obtain run time exponent

$$\max\left\{\frac{1}{2} H\left(\frac{\omega}{4}, \frac{\omega}{4}, \cdot\right), H\left(\frac{\omega}{4}, \frac{\omega}{4}, \cdot\right) - \omega\right\},$$

which improves on Odlyzko's exponent $\frac{1}{2} H(\frac{\omega}{2}, \frac{\omega}{2}, \cdot)$ for every $\omega \in [0, 0.87]$.

Remark 1. We could slightly improve our Rep-0 attack such that the size of $L^{(1)}$ dominates the run time for all $\omega \leq \frac{2}{3}$, i.e. up to random $\mathbf{s} \in \mathcal{T}^n$. As described above, $L^{(2)}$ dominates for $\omega \geq 0.58$. However, such an improvement comes at the cost of adding a third tree layer. As Rep-0 is mainly for didactical reasons to make the reader familiar with the technique, we chose to sacrifice optimality for the sake of a simpler algorithmic description. The Rep-0 results are superseeded anyway in subsequent sections, where we optimize our tree depth.

Theorem 1. *Let* $\mathbf{s}, \mathbf{e}$ *be ternary LWE key with* $\mathbf{s}$ *having weight* $w = \omega n$. *Then* $\mathbf{s}$ *can be found in time and space (neglecting polynomial factors)*

$$3^{\log_q\left(\binom{w/2}{w/4}\right)} \cdot \max\left\{\binom{\frac{n}{2}}{\frac{w}{8}, \frac{w}{8}, \cdot}, \binom{n}{\frac{w}{4}, \frac{w}{4}, \cdot}\binom{\frac{w}{2}}{\frac{w}{4}}^{-2}\right\} \approx 2^{\max\{\frac{1}{2} H(\frac{w}{4}, \frac{w}{4}, \cdot), H(\frac{w}{4}, \frac{w}{4}, \cdot) - \omega\}n}.$$

Proof. We have $R^{(1)} = \binom{w/2}{w/4}^2$ representations. In MEET-LWE we guess in total $r = \lfloor \log_q R^{(1)} \rfloor$ coordinates of $\mathbf{e} \in \mathcal{T}^n$ via some standard MitM approach in time

$$T_g = 3^{r/2} \leq 3^{\log_q\left(\binom{w/2}{w/4}\right)}.$$

The run time T_ℓ of MEET-LWE's list construction is dominated by the maximum of the sizes $L^{(2)}$, $L^{(1)}$ of the lists on level 2 and 1:

$$T_\ell = \max\left\{L^{(2)}, L^{(1)}\right\} = \max\left\{S^{(2)}, \frac{S^{(1)}}{R^{(1)}}\right\} = \max\left\{\binom{\frac{n}{2}}{\frac{w}{8}, \frac{w}{8},\cdot}, \binom{n}{\frac{w}{4}, \frac{w}{4},\cdot}\binom{\frac{w}{2}}{\frac{w}{4}}^{-2}\right\}.$$

MEET-LWE's total run time is $T = T_g \cdot T_\ell$. $\qquad\qquad\qquad\qquad\qquad\square$

Table 4. Non-asymptotic complexity comparison Odlyzko (Sect. 3) vs. REP-0.

	(n,q,w)	Odlyzko	REP-0 [bit]	$\log_S$ REP-0
NTRU	(509,2048,254)	377 bit	$305 = 287 + 18$	0.40
	(677,2048,254)	445 bit	$364 = 347 + 18$	0.41
	(821,4096,510)	643 bit	$520 = 487 + 33$	0.40
NTRU Prime	(653,4621,288)	463 bit	$370 = 352 + 18$	0.40
	(761,4591,286)	502 bit	$408 = 390 + 18$	0.41
	(857,5167,322)	565 bit	$459 = 439 + 20$	0.41
BLISS I+II	(512,12289,154)	299 bit	$247 = 238 + \ 9$	0.41
GLP I	(512,8383489,342)	401 bit	$325 = 314 + 12$	0.41

In Table 4 we computed MEET-LWE's complexity with our REP-0 representations using the exact formula on the left hand side of Theorem 1 (and not the $H(\cdot)$-approximation). In the notation of Sect. 5 we split MEET-LWE's complexity T in the cost T_ℓ of the inner loop for list construction, and T_g of the outer loop for guessing $r/2$ coordinates. E.g. the NTRU instance $(509, 2048, 254)$ has total complexity $T = 305$ bit, which splits in $T_\ell = 287$ bit for list construction, and $T_g = 18$ bit for guessing. Since we round all complexities to the next integers, $T_\ell + T_g$ might deviate from T by one.

We observe that REP-0 already reduces Odlyzko's bit complexities by roughly 18%, resulting in complexity $S^{0.41}$. Due to a large q, key guessing in BLISS and GLP can be performed more efficiently, as can be observed by the small T_g-values of 9 and 12 bit.

7 REP-1: Using Additional Ones

The idea of REP-1 is to represent a weight-w ternary $\mathbf{s} \in \mathcal{T}^n(w/2)$ as the sum of $\mathbf{s}_1^{(1)}, \mathbf{s}_2^{(1)} \in \mathcal{T}^n(w^{(1)})$, where $w^{(1)} > w/4$. In comparison to Sect. 6, this further increases the number R of representations. We build a complete binary search tree T of depth 4, see Fig. 4. In the following, we describe the lists $L_i^{(j)}$ on level j.

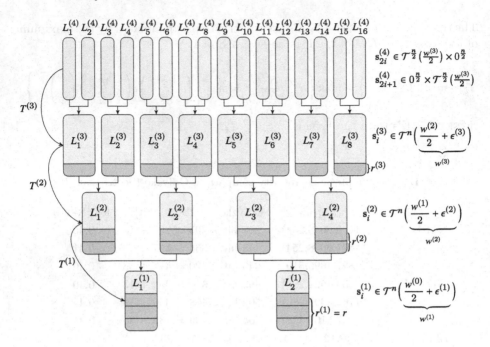

Fig. 4. REP-1 instantiation of MEET-LWE with depth $d = 4$

7.1   Level-1 Lists

Define $w^{(0)} = w/2$ and $w^{(1)} = w^{(0)}/2 + \epsilon^{(1)}$. Let $\mathbf{s}_1, \mathbf{s}_2 \in T^n(w^{(1)})$. Notice that $\mathbf{s}_1 + \mathbf{s}_2 \in T^n(w^{(0)})$ iff in the sum $\epsilon^{(1)}$ many (-1)-coordinates cancel with 1-coordinates, and vice versa. In the terminology of representations, we additionally represent 0 as $(-1) + 1$ and $1 + (-1)$. Recall that in Sect. 6 we represented ± 1 as $\pm 1 + 0$ and 0 ± 1, but 0 was always represented solely as $0 = 0 + 0$.

Therefore, we increase the number of level-1 representations of $\mathbf{s} \in T^n(w^{(0)})$ to

$$R^{(1)} = \left(\frac{w^{(0)}}{\frac{w^{(0)}}{2}}\right)^2 \cdot \binom{n - 2w^{(0)}}{\epsilon^{(1)}, \epsilon^{(1)}, \cdot},$$

where the second factor accounts for our additional representations. On the downside, an increased number $w^{(1)}$ of ± 1 also increases the search space size to

$$S^{(1)} = \binom{n}{w^{(1)}, w^{(1)}, \cdot}.$$

Our goal is to construct two lists $L_1^{(1)}, L_2^{(1)}$ satisfying Eq. (7), both having size $L^{(1)} = S^{(1)}/R^{(1)}$. But as opposed to Sect. 6, due to the increased $S^{(1)}$ we have to construct these lists recursively, until the search space gets small enough to apply a simple MitM construction.

7.2   Level $2 \leq j < d$ Lists

For simplicity of exposition, we perform our analysis for trees of depth $d = 4$, such that the reader may easily follow via Fig. 4. The analysis naturally generalizes to any constant d, see also the full version [May21].

On level $j \in \{1, 2, 3\}$ of our complete binary depth-4 search tree T we construct lists $L_1^{(j)}, \ldots, L_{2^j}^{(j)}$ with vectors $\mathbf{s}_1^{(j)}, \ldots, \mathbf{s}_{2^j}^{(j)}$ of weight $w^{(j)} = w^{(j-1)}/2 + \epsilon^{(j)}$.

This gives us representations and search space size

$$R^{(j)} = \left(\frac{w^{(j-1)}}{\frac{w^{(j-1)}}{2}} \right)^2 \cdot \binom{n - 2w^{(j-1)}}{\epsilon^{(j)}, \epsilon^{(j)}, \cdot} \text{ and } S^{(j)} = \binom{n}{w^{(j)}, w^{(j)}, \cdot}.$$

Let us now describe the level-2 lists more precisely, the level-3 lists are defined analogous. We rewrite Eq. (5) as the following 4-sum for some ternary unknowns $\mathbf{e}_1, \mathbf{e}_2$:

$$A\mathbf{s}_1^{(2)} + A\mathbf{s}_2^{(2)} + \mathbf{e}_1 = \mathbf{b} - A\mathbf{s}_3^{(2)} - A\mathbf{s}_4^{(2)} + \mathbf{e}_2 \bmod q.$$

Let $r^{(1)} := r = \lfloor \log_q R^{(1)} \rfloor$ be the number of guessed coordinates in MEET-LWE (Algorithm 3), and let the fixed target be $\mathbf{t} = \pi_{r^{(1)}}(A\mathbf{s}_1^{(1)} + \mathbf{e}_1) \in \mathbb{Z}_q^{r^{(1)}}$. Let $r^{(2)} = \lfloor \log_q R^{(2)} \rfloor$ be the number of fixed coordinates on level-2, which is a subset of the $r^{(1)}$ fixed coordinates on level 1. Choose two random $\mathbf{t}_1^{(2)}, \mathbf{t}_2^{(2)} \in \mathbb{Z}_q^{r^{(2)}}$. Then the level-2 lists are defined as

$$
\begin{aligned}
L_1^{(2)} &= \{ (\mathbf{s}_1^{(2)}, A\mathbf{s}_1^{(2)}) \mid \pi_{r^{(2)}}(A\mathbf{s}_1^{(2)}) = \mathbf{t}_1^{(2)} \bmod q \}, \\
L_2^{(2)} &= \{ (\mathbf{s}_2^{(2)}, A\mathbf{s}_2^{(2)}) \mid \pi_{r^{(2)}}(A\mathbf{s}_2^{(2)} + \mathbf{e}_1) = \pi_{r^{(2)}}(\mathbf{t}) - \mathbf{t}_1^{(2)} \bmod q \}, \\
L_3^{(2)} &= \{ (\mathbf{s}_3^{(2)}, \mathbf{b} - A\mathbf{s}_3^{(2)}) \mid \pi_{r^{(2)}}(\mathbf{b} - A\mathbf{s}_3^{(2)}) = \mathbf{t}_2^{(2)} \bmod q \}, \\
L_4^{(2)} &= \{ (\mathbf{s}_4^{(2)}, -A\mathbf{s}_4^{(2)}) \mid \pi_{r^{(2)}}(-A\mathbf{s}_4^{(2)} + \mathbf{e}_2) = \pi_{r^{(2)}}(\mathbf{t}) - \mathbf{t}_2^{(2)} \bmod q \}. \quad (8)
\end{aligned}
$$

Let $\mathbf{s}_1^{(1)} = \mathbf{s}_1^{(2)} + \mathbf{s}_2^{(2)}$. Notice that by definition in Eq. (8) and the linearity of π we automatically have

$$\pi_{r^{(2)}}(A\mathbf{s}_1^{(1)} + \mathbf{e}_1) = \pi_{r^{(2)}}(A(\mathbf{s}_1^{(2)} + \mathbf{s}_2^{(2)}) + \mathbf{e}_1) = \pi_{r^{(2)}}(A\mathbf{s}_1^{(2)}) + \pi_{r^{(2)}}(A\mathbf{s}_2^{(2)} + \mathbf{e}_1) = \pi_{r^{(2)}}(\mathbf{t}) \bmod q.$$

Analogous, for $\mathbf{s}_2^{(1)} = \mathbf{s}_3^{(2)} + \mathbf{s}_4^{(2)}$ we obtain $\pi_{r^{(2)}}(\mathbf{b} - A\mathbf{s}_2^{(1)} + \mathbf{e}_2) = \pi_{r^{(2)}}(\mathbf{t}) \bmod q$.

That is, we automatically satisfy our target-$\mathbf{t}$ condition for the level-1 lists $L_1^{(1)}, L_2^{(1)}$ from Eq. (7) on $r^{(2)}$ coordinates. It remains to match the elements in $L_1^{(2)} \times L_2^{(2)}$ and $L_3^{(2)} \times L_4^{(2)}$ on the remaining $r^{(1)} - r^{(2)}$ coordinates.

Eventually, the level-3 lists are constructed via a MitM approach out of level-4 lists, similar to Sect. 6.

7.3   Correctness

Notice that as opposed to the level-1 lists, we compute in (8) the value $\mathbf{As}_i^{(2)}$ instead of the Odlyzko-hashed value $\ell(\mathbf{As}_i^{(2)})$. So whereas on level-1, we compute an approximate matching of vectors via comparing hash values of some locality sensitive hash function, on all other levels $j > 1$ we compute an *exact* (non-hashed) matching of the projected vectors on $r^{(j)}$ coordinates.

On every level $j \geq 1$, our matching ensures that (on expectation) at least one representation of the solution satisfies all conditions. Thus, we expect that the approximate matching of level-1 lists $L_1^{(1)}$ and $L_2^{(1)}$ provides the desired solution in MEET-LWE.

Match-and-Filter. Notice that the sum of vector from $T^n(w^{(j)})$, $1 \leq j < 4$, is in general not in the target distribution $T^n(w^{(j-1)})$. We filter out all vector sums that do not have exactly $w^{(j-1)}$ of each (-1)- and 1-coordinates.

7.4   Run Time

The run time of REP-1 is dominated by constructing all lists of size $L^{(j)}$ on all levels $j \geq 0$.

On level-4, we have sorted lists of size $L^{(4)} = \sqrt{S^{(3)}}$. Ignoring polynomial factors, the construction of each level-4 list costs time $T^{(3)} = L^{(3)}$. Since we match level-4 list elements on $r^{(3)}$ coordinates, the construction of level-3 lists costs on expectation time

$$T^{(3)} = \frac{(L^{(4)})^2}{q^{r^{(3)}}}.$$

Since level-3 list elements already sum to the target $\mathbf{e} = \mathbf{e}_2 - \mathbf{e}_1$ on $r^{(3)}$ coordinates, for the construction of level-2 lists we have to match elements on the remaining $r^{(2)} - r^{(3)}$ coordinates. This can be done in expected time

$$T^{(2)} = \frac{(L^{(3)})^2}{q^{r^{(2)}-r^{(3)}}}.$$

Notice that $\frac{(L^{(3)})^2}{q^{r^{(2)}-r^{(3)}}} \geq L^{(2)}$, since we filter out matching level-3 vector sums that are not in $T^n(w^{(2)})$.

Define $r^{(4)} = 0$. Then in general we can construct every level-j list for $4 > j > 0$ in time

$$T^{(j)} = \frac{(L^{(j+1)})^2}{q^{r^{(j)}-r^{(j+1)}}}.$$

Once we have the level-1 lists $L_1^{(1)}, L_2^{(2)}$ we construct the solution via Odlyzko's approximate matching. Since we already exactly matched elements on $r^{(1)} = \lfloor \log_q R^{(1)} \rfloor$ elements, it remains to approximately match on $n - r^{(1)}$ coordinates. This can be done in time

$$T^{(0)} = \frac{(L^{(1)})^2}{2^{n-r^{(1)}}}.$$

The list construction time T_ℓ and memory complexity M is then in total

$$T_\ell = \max\{T^{(0)}, \ldots, T^{(4)}\} \text{ and } M = \max\{L^{(1)}, \ldots, L^{(4)}\}.$$

The following optimizations balance out the dominating terms $T^{(1)}, T^{(2)}, T^{(3)}$.

7.5   Optimization: Asymptotic and Non-Asymptotic

In Table 5 we optimized for different relative weights ω MEET-LWE's list construction cost T_ℓ, which depends on n and ω only (and not on q). Asymptotically, we can neglect the guessing cost T_g. We write $T_\ell = 2^{c(\omega)n(1+o(1))}$ for some constant $c(\omega)$ that we provide in Table 5, including the optimized additional ones that we add on level j, parametrized by $\bar{\epsilon}^{(j)} = \frac{\epsilon^{(j)}}{n}$.

Table 5. Asymptotics of REP-1 compared to Odlylzko (Sect. 3) and REP-0 (Sect. 6), where we also optimized the search tree depth for REP-0 (see Remark 1).

ω	Odlyz.	REP-0	REP-1	$\log_S T_\ell$	$\bar{\epsilon}^{(1)}, \bar{\epsilon}^{(2)}, \bar{\epsilon}^{(3)}$
0.3	0.591	0.469	0.298	**0.25**	0.054, 0.024, 0.005
0.375	0.665	0.523	0.323	**0.24**	0.056, 0.025, 0.005
0.441	0.716	0.561	0.340	**0.24**	0.061, 0.028, 0.007
0.5	0.750	0.588	0.356	**0.24**	0.062, 0.028, 0.007
0.62	0.790	0.625	0.389	**0.25**	0.069, 0.028, 0.006
0.667	0.793	0.634	0.407	**0.26**	0.068, 0.025, 0.006

Since the REP-I exponent is roughly half of the Odlyzko MitM exponent, the list construction takes about $S^{\frac{1}{4}}$ instead of $S^{\frac{1}{2}}$.

The parameters $\bar{\epsilon}^{(j)}$ are useful starting points for the non-asymptotic analysis in Table 6. Column REP-1 is in a *bit complexity* format $T = T_\ell + T_g$, i.e. the total run time is expressed via T_ℓ for list construction and T_g for guessing. As an example take the first entry $243 = 212 + 31$. List construction takes time $T_\ell = 212$ bit and key guessing $T_g = 31$ bit for a total running time of $T = 243$ bit.

The params-column $4 : 36, 16, 4$ in Table 6 denotes that we construct a search tree of depth 4, where we add 36 additional ± 1 for every level-1 list, 16 additional ± 1 for every level-2 list, and 4 additional ± 1 for every level-3 list. Notice that the relative weight $\omega = 0.5$ in Table 5 has $(\bar{\epsilon}^{(1)}, \bar{\epsilon}^{(2)}, \bar{\epsilon}^{(3)}) = (0.062, 0.028, 0.007)$ and $509 \cdot (\bar{\epsilon}^{(1)}, \bar{\epsilon}^{(2)}, \bar{\epsilon}^{(3)}) \approx (32, 14, 4)$. Therefore, the optimal value $(36, 16, 4)$ is already well approximated by the asymptotic analysis. In fact, the parameters $(32, 14, 4)$ also yield 230 bit complexity.

We optimized every instance with depth-3 and depth-4 search trees. Increasing to depth 5 did not give any further improvements, as predicted by our asymptotic analysis that was also optimal for depth-4 trees.

We observe from Table 6 that for depth-4 trees the list construction bit complexity of T_ℓ (and memory consumption) only—e.g. without T_g—is roughly half

Table 6. Non-asymptotic comparison Odlyzko vs. REP-1.

(n, q, w)	Odly.	REP-1 [bit]	params
NTRU-Encypt			
(509,2048,254)	377	$243 = 212 + 31$	3: 18,4
		$230 = 191 + 38$	4: 36,16,4
(677,2048,254)	445	$281 = 246 + 35$	3: 22,5
		$275 = 229 + 45$	4: 42,19,4
(821,4096,510)	643	$423 = 375 + 49$	3: 24,6
		$393 = 334 + 59$	4: 56,22,6
NTRU Prime			
(653,4621,288)	463	$288 = 254 + 33$	3: 22,5
		$274 = 232 + 42$	4: 42,19,4
(761,4591,286)	502	$313 = 277 + 35$	3: 24,6
		$303 = 257 + 46$	4: 48,22,5
(857,5167,322)	565	$350 = 311 + 39$	3: 27,6
		$338 = 290 + 49$	4: 47,20,3
BLISS I+II			
(512,12289,154)	299	$189 = 169 + 20$	3: 17,4
		$187 = 163 + 24$	4: 27,11,1
GLP I			
(512,8383489,342)	401	$258 = 242 + 16$	3: 16,3
		$241 = 222 + 19$	4: 34,12,4

of Odlyzko's MitM, as predicted by Table 5. On the downside, in comparison to REP-0 in Table 4 the guessing complexity T_g increases quite significantly.

In a nutshell, MEET-LWE uses the additional representations to decrease T_ℓ at the cost of T_g. Since guessing is asymptotically cheaper than list construction, this tradeoff provides in total—already for practical size parameter settings—significant savings.

8   REP-2: Extending the Digit Set with Two

In Sect. 7 we already saw that additional ones lead to a larger number $R^{(1)}$ of representations, thereby significantly improving run times. In this section, we extend the digit set with ± 2, resulting in yet slight improvements.

The benefit of representing ternary $\mathbf{s}$ via $\mathbf{s}_1^{(1)} + \mathbf{s}_2^{(1)}$ with $\mathbf{s}_1^{(1)}, \mathbf{s}_2^{(1)} \in \{-2, -1, 0, 1, 2\}^n$ is that we obtain additionally the following variety of representations for each coordinate of $\mathbf{s}$:

$$
\begin{aligned}
(-1) &= (-2) + 1 = (-1) + 0 = 0 + (-1) = 1 + (-2), \\
1 &= (-1) + 2 = 0 + 1 = 1 + 0 = (-2) + 1, \\
0 &= (-2) + 2 = (-1) + 1 = 0 + 0 = 1 + (-1) = 2 + (-2).
\end{aligned}
\tag{9}
$$

Moreover, REP-2 also allows us for the first time to analyze LWE secrets $\mathbf{s} \in \mathbb{Z}_q^n \cap \{\pm 2, \pm 1, 0\}$, as they appear e.g. in some BLISS instances, see Sect. 8.3.

The benefits of REP-2 come at the price of a quite involved technical analysis, especially for counting the new representations via new optimization parameters. Since REP-2 is algorithmically close to REP-1 from Fig. 4, in the following we only state the results. A detailed analysis including the semantics of our optimization parameters $\epsilon_{k\ell}^{(j)}$ is presented in the full version [May21].

While we obtained significant savings from REP-0 to REP-1, the savings from REP-2 are in comparison quite smallish. This demonstrates that our technique converges quite quickly, once we construct sufficiently many representations. Similar effects were already observed in the subset sum context [HJ10, BCJ11, BBSS20].

8.1 Optimization – Asymptotics

As in Sect. 7.5 we asymptotically neglect the guessing time T_g. The total run time T is dominated by the list construction $T_\ell = 2^{c(\omega)(n+o(n))}$ for some constant $c(\omega)$ that we provide in Table 7. We obtained optimal parameters for depth $d = 4$, further increasing the depth did not improve. As usual, we denote $\bar{\epsilon}_{k\ell}^{(j)} = \frac{\epsilon_{k\ell}^{(j)}}{n}$. In our optimization, we always had $\bar{\epsilon}_{20}^{(2)} = \bar{\epsilon}_{20}^{(3)} = \bar{\epsilon}_{21}^{(3)} = \bar{\epsilon}_{22}^{(3)} = 0$.

Table 7. Asymptotics of REP-2 in comparison to Odlyzko (Sect. 3) and REP-1.

ω	Odlyz.	REP-1	REP-2	$\log_S T_\ell$	$\bar{\epsilon}_{10}^{(1)}, \bar{\epsilon}_{20}^{(1)}, \bar{\epsilon}_{21}^{(1)}, \bar{\epsilon}_{10}^{(2)}, \bar{\epsilon}_{21}^{(2)}, \bar{\epsilon}_{22}^{(2)}, \bar{\epsilon}_{10}^{(3)}$
0.3	0.591	0.298	0.295	**0.25**	50 , 0 , 1 , 26 , 0 , 0, 6 $[10^{-3}]$
0.375	0.665	0.323	0.318	**0.24**	44 , 1 , 3 , 24 , 1 , 1, 7 $[10^{-3}]$
0.441	0.716	0.340	0.334	**0.23**	41 , 1 , 4 , 25 , 1 , 1, 7 $[10^{-3}]$
0.5	0.750	0.356	0.348	**0.23**	40 , 1 , 4 , 25 , 1 , 1, 7 $[10^{-3}]$
0.62	0.790	0.389	0.371	**0.24**	35 , 1 , 5 , 26 , 1 , 1, 7 $[10^{-3}]$
0.667	0.793	0.407	0.379	**0.24**	33 , 0 , 6 , 26 , 1 , 1, 7 $[10^{-3}]$

We see that in the range $\omega \in [\frac{3}{10}, \frac{2}{3}]$, our new run time exponent is smaller than half Odlyzko's run time exponent. Thus, for these ω the asymptotic complexity is less than $S^{\frac{1}{4}}$ (see column $\log_S T_\ell$).

8.2 Optimization – Non-Asymptotic

In the non-asymptotic analysis from Table 8, we still get slight improvements from REP-2 over REP-1. We optimized our algorithm for every instance in depths $d = 3$ and $d = 4$. Take e.g. the NTRU $n = 509$ instance that has level-4 complexities $T_\ell = 189$ for list construction and $T_g = 38$ for guessing.

The params-column with $3 : 14, 1, 4$ gives the parameters $\epsilon_{10}^{(1)}, \epsilon_{21}^{(1)}, \epsilon_{10}^{(2)}$. All other depth-3 parameters were always 0 in the optimization. In our example, we

Table 8. Non-asymptotic comparison REP-1 vs. REP-2

(n, q, w)	$\mathcal{S}$[bit]	REP-1[bit]	REP-2[bit]	params
NTRU-Encypt				
(509,2048,254)	754	$243 = 212 + 31$	$241 = 211 + 30$	3: 14,1,4
		$230 = 191 + 38$	$\mathbf{227} = 189 + 38$	4: 26,2,17,3
(677,2048,254)	891	$281 = 246 + 35$	$281 = 246 + 35$	3: 22,0,5
		$275 = 229 + 45$	$\mathbf{273} = 231 + 42$	4: 32,1,15,1
(821,4096,510)	1286	$423 = 375 + 49$	$419 = 371 + 49$	3: 20,1,6
		$393 = 334 + 59$	$\mathbf{378} = 318 + 60$	4: 34,5,30,6
NTRU Prime				
(653,4621,288)	925	$288 = 254 + 33$	$287 = 254 + 33$	3: 18,1,5
		$274 = 232 + 42$	$\mathbf{272} = 229 + 42$	4: 36,2,22,5
(761,4591,286)	1003	$313 = 277 + 35$	$312 = 277 + 36$	3: 22,1,6
		$303 = 257 + 46$	$\mathbf{301} = 258 + 43$	4: 36,1,17,2
(857,5167,322)	1131	$350 = 311 + 39$	$350 = 310 + 40$	3: 25,1,7
		$\mathbf{338} = 290 + 49$	$338 = 291 + 47$	4: 37,2,19,2
BLISS I+II				
(512,12289,154)	597	$189 = 169 + 20$	$189 - 169 + 20$	3: 17, 4, 0
		$\mathbf{187} = 163 + 24$	$187 = 163 + 24$	4: 27,0,11,1
GLP I				
(512,8383489,342)	802	$258 = 242 + 16$	$257 = 240 + 16$	3: 12,1,4
		$241 = 222 + 19$	$\mathbf{225} = 206 + 20$	4: 22,3,19,4

put on level 1 an amount of 14 additional ± 1 (corresponding to $\epsilon_{10}^{(1)}$), another amount of 1 additional ± 2 (corresponding to $\epsilon_{21}^{(1)}$), and on level 2 an amount of 4 additional ± 1 (corresponding to $\epsilon_{10}^{(2)}$). In the level-4 params column we provide parameters $\epsilon_{10}^{(1)}, \epsilon_{21}^{(1)}, \epsilon_{10}^{(2)}, \epsilon_{10}^{(3)}$, all others were 0.

As a function of the search space size $\mathcal{S}$ we get for all NTRU encryption schemes and BLISS non-asymptotic combinatorial attack complexities around $\mathcal{S}^{0.3}$, for GLP with its large q roughly $\mathcal{S}^{0.28}$. Notice that for all instances the list construction costs T_ℓ are roughly $\mathcal{S}^{\frac{1}{4}}$, as predicted by the asymptotic analysis.

8.3   BLISS with $s \in \{0, \pm 1, \pm 2\}^n$

The BLISS IV parameter set suggests $(n, q) = (512, 12289)$, where the secret s has 230 (± 1)-entries and 30 (± 2)-entries. Asymptotically, such a weight distribution yields $\mathcal{S}^{0.21}$ with REP-2 (adapted to $s \in \{0, \pm 1, \pm 2\}^n$).

Table 9. Non-asymptotic REP-2 on secrets $\mathbf{s} \in \{0, \pm 1, \pm 2\}^n$

Instance	S[bit]	REP-2[bit]	$\epsilon_{10}^{(1)}, \epsilon_{12}^{(1)}, \epsilon_{10}^{(2)}, \epsilon_{10}^{(3)}$
BLISS IV (512,12289,230,30)	890	$246 = 212 + 35$	4: 43, 3, 19, 4

Non-asymptotically, we achieve $S^{0.28}$ from Table 9, where we obtain list construction complexity $T_\ell = 212$ bit and guessing complexity $T_g = 35$ bit.

9 Small Memory Versions

Our new MEET-LWE attack has quite large memory consumption. For all instantiations of MEET-LWE in the previous sections the memory consumption is (almost) as large as the list construction time T_ℓ, i.e. roughly $S^{\frac{1}{4}}$.

We show in this section that our representations REP-0, REP-1, REP-2 used together with Howgrave-Graham's algorithm from Sect. 4 admit small memory versions and simple time-memory tradeoffs. Using Howgrave-Graham's original algorithm instead of MEET-LWE has the advantage that we do not require any key guessing.

Let us rewrite the LWE identity from Eq. (5)

$$A\mathbf{s}_1 + \mathbf{e}_1 = \mathbf{b} - A\mathbf{s}_2 + \mathbf{e}_2 \text{ for some binary } \mathbf{e}_1, \mathbf{e}_2 \in \{0, 1\}^n.$$

We follow the general van Oorschot and Wiener strategy [vW99] that turns a MitM attack memory-less. This strategy was already applied by van Vredendaal [vV16] to Odlyzko's MitM attack from Sect. 3.

Let D be the search space for $\mathbf{s}_1, \mathbf{s}_2$ with size S. Let us define the two functions f_1, f_2 with domain D as

$$f_1 : \mathbf{s}_1 \mapsto \pi_k(\ell(A\mathbf{s}_1)) \text{ and } f_2 : \mathbf{s}_2 \mapsto \pi_k(\ell(\mathbf{b} - A\mathbf{s}_2)).$$

Here $\ell : \mathbb{Z}_q^n \to \{0, 1, 2\}^n$ is Odlyzko's hash function from Eq. (2), changed to ternary labels in the canonical manner (by equipartitioning $\mathbb{Z}_q$), such that it has range size $3^n > S$. Further, π_k is our projection function from Equation (6), where we choose $k = \lceil \log_3(S) \rceil$. Thus, the range of f_1, f_2 is approximately of size S.

Moreover we use an encoding function $h : \{0, 1, 2\}^k \to D$ that encodes the arguments $f_i(\cdot)$ back to D, such that we can iterate functions f_i.

With a cycle-finding algorithm we find in time roughly $\sqrt{S}$ a collision $\mathbf{s}_1, \mathbf{s}_2$ between f_1, f_2, i.e. $f_1(\mathbf{s}_1) = f_2(\mathbf{s}_2)$. This implies

$$\pi_k(\ell(A\mathbf{s}_1)) = \pi_k(\ell(\mathbf{b} - A\mathbf{s}_2)). \tag{10}$$

Let $\mathbf{s}$ be the desired LWE secret key, and let $(\mathbf{s}_1, \mathbf{s}_2)$ be a representation of $\mathbf{s}$, i.e. $\mathbf{s} = \mathbf{s}_1 + \mathbf{s}_2$. By definition of ℓ, any representation $(\mathbf{s}_1, \mathbf{s}_2)$ satisfies Equation

(10). We call a collision (s_1, s_2) *good* iff (s_1, s_2) is a representation of s. Let R be the number of representations of s.

By A's randomness, the functions f_1, f_2 should behave like random functions. Therefore, we expect that there exist roughly $\mathcal{S}$ collisions in total between f_1 and f_2. This in turn implies that we obtain a good collision with probability $p = \frac{R}{\mathcal{S}}$. Since finding any collision takes time $\sqrt{\mathcal{S}}$, we expect overall running time

$$T = \sqrt{\mathcal{S}} p^{-1} = \sqrt{\mathcal{S}} \cdot \frac{\mathcal{S}}{R} = \frac{\mathcal{S}^{\frac{3}{2}}}{R}. \tag{11}$$

van Vredendaal [vV16] chooses Odlyzko's search space size $\mathcal{S} = \sqrt{\binom{n}{w/2, w/2, \cdot}}$ with a unique representation of the solution. Thus, she obtains a polynomial memory algorithm with run time $\mathcal{S}^{\frac{3}{2}} \approx 2^{\frac{3}{4} H(\frac{w}{2}, \frac{w}{2}, \cdot) n}$.

But from Eq. (11) we minimize T by increasing the number R of representations, as long as $\mathcal{S}$ does not grow too fast. We show in the following that this tradeoff between $\mathcal{S}$ and R pays off for our representations REP-0, REP-1, REP-2. To this end, we simply set $\mathcal{S} = \mathcal{S}^{(1)}, R = R^{(1)}$ using the expressions for $\mathcal{S}^{(1)}, R^{(1)}$ derived in Sects. 6 to 8.

We obtain asymptotic runtimes $2^{c(\omega)(n + o(n))}$ for which we state the run time exponents $c(\omega)$ in Table 10. The optimization parameters for REP-1, REP-2 are given in the last two columns.

Table 10. Asymptotic complexities for polynomial memory LWE key search.

ω	Odl.[vV16]	REP-0	REP-1	REP-2	$\bar{\epsilon}^{(1)}$	$\bar{\epsilon}_{10}^{(1)}$	$\bar{\epsilon}_{21}^{(1)}$
0.3	0.886	0.834	**0.772**	0.772	0.032	0.032	0.000
0.375	0.997	0.951	**0.858**	0.858	0.045	0.045	0.000
0.441	1.073	1.031	0.918	**0.918**	0.055	0.056	0.001
0.5	1.125	1.092	0.964	**0.962**	0.061	0.061	0.001
0.621	1.184	1.186	1.043	**1.038**	0.060	0.062	0.003
0.668	1.189	1.211	1.070	**1.064**	0.056	0.058	0.004

In comparison to the previously best results from [vV16], the runtime exponents drop by 10% to 15%.

We may also utilize the well-known time-memory tradeoff provided by Parallel Collision Search (PCS) [vW99]. Let $T_c = \sqrt{\mathcal{S}}$ be the time to find a single collision. Then with PCS using memory M we find M collisions in time $T = \sqrt{M} T_c$. Since we need a total of $p^{-1} = \frac{\mathcal{S}}{R}$ collisions (for finding a good collision), using memory $M \le p^{-1}$ we obtain the time-memory tradeoff

$$T = \frac{p^{-1}}{M} \sqrt{M} T_c = \frac{\mathcal{S}^{\frac{3}{2}}}{\sqrt{M} R}.$$

E.g. if we use full memory $M = p^{-1} = \frac{S}{R}$, we obtain run time $T = \frac{S}{\sqrt{R}}$, which reproduces Howgrave-Graham's run time formula from Sect. 4, albeit with different (better) values of S and R.

10   Hybrid Attack

The presumably best known attack on LWE-type cryptosystems with ternary keys is a combination of lattice reduction and MitM known as the *Hybrid attack*, due to Howgrave-Graham [How07]. Here, we give only a brief outline of the attack. We refer the reader to [How07, Wun19] for more details.

For ease of exposition we describe only the *Plain Hybrid* attack, a dimension reduction method [MS01] that combines lattice reduction with Brute-Force key guessing. Howgrave-Graham [How07] then showed that Brute-Force can be replaced by MitM at the cost of some (often quite smallish) success probability [Wun19, Ngu21].

We write $A = (A_1, A_2) \in \mathbb{Z}_q^{n \times k} \times \mathbb{Z}_q^{n \times (n-k)}$ for some $0 \leq k \leq n$, and the LWE key equation as $A_1 s_1 = b - A_2 s_2 + e$. In *Plain Hybrid* we enumerate all candidates $(s_2, b - A_2 s_2)$. Define the target $t(s_2) := b - A_2 s_2$.

Further, we define a lattice L by the $(n + k)$-dimensional lattice basis

$$B = (\mathbf{b}_1|\mathbf{b}_2|\dots|\mathbf{b}_{n+k}) = \begin{bmatrix} qI_n & A_1 \\ 0 & I_k \end{bmatrix}.$$

Let s_2 be the correct key guess with target $t(s_2)$. L contains the vector $\mathbf{v} = B \cdot (\mathbf{k}, s_1) = (t(s_2) + e, s_1)$ for some suitably chosen $\mathbf{k} \in \mathbb{Z}^n$. Thus $\mathbf{v}$ is close—in distance (e, s_1)—to the known target vector $(t(s_2), 0)$. Hence $\mathbf{v}$ can be recovered by using Babai's *Nearest Plane* algorithm [Bab86], provided we have a sufficiently reduced basis B. Solving such a close vector instance is called Bounded Distance Decoding.

The *Plain Hybrid* approach now balances the cost for enumerating s_2 with the lattice reduction cost for recovering s_1.

Problems when Applying our MitM. It is tempting to replace the key search for s_2 by our MitM approach. However, notice that we have to enumerate *all* vectors s_2. This can surely be done by the MitM attacks from Sects. 3 and 4.

Instead, the strength of our MitM attack is that we do not enumerate all potential keys, but only those that fulfill the LWE key equation on r coordinates. However, we cannot use the LWE key equation anymore for our projected subkey s_2.

Work-around 1: One may introduce *additional* representations $s = s_1 + s_2$ for the lattice and guessing part by letting s_1, s_2 overlap. But our computations so far indicate that the cost of increasing s_1's dimension—and therefore of lattice reduction—is not compensated by the decrease to enumerate s_2 with our improved MitM.

Work-around 2: One may define s_1, s_2 of full length n, but with *different weight*, again introducing additional representations. Especially, by choosing smaller weight for s_2 one can balance the cost of lattice reduction and enumeration. Our computations so far show that such a *Weight Hybrid* is only slightly better than pure lattice reduction.

We leave it as an open problem whether list construction-type algorithms can improve lattice hybrid attacks. Another interesting question is whether we can omit key guessing in our MEET-LWE by using Nearest Neighbor techniques as in [Laa15, MO15].

Acknowledgements. The author wants to thank Elena Kirshanova, John Schank and Andre Esser for discussions and estimations concerning lattice reduction and the Hybrid attack, and the anonymous reviewers for their valuable suggestions.

References

[ABD16] Albrecht, M., Bai, S., Ducas, L.: A subfield lattice attack on overstretched NTRU assumptions. In: Robshaw, M., Katz, J. (eds.) CRYPTO 2016, Part I. LNCS, vol. 9814, pp. 153–178. Springer, Heidelberg (2016). https://doi.org/10.1007/978-3-662-53018-4_6

[ACF+14] Albrecht, M., Cid, C., Faugere, J.C., Fitzpatrick, R., Perret, L.: Algebraic algorithms for LWE problems (2014)

[APS15] Albrecht, M.R., Player, R., Scott, S.: On the concrete hardness of learning with errors. J. Math. Cryptol. **9**(3), 169–203 (2015)

[Bab86] Babai, L.: On lovász'lattice reduction and the nearest lattice point problem. Combinatorica **6**(1), 1–13 (1986)

[BBSS20] Bonnetain, X., Bricout, R., Schrottenloher, A., Shen, Y.: Improved classical and quantum algorithms for subset-sum. In: Moriai, S., Wang, H. (eds.) ASIACRYPT 2020, Part II. LNCS, vol. 12492, pp. 633–666. Springer, Cham (2020). https://doi.org/10.1007/978-3-030-64834-3_22

[BCJ11] Becker, A., Coron, J.-S., Joux, A.: Improved generic algorithms for hard knapsacks. In: Paterson, K.G. (ed.) EUROCRYPT 2011. LNCS, vol. 6632, pp. 364–385. Springer, Heidelberg (2011). https://doi.org/10.1007/978-3-642-20465-4_21

[BCLvV] Bernstein, D.J., Chuengsatiansup, C., Lange, T., van Vredendaal, C.: NTRU prime: round 2 specification (2019)

[BCLvV17] Bernstein, D.J., Chuengsatiansup, C., Lange, T., van Vredendaal, C.: NTRU prime: reducing attack surface at low cost. In: Adams, C., Camenisch, J. (eds.) SAC 2017. LNCS, vol. 10719, pp. 235–260. Springer, Cham (2018). https://doi.org/10.1007/978-3-319-72565-9_12

[BDGL16] Becker, A., Ducas,, L., Gama, N., Laarhoven, T.: New directions in nearest neighbor searching with applications to lattice sieving. In: Krauthgamer, R. (ed.) 27th SODA, ACM-SIAM, pp. 10–24, January 2016

[BDK+17] Bos, J.W., et al.: CRYSTALS-Kyber: a CCA-secure module-lattice-based KEM. Cryptology ePrint Archive (20180716: 135545) (2017)

[BG14] Bai, S., Galbraith, S.D.: Lattice decoding attacks on binary LWE. In: Susilo, W., Mu, Y. (eds.) ACISP 2014. LNCS, vol. 8544, pp. 322–337. Springer, Cham (2014). https://doi.org/10.1007/978-3-319-08344-5_21

[BGPW16] Buchmann, J., Göpfert, F., Player, R., Wunderer, T.: On the hardness of LWE with binary error: revisiting the hybrid lattice-reduction and meet-in-the-middle attack. In: Pointcheval, D., Nitaj, A., Rachidi, T. (eds.) AFRICACRYPT 2016. LNCS, vol. 9646, pp. 24–43. Springer, Cham (2016). https://doi.org/10.1007/978-3-319-31517-1_2

[BJMM12] Becker, A., Joux, A., May, A., Meurer, A.: Decoding random binary linear codes in $2^n/20$: how $1 + 1 = 0$ improves information set decoding. In: Pointcheval, D., Johansson, T. (eds.) EUROCRYPT 2012. LNCS, vol. 7237, pp. 520–536. Springer, Heidelberg (2012). https://doi.org/10.1007/978-3-642-29011-4_31

[BLP+13] Brakerski, Z., Langlois, A., Peikert, C., Regev, O., Stehlé, D.: Classical hardness of learning with errors. In: Boneh, D., Roughgarden, T., Feigenbaum, J. (eds.) 45th ACM STOC, pp. 575–584. ACM Press, June 2013

[CDH+19] Chen, C., et al.: NTRU - algorithm specifications and supporting documentation (2019)

[dBDJW18] de Boer, K., Ducas, L., Jeffery, S., de Wolf, R.: Attacks on the AJPS Mersenne-based cryptosystem. In: Lange, T., Steinwandt, R. (eds.) PQCrypto 2018. LNCS, vol. 10786, pp. 101–120. Springer, Cham (2018). https://doi.org/10.1007/978-3-319-79063-3_5

[DDLL13] Ducas, L., Durmus, A., Lepoint, T., Lyubashevsky, V.: Lattice signatures and bimodal Gaussians. In: Canetti, R., Garay, J.A. (eds.) CRYPTO 2013, Part I. LNCS, vol. 8042, pp. 40–56. Springer, Heidelberg (2013). https://doi.org/10.1007/978-3-642-40041-4_3

[DN12] Ducas, L., Nguyen, P.Q.: Faster Gaussian lattice sampling using lazy floating-point arithmetic. In: Wang, X., Sako, K. (eds.) ASIACRYPT 2012. LNCS, vol. 7658, pp. 415–432. Springer, Heidelberg (2012). https://doi.org/10.1007/978-3-642-34961-4_26

[DRV20] D'Anvers, J.-P., Rossi, M., Virdia, F.: (One) Failure Is Not an Option: bootstrapping the search for failures in lattice-based encryption schemes. In: Canteaut, A., Ishai, Y. (eds.) EUROCRYPT 2020. LNCS, vol. 12107, pp. 3–33. Springer, Cham (2020). https://doi.org/10.1007/978-3-030-45727-3_1

[Gen09] Gentry, C.: Fully homomorphic encryption using ideal lattices. In: Mitzenmacher, M. (ed.) 41st ACM STOC, pp. 169–178. ACM Press, May/June 2009

[GJS15] Guo, Q., Johansson, T., Stankovski, P.: Coded-BKW: solving LWE using lattice codes. In: Gennaro, R., Robshaw, M. (eds.) CRYPTO 2015, Part I. LNCS, vol. 9215, pp. 23–42. Springer, Heidelberg (2015). https://doi.org/10.1007/978-3-662-47989-6_2

[GLP12] Güneysu, T., Lyubashevsky, V., Pöppelmann, T.: Practical lattice-based cryptography: a signature scheme for embedded systems. In: Prouff, E., Schaumont, P. (eds.) CHES 2012. LNCS, vol. 7428, pp. 530–547. Springer, Heidelberg (2012). https://doi.org/10.1007/978-3-642-33027-8_31

[GPV08] Gentry, C., Peikert, C., Vaikuntanathan, V.: Trapdoors for hard lattices and new cryptographic constructions. In: Ladner, R.E., Dwork, C. (eds.) 40th ACM STOC, pp. 197–206. ACM Press, May 2008

[HGSW03] Howgrave-Graham, N., Silverman, J.H., Whyte, W.: A meet-in-the-middle attack on an NTRU private key. Technical report, NTRU Cryptosystems, June 2003

[HJ10]   Howgrave-Graham, N., Joux, A.: New generic algorithms for hard knap-sacks. In: Gilbert, H. (ed.) EUROCRYPT 2010. LNCS, vol. 6110, pp. 235–256. Springer, Heidelberg (2010). https://doi.org/10.1007/978-3-642-13190-5_12

[HKL18] Herold, G., Kirshanova, E., Laarhoven, T.: Speed-ups and time–memory trade-offs for tuple lattice sieving. In: Abdalla, M., Dahab, R. (eds.) PKC 2018, Part I. LNCS, vol. 10769, pp. 407–436. Springer, Cham (2018). https://doi.org/10.1007/978-3-319-76578-5_14

[HNP+03] Howgrave-Graham, N., et al.: The impact of decryption failures on the security of NTRU encryption. In: Boneh, D. (ed.) CRYPTO 2003. LNCS, vol. 2729, pp. 226–246. Springer, Heidelberg (2003). https://doi.org/10.1007/978-3-540-45146-4_14

[How07] Howgrave-Graham, N.: A hybrid lattice-reduction and meet-in-the-middle attack against NTRU. In: Menezes, A. (ed.) CRYPTO 2007. LNCS, vol. 4622, pp. 150–169. Springer, Heidelberg (2007). https://doi.org/10.1007/978-3-540-74143-5_9

[HPS98] Hoffstein, J., Pipher, J., Silverman, J.H.: NTRU: a ring-based public key cryptosystem. In: Buhler, J.P. (ed.) ANTS 1998. LNCS, vol. 1423, pp. 267–288. Springer, Heidelberg (1998). https://doi.org/10.1007/BFb0054868

[KF15]   Kirchner, P., Fouque, P.-A.: An improved BKW algorithm for LWE with applications to cryptography and lattices. In: Gennaro, R., Robshaw, M. (eds.) CRYPTO 2015, Part I. LNCS, vol. 9215, pp. 43–62. Springer, Heidelberg (2015). https://doi.org/10.1007/978-3-662-47989-6_3

[Laa15] Laarhoven, T.: Sieving for shortest vectors in lattices using angular locality-sensitive hashing. In: Gennaro, R., Robshaw, M. (eds.) CRYPTO 2015, Part I. LNCS, vol. 9215, pp. 3–22. Springer, Heidelberg (2015). https://doi.org/10.1007/978-3-662-47989-6_1

[LPR10] Lyubashevsky, V., Peikert, C., Regev, O.: On ideal lattices and learning with errors over rings. In: Gilbert, H. (ed.) EUROCRYPT 2010. LNCS, vol. 6110, pp. 1–23. Springer, Heidelberg (2010). https://doi.org/10.1007/978-3-642-13190-5_1

[Lyu12] Lyubashevsky, V.: Lattice signatures without trapdoors. In: Pointcheval, D., Johansson, T. (eds.) EUROCRYPT 2012. LNCS, vol. 7237, pp. 738–755. Springer, Heidelberg (2012). https://doi.org/10.1007/978-3-642-29011-4_43

[May21] May, A.: How to meet ternary LWE keys. Cryptology ePrint Archive, Report 2021/216 (2021). https://eprint.iacr.org/2021/216

[MO15]   May, A., Ozerov, I.: On computing nearest neighbors with applications to decoding of binary linear codes. In: Oswald, E., Fischlin, M. (eds.) EURO-CRYPT 2015, Part I. LNCS, vol. 9056, pp. 203–228. Springer, Heidelberg (2015). https://doi.org/10.1007/978-3-662-46800-5_9

[MP13]   Micciancio, D., Peikert, C.: Hardness of SIS and LWE with small parame-ters. In: Canetti, R., Garay, J.A. (eds.) CRYPTO 2013, Part I. LNCS, vol. 8042, pp. 21–39. Springer, Heidelberg (2013). https://doi.org/10.1007/978-3-642-40041-4_2

[MS01]   May, A., Silverman, J.H.: Dimension reduction methods for convolution modular lattices. In: Silverman, J.H. (ed.) CaLC 2001. LNCS, vol. 2146, pp. 110–125. Springer, Heidelberg (2001). https://doi.org/10.1007/3-540-44670-2_10

[MU17] Mitzenmacher, M., Upfal, E.: Probability and Computing: Randomization and Probabilistic Techniques in Algorithms and Data Analysis. Cambridge University Press, Cambridge (2017)

[Ngu21] Nguyen, P.Q.: Boosting the hybrid attack on NTRU: torus LSH, permuted HNF and boxed sphere. In: NIST Third PQC Standardization Conference (2021)

[ntr08] 1-2008 - IEEE standard specification for public key cryptographic techniques based on hard problems over lattices (2008)

[NV08] Nguyen, P.Q., Vidick, T.: Sieve algorithms for the shortest vector problem are practical. J. Math. Cryptol. $2(2)$, 181–207 (2008)

[Reg03] Regev, O.: New lattice based cryptographic constructions. In: 35th ACM STOC, pp. 407–416. ACM Press, June 2003

[SS11] Stehlé, D., Steinfeld, R.: Making NTRU as secure as worst-case problems over ideal lattices. In: Paterson, K.G. (ed.) EUROCRYPT 2011. LNCS, vol. 6632, pp. 27–47. Springer, Heidelberg (2011). https://doi.org/10.1007/978-3-642-20465-4_4

[vV16] van Vredendaal, C.: Reduced memory meet-in-the-middle attack against the NTRU private key. LMS J. Comput. Math. 19(A), 43–57 (2016)

[vW99] van Oorschot, P.C., Wiener, M.J.: Parallel collision search with cryptanalytic applications. J. Cryptol. $12(1)$, 1–28 (1999)

[WMM13] Wang, H., Ma, Z., Ma, C.G.: An efficient quantum meet-in-the-middle attack against NTRU-2005. Chin. Sci. Bull. 58(28), 3514–3518 (2013)

[Wun19] Wunderer, T.: A detailed analysis of the hybrid lattice-reduction and meet-in-the-middle attack. J. Math. Cryptol. $13(1)$, 1–26 (2019)

Lattice Reduction with Approximate Enumeration Oracles
Practical Algorithms and Concrete Performance

Martin R. Albrecht[1][✉], Shi Bai[2], Jianwei Li[1], and Joe Rowell[1]

[1] Information Security Group, Royal Holloway, University of London, Egham, UK
martin.albrecht@royalholloway.ac.uk , Jianwei.Li@rhul.ac.uk
[2] Department of Mathematical Sciences, Florida Atlantic University,
Boca Raton, USA

Abstract. This work provides a systematic investigation of the use of approximate enumeration oracles in BKZ, building on recent technical progress on speeding-up lattice enumeration: *relaxing* (the search radius of) enumeration and *extended preprocessing* which preprocesses in a larger rank than the enumeration rank. First, we heuristically justify that relaxing enumeration with certain extreme pruning asymptotically achieves an exponential speed-up for reaching the same root Hermite factor (RHF). Second, we perform simulations/experiments to validate this and the performance for relaxed enumeration with numerically optimised pruning for both regular and extended preprocessing.

Upgrading BKZ with such approximate enumeration oracles gives rise to our main result, namely a practical and faster (wrt. previous work) polynomial-space lattice reduction algorithm for reaching the same RHF in practical and cryptographic parameter ranges. We assess its concrete time/quality performance with extensive simulations and experiments.

1   Introduction

Lattices are discrete subgroups of $\mathbb{R}^m$. A lattice $\mathcal{L}$ in $\mathbb{R}^m$ is represented as a set of all integer linear combinations of n linearly independent vectors $b_0, \ldots, b_{n-1}$ in $\mathbb{R}^m$: $\mathcal{L} = \left\{ \sum_{i=0}^{n-1} x_i \cdot b_i, \ x_i \in \mathbb{Z} \right\}$. The matrix $B := (b_0, \ldots, b_{n-1})$ forms a *basis* of $\mathcal{L}$, and the integer n is the *rank* of $\mathcal{L}$. Any lattice of rank ≥ 2 has infinitely many bases.

A central lattice problem is the *shortest vector problem* (SVP): given a basis of a lattice $\mathcal{L}$ (endowed with the Euclidean norm), SVP is to find a shortest nonzero vector in $\mathcal{L}$. SVP is known to be NP-hard under randomised reductions [3]. The

J. Rowell—This work was supported in part by EPSRC grants EP/S020330/1, EP/S02087X/1, EP/P009301/1, by European Union Horizon 2020 Research and Innovation Program Grant 780701, by Innovate UK grant AQuaSec, by NIST award 60NANB18D216 and by National Science Foundation under Grant No. 2044855. Part of this work was done while MA visited the Simons Institute for the Theory of Computing. The full version of this work is available as [5].

© International Association for Cryptologic Research 2021
T. Malkin and C. Peikert (Eds.): CRYPTO 2021, LNCS 12826, pp. 732–759, 2021.
https://doi.org/10.1007/978-3-030-84245-1_25

hardness of solving SVP and in particular its applications in cryptography have led to the study of approximate variants.

For $\delta \geq 1$, the δ-approximate variant of SVP (δ-SVP) is to find a non-zero vector v in $\mathcal{L}$ such that $\|v\| \leq \delta \cdot \lambda_1(\mathcal{L})$, where $\lambda_1(\mathcal{L}) := \min_{x \in \mathcal{L} \neq 0} \|x\|$ denotes the length of the shortest nonzero vector in $\mathcal{L}$. Solving δ-SVP is also NP-hard for any $\delta \leq n^{c/\log\log n}$ with some constant $c > 0$ under reasonable complexity assumptions [30,32,37,38]. A closely related problem is δ-*Hermite SVP* (δ-HSVP), which asks to find a non-zero vector v in $\mathcal{L}$ such that $\|v\| \leq \delta \cdot \mathrm{vol}(\mathcal{L})^{1/n}$, where $\mathrm{vol}(\mathcal{L})$ denotes the *volume* of $\mathcal{L}$. Many cryptographic primitives base their security on the worst-case hardness of δ-SVP or related lattice problems [2,27,43,46]. Security estimates of these constructions depend on solving δ-HSVP, typically for $\delta = \mathrm{poly}(n)$ [9,10]. The output quality of a δ-HSVP solver in rank n is typically assessed with the so-called *root Hermite factor* (RHF) $\delta^{1/(n-1)}$.[1]

To solve the approximate versions of SVP, the standard approach is *lattice reduction*, which finds reduced bases consisting of reasonably short and relatively orthogonal vectors. Its "modern" history began with the celebrated LLL algorithm [34] and continued with stronger blockwise algorithms [1,4,23,40,49,51]. Lattice reduction has numerous applications in mathematics, computer science and especially cryptanalysis.

Lovász [36] showed that any δ-HSVP solver in rank n can be used to efficiently solve δ^2-SVP in rank n. For random lattices $\mathcal{L}$ of rank n, the classical *Gaussian heuristic* claims $\lambda_1(\mathcal{L}) \approx \mathrm{GH}(\mathcal{L}) := \mathrm{GH}(n) \cdot \mathrm{vol}(\mathcal{L})^{1/n}$. Here, $\mathrm{GH}(n)$ denotes the radius of the unit-volume n-dimensional ball. Thus, any δ-HSVP solver in rank n for $\delta \geq \sqrt{n}$ can possibly be used to solve $(\delta/\sqrt{n})$-SVP in the same rank in practice (see [24, §3.2]).

In this work we consider the practical aspects of solving δ-HSVP using blockwise lattice reduction algorithms. The Schnorr–Euchner BKZ algorithm [51] and its modern incarnations [4,7,12,13,17] provide the best time/quality trade-off in practice. The BKZ algorithm takes a parameter k controlling its time/quality trade-off: the larger k is, the more reduced the output basis, but the running time grows at least exponentially with k. BKZ is commonly available in software libraries (such as FP(y)LLL [21,22], NTL [53] and PBKZ [12]) and has been used in many lattice record computations [7,19,48]. G6K [7,19] currently provides the fastest public BKZ implementation by replacing the enumeration-based SVP oracle in BKZ with a sieving-based oracle. As such, it achieves a running time of $2^{\Theta(k)}$ at the cost of also requiring $2^{\Theta(k)}$ memory. However, this memory requirement may prove prohibitively expensive in some settings. Moreover, in a massively parallelised computation the communication overhead required for sieving may limit its performance advantage.

In this work we reduce the performance gap between enumeration-based and sieving-based BKZ. That is, we focus on enumeration-based lattice reduction for solving δ-HSVP, i.e. the polynomial-memory regime, building on recent technical

---

[1] The normalisation by the $(n-1)$-th root is justified by that the algorithms considered here achieve RHFs that are bounded independently of the lattice rank n.

progress on speeding-up lattice enumeration: *relaxed pruned enumeration* [35] and *extended preprocessing* [4].

Recently, [35] heuristically justified that if relaxing the search radius by a small constant $\alpha > 1$, then enumeration with certain extreme cylinder pruning [25,52] asymptotically achieves an exponential speed-up. Intuitively, this relaxation strategy allows to upgrade the enumeration subroutine for BKZ (2.0) [17,51] with one more optional parameter α. Here and in what follows, we omit pruning parameters due to the use of FP(y)LLL's numerical **pruning** module [21,22].

Concurrently, a variant of BKZ presented in [4] can achieve RHF $\mathrm{GH}(k)^{1/(k-1)}$ in time $k^{k/8+o(k)}$, which is super-exponentially faster than the cost record $k^{k/(2e)+o(k)}$ of [29,31] for reaching the same RHF. The idea behind the BKZ variant [4] is to preprocess in a larger rank than the enumeration rank. That is, [4] upgraded the HSVP-oracle of BKZ to exact (pruned) enumeration in rank k with *extended preprocessing* in rank $\lceil (1+c) \cdot k \rceil$ for some small constant $c \geq 0$. Intuitively, this preprocessing strategy upgrades the enumeration subroutine for BKZ (2.0) [17,51] with an additional optional parameter c.

Contributions. This work investigates the impact of improved enumeration subroutines in BKZ by integrating the relaxation strategy [1,12,35] with the extended preprocessing strategy [4], i.e. we propose the use of *relaxed pruned enumeration with extended preprocessing* in BKZ.

First, in Sect. 3, we justify and empirically validate that relaxed enumeration with certain extreme cylinder pruning [25,52] asymptotically achieves better time/quality trade-offs for certain approximation regimes based on standard heuristics. More precisely, for large enough k, the resulting $\alpha \cdot \mathrm{GH}(k_\alpha)$-HSVP-oracle in rank k_α is exponentially faster than a $\mathrm{GH}(k)$-HSVP-oracle in rank k for any constant $\alpha \in (1,2]$. Here, k_α is the smallest integer greater than k such that the corresponding RHF would not become larger after relaxation:

$$\mathrm{GH}\,(k)^{\frac{1}{k-1}} \geq (\alpha \cdot \mathrm{GH}(k_\alpha))^{\frac{1}{k_\alpha-1}}.$$

Prior work [35] only treated the speed-up of $\alpha \cdot \mathrm{GH}(k)$ compared with $\mathrm{GH}(k)$.

Second, in Sect. 4, we explore the concrete cost estimates of relaxed enumeration with FP(y)LLL's **pruning** module [21,22] with or without extended preprocessing, using simulations and experiments. We validate that with the same preprocessing in rank $\lceil (1+c) \cdot k \rceil$ for $c \in [0, 0.4]$, the resulting $\alpha \cdot \mathrm{GH}(k)$-HSVP-oracle in rank k is exponentially faster than a $\mathrm{GH}(k)$-HSVP-oracle in rank k for constants $\alpha \in (1, 1.3]$.[2]

Third, our main result is a practical BKZ variant presented in Sect. 5, which uses an $(\alpha \cdot \mathrm{GH}(k_\alpha))$-HSVP enumeration oracle in rank k_α with preprocessing in rank $\lceil (1+c) \cdot k_\alpha \rceil$. Intuitively, it upgrades the enumeration subroutine for BKZ (2.0) [17,51] with two more optional parameters (α, c), and generalises the BKZ

---

[2] We also observed a small speed-up of $c = 0.15$ over $c = 0.25$ (claimed to be the "optimal" in [4]) and verified it using the original simulation code from [4] in the full version of this work.

variant in [4] with one more optional parameter α. This additional freedom results in the best current time/quality trade-off for enumeration-based BKZ implementations: our algorithm achieves RHF GH $(k)^{\frac{1}{k-1}}$ in time $\approx 2^{\frac{k \log k}{8} - 0.654\,k + 25.84}$. This improves on the cost record $2^{\frac{k \log k}{8} - 0.547\,k + 10.4}$ given in [4]. As a side result, by setting $c = 0$ (i.e. without extended preprocessing), our algorithm achieves RHF GH $(k)^{\frac{1}{k-1}}$ in time $\approx 2^{\frac{k \log k}{2\,e} - 1.077\,k + 29.12}$, which also improves on the cost for BKZ 2.0 [17] reported in [4]: $2^{\frac{k \log k}{2\,e} - 0.995\,k + 16.25}$. A comparison between our results and those reported in [4] is given in Fig. 1: it illustrates that our BKZ variant is exponentially faster than previous BKZ variants in the polynomial-memory setting. Comparing our best fit with the results reported in [4], we obtain a crossover rank of 145, or approximately 2^{61} operations.[3]

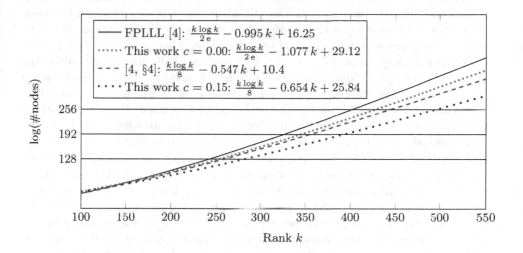

Fig. 1. Cost comparison.

Since our results critically depend on our simulation and implementation results, we provide the complete source code (used to produce our simulation data and experimental verification) with the full version of this work.

Impact on security estimates. Security estimates for lattice-based cryptographic primitives typically rely upon sieving algorithms [6]. In the classical (i.e. non-quantum) setting this is backed by both the asymptotic [14] and concrete [7,19] performance of sieving algorithms. Our results do not affect this

---

[3] To put this into perspective, [55] reports solving 1.05-HSVP in rank 150 using a distributed implementation of an enumeration algorithm. As a result, we expect the speedups demonstrated in this work to be practical.

state of the art.[4] As can be gleaned from Fig. 1, all known enumeration-based algorithms, including those based on the strategies in this work, perform similarly up to rank $k \approx 100$. On the other hand, G6K [7] outperforms FPLLL's implementation of enumeration for ranks $\gtrsim 70$.

In the quantum setting the situation is considerably more complicated. Quantum enumeration algorithms asymptotically produce a quadratic speed-up over classical enumeration algorithms [11] in the "query model", but each such queries may have significant (polynomial) cost, implying that such an estimate is likely a significant underestimate of the true cost. On the other hand, quantum sieving improves the cost from $2^{0.292\,k+o(k)}$ to $2^{0.265\,k+o(k)}$ [33], assuming no depth restriction on quantum computation. In [8] some quantum resource estimates are given for the dominant part of various lattice sieving algorithms. These costs, however, are derived assuming unit cost for accessing quantum accessible RAM, an optimistic assumption. Overall, given the lack of clarity on the cost of the two families of algorithms under consideration in a quantum setting, it is currently not possible to assess the crossover rank when quantum lattice sieving outperforms quantum lattice-point enumeration. This suggests an analogous investigation to [8] for quantum enumeration as a pressing research question.

Faced with the difficulty of assessing the cost of quantum algorithms, the literature routinely relies on rough low bounds to estimate the cost of lattice reduction, see e.g. [15,26,45].[5] In particular, the quantum version of the Core-SVP methodology [10] assigns a cost of $2^{0.265\,k}$ to performing lattice reduction with RHF $GH(k)^{1/(k-1)}$. Now, comparing this figure with a naive square-root of our enumeration costs would give a crossover rank of $k = 547$. Yet, even then, i.e. even presuming the square-root advantage applies as is to our algorithm including preprocessing, accepting the assumptions of suppressing (potentially significant) polynomial factors, no depth restriction on quantum computation and unit-cost qRAM, this would not imply a downward correction of Category 1 NIST PQC Round 3 submission parameters and similar parameters for lattice-based schemes. That is, we stress that this work does *not* invalidate the claimed NIST Security Level of such submissions. This is because a given security level is defined by both a classical and a quantum cost: roughly 2^{λ} classically and $2^{\lambda/2}$ quantumly. For example, for Level 1 this is the cost of classically and quantumly breaking AES-128. Submissions targeting a classical security level 2^{λ} relying on the cost of classical sieving $2^{0.292\,k+o(k)}$ have a quantum security level much higher than $2^{\lambda/2}$ under the $2^{0.265\,k}$ cost model. In other words, this work does not lower the cost of quantum enumeration sufficiently to invalidate NIST Security Level claims since known quantum algorithms provide only a minor speed-up in the chosen cost model over classical algorithms when compared to Grover's algorithm for, say, AES.

---

[4] We discuss the (apparent lack of) applicability of our approach to the sieving setting in the full version of this work.

[5] This does not imply, though, that those works endorse this mode of comparison, e.g. [15] explicates its objections to it.

2   Background

Notation. To be compatible with software implementations such as FP(y)LLL, we let matrix indices start with 0 and use row-representation for both vectors and matrices in this work. Bold lower-case and upper-case letters denote row vectors and matrices respectively. The set of $n \times m$ matrices with coefficients in the ring $\mathbb{A}$ is denoted by $\mathbb{A}^{n \times m}$, and we identify $\mathbb{A}^m$ with $\mathbb{A}^{1 \times m}$. The notations $\log(\cdot)$ and $\ln(\cdot)$ stand for the base 2 and natural logarithms respectively.

2.1   Lattices

Orthogonalisation. Let $B = (b_0, \ldots, b_{n-1}) \in \mathbb{R}^{n \times m}$ be a basis of a lattice $\mathcal{L}$. Lattice algorithms often involve the orthogonal projections $\pi_i : \mathbb{R}^m \mapsto$ span $(b_0, \ldots, b_{i-1})^{\perp}$ for $i = 0, \ldots, n-1$. The *Gram–Schmidt orthogonalisation* (GSO) of B is $B^* = (b_0^*, \ldots, b_{n-1}^*)$, where the Gram–Schmidt vector b_i^* is $\pi_i(b_i)$. Then $b_0^* = b_0$ and $b_i^* = b_i - \sum_{j=0}^{i-1} \mu_{i,j} \cdot b_j^*$ for $i = 1, \ldots, n-1$, where $\mu_{i,j} = \frac{\langle b_i, b_j^* \rangle}{\langle b_j^*, b_j^* \rangle}$. The projected block $(\pi_i(b_i), \pi_i(b_{i+1}), \ldots, \pi_i(b_{j-1}))$ is denoted by $B_{[i,j)}$. Then the volume of the parallelepiped generated by $B_{[i,j)}$ is $\mathrm{vol}(B_{[i,j)}) = \prod_{k=i}^{j-1} \|b_k^*\|$. In particular, $B_{[0,j)} = (b_0, \ldots, b_{j-1})$ and $\mathrm{vol}(\mathcal{L}) = \mathrm{vol}(B) = \prod_{k=0}^{n-1} \|b_k^*\|$.

Hermite's constant. Hermite's constant of dimension n is the maximum $\gamma_n = \max \left(\lambda_1(\mathcal{L})/\mathrm{vol}(\mathcal{L})^{1/n} \right)^2$ over all n-rank lattices $\mathcal{L}$, where $\lambda_1(\mathcal{L}) = \min_{v \in \mathcal{L} \setminus \{0\}} \|v\|$ is the *first minimum* of $\mathcal{L}$. The best asymptotical bounds known are [18,41]: $\frac{n}{2\pi e} + \frac{\log(\pi n)}{2\pi e} \leq \gamma_n \leq \frac{1.744n}{2\pi e} + o(n)$.

Lattice reduction. Let $B = (b_0, \ldots, b_{n-1})$ be a basis of a lattice $\mathcal{L}$.

B is *size-reduced* if $|\mu_{i,j}| \leq \frac{1}{2}$ for all $0 \leq j < i < n$. B is *LLL-reduced* [34] if it is size-reduced and every 2-rank projected block $B_{[i,i+2)}$ satisfies Lovász's condition: $\frac{3}{4} \cdot \|b_i^*\|^2 \leq \|\mu_{i+1,i} \cdot b_i^* + b_{i+1}^*\|^2$ for $0 \leq i \leq n-2$. In practice, the parameter $\frac{3}{4}$ can be replaced with any constant in the interval $(\frac{1}{4}, 1)$.

B is *SVP-reduced* if $\|b_0\| = \lambda_1(\mathcal{L})$. There are two relaxations with $\delta \geq 1$: B is δ-*SVP-reduced* if $\|b_0\| \leq \delta \cdot \lambda_1(\mathcal{L})$; B is δ-*HSVP-reduced* if $\|b_0\| \leq \delta \cdot \mathrm{vol}(\mathcal{L})^{1/n}$.

B is *HKZ-reduced* if it is size-reduced and $B_{[i,n)}$ is SVP-reduced for $i = 0, \ldots, n-1$; B is *k-BKZ-reduced* [49] if it is size-reduced and $B_{[i,\min\{i+k,n\})}$ is SVP-reduced for $i = 0, \ldots, n-1$.

Primitive vector. Let $\mathcal{L}$ be a lattice with basis $(b_0, \ldots, b_{n-1})$. A vector $b = \sum_{i=0}^{n-1} x_i b_i \in \mathcal{L}$ with $x_i \in \mathbb{Z}$ is *primitive* for $\mathcal{L}$ iff it can be extended to a basis of $\mathcal{L}$, or equivalently, $\gcd(x_0, \ldots, x_{n-1}) = 1$ [54, Theorem 32].

HSVP-oracle and RHF. A δ-HSVP-oracle with factor $\delta > 0$ is any algorithm which, given as input an n-rank lattice $\mathcal{L}$ specified by a basis, outputs a primitive vector $\mathbf{v}$ in $\mathcal{L}$ such that $\|\mathbf{v}\| \leq \delta \cdot \mathrm{vol}(\mathcal{L})^{1/n}$. The resulting *root-Hermite-factor* (RHF) is $\left(\frac{\|\mathbf{v}\|}{\mathrm{vol}(\mathcal{L})^{1/n}}\right)^{1/(n-1)}$, which is less than $\delta^{1/(n-1)}$. In other words, the worst-case RHF of this δ-HSVP-oracle on an n-rank lattice is $\delta^{1/(n-1)}$. For instance, any exact SVP-solver working on an n-rank lattice is a $\sqrt{\gamma_n}$-HSVP-oracle, whose corresponding worse-case RHF is $\gamma_n^{\frac{1}{2(n-1)}}$.

Geometric Series Assumption. Let $\mathbf{B} = (\mathbf{b}_0, \ldots, \mathbf{b}_{n-1})$ be a basis. Schnorr's *Geometric Series Assumption* (GSA) [50] says that $\mathbf{B}$ follows the GSA wrt. some constant $r \in [3/4, 1)$ (depending on the reduction algorithm) if its Gram–Schmidt lengths decay geometrically wrt. r, namely $\|\mathbf{b}_{i+1}^*\|/\|\mathbf{b}_i^*\| = r$ for all $i = 0, \ldots, n-2$. In practice, it has been observed that a reduced basis produced by the LLL algorithm [34] satisfies the GSA in an approximate sense when the input basis is sufficiently randomised.

Gaussian heuristic. Given a full-rank lattice $\mathcal{L}$ in $\mathbb{R}^n$ and a measurable set $S \subseteq \mathbb{R}^n$, the cardinality of $S \cap \mathcal{L}$ is approximately $\mathrm{vol}(S)/\mathrm{vol}(\mathcal{L})$. Under the heuristic, there are about α^n points in $\mathcal{L}$ of norm $\leq \alpha \cdot \mathrm{GH}(\mathcal{L})$, and one would expect $\lambda_1(\mathcal{L})$ to be close to $\mathrm{GH}(\mathcal{L})$. Here, $\mathrm{GH}(\mathcal{L}) := \mathrm{GH}(n) \cdot \mathrm{vol}(\mathcal{L})^{1/n}$ with

$$\mathrm{GH}(n) := \frac{\Gamma(n/2+1)^{1/n}}{\sqrt{\pi}} \approx \sqrt{\frac{n}{2\pi e}} \cdot (\pi n)^{\frac{1}{2n}}$$

by Stirling's formula. In fact, for a random lattice $\mathcal{L}$, $\lambda_1(\mathcal{L})$ is close to $\mathrm{GH}(\mathcal{L})$ with high probability [47]; for any lattice $\mathcal{L}$ of rank $n > 24$, it follows from Blichfeldt's inequality $\gamma_n \leq 2 \cdot \mathrm{GH}(n)^2$ [16] that $\lambda_1(\mathcal{L}) \leq \sqrt{2} \cdot \mathrm{GH}(\mathcal{L})$.

2.2   Enumeration: Pruning Plus Relaxation

Enumeration [4,20,31,39,44,51] is the simplest algorithm for solving SVP and requires only polynomial memory: given a full-rank lattice $\mathcal{L}$ in $\mathbb{R}^n$ and a radius $R > 0$, enumeration outputs $\mathcal{L} \cap \mathrm{Ball}_n(R)$ by a depth-first tree search. If $R \geq \lambda_1(\mathcal{L})$, then it is trivial to extract a nonzero lattice vector of length $\leq R$: moreover, by comparing all the norms of vectors in $\mathcal{L} \cap \mathrm{Ball}_n(R)$, one can find a shortest nonzero lattice vector.

Cylinder pruning [25,52] speeds up enumeration by replacing the search region $\mathrm{Ball}_n(R)$ with a (much smaller) subset $\mathrm{P}_f(\mathbf{B}, R)$ defined by a bounding function $f : \{1, \ldots, n\} \to [0,1]$, a basis $\mathbf{B}$ of $\mathcal{L}$ and R:

$$\mathrm{P}_f(\mathbf{B}, R) = \{\mathbf{x} \in \mathbb{R}^n : \|\pi_{n-k}(\mathbf{x})\| \leq f(k) \cdot R \text{ for all } 1 \leq k \leq n\} \subseteq \mathrm{Ball}_n(R).$$

Algorithm 1 recalls enumeration with extreme cylinder pruning, which repeats enumeration with cylinder pruning many times over different subsets $\mathrm{P}_f(\mathbf{B}, R)$ by randomising $\mathbf{B}$. Here, each Step 3 is a single cylinder pruning.

Algorithm 1. Extreme cylinder pruning [25, Algorithm 1]

Require: $(\mathcal{L}, R, f)$, where $\mathcal{L}$ is a full-rank lattice in $\mathbb{R}^n$ specified by a basis, $R > 0$ is
  a radius and f is a bounding function.
Ensure: A nonzero vector in $\mathcal{L} \cap \mathrm{Ball}_n(R)$.
1: **WHILE** no nonzero vector in $\mathcal{L} \cap \mathrm{Ball}_n(R)$ has been found:
2:     Compute a (randomised) reduced basis B by applying basis reduction to a "random" basis of $\mathcal{L}$.
3:     Compute $\mathcal{L} \cap \mathrm{P}_f(B, R)$ by enumeration with cylinder pruning

---

The use of enumeration with extreme cylinder pruning in blockwise lattice reduction requires finding just one nonzero point in $\mathcal{L} \cap \mathrm{P}_f(B, R)$ for some basis B produced at Step 2: it allows to suitably relax radius R for speedup, which was already exploited in solving SVP challenges [48].

Recently, Li and Nguyen [35] clarified the heuristic asymptotic speedup achieved by enumeration with relaxed radius and with certain extreme cylinder pruning. It uses the following two heuristic assumptions as in [25]:

Heuristic 1   *The cost of Algorithm 1 is dominated by enumeration with cylinder pruning at Step 3, rather than the repeated reductions of Step 2.*

Heuristic 2   *All the reduced bases B of Algorithm 1 follow the GSA wrt. the same positive constant.*

Theorem 1 ([35, Theorem 6]). *Let $\mathcal{L}$ be a full-rank lattice in $\mathbb{R}^n$. Let $\alpha \geq 1$ and $\rho \in (0, \frac{1}{2})$ such that $4\,\alpha^4 \cdot \rho \cdot (1 - \rho) < 1$. Let $R = \alpha \cdot \mathrm{GH}(\mathcal{L})$ and*

$$f(i) = \begin{cases} \sqrt{\rho} \ \text{if } 1 \leq i \leq n/2, \\ 1 \quad \text{otherwise.} \end{cases}$$

Under Heuristics 1 and 2, the time complexity $T_{\alpha,\rho}(n)$ of Algorithm 1 on $(\mathcal{L}, R, f)$ equals, up to polynomial factors, $T(n)$ of a full enumeration on $\mathcal{L} \cap \mathrm{Ball}_n(\mathrm{GH}(\mathcal{L}))$ reduced by a multiplicative factor $(4\alpha^2(1 - \rho))^{n/4}$:

$$T_{\alpha,\rho}(n) \approx \frac{T(n)}{(4\alpha^2(1 - \rho))^{n/4}}.$$

Here (and for the remainder of this work) the cost of enumeration is expressed as the number of nodes visited during the enumeration process.

2.3   Schnorr–Euchner's BKZ and its Accelerated Variant in [4]

BKZ. The (original) BKZ algorithm introduced by Schnorr and Euchner [51] is the most widely used lattice reduction algorithm besides LLL [34] and a central tool in lattice-based cryptanalysis. Its performance drives the setting of concrete parameters (such as keysizes) for concrete lattice-based cryptographic primitives (see e.g. [6]).

Originally, the SVP subroutine implemented in [51] was the simplest form of lattice enumeration, but it is now replaced by better subroutines, such as pruned enumeration [25] in BKZ 2.0 [17] and FP(y)LLL [21,22] and (asymptotically) faster sieving in the General Sieve Kernel [7,19]. In practice, BKZ is typically implemented with an approximate (rather than exact) SVP-subroutine. Thus, Algorithm 2 slightly generalises BKZ by allowing the use of a relaxed HSVP-oracle at Step 3, as well as full LLL (instead of partial LLL) at Step 5: both are justified by Li–Nguyen's analysis [35].

At a high level, Algorithm 2 reduces a basis in high rank, using HSVP-oracles in low rank ($\leq k$) as subroutines and running the LLL algorithm [34] to remove the linear dependency right after inserting a lattice vector (found by the oracle) in the current basis.

Algorithm 2. BKZ: Schnorr–Euchner's BKZ algorithm [51]

Require: A block size $k \in (2, n)$, the number of tours $N \in \mathbb{Z}^+$, a relaxation factor $\alpha \geq 1$, and an LLL-reduced basis $\boldsymbol{B} = (\boldsymbol{b}_0, \ldots, \boldsymbol{b}_{n-1})$ of a lattice $\mathcal{L} \subseteq \mathbb{Z}^m$.
Ensure: A new basis of $\mathcal{L}$.
 1: **for** $\ell = 0$ to $N - 1$ **do**
 2:     **for** $j = 0$ to $n - 2$ **do**
 3:         Find a primitive vector $\boldsymbol{b}$ for the sublattice generated by the basis vectors
         $\boldsymbol{b}_j, \ldots, \boldsymbol{b}_{h-1}$ where $h = \min\{j + k, n\}$ s.t. $\|\pi_j(\boldsymbol{b})\| \leq \alpha \sqrt{\gamma_{h-j}} \cdot \mathrm{vol}(\boldsymbol{B}_{[j,h)})^{1/(h-j)}$
 4:         **if** $\|\boldsymbol{b}_j^*\| > \|\pi_j(\boldsymbol{b})\|$ **then**
 5:             LLL-reduce $(\boldsymbol{b}_0, \ldots, \boldsymbol{b}_{j-1}, \boldsymbol{b}, \boldsymbol{b}_j, \ldots, \boldsymbol{b}_{n-1})$ to remove linear dependencies
 6:         **end if**
 7:     **end for**   //A BKZ tour refers to a single execution of Steps 2-7.
 8: **end for**
 9: **return** $\boldsymbol{B}$.

Building on Hanrot–Pujol–Stehlé's analysis of a certain BKZ variant (removing internal LLL calls) [28], Li and Nguyen [35] justified the popular "early termination" strategy in practice of BKZ:

Theorem 2 ([35, Theorem 2]). *Let $n > k \geq 2$ be integers and let $0 < \varepsilon \leq 1 \leq \alpha \leq \frac{2^{(k-1)/4}}{\sqrt{\gamma_k}}$. Given as input a block size k, a relaxation factor α, and an LLL-reduced basis of an n-rank lattice $\mathcal{L} \subset \mathbb{R}^m$, if $N \geq 4(\ln 2)\frac{n^2}{k^2} \log \frac{n^{1.5}}{(4\sqrt{3})\varepsilon}$, then Algorithm 2 outputs a basis $(\boldsymbol{b}_0, \ldots, \boldsymbol{b}_{n-1})$ of $\mathcal{L}$ such that*

$$\|\boldsymbol{b}_0\| \leq (1 + \varepsilon) \cdot (\alpha^2 \gamma_k)^{\frac{n-1}{2(k-1)} + \frac{k \cdot (k-2)}{2n \cdot (k-1)}} \cdot \mathrm{vol}(\mathcal{L})^{1/n}.$$

It was also mentioned in [35] that for $n > k > 8e\pi$, there is a k-BKZ reduced basis $\boldsymbol{B} = (\boldsymbol{b}_0, \ldots, \boldsymbol{b}_{n-1})$ satisfying $\|\boldsymbol{b}_0\| = \left(\frac{k-1}{8e\pi}\right)^{\frac{n-1}{2k}} \cdot \mathrm{vol}(\boldsymbol{B})^{1/n}$. Since $\gamma_k = \Theta(k)$, this means that BKZ with early termination indeed provides bases almost as reduced as the full BKZ algorithm. Theorem 2 has a heuristic version (i.e. [35, Th. 5]), which heuristically models the practical behaviour of BKZ.

The accelerated BKZ variant in [4]. Recently, in [4] a practical and faster BKZ variant within the class of polynomial-space algorithms was introduced, based on the idea that its HSVP-oracle performs an exact enumeration with *extended preprocessing*.

Extended preprocessing is to preprocess in a larger rank than the enumeration rank. Exact enumeration with extended preprocessing refers to the procedure that the $\delta(k)$-HSVP-oracle in "block size" $\lceil (1 + c) \cdot k \rceil$ (for some small constant $c \geq 0$ and an integer $k \geq 2$) first preprocesses a given projected block of rank $\lceil (1+c) \cdot k \rceil$ (using this BKZ variant recursively in lower levels) into a reduced block (say,) C and then performs a (pruned) enumeration for solving SVP exactly on the k-rank head block of C to find a short nonzero vector $v \in \mathcal{L}(C)$.

The performance parameter k dominates the time/quality trade-off:

- Quality aspect: v is a shortest nonzero vector in the lattice generated by the k-rank head block $C_{[0,k)}$ of C, so that $\|v\| \leq \sqrt{\gamma_k} \cdot \mathrm{vol}(C_{[0,k)})^{1/k}$. The BKZ-preprocessing on C ensures that $\mathrm{vol}(C_{[0,k)})/\mathrm{vol}(C)^{k/\lceil(1+c)k\rceil}$ can be upper bounded well, so that $\|v\| \leq \delta(k) \cdot \mathrm{vol}(C)^{1/\lceil(1+c)k\rceil}$.
- Cost aspect: Due to the extended preprocessing on C, the k-rank head block $C_{[0,k)}$ has good quality for enumeration, i.e. $C_{[0,k)}$ almost satisfies the GSA. As a result, enumeration on $C_{[0,k)}$ costs at most $k^{k/8} \cdot 2^{O(k)}$ (matching the Gaussian heuristic estimate under the GSA). Both the GSA shape and the cost estimate were validated by [4]'s simulations and experiments.

We revisit [4, § 4]'s BKZ variant in Algorithms 3 and 4. We refer the reader to [4] for definitions of the functions tail() and pre() called in Algorithm 4.

When $c = 0$, Algorithm 3 is essentially Schnorr-Euchner's BKZ algorithm [51] (i.e. using enumeration but with recursive BKZ preprocessing as an SVP-oracle).

Algorithm 3. BKZ variant in [4, Algorithm 4]

Require: (B, k, c), where $B = (b_0, \ldots, b_{n-1})$ is an LLL-reduced basis of an n-rank lattice $\mathcal{L}$ in $\mathbb{Z}^m$, $k \in [2, n)$ is a performance parameter, $c \geq 0$ is an overshooting parameter and $N \in \mathbb{Z}^+$ is the number of tours.
Ensure: A reduced basis of $\mathcal{L}$.
1: **for** $\ell = 0$ to $N - 1$ **do**
2:     **for** $j = 0$ to $n - 2$ **do**
3:         Find a short nonzero vector v in the lattice $\mathcal{L}_{[j,h)}$ (generated by the projected block $B_{[j,h)}$ where $h = \min\{j + \lceil (1 + c)k \rceil, n\}$), by calling Alg. 4 on $(B_{[j,h)}, k, c)$
4:         **if** $\|b_j^*\| > \|v\|$ **then**
5:             Lift v into a primitive vector b for the sublattice generated by the basis vectors $b_j, \ldots, b_{h-1}$ such that $\|\pi_j(b)\| \leq \|v\|$
6:                 LLL-reduce $(b_0, \ldots, b_{j-1}, b, b_j, \ldots, b_{n-1})$ to remove linear dependencies
7:             **end if**
8:         **end for**
9: **end for**
10: **return** B.

Without formal analysis but with concrete simulations and experiments, [4] reported that the following instantiation of Algorithm 3 seems to provide the best practical performance: $(c, N) = (0.25, 4)$ and Algorithm 4 performing pruned enumeration at both Step 4 and Step 8. The resulting procedure achieves RHF $\approx \mathrm{GH}(k)^{1/(k-1)}$ in time $\approx 2^{\frac{k \log k}{8} - 0.547\,k + 10.4}$, at least up to $k \approx 500$.

2.4   Simulating BKZ

To understand the behaviour of lattice reduction algorithms, a useful approach is to conduct simulations. The underlying idea is to model the practical behaviour of the evolution of the Gram–Schmidt norms during the algorithm execution, without running a costly lattice reduction algorithm. Note that this requires only the Gram–Schmidt norms rather than the basis itself. Chen and Nguyen first provided a BKZ simulator [17] based on the Gaussian heuristic and with an experiment-driven modification for the tail blocks of the basis. It relies on the assumption that each SVP solver on the projected blocks (except the tail ones of the basis) finds a vector whose norm corresponds to the Gaussian heuristic applied to that local block.

We extend/adapt this simulator to also estimate the cost and not only the evolution of the Gram–Schmidt norms. To find the enumeration cost with pruning, we make use of FPyLLL's `pruning` module which numerically optimises pruning parameters for a time/success probability trade-off using a gradient descent. In small block sizes, the enumeration cost is dominated by calls to LLL. In our code, we simply assume that one LLL call in rank k costs the equivalent of visiting k^3 enumeration nodes. While this is clearly not the cost of LLL [42], this choice produces costs that match the observed running times (see e.g. Fig. 4) closest among the choices we experimented with. We hypothesise that this behaviour can be explained by that the basis vectors $\boldsymbol{b}_0, \ldots, \boldsymbol{b}_{j-1}, \boldsymbol{b}_j, \ldots, \boldsymbol{b}_{n-1}$ appearing at, say, Step 6 of Algorithm 3 are already (better than) LLL-reduced. This assumption enables us to bootstrap our cost estimates. BKZ in block size up to (say,) 40 only requires LLL preprocessing, allowing us to estimate the cost of preprocessing with block size up to 40, which in turn enables us to estimate the cost (including preprocessing) for larger block sizes etc. Our simulation source

---

Algorithm 4. An approx-HSVP oracle on $(\boldsymbol{B}_{[j,h)}, k, c)$ using exact enumeration in rank k^* with extended preprocessing in rank $(h - j)$ [4, Algorithm 3]

1: Find the enumeration rank $k^* \leftarrow \mathrm{tail}(k, c, h - j)$
2: Numerically find the preprocessing parameter $k' \leftarrow \mathrm{pre}(k^*, \|\boldsymbol{b}_j^*\|, \ldots, \|\boldsymbol{b}_{h-1}^*\|)$
3: **if** $k' \geq 3$ **then**
4:     Run Alg. 3 on $(\boldsymbol{B}_{[j,h)}, k', c)$ to obtain a reduced basis $\boldsymbol{C} \in \mathbb{Q}^{(h-j) \times m}$ of $\mathcal{L}_{[j,h)}$
5: **else**
6:     LLL-reduce $\boldsymbol{B}_{[j,h)}$ into a basis $\boldsymbol{C} \in \mathbb{Q}^{(h-j) \times m}$ of $\mathcal{L}_{[j,h)}$
7: **end if**   //Steps 3-7 preprocess $\boldsymbol{B}_{[j,h)}$ for the next local enumeration
8: Enumerate on the head block $\boldsymbol{C}_{[0,k^*)}$ of $\boldsymbol{C}$ to find a shortest nonzero vector $\boldsymbol{v}$ in the lattice generated by $\boldsymbol{C}_{[0,k^*)}$

code is available as `simu.py`, as an attachment to the electronic version of the full version of this document.

3   Asymptotic Time/Quality Trade-Offs

In this section, we show asymptotically that relaxed (rather than exact) enumeration with certain extreme cylinder pruning does achieve better time/quality trade-offs for certain approximation regimes, especially for small enough RHFs.

3.1   An Elementary Lemma

We will use the following notation for the remainder of this work:

- δ-HSVP enumeration oracle: it denotes a δ-HSVP-solver using (relaxed) enumeration with (extreme) pruning, i.e. setting the radius $R = \delta \cdot \text{vol}(\mathcal{L})^{1/n}$ for enumeration on a given n-rank lattice $\mathcal{L}$.
- k_α: for real $\alpha \geq 1$ and integer $k \geq 36$, let k_α be the smallest integer greater than k such that

$$\text{GH}(k)^{\frac{1}{k-1}} \geq (\alpha \cdot \text{GH}(k_\alpha))^{\frac{1}{k_\alpha-1}}. \tag{1}$$

The integer k_α is well-defined, due to the following fact:

Fact 3. *With the definition* $\text{GH}(i) = \frac{\Gamma(i/2+1)^{1/i}}{\sqrt{\pi}}$, $\text{GH}(i)^{\frac{1}{i-1}}$ *strictly decreases for integers* $i \geq 36$.

Our following analysis relies on a key observation that the ratio $\frac{k_\alpha}{k}$ "almost" decreases for $k \geq \lceil 2\pi e^2 \rceil = 47$ and tends to 1 as k tends to infinity. More precisely, we will use the following key elementary lemma:

Lemma 1. *Let* $\alpha \geq 1$ *be a real and* $k \geq 36$ *be an integer.*

1. *Monotonicity: For any fixed k, k_α increases with $\alpha \geq 1$.*
2. *Lower bound: $k_\alpha \geq k + \frac{k \log \alpha}{\log k}$.*
3. *Upper bound: If $k \geq (2\pi e^2)^{\frac{\eta}{\eta-2}}$ for some variable $\eta > 2$, then*

$$k_\alpha \leq k + \left\lceil \frac{\eta k \log \alpha}{\log k} \right\rceil.$$

The proofs of Fact 3 and Lemma 1 can be found in the full version of this work.

Lemma 1 indicates that asymptotically for a fixed constant α, the larger the integer k, the smaller we can assign the variable η in Item 3, then the smaller both the upper bound $1 + \frac{\eta \log \alpha}{\log k} + \frac{1}{k}$ and the lower bound $1 + \frac{\log \alpha}{\log k}$ of the ratio $\frac{k_\alpha}{k}$. Figure 2 verifies this numerically for several values of α and k.

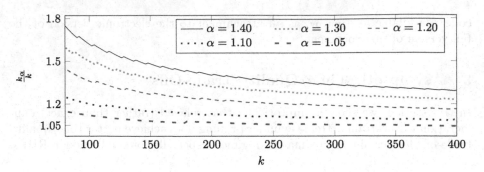

Fig. 2. Evolution of the ratio $\frac{k_\alpha}{k}$ wrt. constant $\alpha \in \{1.05, 1.1, 1.2, 1.3, 1.4\}$ and integer $k = 80, \ldots, 400$.

3.2 Asymptotic Time/Quality Trade-Offs

Theorem 1 implies that with certain extreme cylinder pruning, relaxing enumeration would result in an exponential speedup, with a minor loss in the approximation factor:

Corollary 1. *Let $\mathcal{L}$ be a full-rank lattice in $\mathbb{R}^n$. Let $\alpha \geq 1$ and $\rho \in (0, \frac{1}{2})$ such that $4\alpha^4 \rho(1 - \rho) < 1$. Let $R = \mathrm{GH}(\mathcal{L})$, $R_\alpha = \alpha \cdot \mathrm{GH}(\mathcal{L})$ and*

$$f(i) = \begin{cases} \sqrt{\rho} \text{ if } 1 \leq i \leq n/2, \\ 1 \quad otherwise. \end{cases}$$

Under Heuristics 1 and 2, the heuristic time complexity of Algorithm 1 with radius R_α is less than that of Algorithm 1 with radius R by a multiplicative factor $\alpha^{n/2}$ (up to some polynomial factor).

Proof. Let $T(n)$ denote the standard heuristic estimate for the cost of full enumeration on $\mathcal{L} \cap \mathrm{Ball}_n(\mathrm{GH}(\mathcal{L}))$. It follows from Theorem 1 that the heuristic cost estimates of Algorithm 1 with radius R_α and with radius R are respectively

$$\frac{T(n)}{(4\alpha^2(1 - \rho))^{n/4}} \quad \text{and} \quad \frac{T(n)}{(4(1 - \rho))^{n/4}}$$

up to some polynomial factors. This implies the conclusion. $\qquad\square$

The corollary indicates that, in the same extreme pruning regime (i.e. with the same bounding function f), if one is interested in finding just one short nonzero vector (rather than one shortest nonzero vector) for a given lattice, then it is faster to run a relaxed (rather than exact) enumeration.

A more interesting question is whether such benefits can be carried out without sacrificing the quality. Thus what remains to be established is how the cost gain compares to the corresponding quality loss. For instance, we take $k = 50$ and $\alpha = 2$. For reaching the same RHF GH $(50)^{\frac{1}{49}} \approx 1.012$, it is unlikely that the

$(2 \cdot \mathrm{GH}(152))$-HSVP enumeration oracle in rank 152 is faster than the $\mathrm{GH}(50)$-HSVP enumeration oracle in rank 50. Thus, we now clarify that asymptotically relaxed (rather than exact) enumeration with certain extreme cylinder pruning does achieve better time/quality trade-offs for certain approximation regimes, especially for small enough RHFs. To do so, we compare costs of δ-HSVP enumeration oracles with different factors δ aiming for the same output quality.

More precisely, Lemma 1 allows us to prove that for reaching the same RHF $\mathrm{GH}(k)^{\frac{1}{k-1}}$, the $(\alpha \cdot \mathrm{GH}(k_\alpha))$-HSVP enumeration oracle in rank k_α is exponentially faster than the $\mathrm{GH}(k)$-HSVP enumeration oracle in rank k, provided that k is sufficiently large and $\alpha > 1$ is reasonably small.

Theorem 4. *Let $\alpha > 1$ and $\rho \in (0, \frac{1}{2})$ be constants such that $4\alpha^4 \rho \cdot (1 - \rho) < 1$. Let*

$$f(i) = \begin{cases} \sqrt{\rho} & \text{if } 1 \leq i \leq n/2, \\ 1 & \text{otherwise.} \end{cases}$$

In addition to Heuristics 1 and 2, assume that up to some polynomial factor, the heuristic runtime of full enumeration on any n-rank integer lattice with radius equal to the Gaussian heuristic is $T(n) := n^{c_0 n} \cdot 2^{c_1 n}$ with constant coefficients c_0, c_1 such that $0 < c_0 < \frac{1}{4}$. Let k be an arbitrary positive integer satisfying $k > \max\left\{ (2\pi e^2)^{\frac{1}{1-4c_0}}, 2^{-\frac{c_1}{c_0}} \right\}$. For any real $\eta \in [\frac{2\ln k}{\ln k - \ln(2\pi e^2)}, \frac{1}{2c_0})$, if $1 < \alpha \leq (k^{c_0} \cdot 2^{c_1})^2$, then the $(\alpha \cdot \mathrm{GH}(k_\alpha))$-HSVP enumeration oracle in rank k_α (using Algorithm 1) is exponentially faster than the $\mathrm{GH}(k)$-HSVP enumeration oracle in rank k (using Algorithm 1) by a multiplicative factor of at least

$$\alpha^{\left(\frac{1}{2} - c_0\eta\right)k} \cdot \left(4(1 - \rho) \left(\frac{\sqrt{\alpha}}{(2e)^{c_0} 2^{c_1}} \right)^{4\eta} \right)^{\frac{k \log \alpha}{4 \log k}} \qquad \text{(up to some polynomial factor).}$$

Proof. We omit some polynomial factors in the following complexity analysis. By the assumption, it follows from Theorem 1 that the heuristic runtime of the $(\alpha \cdot \mathrm{GH}(k_\alpha))$-HSVP enumeration oracle in rank k_α and the $\mathrm{GH}(k)$-HSVP enumeration oracle in rank k are respectively

$$T_\alpha \approx \frac{T(k_\alpha)}{(4\alpha^2(1 - \rho))^{k_\alpha/4}} = k_\alpha^{c_0 k_\alpha} \cdot 2^{c_1 k_\alpha} \cdot \alpha^{-k_\alpha/2} \cdot (4(1 - \rho))^{-k_\alpha/4}$$

$$= 2^{\left(c_0 \log k_\alpha + c_1 - \frac{\log \alpha}{2}\right)k_\alpha} \cdot (4(1 - \rho))^{-k_\alpha/4},$$

$$T_1 \approx \frac{T(k)}{(4(1 - \rho))^{k/4}} = k^{c_0 k} \cdot 2^{c_1 k} \cdot (4(1 - \rho))^{-k/4}.$$

For simplicity, let $u_\alpha := k + \phi_\alpha \in \mathbb{Z}^+$ with $\phi_\alpha := \left\lceil \frac{\eta k \log \alpha}{\log k} \right\rceil$. Since $\eta \in [\frac{2\ln k}{\ln k - \ln(2\pi e^2)}, \frac{1}{2c_0})$ and $k > (2\pi e^2)^{\frac{1}{1-4c_0}}$, we have $\eta > 2$ and $k \geq (2\pi e^2)^{\frac{\eta}{\eta-2}} > (2\pi e^2)^{\frac{1}{1-4c_0}}$. Then Item 3 of Lemma 1 implies $k_\alpha \leq u_\alpha$. Since $1 < \alpha \leq (k^{c_0} \cdot 2^{c_1})^2$, Item 2 of Lemma 1 implies $k_\alpha > k \geq \alpha^{\frac{1}{c_0}} 2^{\frac{|c_1|}{c_0}}$. Then $c_0 \log k_\alpha + c_1 - \frac{\log \alpha}{2} > 0$.

Thus,

$$T_\alpha \lesssim 2^{\left(c_0 \log u_\alpha + c_1 - \frac{\log \alpha}{2}\right)u_\alpha} \cdot (4(1-\rho))^{-k_\alpha/4} = u_\alpha^{c_0 u_\alpha} \cdot 2^{c_1 u_\alpha} \cdot \alpha^{-u_\alpha/2} \cdot (4(1-\rho))^{-k_\alpha/4}.$$

As a result, we have

$$\begin{aligned}
\frac{T_1}{T_\alpha} &\gtrsim \frac{k^{c_0 k} \cdot 2^{c_1 k} \cdot \alpha^{u_\alpha/2} \cdot (4(1-\rho))^{k_\alpha/4}}{u_\alpha^{c_0 u_\alpha} \cdot 2^{c_1 u_\alpha} \cdot (4(1-\rho))^{k/4}} \\
&= \frac{\alpha^{(k+\phi_\alpha)/2}}{k^{c_0 \phi_\alpha} \cdot \left(1 + \frac{\phi_\alpha}{k}\right)^{c_0 \cdot (k+\phi_\alpha)} \cdot 2^{c_1 \phi_\alpha}} \cdot (4(1-\rho))^{\frac{(k_\alpha - k)}{4}} \\
&\geq \frac{\alpha^{(k+\phi_\alpha)/2}}{k^{c_0 \phi_\alpha} \cdot e^{c_0 \cdot \phi_\alpha} \cdot \left(1 + \frac{\phi_\alpha}{k}\right)^{c_0 \phi_\alpha} \cdot 2^{c_1 \phi_\alpha}} \cdot (4(1-\rho))^{\frac{(k_\alpha - k)}{4}} \quad \left(\text{using } \left(1 + \frac{\phi_\alpha}{k}\right)^k \leq e^{\phi_\alpha}\right) \\
&\geq \frac{\alpha^{(k+\phi_\alpha)/2}}{k^{c_0 \phi_\alpha} \cdot (2e)^{c_0 \phi_\alpha} \cdot 2^{c_1 \phi_\alpha}} \cdot (4(1-\rho))^{\frac{(k_\alpha - k)}{4}} \quad \left(\text{using } 1 + \frac{\phi_\alpha}{k} \leq 2\right) \\
&\geq \frac{\alpha^{(k+\phi_\alpha)/2}}{\alpha^{c_0 \eta k} \cdot k^{c_0} \cdot (2e)^{c_0 \phi_\alpha} \cdot 2^{c_1 \phi_\alpha}} \cdot (4(1-\rho))^{\frac{(k_\alpha - k)}{4}} \quad \left(\text{using } k^{c_0 \phi_\alpha} \leq \alpha^{c_0 \eta k} \cdot k^{c_0}\right) \\
&\geq \alpha^{\left(\frac{1}{2} - c_0 \eta\right)k} \cdot \left(\frac{\sqrt{\alpha}}{(2e)^{c_0} 2^{c_1}}\right)^{\phi_\alpha} \cdot k^{-c_0} \cdot (4(1-\rho))^{\frac{k \log \alpha}{4 \log k}}. \quad \text{(by Item 2 of Lemma 1)}
\end{aligned}$$

Substituting $\phi_\alpha = \left\lceil \frac{\eta k \log \alpha}{\log k} \right\rceil$, we conclude that

$$\frac{T_1}{T_\alpha} \gtrsim \alpha^{\left(\frac{1}{2} - c_0 \eta\right)k} \cdot \left(\frac{\sqrt{\alpha}}{(2e)^{c_0} 2^{c_1}}\right)^{\frac{\eta k \log \alpha}{\log k}} \cdot (4(1-\rho))^{\frac{k \log \alpha}{4 \log k}}$$

up to some polynomial factor. This completes the proof.   □

By Theorem 4, the smaller the time coefficient c_0 and the larger the relaxation constant α (satisfying both $4\alpha^4 \rho \cdot (1 - \rho) < 1$ and $1 < \alpha \leq (k^{c_0} \cdot 2^{c_1})^2$), the larger the exponential speedup factor $\alpha^{\left(\frac{1}{2} - c_0 \eta\right)k}$. This suggests that if some full enumeration algorithm of time $n^{c_0 n} \cdot 2^{O(n)}$ with smaller coefficient c_0 is found, then relaxing such an algorithm in the certain extreme cylinder pruning regime would result in better time/quality trade-offs for certain (including larger) RHFs. In brief, an enumeration oracle with smaller coefficient c_0 would benefit more from (larger) relaxation.

3.3   Numerical Validation

To validate Corollary 1 for concrete parameters, we simulated enumeration up to rank $k = 500$ when fixing $\rho = 0.01$ for varying α. For this, we first simulated both the output and the corresponding cost of pre-processing with k'-BKZ for some index $k' < k$. We note that for our pre-processing, we always assume a k'-rank SVP oracle inside BKZ. By combining the (recursive) preprocessing cost with the expected (repeated) enumeration cost, we arrive at an expected overall enumeration cost (denoted by $t_\alpha(k)$ in Table 1). For the top-most enumeration, we pick pruning parameters as suggested by Corollary 1 for $\rho = 0.01$ and for all values of α. Our simulation runs a simple linear search for k' such that the total expected cost is minimised. We then used SciPy's scipy.optimize.curve_fit function [56] to fit simulation data into cost functions of form $k^{\frac{k}{2e}} \cdot 2^{c_1 k + c_2}$ with constant coefficients c_1 and c_2. For fitting we use always the indices $k = \lceil \alpha \cdot 100 \rceil, \lceil \alpha \cdot 100 \rceil + 1, \ldots, \lceil \alpha \cdot 250 \rceil$, which depend on α due to numerical stability issues. The results are given in Table 1.

Furthermore, several heuristics (such as the Geometric Series Assumption) are required to hold to instantiate Corollary 1 and Theorem 4. We check these experimentally in the full version of this work. In those experiments, the preprocessing cost is not taken into account and thus these algorithms are hypothetical. As a consequence, they give lower-bound estimates rather than predict costs.

Table 1. Speedups of relaxed enumeration with certain extreme cylinder pruning derived from our simulation for $\rho = 0.01$ and claimed by Corollary 1.

α	$\log t_\alpha(k)$	$\log \frac{t_1(k)}{t_\alpha(k)}$	$\log \frac{t_1(k)}{t_\alpha(k)} \approx \frac{\log \alpha}{2} k$
	Simulation	Simulation	Corollary 1
1.00	$\frac{k \log k}{2e} - 0.581\,k + 9.07$	0.00	0.00
1.05	$\frac{k \log k}{2e} - 0.638\,k + 10.91$	$0.057\,k - 1.84$	$0.035k$
1.10	$\frac{k \log k}{2e} - 0.691\,k + 12.34$	$0.110\,k - 3.27$	$0.069k$
1.15	$\frac{k \log k}{2e} - 0.731\,k + 11.97$	$0.150\,k - 2.90$	$0.101k$
1.20	$\frac{k \log k}{2e} - 0.767\,k + 11.21$	$0.186\,k - 2.14$	$0.132k$
1.25	$\frac{k \log k}{2e} - 0.800\,k + 10.37$	$0.219\,k - 1.30$	$0.161k$
1.30	$\frac{k \log k}{2e} - 0.836\,k + 10.75$	$0.255\,k - 1.69$	$0.189k$

Here, $t_\alpha(k)$ denotes the "expected cost" of the $(\alpha \cdot \mathrm{GH}(k))$-HSVP enumeration oracle in rank $k \in [[\lceil \alpha \cdot 100 \rceil, \lceil \alpha \cdot 250 \rceil]]$, including preprocessing.

4   Practical Approximate Enumeration Oracles

Table 1 highlights the relative speedups obtainable by relaxed enumeration with certain extreme cylinder pruning. It does not, however, present speedups over the state-of-the-art for enumeration, which can be observed by comparing the second column of Table 1 with the known cost $2^{\frac{k \log k}{2e} - 0.995\,k + 16.25}$ of enumeration with optimised BKZ 2.0 [17] preprocessing (see [4, Fig. 2]).

In this section, we provide simulation data – fitted curves and experimental validation – to show that with FP(y)LLL's `pruning` module [21,22] and with or without extended preprocessing, relaxed enumeration does achieve exponential speedups, but with a loss in the approximation factor: it can be viewed as a practical version of Corollary 1. We will consider the performance gain when targeting the same RHF as an exact oracle in Sect. 5. In the full version of this work, we also provide additional experiments to check the accuracy of the underlying cost estimation module in FP(y)LLL, with respect to relaxed pruned enumeration. Furthermore, a curious artefact of our parameters is that they do not suggest extreme pruning. Rather, they imply a small number of repetitions only. We elaborate on this in the full version of this work.

4.1 Simulations and Cost Estimates

As in Sect. 3.3, we run the top-most enumeration as an $(\alpha \cdot \mathrm{GH}(k))$-HSVP-oracle in rank k and perform a linear search over parameter k' ($< k$) for preprocessing such that the overall enumeration cost is minimised. We first simulate calling Algorithm 2 with block size k' (i.e. k'-BKZ) to preprocess a given basis of rank $\lceil(1 + c) \cdot k\rceil$ and then simulate running relaxed enumeration on it. That is, we simulate the "expected cost" of the $(\alpha \cdot \mathrm{GH}(k))$-HSVP enumeration oracle in rank k with preprocessing in rank $\lceil(1 + c) \cdot k\rceil$, i.e. enumeration on a k-rank head block $\boldsymbol{B}$ with FPyLLL's optimised cylinder pruning and with relaxed radius $R = \alpha \cdot \mathrm{GH}(\mathcal{L}(\boldsymbol{B}))$. Here, the "expected cost" of each oracle call includes both the expected (repeated) enumeration cost and all recursive preprocessing costs.

We illustrate the fitted cost estimates in Table 2 (columns "$\alpha' = 1$"), which confirm that relaxed enumeration does achieve exponential speedups. We also give some example data and curve fits in Fig. 3.

Remark 1. In Table 2 we are seeing a slight advantage when picking $c = 0.15$ over picking $c = 0.25$. It slightly deviates from a claim in [4] that for $\alpha = 1$, $c = 0.25$ seems to provide the best performance among $c \geq 0$. We hence reproduce this advantage using the original simulation code from [4] in the full version of this work. This simulation confirms that the choice of $c = 0.15$ also provides a minor performance improvement for $\alpha = 1$.

4.2 Consistency with Experiments

In Fig. 4, we give experimental data comparing our implementation with our simulations of the $(\alpha \cdot \mathrm{GH}(k))$-HSVP enumeration oracle in rank k with preprocessing in rank $\lceil(1 + c) \cdot k\rceil$ for $c \in \{0.00, 0.15, 0.25\}$.[6] It shows that our simulation for cost estimates is reasonably accurate for larger instances with a minor bias towards underestimating the cost. The data should be understood as follows:

---

[6] The reader may consult [4, Fig. 4] for the case $c = 0.00, \alpha = 1.00$.

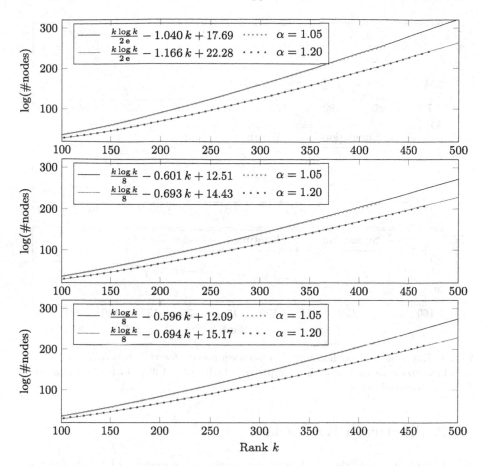

Fig. 3. Selected "expected costs" from simulations for $(\alpha \cdot \mathrm{GH}(k))$-HSVP enumeration oracles in rank k for $c \in \{0.00, 0.15, 0.25\}$ (in turn).

- "Simulation" is the output of our simulation code `simu.py`.
- "Runtime" is the walltime for running FPLLL, converted to "nodes visited" units, assuming 64 CPU cycles per node. It is scaled by $3.3 \cdot 10^9/64$ because it runs on a "Intel(R) Xeon(R) CPU E5-2667 v2 @ 3.30 GHz" (strombenzin).
- "Nodes" is the number of enumeration nodes visited reported by FPLLL. "Runtime" also includes the cost of recursive LLL calls, but "Nodes" does not.

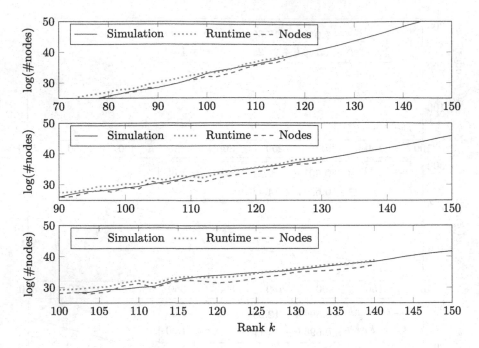

Fig. 4. Experimental verification of simulation results for the $(\alpha \cdot \mathrm{GH}(k))$-HSVP enumeration oracle in rank k with example $\alpha \in \{1.10, 1.20, 1.30\}$ (in turn) and $c = 0.15$. We ran 16 experiments.

5   A Practical BKZ Variant

While Sect. 4 establishes a practical exponential speed-up of relaxed enumeration in the same rank k, it does not yet account for the loss in quality. In this section, we consider relaxed enumeration in rank k_α to obtain a RHF of $\approx \mathrm{GH}(k)^{1/(k-1)}$. This enables us to define a practical variant of the BKZ algorithm utilising relaxed enumeration. This, in turn, enables us to use relaxed enumeration recursively to preprocess bases for relaxed enumeration.

To this end, we present a generalisation of the BKZ variant in [4] with one more optional parameter. This generalisation integrates the idea of extended preprocessing (introduced by [4]) with the relaxation strategy (formalised in [1,35]) on enumeration-based HSVP-oracles. That is, given a performance parameter k (akin to the 'block size' of Algorithm 2), we equip Schnorr–Euchner's BKZ with approximate enumeration oracles as illustrated in Sect. 4, namely an $(\alpha \cdot \mathrm{GH}(k_\alpha))$-HSVP enumeration oracle in rank k_α with preprocessing in rank $\lceil (1 + c) \cdot k_\alpha \rceil$ for some small constant $c \geq 0$ and an optional relaxation constant $\alpha \geq 1$. This BKZ variant uses three parameters (k, c, α), while [4]'s variant relies on two parameters (k, c) and BKZ (2.0) [17,51] uses one parameter k. In particular, our BKZ variant can be viewed as a practical version of Theorem 4.

With extensive experiments and simulations, we investigate the performances of this BKZ variant for both practical and cryptographic parameter ranges: it does achieve better time/quality trade-offs for certain approximation regimes than both [4]'s variant and BKZ 2.0 [17].

Main result. Given as input a performance parameter k—our simulations cover $k \in [100, 400]$—an overshooting parameter $c \in [0, 0.4]$, and a basis of an integer lattice of rank $n \geq (1 + c) \cdot k_{1.3}$, our BKZ variant first picks the "optimal" relaxation constant $\alpha \in \{1, 1.05, 1.1, 1.15, 1.2, 1.25, 1.3\}$ to minimise the expected cost of one oracle call and achieves RHF GH $(k)^{\frac{1}{k-1}}$ with simulated cost estimates:

- Case $c = 0$: the expected cost of one oracle call is about $2^{\frac{k \log k}{2e} - 1.077\,k + 29.12}$, which is lower than BKZ 2.0's record $2^{\frac{k \log k}{2e} - 0.995\,k + 16.25}$ reported in [4, Fig. 2];
- Case $c = 0.25$: the expected cost of one oracle call is about $2^{\frac{k \log k}{8} - 0.632\,k + 21.94}$, which is lower than the record in [4]: $2^{\frac{k \log k}{8} - 0.547\,k + 10.4}$;
- Case $c = 0.15$: the expected cost of one oracle call is about $2^{\frac{k \log k}{8} - 0.654\,k + 25.84}$.

Our results are illustrated in Fig. 1. Our simulations were performed on q-ary lattices of dimensions $n = \lceil (1 + c) \cdot k_\alpha \rceil$ with volume $q^{n/2}$ for $q = 2^{30}$.

5.1 Algorithm

Algorithm 5 is our BKZ variant which, given as input a performance parameter $k \geq 2$, an overshooting parameter $c \geq 0$, a relaxation parameter $\alpha \geq 1$, and a basis of an integer lattice $\mathcal{L}$ of rank $n \geq (1 + c) \cdot k_\alpha$, outputs a reduced basis of $\mathcal{L}$.

It calls the $(\alpha \cdot \mathrm{GH}(k_\alpha))$-HSVP enumeration oracle in rank k_α with preprocessing in rank $\lceil (1 + c) \cdot k_\alpha \rceil$ as an HSVP subroutine. This oracle includes recursive preprocessing: when $\alpha = 1$ then Algorithm 6 is essentially Algorithm 4, and hence calls a function $\mathrm{pre}(\cdot, \cdot)$ for returning the preprocessing parameter. When $(c, \alpha) = (0, 1)$, Algorithm 5 is essentially BKZ 2.0 [17] and Schnorr-Euchner's BKZ algorithm [51].

Restricted to the state-of-the-art power in practice, we choose $c \in [0, 0.4]$ and $\alpha \in \{1.00, 1.05, 1.10, 1.15, 1.20, 1.25, 1.30\}$ for simplicity in our simulations.

Remark 2. In our experiments, the choice of α in Algorithm 5 is determined from an optimised strategy profile built upon our simulated data for each $k \in [2, 400]$. We remark that it is also possible to determine such α on-the-fly based on simulations on the current basis.

Algorithm 5. A new BKZ variant with three parameters (k, c, α)

Require: (B, k, c, α), where $B = (b_0, \ldots, b_{n-1})$ is an LLL-reduced basis of an n-rank
    lattice $\mathcal{L}$ in $\mathbb{Z}^m$, $k \in [2, n)$ is a performance parameter, $c \geq 0$ is an overshooting
    parameter, $\alpha \geq 1$ is a relaxation parameter satisfying $n \geq (1 + c) \cdot k_\alpha$, and $N \in \mathbb{Z}^+$
    denotes the number of tours.
Ensure: A reduced basis of $\mathcal{L}$.
 1: **for** $\ell = 0$ to $N - 1$ **do**
 2:    **for** $j = 0$ to $n - 2$ **do**
 3:        Find a short nonzero vector v in the lattice $\mathcal{L}_{[j,h)}$ (generated by the projected
    block $B_{[j,h)}$ where $h = \min\{j + \lceil(1+c) \cdot k_\alpha\rceil, n\}$), by calling Alg. 6 on $(B_{[j,h)}, k, c, \alpha)$
 4:        **if** $\|b_j^*\| > \|v\|$ **then**
 5:            Lift v into a primitive vector b for the sublattice generated by the basis
    vectors $b_j, \ldots, b_{h-1}$ such that $\|\pi_j(b)\| \leq \|v\|$
 6:            LLL-reduce $(b_0, \ldots, b_{j-1}, b, b_j, \ldots, b_{n-1})$ to remove linear dependencies
 7:        **end if**
 8:    **end for**
 9: **end for**
10: **return** B.

Handling the tail. Just like all known BKZ variants (such as the variant in [4]
and BKZ 2.0 [17]), it is tricky to handle tail projected blocks of the current basis
during execution, because of the decreasing ranks over $d = \lceil(1 + c) \cdot k_\alpha\rceil, \lceil(1 + c) \cdot k_\alpha\rceil - 1, \ldots, 2$. We hence generalise [4]'s tail function $\text{tail}(\cdot, \cdot, \cdot)$ with one more
parameter α for computing the enumeration rank.

For given integer $k \geq 2$, constant $c \geq 0$ and relaxation constant $\alpha \geq 1$, our
approximate enumeration oracle first finds the enumeration rank k^* using the
function $\text{tail}(k, c, \alpha, d)$ for $d = 2, \ldots, \lceil(1 + c) \cdot k_\alpha\rceil$:

$$k^* \leftarrow \text{tail}(k, c, \alpha, d) = \max\left\{\min\left\{d, \left\lceil k_\alpha - \frac{\lceil(1+c) \cdot k_\alpha\rceil - d}{2}\right\rceil\right\}, 2\right\}.$$

Then $k^* = k_\alpha$ when $d = \lceil(1 + c) \cdot k_\alpha\rceil$. It can be checked that k^* is strictly less
than d if d is large enough and is exactly equal to d otherwise:

$$\text{tail}(k, c, \alpha, d) = \begin{cases} k_\alpha + \left\lceil\frac{d - \lceil(1+c) \cdot k_\alpha\rceil}{2}\right\rceil & \text{if } (1 - c) \cdot k_\alpha < d \leq \lceil(1 + c) \cdot k_\alpha\rceil \\ d & \text{if } 2 \leq d \leq (1 - c) \cdot k_\alpha \end{cases} \in [2, k_\alpha].$$
$$(2)$$

Algorithm 5 calls the $(\alpha \cdot \text{GH}(k^*))$-HSVP enumeration oracle in rank k^* with
preprocessing in rank d to reduce each tail projected block, namely Algorithm 6.

Preprocessing parameter. Given a projected block (say,) $(\boldsymbol{b}_0, \ldots, \boldsymbol{b}_{d-1})$ of rank $d \in [2, \lceil (1 + c) \cdot k_\alpha \rceil]$, the preprocessing function $\mathrm{pre}(k^*, \|\boldsymbol{b}_0^*\|, \ldots, \|\boldsymbol{b}_{d-1}^*\|)$ returns the "optimal" preprocessing parameter $k' \in [2, k^*]$, possibly based on simulations, such that the cost of enumeration on the k^*-rank head block is minimised (e.g., at most $k^{k/8} \cdot 2^{O(k)}$ when $c = 0.15$), after preprocessing on $(\boldsymbol{b}_0, \ldots, \boldsymbol{b}_{d-1})$ using Algorithm 5 recursively in lower levels, i.e. equipped with a similar HSVP-oracle with parameters (k', c, α') (instead of the current level (k, c, α)).

Since $k_\alpha \geq k^* \geq k' \geq 2$, each enumeration throughout all recursive levels of Algorithm 5 would not be more expensive than the top-most enumeration-based HSVP-oracle (i.e., the $(\alpha \cdot \mathrm{GH}(k_\alpha))$-HSVP enumeration oracle in rank k_α with preprocessing in rank $\lceil (1 + c) \cdot k_\alpha \rceil$).

5.2   Performance of Our BKZ Variant

Using simulations and data from our implementation, we now validate the performance of our algorithm. We first show that preprocessing with relaxed enumeration has a performance benefit (for $c > 0$) and then validate the output quality of our algorithm. Combining the two, we obtain our main result in Fig. 1, as claimed above.

Algorithm 6. An approx-HSVP oracle on $(\boldsymbol{B}_{[j,h)}), k, c, \alpha)$ using relaxed enumeration in rank k^* with extended preprocessing in rank $(h - j)$

1: Find the enumeration rank $k^* \leftarrow \mathrm{tail}(k, c, \alpha, h - j)$ by Eq. (2)
2: Numerically find the preprocessing parameter $k' \leftarrow \mathrm{pre}(k^*, \|\boldsymbol{b}_j^*\|, \ldots, \|\boldsymbol{b}_{h-1}^*\|)$
3: **if** $k' \geq 3$ **then**
4:     Run Alg. 5 on $(\boldsymbol{B}_{[j,h)}, k', c, \alpha')$ with some $\alpha' \geq 1$ to obtain a reduced basis $\boldsymbol{C} \in \mathbb{Q}^{(h-j) \times m}$ of $\mathcal{L}_{[j,h)}$
5: **else**
6:     LLL-reduce $\boldsymbol{B}_{[j,h)}$ into a basis $\boldsymbol{C} \subset \mathbb{Q}^{(h-j) \times m}$ of $\mathcal{L}_{[j,h)}$
7: **end if**   //Steps 3-7 preprocess $\boldsymbol{B}_{[j,h)}$ for the relaxed enumeration.
8: Call the $(\alpha \cdot \mathrm{GH}(k^*))$-HSVP enumeration oracle in rank k^* on the head block $\boldsymbol{C}_{[0,k^*)}$ of $\boldsymbol{C}$ to find a short nonzero vector $\boldsymbol{v}$ in the lattice $\mathcal{L}_{[j,h)}$

$\alpha \cdot \mathrm{GH}(k)$-**HSVP oracle performance.** In the columns labelled "$\alpha' \geq 1$" in Table 2, we present the speed-ups over $\alpha = 1$ attained by our BKZ variant. That is, the performance of solving $\alpha \cdot \mathrm{GH}(k)$-HSVP when using recursive preprocessing with $\alpha' \geq 1$. We can observe the following from Table 2:

Table 2. Speedups of relaxed enumeration with extreme cylinder pruning derived from our simulation with FPyLLL's optimised cylinder pruning and recursive relaxed enumeration compared with that claimed by Corollary 1.

α	$\log \frac{t_1(k)}{t_\alpha(k)}$ Cor. 1	$\log t_\alpha(k)$ Sim. $(\alpha' = 1)$	$\log \frac{t_1(k)}{t_\alpha(k)}$ Sim. $(\alpha' = 1)$	$\log t_\alpha(k)$ Sim. $(\alpha' \geq 1)$	$\log \frac{t_1(k)}{t_\alpha(k)}$ Sim. $(\alpha' \geq 1)$
			$c = 0.00$		
1.00	0.00	$\frac{k \log k}{2\,e} - 0.994\,k + 17.94$	0.00	$\frac{k \log k}{2\,e} - 0.946\,k + 11.31$	0.00
1.05	$0.035k$	$\frac{k \log k}{2\,e} - 1.040\,k + 17.69$	$0.046\,k + 0.24$	$\frac{k \log k}{2\,e} - 0.984\,k + 9.82$	$0.038\,k + 1.49,$
1.10	$0.069k$	$\frac{k \log k}{2\,e} - 1.088\,k + 18.56$	$0.093\,k - 0.63$	$\frac{k \log k}{2\,e} - 1.027\,k + 9.99$	$0.081\,k + 1.32$
1.15	$0.101k$	$\frac{k \log k}{2\,e} - 1.132\,k + 20.55$	$0.137\,k - 2.61$	$\frac{k \log k}{2\,e} - 1.078\,k + 12.75$	$0.132\,k - 1.45$
1.20	$0.132k$	$\frac{k \log k}{2\,e} - 1.166\,k + 22.28$	$0.171\,k - 4.34$	$\frac{k \log k}{2\,e} - 1.123\,k + 15.73$	$0.176\,k - 4.43$
1.25	$0.161k$	$\frac{k \log k}{2\,e} - 1.193\,k + 23.84$	$0.199\,k - 5.90$	$\frac{k \log k}{2\,e} - 1.157\,k + 17.93$	$0.211\,k - 6.62$
1.30	$0.189k$	$\frac{k \log k}{2\,e} - 1.217\,k + 25.42$	$0.223\,k - 7.48$	$\frac{k \log k}{2\,e} - 1.187\,k + 20.31$	$0.241\,k - 9.00$
			$c = 0.15$		
1.00	0.00	$\frac{k \log k}{8} - 0.552\,k + 12.53$	0.00	$\frac{k \log k}{8} - 0.566\,k + 14.28$	0.00
1.05	$0.035k$	$\frac{k \log k}{8} - 0.601\,k + 12.51$	$0.049\,k + 0.02$	$\frac{k \log k}{8} - 0.617\,k + 14.69$	$0.052\,k - 0.41$
1.10	$0.069k$	$\frac{k \log k}{8} - 0.641\,k + 13.13$	$0.089\,k - 0.60$	$\frac{k \log k}{8} - 0.660\,k + 15.68$	$0.094\,k - 1.40$
1.15	$0.101k$	$\frac{k \log k}{8} - 0.670\,k + 13.79$	$0.118\,k - 1.26$	$\frac{k \log k}{8} - 0.691\,k + 16.71$	$0.126\,k - 2.43$
1.20	$0.132k$	$\frac{k \log k}{8} - 0.693\,k + 14.43$	$0.142\,k - 1.90$	$\frac{k \log k}{8} - 0.716\,k + 17.73$	$0.151\,k - 3.45$
1.25	$0.161k$	$\frac{k \log k}{8} - 0.713\,k + 15.19$	$0.161\,k - 2.66$	$\frac{k \log k}{8} - 0.738\,k + 18.91$	$0.172\,k - 4.63$
1.30	$0.189k$	$\frac{k \log k}{8} - 0.730\,k + 15.95$	$0.178\,k - 3.42$	$\frac{k \log k}{8} - 0.757\,k + 20.01$	$0.191\,k - 5.73$
			$c = 0.25$		
1.00	0.00	$\frac{k \log k}{8} - 0.549\,k + 12.33$	0.00	$\frac{k \log k}{8} - 0.571\,k + 15.39$	0.00
1.05	$0.035k$	$\frac{k \log k}{8} - 0.596\,k + 12.09$	$0.047\,k + 0.24$	$\frac{k \log k}{8} - 0.616\,k + 14.80$	$0.044\,k + 0.60$
1.10	$0.069k$	$\frac{k \log k}{8} - 0.639\,k + 13.15$	$0.090\,k - 0.82$	$\frac{k \log k}{8} - 0.651\,k + 14.84$	$0.080\,k + 0.55$
1.15	$0.101k$	$\frac{k \log k}{8} - 0.669\,k + 14.08$	$0.121\,k - 1.75$	$\frac{k \log k}{8} - 0.683\,k + 15.93$	$0.112\,k - 0.53$
1.20	$0.132k$	$\frac{k \log k}{8} - 0.694\,k + 15.17$	$0.145\,k - 2.84$	$\frac{k \log k}{8} - 0.712\,k + 17.59$	$0.140\,k - 2.20$
1.25	$0.161k$	$\frac{k \log k}{8} - 0.713\,k + 15.92$	$0.164\,k - 3.59$	$\frac{k \log k}{8} - 0.735\,k + 19.09$	$0.164\,k - 3.70$
1.30	$0.189k$	$\frac{k \log k}{8} - 0.728\,k + 16.62$	$0.180\,k - 4.29$	$\frac{k \log k}{8} - 0.755\,k + 20.50$	$0.183\,k - 5.11$

Here, $t_\alpha(k)$ denotes the "expected cost" of the $(\alpha \cdot \mathrm{GH}(k))$-HSVP enumeration oracle in rank $k \in [\lceil \alpha \cdot 100 \rceil, \lceil \alpha \cdot 250 \rceil]$, with preprocessing in rank $\lceil (1 + c)\,k \rceil$, using relaxed enumeration recursively.

- Without extended preprocessing (i.e. setting the overshooting parameter $c = 0$), Table 2 indicates that it is better for preprocessing in rank k to call the $(\alpha' \cdot \mathrm{GH}(k'))$-HSVP enumeration oracle in rank k' with $\alpha' = 1$ than $\alpha' > 1$.
- In contrast, Table 2 indicates that in the case $c > 0$, it is better for preprocessing in rank $\lceil (1 + c) \cdot k \rceil$ to call the $(\alpha' \cdot \mathrm{GH}(k'))$-HSVP enumeration oracle in rank k' with some $\alpha' \geq 1$ than $\alpha' = 1$, i.e. to proceed as outlined above.

Table 2 does not normalise time/quality trade-offs. Thus, in Fig. 5 we illustrate the performance gain of relaxed enumeration for reaching the same RHF.

(a) Expected cost $t_\alpha(k_\alpha)$ of the $(\alpha \cdot \mathrm{GH}(k_\alpha))$-HSVP enumeration oracle in rank k_α for reaching RHF $\mathrm{GH}\,(k)^{\frac{1}{k-1}}$.

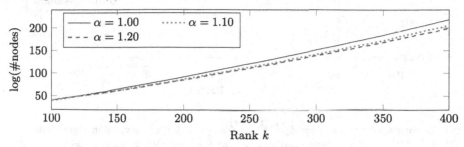

(b) Cost advantage $\log \frac{t_1(k)}{t_\alpha(k_\alpha)}$ of the $(\alpha \cdot \mathrm{GH}(k_\alpha))$-HSVP enumeration oracle in rank k_α for reaching RHF $\mathrm{GH}\,(k)^{\frac{1}{k-1}}$.

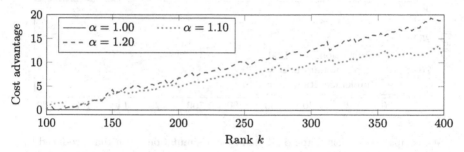

Fig. 5. Expected performance of $(\alpha \cdot \mathrm{GH}(k_\alpha))$-HSVP enumeration oracle in rank k_α; case $c = 0.15$; preprocessing with $\alpha' \geq 1.00$.

Quality. To validate the output quality of our BKZ variant, we compared the RHF predicted by the simulations for BKZ, Algorithm 5 and a self-dual variant of Algorithm 5 in Fig. 6a, following the strategy of [4]. As Fig. 6a illustrates, our variant achieves the same RHF as BKZ, when run in "self-dual" mode.

We also verified the behaviour of the practical implementation of Algorithm 5 against our simulation and give an example in Fig. 6b. As this figure illustrates, our implementation agrees with our simulation except in the tail.

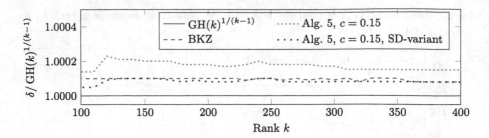

(a) We compare $\delta := \left(\|\boldsymbol{b}_0\|/\mathrm{vol}(\Lambda)^{1/n}\right)^{1/(n-1)}$ as predicted by simulation algorithms to $\mathrm{GH}(k)^{1/(k-1)}$ for $n = 2\,k$ and random q-ary lattices. For "BKZ" we use eight tours of the simulator from [18]. For "Alg. 5, $c = 0.15$" we use eight tours of our simulator. For "Alg. 5, $c = 0.15$, SD-variant" we use our simulator on the dual basis (four tours) followed by the same on the primal basis (four tours).

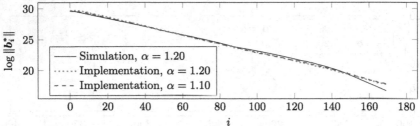

(b) We compare the basis shape predicted by our simulations with that produced by our implementation of Algorithm 5 for q-ary lattices Λ with $q = 2^{24} + 43$, $n = 170$, $\mathrm{vol}(\Lambda) = q^{n/2}$, $k = 60$ and $c = 0.25$. Implementation data is averaged over eight runs.

Fig. 6. Basis quality.

References

1. Aggarwal, D., Li, J., Nguyen, P.Q., Stephens-Davidowitz, N.: Slide reduction, revisited—filling the gaps in SVP approximation. In: Micciancio, D., Ristenpart, T. (eds.) CRYPTO 2020, Part II. LNCS, vol. 12171, pp. 274–295. Springer, Cham (2020). https://doi.org/10.1007/978-3-030-56880-1_10
2. Ajtai, M.: Generating hard instances of lattice problems (extended abstract). In: 28th ACM STOC, pp. 99–108. ACM Press (May 1996)
3. Ajtai, M.: The shortest vector problem in L2 is NP-hard for randomized reductions (extended abstract). In: 30th ACM STOC, pp. 10–19. ACM Press (May 1998)
4. Albrecht, M.R., Bai, S., Fouque, P.A., Kirchner, P., Stehlé, D., Wen, W.: Faster enumeration-based lattice reduction: root Hermite factor $k^{1/(2k)}$ Time $k^{k/8+o(k)}$. In: Micciancio, D., Ristenpart, T. (eds.) CRYPTO 2020, Part II. LNCS, vol. 12171, pp. 186–212. Springer, Cham (2020). https://doi.org/10.1007/978-3-030-56880-1_7
5. Albrecht, M.R., Bai, S., Li, J., Rowell, J.: Lattice reduction with approximate enumeration oracles: practical algorithms and concrete performance. Cryptology ePrint Archive, Report 2020/1260 (2020). https://eprint.iacr.org/2020/1260

6. Albrecht, M.R., et al.: Estimate all the LWE, NTRU schemes!. In: Catalano, D., De Prisco, R. (eds.) SCN 2018. LNCS, vol. 11035, pp. 351–367. Springer, Cham (2018). https://doi.org/10.1007/978-3-319-98113-0_19

7. Albrecht, M.R., Ducas, L., Herold, G., Kirshanova, E., Postlethwaite, E.W., Stevens, M.: The general sieve kernel and new records in lattice reduction. In: Ishai, Y., Rijmen, V. (eds.) EUROCRYPT 2019, Part II. LNCS, vol. 11477, pp. 717–746. Springer, Cham (2019). https://doi.org/10.1007/978-3-030-17656-3_25

8. Albrecht, M.R., Gheorghiu, V., Postlethwaite, E.W., Schanck, J.M.: Estimating quantum speedups for lattice sieves. In: Moriai, S., Wang, H. (eds.) ASIACRYPT 2020, Part II. LNCS, vol. 12492, pp. 583–613. Springer, Cham (2020). https://doi.org/10.1007/978-3-030-64834-3_20

9. Albrecht, M.R., Göpfert, F., Virdia, F., Wunderer, T.: Revisiting the expected cost of solving uSVP and applications to LWE. In: Takagi, T., Peyrin, T. (eds.) ASIACRYPT 2017, Part I. LNCS, vol. 10624, pp. 297–322. Springer, Cham (2017). https://doi.org/10.1007/978-3-319-70694-8_11

10. Alkim, E., Ducas, L., Pöppelmann, T., Schwabe, P.: Post-quantum key exchange - a new hope. In: Holz, T., Savage, S. (eds.) USENIX Security 2016, pp. 327–343. USENIX Association (August 2016)

11. Aono, Y., Nguyen, P.Q., Shen, Y.: Quantum lattice enumeration and tweaking discrete pruning. In: Peyrin, T., Galbraith, S. (eds.) ASIACRYPT 2018, Part I. LNCS, vol. 11272, pp. 405–434. Springer, Cham (2018). https://doi.org/10.1007/978-3-030-03326-2_14

12. Aono, Y., Wang, Y., Hayashi, T., Takagi, T.: Improved progressive BKZ algorithms and their precise cost estimation by sharp simulator. In: Fischlin, M., Coron, J.S. (eds.) EUROCRYPT 2016, Part I. LNCS, vol. 9665, pp. 789–819. Springer, Heidelberg (2016). https://doi.org/10.1007/978-3-662-49890-3_30

13. Bai, S., Stehlé, D., Wen, W.: Measuring, simulating and exploiting the head concavity phenomenon in BKZ. In: Peyrin, T., Galbraith, S. (eds.) ASIACRYPT 2018, Part I. LNCS, vol. 11272, pp. 369–404. Springer, Cham (2018). https://doi.org/10.1007/978-3-030-03326-2_13

14. Becker, A., Ducas, L., Gama, N., Laarhoven, T.: New directions in nearest neighbor searching with applications to lattice sieving. In: Krauthgamer, R. (ed.) 27th SODA, pp. 10–24. ACM-SIAM (January 2016)

15. Bernstein, D.J., et al.: NTRU prime. Tech. rep., National Institute of Standards and Technology (2020). https://csrc.nist.gov/projects/post-quantum-cryptography/round-3-submissions

16. Blichfeldt, H.F.: A new principle in the geometry of numbers, with some applications. Trans. Am. Math. Soc. **16**, 227–235 (1914)

17. Chen, Y., Nguyen, P.Q.: BKZ 2.0: better lattice security estimates. In: Lee, D.H., Wang, X. (eds.) ASIACRYPT 2011. LNCS, vol. 7073, pp. 1–20. Springer, Heidelberg (2011). https://doi.org/10.1007/978-3-642-25385-0_1

18. Conway, J.H., Sloane, N.J.A.: Sphere-Packings, Lattices, and Groups. Springer, Heidelberg (1987). https://doi.org/10.1007/978-1-4757-6568-7

19. Ducas, L., Stevens, M., van Woerden, W.: Advanced lattice sieving on GPUs, with tensor cores (2021). to appear in Eurocrypt 2021. https://eprint.iacr.org/2021/141

20. Fincke, U., Pohst, M.: Improved methods for calculating vectors of short length in a lattice, including a complexity analysis. Math. Comput. **44**(170), 463–471 (1985)

21. FPLLL development team: FPLLL, a lattice reduction library (2019). https://github.com/fplll/fplll

22. FPyLLL development team: FPyLLL, a Python interface to FPLLL (2020). https://github.com/fplll/fpylll

23. Gama, N., Nguyen, P.Q.: Finding short lattice vectors within Mordell's inequality. In: Ladner, R.E., Dwork, C. (eds.) 40th ACM STOC, pp. 207–216. ACM Press (May 2008)

24. Gama, N., Nguyen, P.Q.: Predicting lattice reduction. In: Smart, N.P. (ed.) EUROCRYPT 2008. LNCS, vol. 4965, pp. 31–51. Springer, Heidelberg (2008). https://doi.org/10.1007/978-3-540-78967-3_3

25. Gama, N., Nguyen, P.Q., Regev, O.: Lattice enumeration using extreme pruning. In: Gilbert, H. (ed.) EUROCRYPT 2010. LNCS, vol. 6110, pp. 257–278. Springer, Heidelberg (2010). https://doi.org/10.1007/978-3-642-13190-5_13

26. Garcia-Morchon, O., et al.: Round5. Tech. rep., National Institute of Standards and Technology (2019). https://csrc.nist.gov/projects/post-quantum-cryptography/round-2-submissions

27. Gentry, C., Peikert, C., Vaikuntanathan, V.: Trapdoors for hard lattices and new cryptographic constructions. In: Ladner, R.E., Dwork, C. (eds.) 40th ACM STOC, pp. 197–206. ACM Press (May 2008)

28. Hanrot, G., Pujol, X., Stehlé, D.: Analyzing blockwise lattice algorithms using dynamical systems. In: Rogaway, P. (ed.) CRYPTO 2011. LNCS, vol. 6841, pp. 447–464. Springer, Heidelberg (2011). https://doi.org/10.1007/978-3-642-22792-9_25

29. Hanrot, G., Stehlé, D.: Improved analysis of Kannan's shortest lattice vector algorithm. In: Menezes, A. (ed.) CRYPTO 2007. LNCS, vol. 4622, pp. 170–186. Springer, Heidelberg (2007). https://doi.org/10.1007/978-3-540-74143-5_10

30. Haviv, I., Regev, O.: Tensor-based hardness of the shortest vector problem to within almost polynomial factors. Theory Comput. 8(1), 513–531 (2012). preliminary version in Proceedings of STOC '07

31. Kannan, R.: Improved algorithms for integer programming and related lattice problems. In: 15th ACM STOC, pp. 193–206. ACM Press (April 1983)

32. Khot, S.: Hardness of approximating the shortest vector problem in lattices. J. ACM 52(5), 789–808 (2005). preliminary version in Proceedings of FOCS '04

33. Laarhoven, T.: Search problems in crpytography. Ph.D. thesis, Eindhoven University of Technology (2015)

34. Lenstra, A.K., Lenstra Jr., H.W., Lovász, L.: Factoring polynomials with rational coefficients. Mathematische Annalen 261, 366–389 (1982)

35. Li, J., Nguyen, P.Q.: A complete analysis of the BKZ lattice reduction algorithm (2020). https://eprint.iacr.org/2020/1237.pdf

36. Lovász, L.: An algorithmic theory of numbers, graphs and convexity. Society for Industrial and Applied Mathematics (1986)

37. Micciancio, D.: The shortest vector in a lattice is hard to approximate to within some constant. SIAM J. Comput. 30(6), 2008–2035 (2001). preliminary version in Proceedings of FOCS '98

38. Micciancio, D.: Inapproximability of the shortest vector problem: toward a deterministic reduction. Theory Comput. 8(22), 487–512 (2012). http://www.theoryofcomputing.org/articles/v008a022

39. Micciancio, D., Walter, M.: Fast lattice point enumeration with minimal overhead. In: Indyk, P. (ed.) 26th SODA, pp. 276–294. ACM-SIAM (January 2015)

40. Micciancio, D., Walter, M.: Practical, predictable lattice basis reduction. In: Fischlin, M., Coron, J.S. (eds.) EUROCRYPT 2016, Part I. LNCS, vol. 9665, pp. 820–849. Springer, Heidelberg (2016). https://doi.org/10.1007/978-3-662-49890-3_31

41. Milnor, J., Husemoller, D.: Symmetric Bilinear Forms. Springer, Heidelberg (1973). https://doi.org/10.1007/978-3-642-88330-9

42. Nguên, P.Q., Stehlé, D.: Floating-point LLL revisited. In: Cramer, R. (ed.) EURO-CRYPT 2005. LNCS, vol. 3494, pp. 215–233. Springer, Heidelberg (2005). https://doi.org/10.1007/11426639_13

43. Peikert, C.: Public-key cryptosystems from the worst-case shortest vector problem: extended abstract. In: Mitzenmacher, M. (ed.) 41st ACM STOC, pp. 333–342. ACM Press (May/June 2009)

44. Pohst, M.: On the computation of lattice vectors of minimal length, successive minima and reduced bases with applications. SIGSAM Bull. 15, 37–44 (1981)

45. Poppelmann, T., et al.: NewHope. Tech. rep., National Institute of Standards and Technology (2019). https://csrc.nist.gov/projects/post-quantum-cryptography/round-2-submissions

46. Regev, O.: On lattices, learning with errors, random linear codes, and cryptography. In: Gabow, H.N., Fagin, R. (eds.) 37th ACM STOC, pp. 84–93. ACM Press (May 2005)

47. Rogers, C.A.: The number of lattice points in a set. Proc. Lond. Math. Soc. 3, 305–320 (1956)

48. Schneider, M., Gama, N.: Darmstadt SVP challenges (2010). https://www.latticechallenge.org/svp-challenge/index.php. Accessed 17 Aug 2018

49. Schnorr, C.P.: A hierarchy of polynomial time lattice basis reduction algorithms. Theor. Comput. Sci. 53, 201–224 (1987)

50. Schnorr, C.P.: Lattice reduction by random sampling and birthday methods. In: Alt, H., Habib, M. (eds.) STACS 2003. LNCS, vol. 2607, pp. 145–156. Springer, Heidelberg (2003). https://doi.org/10.1007/3-540-36494-3_14

51. Schnorr, C.P., Euchner, M.: Lattice basis reduction: improved practical algorithms and solving subset sum problems. Math. Program. 66, 181–199 (1994)

52. Schnorr, C.P., Hörner, H.H.: Attacking the Chor-Rivest cryptosystem by improved lattice reduction. In: Guillou, L.C., Quisquater, J.J. (eds.) EUROCRYPT 1995. LNCS, vol. 921, pp. 1–12. Springer, Heidelberg (1995). https://doi.org/10.1007/3-540-49264-X_1

53. Shoup, V.: NTL 11.4.3: number theory c++ library (2020). http://www.shoup.net/ntl/

54. Siegel, C.L.: Lectures on the Geometry of Numbers. Springer, New York (1989). https://doi.org/10.1007/978-3-662-08287-4

55. Teruya, T., Kashiwabara, K., Hanaoka, G.: Fast lattice basis reduction suitable for massive parallelization and its application to the shortest vector problem. In: Abdalla, M., Dahab, R. (eds.) PKC 2018, Part I. LNCS, vol. 10769, pp. 437–460. Springer, Cham (2018). https://doi.org/10.1007/978-3-319-76578-5_15

56. Virtanen, P., et al.: SciPy 1.0: fundamental algorithms for scientific computing in Python. Nat. Methods 17, 261–272 (2020)

Towards Faster Polynomial-Time Lattice Reduction

Paul Kirchner[1(✉)], Thomas Espitau[2], and Pierre-Alain Fouque[1]

[1] IRISA/Inria, Rennes Univ., Rennes, France
{paul.kirchner,pierre-alain.fouque}@irisa.fr
[2] NTT Secure Platform Laboratories, Tokyo, Japan

Abstract. The LLL algorithm is a polynomial-time algorithm for reducing d-dimensional lattice with exponential approximation factor. Currently, the most efficient variant of LLL, by Neumaier and Stehlé, has a theoretical running time in $d^4 \cdot B^{1+o(1)}$ where B is the bitlength of the entries, but has never been implemented. This work introduces new asymptotically fast, parallel, yet *heuristic*, reduction algorithms with their optimized implementations. Our algorithms are recursive and fully exploit fast matrix multiplication. We experimentally demonstrate that by carefully controlling the floating-point precision during the recursion steps, we can reduce euclidean lattices of rank d in time $\tilde{O}(d^\omega \cdot C)$, i.e., almost a constant number of matrix multiplications, where ω is the exponent of matrix multiplication and C is the log of the condition number of the matrix. For cryptographic applications, C is close to B, while it can be up to d times larger in the worst case. It improves the running-time of the state-of-the-art implementation fplll by a multiplicative factor of order $d^2 \cdot B$. Further, we show that we can reduce structured lattices, the so-called knapsack lattices, in time $\tilde{O}(d^{\omega-1} \cdot C)$ with a progressive reduction strategy. Besides allowing reducing huge lattices, our implementation can break several instances of Fully Homomorphic Encryption schemes based on large integers in dimension 2,230 with 4 millions of bits.

1   Introduction

Lattice reduction and cryptanalysis. Lattice reduction is of the utmost importance in public-key cryptanalysis, as testified, for instance, by the extensive survey of Joux and Stern [40]. Indeed, many cryptographic problems are solved by constructing an appropriate lattice and retrieving one of its short vectors. Some standard examples include knapsack problems [40,46,48], breaking linear congruential generators [28,69]), Coppersmith attack [19] against RSA modulus by retrieving small roots of univariate polynomials over $\mathbb{Z}/N\mathbb{Z}$ or bivariate polynomials over $\mathbb{Z}$, or even attacks against the initial versions of the NTRU cryptosystem [4,20,32]. Yet, its field of applications extends way beyond cryptography, as lattice reduction is a cornerstone of many number theoretical algorithms, allowing factoring polynomials over $\mathbb{Z}[X]$ [50], finding integer relations [37], solving simultaneous diophantine approximation problems [45].

© International Association for Cryptologic Research 2021
T. Malkin and C. Peikert (Eds.): CRYPTO 2021, LNCS 12826, pp. 760–790, 2021.
https://doi.org/10.1007/978-3-030-84245-1_26

Essentially, lattice reduction means finding a short and nearly orthogonal basis to a lattice Λ (represented as a $\mathbb{Z}$-basis). For many applications, finding a small non-zero lattice vector, i.e., solving the (approximate) Short Vector Problem (SVP), shall suffice. Since the work of Minkowski, we know that there exists a vector with euclidean norm smaller than $\sqrt{d}(\operatorname{vol}\Lambda)^{\frac{1}{d}}$, but the proof is not constructive. Nonetheless, the LLL algorithm, introduced in 1982 by Lenstra, Lenstra, and Lovász [50] retrieves vector within an exponential factor to the shortest vector of a lattice of dimension d in time $O(d^6 B^3)$ where B is the bit-size of the input representation. One can also prove that the norm of the first vector of an LLL-reduced basis is less than $(\sqrt{4/3})^{\frac{d-1}{2}}(\operatorname{vol}\Lambda)^{\frac{1}{d}}$. The approximation factor $(\|b_1\|/\operatorname{vol}\Lambda)^{1/d}$ is called the *root Hermite factor* (RHF), with b_1 a short vector. Later, Schnorr developed a hierarchy of algorithms to reach better RHF in $\beta^{\frac{1}{2\beta}}$ in time $2^{O(\beta)}$ for large β [62,64]. This family leads to a polynomial-time algorithm with a RHF $2^{\frac{\log\log d}{\log d}}$ [47]. Gama and Nguyen introduced the slide reduction to give an effective take on Mordell's inequality and further improve the RHF [29]. In an orthogonal direction, following Håstad and Lagarias, Seysen proposed a variant of LLL aiming at simultaneously reduces the primal and dual basis [67]. He defines a new reduceness measure which is closely related to the condition number of the matrix [51].

Related work. The two most singular characteristics of lattices appearing in the cryptographic setting are their high dimension and the large bitsize of their matrix representation. As such, the reduction of cryptanalytically relevant lattices is a computationally intensive challenge. While the original LLL implementation works with exact arithmetic on rational entries, Schnorr proposed in 1988 to replace it with floating-point arithmetic [63], significantly improving its efficiency. Since 1996, Shoup maintains a heuristic yet very efficient version in the NTL library with fine control of the float-point precision. This code has been routinely used for more than a decade to break cryptographic schemes. Later, Nguyen and Stehlé precisely analyzed and decreased the asymptotic complexity to $O(d^5(d+B)B)$ in [57], a.k.a. the quadratic LLL or L^2 algorithm. This algorithm has been then implemented in fpLLL [3], which is the current state-of-the-art open-source implementation of LLL. However, despite many *theoretical* improvements to reduce the complexity to quasi-linear in the bitsize using recursive local computation techniques [44,55,58,65] and some attempts [11,13,61] to use only the most significant bits, the practical complexity of the best implementation available remains in $O(d^4 B^2)$. As such, it struggles to reduce lattices with large entries in high dimensions. Consequently, cryptographers still assess their concrete parameters using L^2 as a reference for LLL.

Thus, from a cryptanalytical standpoint, it is interesting to have a fast implementation of lattice reduction (with a controlled approximation factor) even though this algorithm might rely on some heuristics. Since lattice-based cryptography is becoming a strong contender for post-quantum cryptography and offers many interesting functionalities to cryptography, such as efficient Fully Homomorphic Encryption (FHE), new algorithms and implementations of lattice reduction have been designed to give better security estimate for lattice-based cryptography. Some improvements mainly target the BKZ algorithm since it allows to finely adjust the approximation factor [5,14,29,30,35,53]. Others are heuristic and improve sieving technique for solving SVP, use a reduction technique in the lattice dimension [6], exploit subfield structure and symmetries in structured lattices [41,60], or use the tensor core architecture of GPU [26]. Some of them with sieving SVP-oracle [6] are used to perform the security estimation of signatures and KEM, where the dimension are generally lying between 512 and 1024. However, FHE schemes over the integers use extremely large integers (several millions of bits) and high dimensional lattices (typically of a few thousand dimensions), but can be broken with high approximation factors. To deal with such settings, faster algorithms are required, in particular with complexity quasi-linear in the bitsize and not much more costly than matrix multiplication.

Our Contributions. To improve the running time of lattice reduction algorithms, we propose to exploit parallelism with many cores, make full use of computer's cache using block matrix implementation [34], and use a low precision while still controlling the approximation factor at the same time. Our implementation we describe allows reducing lattice in dimensions up to 2,000 with entries of up to millions of bits, which is intractable otherwise.

Our proposal of lattice reduction is a LLL-type algorithm, i.e., using a size-reduction procedure jointly, together with many passes of a rank-2 reduction subprocess. The design rationale is to exploit fast block matrix operations and locality of operations. To do so, we use a block variant of the Cholesky factorization algorithm for computing the QR-decomposition [34]. We replace the size-reduction with a block variant of Seysen's size-reduction, which can be thought of as a rounded version of the multiplication by the inverse of the $\mathbf{R}$ factor of the QR-decomposition. To our knowledge, this algorithm has not been used since 1993. Contrary to the textbook LLL, we do not swap vectors when the Lovász condition is not fulfilled, but we fully reduce the 2-dimensional corresponding projected sublattice, using Schönhage's algorithm. The global design is recursive, as was proposed before by Koy and Schnorr [44] with Segmented LLL and by Neumaier and Stehlé [55]. However, in this work, we do not recurse on overlapping blocks but on separate ones; a technique proposed by Villard to achieve parallelism [73] with even and odd steps, also used recently in [41].

As all the computations are conducted in floating-point arithmetic, a systematic caveat concerns the precision required for computing the correct result. We claim and experimentally verify that on average, it decreases exponentially with the recursion depth as shown in Sect. 4.1, allowing to reduce the overall complexity by a factor d. Additionally, we handle matrice multiplications in the Fourier domain to compute with large numbers. We conjecture and experimentally verify a complexity of approximately $d^\omega \cdot C / \log C$, where ω is the exponent of matrix multiplication, and C is the logarithm of the condition number of the input matrix. We highlight that typically, the complexity of lattice reduction depends on the bitlength B of the input, instead of C. For cryptographic applications (Coppersmith and knapsack-type lattice amid others), C is close to B, while it can be up to d times larger in the worst case. It is well-known that a row-wise diagonal dominant matrice has a condition number bounded by a constant times the ratio beteen the largest diagonal entry and the smallest one, so the logarithm of the condition number will be close to the size of the entries.

Additionally, Sect. 5 shows that one can reduce knapsack lattice in a time approximately equal to the reduction of a random lattice with a bitsize reduced by a factor of d. Such a phenomenon is already known for some algorithms like fp lll [68, 1.5.3], noted [56], and exploited [72]. We present a reduction between the two problems with this property. The idea is to iteratively double the number of columns reduced, and reduce the bitsize of the other ones. It has been implemented and tested.

The complexity of our algorithms can be analyzed in an arithmetic cost model with an analysis similar to [35] (sandpile model) for LLL with even and odd pass as in [42]. However, the specificity of our algorithm is to consider the precision. Without such attention, it would have been impossible to reduce high dimensional lattice with so many bits. In an exact arithmetic cost model, the complexity would have been comparable to previous algorithms, which is not the case in practice. Such heuristic algorithms is interesting, even without a full analysis, to assess the security of cryptographic instances. For instance, many FHE schemes over the integers base their security on the complexity of the best algorithm. However, a rigorous proof of the algorithm with the precision is highly technical in a numerical computational model and escape us so far. Consequently, we decided to present only all the ingredients of our implementation with its applications in this paper and postpone a proof for future work.

Regarding the applications, we first show in Sect. 6 that our implementation is much faster than fp lll with a factor between 30 and 45 on single-thread in all dimensions tractable by fp lll. However, our implementation can exploit multi-core processors and reduce lattices in much higher dimensions. Consequently, we run it on matrices of dimensions a few thousand and inputs of millions of bits, as reported in Table 1. As a result, we attack many instances FHE over the integers to illustrate the efficiency of our code and evaluate its running time on large inputs. For these examples, the wall-clock time is six orders of magnitude smaller than the (estimated) cost of fp lll. We broke knapsack instances from [21] in dimension 2,230 with 4.26 millions of bits in 22h with 18 cores, while the security level was evaluated at 2^{62}. We also broke NTRU instances with overstretched parameters proposed in [31] in 5h (resp. 10 days) in dimension 2560 (resp. 3086) with 111 (resp. 883) bits and RHF $2^{0.1105}$ ($2^{0.018}$, equivalent to BKZ-25). In practice, at the bottom of the recursion tree, we use a small BKZ to improve the approximation factor, whilst not altering too much the running time.

2 Background

2.1 Notations and Conventions

The capitals $\mathbb{Z}$, $\mathbb{Q}$, $\mathbb{R}$ refer to the ring of integers, the field of rational and real. Given a real number x, its integral rounding denoted by $\lfloor x \rceil$ returns its closest integer. The logarithms are log for the binary one and ln for the natural one.

Matrix and norms. We denote by $\mathbb{Q}^{d \times d}$ the space of square matrices of size d over $\mathbb{Q}$, $\mathrm{GL}_d(\mathbb{Q})$ its group of invertible. We use bold fonts for matrices and denote the elementary matrix transformations by $\mathbf{T}_{i,j}(\lambda)$ and $\mathbf{D}_i(\lambda)$ for respectively the transvection (or shear mapping) and the dilatation of parameter λ. We use $\mathrm{Diag}(x_1, \ldots, x_d)$ to refers to a diagonal matrix of elements $x_1, \ldots, x_d$. We generalize this definition to block matrices and overload it to the extraction of the diagonal of a given matrix. A *triangular unipotent* or *unitriangular matrix* is a triangular matrix with ones on the diagonal. We extend the product for any pair of matrices $(\mathbf{A}, \mathbf{B})$: for every matrix $\mathbf{C}$ with compatible size with $\mathbf{A}$ and $\mathbf{B}$, we set: $(\mathbf{A}, \mathbf{B}) \cdot \mathbf{C} = (\mathbf{AC}, \mathbf{BC})$. We adopt the usual conventions for submatrix extraction: for any matrix $\mathbf{M} = (m_{i,j}) \in \mathbb{Q}^{d \times d}$ and $1 \leqslant u < v \leqslant d, 1 \leqslant w < x \leqslant d$, define the submatrix $\mathbf{M}[u : v, w : x] = (m_{i,j})_{u \leqslant i \leqslant v, w \leqslant j \leqslant x}$, while $\mathbf{M}_i$ refers to the i-th column of $\mathbf{M}$. For a vector v (resp. matrix $\mathbf{A} = (a_{i,j})_{1 \leqslant i,j \leqslant d}$), we denote by $\|v\|$ (resp. $\|\mathbf{A}\|$) the Frobenius norm, i.e., $\|\mathbf{A}\| = \sqrt{\sum_{1 \leqslant i,j \leqslant d} a_{i,j}^2}$. The condition number of an invertible matrix $\mathbf{M}$ measures how much the output value of the matrix can change for a small change in the input. It is defined as $\kappa(\mathbf{M}) = \|\mathbf{M}\| \|\mathbf{M}^{-1}\|$ and allows to compute the precision needed during the computation. We deal with block decomposition of matrices, with block of half-dimension. For matrices of odd dimension $2k + 1$, the upper-left block to be of dimension $k + 1$ and the bottom-right one of dimension k.

Computational setting. We use the standard model in algorithmic theory, i.e., the word-RAM with unit cost and logarithmic size register (see [52, Section 2.2] for a comprehensive description). The number of bits in the register is w and the precision during the computation by p. All computations with rational/real values are conducted in floating-point, unless stated otherwise. For a non-negative integer d, we set $\omega(d)$ to be the exponent of matrix multiplication of $d \times d$ matrices. If the dimension d is clear from context we might omit it and write simply $O(d^\omega)$ for this complexity. We can assume that this exponent is not too close to 2, in particular $\omega(d) > 2 + 1/\log(d)$. Due to the conflict with Laudau's small omega notation, we use $\boldsymbol{\omega}$ for the latter symbol.

2.2   Lattices and LLL Reduction

Definition 1 (Lattice). *A d-dimensional (real) lattice $\Lambda \subseteq \mathbb{R}^d$ is the set of integer linear combinations $\sum_{i=1}^{d} b_i \mathbb{Z}$ of some linearly independent vectors $(b_i)_{1 \leqslant i \leqslant d}$.*

The finite family $(b_1, \ldots, b_d) \in \Lambda$ is called a *basis* of Λ. Every basis has the same number of elements called the *rank* of the lattice. A measure of the density of the lattice is its *(co)volume*, defined to be the volume of the torus $\mathbb{R}^d/\Lambda$, which corresponds to the square root of the Gram-determinant of any basis $(b_1, \ldots, b_d)$:

$$\mathrm{vol}\, \Lambda = \sqrt{\det(\langle b_i, b_j \rangle)_{1 \leqslant i,j \leqslant d}}.$$

Two different bases of a lattice Λ are related by a *unimodular transformation*, i.e., a linear transformation represented by an element of $\mathrm{GL}_d(\mathbb{Z})$, the set of $d \times d$ integer-valued matrices of determinant ± 1. In essence, algorithms acting on lattice bases are sequences of unimodular transformations. Among these procedures, reduction algorithms are of the utmost importance. They aim at finding congenial classes of bases, which are *quasi-orthogonal* and with controlled norms. Fundamental constant associated to any rank d lattice Λ are its successive minima $\lambda_1, \ldots, \lambda_d$. The ith minimum $\lambda_i(\Lambda)$ is the radius of the smallest sphere centered in the origin containing i linearly independent lattice vectors.

Orthogonalization, QR-decomposition. Let $\mathbf{B} = (b_1, \ldots, b_d)$ a family of linearly independent vectors. Let π_i the orthogonal projection on $(b_1, \ldots, b_{i-1})^\perp$, with the convention that $\pi_1 = \mathrm{Id}$. The Gram-Schmidt orthogonalization process is an algorithmic method for orthogonalizing $\mathbf{B}$ while preserving the increasing chain of subspaces $(\bigoplus_{j=1}^i b_j \mathbb{R})_{1 \leqslant i \leqslant d}$. It constructs the orthogonal set $\mathbf{B}^* = (\pi_1(b_1), \ldots, \pi_d(b_d))$. For notational simplicity we refer generically to the orthogonalized vectors by b_i^* for $\pi_i(b_i)$. The computation of $\mathbf{B}^*$ can be done inductively as follows: for all $1 \leqslant i \leqslant d$, $b_i^* = b_i - \sum_{j=1}^{i-1} \frac{\langle b_i, b_j^* \rangle}{\langle b_j^*, b_j^* \rangle} b_j^*$. Collect the family $\mathbf{B}$ in a matrix also denoted by the same notation and set $\mathbf{R}_{i,j} = \frac{\langle b_j, b_i^* \rangle}{\|b_i^*\|}$ and $\mathbf{Q} = \left[\frac{b_1^*}{\|b_1^*\|} \middle| \cdots \middle| \frac{b_d^*}{\|b_d^*\|} \right]$. Then, we have $\mathbf{B} = \mathbf{QR}$, with $\mathbf{Q}$ being an orthogonal matrix and $\mathbf{R}$ being upper triangular. This is the QR-decomposition of $\mathbf{B}$. In the following, we work with the $\mathbf{R}$ part only, so that we present the computation of this matrix in the pseudo-code **Orthogonalize** below. We omit considerations on the required fp-precision here, to just focus on the core ideas of the algorithms.

Algorithm 1 — Orthogonalize

Input   Basis $\mathbf{B}$

Output $\mathbf{R}$ part of
           QR-decomposition

for $i = 1$ to d **do**

    for $j = i - 1$ to 1 **do**

        $\mathbf{Q}_i \leftarrow b_i - \frac{\langle b_i, \mathbf{Q}_j \rangle}{\langle \mathbf{Q}_j, \mathbf{Q}_j \rangle} \mathbf{Q}_j$

    end for

end for

return $\mathbf{R} = \left(\frac{\langle \mathbf{Q}_i, b_j \rangle}{\|\mathbf{Q}_i\|} \right)_{1 \leqslant i \leqslant j \leqslant d}$

Algorithm 2 — Size-Reduce

Input   Basis $\mathbf{B}$, $\mathbf{R}$ part of
           QR-decomposition

Output   Tranformation of SR basis

$U = \mathrm{Id}_d$

for $i = 1$ to d **do**

    for $j = i - 1$ to 1 **do**

        $(U, R) \leftarrow (U, R) \cdot \mathbf{T}_{i,j}\left(- \left\lceil \frac{\mathsf{R}[i,j]}{\mathsf{R}[i,i]} \right\rfloor \right)$

    end for

end for

return U

Size-reduction of a family of vectors. Let Λ be a rank d lattice given by a basis $\mathbf{B} = (b_1, \ldots, b_d)$, we might want to use the Gram-Schmidt process. However, since the quotients $\frac{\langle b_i, b_j^* \rangle}{\langle b_j^*, b_j^* \rangle}$ are not integral in general, the vectors b_i^* may not lie in Λ. The size-reduction process instead approximates the result of the

Gram-Schmidt process by rounding to a nearest integer: each vector b_i is replaced by $b_i - \sum_{j=1}^{i-1} \left\lceil \frac{\langle b_i, b_j^* \rangle}{\langle b_j^*, b_j^* \rangle} \right\rfloor b_j$. The whole process takes time $O(d^5 B^2)$ when the input matrix $\mathbf{B}$ is of dimension $d \times d$ with B-bit entries. This process is called *Size-reduction* and corresponds to the following iterative algorithm[1] **Size-reduce**.

2.3   The LLL Reduction Algorithm

Lenstra, Lenstra, and Lovász [50] proposed a notion called LLL-*reduction* and a polynomial-time algorithm that computes an LLL-reduced basis from an arbitrary basis of the same lattice. Their reduction notion is formally defined as follows (presented directly in an algorithmic way with the QR-decomposition):

Definition 2 (LLL reduction). *A basis* $\mathbf{B}$ *of a lattice, admitting the decomposition* $\mathbf{B} = \mathbf{QR}$, *is said to be* δ-LLL-*reduced for* $1/4 < \delta \leqslant 1$, *if the following two conditions are satisfied:*

$$\forall i < j, \quad |\mathbf{R}[i,j]| \leqslant \frac{1}{2} |\mathbf{R}[i,i]| \quad \textit{(Size-Reduction condition)} \tag{1}$$

$$\forall i, \quad \delta \left\| \begin{pmatrix} \mathbf{R}_{j,j} \\ 0 \end{pmatrix} \right\|^2 \leqslant \left\| \begin{pmatrix} \mathbf{R}_{j,j+1} \\ \mathbf{R}_{j+1,j+1} \end{pmatrix} \right\|^2 \quad \textit{(Lovász condition).} \tag{2}$$

The length of vectors and orthogonality defect is related to the parameter δ:

Proposition 1. *Let* $1/4 < \delta \leqslant 1$ *be an admissible* LLL *parameter. Let* $(b_1, \ldots, b_d)$ *a* δ-LLL *reduced basis of rank-d lattice* Λ. *Then for any* $1 \leqslant k \leqslant d$:

$$\mathrm{vol}(b_1, \ldots, b_k) \leqslant (\delta - 1/4)^{-\frac{(d-k)k}{4}} \mathrm{vol}\, \Lambda^{\frac{k}{d}}.$$

In particular, we have that $\mathbf{R}_{i,i} \leqslant (\delta - 1/4)^{-1} \mathbf{R}_{i+1,i+1}$.

We recall that $\mathrm{vol}(\Lambda) = \det(\mathbf{B}) = \prod_{i=1}^{d} \mathbf{R}_{i,i}$ and the log-potential is defined as $\Pi(\mathbf{B}) = \sum_{i=1}^{d} (d-i) \log(\mathbf{R}_{i,i})$. For $k = 1$ and $\delta = 1$, the Hermite approximation factor defined as $\|b_1\| / \det(\mathbf{B})^{1/d}$, will be $(4/3)^{(d-1)/4}$. To find a basis entailing the LLL conditions, it suffices to iteratively modify it at any index violating one of these conditions. This process yields the simplest version of the LLL algorithm. However, we choose to present a different take on this algorithm, closer to the algorithms we introduce later. The first remark is that for a given $1 \leqslant j \leqslant d-1$, the LLL-reduceness conditions correspond to saying that the basis

$$\begin{pmatrix} \mathbf{R}_{j,j} & \mathbf{R}_{j,j+1} \\ 0 & \mathbf{R}_{j+1,j+1} \end{pmatrix}$$

is Gauss–reduced. The global strategy given in Algorithm 3 to reduce a lattice consists of iteratively applying a reduction procedure in rank 2 to projected

---

[1] We choose to present it using the matrix $\mathbf{R}$ and yielding the unimodular transformation matrix, for consistency with the description of our algorithms in Sect. 3.

sublattices, naturally using the Gauss reduction algorithm [35]. We start by reducing the sublattice spanned by b_1, b_2, then the projection onto the orthogonal subspace to b_1 sublattice spanned by b_2, b_3 and so on. When we hit the end of the basis, this iteration restarts afresh until no more progress is achieved.

We replace the outermost **while** loop by a for loop of a fixed number ρ of iterations. This parameter is set to be sufficiently large to ensure the reducedness of the output (using a dynamical system analysis à la [35] after $O(d^2 \log B)$ rounds, a vector within the LLL quality bound is discovered).

We will use a slight generalization of the LLL-reduction notion. In particular, a LLL-reduced basis satisfying the Lovász conditions, is a Siegel reduced basis.

Definition 3 (Siegel reduction). *The Siegel reduction problem consists in, given an integer matrix* $\mathbf{A}$ *of dimension* d *with* $\|\mathbf{A}\|, \|\mathbf{A}^{-1}\| \leqslant 2^B$, *outputting a matrix* $\mathbf{AU}$ *with* $\mathbf{U}$ *a unimodular integer matrix such that with* $\mathbf{QR} = \mathbf{AU}$ *the QR-decomposition, we have for all* i: $\mathbf{R}_{i,i} \leqslant 2\mathbf{R}_{i+1,i+1}$.

————————— Algorithm 3 — Reduction —————————

> **Input**   : Initial basis $\mathbf{B} = (b_1, \ldots, b_d)$
>
> **Output**   : A δ-LLL-reduced basis
>
> 1 **while** $\mathbf{B}$ *is not* LLL-*reduced* **do**
> 2 $\mathbf{R} \leftarrow$ **Orthogonalize($\mathbf{B}$)**
> 3 $\mathbf{U}_i \leftarrow$ **Size-Reduce($\mathbf{R}$)**
> 4 $(\mathbf{B}, \mathbf{R}) \leftarrow (\mathbf{B}, \mathbf{R}) \cdot \mathbf{U}_i$
> 5   **for** $j = 1$ **to** d **do**
> 6 $\mathbf{B}' \leftarrow \mathbf{R}[j : j + 1, j : j + 1]$
> 7 $\mathbf{U}' \leftarrow$**Gauss($\mathbf{B}'$)**
> 8 $(\mathbf{U}_i, \mathbf{B}) \leftarrow (\mathbf{U}_i, \mathbf{B}) \cdot \mathrm{Diag}(\mathbf{Id}_{j-1}, \mathbf{U}', \mathbf{Id}_{d-j-1})$
> 9   **end for**
> 10 **end while**
> 11 **return** $\prod_{i=1}^{\rho} \mathbf{U}_i$ // ρ is the number of passes

---

2.4   Matrices Representation

A matrix $\mathbf{A}$ is represented as $\mathbf{A}'2^e$ where $\mathbf{A}'$ is an integer matrix and $e \leqslant 0$. The quantity $\log(\|\mathbf{A}'\|)$ is the *precision* of the matrix. The standard algorithm for multiplying matrices with large entries consists in transforming the integers in $\mathbf{A}$ and $\mathbf{B}$ into polynomials of degree bounded by $O\left(\frac{p+w}{w}\right)$ (p is the precision and w the number of bits in registers), and computing their evaluations on roots of unity. The matrices of evaluations are then multiplied, and an inverse Fourier transform gives the product of the matrix of polynomials. Carries are then computed to obtain $\mathbf{AB}$. Matrices can be multiplied quickly using the FFT:

Theorem 1. *Given* **A** *and* **B** *two integer matrices of dimension d with* $\log(\|\mathbf{A}\| + \|\mathbf{B}\|) = p$, *the product* **AB** *can be computed in time* $O\left(d^\omega \frac{p+w}{w} + d^2 \frac{p}{w} \log\left(2 + \frac{p}{w}\right)\right)$.

2.5 Fast Inversion of Unitriangular Matrices

We eventually conclude this preliminary section by introducing a natural recursive algorithm to invert unitriangular matrices—working with floating-point approximation. It is a direct application of the computation of Schur's complement in the case of a block triangular matrix, i.e., the observation that:

$$\begin{pmatrix} \mathbf{A} & \mathbf{C} \\ 0 & \mathbf{D} \end{pmatrix}^{-1} = \begin{pmatrix} \mathbf{A}^{-1} & -\mathbf{A}^{-1}\mathbf{C}\mathbf{D}^{-1} \\ 0 & \mathbf{D}^{-1} \end{pmatrix}.$$

As both **A** and **D** are unitriangular, this inversion formula translates naturally in a recursive algorithm. Its base case corresponds to inverting a one dimensional unitriangular matrix, that is (1), which is its own inverse. The corresponding pseudo-code is given in **Invert**. Its complexity is easily analyzed to be asymptotically the cost of a matrix multiplication, as the dominant step of each recursive call is the computation of the complement $-\mathbf{A}^{-1}\mathbf{C}\mathbf{D}^{-1}$.

Algorithm 4 — Invert

Input   : A unitriangular matrix **M**
Output   : A fp-approximation of $\mathbf{M}^{-1}$

1 **if** $dim(\mathbf{M}) = 1$ **then**
2 $\quad$ **return** (1)
3 **end if**
4 $\begin{pmatrix} \mathbf{A} & \mathbf{C} \\ 0 & \mathbf{D} \end{pmatrix} \leftarrow \mathbf{M}$ // with dimension almost halved
5 $\mathbf{A}' \leftarrow$ **Invert**(**A**) ; $\mathbf{D}' \leftarrow$ **Invert**(**D**) // fp-approximations of A^{-1}, D^{-1}
6 $\mathbf{S} \leftarrow -\mathbf{A}'\mathbf{C}\mathbf{D}'$ // Computed in floating-point
7 **return** $\begin{pmatrix} \mathbf{A}' & \mathbf{S} \\ 0 & \mathbf{D}' \end{pmatrix}$

We provide the precise analysis of this inversion. It can be extended to *triangular* matrices, and we consider that **Invert** also computes their inverse.

Lemma 1. *Given an integral unitriangular matrix* **M** *of dimension d, with both* $\|\mathbf{M}\|, \|\mathbf{M}^{-1}\| \leqslant 2^p$ *and* $p \geqslant w + \log(d)$, **Invert** *returns a matrix* **M**' *such that* $\|\mathbf{M}' - \mathbf{M}^{-1}\| \leqslant 2^{-p}$ *with a running time of* $O\left(\frac{d^\omega p}{w} + d^2 p\right)$.

Proof. We set a working precision $p' = 1 + 3p + \lceil \log d \rceil = O(p)$, and by induction on d, let us prove that

$$\|\mathbf{M}'^{-1} - \mathbf{M}\| \leqslant 2\sqrt{d}2^{-p'}.$$

The case $d = 1$ is straightforward, so that we now deal with inductive case $d > 1$. Let $\mathbf{E}$, $\delta\mathbf{A}$ and $\delta\mathbf{D}$ be matrices such that the top-right part of **M**' is $-\mathbf{A}'\mathbf{C}\mathbf{D}' + \mathbf{E}$, $\mathbf{A}'^{-1} = \mathbf{A} + \delta\mathbf{A}$, and $\mathbf{D}'^{-1} = \mathbf{D} + \delta\mathbf{D}$. Consequently, we get: $\mathbf{M}'^{-1} - \mathbf{M} = \begin{pmatrix} \delta\mathbf{A} & -\mathbf{A}'^{-1}\mathbf{E}\mathbf{D}'^{-1} \\ 0 & \delta\mathbf{D} \end{pmatrix}$. We can guarantee that $\|\mathbf{E}\| \leqslant$ $2^{-p'-2p}$ with a computation with intermediary bitsize $O(p')$. This leads to our intermediary result. Now let $\mathbf{M}'^{-1} = \mathbf{M} + \mathbf{F}$, so $\mathbf{M}' = (\mathbf{M}(\mathbf{Id} + \mathbf{M}^{-1}\mathbf{F}))^{-1} =$ $(\mathbf{Id} + \mathbf{M}^{-1}\mathbf{F})^{-1}\mathbf{M}^{-1}$ and $\|\mathbf{M}' - \mathbf{M}^{-1}\| \leqslant \|\mathbf{M}^{-1}\|\|(\mathbf{Id} + \mathbf{M}^{-1}\mathbf{F})^{-1} - \mathbf{Id}\| \leqslant 2^{-p}$. The complexity comes from the matrix multiplication with words of size w.

3 Fast Reduction of Euclidean Lattices

This section is devoted to the description of our block recursive lattice reduction algorithm. In the following, let us fix a Euclidean lattice Λ of rank d, described by a basis collected in a rational matrix $\mathbf{B}$ in the canonical basis of $\mathbb{R}^d$. We generically denote by $\mathbf{R}$ the R-part of the QR-decomposition of this matrix. We recall that computations are conducted in floating-point arithmetic. However, for the sake of readability and ease of presentation, we defer the issue of the necessary precision to Sect. 4.

We turn to a detailed breakdown of the essential parts of the algorithm. Each of the following subsections details and refers to the corresponding lines of Algorithm 5, **Reduce**.

Algorithm 5 — Reduce

Parameter : Relaxation factor $\alpha, \varepsilon > 0$, number of rounds ρ, number of blocks D, $d' = d/D$ block size.

Input : Basis $\mathbf{B} \in \mathbb{Z}^{d \times d}$ of the lattice Λ

Output : A unimodular transformation $\mathbf{U} \in \mathbb{Z}^{d \times d}$, **UB** reduced.

1 **if** $d = 2$ **then return** Schonhage($\mathbf{B}$)
2 **for** $i = 1$ **to** ρ **do**
3     $\mathbf{R} \leftarrow$ **Block-Cholesky**($\mathbf{B}^T\mathbf{B}$)
4     $\mathbf{U}_i \leftarrow$ **Size-Reduce**($\mathrm{Diag}(\mathbf{R})^{-1} \cdot \mathbf{R}$)
5     $(\mathbf{B}, \mathbf{R}) \leftarrow (\mathbf{B}, \mathbf{R}) \cdot \mathbf{U}_i$
6   **for** $j = 1 + (i \mod 2)$ **to** $D/2$ **by step of** 2 **do**
7         $V_1 \leftarrow$ vol($\mathbf{R}[(j-1)d' + 1 : jd', (j-1)d' + 1 : jd']$)
8         $V_2 \leftarrow$ vol($\mathbf{R}[jd' + 1 : (j+1)d' - 1, jd' + 1 : (j+1)d']$)
9   **if** $V_1 \geqslant 2^{2(1+\varepsilon)\alpha(d')^2} V_2$ **then**
10             $\mathbf{U}' \leftarrow$ **Reduce**($\mathbf{R}[jd' : (j+2)d' - 1, jd' : (j+2)d' - 1]$)
11             $(\mathbf{U}_i, \mathbf{B}) \leftarrow (\mathbf{U}_i, \mathbf{B}) \cdot \mathrm{Diag}(\mathbf{Id}_{jd'}, \mathbf{U}', \mathbf{Id}_{d-3jd'})$
12   **end if**
13   **end for**
14 **end for**
15 **return** $\prod_{i=1}^{\rho} \mathbf{U}_i$ // The product is computed from the end

---

3.1   Base Case: Plane Lattices [Line 1]

As in all variants of the LLL algorithm, the *base case* of the reduction boils down to the two-dimensional case, usually handled by the celebrated Lagrange-Gauss reduction or some equivalent transformations. For instance, in the original LLL algorithm, truncated steps of Lagrange-Gauss reduction are conducted on two-dimensional projections of shape $\pi_i(b_i)\mathbb{Z} \oplus \pi_i(b_{i+1})\mathbb{Z}$.

For the sake of efficiency, we adapt Schönhage's algorithm [66], as in the algorithms of [35,41], to reduce these plane lattices. This algorithm is an extension to the bidimensional case of the so-called half-GCD algorithm [54], likewise that Gauss' algorithm is a bidimensional generalization of the classical Euclid's GCD. The original algorithm of Schönhage only deals with the reduction of binary quadratic forms but can be straightforwardly adapted to reduce lattices, as well as returning the corresponding unimodular transformation matrix. In the following, we denote by **Schonhage** this modified procedure. Its complexity is *quasilinear* in the size of its input (which is to be compared with the *quadratic* complexity of the classical Gauss reduction).

3.2   Outer Iteration [Line 2]

To reduce the lattice Λ, we adopt an iterative strategy to progressively modify the basis: for $\rho > 0$ steps, a reduction pass over the current basis is performed, ρ being a parameter set to optimize the complexity of the whole algorithm while still ensuring the reduceness of the basis. We defer the choice of this constant for the moment. This global iterative scheme is similar to the *terminating* variants of the BKZ algorithm, for instance as in [36] or [53], where a polynomial number of rounds is fixed to reduce the input.

3.3   Orthogonalization via Block-Cholesky Decomposition [Line 6]

Gram-Schmidt Orthogonalization is a preliminary step of every LLL-type algorithms, as it computes the so-called *Gram-Schmidt vectors* of the basis, which are ubiquitous in the definition of the reduction itself. On symmetric matrices as the Gram-matrix $\mathbf{B}^T\mathbf{B}$ of the basis, one computes the *Cholesky factorization*, which given a symmetric positive-definite matrix $\mathbf{G}$, the factorization asserts the existence (and unicity) of an upper triangular matrix $\mathbf{R}$ such that $\mathbf{G} = \mathbf{R}^T\mathbf{R}$ which is the some $\mathbf{R}$ in the QR decomposition of $\mathbf{B}$ since $\mathbf{G} = \mathbf{B}^T\mathbf{B} = \mathbf{R}^T\mathbf{R}$.

We use here a *recursive block variant* of the Cholesky factorization algorithm, allowing to compute a floating-point approximation of the matrix $\mathbf{R}$, whose running time is heuristically the cost of a matrix multiplication. It relies heavily on the **Invert** procedure introduced in Sect. 2.5.

Remark 1. Block computations of decompositions seems to be folklore in numerical algebra (see, for instance, the complete monograph of Higham [39] for multiple variants of block orthogonalization, such as modified Gram-Schmidt, Householder transformations, . . .), but oddly, we were unable to find a proper reference to the block Cholesky factorization.

The decomposition is as follows, given as input a symmetric matrix $\mathbf{G}$. We start by block splitting it (with blocks of half size): $\mathbf{G} = \begin{pmatrix} \mathbf{A} & \mathbf{B} \\ \mathbf{B}^T & \mathbf{C} \end{pmatrix}$, where $\mathbf{A}, \mathbf{C}$ are also symmetric. Its Schur complement $\mathbf{S} = \mathbf{C} - \mathbf{B}^T \mathbf{A}^{-1} \mathbf{B}$ is then also symmetric. Suppose that we know the factorization of the $\mathbf{A}$ and $\mathbf{S}$ in say: $\mathbf{A} = \mathbf{R}_A^T \mathbf{R}_A$ and $\mathbf{S} = \mathbf{R}_S^T \mathbf{R}_S$. Then, we set $\mathbf{R} = \begin{pmatrix} \mathbf{R}_A & \mathbf{R}_A^{-T} \mathbf{B} \\ 0 & \mathbf{R}_S \end{pmatrix}$. This matrix is indeed the Cholesky factorization of $\mathbf{G}$, as ensured by the following computation:

$$\mathbf{R}^T \mathbf{R} = \begin{pmatrix} \mathbf{R}_A^T & 0 \\ \mathbf{B}^T \mathbf{R}_A^{-1} & \mathbf{R}_S^T \end{pmatrix} \cdot \begin{pmatrix} \mathbf{R}_A & \mathbf{R}_A^{-T} \mathbf{B} \\ 0 & \mathbf{R}_S \end{pmatrix}$$

$$= \begin{pmatrix} \mathbf{R}_A^T \mathbf{R}_A & \mathbf{R}_A^T \mathbf{R}_A^{-T} \mathbf{B} \\ \mathbf{B}^T \mathbf{R}_A^{-1} \mathbf{R}_A & \mathbf{B}^T \mathbf{R}_A^{-1} \mathbf{R}_A^{-T} \mathbf{B} + \mathbf{R}_S^T \mathbf{R}_S \end{pmatrix} = \begin{pmatrix} \mathbf{A} & \mathbf{B} \\ \mathbf{B}^T & \mathbf{C} \end{pmatrix},$$

since $\mathbf{B}^T \mathbf{R}_A^{-1} \mathbf{R}_A^{-T} \mathbf{B} + \mathbf{R}_S^T \mathbf{R}_S = \mathbf{B}^T \mathbf{A}^{-1} \mathbf{B} + \mathbf{C} - \mathbf{B}^T \mathbf{A}^{-1} \mathbf{B} = \mathbf{C}$ by definition of the Schur complement.

This derivation yields a direct recursive algorithm, whose base case corresponds to the unidimensional instance, i.e., $\mathbf{G} = (g)$, admitting the trivial decomposition $\mathbf{G} = (\sqrt{g})^T (\sqrt{g})$. This observation yields the procedure stated in pseudocode in Algorithm 6 **Block-Cholesky**, computing a floating-point approximation of the Cholesky decomposition.

———— Algorithm 6 — Block-Cholesky ————

> **Input**   : A positive-definite symmetric matrix $\mathbf{G}$
>
> **Output**   : A fp-approx. of a triangular matrix $\mathbf{R}$ s.t. $\mathbf{R}^T \mathbf{R} = \mathbf{G}$
>
> 1   **if** $dim(\mathbf{G}) = 1$ **then return** $\sqrt{\mathbf{G}}$
>
> 2 $\begin{pmatrix} \mathbf{A} & \mathbf{B} \\ \mathbf{B}^T & \mathbf{C} \end{pmatrix} \leftarrow \mathbf{G}$ `// with blocks of half-dimension`
>
> 3 $\mathbf{R}_A \leftarrow$ **Block-Cholesky**$(\mathbf{A})$
>
> 4 $\mathbf{R}_A' \leftarrow$ **Invert**$(\mathbf{R}_A)$
>
> 5 $\mathbf{A}' \leftarrow \mathbf{R}_A'^T \mathbf{R}_A'$
>
> 6 $\mathbf{R}_S \leftarrow$ **Block-Cholesky**$(\mathbf{C} - \mathbf{B}^T \mathbf{A}' \mathbf{B})$
>
> 7   **return** $\begin{pmatrix} \mathbf{R}_A & \mathbf{R}_A'^T \mathbf{B} \\ 0 & \mathbf{R}_S \end{pmatrix}$

3.4   Size-Reduction [Line 4]

As in the LLL algorithm, a size-reduction operation is conducted at each step of the reduction. It allows to control the size of the coefficients and ensures that the running time remains polynomial. However, in our case, we lean on a Seysen-like reduction to perform this operation [67]. Our recursive procedure allows to size-reduce a unitriangular matrix (in our case, the matrix $\mathrm{Diag}(\mathbf{R})^{-1}\mathbf{R}$) in roughly the time of matrix multiplication.

We start from the classical observation that the usual size-reduction process is a discretized version of the iterative Gram-Schmidt process (which is a way of computing the QR-decomposition of a matrix). Over the triangular matrix $\mathbf{R}$, it corresponds to make iteratively the extra diagonal elements as close as possible to 0. However, instead of using an iterative process, we use a lattice reduction algorithm with block matrix operations.

Let us start with a unitriangular matrix $\mathbf{R}$, split in block of half dimension:

Algorithm 7 — Size-Reduce

Input	: A unitriangular matrix $\mathbf{T}$
Output	: An integer unitriangular
	matrix $\mathbf{U}$, $\mathbf{TU}$ reduced

1 **if** $dim(\mathbf{T}) = 1$ **then return** (1)

2 $\begin{pmatrix} \mathbf{A}\ \mathbf{C} \\ \mathbf{0}\ \mathbf{D} \end{pmatrix} \leftarrow \mathbf{R}$ // with half dimension

3 $\mathbf{U}_1 \leftarrow$ **Size-Reduce**$(\mathbf{A})$

4 $\mathbf{U}_2 \leftarrow$ **Size-Reduce**$(\mathbf{D})$

5 $\mathbf{A}' \leftarrow$ **Invert**$(\mathbf{AU}_1)$

6 $\mathbf{W} \leftarrow \lfloor \mathbf{A'CU}_2 \rceil$

7 **return** $\begin{pmatrix} \mathbf{U}_1\ -\mathbf{U}_1\mathbf{W} \\ \mathbf{0}\quad \mathbf{U}_2 \end{pmatrix}$

$\begin{pmatrix} \mathbf{A}\ \mathbf{C} \\ \mathbf{0}\ \mathbf{D} \end{pmatrix}$. Assume for the moment that both unitriangular submatrices $\mathbf{A}$ and $\mathbf{D}$ are already size-reduced. Then, set

$$\mathbf{U} = \begin{pmatrix} \mathrm{Id} & -\lfloor \mathbf{A}^{-1}\mathbf{C} \rceil \\ 0 & \mathrm{Id} \end{pmatrix},$$

which is unimodular as its diagonal elements are all 1. Its action on $\mathbf{R}$ gives by elementary computation: $\mathbf{RU} = \begin{pmatrix} \mathbf{A} & \mathbf{C} - \mathbf{A}\lfloor \mathbf{A}^{-1}\mathbf{C} \rceil \\ 0 & \mathbf{D} \end{pmatrix}$ and the top-right part is of the same magnitude as $\mathbf{A}$. The inverse of $\mathbf{RU}$ is

$$\begin{pmatrix} \mathbf{A}^{-1} & -(\mathbf{A}^{-1}\mathbf{C} - \lfloor \mathbf{A}^{-1}\mathbf{C} \rceil)\mathbf{D}^{-1} \\ 0 & \mathbf{D}^{-1} \end{pmatrix}$$

and the top-right part is of the same magnitude as $\mathbf{D}^{-1}$, ensuring that the norm of this block is controlled. The translation of this process in pseudocode yields Algorithm 7 **Size-reduce**. Note that this algorithm is presented as yielding the *transformation* matrix instead of the reduced matrix, to be consistent with the presentation of **Reduce** (see proof in Appendix A).

Theorem 2. *Given a d-dimensional unitriangular matrix $\mathbf{T}$ such that $\|\mathbf{T}\|$ and $\|\mathbf{T}^{-1}\| \leqslant 2^p$ and $p \geqslant w + \log(d)^2 d$, the algorithm **Size-Reduce** returns an integral unitriangular matrix $\mathbf{U}$ with $\|\mathbf{U}\| \leqslant 2^{O(p)}$ such that $\|\mathbf{TU}\|$, $\|(\mathbf{TU})^{-1}\| \leqslant d^{\lceil \log d \rceil}$ with a running time of $O\left(\frac{d^w p}{w} + d^2 p\right)$.*

3.5   Step Reduction Subroutine [Lines 3–13]

From parallel design of LLL... Let us now describe the step reduction pass, occurring once the size-reduction operation has been performed. As observed in Sect. 2, the LLL algorithm reduces lattice reduction to the reduction of rank two lattices (more precisely, iteratively reduce *orthogonally projected* rank-2 sublattices). A first idea would be to use the same paradigm here and pass over the current basis in a sequence of reduction of projected planar lattices. However, on the contrary to the standard LLL or BKZ-2 algorithms, remark that we are not forced to proceed progressively along the basis, but that we can reduce $\lfloor d/2 \rfloor$ independent (non-overlapping) rank-2 lattices at each step, namely the $(\pi_{2i}(b_{2i}\mathbb{Z} \oplus b_{2i+1}\mathbb{Z}))_{1 \leqslant i < d/2}$ and then, $(\pi_{2i+1}(b_{2i+1}\mathbb{Z} \oplus b_{2i+2}\mathbb{Z}))_{0 \leqslant i < d/2}$. This design enables an efficient parallel implementation which reduces sublattices

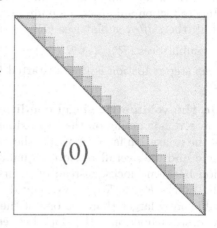

Fig. 1. Illustration of the parallel step reduction on the R-part of the QR-decomposition. Green 2×2 blocks are simultaneously reduced on odd steps and orange ones are reduced on even steps. This strategy is similar to [38].

simultaneously, in the same way that the classical LLL algorithm can be parallelized [38,73]. This technique can also be thought of as a parallelized BKZ [53] or slide-reduction [1] with blocksize 2.

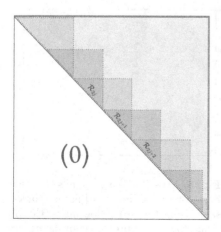

Fig. 2. The block process on the R-part of the basis. Green blocks are *recursively* reduced on odd steps and oranges one are reduced on even steps.

...to recursive block design. A bottleneck with this strategy is that each round needs (at least) a matrix multiplication to be updated. Using a dynamical system analysis similar to [35], such a reduction would require ρ rounds to be a $\Omega(d^2)$ to ensure an LLL approximation factor. This implies a dependency in the running time which would be at *least* quartic in the dimension d. However, one can notice that each round only makes *local* modifications on the basis. As a result, we propose to use a small number D of blocks, and let a round recursively reduces consecutive pairs of blocks of dimension $\frac{d}{D}$. In this setting, the dynamical system analysis of [35] shows that a $O(D^2 \log C)$ bound on the number of iterations ρ is now adequate.

Let us denote by R_j' the extracted submatrix $(R_{a,b})_{(j-1)d'<a,b\leqslant jd'}$, with $d' = d/D$. The lattice $\mathcal{R}_j'$ spanned by R_j' is the projection of $\Lambda_j = \bigoplus_{(j-1)d'<a\leqslant jd'} b_a\mathbb{Z}$ over the orthogonal space to the first $(j-1)d'$ vectors $(b_1,\ldots,b_{(j-1)d'-1})$. The step reduction subprocess simultaneously (and recursively) calls the reduction of all the *shifted* sublattices $(\mathcal{R}_{2j}' \oplus \mathcal{R}_{2j+1}')_{1\leqslant j<\lceil\frac{D}{2}\rceil}$. Then the same is done on the sublattices $(\mathcal{R}_{2j+1}' \oplus \mathcal{R}_{2j+2}')_{0\leqslant j<\lceil\frac{D}{2}\rceil}$ to enable the reduction of cross blocks. This step reduction is then restarted for ρ rounds as indicated in Sect. 3.2.

On the volumetric siegel condition. Remark the use of relaxation parameters $\varepsilon, \alpha > 0$, acting on the approximation factor of the reduction. As an avatar of the relaxation factor δ of LLL, they allow a slight tradeoff between the running time and the overall reduction quality. It is an equivalent of the Siegel condition between blocks: instead of recursively calling the reduction every time on the blocks $\mathcal{R}_{2j} \oplus \mathcal{R}_{2j+1}$, we only do it if the volume of the left block $\mathcal{R}_{2j}$ is sufficiently larger than the one of the right block $\mathcal{R}_{2j+1}$. We *do not* perform a recursive reduction if the slope between the blocks is *already small enough*.

In practice, these values are dependent on the depth of recursion to optimize the global running time. Section 4 addresses this technicality more thoroughly.

4   Complexity Estimation and Supporting Experiments

We now turn to the fine-tuning of the implementation and describe some optimization tricks used. We backed up our choices by supporting experiments and eventually devise an *empirical estimate* of the bit-complexity of our algorithm.

4.1   Needed Precision

Since the implementation of the algorithm is done using floating-point arithmetic, we need to set a precision which is sufficient to handle the internal values during the computation. To do so, we set:

$$p = \log \frac{\max_i \mathbf{R}[i,i]}{\min_i \mathbf{R}[i,i]},$$

where the $\mathbf{R}[i,i]$ encodes the norm of the Gram-Schmidt vectors. As in floating-point variants of LLL [44,55,57,63], it is straightforward that a $O(p)$ is sufficient to handle the computation. However, the remaining question is the evolution of this quantity within the recursive calls. Indeed, as we have more and more recursive calls of the reduction algorithm on

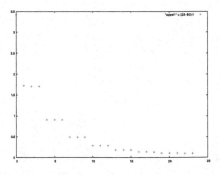

Fig. 3. Abscissa corresponds to the iteration time and ordinates corresponds to the value $\log(\max_i \mathbf{R}[i,i]/\min_i \mathbf{R}[i,i])$. As predicted by heuristic 1 the corresponding graph presents an exponential decay.

projected lattices of smaller dimensions, we would like to reduce them with a limited precision to get an overall faster reduction.

The analysis of [55] bounds the number of rounds, and reaches a complexity in $d^3 C^{1+o(1)}$ with exact arithmetic (C is the log of the condition number), while the non-optimized algorithm [35] uses $\Omega(d^3 \log C)$ local reductions. Consequently, to decrease the complexity of the reduction, we have to reduce the precision in the local operations. The justification of this fact comes from that *in practice*, the values of $\mathbf{R}[i, i]$ decrease roughly exponentially in i both in the input and the output matrices. To define our heuristic, we rely on the notion of *slope* of the basis, which is the opposite of the slope of the linear regression of the log of the norm the Gram-Schmidt vectors. Under the Geometric Series Assumption (GSA), this corresponds to the usual geometric decay factor. Heuristic 1 says that we reduce the slope, i.e. the logarithm potential $\Pi(\mathbf{B}) = \sum_{i=1}^{d}(d-i)\log(\mathbf{R}_{i,i})$. We consider that we have access to an oracle which reduces with a slope parameter of α, namely $\mathbf{R}[i, i]/\mathbf{R}[i+1, i+1] \approx 2^{2\alpha}$. The matrix returned will have a slope parameter of $(1+\varepsilon)\alpha$ for $0 < \varepsilon < 1/2$.

Heuristic 1. *If ρ is even, and $\frac{\rho}{2}(2D-1) \geqslant D^3$, then the slope decreases exponentially quickly towards $(1+\varepsilon)\alpha$, with rate $1 - O(\frac{1}{D^2})$.*

Remark 2. For a smaller ρ, we would have several leaves in the recursion tree, which would be negligible compared to d^3, making it unlikely to reduce the lattice by a significant amount. These values come from an heuristic analysis.

Figure 3 shows the evolution of the slope on a lattice of dimension 1024 where the phenomenon is observable. Heuristic 1 has been tested on various types of lattices (Knapsacks, NTRU-like) in dimensions from 128 to 2048 without failing.

4.2 On the Choice of the Relaxation Parameter ε and Its relation to the Global Complexity

To finely tune our parameters, we need to estimate the decrease of the potential at each recursive call. Using heuristic 1 at any moment in the recursion, when called with a lattice of rank d and working precision $p = \log \frac{\max_i \mathbf{R}_{i,i}}{\min_i \mathbf{R}_{i,i}}$, such that

$$\prod_{i=1}^{d/2} \mathbf{R}_{i,i} > 2^{(1+\varepsilon)\alpha d^2/2} \prod_{i=d/2+1}^{d} \mathbf{R}_{i,i}, \quad \text{(condition)}$$

the output basis has a log-potential reduced by at least $\Omega(d^2 p \varepsilon)$. Calling a recursive reduction only when the condition is fulfilled allows the callee to reduce the slope by a factor of roughly $1+\varepsilon$. If this is actually done, the potential is reduced by $\Omega(\varepsilon(\frac{d}{D})^2 p')$ where p' is the precision used by the callee. The complexity of the callee, if not already in a leaf, and outside of its recursive calls is in

$$O\left(D^2\left((d/D)^\omega(p'/w + 1) + (d/D)^2 p' \frac{\log p'}{w}\right)\right).$$

Keeping only the first term and assuming $p' > w$, we get that the complexity per unit reduction in potential should behave in

$$O\big(D^2(d/D)^{\omega-2}w^{-1}\varepsilon^{-1}\big).$$

This suggests minimizing D, so that we set $D = 2$ and $\rho = 6$; and also we deduce that most of the complexity is at low-depth. While the global complexity is minimized for $D = 2$, considering a larger D leads to better running time when using multithreading (higher number of blocks can be treated in parallel).

If we write d_i and ε_i for their values at depth i, we obtain that the global approximation factor is the one at the leaf multiplied by $\exp(\sum_i \varepsilon_i)$. Also, the main term in the complexity is proportional to $\sum_i d_i^{\omega-2}\varepsilon_i^{-1}$. Thus, we want ε_i proportional to $d_i^{1-\omega/2}$. If we want $\sum_i \varepsilon_i = \Theta(\delta)$, we get

$$\varepsilon_i = \delta(\omega(d) - 2)(d/d_i)^{1-\omega(d_i)/2}.$$

Summing the complexity at all depths, we see that the main term becomes:

$$O\left(\frac{d^\omega C}{w(\omega-2)^2\delta}\right) \quad \text{for any} \quad \delta = O\left(\frac{1}{\omega-2}\right).$$

4.3 Using Small-Dimension Fast Enumeration in the Leaves

Since almost all the complexity concentrates at low recursive depth, we can allocate more time in the leaves of the recursion tree to improve the quality of the reduction without altering much the global complexity. In practice, this means stopping the recursion before reaching rank-2 sublattices and using a stronger reduction process than LLL on these (higher dimensional) leaves.

Some instances of stronger algorithms are the BKZ-type family, which are parameterized by a block size β, and have a complexity exponential in β [2]. This family includes Schnorr's original BKZ algorithm, Terminated-BKZ with less rounds [35], the self-dual BKZ [53] or pressed-BKZ [7]—which is particularly good for low β. If the dimension at the leaf d_l is significantly larger than $\beta \log \beta$, the famous Geometric Series Assumption states that the Gram-Schmidt norms of the reduced basis are well approximated by a geometric series of rate $2^{\Theta\left(\frac{\beta}{\log \beta}\right)}$.

We can assume that the basis was already reduced with a constant slope 2α, so that the potential will overall decrease only by $O(d^3)$. At each leaf, we can use a constant ε_{l-1} and thus expect the log-potential to decrease by at least $\Omega(d_l^3 \frac{\log \beta}{\beta})$. The number of calls is therefore

$$O\left(\frac{d^3\beta}{d_l^3 \log \beta}\right) = O\left(\frac{d^3}{\beta^2}\right)$$

so we can choose any β smaller than $\Omega((\omega-2)\log C)$.

4.4 Complexity Estimation

The sketch of analysis conducted previously let us conjecture that the complexity should have a dominant term in $d^\omega C$. We plot the *single-thread* running time on lattices with dimension $d = 2n$ generated by the columns of the following matrix

$$\begin{pmatrix} q\mathbf{Id}_n & \mathbf{A} \\ 0 & \mathbf{Id}_n \end{pmatrix}$$

with $\mathbf{A}$ sampled uniformly modulo q, and $C = \log(q) \approx n4^{k-1}$ for k from 0 (green) to 3 (blue). The slope of the reduced matrix is $2\alpha \approx 0.065$ (RHF$= 2^{0.032} = 1.02$).

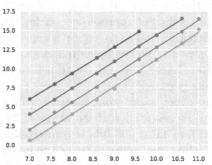

To confirm this hypothesis, we perform a linear regression on the log/log data of the running time in function of the input dimension (ranging from 128 to 2048). The regression reveals a slope of 3.5, that is a complexity in $O(d^{2.5}C)$ as C is linear in d. Given the noise generated by the inherent complexity of the program, its libraries, and the complex processor architecture, this experiment seems to validate our conjectural complexity. Each line corresponds to experiments made with matri-

Fig. 4. Log-Log representation of the running time (in seconds) for increasing dimension, with constant C/d on each line. (Color figure online)

ces with bitsize bounded by (dimension K) [from green (lower) line with $K = 1/4$ to blue (upper) line $K = 16$]. We propose the following complexity for our algorithm, using the small BKZ-enumeration in the leaves.

Analysis 1. *Let $\mathbf{A}$ be a matrix of dimension d with integer entries, with $\kappa(\mathbf{A}) \leqslant 2^C$ such that $C \geqslant d/\log d$. **Reduce**(A) returns the transformation matrix to a basis of $\mathbf{A}\mathbb{Z}^d$ having its first vector of norm bounded by*

$$\max\left(\sqrt{d}, 2^{O\left(d(\omega-2)\frac{\log\log C}{\log C}\right)}\right)\mathrm{vol}A^{\frac{1}{d}}$$

Further, the heuristic running time is

$$O\left(d^\omega \cdot \frac{C}{(\omega-2)^2 \log C} + d^2 C \log C + \frac{d^2 C}{(\omega-2)^2}\right).$$

Remark 3. The values come from a heuristic analysis that we do not develop.

- *In practice*, the entire basis is reduced at the end of the algorithm (as LLL algorithm gives a reduced basis with controlled decay of the Gram-Schmidt).
- When ω is bounded away from 2, and C is not extremely large ($C = 2^{o(d)}$), the complexity simplifies to $O\left(d^\omega \cdot \frac{C}{\log C}\right)$.

- It is better to first reduce with a large δ (say $\min(\log(C/d), \frac{1}{\omega-2})$), and progressively reduce the slope by decreasing δ by a constant, so that the precision used is exponentially decreasing. For $C > d2^{1/(\omega-2)}$, we obtain a heuristic complexity of:

$$O\left(d^\omega \cdot \frac{C}{(\omega-2)\log C} + d^2 C \log C\right).$$

- The dependency in the second term of the complexity (term in $d^2 C \log C$) comes as a direct consequence of the complexity of the Schonhäge algorithm.

The implementation mixes multiple machine representation as it needs to manage efficiently both large and small matrices, with a large range in bit-sizes. On the one hand, the "large matrices", e.g. with of dimension greater than 80 and of coefficient represented on few hundreds bits, are represented in the Fourier domain, that is to say by a collection of complex matrices, one for each evaluation point. The complex matrices are with double-precision floating-point coordinates. Large integers are transformed into polynomials, with between 14 and 16 bits per coefficient.

On the other hand, small matrices (dimension lower than 80) and with small bitsize are represented with an array of MPFR values [27]. A reduction of small matrix with at most 300 bits is computed by repeatedly reducing matrices with at most 39 bits, which are in turned reduced using blocks of dimension 12. These matrices of dimension 12 and with at most 20 bits are reduced with the quadratic L^2 [57] procedure.

Finally, matrices where p is small (around 30) and dimension up to 400 are treated in double precision, thanks to the use of the Householder QR-decomposition and the Seysen size-reduction.

5   Reduction of Structured Knapsack-Like

In this section, we present a progressive strategy to *provably* speed-up the reduction of *almost* triangular matrices. Combined with the reduction of Sect. 3, it gives a heuristic reduction process which estimated running time is essentially a $O\left(d^{\omega-1}\frac{C}{\log C} + Cd\log d\right)$. The general idea is that a knapsack-like matrix of dimension d and with log condition number C can be reduced as quickly as a matrix of dimension d and condition number $2^{C/d}$. As this effect was already known for some algorithms like fplll [68, 1.5.3], noted [56], and used in [72], we aim at giving a general framework to encompass this observation.

5.1   Setting

Definition 4 (Almost triangular matrix). *A matrix* **B** *with d columns and $O(d)$ rows is said to be (asymptotically) almost triangular if* $\mathbf{B}_{i,j} = 0$ *for any $i \geqslant O(j)$, with a uniform constant.*

In order to analyze our strategy we also require the matrices to be well conditioned in the following sense:

Definition 5 (Knapsack-like matrix). *Let* $\mathbf{B} \in \mathbf{Z}^{d \times d}$ *be an almost triangular matrix and set* $C \geqslant d^2$ *such that* $\lambda_k(\mathbf{C}) \leqslant 2^{C/k}$, *for all matrices* $\mathbf{C}$ *whose columns are a subset of those of* $\mathbf{B}$ *of dimension* k. *Set* $\mathbf{R}$ *to be the R-factor of the QR-decomposition of* $\mathbf{B}$. *We say that* $\mathbf{B}$ *is* $C-$knapsack-like *if furthermore* $\|\mathbf{R}^{-1}\| \leqslant 2^{C/d}$ *and* $|\mathbf{R}_{i,j}| \leqslant 2^{C/i}$ *for all* i, j.

Remark 4. The conditions detailed in the previous definition seems apparently strong but such matrices are actually widespread, as corresponding to generic instances of so-called *knapsack* problems or searching integer relations. In practice, one can easily computationally check that these matrices, as well as Hermite Normal Form matrices with decreasing round pivots verify the assumptions with a reasonably small B.

5.2 Iterative Reduction Strategy

Hypothesis 1. *In all of the following suppose that we have access to a lattice reduction oracle* **red-Oracle**, *whose output is a transition matrix to a Siegel-reduced and size-reduced basis. Its running time on a* $d \times d$ *matrix of condition number bounded by* C *is denoted by* $T(d, C)$.

The progressive reduction consists in reducing the first $k = 2^i$ columns of $\mathbf{B}$, for all successive powers of two until reaching d. At step $1 \leqslant i \leqslant \lfloor \log d \rfloor$, we use the—now reduced—first k vectors to size-reduce the remaining columns before concatenating them to the current basis and pursuing the reduction. Hence, the bitsize of the whole matrix is reduced for each i before being actively used in the lattice reduction oracle **red-Oracle**.

Formally, define inductively a family of matrices $\mathbf{B}_i$ which represents the state of the matrix $\mathbf{B}$ computed in the i-th iteration.

Initialization: $\mathbf{B}_0 = \mathbf{B}$.

Induction: Let $i > 0$, and suppose that $\mathbf{B}_i$ is known. We start by reducing *only* the first $k = 2^i$ vectors using **red-Oracle** of $\mathbf{B}_i$ and denote by $\mathbf{B}'_i$ the result. Define $\mathbf{Q}_i \mathbf{R}_i$ to be the QR-decomposition of $\mathbf{B}'_i[:1, k]$. Then, remark that for any x being a column of $\mathbf{B}'_i$ not in the span of $\mathbf{B}'_i[:1, k]$, we can reduce its bitsize by replacing it by $x - \mathbf{B}'_j \lfloor \mathbf{R}_j^{-1} \mathbf{Q}_j^T x \rceil$ for increasing $1 \leqslant j \leqslant k$. Such a size-reduction can be computed on all the columns of $\mathbf{B}_i[k + 1 : d]$ simultaneously using a single matrix multiplication and call $\mathbf{C}$ the corresponding vectors. Eventually set $\mathbf{B}_{i+1}$ to the concatenation $[\mathbf{B}'[:1, k] \mid \mathbf{C}]$.

The corresponding pseudo-code is given in Algorithm 8.

```
──────── Algorithm 8 — Reduction of Knapsack-like lattices ────────
    Parameter : Reduction oracle red-Oracle
    Input     : Matrix B ∈ ℤ^{d×d}
    Output    : A reduced basis of Bℤ

  1  k, i ← 1, 0
  2  B₀ ← B
  3  while k < d do
  4  │   k ← 2k; i ← i + 1
  5  │   Bᵢ[:, 1, k] ← Bᵢ₋₁[:, 1, k]·red-Oracle(Bᵢ₋₁[:, 1, k])
  6  │   Rᵢ ← Block-Cholesky(Bᵢ[:, 1, k]ᵀBᵢ[:, 1, k])
  7  │   Qᵢ ← Bᵢ[:, 1, k] · Rᵢ⁻¹
  8  │   Bᵢ₊₁[1 : k, k + 1 : d] ← Bᵢ[1 : k, k + 1 : d]−
  9  │                         Bᵢ · ⌊Rᵢ⁻¹ · Qᵢᵀ · Bᵢ[1 : k, k + 1 : d]⌉
 10  end while
```

5.3   Complexity Analysis

We now present the complexity analysis of the algorithm presented, under the hypothesis made on the lattice reduction oracle. For readability, we defer the proof to the full version. The following lemma entails that the condition number of the input of the reduction oracle is sufficiently small.

Lemma 2. *Let* **B** *a rank d almost triangular matrix which is C-knapsack-like. For any index* $0 \leqslant i \leqslant \lceil \log d \rceil$, *set* $\mathbf{B}_i$ *to be the matrix computed by the execution of Algorithm 8 on* **B**. *Denote by* $\mathbf{Q}_i\mathbf{R}_i = \mathbf{B}_i[, 1 : 2^i]$ *the QR-decomposition of the matrix of* 2^i *first columns of* $\mathbf{B}_i$. *We get* $\|\mathbf{R}_i\|, \|\mathbf{R}_i^{-1}\| = 2^{O(d + C2^{-i})}$ *for all i.*

From this we have:

Theorem 3. *Let* **B** *a rank d almost triangular matrix which is C-well conditioned,* $C \geqslant d^2$. *We can Siegel-reduce it in time*

$$O\left(\sum_{i=1}^{\log d} T(2^i, O(C2^{-i})) + \frac{d^{\omega-1}}{\omega - 2} \cdot \frac{C}{\log C} + dC \log d\right).$$

Remark 5. • One can use such a procedure to quickly search a putative minimal polynomial; the knapsack-like condition is however not guaranteed.
  • The setting of Theorem 3 includes both modular and integer knapsacks.
  • Assuming algorithm of Sect. 3 has heuristically the right properties (which is the case in all of our extensive experiments), the complexity of the reduction of knapsack like matrices then becomes:

$$O\left(\frac{d^{\omega-1}}{(\omega - 2)^2} \cdot \frac{C}{\log C} + dC \log C\right).$$

6   Applications

Lattice reduction algorithms have numerous applications in mathematics and computer science. We survey here the impact of the implementation our algorithm, starting with cryptanalysis. In particular, we can reduce lattices of dimension in the thousands and with millions of bits. We recall that the Gram-Schmidt norms in the output basis are expected to decrease geometrically with rate $2^{2\alpha}$ so that the Hermite factor in dimension d is $2^{\alpha d}$.

For all the presented experiments, we use an Intel CPU E5-2695 v4 with 18 cores running at 2.10 GHz processors; and 768 GiB of RAM. Some SSD swap was slightly used in the largest computation. For comparison with older timings, we used a machine with an Intel i7-8650U with 4 cores at 1.9 GHz. The program was compiled with Intel's libraries and compiler with the standard -Ofast low-level optimization flag.

6.1   Comparison with State of the Art

We start this section by a comparison with the state-of-the-art implementation of fplll. Its complexity is $O(d^4 B^2)$ in the general case, and its heuristic complexity[2] is $O(d^2 B^2)$ for knapsack matrices, as reported in [68, 1.5.3]. When $d \geqslant 220$, its practical efficiency drops sharply due to the need of multiprecision computations. The following table presents a running time comparison with fplll, in *single-threaded* mode, on classical types of lattices namely knapsack and NTRU matrices. On the all instances, our implementation is sensibly faster than fplll.

Type	Dimension d	Bitsize B	fplll	This work
	128	100 000	88 min	6 min
Knapsack	256	10 000	134 min	4 min
	384	10 000	388 min	13 min
	256	80	24 min	3 min
NTRU	384	70	431 min	10 min
	512	70	1392 min	33 min

6.2   Fully Homomorphic Encryption over the Integers

FHE scheme was first designed by Gentry [33] using number theoretical tools in 2009. Soon after, an equivalent system was presented, using only integer arithmetic [70], and is based on a distant relative [17] of the celebrated Learning

---

[2] This estimation comes from the observation that dB swaps are performed, each taking d^2 operations on B/d bits. There are B/d reduction steps for each new vector, each takes d^2 operations on B bits.

With Error (LWE) problem in dimension one. More precisely, given an integer secret $|s| \leqslant 2^\eta$ (typically a prime), this problem aims at retrieving s from given samples x_i of the form $a_i s + e_i$ where $0 \leqslant a_i \leqslant 2^\gamma / |s|$ and $|e_i| \leqslant 2^\rho$ are sampled uniformly and independently. The parameters verify $\gamma \gg \eta \gg \rho$.

A natural lattice reduction attack consists in collecting d samples $x = (x_i)_{1 \leqslant i \leqslant d}$ and building the matrix $\mathbf{X} = \begin{pmatrix} x_1, \ldots, x_d \\ \mathbf{Id}_d \end{pmatrix}$. The volume of the lattice $\mathcal{X}$ spanned by the columns of $\mathbf{X}$ is $\sqrt{1 + \sum_{i=1}^d x_i^2} \approx 2^\gamma$. Hence, lattice reduction with root Hermite factor 2^α can be used to construct a non-zero vector $y \in \mathbb{Z}^d$ such that $\|y\|, |\langle x, y \rangle| \leqslant 2^{\gamma/d + \alpha d}$. Indeed, any vector in this lattice is of the form $(\langle x, y \rangle, y)$, so that its squared norm is the sum of two contributions: $\|y\|^2 + |\langle x, y \rangle|^2$. It now suffices to remark that norm of a vector found by reduction is smaller than the normalized covolume $2^{\gamma/d}$ times the root Hermite factor $2^{\alpha d}$.

By plugging back the definition of the (x_i), we have $\langle x, y \rangle = s \langle a, y \rangle + \langle e, y \rangle$ where $a = (a_1, \ldots, a_d)$, $e = (e_1, \ldots, e_d)$. Assuming $2^{\gamma/d + \alpha d} \leqslant 2^{\eta - \rho} / \sqrt{d}$, the Cauchy-Schwarz inequality implies that $\langle a, y \rangle = 0$. This is enough to break the scheme; if the $(d-1)$ first vectors of the basis have this length, then the last one must be proportional to a (and is $\pm a$ if the entries are coprime). The first $d - 1$ first vectors are orthogonal to a and are independent, so the last one must be proportional to a since a is in the lattice orthogonal to these vectors. The optimal d – for maximizing α – is therefore close to $\sqrt{\gamma/\alpha}$, leading to the condition $\alpha \leqslant \frac{(\eta - \rho)^2}{4\gamma}$.

A part of the original paper [70] considers security against polynomial-time adversaries, so that they obtain the condition $\gamma = \omega(\eta^2 \log \lambda)$ for a "security parameter" of λ. Another part of the original paper [70, Section 6.3], and almost all follow-ups [15, 21–25], consider however security against adversaries able to do 2^λ operations. However, the condition was copied without change, which possibly explains why a large α was chosen in several implementations[3].

As the lattice reduction algorithm can easily reach $\alpha = 0.04$, this means we can use a smaller d, close to $\frac{\gamma}{\eta - \rho}$ for many instances than the d in the table, which is the dimension where α is maximal. In the instance where $\gamma = 1.02 \cdot 10^6$ and $\eta - \rho = 376$, we used $d = 3600$ so that $\alpha = 0.024$ was needed, and we used a pressed-BKZ-19 in the leaves. This choice was made due to memory concerns.

While the large problems are clearly quite difficult, even the largest instances of the table seem to be within range of (motivated!) academic attackers, with terabytes of SSD memory and perhaps around 2^{65} flop.

6.3   Overstretched NTRU

It is well-known since the work of Albrecht *et al.* [4], Cheon *et al.* [16] and Kirchner and Fouque [43] that an NTRU scheme with a very large modulus q compared to the dimension of the lattice is prone to attacks. However, these

---

[3] Surprisingly, many $\log \lambda$ were "rounded up" to λ in the parameter choices.

Table 1. Examples of schemes attacked, and corresponding reduction algorithm required to break.

Scheme	λ	$\gamma/10^6$	$\eta - \rho$	α	d	Algorithm	Running time
[24]	42	0.16	1072	1.8	299	LLL	5 min
	52	0.86	1608	0.75	1070	LLL	55 min
	62	4.2	2144	0.273	3918	LLL	1030 min
	72	19	2613	0.089	14543	LLL	–
[25]	42	0.061	322	0.43	379	LLL	3 min
	52	0.27	370	0.12	1460	LLL	29 min
	62	1.02	376	0.0347	5426	LLL	27 h
	72	2.2	420	0.02	10476	BKZ-20	–
[22]	42	0.27	929	0.8	290	LLL	13 min
	52	1.1	924	0.2	2380	LLL	176 min
	62	4.2	919	0.051	9140	LLL	–
[15]	52	0.9	1517	0.64	1186	LLL	74 min
	62	4.6	2072	0.24	4440	LLL	1382 min
	72	21	2627	0.082	15988	LLL	–
[21]	52	1	1797	0.82	1104	LLL	67 min
	62	4.26	1987	0.24	4288	LLL	1322 min
	72	18.7	2189	0.0643	17043	LLL	–
	80	63.7	2353	0.0218	54117	BKZ-20	–

cases often happen in NTRU-based Homomorphic encryption schemes such as YASHE [12] or LTV schemes. In 2019, a homomorphic scheme has been proposed by Genise *et al.* [31] with a similar variant of this problem, hoping that the overstretched NTRU only works in algebraic setting using ring of polynomials. Some parameters proposed for performances evaluations have been broken in [49] also showing that the assumptions used is flawed. Here, we break comparable parameters showing that the proposed parameters only achieve a low security level. In [59], Pataki and Tural showed that the volume of any r-dimensional sublattice L' of a lattice L is larger than the product of the r smaller Gram-Schmidt. Kirchner and Fouque combined this result with the fact that in any $2d$-dimensional NTRU lattices, there is a sublattice of dimension d and volume roughly the size of secret-key to the power d, one can deduce that if the volume of the secret key sublattice is of size about the product of the d smaller Gram-Schmidt, it is possible to recover the secret key.

The optimal d is around $\frac{\log(q)}{4\alpha}$, which corresponds to a volume close to $2^{\log(q)^2/16\alpha}$. The scheme of [31] chooses entries in $\mathbf{F}, \mathbf{G}$ as integer Gaussians of standard deviation $\sigma = \sqrt{r/\pi}$ where r is the dimension of their lattice. We can restrict the lattice reduction to the middle $2d$ square matrix, but the volume is conserved. A more precise estimate consists in using the volume of the sublattice, projected orthogonally to the first r vectors of the reduced basis [43]. We expect the i-th Gram-Schmidt norm of the projected basis to be around $\sqrt{r+1-i}\sigma$, so that the volume can be computed with Stirling's formula $\left(\prod_{i=1}^{r}(r+1-i)\sigma^2\right)^{1/2} \approx \left(\frac{\sqrt{r}\sigma}{\sqrt{e}}\right)^r$. Overall we obtain $2^{\log(q)^2/16\alpha} \approx \left(\frac{r}{\sqrt{\pi e}}\right)^r$, from which we can find the α required. The first one necessitates roughly 2^{20} calls to a SVP in dimension 101, and each call currently needs 2^{11} *core*-seconds [6], this translates into a year of computation on our machine. Alternatively, each call can be computed in 2^2 seconds with a GPU [26]. A pressed-BKZ of dimension 29 was used for the second one.

Table 2. Experiments for overstretched NTRU problems. Dimension is the actual dimension of the problem, and effective dimension refers to the dimension required in practice to mount the attack.

Dimension r	$\log q$	α	Effective dimension	Algorithm	Time
1024	42	0.01274	1648	BKZ-101	–
4096	111	0.01799	3086	BKZ-25	233 h
32768	883	0.1105	2560	LLL	263 min

6.4 Miscellaneous

Integral relations. Another use of lattice reduction is the discovery small linear integer relation between reals. It actually corresponds to the setting of Sect. 6.2, where 2^η corresponds the norm of the relation, and γ the precision used to represent the reals. Then clearly, $\gamma \approx d\eta + d^2\alpha$ is enough to perform a search by reduction. In 2001, Bailey and Broadhurst believed [8] that their computation with $\gamma \approx 166000$ and $d = 110$ was the largest performed. It took 44 h, on 32 CPUs of a Cray-T3E (300 MHz). We report this takes 5 min on a laptop, or 600 times fewer cycles. As the task is identical (for large α) to breaking the integer homomorphic schemes, the running time for bigger examples can be found in the previous subsections.

Univariate polynomial factorization. Yet another application is factoring univariate polynomials [10,71] over the integers. The first step is to factor modulo some prime, and the number of factors n is the dimension of the modular vectorial knapsack we have to solve, namely we have to find very short vectors in the lattice generated by $\begin{pmatrix} q\mathbf{Id}_r & \mathbf{A} \\ 0 & \mathbf{Id}_n \end{pmatrix}$. The precision q, and number of coordinates r can essentially be freely chosen. For random polynomials, n is typically very small (e.g. logarithmic) and lattice reduction is not the bottleneck; but it can be as large as half the degree. Our choice is to take r small, say $n/\log n$, and then $r \log q \approx \alpha n^2$ allows (heuristically) to obtain the last Gram-Schmidt norms larger than n^2. Then, this restricts the solutions of the knapsack – known to be shorter than this – to the first few vectors of the reduced basis. At this point, one can recover the factors, and *prove* that they are irreducible. Taking $n = 256$, we get a solution in two minutes on one core of our laptop instead of ten with a 1 GHz Athlon [9]; for $n = 512$ it takes 25 min instead of 500. For ω bounded away from 2, with $\alpha = O\left(\frac{\log \log n}{\log n} \right)$ the heuristic asymptotical complexity is

$$O\left(\frac{n^{\omega+1} \log \log n}{\log^2 n} \right).$$

7   Conclusion and Open Questions

In this work, we introduced a recursive lattice reduction algorithm, whose heuristic complexity is equivalent to a few matrix multiplications. This algorithm and the heuristics used to complete the complexity analysis have been thoroughly tested and applied to reduce lattices of very large dimension. The implementation takes advantage of fast matrix multiplications, and fast Fourier transforms.

This work raises several questions. First of all, the analysis we are making is so far heuristic and empirical. It is possible to get a provable result by mitigating the complexity, in particular it seems difficult to be able to formally prove the heuristic on the decrease of the needed precision, even though this fact is easily checkable in practice. Reaching a *provable bound* in $d^\omega C$ is an open and interesting problem, and our algorithm is a first step in this direction.

A   Proof of Theorem 2

Proof. We use a precision $p' = O(p + \log(d)^2) = O(p)$. We prove by induction on d that $\|\mathbf{TU}\|, \|(\mathbf{TU})^{-1}\| \leqslant d^{\lceil \log d \rceil}$. Initialization is clear, so that we now assume that $d > 1$. We have by direct computation that $\mathbf{TU}$ is

$$\begin{pmatrix} \mathbf{AU}_1 & \mathbf{CU}_2 - \mathbf{AU}_1\mathbf{W} \\ 0 & \mathbf{DU}_2 \end{pmatrix}.$$

The top-right matrix is $\mathbf{AU}_1((\mathbf{AU}_1)^{-1}\mathbf{CU}_2 - \mathbf{W})$ and we have, by setting that $\mathbf{A}' - (\mathbf{AU}_1)^{-1} = \delta\mathbf{A}$:

$$\|(\mathbf{AU}_1)^{-1}\mathbf{CU}_2 - \mathbf{W}\| \leqslant \|\delta\mathbf{ACU}_2\| + \|\mathbf{A}'\mathbf{CU}_2 - \mathbf{W}\|.$$

The first term is bounded by $2^{O(p)}\|\delta\mathbf{A}\|$ and the second by $2d/3$. We choose the precision so that the first term is at most $1/3$ and the result follows directly, as $\|\mathbf{AU}_1\|, \|\mathbf{CU}_2\| \leqslant d^{\lceil\log d\rceil - 1}$.

Next, the matrix $(\mathbf{TU})^{-1}$ is equal to

$$\begin{pmatrix} (\mathbf{AU}_1)^{-1} & -(\mathbf{AU}_1)^{-1}(\mathbf{CU}_2 - \mathbf{AU}_1\mathbf{W})(\mathbf{DU}_2)^{-1} \\ 0 & (\mathbf{DU}_2)^{-1} \end{pmatrix}.$$

The top-right matrix is $((\mathbf{AU}_1)^{-1}\mathbf{CU}_2 - \mathbf{W})(\mathbf{DU}_2)^{-1}$. The first term was already bounded above by d, and $\|(\mathbf{DU}_2)^{-1}\| \leqslant d^{\lceil\log d\rceil - 1}$ and this gives the result.

Finally, we have $\|\mathbf{U}\| = \|\mathbf{T}^{-1}\mathbf{TU}\| \leqslant \|\mathbf{T}^{-1}\|\|\mathbf{TU}\| \leqslant 2^p d^{\lceil\log d\rceil}$.

Remark 6. It is mandatory to have $\mathbf{T}$ well-conditioned if we want a $\mathbf{U}$ which is not much larger than $\mathbf{T}$. This is also true for other variants of LLL (including fplll): outputting the transition matrix may lead to a slow-down by a factor of d.

References

1. Aggarwal, D., Li, J., Nguyen, P.Q., Stephens-Davidowitz, N.: Slide reduction, revisited—filling the gaps in SVP approximation. In: Micciancio, D., Ristenpart, T. (eds.) CRYPTO 2020, Part II. LNCS, vol. 12171, pp. 274–295. Springer, Cham (2020). https://doi.org/10.1007/978-3-030-56880-1_10
2. Becker, A., Ducas, L., Gama, N., Laarhoven, T.: New directions in nearest neighbor searching with applications to lattice sieving. In: SODA , pp. 10–24 (2016)
3. Albrecht, M., Bai, S., Cadé, D., Pujol, X., Stehlé, D.: fpLLL-5.0, a floating-point LLL implementation (2017). http://perso.ens-lyon.fr/damien.stehle
4. Albrecht, M., Bai, S., Ducas, L.: A subfield lattice attack on overstretched NTRU assumptions. In: Robshaw, M., Katz, J. (eds.) CRYPTO 2016, Part I. LNCS, vol. 9814, pp. 153–178. Springer, Heidelberg (2016). https://doi.org/10.1007/978-3-662-53018-4_6
5. Albrecht, M.R., Bai, S., Fouque, P.-A., Kirchner, P., Stehlé, D., Wen, W.: Faster enumeration-based lattice reduction: root Hermite factor $k^{1/(2k)}$ time $k^{k/8+o(k)}$. In: Micciancio, D., Ristenpart, T. (eds.) CRYPTO 2020, Part II. LNCS, vol. 12171, pp. 186–212. Springer, Cham (2020). https://doi.org/10.1007/978-3-030-56880-1_7
6. Albrecht, M.R., Ducas, L., Herold, G., Kirshanova, E., Postlethwaite, E.W., Stevens, M.: The general sieve kernel and new records in lattice reduction. In: Ishai, Y., Rijmen, V. (eds.) EUROCRYPT 2019, Part II. LNCS, vol. 11477, pp. 717–746. Springer, Cham (2019). https://doi.org/10.1007/978-3-030-17656-3_25
7. Bai, S., Stehlé, D., Wen, W.: Measuring, simulating and exploiting the head concavity phenomenon in BKZ. In: Peyrin, T., Galbraith, S. (eds.) ASIACRYPT 2018, Part I. LNCS, vol. 11272, pp. 369–404. Springer, Cham (2018). https://doi.org/10.1007/978-3-030-03326-2_13
8. Bailey, D., Broadhurst, D.: Parallel integer relation detection: techniques and applications. Math. Comput. **70**(236), 1719–1736 (2001)
9. Belabas, K.: A relative van Hoeij algorithm over number fields. J. Symb. Comput. **37**(5), 641–668 (2004)
10. Belabas, K., van Hoeij, M., Klüners, J., Steel, A.: Factoring polynomials over global fields. Journal de théorie des nombres de Bordeaux **21**(1), 15–39 (2009)

11. Bi, J., Coron, J.-S., Faugère, J.-C., Nguyen, P.Q., Renault, G., Zeitoun, R.: Rounding and chaining LLL: finding faster small roots of univariate polynomial congruences. In: Krawczyk, H. (ed.) PKC 2014. LNCS, vol. 8383, pp. 185–202. Springer, Heidelberg (2014). https://doi.org/10.1007/978-3-642-54631-0_11

12. Bos, J.W., Lauter, K., Loftus, J., Naehrig, M.: Improved security for a ring-based fully homomorphic encryption scheme. In: Stam, M. (ed.) IMACC 2013. LNCS, vol. 8308, pp. 45–64. Springer, Heidelberg (2013). https://doi.org/10.1007/978-3-642-45239-0_4

13. Buchmann, J.: Reducing lattice bases by means of approximations. In: Adleman, L.M., Huang, M.-D. (eds.) ANTS 1994. LNCS, vol. 877, pp. 160–168. Springer, Heidelberg (1994). https://doi.org/10.1007/3-540-58691-1_54

14. Chen, Y., Nguyen, P.Q.: BKZ 2.0: better lattice security estimates. In: Lee, D.H., Wang, X. (eds.) ASIACRYPT 2011. LNCS, vol. 7073, pp. 1–20. Springer, Heidelberg (2011). https://doi.org/10.1007/978-3-642-25385-0_1

15. Cheon, J.H., et al.: Batch fully homomorphic encryption over the integers. In: Johansson, T., Nguyen, P.Q. (eds.) EUROCRYPT 2013. LNCS, vol. 7881, pp. 315–335. Springer, Heidelberg (2013). https://doi.org/10.1007/978-3-642-38348-9_20

16. Cheon, J.H., Hhan, M., Lee, C.: Cryptanalysis of middle lattice on the overstretched NTRU problem for general modulus polynomial. Cryptology ePrint Archive, Report 2017/484 (2017). http://eprint.iacr.org/2017/484

17. Cheon, J.H., Stehlé, D.: Fully homomophic encryption over the integers revisited. In: Oswald, E., Fischlin, M. (eds.) EUROCRYPT 2015, Part I. LNCS, vol. 9056, pp. 513–536. Springer, Heidelberg (2015). https://doi.org/10.1007/978-3-662-46800-5_20

18. Cohen, H.: A Course in Computational Algebraic Number Theory. Springer, New York (1993). https://doi.org/10.1007/978-3-662-02945-9

19. Coppersmith, D.: Small solutions to polynomial equations, and low exponent RSA vulnerabilities. J. Cryptol. 10(4), 233–260 (1997)

20. Coppersmith, D., Shamir, A.: Lattice attacks on NTRU. In: Fumy, W. (ed.) EUROCRYPT 1997. LNCS, vol. 1233, pp. 52–61. Springer, Heidelberg (1997). https://doi.org/10.1007/3-540-69053-0_5

21. Coron, J.-S., Lepoint, T., Tibouchi, M.: Practical multilinear maps over the integers. In: Canetti, R., Garay, J.A. (eds.) CRYPTO 2013, Part I. LNCS, vol. 8042, pp. 476–493. Springer, Heidelberg (2013). https://doi.org/10.1007/978-3-642-40041-4_26

22. Coron, J.-S., Lepoint, T., Tibouchi, M.: Scale-invariant fully homomorphic encryption over the integers. In: Krawczyk, H. (ed.) PKC 2014. LNCS, vol. 8383, pp. 311–328. Springer, Heidelberg (2014). https://doi.org/10.1007/978-3-642-54631-0_18

23. Coron, J.-S., Lepoint, T., Tibouchi, M.: New multilinear maps over the integers. In: Gennaro, R., Robshaw, M. (eds.) CRYPTO 2015, Part I. LNCS, vol. 9215, pp. 267–286. Springer, Heidelberg (2015). https://doi.org/10.1007/978-3-662-47989-6_13

24. Coron, J.-S., Mandal, A., Naccache, D., Tibouchi, M.: Fully homomorphic encryption over the integers with shorter public keys. In: Rogaway, P. (ed.) CRYPTO 2011. LNCS, vol. 6841, pp. 487–504. Springer, Heidelberg (2011). https://doi.org/10.1007/978-3-642-22792-9_28

25. Coron, J.-S., Naccache, D., Tibouchi, M.: Public key compression and modulus switching for fully homomorphic encryption over the integers. In: Pointcheval, D.,

Johansson, T. (eds.) EUROCRYPT 2012. LNCS, vol. 7237, pp. 446–464. Springer, Heidelberg (2012). https://doi.org/10.1007/978-3-642-29011-4_27

26. Ducas, L., Stevens, M., van Woerden, W.: Advanced lattice sieving on GPUs, with tensor cores. Cryptology ePrint Archive, Report 2021/141 (2021). https://eprint.iacr.org/2021/141

27. Fousse, L., Hanrot, G., Lefèvre, V., Pélissier, P., Zimmermann, P.: MPFR: a multiple-precision binary floating-point library with correct rounding. ACM Trans. Math. Softw. (TOMS) **33**(2), 13 (2007)

28. Frieze, A.M., Kannan, R., Lagarias, J.C.:. Linear congruential generators do not produce random sequences. In: 25th FOCS, pp. 480–484. IEEE Computer Society Press (1984)

29. Gama, N., Nguyen, P.Q.: Finding short lattice vectors within Mordell's inequality. In: Ladner, R.E., Dwork, C. (eds.) 40th ACM STOC, pp. 207–216 (2008)

30. Gama, N., Nguyen, P.Q., Regev, O.: Lattice enumeration using extreme pruning. In: Gilbert, H. (ed.) EUROCRYPT 2010. LNCS, vol. 6110, pp. 257–278. Springer, Heidelberg (2010). https://doi.org/10.1007/978-3-642-13190-5_13

31. Genise, N., Gentry, C., Halevi, S., Li, B., Micciancio, D.: Homomorphic encryption for finite automata. In: Galbraith, S.D., Moriai, S. (eds.) ASIACRYPT 2019, Part II. LNCS, vol. 11922, pp. 473–502. Springer, Cham (2019). https://doi.org/10.1007/978-3-030-34621-8_17

32. Gentry, C.: Key recovery and message attacks on NTRU-composite. In: Pfitzmann, B. (ed.) EUROCRYPT 2001. LNCS, vol. 2045, pp. 182–194. Springer, Heidelberg (2001). https://doi.org/10.1007/3-540-44987-6_12

33. Gentry, C.: Fully homomorphic encryption using ideal lattices. In: Mitzenmacher, M. (ed.) 41st ACM STOC, pp. 169–178. ACM Press (2009)

34. Golub, G.H., Van Loan, C.F.: Matrix Computations, 3rd edn. The Johns Hopkins University Press, Baltimore (1996)

35. Hanrot, G., Pujol, X., Stehlé, D.: Analyzing blockwise lattice algorithms using dynamical systems. In: Rogaway, P. (ed.) CRYPTO 2011. LNCS, vol. 6841, pp. 447–464. Springer, Heidelberg (2011). https://doi.org/10.1007/978-3-642-22792-9_25

36. Hanrot, G., Pujol, X., Stehlé, D.: Terminating BKZ. Cryptology ePrint Archive, Report 2011/198 (2011). http://eprint.iacr.org/2011/198

37. Håstad, J., Just, B., Lagarias, J.C., Schnorr, C.: Polynomial time algorithms for finding integer relations among real numbers. SIAM J. Comput. **18**(5), 859–881 (1989)

38. Heckler, C., Thiele, L.: Complexity analysis of a parallel lattice basis reduction algorithm. SIAM J. Comput. **27**(5), 1295–1302 (1998)

39. Higham, N.J.: Accuracy and Stability of Numerical Algorithms, vol. 80. SIAM, Philadelphia (2002)

40. Joux, A., Stern, J.: Lattice reduction: a toolbox for the cryptanalyst. J. Cryptol. **11**(3), 161–185 (1998). https://doi.org/10.1007/s001459900042

41. Kirchner, P., Espitau, T., Fouque, P.-A.: Fast reduction of algebraic lattices over cyclotomic fields. In: Micciancio, D., Ristenpart, T. (eds.) CRYPTO 2020, Part II. LNCS, vol. 12171, pp. 155–185. Springer, Cham (2020). https://doi.org/10.1007/978-3-030-56880-1_6

42. Kirchner, P., Espitau, T., Fouque, P.-A.: Algebraic and Euclidean lattices: optimal lattice reduction and beyond. Cryptology ePrint Archive, Report 2019/1436 (2019). https://eprint.iacr.org/2019/1436

43. Kirchner, P., Fouque, P.-A.: Revisiting lattice attacks on overstretched NTRU parameters. In: Coron, J.-S., Nielsen, J.B. (eds.) EUROCRYPT 2017, Part I. LNCS, vol. 10210, pp. 3–26. Springer, Cham (2017). https://doi.org/10.1007/978-3-319-56620-7_1

44. Koy, H., Schnorr, C.P.: Segment LLL-reduction of lattice bases. In: Silverman, J.H. (ed.) CaLC 2001. LNCS, vol. 2146, pp. 67–80. Springer, Heidelberg (2001). https://doi.org/10.1007/3-540-44670-2_7

45. Lagarias, J.C.: The computational complexity of simultaneous diophantine approximation problems. In: 23rd FOCS, pp. 32–39. IEEE Computer Society Press (1982)

46. Lagarias, J.C.: Knapsack public key cryptosystems and diophantine approximation. In: Chaum, D. (ed.) CRYPTO'83, pp. 3–23. Springer, Boston (1984). https://doi.org/10.1007/978-1-4684-4730-9_1

47. Lagarias, J.C., Lenstra, H.W., Schnorr, C.: Korkin-Zolotarev bases and successive minima of a lattice and its reciprocal lattice. Combinatorica **10**(4), 333–348 (1990). https://doi.org/10.1007/BF02128669

48. Lagarias, J.C., Odlyzko, A.M.: Solving low-density subset sum problems. In: 24th FOCS, pp. 1–10. IEEE Computer Society Press, November 1983

49. Lee, C., Wallet, A.: Lattice analysis on MiNTRU problem. Cryptology ePrint Archive, Report 2020/230 (2020). https://eprint.iacr.org/2020/230

50. Lenstra, A.K., Lenstra, H.W.J., Lovász, L.: Factoring polynomials with rational coefficients. Math. Ann. **261**, 515–534 (1982)

51. Maze, G.: Some inequalities related to the Seysen measure of a lattice (2010)

52. Mehlhorn, K., Sanders, P.: Algorithms and Data Structures: The Basic Toolbox. Springer, Heidelberg (2008). https://doi.org/10.1007/978-3-540-77978-0

53. Micciancio, D., Walter, M.: Practical, predictable lattice basis reduction. In: Fischlin, M., Coron, J.-S. (eds.) EUROCRYPT 2016, Part I. LNCS, vol. 9665, pp. 820–849. Springer, Heidelberg (2016). https://doi.org/10.1007/978-3-662-49890-3_31

54. Möller, N.: On Schönhage's algorithm and subquadratic integer GCD computation. Math. Comput. **77**(261), 589–607 (2008)

55. Neumaier, A., Stehlé, D.: Faster LLL-type reduction of lattice bases. In: ISSAC, pp. 373–380 (2016)

56. Nguyen, P.Q., Stehlé, D.: LLL on the average. In: Hess, F., Pauli, S., Pohst, M. (eds.) ANTS 2006. LNCS, vol. 4076, pp. 238–256. Springer, Heidelberg (2006). https://doi.org/10.1007/11792086_18

57. Nguyen, P.Q., Stehlé, D.: An LLL algorithm with quadratic complexity. SIAM J. Comput. **39**(3), 874–903 (2009)

58. Novocin, A., Stehlé, D., Villard, G.: An LLL-reduction algorithm with quasi-linear time complexity. In: 43rd STOC, pp. 403–412. ACM (2011)

59. Pataki, G., Tural, M.: Lattice determinants in reduced bases. arXiv:0804.4014 (2008)

60. Pellet-Mary, A., Hanrot, G., Stehlé, D.: Approx-SVP in ideal lattices with preprocessing. In: Ishai, Y., Rijmen, V. (eds.) EUROCRYPT 2019, Part II. LNCS, vol. 11477, pp. 685–716. Springer, Cham (2019). https://doi.org/10.1007/978-3-030-17656-3_24

61. Morel, I., Stehlé, D., Villard, G.: LLL reducing with the most significant bits. In: Nabeshima, K., Nagasaka, K., Winkler, F., Szántó, Á. (eds.) ISSAC, pp. 367–374. ACM (2014)

62. Schnorr, C.: A hierarchy of polynomial time lattice basis reduction algorithms. Theor. Comput. Sci. **53**, 201–224 (1987)

63. Schnorr, C.: A more efficient algorithm for lattice basis reduction. J. Algorithms **9**(1), 47–62 (1988)
64. Schnorr, C.: Block reduced lattice bases and successive minima. Comb. Probab. Comput. **3**, 507–522 (1994)
65. Schönhage, A.: Factorization of univariate integer polynomials by diophantine approximation and an improved basis reduction algorithm. In: Paredaens, J. (ed.) ICALP 1984. LNCS, vol. 172, pp. 436–447. Springer, Heidelberg (1984). https://doi.org/10.1007/3-540-13345-3_40
66. Schönhage, A.: Fast reduction and composition of binary quadratic forms. In: ISSAC, pp. 128–133. ACM (1991)
67. Seysen, M.: Simultaneous reduction of a lattice basis and its reciprocal basis. Combinatorica **13**(3), 363–376 (1993)
68. Stehlé, D.: Floating-point LLL: theoretical and practical aspects. In: Nguyen, P., Vallée, B. (eds.) The LLL Algorithm, pp. 179–213. Springer, Heidelberg (2009). https://doi.org/10.1007/978-3-642-02295-1_5
69. Stern, J.: Secret linear congruential generators are not cryptographically secure. In: 28th FOCS, pp. 421–426. IEEE Computer Society Press, October 1987
70. van Dijk, M., Gentry, C., Halevi, S., Vaikuntanathan, V.: Fully homomorphic encryption over the integers. In: Gilbert, H. (ed.) EUROCRYPT 2010. LNCS, vol. 6110, pp. 24–43. Springer, Heidelberg (2010). https://doi.org/10.1007/978-3-642-13190-5_2
71. Van Hoeij, M.: Factoring polynomials and the knapsack problem. J. Number Theor. **95**(2), 167–189 (2002)
72. van Hoeij, M., Novocin, A.: Gradual sub-lattice reduction and a new complexity for factoring polynomials. In: López-Ortiz, A. (ed.) LATIN 2010. LNCS, vol. 6034, pp. 539–553. Springer, Heidelberg (2010). https://doi.org/10.1007/978-3-642-12200-2_47
73. Villard, G.: Parallel lattice basis reduction. In: ISSAC, pp. 269–277 (1992)

Lower Bounds on Lattice Sieving and Information Set Decoding

Elena Kirshanova[1,2(✉)] and Thijs Laarhoven[3]

[1] Immanuel Kant Baltic Federal University, Kaliningrad, Russia
[2] Horst Görtz Institute for IT-Security, Ruhr University Bochum, Bochum, Germany
[3] Eindhoven University of Technology, Eindhoven, The Netherlands
mail@thijs.com

Abstract. In two of the main areas of post-quantum cryptography, based on lattices and codes, nearest neighbor techniques have been used to speed up state-of-the-art cryptanalytic algorithms, and to obtain the lowest asymptotic cost estimates to date [May–Ozerov, Eurocrypt'15; Becker–Ducas–Gama–Laarhoven, SODA'16]. These upper bounds are useful for assessing the security of cryptosystems against known attacks, but to guarantee long-term security one would like to have closely matching lower bounds, showing that improvements on the algorithmic side will not drastically reduce the security in the future. As existing lower bounds from the nearest neighbor literature do not apply to the nearest neighbor problems appearing in this context, one might wonder whether further speedups to these cryptanalytic algorithms can still be found by only improving the nearest neighbor subroutines.

We derive new lower bounds on the costs of solving the nearest neighbor search problems appearing in these cryptanalytic settings. For the Euclidean metric we show that for random data sets on the sphere, the locality-sensitive filtering approach of [Becker–Ducas–Gama–Laarhoven, SODA 2016] using spherical caps is optimal, and hence within a broad class of lattice sieving algorithms covering almost all approaches to date, their asymptotic time complexity of $2^{0.292d+o(d)}$ is optimal. Similar conditional optimality results apply to lattice sieving variants, such as the $2^{0.265d+o(d)}$ complexity for quantum sieving [Laarhoven, PhD thesis 2016] and previously derived complexity estimates for tuple sieving [Herold–Kirshanova–Laarhoven, PKC 2018]. For the Hamming metric we derive new lower bounds for nearest neighbor searching which almost match the best upper bounds from the literature [May–Ozerov, Eurocrypt 2015]. As a consequence we derive conditional lower bounds on decoding attacks, showing that also here one should search for improvements elsewhere to significantly undermine security estimates from the literature.

Elena Kirshanova is supported by the "5-100" Russian academic excellence project and by the Young Russian Mathematics scholarship. Thijs Laarhoven is supported by an NWO Veni grant (016.Veni.192.005). Part of this work was done while both authors were visiting the Simons Institute for the Theory of Computing at UC Berkeley for the Spring 2020 program "Lattices: Algorithms, Complexity, and Cryptography".

T. Malkin and C. Peikert (Eds.): CRYPTO 2021, LNCS 12826, pp. 791–820, 2021.
https://doi.org/10.1007/978-3-030-84245-1_27

1   Introduction

Post-quantum cryptography. After Shor's breakthrough work in the 1990s [Sho94], showing that current solutions in public-key cryptography are vulnerable to quantum attacks, many researchers have shifted their attention towards developing new, quantum-safe alternatives. Within the field of post-quantum cryptography, arguably two subfields stand out: *lattice-based cryptography*, offering efficient, small, and versatile solutions [Reg05, Reg10, Gen09, GGH13] and relatively strong security guarantees [AD97, MR07, SSTX09, LPR10]; and *code-based cryptography*, relying on long-studied problems from coding theory, dating back as far as RSA [McE78, RSA78], and having remained unbroken ever since [Lan20]. In both these fields, it is crucial to obtain a good understanding of the true hardness of the underlying hard problems; both by trying to find new techniques that may lead to faster algorithms, and by studying what are the limits of known algorithms, when using algorithmic techniques we are currently aware of.

Hardness estimates for lattices. In the field of lattice-based cryptography, currently the fastest known approach for solving hard lattice problems is commonly referred to as *lattice sieving*. Theoretically, the fastest sieving algorithms for solving e.g. the shortest vector problem (SVP) on random d-dimensional lattices run in time $(3/2)^{d/2+o(d)} \approx 2^{0.292d+o(d)}$ [BDGL16] under plausible heuristic assumptions about random lattices.[1] In practice all recent record-breaking computations on random lattices were done with sieving as well [svp20, ADH+19]. Accurately estimating the true cost of lattice sieving is therefore essential for choosing parameters for lattice-based cryptographic primitives. As the constant $\frac{1}{2}\log_2(\frac{3}{2}) \approx 0.292$ in the exponent has not been improved for several years now (with many improvements happening between 2008 and 2016), one might wonder whether this constant is optimal, and if one can confidently use it as an asymptotic lower bound on the cost of any algorithm trying to break the underlying lattice problem.

Hardness estimates for decoding. In the context of code-based cryptography, the most important algorithms to solve the problem of decoding random binary codes are information set decoding (ISD) algorithms. A random binary code of length d asymptotically has a minimum distance λ of the order $\lambda = \Theta(d)$.[2] In this regime all known ISD algorithms have a single-exponential running time $2^{cd+o(d)}$, where the constant c has been improved over the last 60 years from $c = 0.121$ [Pra62] through a series of works [Ste89, MMT11, BJMM12, MO15] to the current best leading constant $c = 0.0885$ [BM18]. These runtimes hold for

---

[1] The literature on lattice algorithms is divided into two classes: algorithms with provable guarantees on the worst-case complexity for any input lattice [PS09, MV10a, ADRS15]; and algorithms making some heuristic assumptions about the "behavior" of random lattices, to obtain tighter average-case complexity estimates [NV08, GNR10, MV10b, Laa15a, ANSS18].

[2] We choose d to denote the *length* of the code rather than its minimum distance here, to be consistent with lattice and near neighbor literature.

average-case instances and are provable. The recent improvements in ISD come from a combination of various techniques, so it is important to pin down which techniques are already optimal and which should be further explored to see if the current best result from [BM18] can be improved upon.

Note that in this paper, we do not consider the so-called *sparse* error regime in decoding, i.e., when the error weight is promised to be $o(d)$. The aforementioned improvements for ISD do not hold in this regime, and the asymptotically fastest known algorithm for the sparse case is due to Prange's [Pra62].

Lower bounds for cryptanalytic algorithms. Both in the context of lattice algorithms and decoding random binary codes, most work has focused on upper bounds, i.e. constructing algorithms solving these problems as efficiently as possible. However, for applications in cryptography we are equally interested in (tight) lower bounds, stating that any attacker that tries to break the scheme by solving these underlying hard problems needs to spend at least this amount of time to find a solution. Any such lower bound would clearly be conditional on the approach used to solve the problem, but even such conditional lower bounds may already be valuable for choosing parameters in a more conservative manner than optimistically assuming that the current best algorithms are still the best algorithms an attacker can use in 20 years. Unfortunately not much is known about lower bounds in either area, with e.g. [ANSS18] obtaining lower bounds on lattice enumeration.

Nearest neighbor subroutines. Both in lattice sieving and in decoding, an important subroutine in the state-of-the-art algorithms for solving these problems is to solve a nearest neighbor problem in the ℓ_1 and ℓ_2-norms: given a large database of uniformly random vectors, store it in a convenient data structure such that, when given a random query vector, we can efficiently extract nearby vectors (under the corresponding metric) from the database. These relations were explicitly established in [Laa15a, MO15], and especially in lattice sieving many subsequent improvements were directly related to only improving the nearest neighbor subroutine [BGJ15, LdW15, BL16, BDGL16]. As a first step towards finding tight lower bounds on the overall decoding algorithms, we aim at obtaining lower bounds on the nearest neighbor subroutines, so that we can rule out further improvements which only target the nearest neighbor routine.

Nearest neighbor lower bounds. For the applications of interest in this paper (lattice sieving and decoding algorithms), the nearest neighbor methods that have worked best to date are hashing–based solutions, for which lower bounds have previously been studied in e.g. [MNP07, OWZ14, Chr17]. These lower bounds were mostly in a slightly different model than the models which naturally appear in cryptanalysis, and it is therefore unclear whether similar lower bounds apply in the context of cryptography, and whether the best nearest neighbor methods in these other models must also translate to the best methods for the problems of interest in cryptography.

On the strict inequivalence between different models. For the last question, we can explicitly derive a counterexample, showing that a method which is asymptotically optimal in one setting is not necessarily optimal in the other. Namely, for the often-considered *sparse regime*, cross-polytope hashing is known to be asymptotically optimal [TT07, AIL+15], but when applied to lattice sieving it leads to a suboptimal time complexity of $2^{0.298d+o(d)}$, compared to the $2^{0.292d+o(d)}$ obtained via the spherical filters of [BDGL16]. In other words: optimal solutions in other models may be suboptimal in our model, and lower bounds may not carry over to our setting either.

1.1   Contributions

After covering the preliminaries (Sect. 2), and explicitly describing the nearest neighbor search model considered in this paper and how it differs from other models commonly considered in the nearest neighbor literature (Sect. 3), our main contributions are covered in Sects. 4–7:

Nearest neighbor searching on the Euclidean sphere (Sect. 4). For the problem of finding nearest neighbors in data sets uniformly distributed on the sphere, we prove that the best partitioning and filtering approaches – main subroutines in the hash-based Near neighbor searching – must necessarily be based on spherical caps. This shows that the spherical filters introduced in [BDGL16] and further analyzed in [ALRW17, Chr17] are optimal not only in the sparse regime, but also in the dense regime. Note that this result is even stronger than previous optimality results [AINR14, AIL+15, ALRW17], as there are no hidden order terms in the statement that spherical caps are optimal for shaping hash regions.

Application to lattice sieving and lattice-based cryptography (Sect. 5). As a direct application of the above result, we prove that within the framework of running a "pairwise" lattice sieve with some form of hash-based nearest neighbor search (a technique used inside sieves described in e.g., [NV08, Laa15a, BDGL16]), the lattice sieve of Becker–Ducas–Gama–Laarhoven [BDGL16] is optimal, and the associated asymptotic time complexity $2^{0.292d+o(d)}$ is the best possible. Similar optimality results extend to the tuple sieving results of Herold–Kirshanova–Laarhoven [HKL18], the pairwise sieve with quantum speedups [Laa16], and applications to closest vector problems [DLvW20].

Nearest neighbor searching for the Hamming distance (Sect. 6). Moving from ℓ_2 to ℓ_1 norm, we show that spherical caps in Hamming space are optimal in the sparse regime and almost match the lower bound in the dense regime. We point to the source of the small discrepancy between our lower bound and what is achievable by spherical caps.

Application to decoding and code-based cryptography (Sect. 7). Similar to lattices, our lower bound for nearest neighbor searching on the Hamming cube suggests that trying to improve *only* the nearest neighbor subroutine in information set decoding algorithms will not result in a noticeable asymptotic gain. For example, trying to replace a random code, which is used to construct spherical caps, with another code will not improve the overall algorithm.

However, the situation differs from lattices in the fact that near neighbor search is not necessarily the dominant subroutine and its complexity can be rebalanced with other combinatorial steps. This way, Both-May [BM18] were able to improve over [MO15] using the near neighbor routine differently. Thus one should interpret our lower bound as an indication that any faster algorithm for decoding will necessarily require a novel ideal of how (if at all) use near neighbor search.

2 Preliminaries

2.1 Notation

We write (M, d) for a metric space, where M is the underlying set and $d :
M \times M \to \mathbb{R}$ is the distance function (metric) associated to this set. We write $\mathbb{1}\{E\}$ for the indicator function, which is 1 if event E holds and 0 otherwise. For random variables X sampled uniformly from a set S, we may write $X \sim S$. We denote vectors (lowercase) and matrices (uppercase) in boldface. We write $\| \cdot \|_p$ for the ℓ_p-norm, and in this work we will be using both the ℓ_1 and ℓ_2-norms. Throughout, d will always refer to the dimension of the space.

We denote the Euclidean sphere in d dimensions by $\mathcal{S}^{d-1} = \{\mathbf{z} \in \mathbb{R}^d : \|\mathbf{z}\|_2 = 1\} \subset \mathbb{R}^d$. On this sphere we will make use of the uniform surface measure σ which is normalized such that $\sigma(\mathcal{S}^{d-1}) = 1$. We write $\langle \cdot, \cdot \rangle$ for standard dot products.

We denote the Hamming cube in d dimensions by $\{0, 1\}^d$. We define the binary entropy function for $x \in [0, 1]$ as $H(x) = -x \log_2 x - (1-x) \log_2(1-x)$. For asymptotic results on the Hamming cube, we shall be using the approximation for the binomial coefficient $\binom{d}{\alpha d} \approx 2^{H(\alpha)d}$ which holds for constant $\alpha \in (0, 1)$ and large d.

2.2 Lattices

A full-rank lattice $\mathcal{L}(\mathbf{B})$ is a discrete additive subgroup of $\mathbb{R}^d$ generated by the columns of a matrix $\mathbf{B} \in \mathbb{R}^{d \times m}$ (with polynomially-sized entries). Various hard lattice problems have been studied over time, with the shortest and closest vector problems being the classical hard problems. We state the shortest vector problem below, as efficient algorithms for this (exact) problem are often a key ingredient for the best cryptanalytic attacks for lattice-based cryptosystems. For simplicity, one may assume that the rank m below is equal to d.

Definition 1 (The shortest lattice vector problem). *Let d, m be positive integers, and suppose we are given a basis $\mathbf{B} \in \mathbb{R}^{d \times m}$ generating a lattice $\mathcal{L} = \{\mathbf{Bz} : \mathbf{z} \in \mathbb{Z}^m\} \subset \mathbb{R}^d$. Find a vector $\mathbf{s} \in \mathcal{L}$ satisfying $\|\mathbf{s}\|_2 = \min_{\mathbf{v} \in \mathcal{L} \setminus \{0\}} \|\mathbf{v}\|_2$.*

We express complexities for algorithms for solving lattice problems in terms of their main security parameter d, i.e. in the form $2^{\mathsf{c}d + o(d)}$ for a constant c.

2.3   Codes

We refer to a binary linear code $\mathcal{C}$ as a $[d, k, \lambda]$-code, with d being the dimension, k the rank of the code, and λ the minimum distance. While the shortest lattice vector problem is one of the central hard problems on lattices, upon which the security of lattice-based cryptography relies, the following problem is crucial in understanding the security of code-based cryptosystems.

Definition 2 (The information set decoding problem). *Let d, k, λ be positive integers, and suppose we are given a parity check matrix $\mathbf{H} \in \mathbb{F}_2^{(d-k) \times d}$ and a syndrome vector $\mathbf{s} \in \mathbb{F}_2^{d-k}$ satisfying $\mathbf{s} = \mathbf{H}\mathbf{e}$ for some $\mathbf{e} \in \mathbb{F}_2^d$ with Hamming weight $w := \|\mathbf{e}\|_1 \leq \lambda$. Find the error vector $\mathbf{e}$.*

In the analysis of information set decoding algorithms, it is common to relate the parameter w (the error weight) to the rank of the code k and to the dimension d. To do so, we make use of the Gilbert–Varshamov bound which states that $\frac{k}{d} = 1 - H\left(\frac{w}{d}\right)$ as $d \to \infty$. This gives us a way to express w as a function of d and k. Then for any chosen $k \in (0, 1)$, the runtime of an information set decoding algorithm simplifies to the form $2^{cd+o(d)}$ for some constant c. We are interested in the setting when $w = \Theta(d)$, the so-called *dense* regime.

3   Nearest Neighbor Model

3.1   Closest Pairs Problem

For the applications in post-quantum cryptanalysis, which are ultimately the main objective of this study, we are commonly interested in solving the following general closest pairs problem: finding nearby pairs of vectors in a given list of vectors living in some bounded metric space.

Definition 3 (Closest pairs problem). *Let (M, d) be a bounded metric space, and let $r \geq 0$ be a given target distance. Let $L \subset M$ be a finite subset of M, with elements drawn uniformly at random from M. Find almost all[3] pairs $\mathbf{x}, \mathbf{y} \in L$ satisfying $d(\mathbf{x}, \mathbf{y}) \leq r$.*

In the above definition, we assume the list L follows a uniform distribution over the underlying metric space M; in the applications for the Euclidean sphere and Hamming cube it will be clear what this uniform distribution looks like. This is different from various other models in the nearest neighbor literature, where

---

[3] The term "almost all" can intuitively be interpreted as finding at least 90% of all such pairs (or, if only one such pair exists, making sure it is found with probability at least 0.90). Although this minimum success rate is not a hard limit, and the high-level ideas would still work if only e.g. 50% or 10% of all pairs are found, the complexities of these underlying algorithms are usually inversely proportional to the ratio of good pairs that are found in the closest pairs subroutine: finding a smaller ratio of good pairs commonly means having to use bigger lists, which in turn translates to a higher space complexity and a higher overall runtime due to having to search bigger lists.

one might aim to find a solution to the closest pairs problem which works even for worst-case data sets, albeit with a certain approximation factor. In cryptanalytic applications, these uniform distributions appear naturally, and average-case analyses give a better idea of the overall performance than worst-case analyses.

A common approach for solving variants of the closest pairs problem is by first building, and then repeatedly querying a well-chosen nearest neighbor data structure:

1. Initialize a nearest neighbor data structure $\mathcal{D}$;
2. Populate this data structure $\mathcal{D}$ with all elements $\mathbf{x} \in L$;
3. For each $\mathbf{x} \in L$, query the data structure $\mathcal{D}$ to find nearby $\mathbf{y} \in L$, $\mathbf{x} \neq \mathbf{y}$, with $d(\mathbf{x}, \mathbf{y}) \leq r$.

Note that within this framework, we need to index the list L in the data structure $\mathcal{D}$ (corresponding to $|L|$ *insertions*), and we need to run $|L|$ queries on the list L to find almost all closest pairs (corresponding to $|L|$ *queries*). While there is often a trade-off between the insertion and query complexities for such nearest neighbor data structures, this outline naturally tells us that to optimize the overall time complexity for solving the closest pairs problem, we should balance the insertion and query complexities. If insertions and queries can both be done in time $|L|^{\rho + o(1)}$ for some $\rho \in (0, 1)$, then the above algorithm would solve the closest pairs problem in time and memory $|L|^{1+\rho+o(1)}$. There exists memory-efficient version of the above approach that uses only $|L|^{1+o(1)}$ memory [BDGL16] that consists in building $\mathcal{D}$ "on-the-fly".

3.2   Nearest Neighbor Problem

As outlined above, the problem of finding all close pairs in a long list can be solved via the nearest neighbor problem.

Definition 4 (Nearest neighbor problem). *Let (M, d) be a bounded metric space, and let $r \geq 0$ be a given target distance. Let $L \subset M$ be a finite subset of M, with elements drawn uniformly at random from M. Preprocess L in a data structure such that, when later given a uniformly random query $\mathbf{x} \in M$, we can efficiently find almost all vectors $\mathbf{y} \in L$ satisfying $d(\mathbf{x}, \mathbf{y}) \leq r$.*

Similar to the closest pairs problem, we assume that the data set is drawn uniformly at random from the space M, which we therefore assume is bounded. We also assume that the query vector $\mathbf{x} \in M$ is drawn uniformly at random from M, which closely matches the nearest neighbor subroutine that needs to be solved to solve the closest pairs problem defined earlier.

3.3   Hash-Based Nearest Neighbor Searching

While many solutions have been proposed for solving such nearest neighbor problems, the most promising approaches for high-dimensional problem instances all seem to be based around the idea of (randomized) *divide and conquer*: divide the

---

Algorithm 3.1. Hash-based nearest neighbor searching

SCHEME PARAMETERS:
- $t \in \mathbb{N}$ — the number of hash regions
- $r \in \mathbb{R}$ — target distance
- $U_1, \ldots, U_t \subset M$ — hash regions for insertions
- $Q_1, \ldots, Q_t \subset M$ — hash regions for queries

1: **function** INSERT($\mathbf{y}$)   ▷ Add $\mathbf{y}$ to all relevant buckets
2:     **for all** $i \in [t]$ **with** $\mathbf{y} \in U_i$ **do**
3:         $B_i \leftarrow B_i \cup \{\mathbf{y}\}$

4: **function** QUERY($\mathbf{x}$)   ▷ Find near neighbors $\mathbf{y} \in L$ with $d(\mathbf{x}, \mathbf{y}) \leq r$
5:     $C \leftarrow \varnothing$
6:     **for all** $i \in [t]$ **with** $\mathbf{x} \in Q_i$ **do**
7:         **for all** $\mathbf{y} \in B_i$ **with** $d(\mathbf{x}, \mathbf{y}) \leq r$ **do**
8:             $C \leftarrow C \cup \{\mathbf{y}\}$
9:     **return** C

10: **function** PREPROCESS(L)   ▷ Store all $\mathbf{y} \in L$ in the data structure
11:     $B_1, \ldots, B_t \leftarrow \varnothing$
12:     **for all** $\mathbf{y} \in L$ **do**
13:         INSERT($\mathbf{y}$)

14: **function** CLOSESTPAIRS(L)   ▷ Find close pairs $\{\mathbf{x}, \mathbf{y}\} \in L$ with $d(\mathbf{x}, \mathbf{y}) \leq r$
15:     PREPROCESS(L)
16:     $P \leftarrow \varnothing$
17:     **for all** $\mathbf{x} \in L$ **do**
18:         $P \leftarrow P \cup (\{\mathbf{x}\} \times \text{QUERY}(\mathbf{x}))$
19:     **return** P

---

space in regions, and solve the closest pairs problem (nearest neighbor problem) in each region separately. By using well-chosen *hash regions*, and by using many rerandomizations to account for unfortunate separations of nearby vectors, we hope that each pair of nearby vectors will eventually end up in the same hash region at least once.

Formally, with the added generalization that combinations of these hash regions do not necessarily have to form a partition of the space [BDGL16, ALRW17], this leads to the following definition of hash-based nearest neighbor searching.

Definition 5 (Hash-based nearest neighbor searching). *Let the data set $L \subset M$ and target radius $r > 0$ be given. To solve the nearest neighbor problem, hash-based nearest neighbor searching preprocesses the data set L and processes queries $\mathbf{x}$ as outlined in Algorithm 3.1.*

Observe that the pseudocode in Algorithm 3.1 is not quite precise on how we recover the indices $i \in [t]$ with either $\mathbf{y} \in U_i$ (for insertions) or $\mathbf{x} \in Q_i$ (for queries). A naive linear search would take time t, by checking for each i if the condition is satisfied. If there is some additional structure in these hash regions U_i and Q_i, then ideally we may hope for an algorithm finding the set $Y = \{i \in [t] : \mathbf{y} \in U_i\}$ in time $O(|Y|)$, and the set $X = \{i \in [t] : \mathbf{x} \in Q_i\}$ in time $O(|X|)$. Throughout we will often assume the existence of an oracle $\mathcal{O}$ which achieves these optimal time complexities, as the technicalities for implementing this (as in e.g. [BDGL16, ALRW17]) are not necessary for understanding our results, and may distract the reader from the essence of our contributions.

At the end of the query phase, we search the set of candidates $C = \cup_{i:\mathbf{x}\in Q_i} B_i$ for potential nearest neighbors to $\mathbf{x}$. Ideally we would like this set C to only contain nearby vectors in the data set, and not any other vectors. In other words, ideally we would like to guarantee that for random vectors $\mathbf{y} \in L$ the event $\{\mathbf{x} \in Q_i, \mathbf{y} \in U_i\}$ is rare, while for nearby vectors $\mathbf{y} \in L$ the probability of $\{\mathbf{x} \in Q_i, \mathbf{y} \in U_i\}$ happening is large. Therefore, the following quantities are of interest, which capture the probabilities of hash collisions for nearby and random vectors.

Definition 6 (Collision probabilities). *Given a hash-based nearest neighbor scheme, with hash regions $U_1, \ldots, U_t$ and $Q_1, \ldots, Q_t$, and a target distance $r > 0$, we define the following quantities:*

$$p_1 := \sum_{i=1}^{t} p_{1,i}, \qquad p_{1,i} := \Pr_{\mathbf{x},\mathbf{y}\sim M}(\mathbf{x} \in Q_i, \mathbf{y} \in U_i \mid d(\mathbf{x},\mathbf{y}) \le r), \qquad (1)$$

$$p_2 := \sum_{i=1}^{t} p_{2,i}, \qquad p_{2,i} := \Pr_{\mathbf{x},\mathbf{y}\sim M}(\mathbf{x} \in Q_i, \mathbf{y} \in U_i). \qquad (2)$$

To obtain the best performance for a hash-based scheme, we wish to maximize p_1 and minimize p_2. An often considered quantity capturing both these goals is $\rho := \ln p_1 / \ln p_2$. Maximizing p_1 and minimizing p_2 means making the exponent ρ as small as possible, and when the parameters of the scheme are chosen to balance insertion and query costs (and one assumes the existence of an efficient oracle for finding relevant buckets), both these costs can be made equal to $\tilde{O}(n^\rho)$. In general however one can obtain arbitrary trade-offs between the costs of this approach, as described in e.g. [Laa15b, BDGL16, ALRW17]. The shapes of the hash buckets may vary, but intuitively the relative sizes of Q_i and U_i control the trade-off between the query time on the one hand, and the insertion time, preprocessing time, and memory complexity on the other hand as follows:

- For $Q_i \subset U_i$, we are more selective with buckets in the query phase, often leading to better query times but worse insertion and preprocessing complexities, as we will need more buckets to guarantee we still find the nearest neighbors in the few buckets we query for near neighbors.
- For $Q_i \supset U_i$, we are less selective in the query phase, and overall we need a smaller number of buckets t (less memory, better preprocessing time) to make sure we find the nearest neighbor in one of the queried buckets. However, as we also consider "bad quality" hash buckets, we will commonly spend more time in the query phase. (Choosing $Q_i \supset U_i$ is intuitively similar to *probing* in locality-sensitive hashing literature [Pan06, AIL+15].)

– For $Q_i = U_i$, we balance the query and insertion complexities. This is sometimes called the balanced regime, and most lower bounds from the literature
on ρ apply to this regime.

Usually it does not make sense to choose regions U_i and Q_i for which neither
$U_i \subseteq Q_i$ nor $Q_i \subseteq U_i$; we want $\mathbf{x}$ and $\mathbf{y}$ to be as similar as possible, so if we
know $\mathbf{y} \in U_i$ we will want to compare $\mathbf{x}$ to $\mathbf{y}$ only if $\mathbf{x}$ lies in a similar region in
space.

3.4   Assumptions About the Data Set

While most of the above model is still very much in line with most of the existing
(hash-based) nearest neighbor literature, and lower bounds that have previously
appeared, there are some subtle differences we make about the data set, which
warrant the new search for lower bounds in this paper. We will describe the two
key properties below, which have to do with two assumptions about the data
set: the distribution of points, and the size of the data set n relative to d.

The distribution of the data set. As described in the nearest neighbor definitions
above, in this paper we specifically assume that the data set follows a uniform
distribution over the underlying metric space. (Concretely we will consider the
Euclidean sphere and the Hamming cube, for which this uniform distribution is
well-defined.) Most literature on the nearest neighbor problem however makes
no such assumptions, and aims to provide solutions for worst-case data sets. In
practice however it often turns out that these "random data sets" are, in fact,
worst-case data sets for most hash-based solutions [AINR14, AR15, ALRW17].
One may argue that here we are making stronger assumptions about the problem
than in most of the past literature. On the other hand, in most applications the
most natural distribution of points for the data set is uniform, and uniform data
sets are often considered the hardest to deal with anyway. One could therefore
consider this as only a minor additional assumption. Note that without this
additional assumption, we would not be able to strengthen our model compared
to previous work as described in the next paragraph.

The sparsity of data set. Most past work on nearest neighbor searching focused
specifically on the so-called *sparse regime*, where the number of points n in the
data set scales as $n = 2^{o(d)}$, or equivalently $\log n = o(d)$. For $\log n \ll d$, i.e. for
extremely sparse data sets, one can always use a dimension reduction step [JL84]
to obtain $\log n \propto d/\log d$; one can always go from an extremely sparse data set
to a less sparse data set. This is however the limit, and one cannot reduce the
dimensionality to $\log n \propto d$ without losing guarantees on the preservation of
distances between points in the data set. The entire sparse regime can therefore
be reduced by only solving the regime where $\log n \propto d/\log d$, but this leaves
open the regime where $\log n = \Omega(d)$. The latter is exactly the regime of interest
for the cryptanalytic applications in this paper, and unfortunately lower bounds
are specifically tailored to the sparse regime.

To summarize: whereas most past work made no assumptions about the distribution of the data set, it did make assumptions about the sparsity of the data set. In this paper we make no assumptions about the sparsity of the data set, but we do specifically assume that the data set follows a uniform distribution.

3.5   Inapplicability of Existing Lower Bounds

Various lower bounds have previously been derived for (hash-based) nearest neighbor searching in a long line of works [MNP07, PTW10, OWZ14, AR16, Chr17], but all of these have focused on the sparse regime, discussed above. As we are interested in the dense regime of $\log n = O(d)$, one might wonder whether applying the same lower bounds to the dense regime is just a "technicality", and if schemes which are known to be asymptotically optimal in the sparse regime are also optimal in the dense regime.

We can counter this reasoning with an explicit counterexample, showing that indeed the study in this paper is needed. For the sparse regime and for the angular distance (or nearest neighbor searching on the sphere; see Sect. 4), different schemes are known to be optimal:

- The spherical hashing from [AINR14] and the cross-polytope hashing from e.g. [TT09, AIL+15] are both known to be optimal for the sparse regime. They both achieve the optimal scaling of the query exponent ρ for the balanced regime as $\rho \sim 1/(2c^2-1)$ for random data sets, when the target distance r is a factor c less than the average distance on the unit sphere ($\sqrt{2}$). Matching lower bounds are known [AINR14, AR15, AR16, ALRW17] showing their optimality for the sparse regime. When applying these schemes in the context of lattice sieving, where we substitute the nearest neighbor step by these optimized hashing schemes, the best possible time complexity for solving lattice problems in dimension d with both these hash-based approaches becomes $2^{0.297...d+o(d)}$ [LdW15, BL16].
- Later on, spherical filtering was presented in [BDGL16], and further studied in [Laa15b, ALRW17]. Spherical filtering is also known to be optimal in the sparse regime, again obtaining the optimal scaling of $\rho \sim 1/(2c^2 - 1)$, up to lower order terms. When applying these results to lattice sieving however, again substituting this scheme for the nearest neighbor step that needs to be done, the time complexity for solving lattice problems becomes $2^{0.292...d+o(d)}$ [BDGL16]. In other words, using this nearest neighbor scheme leads to a strict asymptotic improvement over the previous results from [LdW15, BL16], even though these other results were also relying on a hash-based scheme which was known to be optimal *in the sparse regime*.

The essence lies exactly in the fact that all existing lower bounds were derived specifically for the sparse regime, and do not necessarily carry over to the dense regime. And as the above situation in lattice sieving shows, indeed asymptotically optimal schemes in the sparse regime may be strictly suboptimal in the dense regime. This motivates the study of this work: to derive lower bounds for the dense regime, which do apply to regimes of interest in cryptanalysis (and potentially in other applications with dense data sets as well).

4   Nearest Neighbor Searching on the Euclidean Sphere

For the Euclidean sphere, we instantiate the metric space (M, d) from Sect. 3 by the Euclidean metric $d(\mathbf{x}, \mathbf{y}) = \|\mathbf{x} - \mathbf{y}\|_2$ and the unit sphere $M = \mathcal{S}^{d-1} = \{\mathbf{x} \in \mathbb{R}^d : \|\mathbf{x}\|_2 = 1\}$. Throughout Sects. 4–5, we will write $\|\cdot\| = \|\cdot\|_2$ for the Euclidean norm.

4.1   The Baernstein–Taylor Rearrangement Inequality

A key ingredient for deriving the optimal hash-based approaches for the Euclidean sphere is the following result of Baernstein–Taylor from the 1970s [BT76]. This inequality is closely related to the Riesz–Sobolev rearrangement inequality [Rie30], but instantiated on the unit sphere rather than the entire real space. The original statement and its proof can be found in [BT76, Theorem 2]. Below σ denotes the normalized surface measure on $\mathcal{S}^{d-1}$, such that $\sigma(\mathcal{S}^{d-1}) = 1$.

Lemma 1 (Baernstein–Taylor inequality for $\mathcal{S}^{d-1}$ [BT76, Theorem 2]). *Let $f, g : \mathcal{S}^{d-1} \to \mathbb{R}$ be arbitrary Lebesgue-integrable functions. Let $h : [-1, 1] \to \mathbb{R}$ be a non-decreasing, bounded, and measurable function. Let $f^*, g^* : \mathcal{S}^{d-1} \to \mathbb{R}$ be functions satisfying the following conditions:*

- *$f^*(\mathbf{z})$ only depends on the first coordinate z_1 of $\mathbf{z}$ and is a non-decreasing function of z_1;*
- *$g^*(\mathbf{z})$ only depends on the first coordinate z_1 of $\mathbf{z}$ and is a non-decreasing function of z_1;*
- *For all $\lambda \in \mathbb{R}$: $\sigma(\{\mathbf{z} \in \mathcal{S}^{d-1} : f^*(\mathbf{z}) > \lambda\}) = \sigma(\{\mathbf{z} \in \mathcal{S}^{d-1} : f(\mathbf{z}) > \lambda\})$;*
- *For all $\lambda \in \mathbb{R}$: $\sigma(\{\mathbf{z} \in \mathcal{S}^{d-1} : g^*(\mathbf{z}) > \lambda\}) = \sigma(\{\mathbf{z} \in \mathcal{S}^{d-1} : g(\mathbf{z}) > \lambda\})$.*

Then:

$$\iint\limits_{\mathcal{S}^{d-1} \times \mathcal{S}^{d-1}} f(\mathbf{x}) g(\mathbf{y}) h(\langle \mathbf{x}, \mathbf{y} \rangle) \, d\sigma(\mathbf{x}) \, d\sigma(\mathbf{y}) \leq \iint\limits_{\mathcal{S}^{d-1} \times \mathcal{S}^{d-1}} f^*(\mathbf{x}) g^*(\mathbf{y}) h(\langle \mathbf{x}, \mathbf{y} \rangle) \, d\sigma(\mathbf{x}) \, d\sigma(\mathbf{y}).$$

4.2   Optimal Hash Collision Probabilities

At first sight it may not be obvious how the above inequality is useful for us. The following corollary shows that with a proper instantiation of the functions f, g, h this naturally leads to an upper bound on collision probabilities for regions on the sphere in the hash-based nearest neighbor framework.

Theorem 1 (Collision probabilities for $\mathcal{S}^{d-1}$). *Let $Q, U \subseteq \mathcal{S}^{d-1}$ be arbitrary subsets of the sphere, and let $\mathcal{C}_Q, \mathcal{C}_U \subseteq \mathcal{S}^{d-1}$ be spherical caps of the following form:*

$$C_Q := \{\mathbf{z} \in \mathcal{S}^{d-1} : z_1 \geq \alpha\}, \quad \text{with } \alpha \in [-1, 1] \text{ such that } \sigma(C_Q) = \sigma(Q),$$

$$C_U := \{\mathbf{z} \in \mathcal{S}^{d-1} : z_1 \geq \beta\}, \quad \text{with } \beta \in [-1, 1] \text{ such that } \sigma(C_U) = \sigma(U).$$

Then, for any $\gamma \in [-1, 1]$ we have:

$$\Pr_{\mathbf{x}, \mathbf{y} \sim \mathcal{S}^{d-1}} [\mathbf{x} \in Q, \mathbf{y} \in U \mid \langle \mathbf{x}, \mathbf{y} \rangle \geq \gamma] \leq \Pr_{\mathbf{x}, \mathbf{y} \sim \mathcal{S}^{d-1}} [\mathbf{x} \in C_Q, \mathbf{y} \in C_U \mid \langle \mathbf{x}, \mathbf{y} \rangle \geq \gamma],$$

$$\Pr_{\mathbf{x}, \mathbf{y} \sim \mathcal{S}^{d-1}} [\mathbf{x} \in Q, \mathbf{y} \in U] = \Pr_{\mathbf{x}, \mathbf{y} \sim \mathcal{S}^{d-1}} [\mathbf{x} \in C_Q, \mathbf{y} \in C_U].$$

Proof. The second equality follows trivially by factoring the joint probability into two individual probabilities, and noting that the spherical caps $\mathcal{C}_Q, \mathcal{C}_U$ have the same volume as the sets Q, U:

$$\Pr_{\mathbf{x}, \mathbf{y} \sim \mathcal{S}^{d-1}} [\mathbf{x} \in Q, \mathbf{y} \in U] = \sigma(Q) \cdot \sigma(U) = \sigma(C_Q) \cdot \sigma(C_U) = \Pr_{\mathbf{x}, \mathbf{y} \sim \mathcal{S}^{d-1}} [\mathbf{x} \in C_Q, \mathbf{y} \in C_U].$$

The first inequality follows almost directly from the Baernstein–Taylor inequality with the proper choice of functions. We define the functions f, g, h as:

$$f(\mathbf{x}) := \mathbb{1}\{\mathbf{x} \in Q\}, \qquad g(\mathbf{y}) := \mathbb{1}\{\mathbf{y} \in U\}, \qquad h(s) := \mathbb{1}\{s \geq \gamma\}.$$

Note that, for $\lambda \in \mathbb{R}$, the functions f and g satisfy:

$$\sigma(\{f > \lambda\}) = \begin{cases} 1, & \lambda < 0; \\ \sigma(Q), & 0 \leq \lambda < 1; \\ 0, & 1 \leq \lambda; \end{cases} \qquad \sigma(\{g > \lambda\}) = \begin{cases} 1, & \lambda < 0; \\ \sigma(U), & 0 \leq \lambda < 1; \\ 0, & 1 \leq \lambda. \end{cases}$$

For the function f^* from Lemma 1 we need $\sigma(\{f^* > \lambda\}) = \sigma(\{f > \lambda\})$ to hold for all $\lambda \in \mathbb{R}$, with f^* only depending on x_1 and being non-decreasing in x_1. To satisfy $f^*(x_1) > 0$ with measure $\sigma(Q)$ and $f^*(x_1) \geq 0$ with measure 1, it follows that $f^*(x_1) = 0$ with measure $1 - \sigma(Q)$. Similarly $f^*(x_1) = 1$ with measure $\sigma(Q)$. This means that $f^*(x_1)$ must be a heaviside step function in one variable $x_1 \in [-1, 1]$, with an increase from 0 to 1 at the value $x_1 = \alpha$ satisfying $\sigma(Q) = \sigma(\{\mathbf{z} \in \mathcal{S}^{d-1} : z_1 \geq \alpha\})$. Defining $C_Q := \{\mathbf{z} \in \mathcal{S}^{d-1} : z_1 \geq \alpha\}$ for the above α, this translates to $\sigma(Q) = \sigma(C_Q)$, and together with a similar derivation for g^* we obtain the expressions:

$$f^*(\mathbf{x}) := \mathbb{1}\{\mathbf{x} \in C_Q\}, \quad \text{with } C_Q = \{\mathbf{z} \in \mathcal{S}^{d-1} : z_1 \geq \alpha\} \text{ such that } \sigma(Q) = \sigma(C_Q);$$

$$g^*(\mathbf{y}) := \mathbb{1}\{\mathbf{y} \in C_U\}, \quad \text{with } C_U = \{\mathbf{z} \in \mathcal{S}^{d-1} : z_1 \geq \beta\} \text{ such that } \sigma(U) = \sigma(C_U).$$

Now, with all conditions for Lemma 1 satisfied, we can instantiate the Baernstein–Taylor inequality for these functions f, f^*, g, g^*, h. Observing that the integrals can be interpreted as probabilities, and combining the indicator functions, we obtain:

$$\Pr_{\mathbf{x},\mathbf{y}\sim\mathcal{S}^{d-1}}[\mathbf{x}\in Q,\mathbf{y}\in U,\langle\mathbf{x},\mathbf{y}\rangle\geq\gamma]=\iint_{\mathcal{S}^{d-1}\times\mathcal{S}^{d-1}}\mathbb{1}\{\mathbf{x}\in Q,\mathbf{y}\in U,\langle\mathbf{x},\mathbf{y}\rangle\geq\gamma\}\,d\sigma(\mathbf{x})\,d\sigma(\mathbf{y})$$

$$\leq\iint_{\mathcal{S}^{d-1}\times\mathcal{S}^{d-1}}\mathbb{1}\{\mathbf{x}\in\mathcal{C}_Q,\mathbf{y}\in\mathcal{C}_U,\langle\mathbf{x},\mathbf{y}\rangle\geq\gamma\}\,d\sigma(\mathbf{x})\,d\sigma(\mathbf{y})=\Pr_{\mathbf{x},\mathbf{y}\sim\mathcal{S}^{d-1}}[\mathbf{x}\in\mathcal{C}_Q,\mathbf{y}\in\mathcal{C}_U,\langle\mathbf{x},\mathbf{y}\rangle\geq\gamma].$$

Note that the above derivation applies for all $\gamma\in[-1,1]$. Now finally, we can easily obtain a similar inequality for the conditional probabilities as follows, where all probabilities are over $\mathbf{x},\mathbf{y}\sim\mathcal{S}^{d-1}$:

$$\Pr[\mathbf{x}\in Q,\mathbf{y}\in U\mid\langle\mathbf{x},\mathbf{y}\rangle\geq\gamma]=\frac{\Pr[\mathbf{x}\in Q,\mathbf{y}\in U,\langle\mathbf{x},\mathbf{y}\rangle\geq\gamma]}{\Pr[\langle\mathbf{x},\mathbf{y}\rangle\geq\gamma]}$$

$$\leq\frac{\Pr[\mathbf{x}\in\mathcal{C}_Q,\mathbf{y}\in\mathcal{C}_U,\langle\mathbf{x},\mathbf{y}\rangle\geq\gamma]}{\Pr[\langle\mathbf{x},\mathbf{y}\rangle\geq\gamma]}=\Pr[\mathbf{x}\in\mathcal{C}_Q,\mathbf{y}\in\mathcal{C}_U\mid\langle\mathbf{x},\mathbf{y}\rangle\geq\gamma].$$

This completes the proof of the first inequality.

The above theorem states that, if we replace the hash regions Q and U by spherical caps of equal volume as Q and U, then (i) uncorrelated pairs of vectors are still equally likely to be found as candidate near neighbors, while (ii) nearby pairs of vectors are at least as likely (and perhaps more likely) to be considered as potential near neighbors. So ignoring e.g. the potential decoding overhead or the cost of membership queries for these different hash regions, this shows that the optimal choice for the hash regions is to use spherical caps. Note that for this optimality to hold, it is crucial that $\mathcal{C}_Q,\mathcal{C}_U$ are spherical caps centered at the same point on the sphere, although the same inequalities hold if both are centered at a different point $\mathbf{v}\in\mathcal{S}^{d-1}$ with $\mathbf{v}\neq\mathbf{e}_1$.

4.3 Optimal Hash-Based Nearest Neighbor Searching

The previous result suggests that using spherical caps is optimal, and the following result formalizes this statement. Here by "optimal" we mean that choosing the hash regions U_i or Q_i of shape different from spherical caps will not improve the performance of Algorithm 3.1.

Theorem 2 (Spherical caps are optimal for $\mathcal{S}^{d-1}$). *Suppose we have access to an efficient decoding oracle for retrieving relevant hash regions. Then to get the best asymptotic performance for hash-based nearest neighbor searching, the following choice of hash regions is asymptotically optimal:*

- *Choose $t\in N$, and for each $i\in[t]$ choose thresholds $\alpha_i,\beta_i\in[-1,1]$ and draw $\mathbf{v}_i\sim\mathcal{S}^{d-1}$;*
- *Define $Q_i=\{\mathbf{z}\in\mathcal{S}^{d-1}:\langle\mathbf{z},\mathbf{v}_i\rangle\geq\alpha_i\}$ and $U_i=\{\mathbf{z}\in\mathcal{S}^{d-1}:\langle\mathbf{z},\mathbf{v}_i\rangle\geq\beta_i\}$.*

Proof. First, observe that with access to an efficient decoding algorithm, the costs of the hash-based nearest neighbor search are equal for two schemes which use regions of equal size; the data set and queries are assumed to be uniform, and therefore the number of hash collisions within each bucket and the number of buckets to check only depend on their volumes, and not on their shapes. Given the volumes of the regions, and the number of regions, the costs in terms of having to compare a query $\mathbf{x}$ with random vectors $\mathbf{y} \in L$ which are not near neighbors, does not depend on the shapes of the regions. The only thing that is influenced by the (relative) shapes of the regions is the probability of finding nearby vectors in the list: given a query $\mathbf{x} \sim \mathcal{S}^{d-1}$, the probability of finding a nearby vector $\mathbf{y} \in L$ with $\langle \mathbf{x}, \mathbf{y} \rangle \geq \gamma$ in at least one of the t potential buckets.

Recall that the hash collision probabilities for nearby vectors can be expressed in terms of probabilities of inserting and querying the same bucket, for at least one of the indices $i = 1, \ldots, t$. Letting $E_i = \{\mathbf{x} \in Q_i, \mathbf{y} \in U_i \mid \langle \mathbf{x}, \mathbf{y} \rangle \geq \gamma\}$ denote the event that for a nearby vector $\mathbf{y}$ to the query $\mathbf{x}$, we insert $\mathbf{y}$ into bucket U_i and we later query Q_i for $\mathbf{x}$ in the query phase. Then we have:

$$p_1 = \Pr\left[\bigcup_{i=1}^{t} E_i\right] \leq \sum_{i=1}^{t} \Pr[E_i] = \sum_{i=1}^{t} \Pr_{\mathbf{x},\mathbf{y} \sim \mathcal{S}^{d-1}} \left[\mathbf{x} \in Q_i, \mathbf{y} \in U_i \mid \langle \mathbf{x}, \mathbf{y} \rangle \geq \gamma\right]. \quad (3)$$

The first inequality becomes more of an equality when the events are more disjoint; this tells us that ideally we should minimize the probabilities that two events E_i and E_j happen at the same time, e.g. by carefully spreading out these hash regions over the unit sphere[4]. Note that asymptotically, as analyzed in e.g. [BDGL16, Laa15b], we do indeed have $\Pr\left[\bigcup_{i=1}^{t} E_i\right] = \sum_{i=1}^{t} \Pr[E_i] \cdot (1 + o(1))$ for all common parameter choices, as it is extremely unlikely that multiple events E_i happen at the same time for random $\mathbf{v}_i$. So the right hand side of (3) is asymptotically equal to p_1.

Finally, by Theorem 1 the right hand side of (3) is maximized when the shapes of the regions are spherical caps. So the probability of finding nearby vectors is maximized when the Q_i and U_i are spherical caps centered around the same vector $\mathbf{v}_i$ on the sphere. With the other collision probability p_2 being invariant under these replacements of arbitrary regions by equal-volume spherical caps, and with the decoding costs assumed to be not an issue, this shows that up to lower order terms, this hash-based scheme is optimal.

All that now remains is choosing the thresholds α_i and β_i. The following result shows that all the β_i's should be equal to get the best asymptotic performance, and that their optimal value is determined purely by the list size n. For the α_i we also derive that they should all be equal to the same value α, but together with t this parameter allows us to obtain trade-offs between the query and update complexities of the underlying hash-based scheme.

---

[4] This further illustrates the need for good spherical codes for determining where to place these vectors $\mathbf{v}_i$ to obtain the best performance in practice [AI06, TT07, AIL+15, Laa20].

In the following theorem by "optimal" we mean that choosing the spherical caps U_i's (or Q_i's) of different sizes for different i will not improve the performance of Algorithm 3.1.

Theorem 3 (Equal spherical caps are optimal for $\mathcal{S}^{d-1}$). *Suppose we have access to an efficient decoding oracle for retrieving relevant hash regions. Then to get the best asymptotic performance for hash-based nearest neighbor searching, the following choice is asymptotically optimal:*

- *Choose $t \in \mathbb{N}$, choose $\alpha \in [-1, 1]$ and compute β such that it satisfies the relation $\sigma(\{\mathbf{z} \in \mathcal{S}^{d-1} : z_1 \geq \beta\}) \approx 1/n$;*
- *For each $i \in [t]$ draw $\mathbf{v}_i \sim \mathcal{S}^{d-1}$;*
- *Define $Q_i = \{\mathbf{z} \in \mathcal{S}^{d-1} : \langle \mathbf{z}, \mathbf{v}_i \rangle \geq \alpha\}$ and $U_i = \{\mathbf{z} \in \mathcal{S}^{d-1} : \langle \mathbf{z}, \mathbf{v}_i \rangle \geq \beta\}$.*

Proof. Compared to the optimality result from Theorem 2 we need to prove that (1) fixing one parameter β, rather than choosing each separately, cannot decrease the asymptotic performance; and (2) with β fixed, it does not make sense to use different values α_i for the different buckets.

Fixing $\beta_i \equiv \beta$. For populating the buckets B_i, observe that we do not want most buckets to be empty (which happens when β_i is too large). In that case the overhead of retrieving these hash buckets will be much larger than the actual comparisons with potential near neighbors, as the number of buckets is larger than the number of vectors in these buckets. If many buckets are empty, we would be better off creating larger buckets, corresponding to larger spherical caps, until these buckets contain at least a few vectors each, decreasing the decoding cost and not affecting other costs more than $n^{o(1)}$. So we never want to choose β_i such that $\sigma(\{\mathbf{z} \in \mathcal{S}^{d-1} : z_1 \geq \beta\}) \ll 1/n$.

On the other hand, if we use spherical caps with too small parameters β_i, then these buckets will contain $n^{\Theta(1)}$ vectors each. Note that such a bucket corresponds to a spherical cap, which can essentially be seen as a sphere of one dimension less, with a smaller radius, and where again the vectors in this bucket are uniformly distributed over this lower-dimensional sphere. This is again a NNS instance on a smaller sphere, and we can do better than to put all $n^{\Theta(1)}$ vectors in one big list and having to query the whole list when we want to search this region for near neighbors. It cannot be worse to partition this bucket into smaller buckets, so that we can either choose α so large that the entire list is queried (if necessary), or we can choose α larger to only query some of these smaller buckets. So we also do not want to choose β_i too small, such that $\sigma(\{\mathbf{z} \in \mathcal{S}^{d-1} : z_1 \geq \beta\}) \gg 1/n$.

In other words, we want each β_i to satisfy $\sigma(\{\mathbf{z} \in \mathcal{S}^{d-1} : z_1 \geq \beta\}) \propto 1/n$. Small deviations in individual bucket sizes may not be worse in practice, but asymptotically we need all β_i to be approximately equal to the β satisfying $\sigma(\{\mathbf{z} \in \mathcal{S}^{d-1} : z_1 \geq \beta\}) = 1/n$.

Fixing $\alpha_i \equiv \alpha$. With all β_i fixed to the same value β, and with all buckets containing (in expectation) a small number of vectors, the parameters α_i now control when buckets are queried. Note that for a fixed β, all buckets are identically shaped as a spherical cap of a fixed size, and with the data set being uniform on the sphere, all buckets are essentially equivalent. For a given query $\mathbf{x}$ however, the distribution of dot products $\langle \mathbf{x}, \mathbf{y} \rangle$ for vectors $\mathbf{y} \in B_i$ depends on $\langle \mathbf{x}, \mathbf{v}_i \rangle$: if $\mathbf{x}$ is almost equal to $\mathbf{v}_i$, we have a stronger guarantee that the vectors in this bucket (which are uniform in a spherical cap centered at $\mathbf{y}_i$) are close to $\mathbf{x}$ as well. On the other hand, if $\langle \mathbf{x}, \mathbf{v}_i \rangle$ is relatively small, then the vectors centered around $\mathbf{v}_i$ will on average be further away from $\mathbf{x}$. As each bucket contains equally many vectors, we therefore want to select only the buckets with the best potential for near neighbors, i.e. those buckets for which $\langle \mathbf{x}, \mathbf{v}_i \rangle$ is largest. Sorting the buckets by $\langle \mathbf{x}, \mathbf{v}_i \rangle$ and only going through the highest-quality buckets is equivalent to selecting a single appropriate parameter α and only checking those buckets for which $\langle \mathbf{x}, \mathbf{v}_i \rangle \geq \alpha$.

So ultimately, we may set $\beta_i \equiv \beta$ to one fixed value, determined immediately by n and d, and fix $\alpha_i \equiv \alpha$ to one value which together with t then trades off the space and query complexities.

Note that the optimal choice of α is not obvious. The free parameters α and t together control the trade-off between the query time complexity and the update complexity. Concretely we can minimize for the query time by choosing both α and t to be large (generate a large number of buckets, and only query the buckets for which $\mathbf{v}_i$ is almost identical to $\mathbf{x}$), or we can minimize for the update and space complexities by choosing α and t to be small (using fewer hash buckets, but being less selective in the query phase and visiting most of these buckets).

Summarizing, the asymptotically optimal scheme (up to order terms) is now written all the way down up to selecting the best parameters t, α, and implementing such an efficient decoding oracle. This problem has previously been studied in [BDGL16, Laa15b, ALRW17], and here we will merely state that the schemes analyzed in these works are therefore optimal.

Theorem 4 (Spherical filtering is optimal for $\mathcal{S}^{d-1}$). *The hash-based near neighbor schemes studied in [Laa15b, BDGL16, ALRW17] are optimal within the hash-based framework for uniformly random data sets on the sphere.*

4.4 Results for Dense Data Sets

Note that [ALRW17] already claimed optimality of the filtering approach described in [BDGL16, ALRW17], by proving matching lower bounds *in the sparse regime*. For the dense regime, no lower bounds were previously known, and as explained in Sect. 3.4 this was not just a matter of applying optimal algorithms from the sparse regime to the dense regime and claiming optimality in the dense regime as well. Our results settle the issue for uniformly random data sets, showing that spherical caps of specific sizes are indeed optimal.

The resulting optimal complexities for the dense regime can be found in e.g. [Laa15b, Theorem 2], where the parameters α and t were optimized to obtain the best performance. We restate these upper bounds below, where based on our lower bounds we now add that these trade-offs are optimal for the dense regime.

Theorem 5 (Trade-offs for the dense regime). *Let $\theta \in (0, \frac{1}{2}\pi)$, let the target dot product be $\langle \mathbf{x}, \mathbf{y} \rangle \geq \cos\theta$, and let the data set consist of $n = 2^{\Theta(d)}$ random points on the unit sphere. Then to obtain asymptotically optimal trade-offs for the query and update complexities, we should choose $u \in [\cos\theta, 1/\cos\theta]$ and set the parameters as:*

$$\alpha = u \cdot \sqrt{1 - n^{-2/d}}, \qquad\qquad \beta = \sqrt{1 - n^{-2/d}}.$$

We can then find nearest neighbors on the Euclidean sphere with query and update exponents:

$$\rho_q = \frac{-d}{2\log n} \log\left[1 - \left(1 - n^{-2/d}\right)\frac{1 + u^2 - 2u\cos\theta}{\sin^2\theta}\right] + \frac{d}{2\log n}\log\left[1 - \left(1 - n^{-2/d}\right)u^2\right],$$

$$\rho_u = \frac{-d}{2\log n}\log\left[1 - \left(1 - n^{-2/d}\right)\frac{1 + u^2 - 2u\cos\theta}{\sin^2\theta}\right] - 1.$$

The resulting algorithm has a query time complexity $\tilde{O}(n^{\rho_q})$, an update time complexity $\tilde{O}(n^{\rho_u})$, a preprocessing time complexity $\tilde{O}(n^{1+\rho_q})$, and a total space complexity of $\tilde{O}(n^{1+\rho_q})$. The total number of filters scales as $t = \tilde{O}(n^{1+\rho_q})$.

While the above formulas are a bit more technical, note that the query and update exponents only involve the input parameters d, n, θ and the trade-off parameter u. Choosing $u = 1$ leads to a "balanced" trade-off with $\rho_q = \rho_u$, and e.g. for the lattice sieving regime of the next section, where $\theta = \frac{\pi}{2}$ and $n = (4/3)^{d/2+o(d)}$, for $u = 1$ we obtain $\rho_q = \rho_u = \log(9/8)/\log(4/3)$ with query complexity $n^\rho = (9/8)^{d/2+o(d)}$ and closest pairs complexity $n^{1+\rho} = (3/2)^{d/2+o(d)}$.

5   Application to Lattice Sieving and Lattice-Based Cryptography

With the results from Sect. 4 in mind, showing that the best hash-based nearest neighbor search technique is what has already been studied in the context of lattice cryptanalysis, we immediately get conditional optimality results for various current lattice sieving approaches. These optimality results are all under the assumption that we are only allowed to make tweaks to the nearest neighbor subroutine within these algorithms.

5.1   Lattice Sieving

The lattice sieving approach introduced by Ajtai–Kumar–Sivakumar [AKS01] is currently the best known method for solving the shortest vector problem in practice on random high-dimensional lattices. For a d-dimensional lattice, the time and memory complexity are both of the order $2^{\Theta(d)}$, compared to a time complexity of $2^{\Omega(d\log d)}$ for enumeration-based approaches [Kan83, FP85, GNR10].

Given as input an arbitrary basis **B** of a lattice, sieving algorithms start by sampling an exponentially long list L of lattice vectors using efficient discrete Gaussian sampling procedures like [Kle00, GPV08]. Note that sampling exactly from a discrete Gaussian is not important; all that matters is that the sampled points are distinct, and are as short as possible. The points from the list are then combined to produce new shorter vectors $\mathbf{z} = \mathbf{x} - \mathbf{y}$ where $\mathbf{x}, \mathbf{y} \in L$. Note that $\mathbf{z}$ is short if and only if $\mathbf{x}$ and $\mathbf{y}$ are "near neighbors" in space, and this naturally leads us to using closest pairs algorithms for performing these sieving steps. The process of sieving is then executed iteratively with the new and shorter vectors added to the list (and longer vectors getting removed from the list), until we ultimately find a shortest vector in our list.

The complexity of sieving algorithms is determined by the size of the starting list required for the iterative process to succeed, and by the complexity of finding short pairwise combinations of vectors in the list to form new short vectors. Note that by volume arguments over the sphere, if all lattice vectors in the list L have roughly the same norm, then (i) for a list of size $n = |L| \ll (4/3)^{d/2+o(d)}$ we expect the number of nearby pairs $\mathbf{x}, \mathbf{y} \in L$ with $\|\mathbf{x}-\mathbf{y}\| < \|\mathbf{x}\|$ to be significantly less than n, while (ii) for a list of size $n = (4/3)^{d/2+o(d)}$ we do expect the number of such pairs to be proportional to n. So if we wish to repeat this sieving step a polynomial number of times and end up with sufficiently many new vectors each time, we need the input list to be of size $n = (4/3)^{d/2+o(d)}$. The closest pairs subroutine then consists of: given a list of n vectors of roughly equal norms as input, find all pairs of vectors whose mutual distance is shorter than their individual norms. This translates to a target angle of $\pi/3$.

The above requirements on the algorithm lead to the following results, where we know that within the hash-based nearest neighbor framework, the results from Theorem 5 are optimal. So unless we modify other parts of the algorithm, or solve the closest pairs problem differently, these complexities are optimal for the standard pairwise sieving framework.

Theorem 6 (Classical sieve, heuristic). *Suppose we use a pairwise sieve with a hash-based nearest neighbor search subroutine to solve the closest pairs problem. Then the following time and space complexities of Becker–Ducas–Gama–Laarhoven [BDGL16] are asymptotically optimal:*

$$T = \left(\frac{3}{2}\right)^{d/2+o(d)} \approx 2^{0.292d+o(d)}, \qquad S = \left(\frac{4}{3}\right)^{d/2+o(d)} \approx 2^{0.208d+o(d)}.$$

Lattice sieving variants. Various variants of lattice sieving have been studied, aiming to solve slightly different problems or optimizing other parts of the underlying algorithm. We will briefly cover three of these variants: (i) quantum sieving [LMvdP15, Laa16, KMPM19], (ii) tuple sieving [BLS16, HK17, Laa17, HKL18], and (iii) sieving for the closest vector problem with preprocessing [Laa21, DLvW20]. Almost all these algorithms (with the exception being the tuple sieve from [BLS16]) use near neighbor routines. Therefore, our lower bounds apply: if we are only allowed to replace the nearest neighbor subroutine by some other hash-based nearest neighbor subroutine, then asymptotically we cannot do better than using spherical cap regions. Of course, this does not rule out potential improvements coming from other modifications.

Relevance for lattice-based cryptography. As a take-away for cryptographic applications, one can view our lower bounds on sieving with nearest neighbor searching as a further motivation for most concrete parameter selection methods currently used in practice, which assume that the leading time complexity exponents 0.292 and 0.265 are the best an attacker can do [BDK+18, BGML+18, BCD+16]. There is always the possibility that faster algorithms will be found, but if an attacker uses sieving with some form of nearest neighbor searching, they will not be able to improve upon these exponents.

The question remains how to estimate concrete costs in e.g. dimension 768 or 1024, as our lower bounds and most asymptotic analyses of upper bounds are asymptotic: the exponent scales as $0.292d + o(d)$ for large d (or $0.265d + o(d)$ quantumly), but the $o(d)$ may be arbitrarily small or large when d is fixed. Some past work has looked at trying to estimate the $o(d)$-term of the best upper bounds [Sch19, AGPS19].

Observe that when studying concrete attack costs in fixed dimensions d, it is also necessary to take into account further potential subexponential speedups, proposed in e.g. [Duc18, ADH+19, DLdW20]. Furthermore it may not be sufficient to only look at the asymptotically fastest approaches: in a fixed dimension d, another nearest neighbor method may have less overhead in practice and lead to better time and space complexities than the spherical filters, which match our asymptotic lower bounds. Especially here, where the gap between the time complexities for sieving with spherical filtering ($0.292d + o(d)$) and cross-polytope hashing ($0.298d + o(d)$) is so small, there is no guarantee that spherical filtering will be faster than cross-polytope hashing.

6   Nearest Neighbor Searching on the Hamming Cube

We instantiate the nearest neighbor problem from Definition 4 with the Hamming cube $M = \{0, 1\}^d$ and the Hamming metric $d(\mathbf{x}, \mathbf{y}) = |\{i \in [d] : x_i \neq y_i\}| = \|\mathbf{x} - \mathbf{y}\|_1$. Throughout Sects. 6–7, we will write $\|\cdot\| = \|\cdot\|_1$ for the Hamming distance, and for the Hamming weight of vectors on the Hamming cube. It will further be easier to work with dimensionless versions of Hamming distances. In particular, we will denote the dimensionless target distance of the nearest neighbor problem by γ, i.e., $\gamma := r/d$. This applies to other distances we introduce below.

We start this section by obtaining a lower bound on nearest neighbor search using the result of Andoni–Razenstein [AR16]. Next we show that the algorithm of May–Ozerov [MO15] matches this lower bound in the sparse regime and comes extremely close to it in the dense regime.

6.1   The Andoni–Razenshteyn Lower Bound

Following [AR16], for $\mathbf{x} \in \mathbb{F}_2^d$ and $0 \leq \gamma < 1/2$, let us denote by $N_\gamma(\mathbf{x})$ a vector from $\mathbb{F}_2^n$ such that $(N_\gamma(\mathbf{x}))_i = x_i$ with probability $1 - \gamma$ and $(N_\gamma(\mathbf{x}))_i = x_i \oplus 1$ with probability γ. So for any $\mathbf{x}$ and $N_\gamma(\mathbf{x})$, the Hamming distance between them is on expectation $\gamma \cdot d$. For any hash function h, define

$$p_1 = \Pr_{\substack{\mathbf{x} \sim \mathbb{F}_2^d \\ \mathbf{y} \sim N_\gamma(\mathbf{x})}} [h(\mathbf{x}) = h(\mathbf{y})], \qquad p_2 = \Pr_{\mathbf{x}, \mathbf{y} \sim \mathbb{F}_2^d} [h(\mathbf{x}) = h(\mathbf{y})].$$

We are interested in the quantity $\rho = \ln p_1 / \ln p_2$, which defines the complexity of the nearest neighbor search when applied to the closest pairs problem. In particular, we are interested in a lower bound on ρ given in the following lemma.

Lemma 2 (Collision probabilities for $\{0, 1\}^d$ [AR16, Lemma 5]). *For every hash function $h : \{0, 1\}^n \to \mathbb{Z}$ and every $0 \leq \gamma \leq 1/2$:*

$$\Pr_{\substack{\mathbf{x} \sim \mathbb{F}_2^n \\ \mathbf{y} \sim N_\gamma(\mathbf{u})}} [h(\mathbf{x}) = h(\mathbf{y})] \leq \Pr_{\mathbf{x}, \mathbf{y} \sim \mathbb{F}_2^n} [h(\mathbf{x}) = h(\mathbf{y})]^{\frac{\gamma}{1-\gamma}}. \tag{4}$$

This lemma gives the relation between the probabilities p_1, p_2 and thus, tells what is the best sensitivity parameter ρ we can hope for. Namely, for the target distance $r = \gamma d$, using the above lemma we obtain the lower bound $\rho \geq \gamma/(1-\gamma)$. So the best we could achieve is the query time $T^{\mathtt{Query}} = |L|^\rho$ and the total runtime of the nearest neighbor problem is $T = |L|^{1+\rho}$, which is the runtime of both the preprocessing step and the query step, when the number of queries is $|L|$. Taking the logarithm, we obtain the following lower bound:

$$\log_2 T = \frac{1}{1 - \gamma} \log_2 |L|. \tag{5}$$

Next we compare the obtained lower bound with what is achieved in [MO15].

6.2   Spherical Caps on the Hamming Cube

For the dense case, the best known algorithm for the nearest neighbor problem is due to May–Ozerov [MO15] (see a recent result of Esser et al. [EKZ21] for a different analysis of this algorithm). At the heart of May–Ozerov is a hashing technique analogous to the one defined in Theorem 3, which is based on spherical caps in the Hamming space. As the main application of this hashing technique is to solve the closest pairs problem, we shall describe it the setting when the insert regions U_i and the query regions Q_i are the same.

The set up for the nearest neighbor data structure is as follows. An insertion region is defined by a center $\mathbf{v}_i \subseteq \mathbb{F}_2^d$ of the spherical cap $U_i = \{\mathbf{z} \in \mathbb{F}_2^n : \|\mathbf{z} - \mathbf{v}_i\| \leq \beta\} \subseteq \mathbb{F}_2^d$, where β is the insertion parameter subject to optimization. The purpose of these regions is similar to the Euclidean metric case: when two vectors end up in the same region, i.e., both are close to some $\mathbf{v}_i$, then these vectors are also likely to be nearby to one another on the cube.

Given on input a list $L \subset \mathbb{F}_2^d$, the nearest neighbor search assigns each $\mathbf{y} \in L$ to its regions thus defining the buckets as $B_i = U_i \cap L$. The nearest neighbor data structure $\mathcal{D}$ consists of the union of all these buckets. Given a query $\mathbf{x}$ we then look at all buckets B_i that are α-close to $\mathbf{x}$ (i.e., all $\mathbf{v}_i$ with $\|\mathbf{x} - \mathbf{v}_i\| \leq \alpha$), and we check if any of the vectors $\mathbf{y}$ stored in these buckets gives a solution to the nearest neighbor problem with parameter γ.

Similar to Theorem 3, we assume that we can efficiently find all relevant centers to a given point. An efficient procedure for that is called the 'stripes technique' and is described in [MO15]. The idea is to make the filter vectors structured (i.e., a concatenation of several codewords from some lower-dimensional codes). We will not describe this technique here in detail (for that, see [BDGL16, MO15]), but remark the main advantage of such a construction: it allows us find all close buckets in time (up to lower-order terms) equal to the output size.

When nearest neighbor searching is applied to the closest pairs problem, the number of queries is equal to $|L|$. In this case, the optimal choice of parameters is $\alpha = \beta = H^{-1}(1 - \log_2 |L|/d)$ so that the runtime T of the nearest neighbor search step are determined by the total number of buckets $|U_i|$ which we denote as t. This number is computed in [MO15, Theorem 1].

Theorem 7 (Hash-based complexities for $\{0,1\}^d$ [MO15, Thm. 1]). *To solve the nearest neighbor problem in the Hamming metric with some fixed target $0 \leq \gamma \leq 1/2$, with $\gamma = \Theta(d)$, the May–Ozerov algorithm uses a number t of hash regions satisfying:*

$$\log_2 t = (1 - \gamma)\left(1 - H\left(\frac{H^{-1}(1 - \log_2 |L|/d) - \gamma/2}{1 - \gamma}\right)\right). \tag{6}$$

The following observation is important for our result: when the list size $|L|$ becomes subexponential in the dimension d, then the number of hash regions given above converges to $|L|^{\frac{1}{1-\gamma}}$. More precisely, [MO15, Corollary 1] shows that:

$$\lim_{\frac{1}{d}\log_2|L| \to 0} \frac{\log_2 t}{\log_2 |L|} = \frac{1}{1 - \gamma}. \tag{7}$$

We shall next compare the lower and upper bounds for nearest neighbor searching on the Hamming cube.

6.3   Comparison Between Upper and Lower Bounds

Notice first that the lower bound given in Eq. 5 matches exactly the performance of the May–Ozerov upper bound in the setting when the input list size is subexponential in the dimension, i.e., in the *sparse* regime.

Decoding algorithms we discuss in the next section work in the *dense* regime, i.e., when $|L| = 2^{cd}$ for a constant c. In this regime the above lower bound does not exactly match the complexity of May–Ozerov given in Eq. (6) as one can see from the plot given in Fig. 1, where we compare the two nearest neighbor search runtimes given in Eq. (5). For a given target distance γ we set $|L| = 2^{\frac{1}{2} - \frac{1}{2}H(\gamma)}$, so we expect only sub-exponentially many pairs from L to satisfy the target distance condition, assuming L consists of uniformly randomly vectors. Notice that the larger γ is, the smaller the list sizes we choose and the closer both bounds are to each other. This is consistent with the fact that May–Ozerov is optimal in the sparse regime.

One source of the discrepancy between the upper bound of May–Ozerov and the lower bound based on the Andoni–Razensteyn result is that the latter uses the probabilistic distance between the two close vectors $\mathbf{x}, \mathbf{y}$, namely the distance follows a binomial distribution with expected value $\gamma \cdot d$, while the algorithm of [MO15] targets to find $\mathbf{x}, \mathbf{y}$ whose distance is *at most* $\gamma \cdot d$ (with high concentration at the boundary). The tails of the distributions of the distances differ in these two cases leading to a gap between the bounds.

Another source of the gap lies in an inequality which Andoni–Razensteyn used in the proof of Lemma 2. In particular, they use the fact (see [KV15] for a proof) that for an arbitrary set $A \subseteq \mathbb{F}_2^d$, $\Pr_{\mathbf{x} \sim \mathbb{F}_2^d, \mathbf{y} \sim N_\gamma(\mathbf{u})} [\mathbf{x} \in A \mid \mathbf{y} \in A] \leq (|A|/2^d)^{\gamma/(1-\gamma)}$. This inequality is not tight when A is chosen to be Region$_c$ – a spherical cap in the Hamming space. This leaves the question of whether one can construct a set A, which would be useful for nearest neighbor searching (that is, it would have an efficient membership oracle), and for which the inequality holds with equality. That would give an improvement to nearest neighbor searching in the dense regime, albeit a very small one, as we shall see in the next section.

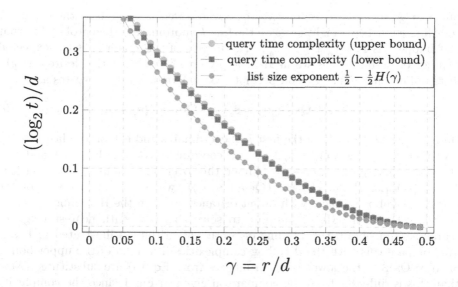

Fig. 1. Nearest neighbor search runtime exponents (dimensionless) for the target distance γ for lists of sizes $2^{\left(\frac{1}{2} - \frac{1}{2}H(\gamma)\right)d}$, i.e., we expect sub-exponentially many solutions. Upper bounds are determined by the number of hash regions t and follow from Eq. (6), while lower bounds are based on Eq. (5).

7   Application to Decoding and Code-Based Cryptography

All currently known fastest information set decoding algorithms for the *dense* setting make use of nearest neighbor searching. The goal of this chapter is to see how far down we could push the complexity of these decoding algorithms if we had a nearest neighbor search technique that matches the lower bound derived in the previous section.

In this section we will consider two algorithms: Stern's algorithm [Ste89], and the most recent algorithm of Both–May [BM18]. The first is the simplest information set decoding algorithm where nearest neighbor searching can be applied, while the second is the one that achieves the best currently known asymptotic time complexities.

7.1   Stern's Algorithm

Recall from Definition 2, that as input the information set decoding problem receives a parity check matrix $\mathbf{H} \in \mathbb{F}_2^{d-k \times d}$ and a syndrome $\mathbf{s} \in \mathbb{F}_2^{d-k}$. Stern's algorithm transforms the parity check matrix $\mathbf{H}$ into systematic form $[\mathbf{Q} \mid \mathbb{I}_{d-k}]$ (provided the last $d - k$ columns of $\mathbf{H}$ form an invertible matrix, which happens with constant success probability). The same transformation is applied to the syndrome $\mathbf{s}$ giving a new syndrome $\bar{\mathbf{s}}$. So the task is to find $\mathbf{e}$ that satisfies the equation:

$$[\mathbf{Q} \mid \mathbb{I}_{d-k}] \cdot \mathbf{e} = \bar{\mathbf{s}} \quad \text{for } \mathbf{Q} \in \mathbb{F}_2^{d-k \times k}. \tag{8}$$

Stern's algorithm searches for a vector $\mathbf{e}$ whose weight is $p > 0$ on the last $d - k$ coordinates (hence, weight $w - p$ on the first k coordinates). The probability that this happens is $P = \binom{k}{p}\binom{d-k}{w-p}/\binom{d}{w}$. The inverse of this quantity is the expected number of permutations we need to apply on $\mathbf{H}$ to obtain the desired weight distribution on $\mathbf{e}$. Once a good permutation is found, Eq. (8) rewrites as:

$$\mathbf{Q}\mathbf{e}_1 + \mathbf{Q}\mathbf{e}_2 + \mathbf{e}_3 = \bar{\mathbf{s}} \implies \mathbf{Q}\mathbf{e}_1 \approx \mathbf{Q}\mathbf{e}_2 + \bar{\mathbf{s}}. \tag{9}$$

Here $\mathbf{e}_1$ has weight $p/2$ on the first $k/2$ coordinates and is 0 on the last $d - k/2$ coordinates, $\mathbf{e}_2$ has weight $p/2$ on the coordinates $\{k/2 + 1, \ldots, k\}$ and is 0 elsewhere, and $\|\mathbf{e}_3\| = w - p$. Enumerating over all $\mathbf{e}_1$ and $\mathbf{e}_2$ into the lists $L_1 = \{(\mathbf{Q}\mathbf{e}_1, \mathbf{e}_1)\}$ and $L_2 = \{(\mathbf{Q}\mathbf{e}_2 + \mathbf{s}, \mathbf{e}_2)\}$, we receive an instance of the nearest neighbor problem with target distance $w - p$ in the Hamming metric.

May–Ozerov in [MO15] propose to solve this task with nearest neighbor searching and obtain the runtime of Stern's algorithm as illustrated in Fig. 2. We compare this with the decoding complexities if instead of the upper bound of May–Ozerov, the lower bound runtimes from Eq. (5) are substituted. Note that this is different from the comparison given in Fig. 1 since the complexity of Stern's algorithm is not only determined by the complexity of the nearest neighbor subroutine, but also by the number of permutations. For various code rates k, Fig. 2 compares the runtime exponents c for Stern's algorithm when (i) the nearest neighbor technique of [MO15] as in Eq. (6) is used, or (ii) the lower

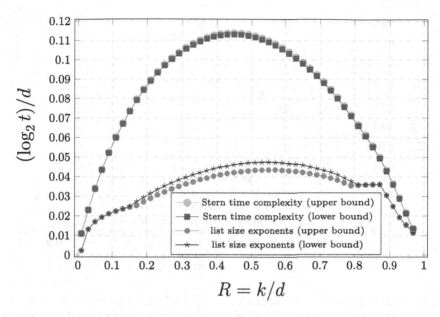

Fig. 2. Runtime exponents for Stern's information set decoding algorithm when either May–Ozerov's nearest neighbor search approach is used (blue circles), or when the lower bound is implemented (red squares). The code rate R is on the horizontal axis. The other two plots show the list size exponents that Stern's algorithm runs the nearest neighbor step on. The faster nearest neighbor searching (the lower bound) allows lager lists, hence there is a bigger gap between the list sizes in the most dense regime (around $R = 0.5$). The larger or the smaller the code rate is, the closer we are to the sparse setting, so the closer lower and upper bounds to each other.

bound for nearest neighbor searching is used. It also gives corresponding list sizes $|L_1| = |L_2| = \binom{k}{p} \approx 2^{kH(p/k)}$, but note that the optimal value for p slightly differs between the two runtimes. As the nearest neighbor search step becomes cheaper, the p is allowed to increase leading to larger lists.

7.2 The Both–May Algorithm

The recent information set decoding algorithm due to Both–May [BM18] significantly improves Stern's algorithm, and is currently the fastest algorithm for solving the information set decoding problem in the dense regime. We shall not describe the algorithm here but point out that the algorithm uses two-step nearest neighbor searching.

Similar to Stern's algorithm we compare the runtime of the Both–May algorithm when for the nearest neighbor steps, either (i) the best known nearest neighbor approach of May–Ozerov is used, or (ii) the lower bound given in Eq. (5) is used. Optimal runtimes for each code rate k are given in Fig. 3. We notice that the Both–May algorithm, while being quite close to the lower bound, leaves more potential for improvement than Stern's algorithm. This can be explained by looking at the lists sizes: the Both–May algorithm allows for larger lists that Stern's

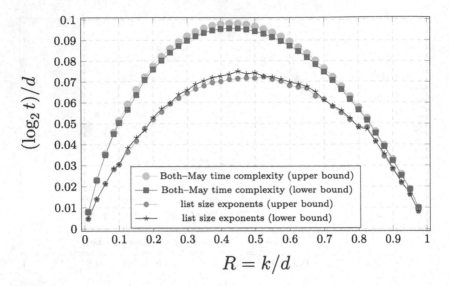

Fig. 3. Runtime exponents for the Both–May [BM18] algorithm when either the May–Ozerov [MO15] upper bound is used (blue circles), or our lower bound is substituted (red squares). The other two plots show the list size exponents that nearest neighbor searching receives on input. The code rate R is on the X-axis.

algorithm, thus making the contribution of the nearest neighbor subroutine more substantial. Still, our conclusion is that a potential improvement in the nearest neighbor subroutine will not significantly improve the overall algorithm.

7.3 Relevance for Code-Based Cryptography

The hardness of the information set decoding problem is essential for the security of prominent code-based cryptosystems, such as the McEliece cryptosystem [McE78]. All proposed constructions for the NIST standardization competition [BCL+19] work in the regime where the error is of weight sub-linear in d, thus making Stern's algorithm and other faster information set decoding algorithms like [BM18] *asymptotically* irrelevant [CTS16]. This does not imply, however, that these information set decoding algorithms are *practically* irrelevant for concrete parameters. To the best of our knowledge, the question of the exact complexity of the fastest information set decoding algorithms using recent improvements has not been investigated. This leaves the possibility that information set decoding algorithms which do use nearest neighbor techniques will eventually be recognized as being actually applicable to cryptographic parameters as well, in which case our lower bounds may serve as conservative estimates for potential attack costs, and for choosing parameters.

References

[AD97] Ajtai, M., Dwork, C.: A public-key cryptosystem with worst-case/average-case equivalence. In: STOC, pp. 284–293 (1997)

[ADH+19]   Albrecht, M.R., Ducas, L., Herold, G., Kirshanova, E., Postlethwaite, E.W., Stevens, M.: The general sieve kernel and new records in lattice reduction. In: Ishai, Y., Rijmen, V. (eds.) EUROCRYPT 2019. LNCS, vol. 11477, pp. 717–746. Springer, Cham (2019). https://doi.org/10.1007/978-3-030-17656-3_25

[ADRS15]   Aggarwal, D., Dadush, D., Regev, O., Stephens-Davidowitz, N.: Solving the shortest vector problem in 2^n time via discrete Gaussian sampling. In: STOC, pp. 733–742 (2015)

[AGPS19]   Albrecht, M.R., Gheorghiu, V., Postlethwaite, E.W., Schanck, J.M.: Estimating quantum speedups for lattice sieves. Cryptology ePrint Archive 2019/1161 (2019)

[AI06]   Andoni, A., Indyk, P.: Near-optimal hashing algorithms for approximate nearest neighbor in high dimensions. In: FOCS, pp. 459–468 (2006)

[AIL+15]   Andoni, A., Indyk, P., Laarhoven, T., Razenshteyn, I., Schmidt, L.: Practical and optimal LSH for angular distance. In: NIPS, pp. 1225–1233 (2015)

[AINR14]   Andoni, A., Indyk, P., Nguyên, H.L., Razenshteyn, I.: Beyond locality-sensitive hashing. In: SODA, pp. 1018–1028 (2014)

[AKS01]   Ajtai, M., Kumar, R., Sivakumar, D.: A sieve algorithm for the shortest lattice vector problem. In: STOC, pp. 601–610 (2001)

[ALRW17]   Andoni, A., Laarhoven, T., Razenshteyn, I., Waingarten, E.: Optimal hashing-based time-space trade-offs for approximate near neighbors. In: SODA, pp. 47–66 (2017)

[ANSS18]   Aono, Y., Nguyen, P.Q., Seito, T., Shikata, J.: Lower bounds on lattice enumeration with extreme pruning. In: Shacham, H., Boldyreva, A. (eds.) CRYPTO 2018. LNCS, vol. 10992, pp. 608–637. Springer, Cham (2018). https://doi.org/10.1007/978-3-319-96881-0_21

[AR15]   Andoni, A., Razenshteyn, I.: Optimal data-dependent hashing for approximate near neighbors. In: STOC, pp. 793–801 (2015)

[AR16]   Andoni, A., Razenshteyn, I.: Tight lower bounds for data-dependent locality-sensitive hashing. In: SOCG, pp. 1–15 (2016)

[BCD+16]   Bos, J., et al.: Frodo: take off the ring! practical, quantum-secure key exchange from LWE. In: CCS, pp. 1006–1018 (2016)

[BCL+19]   Bernstein, D.J., et al.: Classic McEliece: conservative code-based cryptography (2019)

[BDGL16]   Becker, A., Ducas, L., Gama, N., Laarhoven, T.: New directions in nearest neighbor searching with applications to lattice sieving. In: SODA, pp. 10–24 (2016)

[BDK+18]   Bos, J., et al.: CRYSTALS - Kyber: a CCA-secure module-lattice-based KEM. In: Euro S&P, pp. 353–367 (2018)

[BGJ15]   Becker, A., Gama, N., Joux, A.: Speeding-up lattice sieving without increasing the memory, using sub-quadratic nearest neighbor search. Cryptology ePrint Archive, Report 2015/522, pp. 1–14 (2015)

[BGML+18]   Bhattacharya, S., et al.: Round5: compact and fast post-quantum public-key encryption. Cryptology ePrint Archive, Report 2018/725 (2018)

[BJMM12]   Becker, A., Joux, A., May, A., Meurer, A.: Decoding random binary linear codes in $2^{n/20}$: how $1 + 1 = 0$ improves information set decoding. In: Pointcheval, D., Johansson, T. (eds.) EUROCRYPT 2012. LNCS, vol. 7237, pp. 520–536. Springer, Heidelberg (2012). https://doi.org/10.1007/978-3-642-29011-4_31

[BL16]   Becker, A., Laarhoven, T.: Efficient (ideal) lattice sieving using cross-polytope LSH. In: Pointcheval, D., Nitaj, A., Rachidi, T. (eds.) AFRICACRYPT 2016. LNCS, vol. 9646, pp. 3–23. Springer, Cham (2016). https://doi.org/10.1007/978-3-319-31517-1_1

[BLS16] Bai, S., Laarhoven, T., Stehlé, D.: Tuple lattice sieving. In: ANTS, pp. 146–162 (2016)

[BM18]   Both, L., May, A.: Decoding linear codes with high error rate and its impact for LPN security. In: Lange, T., Steinwandt, R. (eds.) PQCrypto 2018. LNCS, vol. 10786, pp. 25–46. Springer, Cham (2018). https://doi.org/10.1007/978-3-319-79063-3_2

[BT76]   Baernstein, A., Taylor, B.A.: Spherical rearrangements, subharmonic functions, and *-functions in n-space. Duke Math. J. **43**(2), 245–268 (1976)

[Chr17] Christiani, T.: A framework for similarity search with space-time tradeoffs using locality-sensitive filtering. In: SODA, pp. 31–46 (2017)

[CTS16] Torres, R.C., Sendrier, N.: Analysis of information set decoding for a sub-linear error weight. In: Takagi, T. (ed.) PQCrypto 2016. LNCS, vol. 9606, pp. 144–161. Springer, Cham (2016). https://doi.org/10.1007/978-3-319-29360-8_10

[DLdW20] Doulgerakis, E., Laarhoven, T., de Weger, B.: Sieve, enumerate, slice, and lift: hybrid lattice algorithms for SVP via CVPP. In: Nitaj, A., Youssef, A. (eds.) AFRICACRYPT 2020. LNCS, vol. 12174, pp. 301–320. Springer, Cham (2020). https://doi.org/10.1007/978-3-030-51938-4_15

[DLvW20] Ducas, L., Laarhoven, T., van Woerden, W.: The randomized slicer for CVPP: sharper, faster, smaller, batchier. In: PKC, pp. 3–36 (2020)

[Duc18] Ducas, L.: Shortest vector from lattice sieving: a few dimensions for free. In: Nielsen, J.B., Rijmen, V. (eds.) EUROCRYPT 2018. LNCS, vol. 10820, pp. 125–145. Springer, Cham (2018). https://doi.org/10.1007/978-3-319-78381-9_5

[EKZ21] Esser, A., Kübler, R., Zweydinger, F.: A faster algorithm for finding closest pairs in hamming metric (2021)

[FP85]   Fincke, U., Pohst, M.: Improved methods for calculating vectors of short length in a lattice. Math. Comput. **44**(170), 463–471 (1985)

[Gen09] Gentry, C.: Fully homomorphic encryption using ideal lattices. In: STOC, pp. 169–178 (2009)

[GGH13] Garg, S., Gentry, C., Halevi, S.: Candidate multilinear maps from ideal lattices. In: Johansson, T., Nguyen, P.Q. (eds.) EUROCRYPT 2013. LNCS, vol. 7881, pp. 1–17. Springer, Heidelberg (2013). https://doi.org/10.1007/978-3-642-38348-9_1

[GNR10] Gama, N., Nguyen, P.Q., Regev, O.: Lattice enumeration using extreme pruning. In: Gilbert, H. (ed.) EUROCRYPT 2010. LNCS, vol. 6110, pp. 257–278. Springer, Heidelberg (2010). https://doi.org/10.1007/978-3-642-13190-5_13

[GPV08] Gentry, C., Peikert, C., Vaikuntanathan, V.: Trapdoors for hard lattices and new cryptographic constructions. In: STOC, pp. 197–206 (2008)

[HK17]   Herold, G., Kirshanova, E.: Improved algorithms for the approximate k-list problem in Euclidean norm. In: Fehr, S. (ed.) PKC 2017. LNCS, vol. 10174, pp. 16–40. Springer, Heidelberg (2017). https://doi.org/10.1007/978-3-662-54365-8_2

[HKL18]   Herold, G., Kirshanova, E., Laarhoven, T.: Speed-ups and time–memory trade-offs for tuple lattice sieving. In: Abdalla, M., Dahab, R. (eds.) PKC 2018. LNCS, vol. 10769, pp. 407–436. Springer, Cham (2018). https://doi.org/10.1007/978-3-319-76578-5_14

[JL84]   Johnson, W.B., Lindenstrauss, J.: Extensions of Lipschitz mappings into a Hilbert space. Contemp. Math. **26**(1), 189–206 (1984)

[Kan83]   Kannan, R.: Improved algorithms for integer programming and related lattice problems. In: STOC, pp. 193–206 (1983)

[Kle00]   Klein, P.: Finding the closest lattice vector when it's unusually close. In: SODA, pp. 937–941 (2000)

[KMPM19]   Kirshanova, E., Mårtensson, E., Postlethwaite, E.W., Moulik, S.R.: Quantum algorithms for the approximate k-list problem and their application to lattice sieving. In: Galbraith, S.D., Moriai, S. (eds.) ASIACRYPT 2019. LNCS, vol. 11921, pp. 521–551. Springer, Cham (2019). https://doi.org/10.1007/978-3-030-34578-5_19

[KV15]   Khot, S.A., Vishnoi, N.K.: The unique games conjecture, integrality gap for cut problems and embeddability of negative-type metrics into ℓ_1. J. ACM **62**(1), 1–39 (2015)

[Laa15a]   Laarhoven, T.: Sieving for shortest vectors in lattices using angular locality-sensitive hashing. In: Gennaro, R., Robshaw, M. (eds.) CRYPTO 2015. LNCS, vol. 9215, pp. 3–22. Springer, Heidelberg (2015). https://doi.org/10.1007/978-3-662-47989-6_1

[Laa15b]   Laarhoven, T.: Tradeoffs for nearest neighbors on the sphere. arXiv:1511.07527 [cs.DS], pp. 1–16 (2015)

[Laa16]   Laarhoven, T.: Search problems in cryptography. Ph.D. thesis, Eindhoven University of Technology (2016)

[Laa17]   Laarhoven, T.: Faster tuple lattice sieving using spherical locality-sensitive filters. arXiv:1705.02828 [cs.DS], pp. 1–14 (2017)

[Laa20]   Laarhoven, T.: Polytopes, lattices, and spherical codes for the nearest neighbor problem. In: ICALP (2020)

[Laa21]   Laarhoven, T.: Approximate Voronoi cells for lattices, revisited. J. Math. Cryptol. **15**, 1–21 (2021)

[Lan20]   Lange, T.: Overview of code-based crypto assumptions. Talk at Quantum Cryptanalysis of Post-Quantum Cryptography (2020)

[LdW15]   Laarhoven, T., de Weger, B.: Faster sieving for shortest lattice vectors using spherical locality-sensitive hashing. In: Lauter, K., Rodríguez-Henríquez, F. (eds.) LATINCRYPT 2015. LNCS, vol. 9230, pp. 101–118. Springer, Cham (2015). https://doi.org/10.1007/978-3-319-22174-8_6

[LMvdP15]   Laarhoven, T., Mosca, M., van de Pol, J.: Finding shortest lattice vectors faster using quantum search. Des. Codes Crypt. **77**(2), 375–400 (2015)

[LPR10]   Lyubashevsky, V., Peikert, C., Regev, O.: On ideal lattices and learning with errors over rings. In: Gilbert, H. (ed.) EUROCRYPT 2010. LNCS, vol. 6110, pp. 1–23. Springer, Heidelberg (2010). https://doi.org/10.1007/978-3-642-13190-5_1

[McE78]   McEliece, R.J.: A public-key cryptosystem based on algebraic coding theory. The Deep Space Network Progress Report, pp. 114–116 (1978)

[MMT11]   May, A., Meurer, A., Thomae, E.: Decoding random linear codes in $\tilde{\mathcal{O}}(2^{0.054n})$. In: Lee, D.H., Wang, X. (eds.) ASIACRYPT 2011. LNCS, vol. 7073, pp. 107–124. Springer, Heidelberg (2011). https://doi.org/10.1007/978-3-642-25385-0_6

[MNP07]   Motwani, R., Naor, A., Panigrahy, R.: Lower bounds on locality sensitive hashing. SIAM J. Discret. Math. **21**(4), 930–935 (2007)

[MO15] May, A., Ozerov, I.: On computing nearest neighbors with applications to decoding of binary linear codes. In: Oswald, E., Fischlin, M. (eds.) EUROCRYPT 2015. LNCS, vol. 9056, pp. 203–228. Springer, Heidelberg (2015). https://doi.org/10.1007/978-3-662-46800-5_9

[MR07] Micciancio, D., Regev, O.: Worst-case to average-case reductions based on Gaussian measures. SIAM J. Comput. **37**(1), 267–302 (2007)

[MV10a] Micciancio, D., Voulgaris, P.: A deterministic single exponential time algorithm for most lattice problems based on Voronoi cell computations. In: STOC, pp. 351–358 (2010)

[MV10b] Micciancio, D., Voulgaris, P.: Faster exponential time algorithms for the shortest vector problem. In: SODA, pp. 1468–1480 (2010)

[NV08] Nguyên, P.Q., Vidick, T.: Sieve algorithms for the shortest vector problem are practical. J. Math. Cryptol. **2**(2), 181–207 (2008)

[OWZ14] O'Donnell, R., Wu, Y., Zhou, Y.: Optimal lower bounds for locality-sensitive hashing (except when q is tiny). ACM Trans. Comput. Theory **6**(1), 5:1–5:13 (2014)

[Pan06] Panigrahy, R.: Entropy based nearest neighbor search in high dimensions. In: SODA, pp. 1186–1195 (2006)

[Pra62] Prange, E.: The use of information sets in decoding cyclic codes. IRE Trans. Inf. Theory **8**, 5–9 (1962)

[PS09] Pujol, X., Stehlé, D.: Solving the shortest lattice vector problem in time $2^{2.465n}$. Cryptology ePrint Archive, Report 2009/605, pp. 1–7 (2009)

[PTW10] Panigrahy, R., Talwar, K., Wieder, U.: Lower bounds on near neighbor search via metric expansion. In: FOCS, pp. 805–814, October 2010

[Reg05] Regev, O.: On lattices, learning with errors, random linear codes, and cryptography. In: STOC, pp. 84–93 (2005)

[Reg10] Regev, O.: The learning with errors problem (invited survey). In: CCC, pp. 191–204 (2010)

[Rie30] Riesz, F.: Sur une inégalité intégrale. J. London Math. Soc. **s1-5**(3), 162–168 (1930)

[RSA78] Rivest, R.L., Shamir, A., Adleman, L.: A method for obtaining digital signatures and public-key cryptosystems. Commun. ACM **21**(2), 120–126 (1978)

[Sch19] Schanck, J.: Sieve tables (2019)

[Sho94] Shor, P.W.: Algorithms for quantum computation: discrete logarithms and factoring. In: FOCS, pp. 124–134 (1994)

[SSTX09] Stehlé, D., Steinfeld, R., Tanaka, K., Xagawa, K.: Efficient public key encryption based on ideal lattices. In: Matsui, M. (ed.) ASIACRYPT 2009. LNCS, vol. 5912, pp. 617–635. Springer, Heidelberg (2009). https://doi.org/10.1007/978-3-642-10366-7_36

[Ste89] Stern, J.: A method for finding codewords of small weight. In: Cohen, G., Wolfmann, J. (eds.) Coding Theory 1988. LNCS, vol. 388, pp. 106–113. Springer, Heidelberg (1989). https://doi.org/10.1007/BFb0019850

[svp20] SVP challenge (2020). http://latticechallenge.org/svp-challenge/

[TT07] Terasawa, K., Tanaka, Y.: Spherical LSH for approximate nearest neighbor search on unit hypersphere. In: Dehne, F., Sack, J.-R., Zeh, N. (eds.) WADS 2007. LNCS, vol. 4619, pp. 27–38. Springer, Heidelberg (2007). https://doi.org/10.1007/978-3-540-73951-7_4

[TT09] Terasawa, K., Tanaka, Y.: Approximate nearest neighbor search for a dataset of normalized vectors. IEICE Trans. Inf. Syst. **92**(9), 1609–1619 (2009)

Author Index

Printed in the United States
by Baker & Taylor Publisher Services